Principles of Marketing

We work with leading authors to develop the
strongest educational materials in marketing,
bringing cutting-edge thinking and best learning
practice to a global market.

Under a range of well-known imprints, including
Financial Times Prentice Hall, we craft high quality
print and electronic publications which help
readers to understand and apply their content,
whether studying or at work.

To find out more about the complete range of our
publishing please visit us on the World Wide Web at:
www.pearsoneduc.com

Third European Edition

Principles of
Marketing

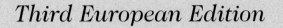

Philip Kotler

Gary Armstrong

John Saunders

Veronica Wong

 Prentice Hall
FINANCIAL TIMES

An imprint of Pearson Education

Harlow, England • London • New York • Boston • San Francisco • Toronto
Sydney • Tokyo • Singapore • Hong Kong • Seoul • Taipei • New Delhi
Cape Town • Madrid • Mexico City • Amsterdam • Munich • Paris • Milan

Pearson Education Limited
Edinburgh Gate
Harlow
Essex CM20 2JE
England

and Associated Companies throughout the world

Visit us on the World Wide Web at:
www.pearsoneduc.com

First European Edition published 1996
Second European Edition published 1999 by Prentice Hall Europe
under the Prentice Hall imprint
Third European Edition 2002

© Prentice Hall Europe 1996, 1999
© Pearson Education Limited 2002

ISBN 0 273 64662 1

British Library Cataloguing-in-Publication Data
A catalogue record for this book is available from the British Library

10 9 8 7 6 5 4 3
06 05 04 03 02

Typeset by 35
Printed and bound by Rotolito Lombarda, Italy

**To Carolyne and Paul:
our reasons for being.**

brief contents

contents

part two

The marketing setting 114

chapter four
The marketing environment 116

chapter five
The global marketplace 152

part three

Core strategy 312

chapter nine
Market segmentation and targeting:
satisfying human needs 314

chapter ten
Positioning 355

chapter eleven
Building customer relationships: customer
satisfaction, quality, value and service 389

chapter fifteen
Marketing services 533

part five

Price 564

chapter sixteen
Pricing considerations and approaches 566

chapter seventeen
Pricing strategies 596

part six

Promotion 622

preface

The past few years have brought vast changes to European marketing. Besides the usual ebb and flow of markets and the intensification of international competition, European and global integration has heralded an exponential increase in cross-border and domestic mergers and acquisitions. Since 1997, the value of European mergers and acquisitions has increased fourfold to over €2,000bn. The style, concentration and aggression of European business is clearly changing, and marketing must change as well alongside this new business environment. This book will seek to address such changes in European business and will explore their implications for marketing strategies.

While European industry has undergone a process of restructuring in recent years, the sudden explosion in e-commerce has further intensified the reinvention of marketing at the dawn of a new century. So far, Europe has lagged behind the US in the rush into the electronic age, but that has not immunised the continent from the recent dramatic swings of e-boom and bust. Behind the headline-grabbing business-to-consumer (B2C) e-flops, business-to-business (B2B) e-commerce is changing the way businesses trade. Indeed, the very foundation of trade is changing, as is, for that matter, the nature of money. This is manifest not just in the decline of local currencies as the euro grows, but also in the growth of safe and encrypted electronic financial exchanges.

While a number of European companies, such as Nokia and Vodafone, have flourished in the new e-economy, many traditional industry leaders have floundered. After years as the country's most admired retailer, Britain's Marks & Spencer is struggling to survive in the middle ground between discounters and agile, global retail chains. Moreover, more traditional problems also continue to beset manufacturing industry. For instance, car manufacturers, such as General Motors and Ford, have had to restructure production to cope with global overcapacity.

Principles of Marketing has changed to reflect the new faces of marketing. All the highlights and cases have been revised or completely changed to embrace the growth in e-commerce. It is a sign of the times that many people will use *Principles of Marketing* alongside its associated MYPHLIP Web Site. An increasing number of references are now website addresses that anyone can access from their PC, and each chapter now has Web-based exercises. Yet amid this turmoil some issues remain the same. As always, while many products and brands change at a breathless pace, many others remain familiar to us over the years, including Coca-Cola, Nokia, Sony, BMW, Vodafone and Shell. Such companies' continued high level of brand recognition will be discussed in the coming chapters.

Marketing is changing to meet the changing world. Marketing remains the business activity that identifies an organisation's customer needs and wants. Marketing determines which target markets a company can serve best, and marketing helps the design of appropriate products, services and programmes to serve these markets. However, marketing is much more than an isolated business function; it is a philosophy that guides the entire organisation. The goal of marketing is to create customer satisfaction profitably by building valued relationships with customers. Marketers cannot accomplish this goal by themselves. They must work closely with other people in their company and with other organisations in their value chain, to provide superior value to customers. Thus marketing calls upon everyone in the organisation to 'think customer' and to do all that they can to help create and deliver superior customer value and satisfaction. As Professor Stephen Burnett says, 'In a truly great marketing organisation, you can't tell who's in the marketing department. Everyone in the organisation has to make decisions based on the impact on the consumer.'

Marketing is not solely about advertising or selling. Real marketing is less about selling and more about knowing what to make! Organisations gain market leadership by understanding customer needs and finding solutions that satisfy or even delight through superior value, quality and service. No amount of advertising or selling can compensate for a lack of customer satisfaction. Marketing is also about applying that same process of need fulfilment to groups other than the final consumer. Paying customers are only one group of stakeholders in our society. We have to reach out to others sharing our world.

Marketing is all around us. 'We are all customers now', notes the author Peter Mullen, 'in every area of customer inter-relationship from the supply and consumption of education and health care to the queue in the Post Office and the ride in an inter-city express, and in every financial transaction from the buying of biscuits to the purchase of a shroud.' Marketing is not only for manufacturing companies, wholesalers and retailers but for all kinds of individuals and organisations. Lawyers, accountants and doctors use marketing to manage demand for their services. So do hospitals, museums and performing arts groups. No politician can get the required votes and no resort the necessary tourists, without developing and carrying out marketing plans. *Principles of Marketing* helps students learn and apply the basic concepts and practices of modern marketing as used in a wide variety of settings: in product and service firms, consumer and business markets, profit and non-profit organisations, domestic and global companies and small and large businesses.

People in such organisations need to know how to define and segment markets and how to position themselves by developing need-satisfying products and services for their chosen target segments. Marketers must know how to price their offerings attractively and affordably, and how to choose and manage the marketing channel that delivers products to customers. They need to know how to advertise and promote products so that customers will know about and want them. All of these demand a broad range of skills to sense, serve and satisfy consumers.

We need to understand marketing from the point of view of consumers and citizens. Someone is always trying to sell us something, so we need to recognise the methods they use. When we seek employment we need in effect to market ourselves. Many of us will start our careers within a salesforce, in retailing, in advertising, in research or in one of the many other marketing areas.

approach and objectives

Principles of Marketing takes a practical, managerial approach to marketing. It is rich in practical examples and applications, showing the major decisions that marketing managers face in their efforts to balance an organisation's objectives and resources against needs and opportunities in the global marketplace. Each chapter opens with a preview case, a major example describing a market situation. Boxed Marketing Highlights, short examples, company cases and colour illustrations highlight key ideas, stories and marketing strategies.

Principles of Marketing tells the stories that reveal the drama of modern marketing: Nike's powerful marketing; BMW's entry into the off-the-road market; the Swatchmobile; Absolut Vodka's startling success in finding new ways to grow globally; French wine growers' struggle against 'new world wines'; Sony's legendary successful PS2; MTV's segmentation of the European music market; Virgin's lifestyle marketing;

LVMH's focus on luxury products; and Nestlé's difficulty with pressure groups. These and dozens of other examples and illustrations throughout each chapter reinforce key concepts and bring marketing to life.

Principles of Marketing provides a comprehensive and innovative managerial and practical introduction to marketing. Its style and extensive use of examples and illustrations make the book straightforward, easy to read, lively and enjoyable.

the third european edition

The Third European Edition of *Principles of Marketing* offers significant improvements in perspective, in organisation, content and style. Recognising Europe's internationalism and the growth of globalisation, examples and cases are drawn, not from Europe alone, but from the US, Japan, South-east Asia and Africa. Some examples and cases concentrate on national issues, but even these have been selected to reflect issues of interest to students worldwide. Many involve developments in e-commerce, mobile communications, fashion and entertainment.Although such cases cover many markets and products, the brands and customers used are close to the experience or aspiration of readers.

This book is divided into eight parts that first cover marketing concepts and strategy and then the marketing mix. A final chapter is devoted to new developments in Internet marketing, although e-commerce is emphasised throughout the text.

Part 1 MARKETING AND THE MARKETING PROCESS introduces marketing in a changing world and then immediately addresses the important issues of marketing and society, social responsibility and marketing ethics. Chapter 3, Strategic Marketing Planning, then provides an early framework for marketing thinking, shows the links between the chapters that follow and sets the stage for the remainder of the text.

Part 2 THE MARKETING SETTING examines the environment in which modern firms compete and how to gather information on the markets. Chapters 4 and 5 cover the dimensions of the marketing environment and the global marketplace. The next two chapters cover consumer marketing and industrial marketing, which includes selling to international government agencies. Chapter 8 considers marketing information and marketing research.

Part 3 CORE STRATEGY begins with a chapter on market segmentation and targeting. This is followed by a separate chapter on positioning. The next two chapters then show how to build relationships with customers through customer satisfaction, quality, value and service, ways of creating competitive advantage and how to compete.

The final four parts cover the marketing mix.

Part 4 PRODUCT has two chapters on designing the product, new-product development, product life cycle, products, brands, packaging and service. The final chapter focuses on the increasingly important area of marketing services.

Part 5 PRICE has two chapters: one on pricing consideration and approaches and the other on pricing strategies.

Part 6 PROMOTION has a chapter on communication and promotional strategy and two more on parts of the communications mix: advertising, sales promotion and public relations, then personal selling and sales management.

Part 7 PLACE represents the last stage in getting products or services to the buyer. It starts with the traditional flow through distribution channels and logistics management to retailing and wholesaling. It then examines the huge new developments in direct marketing and in marketing using the Internet.

learning aids

Many aids to student learning come within this book. These include:

+ **Chapter objectives** say what students will be able to do after completing each chapter.
+ **Forty-four cases** appear, each with **questions graded** in difficulty from direct first questions to more demanding later ones:

     Preview cases. Each chapter begins with a short preview case that gives an example of marketing in practice and poses questions that introduce the chapter.

     Cases. Case studies for class or written discussion are provided at the end of each chapter. These cases challenge students to apply marketing principles to real companies in real situations.

+ **Key phrases** and **words** are highlighted throughout the text to allow easy reference and signposting.
+ **Full-colour** coded figures, photographs, advertisements and illustrations appear throughout the text. In each chapter key concepts and applications are illustrated with strong, full-colour visual materials.
+ **Marketing Highlights**. Additional examples and important information appear in Marketing Highlight exhibits throughout the text. Many of these are e-commerce applications.
+ **Summaries**. Each chapter ends with a summary that wraps up the main points and concepts.
+ **Discussing the Issues**. At the end of each chapter the discussion issues are presented as questions for use in lectures, seminars or tutorials.
+ **Applying the Concepts**. These exercises are for use in seminars or as practical assignments. Each chapter has at least one exercise involving Internet access.
+ **Glossary**. An extensive glossary provides quick reference to the key terms in the book. These terms are printed in bold at their first or key reference.
+ **Indexes**. Subject, company and author indexes reference all information and examples in the book.

supplements

A successful marketing course requires more than a well-written book. Today's class-room requires a dedicated teacher and a fully integrated teaching system. *Principles of Marketing* is supported by an extensive system of supplemental learning and teaching aids:

■ For instructors

+ **Instructor's MYPHLIP Web Site** provides password-protected electronic versions of the Instructor's Manual and PowerPoint slides as well as a **Syllabus Manager**. Available to adopters at www.booksites.net/kotler. Please contact your local sales representative for a password.

+ **Instructor's Resource Manual**. This helpful online teaching resource, prepared by Jim Blythe of Glamorgan University, contains:

  chapter outlines; class exercises with questions and suggested answers; suggested essay titles; practical projects; model answers to the preview cases within the text and ways of discussing the issues within each case, including tips, themes, challenging questions, new ways of approaching old topics and teaching tips; suggestions for stimulating debate.

+ **PowerPoint slides**. The full-colour slides include tables and figures prepared to ensure clear classroom presentation.

+ **Marketing Plan Pro** – the student version of this commercial software from Palo Alto Software is also available to lecturers who adopt this text. Marketing Plan Pro is totally interactive and features ten sample marketing plans, customisable charts, and professional-looking colour printouts. Students can customise their marketing plans, budget and forecast; track their progress from strategy to implementation; and then print out the final results. Available for WebCT, Blackboard, and Pearson's own Course Compass online platform. Please contact your local Pearson sales representative for further details.

■ For students

+ **Student's MYPHLIP Web Site**: Expertly written by Sukhbinder Barn of Middlesex University, this takes students beyond the text and includes chapter objectives, interactive multiple choice questions (30 per chapter), case studies with discussion questions, suggested solutions to these, key concepts and hotlinks to related sites. All these are provided with a search facility for the site and an opportunity to feed back ideas for the future development of the text and site. Instructors can also give students limited-access material they have produced on **Syllabus Manager**. Available at www.booksites.net/kotler.

myPHLIP Web Site

A **myPHLIP** Web Site
accompanies
Principles of Marketing, Third European Edition
by Kotler, Armstrong, Saunders and Wong

Visit the *Principles of Marketing* myPHLIP Web Site at www.booksites.net/kotler to find valuable and customisable teaching and learning material, including:

For students:
+ Resources specially written by Sukhbinder Barn, Middlesex University, including:
    + Learning objectives to guide you through your course
    + Key concepts highlighting the core knowledge you need to acquire
    + Case studies with discussion questions promoting deeper learning in the real world
    + Multiple choice questions (35 per chapter) enabling you to test your understanding
    + Hotlinks to further your research

For lecturers, comprehensive resources including:

+ A secure, password protected site with teaching material
+ Instructor's Manual (written by Jim Blythe, University of Glamorgan) and containing for each chapter:
    + Chapter outline
    + Class exercise with questions and suggested answers
    + Suggested essay titles
    + Practical projects
    + Preview cases – suggested answers
    + Discussing the Issues – tips, themes, challenging questions, new ways of approaching old topics – based on preview cases.
    + Applying the Concepts – stimulating debate
+ PowerPoint slides of figures from the text
+ Suggested solutions to the case studies found on the student side of the site
+ The myPHLIP syllabus manager allowing you to create a dynamic, personalised and integrated syllabus on line.

Chapter introductions *outline the core content of the chapter and explain how the chapter fits into the larger structure of the book.*

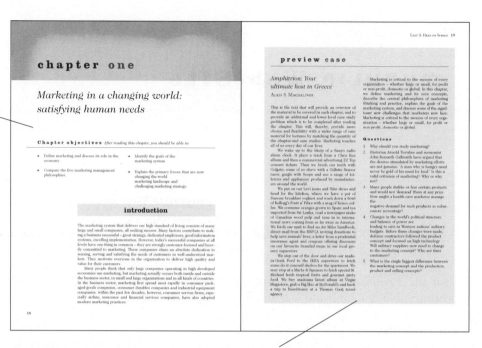

Preview cases *serve as an introduction by example to the chapter, providing additional and straightforward information about marketing in practice that illustrates the chapter to come. Preview cases provide lecturers and students with a greater range and flexibility in using case material for teaching and learning.*

Marketing highlights *can be used as additional case studies to stimulate discussion and to illuminate, in an advanced fashion, marketing in practice issues to emerge from the chapter.*

Margin notes *provide easy to understand definitions of key terms highlighted in the text.*

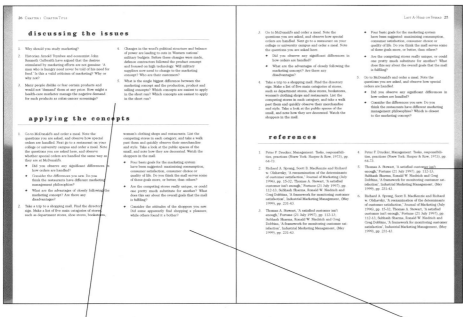

Discussing the issues

These provide lecturers and students with ideas for further debate and possible questions for further written work. Issues and questions have been chosen to challenge students and to encourage further reflection on the concepts dealt with in the chapter.

Applying the concepts

These tasks and questions ask students to think in theoretical and conceptual terms while investigating real issues faced by marketers in practice.

References

are listed to guide students and lecturers to further reading and to underpin the core ideas discussed in the text.

myPHLIP online learning resource for lecturers and students

www.booksites.net/kotler

Hyperlinks

to the resources for this book

Multiple-choice quiz bank

designed to test students' understanding of the concepts covered within this chapter

Case study *taken from the Financial Times or the Guardian. Lecturer view includes suggested answers*

Full downloadable Instructor's Manual

(written by Jim Blythe, University of Glamorgan)

Downloadable powerpoint presentation Manual

Utilising figures and tables from the book.

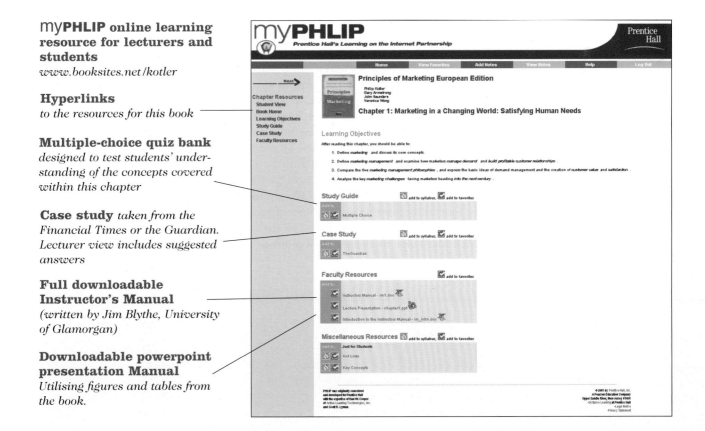

acknowledgements

No book is the work only of its authors. We owe much to the pioneers of marketing who first identified its major issues and developed its concepts and techniques in Europe. We are particularly indebted to a trio of colleagues who have led and inspired marketing research and teaching to the great benefit of many students, researchers and practitioners: Peter Doyle, Malcolm Macdonald and Michael Baker. Our thanks also go to our colleagues at the J. L. Kellogg Graduate School of Management, Northwestern University; the Kenan-Flagler Business School, University of North Carolina at Chapel Hill; Aston Business School; and The Business School, Loughborough University, for ideas, encouragement and suggestions. Also thanks to all our friends in the Academy of Marketing, European Marketing Academy, Informs, the American Marketing Association, the Chartered Institute of Marketing and the European Foundation for Management Development who have stimulated and advised us over the years. It has been an honour to work with so many people who have helped pioneer marketing in Europe.

Special thanks also to Maria del Mar Souza Fontan, of Aston Business School, who has helped with many parts of the book. Thanks to Pedro Quelhas Brito, Ann Torres, John Thornhill, Thomas Helgesson, Robert A. Vander Zwart, Samual Pronk, Kevin Done and Marcel Cohen who have contributed excellent cases to this edition. Also many thanks to Jim Blythe for his patience and work on the Instructor's Manual, and to Sukhbinder Barn for the construction and vitality of the MYPHLIP Web Site.

We were aided in our revision of this edition by over a hundred reviewers from universities and colleges throughout Europe who responded to Pearson Education's questionnaires and to whom we extend our thanks.

We also owe a great deal to the people at Pearson Education who have worked so hard to help us develop and produce this book: Bridget Allen, Project Manager Production; Kevin Ancient, Designer; Lynn Brandon, Acquisitions Editor; Patrick Brindle, Development Editor; Tina Cadle, Managing Editor; David Harrison, Web Editor; Liz Johnson, Editorial Administrator; Martin Klopstock, Head of Production; Simon Lake, Product Development Director; Jacqueline Senior, former Development Editor; Liz Sproat, former Acquisitions Editor; Alison Stanford, Editorial Manager; and Amanda Thomas, Senior Production Executive. We should thank also Annette Abel, freelance copy editor; Patrick Bonham, freelance proof-reader; Lynette Miller, freelance permissions editor; and Sue Williams, freelance picture researcher. A special mention should also go to Melinda Welch at Design Deluxe for producing such a wonderful text design.

PHILIP KOTLER
GARY ARMSTRONG
JOHN SAUNDERS
VERONICA WONG

Publisher's acknowledgements

We are grateful to the following for permission to reproduce copyright material:

Text extracts: Chapter 10, Case 10 from Herbal hedonism with coke's fizz, © *Financial Times*, 27 October, 2000; Chapter 11, preview case, from Facile's seriously rich barmen in Trying to make selling spirits seriously easy, © *Financial Times*, 11 September, 2000; Chapter 13, Table in Marketing Highlight 13.1 from Coca-Cola loses its fizz, © *Financial Times*, 18 July, 2000; Chapter 15, end case, Inside Track: In defence of the NSPCC from *Financial Times* Limited, 14 December 2000 © Anderson, Q.M.C. Quentin Anderson is CEO of Addison Corporate Marketing, a WPP company; Chapter 16, end case, from Budget airlines lured by hope of skyhigh profits, © *Financial Times*, 11 November, 2000; Chapter 20, preview case, based on Mogens Bjerre, MD Foods AMBA: A anew world of sales and marketing, in *Understanding marketing: A European casebook*, Celia Phillips, Ad Pruyn and Marie-Paule Kestemont (eds), pp. 30–41, reproduced with permission © John Wiley & Sons Limited, Chichester, UK, 2000; Chapter 22, end case and ads. based on company data provided by Cool Diamonds; material supplied by Molly McKellar Public Relation, London.

Plates (new edition): 3 Suisses (http://www.3suissesfr) for plate on p. 793 (top); Abbey National plc, agency Euro RSCG WNEK Gosper for plate on p. 612; Advertising Archives for plates on p. 32, p. 84, p. 420, p. 467 (agency Saatchi & Saatchi, photographer Jo Magrean), p. 562, p. 573, p. 599, p. 601 and p. 671; ASA, London for plate on p. 47; Airbus, agency Euro RSCG WNEK Gosper for plate on p. 431; Aiwa for plate on p. 711; Associated Press for plate on p. 157; Atlas Commerce for plate on p. 27 and p. 400; BMW, photographer Tif Hunter for plate on p. 468; Boots/Inspiral Condoms/Rockland Corporation, agency Big Fish design solutions, designed by Paul Labeter for plate on p. 208; Breitling SA for plate on p. 374; Carlsberg Breweries AS, agency Publicis Torma Finland for Carlesberg Norway, 1999 for plate on p. 366; CoShopper (http://www.coshopper.com) for plate on p. 785 (bottom); Daimler Chrysler UK Ltd., agency Partners BDDH, photographer Slater Kinney for plate on p. 8; Daimler Chrysler AG, agency Springer & Jacoby for plate on p. 96; Dixons Group/Advertising Archives for plate on p. 599; Dolphin Telecom for plate on p. 574; Food Brokers Ltd., agency Scholz and friends for plate on p. 635; Ford Motor Company, agency Young & Rubicam for plate on p. 569; Four Seasons Hotels and Resorts, agency Ammirati Puris Lintas for plate on p. 627; Geneva's Private Bankers, agency The Creative Factory for plate on p. 726; The Gillette Company/Advertising archives, agency BDDO New York for plate on p. 601; Hewlett Packard, agency Publicis/SF Goodbee for plate on p. 482; Hjemmet Mortensen AS for plate on p. 376, HSBC Investment Bank plc., agency KBW Ltd. for plate on p. 399; Inchon International Airport Corporation, Korea, agency Dentsu Young and Rubicam, Korea for plate on p. 59; Infineon, agency J. Walter Thompson for plate on p. 270; IBM UK, agency Ogilvy One for plate on p. 176; J.P Gaultier/Advertising archives for plate on p. 671; KPNQwest, agency PPGH JWL Colors, photographer Jan Willem Scholten for plate on p. 362; Lacoste, agency Pentland Group for plate on p. 365 (left); La Redoute (http://www.redoute.com) for plate on p. 793 (bottom); lastminute.com (http://www.lastminute.com) for plate on p. 805; The London Clinic (http://www.thelondonclinic.co.uk) for plate on p. 803; Mann (Norway), Oct. 2000 for plate on p. 376; Marks & Spencer for plate on p. 143; Marriott Hotels, Resorts & Suites, agency McCann-Erikson, London for plate on p. 544; Michelin for plate on p. 78; Mont Blanc/Advertising archives for plate on p. 84; Moulinex (Denmark), agency DDB Needham for plate on p. 643; Nationwide for plate on p. 588; Nokia (http://www.nokia.com) for plate on p. 785 (top); NSPCC, photographer Matt Harris for plate on p. 32 and on p. 562; Orange for plate on p. 22; Packard Bell, agency Fred Fisher Associates for plate on p. 212; Peugeot Motor Company plc, agency Euro RSCG WNEK Gosper for plate on p. 670; Philips Consumer Electronics, agency Interface Marketing Communications for plate on p. 365 (right); Pillsbury UK Ltd., agency Euros for plate on p. 367; Regent International Hotels for plate on p. 363 and p. 706; Robocom Systems (http://www.robocom.com) for plate on p. 765; Rockwell Automation, agency Chilworth Communications for plate on p. 464; Royal Mail, agency Bates UK for plate on p. 631; SAS, agency Mason Zimbler for plate on p. 252; Scandinavian Airlines, agency Admaker for plate on p. 543; Sekonda for plate on p. 198; Shell International Petroleum Co. Ltd., agency J. Walter Thompson for plate on p. 57 and p. 144; Star Alliance for plate on p. 28, agency Y and R Europe; Unilever/ Advertising archives for plate on p. 420; Viking Footwear for plate on p. 376; VNU Tijdschriften, *Cosmopolitan* Nov. 2000, (Netherlands) for plate on p. 203; Weekbladpers, Men's Health) for plate on p. 603; Zumtobel Staff/Cash, Public Animation for plate on p. 444.

Plates (old edition): American Express Incentive Services for plates on p. 6 and 718; American Honda Motor Co., Inc. for plate on p. 210; Bartle Bogle Hegarty (BBH) for plate on p. 427; Benetton Group SPA for plate on p. 641; Bord Fáilte – Irish Tourist Board for plate on p. 465; Corbis Stock Market, photographer Jon Feingersh for plate on p. 246; Corbis Stock Market, photographer Richard Steedman for plate on p. 246; Duck Head Apparel Co. for plate on p. 329; Fujitsu Ltd for plate on p. 238; GettyOne for plate on p. 723; The Gillette Company for plates on p. 678; Guinness Ltd for plates on p. 372 and p. 378; Hewlett-Packard Company for plate on p. 237; The Image Works, photographer Fritz Hoffmann for plate on p. 165; Lever Fabergé for plate on p. 63; Liaison Agency for plate on p. 506; Lofthouse of Fleetwood Ltd for plate on p. 445; 3M for plate on p. 78 and plate on p. 505; Kommünalverband Rührgebiet for plate on p. 377; Marketing Week, Centaur Communications Ltd for plates on p. 477 and p. 687; MCC Smart GmbH for plate on p. 487; McDonald's Corporation for plate on p. 142; Network Aspen, photographer Jeffrey Aaronson for plate on p. 30; Nikon, Inc for plate on p. 219; NOP Research Group Ltd for plate on p. 295; Pirelli and C. for plate on p. 175; Roper Starch Worldwide, Inc. for plate on p. 301; Siemens Medical Solutions for plate on p. 136; Stock Boston, photographer Charles Gupton for plate on p. 767; Swatch AG for plate on p. 522; TENCEL® for plate on p. 236; Trillium Studios, photographer Cary Wolinsky for plate on p. 164; Triumph International Ltd for plate on p. 392; UNIQ plc for plate on p. 665; Virgin Management Ltd, photographer Tierry Boccon-Gibod for plates on p. 158; Volkswagen of American, Arnold Worldwide for plate on p. 638.

Figures, exhibits and tables: Exhibits 1.1 and 1.3 from *CBCL Manufacturer Performance, AGB Superpanel*, Taylor Nelson Sofres 1994; Figure 2.1 from Beyond Greening: Strategies for a Sustainable World in *Harvard Business Review* January-February, copyright © 1997 by the President and Fellows of Harvard College, all rights reserved (Hart, S. 1997); Figure 4.6 from Too Many or Too Few in *The Economist* 25 September 1999, © The Economist Newspaper Ltd; Figure 4.7 from *European Marketing Pocket Book 2000*, reprinted with permission of NTC Publications Ltd; Figure 4.8 from Emerging Market Indicators in *The Economist* 29 January 2000, © The Economist Newspaper Ltd, London; Table 6.1 from *National Statistics – Socioeconomic Classification* (ONS). Crown Copyright material is reproduced under Class Licence Number C01W0000039 with the permission of the Controller of HMSO; Figure 6.3 adapted from Reference Group Influence on Product and Brand Purchase Decisions in *Journal of Consumer Research* September, The University of Chicago Press (Bearden, W. O. and Etzel, M. J. 1982); Table 6.3 from The Concept and Application of Lifestyle Segmentation *Journal of Marketing*, January, American

Marketing Association (Plummer, J. T. 1974); Figure 6.4 adapted from *Motivation and Personality*, Second Edition, Pearson Education, Inc. (Maslow, A. H. 1970); Figure 6.5 adapted from *Consumer Behaviour and Marketing Action*, Sixth Edition, p. 67, reprinted with permission from the author (Assael, H. 1987); Figure 6.8 redrawn from *Diffusion of Innovations*, Fourth Edition, The Free Press, a Division of Simon and Schuster, Inc. (Rogers, E. M. 1995). Copyright © 1995 by Everett M. Rogers. Copyright © 1962, 1971, 1983 by The Free Press; Table 8.2 adapted from *Market Research: Measurement and Method*, Sixth Edition, pub Macmillan Publishing Co., reprinted with permission from the author (Tull, D. S. 1993); Exhibit 8.2 reproduced with permission of Galway Chamber of Commerce and Industry; Table 8.3 from www.esomar.nl/press/industryreport01.htm, reprinted with permission from ESOMAR; Exhibits 9.3 and 9.4 from *National Food Survey*, pub MAFF. Crown Copyright material is reproduced under Class Licence Number C01W0000039 with the permission of the Controller of HMSO; Figure 10.5 from The Finnish Tourist Board in *Case Studies in International Marketing* edited by P. Doyle and N. Hart, Heinemann Educational Publishers (Hooley, G. 1982); Figure 11.2 from *Competitive Advantage: Creating and Sustaining Superior Performance*, The Free Press, a Division of Simon & Schuster, Inc., copyright © 1985, 1998 by Michael E. Porter (Porter, M. E. 1985); Figure 11.6 from Quality as a Strategic Weapon: Measuring Relative Quality, Value and Market Differentiation in *European Business Journal 2*, 4, Whurr Publishers Ltd (Luchs, B. 1990); Table 12.1 from *Fortune*, 2 August 1999, © 1999 Time, Inc. All rights reserved; Figure 12.2 from *Winning on the Marketing Front*, pub John Wiley & Sons, Inc., reprinted with permission from Ann Elmo Agency, Inc. (Cohen, W. A. 1986); Table 14.2 from *Marketing Management: Analysis, Planning, Implementation and Control*, Ninth Edition, Pearson Education, Inc (Kotler, P. 1997); Figure 16.7 from *The Strategy and Tactics of Pricing*, Third Edition, Prentice-Hall, Inc. (Nagle, T. T. and Holden, R. K. 1995); Figure 17.2 redrawn from a working paper, reprinted with permission from the author (Trapp, R. J. 1964); Figure 20.2 from *Dartnell Corporation, 30th Sales Force Compensation Survey*, reprinted with permission from The Dartnell Corporation; Figure 21.7 from Grocery retailers in Europe: The super league in *The Times* 1 September, 1999, © Times Newpapers Limited; Table 22.2 from *The One-to-One Future*, © 1993 by Don Peppers and Martha Rogers, Ph.D, used by permission of Doubleday, a division of Random House, Inc. (D. Peppers and M. Rogers, 1993); Figure 22.1 and Table 22.2 from E-Commerce Survey in *The Economist* 26 February 2000, © The Economist Ltd, London; Figures 22.2(a) and 22.2(b) from *e.Business* February 2000, Crimson Publishing; Figure 22.3 from Netymology in *The Economist*, 9 October 1999, © The Economist Ltd, London; Figure in MH 1.2 from The Millennium of the West in *The Economist*, 31 December 1999, The Economist Ltd, London; Table 1 in MH 9.2 from CACI Market Analysis Group, © CACI Ltd 2001. All rights reserved. Exhibit 1 in MH22.2 from Analysys 2000, reproduced with permission of Katrina Bond, Analysys.

Whilst every effort has been made to trace the owners of copyright material, in a few cases this has proved impossible and we take this opportunity to offer our apologies to any copyright holders whose rights we may have unwittingly infringed.

about the authors

Philip Kotler is S. C. Johnson & Son Distinguished Professor of International Marketing at the J. L. Kellogg Graduate School of Management, Northwestern University. He received his master's degree at the University of Chicago and his PhD at MIT, both in Economics. Dr Kotler is author of *Marketing Management: Analysis, Planning, Implementation and Control* (Prentice Hall). He has authored several other successful books and he has written over 100 articles for leading journals. He is the only three-time winner of the Alpha Kappa Psi award for the best annual article in the *Journal of Marketing*. Dr Kotler's numerous major honours include the Paul D. Converse Award given by the American Marketing Association to honour 'outstanding contributions to the science of marketing' and the Stuart Henderson Brit Award as Marketer of the Year. In 1985, he was named the first recipient of two major awards: the Distinguished Marketing Educator of the Year Award, given by the American Marketing Association, and the Philip Kotler Award for Excellence in Health Care Marketing. Dr Kotler has served as a director of the American Marketing Association. He has consulted with many major US and foreign companies on marketing strategy.

Gary Armstrong is Professor and Chair of Marketing in the Kenan-Flagler Business School at the University of North Carolina at Chapel Hill. He received his PhD in marketing from Northwestern University. Dr Armstrong has contributed numerous articles to leading research journals and consulted with many companies on marketing strategy. But Dr Armstrong's first love is teaching. He has been very active in Kenan-Flagler's undergraduate business programme and he has received several campus-wide and business schools teaching awards. He is the only repeat recipient of the School's highly regarded Award for Excellence in Undergraduate Teaching, which he won for the third time in 1993.

John Saunders, BSc (Loughborough), MBA (Cranfield), PhD (Bradford), FBAM, FCIM, FRSA is Professor of Marketing and Head of Aston Business School. Previously, he worked for Hawker Siddeley and British Aerospace and has acted as a consultant for many leading organisations, including Rolls-Royce, Unilever, Nestlé, Ford, the European Commission, the Cabinet Office and the Singapore Government. He is a member of the BAM's fellowship committee, the CIM's senate and the steering committee of the EFMD. He is currently leading the CIM's Research Initiative and is a panel member for Britain's Research Assessment Exercise. His publications include *The Marketing Initiative* and co-authorship of *Marketing Strategy* and *Competitive Positioning*. He has published over seventy refereed journal articles, including publications in the *Journal of Marketing*, *Journal of Marketing Research* and *Marketing Science*.

Veronica Wong, Bachelor of Science, Master of Business Administration (Bradford), Doctor of Philosophy (Manchester), Fellow of the Royal Society of Arts, is Professor of Marketing and Innovation Management and Coordinator of the Marketing and Retailing Research Group at Loughborough University Business School. She was born in Malaysia where she studied until her first degree. Previously, Dr Wong worked at the University of Warwick. She has also taught in Malaysia and worked for Ciba Laboratories, UK. She has worked with a wide range of international firms and government bodies concerned with product innovation and its management, including Britain's Department of Trade and Industry (DTI) Innovation Advisory Unit. She wrote the DTI's manual on *Identifying and Exploiting New Market Opportunities*. She has also published over sixty articles in refereed journals and conferences, including the *Journal of International Business Studies*, the *Journal of Product Innovation Management* and *Industrial Marketing Management*.

part one

Marketing and the marketing process

'No profit grows where is no pleasure taken.'

WILLIAM SHAKESPEARE

part introduction

PART ONE OF *PRINCIPLES OF MARKETING* examines marketing's role in society and the organisations that use it.

Chapter 1 shows how marketing is everywhere. It also tells how marketing has grown as the belief that organisations do best by caring for their customers. This understanding is expanded in Chapter 2, which looks beyond buying and selling to examine marketing's role and responsibilities in society. Together these chapters examine marketing as 'the place where the selfish interests of the manufacturer coincide with the interest of society', as the advertising guru David Ogilvy put it.

Chapter 3 takes the discussion from what marketing does to how marketing is done. In developing the strategic marketing planning process, it looks at how marketing fits with other business activities and how it is organised. Most importantly, it introduces the marketing activities appearing elsewhere in *Principles of Marketing* and shows how they combine to make modern marketing.

Chapter 1

Marketing in a changing world: satisfying human needs

Chapter 2

Marketing and society: social responsibility and marketing ethics

Chapter 3

Strategic marketing planning

1

chapter one

Marketing in a changing world: satisfying human needs

Chapter objectives *After reading this chapter, you should be able to:*

- Define *marketing* and discuss its core concepts.

- Define marketing management and examine how marketers manage demand and build profitable customer relationships.

- Explain the relationships between *customer value*, *satisfaction* and *quality*.

- Compare the five *marketing management philosophies*.

- Analyse the key marketing challenges facing marketers heading into the twenty-first century.

introduction

Today's successful companies at all levels have one thing in common – like Nike, featured in the preview case opposite, their success is founded upon a strong customer focus and heavy commitment to marketing. These companies share an absolute dedication to sensing, serving and satisfying the needs of customers in well-defined target markets. They motivate everyone in the organisation to deliver high quality and superior value for their customers, leading to high levels of customer satisfaction. These organisations know that if they take care of their customers, market share and profits will follow.

Marketing, more than any other business function, deals with customers. Customers are an essential component of a marketing system. Each and every one of us is a customer in every area of human interrelation, from the consumption of education and health care and the queue in the post office to the ride on the Intercity express, and in every financial transaction, from the buying of biscuits to the purchase of a mobile phone. Creating customer value and satisfaction is at the very heart of modern marketing thinking and practice. Although we will explore more detailed definitions of marketing later in this chapter, perhaps the simplest definition is this one: Marketing is the delivery of customer satisfaction at a profit. The goal of marketing is

preview case

Nike

Nike has built the ubiquitous 'SWOOSH' (which represents the wing of Nike, the Greek goddess of victory) into one of the best-known brand symbols on the planet.

The power of its brand and logo speaks loudly to Nike's superb marketing skills. The company's strategy of building superior products around popular athletes and its classic 'Just do it!' ad campaign have forever changed the face of sports marketing. Nike spends hundreds of millions of dollars annually on big-name endorsements, splashy promotional events and lots of attention-getting ads. Nike has associated itself with some of the biggest names in sports: heroic images of Michael Jordan, Tiger Woods and Agassi made many people who wear the swoosh feel as if they were winners!

Nike's initial success resulted from the technical superiority of its running and basketball shoes. But Nike gives its customers more than just good athletic gear. As the company notes on its Web page (www.nike.com): 'Nike has always known the truth – it's not so much the shoes but where they take you.' Beyond shoes, apparel and equipment, Nike markets a way of life, a sports culture, a 'Just do it!' attitude. The company was built on a genuine passion for sports, a maverick disregard for convention, hard work and serious sports performance. Nike is athletes, athletes are sports, *Nike is sports*.

Over the past decade, Nike's revenues grew at an incredible annual rate of 21 per cent. Nike, with a 27 per cent share internationally, dominates the world's athletic footwear market.

Nike also moved aggressively into new markets, from baseball and golf to inline skating and wall climbing. Its familiar swoosh logo is now found on everything from sports apparel, sunglasses and footballs to batting gloves and hockey sticks.

In 1998, however, Nike stumbled and its sales slipped. Many factors contributed to the company's woes. The 'brown shoe' craze for hiking and rugged, outdoor styles such as Timberland, Hush Puppies and Doc Martens ate into the athletic footwear business. Nike also faced increasing competition from Adidas, Germany's venerable sporting goods company, and from clothing designers such as Tommy Hilfiger and Ralph Lauren. In Europe, Nike and Adidas maintain a fierce battle for leadership with about 24 per cent market share each. To make matters worse, college students and consumer groups at home have protested against Nike for its alleged exploitation of child labour in Asia and its commercialisation of sports.

But Nike's biggest obstacle may be its own incredible success. A Nike executive admits that Nike has moved from maverick to mainstream, and the swoosh is becoming too common to be cool. To address these problems, Nike returned to the basics – focusing on innovation and introducing new sub-brands (e.g. the Michael Jordan line with its 'jumping man' logo and the ACG [All Condition Gear] line of outdoor and hiking styles). Recent advertising de-emphasises the swoosh, re-focusing on product performance and using only the Nike script logo name. Nike is also focusing on expanding sales in overseas markets, which now represent about 38 per cent of its total sales. However, to dominate globally, Nike must dominate in soccer, the world's most popular sport. This multi-billion-dollar market currently accounts for only 3 per cent of its sales. Nike has set World Cup 2002 as its deadline for becoming the world's no. 1 supplier of football boots, clothing and equipment.

Elbowing its way to the top by 2002 won't be easy. Adidas has long dominated, with an 80 per cent global market share in football gear. Moreover, Nike must deliver worldwide quality, innovation and value and earn consumers' respect on a country-by-country basis. No longer the rebellious, anti-establishment upstart, huge Nike must continually reassess its relationships with customers. Says its founder and chief executive, Phil Knight, 'Now that we've [grown so large], there's a fine line between being a rebel and being a bully. [To our customers,] we have to be beautiful as well as big.'[1]

Questions

1. What would you consider to be Nike's 'superb marketing skills'?

2. Why does Nike require these skills to compete in the marketplace?

3. Show how marketing principles and practices will enable Nike to satisfy these needs, bearing in mind the diverse range of product and geographic markets the company operates in.

to attract new customers by promising superior value, and to keep current customers by delivering satisfaction.

Many people think that only large companies operating in highly developed economies use marketing, but sound marketing is critical to the success of every organisation, whether large or small, domestic or global. In the business sector, marketing first spread most rapidly in consumer packaged-goods companies, consumer durables companies and industrial equipment companies. Within the past few decades, however, consumer service firms, especially airline, insurance and financial services companies, have also adopted modern marketing practices. Business groups such as lawyers, accountants, physicians and architects, too, have begun to take an interest in marketing and to advertise and price their services aggressively. Marketing has also become a vital component in the strategies of many non-profit organisations, such as schools, charities, churches, hospitals, museums, performing arts groups and even police departments.

Today, marketing is practised widely all over the world. Most countries in North and South America, western Europe and Asia have well-developed marketing systems. Even in eastern Europe and the former Soviet republics, where marketing has long had a bad name, dramatic political and social changes have created new opportunities for marketing. Business and government leaders in most of these nations are eager to learn everything they can about modern marketing practices.

You already know a lot about marketing – it's all around you. You see the results of marketing in the abundance of products that line the store shelves in your nearby shopping centre. You see marketing in the advertisements that fill your TV, spice up your magazines, come through your letterbox or enliven your Internet pages. At home, at college, where you work, where you play – you are exposed to marketing in almost everything you do. Yet, there is much more to marketing than meets the consumer's casual eye. Behind it all is a massive network of people and activities competing for your attention and money.

This book will give you a more complete and formal introduction to the basic concepts and practices of today's marketing. In this chapter, we begin by defining marketing and its core concepts, describing the major philosophies of marketing thinking and practice, and discussing some of the major new challenges that marketers face as we whirl into the new millennium.

what is marketing?

What does the term *marketing* mean? Many people think of marketing only as selling and advertising. And no wonder, for every day we are bombarded with television commercials, newspaper ads, direct mail campaigns, Internet pitches and sales calls. Although they are important, they are only two of many marketing functions and are often not the most important ones.

Today, marketing must be understood not in the old sense of making a sale – 'telling and selling' – but in the new sense of satisfying customer needs. Selling occurs only after a product is produced. By contrast, marketing starts long before a company has a product. Marketing is the homework that managers undertake to assess needs, measure their extent and intensity and determine whether a profitable opportunity exists. Marketing continues throughout the product's life, trying to find new customers and keep current customers by improving product appeal and performance, learning from product sales results and managing repeat performance.

Everyone knows something about 'hot' products. When Sony designed its first Walkman cassette and disc players, when Nintendo first offered its improved video

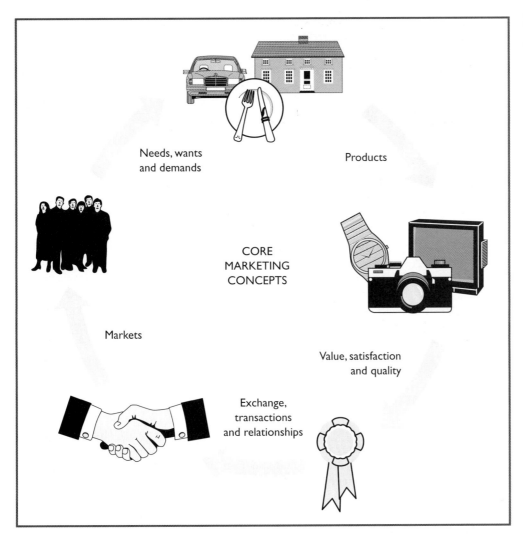

Figure 1.1

Core marketing concepts

game console, and when The Body Shop introduced animal-cruelty-free cosmetics and toiletries, these manufacturers were swamped with orders. They had designed the 'right' products: not 'me-too' products, but ones offering new benefits. Peter Drucker, a leading management thinker, has put it this way: 'The aim of marketing is to make selling superfluous. The aim is to know and understand the customer so well that the product or service fits . . . and sells itself.'[2] If the marketer does a good job of identifying customer needs, develops products that provide superior value, distributes and promotes them effectively, these goods will sell very easily. This does not mean that selling and advertising are unimportant. Rather, it means that they are part of a larger marketing mix – a set of marketing tools that work together to affect the marketplace.

We define **marketing** as: *a social and managerial process by which individuals and groups obtain what they need and want through creating and exchanging products and value with others*.[3] To explain this definition, we examine the following important terms: *needs, wants* and *demands; products* and *services; value, satisfaction* and *quality; exchange, transactions* and *relationships*; and *markets*. Figure 1.1 shows that these core marketing concepts are linked, with each concept building on the one before it.

Marketing

A social and managerial process by which individuals and groups obtain what they need and want through creating and exchanging products and value with others.

This ad assures card members that American Express World Service representatives go beyond the call of duty to solve their unexpected problems.

Source: American Express

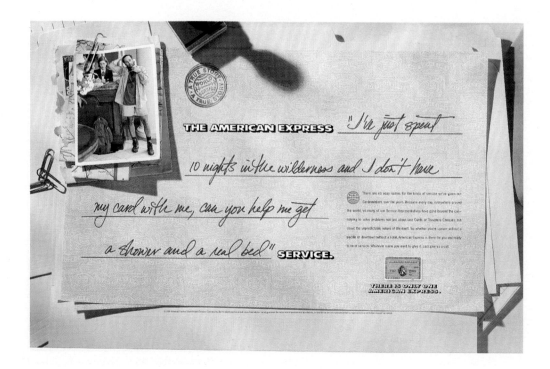

needs, wants and demands

Human need
A state of felt deprivation.

The most basic concept underlying marketing is that of human needs. **Human needs** are states of felt deprivation. They include basic *physical* needs for food, clothing, warmth and safety; *social* needs for belonging and affection; and *individual* needs for knowledge and self-expression. These needs were not invented by marketers; they are a basic part of the human make-up. When a need is not satisfied, a person will do one of two things:

1. look for an object that will satisfy it; or
2. try to reduce the need.

People in industrial societies may try to find or develop objects that will satisfy their desires. People in less developed societies may try to reduce their desires and satisfy them with what is available.

Human want
The form that a human need takes as shaped by culture and individual personality.

Wants are the form human needs take as they are shaped by culture and individual personality. A hungry person in Mauritius may want a mango, rice, lentils and beans. A hungry person in Eindhoven may want a ham and cheese roll, salad and a beer. A hungry person in Hong Kong may want a bowl of noodles, 'char-siu' pork and jasmine tea. Wants are shaped by one's society and are described in terms of objects that will satisfy needs. As a society evolves, the wants of its members expand. As people are exposed to more objects that arouse their interest and desire, producers try to provide more want-satisfying products and services.

Demands
Human wants that are backed by buying power.

People have narrow, basic needs (e.g. for food or shelter), but almost unlimited wants. However, they also have limited resources. Thus they want to choose products that provide the most satisfaction for their money. When backed by an ability to pay – that is, buying power – wants become **demands**. Consumers view products as bundles of benefits and choose products that give them the best bundle for their money. Thus a Honda Civic means basic transportation, low price and fuel economy. A Mercedes means comfort, luxury and status. Given their wants and resources, people demand products with the benefits that add up to the most satisfaction.

Outstanding marketing companies go to great lengths to learn about and understand their customers' needs, wants and demands. They conduct consumer research about consumer likes and dislikes. They analyse customer complaint, enquiry, warranty and service data. They observe customers using their own and competing products and train salespeople to be on the lookout for unfulfilled customer needs. Understanding customer needs, wants and demands in detail provides important input for designing marketing strategies.

products and services

People satisfy their needs and wants with products. A **product** is anything that can be offered to a market to satisfy a need or want. The concept of *product* is not limited to physical objects, such as a car, a television set or a bar of soap – anything capable of satisfying a need can be called a product. In addition to tangible goods, products include **services**, which are activities or benefits offered for sale that are essentially intangible and do not result in the ownership of anything. Examples include banking, airline, hotel and home repair services. Broadly defined, products also include other entities such as *experiences, persons, places, organisations, information* and *ideas*. EuroDisney is an experience; so is a visit to the Grand Canyon. In fact, as products and services increasingly become commodities, experiences have emerged for many firms as the next step in differentiating the company's offer. Thus, the term *product* includes much more than just physical goods or services. Consumers decide which entertainers to watch on television, which political party to vote for, which places to visit on holiday, which charity organisations to support through contributions and which ideas to adopt. To the consumer, these are all products. If at times the term *product* does not seem to fit, we could substitute other terms such as *satisfier, resource* or *marketing offer*.

Many sellers make the mistake of paying more attention to the specific products they offer than to the benefits produced by these products. They see themselves as selling a product rather than providing a solution to a need. The importance of physical goods lies not so much in owning them as in the benefits they provide. A manufacturer of drill bits may think that the customer needs a drill bit, but what the customer really needs is a hole. These sellers may suffer from 'marketing myopia'.[4] They are so taken with their products that they focus only on existing wants and lose sight of underlying customer needs. They forget that a physical product is only a tool to solve a consumer problem. These sellers have trouble if a new product comes along that serves the need better or less expensively. The customer with the same *need* will *want* the new product.

value, satisfaction and quality

Consumers usually face a broad array of products and services that might satisfy a given need. How do they choose among these many products? Consumers make buying choices based on their perceptions of the value that various products and services deliver.

The guiding concept is **customer value**. Customer value is the difference between the values the customer gains from owning and using a product and the costs of obtaining the product. For example, Mercedes-Benz customers gain a number of benefits. The most obvious is a well-engineered and reliable car. However, customers may also receive some status and image values. Owning or driving a Mercedes-Benz may make them feel more important. When deciding whether to buy the desired model, customers will weigh these and other values against what it costs to buy the car. Moreover,

Product
Anything that can be offered to a market for attention, acquisition, use or consumption that might satisfy a want or need. It includes physical objects, services, persons, places, organisations and ideas.

Services
Activities, benefits or satisfactions that are offered for sale.

Customer value
The consumer's assessment of the product's overall capacity to satisfy his or her needs.

Sheer delight and satisfaction: This ad for the new Mercedes C-Class seeks to convey just how great it feels to drive the car.

SOURCE: Daimler Chrysler UK Ltd. *Agency:* Partners BDDH. *Photographer:* Slater Kinney

The next time someone tells you to get lost, take them up on it.

Go somewhere you've never been before. Burn the map. Ignore the road signs. Don't stop to ask directions. And take the long way back.

The New C, from £20,740. Life's what you make it.

www.thenewc.co.uk

Mercedes-Benz

Customer satisfaction
The extent to which a product's perceived performance matches a buyer's expectations. If the product's performance falls short of expectations, the buyer is dissatisfied. If performance matches or exceeds expectations, the buyer is satisfied or delighted.

Total quality management (TQM)
Programmes designed to constantly improve the quality of products, services, and marketing processes.

they will compare the value of owning a Mercedes against the value of owning other comparable manufacturers' models – Lexus, Audi, BMW – and select the one that gives them the greatest delivered value.

Customers often do not judge product values and costs accurately or objectively. They act on *perceived* value. Customers perceive Mercedes-Benz to provide superior performance, and are hence prepared to pay the higher prices that the company charges. **Customer satisfaction** depends on a product's perceived performance in delivering value relative to a buyer's expectations. If the product's performance falls short of the customer's expectations, the buyer is dissatisfied. If performance matches expectations, the buyer is satisfied. If performance exceeds expectations, the buyer is delighted. Outstanding marketing companies go out of their way to keep their customers satisfied. They know that satisfied customers make repeat purchases, and they tell others about their good experiences with the product. The key is to match customer expectations with company performance. Smart companies aim to delight customers by promising only what they can deliver, then delivering more than they promise.[5]

Customer satisfaction is closely linked to quality. In recent years, many companies have adopted **total quality management** (TQM) programmes, designed constantly to improve the quality of their products, services and marketing processes. Quality has a direct impact on product performance, and hence on customer satisfaction.

In the narrowest sense, quality can be defined as 'freedom from defects'. But most customer-centred companies go beyond this narrow definition of quality. Instead, they define quality in terms of customer satisfaction. For example, Motorola, a company that pioneered total quality efforts, stresses that 'Quality has to do something for the customer – Our definition of a defect is "if the customer doesn't like it, it's a defect".' Customer-focused definitions of quality suggest that a company has achieved total quality only when its products or services meet or exceed customer expectations. Thus, the fundamental aim of today's *total quality* movement has become *total customer satisfaction*. Quality begins with customer needs and ends with customer satisfaction. Moreover, in order to retain customers, companies must ensure they are consistent in delivering these satisfactions. Consider, for example, Coca-Cola, a globally known brand name. In 1999, Coke had its European customers' trust shattered, in part because one plant in Belgium failed to deliver the quality product in which those customers had come to believe.

Today, consumer-behaviourists have gone far beyond narrow economic assumptions about how consumers form value judgements and make product choices. Smart companies pay greater attention to understanding what and how their customers want to buy, not how the firm wants to sell. They get into their customers' mind. Take, for example, McDonald's, the fast burger chain. McDonald's management is aware that mothers do not kid themselves: mums do not count on McDonald's to deliver the best in quality food. They count on McDonald's consistency – clean toilets, consistent food – anywhere in the world.

We will look at modern theories of consumer-choice behaviour in Chapter 6. In Chapter 11, we will examine more fully customer satisfaction, value and quality.

exchange, transactions and relationships

Marketing occurs when people decide to satisfy needs and wants through exchange. **Exchange** is the act of obtaining a desired object from someone by offering something in return. Exchange is only one of many ways people can obtain a desired object. For example, hungry people can find food by hunting, fishing or gathering fruit. They could beg for food or take food from someone else. Finally, they could offer money, another good or a service in return for food.

As a means of satisfying needs, exchange has much in its favour. People do not have to prey on others or depend on donations. Nor must they possess the skills to produce every necessity for themselves. They can concentrate on making things they are good at making and trade them for needed items made by others. Thus exchange allows a society to produce much more than it would with any alternative system.

Exchange is the core concept of marketing. For an exchange to take place, several conditions must be satisfied. Of course, at least two parties must participate and each must have something of value to offer the other. Each party must also want to deal with the other party and each must be free to accept or reject the other's offer. Finally, each party must be able to communicate and deliver.

These conditions simply make exchange *possible*. Whether exchange actually *takes place* depends on the parties coming to an agreement. If they agree, we must conclude that the act of exchange has left both of them better off or, at least, not worse off. After all, each was free to reject or accept the offer. In this sense, exchange creates value just as production creates value. It gives people more consumption choices or possibilities.

Whereas exchange is the core concept of marketing, a transaction is marketing's unit of measurement. A **transaction** consists of a trading of values between two parties: one party gives X to another party and gets Y in return. For example, you pay a retailer 500 euros for a television set or the hotel 120 euros a night for a room. This is a classic monetary transaction, but not all transactions involve money. In a barter transaction, you might trade your old refrigerator in return for a neighbour's second-hand television set. Or, a lawyer writes a will for a doctor in return for a medical examination.

In the broadest sense, the market tries to bring about a response to some offer. The response may be more than simply 'buying' or 'trading' goods and services. A political candidate, for instance, wants a response called 'votes', a church wants 'membership', and a social-action group wants 'idea acceptance'. Marketing consists of actions taken to obtain a desired response from a target audience towards some product, service, idea or other object.

Transaction marketing is part of the larger idea of **relationship marketing**. Beyond creating short-term transactions, smart marketers work at building long-term

Exchange
The act of obtaining a desired object from someone by offering something in return.

Transaction
A trade between two parties that involves at least two things of value, agreed-upon conditions, a time of agreement and a place of agreement.

Relationship marketing
The process of creating, maintaining and enhancing strong, value-laden relationships with customers and other stakeholders.

relationships with valued customers, distributors, dealers and suppliers. They build strong economic and social connections by promising and consistently delivering high-quality products, good service and fair prices. Increasingly, marketing is shifting from trying to maximise the profit on each individual transaction to maximising mutually beneficial relationships with consumers and other parties. In fact, ultimately, a company wants to build a unique company asset called a marketing network. A marketing network consists of the company and all of its supporting stakeholders: customers, employees, suppliers, distributors, retailers, ad agencies, and others with whom it has built mutually profitable business relationships. Increasingly, competition is not between companies but rather between whole networks, with the prize going to the company that has built the best network. The operating principle is simple: build a good network of relationships with key stakeholders, and profits will follow.[6] Chapter 11 will further explore relationship marketing and its role in creating and maintaining customer satisfaction.

markets

Market

The set of all actual and potential buyers of a product or service.

The concepts of exchange and relationships lead to the concept of a market. A **market** is the set of actual and potential buyers of a product. These buyers share a particular need or want that can be satisfied through exchanges and relationships. Thus, the size of a market depends on the number of people who exhibit the need, have resources to engage in exchange, and are willing to offer these resources in exchange for what they want.

Originally the term *market* stood for the place where buyers and sellers gathered to exchange their goods, such as a village square. Economists use the term to refer to a collection of buyers and sellers who transact in a particular product class, as in the housing market or the grain market. Marketers, however, see the sellers as constituting an industry and the buyers as constituting a market. The relationship between the *industry* and the *market* is shown in Figure 1.2. The sellers and the buyers are connected by four flows. The sellers send products, services and communications to the market; in return, they receive money and information. The inner loop shows an exchange of money for goods; the outer loop shows an exchange of information.

Modern economies operate on the principle of division of labour, where each person specialises in producing something, receives payment, and buys needed things with this money. Thus, modern economies abound in markets. Producers go to resource markets (raw material markets, labour markets, money markets), buy resources, turn them into goods and services, and sell them to intermediaries, who sell them to consumers. The consumers sell their labour, for which they receive income to pay for the goods and services they buy. The government is another market that plays several roles. It buys goods from resource, producer and intermediary markets; it pays

Figure 1.2

A simple marketing system

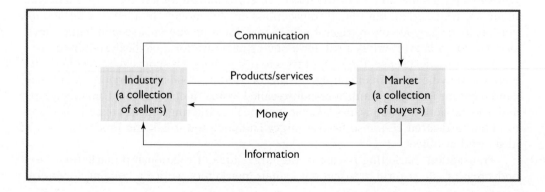

them; it taxes these markets (including consumer markets); and it returns needed public services. Thus each nation's economy and the whole world economy consist of complex interacting sets of markets that are linked through exchange processes.

In advanced societies, markets need not be physical locations where buyers and sellers interact. With modern communications and transportation, a merchant can easily advertise a product on a late evening television programme, take orders from thousands of customers over the phone, and mail the goods to the buyers on the following day without having had any physical contact with them.

marketing

The concept of markets finally brings us full circle to the concept of marketing. Marketing means managing markets to bring about exchanges and relationships for the purpose of creating value and satisfying needs and wants. Thus, we return to our definition of marketing as a process by which individuals and groups obtain what they need and want by creating and exchanging products and value with others.

Exchange processes involve work. Sellers must search for buyers, identify their needs, design good products and services, promote them, and store and deliver them. Activities such as product development, research, communication, distribution, pricing and service are core marketing activities. Although we normally think of marketing as being carried on by sellers, buyers also carry on marketing activities. Consumers do marketing when they search for the goods they need at prices they can afford. Company purchasing agents do marketing when they track down sellers and bargain for good terms. A *sellers' market* is one in which sellers have more power and buyers must be the more active 'marketers'. In a *buyers' market*, buyers have more power and sellers have to be more active 'marketers'.

Figure 1.3 shows the main elements in a modern marketing system. In the usual situation, marketing involves serving a market of end users in the face of competitors. The company and the competitors send their respective products and messages directly to consumers or through marketing intermediaries to the end users. All of the actors in the system are affected by major environmental forces – demographic, economic, physical, technological, political/legal, social/cultural. We will address these forces that affect marketing decisions in Chapter 4.

Each party in the system adds value for the next level. Thus, a company's success depends not only on its own actions, but also on how well the entire value chain serves the needs of final consumers. IKEA, the Swedish furniture retailer, cannot fulfil its promise of low prices unless its suppliers provide merchandise at low costs. Neither can Toyota deliver high quality to car buyers unless its dealers provide outstanding service.

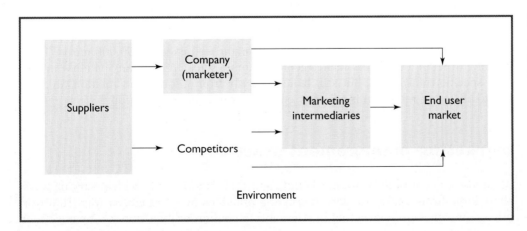

Figure 1.3

Main actors and forces in a modern marketing system

marketing management

Marketing management
The analysis, planning, implementation and control of programmes designed to create, build and maintain beneficial exchanges with target buyers for the purpose of achieving organisational objectives.

We define **marketing management** as the analysis, planning, implementation and control of programmes designed to create, build and maintain beneficial exchanges with target buyers for the purpose of achieving organisational objectives. Thus, marketing management involves managing demand, which in turn involves managing customer relationships.

demand management

Most people think of marketing management as finding enough customers for the company's current output, but this is too limited a view. The organisation has a desired level of demand for its products. At any point in time, there may be no demand, adequate demand, irregular demand or too much demand, and marketing management must find ways to deal with these different demand states. Marketing management is concerned not only with finding and increasing demand, but also with changing or even reducing it.

Demarketing
Marketing to reduce demand temporarily or permanently – the aim is not to destroy demand, but only to reduce or shift it.

For example, Disney World is badly overcrowded in the summertime and restaurants sometimes have trouble meeting demand during peak usage periods. In these and other cases of excess demand, the needed marketing task, called **demarketing**, is to reduce demand temporarily or permanently. The aim of demarketing is not to destroy demand, but only to reduce or shift it. Thus, marketing management seeks to affect the level, timing and nature of demand in a way that helps the organisation achieve its objectives. Simply put, marketing management is *demand management*.

building profitable customer relationships

Managing demand means managing customers. A company's demand comes from two groups: new customers and repeat customers. Traditional marketing theory and practice have focused on attracting new customers and creating transactions – making the sale. In today's marketing environment, however, changing demographic, economic and competitive factors mean that there are fewer new customers to go around. The costs of *attracting* new customers are rising. In fact, it costs five times as much to attract a new customer as it does to keep a current customer satisfied.[7] Thus, although finding new customers remains very important, the emphasis is shifting towards *retaining* profitable customers and building lasting *relationships* with them.

Companies have also discovered that losing a customer means losing not just a single sale, but also a lifetime's worth of purchases and referrals. For example, the *customer lifetime value* of a Ford customer might well exceed 350,000 euros. Thus, working to retain customers makes good economic sense. A company can lose money on a specific transaction, but still benefit greatly from a long-term relationship. The key to customer retention is superior customer value and satisfaction.

marketing management practice

All kinds of organisations use marketing, and they practise it in widely varying ways. Many large firms apply standard marketing practices in a formalised way. However, other companies use marketing in a less formal and orderly fashion. Companies such as Virgin Atlantic Airways and Harley-Davidson achieved success by seemingly breaking all the rules of marketing. Instead of commissioning expensive marketing research, spending huge sums on mass advertising and operating large marketing departments, these companies practised *entrepreneurial marketing*. Their founders, typically, live by their wits. They visualise an opportunity and do what it takes to gain attention. They build a successful organisation by stretching their limited resources, living close to their customers and creating more satisfying solutions to customer needs. Companies such as Virgin Atlantic Airways and Harley-Davidson formed buyers' clubs, used creative public relations and focused on delivering high product quality and winning long-term customer loyalty. It seems that not all marketing must follow in the footsteps of marketing giants such as Procter & Gamble.[8]

However, entrepreneurial marketing often gives way to *formulated marketing*. As small companies achieve success, they inevitably move towards more formulated marketing. They begin to spend more on television advertising in selected markets. They may also expand their sales force and establish a marketing department that carries out market research. They embrace many of the tools used in so-called professionally run marketing companies. Before long, these companies grow to become large and, eventually, mature companies. They get stuck in formulated marketing, poring over the latest Nielsen numbers, scanning market research reports and trying to fine-tune dealer relations and advertising messages. These companies sometimes lose the marketing creativity and passion that they had at the start. They now need to re-establish within their companies the entrepreneurial spirit and actions that made them successful in the first place. They need to practise *intrepreneurial marketing*, that is, to encourage more initiative and 'intrepreneurship' at the local level. Their brand and product managers need to get out of the office, start living with their customers and visualise new and creative ways to add value to their customers' lives.

The bottom line is that effective marketing can take many forms. There will be a constant tension between the formulated side of marketing and the creative side. It is easier to learn the formulated side of marketing, which will occupy most of our attention in this book. But we will also see how real marketing creativity and passion operate in many companies – whether small or large, new or mature – to build and retain success in the marketplace.

marketing management philosophies

We describe marketing management as carrying out tasks to achieve desired exchanges with target markets. What *philosophy* should guide these marketing efforts? What weight should be given to the interests of the organisation, customers and society? Very often these interests conflict. Invariably, the organisation's marketing management philosophy influences the way it approaches its buyers.

There are five alternative concepts under which organisations conduct their marketing activities: the *production*, *product*, *selling*, *marketing* and *societal marketing* concepts.

the production concept

The **production concept** holds that consumers will favour products that are available and highly affordable, and that management should therefore focus on improving production and distribution efficiency. This concept is one of the oldest philosophies that guides sellers.

Production concept
The philosophy that consumers will favour products that are available and highly affordable, and that management should therefore focus on improving production and distribution efficiency.

The production concept is a useful philosophy in two types of situation. The first occurs when the demand for a product exceeds the supply. Here, management should look for ways to increase production. The second situation occurs when the product's cost is too high and improved productivity is needed to bring it down. For example, in the early years of the Ford Motor Company, Henry Ford's whole philosophy was to perfect the production of the Model T so that its cost could be reduced and more people could afford it. He joked about offering people a car of any colour as long as it was black. The company won a big share of the automobile market with this philosophy. However, companies operating under a production philosophy run a big risk of focusing too narrowly on their own operations. After some time, Ford's strategy failed. Although its cars were priced low, customers did not find them very attractive. In its drive to bring down prices, the company lost sight of something else that its customers wanted – namely, *attractive*, affordable vehicles. The gap left by Ford gave rise to new market opportunities which rival General Motors was quick to exploit.

the product concept

Product concept
The idea that consumers will favour products that offer the most quality, performance and features, and that the organisation should therefore devote its energy to making continuous product improvements.

Another important concept guiding sellers, the **product concept**, holds that consumers will favour products that offer the most quality, performance and innovative features, and that an organisation should thus devote energy to making continuous product improvements. Some manufacturers believe that if they can build a better mousetrap, the world will beat a path to their door.[9] But they are often rudely shocked. Buyers may well be looking for a better solution to a mouse problem, but not necessarily for a better mousetrap. The solution might be a chemical spray, an exterminating service or something that works better than a mousetrap. Furthermore, a better mousetrap will not sell unless the manufacturer designs, packages and prices it attractively; places it in convenient distribution channels; and brings it to the attention of people who need it and convinces them that it is a better product. A product orientation leads to obsession with technology because managers believe that technical superiority is the key to business success.

The product concept also can lead to 'marketing myopia'. For instance, railway management once thought that users wanted *trains* rather than *transportation* and overlooked the growing challenge of airlines, buses, trucks and cars. Building bigger and better trains would not satisfy consumers' demand for transportation, but creating other forms of transportation and extending choice would.

the selling concept

Selling concept
The idea that consumers will not buy enough of the organisation's products unless the organisation undertakes a large-scale selling and promotion effort.

Many organisations follow the **selling concept**, which holds that consumers will not buy enough of the organisation's products unless it undertakes a large-scale selling and promotion effort. The concept is typically practised with *unsought goods* – those that buyers do not normally think of buying, such as encyclopaedias and funeral plots. These industries must be good at tracking down prospects and convincing them of product benefits.

The selling concept is also practised in the non-profit area. A political party, for example, will vigorously sell its candidate to voters as a fantastic person for the job. The candidate works hard at selling him or herself – shaking hands, kissing babies, meeting supporters and making speeches. Much money also has to be spent on radio and television advertising, posters and mailings. Candidate flaws are often hidden from the public because the aim is to get the sale, not to worry about consumer satisfaction afterwards.

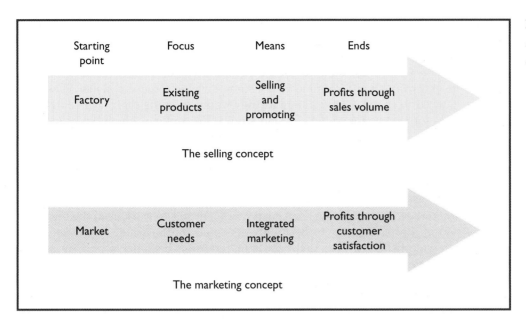

Figure 1.4

The selling and marketing concepts contrasted

Most firms practise the selling concept when they have overcapacity. Their aim is to sell what they make rather than make what the market wants. Such marketing carries high risks. It focuses on creating sales transactions in the short term, rather than on building long-term, profitable relationships with customers. It assumes that customers who are coaxed into buying the product will like it. Or, if they don't like it, they may forget their disappointment and buy it again later. These are usually poor assumptions to make about buyers. Most studies show that dissatisfied customers do not buy again. Worse yet, while the average satisfied customer tells three others about good experiences, the average dissatisfied customer tells ten others of his or her bad experiences.[10]

the marketing concept

The **marketing concept** holds that achieving organisational goals depends on determining the needs and wants of target markets and delivering the desired satisfactions more effectively and efficiently than competitors do.

The selling concept and the marketing concept are frequently confused. Figure 1.4 compares the two concepts. The selling concept takes an *inside-out* perspective. It starts with the factory, focuses on the company's existing products and calls for heavy selling and promotion to obtain profitable sales. It focuses on customer conquest – getting short-term sales with little concern about who buys or why.

In contrast, the marketing concept takes an *outside-in* perspective. It starts with a well-defined market, focuses on customer needs, coordinates all the marketing activities affecting customers and makes profits by creating long-term customer relationships based on customer value and satisfaction. Under the marketing concept, customer focus and value are the paths to sales and profits.

Many successful and well-known global companies have adopted the marketing concept. IKEA, Procter & Gamble, Marriott, Nordström and Wal-Mart follow it faithfully. Toyota, the highly successful Japanese car manufacturer, is also a prime example of an organisation that takes a customer- and marketing-oriented view of its business.

Marketing concept
The marketing management philosophy which holds that achieving organisational goals depends on determining the needs and wants of target markets and delivering the desired satisfactions more effectively and efficiently than competitors do.

Toyota is intent on getting deep into the hearts and minds of its customers, to establish precisely what they want and subsequently find ways to fulfil their wishes. In Japan, Toyota's 14-storey Amlux building, resembling a blue and black striped rocket, attracts millions of visitors. These could be potential customers or people with ideas on how the company should respond to consumers' vehicle requirements. These visitors are allowed to spend as much time as they want designing their own vehicles on computer/TV screens in the vehicle-design studio. Visitors can obtain specific information about the company, its dealers or products. The visitors are also allowed to expound, at length, on what they think Toyota should be doing or making. Meanwhile, Toyota's attentive note-taking staff ensure that the entire Amlux complex is dedicated to involving potential customers who can give them close insights into how their car needs can be satisfied.

In marketing-led organisations, real customer focus has to work from the top down and the bottom up, and it has to be totally accepted by the whole workforce. This organisation-wide belief ensures that customer retention becomes a priority and all staff are committed to building lasting relationships with the customer. To achieve successful implementation of the marketing concept, the organization therefore focuses on how best to tap and channel the knowledge and understanding, the motivation, the inspiration and the imagination of all staff to deliver products and services that meet exactly what the customer requires from the organisation.

Many companies claim to practise the marketing concept, but do not. They have the *forms* of marketing – such as a marketing director, product managers, marketing plans and marketing research – but this does not mean that they are *market-focused* and *customer-driven* companies. The question is whether they are finely tuned to changing customer needs and competitor strategies. Great companies – Philips, Marks & Spencer, IBM – have lost substantial market share in the past because they failed to adjust their marketing strategies to the changing marketplace.

Implementing the marketing concept often means more than simply responding to customers' stated desires and obvious needs. Customer-driven companies research current customers to learn about their desires, gather new product and service ideas and test proposed product improvements. Such customer-driven marketing usually works well when there exists a clear need and when customers know what they want. In many cases, however, customers don't know what they want or even what is possible. Such situations call for *customer-driving* marketing – understanding customer needs even better than customers themselves do, and creating products and services that will meet existing and latent needs now and in the future.

> Customers are notoriously lacking in foresight. Twenty years ago, how many of us were asking for mobile phones, fax machines and copiers at home, cars with on-board navigation systems, hand-held global satellite positioning receivers, cyber-cafés or interactive television shopping networks? As the late Akio Morita, Sony's visionary leader once said: 'Our plan is to lead the public with new products rather than ask them what kinds of products they want. The public does not know what is possible, but we do. So, instead of doing a lot of market research, we refine our thinking on a product and its use and try to create a market for it by educating and communicating with the public.'[11]

Years of hard work are needed to turn a sales-oriented company into a marketing-oriented company. The goal is to build customer satisfaction into the very fabric of the firm. However, the marketing concept does not mean that a company should try to give *all* consumers *everything* they want. The purpose of marketing is not to *maximise* customer satisfaction, but to meet customer needs profitably. Marketers must therefore seek to achieve the very delicate balance between creating more value for customers and making profits for the company.

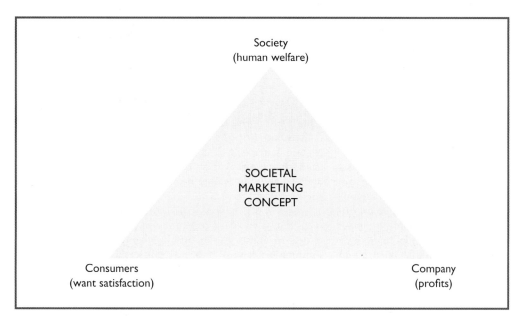

Figure 1.5

Three considerations
underlying the societal
marketing concept

the societal marketing concept

The **societal marketing concept** holds that the organisation should determine the needs, wants and interests of target markets. It should then deliver the desired satisfactions more effectively and efficiently than competitors in a way that maintains or improves the consumer's *and the society's* well-being. The societal marketing concept is the newest of the five marketing management philosophies.

The societal marketing concept questions whether the pure marketing concept is adequate in an age of environmental problems, resource shortages, worldwide economic problems and neglected social services. It asks if the firm that senses, serves and satisfies individual wants is always doing what's best for consumers and society in the long run. According to the societal marketing concept, the pure marketing concept overlooks possible conflicts between short-run consumer *wants* and long-run consumer *welfare*.

Consider the fast-food industry. Most people see today's giant fast-food chains as offering tasty and convenient food at reasonable prices. Yet certain consumer and environmental groups have voiced concerns. Critics point out that hamburgers, fried chicken, French fries and most other foods sold by fast-food restaurants are high in fat and salt. The products are wrapped in convenient packaging, but this leads to waste and pollution. Thus, in satisfying consumer wants, the highly successful fast-food chains may be harming consumer health and causing environmental problems.

Such concerns and conflicts led to the societal marketing concept. As Figure 1.5 shows, the societal marketing concept calls upon marketers to balance three considerations in setting their marketing policies: company profits, consumer wants and society's interests. Originally, most companies based their marketing decisions largely on short-run company profit. Eventually, they began to recognise the long-run importance of satisfying consumer wants, and the marketing concept emerged. Now many companies are beginning to think of society's interests when making their marketing decisions.

Increasingly, firms also have to meet the expectations of society as a whole. For example, society expects businesses genuinely to uphold basic ethical and environmental standards. Not only should they have ethics and environmental policies, they must also back these with actions (see Marketing Highlight 1.1).

Societal marketing concept
The idea that the organisation should determine the needs, wants and interests of target markets and deliver the desired satisfactions more effectively and efficiently than competitors in a way that maintains or improves the consumer's and society's well-being.

marketing highlight 1.1

The citizen brands

Consumer activism and government vigilance in monitoring the impact of business on society are on the rise. Many companies, particularly the very large ones, are having to reflect a greater sense of corporate responsibility, ensuring that they are readily accountable to consumers, employees, shareholders and society at large. Corporate citizenship is cast as a new model for today's businesses. Many companies are thinking hard about how to build and maintain strong *citizen* brands. Companies whose business strategies include corporate citizenship activities will realise their investment in the form of reinforcement of brand values and enhanced customer loyalty.

This is what London's Capital Radio, with a long history of corporate citizenship, believe will sustain the popularity of their brand. Capital Radio, launched over two decades ago, offered a service to the community through help-lines, flat-share and support services. Partnering their *citizen* brand – *Capital* – in doing good is *Floodlight*, an education publication which is a market leader in the further education and part-time education directories market. Capital Radio and a sister station, Capital Gold, run commercials which encourage listeners to pick up a copy of the publication. The idea behind the publication was to help listeners advance themselves through education.

Other companies are addressing the need to build social, including employee, welfare and ethical considerations into their business practices. Berated by activists in the past, big sporting goods firm Nike sees it as part of its corporate mission to raise standards within the company and in countries where it operates. For example, Nike has absorbed much of the cost incurred in raising the minimum wage paid to local workers by its Indonesian supplier-factories in 1999. The company would like to see its factories be places where workers' health actually improves, through better education and care, and where the status of women is raised.

Oil company Shell suffered two blows to its reputation in 1995. One was from its attempt to dispose of the Brent Spar oil rig in the North Sea, and the other over its failure to oppose the Nigerian government's execution of Ken Saro-Wiwa, a human-rights activist in a part of Nigeria where Shell had extensive operations. Since then, the company has rewritten its business principles and created an elaborate mechanism to implement them.

Coca-Cola has recently embarked on a £670m (€1,099m) five-year programme to promote diversity in efforts to address problems highlighted by a race discrimination lawsuit lodged against the firm in 1999. The programme, applauded by analysts and civil rights groups, will double the amount Coke invested in enterprises owned by ethnic minorities and women over the next five years, to $160m a year. The company is also addressing areas where minority groups can participate in the bottling system. It is spending some $50m to expand its community partnership programmes with urban communities. Inside the company, management is also compelled to work harder to maintain equality of treatment and opportunities for ethnic minorities and female workers.

The trend towards corporate citizenship is further illustrated by NatWest Bank's *Community Bond*. A NatWest customer makes a contribution (a loan) and becomes a bond-holder. The money funds charitable projects. The loan is repaid to the bond-holder who can choose a lower rate of return, triggering a donation from NatWest to a network of regional charitable loan funds. The NatWest Community Bond creates 'social capital' for the brand. It helps the bank to promote and sustain relationships with its customers and partners in the charity sector. And, by aligning corporate and community values, it gives NatWest status as a citizen brand.

SOURCES: 'Doing well by doing good', *The Economist* (22 April 2000), pp. 83–6; Linda Bishop, 'The corporate citizen', *Marketing Business* (April 2000), pp. 16–9; Betty Liu, 'Coca-Cola launches £670m push to promote diversity', *Financial Times* (Wednesday 17 May 2000), p. 25; also see: Wally Ollins, Trading identities: why countries and companies are taking on each other's roles, which is available from the Foreign Policy Centre at www.fpc.org.uk, and visit www.un.org/partners/business for further information.

marketing challenges in the new 'connected' millennium

As the world spins into the first decade of the twenty-first century, dramatic changes are occurring in the world of marketing. Business pundits and politicians are referring to a new economy (see Marketing Highlight 1.2) within which firms have to think afresh about their marketing objectives and practices. Rapid changes can quickly make yesterday's winning strategies out of date. As management thought-leader Peter Drucker once observed, a company's winning formula for the last decade will probably be its undoing in the next decade. The rapid pace of change means that the firm's ability to change will become a competitive advantage.

The major marketing developments as we enter the new millennium can be summed up in a single theme: *connectedness*. Now, more than ever before, we are all connected to each other and to things near and far in the world around us. Moreover, we are connecting in new and different ways. Where it once took weeks to travel across Europe, we can now travel around the globe in days, even hours. Where it once took days or even weeks to receive news about important world events, we now see them as they are occurring through live satellite broadcasts. Where it once took days to correspond with others in distant places, they are now only moments away by phone or the Internet. In this section, we examine the major trends and forces that are changing the marketing landscape and challenging marketing strategy in this new, connected millennium. As shown in Figure 1.6 and discussed in the following pages, sweeping

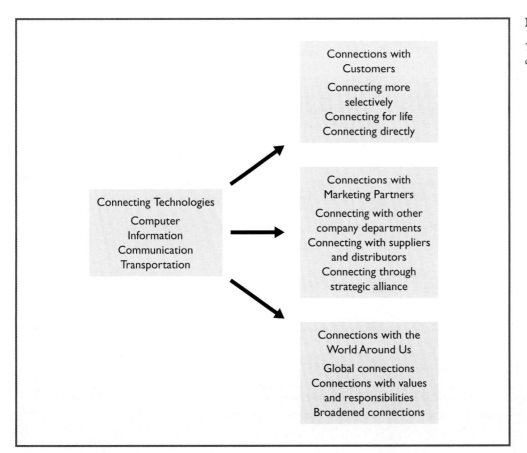

Figure 1.6

Today's marketing connections

marketing highlight 1.2

A new Europe's dawning

Western Europe's material prosperity has soared more in the past 250 years than in the previous 1,000 (see Exhibit 1), thanks to industrialisation. Arguably, this remarkable phenomenon may not live on forever, given that the frontiers of technology and science are moving closer. Or, natural or man-made environmental disasters may intervene. Nonetheless, scientific progress today seems certain to continue, harnessing technological progress which, in turn, sustains economic growth and improves living standards. For example, America's recent economic 'miracle' – rapid growth, subdued inflation and low unemployment – has been attributed to the information technology revolution. As the new century dawns, will western Europe also partake of a 'new economy' and, if so, what is the shape of things to come?

Knowledge? Service? E-conomy? M-economy?

Business pundits and politicians say that our countries' economic welfare will increasingly rely on wealth creation in knowledge-based, high value-added industries, such as computing, software and telecommunications, and those employing highly skilled workers, such as finance and education. Many talk about the 'knowledge economy', driven by sky-rocketing investment in knowledge. Witness the acceleration in the number of patents filed in the last decade. Thanks to landmark legal battles, businesses across Europe and the US can now patent a raft of new areas of technology, from biotechnology,

genes and financial services, to consulting, software, business methods and the Internet.

Rough-and-ready measures used by the OECD to gauge knowledge investment show that Sweden, which currently spends 3.85 per cent of GDP on R&D, tops the international league table, followed by Finland (just under 3.0 per cent), then Japan (2.92 per cent) and the US (2.79 per cent). Switzerland, Germany, France, Netherlands, Denmark and Britain all spent more than the EU average (1.83 per cent). Combining spending on R&D, investment in software and both public and private spending on education, Sweden tops the list again, with an investment reaching 10.6 per cent of its GDP, followed by France (10.0 per cent), Britain (8.3 per cent) and the US (8.0 per cent). Japan's investment of 6.6 per cent is puny compared to the EU's average spend of just under 8.0 per cent of GDP. Moreover, the EU's burgeoning knowledge economy is evident from the 48.6 per cent of *total* business output accounted for by knowledge-based industries.

Notwithstanding the inevitable imperfections in definitions and measurements, the OECD suggests that the proportion of business R&D spending accounted for by services rose nearly five-fold to 19.5 per cent over the past two decades. Moreover, nearly 20 per cent of global trade is now in services, rather than manufactured goods. According to the World Trade Organisation [WTO], global exports of commercial services totalled $1.30 trillion in 1999, of which the EU accounts for some 40 per cent, compared to

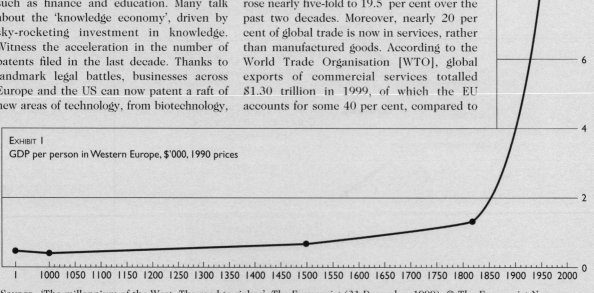

EXHIBIT 1
GDP per person in Western Europe, $'000, 1990 prices

SOURCE: 'The millennium of the West. The road to riches', *The Economist* (31 December 1999). © The Economist Newspaper Ltd., London.

the US with a 19.0 per cent share. Western Europe seems to be advancing not only towards a knowledge, but an increasingly dominant service, economy.

What of the Internet and 'E'-conomy? Although western European firms are increasing their investment in information technology (IT), the EU, with current investment of nearly 5.5 per cent of GDP on IT, lags behind America, which spends 8.0 per cent of GDP. The US also has five times as many people per 1,000 population with access to the Internet. With some exceptions (e.g. Finland), e-commerce is currently less developed in Europe. However, the region as a whole is ahead of the US in 'wireless technology'. With a much higher use of mobile phones, which are touted to become the most widely used link to the Internet, M (mobile)-commerce is expected to flourish.

To reap the benefits of the E- or M-economy, EU politicians are having to make far-reaching structural, tax, labour market and capital market reforms. These will create flexible, open and efficient markets where business entrepreneurship and innovation can flourish. Europe is changing for that matter. The euro, introduced in January 1999, creates a big single capital market, facilitating business's efforts to raise money for investment. *Slowly*, things are moving in the right direction: tax cuts in Germany, France and the Netherlands; deregulation of industries, such as utilities and telecommunications; and countries like Spain are making their labour markets more flexible.

Just how much the EU is changing is also evident in the recent merger and acquisition boom. These totalled $1.3 trillion (€1.46 trillion) in 1999 alone, a rise of 50 per cent over 1998. Of these, half were cross-border deals. Striking deals include the mega-merger between Pearson, the UK's media group, CLT-Ufa, the pan-European broadcaster, owned jointly by Bertelsmann, the German media group, and Audiofina, a Belgian holding company. Hostile takeovers, once taboo, have also recently succeeded in Italian telecommunications and insurance, French banking and energy. Britain's VodafoneAirTouch's hostile, and successful, $190 billion bid for the German Mannesman in 2000 was hailed as the biggest, most visible testimony of rising 'shareholder power that promises to remake European capitalism'.

Many forces are working together to direct the EU's business revolution. From the Internet and information technology, to the pressures for restructuring and deregulation, responsive countries and businesses will emerge the winners. Call it what we like – knowledge, service, E- or M- economy, Europe's economic transformation may hope to yield a capitalism that is more transparent, efficient and, most importantly, more rewarding for all that partake in it.

Sources: 'Wo ist Goldilocks?', *The Economist* (5 February 2000), pp. 95–6; 'Post-Fordism', *The Economist* (29 April 2000), p. 31; 'Trade in services', *The Economist* (29 April 2000), p. 131; 'Toiling from there to here', *The Economist* (31 December 1999), p. 28; 'The road to riches', *The Economist* (31 December 1999), pp. 10–12; 'Knowledge gap', *The Economist* (16 October 1999), pp. 142 and 145; 'Research and development', *The Economist* (28 August 1999), p. 89; 'Patent wars', *The Economist* (8 April 2000), pp. 95–9; 'Who owns the knowledge economy?', *The Economist* (8 April 2000), p. 19; 'Internet Economics: a thinkers' guide', *The Economist* (1 April 2000), pp. 77–9; James Harding, 'Pearson set for £12bn TV deal', *Financial Times* (Friday 7 April 2000), p. 23.

changes in connecting technologies are causing marketers to redefine how they are connecting with the marketplace – with their customers, with marketing partners inside and outside the company and the world around them. We first examine the dramatic changes that are occurring in the connecting technologies. Then, we look at how these changes are affecting marketing connections.

technologies for connecting

The major force behind the new connectedness is technology. Explosive advances in computer, telecommunications and information, transportation and other connecting technologies have had a major impact on the way companies bring value to their customers. The technology boom has created exciting new ways to learn about and track customers, create products and services tailored to meet customer needs, distribute products more efficiently and effectively, and communicate with customers in large groups or one-to-one. For example, through videoconferencing, marketing researchers at a company's headquarters in London can look in on focus groups in New York or Paris without ever stepping on to a plane. With only a few clicks of a mouse button, a direct marketer can tap into online data services to learn anything from what car you

The Internet and wireless technologies are paving the way for a new model for doing business. Orange used this ad to promote Wirefree™ working allowing employees in a company to keep in touch wherever they are.

SOURCE: Orange

drive to what you read to what flavour of ice cream you prefer. Consider also the rapidly changing face of personal selling. Many companies now equip their salespeople with the latest sales automation tools, including the capacity to produce individualised multimedia presentations and to develop customised market offerings contracts. Many buyers now prefer to meet salespeople on their computer screens rather than in the office. An increasing amount of personal selling is occurring through videoconferences or live Internet presentations, where buyers and sellers can interact across great distances without the time, costs or delays of travel.

Using today's vastly more powerful computers, marketers create detailed databases and use them to target individual customers with offers designed to meet their specific needs and buying patterns. With a new wave of communication and advertising tools – ranging from cell phones, fax machines and CD-ROMs to interactive TV, video kiosks, Internet access stations at hotels, airports and retail outlets – marketers can zero in on selected customers with carefully targeted messages. Through electronic commerce, customers are increasingly able to design, order and pay for products and services – all without ever leaving home. Then, through the marvels of express delivery, they can receive their purchases in less than 24 hours.

the internet

Internet (the Net)
A vast global computer network that enables computers, with the right software and a modem (a telecommunications device that sends data across telephone lines), to be linked together so that their users can obtain or share information and interact with other users.

Perhaps the most dramatic new technology driving the connected age is the **Internet,** a vast and burgeoning global web of computer networks, with no central management or ownership. It was created during the late 1960s by the US Department of Defense, initially to link government labs, contractors and military installations. Today, the Internet links computer users of all types around the world. Anyone with a PC, a modem and the right software – or a TV with a set-top 'Web box' – can browse the Internet to obtain or share information on almost any subject and to interact with other users.[12] However, technology is not standing still. Advances in digital, mobile phone technology mean that mobile phones may become the most widely used apparatus to link to the Internet. Particularly in Europe, which leads in wireless technology, there is a much higher use of mobile phones, thanks to its adoption of a single standard for them. Finland, home of Nokia, the world's most successful mobile-phone manufacturer, has the highest ownership of mobile phones in the world, at some 63 per cent of the population.[13]

The Internet has been hailed as the technology behind a new model for doing business. It allows anytime, anywhere connections to information, entertainment and communication. Companies are using the Internet to link employees in remote offices, distribute sales information more quickly, build closer relationships with customers and suppliers, and sell and distribute their products more efficiently and effectively. They are rapidly converting from '*snail mail*' and the telephone to the *Internet* (connecting with customers), *intranets* (connecting with others in the company) and *extranets* (connecting with strategic marketing partners, suppliers and dealers). Beyond competing in traditional *marketplaces*, they now have access to exciting new *marketspaces*.

Internet usage surged in the 1990s with the development of the user-friendly World Wide Web. The US leads with its Internet population growing from around 40 million users in 1997 to more than 100 million today; it will grow to a projected 170 million users by 2003. Lagging behind is the European Union (EU), with fewer than half as many Internet hosts per 1,000 inhabitants as in the US. According to Forrester Research, Internet adoption in western Europe will double from 33.6 million in 2000 to 60 million users by 2003. Fast catching up, however, are the newly industrialising Asian 'tigers', where the Internet population is forecast to grow explosively, rising from the current 40 million to over 200 million, overtaking America, by 2003.[14] The Internet is truly a global phenomenon.

Analysts project that, worldwide, Internet-based or e-commerce will grow from $657 billion in 2000 to over $6,789 billion in 2004. In western Europe, the e-commerce market is forecast to reach 600 trillion euros by 2003.[15] It would seem that almost every business, from small start-ups to established giants, is racing to explore and exploit the Web's possibilities for marketing, shopping and browsing for information. This cyber race has even spawned a whole new industry of Net incubators – companies that help to 'breed' Internet start-up firms by providing the latter with seed capital, management and accounting skills, personnel and legal advice, in exchange for equity. Examples include Idealab, based near Los Angeles, the first Internet incubator started in 1996, Speed Ventures in Sweden, and Dawnay, Day Lander (DDL) in the UK.

However, for all its potential, the Internet does have drawbacks. It is yet to be seen how many of the millions of Web browsers will become actual buyers. Although the value of a website is difficult to measure, the reality is that few companies have made much money from their Internet efforts. According to one analyst, Michael Whitaker, chief executive of internet 'incubator' NewMedia Spark, more than 70 per cent of current Internet-related companies will go out of business within two years.[16] (See Marketing Highlight 1.3.)

The Web also poses security problems. Companies that link their internal computer networks to the outside world expose their systems to possible attacks by vandals. Similarly, consumers are wary about sending credit card account numbers or other confidential information that may be intercepted in cyberspace and misused. Finally, using the Web can be costly. For companies to make the most of the Internet, they must invest heavily in leased telephone lines, powerful computers and other technologies and Internet specialists.

However, given the lightning speed at which Internet technology and applications are developing, it's unlikely that these drawbacks will deter the millions of businesses and consumers who are logging on to the Net each day. Thus, marketers have to stay in touch and respond appropriately to the changes in connecting technologies which are providing exciting new opportunities for their company. We will examine these developments in connecting technologies and implications for marketing management more fully in Chapter 22. Next, we look briefly at the ways these changes are affecting how companies connect with their customers, marketing partners and the world around us.

marketing highlight 1.3

Bye-Bye! Boo-Boo?

Boo.com was launched in January 1999 in a blaze of publicity hailing it as one of the rising stars of the European Internet scene. Its founders, two attractive Swedes – Ernst Malmsten, a former book critic, and Kajsa Leander, a former model – had drawn up an audacious business plan to create a leading global retailer of trendy sportswear that would be at the technological cutting edge. The plan was to launch in 18 countries simultaneously, supported by some $135 million (€152 million) which the founders had successfully raised from distinguished names such as Groupe Arnault, the French entrepreneur, the Benetton family and J.P. Morgan, the US investment bank. The company was certainly seen as one of the highest profile and best-funded Internet start-ups in Europe. Its founders even posed on the cover of *Fortune* magazine.

But, on 17 May 2000, Boo.com called in KPMG to liquidate the business, which was on the verge of bankruptcy after investors refused to pump in more money. Boo had exhausted all but $500,000 of the venture capital funding it had raised since early 1999. Thanks to Fashionmall.com, a New York-based online fashion portal, Boo.com's brand name may live on: the fashion portal bought the failed sportswear retailer's brand and Internet domain from the liquidators, pledging to position Boo as the ultimate global fashion portal. The technology side of Boo.com was concurrently sold to Bright Station, a software and e-business company, for £250,000 (€410,000).

Boo became Europe's first big Internet casualty. Its demise coincided with other high-profile business-to-consumer Internet downfalls – not least World Online, the Dutch Internet service provider, and Lastminute.com, the UK-based e-tailer, who have seen their share prices plunge recently, amidst anxieties concerning the immaturity of the European Internet sector and the shortcomings of those running Europe's so-called new economy.

Boo's collapse has been attributed to a combination of poor financial controls, insufficient good management and too much ambition. Dogged by technical problems, its website was launched five months late, but the company had no revenues to offset these costs. About $6 million were spent on spring/summer fashionwear, which was unfashionable by the time the site was launched (in November) and had to be heavily discounted! The company was burning $1 million a week, spending on maintaining a technologically innovative platform, costly marketing and paying expensive salaries to its 400 employees across 18 countries.

In January 2000, Mr Malmsten realised that Boo had to cut costs, but its investors were becoming concerned as Boo's valuation started to suffer. For Boo, time and money was fast running out.

Boo's early collapse shows that the Internet is not the magic money machine that some investors think. However, it does not herald a general, insurmountable malaise for all such dotcoms. There are stark lessons to be learnt. Like most start-ups that do get to profitability, financial controls must be in place to avoid going bust on the way. It may be important to spend to get big, but start-ups have to pay attention to good management of their inventory and cost control. While seeking to be bold and spend to stay in front of the pack, founders must also be wary of the difficulty of executing marketing in this *space*. Online flair must be matched by conventional, offline business skills! While it looks like it may not be bye-bye forever to Boo, let the lessons from Europe's first big e-tailing flop be a lasting legacy for the many more dotcoms to follow.

SOURCE: Thorold Barker and Caroline Daniel, 'Boo.com collapses as investors refuse funds', *Financial Times* (18 May 2000), p. 1 and 'Boo ends with a bang as the money runs out', *Financial Times* (18 May 2000), p. 28; 'Dotcom boo-boo', *Financial Times* (18 May 2000), p. 24; Thorold Barker, Caroline Daniel and Anna Minton, 'Mideast backers are big losers in Boo.com failure', *Financial Times* (19 May 2000), p. 1; Caroline Daniel and Thorold Barker, 'Boo's next', *Financial Times* (19 May 2000), p. 26; 'Tech stocks suffer heavy falls', *Financial Times* (20/21 May 2000), p. 1; 'On the last minutes of Boo.com', *Financial Times* (20/21 May 2000), p. 2. Also based on 'Is the future grim for e-trading?', discussed in the discussion forum at www.ft.com, May 2000; Thorold Barker, 'US portal's pledge on Boo', *Financial Times* (2 June 2000), p. 26 and 'Beyond the grave', *Connectis* (October 2000) Issue 5, pp. 42–5.

connections with customers

The most profound new developments in marketing involve the ways in which today's companies are connecting with their customers. Yesterday's companies focused on mass marketing to all customers at arm's length. Today's companies are selecting their customers more carefully and building more lasting and direct relationships with these carefully targeted customers.

■ Connecting with more carefully selected customers

Few firms today practise true mass marketing – selling in a standardised way to any customer who comes along. The EU – in fact, the world – resembles a 'salad bowl' of diverse cultural, social, ethnic and locational groups. The EU is far from representing a homogeneous marketplace. There is increasing pressure on firms within member countries to adjust to evolving deregulation and the trend is towards more universal trading conditions within the single market. The notion of nationally separate markets is vaporising, but only very slowly. On the one hand, customers across the EU, and the globe, maintain diversity by keeping and valuing important differences. On the other, customers themselves are also connecting in new ways to form specific 'consumer communities', in which buyers connect with each other by common interests, situations and activities.

Greater diversity and these new consumer connections have meant greater market fragmentation. In response, most firms have moved from mass marketing to segmented marketing, in which they target carefully chosen sub-markets or even individual buyers. 'One-to-one marketing' has become the order of the day for some marketers. They build extensive customer databases containing rich information on individual customer preferences and purchases. Then, they mine these databases to gain segment and customer insights by which they can 'mass-customise' their offerings to deliver greater value to individual buyers.

At the same time that companies are finding imaginative, new ways to deliver more value *to* customers, however, they are also beginning to assess carefully the value *of* customers to the firm. They want to connect only with customers that they can serve *profitably*. Once they identify profitable customers, firms can create attractive offers and special handling to capture these customers and earn their loyalty.

■ Connecting for a customer's lifetime

At the same time that companies are being more selective about which customers they choose to serve, they are serving those they choose in a deeper, more lasting way. In the past, many companies have focused on finding *new customers* for their products and closing *sales* with them. In recent years, this focus has shifted towards keeping *current customers* and building lasting *relationships* based on superior customer satisfaction and value. Increasingly, the goal is shifting from making a profit on each sale to making long-term profits by managing the lifetime value of a customer.

In turn, as businesses do a better and better job of keeping old customers, competitors find it increasingly difficult to acquire new customers. As a result, marketers now spend less time figuring out how to increase 'share of market' and more time trying to grow 'share of customer'. They offer greater variety to current customers and train employees to cross-sell and up-sell in order to market more products and services to existing customers. For example, Amazon.com began as an online bookseller, but now offers music, videos, gifts, toys, consumer electronics and even an online auction as well, increasing per-customer sales. In addition, based on each customer's purchase history, the company recommends related books, CDs or videos that might be of interest. In this way, Amazon.com captures a greater share of each customer's leisure and entertainment budget.

■ Connecting directly

Today, beyond connecting more deeply, many companies are also taking advantage of new technologies that let them connect more *directly* with their customers. In fact, direct marketing is booming. Virtually all products are now available without going to a store – by telephone, mail-order catalogues, kiosks and electronic commerce. Customers surfing the Internet can view pictures of almost any product, read the specs, shop among online vendors for the best prices and terms, speak with online vendors' shopping consultants and even place and pay for their orders – all with only a few mouse clicks. Business-to-business (B2B) purchasing over the Internet has increased even faster than online consumer buying. Business purchasing agents routinely shop on the Web for items ranging from standard office supplies to high-priced, high-tech computer equipment.

Some companies sell *only* via direct channels – firms such as Direct Line (a household and motor insurance company), Dell Computer and Amazon.com, to name only a few. Other companies use direct connections as a supplement to their other communications and distribution channels. For example, companies such as Lever Brothers and Procter & Gamble (P&G) sell packaged consumer products through retailers, supported by heavy spending on mass-media advertising. However, these companies also use their www.com websites to build relationships with consumers by providing information and advice on a host of product and consumption-related issues.

Direct marketing is redefining the buyer's role in connecting with sellers. Instead of being the targets of a company's one-way marketing efforts, customers have now become active participants in shaping the marketing offer and process. Many companies now let customers design their own desired products online. For example, shoppers at the Lands' End site (www.LandsEnd.com) can build a 'personal model' with their own hair colour, height and shape. They then visit an online dressing room, where they can try clothes on the model to see how they would look in them. The site also gives buyers tips on how best to dress given their individual body styles.

Some marketers have hailed direct marketing as the 'marketing model of the next millennium'. They envisage a day when all buying and selling will involve direct connections between companies and their customers. Others, while agreeing that direct marketing will play a growing and important role, see it as not a substitute, but just one more way to approach the marketplace. We will examine the exploding world of direct marketing in more detail in Chapter 22.

connections with marketing's partners

In these ever more connected times, major changes are occurring in how marketers connect with others inside and outside the company to bring greater value jointly to customers.

■ Connecting inside the company

Traditionally, marketers have played the role of intermediary, charged with understanding customer needs and representing the customer to different company departments, which then acted upon these needs. The old thinking was that marketing is done only by marketing, sales, and customer support people. However, in today's connected world, every functional area can interact with customers, especially electronically. Marketing no longer has sole ownership of customer interactions. The new thinking is that every employee must be customer-focused.

Today's forward-looking companies are reorganising their operations to align them better with customer needs. Rather than letting each department pursue its own objectives, firms are linking all departments and forming cross-functional customer teams in the cause of creating customer value.

Here, Atlas Commerce offers software products that link the entire supply chain, helping firms to reduce inventories and improve process efficiency.

SOURCE: Atlas Commerce

■ Connecting with outside partners

Rapid changes are also occurring in how marketers connect with their suppliers, channel partners and even competitors. Most companies today are networked companies, relying heavily on partnerships with other firms.

Supply chain management Marketing channels consist of distributors, retailers and others who connect the company to its buyers. The *supply chain* describes a longer channel, stretching from raw materials to components to final products that are carried to final buyers. For example, the supply chain for personal computers consists of suppliers of computer chips and other components, the computer manufacturer, and the distributors, retailers and others who sell the computers to businesses and final customers. Each member of the supply chain creates and captures only a portion of the total value generated by the supply chain.

Through *supply chain management*, many companies today are strengthening their connections with partners all along the supply chain. They recognise that their fortunes rest not just on how well they perform, but also on how well their entire supply chain performs against competitors' supply chains. Rather than treating suppliers as vendors and distributors as customers, it treats both as partners in delivering value to consumers. For example, suppliers like Nestlé, Lever Brothers, Danone and Procter & Gamble are working with supermarkets to streamline logistics and reduce joint distribution costs, resulting in lower prices to consumers. Car manufacturers such as Toyota, Ford and Mercedes-Benz, on the one hand, have to work closely with carefully selected suppliers to ensure quality and operations efficiency. On the other hand, they have to work with their franchise dealers to provide top-grade sales and service support that will bring customers through the door and keep them coming back.

Airline companies have joined forces with the aim of delivering superior value to target customers, as reflected in this ad.

Source: Star Alliance. *Agency:* Y and R Europe

Strategic alliances Beyond managing the supply chain, today's companies are also discovering that they need *strategic* partners if they hope to be effective. In the new global environment, with greater competition from more and more products and choices, going it alone is going out of style. *Strategic alliances* are gaining importance across the entire spectrum of industries and services. Smart companies are forming strategic alliances with customers, suppliers and other partners. They are replacing *go-it-alone* strategies with *do-it-together* strategies. Reliance on partnering means leveraging the strengths of a business partner to create more value and build more sales than either company could do alone. Large companies often count on technological breakthroughs from tiny focused partners who, in turn, need large partners to reach international markets and build credibility. Every search for ways to build sales should include a search for partners who can help reach that goal faster.[17]

Many strategic alliances take the form of *marketing alliances*. These may be *product* or *service alliances* in which one company licenses another to produce its product, or two companies jointly market their complementary products. For instance, toy manufacturer Lego joined with Microsoft to co-design, co-manufacture, and co-market new digital toys. Through *promotional alliances*, one company agrees to join in a promotion for another company's product or service. For example, McDonald's teamed up with Ty to offer an incredibly successful Beanie Babies promotion for its value meals. Companies may form *logistics alliances* in which one company offers distribution services for another company's product. One example of how distribution partnerships can help to expand market reach is the recent tie-up between Yahoo! and the BBC's Internet news service, News Online.

BBC's news content will be carried by Yahoo! The venture brings together two of the key drivers in web development – content and portal – and two of the most respected brands in the world – the BBC and Yahoo! Given Yahoo! UK and Ireland enjoys over 253 million page views per month, compared to the 75 million viewers who visit the BBC News Online, the venture will certainly help to raise BBC News reach, enabling the BBC to make its online news service more accessible. At the same time, Yahoo! will be fed stories on the UK and world news, politics, business, science, technology and sport, with the service updated every five minutes. Yahoo! has also agreed to keep pages hosting BBC news advertising-free in order to uphold the corporation's public service status and editorial independence. Deals with commercial partners are believed to be crucial to the BBC if it were to survive in the face of new competition. For Yahoo!, an internal spokesperson acknowledges that it reflects continual progress in the firm's commitment to provide Yahoo! customers with quality, independent content and two of the strongest brands on the web.[18]

Finally, one or more companies may join in special *pricing alliances*, as when hotel and rental car companies join forces to offer mutual price discounts.[19]

connections with the world around us

Beyond redefining their relationships with customers and partners, marketers are taking a fresh look at the ways in which they connect with the broader world around them. Here we look at trends towards increasing globalisation, more concern for social environmental responsibility and greater use of marketing by non-profit and public-sector organisations.

■ Global connections

In an increasingly *smaller* world, many marketers are now connected *globally* with their customers and marketing partners. The world economy has undergone radical change during the past two decades. Geographical and cultural distances have shrunk with the advent of jumbo-jet planes, global computer and telephone hook-ups, world television satellite and cable broadcasts and other technical advances. This has allowed companies to greatly expand their geographical market coverage, purchasing and manufacturing. The result is a vastly more complex marketing environment for both companies and consumers.

Today, almost every company, large or small, is touched in some way by global competition – from the neighbourhood florist that buys its flowers from local nurseries to the electronics firm that competes in the home market with giant multinational rivals; from the fledgling Internet retailer that finds itself receiving orders from all over the world to the large consumer goods producer that introduces new products into emerging markets abroad. European firms have been challenged at home by the skilful marketing of new entrants from the US, Japan and other Asian countries. Similarly, European companies in a wide range of industries have found new opportunities abroad, challenging their overseas rivals in their home territories. Many companies are moving aggressively to take advantage of international marketing opportunities. Nestlé, Asea Brown Boveri, IKEA, Philips and many others have sought to develop global operations, making and selling their products or services worldwide. Notable success cases include Nokia, a dominant player in the global mobile-phone market, and the German media group Bertelsmann, which has become the number two operator and a powerhouse in what is regarded as one of the world's most challenging markets – the US music industry.

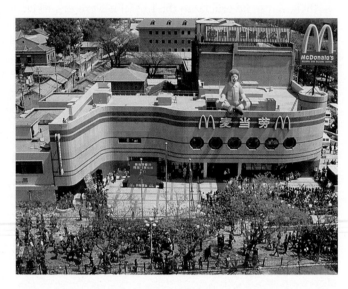

Looking for growth, McDonald's repeats its phenomenal success abroad, here in the world's largest McDonald's restaurant in Beijing.

Source: (left) © Jeffrey Aaronson/Network Aspen; (right) Kees/Sygma

Today, companies are not only trying to sell more of their locally produced goods in international markets; they are also buying more components and supplies abroad. Increasingly, international firms have to coordinate functional operations across borders and to increase efficiency. Consequently, many domestically purchased goods and services are 'hybrids', with design, material purchases, manufacturing and marketing taking place in several countries. For example, a fashion clothing designer in France may choose cloth woven from Swiss cotton with designs printed in Italy. She designs a dress and sends the drawing online to a Hong Kong agent, who will place the order with a Chinese factory in Macau. Finished dresses will be air-freighted to London, New York and other major cities, where they will be redistributed to boutiques and department stores around the world. Luxury cars are another case in point.

Thus managers in countries around the world are increasingly taking a global, not just local, view of the company's industry, competition and opportunities. They are asking: What is global marketing? How does it differ from domestic marketing? How do global competitors and forces affect our business? To what extent should we 'go global'? Many companies are forming strategic alliances with foreign companies, even competitors, who serve as suppliers or marketing partners. Winning companies in the decade ahead may well be those that have built the best global networks. We will examine global marketing management issues in greater detail in Chapter 5.

■ Connections with our values and social responsibilities

Marketing managers are re-examining their connections with social values and responsibilities and with the very earth that sustains us. As the worldwide consumerism and environmentalism movements mature, today's marketers are compelled to take greater responsibility for the social and environmental impact of their actions. Corporate ethics has become a hot topic in almost every business arena, from the corporate boardroom to the business school classroom. In addition, few companies can ignore the renewed and very demanding environmental movement. In the former Eastern bloc and many Asian countries, air, water and soil pollution has added to our environmental concerns. These and other governments across the world must consider how to handle such problems as the destruction of rainforests, global warming, endangered species and other environmental threats. The pressure is on businesses to 'clean up' our environment. In the future, companies will be held to an increasingly high standard of environmental responsibility in their marketing and manufacturing activities.[20]

Some companies may continue to resist the ethics and environmental movements, budging only when forced by legislation or consumer outcries. More forward-looking companies, however, readily accept their responsibilities to the world around them. They view socially responsible actions as an opportunity to do well by doing good and to profit by serving the best long-term interests of their customers and communities. Some businesses, such as Ben & Jerry (recently acquired by Unilever), The Body Shop and others, are practising 'caring capitalism'. They build social responsibility and action into their company value and mission statements. For example, Ben & Jerry's mission statement challenges all employees, from top management to ice-cream scoopers in each store, to include concern for individual and community welfare in their day-to-day decisions.[21]

In Chapter 2 we will take a closer look at marketing ethics and social responsibility.

■ Broadening connections

More and more different kinds of organisations are using marketing to connect with customers and other important constituencies. In the past, marketing has been most widely applied in the business sector. In recent years, however, marketing also has become a major component in the strategies of many non-profit organisations. Consider the following examples:

> Faced with the daunting task of selling the single currency to European citizens, many of whom appeared disturbed by the economic sacrifices involved, the European Commission turned to marketing and media experts to develop a strategy to promote the 'euro'. Pan-European advertising campaigns were also launched to reinforce national initiatives to influence public opinion in favour of replacing national currencies.[22]

> To stem the falling number of church-goers, many of Britain's church groups are seeking more effective ways to attract members and maintain financial support. Increasingly, and despite the controversy, preachers are using the press, television and radio to advertise religion to the general public. They are conducting marketing research to better understand member needs and are redesigning their 'service offerings' accordingly. Some evangelical groups even have their own radio and television stations. The Vatican has also employed advertising agencies such as Saatchi and Saatchi to run television campaigns to promote its cause.[23]

> Over the past decade, many charities have moved on from tin-rattling and tombolas to employing some of the most sophisticated marketing tools, to win support for their causes. For example, the Royal Society for the Protection of Birds (RSPB) is Europe's largest wildlife conservation charity, dealing with issues as wide-ranging as biodiversity, protection of wildlife sites, and marine life. The charity has run awareness advertising campaigns to attract new members and uses direct marketing activity to reinforce its communications with its target market.

Charities such as the NSPCC (National Society for the Prevention of Cruelty to Children) also use marketing techniques to raise public awareness of, and their support for, their work.

SOURCE: NSPCC. *Photographer*: Matt. Harris

Many long-standing non-profit organisations – the YMCA, the Red Cross, the Salvation Army, the Girl Scouts – are modernising their missions and 'products' to attract more members and donors.[24]

Finally, government agencies also practise marketing. Some have designed *social marketing campaigns* to encourage energy conservation and concern for the environment, or to discourage smoking, excessive drinking and drug use.[25]

The continued growth of non-profit and public sector marketing presents new and exciting challenges for marketing managers.

the new connected world of marketing

So, today, smart marketers of all kinds are taking advantage of new opportunities for connecting with their customers, marketing partners and the world around them. Table 1.1 compares the old marketing thinking to the new. The old thinking saw marketing as little more than selling and advertising. It viewed marketing as customer acquisition rather than customer nurturing and care. It emphasised trying to make a profit on each sale rather than trying to profit by managing customer lifetime value. And it concerned itself with trying to sell products rather than to understand, create, communicate and deliver real value to customers.

Fortunately, this old marketing thinking is now giving way to newer ways of thinking. Today, smart marketing companies are improving their customer knowledge and customer connections. They are targeting profitable customers, then finding innovative ways to capture and keep these customers. They are forming more direct connections

The old marketing thinking	The new marketing thinking
Connections with customers	
Be sales and product centred	Be market and customer centred
Practise mass marketing	Target selected market segments or individuals
Focus on products and sales	Focus on customer satisfaction and value
Make sales to customers	Develop customer relationships
Get new customers	Keep old customers
Grow share of market	Grow share of customer
Serve any customer	Serve profitable customers, 'fire' losing ones
Communicate through mass media	Connect with customers directly
Make standardised products	Develop customised products
Connections with marketing partners	
Leave customer satisfaction and value to sales and marketing	Enlist all departments in the cause of customer satisfaction and value
Go it alone	Partner with other firms
Connections with the world around us	
Market locally	Market locally *and* globally
Assume profit responsibility	Assume social and environmental responsibility
Market for profits	Market for non-profits
Conduct commerce in market*places*	Conduct e-commerce in market*spaces*

Table 1.1 Marketing connections in transition

with customers and building lasting customer relationships. They are using more targeted media and integrating their marketing communications to deliver meaningful and consistent messages through every customer contact. They are employing more technologies such as videoconferencing, sales automation software and the Internet, intranets and extranets. They see their suppliers and distributors as partners, not adversaries. In sum, they are forming new kinds of connections for delivering superior value to their customers.

We will explore all of these developments in more detail in future pages. For now, we must recognise that marketing will continue to change dramatically in the twenty-first century. The new millennium offers many exciting opportunities for forward-thinking marketers.

summary

Today's successful companies – whether large or small, for-profit or non-profit, domestic or global – share a strong focus and a heavy commitment to marketing. Many people think of marketing as only selling or advertising. But marketing combines many activities – marketing research, product development, distribution, pricing, advertising, personal selling and others – designed to sense, serve and satisfy consumer needs while meeting the organisation's goals. Marketing seeks to attract new customers by promising superior value, and to keep current customers by delivering satisfaction.

We defined marketing as *a social and managerial process by which individuals and groups obtain what they need and want through creating and exchanging products and value with others*. The core concepts of marketing are *needs*, *wants* and *demands*; *products* and *services*; *value, satisfaction* and *quality*; *exchange, transactions* and *relationships*; and *markets*. Wants are the form assumed by human needs when shaped by culture and individual personality. When backed by buying power, wants become demands. People satisfy their needs, wants and demands with products and services. A product is anything that can be offered to a market to satisfy a need, want or demand. Products also include services and other entities such as persons, places, organisations, activities and ideas.

We explained the relationships between customer value, satisfaction and quality. In deciding which products and services to buy, consumers rely on their perception of relative value. *Customer value* is the difference between the values the customer gains from owning and using a product and the costs of obtaining and using the product. *Customer satisfaction* depends on a product's perceived performance in delivering value relative to a buyer's expectations. Customer satisfaction is closely linked to *quality*, leading many companies to adopt *total quality management (TQM)* practices. Marketing occurs when people satisfy their needs, wants and demands through exchange. Beyond creating short-term exchanges, marketers need to build long-term relationships with valued customers, distributors, dealers and suppliers.

We then defined marketing management and examined how marketers manage demand and build profitable customer relationships. *Marketing management* is the analysis, planning, implementation and control of programmes designed to create, build and maintain beneficial exchanges with target buyers for the purpose of achieving organisational objectives. Marketing is at times also concerned with changing or even reducing demand. Beyond designing strategies to *attract* new customers and create *transactions* with them, today's companies are focusing on *retaining* current customers and building lasting relationships through offering superior customer value and satisfaction.

The five marketing management philosophies were compared. The *production concept* holds that consumers favour products that are available and highly affordable; management's task is to improve production efficiency and bring down prices. The *product concept* holds that consumers favour products that offer the most quality, performance and innovative features; thus, little promotional effort is required. The *selling concept* holds that consumers will not buy enough of the organisation's products unless it undertakes a large-scale selling and promotion effort. The *marketing concept* holds that achieving organisational goals depends on determining the needs and wants of target markets and delivering the desired satisfactions more effectively and efficiently than competitors do. The *societal marketing concept* holds that the company should determine the needs, wants and interests of target markets. Generating customer satisfaction *and* long-run societal well-being are the keys to achieving both the company's goals and its responsibilities.

Finally, dramatic changes in the marketplace create opportunities and challenges for marketers. Major marketing developments can be summed up in a single theme: *connections*. The explosive growth in connecting technologies – computer, telecommunications, information, wireless and transportation technologies – has created exciting new ways for marketers to learn about and serve consumers, in large groups or one-to-one. Marketers are redefining how they connect with their customers, with their marketing partners and with the world around them. They are choosing their customers more carefully and developing closer, more direct, and more lasting connections with them. They are also connecting more closely with other company departments and other firms in an integrated effort to bring more value to customers. They are taking a fresh look at the ways in which they connect with the broader world, resulting in increased globalisation, growing attention to social and environmental responsibilities, and greater use of marketing by non-profit and public-sector organisations. The new, connected millennium offers exciting possibilities for forward-thinking marketers.

discussing the issues

1. Discuss why you should study marketing.

2. As the preview case implies, the marketing efforts of organisations seek to fulfil consumer needs. How genuine are the needs targeted by Nike's marketing efforts? Critically evaluate the role that marketing plays in satisfying human desires.

3. What is the single biggest difference between the marketing concept and the production, product and selling concepts? Which concepts are easiest to apply in the short run? Which concept can offer the best long-term success?

4. Using practical examples, discuss the key challenges facing companies in the twenty-first century. What actions might marketers take to ensure they continue to survive and thrive in the new connected world of marketing?

5. According to economist Milton Friedman, 'Few trends could so thoroughly undermine the very foundations of our free society as the acceptance by corporate officials of a social responsibility other than to make as much money for their stockholders as possible.' Do you agree or disagree with Friedman's statement? What are some drawbacks of the societal marketing concept?

applying the concepts

1. Go to McDonald's and order a meal. Note the questions you are asked, and observe how special orders are handled. Next go to a restaurant on your college or university campus and order a meal. Note the questions you are asked here, and observe whether special orders are handled the same way as they are at McDonald's.

    ✦ Did you observe any significant differences in how orders are handled?

    ✦ Consider the differences you saw. Do you think the restaurants have different marketing management philosophies? Which is closest to the marketing concept? Is one closer to the selling or production concept?

    ✦ What are the advantages of closely following the marketing concept? Are there any disadvantages?

2. Take a trip to a shopping mall. Find the directory sign. List five major categories of store, such as department stores, shoe stores, bookstores, women's clothing shops and so forth. List the competing stores in each category, walk past them and quickly observe their merchandise and style. Look at the public

spaces of the mall, and note how they are decorated. Watch the shoppers in the mall.

    ✦ Are the competing stores really unique, or could one pretty much substitute for another? What does this say about the overall goals that the mall is fulfilling?

    ✦ Consider the attitudes of the shoppers you saw. Did some apparently find shopping a pleasure, while others found it a bother?

    ✦ A major goal for marketing is to maximise consumer satisfaction. Discuss the extent to which the mall serves this goal.

Now, take a trip to an electronic mall of your choice.

    ✦ Note the categories of merchandise and store layout and comment on the overall goals that the mall is fulfilling. What are the major differences between a traditional and electronic mall?

    ✦ To what extent is the shopping experience similar or different across the traditional and online shopping environment?

    ✦ Contrast the ways in which the two mall formats seek to maximise consumer satisfaction.

references

1. Linda Himelstein, 'The swoosh heard "round the world"', *Business Week* (12 May 1997), p. 76; Bill Saporito, 'Can Nike get unstuck?', *Time* (30 March 1998), pp. 48–53; Jolie Solomon, 'When cool goes cold', *Newsweek* (30 March 1998), pp. 36–7; Jerry Edgerton, 'Can Nike still play above the Rim?' *Money* (May 1999), p. 48; Nicholas Moss, 'Shoe giants are caught on the hop', *The European* (30 March–5 April 1998), p. 24; John Wyatt, 'Is it time to jump on Nike?', *Fortune* (26 May 1997), pp. 185–6; Patrick Harverson, 'Showing a clean pair of heels', *Financial Times* (17/18 January 1998), p. 6; Patricia Sellers,

'Four reasons Nike's not cool', *Fortune* (30 March 1998), pp. 26–7; Ore Beaverton, 'Nike battles backlash from overseas sweatshops', *Marketing News* (9 November 1999), p. 14; Uta Harnischfeger, 'Adidas reports sharp nine-month profit fall', *Financial Times* (3 November 2000), p. 28; 'Thanks, Mike: Phil Knight on Michael Jordan's retirement', Nike press release, www.nikebiz.com (13 January 1999); and Nike's Web page at www.nike.com (September 1999).

2. Peter F. Drucker, *Management: Tasks, responsibilities, practices* (New York: Harper & Row, 1973), pp. 64–5.

3. Here are some other definitions: 'Marketing is the performance of business activities that direct the flow of goods and services from producer to consumer or user.' 'Marketing is selling goods that don't come back to people that do.' 'Marketing is getting the right goods and services to the right people at the right place at the right time at the right price with the right communication and promotion.' 'Marketing is the creation and delivery of a standard of living.' 'Marketing is the creation of time, place and possession utilities.' The American Marketing Association approved the definition: 'Marketing is the process of planning and executing the conception, pricing, promotion, and distribution of ideas, goods, and services to create exchanges that satisfy individual and organisational objectives.' As you can see, there is no single, universally agreed definition of marketing. There are definitions that emphasise marketing as a process, a concept or philosophy of business, or an orientation. The diversity of views adopted by authors is reflected in the wide selection of marketing definitions in common use. See Barbara R. Lewis and Dale Littler, 'The Blackwell Encyclopaedic Dictionary of Marketing', *Reference Reviews*, **12**, 4 (1998), p. 18.

4. See Theodore Levitt's classic article, 'Marketing myopia', *Harvard Business Review* (July–August 1960), pp. 45–56; Dhananjayan Kashyap, 'Marketing myopia revisited: a look through the "colored glass of a client"', *Marketing and Research Today* (August 1996), pp. 197–201; Colin Grant, 'Theodore Levitt's marketing myopia', *Journal of Business Ethics* (February 1999), pp. 397–406.

5. Richard A. Spreng, Scott B. MacKenzie and Richard W. Olshavsky, 'A reexamination of the determinants of customer satisfaction', *Journal of Marketing* (July 1996), pp. 15–32; Banwari Mittal and Walfried M. Lassar, 'Why do customers switch? The dynamics of satisfaction versus loyalty', *Journal of Services Marketing*, **12**, 3 (1998), pp. 177–94; Subhash Sharma, Ronald W. Niedrich and Greg Dobbins, 'A framework for monitoring customer satisfaction', *Industrial Marketing Management* (May 1999), pp. 231–43.

6. See James C. Anderson, Hakan Hakansson and Jan Johanson, 'Dyadic business relationships within a business network context', *Journal of Marketing* (October 1994), pp. 1–15. For more discussion of relationship marketing, see Thomas W. Gruen, 'Relationship marketing: the route to marketing efficiency and effectiveness', *Business Horizons* (November–December 1997), pp. 32–8 and John V. Petrof, 'Relationship marketing: the emperor in used clothes', *Business Horizons* (March–April 1998), pp. 79–82.

7. For more on assessing customer value, see Thomas O. Jones and W. Earl Sasser, 'Why satisfied customers defect', *Harvard Business Review* (November–December 1995), pp. 88–99; Paul D. Berger, 'Customer lifetime value: marketing models and applications', *Journal of Interactive Marketing* (Winter 1998), pp. 17–30; and Libby Estell, 'This call center accelerates sales', *Sales & Marketing Management* (February 1999), p. 72.

8. Sam Hill and Glenn Rifkin, *Radical Marketing* (New York: Harper Business, 1999).

9. Ralph Waldo Emerson offered this advice: 'If a man . . . makes a better mousetrap . . . the world will beat a path to his door.' Several companies, however, have built better mousetraps yet failed. One was a laser mousetrap costing $1,500. Contrary to popular assumptions, people do not automatically learn about new products, believe product claims, or willingly pay higher prices.

10. Barry Farber and Joyce Wycoff, 'Customer service: evolution and revolution', *Sales and Marketing Management* (May 1991), p. 47.

11. Gary Hamel and C.K. Prahalad, 'Seeing the future first', *Fortune* (5 September 1994), pp. 64–70. Also see Philip Kotler, *Kotler on Marketing* (New York: Free Press, 1999), pp. 20–4.

12. For more on the basics of using the Internet, see Raymond D. Frost and Judy Strauss, *The Internet: A new marketing tool* (Upper Saddle River, NJ: Prentice Hall, 1997). Also see Malcolm McDonald and Hugh Wilson, *e-Marketing: Improving marketing effectiveness in a digital world* (Harlow: Pearson Education, 1999).

13. 'A survey of telecommunications: The world in your pocket', *The Economist* (9 October 1999); 'Wo ist Goldilocks?', *The Economist* (5 February 2000), pp. 95–6.

14. Amy Cortese, 'A census in cyberspace', *Business Week* (5 May 1997), p. 84. For the most recent statistics, check the results of an ongoing survey of Internet usage conducted by CommerceNet and Nielsen Media Research, www.commerce.net/nielsen/; 'The tiger and the tech', *The Economist* (5 February 2000), pp. 91–3.

15. Internet usage and buying statistics provided by Forrester Research, 2000-05-05. Also see: Kim Benjamin, 'Internet technologies grow in Europe', *e.Business* (February 2000), pp. 17–18.

16. Thorold Barker and Caroline Daniel, 'Boo.com collapses as investors refuse funds', *Financial Times* (18 May 2000), p. 1.

17. Philip Kotler, *Kotler on Marketing* (New York: Free Press, 1999), p. 20.

18. Andrew Ward, 'Yahoo! in deal to carry news from the BBC', *Financial Times* (16 May 2000), p. 32.

19. Rosabeth Moss Kanter, 'Why collaborate?', *Executive Excellence* (April 1999), p. 8; and Philip Kotler, *Marketing Management: Analysis, planning, implementation, and control* (Upper Saddle River, NJ: Prentice Hall, 2000), p. 82. For more on strategic alliances, see Peter Lorange and Johan Roos, *Strategic Alliances: Formation, implementation and evolution* (Cambridge, MA: Blackwell, 1992); Frederick E. Webster, Jr, 'The changing role of marketing in the corporation', *Journal of Marketing* (October 1992), pp. 1–17; and Gabor Gari, 'Leveraging the rewards of strategic alliances', *The Journal of Business Strategy* (April 1999), pp. 40–3.

20. Stuart L. Hart, 'Beyond greening: strategies for a sustainable world', *Harvard Business Review* (January–February 1997), pp. 67–76.

21. See Ben & Jerry's full mission statement online at www.benjerry.com. For more reading, see Stuart L. Hart, 'Beyond greening: strategies for a sustainable world', *Harvard Business Review* (January–February 1997), pp. 67–76.

22. Victor Smart, 'Brussels ask admen how to sell the euro', *The European* (18–24 January 1996), p. 1.

23. Martin Wroe, 'Ministries, missions and markets', *Marketing Business* (October 1993), pp. 8–11; Peter Mullen, 'The intoxication of belief', *The Guardian* (20 May 1995), p. 18.

24. For more examples, see Philip Kotler and Karen Fox, *Strategic Marketing for Educational Institutions*, 5th edn (Upper Saddle River, NJ: Prentice Hall, 1995); Norman Shawchuck, Philip Kotler, Bruce Wren and Gustav Rath, *Marketing for Congregations: Choosing to serve people more effectively* (Nashville, TN: Abingdon Press, 1993); Joanne Scheff and Philip Kotler, 'How the arts can prosper', *Harvard Business Review* (January–February 1996), pp. 56–62; George Pitcher, 'God help those who confuse advertising and PR disasters', *Marketing Week*, **21**, 44 (1999), p. 33.

25. Philip Kotler and Eduardo Roberto, *Social Marketing: Strategies for changing public behaviour* (New York: Free Press, 1990).

case 1

KitKat: Have a break . . .

Sylvie Laforet* and Andy Hirst**

SONIA NG SAT DOWN TO HAVE a cup of tea with her friend, David Johnson, in the company's dimly lit canteen in York, England. She unwrapped the bright red paper band from a KitKat, then ran a finger down the foil between the two biscuits. She snapped the biscuits apart, handed one to David and sighed: 'This KitKat is not going to be like any I have eaten before.' As a new assistant brand manager, Sonia had to prepare the brand plan for KitKat. It was a great break for her as KitKat was the company's top confectionery brand. Her first action was to gather what information she could about the brand, then talk to managers who knew about it.

Rowntree launched KitKat in August 1935 as 'Chocolate Crisp'. Renamed twice – in 1937 as 'KitKat Chocolate Crisp' and in 1949 as 'KitKat' – by 1950 it was Rowntree's biggest brand and it has remained so ever since. The name KitKat has favourable onomatopoeic qualities that help the association of the wafer biscuit with a dry, soft snapping or cracking, as of the biscuit being broken or bitten. Other Rowntree brands include Rowntree's Fruit Pastilles (launched 1881), Rowntree's Fruit Gums (1893), Black Magic (1933), Aero (1935), Dairy Box (1936), Smarties (1937), Polo (1948) and After Eight (1962).

Rowntree is a large exporter of chocolate and sugar confectionery, selling to over 120 countries. The most important markets are Europe and the Middle East. Besides the UK, the European markets include France, Germany, Belgium, Holland, Italy and Ireland. The chocolate biscuit countline (CBCL) market is not as large in the rest of Europe as it is in the UK. The

* Research Associate, Birmingham University, Birmingham, UK
** Research Associate, Loughborough University Business School, Loughborough, UK.

proportions of KitKat volume sales are 67 per cent for the UK, 10.6 for Germany and 5.6 for France. And over the last decade overseas markets have grown by more than 50 per cent.

Net operating profits, return on capital employed (ROCE) and market shares drive the company. Each product group has objectives. The company has a cascade system so that each brand has its objectives as well. Each has a brand plan – business plans for each brand. One of the strategic objectives is to increase sales across the European markets. Often the marketing managers are not always able to put in capital to supply across Europe. To do this the company has a penetration strategy, which means that the margins are lower and this has a depressing effect on the group's ROCE.

The company's long-term aims are to become the clear leader in the UK confectionery industry and to generate real growth in the profitability and productivity of its confectionery business. It also aims to increase the efficiency of its supply chain and so improve customer service.

Business strategy

The company's strategy is to pursue the company's objectives rather than to defend its position against competitors. For example, some countlines are 'below threshold size'. The objective for these is to improve the performance up to the threshold level. Rod Flint, the director of J. Walter Thompson, which is responsible for KitKat's advertising, comments: 'Their objective is not always driven by the stock market. They are highly global in their approach now, since they are also organising their European marketing department.'

Basic principles drive the company's brand strategy. It believes in offering the consumer value for money. It also believes in developing long-term brands and aims to differentiate its products from one another within the brand portfolio, which the company thinks will offer a competitive advantage over those of its competitors. The company works to ensure that its brands maintain clear positions in order to prevent cannibalisation. Up to now, the best way to achieve this has been stand-alone product brands, as opposed to umbrella brands. More recently, however, the cost of establishing new brands has increased very dramatically. The company is continually looking for ways to leverage the brand across the confectionery business and other product categories. Part of the company's brand policy is also to dedicate significant sums of money to advertising and promotions. This helps to build customer loyalty and block the entrance of new competitors. On average, 10 per cent of the sales value of the brand goes on advertising and promotions.

KitKat

When launched, KitKat entered a market already dominated by Cadbury's Dairy Milk. From its beginning, KitKat was positioned as both a confectionery and a snack. It is now positioned halfway between a snack and an indulgence. In the consumers' eyes, however, KitKat is essentially a snack product and its slogan 'Have a break, have a KitKat' is widely known through long-running ads on TV and in other media.

The KitKat brand has two formats in the UK. The two-finger format is bought in multipack (packs of eight or more) at large grocers by parents for their children. In contrast, the four-finger format is bought individually by 16–24-year-olds for their consumption (Exhibit 1.1). The two-finger format's £112m (€184m) annual sales is part of the £535m per annum CBCL sector whose sales are for non-personal and 'family' consumption, as well as for snack and kids' consumption. The four-finger format is part of the £1,865m per annum general chocolate

Exhibit 1.1 CBCL competitor performance

Manufacturer	% share	% change year on year
Rowntree	25.3	−2.6
United Biscuits	17.4	−15.7
Jacobs Bakery	12.0	−1.5
Mars Confectionery	3.3	−14.0
Burtons	7.1	−14.3
Thomas Tunnocks	3.8	−3.5
Fox's	7.8	51.8
Others	5.7	3.6
Cadbury	2.2	n/a
Private label	15.3	25.6
Total market		0.9

Source: AGB Superpanel.

countline sector whose products are for personal consumption, broad usage and the 'adults' and 'self-eats' categories. The four-finger format was the main volume format, but its £96m sales have been overtaken by the two-finger format as the grocery sector rose at the expense of the CTNs (confectioner/tobacconist/newsagent). About 18 per cent of KitKat two-finger's volume goes through cash-and-carry to CTN, compared with 80 per cent of the four-finger format.

The company divides the chocolate market into three categories: chocolate box assortments (a gift-oriented marketplace), the countline market (a 'self-eat' market, i.e. KitKat four-finger) and CBCL, a sector that the company created. KitKat is marketed as a countline product in its four-finger format and as a CBCL in its two-finger format. This helped KitKat cover two sections in stores, one selling confectionery and the other selling biscuits.

The reason for the promotion of KitKat as a CBCL is the growing power of the multiple grocers (Exhibit 1.2). There has been a shift from a less structured retail sector into multiple businesses that are sophisticated and powerful. The company produces different packs for the multiple grocers and the independent sector. This avoids direct price and value comparison by the consumer and, therefore, restricts the power of the multiple retailers in their negotiations to increase their profitability.

KitKat two-finger is market leader with 19.5 per cent of the CBCL market (Exhibit 1.3). KitKat's nearest competitors are Mars Bars and Twix, both Mars' products. Twix was launched as a countline product, but is now marketed as single fingers in the multipack format in the CBCL category. KitKat two-finger's main CBCL competitors are United Biscuits and Jacobs; in the general chocolate countline category, KitKat four-finger's main competitors are Mars and Cadbury.

The market

The chocolate confectionery market is concentrated, stable and very competitive. The leading suppliers are Cadbury (28 per cent market share), Rowntree (25), Mars (21) and Terry's Suchard (5). KitKat has the biggest advertising expenditure in the UK confectionery market.

Exhibit 1.2 KitKat sales by pack and sector: tonnes (change over last five years)

	2-finger			4-finger	
	Singles	Multipacks	Other	Singles	Multipacks
Multiple retail	50 (0%)	21,200 (13%)	50 (−50%)	1,900 (6%)	3,600 (31%)
Wholesale/independent	650 (−41%)	1,950 (−2%)	50 (−75%)	13,950 (15%)	150 (−40%)

Sources: Internal.

Exhibit 1.3 CBCL brand performance

	% SHARE (EXPENDITURE)	% CHANGE (YEAR ON YEAR)
KitKat 2-finger	19.5	2.5
Penguin	8.8	7.4
Club	9.0	−7.7
Twix	3.3	−13.6
Rocky	4.1	159.3
Blue Riband	2.7	−4.0
Breakaway	2.7	−7.9
Wagon Wheel	4.7	−15.3
Tunnocks CW	3.4	−2.1
Classic	2.4	−11.2
Trio	2.2	−5.3
Private label	15.3	25.6

Source: AGB Superpanel.

Exhibit 1.4 Countline brand performance

	% SHARE (EXPENDITURE)	% CHANGE (YEAR ON YEAR)
Mars Bar	13.9	0.8
Snickers	7.5	−0.3
KitKat 4-finger	6.7	−0.1
Twix	4.9	0
Twirl	3.3	−0.2
Time Out	2.7	−0.3
Drifter	1.3	0

Source: AC Nielsen (countlines and filled blocks excluding CBCL multis).

The £1.5 billion confectionery snack market, including countlines and chocolate blocks, is 38 per cent of the confectionery market. This market has grown by 20 per cent over the past five years, following the rise in popularity of snacking. Growth in both the countline market and the CBCL sector has now stabilised. As market leader, KitKat has retained a price premium and set prices for its competitors to follow. There is a risk to volume if the market does not follow. The market share for KitKat four-finger was 7 per cent of the general countline market. KitKat four-finger had lost some of its market share to Mars Bar (Exhibit 1.4) and is a weak no. 3, competing with three strong Mars products: Mars bars, Twix and Snickers.

New-product development, which fuelled countline growth, has seen a number of new entrants. Firstly, the CBCL market has seen the entrance of Fox's Rocky bar. Rocky has claimed 4.1 per cent of the market. Cadbury has made the second major new-product development. It launched the Fuse bar – a mixture of chocolate, fudge and raisins. It cost £7 million to create, sold 40 million bars in its first week and was becoming the second most popular chocolate bar in the UK.

Pressure will continue to be on the countline market as the population of 15–24-year-olds declines. The KitKat two-finger sales are biased towards the C1 and C2 socio-economic and the 35–44 age groups. There is also a high penetration of very young consumers, particularly in the 12–15 age group. The four-finger format has a smarter image, inclines more towards 'chocolate occasions' consumption, and is consumed on the street. Consumption is heavily biased towards female buyers. The two-finger format ads aim at the 35–44-year-olds through morning television. Children are not specifically targeted. The four-finger format ads target the 16–24-year-olds through TV and youth press. The ad strategy for this format is different from that of the two-finger. The company puts an emphasis on updating KitKat's brand image by making it appeal to the younger generation through advertising in trendy and young people's magazines and independent radio.

The promotions for the two-finger format are value- and grocery-trade-oriented (for example, 'one bar free' activity, or repeat purchase incentives). For the four-finger format, the promotions are different because of the different segments targeted (for example, 1p off). However, there is an annual pan-promotion for KitKat as a whole that consists of big promotions, price and emphasis on brand awareness. There is a price differentiation between the two formats. KitKat four-finger is 'twin-priced' in parallel with Twix, and 2p below the Mars Bar. This is because KitKat is 'snacky' and not as hunger satisfying as the Mars Bar. If the company deviated from this pricing strategy, its volume share might drop. The two-finger format is not as price-sensitive as the four-finger. As a market leader within the CBCL category, it can more or less dictate price. Thus its competitor Penguin is priced 2p below KitKat two-finger. According to KitKat's brand managers, 'The objective for KitKat is to maintain customer loyalty by being innovative, and to remain *the* number one UK confectionery brand.' There is evidence of relative brand loyalty for KitKat. However, people who buy KitKat two-finger will also be likely to buy other brands, such as Classic, Club Orange, Penguin, Twix, Blue Riband and Gold. According to Brian Ford, the brand manager for the KitKat two-finger: 'Although they have tried to differentiate the two formats of KitKat in its segmentation and positioning strategies, the consumer sees no difference in the total brand.'

In light of the recent developments, KitKat has worked hard to maintain its position as the market leader. When KitKat Orange was launched as a limited edition, the first flavour variant in its 59-year history, the success of the product was so phenomenal that customers were writing letters to have the product re-released. A second new mint variant has been even more popular in trials.

Competition

Competition is likely to come from small brands, grocery retailers' own labels and other lines coming into the UK. There is also a crossover between the chocolate countline and the CBCL sector. Cadbury has recently encroached into KitKat's 'Have a break' territory with Time Out – a bar aimed at the CBCL sector. Time Out aims to bridge the gap between chocolate snack bars, such as Twirl, and wafer-based snacks, such as KitKat. It will compete with KitKat and Twix and should take sales away from brands with a 'heavy sweet' product image, like Spira and Twix.

Competition from other European confectioners has intensified with the growth of discounters such as Aldi and Netto. This might lead to a price-cutting war in the multiple grocery sector, especially among KwikSave, Lo-Cost and Asda. Aldi is a particular concern because it is importing bags of KitKat minis from Germany. Although Rowntree sells many of its countlines as minis, it does not make or sell KitKat in that format. Besides losing it revenue, Aldi's KitKat minis cause other problems: first, large grocers, like Sainsbury and Tesco, now want supplies of minis like Aldi's; second, the biscuit and chocolate used to make the German KitKat are distinctly different from those used in Britain.

Outside the UK, the four-finger format sells more than the two-finger format. European retailers outside the UK also emphasise minis (Aldi imports only that form). Rowntree does sell minis in the UK, but these are very low-volume products and appear only in variety packs with other minis. The company does not see them as a threat to its existing brands as the volume of minis is relatively low in comparison.

The company is now producing to capacity. The problem is managing demand in the marketplace. 'We can't give them any more, so we use price to limit demand and to get maximum profit return on the amount we produce', explains Ford. In his opinion, this is easier for the two-finger format because it is the market leader in the CBCL category, but is less easy in the four-finger case. 'It is not the market leader in the chocolate countline sector, therefore we cannot dictate price.'

Brand pressures

For generations Rowntree had succeeded in the marketplace by making highly differentiated products that the competition found hard to copy. This contrasted with Mars whose products were strong brands but easy to make. Recently the company's confidence had been battered by the failure of Secret, a countline that used a new process to spin chocolate threads round a caramel core. After two new production lines were built and the product heavily advertised using a highly atmospheric campaign based on a Secret Agent theme, the product failed in the marketplace and proved too expensive to make. As a failure, the Secret story came very close to the flop of an equally differentiated Savanna, a pyramid-shaped boxed chocolate, that had occurred a few years earlier. The company had also failed in their launch of the Italian market-leading boxed chocolate Baci on to the UK market. Targeted head-on against the successful Ferrero Rocher chocolates and given a powerful Italian theme (Verdi . . . Ferrari . . . Baci), customers had stuck to the established brand.

Following the failures, the new product emphasis had shifted to levering existing brands rather than developing new ones. One idea was to follow Mars' lead and launch a KitKat iced confectionery. Another was to launch KitKat Chunky, a thick, single finger of KitKat about the size of a Snickers bar. This would be a 'hunger satisfier' like Mars' market-leading countlines.

To fit the regulations across Europe, some KitKats produced have different chocolate from others. Although they taste different, most consumers cannot tell the difference. The management of so many internationally important brands limits the company's freedom of action outside the UK. The pricing relationships between, say, France, Germany and the UK need careful controlling. At the same time, the company needs to achieve its UK business objectives. The marketing of brands will be different because these brands are at different product life-cycle states in different markets. 'The UK is probably the most sophisticated confectionery market in Europe', claims Robertson. 'Therefore, for example, the company's advertising style for KitKat is not directly transferable to Germany. The German consumer does not understand the British sense of humour', explains Robertson. 'So, from the business perspective, there is a pulling together in Europe, while from the consumer perspective, there are still marked differences between different types of consumers, and that is the biggest problem.'

The packing used for KitKat in the UK is different from that used elsewhere. So KitKat exported to Germany does not have UK packaging and vice versa. Germany's KitKat is flow-wrapped, whereas the UK has a foil and band. This relatively expensive format appeared because of the early competition with Cadbury, whose market-leading milk chocolate bars had blue foil and a blue wrapper. To differentiate it from Cadbury, the KitKat pack is a silver foil with a visually strong red band wrapped end to end.

Standardisation to less expensive flow wrap had been resisted in the UK because of the ritualistic way that UK consumers eat KitKat. Often they eat KitKat socially over a cup of tea. When eating KitKat, many consumers first take off the red wrapper, then run a finger down the foil between two biscuits. With the top of the foil broken, the KitKat fingers are snapped off and then eaten one by one, just as KitKat's new assistant brand manager, Sonia Ng, did. Her job was to develop a brand plan for KitKat while the whole tradition of KitKat was being challenged. After a series of product failures top management had decided to revitalise the business by:

◆ focusing more on major brands, reducing the overall brand portfolio;

◆ using existing brands for innovation where possible;

◆ making sure that much more emphasis went into meeting customers' expectations, through improving performance versus price;

◆ boosting trade cooperation and becoming more category focused.

KitKat was one of five brands identified for innovation. After years of relatively minor development of KitKat, a senior product manager and the ad agency had 'dug out ideas from the drawers'. Among them was KitKat Chunky. In the past, barriers to its introduction had been centred on the company's view of what the brand stood for, with a great emphasis on the physical format and packaging of the product. As Sonia ritualistically consumed her KitKat she pondered that her new job was a great break, but not an easy one.

Questions

1. Has KitKat taken a marketing-oriented approach to developing its confectionery brand? What elements of marketing orientation, if any, are missing?

2. What is the situation facing KitKat: the strengths and weaknesses of the brand and the opportunities and threats it faces?

3. How and why are the KitKat two-fingers and four-fingers marketed differently?

4. What are the barriers to the brand's standardisation across Europe and should the company now move towards standardising its brand and packaging across Europe?

5. How would you describe the organisational structure of the company and its marketing department? In what alternative ways could the company organise the management of its wide range of confectionery?

6. Should the launch of KitKat Chunky be once again rejected?

SOURCES: Prepared with assistance from: the advertising agency J. Walter Thompson, London; Nestlé Rowntree, York; and Nestec, Vevey, Switzerland and reference to Nicholas Whitaker, *Sweet Talk: A secret history of confectionery* (Victor Gollancz, London, 1988); Kamran Kashani (ed.), *A Virtuous Cycle: Innovation, consumer value, and communication* (European Brands Association, London, 2000) and kitkat.co.uk; names, statistics and some details have been changed for commercial reasons.

internet exercises

Internet exercises for this chapter can be found on the student site of the MYPHLIP Web Site at www.booksites.net/kotler.

chapter two

Marketing and society: social responsibility and marketing ethics

Chapter objectives *After reading this chapter, you should be able to:*

- List and respond to the social criticisms of marketing.

- Define *consumerism* and *environmentalism* and explain how they affect marketing strategies.

- Describe the principles of socially responsible marketing.

- Explain the role of ethics in marketing.

introduction

Responsible marketers discover what consumers want and respond with the right products, priced to give good value to buyers and profit to the producer. The *marketing concept* is a philosophy of customer service and mutual gain. Its practice leads the economy by an invisible hand to satisfy the many and changing needs of millions of consumers. But does social responsibility and morality have any role to play? Or is it incompatible with commercial survival in a competitive global marketplace?

Those are the sorts of questions that used to be asked only in classrooms and communes. Today's consumers care about more than price and quality. In the Prince of Wales Trust's Millennium Survey of 25,000 consumers across 20 countries, more people gave higher priority to social responsibility (49 per cent) than brand quality (40 per cent) in choosing products. In an era when the consumer is wiser to much more of a company's practice, and when there are increasingly wide concerns about environmental issues, race and gender equality, animal testing and human rights, the need for social responsibility and sound ethics in marketing has become crucial. Any number of these sensitivities can be picked up and how companies behave in the broadest sense will have an impact on their reputation and how people view their products and services.

Not all marketers follow the marketing concept. In fact, some companies use questionable marketing practices, and some marketing actions that seem innocent in themselves strongly affect the larger society. Consider the sale of sensitive products such as cigarettes. On the face of it, companies should be free to sell cigarettes, and smokers

preview case

Euro Tobacco's last gasp!

SCARCELY A WEEK PASSES WITHOUT a tobacco company being assaulted by a fearsome writ. If you want to keep count, log into the 'courtroom' section of the website of tobacco companies such as the Anglo-American British American Tobacco's (BAT) subsidiary, Brown and Williamson, to keep an exact count. Today, tobacco companies are more vulnerable than they have ever been. The directors of Europe's largest tobacco companies, from Seita in France to Imperial in Britain, have been bracing themselves for tough times ahead – moral panic, political wrangling and legal battles are the order of the day.

Legal action against tobacco companies seemingly worked in America. In June 1997, US tobacco companies, after some 30 years of 'foot-dragging', agreed health damages of \$368 billion (€413 billion) to compensate smoking victims. At the time, Martin Broughton, the chief executive of BAT, described the agreement as a 'uniquely American situation and a uniquely American solution to it'. He has been proven wrong. On 12 February 1998, a landmark ruling by the British court of appeal set the stage for what was seen as the most significant legal challenge yet to the UK tobacco industry. Fifty British lung cancer victims were suing UK tobacco companies Imperial Tobacco and Gallaher, who control more than 70 per cent of the British tobacco market, for allegedly failing to reduce the tar content of cigarettes after learning in the late 1950s of the link between smoking and lung cancer. According to the victims' lawyers, by 1957, the companies had the technology necessary to reduce nicotine levels in cigarettes on a sliding-scale basis, but they chose not to, preferring to keep the smokers addicted. If the cases succeed, the tobacco industry could face thousands of similar claims and multi-million-pound compensation bills. It could also have potentially alarming consequences for themselves and their peers across the rest of Europe, if new cases are brought on a similar scale.

The emergence of medical evidence suggesting that smoking is a health hazard has triggered reactions from anti-smoking groups. The lobbying efforts of cigarette prohibitionists, over the 1980s, led to enforcement of tighter restrictions throughout Europe, notably on tobacco advertising. Cigarette companies are prohibited from advertising on television in many European markets. To stave off more draconian legislation, they have agreed to a number of other measures, from stopping advertising in the cinema, on shop fronts or on posters near schools to avoiding any hint that smoking brings social or sexual success. This does not stop advertisers, though, from using cryptic pictures, like *red* motorcycles – the clue that told consumers to rush out and buy 'Marlboro' (red is the Marlboro brand colour).

More recent plans have been supported by the European parliament for significantly increasing the size of health warnings on cigarette packets. Members of the European Parliament have voted for health warnings with starkly worded warnings including statements such as 'Smoking causes cancer' or 'If you smoke, you are killing yourself'. Other measures include new EU-wide limits on tar, nicotine and carbon monoxide content in cigarettes, and banning ammonia compounds added to cigarettes to increase their addictive effect. The plans reflect EU ministers' and parliament's response to the call for tighter health controls on cigarettes through a regulatory framework which ensures a maximum of consumer information and transparency and which raises consumer knowledge on what is in tobacco products.

Ironically, as court cases catch newspaper headlines and the EU wrestles with 'its conscience', the global tobacco companies have their eyes on other markets. Across the Union, average cigarette consumption per capita is falling steadily, but outside the region, the larger firms are growing. They are moving into the developing countries such as central and eastern Europe, Latin America and China. In search of new customers, cigarette manufacturers are also targeting females. In France, Spain, Germany and Britain, between a quarter and a third of smokers are women. In Sweden, they form a majority of smokers. In some countries, like India and Hong Kong, women-only brands have been launched. Worse, tobacco firms are preying on children. Their aggressive campaigns in the less developed Far Eastern countries, with fewer consumer protection laws, are also cause for concern.[1]

Questions

You should attempt these questions only after completing your reading of this chapter.

1. Should tobacco firms take greater responsibility for regulating the sale of cigarettes and practise more socially responsible marketing?

2. Can customers and society, at large, be left to develop their own sense of personal responsibility – to avoid harmful products – even if firms don't? Discuss.

3. Should legislators be the ultimate force that protects innocent consumers from unsavoury marketing?

should be free to buy them. But this transaction affects the public interest. First, the smoker may be shortening his or her own life. Second, smoking places a burden on the smoker's family and on society at large. Third, other people around the smoker may have to inhale the smoke and may suffer discomfort and harm from second-hand smoke. This is not to say that cigarettes should be banned, although the anti-smoking zealots would welcome that. Rather, it shows that private transactions may involve larger questions of public policy. In practice, the answers are by no means always clear cut. It may be ethical for tobacco firms to stop peddling cigarettes altogether, but this, while seen by absolute moralists as 'the right thing' to do, will lead to companies' demise, job losses and the repercussions of increased unemployment on the wider community.

Marketers face difficult decisions when choosing to serve customers profitably, on the one hand, and seeking to maintain a close fit between consumers' wants or desires and societal welfare, on the other. In this chapter, we examine the social effects of private marketing practices. We discuss marketing in the context of society, the need for integrity, social responsibility and sound ethics, and the dilemmas that marketing people face. We ask several questions: What are the most frequent social criticisms of marketing? What steps have private citizens taken to curb marketing ills? What steps have legislators and government agencies taken to curb marketing ills? What steps have enlightened companies taken to carry out socially responsible and ethical marketing?

social criticisms of marketing

Marketing receives much criticism. Some of this criticism is justified; much is not.[2] Social critics claim that certain marketing practices hurt individual consumers, society as a whole and other business firms.

marketing's impact on individual consumers

Consumers have many concerns about how well marketing and businesses, as a whole, serve their interests. Consumer advocates, government agencies and other critics have accused marketing of harming consumers through high prices, deceptive practices, high-pressure selling, shoddy or unsafe products, planned obsolescence and poor service to disadvantaged consumers.

■ High prices

Many critics charge that marketing practices raise the cost of goods and cause prices to be higher than they would be if clever marketing were not applied. They point to three factors: *high costs of distribution*, *high advertising and promotion costs*, and *excessive mark-ups*.

High costs of distribution   A long-standing charge is that greedy intermediaries mark up prices beyond the value of their services. Critics charge either that there are too many intermediaries, or that intermediaries are inefficient and poorly run, provide unnecessary or duplicate services, and practise poor management and planning. As a result, distribution costs too much and consumers pay for these excessive costs in the form of higher prices.

How do retailers answer these charges? They argue that intermediaries do work which would otherwise have to be done by manufacturers or consumers. Mark-up reflects improved services that consumers themselves want – more convenience, larger stores and assortment, longer store opening hours, return privileges and others. More-over, the costs of operating stores keep rising, forcing retailers to raise their prices. In fact, they argue, retail competition is so intense that margins are actually quite low: for example, after taxes, supermarket chains are typically left with barely 1 per cent profit on their sales. If some resellers try to charge too much relative to the value they add, other resellers will step in with lower prices. Low-price stores and other discounters pressurise their competitors to operate efficiently and keep their prices down.

High advertising and promotion costs Modern marketing is also accused of pushing up prices because of heavy advertising and sales promotion. For example, a dozen tablets of a heavily promoted brand of aspirin sell for the same price as 100 tablets of less promoted (often termed 'generic') brands. Differentiated products – cosmetics, detergents, toiletries – include promotion and packaging costs that can amount to 40 per cent or more of the manufacturer's price to the retailer. Critics charge that much of the packaging and promotion adds only psychological value to the product rather than real functional value. Retailers use additional promotion – advertising, displays and sweepstakes – that add even more to retail prices.

Marketers respond by saying that consumers can usually buy functional versions of products at lower prices. However, they *want* more than the merely functional qualities of products. They are often willing to pay more for products that also provide desired psychological benefits – that make them feel wealthy, beautiful or special. Brand-name products may cost more, but branding gives buyers confidence. Heavy advertising adds to product costs but is needed to inform millions of potential buyers of the merits of a brand. If consumers want to know what is available on the market, they must expect manufacturers to spend large sums of money on advertising. Also, heavy advertising and promotion may be necessary for a firm to match competitors' efforts. The business would lose 'share of mind' if it did not match competitive spending. At the same time, companies are cost conscious about promotion and try to spend their money wisely.

Excessive mark-ups Critics also charge that some companies mark up goods excessively. They point to the drug industry, where a pill costing €0.10 to make may cost the consumer €4.0 to buy. Or to the pricing tactics of perfume manufacturers, who take advantage of customers' ignorance of the true worth of a 50 g bottle of Chanel perfume, while preying on their desire to fulfil emotional needs.

Marketers respond that most businesses try to deal fairly with consumers because they want repeat business. Most consumer abuses are unintentional. When shady marketers do take advantage of consumers, they should be reported to industry watchdogs and to other consumer-interest or consumer-protection groups. Marketers also stress that consumers often don't understand the reason for high mark-ups. For example, pharmaceutical mark-ups must cover the costs of purchasing, promoting and distributing existing medicines, plus the high research and development costs of finding new medicines.

■ Deceptive practices

Marketers are sometimes accused of deceptive practices that lead consumers to believe they will get more value than they actually do. Deceptive marketing practices fall into three groups: *deceptive pricing*, *promotion* and *packaging*. Deceptive pricing includes practices such as falsely advertising 'factory' or 'wholesale' prices or a large price reduction from a phoney high retail list price. Deceptive promotion includes practices such as overstating the product's features or performance, luring the customer to the store for a bargain that is out of stock, or running rigged contests. Deceptive packaging includes exaggerating package contents through subtle design, not filling the package to the top, using misleading labelling, or describing size in misleading terms.

Deceptive practices have led to legislation and other consumer-protection actions. Positive steps have already been taken, for example, with regard to European directives aimed at a number of industries. For example, since the introduction of Council Directive 93/35/EEC on 14 June 1993, far-reaching changes have been made to cosmetic laws. The legislation controls the constituents of cosmetic products and their associated instructions and warnings about use, and specifies requirements relating to the marketing of cosmetic products, which cover product claims, labelling, information on packaging and details about the product's intended function. Where a product claims to remove 'unsightly cellulite' or make the user look '20 years younger', proofs must be documented and made available to the enforcement authorities. These laws also require clear details specifying where animal testing has been carried out on both the finished product and/or its ingredients. The EU has recognised increased public resistance to animal testing and has proposed a limited ban on animal testing for cosmetic ingredients since 1 January 1998.

Similar directives are found to regulate industry practices in the United States. The Federal Trade Commission (FTC), which has the power to regulate 'unfair or deceptive acts or practices', has published several guidelines listing deceptive practices. The toughest problem is defining what is 'deceptive'. For example, some years ago, Shell Oil advertised that Super Shell petrol with platformate gave more mileage than did the same fuel without platformate. Now this was true, but what Shell did not say is that almost *all* petrol includes platformate. Its defence was that it had never claimed that platformate was found only in Shell petroleum fuel. But even though the message was literally true, the FTC felt that the ad's *intent* was to deceive.

Marketers argue that most companies avoid deceptive practices because such practices harm their business in the long run. If consumers do not get what they expect, they will switch to more reliable products. In addition, consumers usually protect themselves from deception. Most consumers recognise a marketer's selling intent and are careful when they buy, sometimes to the point of not believing completely true product claims. Theodore Levitt claims that some advertising puffery is bound to occur – and that it may even be desirable:

> There is hardly a company that would not go down in ruin if it refused to provide fluff, because nobody will buy pure functionality . . . Worse, it denies . . . man's honest needs and values . . . Without distortion, embellishment and elaboration, life would be drab, dull, anguished and at its existential worst . . .[3]

■ High-pressure selling

Salespeople are sometimes accused of high-pressure selling that persuades people to buy goods they had no thought of buying. It is often said that cars, insurance, property and home improvement plans are *sold*, not *bought*. Salespeople are trained to deliver smooth, canned talks to entice purchase. They sell hard because commissions and sales contests promise big prizes to those who sell the most.

Marketers know that buyers can often be talked into buying unwanted or unneeded things. A key question is whether industry self-regulatory or trading standards bodies, consumer-protection laws and consumer-interest groups are sufficiently effective in checking and curbing unsavoury sales practices. In this modern era, it is encouraging to note that one or more of these can work to the advantage of consumers. Or, where malpractices are pervasive, regulators will catch out wrongdoers, who will invariably pay the penalties for irresponsible marketing (see Marketing Highlight 2.1). In most cases, marketers have little to gain from high-pressure selling. Such tactics may work in the short run but will damage the marketer's long-run relationships with customers.

■ Shoddy or unsafe products

Another criticism is that products lack the quality they should have. One complaint is that products are not made well and services not performed well. A second complaint is that some products deliver little benefit. In an attempt to persuade customers to buy their brand rather than any other, manufacturers sometimes make claims that are not fully substantiated. In the United Kingdom, for example, the Independent Television Commission (ITC) introduced new rules covering the advertising of medicines and treatments, health claims, and nutrition and dietary supplements, including slimming products. The move, which followed the publication of new advertising rules by the Advertising Standards Authority (ASA), brings the ITC in line with public and private sector opinion, and recent European Union legislation governing the advertising and sales of these products. Health claims for food, for example, must now be fully substantiated. Creative ads must guard against encouraging overindulgence in products such as confectionery, so advertisers must pay attention to health implications.[4]

In markets where many brands are promising a wide array of product benefits, consumers are often left confused. In fact, consumers often end up paying more for product benefits that do not exist.

A third complaint concerns product safety. Product safety has been a problem for several reasons, including manufacturer indifference, increased production complexity, poorly trained labour and poor quality control. Consider the following cases of costly and image-damaging crises brought upon vehicle manufacturers:

> The Ford Pinto became the symbol of automotive disaster when several people died during the 1970s in fuel tank fires allegedly linked to a design fault. In the late 1990s, Chrysler issued one of the largest product recall notices in the history of the motoring industry, calling back 900,000 vehicles, ranging from pick-ups to a selection of 'people carriers' including the Voyager, Wrangler and Jeep Cherokee models, for a variety of reasons in seven different recalls. Another example is provided by VW which recalled 350,000 of its models world-wide because of a potentially faulty electric cable, as well as some 950,000 Golfs, Jettas, Passats and Corrados because of problems, including a cooling system fault, which could potentially damage engines and injure passengers. Even Rolls-Royce was forced to check some of its Bentley Continental T sports coupés (at €360,000 apiece) because of concerns that airbags were firing unexpectedly.[5]

For years, consumer protection groups or associations in many countries have regularly tested products for safety, and have reported hazards found in tested products, such as electrical dangers in appliances, and injury risks from lawnmowers and faulty

marketing highlight 2.1

We have ways of making you buy!

In the early 1990s, LAUTRO, the body that regulated the selling of life insurance, fined at least a dozen life assurance companies a total of nearly £1 million (€164m) for failing to ensure that potential customers were fully informed about different policies. Those singled out, including Scottish Widows, Guardian Royal Exchange, General Accident, Commercial Union and Norwich Union, were severely reprimanded for mis-selling, offering poor value to customers who surrender their policies early and exploiting customers' ignorance – in short, for breaking the rules!

Later, the Office of Fair Trading (OFT), a government watchdog, got it in for some 60 of the United Kingdom's largest life insurance firms. Many household names, the symbols of probity and financial solidity, were severely criticised for short-changing customers who surrendered long-term policies early. For a number of policies investigated, the OFT found that the insurers offered *zero* surrender value – that is, the insured received no money should she or he decide to terminate the policy – at the end of the first year. Also, wide disparities occurred in the surrender values of life insurance policies, but information was seldom disclosed to buyers.

Why should companies be penalised because their investors want to cash in earlier on long-term savings plans? Regulators argue that life insurers had exploited customers' ignorance and vulnerability, selling them products that generated big profits for the sellers, but were unsuited to the buyer. Up to one-third of all policies were cashed in during the first two years alone. Companies profited from early lapse rates, and many people holding policies with companies which have relatively high lapse rates were actually worse off than if they had no policy at all. Lapses are insurers' profits!

Sales 'tricks' were not unusual in the industry. For example, some salespeople sent letters to married women, talking about their company and appending a blank form with a piece of paper telling the woman: 'This is what you get when your husband dies.' Although many independent financial advisers ensure that clients get good value for money from respectable insurers, there are many others who are forced to sell poor-quality products, because they are trapped in a commission structure that requires them to sell or starve. One insurance sales representative says: 'You would see that some prospective clients might have to struggle to pay the premiums, but because your livelihood depended on it, you would play on their emotions to try to sell them something.'

Having had their knuckles rapped, insurers did improve the surrender values offered to their clients. However, they responded that customers have the product literature to help them assess their policies. The OFT argues that the idea that customers could understand readily the surrender values of their policies simply by reading the product literature is quite false. 'These things are not only obscure to the average consumer but to the informed consumer as well', says the OFT's consumer policy division. The argument stands: not nearly as many people would have bought life insurance if the products had not been actively sold to them.

The subsequent introduction of disclosure rules compel salespeople to inform the consumer how much commission they take for selling a given policy. The authorities also called for wrongdoers to compensate those they've wronged!

After years of deliberately confusing jargon and pushy sales techniques, the industry has had to work harder to redeem the public's trust. Meanwhile, life's got tougher as new entrants, such as Direct Line, Marks & Spencer and Virgin Direct, with their 'cleaner images', have made inroads, driving down prices and capturing market share.

The moral of the story? Sales tricks do not make sound marketing sense. You cannot sell something nobody wants, no matter how you push it!

SOURCES: Alison Smith, 'Standard Life's surrender bonus', *Financial Times* (21 November 1994), p. 22; Alison Smith, 'OFT names insurers offering zero first year surrender value', *Financial Times* (9–10 July 1994), p. 1; Alison Smith, 'Back from the brink', *Financial Times* (23 June 1994), p. 16; Norma Cohen, 'Life insurers criticised for poor surrender values', 'Your lapses are their profits', *Financial Times* (18–19 June 1994), pp. I, III; Peter Marsh, 'We have ways of making you buy', *Financial Times* (14 June 1994), p. 18; Peter Marsh, 'When he dies, my dear, all this will be yours', *Financial Times* (11–12 June 1994), pp. I, XII; 'All life's troubles', *The Economist* (17 July 1993), pp. 76–7; Sean Brierley, 'A matter of life and death', *Marketing Week* (28 June 1995); Andrew Duffy, 'Great British pensions disaster', *Business Age* (5 July 1995), pp. 40–3; Alan Mitchell, 'Swimming with the sharks', *Marketing Business* (September 1997), pp. 26–30.

car design. The testing and reporting activities of these organisations have helped consumers make better buying decisions and have encouraged businesses to eliminate product flaws. Marketers may sometimes face dilemmas when seeking to balance consumer needs and social responsibility. For example, no amount of test results can guarantee product safety in cars if consumers value speed and power more than safety features. Buyers might choose a less expensive chain-saw without a safety guard, although society or a government regulatory agency might deem it irresponsible and unethical for the manufacturer to sell it.

However, most responsible manufacturers *want* to produce quality goods. Companies selling poor-quality or unsafe products risk damaging conflicts with consumer groups and regulators. Moreover, unsafe products can result in product liability suits and large awards for damages. Consumers who are unhappy with a firm's products may avoid future purchases and talk other consumers into doing the same. More fundamentally, today's marketers know that self-imposed standards, which accompany customer-driven quality, result in customer satisfaction, which in turn creates profitable customer relationships.

■ Planned obsolescence

Planned obsolescence
A strategy of causing products to become obsolete before they actually need replacement.

Critics have charged that some producers follow a programme of **planned obsolescence**, causing their products to become obsolete before they need replacement. For example, some critics charge that some producers continually change consumer concepts of acceptable styles in order to encourage more and earlier buying. An obvious example is constantly changing clothing fashions. Producers have also been accused of holding back attractive functional features, then introducing them later to make older models obsolete. Critics claim that this practice is frequently found in the consumer electronics and computer industry. The Japanese camera, watch and consumer electronics companies frustrate consumers because rapid and frequent model replacement has created difficulties in obtaining spare parts for old models; dealers refuse to repair outdated models and planned obsolescence rapidly erodes basic product values. Finally, producers have been accused of using materials and components that will break, wear, rust or rot sooner than they should. For example, many drapery manufacturers are using a higher percentage of rayon in their curtains. They argue that rayon reduces the price of the curtains and has better holding power. Critics claim that using more rayon causes the curtains to fall apart sooner.

Marketers respond that consumers *like* style changes; they get tired of the old goods and want a new look in fashion or a new design in cars. No one has to buy the new look, and if too few people like it, it will simply fail. Companies frequently withhold new features when they are not fully tested, when they add more cost to the product than consumers are willing to pay, and for other good reasons. But they do so at the risk that a competitor will introduce the new feature and steal the market. Moreover, companies often put in new materials to lower their costs and prices. They do not design their products to break down earlier, because they do not want to lose their customers to other brands. Instead, they implement total quality programmes to ensure that products will consistently meet or exceed customer expectations. Thus, much so-called planned obsolescence is the working of the competitive and technological forces in a free society – forces that lead to ever-improving goods and services.[6]

■ Poor service to disadvantaged consumers

Finally, marketing has been accused of poorly serving disadvantaged consumers. Critics claim that the urban poor often have to shop in smaller stores that carry inferior goods and charge higher prices. Marketing's eye on profits also means that disadvantaged consumers are not viable segments to target. The high-income consumer is the preferred target.

Clearly, better marketing systems must be built in low-income areas – one hope is to get large retailers to open outlets in low-income areas. Moreover, low-income people clearly need consumer protection. Consumer-protection agencies should take action against suppliers who advertise false values, sell old merchandise as new, or charge too much for credit. Offenders who deliver poor value should be expected to compensate customers, as in the case of many UK pensions providers, who were required to meet mis-selling compensation targets following the disclosure of malpractices by an Office of Fair Trading (OFT) investigation.

We now turn to social critics' assessment of how marketing affects society as a whole.

marketing's impact on society as a whole

The marketing system, as we – in Europe and other developed economies such as North America – are experiencing it, has been accused of adding to several 'evils' in our society at large. Advertising has been a special target. It has been blamed for creating false wants, nurturing greedy aspirations and inculcating too much materialism in our society.

■ False wants and too much materialism

Critics have charged that the western marketing system urges too much interest in material possessions. People are judged by what they *own* rather than by what they *are*. To be considered successful, people must own a large home or smart-looking apartment in a prime residential site, expensive cars and the latest designer-label clothes and consumer electronics.

Critics view this interest in material things not as a natural state of mind, but rather as a matter of false wants created by marketing. Businesses stimulate people's desires for goods through the force of advertising, and advertisers use the mass media to create materialistic models of the good life. People work harder to earn the necessary money. Their purchases increase the output of the nation's industry, and industry, in turn, uses the advertising media to stimulate more desire for its industrial output. Thus marketing is seen as creating false wants that benefit industry more than they benefit consumers.

However, these criticisms overstate the power of business to create needs. People have strong defences against advertising and other marketing tools. Marketers are most effective when they appeal to existing wants rather than when they attempt to create new ones. Furthermore, people seek information when making important purchases and often do not rely on single sources. Consumers ultimately display rational buying behaviour: even minor purchases that may be affected by advertising messages lead to repeat purchases only if the product performs as promised. Finally, the high failure rate of new products shows that companies are not always able to control demand.

On a deeper level, our wants and values are influenced not only by marketers, but also by family, peer groups, religion, ethnic background and education. If societies, wherever they exist, are highly materialistic, these values arose out of basic social-isation processes that go much deeper than business and mass media could produce alone. The importance of wealth and material possessions to the overseas Chinese, for example, is explained more by cultural and socialisation factors than by sustained exposure to western advertising influences. Moreover, in affluent economies such as America, some social critics see materialism as a positive and rewarding force:

> When we purchase an object, what we really buy is meaning. Commercialism is the water we swim in, the air we breathe, our sunlight and our shade. . . . Materialism is a vital source of meaning and happiness in the modern world. . . . We have not just asked to go this way, we have demanded. Now most of the world is lining up, pushing and shoving, eager to elbow into the mall. Getting and spending has become the most passionate, and often the most imaginative, endeavor of modern life. While this is dreary and depressing to some, as doubtless it should be, it is liberating and democratic to many more.[7]

■ Too few social goods

Business has been accused of overselling private goods at the expense of public goods. As private goods increase, they require more public services that are usually not forthcoming. For example, an increase in car ownership (private good) requires more roads, traffic control, parking spaces and police services (public goods). The overselling of private goods results in 'social costs'. For cars, the social costs include excessive traffic congestion, air pollution, and deaths and injuries from car accidents.

A way must be found to restore a balance between private and public goods. One option is to make producers bear the full social costs of their operations. For example, the government could require car manufacturers to build cars with even more safety features and better pollution-control systems. Car makers would then raise their prices to cover extra costs. If buyers found the price of some cars too high, however, the producers of these cars would disappear, and demand would move to those producers that could support both the private and social costs.

A second option is to make consumers pay the social costs. For example, highway authorities around the world are starting to charge 'congestion tolls' in an effort to reduce traffic congestion.

> Norway, Singapore and France are managing traffic with varying tolls. In southern California, drivers are being charged premiums to travel in underused car pool lanes. Peak surcharges are being considered for roads around New York, San Francisco, Los Angeles and other American cities. Economists point out that traffic jams are caused when drivers are not charged the costs they impose on others, such as delays. The solution: Make 'em pay![8]

More generally, if the costs of driving rise high enough, consumers will travel at non-peak times or find alternative transportation modes.

■ Cultural pollution

Critics charge the marketing system with creating *cultural pollution*. Our senses are being assaulted constantly by advertising. This devious practice is inflicted on our kids every day. Commercials interrupt serious programmes; pages of ads obscure printed matter; billboards mar beautiful scenery. These interruptions continuously pollute people's minds with messages of materialism, sex, power or status. Children's constant exposure to advertising, the protectionists argue, creates mercenary kids, experts in 'pester power', who force their downtrodden and beleaguered parents into spending enormous sums of money on branded goods and the latest crazes. Although most people do not find advertising overly annoying (some even think it is the best part of television programming), some critics call for sweeping changes.

Marketers answer the charges of 'commercial noise' with the following arguments. First, they hope that their ads reach primarily the target audience. But because of mass-communication channels, some ads are bound to reach people who have no interest in the product and are therefore bored or annoyed. As for TV advertising's influence on children, free marketers point to European research that shows that parents and peers influence children more than advertising. Trend products like yoyos, Beanie Babies and Furbies have reached the top without a penny spent on TV commercials. Children are not empty vessels helplessly vulnerable to marketers' wiles.[9] People who buy magazines slanted towards their interests – such as *Vogue, Bliss, Heat* or *Fortune* – rarely complain about the ads because the magazines advertise products of interest. Second, ads make much of television and radio free, and keep down the costs of magazines and newspapers. Most people think commercials are a small price to pay for these benefits. Finally, consumers have alternatives: they can zip and zap TV commercials or avoid them altogether on many cable and satellite channels. Thus advertisers are making their ads more entertaining and informative.

■ Too much political power

Another criticism is that business wields too much political power. 'Oil', 'tobacco', 'pharmaceuticals', 'financial services' and 'alcohol' have the support of important politicians and civil servants, who look after an industry's interests against the public interest. Advertisers are accused of holding too much power over the mass media, limiting their freedom to report independently and objectively.

The setting up of citizens' charters and greater concern for consumer rights and protection over the 1990s will see improvements, not regression, in business accountability in the twenty-first century. Fortunately, many powerful business interests once thought to be untouchable have been tamed in the public interest. For example, in both western Europe and the United States, consumerism campaigns have caused legislation that forced the car industry to build more safety into its cars and cigarette companies have long been compelled to put health warnings on their packages. More recently, giants such as Coca-Cola, Microsoft and Intel have felt the impact of regulators seeking to balance the interests of big business against those of the public. Moreover, because the media receive advertising revenues from many different advertisers, it is easier to resist the influence of one or a few of them. Too much business power tends to result in counterforces that check and offset these powerful interests.

Let us now take a look at the criticisms that business critics have levelled at companies' marketing practices.

marketing's impact on other businesses

Critics also charge that companies' marketing practices can harm other companies and reduce competition. Three problems are involved: acquisition of competitors, marketing practices that create barriers to entry, and unfair competitive marketing practices.

Critics claim that firms are harmed and competition reduced when companies expand by acquiring competitors rather than by developing their own new products. The large number of acquisitions and rapid pace of industry consolidation over the past two decades have caused concern that vigorous young competitors will be absorbed and that competition will be reduced. In virtually every major industry – financial services, utilities, transportation, motor vehicles, telecommunications, entertainment – the number of major competitors is shrinking.

Acquisition is a complex subject. Acquisitions can sometimes be good for society. The acquiring company may gain economies of scale that lead to lower costs and lower prices. A well-managed company may take over a poorly managed company and improve its efficiency. An industry that was not very competitive might become more competitive after the acquisition. But acquisitions can also be harmful and are therefore closely regulated by the government.

Critics have also claimed that marketing practices bar new companies from entering an industry. The use of patents and heavy promotion spending can tie up suppliers or dealers to keep out or drive out competitors. People concerned with antitrust regulation recognise that some barriers are the natural result of the economic advantages of doing business on a large scale. Other barriers could be challenged by existing and new laws. For example, some critics have proposed a progressive tax on advertising spending to reduce the role of selling costs as a substantial barrier to entry.

Finally, some firms have in fact used unfair competitive marketing practices with the intention of hurting or destroying other firms. They may set their prices below costs, threaten to cut off business with suppliers, or discourage the buying of a competitor's products. Various laws work to prevent such predatory competition. It is difficult, however, to prove that the intent or action was really predatory.

Take, for example, the case of Microsoft, the world's biggest software company, which has recently been accused by the US Justice Department of predatory practices and abusing its monopoly over personal computer software.

In 1998, Microsoft's $3.4 billion (€3.82b) in net income accounted for 41 per cent of the profits of the 10 largest publicly traded software companies. Its reach extends beyond the PC into everything from computerised toys and TV set-top boxes to selling cars and airline tickets over the Internet. In its zeal to become a leader not just in operating systems but on the Internet, the company bundled its Internet Explorer browser into its Windows software. This move sparked an antitrust suit by the government, much to the delight of Microsoft's rivals. After all, web-browsing innovator Netscape has seen its market share plummet as it tries to sell what Microsoft gives away for free. After a two-year trial, the antitrust authorities emerged victors, when the judge who heard the landmark case against the software giant ruled that Microsoft broke antitrust laws and behaved illegally by tying its web browser to its best-selling Windows operating system. The antitrust officials demanded Microsoft to be broken up into two separate businesses – one to run its Windows operating system and the other to manage its application software products such as word processing and spreadsheets. The company was also required to implement a host of remedies aimed at curbing any abuse of its dominant position. Microsoft continues to protest its innocence, taking its appeal to the higher courts.

While the appeal process in the US is under way, in Brussels, the European Commission is looking into the implications of the US ruling on Microsoft for its own investigations into the company's dominant position in the EU. The Commission is still far from concluding its enquiries. The Commission has five enquiries under way into different aspects of Microsoft's behaviour. These range from its monopoly of the PC operating system market, following complaints from rival firms such as Sun Microsystems, predatory behaviour associated with Windows 2000, to the company's pricing policy for French software, where the firm allegedly sold software more cheaply in Canada than in France. Meanwhile, problems brew further afield for the global firm, with lawyers seeking to expand the case against Microsoft by claiming damages for worldwide customers. They argue that international curbs against anti-competitive commercial activity have become so prevalent that they must be deemed to rise to the level of the law of nations. They also claim to have the support from a mixture of United Nations statements of principles on competition and recommendations from the Organisation for Economic Cooperation and Development (OECD).[10]

Another example which reminds us of the vulnerability of firms, particularly dominant, global companies, to competition authorities is Coca-Cola's recent experience. Spurred by its acquisition of Cadbury's soft-drinks brands outside America, competition authorities from Chile to Australia to Europe scrutinised Coke's market share and business practices. In Europe, the European Commission had launched an investigation into Coke's alleged anti-competitive practices in Germany, Denmark and Austria: one common anti-competitive practice is to give retailers and restaurants free fridges or soda fountains if they refuse to sell soft drinks from rival firms. Another is to offer them special prices if they stock the complete range of Coke's products, including Sprite and Fanta. A third offers retailers rebates and volume discounts for sales growth.[11]

Although competitors and governments charge that the actions of companies such as Coca-Cola and Microsoft are predatory and illegal, the fundamental question remains: Is this unfair competition or the healthy competition of a more efficient company against the less efficient?

citizen and public actions to regulate marketing

Because some people view business as the cause of many economic and social ills, grassroots movements have arisen from time to time to keep business in line. The two main movements have been consumerism and environmentalism.

consumerism

Western business firms have been the targets of organised consumer movements on three occasions. Consumerism has its origins in the United States. The first consumer movement took place in the early 1900s. It was fuelled by rising prices, Upton Sinclair's writings on conditions in the meat industry, and scandals in the drug industry. The second consumer movement, in the mid-1930s, was sparked by an upturn in consumer prices during the Great Depression and another drug scandal.

The third movement began in the 1960s. Consumers had become better educated, products had become more complex and potentially hazardous, and people were unhappy with western (usually meaning American) institutions. Ralph Nader appeared on the scene in the 1960s to force many issues, and other well-known writers accused big business of wasteful and unethical practices. President John F. Kennedy declared that consumers have the right to safety and to be informed, to choose and to be heard. The American Congress investigated certain industries and proposed consumer-protection legislation. Since then, many consumer groups have been organised and several consumer laws have been passed. The consumer movement has spread internationally and has become very strong in Europe.[12]

But what is the consumer movement? **Consumerism** is an organised movement of citizens and government agencies to improve the rights and power of buyers in relation to sellers. Traditional sellers' rights include the following:

Consumerism
An organised movement of citizens and government agencies to improve the rights and power of buyers in relation to sellers.

✦ The right to introduce any product in any size and style, provided it is not hazardous to personal health or safety; or, if it is, to include proper warnings and controls.

✦ The right to charge any price for the product, provided no discrimination exists among similar kinds of buyer.

✦ The right to spend any amount to promote the product, provided it is not defined as unfair competition.

✦ The right to use any product message, provided it is not misleading or dishonest in content or execution.

✦ The right to use any buying incentive schemes, provided they are not unfair or misleading.

Traditional buyers' rights include the following:

✦ The right not to buy a product that is offered for sale.
✦ The right to expect the product to be safe.
✦ The right to expect the product to perform as claimed.

Comparing these rights, many believe that the balance of power lies on the sellers' side. True, the buyer can refuse to buy. But critics feel that the buyer has too little

information, education and protection to make wise decisions when facing sophisticated sellers. Consumer advocates call for the following additional consumer rights:

+ The right to be well informed about important aspects of the product.
+ The right to be protected against questionable products and marketing practices.
+ The right to influence products and marketing practices in ways that will
  improve the 'quality of life'.

Each proposed right has led to more specific proposals by consumerists. The right to
be informed includes the right to know the true interest on a loan (truth in lending),
the true cost per unit of a brand (unit pricing), the ingredients in a product (ingredient labelling), the nutrition in foods (nutritional labelling), product freshness (open
dating) and the true benefits of a product (truth in advertising). Proposals related to
consumer protection include strengthening consumer rights in cases of business fraud,
requiring greater product safety and giving more power to government agencies.
Proposals relating to quality of life include controlling the ingredients that go into certain products (detergents) and packaging (soft-drink containers), reducing the level of
advertising 'noise' and putting consumer representatives on company boards to protect consumer interests.

Consumers have not only the *right* but also the *responsibility* to protect themselves instead of leaving this function to someone else. Consumers who believe that
they got a bad deal have several remedies available, including writing to the company
heads or to the media, contacting government or private consumer-interest/protection
initiatives or agencies, and going to small-claims courts.

environmentalism

Environmentalism
*An organised movement
of concerned citizens
and government
agencies to protect
and improve people's
living environment.*

Whereas consumerists consider whether the marketing system is efficiently serving
consumer wants, environmentalists are concerned with marketing's effects on the
environment and the costs of serving consumer needs and wants. **Environmentalism**
is an organised movement of concerned citizens and government agencies to protect
and improve people's living environment. Environmentalists are not against marketing
and consumption; they simply want people and organisations to operate with more
care for the environment, not to maximise consumption, consumer choice or consumer
satisfaction, but rather to maximise life quality. 'Life quality' means not only the
quantity and quality of consumer goods and services, but also the quality of the environment. Environmentalists want environmental costs to be included in both producer
and consumer decision making.

The first wave of modern environmentalism was driven by environmental groups
and concerned consumers in the 1960s and 1970s. They were concerned with damage
to the ecosystem caused by strip mining, forest depletion, acid rain, loss of the atmosphere's ozone layer, toxic wastes and litter. They were also concerned with the loss
of recreational areas and with the increase in health problems caused by bad air,
polluted water and chemically treated food.

The second wave was driven by governments, which passed laws and regulations
during the 1970s and 1980s governing industrial practices impacting the environment.
This wave hit some industries hard. Heavy industry, public utilities, and chemical and
steel companies had to spend heavily on clean-up technology, waste management and
other pollution-control equipment. The car industry has had to introduce expensive
emission controls in cars. In some countries, governments have introduced tough
regulations on car makers to deal with environmental problems, as in the case of
Germany, where the car industry has to grapple with laws to create a car recycling

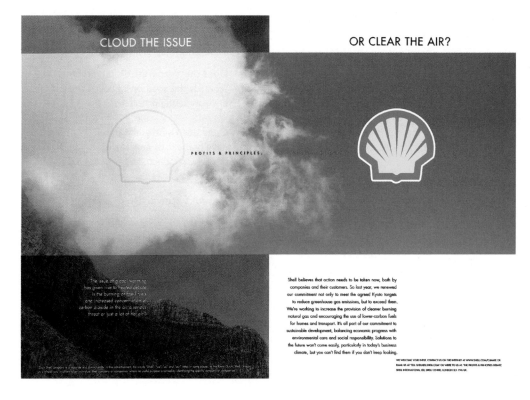

CLOUD THE ISSUE

OR CLEAR THE AIR?

PROFITS & PRINCIPLES.

The issue of global warming
has given rise to heated debate.
Is the burning of fossil fuels
and increased concentration of
carbon dioxide in the air a serious
threat or just a lot of hot air?

Shell believes that action needs to be taken now, both by
companies and their customers. So last year, we renewed
our commitment not only to meet the agreed Kyoto targets
to reduce greenhouse gas emissions, but to exceed them.
We're working to increase the provision of cleaner burning
natural gas and encouraging the use of lower-carbon fuels
for homes and transport. It's all part of our commitment to
sustainable development, balancing economic progress with
environmental care and social responsibility. Solutions to
the future won't come easily, particularly in today's business
climate, but you can't find them if you don't keep looking.

Here Shell demonstrates its commitment to reduce greenhouse gas emissions, hence contributing to the control of global warming.

SOURCE: Shell International Petroleum Co. Ltd. *Agency:* J. Walter Thompson

system.[13] The packaging industry has had to find ways to reduce litter and energy consumption. The petroleum industry has had to create new low-lead and unleaded petrols. These industries often resent environmental regulations, especially when they are imposed too rapidly to allow companies to make proper adjustments. These companies have absorbed large costs that they pass on to buyers.

In the twenty-first century, the first two environmentalism waves are merging into a third and stronger wave in which companies are accepting responsibility for doing no harm to the environment. They are shifting from protest to prevention, and from regulation to responsibility. More and more companies are adopting **environmental sustainability** – developing strategies that both sustain the environment and produce profits for the company.

Figure 2.1 shows a grid that companies can use to gauge their progress towards environmental sustainability. At the most basic level, a company can practise *pollution prevention*. This involves more than pollution control – cleaning up waste after it has been created. Pollution prevention means eliminating or minimising waste before it is created. Companies emphasising prevention have responded with 'green marketing' programmes – developing ecologically safer products, recyclable and biodegradable packaging, better pollution controls and more energy-efficient operations. They are finding that they can be both green and competitive. Consider how the Dutch flower industry has responded to its environmental problems:

> Intense cultivation of flowers in small areas was contaminating the soil and groundwater with pesticides, herbicides and fertilizers. Facing increasingly strict regulation, the Dutch growers understood that the only effective way to address the problem would be to develop a closed-loop system. In advanced Dutch greenhouses, flowers now grow in water and rock wool, not soil. This lowers the risk of infestation, reducing the need for fertilizers and pesticides, which are delivered in water that circulates and is re-used. The closed-loop system also reduces variation in growing

Environmental sustainability
A third environmentalism wave in which companies seek to produce profits for the company while sustaining the environment.

Figure 2.1

The environmental sustainability grid

SOURCE: Harvard Business School Publishing. Reprinted by permission of *Harvard Business Review*, The sustainability portfolio from 'Beyond Greening: strategies for a sustainable world' by Stuart Hart, Jan–Feb 1997. Copyright © 1997 by the President and Fellows of Harvard College; all rights reserved

	Internal	External
Tomorrow	**New environmental technology** Is the environmental performance of our products limited by our existing technology base? Is there potential to realise major improvements through new technology?	**Sustainability vision** Does our corporate vision direct us towards the solution of social and environmental problems? Does our vision guide the development of new technologies, markets, products and processes?
Today	**Pollution prevention** Where are the most significant waste and emission streams from our current operations? Can we lower costs and risks by eliminating waste at the source or by using it as useful input?	**Product stewardship** What are the implications for product design and development if we assume responsibility for a product's entire life cycle? Can we add value or lower costs while simultaneously reducing the impact of our products?

> conditions, thus improving product quality. Handling costs have reduced because the flowers are cultivated on specially designed platforms. The net result is not only dramatically lower environmental impact but also lower costs, better quality and enhanced global competitiveness.[14]

At the next level, companies can practise *product stewardship* – minimising not just pollution from production but all environmental impacts throughout the full product life cycle. Many companies are adopting design for environment (DFE) practices, which involve thinking ahead in the design stage to create products that are easier to recover, reuse or recycle. DFE not only helps to sustain the environment, it can be highly profitable:

> Consider Xerox Corporation's Asset Recycle Management (ARM) programme, which uses leased Xerox copiers as sources of high-quality, low-cost parts and components for new machines. A well-developed [process] for taking back leased copiers combined with a sophisticated re-manufacturing process allows components to be reconditioned, tested and then reassembled into 'new' machines. Xerox estimates that ARM savings in raw materials, labour and waste disposal fall in the €300-million to €400-million range. By redefining product-in-use as part of the company's asset base, Xerox has discovered a way to add value and lower costs. It can continually provide lease customers with the latest product upgrades, giving them state-of-the-art functionality with minimum environmental impact.[15]

At the third level of environmental sustainability, companies look to the future and plan for *new environmental technologies*. Many organisations that have made good headway in pollution prevention and product stewardship are still limited by existing technologies. To develop fully sustainable strategies, they will need to develop new technologies. For example, some chemicals firms are shifting their agricultural technology base from bulk chemicals to biotechnology. By controlling plant growth and

Travelers have always relied on the stars...

Inchon International Airport, Korea - The Winged City,
Seoul's new international airport

The 21ˢᵗcentury airport of your dreams, gateway to all of Asia

The dream airport for airline operations, with the emphasis on efficiency and cost effectiveness
- 24 hours, around the clock flight operations, handling 27 million passengers and 1.7 million tons of cargo annually.
- Connects North America and Europe to 40 Asian cities, each with more than one million population, that are within 3.5 hours flying time.
- At 15 kilometers offshore from Korea's West Coast, IIA is environmentally friendly, with no noise pollution problems.

The dream airport for passengers, with the emphasis on comfort and convenience
- On arrival, baggage delivery within five minutes.   - Entries and exits completed within 30 minutes.
- 24 hour fine dining and shopping(including fashion boutique) - 24 hour sauna and fitness center
- 24 hour video rooms and entertainment center   - 24 hour business center and hotel
- Environmentally sensitive, with 30% of entire space devoted to landscaping and gardens with waterfalls.

inchon www.wingedcity.com

The Winged City

The boom in environmentalism has reached such dimensions that even Seoul's International Airport claims to be environmentally friendly.

SOURCE: Inchon International Airport Corporational, Korea. *Agency*: Dentsu Young and Rubicam, Korea

pest resistance through bio-engineering rather than through the application of pesticides or fertilisers, these companies hope to find environmentally sustained paths to increased agricultural yields.

Environmentalism creates special challenges for global marketers. As international trade barriers come down and global markets expand, environmental issues will continue to have an ever-greater impact on international trade. Global companies have to operate in accordance with stringent environment regulations that are being developed in countries across North America, Western Europe and other developed regions. For example, the EU's Eco-Management and Audit Regulation has provided guidelines for environmental self-regulation. Similarly, a side accord to the North American Free Trade Agreement (NAFTA) set up a commission for resolving environmental matters.[16]

Marketers' lives will become more complicated. They must raise prices to cover environmental costs, knowing that the product will be harder to sell. Yet environmental issues have become so important in our society that there is no turning back to the time when few managers worried about the effects of product and marketing decisions on environmental quality.[17]

However, environmental policies still vary widely from country to country, and uniform worldwide standards are not expected for many years. Although countries such as Denmark, Germany, Japan and the United States have fully developed environmental policies and high public expectations, major countries such as China, India, Brazil and Russia are in only the early stages of developing such policies. Moreover, environmental factors that motivate consumers in one country may have no impact on consumers in another. For example, PVC soft-drink bottles cannot be used in Switzerland or Germany. However, they are preferred in France, which has an extensive recycling process for them. Thus, international companies are finding it difficult to develop standard environmental practices that work around the world. Instead, they are creating general policies, and then translating these policies into tailored programmes that meet local regulations and expectations.

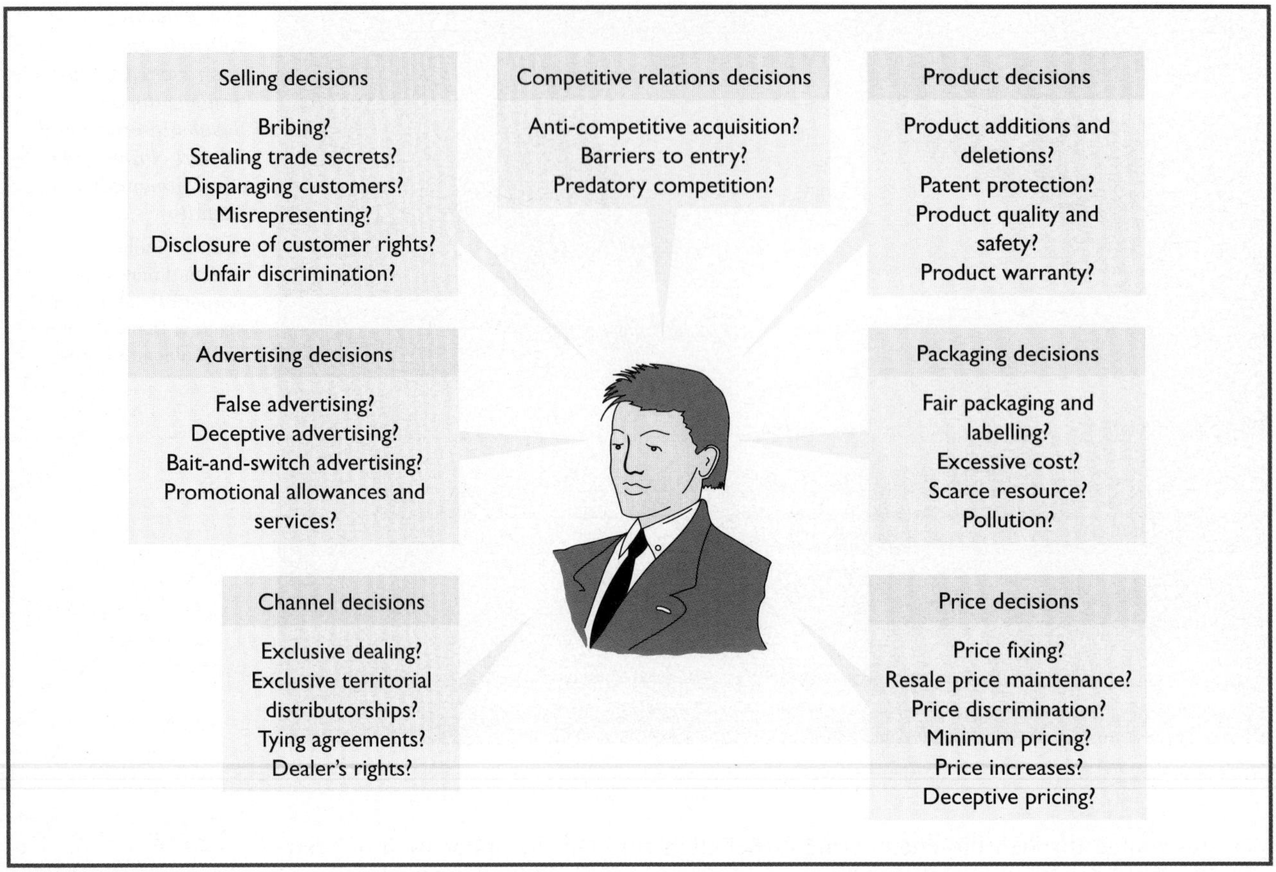

Selling decisions

Bribing?
Stealing trade secrets?
Disparaging customers?
Misrepresenting?
Disclosure of customer rights?
Unfair discrimination?

Competitive relations decisions

Anti-competitive acquisition?
Barriers to entry?
Predatory competition?

Product decisions

Product additions and
deletions?
Patent protection?
Product quality and
safety?
Product warranty?

Advertising decisions

False advertising?
Deceptive advertising?
Bait-and-switch advertising?
Promotional allowances and
services?

Packaging decisions

Fair packaging and
labelling?
Excessive cost?
Scarce resource?
Pollution?

Channel decisions

Exclusive dealing?
Exclusive territorial
distributorships?
Tying agreements?
Dealer's rights?

Price decisions

Price fixing?
Resale price maintenance?
Price discrimination?
Minimum pricing?
Price increases?
Deceptive pricing?

Figure 2.2

Legal issues facing
marketing management

public actions to regulate marketing

Citizen concerns about marketing practices will usually lead to public attention and
legislative proposals. New bills will be debated – many will be defeated, others will be
modified and a few will become workable laws.

Figure 2.2 illustrates the principal legal issues facing marketing management.
Individual country laws exist which affect marketing. The task is to translate these
laws into the language that marketing executives understand as they make decisions
about competitive relations, products, price, promotion and channels of distribution.

Having discussed citizen and public actions to regulate marketing, consumerism,
environmentalism and regulation – and the way they affect marketing – we will next
examine the business actions towards socially responsible marketing that lead to different philosophies of enlightened marketing and the fostering of marketing ethics.

business actions towards socially responsible marketing

Today, most companies have grown to accept the new consumer rights, at least in principle. They might oppose certain pieces of legislation as inappropriate ways to solve

certain consumer problems, but they recognise the consumer's right to information and protection.

enlightened marketing

The philosophy of **enlightened marketing** holds that a company's marketing should support the best long-run performance of the marketing system. Enlightened marketing consists of five principles: consumer-oriented marketing, innovative marketing, value marketing, sense-of-mission marketing and societal marketing. Enlightened marketers also ensure that their marketing approach reflects corporate ethics.

■ Consumer-oriented marketing

Consumer-oriented marketing means that the company views and organises its marketing activities from the consumer's point of view. It works hard to sense, serve and satisfy the needs of a defined group of customers.

■ Innovative marketing

The principle of **innovative marketing** requires that the company continuously seek real product and marketing improvements. The company that overlooks new and better ways to do things will eventually lose customers to another company that has found a better way.

> Ola Ivarsson is the environmental director at Scandic Hotels and his drive to transform the chain into an eco-friendly business has started to revolutionize Europe's leisure industry.
>
> Under Ivarsson's direction, Scandic Hotels has made design improvements that have drastically improved the company's environmental impact. The hotel chain's annual consumption of plastic, metal usage, and the discharge of harmful chemicals has fallen dramatically in recent years; the quantity of unsorted waste produced by the chain has been reduced by a whopping 50 per cent. At the same time, Ivarsson's programme has boosted the chain's popularity, which has helped lift Scandic out of the difficulties it experienced in the early 1990s.
>
> The centrepiece of this design revolution is the 'recyclable room' that Ivarsson created with the help of his team of in-house architects. They managed to make the room a remarkable 97 per cent recyclable, and since then Scandic has built 2,700 more worldwide.
>
> Ivarsson explains, 'We identified our customers' most repetitive activities and found ways of making these less damaging to the environment.' Ivarsson found that many of the best solutions were the least complicated. 'The most creative ideas were deceptively simple', he says. 'For example, we used to provide soap in miniature bars and shampoo in 50 ml bottles. But most customers only use a tiny fraction of these quantities during their stay, so we decided to offer soap and shampoo using dispensers instead. It saves us more than 25 tonnes of soap and shampoo each year.'
>
> Scandic's dispenser system and other innovations, such as the chain's use of natural, renewable materials (wood, wool and cotton), are beginning to catch on among European hoteliers, and the benefits of these materials have been both environmental and economic.

Enlightened marketing
A marketing philosophy holding that a company's marketing should support the best long-run performance of the marketing system; its five principles are consumer-oriented marketing, innovative marketing, value marketing, sense-of-mission marketing and societal marketing.

Consumer-oriented marketing
A principle of enlightened marketing which holds that a company should view and organise its marketing activities from the consumers' point of view.

Innovative marketing
A principle of enlightened marketing which requires that a company seek real product and marketing improvements.

'But customers don't have to be less comfortable', Ivarsson says. 'Our recyclable rooms are at least as comfortable as the others, and they are always booked up first. It's not difficult to see why they're popular. If you look at all that wood, you get a lovely homey, hearty, welcoming feeling – it is beautiful.'[18]

■ Value marketing

Value marketing

A principle of enlightened marketing which holds that a company should put most of its resources into value-building marketing investments.

According to the principle of **value marketing**, the company should put most of its resources into value-building marketing investments. Many things marketers do – one-shot sales promotions, minor packaging changes, advertising puffery – may raise sales in the short run, but add less *value* than would actual improvements in the product's quality, features or convenience. Enlightened marketing calls for building long-run consumer loyalty, by continually improving the value that consumers receive from the firm's marketing offer.

The computer company Dell, which pioneered mail-order selling of personal computers in the late 1980s, is a good example of a value-based marketer. The company recognised that PC buyers were becoming more knowledgeable about computers and the software they wanted, and were confident about making a purchase decision without the need for salespeople's advice and interference. They wanted fast delivery and reliable after-sales service and maintenance support. They did not require the intermediary. Dell bypassed traditional distribution channels used by the competition and, in selling direct to customers, created a unique selling point (USP) based on its innovative distribution arrangements. The approach was so successful that many competitors followed suit. Today, Dell continues to maintain a direct relationship with consumers that enables the company to deliver superior value to buyers by listening better, learning faster and becoming more agile in responding to their changing and differing needs.[19]

■ Sense-of-mission marketing

Sense-of-mission marketing

A principle of enlightened marketing which holds that a company should define its mission in broad social terms rather than narrow product terms.

Sense-of-mission marketing means that the company should define its mission in broad *social* terms rather than narrow *product* terms. When a company defines a social mission, employees feel better about their work and have a clearer sense of direction. For example, defined in narrow product terms, the British Co-operative Bank's mission might be to sell banking services, but the company has taken a firm decision to promote a broader mission – to be an ethical bank, refraining from doing business with those companies that engage in so-called unsavoury business practices, from companies that are involved in the fur trade to tobacco product manufacturers.

■ Societal marketing

Societal marketing

A principle of enlightened marketing which holds that a company should make marketing decisions by considering consumers' wants, the company's requirements, consumers' long-run interests and society's long-run interests.

Following the principle of **societal marketing**, an enlightened company makes marketing decisions by considering consumers' wants and long-run interests, the company's requirements and society's long-run interests. The company is aware that neglecting consumer and societal long-term interests is a disservice to consumers and society. In many cases customer needs, customer wants and customer long-run interests are the same things, and customers are the best judges of what is good for them. However, customers do not invariably make decisions that are good for them. People want to eat fatty food, which is bad for their health; some people want to smoke cigarettes knowing that smoking can kill them and damage the environment for others; many enjoy drinking alcohol despite its ill effects. To control some of the potential evils of marketing there has to be access to the media for the counter-argument – the counter-argument against smoking, against fatty foods, against alcohol. There is also a need for regulation – self if not statutory – to check unsavoury demand.

A second problem is that what consumers want is sometimes at odds with societal welfare. If marketing's job is to fulfil customers' wants, unsavoury desires leave

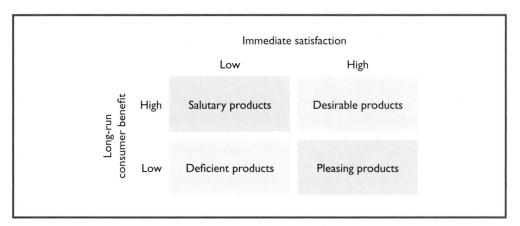

Figure 2.3

Societal classification
of new products.

marketers with a dilemma. Consumers want the convenience and prestige of hardwood window frames, doors and furniture, but society would also like to keep the Amazon rainforest; consumers want the comfort of air-conditioning, yet we need the ozone layer; consumers worldwide should be using lead-free petrol, yet not all bother. Marketing has to be more alert to the inconsistencies between consumer wants and society's welfare. Where there is insufficient drive from within the consumer movement and consumers' own sense of responsibility, marketers would do better to control or regulate their own behaviour in providing goods or services that are undesirable for society at large. If not, legislation is likely to do that for them.

A societally oriented marketer should design products that are not only pleasing but also beneficial. The difference is shown in Figure 2.3. Products can be classified according to their degree of immediate consumer satisfaction and long-run consumer benefit. **Desirable products** such as a tasty and nutritious breakfast food give both high immediate satisfaction and high long-run benefits. **Pleasing products** give high immediate satisfaction, but may hurt consumers in the long run. Examples are indulgence goods like confectionery, alcohol and cigarettes. **Salutary products** have low appeal, but benefit consumers in the long run, for instance seat belts and airbags in cars. Finally, **deficient products**, such as bad-tasting and ineffective medicines, have neither immediate appeal nor long-run benefits.

Companies should try to turn all of their products into desirable products. The international office furniture maker Herman Miller sets itself this goal and has succeeded in

Desirable products
Products that give both high immediate satisfaction and high long-run benefits.

Pleasing products
Products that give high immediate satisfaction but may hurt consumers in the long run.

Salutary products
Products that have low appeal but may benefit consumers in the long run.

Deficient products
Products that have neither immediate appeal nor long-term benefits.

Pears promote their product as being at one with nature – a strategy used more often in this age of heightened environmental awareness.

SOURCE: Pears Soap is manufactured by Lever Fabergé

winning numerous awards for its ecologically friendly products and business practices: its Avian office chair, for example, has the lowest possible environmental impact and is 100 per cent recyclable. The challenge posed by pleasing products is that they sell very well, but may end up hurting the consumer. The product opportunity, therefore, is to add long-run benefits without reducing the product's pleasing qualities. For example, the British drug and household product manufacturer Reckitt & Coleman developed a phosphate-free laundry detergent that was relatively more effective than existing 'green' detergents. The challenge posed by salutary products is to add some pleasing qualities so that they will become more desirable in the consumers' minds. For example, synthetic fats and fat substitutes, such as NutraSweet's Simplesse and P&G's Olese, promise to improve the appeal of low-calorie and low-fat foods.

marketing ethics

Ethics, in the broadest sense of the word, is rising to the top of the corporate agenda. Scarcely a week goes by without a leading company coming under attack, rightly or wrongly, for alleged unethical business practices, whether it is Shell UK dumping its redundant oil platform, Brent Spar, in the North Sea or McVities' use of fish oil from sand eels, an endangered species and puffins' staple diet.

However far from reality the accusations of manufacturers' unethical business practices are, companies under attack risk tarnishing their reputation. And those found guilty of wrongdoing face hefty legal penalties, as in the recent cases of Swiss and German companies that were sued for Holocaust compensation and the world's largest vitamin companies for price-fixing. High-publicity scandals, which made international news, such as the case of Union Carbide's plant in Bhopal, India, which negligently released toxic fumes, killing 25,000 people, serve to remind society of the pressing imperatives for corporations to act in an ethical manner.

Conscientious marketers, however, face many moral dilemmas. The best thing to do is often unclear. Because not all managers have fine moral sensitivity, companies need to develop *corporate marketing ethics policies* – broad guidelines that everyone in the organisation must follow. They cover distributor relations, advertising standards, customer service, pricing, product development and general ethical standards. The finest guidelines cannot resolve all the difficult ethical situations the marketer faces. However, managers need a set of principles that will help them figure out the moral importance of each situation and decide how far they can go in good conscience.

But *what* principle should guide companies and marketing managers on issues of ethics and social responsibility? One philosophy is that such issues are decided by the free market and legal system. Under this principle, companies and their managers are not responsible for making moral judgements. Companies can in good conscience do whatever the system allows.

A second philosophy puts responsibility not in the system, but in the hands of individual companies and managers. This more *enlightened philosophy* suggests that a company should have a 'social conscience'. Companies and managers should apply high standards of ethics and morality when making corporate decisions, regardless of 'what the system allows'. They must work out a philosophy of socially responsible and ethical behaviour. Consistent with the societal marketing concept, each manager must look beyond what is legal and allowed, and develop standards based on personal integrity, corporate conscience and long-run consumer welfare. A clear and responsible philosophy will help the marketing manager deal with the many knotty questions posed by marketing and other human activities.

In searching for ethical standards for marketing, marketing managers may also draw upon postmodernist thinking and philosophies that date back well beyond marketing itself. Marketing Highlight 2.2 introduces some of this.[20]

marketing highlight 2.2

From Plato's Republic to supermarket slavery

There is good reason to search a long way back for the ethics to guide marketing. As the British philosopher Alfred North Whitehead (1861–1947) commented, 'all Western philosophy is really no more than a footnote to Plato's (428–354 BC) great work *The Republic*'. If that were true, our thinking on 'marketing ethics' is little more than a smudge on that footnote.

The ancients were also practical, as Plato's student explained:

> Ethics is a rough and ready business determined by ordinary practical men of common sense, not by inbred ascetic 'experts' with their heads in a remote and austere world.
>
> Aristotle (384–322 BC)

Thinking's the thing

A lot of thinking went on in ancient Athens, a city state of only about 400,000 people. Socrates (469–399 BC) thought that the most important thing about human beings is that they ask questions. He also thought that real moral knowledge existed and was worth pursuing. He did not think morality could be tough, but said that it was more than just obeying the law. The newly democratic Athenians did not like this questioning of state morality, so they condemned him to death by poisoning.

Good for the state and good for you too

Plato thought that Athens' experiments with democracy were a shambles and left town. He believed in moral absolutes that were separate from the more sordid world. This led him to idealise regimes where right and wrong were well defined. He thought militaristic and disciplined Sparta was a much better place than free-thinking Athens and that people should do what is good for the state. Lots of leaders have tried this and very nasty it is too.

Choosing the happy medium

Aristotle rejected his teachers' concern for absolute truths, suggesting that people take a middle road and learn how to behave from experience. People learn to become good citizens, and from that achieve contentment. Well, most people! And how about being a good citizen of a gang of hooligans?

It was a long time before western philosophy recovered from these Greeks, but the Renaissance got things going again. Machiavelli was born in another city state: Florence.

He may be dung, but at least he's our dung

Machiavelli (1469–1527) was an observer rather than a philosopher. After he saw what succeeded, he recognised that politics and morality mix badly. This is a convenient view for business leaders who think there should be two sets of moral standards: one for public life and one for private life. In political and business life it is necessary to be pragmatic and prudent – in other words, unethical – while retaining a different private ethic. As recent politicians have found, life does not always divide so easily.

Solitary, poor, nasty, brutish and short

The English Royalist Hobbes (1588–1678) is even more depressing than Machiavelli. People are awful and are prevented from degenerating into our natural brutish behaviour only by realising that everyone behaving that way would make life unbearable. People therefore establish a 'social contract' (which parents call 'bringing up') that has to be enforced by a neutral third party (government contract). Franco-Swiss Rousseau (1712–78) had the opposite view that humanity is essentially good, but is corrupted by society to want things like smart clothes, carriages and Nike trainers.

Sum happiness

English Utilitarians Bentham (1748–1832) and Mill (1806–73) invented a form of moral calculus. Bentham thought his country's laws were in a mess because they lacked a scientific foundation. He saw human beings as pleasure–pain machines, so he suggested that law makers should balance the sum of the pain and pleasure to achieve 'the greatest happiness of the greatest number'. This has two consequences: means justifying ends, and problems for minority groups. Mills worried about this 'tyranny of the majority'. He preferred talking about happiness rather than pleasure, tolerated individual lifestyles and thought that the 'happiness sums' varied and were for individuals as well as law makers.

Bah, happiness

Kant (1724–1804) had little time for happiness. The German idealist's ethics had categorical imperatives. He believed that a moral action was one done out of a sense of duty. Ethics was about finding out our duties and living by them. Kant deduced a 'universality test' to find the compulsory rules. He asked people to imagine what it would be like if everybody did what they themselves wanted to do. Using this mind model, we deduce that if people sold shoddy goods habitually, life would be chaotic and, therefore, people have a duty not to sell shoddy goods.

And justice for all

Living American John Rawls (1921–) has greatly influenced modern liberal thinking. He has a mind model based on imagining a group of people brought together with no knowledge of what place they will have in society. They have to invent a series of rules that will make their community just and fair. Then they have to live in it.

Don't know; can't know

This rationalist claim to understanding 'truths' started being undermined by Scotsman David Hume (1711–76). His 'meta-ethics' does not offer any advice, but recognises an 'is–ought gap' between what we experience (is) and the conclusion we try to draw from that (ought). Even though we know that bull bars on cars kill children (is), we can only produce a false argument that they should not be sold (ought). Developing similar insights, it follows that any moral argument between people is 'utterly futile, unsolvable and irrational' (A. J. Ayers, 1910–89).

The age of unreason

Postmodernists have pursued this ethical scepticism to new levels. Reason fails because of its dependence on language. What passed as reason in the past has caused so much human suffering. This level of ethical uncertainty is not new; it is close to the Sophist views that Plato argued against. Postmodernists despair at the society they see coming: a kaleidoscope of consumerist images that hypnotise citizens into accepting the morality of capitalism; where individual morality ceases to exist, where all that remains is supermarket slavery and where the only choice is by consumers between products – marketing.

Meanwhile Alisdair MacIntyre looks back to the Aristotelian idea that we should concentrate less on the individual and more on people and what is good for the society.

SOURCES: J. Ackrill, *Aristotle and the Philosophers* (Oxford, 1981); G. Kerner, *Three Philosophical Moralists* (Oxford, 1990); A. MacIntyre, *A Short History of Ethics* (Routledge, 1987); D. Robinson and C. Garratt, *Ethics for Beginners* (Icon, 1996); B. Russell, *A History of Western Philosophy* (Oxford, 1945); P. Singer, *Practical Ethics* (Oxford, 1993).

As with environmentalism, the issue of ethics provides special challenges for international marketers. Business standards and practices vary a great deal from one country to the next. Imagine you are trying to win a big public contract in a developing country. The minister in charge makes unmistakable references to the disgracefully low pay of local civil officials and the benefits his own children would enjoy if they could study abroad. The cost of providing this (concealed as a 'scholarship' paid for by your company) is minute compared with the value of the contract. Your competitors, given the chance, would assuredly find the money. Do you pull out, or pay up?

Most businesspeople in such situations find that their scruples are soon swallowed. So do most governments. Germany is one of several European countries where bribes paid abroad are tax-deductible (although the tax office may want proof that the person paid is not liable for German income tax). The United States is harsher – under the Foreign Corrupt Practices Act, executives can face jail for paying bribes. But it is hard to prove; and many firms may get third-party consultancies to do their bribing for them. So, across the globe, national cultures naturally impose different standards of behaviour on individuals and organisations. In the European Union, each market sector in each country is still characterised by a mixture of accepted commercial practices, codes of practice and formalised legislation. What is considered an acceptable practice in one country may be illegal in another (see Marketing Highlight 2.3). The EU may eventually move towards a pan-European business ethics policy and codes of conduct, but that day is still some way off.[21]

The question arises as to whether a company must lower its ethical standards to compete effectively in countries with lower standards. In a recent study, two

marketing highlight 2.3

Frequent flyer: perks or bribes?

A high-ranking official at the Swedish Board of Health and Welfare faced prosecution for allegedly violating regulations prohibiting public sector employees from making private use of airline bonus points gained on business trips. The official was suspended for using bonus points accumulated on regular business flights under Scandinavian Airlines System's EuroBonus scheme to fund private holidays. A similar case has also been reported from Finland, where strict anti-corruption laws also prevent employees from accepting inducements.

The incidents reflect tensions between employers and SAS over the frequent-flyer programme, which, companies say, inflates ticket prices, restricts competition and encourages staff to make unnecessary trips in order to amass bonus points.

Public organisations have declared that the benefits constitute illegal inducements when offered to business travellers, and have issued instructions to employees banning private use of frequent-flyer benefits. In the private sector, personal use of bonus points has also been deemed unlawful unless sanctioned by the employer. Ulf Franke, of the Stockholm-based Institute Against Corruption, a private watchdog, said: 'Giving private benefits to business travellers is just like sending them a cheque. The law is absolutely clear, it is corrupt behaviour.'

But employers say it is practically impossible to track down individuals who contravene the regulations. The Swedish parliament said state bodies and companies were powerless to intervene because the frequent-flyer programme was a private contract between airline and traveller. The parliament is among a growing number of public and private sector employers that have protested to SAS, urging it to modify the system by allowing them to handle the bonus points on behalf of their workers. SAS has rejected the pleas out of hand as the key object of the scheme is to cultivate the loyalty of individual passengers.

Instead, business travellers' associations in Sweden and Denmark turned to the European Commission in Brussels, urging it to rule frequent-flyer schemes unlawful on competition grounds. The Swedish Business Travellers' Association spokesperson said that bonus programmes discriminated against smaller carriers. 'Only the biggest companies have the resources to fund these schemes. If a carrier does not have a large number of routes, it is forced out of the market.'

SAS insists that its frequent-flyer programme does not prompt staff to make unnecessary journeys, but simply encourages them to fly more with SAS. With 800,000 members, the SAS EuroBonus scheme is expanding at the rate of 150,000 new subscriptions per year. The airline brushes off talk of illegal inducements. It is up to employers to clamp down on abuses.

'It is not up to us to be a police force', said Knut Lovstuhagen, SAS's director of corporate communications.

Source: Greg McIvor, 'Swedes say frequent-flyer perks are bribes', *The European* (15–21 February 1996), p. 17.

---

researchers posed this question to chief executives of large international companies and got a unanimous response: No.[22] For the sake of all the company's stakeholders – customers, suppliers, employees, shareholders and the public – it is important to make a commitment to a common set of standards worldwide. Some western firms have already done so. For example, the ethical code of Levi Strauss, a jeans manufacturer, forbids bribes, whether or not prevalent or legal in the foreign country involved.

Many industrial and professional associations have suggested codes of ethics. Efforts have also been made to develop 'global' standards. One example is the Social Accountability standard called SA8000, launched in 1998 by an independent US-based agency, the Council on Economic Priorities. SA8000 verifies the ethical stance of businesses in the production and sourcing of goods from the developing countries. Businesses applying for the standard are accredited by SGS-ICS, the Swiss company that is the world's largest certification agency. Many companies are now adopting their own codes of ethics.[23] Companies have set up ethics committees and are also developing programmes, workshops and seminars to teach managers about important ethics issues and help them find the proper responses.[24] Further, more and more international companies have appointed high-level ethics officers to champion ethics issues and to help resolve problems and concerns facing employees.

Still, written codes and ethics programmes do not ensure ethical behaviour. The code of the Prudential Corporation, a life-insurance-to-property group, pledges to work for the good of its shareholders, customers and staff. It notes that 'in providing its business, the Prudential aims are to abide by the spirit of laws as well as their letter and to be a significant contributor to the development and well-being of the wider community in which we operate'. The guidelines are well meaning but too abstract to direct action when the interests of the company diverge sharply from those of its employees, customers or the local community. There have to be precise statements that spell out what employees must do in specific dilemmas, such as bribes and gifts, whether being offered or asked for. There should also be sanctions to enforce the code, so that ethical pledges are more than mere PR 'puff'.

Ethics and social responsibility require a total corporate commitment. They must be components of the overall corporate culture. Ethics programmes or seminars for employees help to imbue corporate ethics and codes of conduct among staff, while ethical and social audits may be used to monitor and evaluate business conduct and to use the lessons to guide both policy and behaviour:

> In the final analysis, 'ethical behaviour' must be an integral part of the organization, a way of life that is deeply ingrained in the collective corporate body . . . In any business enterprise, ethical behaviour must be a tradition, a way of conducting one's affairs that is passed from generation to generation of employees at all levels of the organization. It is the responsibility of management, starting at the very top, to both set the example by personal conduct and create an environment that not only encourages and rewards ethical behaviour, but which also makes anything less totally unacceptable.[25]

The future holds many challenges and opportunities for marketing managers as they move into the twenty-first century. Technological advances in every area, from telecommunications information technology and the Internet to health care and entertainment, provide abundant marketing opportunities. However, forces in the socioeconomic, cultural and natural environments increase the limits within which marketing can be carried out. Companies that are able to create new customer value in a socially responsible way will have a world to conquer.

summary

In this chapter, we have examined many important concepts involving marketing's sweeping impact on individual consumers, other businesses and society as a whole. Responsible marketers discover what consumers want and respond with the right products, priced to give good value to buyers and profit to the company. A marketing system should sense, serve and satisfy consumer needs and improve the quality of consumers' lives. In working to meet consumer needs, marketers may take some actions that are not to everyone's liking or benefit. Marketing managers should be aware of the main *criticisms of marketing*.

Marketing's *impact on individual consumer welfare* has been criticised for its *high prices, deceptive practices, high-pressure selling, shoddy or unsafe products, planned obsolescence* and *poor service to disadvantaged consumers*. Marketing's *impact on society* has been criticised for *creating false wants* and *too much materialism, too few social goods, cultural pollution* and *too much political power*. Critics have also criticised marketing's *impact on other businesses* for *harming competitors* and *reducing competition* through acquisitions, practices that create barriers to entry, and unfair competitive marketing practices.

Concerns about the marketing system have led to *citizen action movements*. *Consumerism* is an organised social movement intended to strengthen the rights and power of consumers relative to sellers. Alert marketers view it as an opportunity to serve consumers better by providing more consumer information, education and protection.

Environmentalism is an organised social movement seeking to minimise the harm done to the environment and quality of life by marketing practices. The first wave of modern environmentalism was driven by environmental groups and concerned consumers, whereas the second was driven by government, which passed laws and regulations governing practices impacting the environment. Moving into the twenty-first century, the first two environmentalism waves are merging into a third and stronger wave in which companies are accepting responsibility for doing no environmental harm. Companies now are adopting policies of environmental sustainability – developing strategies that both sustain the environment and produce profits for the company.

Many companies originally opposed these social movements and laws, but most of them now recognise a need for positive consumer information, education and protection. Some companies have followed a policy of enlightened marketing based on the principles of *consumer orientation, innovation, value creation, social mission* and *societal marketing*.

Increasingly, companies are responding to the need to provide company policies and guidelines to help their employees deal with questions of *marketing ethics*. Of course, even the best guidelines cannot resolve all the difficult ethical decisions that individuals and firms must make. However, there are some principles that marketers can choose among. One principle states that such issues should be decided by the free market and legal system. A second, and more enlightened principle puts responsibility not in the system but in the hands of individual companies and managers. Each firm and marketing manager must work out a philosophy of socially responsible and ethical behaviour. Under the societal marketing concept, managers must look beyond what is legal and allowable and develop standards based on personal integrity, corporate conscience and long-term consumer welfare.

discussing the issues

1. Marketing receives much criticism, some justified and much not. Which of the major criticisms of marketing discussed in the chapter do you think are most justified? Which are least justified? Explain.

2. You have been invited to appear along with an economist on a panel assessing marketing practices in the soft-drink industry. You are surprised when the economist opens the discussion with a long list of criticisms (focusing especially on the unnecessarily high marketing costs and deceptive promotional practices). Abandoning your prepared comments, you set out to defend marketing in general and the beverage industry in particular. How would you respond to the economist's attack?

3. Comment on the state of consumers' rights on the Internet and in e-commerce. Design a 'Bill of Rights' that would protect consumers while they shop for products and services on the Internet. Consider such issues as government regulation, ease and convenience of use, solicitation, privacy and cost-efficient commerce.

4. You are the marketing manager for a small firm that makes kitchen appliances. While conducting field tests, you discover a design flaw in one of your most popular models that could potentially cause harm to a small number of consumers. However, a product recall is likely to bankrupt your company, leaving all of the employees (including you) jobless. What would you do?

5. The issue of ethics provides special challenges for international marketers as business standards and practices vary a great deal from one country to the next. Should a company adapt its ethical standards to compete effectively in countries with different standards? (Bribes, use of child labour, low wages, positive discrimination against female workers and members from ethnic minorities might be examples of values/practices which vary across countries/cultures in different corners of the globe and can be used to focus your discussion.)

applying the concepts

1. Changes in consumer attitudes, especially the growth of consumerism and environmentalism, have led to more societal marketing – and to more marketing that is *supposedly* good for society, but is actually close to deception.

   ✦ List three examples of marketing campaigns that you feel are genuine societal marketing. If possible, find examples of firm communications, including advertising or packaging that support these campaigns. You may also visit relevant websites of companies of your choice to gather more specific information on these campaigns.

   ✦ Find three examples of deceptive or borderline imitations of societal marketing. How are you able to tell which campaigns are genuine and which are not?

   ✦ What remedies, if any, would you recommend for this problem?

2. As a small child you were probably taught that 'it is better to give than to receive'. This advice is one of the cornerstones of philanthropy, including corporate philanthropy. Given the new environmentalism and social responsibility in western societies today, explain what should be an organisation's view towards charitable giving. What are the marketing ramifications of an organisation's philanthropic activities? Many corporations support worthy causes and contribute generously to their communities. Check out the websites of one of the following or some other company and report on its philanthropic and socially responsible activities: Nestlé (www.nestlé.com), Johnson & Johnson (www.jnj.com), Nike (www.nikebiz.com), Coca-Cola (www.cocacola.com) and Prudential Life Insurance (www.prudential.com). How does philanthropy by corporations relate to the social criticisms of marketing?

references

1. See Neil Buckley, 'New tobacco regulations on health supported', *Financial Times* (15 June 2000), p. 10; Warren Giles and John Thornhill, 'Gloves off in WHO tobacco campaign', *Financial Times* (22 September 2000), p. 10; John Mason, 'Victims can sue tobacco companies', *Financial Times* (13 February 1998), p. 1; Julian Coman, 'Tobacco's last gasp', *The European* (23 February–1 March 1998), pp. 8–12; Andrew Edgecliffe-Johnson, 'Tobacco companies refuse to settle lawsuits', *Financial Times* (1 May 2000), p. 6; David Brierley, 'A woman's place is in the pub, smoking', *The European* (20–6 June 1996), p. 29; 'The tobacco wars: Looking for a landmark', *The Economist* (11 July 1998), pp. 88 and 91. For more discussion about the gains and losses in a total ban on tobacco advertising, see Stephanie Bentley, 'Stubbing out advertising', *Marketing Week* (5 January 1996), pp. 18–21; 'Chewing up tobacco', *The Economist* (20 September 1997), p. 106.

2. See Steven H. Star, 'Marketing and its discontents', *Harvard Business Review* (November–December 1989), pp. 148–54; Miriam Catterall, Pauline Maclaran and Lorna Stevens, 'Critical marketing in the classroom: possibilities and challenges', *Marketing Intelligence and Planning*, **17**, 7 (1999), pp. 344–53.

3. Excerpts from Theodore Levitt, 'The morality(?) of advertising', *Harvard Business Review* (July–August 1970), pp. 84–92; Ben Abrahams, 'The ASA: Older and wiser', *Marketing* (10 July 2000), p. 3.

4. 'ITC unveils new rules on food, drugs', *Marketing Week* (3 February 1995), p. 9.

5. 'When quality control breaks down', *The European* (6–12 November 1997), p. 29. For more discussion on managing product recalls, see N. Craig Smith, Robert J. Thomas and John A. Quelch, 'A strategic approach to managing product recalls', *Harvard Business Review* (September–October 1996), pp. 102–12.

6. For a thought-provoking short case involving planned obsolescence, see James A. Heely and Roy L. Nersesian, 'The case of planned obsolescence', *Management Accounting* (February 1994), p. 67. Also see Joel Dreyfuss, 'Planned obsolescence is alive and well', *Fortune* (15 February 1999), p. 192.

7. James Twitchell, 'Two cheers for materialism', *The Wilson Quarterly*, Spring 1999, pp. 16–26; and Twitchell, *Lead Us into Temptation: The triumph of American materialism* (New York: Columbia University Press, 1999).

8. Kim Clark, 'Real-World-O-Nomics: How to make traffic jams a thing of the past', *Fortune* (31 March 1997), p. 34.

9. Gail Kemp, 'Commercial break: Should kids' TV ads be banned?', *Marketing Business* (September 1999), pp. 16–18; John Clare, 'Marketing's "material girls" aged only three', *The Daily Telegraph* (23 November 1999), p. 9.

10. Richard Wolffe, 'Lawyers try to expand case against Microsoft', *Financial Times* (17/18 June 2000), p. 9; Deborah Hargreaves, 'European Commission to continue inquiry', *Financial Times* (9 June 2000), p. 11; Richard Wolffe and Fiona Harvey, 'Door left open for Microsoft talks', *Financial Times* (9 June 2000), p. 11; Richard Wolffe, Andrew Hill and Lesia Ruda Kewych, 'Judge rules against Microsoft', *Financial Times* (4 April 2000), p. 1; Steve Hamm, 'Microsoft's future', *Business Week* (19 January 1998), pp. 58–68; Ronald A. Cass, 'Microsoft, running scared', *The New York Times* (28 June 1999), p. 17.

11. 'Going for Coke', *The Economist* (14 August 1999), pp. 55–6; 'Coke is hit again', *The Economist* (24 July 1999), pp. 70–1.

12. For more details, see Paul N. Bloom and Stephen A. Greyser, 'The maturing of consumerism', *Harvard Business Review* (November–December 1981), pp. 130–9; Douglas A. Harbrecht, 'The second coming of Ralph Nader', *Business Week* (6 March 1989), p. 28; George S. Day and David A. Aaker, 'A guide to consumerism', *Marketing Management* (Spring 1997), pp. 44–8; Benet Middleton, 'Consumerism: a pragmatic ideology', *Consumer Policy Review* (November/December 1998), pp. 213–7; Colin Brown, 'Consumer activism in Europe', *Consumer Policy Review*, **8**, 6 (1998), pp. 209–12.

13. Michael Lindemann, 'Green light begins to flash for recyclable cars in Germany', *Financial Times* (3 August 1994), p. 2; Udo Mildenberger and Anshuman Khare, 'Planning for an environmentally-friendly car', *Technovation*, **20**, 4 (2000), pp. 205–14.

14. Michael E. Porter and Claas van der Linde, 'Green and competitive: Ending the stalemate', *Harvard Business Review* (September–October 1995), pp. 120–34. See also Andrea Prothero, 'Green marketing: The "fad" that won't slip away', *Journal of Marketing Management*, **14**, 6 (1998), pp. 507–12.

15. Stuart L. Hart, 'Beyond greening: Strategies for a sustainable world', *Harvard Business Review* (January–February 1997), pp. 66–76; for other examples, see Jacquelyn Ottman, 'Environmental winners show sustainable strategies', *Marketing News* (27 April 1998), p. 6.

16. Lars K. Hallstrom, 'Industry versus ecology: Environment in the New Europe', *Futures* (February 1999), pp. 25–38; Andreas Diekmann and Axel Frannzen, 'The wealth of nations and environmental concern', *Environment and Behavior* (July 1999), pp. 540–9; John Audley, *Green Politics and Global Trade: NAFTA and the future of environmental politics* (Georgetown University Press, 1997).

17. For more details on the 'green' debate, see R. Schuster, *Environmentally Oriented Consumer Behaviour in Europe* (Hamburg: Kovac, 1992); R. Worcester, *Public and Elite Attitudes to Environmental Issues* (London: MORI, 1993); Ian Hamilton Fazey, 'Paints and the environment', survey, *Financial Times* (8 April 1994); Stavros P. Kalafatis, Michael Pollard, Robert East and Markos H. Tsogas, 'Green marketing and Azjen's theory of planned behaviour: a cross-market examination', *Journal of Consumer Marketing*, **16**, 5 (1999), pp. 441–60.

18. Nathan Yates, 'Now recycle your room', *The European Magazine* (24–30 April 1997), p. 13.

19. Alan Mitchell, 'Changing channels', *Marketing Business* (February 1995), pp. 10–13.

20. 'Who will listen to Mr Clean?', *The Economist* (2 August 1997), p. 58.

21. See Susan Norgan, *Marketing Management: A European perspective* (Wokingham, Berks: Addison-Wesley, 1994), p. 49; David Murphy, 'Cross-border conflicts', *Marketing* (11 February 1999), pp. 30–3.

22. John F. Magee and P. Ranganath Nayak, 'Leaders' perspectives on Business Ethics', *Prism*, Arthur D. Little, Inc., Cambridge, MA, first quarter, 1994, pp. 65–77; see also Kumar C. Rallapali, 'A paradigm for development and promulgation of a global code of marketing ethics', *Journal of Business Ethics* (January 1999), pp. 125–37.

23. Simon Buckby, 'Standard to verify business ethics launched', *Financial Times* (11 June 1998), p. 9; Bodo Schlegelmilch, 'A review of marketing ethics: An international perspective', *International Marketing Review*, **16**, 3 (1999), pp. 1–7.

24. 'Good takes on greed', *The Economist* (17 February 1990), pp. 87–9; Patrick Maclagan, 'Education and development for corporate ethics: An overview', *Industrial and Commercial Training*, **26**, 4 (1994), pp. 3–7.

25. From 'Ethics as a practical matter', a message from David R. Whitman, chairman of the board of Whirlpool Corporation, as reprinted in Ricky E. Griffin and Ronald J. Ebert, *Business* (Englewood Cliffs, NJ: Prentice Hall, 1989), pp. 578–9. For more discussion, see Thomas Donaldson, 'Values in tension', *Harvard Business Review* (September–October 1996), pp. 48–62.

case 2

Nestlé: singled out again and again

'During the first few months, the mother's milk will always be the most natural nutriment, and every mother able to do so, should herself suckle her children.'

HENRI NESTLÉ, 1869

The corporate affairs department at Nestlé UK's head-quarters were bracing themselves for another burst of adverse publicity. At the forthcoming General Synod of the Church of England a motion would call for a contin-ued ban on Nescafé by the Church. They also wanted the Church Commissioners to disinvest their £1.1m (€1.8m) in Nestlé. The Church's much publicised boy-cott of Nescafé first occurred, amid much ridicule, in 1991, as a protest against the use of breast milk substi-tutes in the Third World countries. In the aftermath of the 1991 vote, Nescafé claimed that its sales increased, although many churchgoers said they stopped using the brand-leading coffee. The new protest would be one of many the company had faced from activist protesters in the last 25 years although, according to Nestlé, the protesters' complaints had no foundation.

Nestlé SA, whose headquarters are in Vevey, Switzerland, is the world's largest food company, with annual sales of CHF75 billion (€52b), 509 factories and 230,000 employees worldwide. Henri Nestlé invented manufactured baby food 'to save a child's life' and the company have been suppliers ever since. Then, in the late 1970s and early 1980s, Nestlé came under heavy fire from activists who charged the company with encouraging Third World mothers to give up breast feed-ing and use a company-prepared formula. In 1974 the British charity, War on Want, published a pamphlet, *The Baby Killer*, that criticised Unigate and Nestlé's ill-advised marketing efforts in Africa. While War on Want criticised the entire infant formula industry, the German-based Third World Action Group issued a 'translation' of the original pamphlet retitled *Nestlé Kills Babies*, which singled out the company for 'unethical and immoral behaviour'. The pamphlets generated much publicity. Enraged at the protest, Nestlé sued the activists for defamation. The two-year case kept media attention on the issue. 'We won the legal case, but it was a public-relations disaster,' commented a Nestlé executive.

In 1977, two American social-interest groups, the Interfaith Center on Corporate Responsibility and the Infant Formula Action Coalition (INFACT), spearheaded a worldwide boycott against Nestlé. The campaign con-tinued despite the fact that many organisations rejected the boycott. The US United Methodist Church con-cluded that the activists were guilty of 'substantial and sometimes gross misrepresentation', of 'inflammatory rhetoric', and of using 'wildly exaggerated figures'. The boycott was called off in 1984 when the activists accepted that the company was complying with an infant formula marketing code adopted by the World Health Organisation (WHO). Since then, church, uni-versity, local government and other action groups peri-odically rediscover the controversy and create publicity by calling for a boycott.

In the 1990s the main accusation became Nestlé's use of promotions that persuaded hundreds of thou-sands of poverty-stricken, poorly educated mothers that formula feeding was better for their children. One issue predominated: the donation of free or low-cost supplies of infant formula to maternity wards and hospitals in developing countries. Formula feeding is usually an unwise practice in such countries because of poor living conditions and habits; people cannot or do not clean bottles properly and often mix formula with impure water. Income level does not permit many families to buy sufficient quantities of formula. Protesters hit out at several industry practices, keeping Nestlé as their prime target:

✦ Promotional baby booklets ignoring or de-emphasising breast feeding.

✦ Misleading advertising encouraging mothers to bottle feed their babies and showing breast feeding to be old-fashioned and inconvenient.

✦ Gifts and samples inducing mothers to bottle feed their infants.

✦ Posters and pamphlets in hospitals.

✦ Endorsements of bottle feeding by milk nurses.

✦ Formula so expensive that poor customers dilute to non-nutritious levels.

A WHO code eliminates all promotional efforts, requiring companies to serve primarily as passive 'order takers'. It prohibits advertising, samples and direct con-tact with consumers. Contacts with professionals (such as doctors) occur only if professionals seek such con-tact. Manufacturers can package products with some form of visual corporate identity, but they cannot pic-ture babies. The WHO code effectively allows almost no marketing. However, the code contains only *recom-mended* guidelines. They become *mandatory* only if individual governments adopt national codes through their own regulatory mechanisms.

WHO allows the donation of free or low-cost supplies of infant formulas for infants who cannot be breast-fed.

However, the International Association of Infant Food Manufacturers (IFM) is working with WHO and UNICEF to secure country-by-country agreements with countries to end free and low-cost supplies. By the end of 1994, only one small developing country had not agreed to the change.

Nestlé itself has a policy on low-cost supplies in developing countries, as follows:

✦ Where there is government agreement, Nestlé will strictly apply the terms of that agreement.

✦ Where there is no agreement Nestlé, in cooperation with others, will be active in trying to secure early government action.

✦ Where other companies break an agreement, Nestlé will work with IFM and governments to stop the breach.

✦ Nestlé will take disciplinary measures against any Nestlé personnel or distributors who deliberately violate Nestlé policy.

Given the repeated public relations problems that Nestlé faces, why does it not take unilateral action in ending free supplies? Since the Third World infant formula market is so small compared with Nestlé's worldwide interests, why bother with it? Part of the answer is in Henri Nestlé's desire 'to save a child's life'. The European Commission's directive on baby food concludes that infant formula is 'the only processed foodstuff that wholly satisfies the nutritional requirements of infants' first four to six months of life'.

Few mothers in countries with very high infant mortality rates use anything other than breast milk. However, Kenya is probably typical of what happens when mothers do supplement breast milk with something else:

✦ 33 per cent use uji, a local food made from maize;

✦ 33 per cent use cow's milk;

✦ 28 per cent use water;

✦ 14 per cent use glucose;

✦ 11 per cent use milk powder, of which some is infant formula;

✦ 3 per cent use tea.

A study in the Ivory Coast shows the sort of problems that arise when Nestlé withdraws unilaterally. Other companies replaced the supplies to the affluent private nurseries, but supplies for mothers in need collapsed. As a result the main hospital was not able to 'afford to buy enough to feed abandoned babies or those whose mothers are ill'.

Questions

1. Was and is Nestlé's and the other IFM members' marketing of infant formula 'unethical and immoral'?

2. Is it the case that ethical standards should be the responsibility of organisations such as WHO and UNESCO, and that the sole responsibility of firms is to work within the bounds set?

3. Is Nestlé just unlucky or did its actions precipitate its being singled out by activists? Is the activists' focus on Nestlé unjust and itself dangerous? What accounts for Nestlé's continuing in the infant formula market despite the protests?

4. Did Nestlé benefit from confronting the activists directly in court and winning? Should firms ever confront activists directly? What other forms of action are available to the company? Should firms withdraw from legitimate markets because of the justified or unjustified actions of pressure groups?

5. The WHO code is a recommendation to government. Is it Nestlé's responsibility to operate according to the national legislation of any given country, or to follow WHO's recommendations to that country? Do international bodies setting international standards, such as WHO and UNICEF, have a moral responsibility to make those standards clearly understood by all parties and to demand action by national governments to enact them?

6. How should Nestlé respond to the threats from the General Synod in 1994? Since Nestlé claimed sales increased after the Nescafé boycott in 1991, should it just ignore the problem?

Sources: John Sparks, 'The Nestlé controversy – anatomy of a boycott', Public Policy Education Fund, Inc. (June 1981); Robert F. Hartley, *Marketing Mistakes* (Chichester, UK: Wiley, 1986); European Commission, Commission Directive on Infant Formula and Follow-on Formula, 91/321/EEC; UNICEF, *The State of the World's Children* (1992); RBL, *Survey of Baby Feeding in Kenya* (1992); Nestlé, *Nestlé and Baby Milk* (1994); Andrew Brown, 'Synod votes to end Nestlé boycott after passionate debate', *Independent* (12 July 1994), 'Church boycott of Nescafé ends', *The Times* (12 July 1994); Damion Thompson, 'Synod rejects disestablishment move', *The Daily Telegraph* (12 July 1994); 'Clear conscience for Nescafé drinkers', *Church Times* (17 July 1994). Also see Nestlé's infant formula website nestle.com/in_your_life/ and that of the protesters at infactcanada.ca/newsletters/spring95/boycott.htm and zmag.org/Bulletins/pnest.htm.

internet exercises

Internet exercises for this chapter can be found on the student site of the MYPHLIP Web Site at www.booksites.net/kotler.

chapter three

Strategic marketing planning

Chapter objectives *After reading this chapter, you should be able to:*

- ✦ Explain company-wide strategic planning and its principal steps.

- ✦ Describe how companies develop mission statements and objectives.

- ✦ Explain how companies evaluate and develop their business portfolios.

- ✦ Explain marketing's role in strategic planning.

- ✦ Describe the marketing management process.

- ✦ Show how marketing organisations are changing.

introduction

Just like the luxury-goods makers in the preview case opposite, all companies need strategies to meet changing markets. No one strategy is best for all companies. Each company must find the way that makes most sense, given its situation, opportunities, objectives and resources. Marketing plays an important role in strategic planning. It provides information and other inputs to help prepare the strategic plan. Strategic planning is also the first stage of marketing planning and defines marketing's role in the organisation. The strategic plan guides marketing, which must work with other departments in the organisation to achieve strategic objectives.

Here we look at the three stages of strategic market planning: first, the strategic plan and its implications for marketing; second, the marketing process; and third, ways of putting the plan into action.

strategic planning

overview of planning

Many companies operate without formal plans. In new companies, managers are sometimes too busy for planning. In small companies, managers may think that only large

preview case

Poor little rich brands

'We prefer the Blue Circle Café to the Sotto Vento', exclaims Sten, the son of a Norwegian millionaire. The Sotto Vento is on the exclusive Costa Smeralda, and is Sardinia's most famous disco but, says Sten, 'is already being invaded by "the Rolex crowd"'.

Sten has a point. While most people never aspire to owning a pair of €2,000 Gucci crocodile skin loafers, many do. According to Sten, those who want to show off such belongings go to Antibes or St Tropez. Costa Smeralda is somewhat different. The likes of Sylvester Stallone, David Bowie, Tom Cruise and Nicole Kidman go there so as not to be seen. They do not wear Gucci, Prada or Versace to display their success but because that is what their local store sells. Whereas luxury brands bestow glamour to ordinary mortals, the super rich who holiday at Costa Smeralda bestow glamour to the luxury brands. Similarly, the Aga Khan's original investment in the Costa Smeralda became attractive to the super *nouveau riche* after Prince Rainier of Monaco, Prince Juan Carlos of Spain and Britain's Princess Margaret became regular visitors.

Costa Smeralda retains its exclusivity by staying small, being well guarded and being only accessible by helicopter or cabin cruiser. However, life has recently not been so easy for the luxury brands that adorn its visitors. Many of the luxury-brand makers were founded in the 1950s by mainly Italian entrepreneur designers who are now ageing and whose families lack the design and management skills to run an increasingly competitive business. Luxury-goods sales have also been hit hard by recessions in south-east Asia and Japan which, for example, account for 70 per cent of the sales of some companies.

The 'new idea' for luxury-goods makers is to control the whole value chain, from manufacture to distribution, retailing and marketing. This comes expensive where advertising costs approach 35 per cent of sales and the rental of the prime retail site they need can cost up to €10,000 per square metre. Covering such costs requires the sales volume and working capital that many of the family firms lack. According to Cedric Magnelia, of Credit Suisse First Boston, gaining sales by brand extensions into such obvious areas as perfumes has been 'done to death'. There also seems little further to gain from the 'old idea' of designers creating stunning but hugely loss-making *haute couture* while money was made from licensees selling perfumes, handbags and scarves. Luxury brands are easily tainted by down-market asso-

ciations, as occurred when Tiffany's was briefly owned by Avon. TAG Heuer and Porsche both tried stretching their product ranges down-market. Both increased sales, tarnished their luxury brand names and retreated back up-market.

The formation of luxury conglomerates has become part of the 'new idea'. These offer negotiating power in obtaining retail space, skills in areas where brands could be extended, access to capital and managerial skills. Two of the biggest of these are French LVHM, who own Louis Vuitton, Christian Dior, Givenchy and others, and Swiss Richemont, whose brands include Cartier, Dunhill and Piaget. The recognition of the conglomerate strategy has led to a feeding frenzy as Gucci consume Italian shoemaker Sergio Rossi, LVHM and Prada jointly share out Fendi with its famous Baguette handbag, and LVHM bid for Gucci. Laurent Paichot, of the Federation of Swiss Watch Makers, thinks being bought by a conglomerate is the only alternative for many small watchmakers: 'Due to globalisation everything is expensive – especially advertising.' He continues, 'Bigger companies have the economic power to really push the product and consumers will buy from a brand they know well.'

However, in this industry, synergy is hard to find. Morgan Stanley Dean Witter's Claire Kent says, 'cost savings in a takeover in this industry are spurious'. How can synergy be achieved in a market where the appeal is the idiosyncratic way products are designed, made and marketed? Hermès boasts that it takes them longer to make their Kelly bags than it takes BMW to assemble a car! Even where cost savings are easy and logical to find, they can endanger brands. Richemont is eager to clarify that Cartier pens are not made at Mont Blanc factories.

A few luxury-goods makers, such as Rolex, Mondane Watch and Prada, are holding out against the force of the 'new idea'. Mondane intends to remain a speciality watchmaker, having joined with Camel and Bally to use their brand names. Meanwhile, Rolex is adamant that it will remain independent, although it seems unlikely that Sten will be wearing one.[1]

Questions

1. What makes a luxury good or service desirable?

2. Is the economic drive for scale inconsistent with consumers' desires in the €60 billion luxury-goods industry?

3. Does Sten's sneering at 'the Rolex crowd' suggest that Rolex is failing in its desire to remain an independent luxury-goods maker?

corporations need planning. In mature companies, many managers argue that they have done well without formal planning, so it cannot be very important. They may resist taking the time to prepare a written plan. They may argue that the marketplace changes too fast for a plan to be useful – that it would end up collecting dust.[2]

Failing to plan means planning to fail.[3] Moreover, formal planning yields benefits for all types of company, large and small, new and mature. It encourages systematic thinking. It forces the company to sharpen its objectives and policies, leads to better coordination of company efforts, and provides clearer performance standards for control. The argument that planning is less useful in a fast-changing environment makes little sense. The opposite is true: sound planning helps the company to anticipate and respond quickly to environmental changes, and to prepare better for sudden developments. Such planning could have helped Carrefour,[4] Europe's largest retailer, avoid their share price collapse after they were first dismissive of the impact of the Internet on their business and then announced a vague, €1 billion e-commerce strategy.[5]

Companies usually prepare annual plans, long-range plans and strategic plans:

Annual plan

A short-term plan that describes the company's current situation, its objectives, the strategy, action programme and budgets for the year ahead, and controls.

✦ The **annual plan** is a short-term plan that describes the current situation, company objectives, the strategy for the year, the action programme, budgets and controls.

Long-range plan

A plan that describes the principal factors and forces affecting the organisation during the next several years, including long-term objectives, the chief marketing strategies used to attain them and the resources required.

✦ The **long-range plan** describes the primary factors and forces affecting the organisation during the next several years. It includes the long-term objectives, the main marketing strategies used to attain them and the resources required. This long-range plan is reviewed and updated each year so that the company always has a current long-range plan. The company's annual and long-range plans deal with current businesses and how to keep them going.

✦ The **strategic plan** involves adapting the firm to take advantage of opportunities in its constantly changing environment. It is the process of developing and maintaining a strategic fit between the organisation's goals and capabilities and its changing marketing opportunities.

Strategic plan

A plan that describes how a firm will adapt to take advantage of opportunities in its constantly changing environment, thereby maintaining a strategic fit between the firm's goals and capabilities and its changing market opportunities.

Strategic planning sets the stage for the marketing plan. It starts with its overall purpose and mission. These guide the formation of measurable corporate objectives. A corporate audit then gathers information on the company, its competitors, its market and the general environment in which the firm competes. A SWOT analysis gives a summary of the strengths and weaknesses of the company together with the opportunities and threats it faces. Next, headquarters decides what portfolio of businesses and products is best for the company and how much support to give each one. This helps to provide the strategic objectives that guide the company's various activities. Then each business and product unit develops detailed marketing and other functional plans to support the company-wide plan. Thus marketing planning occurs at the business-unit, product and market levels. It supports company strategic planning with more detailed planning for specific marketing opportunities. For instance Nestlé, the world's largest food manufacturer, develops an overall strategic plan at its headquarters in Vevey, Switzerland. Below that, each strategic group, such as confectionery, develops subordinate strategic plans. These feed into the strategic plan's national operations. At each level, marketing and other functional plans will exist. At the final level, brand plans cover the marketing of brands such as KitKat, Lion and Quality Street in national markets.

the planning process

Putting plans into action involves four stages: analysis, planning, implementation and control. Figure 3.1 shows the relationship between these functions, which are common to strategic planning, marketing planning or the planning for any other function.

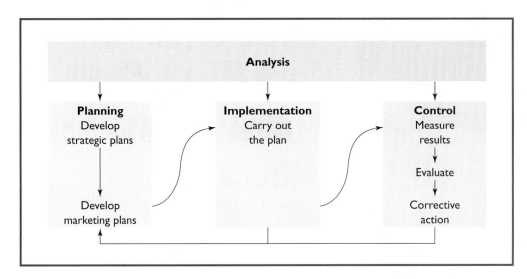

Figure 3.1

Market analysis, planning, implementation and control

Analysis   Planning begins with a complete analysis of the company's situation. The company must analyse its environment to find attractive opportunities and to avoid environmental threats. It must analyse company strengths and weaknesses, as well as current and possible marketing actions, to determine which opportunities it can best pursue. Analysis feeds information and other inputs to each of the other stages.

Planning   Through strategic planning, the company decides what it wants to do with each business unit. Marketing planning involves deciding marketing strategies that will help the company attain its overall strategic objectives. Marketing, product or brand plans are at the centre of this.

Implementation   Implementation turns strategic plans into actions that will achieve the company's objectives. People in the organisation who work with others, both inside and outside the company, implement marketing plans.

Control   Control consists of measuring and evaluating the results of plans and activities, and taking corrective action to make sure objectives are being achieved. Analysis provides information and evaluations needed for all the other activities.

the strategic plan

The strategic plan contains several components: the mission, the strategic objectives, the strategic audit, SWOT analysis, portfolio analysis, objectives and strategies. All of these feed from and feed into marketing plans.

the mission

A mission states the purpose of a company. Firms often start with a clear mission held within the mind of their founder. Then, over time, the mission fades as the company acquires new products and markets. A mission may be clear, but forgotten by some managers. An extreme case of this was the Anglican Church Commissioners, who thought they had the 'Midas touch' when they started speculating on the international property market. They found out that markets go down as well as up and lost a third

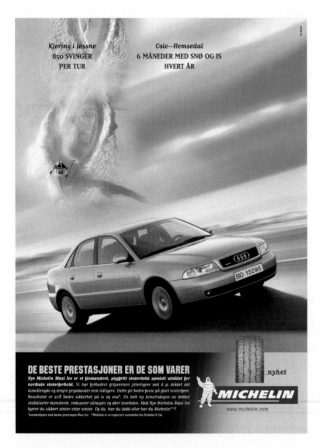

Setting company objectives and goals. Michelin defines its mission as 'service to people and their transportation', rather than reducing its purpose to the mere production of tyres. This mission leads to specific business and marketing objectives. 3M has held on to its mission to be innovative through product generations.

Source: (left) Michelin and Hjemmet Mortensen AS; (right) Advertising courtesy of 3M

of the Church's ancient wealth in the process. Other problems can occur when the mission may remain clear, but no longer fits the environment. The luxury-goods firms in the preview case are struggling with that problem.

When an organisation is drifting, the management must renew its search for purpose. It must ask, What business are we in? What do consumers value? What are we in business for? What sort of business are we? What makes us special? These simple-sounding questions are among the most difficult that the company will ever have to answer. Successful companies continuously raise these questions and answer them. Asking such basic questions is a sign of strength, not uncertainty.

Many organisations develop formal mission statements that answer these questions. A **mission statement** is a statement of the organisation's purpose – what it wants to accomplish in the larger environment. A clear mission statement acts as an 'invisible hand' that guides people in the organisation, so that they can work independently and yet collectively towards overall organisational goals.

Traditionally, companies have defined their business in product terms ('we manufacture furniture'), or in technological terms ('we are a chemical-processing firm'). But mission statements should be *market-oriented*.

Mission statement
A statement of the organisation's purpose – what it wants to accomplish in the wider environment.

What business are we in?   Asking this question helps. Market definitions of a business are better than product or technological definitions. Products and technologies eventually become outdated, but basic market needs may last for ever. A market-oriented mission statement defines the business based on satisfying basic customer needs. Thus

Rolls-Royce is in the power business, not the aero-engine business. Visa's business is not credit cards, but allowing customers to exchange value – to exchange assets, such as cash on deposit or equity in a home, for virtually anything, anywhere in the world. Creative 3M does more than just make adhesives, scientific equipment and healthcare products; it solves people's problems by putting innovation to work for them.

Who are our customers?   This is a probing question. Who are the customers of Rolls-Royce's new Trent aero-engine? At one level it is the airframers, like Boeing and European Airbus. If Rolls-Royce can get an airframer to launch a new aircraft with a Rolls-Royce engine, this saves development costs and makes early orders likely. Is it the airline or leasing companies that eventually buy the engines? They will certainly have to sell to them as well. Is it the pilot, the service crew or even the passenger? Unlike the competition, Rolls-Royce has a brand name that is synonymous with prestige and luxury.

What are we in business for?   This is a hard question for non-profit-making organisations. Do universities exist to educate students or to train them for industry? Is the pursuit of knowledge by the faculty the main reason for their existence? If so, is good research of economic value or is pure research better?

What sort of business are we?   This question guides the strategy and structure of organisations. Companies aiming at *cost leadership* seek efficiency. These firms, like Aldi or KwikSave, run simple, efficient organisations with careful cost control. These contrast with *differentiators*, like Sony, who aim to make profits by inventing products, such as the Walkman, whose uniqueness gives a competitive edge. *Focused* companies concentrate upon being the best at serving a well-defined target market. They succeed by tailoring their products or services to customers they know well. In Britain, Coutts & Co., a National Westminster Bank subsidiary, does this by providing 'personal banking' to the very wealthy. Michael Porter[6] describes a fourth option that occurs if firms do not define how they are to do business: *stuck in the middle*.

Management should avoid making its mission too narrow or too broad. A lead-pencil manufacturer that says it is in the communication equipment business is stating its mission too broadly. A mission should be:

+ *Realistic.* Singapore International Airlines is excellent, but it would be deluding itself if its mission were to become the world's largest airline.

+ *Specific.* It should fit the company and no other. Many mission statements exist for public-relations purposes, so lack specific, workable guidelines. The statement 'We want to become the leading company in this industry by producing the highest-quality products with the best service at the lowest prices' sounds good, but it is full of generalities and contradictions. Such motherhood statements will not help the company make tough decisions.

+ Based on *distinctive competencies.* Bang & Olufsen has the technology to build microcomputers, but an entry into that market would not take advantage of its core competencies in style, hi-fi and exclusive distribution.

+ *Motivating.* It should give people something to believe in. It should get a 'Yeah!', not a yawn or a 'Yuck!'. A company's mission should not say 'making more sales or profits' – profits are only a reward for undertaking a useful activity. A company's employees need to feel that their work is significant and that it contributes to people's lives. Contrast the missions of the two computer giants IBM and Apple. When IBM sales were $50 billion, president John Akers said that IBM's goal was to become a $100 billion company by the end of the century. Meanwhile, Apple's long-term goal has been to put computer power into the hands of every person. Apple's mission is much more motivating than IBM's.

Strategy	Competitive strength	Achieve a sustained leading position worldwide
Identity	Progress	Technological, social and marketing competences focused on progress
Entrepreneurial style	Will to lead	Agree on clear objectives and vigorously transform them into competitive advantage
Managers	Entrepreneurship	Managers and employees think and act as if it were their own company
Executive decision making	Speed	Faster decision making through integrated business functions
New organisation	Close to the customer	Marketing-oriented business functions create entrepreneurial freedom
Strength	Systems integration	Integrate competitive products into problem-solving systems

Figure 3.2

Siemens' seven core statements

Visions guide the best missions. A vision is a contagious dream, a widely communicated statement or slogan that captures the needs of the time. Sony's president, Akio Morita, wanted everyone to have access to 'personal portable sound', and his company created the Walkman. Richard Branson thought 'flying should be fun', so he founded Virgin Airlines. Julian Richer has become a business guru after making his Richer Sounds hi-fi dealer the 'Friendliest, cheapest, busiest', most profitable and productive in the industry.[7]

The company's mission statement should provide a vision and direction for the company for the next 10–20 years. They do not change every few years in response to each new turn in the environment. Still, a company must redefine its mission if that mission has lost credibility or no longer defines an optimal course for the company.[8] The hostile environment caused Siemens, the German electronics giant, to review its strategy. Its seven core statements (Figure 3.2) provided strong communications to drive its strategy, structure and style of management.

from mission to strategic objectives

The company's mission needs to be turned into strategic objectives to guide management. Each manager should have objectives and be responsible for reaching them. For example, its fertiliser business unit is one of International Minerals & Chemical Corporation's many activities. The fertiliser division does not say that its mission is to produce fertiliser. Instead, it says that its mission is to 'increase agricultural productivity'. This mission leads to a hierarchy of objectives, including business objectives and marketing objectives. The mission of increasing agricultural productivity leads to the company's business objective of researching new fertilisers that promise higher yields. Unfortunately, research is expensive and requires improved profits to plough back into research programmes. So improving profits becomes another key business objective.

Profits are improved by increasing sales or reducing costs. Sales increase by improving the company's share of the domestic market, or by entering new foreign markets, or both. These goals then become the company's current marketing objectives. The objective to 'increase our market share' is not as useful as the objective to 'increase our market share to 15 per cent in two years'. The mission states the philosophy and direction of a company, whereas the strategic objectives are measurable goals.

strategic audit

'Knowledge is power': so stated Francis Bacon, the sixteenth-century philosopher, while according to the ancient Chinese strategist Sun Zi, 'The leader who does not want to buy information is inconsiderate and can never win.' The strategic audit covers the gathering of this vital information. It is the intelligence used to build the detailed objectives and strategy of a business. It has two parts: the external and internal audit.

The **external audit** or marketing environment audit examines the macroenvironment and task environment of a company. EuroDisney's problems can be partly explained by an excessive faith in company strengths and too little attention being paid to the macroenvironment. French labour costs make the park much more expensive than in America, Europe's high travel costs add to guests' total bill and the north European climate takes the edge off all-year-round operations. EuroDisney contrasts with the success of Center Parcs. This Dutch company's resort hotels offer north Europeans undercover health and leisure facilities that they can enjoy all year round.

The **internal audit** examines all aspects of the company. It covers the whole *value chain* described by Michael Porter.[9] It includes the primary activities that follow the flow of goods or services through the organisation: inbound logistics, operations, outbound logistics, sales and marketing, and after-sales services. In addition, it extends to the support activities on which the primary activities depend: procurement, technology development, human resource management and the infrastructure of the firm. These go beyond traditional marketing activities, but marketing strategy depends on all of them. A key to the Italian Benetton's international success is a system that allows it to change styles and colours rapidly. Unlike traditional mass-clothing manufacturers, which have to order fabrics in colours and patterns over a year ahead of seasons, Benetton's design and manufacturing technology allows it to change within a season.

Reading financial statements is basic to understanding the state of a company and seeing how it is developing. The operating statement and the balance sheet are the two main financial statements used. The **balance sheet** shows the assets, liabilities and net worth of a company at a given time. The **operating statement** (also called profit-and-loss statement or income statement) is the more important of the two for marketing information. It shows company sales, cost of goods sold, and expenses during a specified time period. By comparing the operating statement from one time period to the next, the firm can spot favourable or unfavourable trends and take appropriate action. Marketing Highlight 3.1 describes these statements in more detail and explains their construction.

SWOT analysis

SWOT analysis draws the critical strengths, weaknesses, opportunities and threats (SWOT) from the strategic audit. The audit contains a wealth of data of differing importance and reliability. SWOT analysis distils these data to show the critical items from the internal and external audit. The number of items is small for forceful communications, and they show where a business should focus its attention.

External audit
A detailed examination of the markets, competition, business and economic environment in which the organisation operates.

Internal audit
An evaluation of the firm's entire value chain.

Balance sheet
A financial statement that shows assets, liabilities and net worth of a company at a given time.

Operating statement (profit-and-loss statement or income statement)
A financial statement that shows company sales, cost of goods sold and expenses during a given period of time.

SWOT analysis
A distillation of the findings of the internal and external audit which draws attention to the critical organisational strengths and weaknesses and the opportunities and threats facing the company.

marketing highlight 3.1

Albumart.com: But will we make money?

Table 1 shows the 2000 operating statement for Albumart.com, a start-up that has avoided the big bucks and bust of Boo.com and others. They market specialised picture frames designed to display 'album art'. They enable people to make a wall decoration by slotting an old favourite vinyl album or CD cover directly into the frame. This statement is for a retailer; the operating statement for a manufacturer would be somewhat different. Specifically, the section on purchases within the 'Cost of goods sold' area would be replaced by 'Cost of goods manufactured'.

The outline of the operating statement follows a logical series of steps to arrive at the firm's €25,000 net profit figure:

Net sales	€300,000
Cost of goods sold	−175,000
Gross margin	€125,000
Expenses	−100,000
Net profit	€25,000

The first part details the amount that Albumart.com received for the goods sold during the year. The sales figures consist of three items: gross sales, returns or allowances, and net sales. *Gross sales* is the total amount charged to customers during the year for merchandise purchased from Albumart.com. Some customers returned merchandise. If the customer gets a full refund or full credit on another purchase, we call this a return. Other customers may decide to keep the item if Albumart.com will reduce the price. This is called an allowance. By subtracting returns and allowances from gross sales:

Gross sales	€325,000
Returns and allowances	−25,000
Net sales	€300,000

The second part of the operating statement calculates the amount of sales revenue that Albumart.com retains after paying the costs of the merchandise. We start with the inventory in the store at the beginning of 2000. During the year, Albumart.com aim to buy €150,000 worth of frames. Albumart.com also has to pay an additional €10,000 to get the products delivered,

Gross sales			325,000
less: Sales returns and allowances			25,000
Net sales			300,000
Cost of goods sold			
Beginning inventory, 1 January 2000, at cost		60,000	
Purchases	150,000		
plus: Freight-in	10,000		
Net cost of delivered purchases		160,000	
Cost of goods available for sale		220,000	
less: Ending inventory, 31 December 2000, at cost		45,000	
Total cost of goods sold			175,000
Gross margin			125,000
Expenses			
Selling expenses:		50,000	
Administrative expenses:		30,000	
General expenses:		20,000	
Total expenses			100,000
Net profit			25,000

Table 1   Operating statement for Albumart.com for year ending 31 December 2000 (€)

giving the firm a net cost of €160,000. Adding the beginning inventory, the cost of goods available for sale amounted to €220,000. The €45,000 ending inventory on 31 December 2000 is then subtracted to come up with the €175,000 *cost of goods sold*.

The difference between what Albumart.com paid for the merchandise (€175,000) and what it sold it for (€300,000) is called the *gross margin* (€125,000).

In order to show the profit Albumart.com 'cleared' at the end of the year, we must subtract from the gross margin the expenses incurred while doing business. *Selling expenses* included two employees, advertising in music magazines and the cost of mailing the merchandise. Selling expenses totalled €50,000 for the year. *Administrative expenses* included the salary for an office manager, office supplies such as stationery and business cards, and miscellaneous expenses including an administrative audit conducted by an outside consultant. Administrative expenses totalled €30,000 in 1995. Finally, the *general expenses* of rent, utilities, insurance, and depreciation came to €20,000. Total expenses were therefore €100,000 for the year. By subtracting expenses (€100,000) from the gross margin (€125,000), we arrive at the *net profit* of €25,000 for Albumart.com during 2000. Not a lot, but not a loss.

■ Opportunities and threats

Managers need to identify the main threats and opportunities that their company faces. The purpose of the analysis is to make the manager anticipate important developments that can have an impact on the firm. A large pet food division of a multinational company could list the following.

Opportunities:
+ *Economic climate*. Because of improved economic conditions, pet ownership is increasing in almost all segments of the population.
+ *Demographic changes*. (1) Increasing single parenthood, dual-income families and ageing will increase the trend towards convenient pet foods (from wet to dry); and (2) the aged population will grow and increasingly keep pets as company.
+ *Market*. The pet food market will follow the human market in the concern for healthy eating and pre-prepared luxury foods.
+ *Technology*. New forms of pet food that are low in fat and calories, yet highly nutritious and tasty, will soon emerge. These products will appeal strongly to many of today's pet food buyers, whose health concerns extend to their pets.

Threats:
+ *Competitive activity*. A large competitor has just announced that it will introduce a new premium pet food line, backed by a huge advertising and sales promotion blitz.
+ *Channel pressure*. Industry analysts predict that supermarket chain buyers will face more than 10,000 new grocery product introductions next year. The buyers accept only 38 per cent of these new products and give each one only five months to prove itself.
+ *Demographic changes*. Increasing single parenthood and dual-income families (1) will encourage the trend towards pets that need little care (cats rather than dogs), and (2) will encourage the trend towards smaller pets that eat less.
+ *Politics*. European Union legislation will force manufacturers to disclose the content of their pet food. This will adversely affect the attractiveness of some ingredients like kangaroo and horsemeat.

Not all threats call for the same attention or concern – the manager should assess the likelihood of each threat and the potential damage each could cause. The manager

Mont Blanc competes in the exquisite accessories market capitalising on its strength in exclusive design and making high-quality products.

SOURCE: Mont Blanc and the Advertising Archives

New Look. New Mood. New Times.

New: Meisterstück Sport Chronograph Stainless Steel Automatic with Rubber Strap and Security Clasp

Meisterstück Solitaire Stainless Steel Doué Ballpoint Pen

THE ART OF WRITING YOUR LIFE
Writing Instruments · Watches · Leather · Jewellery · Eyewear

Montblanc Boutiques. 60/61 Burlington Arcade. 10/11 Royal Exchange. Canada Place, Canary Wharf. Harrods, Knightsbridge. Selfridges, Oxford Street. Call 020 7663 4830 for further details and national stockists.

should then focus on the most probable and harmful threats and prepare plans in advance to meet them.

Opportunities occur when an environmental trend plays to a company's strength. The manager should assess each opportunity according to its potential attractiveness and the company's probability of success. Companies can rarely find ideal opportunities that exactly fit their objectives and resources. The development of opportunities involves risks. When evaluating opportunities, the manager must decide whether the expected returns justify these risks. A trend or development can be a threat or an opportunity depending on a company's strengths. The development of the steel-braced radial tyre was an opportunity for Michelin, which used its technological lead to gain market share. To the rest of the industry, the new technology was a threat because the tyre's longer life reduced total demand and the new technology made their plant obsolete.

■ Strengths and weaknesses

Critical success factors
The strengths and weaknesses that most critically affect an organisation's success. These are measured relative to competition.

The strengths and weaknesses in the SWOT analysis do not list all features of a company, but only those relating to **critical success factors**. A list that is too long betrays a lack of focus and an inability to discriminate what is important. The strengths or weaknesses are *relative*, not absolute. It is nice to be good at something, but it can be a weakness if the competition is stronger. Mercedes is good at making reliable luxury cars with low depreciation, but this stopped being a strength when Honda's Acura and Toyota's Lexus beat Mercedes on all three fronts in the American market. The Japanese products were not cheap, but they were styled for the American market and came with all the extras that buyers of German luxury cars had to pay for. Finally, the strengths should be *based on fact*. In buying Skoda, VW has acquired a well-known brand name, but is the name a strength? A failure to understand true strengths can be dangerous. A well-known aircraft manufacturer for years promoted the quality of its after-sales service. Only after another company acquired it did it find out that its reputation was the worst in the industry.

A major pet food manufacturer could pitch the following strengths and weaknesses against the opportunities and threats.

Strengths:
+ Market leader in the dry cat food market.
+ Access to the group's leading world position in food technology.
+ Market leader in luxury pet foods.
+ The group's excellent worldwide grocery distribution.
+ Pet food market leader in several big markets, including France, Italy, Spain and South America.

Weaknesses:
+ Number three in the wet pet food market.
+ Excessive product range with several low-volume brands.
+ Most brand names are little known, and are cluttered following acquisitions.
+ Relatively low advertising and promotions budget.
+ Product range needs many manufacturing skills.
+ Poor store presence in several large markets: Germany, UK, USA and Canada.
+ Overall poor profit performance.

The pet food company shows how some parts of the SWOT balance. The strengths in dry and luxury pet foods match demographic trends, so this looks like an opportunity for growth. Access to food technology should also help the company face changing consumer tastes and legislation. The weaknesses suggest a need for more focus. Dropping some uneconomic lines in the mass wet pet food market, simplifying the brand structure and concentrating on fewer manufacturing processes could release resources for developing the dry and luxury markets. By using its access to worldwide grocery distribution, the company could become profitable and focused.

the business portfolio

The **business portfolio** is the collection of businesses and products that make up the company. It is a link between the overall strategy of a company and those of its parts. The best business portfolio is the one that fits the company's strengths and weaknesses to opportunities in the environment. The company must (1) analyse its *current* business portfolio and decide which businesses should receive more, less or no investment, and (2) develop growth strategies for adding *new* products or businesses to the portfolio.

Business portfolio
The collection of businesses and products that make up the company.

■ Analysing the current business portfolio

Portfolio analysis helps managers evaluate the businesses making up the company. The company will want to put strong resources into its more profitable businesses and phase down or drop its weaker ones. Sweden's Volvo is disposing of its non-core businesses to strengthen its portfolio, selling its interests in consumer products (holdings

Portfolio analysis
A tool by which management identifies and evaluates the various businesses that make up the company.

Figure 3.3

The BCG growth–share matrix

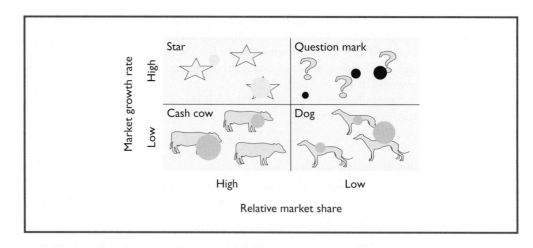

in BCP), pharmaceuticals (28 per cent of Pharmacia), stock brokering, property and investment. The tighter portfolio will allow Volvo to concentrate on revitalising its passenger car, truck and bus operations.

Management's first step is to identify the key businesses making up the company. These are strategic business units. A **strategic business unit (SBU)** is a unit of the company that has a separate mission and objectives, and which can be planned independently from other company businesses. An SBU can be a company division, a product line within a division, or sometimes a single product or brand.

The next step in business portfolio analysis calls for management to assess the attractiveness of its various SBUs and decide how much support each deserves. In some companies, this occurs informally. Management looks at the company's collection of businesses or products and uses judgement to decide how much each SBU should contribute and receive. Other companies use formal portfolio-planning methods.

The purpose of strategic planning is to find ways in which the company can best use its strengths to take advantage of attractive opportunities in the environment. So most standard portfolio-analysis methods evaluate SBUs on two important dimensions: the attractiveness of the SBU's market or industry, and the strength of the SBU's position in that market or industry. The best-known portfolio-planning methods are from the Boston Consulting Group, a leading management consulting firm, and by General Electric and Shell.

The Boston Consulting Group box   Using the Boston Consulting Group (BCG) approach, a company classifies all its SBUs according to the **growth–share matrix** shown in Figure 3.3. On the vertical axis, *market growth rate* provides a measure of market attractiveness. On the horizontal axis, *relative market share* serves as a measure of company strength in the market. By dividing the growth–share matrix as indicated, four types of SBU can be distinguished:

1. **Stars.** Stars are high-growth, high-share businesses or products. They often need heavy investment to finance their rapid growth. Eventually their growth will slow down, and they will turn into cash cows.

2. **Cash cows.** Cash cows are low-growth, high-share businesses or products. These established and successful SBUs need less investment to hold their market share. Thus they produce cash that the company uses to pay its bills and to support other SBUs that need investment.

3. **Question marks.** Question marks are low-share business units in high-growth markets. They require cash to hold their share, let alone increase it. Management

---

Strategic business unit (SBU)
A unit of the company that has a separate mission and objectives and that can be planned independently from other company businesses. An SBU can be a company division, a product line within a division, or sometimes a single product or brand.

Stars
High-growth, high-share businesses or products that often require heavy investment to finance their rapid growth.

Cash cows
Low-growth, high-share businesses or products; established and successful units that generate cash that the company uses to pay its bills and support other business units that need investment.

Question marks
Low-share business units in high-growth markets that require a lot of cash in order to hold their share or become stars.

has to think hard about question marks – which ones they should build into stars and which ones they should phase out.

4. **Dogs.** Dogs are low-growth, low-share businesses and products. They may generate enough cash to maintain themselves, but do not promise to be large sources of cash.

The ten circles in the growth–share matrix represent a company's ten current SBUs. The company has two stars, two cash cows, three question marks and three dogs. The areas of the circles are proportional to the SBUs' sales value. This company is in fair shape, although not in good shape. It wants to invest in the more promising question marks to make them stars, and to maintain the stars so that they will become cash cows as their markets mature. Fortunately, it has two good-sized cash cows whose income helps finance the company's question marks, stars and dogs. The company should take some decisive action concerning its dogs and its question marks. The picture would be worse if the company had no stars, or had too many dogs, or had only one weak cash cow.

Once it has classified its SBUs, the company must determine what role each will play in the future. There are four alternative strategies for each SBU. The company can invest more in the business unit to *build* its share. It can invest just enough to *hold* the SBU's share at the current level. It can *harvest* the SBU, milking its short-term cash flow regardless of the long-term effect. Finally, the company can *divest* the SBU by selling it or phasing it out and using the resources elsewhere.

As time passes, SBUs change their positions in the growth–share matrix. Each SBU has a life cycle. Many SBUs start out as question marks and move into the star category if they succeed. They later become cash cows as market growth falls, then finally die off or turn into dogs towards the end of their life cycle. The company needs to add new products and units continuously, so that some of them will become stars and, eventually, cash cows that will help finance other SBUs.

The General Electric grid   General Electric introduced a comprehensive portfolio planning tool called a **strategic business-planning grid** (see Figure 3.4). It is similar to Shell's *directional policy matrix*. Like the BCG approach, it uses a matrix with two dimensions – one representing industry attractiveness (the vertical axis) and one representing company strength in the industry (the horizontal axis). The best businesses are those located in highly attractive industries where the company has high business strength.

The GE approach considers many factors besides market growth rate as part of *industry attractiveness*. It uses an industry attractiveness index made up of market size, market growth rate, industry profit margin, amount of competition, seasonality

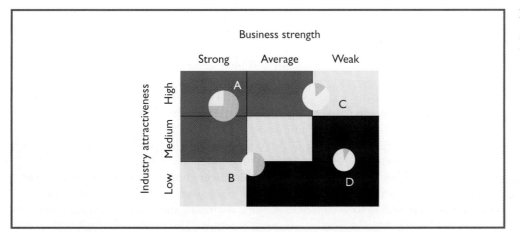

Figure 3.4

GE's strategic business-planning grid

and cycle of demand, and industry cost structure. Each of these factors is rated and combined in an index of industry attractiveness. For our purposes, an industry's attractiveness is high, medium or low. As an example, the Kraft subsidiary of Philip Morris has identified numerous highly attractive industries – natural foods, speciality frozen foods, physical fitness products and others. It has withdrawn from less attractive industries, such as bulk oils and cardboard packaging. The Dutch chemical giant Akzo Nobel has identified speciality chemicals, coatings and pharmaceuticals as attractive. Its less attractive bulk chemical and fibre businesses are being sold.

For *business strength*, the GE approach again uses an index rather than a simple measure of relative market share. The business strength index includes factors such as the company's relative market share, price competitiveness, product quality, customer and market knowledge, sales effectiveness and geographic advantages. These factors are rated and combined in an index of business strengths described as strong, average or weak. Thus, Kraft has substantial business strength in food and related industries, but is relatively weak in the home appliances industry.

The grid has three zones. The green cells at the upper left include the strong SBUs in which the company should invest and grow. The amber diagonal cells contain SBUs that are medium in overall attractiveness. The company should maintain its level of investment in these SBUs. The three red cells at the lower right indicate SBUs that are low in overall attractiveness. The company should give serious thought to harvesting or divesting these SBUs.

The circles represent four company SBUs; the areas of the circles are proportional to the relative sizes of the industries in which these SBUs compete. The pie slices within the circles represent each SBU's market share. Thus circle A represents a company SBU with a 75 per cent market share in a good-sized, highly attractive industry in which the company has strong business strength. Circle B represents an SBU that has a 50 per cent market share, but the industry is not very attractive. Circles C and D represent two other company SBUs in industries where the company has small market shares and not much business strength. Altogether, the company should build A, maintain B and make some hard decisions on what to do with C and D.

Management would also plot the projected positions of the SBUs with and without changes in strategies. By comparing current and projected business grids, management can identify the primary strategic issues and opportunities it faces. One of the aims of portfolio analysis is to direct firms away from investing in markets that look attractive, but where they have no strength:

In their rush away from the declining steel market, four of Japan's 'famous five' big steel makers (Nippon, NKK, Kawasaki, Sumitomo and Kobe) diversified into the microchip business. They had the misplaced belief that chips would be to them in the future what steel had been to the 1950s and that they had to be part of it. The market was attractive but it did not fit their strengths. So far, none have made money from chips. The misadventure also distracted them from attending to their core business. They said they would reduce fixed costs by 30 per cent but they retained their tradition of lifelong employment and their 'salary-men' stayed in place. In reality their costs rose and their losses mounted. For Japanese firms the unthinkable is happening. Cross-keiretsu (keiretsu are Japan's huge multi-industry holding companies) mergers look likely and lifelong employment is no more!

The 'famous five's' failure contrasts with Eramet, a focused French company who are the world's biggest producer of Ferro-nickel and high-speed steels. They owe their number one position to their decision to invest their profits in a 'second leg' that would be a logical industrial and geographical diversification for them. They bought French Commentryene and Swedish Kloster Speedsteel. They quickly integrated them and, according to Yves Rambert, their chairman and chief executive, 'found that the French and the Swedes can work together'. The unified international marketing team is doing better than when the companies were separate. Eramet are now looking for a 'third industrial leg' that will have customers and technologies with which the group's management are familiar but does not compete for their present customers.[10]

■ Problems with matrix approaches

The BCG, GE, Shell and other formal methods revolutionised strategic planning. However, such approaches have limitations. They can be difficult, time consuming and costly to implement. Management may find it difficult to define SBUs and measure market share and growth. In addition, these approaches focus on classifying *current* businesses, but provide little advice for *future* planning. Management must still rely on its judgement to set the business objectives for each SBU, to determine what resources to give to each and to work out which new businesses to add.

Formal planning approaches can also lead the company to place too much emphasis on market-share growth or growth through entry into attractive new markets. Using these approaches, many companies plunged into unrelated and new high-growth businesses that they did not know how to manage – with very bad results. At the same time, these companies were often too quick to abandon, sell or milk to death their healthy, mature businesses. As a result, many companies that diversified in the past are now narrowing their focus and getting back to the industries that they know best (see Marketing Highlight 3.2).

Despite these and other problems, and although many companies have dropped formal matrix methods in favour of customised approaches better suited to their situations, most companies remain firmly committed to strategic planning.

Such analysis is no cure-all for finding the best strategy. Conversely, it can help management to understand the company's overall situation, to see how each business or product contributes, to assign resources to its businesses, and to orient the company for future success. When used properly, strategic planning is just one important aspect of overall strategic management, a way of thinking about how to manage a business.[11]

developing growth strategies

The product/market expansion grid,[12] shown in Figure 3.5, is a useful device for identifying growth opportunities. This shows four routes to growth: market development, new markets, new products and diversification. We use the grid to explain how Mercedes-Benz, the luxury car division of DaimlerChrysler, hoped to return to profits after its €1bn loss in mid-1990.[13]

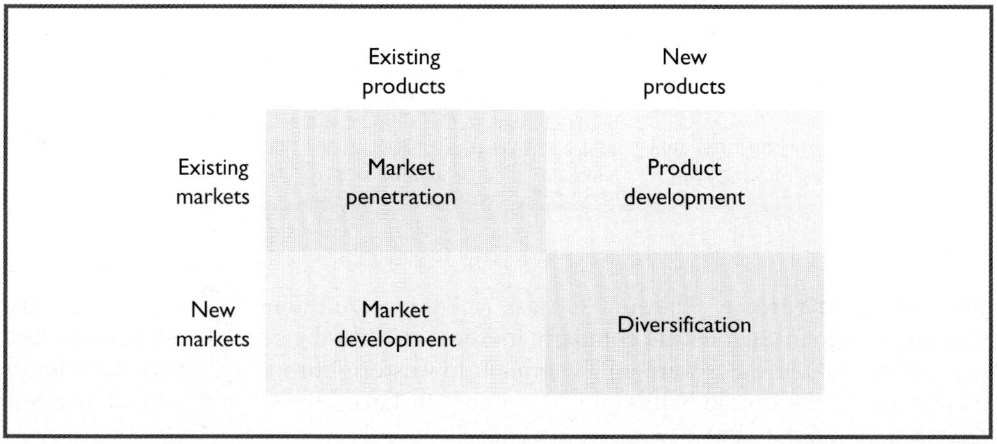

Figure 3.5

Product/market expansion grid

	Existing products	New products
Existing markets	Market penetration	Product development
New markets	Market development	Diversification

marketing highlight 3.2

KISS (Keep It Simple Stupid)

Once upon a time, strategic planners caught expansion fever. Big was beautiful and everyone wanted to get bigger and grow faster by broadening their business portfolios. Companies milked their stodgy core businesses to get the cash needed to acquire glamorous businesses in more attractive industries. It did not seem to matter that many of the acquired businesses fitted poorly with old ones, or that they operated in markets unfamiliar to company management.

Many firms exploded into conglomerates, sometimes containing hundreds of unrelated products and businesses. Extreme cases involved French banks and Japanese electronics companies buying Hollywood film studios. Managing these 'smorgasbord' portfolios proved difficult. Eventually managers realised that it was tough to run businesses they knew little about. Many newly acquired businesses were also bogged down under added layers of corporate management and administrative costs. Meanwhile, the profitable core businesses withered from lack of investment and management attention.

Encumbered with the burden of their scattergun diversification, acquisition fever gave way to a new philosophy of keeping things simple: 'narrowing the focus', 'sticking to your knitting', 'the urge to purge'. They all mean narrowing the company's market focus and returning to the idea of serving one or a few core industries that the firm knows and can be strong. Companies are shedding businesses that do not fit their narrowed focus and rebuilding by concentrating resources on other businesses that do. Examples are Royal Dutch/Shell's sale of their coal division or Lucas selling swathes of peripheral and underperforming activities to refocus on its core of automotive, aerospace and electronic components. The result is a smaller, but more focused company; a stronger firm serving fewer markets, but serving them much better. Other firms, like LloydsTSB, Coca-Cola and McDonald's, never lost their focus but gained in strength while their competitors squandered their energy elsewhere.

When Cor Boonstra joined Philips, as the first outsider to become President of the then loss-making Dutch consumer electronics company, he was horrified at what he found. Philips was the world's number one in lighting, number two in television tubes and number eight in semiconductors but had lots of other activities bleeding cash and managerial time. Its lighting and tubes were under huge pressure from manufacturers from South Korea and Taiwan but the ability to compete was being swamped by numerous unconnected and loss-making businesses. Boonstra also inherited a 'hopelessly bureaucratic' business with layers and layers of management between factory and consumer. His strategy was to take the company back to its core strengths in 'high-volume consumer electronics'. Marketing expenditure in the core businesses was to increase while the strategy was to 'close, fix or sell' the 'bleeders'. Among the non-core businesses sold are Polygram, a music and film business, a chain of video stores and massively loss-making Grundig. In his first two years Boonstra sold off 40 businesses, losing 28,000 workers but bringing in €8bn to invest in the core. The company shrunk to a less bloated eight divisions with 80 businesses from 120 businesses in 11 divisions, but many more factories have to go. However, all is not gloom. While becoming a less complex company, Philips is gaining market share in its major markets and profits are growing.

Philips is now facing a dilemma that concentration forces on many businesses. Should it sell the very business on which it was founded? Reckitt & Colman did that when they sold Colman's mustard. Lighting is profitable and strong business but it is far from its chosen future in consumer electronics.

SOURCES: Brian Bremner, 'The age of consolidation', *Business Week* (14 October 1991), pp. 86–94; 'The Lloyds money machine', *The Economist* (17 January 1998), pp. 81–2; 'Oil and Coal: Downcast', *The Economist* (4 September 1999), p. 81; Paul Cheeseright, 'Simpson aims to accelerate change at Lucas', *Financial Times* (11 October 1994), p. 21; Barbara Smirt, 'Philips to focus on consumer electronics', *Financial Times* (13 February 1998), p. 29; 'Philips: The shrinking company', *The Economist* (8 May 1999), pp. 98–9.

Market penetration The new C-class (medium-sized family saloon) and E-class (Executive saloon) helped the company increase its sales by 23 per cent besides costing less to produce. Sales were up 40 per cent in western Europe (excluding Germany), 34 per cent in the United States and 30 per cent in Japan. In Germany, the 38 per cent growth gave a 2 per cent rise in market share.

Market development   With its A-class small family saloon, and even smaller Smart car, Mercedes will enter the small car market. German reunification gave the company a sales boost. In eastern Europe and China, the brand's image and reputation for reliability and quality have made it *the* transport for the new rich. Besides offering cost savings, the formation of DaimlerChrysler in 1998 gave the company a chance to develop lower-price brands worldwide through products like the Chrysler Neon and Voyager. However, there is some worry that association with such down-market products is tarnishing Mercedes' reputation for safety and quality.

Diversification   Diversification is an option taken by Mercedes' parent company. It has rapidly moved into aerospace by buying Dornier, Motoren Turbinen Union (MTU) and a 51 per cent stake in Messerschmitt-Bölkow-Blohm (MBB). Its Deutsche Aerospace (DASA) subsidiary is now Germany's biggest aerospace and defence group, although tiny by world standards. The motives behind the strategy were to offset stagnating vehicle sales and to use high technology from the acquisitions in cars and trucks. Like many other firms, DaimlerChrysler found diversification difficult. Shortly after consolidating the acquisitions, the 'peace dividend' damaged the defence sector and the international airline industry was in recession. Observers now question the logic of the acquisitions and doubt whether even a company with Daimler's management and financial strength can handle such a radical diversification. Part of its hope now is to sell off or find a partnership for its most loss-making subsidiaries, such as rail equipment maker Adtranz.[14]

marketing within strategic planning

planning functional strategies

The company's strategic plan establishes what kinds of business the company will be in and its objectives for each. Then, within each business unit, more detailed planning takes place. The main functional departments in each unit – marketing, finance, accounting, buying, manufacturing, personnel and others – must work together to accomplish strategic objectives.

Each functional department deals with different publics to obtain resources such as cash, labour, raw materials, research ideas and manufacturing processes. For example, marketing brings in revenues by negotiating exchanges with consumers. Finance arranges exchanges with lenders and stockholders to obtain cash. Thus the marketing and finance departments must work together to obtain needed funds. Similarly, the personnel department supplies labour, and the buying department obtains materials needed for operations and manufacturing.

marketing's role in strategic planning

There is much overlap between overall company strategy and marketing strategy. Marketing looks at consumer needs and the company's ability to satisfy them; these factors guide the company mission and objectives. Most company strategic planning deals with marketing variables – market share, market development, growth – and it is sometimes hard to separate strategic planning from marketing planning. Some companies refer to their strategic planning as 'strategic marketing planning'.

Marketing plays a key role in the company's strategic plans in several ways. First, marketing provides a guiding *philosophy* – company strategy should revolve around serving the needs of important consumer groups. Second, marketing provides *inputs* to strategic planners by helping to identify attractive market opportunities and by assessing the firm's potential to take advantage of them. Finally, within individual business units, marketing designs *strategies* for reaching the unit's objectives.

Within each business unit, marketing management determines how to help achieve strategic objectives. Some marketing managers will find that their objective is not to build sales. Rather, it may be to hold existing sales with a smaller marketing budget, or even to reduce demand. Thus marketing management must manage demand to the level decided upon by the strategic planning prepared at headquarters. Marketing helps to assess each business unit's potential, set objectives for it and then achieve those objectives.

marketing and the other business functions

In some firms, marketing is just another function – all functions count in the company and none takes leadership. At the other extreme, some marketers claim that marketing is the *principal* function of the firm. They quote Drucker's statement: 'The aim of the business is to create customers.' They say it is marketing's job to define the company's mission, products and markets, and to direct the other functions in the task of serving customers.

More enlightened marketers prefer to put the *customer* at the centre of the company. These marketers argue that the firm cannot succeed without customers, so the crucial task is to attract and hold them. Customers are attracted by promises and held by satisfaction. Marketing defines the promise and ensures its delivery. However, because actual consumer satisfaction is affected by the performance of other departments, *all* functions should work together to sense, serve and satisfy customer needs. Marketing plays an integrative role in ensuring that all departments work together towards consumer satisfaction.

conflict between departments

Each business function has a different view of which publics and activities are most important. Manufacturing focuses on suppliers and production; finance addresses stockholders and sound investment; marketing emphasises consumers and products, pricing, promotion and distribution. Ideally, all the different functions should blend to achieve consumer satisfaction. In practice, departmental relations are full of conflicts and misunderstandings. The marketing department takes the consumer's point of view. But when marketing tries to develop customer satisfaction, it often causes other departments to do a poorer job *in their terms*. Marketing department actions can increase buying costs, disrupt production schedules, increase inventories and create budget headaches. Thus the other departments may resist bending their efforts to the will of the marketing department.

Despite the resistance, marketers must get all departments to 'think consumer' and to put the consumer at the centre of company activity. Customer satisfaction requires a total company effort to deliver superior value to target customers.

Creating value for buyers is much more than a 'marketing function'; rather, it is 'analogous to a symphony orchestra in which the contribution of each subgroup is tailored and integrated by a conductor – with a synergistic effect. A seller must draw upon and integrate effectively . . . its entire human and other capital resources . . . [Creating superior value for buyers] is the proper focus of the entire business and not merely of a single department in it.'[15]

Swiss Swedish company ABB shows the benefits of a customer focus programme. It was initially a regional effort stressing time-based management to quicken response to customers by cutting total customer order to delivery time. The customer focus programme has since extended to all its operations. It encourages people in all its 5,000 plus profit centres to 'think customer', track customer satisfaction and find ways to continually improve customer service. The company keeps 'close to the customer' by extreme decentralization and a flat, team driven organization. Sune Karlsson, who is responsible for the customer focus programme, says: 'the people in our many small groups are close to the customer, are more sensitive to their needs, and are more able to respond to those needs'. The role of keeping the customer satisfied and happy is not just the role of marketing people. Employees work together to develop a system of functional plans and then use cross-border co-ordination to accomplish the company's overall objectives. Furthermore, Karlsson suggests, 'We have learned that the customer focus programme reduces the optimal size of an operation (that is, improves efficiency). It ensures that the customer is better served and brings us closer to the ultimate goal of partnering (that is, long-term relationships).'[16]

the marketing process

The strategic plan defines the company's overall mission and objectives. Within each business unit, marketing plays a role in helping to accomplish the overall strategic objectives. Marketing's role and activities in the organisation are shown in Figure 3.6, which summarises the **marketing process** and the forces influencing marketing strategy, giving the numbers of the chapters covering them in this text.

marketing strategy

Target consumers are at the centre of the **marketing strategy**. The company identifies the total market, divides it into smaller segments, selects the most promising segments and focuses on serving them. It designs a marketing mix using mechanisms under its control: product, price, place and promotion. The company engages in marketing analysis, planning, implementation and control to find the best marketing mix and to take action. The company uses these activities to enable it to watch and adapt to the marketing environment. We will now look briefly at each factor in the marketing process and say where it is developed elsewhere in this book.

■ Target consumers

To succeed in today's competitive marketplace, companies must be customer centred – winning customers from competitors by delivering greater value. However, before it can satisfy consumers, a company must first understand their needs and wants. So, sound marketing requires a careful analysis of consumers. An understanding of buyer behaviour, discussed in Chapters 6 and 7, guides this process. Companies know that they cannot satisfy all consumers in a given market – at least, not all consumers in the same way. There are too many kinds of consumer with too many kinds of need, and some companies are in a better position to serve certain segments of the market. As a consequence, each company must divide the total market, choose the best segments and design strategies for profitably serving chosen segments better than its competitors do. This process involves five steps: demand measurement and forecasting, market segmentation, market targeting, market positioning and competitive positioning.

Marketing process
The process of (1) analysing marketing opportunities; (2) selecting target markets; (3) developing the marketing mix; and (4) managing the marketing effort.

Marketing strategy
The marketing logic by which the business unit hopes to achieve its marketing objectives.

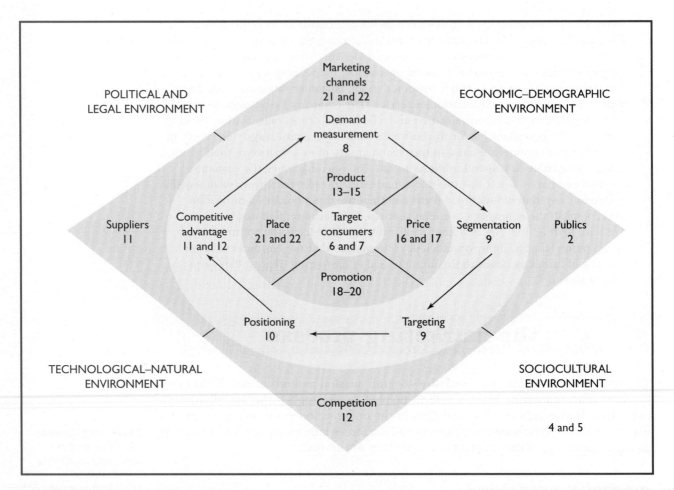

Figure 3.6

Influences on marketing strategy, showing the numbers of the chapters in which they appear in this text

■ The competitive environment

Companies aim to serve their customers, but they must do so in an environment with many other influences. At the widest level is the *macroenvironment* of Political, Economic, Social and Technological (PEST) influences that all organisations face. Besides this, companies also face a unique microenvironment, including suppliers, competitors, channels of distribution and publics – such as employees and the media – that are not necessarily customers. Chapters 4 and 5 explore these environments and their increasingly global dimensions.

■ Demand measurement and forecasting

Suppose a company is looking at possible markets for a potential new product. First, the company needs to estimate the current and future size of the market and its segments. To estimate current market size, the company would identify all competing products, estimate the current sales of these products, and determine whether the market is large enough to support another product profitably. Chapter 8 explores ways of doing this and other types of marketing research and information systems.

Equally important is future market growth. Companies want to enter markets that show strong growth prospects. Growth potential may depend on the growth rate of certain age, income and nationality groups that use the product. Growth may also relate to larger developments in the environment, such as economic conditions, the crime rate and lifestyle changes. For example, the future markets for quality children's toys and clothing relate to current birth rates, trends in consumer affluence and projected family lifestyles. Forecasting the effect of these environmental forces is difficult, but it is necessary in order to make decisions about the market. The company's marketing information specialists will probably use complex techniques to measure and forecast demand.

■ Market segmentation

If the demand forecast looks good, the company next decides how to enter the market. The market consists of many types of customers, products and needs. The marketer has to determine which segments offer the best opportunity for achieving company objectives. Consumers are grouped in various ways based on geographic factors (countries, regions, cities); demographic factors (sex, age, income, education); psychographic factors (social classes, lifestyles); and behavioural factors (purchase occasions, benefits sought, usage rates). The process of dividing a market into groups of buyers with different needs, characteristics or behaviour, who might require separate products or marketing mixes, is **market segmentation**.

Every market has market segments, but not all ways of segmenting a market are equally useful. For example, Panadol would gain little by distinguishing between male and female users of pain relievers if both respond the same way to marketing stimuli. A **market segment** consists of consumers who respond in a similar way to a given set of marketing stimuli. In the car market, for example, consumers who choose the biggest, most comfortable car regardless of price make up one market segment. Another market segment would be customers who care mainly about price and operating economy. It would be difficult to make one model of car that was the first choice of every consumer. Companies are wise to focus their efforts on meeting the distinct needs of one or more market segments.

■ Market targeting

After a company has defined market segments, it can enter one or many segments of a given market. **Market targeting** involves evaluating each market segment's attractiveness and selecting one or more segments to enter. A company should target segments in which it has a differential advantage over its competitors; where it can generate the greatest customer value and sustain it over time. A company with limited resources might decide to serve only one or a few special segments; this strategy limits sales, but can be very profitable. Alternatively, a company might choose to serve several related segments – perhaps those with different kinds of customer, but with the same basic wants. Or perhaps a large company might decide to offer a complete range of products to serve all market segments. The closely linked processes of market segmentation and targeting are both developed in Chapter 9.

Most companies enter a new market by serving a single segment, and if this proves successful, they add segments. Large companies eventually seek full market coverage. They want to be the 'General Motors' (GM) of their industry. America's GM says that it makes a car for every 'person, purse, and personality'. Similarly, Japan's Seiko is proud of its range of 2,500 watches designed to cover consumer segments across the world. The leading company normally has different products designed to meet the special needs of each segment.

■ Positioning

After a company has decided which market segments to enter, it must decide what 'position' it wants to occupy in those segments. A **product's position** is the place the product occupies in consumers' minds. If a product were perceived to be exactly like another product on the market, consumers would have no reason to buy it.

Market segmentation
Dividing a market into distinct groups of buyers with different needs, characteristics or behaviour, who might require separate products or marketing mixes.

Market segment
A group of consumers who respond in a similar way to a given set of marketing stimuli.

Market targeting
The process of evaluating each market segment's attractiveness and selecting one or more segments to enter.

Product position
The way the product is defined by consumers on important attributes – the place the product occupies in consumers' minds relative to competing products.

*Market positioning:
Mercedes-Benz positions
on high-quality luxury
cars, targeting those
who are looking for
something more than
an economic and
functional means of
transport.*

Source: Daimler Chrysler
AG. Agency: Springer &
Jacoby

Market positioning

*Arranging for a product
to occupy a clear,
distinctive and
desirable place relative
to competing products
in the minds of target
consumers. Formulating
competitive positioning
for a product and a
detailed marketing mix.*

Market positioning gives a product a clear, distinctive and desirable place in the minds of target consumers compared with competing products. Marketers plan positions that distinguish their products from competing brands and give them the greatest strategic advantage in their target markets. For example, Ford says, 'Everything we do is driven by you'. Renault builds cars that 'take your breath away'. BMW is 'the ultimate driving machine' while Jaguar is a 'blend of art and machine'. Rolls-Royce cars are 'Strictly for the wealthy arrived individual', while 'you don't Park, you position' the equally luxurious Bentley. Such simple statements are the backbone of a product's marketing strategy.

In positioning its product, the company first identifies possible competitive advantages upon which to build the position. To gain competitive advantage, the company must offer greater value to chosen target segments, either by charging lower prices than competitors or by offering more benefits to justify higher prices. However, if the company positions the product as *offering* greater value, it must *deliver* greater value. Effective positioning begins with actually *differentiating* the company's marketing offer so that it gives consumers more value than is offered by the competition.

The company can position a product on only one important differentiating factor or on several. However, positioning on too many factors can result in consumer confusion or disbelief. Once the company has chosen a desired position, it must take steps to deliver and communicate that position to target consumers. Chapter 10 focuses on positioning and tells how the company's entire marketing programme should support the chosen positioning strategy.

marketing strategies for competitive advantage

To be successful, the company must do a better job than its competitors of satisfying target consumers. Chapter 11 shows how this increasingly depends upon establishing relationships with customers and other participants in the value chain by providing them with quality, value and service. Recently there has been a major shift from marketing as a single transaction between supplier and buyer to establishing a longer-term relationship with customers through loyalty schemes and data-based marketing. These recognise that it is far more expensive to obtain customers than to retain them.

Providing excellent value and customer service is a necessary but not sufficient means of succeeding in the marketplace. Besides embracing the needs of consumers, marketing strategies must build an advantage over the competition. The company must consider its size and industry position, then decide how to position itself to gain the strongest possible competitive advantage. Chapter 12 explains how to do this.

The design of competitive marketing strategies begins with competitor analysis. The company constantly compares the value and customer satisfaction delivered by its products, prices, channels and promotion with those of its close competitors. In this way it can discern areas of potential advantage and disadvantage. The company must formally or informally monitor the competitive environment to answer these and other important questions: Who are our competitors? What are their objectives and strategies? What are their strengths and weaknesses? How will they react to different competitive strategies we might use?

Which competitive marketing strategy a company adopts depends on its industry position. A firm that dominates a market can adopt one or more of several **market leader** strategies. Well-known leaders include Nescafé, Perrier, Swatch, Chanel, Johnnie Walker, Coca-Cola, McDonald's, Marlboro, Komatsu (large construction equipment), Sony, Nokia, Lego and Shell.

Market challengers are runner-up companies that aggressively attack competitors to get more market share. For example, Lexus challenges Mercedes, Adidas challenges Nike, and Airbus challenges Boeing. The challenger might attack the market leader, other firms of its own size, or smaller local and regional competitors. Some runner-up firms will choose to follow rather than challenge the market leader. Firms using **market follower** strategies seek stable market shares and profit by following competitors' product offers, prices and marketing programmes.[17] Smaller firms in a market, or even larger firms that lack established positions, often adopt **market nicher** strategies. They specialise in serving market niches that large competitors overlook or ignore. Market nichers avoid direct confrontations with the big companies by specialising along market, customer, product or marketing-mix lines. Through clever niching, low-share firms in an industry can be as profitable as their large competitors. Two regions of Europe are particularly strong in cultivating strong niche players: Germany for medium-sized specialist engineering firms and northern Italy's fashion industry.

developing the marketing mix

Once the company has chosen its overall competitive marketing strategy, it is ready to begin planning the details of the marketing mix. The marketing mix is one of the dominant ideas in modern marketing. We define **marketing mix** as the set of controllable tactical marketing tools that the firm blends to produce the response it wants in the target market. The marketing mix consists of everything the firm can do to influence the demand for its product. The many possibilities gather into four groups of variables known as the 'four Ps': product, price, place and promotion.[18] These are the subject of the second part of this book, Chapters 13–22. Figure 3.7 shows the particular marketing tools under each P.

Product means the totality of 'goods and services' that the company offers the target market. The Honda Civic 'product' is nuts, bolts, spark plugs, pistons, headlights and many other parts. Honda offers several Civic styles and dozens of optional features. The car comes fully serviced, with a comprehensive warranty and financing that

Market leader
The firm in an industry with the largest market share; it usually leads other firms in price changes, new product introductions, distribution coverage and promotion spending.

Market challenger
A runner-up firm in an industry that is fighting hard to increase its market share.

Market follower
A runner-up firm in an industry that wants to hold its share without rocking the boat.

Market nicher
A firm in an industry that serves small segments that the other firms overlook or ignore.

Marketing mix
The set of controllable tactical marketing tools – product, price, place and promotion – that the firm blends to produce the response it wants in the target market.

Product
Anything that can be offered to a market for attention, acquisition, use or consumption that might satisfy a want or need. It includes physical objects, services, persons, places, organisations and ideas.

Figure 3.7

The four Ps: the marketing mix

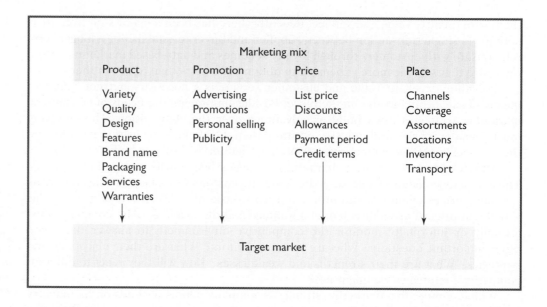

is as much a part of the product as the exhaust pipe. Increasingly, the most profitable part of the business for car companies is the loan that they offer to car buyers.

Price

The amount of money charged for a product or service, or the sum of the values that consumers exchange for the benefits of having or using the product or service.

Price is what customers pay to get the product. Honda suggests retail prices that its dealers might charge for each car, but dealers rarely charge the full asking price. Instead, they negotiate the price with each customer. They offer discounts, trade-in allowances and credit terms to adjust for the current competitive situation and to bring the price into line with the buyer's perception of the car's value.

Place

All the company activities that make the product or service available to target customers.

Place includes company activities that make the product available to target consumers. Honda maintains a body of independently owned dealerships that sell the company's cars. They select dealers carefully and support them strongly. The main dealers keep a stock of Hondas, demonstrate them to potential buyers, negotiate prices, close sales, arrange finance, and service the cars after the sale.

Promotion

Activities that communicate the product or service and its merits to target customers and persuade them to buy.

Promotion means activities that communicate the merits of the product and persuade target customers to buy it. Honda spends millions on advertising each year to tell consumers about the company and its products. Dealership salespeople assist potential buyers and persuade them that a Honda is the car for them. Honda and its dealers offer special promotions – sales, cash rebates, low financing rates – as added purchase incentives.

An effective marketing programme blends the marketing mix elements into a co-ordinated programme designed to achieve the company's marketing objectives. The marketing mix constitutes the company's tactical tool kit for establishing strong positioning in target markets. However, note that the four Ps represent the sellers' view of the marketing tools available for influencing buyers. From a consumer viewpoint, each marketing tool must deliver a customer benefit. One marketing expert suggests that companies should view the four Ps as the customer's four Cs:[19]

FOUR PS	FOUR CS
Product	Customer needs and wants
Price	Cost to the customer
Place	Convenience
Promotion	Communication

Winning companies are those that meet customer needs economically and conveniently and with effective communication.

Table 3.1

Contents of a
marketing plan

Section	Purpose
Executive summary	Presents a quick overview of the plan for quick management review.
Current marketing situation	The marketing audit that presents background data on the market, product, competition and distribution.
SWOT analysis	Identifies the company's main *strengths* and *weaknesses* and the main *opportunities* and *threats* facing the product.
Objectives and issues	Defines the company's objectives in the areas of sales, market share and profits, and the issues that will affect these objectives.
Marketing strategy	Presents the broad marketing approach that will be used to achieve the plan's objectives.
Action programmes	Specifies *what* will be done, *who* will do it, *when* it will be done and *what* it will cost.
Budgets	A projected profit-and-loss statement that forecasts the expected financial outcomes from the plan.
Controls	Indicates how the progress of the plan will be monitored.

the marketing plan

Each business, product or brand needs a detailed marketing plan. What does a marketing plan look like? Our discussion focuses on product or brand plans that are a development of the general planning process in Figure 3.1. A product or brand plan should contain the following sections: executive summary, current marketing situation, threats and opportunities, objectives and issues, marketing strategies, action programmes, budgets and controls (see Table 3.1).[20]

executive summary

The marketing plan should open with a short summary of the main goals and recommendations in the plan. Here is a short example:

> The 2000 Marketing Plan outlines an approach to attaining a significant increase in company sales and profits over the preceding year. The sales target is €24 million – a planned 20 per cent sales gain. We think this increase is attainable because of the improved economic, competitive, and distribution picture. The target operating margin is €2.5 million, a 25 per cent increase over last year. To achieve these goals, the sales promotion budget will be €500,000, or 2 per cent of projected sales. The advertising budget will be €720,000, or 3 per cent of projected sales . . . [more details follow]

The executive summary helps top management to find the plan's central points quickly. A table of contents should follow the executive summary.

marketing audit

The **marketing audit** is a systematic and periodic examination of a company's environment, objectives, strategies and activities to determine problem areas and opportunities.

Marketing audit
A comprehensive, systematic, independent and periodic examination of a company's environment, objectives, strategies and activities to determine problem areas and opportunities, and to recommend a plan of action to improve the company's marketing performance.

The macroenvironment
1. *Demographic.* What primary demographic trends pose threats and opportunities for this company?
2. *Economic.* What developments in income, prices, savings and credit will impact on the company?
3. *Natural.* What is the outlook for costs and availability of natural resources and energy? Is the company environmentally responsible?
4. *Technology.* What technological changes are occurring? What is the company's position on technology?
5. *Political.* What current and proposed laws will affect company strategy?
6. *Cultural.* What is the public's attitude towards business and the company's products? What changes in consumer lifestyles might have an impact?

The task environment
1. *Markets.* What is happening to market size, growth, geographic distribution and profits? What are the large market segments?
2. *Customers.* How do customers rate the company on product quality, service and price? How do they make their buying decisions?
3. *Competitors.* Who are the chief competitors? What are their strategies, market shares, and strengths and weaknesses?
4. *Channels.* What main channels does the company use to distribute products to customers? How are they performing?
5. *Suppliers.* What trends are affecting suppliers? What is the outlook for the availability of key production resources?
6. *Publics.* What key publics provide problems or opportunities? How should the company deal with these publics?

Marketing strategy audit
1. *Mission.* Is the mission clearly defined and market-oriented?
2. *Objectives.* Has the company set clear objectives to guide marketing planning and performance? Do these objectives fit with the company's opportunities and strengths?
3. *Strategy.* Does the company have a sound marketing strategy for achieving its objectives?
4. *Budgets.* Has the company budgeted sufficient resources to segments, products, territories and marketing-mix elements?

Marketing organisation audit
1. *Formal structure.* Does the chief marketing officer have adequate authority over activities affecting customer satisfaction? Are activities optimally structured along functional, product, market and territory lines?
2. *Functional efficiency.* Do marketing, sales and other staff communicate effectively? Are the staff well trained, supervised, motivated and evaluated?
3. *Interface efficiency.* Do staff work well across functions: marketing with manufacturing, R&D, buying, personnel, etc.?

Marketing systems audit
1. *Marketing information system.* Is the marketing intelligence system providing accurate and timely information about developments? Are decision makers using marketing research effectively?
2. *Planning system.* Does the company prepare annual, long-term and strategic plans? Are they used?
3. *Marketing control system.* Are annual plan objectives being achieved? Does management periodically analyse the sales and profitability of products, markets, territories and channels?
4. *New-product development.* Is the company well organised to gather, generate and screen new-product ideas? Does it carry out adequate product and market testing? Has the company succeeded with new products?

Productivity audit
1. *Profitability analysis.* How profitable are the company's different products, markets, territories and channels? Should the company enter, expand or withdraw from any business segments? What would be the consequences?
2. *Cost-effectiveness analysis.* Do any activities have excessive costs? How can costs be reduced?

Marketing function audit
1. *Products.* Has the company developed sound product-line objectives? Should some products be phased out? Should some new products be added? Would some products benefit from quality, style or feature changes?
2. *Price.* What are the company's pricing objectives, policies, strategies and procedures? Are the company's prices in line with customers' perceived value? Are price promotions used properly?
3. *Distribution.* What are the distribution objectives and strategies? Does the company have adequate market coverage and service? Should existing channels be changed or new ones added?
4. *Advertising, sales promotion and publicity.* What are the company's promotion objectives? How is the budget determined? Is it sufficient? Are advertising messages and media well developed and received? Does the company have well-developed sales promotion and public relations programmes?
5. *Sales force.* What are the company's sales force objectives? Is the sales force large enough? Is it properly organised? Is it well trained, supervised and motivated? How is the sales force rated relative to those of competitors?

Table 3.2 Marketing audit questions

The first main section of the plan describes the target market and the company's position in it (Table 3.2 gives the questions asked). It should start with the strategic imperatives: the pertinent objectives, policies and elements of strategy passed down from broader plans. In the **current marketing situation** section, the planner provides information about the market, product performance, competition and distribution. It includes a *market description* that defines the market, including chief market segments. The planner shows market size, in total and by segment, for several past years, and then reviews customer needs together with factors in the marketing environment that may affect customer purchasing. Next, the *product review* shows sales, prices and gross margins of the principal products in the product line. A section on *competition* identifies big competitors and their individual strategies for product quality, pricing, distribution and promotion. It also shows the market shares held by the company and each competitor. Finally, a section on *distribution* describes recent sales trends and developments in the primary distribution channels.

> **Current marketing situation**
> *The section of a marketing plan that describes the target market and the company's position in it.*

Managing the marketing function would be hard enough if the marketer had to deal only with the controllable marketing-mix variables. Reality is harder. The company is in a complex marketing environment consisting of uncontrollable forces to which the company must adapt. The *environment* produces both threats and opportunities. The company must carefully analyse its environment so that it can avoid the threats and take advantage of the opportunities.

The company's marketing environment includes forces close to the company that affect its ability to serve its consumers, such as other company *departments*, *channel members*, *suppliers*, *competitors* and other *publics*. It also includes broader *demographic* and *economic* forces, *political* and *legal* forces, *technological* and *ecological* forces, and *social* and *cultural* forces. The company must consider all of these forces when developing and positioning its offer to the target market.

SWOT analysis

The SWOT analysis section draws from the market audit. It is a brief list of the critical success factors in the market, and rates strengths and weaknesses against the competition. The SWOT analysis should include costs and other non-marketing variables. The outstanding opportunities and threats should be given. If plans depend upon assumptions about the market, the economy or the competition, they need to be explicit.

objectives and issues

Having studied the strengths, weaknesses, opportunities and threats, the company sets objectives and considers issues that will affect them. The objectives are goals that the company would like to attain during the plan's term. For example, the manager might want to achieve a 15 per cent market share, a 20 per cent pre-tax profit on sales and a 25 per cent pre-tax profit on investment. If current market share is only 10 per cent, the question needs answering: Where are the extra sales to come from? From the competition, by increasing usage rate, by adding, and so on?

marketing strategy

In this section of the marketing plan, the manager outlines the broad marketing strategy or 'game plan' for attaining the objectives. Marketing strategy is the marketing logic by which the business unit hopes to achieve its marketing objectives. It shows how strategies for target markets and positioning build upon the firm's differential advantages. It should detail the market segments on which the company will focus. These segments differ in their needs and wants, responses to marketing, and profitability. The company should put its effort into those market segments it can best serve from a competitive point of view. It should develop a marketing strategy for each targeted segment.

marketing mix

The manager should also outline specific strategies for such marketing mix elements in each target market: new products, field sales, advertising, sales promotion, prices and distribution. The manager should explain how each strategy responds to the threats, opportunities and critical issues described earlier in the plan.

action programmes

Marketing strategies become specific action programmes that answer the following questions: *What* will be done? *When* will it be done? *Who* is responsible for doing it? *How much* will it cost? For example, the manager may want to increase sales promotion as a key strategy for winning market share. A sales promotion action plan should outline special offers and their dates, trade shows entered, new point-of-purchase displays and other promotions. The action plan shows when activities will start, be reviewed and be completed.

budgets

Action plans allow the manager to make a supporting marketing budget that is essentially a projected profit and loss statement. For revenues, it shows the forecast unit sales and the average net price. On the expense side, it shows the cost of production, physical distribution and marketing. The difference is the projected profit. Higher management will review the budget and either approve or modify it. Once approved, the budget is the basis for materials buying, production scheduling, personnel planning and marketing operations. Budgeting can be very difficult and budgeting methods range from simple 'rules of thumb' to complex computer models.

controls

The last section of the plan outlines the controls that will monitor progress. Typically, there are goals and budgets for each month or quarter. This practice allows higher management to review the results of each period and to spot businesses or products that are not meeting their goals. The managers of these businesses and products have to explain these problems and the corrective actions they will take.

implementation

Marketing implementation
The process that turns marketing strategies and plans into marketing actions in order to accomplish strategic marketing objectives.

Planning good strategies is only a start towards successful marketing. A brilliant marketing strategy counts for little if the company fails to implement it properly. **Marketing implementation** is the process that turns marketing strategies and *plans* into marketing *actions* to accomplish strategic marketing objectives. Implementation involves day-to-day, month-to-month activities that effectively put the marketing plan to work. Whereas marketing planning addresses the *what* and *why* of marketing activities, implementation addresses the *who, where, when* and *how*.

marketing organisation

The company must have people who can carry out marketing analysis, planning, implementation and control. If the company is very small, one person might do all the marketing work – research, selling, advertising, customer service and other activities. As the company expands, organisations emerge to plan and carry out marketing activities. In large companies there can be many specialists: brand managers, salespeople and sales managers, market researchers, advertising experts and other specialists.

Modern marketing activities occur in several forms. The most common form is the *functional organisation*, in which functional specialists head different marketing activities – a sales manager, advertising manager, marketing research manager, customer service manager, new-product manager. A company that sells across the country or internationally often uses a *geographic organisation*, in which its sales and marketing people run specific countries, regions and districts. A geographic organisation allows salespeople to settle into a territory, get to know their customers, and work with a minimum of travel time and cost.

Companies with many, very different products or brands often create a *product management* or *brand management* organisation. Using this approach, a manager develops and implements a complete strategy and marketing programme for a specific product or brand. Product management first appeared in Procter & Gamble in 1929. A new soap, Camay, was not doing well, and a young P&G executive was assigned to give his exclusive attention to developing and promoting this brand. He was successful, and the company soon added other product managers. Since then, many organisations, especially in the food, soap, toiletries and chemical industries, have introduced the brand management system, which is in widespread use today. Dramatic changes in competitive intensity and distribution are causing companies to rethink their marketing organisation. Marketing Highlight 3.3 tells what leading companies are trying and shows that, so far, no single new structure dominates.

marketing control

Because many surprises occur during the implementation of marketing plans, the marketing department must engage in constant marketing control. **Marketing control** is the process of measuring and evaluating the results of marketing strategies and plans and taking corrective action to ensure the achievement of marketing objectives. It involves the four steps shown in Figure 3.8. Management first sets specific marketing goals. It then measures its performance in the marketplace and evaluates the causes of any differences between expected and actual performance. Finally, management takes corrective action to close the gaps between its goals and its performance. This may require changing the action programmes or even changing the goals.

Operating control involves checking ongoing performance against the annual plan and taking corrective action when necessary. Its purpose is to ensure that the company achieves the sales, profits and other goals set out in its annual plan. It also involves determining the profitability of different products, territories, markets and channels. **Strategic control** involves looking at whether the company's basic strategies match its opportunities and strengths. Marketing strategies and programmes can quickly become outdated and each company should periodically reassess its overall approach to the marketplace. Besides providing the background for marketing planning, a *marketing audit* can also be a positive tool for strategic control. Sometimes it

Marketing control
The process of measuring and evaluating the results of marketing strategies and plans, and taking corrective action to ensure that marketing objectives are attained.

Operating control
Checking ongoing performance against annual plans and taking corrective action.

Strategic control
Checking whether the company's basic strategy matches its opportunities and strengths.

marketing highlight 3.3

New challenges; new marketing organisation

Today's consumers have more choice and are more deal-prone than brand-prone. In response, companies are shifting away from national advertising in favour of pricing and other promotions. Growing retailer power is also affecting brand management. Larger and better-informed retailers are also demanding trade promotions in exchange for their shelf space. This all leaves fewer resources for advertising, the brand manager's traditional marketing tool.

To cope with these changes, Campbell Soups created *brand sales managers* charged with brand management as well as handling brands in the field, working with the trade, and designing localised brand strategies. These managers spend more time in the field working with salespeople, learning what is happening in stores, and getting closer to the customer.

Other companies, including Colgate-Palmolive, Procter & Gamble and Kraft, have *category management* where brands are grouped according to the sections or aisles in stores. Here, brand managers report to a category manager who has total responsibility for a category. For example, at Procter & Gamble, the brand manager for Dawn reports to a manager who is responsible for Dawn, Ivory, Joy and all other light-duty liquid detergents. The light-duty liquid manager then reports to a manager who is responsible for all of P&G's packaged soaps and detergents. This offers advantages. First, the category managers have broader planning perspectives than brand managers. Second, it matches the buying processes of retailers. Retailers have begun making their individual buyers responsible for working with *all* suppliers of a specific product category. The aim of a supplier is to become a *category leader* who works closely with the retailer to increase category sales rather than that of one brand. These category leaders have considerable power and responsibility.

Nabisco combines category management with *brand teams* or *category teams*. Instead of having several brand managers, Nabisco has three teams covering adult rich, nutritional and children's biscuits. Headed by a category manager, each team includes marketing people: brand managers, a sales planning manager and a marketing information specialist handling brand strategy, advertising, and sales promotion. Also in the team are a finance manager, a research and development specialist, and representatives from manufacturing, engineering and distribution. Thus category managers act as a small business, with responsibility for the performance of the category and with a full complement of people to help them plan and implement strategies.

Market management organisations can suit companies selling a product line to markets that have different needs and preferences. Market managers are responsible for developing long-range and annual plans for the sales and profits in their markets. This system's main advantage is that the company is organised around the needs of specific customer segments.

Elida Gibbs, Unilever's personal care products division, has many strong brands, including Pears, Fabergé, Brut, Signal and Timotei, but seeks to improve its service to retailers and pay more attention to developing the brands. To do this it created two new roles: brand development managers and customer development managers. *Customer development managers* work with customers and have also taken over many of the old responsibilities of brand management. This provides an opportunity for better coordination of sales, operations and marketing campaigns. The change leaves *brand development managers* with more time to spend on the strategic development of brands and innovation. They have the authority to pull together technical and managerial resources to see projects through to their completion.

Elida Gibbs' reorganisation goes beyond sales and marketing. Cross-functional teamwork is central to the approach and this extends to the shop floor. The company is already benefiting from the change. Customer development managers have increased the number of correctly completed orders from 72 per cent to 90 per cent. In addition, brand development managers developed Aquatonic – an aerosol deodorant – in six months, less than half the usual time.

SOURCES: See Robert Dewar and Don Schultz, 'The product manager: an idea whose time has gone', *Marketing Communications* (May 1989), pp. 28–35; Betsey Spethman, 'Category management multiplies', *Advertising Age* (11 May 1992), p. 42; Guy de Jonquières, 'A clean break with tradition', *Financial Times* (12 July 1993), p. 12; Belinda Dewsnap and David Jobber, 'The sales–marketing interface in consumer packaged-goods companies: a conceptual framework', *The Journal of Personal Selling & Sales Management*, **20**, 2 (2000), pp. 109–19.

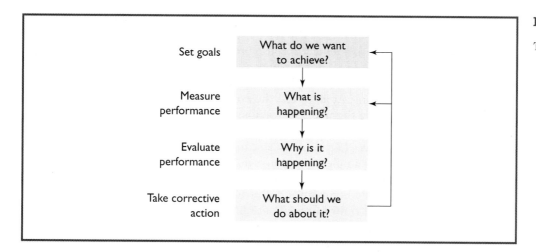

Figure 3.8

The control process

is conducted by an objective and experienced outside party who is independent of the marketing department. Table 3.2 shows the kind of questions the marketing auditor might ask. The findings may come as a surprise – and sometimes as a shock – to management. Management then decides which actions make sense and how and when to implement them.

implementing marketing

Implementation is difficult – it is easier to think up good marketing strategies than it is to carry them out.

Many managers think that 'doing things right' (implementation) is as important as, or even more important than, 'doing the right things' (strategy). The fact is that both are critical to success.[21] However, companies can gain competitive advantages through effective implementation. One firm can have essentially the same strategy as another yet win in the marketplace through faster or better execution.

In an increasingly connected world, people at all levels of the marketing system must work together to implement marketing plans and strategies. At Bosch, for example, marketing implementation for the company's power tool products requires day-to-day decisions and actions by thousands of people both inside and outside the organisation. Marketing managers make decisions about target segments, branding, packaging, pricing, promoting, and distributing. They connect with people elsewhere in the company to get support for their products and programmes. They talk with engineering about product design, with manufacturing about production and inventory levels, and with finance about funding and cash flows. They also connect with outside people, such as advertising agencies to plan ad campaigns and the media to obtain publicity support. The sales force urges retailers to advertise Bosch products, provide ample shelf space, and use company displays.

Successful marketing implementation depends on how well the company blends its people, organisational structure, decision and reward systems, and company culture into a cohesive action programme that supports its strategies. At all levels, the company must be staffed by people who have the needed skills, motivation, and personal characteristics. Before a company can hope to obtain and retain its customers, it must learn how to gain, train and retain its staff. A major recent study shows, within industries, human resource management and the quality of management training (particularly to MBA level) to be the largest indicator of company performance.

Another factor affecting successful implementation is the company's **decision-and-reward systems** – formal and informal operating procedures that guide planning,

Decision-and-reward systems
Formal and informal operating procedures that guide planning, targeting, compensation and other activities.

budgeting, compensation and other activities. For example, if a company compensates managers for short-run results, they will have little incentive to work towards long-run objectives. Companies recognising this are broadening their incentive systems to include more than sales volume. For instance, Xerox rewards include customer satisfaction and Ferrero's the freshness of its chocolates in stores. Effective implementation also requires careful planning. At all levels, the company must fill its structure and systems with people who have the necessary skills, motivation and personal characteristics. In recent years, more and more companies have recognised that long-run human resources planning can give the company a strong competitive advantage.

Finally, for successful implementation, the firm's marketing strategies must fit with its culture. *Company culture* is a system of values and beliefs shared by people in an organisation. It is the company's collective identity and meaning. The culture informally guides the behaviour of people at all company levels. Marketing strategies that do not fit the company's style and culture will be difficult to implement. Because managerial style and culture are so hard to change, companies usually design strategies that fit their current cultures rather than trying to change their styles and cultures to fit new strategies.[22]

Thus successful marketing implementation depends on how well the company blends five elements – action programmes, organisation structure, decision-and-reward systems, human resources and company culture – into a cohesive programme that supports its strategies.

summary

Strategic planning involves developing a strategy for long-run survival and growth. Marketing helps in strategic planning, and the overall strategic plan defines marketing's role in the company. Not all companies use formal planning or use it well, yet formal planning offers several benefits. Companies develop three kinds of plan: *annual plans*, *long-range plans* and *strategic plans*.

Strategic planning sets the stage for the rest of company planning. The strategic planning process consists of developing the company's mission, understanding a company's strengths and weaknesses, its environment, business portfolio, objectives and goals, and functional plans. Developing a sound *mission statement* is a challenging undertaking. The mission statement should be market-oriented, feasible, motivating and specific, if it is to direct the firm to its best opportunities.

Companies have plans at many levels: global, regional, national and so forth. The higher-level plans contain objectives and strategies that become part of subordinate plans. These *strategic imperatives* are objectives or defined practices. At each level a *strategic audit* reviews the company and its environment. A *SWOT analysis* summarises the main elements of this audit into a statement of the company's strengths and weaknesses and the chief threats and opportunities that exist.

From here, strategic planning calls for analysing the company's *business portfolio* and deciding which businesses should receive more or fewer resources. The company might use a formal portfolio-planning method like the *BCG growth–share matrix* or the *General Electric grid*. However, most companies are now designing more customised portfolio-planning approaches that better suit their unique situations.

This analysis and mission lead to strategic objectives and goals. Management must decide how to achieve growth and profits objectives. The *product/market expansion grid* shows four avenues for market growth: *market penetration*, *market development*, *product development* and *diversification*.

Once strategic objectives and strategies are defined, management must prepare a set of *functional plans* that coordinate the activities of the marketing, finance, manufacturing and other departments. Each of the company's *functional departments* provides inputs for strategic planning. Each department has a different idea about which objectives and activities are most important. The marketing department stresses the consumer's point of view. Marketing managers must understand the point of view of the company's other functions and work with other functional managers to develop a system of plans that will best accomplish the firm's overall strategic objectives.

To fulfil their role in the organisation, marketers engage in the *marketing process*. Consumers are at the centre of the marketing process. The company divides the total market into smaller segments and selects the segments it can best serve. It then designs its *marketing mix* in order to differentiate its marketing offer and to position this offer in selected target segments. To find the best mix and put it into action, the company engages in marketing analysis, marketing planning, marketing implementation and marketing control.

Each business must prepare marketing plans for its products, brands and markets. The main components of a *marketing plan* are the executive summary, current marketing situation, threats and opportunities, objectives and issues, marketing strategies, action programmes, budgets and controls. To plan good strategies is often easier than to carry them out. To be successful, companies must implement the strategies effectively. *Implementation* is the process that turns marketing strategies into marketing actions. The process consists of five key elements:

1. The *action programme* identifies crucial tasks and decisions needed to implement the marketing plan, assigns them to specific people and establishes a timetable.

2. The *organisation structure* defines tasks and assignments and coordinates the efforts of the company's people and units.

3. The company's *decision-and-reward systems* guide activities such as planning, information, budgeting, training, control and personnel evaluation and rewards. Well-designed action programmes, organisation structures and decision-and-reward systems can encourage good implementation.

4. Successful implementation also requires careful *human resources planning*. The company must obtain, maintain and retain good people.

5. The firm's *company culture* can also make or break implementation. Company culture guides people in the company; good implementation relies on strong, clearly defined cultures that fit the chosen strategy.

Most of the responsibility for implementation goes to the company's marketing department. Modern marketing activities occur in a number of ways. The most common form is the *functional marketing organisation*, in which marketing functions are directed by separate managers who report to the marketing director. The company might also use a *geographic organisation*, in which its sales force or other functions specialise by geographic area. The company may also use the *product management organisation*, in which products are assigned to product managers who work with functional specialists to develop and achieve their plans. Another form is the *market management organisation*, in which main markets are assigned to market managers who work with functional specialists.

Marketing organisations carry out marketing control. *Operating control* involves monitoring results to secure the achievement of annual sales and profit goals. It also calls for determining the profitability of the firm's products, territories, market segments and channels. *Strategic control* makes sure that the company's marketing objectives, strategies and systems fit with the current and forecast marketing environment. It uses the *marketing audit* to determine marketing opportunities and problems, and to recommend short-run and long-run actions to improve overall marketing performance. The company uses these resources to watch and adapt to the marketing environment.

discussing the issues

1. What are the benefits of a long-range plan? Does it have any role when forces, such as e-commerce, are changing markets so rapidly?

2. Many companies undertake a marketing audit to identify the firm's strengths and weaknesses relative to competitors, and in relation to the opportunities and threats in the external environment. Why is it important that such an analysis should address relative, not absolute, company strengths and weaknesses?

3. A tour operator has its own charter airline that is also used by other tour operators. The subsidiary is smaller and less profitable than are the competing charter airlines. Its growth rate has been below the industry average during the past five years. Into what cell of the BCG growth–share matrix does this strategic business unit fall? What should the parent company do with this SBU?

4. A consumer electronics company finds that sales in its main product line – CD players – are beginning to stabilise. The market is reaching maturity. What growth strategies might the firm pursue for this product line? How might the strategic-focus tool help managers examine the growth opportunities for this line?

5. The General Electric strategic business-planning grid gives a broad overview that can be helpful in strategic decision making. For what types of decision would this grid be helpful? For what types of strategic decision would it be less useful?

6. Sony's PlayStation is a market leader. Discuss how a competitor would use market-challenger, market-follower and market-nicher strategies to compete effectively with Sony.

applying the concepts

1. Think of a product or service that has presented you with difficulties in recent weeks (such as late delivery or hard to locate products), then:

   ✦ Use the Web to identify Internet-enhanced suppliers of that product or service.

   ✦ Evaluate the strengths and weaknesses of Web providers in their ability to overcome the problem you faced.

   ✦ Suggest alternative ways that the Internet could be used to overcome the product or service failure you faced.

2. Take a product or service organisation you are familiar with.

   ✦ List the key external environmental opportunities or threats that face the organisation.

   ✦ What do you think are the organisation's main strengths and weaknesses?

   ✦ Suggest ways in which the organisation might respond to the external forces.

   ✦ Recommend a possible marketing strategy which will ensure that the organisation matches its internal capabilities with external opportunities.

references

1. Saskia Sisson, 'Billionaire beach', *The European* (24–30 July 1997), pp. 56–7; Victoria McCubbine, 'Predators stalk the gnomes', *Eurobusiness* (May 2000), pp. 29–30; Mike London, 'Breaking into the audio industry', *Eurobusiness* (May 2000), pp. 82–4; 'Families out of fashion', *The Economist* (4 March 2000), p. 92; 'LVHM and Gucci: Don't mix your designers', *The Economist* (16 January 1999), pp. 70–1; 'Luxury goods: Snob appeal', *The Economist* (13 February 1999), pp. 85–6; 'The cashmere revolutionary', *The Economist* (15 July 2000), p. 94.

2. Malcolm MacDonald investigates the barriers to marketing planning in his article 'Ten barriers to marketing planning', *Journal of Marketing Management*, **5**, 1 (1989), pp. 1–18; Sean Ennis, 'Marketing planning in the smaller evolving firm: empirical evidence and reflections', *Irish Marketing Review*, **11**, 2 (1998), pp. 49–61.

3. See Philip Kotler, *Kotler on Marketing* (New York: Free Press, 1999), pp. 165–6.

4. Susanna Voyle, 'Carrefour fails to satisfy its investors' appetites', *Financial Times* (5 April 2000), p. 34.

5. To see how planning and entrepreneurship exist side by side and how the best-performing companies have balanced orientation towards marketing and technology, see Veronica Wong and John Saunders, 'Business orientation and corporate success', *Journal of Strategic Marketing*, **1**, 1 (1993), pp. 20–40.

6. Michael E. Porter, *Competitive Advantage: Creating and sustaining competitive performance* (New York: Free Press, 1985); Nicholas J. O'Shaughnessy, 'Michael's Porter competitive advantage revisited', *Management Decision*, **34**, 6 (1996), pp. 12–20.

7. David Reed, 'Sound advice', *Marketing Business* (November 1997), pp. 24–9.

8. For more on mission statements, see G. Hooley and Laura Nash, 'Mission statements – mirrors and windows', *Harvard Business Review* (March–April 1988), pp. 155–6; Fred R. David, 'How companies define their mission', *Long Range Planning*, **22**, 1 (1989), pp. 90–7.

9. Michael Porter popularised his view of value chains through his book *Competitive Advantage*, op. cit.

10. 'Mitsubishi Heavy Industries', *The Economist* (23 October 1999), pp. 119–20; 'Just possibly, something to sing about', *The Economist* (18 March 2000), pp. 97–9; Kenneth Goading, 'High speed steel group rolls towards flotation', *Financial Times* (24 June 1994), p. 27.

11. Richard G. Hamermesh, 'Making planning strategic', *Harvard Business Review*, **64**, 4 (1986), pp. 115–20; Hayley Carter, 'Strategic planning reborn', *Work Study*, **48**, 2 (1999), p. 104.

12. H. Igor Ansoff, 'Strategies for diversification', *Harvard Business Review* (September–October 1957), pp. 113–24; Ade S. Olusoga, 'Market concentration versus market diversification and internationalization: implications for MNE performance', *International Marketing Review*, **10**, 2 (1993), pp. 40–59.

13. Information taken from: Guy de Jonquières, 'Pell-mell expansion has sparked controversy', *Financial Times* (11 June 1991), p. 8; Christopher Parkes, 'New car plant will be test for "lean production"', *Financial Times* (25 June 1992), p. 4.

14. 'DaimlerChrysler: crunch time', *The Economist,* (25 September 1999), pp. 107–8; 'Transatlantic aerobatics', *The Economist* (5 June 1999), pp. 87–8; Haig Simonian, 'Bombardier lined up to buy Adtranz', *Financial Times* (20 July 2000), p. 29.

15. Nigel Piercy, *Market-Led Strategic Change: Transforming the process of going to market* (Oxford: Butterworth-Heinemann, 1997).

16. 'Quality '93: empowering people with technology', advertising supplement, *Fortune* (20 September 1993). For more reading, see Yoram Wind, 'Marketing and the other business functions', in Jagdish N. Sheth (ed.), *Research in Marketing*, vol. 5 (Greenwich, CT: JAL Press, 1981), pp. 237–56; Robert W. Ruekert and Orville C. Walker, Jr, 'Marketing's interaction with other functional units: a conceptual framework and empirical evidence', *Journal of Marketing* (January 1987), pp. 1–19; Belinda Dewsnap and David Jobber, 'The sales–marketing interface in consumer packaged-goods companies: a conceptual framework', *The Journal of Personal Selling & Sales Management* **20**, 2 (2000), pp. 109–19.

17. For more on follower strategies, see Daniel W. Haines, Rajan Chandran and Arvind Parkhe, 'Winning by being first to market . . . or second?', *Journal of Consumer Marketing* (Winter 1989), pp. 63–9.

18. The four-P classification was first suggested by E. Jerome McCarthy, *Basic Marketing: A managerial approach* (Homewood, IL: Irwin, 1960). For more discussion of this classification scheme, see Walter van Waterschoot and Christophe Van den Bulte, 'The 4P classification of the marketing mix revisited', *Journal of Marketing* (October 1992), pp. 83–93; T.C. Melewar and John Saunders, 'Global corporate visual identity systems: using an extended marketing mix', *European Journal of Marketing*, **34**, 5/6 (2000), pp. 538–50; Christian Gronroos, 'Keynote paper: From marketing mix to relationship marketing – towards a paradigm shift in marketing', *Management Decision* **35**, 4 (1997), pp. 322–39.

19. Robert Lauterborn, 'New marketing litany: four Ps passé; C-words take over', *Advertising Age* (1 October 1990), p. 26.

20. Harry Macdivitt, 'Plan', Chapter 3 in Chartered Institute of Marketing, *Marketing Means Business for the CEO*, 2000, pp. 54–61.

21. For a good discussion of gaining advantage through implementation effectiveness versus strategic differentiation, see Michael E. Porter, 'What is strategy?', *Harvard Business Review* (November–December 1996), pp. 61–78.

22. For more on company cultures, see Rohit Deshpande and Frederick E. Webster, Jr, 'Organizational culture and marketing: defining the research agenda', *Journal of Marketing* (January 1989), pp. 3–15; Brian Dumaine, 'Creating a new company culture', *Fortune* (15 January 1990), pp. 127–31; John P. Kotter and James L. Heskett, *Corporate Culture and Performance* (New York: Free Press, 1992).

case 3

Look out Lipton, here comes Oolong!

Heating up an old product

Chinese Emperor Shen Nung was boiling water under a *Camellia sinensis* tree in 2737 BC. When some leaves fell into the pot, he found the resulting infusion pleasant. So, the legend has it, tea was born. From this accident flowed the Opium Wars, the annexation of Hong Kong and rituals that have made tea far more than just a drink in the great tea-drinking nations of China, Japan and Britain.

Thomas J. Lipton Company has been in the tea business ever since *Cutty Sark* and other tea clippers raced around Cape Horn and the Cape of Good Hope to be the first to the European and American coffeehouses with their crop from the Orient. By the 1990s the excitement had left the declining tea market. To enliven the old-fashioned product market leader, Unilever resorted to selling Lipton, along with its other leading brands, Brooke Bond, PG Tips, Red Label and Taaza, using frantic sales promotions and comical characters. Then, the boring business heated up by cooling down.

Chalk up the change to those fickle consumers. Forget soft drinks. They were the rage of the 1980s, as the cola companies added 'diet everything' to their lines and experimented with all sorts of flavours. Forget sports drinks. They became the glamour drinks of the early 1990s as the soft-drink market levelled and the cola companies searched for growth opportunities. Forget those flavoured sparkling waters, like Oasis and Perrier. They had a wild ride in the early 1990s and became a health sensation. Forget coffee. After being battered by soft drinks, the venerable standby has risen as people have begun to turn away from alcoholic drinks and entrepreneurs have rediscovered the coffeehouse. However, today's hot drink is iced tea. Yes, iced tea. In fact, it's iced tea in a bottle or can, already prepared and ready to drink. No fuss, no boiling and no tea bags.

Iced tea is not new. We can trace iced tea's invention to the 1904 World's Fair in St Louis. Richard Blechynden, a promoter of Indian and Ceylon tea, found it impossible to peddle his hot tea in the stifling Missouri heat. In desperation he dumped some ice cubes into his tea and discovered that the spectators were willing to gulp anything cold. Iced tea in a can isn't new either. That's been around since the early 1970s, but it had never been more than a blip on the beverage market's radar screen.

Adding flavour

Flavour is what's new. Snapple started the trend by building a regional cult following based on bottled iced teas that featured zany flavours like cranberry, peach and raspberry. Snapple's flavoured, hot-filled tea (the manufacturer bottles the tea while it is still warm from brewing) offered consumers a better-tasting tea. Before Snapple, Lipton and others offered iced teas in plain and lemon flavour. Young, trend-setting consumers bought Snapple directly from ice cabinets in convenience stores and delicatessens and drank it straight from the bottle.

The flavoured teas hit a bull's-eye with consumers. They were willing to move away from traditional colas in search of new flavours. Consumers seemed to have a short attention span for new products and were willing to try new drinks. They were interested in so-called 'New Age' beverages – drinks that appealed to their desire for healthier, lighter refreshment. Consumers responded to the all-natural, no-calorie, relaxing and refreshing claims that the new-age beverages made. Increasingly on the go, consumers also liked the convenience and availability of ready-to-drink teas.

Forming teams

Despite the small size of the iced tea market, the big players noticed the growth rate and jumped in. Coca-Cola made the first move by teaming up with Nestlé to form Coca-Cola Nestlé Refreshments, combining Coca-Cola's powerful distribution network with Nestlé's tea expertise and its Nestea brand. Pepsi-Cola followed by joining forces with Thomas J. Lipton Company. Barq's energised its Luzianne tea brand, A&W announced it would make and distribute Tetley tea, Cadbury uncovered little-known All Seasons to serve as its tea partner and Perrier joined forces with Celestial Seasonings.

Lipton was already no. 1 in the tea market, but like Coca-Cola, Pepsi's top management argued that the company's alliance with Lipton would leverage Pepsi's distribution strength with Lipton's leadership in tea to produce a can't-miss proposition. Lipton's president observed that the new partnership would make Lipton 'as widely available as Pepsi'.

The entrance of Pepsi, Coca-Cola and their competitors should invigorate the ready-to-drink tea market. One observer noted that the iced-tea market was still a small market and it was getting very overcrowded: almost 200 new ready-to-drink teas. The competitors hoped to generate growth by dusting off tea's boring image and recasting it as a natural, better-for-you beverage. Further, scientific evidence emerged that tea inhibited certain types of cancer in laboratory mice and seemed to be linked to lower cholesterol rates. Lipton, Nestea and Snapple lured customers with new flavours and pointed out that lack of carbonation makes iced tea easier to drink rapidly and in quantity.

Although Coca-Cola/Nestlé's Nestea sales soared, Snapple's and Lipton's have grown even faster. As a result, Nestea narrowed its promotion to target 18- to 29-year-olds with a promotional blitz consisting of sponsorships and sampling. It dispatched five 18-wheeler demonstration trucks, which it called its 'Cool Out Caravans', to sporting events, theme parks and beaches in 60 markets.

Pepsi continued its cola-style marketing for Lipton teas. Its radio ads argued that Snapple is 'mixed up from a powder', but Lipton is 'real brewed'. Pepsi also promoted Lipton in supermarkets by offering customers 'value packs' that contained one bottle each of three new drinks: Lipton Original, Ocean Spray Lemonade and AllSport sports drink. Pepsi also pursued sponsorship of a Rolling Stones concert tour, to which it would link a massive sampling programme.

Because of its efforts, Lipton's teas seemed ready to unseat Coca-Cola/Nestlé which, despite its early market entry, was falling behind in the iced-tea wars. Lipton was taking market share from both Snapple and Nestea. One observer noted that Pepsi had done a better job with Lipton and new-age beverages than the Coke system had. Perhaps as a result, Coca-Cola and Nestlé announced they were dissolving their relationship. Coca-Cola would take the primary responsibility for marketing ready-to-drink Nestea, while Nestlé would focus on ready-to-drink coffees. Analysts suggested that the new arrangement would give Coca-Cola more speed and flexibility because it would not have to deal with Nestlé on every decision.

Oolong enters from the East

Just as Lipton seems to be pulling ahead in the 'new tea' market, a threat looms from tea's homeland. Shin Shii Industrial Company, a little-known beverage company based in a dusty industrial city in southern Taiwan, has emerged as a giant-killer in the Taiwanese beverage market. Shin Shii originally launched Kai Shii oolong tea, a canned ready-to-drink iced tea. Although iced tea was popular in other Pacific Rim countries like Japan, the Taiwanese had never heard of iced tea. They drank only fresh-brewed hot tea.

Shin Shii and its advertising agency Metaphysical Punctuality Advertising Company used an offbeat multi-million-dollar advertising campaign to propel Kai Shii from back shelves in mom-and-pop stores to prominent spots in rapidly growing convenience-store chains, grocery stores, hypermarkets and warehouse clubs. The ads proclaimed that Kai Shii was the choice of a 'new breed of people' in a 'new world' and featured 'neo-people' who spanned all age groups, even the tradition-bound older generation. The ads presented Kai Shii as a natural drink that fits with people's concerns for their health and the environment. Some ads made fun of inebriated businesspeople that drank foreign liquors, picturing them alongside fresh-faced Kai Shii tea drinkers.

Next, Kai Shii's advertising team travelled to China to film scenes of Chinese peasants clad in colourful traditional costumes. They put these scenes in Kai Shii ads that played on the emotions generated by Taiwan's growing ties with mainland China. The ads won a first-place award at the Cannes Film festival.

Through aggressive advertising, Kai Shii now dominates the nearly 100 brands in the Oolong sector of Taiwan's ready-to-drink tea market. Kai Shii doubled its share to 25 per cent of the overall market and 70 per cent of the Oolong tea segment.

Furthermore, consumer demand for ready-to-drink iced tea has cut sharply into sales of carbonated soft drinks. Soft-drink sales in Taiwan have plummeted by 16 per cent, while ready-to-drink sales have more than doubled. The sales trend hit Coke and Pepsi especially hard, and Pepsi said it would move to reduce costs.

Next, Kai Shii's ads went global, featuring young Chinese living in New York City and Europeans living in London and Paris. These ads were just the opening salvos as Shin Shii turned its sights on foreign markets. Its managers plan to use the skills they have honed in Taiwan to enter the US market.

In entering western markets, Shin Shii will face the challenge of introducing consumers to the smooth-tasting, amber-coloured oolong tea. Lipton and Pepsi will face the challenge of a new competitor that has already shown it can succeed in selling iced tea and in taking share from soft drinks. The local producers are not standing still. They now intend to use hot tea to displace colas and other soft drinks sold to people to consume 'on the hoof'. Unilever are now adding to its Liptonice with a radical new way of selling hot tea. Having spent £10 million (€16.6 million) developing hot cans to be sold in convenience stores and petrol stations, it was ready to test-market the product in Manchester, England. Brooke Bond's PG Tips will be sold in ring-pull tins kept at 56 °C in a heated cabinet on shop counters. On sale alongside PG Tips, with or without sugar, will be Red Mountain coffee, sweetened or unsweetened, and Choky, the leading French hot chocolate brand. Watch out Oolong, Brooke Bond's waiting!

Questions

1. What bases can companies use to segment the iced-tea market?

2. What potential market segments can you identify?

3. How would you go about forecasting demand in the iced-tea market and in any given segment?

4. Which type of market coverage strategy should Pepsi/Lipton adopt? Why? How should they position Lipton iced teas and Brooke Bond canned teas?

5. If you were advising Shin Shii, what marketing strategy recommendations would you make concerning its entry into the market?

6. How should it position Kai Shii?

SOURCES: Sally D. Goll, 'Taiwan soft drink sales break for tea', *Wall Street Journal* (29 July 1994), p. A7B, used with permission of *Wall Street Journal*. See also: Laurie M. Grossman, 'Coca-Cola, Nestlé are ending venture in tea and coffee but plan other ties', *Wall Street Journal* (30 August 1994), p. B3; Laura Bird, 'Trouble is brewing for Snapple as rivals fight for iced tea sales', *Wall Street Journal* (9 June 1994), p. B4; Eric Sfiligoj, 'Ladies and gentlemen and beverages of all ages', *Beverages World* (April 1994), pp. 42–7; Gerry Khermouch, 'Nestea iced tea plans summer push', *Adweek* (21 March 1994), p. 13; Michael J. McCarthy, 'Competition heats up iced-tea industry', *Wall Street Journal* (15 June 1993), p. B1; Kevin Goldman, 'Snapple goes big time for new age drink', *Wall Street Journal* (20 April 1993), p. B6; Greg W. Prince, 'Tea for all', *Beverage World* (April 1992), pp. 24–32; Maggie Urry, 'Tea in a can is hot tip from Brooke Bond', *Financial Times* (13 December 1997), p. 4; Gary Mead, 'Brewing a healthier image for tea', *Financial Times*, 7 April 1997 (FT web archives); 'Twinings', http://www.cuttsark.org.uk/twining; 'Lipton', http://www.lipton.com; 'Tea Council', http://www.teacouncil.co.uk.

internet exercises

Internet exercises for this chapter can be found on the student site of the MYPHLIP Web Site at www.booksites.net/kotler.

part two

The marketing setting

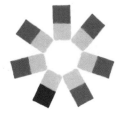

'Let the great world spin for ever down the ringing grooves of change.'

ALFRED LORD TENNYSON

part introduction

PART TWO OF *PRINCIPLES OF MARKETING* looks at the environment in which marketing operates, customer behaviour and how information from the environment is fed into the marketing decision-making process. It has five chapters.

Chapter 4 looks at the environment in two parts: the *microenvironment* that is specific to an organisation's operation, such as suppliers and competitors; and the *macroenvironment* of wider forces that shape society, such as the natural and political environment. Global markets make it even harder to understand the social environment of marketing. Chapter 5 looks at these and forces us to see how much we have to change to succeed in international markets.

Chapter 6 explores ways of understanding consumer markets: individuals and households who buy goods and services for final consumption. The many ways of doing this give insights that can help in the design of marketing research and guide marketing decision making. Although consumer marketing is the most visible, the majority of marketing is to other organisations. These include retailers that sell on to final consumers, sellers of capital equipment – such as trucks, raw materials, components or business services. Chapter 7 reviews this wide range of business markets.

As Gunther Grass recognised, 'Information networks straddle the world. Nothing remains concealed. But the sheer volume of information dissolves the information. We are unable to take it all in.' Chapter 8 shows how *marketing information systems* gather, process and present this overwhelming flow of information to support marketing decision making.

chapter four

The marketing environment

Chapter objectives *After reading this chapter, you should be able to:*

✦ Describe the environmental forces that affect the company's ability to serve its customers.

✦ Explain how changes in the demographic and economic environments affect marketing decisions.

✦ Identify the main trends in the firm's natural and technological environments.

✦ Explain the key changes that occur in the political and cultural environments.

✦ Discuss how companies can react to the marketing environment.

introduction

Companies succeed as long as they have matched their products or services to today's marketing environment. This chapter addresses the key forces in the firm's marketing environment and how they affect its ability to maintain satisfying relationships with target customers. Moreover, as noted in Chapter 1, marketers operate in an increasingly connected world. Today's marketers must connect effectively with customers, others in the company and external partners in the face of major environmental forces that buffer all of these actors.

Marketing environment
The actors and forces outside marketing that affect marketing management's ability to develop and maintain successful transactions with its target customers.

A company's **marketing environment** consists of the actors and forces outside marketing that affect marketing management's ability to develop and maintain successful transactions with its target customers. The marketing environment offers both opportunities and threats. Successful companies know the vital importance of constantly watching and adapting to the changing environment. Too many other companies, unfortunately, fail to think of change as opportunity. They ignore or resist critical changes until it is almost too late. Their strategies, structures, systems and culture grow increasingly out of date. Corporations as mighty as IBM and General Motors have faced crises because they ignored environmental changes for too long.

As we enter the new millennium, both consumers and marketers wonder what the future will bring. The environment continues to change at a rapid pace. For example, think about how you buy groceries today. How will your grocery buying change during the next few decades? What challenges will these changes present for marketers?

preview case

Volkswagen: a drive down memory lane

As we hurtle into the new millennium, social experts are busier than ever assessing the impact of a host of environmental forces on consumers and the marketers who serve them. Some experts observe how 'millennial fever' is driving consumer behaviour in all sorts of interesting ways.

Today, people of all ages seem to feel a bit over-worked, overstimulated and overloaded. While they hail the benefits of the wired 90s, they are also overwhelmed by the breathtaking onrush of the Information Age, with its high-speed modems, cell phones and pagers. The result of this 'millennial fever' is a yearning to turn back the clock, to return to simpler times. This yearning has in turn produced a massive nostalgia wave to which marketers of all kinds have responded by re-creating products and images that help take consumers back to 'the good old days'. Examples of such flirtations with nostalgia include retro roadsters such as the Porsche Boxter, DaimlerChrysler's PT (personal transportation) Cruiser and the new Mini. The singer Aretha Franklin re-recorded 'Rescue Me' as 'Deliver Me' for a Pizza Hut commercial, a recent Pepsi commercial rocks to the Rolling Stones' 'Brown Sugar', while Janis Joplin's raspy voice crows, 'Oh Lord, won't you buy me a Mercedes-Benz?'

Perhaps no company has more riding on the nostalgia wave than Volkswagen. Back in the 1950s, the original Volkswagen Beetle, with its simple, bug-like design, no-frills engineering and economical operation, was the antithesis of American brash, chrome-laden gas guzzlers. Although most owners would readily admit that their Beetles were under-powered, noisy, cramped and freezing in the winter, they saw these as endearing qualities. Overriding these minor inconveniences, the Beetle was cheap to buy and own, dependable, easy to fix, fun to drive and anything but flashy.

During the booming 1960s, demand exploded and the Beetle blossomed into an unlikely icon. Bursting with personality, the understated Bug came to personify an era of rebellion against conventions. By the late 1970s, however, the 'baby boomers' (babies born post World War II, that is, between 1946 and 1964) had moved on, Bug mania had faded. Still, more than 20 years later, allusion to these chugging oddities evokes smiles and strong emotions.

Now, in an attempt to surf the nostalgia wave, Volkswagen has introduced a New Beetle. Outwardly, the re-born Beetle resembles the original, tapping the strong emotions and memories of times gone by. Underneath the New Beetle is none other than a fourth generation VW Golf – packed with modern features, but wrapped up in an old-style package. Built into the dashboard is a bud vase perfect for a daisy plucked straight from the 1960s. But right next to it is a high-tech multi-speaker stereo. It also comes with airbags and power outlets for mobile phones – and options like power windows, cruise control and a power sunroof make it a very different car from the rattly old Bug.

With a familiar bubble shape that still makes people smile as it skitters by, the new Beetle offers a pull that is purely emotional. Advertising for the New Beetle plays strongly on the nostalgia theme, while also refreshing the old Beetle heritage. 'If you sold your soul in the '80s,' tweaks one ad, 'here's your chance to buy it back.' Other ads read, 'Less flower, more power', and 'Comes with wonderful new features. Like heat.' Still another ad declares '0 to 60? Yes.' The car's Web page (www3.vw.com/cars/newbeetle/main.html) summarises: 'The New Beetle has what any Beetle always had. Originality. Honesty. A point of view. It's an exhaustive and zealous rejection of banality. Isn't the world ready for that kind of car again?'

'Millennial fever' results from the convergence of a wide range of forces in the marketing environment – from technological, economic and demographic forces to cultural, social and political ones. Most trend analysts believe that the nostalgia craze will only grow as the baby boomers, whose emotions are tied closely to the Beetle, continue to age. Says another trend analyst, the New Beetle 'is our romantic past, reinvented for our hectic here-and-now. Different, yet deeply familiar – a car for the times.'[1]

Questions

1. What factors govern the effective use of nostalgia marketing? Do you agree with the suggestion that the Beetle nostalgia craze will grow as the 'baby boomers' continue to age? Explain.

2. In addition to watching and responding to consumer trends, what other actors and forces in the marketing environment should be considered by companies in order to develop and maintain successful relationships with their customers?

3. To what extent are companies such as Volkswagen able to forecast future trends in the marketing environment?

Some futurists predict that we will not be shopping in multi-aisle supermarkets in 2025. The growth of e-commerce and the rapid speed of the Internet will lead to online ordering of lower-priced, non-perishable products, from strawberry jam to coffee filters. Retailers will become 'bundlers', combining these orders into large packages of goods for each household and delivering them efficiently to their doorsteps. As a result we will see mergers between retailing and home-delivery companies. Consumers will not waste time searching for the best-priced bundle. Online information agents will do it for them, comparing prices among competitors.

Another futuristic view sees computers in 2025 as being as smart as humans. Consumers will use them to exchange information with on-screen electronic agents that ferret out the best deals online. Thanks to embedded-chip technology in the pantry, products on a continuous household replenishment (CHR) list, like paper towels and pet food, will sense they are running low and reorder themselves automatically. If the information agent finds a comparable but cheaper substitute for a CHR product, the item will be switched instantly.[2]

Such pictures of the future give marketers plenty to think about. A company's marketers take the major responsibility of identifying significant changes in the environment. More than any other group in the company, marketers must be the trend trackers and opportunity seekers. Although every manager in an organisation needs to observe the outside environment, marketers have two special aptitudes. They have disciplined methods – marketing intelligence and marketing research – for collecting information about the marketing environment. They also normally spend more time in the customer and competitor environment. By conducting systematic environmental scanning, marketers are able to revise and adapt marketing strategies to meet new challenges and opportunities in the marketplace.

Microenvironment
The forces close to the company that affect its ability to serve its customers – the company, market channel firms, customer markets, competitors and publics, which combine to make up the firm's value delivery system.

Macroenvironment
The larger societal forces that affect the whole microenvironment – demographic, economic, natural, technological, political and cultural forces.

The marketing environment consists of a microenvironment and a macroenvironment. The **microenvironment** consists of the forces close to the company that affect its ability to serve its customers – the company, suppliers, marketing channel firms, customer markets, competitors and publics. The **macroenvironment** consists of the larger societal forces that affect the whole microenvironment – demographic, economic, natural, technological, political and cultural forces. We look first at the company's microenvironment.

the company's microenvironment

Marketing management's job is to attract and build relationships with customers by creating customer value and satisfaction. However, marketing managers cannot accomplish this task alone. Their success will depend on other actors in the company's microenvironment – other company departments, suppliers, marketing intermediaries, customers, competitors and various publics, which combine to make up the company's value delivery system (see Figure 4.1).

Figure 4.1

Principal actors in the company's microenvironment

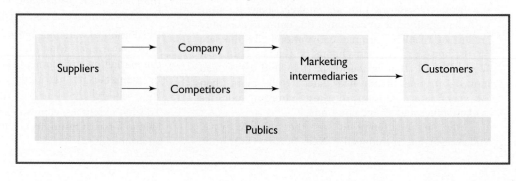

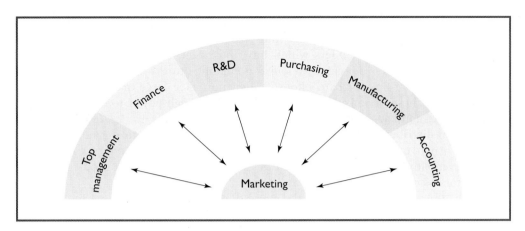

Figure 4.2

The company's internal
environment

the company

In designing marketing plans, marketing management should take other company
groups, such as top management, finance, research and development (R&D), purchasing, manufacturing and accounting, into consideration. All these interrelated groups
form the internal environment (see Figure 4.2). Top management sets the company's
mission, objectives, broad strategies and policies. Marketing managers make decisions
consistent with the plans made by top management, and marketing plans must be
approved by top management before they can be implemented.

Marketing managers must also work closely with other company departments.
Finance is concerned with finding and using funds to carry out the marketing plan. The
R&D department focuses on the problems of designing safe and attractive products.
Purchasing worries about getting supplies and materials, whereas manufacturing is
responsible for producing the desired quality and quantity of products. Accounting has
to measure revenues and costs to help marketing know how well it is achieving its
objectives. Together, all of these departments have an impact on the marketing department's plans and actions. Under the marketing concept, all of these functions must
'think customer' and they should work in harmony to provide superior customer value
and satisfaction.

suppliers

Suppliers are an important link in the company's overall customer 'value delivery
system'. They provide the resources needed by the company to produce its goods
and services. Supplier developments can seriously affect marketing. Marketing managers must watch supply availability – supply shortages or delays, labour strikes and
other events can cost sales in the short run and damage customer satisfaction in the
long run. Marketing managers must also monitor the price trends of their key inputs.
Rising supply costs may force price increases that can harm the company's sales
volume.

marketing intermediaries

Marketing intermediaries are firms that help the company to promote, sell and distribute its goods to final buyers. They include *resellers*, *physical distribution firms*,

Suppliers
*Firms and individuals
that provide the
resources needed by
the company and its
competitors to produce
goods and services.*

**Marketing
intermediaries**
*Firms that help the
company to promote,
sell and distribute its
goods to final buyers;
they include physical
distribution firms,
marketing-service
agencies and financial
intermediaries.*

Resellers
The individuals and organisations that buy goods and services to resell at a profit.

Physical distribution firms
Warehouse, transportation and other firms that help a company to stock and move goods from their points of origin to their destinations.

Marketing services agencies
Marketing research firms, advertising agencies, media firms, marketing consulting firms and other service providers that help a company to target and promote its products to the right markets.

Financial intermediaries
Banks, credit companies, insurance companies and other businesses that help finance transactions or insure against the risks associated with the buying and selling of goods.

marketing services agencies and *financial intermediaries*. **Resellers** are distribution channel firms that help the company find customers or make sales to them. These include wholesalers and retailers which buy and resell merchandise. Selecting and working with resellers is not easy. No longer do manufacturers have many small, independent resellers from which to choose. They now face large and growing reseller organisations. These organisations frequently have enough power to dictate terms or even shut the manufacturer out of large markets.

Physical distribution firms help the company to stock and move goods from their points of origin to their destinations. Working with warehouse and transportation firms, a company must determine the best ways to store and ship goods, balancing such factors as cost, delivery, speed and safety.

Marketing services agencies are the marketing research firms, advertising agencies, media firms and marketing consultancies that help the company target and promote its products to the right markets. When the company decides to use one of these agencies, it must choose carefully because the firms vary in creativity, quality, service and price. The company has to review the performance of these firms regularly and consider replacing those that no longer perform well.

Financial intermediaries include banks, credit companies, insurance companies and other businesses that help finance transactions or insure against the risks associated with the buying and selling of goods. Most firms and customers depend on financial intermediaries to finance their transactions. The company's marketing performance can be seriously affected by rising credit costs and limited credit.

Like suppliers, marketing intermediaries form an important component of the company's overall value delivery system. In its quest to create satisfying customer relationships, the company must do more than just optimise its own performance. It must partner effectively with suppliers and marketing intermediaries to optimise the performance of the entire system.

customers

The company must study its customer markets closely. Figure 4.3 shows six types of customer market. *Consumer markets* consist of individuals and households that buy goods and services for personal consumption. *Business markets* buy goods and services for further processing or for use in their production process, whereas *reseller markets* buy goods and services to resell at a profit. *Institutional markets* are made up of schools, hospitals, nursing homes, prisons and other institutions that provide goods

Figure 4.3

Types of customer market

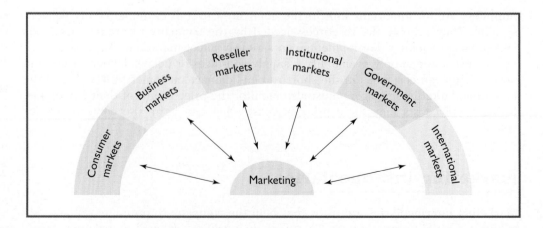

and services to people in their care. *Government markets* are made up of government agencies that buy goods and services in order to produce public services or transfer the goods and services to others who need them. Finally, *international markets* consist of buyers in other countries, including consumers, producers, resellers and governments. Each market type has special characteristics that call for careful study by the seller. At any point in time, the firm may deal with one or more customer markets: for example, as a consumer packaged goods manufacturer, Unilever has to communicate brand benefits to consumers as well as maintaining a dialogue with retailers that stock and resell its branded products.

competitors

The marketing concept states that, to be successful, a company must provide greater customer value and satisfaction than its competitors. Thus, marketers must do more than simply adapt to the needs of target consumers. They must also gain strategic advantage by positioning their offerings strongly against competitors' offerings in the minds of consumers.

No single competitive marketing strategy is best for all companies. Each firm should consider its own size and industry position compared to those of its competitors. Large firms with dominant positions in an industry can use certain strategies that smaller firms cannot afford. But being large is not enough. There are winning strategies for large firms, but there are also losing ones. And small firms can develop strategies that give them better rates of return than large firms enjoy.

publics

The company's marketing environment also includes various publics. A **public** is any group that has an actual or potential interest in or impact on an organisation's ability to achieve its objectives. Figure 4.4 shows seven types of public:

Public
Any group that has an actual or potential interest in or impact on an organisation's ability to achieve its objectives.

1. *Financial publics.* Financial publics influence the company's ability to obtain funds. Banks, investment houses and stockholders are the principal financial publics.
2. *Media publics.* Media publics are those that carry news, features and editorial opinion. They include newspapers, magazines and radio and television stations.

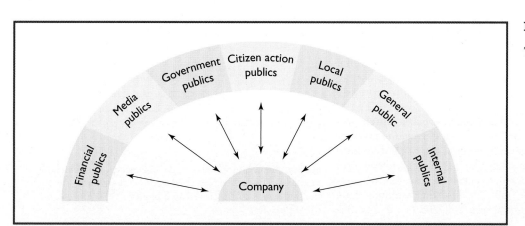

Figure 4.4

Types of public

marketing highlight 4.1

We shall be heard!

The Irish pop band Westlife, together with their manager Ronan Keating, the lead singer of the group BoyZone, joined several celebrities, including footballers Michael Owen, Robbie Fowler and Paul Ince, to back a boycott. This time it is a campaign urging people not to buy Bell's Whisky, Guinness, Burger King burgers and Haagen-Dazs ice-cream, until the company meets UK Thalidomide victims' demands for increased compensation. What's all this about?

Thalidomide, the drug that led to hundreds of children being born without limbs, was withdrawn in 1961, when the side-effects of the drug taken by pregnant women were discovered. Distillers, the company that marketed the drug, had to make annual payments to 450 Thalidomide victims, with payments expiring in 2009. However, the health of many beneficiaries has been deteriorating. The predicament of these long-suffering victims led to the launch of a consumer boycott by Thalidomide UK, a support group for victims. The target? Distillers parent, Diageo, formed in 1997 after the merger of Grand Metropolitan and Guinness, which previously acquired Distillers. Thalidomide UK had pressed for extra funds to be provided by Diageo to cover the increased costs of victims' deteriorating health and proposed that payments should be extended ten years, taking most victims up to their retirement age. Frustration with the lack of progress in Diageo's resolve to meet the group's proposals saw an intensification of the campaign, amid claims by Thalidomide UK of Diageo's attempt to dissuade celebrities from backing the offensive.

Publicity of this nature can tarnish a company's image. Diageo continued to defend its policy on thalidomide. A Diageo spokesperson responded: 'We recognise that there will always be issues of serious concern arising from the tradegy of thalidomide . . . their resolution can be neither swift nor simple.' No matter how these concerns are ultimately resolved, one thing is certain. The company cannot afford to ignore public forces: like a voice from the past, Thalidomide UK will relentlessly knock on its conscience.

Consider another example. Nutricia, a Dutch producer of baby foods and powders and a leading investor in biotechnology research, entered into a joint venture with the Dutch subsidiary of US biotechnology firm GenPharm International, to carry out research to genetically engineer cows' milk. By inserting a human gene into the genetic material of a bull, the two companies hoped that the milk produced by the bull's female descendants would contain large amounts of lactoferrine, a substance normally found in human milk. The Dutch Society for the Protection of Animals (DSPA) subsequently launched a campaign in the form of a series of shock posters. One showed a starry-eyed cow with the question posed: 'Soon to be marketed with blonde hair and blue eyes?' A second depicted a woman's naked chest with two neat rows of udders. Campaigners threatened to call an all-out boycott of Nutricia products.

The Dutch government, which has introduced 'never unless' rules to regulate genetic manipulation of animals, exceptionally permitted the Nutricia project to go ahead as scientists argued that large-scale production of lactoferrine serves unique medical goals. The DSPA, however, stressed that the Nutricia project's motive was purely commercial – to manufacture the equivalent of mother's milk on an agribusiness scale at potential cost to animal welfare.

Under mounting pressure from the interest groups, the project was ultimately abandoned. Nutricia said it would handle such pioneering efforts in genetic modification more carefully in the future. Dutch pressure groups declare that they have effectively scared investors from venturing into the most delicate and controversial field of modern biotechnology. According to a spokesman for NIABA, a group representing the Dutch food industry for biotechnology matters, 'The animal rights and environmental pressure groups may not represent a very large section of opinion, but their blackmailing tactics have been known to work in the past. Any company that ignores their signals takes a very big chance.'

SOURCE: Jimmy Burns, 'Diageo defends policy on thalidomide', *Financial Times* (9 March 2000), p. 6; Barbara Smit, 'Herman the Bull scares off Dutch research pioneers', *The European* (22–8 July 1994), p. 25.

Communicating with publics:
Unilever magazine communicates
news and information to employees.
SOURCE: Unilever plc

3. *Government publics*. Management must take government developments into account. Marketers must often consult the company's lawyers on issues of product safety, truth in advertising and other matters.

4. *Citizen action publics*. A company's marketing decisions may be questioned by consumer organizations, environmental groups, minority groups and other pressure groups (see Marketing Highlight 4.1). Its public relations department can help it stay in touch with consumer and citizen groups.

5. *Local publics*. Every company has local publics, such as neighbourhood residents and community organisations. Large companies usually appoint a community-relations officer to deal with the community, attend meetings, answer questions and contribute to worthwhile causes.

6. *General public*. A company needs to be concerned about the general public's attitude towards its products and activities. The public's image of the company affects its buying. Thus, many large corporations invest huge sums of money to promote and build a healthy corporate image.

7. *Internal publics*. A company's internal publics include its workers, managers, volunteers and the board of directors. Large companies use newsletters and other means to inform and motivate their internal publics. When employees feel good about their company, this positive attitude spills over to their external publics.

A company can prepare marketing plans for these publics as well as for its customer markets. Suppose the company wants a specific response from a particular public, such as goodwill, favourable word-of-mouth, or donations of time or money. The company would have to design an offer to this public that is attractive enough to produce the desired response.

We have looked at the firm's immediate or microenvironment. Next we examine the larger macroenvironment.

Figure 4.5

Influential forces
in the company's
macroenvironment

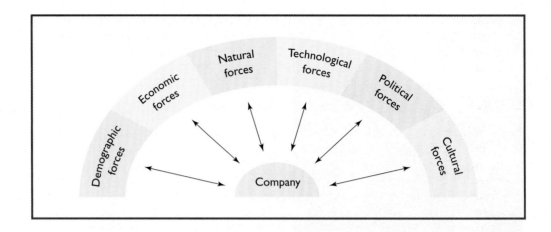

the company's macroenvironment

The company and all the other actors operate in a larger macroenvironment of forces
that shape opportunities and pose threats to the company. Figure 4.5 shows the six
most influential forces in the company's macroenvironment. The remaining sections
of this chapter examine these forces and show how they affect marketing plans.

demographic environment

Demography

*The study of human
populations in terms of
size, density, location,
age, sex, race,
occupation and
other statistics.*

Demography is the study of human populations in terms of size, density, location, age,
gender, race, occupation and other statistics. The demographic environment is of
considerable interest to marketers because it involves people, and people make up
markets. Here, we discuss the most important demographic characteristics and trends
in the largest world markets.

■ Population size and growth trends

In any geographic market, population size and growth trends can be used to gauge its
broad potential for a wide range of goods and services. The European Union (EU),
together with members of the European Free Trade Area (EFTA), has a population of
around 376 million. With another 120 million from eastern Europe and 280 million
from the former USSR, the overall European market is significantly larger than the
North America Free Trade Area – the United States, Canada and Mexico – with a
population of 370 million and Japan with 127 million. Marketers also view China, with
1.2 billion people, as a potentially lucrative growth market.[3]

The world population now totals more than 6 billion and is forecast to grow to
about 8 billion by 2040, thanks to falling mortality rates, especially among infants, and
improved life expectancy. A growing population means growing human needs to
satisfy, offering marketers an indication of demand for certain goods and services.
Depending on purchasing power, it may also mean growing market opportunities. For
example, to curb its skyrocketing population, the Chinese government passed regulations limiting families to one child each. As a result, Chinese children tended to be
spoiled and fussed over as never before. They are being showered with everything from
sweets to computers as a result of what is known as the 'six-pocket syndrome'. As
many as six adults – including parents and two sets of doting grandparents – may be

indulging the whims of each child. Parents in the average Beijing household now spend about 40 per cent of their income on their cherished only child. This trend has encouraged toy companies such as Denmark's Lego Group, Japan's Bandai Company and America's Mattel to enter the Chinese market.[4]

■ Changing age structure of a population

The single most noticeable demographic trend in Europe and other industrialised countries, including the US and affluent Asian countries, is the changing age structure of the population. The post World War II baby boom produced the *baby boomers*, born between 1946 and 1964. The boomers have presented a moving target, creating new markets as they grew from infancy to their pre-adolescent, teenage, young-adult and now middle-age to mature years. Baby boomers cut across all walks of life. But marketers typically have paid the most attention to the smaller upper crust of the boomer generation – its more educated, mobile and wealthy segments. These segments have gone by many names. In the 1980s, they were called 'yuppies' (young urban professionals), 'yummies' (young upwardly mobile mommies), and 'DINKIES' (from DINKY, dual-income, no kids yet). In the 1990s, however, yuppies and DINKIES gave way to a new breed, with names such as DEWKs (dual-earners with kids) and SLOPPIES (slightly older urban professionals).

The oldest boomers are now in their fifties; the youngest are in their mid-to-late thirties. They are also reaching their peak earning and spending years. Thus, they constitute a lucrative market for housing, furniture and appliances, healthful foods and beverages, physical fitness products, high-priced cars, convenience products and travel and financial services.

The maturing boomers are experiencing the pangs of midlife and rethinking the purpose and value of their work, responsibilities and relationships. They are approaching life with a new stability and reasonableness in the way they live, think, eat and spend. As they continue to age, they will create a large and important seniors market.

The baby boom was followed by a 'birth dearth' creating another generation of people born between 1965 and 1976. The *Generation Xers* tend to be the children of parents who both held jobs. Increasing divorce rates and higher employment for their mothers made them the first generation of latchkey kids. They want to build more traditional families and to be more available to their children. Whereas the boomers created a sexual revolution, the GenXers have lived in the age of AIDS. Having grown up during times of recession and corporate downsizing, they have developed a more cautious economic outlook. As a result, the GenXers are a more sceptical bunch, cynical of frivolous marketing pitches that promise easy success. Their cynicism makes them more savvy shoppers, and their financial pressures make them more value conscious. They like lower prices and a more functional look. The GenXers respond to honesty in advertising. They like irreverence and sass and ads that mock the traditional advertising approach.

GenXers share new cultural concerns. They care about the environment and respond favourably to socially responsible companies. Although they seek success, they are less materialistic, they prize experience, not acquisition. They are cautious romantics who want a better quality of life and are more interested in job satisfaction than in sacrificing personal happiness and growth for promotion.

The GenXers are now growing up and beginning to take over. They are the first generation to have grown up with computers and surf the Net more than other groups, but with serious intent. By 2010, they will have overtaken the baby boomers as a primary market for almost every product category.

Both the baby boomers and GenXers will one day be passing the reins to the latest demographic group, the *echo boomers* (the baby boomlet generation). Born between 1977 and 1994, and ranging from pre-teens to twenties, the echo boomer

To serve the large and growing 'kid market', many retailers are opening separate children's chains. For example, Toys 'Я' Us opened Kids 'Я' Us.

SOURCE: Toys 'Я' Us

generation is still forming its buying preferences and behaviours. The baby boomlet has created large and growing kid and teens markets. Teens and pre-teens under 20 years of age are high spenders, or at least greatly influence their parents' spending.[5] After years of bust, markets for children's toys and games, clothes, furniture and food are enjoying a boom. For instance, Sony and other electronics firms are now offering products designed especially for children. In recent years, designers and retailers have created new lines, new products and even new stores devoted to children and teens – DKNY, Gap, Kids 'Я' Us and Guess, to name just a few. Banks too are offering banking and investment services for kids.

Like the trailing edge of the Generation Xers ahead of them, one distinguishing characteristic of the echo boomers is their utter fluency and comfort with computer, digital and Internet technology. For this reason, one analyst has christened them the Net-Gens (or N-gens). He observes:

> What makes this generation different . . . is not just its demographic muscle, but it is the first to grow up surrounded by digital media. Computers and other digital technologies, such as digital cameras, are commonplace to N-Gen members. They work with them at home, in school, and they use them for entertainment. Increasingly these technologies are connected to the Internet. . . . Constantly surrounded by technology, today's kids are accustomed to its strong presence in their lives. [They] are so bathed in bits that they are no more intimidated by digital technology than a VCR or a toaster. And it is through their use of the digital media that N-Gen will develop and superimpose its culture on the rest of society. Boomers stand back. Already these kids are learning, playing, communicating, working, and creating communities very differently than did their parents. They are a force for social transformation.[6]

Do marketers have to create separate products and marketing programmes for each generation? Some experts caution that each generation spans decades of time and many socioeconomic levels. So, they do not constitute meaningful target markets. As such, marketers should form more precise age-specific segments within each group. Others warn that marketers have to be careful about turning off one generation each time they craft a product or message that appeals effectively to another. Marketers should carefully develop their product brands such as to be broadly inclusive, offering each generation something specifically designed for it.

In most rich countries though, national populations are getting older, and the trend is forecast to continue over the next 50 years. The ageing population structure reflects two influences. First is a declining birth rate. Although official forecasts suggest that the world's population is growing, the United Nations Population Fund (UNFPA) points

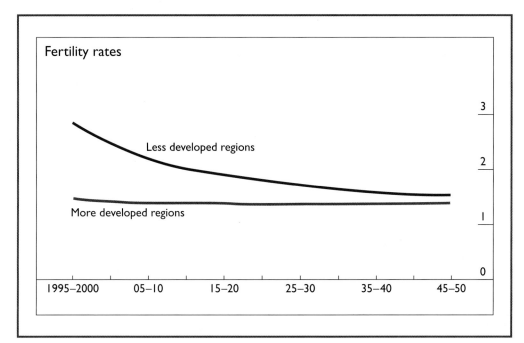

Figure 4.6

Fertility rates: developed and less developed nations

SOURCE: United Nations. Based on article published in 'Too many or too few', *The Economist* (25 September 1999). © The Economist Newspaper Ltd., London

to a reality – the world's population is growing more slowly, and it could soon start to decline. UN demographers and a number of specialists in demographics suggest that this steady decline will occur around 2040, mostly because fertility levels are dropping sharply in all rich countries, and in most poor ones (see Figure 4.6), in part due to the devastation being wrought by AIDS in Africa. A low fertility rate implies that the number of babies born into the world will fall below the number needed for replacement. EU countries, with the exception of Ireland, rank below the 2.1 children per woman (fertility) level found in the United States, and well below the 3.3 world average. Italy, reporting 1.3 children per woman, has the lowest fertility level in the world. Fertility rates in Japan, Singapore, South Korea and Hong Kong have declined steadily over the past two decades, and all lie below America's 2.1 average. In countries such as India, fertility too has fallen fast, from 4.5 children per woman in the 1980s to just around 3 children per woman at the turn of the millennium. This 'birth-dearth' linked to smaller family sizes is due to people's desire to improve personal living standards, women's desire to work outside the home, and widely available and effective birth control practices.[7]

Secondly, ageing trends are influenced by life expectancy increases (see Figure 4.7). Official forecasts in the EU countries suggest that, by 2031, 38 per cent of the UK population will be over 50 years old, compared with 32 per cent in 1991 and only 28 per cent in 1951. In Germany, the balance of people over 65 years of age to persons of working age (or the *dependency ratio*) is expected to exceed 1:1 by 2031. Italy is forecast to face the most severe ageing. Put more colourfully by the historian and demographer Peter Laslett, 'Europe and the West are growing older and will never be young again.'

The picture is repeated in developed Asian countries. The rapid ageing of the Japanese population is one of the government's biggest long-term worries.[8] Further, the demographic change of longer life is not confined to advanced countries. In Latin America and most of Asia, the share of over-60s is set to double between now and 2030, to 14 per cent. In China, it will increase from less than 10 per cent now to around 22 per cent in 2030.

Demographic shifts have important implications for marketing managers. The rising ageing population, for example, will imply a growing demand for healthcare

Figure 4.7

Europe's ageing population: forecast growth rates to 2020

SOURCE: National statistical offices. *European Marketing Pocket Book*, 2000 (Henley-on-Thames, UK: NTC Publications, 2000), p. 10. NTC Publications Ltd

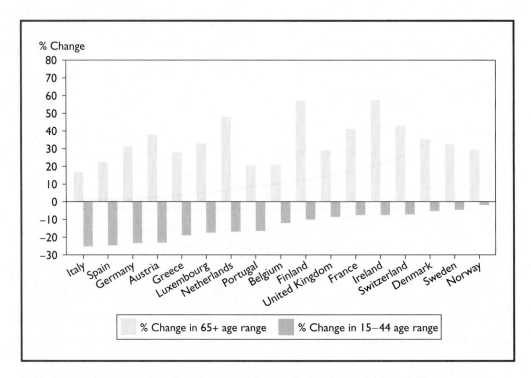

products and services tailored to the needs of this group of consumers. Marketers must track demographic trends and moves carefully in order to identify new product and market opportunities for their company.

■ The changing family

The notion of the ideal family – mum, dad and two kids – has lately been losing some of its lustre. People are marrying later and having fewer children. The specific figures may vary among countries, but the general trend is towards fewer married couples with children. In fact, couples with children under 18 now make up a small proportion of all families. These are worrying trends too for wealthy Asian countries like Singapore, Japan and Hong Kong.

Also, the number of working women, including mothers, is increasing. This trend has spawned the child day-care business, cleaning and catering services, increased consumption of convenience foods, career-oriented women's clothing and many other business opportunities (see Marketing Highlight 4.2). Marketers of goods ranging from cars, insurance and travel to financial services are increasingly directing their advertising to working women. For some products such as jewellery, typically bought by men and worn by women, retailers have also seen a move towards more professional women buying jewellery for themselves simply for their own pleasure and interest. Moreover, as a result of the shift in the traditional roles and values of husbands and wives, with male partners assuming more domestic functions such as shopping and child care, more food and household appliance marketers are targeting this group of individuals.

Finally, the number of one-person and non-family households will represent a sizeable proportion of all households. These reflect 'non-traditional' or 'diverse' households consisting of single-live-alones, adult live-togethers of one or both sexes, single-parent families, childless married couples or empty-nesters. More married people are divorcing or separating, choosing not to marry, marrying later or marrying without intention to have children. In countries such as Sweden, Germany, Denmark and Switzerland,

marketing highlight 4.2

A woman's place is at work!

'How much more respectable is the woman who earns her own bread by fulfilling any duty than the most accomplished beauty!' Early British feminist Mary Wollstonecraft's view of working women was somewhat ahead of her time. But in the past few decades, women in paid jobs have become the norm. The trend is unlikely to abate. Moreover, a growing ageing population and declining birth rates and workforce in rich countries mean that, barring large-scale immigration and later retirement, the only source of extra labour for these countries will be women. True, single women have always worked either up until marriage or until the birth of the first child. What's new is that a growing number of married women have jobs.

Combining work and family, however, makes for hectic lives. A major concern is how to maintain a balance between work and private life. On the one hand, governments wish to see as many women as possible, whether single or with kids, at work, not least to help pay for the pensions of the rapidly growing number of retired people. On the other, inflexible work regimes deter women from returning to work after having children.

The dilemma has recently triggered the launch of fresh initiatives, such as Employers for Work–Life Balance campaign, a joint campaign between the British government and employers, to promote flexible work practices.

Entrepreneurial start-ups to address the very problem – maintaining balance in work and home lives – have also sprouted. One such business is Flametree, a new online business, founded by Jayne Buxton (a mother and a former strategy consultant with Gemini Consulting) and Rosemary Leith (a mother and a former specialist in media companies at investment company Talisman Management). Flametree's mission is to help people balance the demands of home and career. This it does through flametree.co.uk, a website devoted to helping people have both a career and a life. The website covers everything from negotiating flexible hours or starting a business to finding childcare or coping with stress. It conveys individual experiences of how to juggle work and family and case studies of creative solutions.

What is intriguing is that Flametree's team of nine people (not all have children) all practise what they preach. The founding partners were determined not to let the business take over their lives completely, even at the height of 'pre-launch mania'. They left work at 6 pm, to put their children to bed every night. They did their domestic chores, then resumed business in the early hours. Sometimes, married partners took it in turns to look after the children or to get some rest at weekends. The customer service team is a job-share, and the website editor (a digital publishing expert and mother with kids) works a four-day week. A flexible support structure means that staff can cover for each other when needed.

The rules? Maintaining balance in lives requires absolute determination and commitment not to slip into working the 100-hour weeks that have become the norm in the dotcom world! Ms Buxton offers another pointer on surviving the dotcom world without crazy hours. You can do it by developing the discipline to carve out that time for the family, an attitude that Ms Buxton believes has to be forcefully cultivated. It does take effort, but she offers one stark reminder of the demise of Boo.com, the defunct online fashion retailer: 'I don't think long hours can stop you making mistakes. Boo was an example of people racing and racing and forgetting the fundamentals in terms of financial control.'

SOURCES: Alison Maitland and Rosemary Bennet, 'Promoting a flexible work regime', *Financial Times* (9 March 2000), p. 6; Alison Maitland, 'Putting work in its place', *Financial Times* (13 July 2000), p. 16; 'A survey of women and work', *The Economist* (18 July 1998), pp. 3–5; More details on Employers for Work–Life Balance can be obtained from the website: www.Employersfor-Work-LifeBalance.org.uk.

---

for example, one-person households now account for over 30 per cent of all homes. In the United States, the proportion of single households is a staggering 47 per cent. Marketers must increasingly consider the special needs of non-traditional households since they are now growing more rapidly than traditional households. Each group has a distinctive set of needs and buying habits. For example, people in the SSWD (single, separated, widowed, divorced) group need smaller apartments, inexpensive and smaller appliances, furniture and furnishings, and food that is packaged in smaller sizes.[9]

■ Rising number of educated people

The percentage of a country's population that has been educated – that is, have upper secondary and university-level education – varies across countries, but some trends can be discerned in the EU and other industrialised nations as a whole. According to OECD statistics, there has been a narrowing trend in the gap between the number of men and women who have a university education in member countries. In most countries, equal education has been attained among men and women belonging to the 25–34 age group. Gaps remain in some countries – Britain, Germany and Switzerland, for example – where more men still go to university than women. As economies in eastern Europe and Asia develop, we may expect to see rising investment in education and an increasingly more educated population. The rising number of educated people will increase the demand for quality products, books, magazines, travel, personal computers and Internet services.[10]

■ Increasing diversity

The 1990s saw an escalation of efforts towards European nation integration. The EU now comprises 15 member states – France, Luxembourg, Italy, Germany, with East Germany on unification, Netherlands, Belgium, Denmark, Ireland, United Kingdom, Greece, Spain, Portugal, Sweden, Austria and Finland. Further economic integration has occurred with the launch of the single currency, the euro, in January 1999, with eleven of the 15 EU nations currently having joined the single-currency or 'euro zone'. The EU's enlargement programme is still high on politicians' agendas. Eastern and central European countries, including former Soviet bloc states, are seeking to participate in the EU, which, in the longer term, could become a reality.

The EU, in its present state, and in a potentially enlarged form, presents huge challenges and opportunities for domestic and international marketers. We will discuss international marketing issues in more detail in Chapter 5.

In general, marketers operating in the vastly expanded EU must recognise the great diversity across member states. Unification strives to achieve harmonisation of rules and regulations, which will affect business practices across the Union. Many marketers believe the single European market encourages convergence in consumer tastes, propagating the idea of the 'Euroconsumer'. Converging lifestyles, values, beliefs, habits and tastes may often not mean converging needs. These may differ across individual country markets, just as spending power and consumption patterns are likely to vary. Europe remains a pot-pourri of cultures and systems, which present immense marketing opportunities for sellers. Although social and demographic factors and the marketing strategies of multinational consumer goods companies may combine to make lifestyles of different European (and rising wealthy Asian) nations more alike, diversity will feature just as much as convergence in the new world economy. Businesses will do well to identify regional, national and local differences, and to develop appropriate marketing strategies that take on board this diversity. Where European consumers display similar cultural values and homogeneous tastes for particular goods and services, then pan-European strategies may be more cost-effective. For example, the internationalism of snob items, such as Rolex watches or Cartier jewellery, which appeal to a small number of like-minded consumers, or high-fashion purchases like Swatch watches and DKNY clothes, which pander to the younger generation of dedicated fashion followers, lend themselves to pan-European marketing or advertising.

In most markets, however, firms have found that the 'one sight, one sound, one sell' dictum loses out to the more effective strategy of customisation. Even Coca-Cola, arch exponent of globalism, tailors the marketing of its drinks to suit different markets. Kronenbourg, France's most popular beer, is sold to a mass market with the eternal images of France, like cafés, boules and Citroën 2CVs. In the United Kingdom, Kronenbourg is presented as a drink for 'yuppies'. Unilever customises its advertisements for Impulse, a body spray. In the UK, the handsome young fellow who gets a whiff of Impulse from the woman nearby presents her with a bunch of flowers. In the Italian version, Romeo offers the woman a rose.

Ultimately, marketers must address a marketing basic: identify consumer needs and respond to them. Companies that overlook diversity in favour of pan-European or global strategies must carefully develop and execute their standardised approaches.[11] We discuss pan-European versus standardised marketing practices in greater depth in the next chapter.

economic environment

Markets require buying power as well as people. The **economic environment** consists of factors that affect consumer purchasing power and spending patterns. Nations vary greatly in their levels and distribution of income. Some countries have *subsistence economies* – they consume most of their own agricultural and industrial output. At the other extreme are *industrial economies*, which constitute rich markets for different kinds of goods. Marketers must pay close attention to major trends and consumer spending patterns both across and within their world markets.

Economic environment
Factors that affect consumer buying power and spending patterns.

■ Income distribution and changes in purchasing power

Global upheavals in technology and communications in the last decade brought about a shift in the balance of economic power from the West (mainly North American, Canadian and western European nations) towards the rapidly expanding economies of Asia and the Pacific Rim. Up until the Asian economic and financial crisis in 1997, many of the Asian 'tiger' economies, notably South Korea, Taiwan, Thailand, Malaysia, Indonesia and Singapore, were enjoying annual growth rates in excess of 7 per cent, compared to the 2–3 per cent found in western Europe and the USA.[12]

Official statistics have adjusted downwards the annual growth rates of these economies, in the first decade of the new millennium. However, rapid economic recovery in Singapore, Taiwan and South Korea means purchasing power income per head will exceed that of the US and western Europe.[13]

In view of the rising importance of overseas markets as a source of growth for many western businesses, the uncertain economic climate in the Asian economies has important implications for international marketers. They must determine how changing incomes affect purchasing power and how they translate into marketing threats and opportunities for the firm.

Where consumer purchasing power is reduced, as in countries experiencing economic collapse or in an economic recession, financially squeezed consumers tend to spend more carefully and seek greater value in the products and services they buy. For example, 'thrift shops' are booming in Japan, whose economy is stumbling into recession. *Value marketing* becomes the watchword for many marketers. Rather than offering high quality at a high price, or lesser quality at very low prices, marketers have to look for ways to offer the more financially cautious buyers greater value – just the right combination of product quality and good service at a fair price.

Marketers should also pay attention to *income distribution* as well as average income. Consumers with the greatest purchasing power are likely to belong to the higher socioeconomic groups, whose rising incomes mean that their spending patterns are less susceptible to economic downturns than lower-income groups. The *upper* economic strata of a society become primary targets for expensive luxury goods. The comfortable, *middle* income groups are more careful about their spending, but can usually afford the good life some of the time. The *lower* strata will stick close to the basics of food, clothing and shelter needs. In some countries, an *underclass* exists – people permanently living on state welfare and/or below the poverty line – which has little purchasing power, often struggling to make even the most basic purchases.

■ Changing consumer spending patterns

Generally, the total expenditures made by households tend to vary for essential categories of goods and services, with food, housing and transportation often using up most household income. However, consumers at different income levels have different spending patterns. Some of these differences were noted over a century ago by Ernst Engel, who studied how people shifted their spending as their income rose. He found that as family income rises, the percentage spent on food declines, the percentage spent on housing remains constant (except for such utilities as gas, electricity and public services, which decrease), and both the percentage spent on other categories and that devoted to savings increase. **Engel's laws** have generally been supported by later studies.

Changes in major economic variables such as income, cost of living, interest rates, and savings and borrowing patterns have a large impact on the marketplace. Companies watch these variables by using economic forecasting. Businesses do not have to be wiped out by an economic downturn or caught short in a boom. With adequate warning, they can take advantage of changes in the economic environment.

natural environment

The **natural environment** involves the natural resources that are needed as inputs by marketers or that are affected by marketing activities. Environmental concerns have grown steadily during the past three decades. Protection of the natural environment will remain a crucial worldwide issue facing business and the public. In many cities around the world, air and water pollution have reached dangerous levels. World concern continues to mount about the depletion of the earth's ozone layer and the resulting 'greenhouse effect', a dangerous warming of the earth. And many of us fear that we will soon be buried in our own rubbish. Marketers should be aware of four trends in the natural environment.

■ Shortages of raw materials

Air and water may seem to be infinite resources, but some groups see long-run dangers. Air pollution chokes many of the world's large cities and water shortages are already a big problem in some parts of the world. Renewable resources, such as forests and food, also have to be used wisely. Non-renewable resources such as oil, coal and various minerals pose a serious problem. Firms making products that require these scarce resources face large cost increases, even if the materials do remain available. They may not find it easy to pass these costs on to the consumer. However, firms engaged in research and development and in exploration can help by developing new sources and materials.

■ Increased cost of energy

One non-renewable resource – oil – has created the most serious problem for future economic growth. The large industrial economies of the world depend heavily on oil, and until economical energy substitutes can be developed, oil will continue to dominate the world political and economic picture. Many companies are searching for practical ways to harness solar, nuclear, wind and other forms of energy. Others are directing their research and development efforts to produce high energy-efficient

Engel's laws
Differences noted over a century ago by Ernst Engel in how people shift their spending across food, housing, transportation, health care, and other goods and services categories as family income rises.

Natural environment
Natural resources that are needed as inputs by marketers or that are affected by marketing activities.

technologies to meet customers' needs. For example, the tyre company Michelin introduced *Energy* low-resistance tyres that offer a 5 per cent reduction in fuel consumption. Car makers Ford, Volkswagen, Opel and Peugeot-Citroën have all introduced new, sophisticated compact cars whose small dimensions and low weight make them the front-runners in the race towards the environmentalists' 'year-2000 holy grail' – fuel consumption of just 3 litres per 100 km.[14]

■ Increased pollution

Industry has been largely blamed for damaging the quality of the natural environment. The 'green' movement draws attention to industry's 'dirty work': the disposal of chemical and nuclear wastes, the dangerous mercury levels in the ocean, the quantity of chemical pollutants in the soil and food supply, and the littering of the environment with non-biodegradable bottles, plastics and other packaging materials.

Many companies, especially those at the 'grubbier' ends of manufacturing, often complain about the cost of fulfilling their obligations to 'clean up' regulations or to produce new greener technologies.[15] On the other hand, more alert managers are responding to public environmental concerns with more ecologically sensitive goods, recyclable or biodegradable packaging, improved pollution controls and more energy-efficient operations.

Environmental pressures may be one firm's expensive obligation, but another's chance for profit. The increase in demand for waste management – collecting, transporting and disposal of solid rubbish – and recycling has also led to a growing industry worth billions of euros. Europe's environmental industry has been growing at 7 per cent a year over the last decade, the industry attracting big players, including America's Waste Management, Asea Brown Boveri's Flakt, and Lurgi, a part of Germany's Metallgesellschaft. Some big operators in sewage treatment, like France's Générales des Eaux, Lyonnaise des Eaux Dumez and Saur, Bouygues's subsidiary, have expanded abroad and give public authorities in European countries a one-stop shop: that is, they finance, build and operate water-treatment plants.

The complexity of EU green directives and national laws also makes for a booming business in environmental consultancy, particularly in the areas of environmental auditing and risk management. As the green business grows, with it will flourish clever companies that have learnt to turn trash into cash![16]

In consumer markets, niche green segments, where environmentally sensitive consumers are prepared to pay a premium price for green benefits, have emerged in categories ranging from cosmetics, toiletries and detergents to passenger cars. However, most consumers worldwide are more likely to make trade-offs between green advantages and product quality and performance benefits in their purchasing decision.

For example, in a recent international poll, two-thirds of respondents in Venezuela and half those in China, India and Egypt agreed strongly that they were willing to pay a 10 per cent premium for a greener product. Though consumers may tell pollsters they will pay a premium to support the environment, getting them to do so at the shop may be trickier. The Body Shop, the British firm known for its ecologically sensitive beauty products, has used green strategies in overseas markets with mixed success.[17] Customers still consider non-green attributes more important in making purchase decisions. So, although environmental pressures upon businesses in the decade ahead are expected to escalate, firms must seek to balance both the ecological and performance benefit expectations of the mass of consumers.[18]

■ Government intervention in natural resource management

The governments of different countries vary in their concern and efforts to promote a clean environment. Some countries have adopted policies that have a stronger,

Figure 4.8

Environmental
sustainability index

SOURCE: 'Emerging-market
indicators', *The Economist*
(29 January 2000), p. 150.
© The Economist
Newspaper Ltd., London

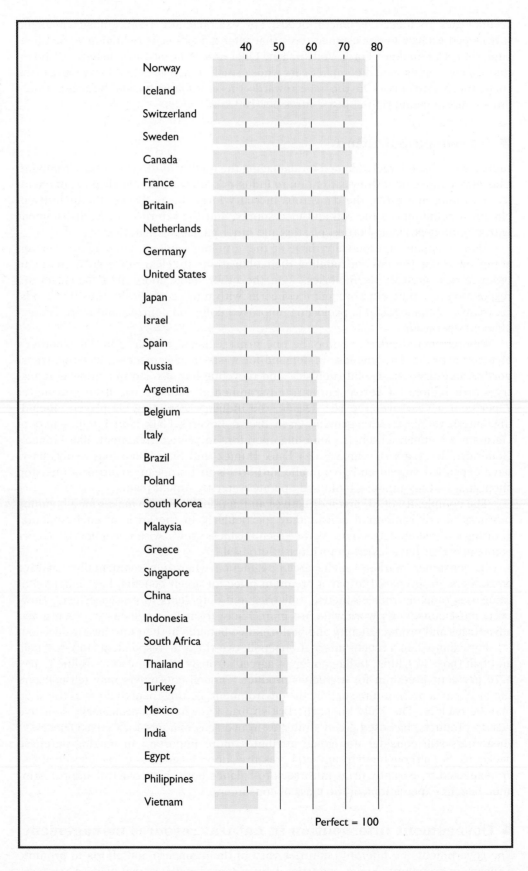

positive impact on environmental sustainability than others. A recent report which ranks countries by five criteria of environmental sustainability, such as whether their main environmental systems are flourishing and how well they cooperate with other countries in managing common environmental problems, place the Nordic countries at the top of the league. Belgium, Italy and Greece, by contrast, do remarkably badly (Figure 4.8).[19] Whereas some governments vigorously pursue environmental quality, others, especially many poorer nations, do little about it, largely because they lack the needed funds or political will. Even the richer nations lack the vast funds and political accord needed to mount a worldwide environmental effort. The general hope is that companies around the world will accept more social responsibility, and that less expensive devices can be found to control and reduce pollution.

In most countries, industry has been pressured rather than persuaded to 'go green'. Environment protection agencies of one sort or another have been established to enforce pollution standards and to conduct pollution research. Environmental legislation has toughened up in recent years and businesses can expect this to continue in the foreseeable future. Governments have also looked at the potential of voluntary agreements with industry. The idea is to help industry meet environmental standards cost-effectively.

> A successful case is Holland's National Environmental Policy Plan (NEPP), which set tight targets for pollution reduction. Some industries agreed to tougher pollution controls in return for greater government flexibility over their implementation. Although firms knew that failure to co-operate meant harsher laws would follow, the NEPP provided a channel for government–industry dialogue and co-operation. Detailed plans were agreed with sectors accounting for 60–70 per cent of Holland's environmental pollution. Deals with oil refineries in Rotterdam helped to cut smog and sulphur dioxide emissions. Agreements with packaging firms have led to a decline in the volume of municipal waste. Ammonia output also declined sharply.[20]

In most developed western nations, well-organised sectors, such as oils, chemicals, pharmaceuticals and food, are more likely to reach common agreements with government agencies and their plans for environmental control. Enlightened companies, however, go beyond what government regulations dictate. They are developing *environmentally sustainable* strategies and practices in an effort to create a world economy that the planet can support indefinitely. They are responding to consumer demands with ecologically safer products, recyclable or biodegradable packaging, better pollution controls and more energy-efficient operations. Many of these companies, from IKEA, Lego and McDonald's to 3M, IBM and BMW, are recognising the link between a healthy economy and a healthy ecology.[21]

technological environment

The **technological environment** is perhaps the most dramatic force now shaping our destiny. Technology has released such wonders as penicillin, organ transplants, notebook computers and the Internet. It has also released such horrors as the nuclear bomb, chemical weapons and assault rifles, and such mixed blessings as cars, televisions and credit cards. Our attitude towards technology depends on whether we are more impressed with its wonders or its blunders.

New technologies create new markets and opportunities. However, every new technology replaces an older technology. Transistors hurt the vacuum-tube industry, xerography killed the carbon-paper business, cars and roads hurt the railways, and compact discs hurt vinyl records. When old industries fought or ignored new technologies, their businesses declined.

Technological environment
Forces that create new technologies, creating new product and market opportunities.

The technological environment is changing rapidly. Marketers should watch the following trends in technology.

■ Fast pace of technological change

Many of today's common products were not available a hundred years ago: televisions, home freezers, automatic dishwashers, contraceptives, earth satellites, personal computers, compact disc players, digital video discs, facsimile machines, mobile phones. The list is unending! Companies that fail to anticipate and keep up with technological change soon find their products outdated. But keeping pace with technological change is becoming more challenging for firms today. *Technology life cycles* are getting shorter. Take the typewriter. The first-generation modern mechanical typewriter dominated the market for 25 years. Subsequent generations had shorter lives – 15 years for electromechanical models, 7 years for electronic versions and 5 years for first-generation microprocessor-based ones. Other examples of fast technological change are found. The average life of some computer software products, for example, is now well under one year. Moreover, technology trends can be very fickle. Consider the ever-changing world of children's games consoles. It may have been only a few months since kids of all ages were clamouring for a Sega Dreamcast. Then, Sony's Playstation 2 became the next hit. By Christmas 2000, the craze turned to Nintendo's Dolphin and Microsoft's X-Box systems. One thing's for sure – many of these will end up as obsolete appliances before the next Christmas season!

Firms must track technological trends and determine whether or not these changes will affect their products' continued ability to fulfil customers' needs. Technologies arising in unrelated industries can also affect the firm's fortunes. The mechanical watch industry was overtaken by manufacturers of electronic components seeking new applications and growth opportunities for their quartz technology. Businesses must assiduously monitor their technological environment to avoid missing new product and market opportunities.

As this Siemens ad suggests, research and development has changed considerably over the years. Lone inventors have been replaced by research teams employed by large companies or other organisations.

SOURCE: Reproduced courtesy of Siemens Medical Solutions

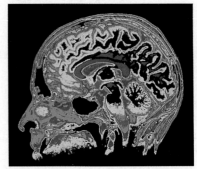

■ High R&D budgets

Technology and innovations require heavy investments in research and development. It is not uncommon for pharmaceuticals companies, for example, to spend €350–450 million to develop a new drug. High R&D spending is also a feature of many industries, including cars, communications, computers, aerospace, engineering, entertainment and consumer electronics.

In recent years, there has been a marked increase in collaborative technological research efforts between western governments and industries. In Europe, this mood spawned subsidised programmes, such as Esprit, Eureka and Jessi, and in the USA schemes such as Sematech and MCC. These programmes stemmed from two main concerns: first, the soaring cost of R&D and the difficulty, even for big companies, of mastering a wide range of technologies; and second, the increasing international competition, mainly from Japan, in electronics and related industries. There are mixed views on the success of these programmes, although collaboration has helped break down barriers between rival firms and stimulated the dissemination of know-how.[22]

■ Concentration on minor improvements

As a result of the high cost of developing and introducing new technologies, many companies are tinkering – making minor product improvements – instead of gambling on substantial innovations. The high costs and risks of commercialisation failure make firms take this cautious approach to their R&D investment. Most companies are content to put their money into copying competitors' products, making minor feature and style improvements, or offering simple extensions of current brands. Thus much research is in danger of being defensive rather than offensive.

■ Increased regulation

As products become more complex, people need to know that they are safe. Thus, government agencies investigate and ban potentially unsafe products. In the EU and America, complex regulations exist for testing new drugs. The US Federal Food and Drug Administration, for example, is notorious for its strict enforcement of drug testing and safety rules. Statutory and industry regulatory bodies exist to set safety standards for consumer products and penalise companies that fail to meet them. Such regulations have resulted in much higher research costs and in longer times between new-product ideas and their introductions. Marketers should be aware of these regulations when seeking and developing new products.

Marketers need to understand the changing technological environment and the ways that new technologies can serve customer and human needs. They need to work closely with R&D people to encourage more market-oriented research. They must also be alert to the possible negative aspects of any breakthroughs (like the sequencing of the human genome[23]) or innovations (like Viagra, the anti-impotence drug) that might harm users or arouse opposition.

political environment

Marketing decisions are strongly affected by developments in the political environment. The **political environment** consists of laws, government agencies and pressure groups that influence and limit various organisations and individuals in a given society.

Political environment
Laws, government agencies and pressure groups that influence and limit various organisations and individuals in a given society.

■ Legislation regulating business

Even the most liberal advocates of free-market economies agree that the system works best with at least some regulation. Well-conceived regulation can encourage competition and ensure fair markets for goods and services. Thus governments develop *public policy* to guide commerce – sets of laws and regulations that limit business for the good of society as a whole. Almost every marketing activity is subject to a wide range of laws and regulations.

Legislation affecting business around the world has increased steadily over the years. The European Commission has been active in establishing a new framework of laws covering competitive behaviour, product standards, product liability and commercial transactions for the nations of the EU. Similarly, the US has many laws covering issues such as competition, fair trade practices, environmental protection, product safety, truth in advertising, packaging and labelling, pricing and other important areas. Several countries have passed strong consumerism legislation. For example, Norway bans several forms of sales promotion – trading stamps, contests, premiums – as being inappropriate or unfair ways of promoting products. Thailand requires food processors selling national brands to market low-price brands also, so that low-income consumers can find economy brands on the shelves. In India, food companies must obtain special approval to launch brands that duplicate those already existing on the market, such as additional cola drinks or new brands of rice.

Understanding the public policy implications of a particular marketing activity is not a simple matter. First, there are many laws created at different levels: for example, in the EU, business operators are subject to European Commission, individual member state and specific local regulations; in the USA, laws are created at the federal, state and local levels, and these regulations often overlap. Second, the regulations are constantly changing – what was allowed last year may now be prohibited, and what was prohibited may now be allowed. In the single European market, deregulation and ongoing moves towards harmonisation are expected to take time, creating a state of flux, which challenges and confuses both domestic and international marketers. They must therefore work hard to keep up with these changes in the regulations and their interpretations.

In many developed economies, business legislation has been enacted for a number of reasons. The first is to *protect companies* from each other. Although business executives may praise competition, they sometimes try to neutralise it when it threatens them. Antitrust agencies, competition authorities and monopolies and mergers commissions have surfaced to enforce laws, typically passed to define and prevent unfair competition. For example, the European Commission recently introduced new competition laws to promote a level playing field for firms in the telecommunications sector. These laws have a number of aims, from seeking to establish a better pricing balance to forcing incumbent telecoms operators to open up local markets to new market entrants. The EU's competition authorities have also been known to block many merger deals, one example being its decision to veto Volvo's recent proposal to merge with Scania, its Swedish truck rival.[24]

The second purpose of government regulation is to *protect consumers* from unfair business practices. Some firms, if left alone, would make shoddy products, tell lies in their advertising and deceive consumers through their packaging and pricing. Unfair business practices have been defined and are enforced by various agencies.

The third purpose of government regulation is to *protect the interests of society* against unrestrained business behaviour. Profitable business activity does not always create a better quality of life. Regulation arises to ensure that firms take responsibility for the social costs of their production or products.

New laws and their enforcement are likely to continue or increase. Business executives must watch these developments when planning their products and marketing programmes. International marketers will additionally encounter dozens, even hundreds, of agencies set up to enforce trade policies and regulations. Importantly, they need to understand these laws at the local, country, regional and international levels.

■ Growth of public interest groups

The number and power of public interest groups have increased during the past two decades. In Chapter 2 we discussed a broad range of societal marketing issues. Consumerism, a powerful force that has its roots in the US, has spilled over to countries in western Europe and other developed market economies such as Australia. Hundreds of other consumer interest groups, private and governmental, operate at all levels – regional, national and local levels. Other groups that marketers need to consider are those seeking to protect the environment and to advance the rights of various groups such as women, children, ethnic minorities, senior citizens and the handicapped. As we saw in the case of Diageo's defence of thalidomide and Nutricia's failed biotechnology project (see Marketing Highlight 4.1), companies cannot afford to ignore the views of public interest groups.

■ Increased emphasis on ethics and socially responsible actions

Written regulations cannot possibly cover all potential marketing abuses, and existing laws are often difficult to enforce. However, beyond written laws and regulations, business is also governed by social codes and rules of professional ethics. Enlightened companies encourage their managers to look beyond what the regulatory system allows and simply to 'do the right thing'. These socially responsible firms actively seek out ways to protect the long-run interests of their consumers and the environment.

The recent rash of business scandals and increased concerns about the environment have created fresh interest in the issues of ethics and social responsibility. Almost every aspect of marketing involves such issues. Unfortunately, because these issues usually involve conflicting interests, well-meaning people can disagree honestly about the right course of action in a particular situation. Thus many industrial and professional trade associations have suggested codes of ethics, and many companies are now developing policies and guidelines to deal with complex social responsibility issues.

The boom in e-commerce and Internet marketing has created a new set of social and ethical issues. Privacy issues are the primary concern. For example, website visitors often provide extensive personal information that might leave them open to abuse by unscrupulous marketers. Moreover, both Intel and Microsoft have been accused of covert, high-tech computer chip and software invasions of customers' personal computers to obtain information for marketing purposes.

Another cyberspace concern is that of access by vulnerable or unauthorised groups. For example, marketers of adult-oriented materials have found it difficult to restrict access by minors. In a more specific example, sellers using eBay.com, the online auction website, recently found themselves the victims of a 13-year-old boy who had bid on and purchased more than €3 million worth of high-priced antiques and rare art works on the site. eBay has a strict policy against bidding by anyone under 18 but works largely on the honour system. Unfortunately, this honour system did little to prevent the teenager from taking a cyberspace joy ride.[25]

In Chapter 2, we discussed in greater depth the public and social responsibility issues surrounding key marketing decisions, the legal issues that marketers should understand, and the common ethical and societal concerns that marketers face.

cultural environment

Cultural environment
Institutions and other forces that affect society's basic values, perceptions, preferences and behaviours.

The **cultural environment** is made up of institutions and other forces that affect society's basic values, perceptions, preferences and behaviours. People grow up in a particular society that shapes their basic beliefs and values. They absorb a world-view that defines their relationships with others. The following cultural characteristics can affect marketing decision making. Marketers must be aware of these cultural influences and how they vary across societies within the markets served by the firm.

■ Persistence of cultural values

People in a given society hold many beliefs and values. Their core beliefs and values have a high degree of persistence. For example, most of us believe in working, getting married, giving to charity and being honest. These beliefs shape more specific attitudes and behaviours found in everyday life. *Core* beliefs and values are passed on from parents to children and are reinforced by schools, religious groups, business and government.

Secondary beliefs and values are more open to change. Believing in marriage is a core belief; believing that people should get married early in life is a secondary belief. Marketers have some chance of changing secondary values, but little chance of changing core values. For example, family-planning marketers could argue more effectively that people should get married later than that they should not get married at all.

■ Shifts in secondary cultural values

Although core values are fairly persistent, cultural swings do take place. Consider the impact of popular music groups, movie personalities and other celebrities on young people's hair styling, clothing and sexual norms. Marketers want to predict cultural shifts in order to spot new opportunities or threats. Such information helps marketers cater to trends with appropriate products and communication appeals.

The principal cultural values of a society are expressed in people's views of themselves and others, as well as in their views of organisations, society, nature and the universe.

People's views of themselves People vary in their emphasis on serving themselves versus serving others. Some people seek personal pleasure, wanting fun, change and escape. Others seek self-realisation through religion, recreation or the avid pursuit of careers or other life goals. People use products, brands and services as a means of self-expression and buy products and services that match their views of themselves.

In the last decade or so, personal ambition and materialism increased dramatically, with significant marketing implications. In a 'me-society', people buy their 'dream cars' and take their 'dream vacations'. They tend to spend to the limit on self-indulgent goods and services. Today, people are adopting more conservative behaviours and ambitions. They are more cautious in their spending patterns and more value-driven in their purchases. Moving into the new millennium, materialism, flashy spending and self-indulgence have been replaced by more sensible spending, saving, family concerns and helping others. This suggests a bright future for products and services that serve basic needs and provide real value rather than those relying on glitz and hype.

People's views of others More recently, observers have noted a shift from a 'me-society' to a 'we-society', in which more people want to be with and serve others. Notes one trend tracker, 'People want to get out, especially those . . . working out of their home and feeling a little cooped-up [and] all those shut-ins who feel unfulfilled by the cyberstuff that was supposed to make them feel like never leaving home.'[26] Other surveys showed that more people are becoming involved in charity, volunteer work and social service activities.[27] These trends suggest greater demand for 'social support' products and services that improve direct communication between people, such as health clubs, family vacations and games.

People's views of organisations   People vary in their attitudes towards corporations, government agencies, trade unions, universities and other organisations. By and large, people are willing to work for big organisations and expect them, in turn, to carry out society's work. In recent years, there has been a decrease in confidence in, and loyalty towards, business and political organisations and institutions. In the workplace, there has been an overall decline in organisational loyalty. Recent waves of company downsizing, for example, have bred cynicism and distrust. Many people today see work not as a source of satisfaction, but as a required chore to earn money to enjoy non-work hours.

This trend suggests that organisations need to find new ways to win consumer confidence and employee confidence. They need to review their advertising communications to make sure their messages are honest. Also, they need to review their various activities to make sure that they are coming across as 'good corporate citizens'. More companies are linking themselves to worthwhile causes, measuring their images with important publics and using public relations to build more positive images (see Marketing Highlight 4.3).

People's views of society   People vary in their attitudes toward their society – from patriots who defend it, to reformers who want to change it, and malcontents who want to leave it. People's orientation to their society influences their consumption patterns, levels of savings and attitudes toward the marketplace.

In the affluent and industrialising Asian nations, consumers aspire to achieve the high living standards and lifestyles of people in the more advanced western countries. The display of conspicuous consumption and fondness for expensive western brands – the common label for achievement and westernisation – are highly acceptable behaviour. Consumer patriotism, for example, is not an issue, since locally made goods are often viewed as inferior or less desirable than foreign imported brands. Consumers' predispostion towards western brands suggest a greater demand for goods marketed by companies of western origin, hence creating new marketing opportunities for these firms. By contrast, in the western developed countries, the last two decades saw an

marketing highlight 4.3

Ronald McDonald Children's Charities: playing a role in local communities

Ronald McDonald Children's Charities (RMCC) was founded in 1984 in the United States. It was established in memory of Ray Kroc, founder of McDonald's Corporation. He believed that 'It is important to have an involvement in the life and spirit of a community and the people around you.' This belief lives on in the McDonald's system and is evident in a variety of community programmes practised by McDonald's the world over. In 1989, for example, RMCC was set up in the United Kingdom, and through the efforts of McDonald's Restaurants Limited, its staff, customers and suppliers, over £3 million (€4.92m) has since been raised for a wide variety of charitable causes that help children.

RMCC grants have been awarded to programmes which help young people reach their full potential and make a real difference for children and their well-being. The 'Ronald McDonald House' is a cornerstone of RMCC.

*"It is
important
to have an
involvement
in the life
and spirit of
a community
and the people
around you."*

Ray A Kroc
Founder
McDonald's Corporation

What is McDonald's Involvement?

As well as their generous £1 million donation, McDonald's has lent expertise in setting up the House along with legal, design and construction advice. McDonald's is totally committed to working with representatives of the hospital and parents through the Alder Hey Family House Trust Ltd, a registered charity, which is responsible for raising funds and running the House now it is open.

Paul Preston, McDonald's UK President, explains: "With diminishing public-sector resources, it is vital that private enterprise plays a role in developing concepts such as the Ronald McDonald House where, at long last, parents can live in home-like surroundings whilst their child undergoes treatment. Hopefully the days in which parents have to camp out in the hospital are numbered.

"Ronald McDonald House is the result of team effort; a caring partnership between McDonald's, the Hospital staff and the families of the children."

The Tree of Life

The "Tree of Life" which is on display at the house. A visible thank-you to those who support the Trust.

McDonald's plays its role in the life and spirit of the surrounding local communities.

SOURCE: With permission from McDonald's Corporation

The first was built at Philadelphia in the United States in 1974, close to the Philadelphia Children's Hospital. When a child is taken seriously ill and has to spend some time in hospital, families are usually faced with the problem of where to stay to be close at hand. The Ronald McDonald House has a set number of beds for parents to stay overnight and a family accommodation block. This means that the family can be together again as a unit, while also providing a brief respite in a family environment.

There are now over 160 Ronald McDonald Houses in the United States, Canada, Australia, Japan and Europe. Each House is a 'home away from home' with the feel, aesthetics and comfort of family living. Families are able to prepare their own meals, relax and rest in privacy or enjoy the company of others living in when they so desire. The House is the result of a team effort between the hospital doctors and staff, the parents of the children and McDonald's. Each House is run by a separate charitable trust set up to oversee fund raising and to manage the house. The boards of these trusts are made up of parents, hospital representatives and senior management of McDonald's. The trusts initiate their own fund-raising events. Throughout the year, McDonald's own restaurant staff are involved in local events to raise

money for RMCC, and collecting boxes for donations from customers are placed in every restaurant. McDonald's Restaurants Limited, its franchisees and also its suppliers all donate to RMCC. Other recipients of money raised by RMCC include children's charities – such as hospitals, youth organisations, schools and many more worthy causes.

McDonald's restaurants not only display posters and collecting boxes for the RMCC programme, but also provide customers with information leaflets to disseminate information about their community involvement. These leaflets also sometimes contain requests for funds and/or volunteers who may be interested in helping in specific campaigns. This type of communication effort is also designed to raise customers' as well as other local and general publics' awareness of Ray Kroc's philosophy of 'giving something back to the communities that give so much to us [McDonald's Corporation]'.

SOURCES: 'Your questions answered', Ronald McDonald Children's Charities, London; The Public Relations Department, McDonald's Restaurants Limited, London.

Companies are increasingly seeking to improve their positive impact on society. Here, Marks & Spencer's award-winning Children's Promise campaign reinforces the company's commitment to supporting the local community.

SOURCE: Marks & Spencer

increase in consumer patriotism. European consumers reckoned that sticking to locally produced goods would save and protect jobs. Similarly, many US companies also responded to American patriotism with 'made in America' themes and flag-waving promotions, such as Chevrolet is 'the heartbeat of America' and the textile industry's 'Crafted with Pride in the USA' advertising campaign, which insisted that 'made in the USA' matters.[28]

People's views of nature People vary in their attitudes towards the natural world. Some feel ruled by it, others feel in harmony with it and still others seek to master it. A long-term trend has been people's growing mastery over nature through technology and the belief that nature is bountiful. More recently, however, people have recognised that nature is finite and fragile – that it can be destroyed or spoiled by human activities.

Love of nature is leading to more camping, hiking, boating, fishing and other outdoor activities. Business has responded by offering more products and services catering to these interests. Tour operators are offering more tours to wilderness areas and retailers are offering more fitness gear and apparel. Food producers have found growing markets for 'natural' products like natural cereal, natural ice-cream, organically farmed produce and a variety of health foods. Marketing communicators are using appealing natural backgrounds in advertising their products. Yet others have succeeded in building their fortunes by emphasising simplicity and inspiration drawn from nature.

Consider, for example, Marimekko, a small Finnish company that sells clothing, bags, interior textiles and accessories. Back in the 1960s, the company made sensational news in the US because Jacqueline Kennedy, then First Lady, had chosen to buy some maternity dresses from the little known clothing designer over an American one. The company, however, was bought by Amer, the Finnish conglomerate, in 1985, but suffered six years of losses, until it was bought back by Kirsti Paakkanen, in 1991. Over the last decade, Ms Paakkanen has steadily rebuilt

Marimekko's financial strength, capitalising on its trademark of bold colours, bright patterns and distinctive stripes. Marimekko sees itself as a lifestyle company, synoymous with the best of Finnish design, with an emphasis on simplicity and inspiration drawn from Finnish nature. The simple, horizontally-striped T-shirts epitomise Marimekko's quality, functionality and practicality. According to Ms Paakkanen, the secrets of the company's success today are a clear set of values: community spirit, respect and caring – values that are set out clearly in the company's annual report. There is also a steadfast support of employees, particularly a refusal to stifle the creativity of its designers. Maybe, this is one reason why the company enjoys exceptionally strong employee loyalty – some 40 per cent of employees who joined in the 1950s and 1960s are still with the company. Marimekko will celebrate its 50th anniversary in 2001, against a forecast of steady growth, both at home and in markets across the EU, US and Japan. What is remarkable is that the company is achieving higher sales abroad, despite the problems that have afflicted so many international retailers when expanding outside their own countries. Bright and breezy, big and bold, Marimekko is set to remain one of Finland's best known international brands, after Nokia. There is no better reminder of that than a recent headline on a *New York Times* article about Scandinavian design: 'Marimekko, I think I love you.'[29]

People's views of the universe   Finally, people vary in their beliefs about the origin of the universe and their place in it. While the practice of religion remains strong in many parts of the world, religious conviction and practice have been dropping off through the years in certain countries, notably in the United States and Europe where, for example, church attendance is on the decline. However, some futurists have noted an emerging renewal of interest in religion, perhaps as part of a broader search for a new inner purpose. People have been moving away from materialism and dog-eat-dog ambition to seek more permanent values and a more certain grasp of right and wrong. The 'new realists' reflect a move away from overt consumerism. Some experts observe

Businesses today face great pressure to balance economic progress with social responsibility. In this ad, the multinational company Shell seeks to reassure its publics and other stakeholders of its commitment to support fundamental human rights.

Source: Shell International Petroleum Co. Ltd. *Agency*: J. Walter Thompson

that this trend reflects a 'new spiritualism' which is affecting consumers in everything, from the television shows they watch and the books they read, to the products and services they buy. 'Since consumers don't park their beliefs and values on the bench outside the marketplace,' adds one expert, 'they are bringing this awareness to the brands they buy. Tapping into this heightened sensitivity presents a unique marketing opportunity for brands.'[30]

However, in many overseas markets where western companies seek to expand, such as India, China and south-east Asia, society's value systems place great importance on economic achievement and material possession. The values of these 'enthusiastic materialists' are also shared by the developing markets of Europe, such as Turkey, and some Latin American countries.[31]

responding to the marketing environment

Many companies view the marketing environment as an 'uncontrollable' element to which they must adapt. They passively accept the marketing environment and do not try to change it. They analyse the environmental forces and design strategies that will help the company avoid the threats and take advantage of the opportunities the environment provides.

Other companies take an **environmental management perspective**.[32] Rather than simply watching and reacting, these firms take aggressive actions to affect the publics and forces in their marketing environment. Such companies hire lobbyists to influence legislation affecting their industries and stage media events to gain favourable press coverage. They run 'advertorials' (ads expressing editorial points of view) to shape public opinion. They take legal action and file complaints with regulators to keep competitors in line. They also form contractual agreements to control their distribution channels better.

Marketing management cannot always affect environmental forces. In many cases, it must settle for simply watching and reacting to the environment. For example, a company would have little success trying to influence geographic population shifts, the economic environment or important cultural values. But whenever possible, smart marketing managers will take a *proactive* rather than *reactive* approach to the marketing environment.

Environmental management perspective
A management perspective in which the firm takes aggressive actions to affect the publics and forces in its marketing environment rather than simply watching it and reacting to it.

summary

Companies must constantly watch and adapt to the *marketing environment* in order to seek opportunities and ward off threats. This environment comprises all the actors and forces that affect the company's ability to transact effectively with its target market.

The company's marketing environment can be divided into the microenvironment and the macroenvironment. The *microenvironment* consists of five actors or components close to the company that combine to form the company's value delivery system. The first is the company's *internal environment* – its departmental and managerial structure, which affects marketing management's decision making. The second component – the marketing channel firms – cooperate to create value. These include the firm's suppliers and marketing intermediaries (resellers, physical distribution firms, financial intermediaries, marketing services agencies). The third component refers to the five types of *market* in which the company can sell: the consumer, producer, reseller, government and international markets. The *competitors*, who vie with the company in an effort to serve customers better, make up the fourth component. Finally, various *publics* – financial, media, government, citizen action, local, general and internal publics – have an actual or potential interest in or impact on the organisation's ability to achieve its objectives.

The company's *macroenvironment* consists of six primary forces that shape opportunities and pose threats to the company. These include demographic, economic, natural, technological, political and cultural forces.

We considered how changes in the demographic and economic environments affect marketing decisions. In the more developed western economies, today's *demographic environment* shows a changing age structure, shifting family profiles, trends towards a better educated and increasing diverse population. The *economic environment* shows changing patterns of real income and shifts in consumer spending patterns.

Major trends in the firm's natural and technological environments have been addressed. The *natural environment* shows the following trends: shortages of certain raw materials, increased energy costs, higher pollution levels, more government intervention in natural resource management and higher levels of citizen concern and activism about these issues. The *technological environment* reveals rapid technological change, high R&D budgets, the concentration by companies on minor product improvements rather than radical innovations and increased government regulation.

Key changes are also observed in the political and cultural environments. The *political environment* consists of laws, agencies and groups that influence or limit marketing actions. The political environment has undergone three changes that affect marketing actions: increasing legislation regulating business, the rising importance of public interest groups and increased emphasis on ethics and socially responsible actions. The *cultural environment* suggests long-term trends towards a 'we-society', a cautious trust of institutions, increasing patriotism and conservatism, greater appreciation for nature, a new realism and search for more meaningful and enduring values.

Companies can passively accept the marketing environment as an uncontrollable element to which they must adapt, avoiding threats and taking advantage of opportunities as they arise. Or they can take an environmental management perspective, proactively working to change the environment rather than simply reacting to it.

discussing the issues

1. Select a sports and leisure footwear company. What microenvironmental trends will affect the success of the company in the decade ahead? What marketing plans would you make to respond to these trends?

2. Demographers note the growing importance of two demographic groups, the 'Generation Xers' and 'Baby boomlets'. If you were in charge of marketing in a consumer healthcare company, how would you deal with the potential opportunities presented by these two consumer groups?

3. Pressure groups, lobbyists and public interest groups play an important role in defending society's interests. Select one such group you are familiar with and describe its cause. Suggest ways in which goods or services providers targeted by the group might satisfactorily address the demands or pressures imposed by the group.

4. Younger customers are becoming more concerned about the natural environment. How would this trend affect a company that markets plastic sandwich bags? Discuss some effective responses to this trend.

5. Some marketing goals, such as improved quality, require strong support from an internal public – a company's own employees. But surveys show that employees increasingly distrust management and that company loyalty is eroding. How can a company market internally to help meet its goals?

applying the concepts

1. Changes in the marketing environment mean that marketers must meet new consumer needs that may be quite different – even directly opposite – from those in the past. You can track changes in the marketing environment by looking at how companies modify their products. Where appropriate, you could visit selected companies' websites to gain details about their products.

    ◆   Make a list of the products you encounter in one day that claim to be 'low' or 'high' in some ingredient, such as low-tar cigarettes or high-fibre cereal.

    ◆   Write down similar products that seem to offer the opposite characteristics.

    ◆   In each case, which product do you think came first? Do you think that this is an effective response to a changing marketing environment? Why? Why not?

2. The political environment can have a direct impact on marketers and their plans. Thinking about a recent major political environmental change in a country of your choice, consider the following:

    ◆   Name three industries that will probably have their marketing plans and strategies affected by the political changes.

    ◆   For each of the industries that you named, list three potential strategies to help adapt to the coming changes in the political environment.

    ◆   Although environmental changes appear likely, are they certain? How should companies plan for unsettled conditions?

references

1. Quotes from Keith Naughton and Bill Vlasic, 'The nostalgia boom: why the old is new again', *Business Week* (23 March 1998), pp. 58–64; 'New Beetles: drivers wanted', accessed online at www.vw.com/cars/newbeetle/main.html (11 August 1998). Also see Stuart Marshall, 'A drive down memory lane', *Financial Times Weekend* (10 and 11 January 1998), p. xiii; Stuart Marshall, 'Nostalgic flirtations turn into full-blown affair', *Financial Times Weekend* (7 and 8 October 2000), p. xvi; Graham Bowley, 'Beetles want Beatles, if VW can afford', *Financial Times* (5 February 1998), p. 25; Greg Farrell, 'Getting the Bugs out', *Brandweek* (6 April 1998), pp. 30–40; 'Beetle mania', *Adweek* (13 July 1998), p. 24.

2. Jennifer Lach, 'Dateline America: May 1, 2025', *American Demographics* (May 1999), pp. 19–20.

3. The *UN World Population Prospects* gives population details for individual countries.

4. Lorien Holland, 'Baby boom', *Far Eastern Economic Review* (24 June 1999), p. 61; Sally D. Goll, 'Marketing: China's (only) children get the royal treatment', *Wall Street Journal* (8 February 1995), pp. B1, B3; for continuously updated projections of the world population, consult the US Census Bureau's website, www.census.gov.

5. See Philip Kotler, *Marketing Management: Analysis, planning, implementation, and control*, 10th edn (Upper Saddle River, NJ: Prentice Hall, 2000), p. 141.

6. Accessed online from www.growingupdigital.com/flecho.html, October 1999. Also see Diane Summers, 'Generation X comes of age', *Financial Times* (16 February 1998), p. 16; and Douglas Tapscott, *Growing Up Digital: The Rise of the Net Generation* (New York: McGraw-Hill, 1999).

7. 'A survey of the 20th century. On the yellow brick road', *The Economist* (11 September 1999), p. 6; 'Too many or too few', *The Economist* (25 September 1999), p. 19; 'Like herrings in a barrel', *The Economist* (31 December 1999), pp.13–14.

8. Stephen Fidler, 'Problem of ageing "underestimated"', *Financial Times* (17/18 June 2000), p. 7; 'Fewer and wrinklier Europeans', *The Economist* (15 January 2000), p. 42; 'Fings ain't wot they used to be', *The Economist* (28 May 1994), pp. 77–8; European Commission, *Demographic Statistics*, UN Population Division and OECD are further sources of population statistics and projections.

9. David Short, 'A different taste of things to come', *The European* (14–20 October 1994), p. 21; for an outstanding discussion of the changing nature of American households, see *American Households*, American Demographics Desk Reference Series, no. 3 (July 1992).

10. 'Education. The uses of literacy', *The Economist* (17 June 2000), pp. 34–5; 'Dorothy's dream', The Economist 20th Century Survey, *The Economist* (11 September 1999), pp. 34–8.

11. Alan Mitchell, 'Brands play for global domination', *Marketing Week* (2 February 1996), pp. 26–7; 'The myth of the Euro-consumer', *The Economist* (4 November 1989), pp. 107–8.

12. 'Living under an Asian cloud', *Financial Times* (27–8 December 1997), p. 7; 'The day the miracle came to an end', *Financial Times* (12 January 1998), p. 8; John Ridding and James Kynge, 'Complacency gives way to contagion', *Financial Times* (13 January 1998), p. 8.

13. See 'Can Europe compete? Balance of economic power begins to shift', *Financial Times* (9 March 1994), p. 14; 'Emerging-market indicators', *The Economist* (18 May 1999), p. 142; data on Gross Domestic Product (GDP) of countries, including GDP at purchasing power parity, are obtained from the following sources: Eurostat (National Statistics Office), World Bank, International Monetary Fund. Data are also available to subscribers to *The Economist* at www.economist.com.

14. Tony Lewin, 'Car makers line up for next baby boom', *The European* (30 May 1996), p. 30.

15. Michael Smith and Leyla Boulton, 'Oil v. autos in fight over cost of pollution', *Financial Times* (17 February 1998), p. 2; Casper Henderson, 'Might PVC be PC after all?', *Financial Times* (7 June 2000), p. 17.

16. John-Paul Flintoff, 'Stinking rich in Holland Park', *The Business Weekend FT Magazine* (29 April 2000), pp. 28–31; 'Pollution: the money in Europe's muck', *The Economist* (20 November 1993), pp. 109–10.

17. 'How green is your market?', *The Economist* (8 January 2000), p. 77.

18. For more discussion about consumers' environmental consciousness and consumers' environmental decisions, see Veronica Wong, William Turner and Paul Stoneman, 'Marketing strategies and market prospects for environmentally-friendly consumer products', *British Journal of Management* (1996), pp. 263–81; Sabine Dembkowski and Stuart Hanmer-Lloyd, 'The environmental value–attitude–system model: a framework to guide the understanding of environmentally-conscious consumer behaviour', *Journal of Marketing Management* (October 1994), pp. 593–603.

19. 'Emerging-market indicators. Green growth', *The Economist* (29 January 2000), p. 150.

20. 'Going Dutch', *The Economist* (20 November 1993), p. 110.

21. For more discussion, see Michael E. Porter and Claas van der Linde, 'Green *and* competitive: ending the stalemate', *Harvard Business Review* (September–October 1995), pp. 120–34; Stuart L. Hart, 'Beyond greening: strategies for a sustainable world', *Harvard Business Review* (January–February 1997), pp. 67–76; Jacquelyn Ottman, 'Environment winners show sustainable strategies', *Marketing News* (27 April 1998), p. 6; and Forest L. Reinhardt, 'Bringing the environment down to earth', *Harvard Business Review* (July–August 1999), pp. 149–57.

22. Guy de Jonquières, 'Shortcomings of joint research', *Financial Times* (16 October 1990), p. 18.

23. David Pilling, Clive Cookson and Victoria Griffith, 'Human blueprint is revealed', *Financial Times* (27 June 2000), p. 1; Clive Cookson, 'Book of life that rewrites existence', *Financial Times* (27 June 2000), p. 15; Victoria Griffith, 'Advance is a mixed blessing', *Financial Times* (27 June 2000), p. 15.

24. Michael Smith, 'Brussels acts over telecoms pricing and unveils competition blueprint', *Financial Times* (13 April 2000), p. 1; Christopher Brown-Humes, 'Volvo attacks Brussels over Scania ruling', *Financial Times* (9 March 2000), p. 33.

25. '13-year-old bids over $3M for items in eBay auctions', *USA Today* (30 April 1999), p. 10B.

26. See Cyndee Miller, 'Trendspotters: "Dark Ages" ending; so is cocooning', *Marketing News* (3 February 1997), pp. 1 and 16.

27. Adrienne Ward Fawcett, 'Lifestyle study', *Advertising Age* (18 April 1994), pp. 12–13.

28. See Bill McDowell, 'New DDB Needham report: consumers want it all', *Advertising Age* (November 1996), pp. 32–3.

29. Christopher Brown-Humes, 'Big designs on practicality' in supplement on Finland, *Financial Times* (10 July 2000), p. vi.

30. Myra Stark, 'Celestial season', *Brandweek* (16 November 1998), pp. 25–6; also see David B. Wolfe, 'The psychological center of gravity', *American Demographics* (April 1998), pp. 16–19; and Richard Cimino and Don Lattin, 'Choosing my religion', *American Demographics* (April 1999), pp. 60–5.

31. Dyan Machan, 'A more tolerant generation', *Forbes* (8 September 1997), pp. 46–7; William Davis, 'Opinion', *Marketing Business* (March 1996), p. 6.

32. See Carl P. Zeithaml and Valerie A. Zeithaml, 'Environmental management: revising the marketing perspective', *Journal of Marketing* (Spring 1984), pp. 46–53.

case 4

Unilever: power?

'My God! They're really going to use it!' Nabil Sakkab, Procter & Gamble's European head of laundry products development, exclaimed to colleagues as he looked closely at the myriad, tiny pink crystals scattered among a heap of detergent he'd just poured on to his desk. It was mid-March 1994 – the beginning of a protracted nightmare for Unilever, when arch rival P&G discovered the secret ingredient in its super-concentrated Power, a new, revolutionary washing powder: Omo Power in the Netherlands, Persil Power in the United Kingdom and Skip Power in France. Power was the biggest advance in fabric detergents in 15 years, and sales of Power were leaping in the three European countries where it had been launched. It worried P&G not just because the rivals were doing so well, but because Power contained a manganese catalyst, known as the 'accelerator', which is 'unkind' to clothes – it attacks fabrics! P&G had dropped the defective manganese as a possible ingredient ten years ago for that reason.

The question P&G posed was 'WHY?' With that, the Great Soap War over Unilever's Power detergent began.

Power, the culmination of five years of developmental work, lay behind Unilever's strategy to salvage its market position in the €10 billion European fabric detergent market, in which P&G had long since overtaken it. Power was the company's second entry into the concentrated fabric detergent market. It had to be the trailblazer in the industry, a quantum leap in detergent effectiveness, to win back the lead. Unilever planned to launch Power in 11 countries in short order – a marketing blitzkrieg without precedent in Europe. For Niall Fitzgerald, Unilever's global coordinator of detergents, much was riding on Power's success. Turning round Unilever's ailing detergents business could mean eventual ascent to the joint chairmanship of the group.

A private warning

Ed Artzt, P&G's chairman, also nicknamed the Prince of Darkness, had a well-earned reputation for responding rapidly and ruthlessly when he felt P&G's interests were threatened. Power's success posed a significant threat to the company's current and imminent new products – Ariel Future was due for launch in late 1994. The Power detergent was claiming a technological lead based on what he knew was a fundamentally flawed formula. Sakkab and his colleagues at P&G's European Technology Centre not only found that some dark dyes in cotton and viscose fabrics reacted badly to the detergent, they also discovered holes in clothes washed in Power.

On 31 March 1994 Artzt urged top executives at Unilever House, London, to withdraw their new detergent. This was a private warning. For all the aggression in the market, P&G and Unilever have been known in private to alert one another to product flaws and work together to solve problems. This time, however, Unilever executives ignored this private warning, suspecting that Artzt was on a spoiling mission to undermine Power. Fitzgerald saw no need to take the costly and humiliating step of withdrawing Power, which had already been tested by scientists and over 60,000 consumers for two years without incident.

A story in the Dutch press on 27 April 1994 quoted a P&G spokesman who alluded to fabric damage caused by Power. Unilever held a press conference on 29 April denying P&G's claims, while issuing two writs for product defamation and trademark infringement, and seeking an injunction to stop P&G using the term 'Power' for its own detergents. Things were getting 'grubbier' by this time!

P&G not only hired the PR firm, The Rowland Company (a Saatchi & Saatchi subsidiary), to run its campaign of public vilification, but also started a ruthlessly well-organised knocking-copy campaign – running around Europe to consumers' associations, washing machine manufacturers, retailers and anybody else who would listen, giving them very extensive technical briefings with lots of pictures of Power-damaged clothes.

Unilever on the defensive

Power sales fell after every P&G onslaught. Although Unilever was able to rebuild them with advertising and special offers, this defence could not hold out for long. Leading supermarket chains in various countries were considering emptying their shelves of Power, even though Unilever stood firmly behind its products, denying that there was a problem.

On 3 June 1994 Unilever announced that it would:

♦ drop the lawsuits against P&G (after P&G assured Unilever that its spokesman had been misquoted);

♦ reformulate Power, and reduce the level of the accelerator in the powder by 80 per cent.

Meanwhile, P&G persisted in proving its point, releasing to the press pictures of clothes damaged by Power, plus results from six test institutes, all of which became front-page news in several European countries. Consumers' associations damned Power detergents; environmental campaigners in Sweden accused Power of putting the nation's clothes in imminent jeopardy! Unilever remained defensive with both the press and the public, failing to find an effective counter to criticisms from all sides.

Unilever's climbdown

Unilever revamped and relaunched Power products, while also retreating from its original broad market positioning to a more specialised niche – the package was changed to concentrate use of the product in lower temperatures and on white fabrics. The company attempted to reassure consumers through advertisements that guaranteed the safety of its revamped product. But then the Dutch consumers' union confirmed the damaging effects of the upgraded Power.

In late 1994, Unilever management finally admitted: 'We made a mistake. We launched a product which had a defect which we had not detected. We were very enthusiastic about an exciting new product and did not look closely enough at the negatives. Somewhere between research and marketing something went wrong – under the normal pressure to be first to the market.'

Unilever obviously failed to anticipate how violently its arch rival would react. By the end of the year, new independent tests, including the UK Consumers' Association *Which?* investigation, confirmed everybody's suspicions – that Power, even the reformulated version with reduced manganese, was defective.

Costs of the Power fiasco to Unilever?

After spending more than €300 million on developing, manufacturing and marketing Power products, Unilever remains a poor second to P&G in the European detergent market. A heavy price was extracted on reputations – the company's and those of the Persil and Omo brands. Unilever's image as a shrewd marketer and innovator was undermined. The whole affair has exacerbated consumers' scepticism towards manufacturers; as one retailer said, 'the whole [detergents] sector is drowning

in over-claiming and publicity which leaves consumers confused'.

Power products were eventually withdrawn from all markets. There were painful lessons to be learnt by management. Not least, the company has to try harder to develop new products that satisfy changing customer needs profitably. In 1998, the company beat rival P&G to the launch of revolutionary Persil tablets. Revolutionary because the concept of tablets (in this case, two to be used in each wash) for the first time offers consumers the benefits of no mess, no waste and no confusion about the amount used.

Questions

1. Identify the key actors and forces in the company's marketing environment that affect its ability to serve its target customers effectively.

2. What were the most critical actors or forces that accounted for Persil/Omo Power's final downfall?

3. Show how each of the actors/forces you have identified in question 2 directly (or indirectly) impacted on Unilever's final decision to revamp and relaunch the defective Omo/Persil Power.

4. Critically evaluate the motives of P&G.

5. What are the key lessons for management?

6. Could the problems have been anticipated and avoided? How?

SOURCES: John Willman, 'Start taking the tablets for a more convenient wash', *Financial Times* (28 April 1998), pp. 14–15; George Pitcher, 'Sham "soap wars" signal fierce battle to capture market share', *Marketing Week* (3 May 1996), p. 29; 'Soap and chips', *Financial Times* (27 December 1994), p. 15; Roderick Oram, 'Washing whiter proves a murky business', *Financial Times* (21 December 1994), p. 8; Diane Summers, 'Procter set for rap on soap advert', *Financial Times* (1 December 1994), p. 9; Roderick Oram, 'P&G, Unilever soap wars leave market spinning', *Financial Times* (1 November 1994), p. 29; 'Persil Power "no better than others"', *Financial Times* (6 October 1994), p. 11; Barbara Smit, 'Unilever comes clean over detergent', *The European* (30 September–6 October 1994), p. 18; Diane Summers, 'Unilever detergent comes under renewed criticism', *Financial*

Times (24–5 September 1994), p. 26; Roderick Oram, 'Unilever concedes detergent damaged clothing', *Financial Times* (23 September 1994), p. 1; 'Tale from the washroom', *The Economist* (11 June 1994), p. 89; David Short, 'Dirty fighting in soap wars', *The European* (5–11 August 1994), p. 17; Diane Summers, 'Procter steps up attack on Unilever's Persil Power', *Financial Times* (30–1 July 1994), p. 24; Barbara Smit, 'Unilever sticks by Omo', *The European* (10–16 June 1994); Tony Jackson, 'Dirty tricks alleged in soap war', *Financial Times* (3 May 1994), p. 9; 'Unilever takes Procter to court in row over "super" detergent', *Financial Times* (30 April–1 May 1994), p. 1.

internet exercises

Internet exercises for this chapter can be found on the student site of the мyPHLIP Web Site at www.booksites.net/kotler.

chapter five

The global marketplace

Chapter objectives *After reading this chapter, you should be able to:*

✦ Discuss how the international trade system, economic, political–legal and cultural environments affect a company's international marketing decisions.

✦ Describe three key approaches to entering international markets.

✦ Explain how companies adapt their marketing mixes for international markets.

✦ Distinguish between the three major forms of international marketing organisations.

introduction

The world is shrinking rapidly with the advent of faster communication, transportation and financial flows. Brands or products originating from one country – Gucci handbags, Mont Blanc pens, German BMWs, McDonald's hamburgers, Japanese sushi – are finding enthusiastic acceptance in other countries. International trade is booming. Since 1969, the number of multinational corporations in the world's richest countries has more than tripled from 7,000 to 24,000. Experts predict that by 2005, world exports of goods and services will reach 28 per cent of world gross domestic product, up from only 9 per cent 20 years ago. The US exported more than any other single country, with foreign sales of $695 billion (€781 bn) or 12.4 per cent of world exports in 1999. However, the EU, with exports of nearly €800 billion in 1999, took a bigger share (18.9 per cent) of world trade.[1]

This chapter discusses the importance of global marketing and explains the key elements of the planning process: analysing the global environment; deciding whether or not to go international; deciding which markets to enter and how to enter; deciding the global marketing programme; and determining the global marketing organisation.

preview case

Barco: new life abroad

THE JAPANESE POST-WAR CONSUMER ELECTRONICS BOOM left many European rivals gasping for air. But one Belgian company saw it as an opportunity to breathe new life into a tired range.

Barco, a thriving Bel-20 niche-market electronics group, is now seen as an innovative high-tech growth company and a solid profit-generator. It is one of a new breed of Belgian companies that have looked outside the country's narrow borders and captured a significant market share overseas.

In 1980, Barco, based in Kortrijk, near the French border, was a simple manufacturer of television sets. Its margins were low in a mass market sector increasingly dominated by Japanese brands. A radical change in direction was needed.

'In 20 years we have made a totally different company. And it will continue to change', says Hugo Vandamme, chief executive officer. A Barco employee for 25 years and chief executive officer (CEO) since 1989, he has overseen a switch to making high-technology image-related products. The transformation went a step further in 1999 when the company's activities, which include projection systems, Internet via cable, medical imaging, packaging and digital cinema, were focused into six separate divisions, each setting the target of retaining number one positions in the world in their sub-sectors.

Barco's flagship products include the huge screens seen on the tops of buildings in city centres to display news, advertisements and stock prices. The company provides both the screens and an Internet-based system that links the content of the screens to synchronise them across the world.

The changes propelled Barco to a stock market listing in 1986 and a Bel-20 spot by the early 1990s. Its employee numbers have grown from 1,000 in 1980 to 5,000 today. Its market capitalisation of around €2 billion reflects rising profits since its initial public offering. Its pre-tax profits for the first half of 2000 were €51.6 million, a 15 per cent increase on the year before. Barco expects full year profits to be €190 million by 2004. These projections are backed up by the company's strengths in overseas markets.

Nearly 30 per cent of Barco's revenues come from North America, a legacy of the company's founder who sold radio sets to the US at the company's inception in 1936. Even Barco's name – Belgian-American Radio Corporation – underscores the fact that it has never positioned itself as a Belgian or even European group. 'We never look to develop a product that [purely] would fit the Belgian or European market. I tell our marketing and product managers to always think worldwide', says Mr Vandamme. This strategy includes a shift to manufacturing in low-cost countries such as India.

Such flexibility, once a rarity among Belgian companies, has helped Barco withstand pressure from high-profile rivals such as NEC and Sony, in the projector sector. And, with a weak euro, Barco believes that it can expand its proportion of sales to non-euro-zone countries and to the US, in particular.

With growth in mind, the Barco board plans to split off and float each of the six divisions over the next decade, with the aim of raising capital for acquisitions and realising the full value of each of the businesses concerned. These acquisitions are most likely to be in the US and UK, but could be elsewhere. The recent creation of Euronext, the merger of the Paris, Brussels and Amsterdam bourses, goes some way to facilitate Barco's expansion plans. The company's products are now widely seen as best-in-class. However, new life abroad for these products would require not only financial resources, but also the need to consider a number of critical international marketing issues.[2]

Questions

You should attempt these questions only after completing your reading of this chapter.

1. What are the key factors that Barco should consider when deciding on which new country-markets to enter?

2. Barco seeks to grow through acquisitions. What other modes of market entry might Barco consider when expanding into foreign markets? Assess their merits and disadvantages.

3. What constitutes an effective global marketing programme for a company such as Barco?

global marketing in the twenty-first century

Companies pay little attention to international trade when the home market is big and teeming with opportunities. The home market is also much safer. Managers do not need to learn other languages, deal with strange and changing currencies, face political and legal uncertainties or adapt their products to different customer needs and expectations. This has been the attitude of many western companies, which saw little need to sell in overseas markets because their domestic market alone seemed to offer attractive opportunities for growth.

Today, however, the business environment is changing and firms cannot afford to ignore international markets. The increasing dependency of nations around the world on each other's goods and services has raised awareness among companies of the need for a more international outlook in their approach to business. International markets are important because most firms are geared towards growth and so must seek new opportunities in foreign countries as their domestic markets mature. As international trade becomes more liberalised, firms are facing tougher foreign competition in the domestic market. They must develop the ability to fight off competitors on their own home ground, or to exploit business opportunities in foreign markets.

True, many companies have been carrying on international activities for decades. Across western Europe and North America, names such as Toyota, Sony and Toshiba have become household words in the same way McDonald's, Toys 'R' Us, Nestlé, Philips and IKEA are familiar names to most consumers in Asian countries like Japan, Singapore and Hong Kong. But, today, global competition is intensifying. Foreign firms are expanding aggressively into new international markets and home markets are no longer as rich in opportunity. Local companies that never thought about foreign competitors suddenly find these competitors in their own backyards. The firm that stays at home to play it safe not only misses the opportunity to enter other markets, but also risks losing its home market.

Although some companies would like to stem the tide of foreign imports through protectionism, in the long run, this would only raise the cost of living and protect inefficient domestic firms. The better way for companies to compete is to improve their products continuously at home and expand into foreign markets.

The longer companies delay taking steps towards internationalising, the more they risk being shut out of growing markets around the world. Domestic firms that thought that they were safe now find companies from neighbouring countries invading their home markets. All companies will have to answer some basic questions: What market position should we try to establish in our country, in our economic region (e.g. western Europe, eastern Europe, North America, Asia, Pacific Rim) and globally? Who will our global competitors be, and what are their strategies and resources? Where should we produce or source our products? What strategic alliances should we form with other firms around the world?

Ironically, although the need for companies to go abroad is greater today than in the past, so are the risks. Companies that go global confront several major problems. High debt, inflation and unemployment in many countries have resulted in highly unstable governments and currencies, which limit trade and expose foreign firms to many risks. For example, in 1998, Russia created a global economic crisis when it devalued the ruble, effectively defaulting on its global debts. A more widespread Asian economic downturn had a far-reaching impact on Western businesses with significant markets or investments there.

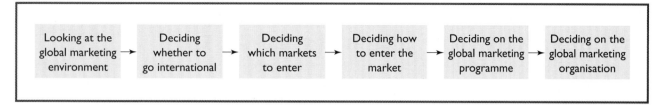

Figure 5.1

Major decisions in international marketing

Governments are placing more regulations on foreign firms, such as requiring joint ownership with local partners, mandating the hiring of foreign nationals and limiting profits that can be taken from the country. Moreover, some governments often impose high tariffs or trade barriers in order to protect their own industries. Finally, corruption is an increasing problem – officials in several countries often award business not to the best bidder, but to the highest briber.

Still, companies selling in global industries have no choice but to internationalise their operations and strive to be a global firm. A **global industry** is one in which the strategic positions of competitors in given geographic or national markets are affected by their overall global positions. A **global firm** is one that, by operating in more than one country, gains research and development, production, marketing and financial advantages that are not available to purely domestic competitors. The global company sees the world as one market. It minimises the importance of national boundaries, and raises capital, obtains materials and components, and manufactures and markets its goods wherever it can do the best job. For example, Ford's 'world truck' sports a cab made in Europe and a chassis built in North America. It is assembled in Brazil and imported to the United States for sale. Thus global firms gain advantages by planning, operating and coordinating their activities on a worldwide basis. These gains are a key reason behind recent global restructuring programmes undertaken by leading German car producers, BMW and Mercedes-Benz. **Global marketing** is concerned with integrating or standardising marketing actions across a number of geographic markets. This does not rule out adaptation of the marketing mix to individual countries, but suggests that firms, where possible, ignore traditional market boundaries and capitalise on similarities between markets to build competitive advantage.

Because firms around the world are globalising at a rapid rate, domestic firms in global industries must act quickly before the window closes. This does not mean that small and medium-size firms must operate in a dozen countries to succeed. These firms can practise global niching. In fact, companies marketing on the Internet may find themselves going global whether they intend it or not. In many cases, they may run up against unexpected problems, especially governmental or cultural restrictions. Even established Internet marketers are only beginning to discover the reality of global cyber marketing (see Marketing Highlight 5.1). The world, however, is becoming smaller and every business operating in a global industry – whether large or small, online or offline – must assess and establish its place in world markets.

As shown in Figure 5.1, a company faces six major decisions in international marketing. Each decision will be discussed in detail.

Global industry
An industry in which the strategic positions of competitors in given geographic or national markets are affected by their overall global positions.

Global firm
A firm that, by operating in more than one country, gains R&D, production, marketing and financial advantages that are not available to purely domestic competitors.

Global marketing
Marketing that is concerned with integrating or standardising marketing actions across different geographic markets.

looking at the global marketing environment

Doing international business successfully requires firms to take a broad market perspective.

marketing highlight 5.1

WWW.The world is your oyster.com: global rhetoric versus reality

More and more companies have made a strategic decision to take advantage of cyberspace's vanishing national boundaries. Despite encouraging e-commerce developments in the US, Europe and Asia, the reality of the global Internet market depends on each country's economic, technical, cultural, political and regional dynamics. Technological challenges abound. Response times overseas can be dismal. Many countries remain technologically underdeveloped and have a low-income citizenry lacking PCs or even phone connections. Other countries have acceptable phone and PC penetrations, but high subscription and connection costs sharply restrict casual uses such as surfing on the Internet.

In addition, the global marketer may run up against governmental or cultural restrictions. In Germany, a vendor cannot accept payment via credit card until two weeks after an order has been sent. Also, it is against the law for credit card companies and direct-marketing firms to gather certain types of data on potential applicants. Such restrictions, sometimes combined with underdeveloped banking systems, have limited credit-card and direct-mail usage in many countries. The issue of who pays taxes and duties on global e-commerce is murkier still. Subsequently, marketers have to find alternative marketing and collection approaches.

Consider another example – France. Recently, two French anti-racism groups sued Yahoo! to remove collectibles such as swastika flags and Nazi uniforms from its American website, as it is illegal in France to display or sell objects that incite racial hatred. A French judge subsequently ruled that Yahoo!, the leading Web portal, must block French users from viewing and buying Nazi memorabilia on its American auction site, or else pay a fine. Although there was a remote chance that such a ruling will ever be enforced for technical as well as legal reasons, the decision sets a precedent for the way in which national governments might impose their own laws in an online world that has seemingly transcended country borders. As Yahoo!'s site can be reached by French users, the judge ruled that Yahoo! had to make it impossible for French Web surfers to reach auctions of this illegal merchandise. Although it was possible to block French online users by getting them to complete a 'declaration of nationality' online or using a technology to track users' computer identities on the Internet (that is, their Internet service provider's IP address), technical experts say that users could easily avoid having their IP addresses tracked, by using services which replace them with fictitious addresses. Furthermore, it is hard for Yahoo! to decide on which of its millions of auctions to block. Putting an electronic wall around pages that contain keywords such as 'SS' or 'Nazi' may keep users from bidding for legal goods such as *The Diary of Anne Frank*.

Although some are quick to dismiss the ruling against Yahoo! as an amusing French attempt to defy commercial reality, many fear that the decision will incite other countries to try to impose laws on foreign Web services. This could mean costly reprogramming of sites to comply with many different jurisdictions. These fears are not unfounded. The Brussels Convention is a recent measure considered by the European Union which will allow European consumers to sue, in their local courts, any Internet site in Europe that is marketing its services in the consumer's home country.

Meanwhile, businesses need to realise that the Web does not offer complete solutions for transacting global business – and it probably never will. Most companies will always find it difficult to complete a big business-to-business deal via e-mail. The Internet will not surmount customs red tape or local regulations regarding import or export of certain goods. Despite the barriers, however, global Internet enterprise is growing rapidly. For companies that wish to go or stay global, the Internet and online services can represent an easy way to get started, or to reinforce other efforts.

SOURCES: Anna Chalmers, 'Feelings run high on Nazi issue', *Financial Times IT Review* (6 December 2000), p. xxiii; 'The Internet: Vive la liberté', *The Economist* (25 November 2000), pp. 120 and 125; Shannon Oberndorf, 'Europe jumps online', *Catalog Age* (June 1999), p. 10; and Bill Spindle, 'E-commerce (a special report)', *Wall Street Journal* (12 July 1999), p. R22; 'First America, then the world', *The Economist. E-Commerce Survey* (26 February 2000), pp. 35–6 and 41.

Asia: a growing market. China's booming mobile telephone market has become the focus of intense competition among western telecommunications equipment companies such as Nokia, Ericsson and Motorola.

Source: Associated Press

understanding the global environment

Before deciding whether or not to sell abroad, a company must thoroughly understand the international marketing environment. That environment has changed a great deal in the past two decades, creating both new opportunities and new problems. The world economy has globalised. First, world trade and investment have grown rapidly, with many attractive markets opening up in western and eastern Europe, China, the Pacific Rim, Russia and elsewhere. Official sources suggest that the volume of world goods trade grew by 6.5 per cent in 2000, from 4.5 per cent annually in the past two years. During the past decade, international trade has also risen faster than world output.[3] There has been a growth of global brands in motor vehicles, food, clothing, electronics and many other categories. The number of global companies has grown dramatically. The international financial system has become more complex and volatile. In some country markets, foreign companies face increasing trade barriers, erected to protect domestic markets against outside competition.

■ The international trade system

Companies looking abroad must develop an understanding of the international trade system. When selling to another country, the firm faces various trade restrictions. The most common is the **tariff**, which is a tax levied by a foreign government against

Tariff
A tax levied by a government against certain imported products. Tariffs are designed to raise revenue or to protect domestic firms.

Many companies have made the world their market: opening the megastore in Milan (top left) and Virgin megastores in London, Los Angeles, Vienna and Tokyo.

Source: Virgin Management Ltd.
Photographer: Tierry Boccon-Gibod
(Paris 331 4254 2370)

Quota
A limit on the amount of goods that an importing country will accept in certain product categories; it is designed to conserve on foreign exchange and to protect local industry and employment.

Embargo
A ban on the import of a certain product.

Exchange controls
Government limits on the amount of its country's foreign exchange with other countries and on its exchange rate against other currencies.

Non-tariff trade barriers
Non-monetary barriers to foreign products, such as biases against a foreign company's bids or product standards that go against a foreign company's product features.

certain imported products. The tariff may be designed either to raise revenue or to protect domestic firms: for example, those producing motor vehicles in Malaysia and whisky and rice in Japan. The exporter also may face a **quota**, which sets limits on the amount of goods the importing country will accept in certain product categories. The purpose of the quota is to conserve foreign exchange and to protect local industry and employment. An **embargo** or boycott, which totally bans some kinds of import, is the strongest form of quota.

Firms may face **exchange controls** that limit the amount of foreign exchange and the exchange rate against other currencies. The company may also face **non-tariff trade barriers**, such as biases against company bids or restrictive product standards that favour or go against product features.[4]

At the same time, certain forces help trade between nations. Examples are the General Agreement on Tariffs and Trade and various regional free trade agreements.

■ The World Trade Organisation and GATT

The General Agreement on Tariffs and Trade (GATT) is a 50-year-old treaty designed to promote world trade by reducing tariffs and other international trade barriers. Since the treaty's inception in 1948, member nations (currently numbering more than 130, with China joining in 2001) have met in eight rounds of GATT negotiations to reassess trade barriers and set new rules for international trade. The first seven rounds of negotiations reduced average worldwide tariffs on manufactured goods from 45 per cent to just 5 per cent.

The most recently completed GATT negotiations, dubbed the Uruguay round, dragged on for seven long years before concluding in 1993. The benefits of the Uruguay round will be felt for many years as the new accord promotes long-term global trade growth. It reduced the world's remaining manufactured goods tariffs by 30 per cent, which could boost global merchandise trade by up to 10 per cent, or nearly €320 billion, by 2002. The new round also extended GATT to cover trade in agriculture and a wide range of services, and it toughened international protection of copyrights, patents, trademarks and other intellectual property.[5]

The Uruguay round did much more than reducing trade barriers and setting international standards for trade; it established the World Trade Organisation (WTO) to enforce GATT rules. One of the WTO's first major tasks was to host negotiations on the General Agreement on Trade in Services, which deals with worldwide trade in banking, securities and insurance services. In general, the WTO acts as an umbrella organisation, overseeing GATT, the General Agreement on Trade in Services and a similar agreement governing intellectual property. In addition, the WTO mediates global disputes and imposes trade sanctions, authorities that the previous GATT organisation never possessed.[6] A fresh round of talks began in late 1999.

■ Regional free-trade zones

Some countries have formed free-trade zones or economic communities – groups of nations organised to secure common goals in the regulation of international trade. One such community is the European Union, which aims to create a single European market by reducing barriers to the free flow of products, services, finances and labour among member countries and developing policies on trade with non-member nations.

European unification offers tremendous trade opportunities for non-European firms. However, it also poses threats. As a result of increased unification, European companies will grow bigger and more competitive. Perhaps an even bigger concern, however, is that lower barriers *inside* Europe will only create thicker *outside* walls. Some observers envision a 'Fortress Europe' that heaps favours on firms from EU countries but hinders outsiders by imposing obstacles such as stiffer import quotas, local content requirements and other non-tariff barriers.

Progress towards European unification has been slow – many doubt that complete unification will ever be achieved. However, on 1 January 1999, 11 of the 15 member nations took a significant step toward unification by adopting the euro as a common currency. These 11 nations represent 290 million people and a €7.7 trillion market. Currencies of the individual countries will be phased out gradually until 1 January 2002, when the euro will become the only currency. Adoption of the euro will decrease much of the currency risk associated with doing business in Europe, making member countries with previously weak currencies more attractive markets. In addition, by removing currency conversion hurdles, the switch will likely increase cross-border trade and highlight differences in pricing and marketing from country to country.[7]

Even with the adoption of the euro as a standard currency, from a marketing viewpoint, creating an economic community will not create a homogeneous market. As one international analyst suggests, 'Even though you have fiscal harmonisation, you can't go against 2,000 years of tradition.' With 14 different languages and distinctive national customs, it is unlikely that the EU will ever become the 'United States of Europe'.[8] Although economic and political boundaries may fall, social and cultural differences will remain, and companies marketing in Europe will face a daunting mass of local rules. Still, even if only partly successful, European unification will make a more efficient and competitive Europe a global force with which to reckon.[9]

In North America, the United States and Canada phased out trade barriers in 1989. In January 1994, the *North American Free Trade Agreement (NAFTA)* established a free-trade zone among the United States, Mexico and Canada. The agreement created a single market of 360 million people who produce and consume $6.7 trillion (€7.53 trillion) worth of goods and services. As it is implemented over a 15-year period, NAFTA will eliminate all trade barriers and investment restrictions among the three countries. Prior to NAFTA, tariffs on American products entering Mexico averaged

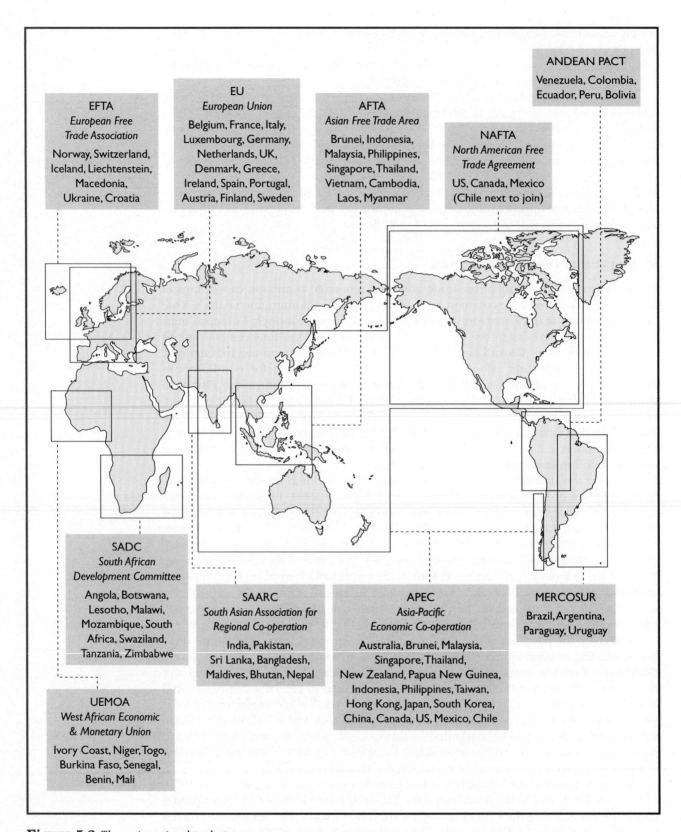

Figure 5.2 The main regional trade groups

Developing economies: ads like this one appearing in Hungarian magazines cater to a new class of buyers with dreams of the good life – and buying habits to match, who are eager to snap up everything from the high fashions to the latest cell phones.

SOURCE: Young and Rubicam Inc.

13 per cent, whereas US tariffs on Mexican goods averaged 6 per cent. Thus far, the agreement has allowed trade between the countries to flourish. Each day the United States exchanges more than $1 billion in goods and services with Canada, its largest trading partner. Over the past four years, exports from the United States to Mexico have increased 116 per cent. In 1998, Mexico passed Japan to become America's second largest trading partner.[10]

Other free-trade areas have formed in Latin America and South America. For example, MERCOSUR now links six members, including full members Argentina, Brazil, Paraguay and Uruguay and associate members Bolivia and Chile. With a population of more than 200 million and a combined economy of more than €1.19 trillion a year, these countries make up the largest trading bloc after NAFTA and the European Union. There is talk of a free-trade agreement between the EU and MERCOSUR.[11]

Other free-trade communities exist (see Figure 5.2). In fact, almost every member of the WTO is also a member of one or more such communities. And, of the 100 or so free-trade arrangements listed by the WTO, over half have come into being in the 1990s.

Each nation has unique features that must be understood. A country's readiness for different products and services and its attractiveness as a market to foreign firms depend on its economic, political–legal and cultural environments. We address these environmental influences next.

■ Economic environment

The international marketer must study each country's economy. Two economic factors reflect the country's attractiveness as a market: the country's *industrial structure* and its *income distribution*.

The country's industrial structure shapes its product and service needs, income levels and employment levels. Four types of industrial structure should be considered:

1. *Subsistence economies.* In a subsistence economy, the vast majority of people engage in simple agriculture. They consume most of their output and barter the rest for simple goods and services. They offer few market opportunities.

2. *Raw-material-exporting economies.* These economies are rich in one or more natural resources, but poor in other ways. Much of their revenue comes from exporting these resources. Examples are Chile (tin and copper), The Democratic

Republic of Congo (formerly Zaire) (copper, cobalt and coffee) and Saudi Arabia (oil). These countries are good markets for large equipment, tools and supplies, and trucks. If there are many foreign residents and a wealthy upper class, they are also a market for luxury goods.

3. *Industrialising economies*. In an industrialising economy, manufacturing accounts for 10–20 per cent of the country's economy. Examples include the Philippines, India and Brazil. As manufacturing increases, the country needs more imports of raw textile materials, steel and heavy machinery, and fewer imports of finished textiles, paper products and motor vehicles. Industrialisation typically creates a new rich class and a small but growing middle class, both demanding new types of imported goods. In these countries, people with rising disposable income want to spend on items such as fashion, video recorders, CD players and instant coffee.

4. *Industrial economies*. Industrial economies are large exporters of manufactured goods and investment funds. They trade goods among themselves and also export them to other types of economy for raw materials and semi-finished goods. The varied manufacturing activities of these industrial nations and their large middle class make them rich markets for all sorts of goods. Asia's newly industrialised economies, such as Taiwan, Singapore, South Korea and Malaysia, fall into this category.

The second economic factor is the country's income distribution. Countries with subsistence economies may consist mostly of households with very low family incomes. In contrast, industrialised economies may have low-, medium- and high-income households. Still other countries may have households with only either very low or very high incomes. However, in many cases, poorer countries may have small but wealthy segments of upper-income consumers. Also, even in low-income and developing countries, people may find ways to buy products that are important to them:

> Philosophy professor Nina Gladziuk thinks carefully before shelling out her hard-earned zlotys for Poland's dazzling array of consumer goods. But spend she certainly does. Although she earns just €700 a month from two academic jobs, Gladziuk, 41, enjoys making purchases: They are changing her lifestyle after years of deprivation under communism. In the past year, she has furnished a new apartment in a popular neighborhood near Warsaw's Kabaty Forest, splurged on foreign-made beauty products, and spent a weekend in Paris before attending a seminar financed by her university. . . . Meet Central Europe's fast-rising consumer class. From white-collar workers like Gladziuk to factory workers in Budapest, to hip young professionals in Prague, incomes are rising and confidence surging as a result of four years of economic growth. In the region's leading economies – the Czech Republic, Hungary and Poland – the new class of buyers is growing not only in numbers but also in sophistication. . . . In Hungary, ad agency Young & Rubicam labels 11 per cent of the country as 'aspirers', with dreams of the good life and buying habits to match. Nearly one-third of all Czechs, Hungarians and Poles – some 17 million people – are under 30 years old, eager to snap up everything from the latest fashions to compact disks.[12]

Thus, international marketers face many challenges in understanding how the economic environment will affect decisions about which global markets to enter and how.

■ Political–legal environment

Nations differ greatly in their political–legal environments. At least four political–legal factors should be considered in deciding whether to do business in a given country:

attitudes towards international buying, political stability, monetary regulations and government bureaucracy. We will consider each of these in turn.

Attitudes towards international buying   Some nations are quite receptive to foreign firms, and others are quite hostile. Western firms have found newly industri- alised countries in the Far East, such as Singapore, Thailand and the Philippines, attractive overseas investment locations. In contrast, others like India are bothersome with their import quotas, currency restrictions and limits on the percentage of the management team that can be non-nationals.

Government bureaucracy   This is the extent to which the host government runs an efficient system for helping foreign companies: efficient customs handling, good market information, and other factors that aid in doing business.

Political stability   Governments change hands, sometimes violently. Even without a change, a government may decide to respond to new popular feelings. The foreign company's property may be taken, its currency holdings may be blocked, or import quotas or new duties may be set. International marketers may find it profitable to do business in an unstable country, but the unsteady situation will affect how they handle business and financial matters.

Monetary regulations   Sellers want to take their profits in a currency of value to them. Ideally, the buyer can pay in the seller's currency or in other world currencies. Short of this, sellers might accept a blocked currency – one whose removal from the country is restricted by the buyer's government – if they can buy other goods in that country that they need themselves or can sell elsewhere for a needed currency. Besides currency limits, a changing exchange rate, as mentioned earlier, creates high risks for the seller.

Most international trade involves cash transactions. Yet many nations have too little hard currency to pay for their purchases from other countries. They may want to pay with other items instead of cash, which has led to a growing practice called **coun- tertrade**. Countertrade now accounts for more than one-half of all international trade.

Countertrade takes several forms. *Barter* involves the direct exchange of goods or services. For example, British coal mining equipment has been 'sold' for Indonesian plywood; Volkswagen cars were swapped for Bulgarian dried apricots; and Boeing 747s, fitted with Rolls-Royce engines, were exchanged for Saudi oil. Another form is *com- pensation* (or *buyback*), whereby the seller sells a plant, equipment or technology to another country and agrees to take payment in the resulting products. Thus, Goodyear provided China with materials and training for a printing plant in exchange for finished labels. Another form is *counterpurchase*. Here the seller receives full payment in cash, but agrees to spend some portion of the money in the other country within a stated time period. For example, Pepsi sells its syrup to Russia for roubles, and agrees to buy Russian vodka for reselling in the United States.

Countertrade deals can be very complex. For example, DaimlerChrysler recently agreed to sell 30 trucks to Romania in exchange for 150 Romanian jeeps, which it then sold to Ecuador for bananas, which were in turn sold to a German supermarket chain for German currency. Through this roundabout process, DaimlerChrysler finally obtained payment in German money.[13]

> **Countertrade**
> *International trade involving the direct or indirect exchange of goods for other goods instead of cash. Forms include barter compensation (buyback) and counterpurchase.*

■ Cultural environment

Each country has its own traditions, norms and taboos. The seller must examine the way consumers in different countries think about and use certain products before planning a marketing programme. The cultural barriers in target country markets must

Overlooking cultural differences can result in embarrassing mistakes. When it learned that this stylised 'Air' logo resembled 'Allah' in Arabic script, Nike apologised and pulled the shoes from distribution.

Source: Trillium Studios/Cary Wolinsky

Culture
The set of basic values, perceptions, wants and behaviours learned by a member of society from family and other important institutions.

be identified. **Culture** is defined simply as *the learned distinctive way of life of a society*. The dimensions of culture include the social organisation of society (e.g. the class system in the United Kingdom, the caste system in India, the heavy reliance on social welfare in Sweden or the lack of it in Japan); religion (ranging from the Islamic fundamentalism of Iran to the secular approaches of western countries such as the United Kingdom); customs and rituals; values and attitudes towards domestic and international life; education provision and literacy levels; political system; aesthetic systems (e.g. folklore, music, arts, literature); and language.

Culture and people's general behaviour influence the customer's actions in the marketplace, which, in turn, impact upon the firm's marketing decisions. There are often surprises. For example, the average Frenchman uses almost twice as many cosmetics and beauty aids as does his female partner. The Germans and the French eat more packaged, branded spaghetti than do Italians. Italian children like to eat chocolate bars between slices of bread as a snack. Women in Tanzania will not give their children eggs for fear of making them bald or impotent. A good example of cultural differences is the case of a Scandinavian company wishing to sell baby clothes in Belgium. It discovered its clothes were virtually unsaleable because, in most regions, clothes for baby girls are trimmed with blue and those for baby boys with pink.

Business norms and behaviour also vary from country to country. Business executives need to be briefed on these factors before conducting business in another country. Here are some examples of different global business behaviour:

✦ In face-to-face communications, Japanese business executives rarely say 'no' to the western business executive. Thus westerners tend to be frustrated and may not know where they stand. Where westerners come to the point quickly, Japanese business executives may find this behaviour offensive.

- In France, wholesalers don't want to promote a product. They ask their retailers what they want and deliver it. If a foreign company builds its strategy around the French wholesaler's cooperation in promotions, it is likely to fail.

- When British executives exchange business cards, each usually gives the other's card a cursory glance and stuffs it in a pocket for later reference. In Japan, however, executives dutifully study each other's cards during a greeting, carefully noting company affiliation and rank. They hand their card to the most important person first.

- In the United Kingdom and the United States, business meals are common. In Germany, these are strictly social. Foreigners are rarely invited to dinner and such an invitation suggests a very advanced association. The opposite applies in Italy where entertaining is an essential part of business life (guests should offer to pay but, in the end, should defer to their Italian host). In France, watch out. There are two kinds of business lunch – one for building up relations, without expecting anything in return, and the other to discuss a deal in the making or to celebrate a deal afterwards. Deals, however, should be concluded in the office, never over a lunch table.

- Shaking hands on meeting and on parting is common in Germany, Belgium, France and Italy. Ignoring this custom, especially in France, causes offence. In France, it is advisable to shake hands with everyone in a crowded room.

By the same token, companies that understand cultural nuances can use them to advantage when positioning products internationally. For example, consider French cosmetics giant, L'Oréal:

It's a sunny afternoon outside Parkson's department store in Shanghai, and a marketing battle is raging for the attention of Chinese women. Tall, pouty models in beige skirts and sheer tops pass out flyers promoting Revlon's new spring colours. But their effort is drowned out by L'Oréal's eye-catching show for its

Companies that understand cultural nuances can use them to advantage. L'Oréal's winning formula is to convey the allure of different cultures through its many products.

Source: Fritz Hoffmann/The Image Works

Maybelline brand. To a pulsing rhythm, two gangly models in shimmering lycra tops dance on a podium before a large backdrop depicting the New York City skyline. The music stops, and a makeup artist transforms a model's face while a Chinese saleswoman delivers the punch line. 'This brand comes from America. It's very trendy', she shouts into her microphone. 'If you want to be fashionable, just choose Maybelline'. Few of the women in the crowd realize that the trendy 'New York' Maybelline brand belongs to French cosmetics giant L'Oréal. . . . Blink an eye and L'Oréal has just sold 85 products around the world, from Redken hair care and Ralph Lauren perfumes to Helena Rubinstein cosmetics. In the battle for global beauty markets, L'Oréal has developed a winning formula: . . . conveying the allure of different cultures through its many products. Whether it's selling Italian elegance, New York street smarts, or French beauty through its brands, L'Oréal is reaching out to a vast range of people across incomes and cultures.[14]

Thus, the key to success for the international marketer lies in assiduously researching and understanding a country's cultural traditions, preferences and behaviours. Building *cultural empathy* in this way helps companies to avoid embarrassing mistakes and to take advantage of cross-cultural opportunities.

deciding whether to go international

Not all companies need to venture into international markets to survive. For example, many companies are local businesses that need to market well only in the local marketplace. Operating domestically is easier and safer. Managers need not learn another country's language and laws, deal with volatile currencies, face political and legal uncertainties, or redesign their products to suit different customer needs and expectations. However, companies that operate in global industries, where their strategic positions in specific markets are affected strongly by their overall global positions, must compete on a worldwide basis if they are to succeed.

Any of several factors might draw a company into the international arena. Global competitors might attack the company's domestic market by offering better products or lower prices. The company might want to counterattack these competitors in their home markets to tie up their resources. Or the company might discover foreign markets that present higher profit opportunities than the domestic market does. The company's domestic market might be stagnant or shrinking, or the company might need an enlarged customer base in order to achieve economies of scale. The company might want to reduce its dependence on any one market so as to reduce its risk. Finally, the company's customers might be expanding abroad and require international servicing.

Before going abroad, the company must weigh several risks and answer many questions about its ability to operate globally. Can the company learn to understand the preferences and buyer behaviour of consumers in other countries? Can it offer competitively attractive products? Will it be able to adapt to other countries' business cultures and deal effectively with foreign nationals? Do the company's managers have the necessary international experience? Has management considered the impact of regulations and the political environments of other countries?

Because of the risks and difficulties of entering international markets, most companies do not act until some situation or event thrusts them into the global arena. Someone – a domestic exporter, a foreign importer, a foreign government – may ask the company to sell abroad. Or the company may be saddled with overcapacity and must find additional markets for its goods.

deciding which markets to enter

Before going abroad, the company should define its international *marketing objectives* and *policies*. First, it should decide what *volume* of foreign sales it wants. Most companies start small when they go abroad. Some plan to stay small, seeing foreign sales as a small part of their business. Other companies have bigger plans, seeing foreign business as equal to or even more important than their domestic business. Second, the company must choose *how many* countries it wants to market in. Generally, it makes better sense to operate in fewer countries with deeper penetration in each. Third, the company must decide on the *types* of country to enter. A country's attractiveness depends on the product, geographical factors, income and population, political climate and other factors. The seller may prefer certain country groups or parts of the world. In recent years, many major new markets have emerged, offering both substantial opportunities and daunting challenges (see Marketing Highlight 5.2).

marketing highlight 5.2

Emerging markets: going east

China and India each have over a billion consumers, presenting tempting prospects for international companies. The experience of international companies suggests that, despite the attractiveness of these emerging markets, their consumers remain an elusive target. Many dominant brands – from Unilever, Sony and Mercedes to Levi, Kellogg and Ford – have all struggled to deliver on the promise of the 'billion-consumer' markets.

A common fallacy lies in the thinking that there are huge margins to be gained from skimming the 3 or 5 per cent of affluent consumers in emerging markets who have global preferences for 'luxury goods' and purchasing power. In India, Coca-Cola came in at the top and tried to trickle down. It launched pricey 350 ml bottles instead of offering cheaper smaller ones. Rather than concentrating on the main towns, it went for the whole of India with a single size and price, using expensive and flawed distribution and advertising. Ford and other motor manufacturers also misjudged the Indian market. They started with medium-sized cars in a market dominated by small ones, and expected to compete with nearly 70 per cent overcapacity in medium-sized car manufacturing. Kellogg's offered premium-priced cereals supported by expensive marketing. They soon learnt that, although market research showed that India was the largest cereal-eating nation on earth, consumers were choosing to buy Champion's products costing a fifth the price of Kellogg's. By contrast, Akai, the Japanese consumer electronics producer, stole a march on global giant Sony, by offering cheaper televisions and taking customers' old sets in part-exchange.

Analysts argue that it is important to define the Indian market not by income alone, but by consumption. A disaggregation will yield a demographic pyramid of five layers: the destitute, climbers, aspirants, consumers and the rich (who are the 1 million households earning more than Rs 1 million (€25,600) a year). The 30m people normally identified as consumers have less disposable income than the groups below them, because they tend to spend more on education. The bottom of the pyramid, especially the aspirants, is more attractive because of rising incomes. Unilever's Indian subsidiary, Hindustan Lever, designed products for each of the five tiers. It began moving goods by road instead of rail, building a network of 40,000 wholesalers and 500,000 retailers and supplying it with credit. Levi initially aggregated the 156m people aged 12 to 19, but 111m of these live in rural India. Targeting the top tier leaves a meagre 500,000 rich urban consumers, potentially yielding slim pickings.

The key to success lies in developing products for each or most of the five consumption segments, instead of targeting the 'affluent global consumer'. But segmentation of this nature is costly and only justified if consumers are able and willing to pay for specialised products. The experience of SmithKline Beecham (SB) in India points to the power of targeting local consumers. But fine segmentation does not have to come at a cost. Horlicks, its flagship product in India, has long been positioned as 'the great family nourisher'. It caught on because of milk shortages and poor health conditions and people saw a need for a nutritional supplement. SB built its own supply chain, worked hard at paring costs and pricing and markets its drink as a nutrient for all seasons and all types. Its supply chain now reaches 375,000 outlets across India. Horlicks refill packages and Horlicks biscuits give consumers the same nutrition at a fraction of the cost of a jar. The Horlicks brand has also been launched into new areas, from Junior Horlicks and Mothers' Horlicks for pregnant or breast-feeding women, to Horlicks for sports, convalescence, the elderly or kids during the monsoon fever period.

Unilever's early, troubled decade and a half in China culminated in recent sweeping restructuring of its Chinese operations, and careful adaptation to the vagaries of operating in this populous market. Its 14 joint ventures with local companies in sectors ranging from detergents, food and wine to ice-creams, toothpaste and chemicals are now brought under three companies: home and personal care; ice-cream; and food and beverages. A crucial change has been to become more local. R&D is adapted to Chinese tastes and local remedies. Drawing from Hindustan Lever's considerable expertise on selling in rural India, Unilever now targets consumers well beyond China's largest cities and has been increasing the range of prices for its various brands, tapping particularly the lower end of the mar-ket. For example, Unilever sells pricier Omo laundry detergents to the wealthy, urban consumer who has a washing machine and is prepared to pay a premium for the detergent. To compete with low-priced mass market offerings from local upstarts, it also offers its cheaper Sunlight soap to consumers with more modest means.

Increasingly, multinational companies such as Unilever, Procter & Gamble, Nestlé and Coca-Cola are discovering that consumers in emerging markets such as India and China will remain hard to get unless they develop value propositions that appeal to the mass market. Products transplanted from affluent, developed nations tend to appeal to a relatively small elite. International companies have to delve deeper into the local consumer base in order to tap the potential of the 'billion-consumer' markets.

SOURCES: Niraj Dawar and Amitava Chattopadhyay, 'The new language of emerging markets', *Financial Times, Mastering Management* (13 November 2000), pp. 6–7; David Gardner, 'Slim pickings for the international brand in India', *Financial Times* (10 October 2000), p. 19; 'How Horlicks won an empire', *Financial Times* (10 October 2000), p. 19; Rahul Jacob, 'A Chinese clean-up operation', *Financial Times* (18 May 2000), p. 18; Niraj Dawar and Tony Frost, 'Competing with giants: Survival strategies for emerging market companies', *Harvard Business Review* (March–April 1999), pp. 119–29.

Table 5.1

Indicators of market potential

1. Demographic characteristics	**4. Technological factors**
Size of population	Level of technological skills
Rate of population growth	Existing production technology
Degree of urbanisation	Existing consumption technology
Population density	Education levels
Age structure and composition of the population	
	5. Sociocultural factors
2. Geographic characteristics	Dominant values
Physical size of a country	Lifestyle patterns
Topographical characteristics	Ethnic groups
Climate conditions	Linguistic fragmentation
3. Economic factors	**6. National goals and plans**
GDP per capita	Industry priorities
Income distribution	Infrastructure investment plans
Rate of growth of GNP	
Ratio of investment to GNP	

SOURCE: Susan P. Douglas, C. Samuel Craig and Warren Keegan, 'Approaches to assessing international marketing opportunities for small and medium-sized businesses', *Columbia Journal of World Business*, Fall 1982, pp. 26–32. Copyright 1982, 1999, *Columbia Journal of World Business*. Reprinted with permission. Also see Tamer S. Cavusil, 'Measuring the potential of emerging markets: an indexing approach', *Business Horizons*, January–February 1997, pp. 87–91.

After listing possible international markets, the company must screen and rank each one on several factors, including market size, market growth, cost of doing business, competitive advantage and risk level. The goal is to determine the potential of each market, using indicators like those shown in Table 5.1. Then the marketer must decide which markets offer the greatest long-run return on investment.

Making the 'go' or 'no-go' decision requires management to invest time and effort in researching the potential challenges and opportunities facing the company. Increasingly, a vast array of resources is available on the Internet. These resources offer managers a way to research prospective target markets and customers as well as gain critical information about doing business in unfamiliar countries and market environments. Market research, therefore, is key to understanding how the company may break into overseas markets or to improve their existing international marketing practices and contacts.[15]

deciding how to enter the market

Once a company has decided to market in a foreign country, it must determine the best mode of entry. Its choices are exporting, joint venturing and direct investment. Figure 5.3 shows these routes to servicing foreign markets, along with the options that each one offers. As we can see, each succeeding strategy involves more commitment and risk, but also more control and potential profits.

exporting

The simplest way to enter a foreign market is through exporting. The company may passively export its surpluses from time to time, or it may make an active commitment to expand exports to a particular market. In either case, the company produces all its goods in its home country. It may or may not modify them for the export market. Exporting involves the least change in the company's product lines, organisation, investments or mission.

■ Indirect exporting

Companies typically start with indirect exporting, working through independent home-based international marketing intermediaries. Indirect exporting involves less

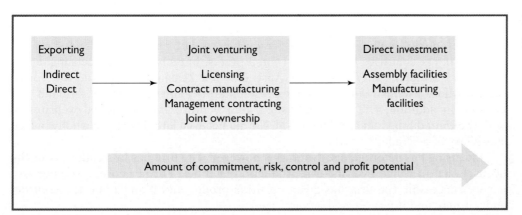

Figure 5.3

Market entry strategies

investment because the firm does not require an overseas sales force or set of contacts. It also involves less risk. These home-based intermediaries – export merchants or agents, cooperative organisations, government export agencies and export-management companies – bring know-how and services to the relationship, so the seller normally makes fewer mistakes.

■ Direct exporting

Sellers may eventually move into direct exporting, whereby they handle their own exports. The investment and risk are somewhat greater in this strategy, but so is the potential return. A company can conduct direct exporting in several ways. It can set up a domestic export department that carries out export activities. Or it can set up an overseas sales branch that handles sales, distribution and perhaps promotion. The sales branch gives the seller more presence and programme control in the foreign market and often serves as a display centre and customer service centre. Or the company can send home-based salespeople abroad at certain times in order to find business. Finally, the company can do its exporting either through foreign-based distributors that buy and own the goods or through foreign-based agents that sell the goods on behalf of the company.

joint venturing

Joint venturing

Entering foreign markets by joining with foreign companies to produce or market a product or service.

A second method of entering a foreign market is **joint venturing** – joining with foreign companies to produce or market products or services. Joint venturing differs from exporting in that the company joins with a partner to sell or market abroad. It differs from direct investment in that an association is formed with someone in the foreign country. There are four types of joint venture: licensing, contract manufacturing, management contracting and joint ownership.

■ Licensing

Licensing

A method of entering a foreign market in which the company enters into an agreement with a licensee in the foreign market, offering the right to use a manufacturing process, trademark, patent, trade secret or other item of value for a fee or royalty.

Licensing is a simple way for a manufacturer to enter international marketing. The company enters into an agreement with a *licensee* in the foreign market. For a fee or royalty, the licensee buys the right to use the company's manufacturing process, trademark, patent, trade secret or other item of value. The company thus gains entry into the market at little risk; the licensee gains production expertise or a well-known product or brand name without having to start from scratch.

East European brewers such as Czech Republic's Pilsner Urquell and the Budvar Company have sought to strengthen their international market positions through licensing the production of their beer brands in breweries abroad. Coca-Cola markets internationally by licensing bottlers around the world and supplying them with the syrup needed to produce the product. And in an effort to bring online retail investing to people abroad, online brokerage E*Trade has to date launched E*Trade-branded websites in six countries outside the United States, initially forming licensing agreements and launching sites in Canada, Australia–New Zealand, France and the Nordic region, whose Swedish site also serves residents of Denmark, Norway, Finland and Iceland. In addition, E*Trade established joint ventures and launched websites in both the United Kingdom and Japan. The Nordic licensee later became a wholly owned subsidiary of E*Trade.[16]

Licensing has potential disadvantages, however. The firm has less control over the licensee than it would over its own production facilities. Furthermore, if the licensee is very successful, the firm has given up these profits, and if and when the contract ends, it may find it has created a competitor.

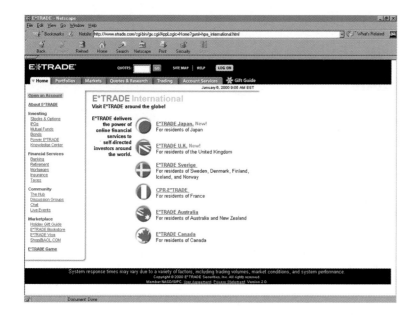

Online brokerage E*Trade used licensing agreements to launch sites in Canada, Australia–New Zealand, France and the Nordic region, whose Swedish site also serves residents of Denmark, Norway, Finland and Iceland.

SOURCE: E*Trade Securities, Inc.

■ Contract manufacturing

Another option is **contract manufacturing**. The company contracts with manufacturers in the foreign market to produce its product or provide its service. Many western firms have used this mode for entering Taiwanese and South Korean markets.

The drawbacks of contract manufacturing are the decreased control over the manufacturing process and the loss of potential profits on manufacturing. The benefits are the chance to start faster, with less risk, and the later opportunity either to form a partnership with or to buy out the local manufacturer.

Contract manufacturing
A joint venture in which a company contracts with manufacturers in a foreign market to produce the product.

■ Management contracting

Under **management contracting**, the domestic firm supplies management know-how to a foreign company that supplies the capital. The domestic firm exports management services rather than products. Hilton uses this arrangement in managing hotels around the world. Management contracting is a low-risk method of getting into a foreign market, and it yields income from the beginning. The arrangement is even more attractive if the contracting firm has an option to buy a share in the managed company later on. The arrangement is not sensible, however, if the company can put its scarce management talent to better uses or if it can make greater profits by undertaking the whole venture. Management contracting also prevents the company from setting up its own operations for a period of time.

Management contracting
A joint venture in which the domestic firm supplies the management know-how to a foreign company that supplies the capital; the domestic firm exports management services rather than products.

■ Joint ownership

Joint-ownership ventures consist of one company joining forces with foreign investors to create a local business in which they share joint ownership and control. A company may buy an interest in a local firm, or the two parties may form a new business venture. Joint ownership may be needed for economic or political reasons. A foreign government may require joint ownership as a condition for entry. Or the firm may lack the financial, physical or managerial resources to undertake the venture alone.

Joint ownership has certain drawbacks. The partners may disagree over investment, marketing or other policies. To enjoy partnership benefits, collaborators must

Joint ownership
A joint venture in which a company joins investors in a foreign market to create a local business in which the company shares joint ownership and control.

clarify their expectations and objectives and work hard to secure a win–win outcome for all parties concerned.

direct investment

Direct investment
Entering a foreign market by developing foreign-based assembly or manufacturing facilities.

The biggest involvement in a foreign market comes through **direct investment** – the development of foreign-based assembly or manufacturing facilities. If a company has gained experience in exporting, and if the foreign market is large enough, foreign production facilities offer many advantages:

1. The firm may have lower costs in the form of cheaper labour or raw materials, foreign government investment incentives and freight savings.
2. The firm may improve its image in the host country because it creates jobs.
3. Generally, a firm develops a deeper relationship with government, customers, local suppliers and distributors, allowing it to adapt its products better to the local market.
4. Finally, the firm keeps full control over the investment and therefore can develop manufacturing and marketing policies that serve its long-term international objectives.

The main disadvantage of direct investment is that the firm faces many risks, such as restricted or devalued currencies, declining markets or government takeovers. In some cases, a firm has no choice but to accept these risks if it wants to operate in the host country.

There are therefore direct and indirect ways of entering a foreign market. Firms seeking to market goods and services in a foreign market should evaluate the alternative modes of entry and decide upon the most cost-effective path that would ensure long-term performance in that market.

deciding on the global marketing programme

Standardised marketing mix
An international marketing strategy for using basically the same product, advertising, distribution channels and other elements of the marketing mix in all the company's international markets.

The marketing programme for each foreign market must be carefully planned. Managers must first decide on the precise customer target or targets to be served. Then managers have to decide how, if at all, to adapt the firm's marketing mix to local conditions. To do this requires a good understanding of country market conditions as well as cultural characteristics of customers in that market. We have already addressed the need for cultural sensitivity. This section will discuss reasons for standardisation versus adaptation for the global market before highlighting specific international marketing mix decisions.

Adapted marketing mix
An international marketing strategy for adjusting the marketing-mix elements to each international target market, bearing more costs but hoping for a larger market share and return.

standardisation or adaptation for international markets?

At one extreme are companies that use a **standardised marketing mix** worldwide, selling largely the same products and using the same marketing approaches worldwide. At the other extreme is an **adapted marketing mix**. In this case, the producer adjusts the marketing mix elements to each target, bearing more costs but hoping for a larger market share and return.

The question of whether to adapt or standardise the marketing mix has been much debated in recent years. The marketing concept holds that marketing programmes will be more effective if tailored to the unique needs of each targeted customer group. If this concept applies within a country, it should apply even more in international markets. Consumers in different countries have widely varied cultural backgrounds, needs and wants, spending power, product preferences and shopping patterns. Because these differences are hard to change, most marketers adapt their products, prices, channels and promotions to fit consumer desires in each country.

However, some global marketers are bothered by what they see as too much adaptation, which raises costs and dilutes global brand power. As a result, many companies have created so-called world brands – more or less the same product sold the same way to all consumers worldwide. Marketers at these companies believe that advances in communication, transportation and travel are turning the world into a common marketplace. These marketers claim that people around the world want basically the same products and lifestyles. Despite what consumers say they want, all consumers want good products at lower prices.

Such arguments ring true. The development of the Internet, the rapid spread of cable and satellite TV around the world, and the creation of telecommunications networks linking previously remote places have all made the world a smaller place. For instance, the disproportionately American programming beamed into homes in the developing nations has sparked a convergence of consumer appetites, particularly among youth. One economist calls these emerging consumers the 'global MTV generation'. 'They prefer Coke to tea, Nikes to sandals, Chicken McNuggets to rice, and credit cards to cash', he says.[17] Fashion trends spread almost instantly, propelled by TV and Internet chat groups. Around the world, news and comment on almost any topic or product is available at the click of a mouse or twist of a dial. The resulting convergence of needs and wants has created global markets for standardised products, particularly among the young middle class.

Proponents of global standardisation claim that international marketers should adapt products and marketing programmes only when local wants cannot be changed or avoided. Standardisation results in lower production, distribution, marketing and management costs, and thus lets the company offer consumers higher quality and more reliable products at lower prices. In fact, some companies have successfully marketed global products – for example, McDonald's hamburgers, Philips razors and Sony Walkmans.

However, even for these 'global' brands, companies make some adaptations. Moreover, the assertion that global standardisation will lead to lower costs and prices, causing more goods to be snapped up by price-sensitive consumers, is debatable. Consider, for example, MTV.

MTV, with its largely global programming, has retrenched along more local lines. Pummelled by dozens of local music channels in Europe, such as Germany's *Viva*, Holland's *The Music Factory*, and Scandinavia's *ZTV*, MTV Europe has had to drop its pan-European programming, which featured a large amount of American and British pop along with local European favourites. In its place, the division created regional channels broadcast by four separate MTV stations – MTV: UK & Ireland, MTV: Northern Europe, MTV: Central Europe, and MTV: Southern Europe. Each of the four channels shows programmes tailored to music tastes of its local market, along with more traditional pan-European pop selections. Within each region, MTV further subdivides its programming. For example, within the United Kingdom, MTV offers sister stations M2 and VH-1, along with three new digital channels: MTV Extra, MTV Base and VH-1 Classic. Says the head of MTV Europe, 'We hope to offer every MTV fan something he or she will like to watch any time of the day.'[18]

In these cases, incremental revenues from adapting products far exceeded the incremental costs.

So which approach is best – global standardisation or adaptation? Clearly, global standardisation is not an all-or-nothing proposition but rather a matter of degree. Companies should look for more standardisation to help keep down costs and prices and to build greater global brand power. But they must not replace long-run marketing thinking with short-run financial thinking. Although standardisation saves money, marketers must make certain that they offer what consumers in each country want.[19]

Many possibilities exist between the extremes of standardisation and complete adaptation. For example, although Philips dishwashers, clothes washers and other major appliances share the same interiors worldwide, their outer styling and features are designed to meet the preferences of consumers in different countries. Coca-Cola sells virtually the same Coke beverage worldwide, and it pulls advertisements for specific markets from a common pool of ads designed to have cross-cultural appeal. However, Coca-Cola is less sweet or less carbonated in certain countries. The company also sells a variety of other beverages created specifically for the tastebuds of local markets and modifies its distribution channels according to local conditions.

Similarly, McDonald's uses the same basic operating formula in its restaurants around the world but adapts its menu to local tastes. For example, it uses chili sauce instead of ketchup on its hamburgers in Mexico. In India, where cows are considered sacred, McDonald's serves chicken, fish, vegetable burgers and the Maharaja Mac – two all-mutton patties, special sauce, lettuce, cheese, pickles, onions on a sesame-seed bun. In Vienna, its restaurants include 'McCafes', which offer coffee blended to local tastes, and in Korea, it sells roast pork on a bun with a garlicky soy sauce.

The decision about which aspects of the marketing mix to standardise and which to adapt should be taken on the basis of target market conditions. Firms are often unwilling to modify their product offering for foreign markets because of 'cultural arrogance'. German and American machine-tool manufacturers, for example, saw their world market shares dive over the 1980s due, in part, to their reluctance to adapt products and marketing approaches in the face of changing customer needs in their home and foreign markets. 'What's good for Germany is good enough for the world market' was the view typifying a large proportion of German machine-tool producers which formed the focus of a study into international marketing strategies in the UK market. This cultural arrogance has been termed the 'self-reference criterion' and has been a significant factor in accounting for poor export performance.[20]

Some international marketers suggest that companies should 'think globally but act locally'. They advocate a 'glocal' strategy in which the firm standardises certain core marketing elements and localises others. The corporate level gives strategic direction; local units focus on the individual consumer differences. They conclude: global marketing, yes; global standardisation, not necessarily.

Let us now examine marketing mix decisions with regard to global marketing planning.

product

Five strategies allow for adapting product and promotion to a foreign market (see Figure 5.4).[21] We first discuss the three product strategies and then turn to the two promotion strategies.

Straight product extension
Marketing a product in a foreign market without any change.

Straight product extension means marketing a product in a foreign market without any change. Straight extension has been successful in some cases. Coca-Cola, Kellogg cereals, Heineken beer and Black & Decker tools are all sold successfully in about the same form around the world. Straight extension is tempting because it involves no additional product-development costs, manufacturing changes or new

The Italian execution of a Pirelli campaign shows the global application of many of today's ads.
SOURCE: Pirelli & C

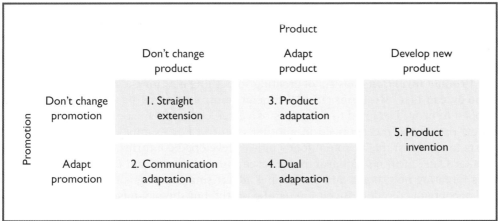

Figure 5.4

Five international product and promotion strategies

promotion. But it can be costly in the long run if products fail to satisfy foreign consumers.

Product adaptation involves changing the product to meet local conditions or wants. For example, Philips began to make a profit in Japan only after it reduced the size of its coffee makers to fit into smaller Japanese kitchens and its shavers to fit smaller Japanese hands. The Japanese construction machinery maker, Komatsu, had to alter the design of the door handles of earth movers sold in Finland: drivers wearing thick gloves in winter found it impossible to grasp the door handles, which were too small (obviously designed to fit the fingers of the average Japanese, but not the double-cladded ones of larger European users!). And Nokia customised its 6100 series cellular phone for every major market. It built in rudimentary voice recognition for Asia

Product adaptation
Adapting a product to meet local conditions or wants in foreign markets.

IBM Global Services communicates its global reach by using a standardised advertising theme in dozens of countries around the world: 'People Who Think. People Who Do. People Who Get It.' These ads are from Canada and the United Kingdom.

SOURCE: (right) IBM UK. *Agency:* Ogilvy One

where keyboards are a problem and raised the ring volume so the phone could be heard on crowded Asian streets.[22]

Product invention

Creating new products or services for foreign markets.

Product invention consists of creating something new for the foreign market. This strategy can take two forms. It might mean reintroducing earlier product forms that happen to be well adapted to the needs of a given country. Or a company might create a new product to meet a need in another country. For example, an enormous need exists for low-cost, high-protein foods in less developed countries. Companies such as Quaker Oats, Swift and Monsanto are researching the nutrition needs of these countries, creating new foods, and developing advertising campaigns to gain product trial and acceptance. Product invention can be costly, but the pay-offs are worthwhile.

promotion

Companies can either adopt the same promotion strategy in different countries or change it for each local market.

Consider advertising messages. Some global companies use a standardised advertising theme around the world. For example, IBM Global Services runs virtually identical 'People Who Think. People Who Do. People Who Get It.' ads in dozens of countries around the world.

Sometimes the copy is varied in minor ways to adjust for language differences. Colours may also be changed to avoid taboos in other countries. For example, in Spain, packaging that uses red and yellow, the colours of the Spanish flag, may be seen as an offence to Spanish patriotism. In Greece, purple should be avoided as it has funeral

marketing highlight 5.3

Mind your language

Many global companies have had difficulty crossing the language barrier, with results ranging from mild embarrassment to outright failure. Seemingly innocuous brand names and advertising phrases can take on unintended or hidden meanings when translated into other languages. Careless translations can make a marketer look downright foolish to foreign consumers.

We've all run across examples when buying products from other countries. Here's one from a firm in Taiwan attempting to instruct children on how to install a ramp on a garage for toy cars: 'Before you play with, fix waiting plate by yourself as per below diagram. But after you once fixed it, you can play with as is and no necessary to fix off again.'

Many western firms are guilty of such atrocities when marketing abroad. The classic language blunders involve standardised brand names that do not translate well. When Coca-Cola first marketed Coke in China in the 1920s, it developed a group of Chinese characters that, when pronounced, sounded like the product name. Unfortunately, the characters actually translated to mean 'bite the wax tadpole'. Now, the characters on Chinese Coke bottles translate as 'happiness in the mouth'.

Car-maker Rolls-Royce avoided the name Silver Mist in German markets, where *mist* means 'manure'. Sunbeam, however, entered the German market with its Mist Stick hair curling iron. As should have been expected, the Germans had little use for a 'manure wand'. A similar fate awaited Colgate when it introduced a toothpaste in France called Cue, the name of a notorious porno magazine. One well-intentioned firm sold its shampoo in Brazil under the name Evitol. It soon realised it was claiming to sell a 'dandruff contraceptive'.

Interbrand of London, the firm that created household names such as Prozac and Acura, recently developed a brand-name 'hall of shame' list, which contained these and other foreign brand names that are unlikely to cross the English language barrier: Krapp toilet paper (Denmark), Crapsy Fruit cereal (France), Happy End toilet paper (Germany), Mukk yogurt (Italy), Zit lemonade (Germany), Poo curry powder (Argentina) and Pschitt lemonade (France).

Travellers often encounter well-intentioned advice from service firms that takes on meanings very different from those intended. The menu in one Swiss restaurant proudly stated: 'Our wines leave you nothing to hope for.' Signs in a Japanese hotel pronounced: 'You are invited to take advantage of the chambermaid.' At a laundry in Rome, it was: 'Ladies, leave your clothes here and spend the afternoon having a good time.' The brochure at a Tokyo car rental offered this sage advice: 'When passenger of foot heave in sight, tootle the horn. Trumpet him melodiously at first, but if he still obstacles your passage, tootle him with vigour.' And a Chinese grocery retailer in Kuala Lumpur offers to sell all sorts of sundry goods, although foreign visitors may be somewhat wary about stepping into the store. Why? Because it is called 'Sin Tit'.

Advertising themes often lose – or gain – something in the translation. The Coors beer slogan 'get loose with Coors' in Spanish came out as 'get the runs with Coors'. Coca-Cola's 'Coke adds life' theme in Japanese translated into 'Coke brings your ancestors back from the dead'. In Chinese, the KFC slogan 'finger-lickin' good' came out as 'eat your fingers off'. Even when the language is the same, word usage may differ from country to country. Thus, the British ad line for Electrolux vacuum cleaners – 'Nothing sucks like an Electrolux' – would capture few customers in the United States.

SOURCES: See Matt Forney, Dimon Fluendy and Emily Thornton, 'A matter of wording', *Far Eastern Economic Review* (10 October 1996), pp. 72–3; David A. Ricks, 'Products that crashed into the language barrier', *Business and Society Review* (Spring 1983), pp. 46–50; David A. Ricks, 'Perspectives: Translation blunders in international business', *Journal of Language for International Business*, **7**, 2 (1996), pp. 50–5; Ken Friedenreich, 'The lingua too France', *World Trade* (April 1998), p. 98; and Richard P. Carpenter, 'What they meant to say was . . .', *Boston Globe* (2 August 1998), p. M6.

associations. Black is an unlucky colour for the Chinese, white is a mourning colour in Japan, and green is associated with jungle sickness in Malaysia. Even names must be changed. In Sweden, Helene Curtis changed the name of its 'Every Night Shampoo' to 'Every Day' because Swedish consumers usually wash their hair in the morning. (See Marketing Highlight 5.3 for more on language blunders in international marketing.)

Other companies follow a strategy of **communication adaptation**, fully adapting their advertising messages or techniques to local markets. Mass media communications are

Communication adaptation
A global communication strategy of fully adapting advertising messages to local markets.

less effective in emerging markets such as China or India. Their vast rural population is dispersed and has limited access to broadcast media. Unilever used video vans that toured the villages screening films in the local language, interspersed with advertising for Unilever products.

Media also need to be adapted internationally because media availability varies from country to country. TV advertising time varies across Europe, for instance, ranging from four hours a day in France to none in Scandinavian countries, where print advertising is preferred to TV ads. Advertisers must buy time months in advance, and they have little control over air times. The types of print media also vary in effectiveness. For example, magazines are a popular medium in Italy and a minor one in Austria. Newspapers are national in the United Kingdom, but are only local in Spain.

Companies adopt a dual adaptation strategy when both the product and communication messages have to be modified to meet the needs and expectations of target customers in different country markets.

> For example, the French food multinational, Danone, not only had to bring its products closer to consumer tastes, but also adapted advertising messages to suit different European market expectations. In France, yoghurt is typically sold as a plain yoghurt, a symbol of good health. Fruit and flavourings come later. Advertising emphasises the health logic. In the UK, the product is associated with pleasure, of a sort enjoyed by adults. Fruits add to the pleasure of eating yoghurt. Plain, flavoured yoghurt (without the fruit) is considered a lesser yoghurt, one without the pleasure. In Spain or Portugal, where fruit is abundant, consumers prefer plain yoghurt, eaten as much by children as by adults. In Italy, consumers prefer blended yoghurt, while flavoured varieties are positioned for very young children. Advertising messages are therefore adjusted accordingly to reflect these preferences.

price

Companies also face many problems in setting their international prices.

Regardless of how companies go about pricing their products, their foreign prices will probably be higher than their domestic prices. A Gucci handbag may sell for 150 euros in Italy and 250 euros in Singapore. Why? Gucci faces a price escalation problem. It must add the cost of transportation, tariffs, importer margin, wholesaler margin and retailer margin to its factory price. Depending on these added costs, the product may have to sell for two to five times as much in another country to make the same profit.

Another problem involves setting a price for goods that a company ships to its foreign subsidiaries. If the company charges a foreign subsidiary too much, it may end up paying higher tariff duties even while paying lower income taxes in that country. If the company charges its subsidiary too little, it can be charged with *dumping* – that is, pricing exports at levels less than their costs or less than the prices charged in its home market. For example, the EU imposed anti-dumping duties of as much as 96.0 per cent on imports of broadcasting cameras made by some Japanese companies after an investigation by the European Commission found that Japanese exporters had, through unfair pricing, increased their share of the EU studio video camera market in the early 1990s.[23]

Recent economic and technological forces have had an impact on global pricing. For example, in the EU, the move by 11 member countries to a single currency will certainly reduce the amount of price differentiation. In 1998, for instance, a bottle of Gatorade cost 3.5 ecus (European Currency Units) in Germany but only about 0.9 in Spain. Once consumers recognise price differentiation by country, companies will be forced to harmonise prices throughout the countries that have adopted the single

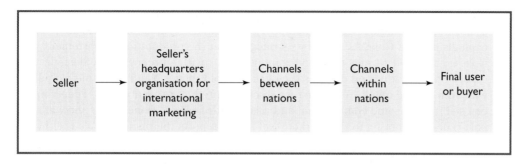

Figure 5.5

Whole-channel concept
for international
marketing

currency. Companies and marketers that offer the most unique or necessary products or services will be least affected by such 'price transparency'. For instance, Mail Boxes, Etc., which has 350 stores in Europe, believes that customers who need to send faxes won't refuse to do so because it costs more in Paris than in Italy.[24]

The Internet will also make global price differences more obvious. When firms sell their wares over the Internet, customers can see how much products sell for in different countries. They might even be able to order a given product directly from the company location or dealer offering the lowest price. This will force companies toward more standardised international pricing.[25]

distribution channels

The international company must take a *whole-channel* view of the problem of distributing products to final consumers. Figure 5.5 shows the three main links between the *seller* and the *final buyer*. The first link, the *seller's headquarters organisation*, supervises the channels and is part of the channel itself. The second link, *channels between nations*, moves the products to the borders of the foreign nations. The third link, *channels within nations*, moves the products from their foreign entry point to the final consumers. Some manufacturers may think their job is done once the product leaves their hands, but they would do well to pay more attention to its handling within foreign countries.

Channels of distribution within countries vary greatly from nation to nation. First, there are the large differences in the *numbers and types of intermediaries* serving each foreign market.

> For example, a European company marketing in China must operate through a frustrating maze of state-controlled wholesalers and retailers. Chinese distributors often carry competitors' products and frequently refuse to share even basic sales and marketing information with their suppliers. Hustling for sales is an alien concept to Chinese distributors, who are used to selling all they can obtain. Working with or getting around this system sometimes requires substantial time and investment.[26]

When Coke first entered China, for example, customers bicycled up to bottling plants to get their soft drinks. Many shopkeepers still don't have enough electricity to run soft-drink coolers. Now, Coca-Cola is setting up direct-distribution channels, investing heavily in refrigerators and trucks, and upgrading wiring so that more retailers can install coolers. Moreover, it is always on the lookout for innovative distribution approaches:

> Stroll through any residential area in a Chinese city and sooner or later you'll encounter a senior citizen with a red arm band eyeing strangers suspiciously. These are the pensioners who staff the neighborhood committees, which act as street-level

watchdogs for the ruling Communist Party. In Shanghai, however, some of these socialist guardians have been signed up by the ultimate symbol of American capitalism, Coca-Cola. As part of its strategy to get the product to the customer, Coke approached 14 neighborhood committees . . . with a proposal. The head of Coke's Shanghai division outlines the deal: 'We told them, "You have some old people who aren't doing much. Why don't we stock our product in your office? Then you can sell it, earn some commission, and raise a bit of cash."' Done. So . . . how are the party snoops adapting to the market? Not badly, reports the manager. 'We use the neighborhood committees as a sales force,' he says. Sales aren't spectacular, but because the committees supervise housing projects with up to 200 families, they have proved to be useful vehicles for building brand awareness.[27]

Another difference lies in the size and character of retail units abroad. Whereas large-scale retail chains dominate the British and US scene, most retailing in the rest of Europe and other countries, such as Japan and India, is done by many small independent retailers. Getting to grips with a foreign country's distribution structure is often crucial to achieving effective market access. The international firm must therefore invest in acquiring knowledge about each foreign market's channel features and decide on how best to break into complex or entrenched distribution systems.

deciding on the global marketing organisation

The key to success in any marketing strategy is the firm's ability to implement the chosen strategy. Because of the firm's distance from its foreign markets, international marketing strategy implementation is particularly difficult. The firm must have an organisation structure that fits with the international environment.

Companies manage their international marketing activities in at least three different ways. Most companies first organise an export department, then create an international division and finally become a global organisation.

export department

Export department
A form of international marketing organisation that comprises a sales manager and a few assistants whose job is to organise the shipping out of the company's goods to foreign markets.

A firm normally gets into international marketing by simply shipping out its goods. If its international sales expand, the company organises an **export department** with a sales manager and a few assistants. As sales increase, the export department can then expand to include various marketing services, so that it can actively go after business. If the firm moves into joint ventures or direct investment, the export department will no longer be adequate.

international division

International division
A form of international marketing organisation in which the division handles all of the firm's international activities. Marketing, manufacturing, research, planning and specialist staff are organised into operating units according to geography or product groups, or as an international subsidiary responsible for its own sales and profitability.

Many companies get involved in several international markets and ventures. A company may export to one country, license to another, have a joint-ownership venture in a third and own a subsidiary in a fourth. Sooner or later it will create an **international division** or subsidiary to handle all its international activities.

The international division's corporate staff consists of marketing, manufacturing, research, finance, planning and personnel specialists. They plan for and provide services to various operating units. Operating units may be organised in one of three ways. They may be *geographical* organisations, with country managers who are responsible for salespeople, sales branches, distributors and licensees in their respective countries. Or the operating units may be *world product groups*, each responsible for worldwide sales of different product groups. Finally, operating units may be *international subsidiaries*, each responsible for its own sales and profits.

global organisation

Several firms have passed beyond the international division stage and become truly **global organisations**. They stop thinking of themselves as national marketers that sell abroad and start thinking of themselves as global marketers. The top corporate management and staff plan worldwide manufacturing facilities, marketing policies, financial flows and logistical systems. The global operating units report directly to the chief executive or executive committee of the organisation, not to the head of an international division. Executives are trained in worldwide operations, not just domestic or international. The company recruits management from many countries, buys components and supplies where they cost the least, and invests where the expected returns are greatest.

Moving into the twenty-first century, major companies must become more global if they hope to compete. As foreign companies successfully invade the domestic market, domestic companies must move more aggressively into foreign markets. They will have to change from companies that treat their foreign operations as secondary concerns, to companies that view the entire world as a single borderless market.[28]

Global organisation
A form of international organisation whereby top corporate management and staff plan worldwide manufacturing or operational facilities, marketing policies, financial flows and logistical systems. The global operating unit reports directly to the chief executive, not to an international divisional head.

summary

Companies today can no longer afford to pay attention only to their domestic market, regardless of its size. Many industries are global industries, and those firms that operate globally achieve lower costs and higher brand awareness. At the same time, *global marketing* is risky because of variable exchange rates, unstable governments, protectionist tariffs and trade barriers, and several other factors. Given the potential gains and risks of international marketing, companies need to adopt a systematic approach to making international marketing decisions. We examined six major international marketing decisions.

First, managers must understand the *global marketing environment*, especially the *international trade system*. The company must assess each foreign market's *economic*, *political–legal* and *cultural characteristics*. Second, it must decide whether to go international based on a consideration of the potential risks and benefits. Third, it must decide on the volume of international sales it wants, how many countries it wants to market in, and which specific *country markets* it wants *to enter*. This decision calls for weighing the probable rate of return on investment against the level of risk.

Fourth, the company must *decide how to enter* each chosen market – whether through *exporting*, *joint venturing* or *direct investment*. Many companies start as exporters, move to joint ventures and finally make a direct investment in foreign markets. Increasingly, however, firms – domestic or international – use joint ventures and even direct investments to enter a new country market for the first time. In *exporting*, the company enters a foreign market by sending and selling products through international marketing intermediaries (indirect exporting) or the company's own department, branch, or sales representative or agents (direct exporting). When establishing a *joint venture*, a company enters foreign markets by joining with foreign companies to produce or market a product or service. In *licensing*, the company enters a foreign market by contracting with a licensee in the foreign market, offering the right to use a manufacturing process, trademark, patent, trade secret, or other item of value for a fee or royalty.

Fifth, the company must decide on its global marketing programme. Managers must decide on the level of *adaptation* or *standardisation* of their *product, promotion, price* and *distribution channels* for each foreign market. At one extreme, global companies use a *standardised marketing mix* worldwide. Others use an *adapted marketing mix*, in which they adjust the marketing mix to each target market, bearing more costs but hoping for a larger market share and return.

Finally, the firm must develop an effective organisational structure for international marketing. Most firms start with an *export department* and graduate to an *international division*. A few become *global organisations*, with worldwide marketing planned and managed by the top officers of the company, who view the entire world as a single borderless market.

discussing the issues

1. The world is shrinking rapidly with the advent of faster communication, transportation, and financial flows. The terms *global industry* and *global firm* are becoming more common. Define these terms and provide an example of each. Explain your examples.

2. When exporting goods to a foreign country, a marketer may be faced with various trade restrictions. Discuss the effects these restrictions might have on an exporter's marketing mix: (a) tariffs, (b) quotas and (c) embargoes.

3. With all the problems facing companies that 'go global', why are so many companies choosing to expand internationally? What are the advantages of expanding beyond the domestic market?

4. Imported products are usually more expensive, but not always: a Nikon camera is cheaper in London than in Tokyo. Why are foreign prices sometimes higher and sometimes lower than domestic prices for exports?

5. Before going abroad, a company should try to define its international marketing objectives, policies and modes of entry. Assume that you are a product manager for Nokia. Outline a plan for expanding your operations and marketing efforts into Africa.

6. Which type of international marketing organisation would you suggest for the following companies: (a) Xerox selling a wide range of photocopying and document processing systems across the globe; (b) a European perfume manufacturer that plans to expand into Asia; and (c) Ericsson selling its full line of products in the Far East?

applying the concepts

1. 'Defend Our Forests—Clear-cut the WTO!', 'WTO Breeds Greed', 'WTO: Fix It or Nix It!' These statements were issued by protesters at the 1999 World Trade Organisation talks in Seattle, Washington. The protests even led to riots, and the National Guard had to be called to restore order. Why all the mobilisation against globalisation? It used to be that free trade and globalisation talks involved mostly discussions about tariffs and quotas. Now the two equate with culture, sovereignty and power.

Trade talks were once held in smoke-filled rooms by diplomats. Today, they are conducted via television and the World Wide Web. The Seattle protesters feel damaged by globalisation. They argue that globalisation is about exploitation and environmental destruction. They feel that it will result in the assimilation of people, markets and cultures into a more generic whole. For more information, visit the following websites: the International Trade Association (www.ita.doc.gov), the *1998 World*

Fact Book, a CIA publication (www.odic.gov/cia/publications/factbook/index.html), the World Bank (www.worldbank.org) and the World Trade Organisation (www.wto.org); also visit www.paris21.org/betterworld for more information on 'A better world for all' that reflects the ongoing concerns about globalisation. The report is prepared jointly by the UN, World Bank, IMF and OECD.

✦ What does the World Trade Organisation attempt to do? Who are the member nations?

✦ Why were there so many protesters against globalisation at the WTO's Seattle conference? How should the WTO proceed in the face of such protests?

✦ Write a short position paper either defending or rejecting globalisation.

✦ What are the ramifications of China joining the World Trade Organisation?

2. Nowhere is international competition more apparent than in the digital camera market. Overnight, the advent of digital cameras has changed the way many photographers view their equipment. Digital cameras offer opportunities for reproduction and Internet viewing unrivalled by more traditional products. However, the market is also uncharted, chaotic, and increasingly crowded, with more than 20 manufacturers worldwide. The latest entrant is film giant Fuji (www.fujifilm.com). As the world's number-two producer, Fuji now plans to meet or beat Kodak (www.kodak.com), Sony (www.sony.com), Olympus (www.olympus.com), and Konica (www.konica.com) in digital camera products. Fuji introduced its first digital cameras in its own backyard – Japan, which is also a Sony stronghold. One factor motivating the move into digital cameras was its inability to erode Kodak's worldwide share of the film market. If the wave of the future turns out to be digital, Fuji plans to ride the wave's crest for as long as it can.

✦ Analyse Fuji's strategy of entering the digital camera market. What challenges is Fuji most likely to face in the digital camera market? How might Fuji's traditional strengths in film aid its efforts in the new digital camera market?

✦ What world markets should Fuji consider after Japan? Explain.

✦ If you were the marketing manager of Fuji, what advertising strategy would you suggest for Fuji's new product venture? What distribution strategy?

✦ What actions will Kodak, Olympus, Konica and Sony probably take to counter Fuji's entry?

references

1. 'Financial Indicators. Top exporters', *The Economist* (15 April 2000), p. 145.

2. Taken from Philip Davis, 'New life abroad for niche products', Financial Times Survey: Belgium, p. V, in *Financial Times* (21 November 2000).

3. 'WTO predicts global trade to rise 6.5%', *Financial Times* (14 April 2000), p. 12; 'All free traders now?', *The Economist* (7 December 1996), pp. 25–9.

4. For more on non-tariff and other barriers, see Carla Rapoport, 'The big split', *Fortune* (6 May 1991), pp. 38–48; Mark Maremont, 'Protectionism is king of the road', *Business Week* (13 May 1991), pp. 57–8.

5. Douglas Harbrecht and Owen Ullmann, 'Finally GATT may fly', *Business Week* (29 December 1993), pp. 36–7; Jon Marks, 'New kids on the Eurotrading bloc', *Financial Times, FT Exporter*, 11 (Spring 1996), p. 7; 'Special article: World trade: Fifty years on', *The Economist* (16 May 1998), pp. 21–3; and Helene Cooper, 'The millennium – Trade & Commerce: Trading blocks', *Wall Street Journal* (11 January 1999), p. R50.

6. Martin Wolf, 'Welcoming China to the world', *Financial Times* (17 May 2000), p. 23; James Kynge, 'Rising giant "enters the world"', *Financial Times Survey* (13 November 2000), p. I; 'Fifty years on', *The Economist* (16 May 1998), pp. 21–5; 'School's brief: trade winds', *The Economist* (8 November 1997), pp. 124–5; 'All free traders now', *The Economist* (7 December 1996), pp. 25–7.

7. Stanley Reed, 'We have lift off! The strong launch of the euro is hailed around the world', *Business Week* (18 January 1999), pp. 34–7; Quentin Peel, 'Mapping Europe's future', *Financial Times* (19 June 2000), p. 26.

8. James Welsh, 'Enter the Euro', *World Trade* (January 1999), pp. 34–8.

9. See 'Around Europe in 40 years', *The Economist* (31 May 1999), p. S4; Colin Egan and Peter McKiernan, *Inside Fortress Europe: Strategies for the single market*, the EIU series (Wokingham, Berks: Addison-Wesley, 1994); Brian Rothery, *What Maastricht Means for Business* (Aldershot: Gower, 1993).

10. Aaron Robertson, 'North America: Trade brisk despite bumps in the road', *World Trade* (May 1999), pp. 28–32; and Tom Foster, 'The NAFTA Gateway', *Logistics Management and Distribution Report* (May 1999), pp. S10–S11.

11. Larry Rohter, 'Latin America and Europe to talk trade', *New York Times* (26 June 1999), p. 2; David M. Gould, 'Has NAFTA changed North American trade?', *Economic Review – Federal Reserve Bank of Dallas* (First Quarter 1998), pp. 12–23.

12. David Woodruff, 'Ready to shop until they drop', *Business Week* (22 June 1998), pp. 104–8.

13. For further reading, see Leo G. B. Welt, *Trade Without Money: Barter and countertrade* (New York: Harcourt Brace Jovanovic, 1984); Demos Vardiabasis, '"Countertrade": new ways of doing business', *Business to Business* (December 1985), pp. 67–71; Louis Kraar, 'How to sell to cashless buyers', *Fortune* (7 November 1988), pp. 147–54; 'Pepsi to get ships, vodka in $3 billion deal', *Durham Morning Herald* (10 May 1990), p. B5; Cyndee Miller, 'Worldwide money crunch fuels more international barter', *Marketing News* (2 March 1992), p. 5.

14. Gail Edmondson, 'The beauty of global branding', *Business Week* (28 June 1999), pp. 70–5.

15. Websites such as these may be of use to exporters and international marketers seeking market information about exporting. Some are officially sanctioned by government agencies, others are commercial in nature, offering research material and contact opportunities on a subscription basis. The British Chambers of Commerce (www.britishchambers.org.uk/exportzone), British Trade International (www.brittrade.com/emic), Trade UK (www.tradeuk.com), The United States–Asia Environmental Partnership (www.usaep.org/export/index.htm/), Asia Market Research Dot Com (www.asiamarketresearch.com), and Cyberatlas (http://cyberatlas.internet.com) give a global overview of the state of the online marketplace.

16. Robert Neff, 'In Japan, they're goofy about Disney', *Business Week* (12 March 1990), p. 64; and 'In brief: e-trade licensing deal gives it an Israeli link', *American Banker* (11 May 1998).

17. Lawrence Donegan, 'Heavy job rotation: MTV Europe sacks 80 employees in the name of "regionalisation"', *The Guardian* (21 November 1997), p. 19.

18. Karen Benezra, 'Fritos "Round the world"', *Brandweek* (27 March 1995), pp. 32, 35; Cyndee Miller, 'Chasing global dream', *Marketing News* (2 December 1996), pp. 1, 2; and Christian Lorenz, 'MTV Europe launches channels', *Billboard* (27 February 1999), p. 48.

19. See Theodore Levitt, 'The globalization of markets', *Harvard Business Review* (May–June 1983), pp. 92–102; David M. Szymanski, Sundar G.

Bharadwaj and Rajan Varadarajan, 'Standardization versus adaptation of international marketing strategy: An empirical investigation', *Journal of Marketing* (October 1993), pp. 1–17; Ashish Banerjee, 'Global campaigns don't work; multinationals do', *Advertising Age* (18 April 1994), p. 23; Jeryl Whitelock and Carole Pimblett, 'The standardization debate in international marketing', *Journal of Global Marketing* (1997), p. 22; and David A. Aaker and Ericj Joachimsthaler, 'The lure of global branding', *Harvard Business Review* (November–December 1999), pp. 137–44.

20. See George S. Yip, 'Global strategy . . . in a world of nations?', *Sloan Management Review* (Fall 1989), pp. 29–41; Kamran Kashani, 'Beware the pitfalls of global marketing', *Harvard Business Review* (September–October 1989), pp. 91–8; Saeed Saminee and Kendall Roth, 'The influence of global marketing standardization on performance', *Journal of Marketing* (April 1992), pp. 1–17.

21. See Keegan, *Global Marketing Management*, op. cit., pp. 378–81. See also see Peter G. P. Walters and Brian Toyne, 'Product modification and standardization in international markets: strategic options and facilitating policies', *Columbia Journal of World Business* (Winter 1989), pp. 37–44.

22. See Andrew Kupfer, 'How to be a global manager', *Fortune* (14 March 1988), pp. 52–8; Jack Neff, 'Test it in Paris, France, launch it in Paris, Texas', *Advertising Age* (31 May 1999), p. 28.

23. See Guy de Jonquières, 'High duties against Japan', *Financial Times* (4 May 1994), p. 7.

24. Maricris G. Briones, 'The Euro starts here', *Marketing News* (20 July 1998), pp. 1, 39.

25. Ram Charan, 'The rules have changed', *Fortune* (16 March 1998), pp. 159–62.

26. See Maria Shao, 'Laying the foundation for the great mall of China', *Business Week* (25 January 1988), pp. 68–69; and Mark L. Clifford and Nicole Harris, 'Coke pours into China', *Business Week* (28 October 1996), p. 73.

27. Richard Tomlinson, 'The China card', *Fortune* (25 May 1998), p. 82; and Paul Mooney, 'Deals on wheels', *Far East Economic Review* (20 May 1999), p. 53.

28. See Kenichi Ohmae, 'Managing in a borderless world', *Harvard Business Review* (May–June 1989), pp. 152–61; William J. Holstein, 'The stateless corporation', *Business Week* (14 May 1990), pp. 98–105; John A. Byrne and Kathleen Kerwin, 'Borderless management', *Business Week* (23 May 1994), pp. 24–6.

case 5

Making the global tipple: soil, climate, aspect and mystique

'A few decades ago it was not difficult to know about wine', explained Ivor Trink, one of Australia's new breed of flash, flying wine makers. 'There was claret, burgundy, champagne, port, sherry and loads of gut rot.' Dr Trink had been invited, and paid a fat fee, to talk to a gathering of some of Bordeaux's 12,000 wine producers. He continued, 'You are the guardians of the *terrier*, that combination of soil, climate and aspect shaped by two millennia of expertise that signal a wine's excellence. Australian wine producers are resigned to French producers continuing to dominate the great heights of wine making, trophy wines selling for hundreds of Euros a bottle.' 'Of course', heckled one distinguished wine grower, 'but we don't need you to tell us that.'

Undeterred, Dr Trink continued and started to win over his sceptical audience. He showed a chart (Exhibit 5.1) that showed how the main European exporters, which he called the 'old world', dominated the world's wine exports. 'You have the advantage,' he continued, 'as your own Baroness Philippine de Rothschild told me, "Winemaking is easy. Only the first 200 years are difficult." And you certainly have experience. The museum at Château Mouton Rothschild traces wine making back to Roman times and has a cellar devoted to mid-nineteenth-century vintages. The whole place reeks as much of history as wine.

'In a market that is very fragmented, the world market leader – France's luxury goods giant LVHM – has less than 1 per cent of the world market, and the number of "old world" winemakers swamp those from the new world. Italy alone has 1 million winemakers and this region, Bordeaux, makes more wine than the whole of Australia.

'You have the mystique beloved of wine enthusiasts. As the author and wine guru Hugh Johnson proclaims: "Why is wine so fascinating? Because there are so many different kinds, and every single one is different." The prices of the world's most costly wines show France's dominance. While Château d'Yquem (1811) sauternes has sold for $26,500 (€30,000), Moët & Chandon Esprit de Siècle champagne for $10,000 and Château Mouton Rothschild (1945) for $4,200, the best that the rest of the world can manage is $1,400 for Australian Grange (1955) and $1,000 for Californian Screaming Eagle (1995).

'In addition you have the *appellation contrôlée* that protects your wine's identity through a plethora of rigidly enforced regulations covering the grapes that can be used in a region's blend, the way they are picked, the way the wines are planted, their irrigation, the wine's alcoholic content, the labelling and much more. Your "brands", if you will excuse my use of the word, are the most protected in the world.

'You also have amazingly loyal customers. For example, France is one of the world's greatest consumers of wine and yet imports account for less than 5 per cent of sales. As Françoise Brugière, of the Office National Introprofessionel des Vins, explained to me, "It's no accident that Chauvin was a Frenchman." And the French are not alone in their loyalty. Italian and Spanish wine drinkers are just as loyal to wine made in their own country. Even in Australia over 90 per cent of the wine consumed is home grown.

'Your position in the wine world is pre-eminent. Through your combined strength you have already given bloody noses to the big conglomerates moving into your markets. Remember the fanfare when Coca-Cola introduced their new beverage category, wine, in 1976. It took them four years of losses to learn that Coke is no Grand Cru and make an ignominious exit in 1980. Having not learned from your victory over Coca-Cola, Nestlé, Philip Morris and RJR Nabisco all entered the wine trade, lost their shirts and quit the wine trade in the 1980s. True, some global companies are still dabbling in wine but they are finding it tough. Seagram has just sold off its champagne brands. Only Diageo is hanging on but they are dismissive of the role of wine in their overall strategy. As one manager joked: "Two millennia ago a miracle changes water into wine. We're still waiting for the second miracle: turning wine into profits!".'

EXHIBIT 5.1: REGIONAL SHARE OF WORLD EXPORTS (1997)

REGION	% SHARE
Main European exporters: France, Italy, Portugal and Spain	72
Other Western Europe	7
Other major southern hemisphere exporters: Argentina, Brazil, Chile, New Zealand, South Africa and Uruguay	7
European Transitional economies: Central and Eastern Europe and the former Soviet Union	6
Australia	5
North America	3
Rest of World	Less than 1

The audience was getting to like Dr Tipple but their mood was about to change. 'Yes, you are confidently on top of the pile now but, unless you shape up, Bordeaux will be as much a wine-making joke as Britain. For too long you have ignored customers. You think you are so special, custodians of a grand heritage that defines your nation. You are wrong. You are mostly outdated business, yes business, who for generations have operated more for your own convenience than that of the customers.

'You may have 95 per cent of the French market but the market is, literally, dying on you and you are losing ground elsewhere. Over the past 30 years France's wine consumption has halved and the average age of the regular wine consumer, who drinks at least a glass a day, has risen from 35 to 55. You have lost touch with the youth market. Go to Paris and you will find the bars full of young people drinking. Drinking, yes, but not French wine or wine from any other country. Their drink is foreign beer or whisky.

'The situation in your traditional export markets is equally dire. In the late 1980s, France and Europe's other three big exporters (Exhibit 5.1) accounted for 85 per cent of the world's exports. They are now down to about 70 per cent. The British market is a good example of what is happening outside the wine-producing countries. Only six years ago, French, German and Italian wines accounted for two-thirds of the wine the Brits consumed. Their combined share is now less than 50 per cent and declining.

'France, Italy and Spain may be holding onto their share of their declining markets but, elsewhere, new-world wines are driving out the old. And it is in these non-wine-growing areas that wine consumption is growing. While the share of world exports, excluding intra-EU trade, of the main European exporters has slipped from 75 per cent to 55 per cent over the last 10 years, sales of new-world exporters have soared. This table (Exhibit 5.2) shows how percentage points in world exports have changed.

Exhibit 5.2: Change in percentage share of world exports, excluding intra-EU (1997–1998)

Region	% point change in share
Main European exporters: France, Italy, Portugal and Spain	–20
Other Western Europe	–1
Other major southern hemisphere exporters: Argentina, Brazil, Chile, New Zealand, South Africa and Uruguay	10
European Transitional economies: Central and Eastern Europe and the former Soviet Union	5
Australia	5
North America	4
Rest of World	1

'You may claim that the new world's gains have been made because of their heavy advertising but that is only part of the story. New-world wine producers are producing brands but a large part of their success is because they understand what brands are. For a brand to succeed consumers have got to recognise and enjoy what they are getting. For a long time, that has not been true of old-world wines. The quality of old-world wines can be outstanding but often it is not. One old-world wine buff was close to the truth when he joked: "It costs £20 (€33) for a good bottle of burgundy, but to enjoy a great bottle of burgundy it cost £200 plus £1800 for the other nine bottles that were not."

'The old world are still trying to use the old SCAM of Soil, Climate, Aspect and Mystique but are losing out to the new world's appliance of science and professionalism. That is what accounted for the "Judgement of Paris" as long ago as 1976. On that occasion the Paris-based wine merchant Steven Spurrier brought together 15 of the most influential French wine critics to compare Californian and French wines in a blind test. These critics were shocked and there was a national outcry when, without the benefit of labels and bottles to guide them, the critics chose the Californian wine over the French. After cries that the test was rigged it was rerun two years later and, once again, gave the same results!

'It seems that your great wine heritage now accounts for little, according to the world's leading wine critics. Australia's Grange, first produced in 1950, "has replaced Bordeaux's Pétrus as the world's most exotic and concentrated wine" and it is argued that New Zealand sauvignon blanc, first produced in 1970, is "arguably, the best in the world". Price comparisons in the UK market show how consumers are voting. Besides gaining sales, new-world wines carry higher prices than European producers: the average price paid for a bottle of New Zealand wine is over £5 (€8.20), for Australian and US wines over £4 a bottle, the average French bottle is about £3.50 and the average German bottle a little over £2.50.

'How has the new world achieved this success? The answer is the appliance of science in wine making and marketing. As John Worontschak, a fellow Australian who lives in Bordeaux, so eloquently explains: "It's because we're open to new ideas, and we're not full of pretentious bullshit." Australia, California and New Zealand do not strive to uphold wine-making traditions supported by state subsidies, but strive to make good, consistent, keenly priced wines, carefully crafted to fit consumers' tastes and expectations. An indication of their scientific endeavour is the production of scientific papers on wine making. Although Australia and New Zealand have only a fraction of the world market they already produce 20 per cent of the scientific papers on wine making. That investment has made them good but also means they are getting better.

'The new world's more enlightened regulations enable them to make both consistent and excellent wines in a way that your *appellation contrôlée* blocks. Their wines are consistent because they can use different irrigation methods and take grapes from different areas to make the taste right. If in one year the conditions are perfect to produce an excellent strong vintage, they will do it and win international prizes for their efforts; your *appellation contrôlée* would prevent you making the superb wines above the regulated strength. If the vintage needs it, they will put oak chips in a barrel to bring out the flavour while you would have to hope for the vagaries of the oak barrel and your variable climate. Yes, your love of the old ways, cottage industries and *appellation contrôlée* are great gifts to the new world.

'Our final great advantage is marketing, but that is more than big budgets. It is finding out what people want and respecting their views. For instance we know that, once people have decided not to buy the cheapest wine, their choice is influenced by four main factors: past experience of wines, the country of origin of the wine, the variety of grape and brand. Too often the wine labels in the old world are designed to look grand and regulate, rather than elucidate. As Hugh Johnson comments on German wine labels: ". . . laws have introduced ambiguities which only the most dogged use of a reference book can elucidate. Whether there was a publisher on the committee that framed them I don't know. But there can't have been a customer."

'In pandering to customers, not custom, new-world growers understand the importance of consistency and rewarding customers with a taste they like. You may find it amazing but many potential customers are attracted to the sophistication of wine drinking but don't like the taste. Rather than rejecting these lost causes, Californians have invested in wine coolers (a mixture of wine and fruit juices) and fruit-flavoured wines. It is consistently giving customers what they want that allows inexpensively produced new-world wines to sell at a higher price than old-world bottles.

'It is also important to recognise the importance of country of origin. Many of the new-world wines come from young countries with a youthful, fun-loving image. There are also linguistic and historic links with the new world. To English-speaking people, Screaming Eagle is a lot easier to remember and sounds more fun than Veuve Clicquot-Ponsardin or Regierungsbezirk. These links really do matter in the wine trade. For example, the historical links are helping South African wines in the Netherlands while "brand Australia" is struggling in Germany. Eventually Australia will have to do in Germany what they did for the UK market, use focus groups to come up with attractive Australian-sounding names – like Barramundi – that appeal to the local consumer.

'Californians started putting grape varieties on their wine to help give consumers a clue to taste. It is a trick that has since been adopted from New Zealand's superb sauvignon blanc to Chile's merlot. The grape variety constrains the taste that can be constructed but is a useful shorthand valued by mid-range consumers.

'Branding is the real spirit of new-world wines. It demands the simple labelling, consistency and quality that new-world wines give. In using these marketing techniques, the scale of new-world wine makers gives them an advantage. Although globally no single wine-grower has the dominance of Diageo in the spirits market or Coca-Cola in soft drinks, new-world producers are huge compared with Europe's fragmented industry. In Australia four companies have 80 per cent of wine production and in the huge US market the five biggest producers account for 62 per cent of the market. Like it or not, the big brands are coming. Yes, wine is special to the producers and drinkers, but no more special than globally marketed Highland Park malt whisky or Guinness beer. As the wine journalist Andrew Jefford complained, Australian brands, like Jacob's Creek and Nottage Hill, are "becoming the equivalent of cans of lager; standardised, consistent, reliable, risk-free, challenge-free". Why does he complain? What's wrong with that? The longer you and he fight the march of progress, the sooner you'll die.'

Questions

1. What accounts for the new world's recent success over the old world's wine producers?

The remaining questions for this case ask you to evaluate alternative courses of action suggested in a discussion by the Bordeaux winemakers following Dr Tipple's presentation.

2. Stick to what we have always been doing and build upon our unique *terrier*. Great wines are beyond the marketing babble of the multinationals. We have defeated Coca-Cola, Nestlé and the like, and will defeat this new challenge from much smaller new-world wine makers who are a fraction of the size of those we have already beaten. After all, the world's wine critics, wine enthusiasts the world over and our local customers remain discerning and are loyal to our wines.

3. Adopt Australian methods of wine production and branding for international markets, like several local wine-makers have done. We must be humble and learn from British Diageo in developing an accessible French brand, such as their Le Piat d'Or, or American Australian Southcorp with Vichon.

4. Follow the lead taken by France's LVHM and Pernod Ricard and buy into the new-world wines' positioning and expertise. LVHM own Australian Green Point and Californian Domaine Chandon while Pernod Ricard owns Australian Jacob's Creek and South African Long Mountain.

5. Seek the disestablishment of *appellation contrôlée* for many of our wine-growing areas so that we can develop the global French brands we need.

6. Follow the lead shown by our farming colleagues to protect our consumers from practices that undermine our European heritage. We have fought against hormones in American beef, genetically modified soya beans and bananas from the Windward Islands. We need to use our political clout in the EU as well as our own parliament.

Sources: 'The globe in a glass', *The Economist* (18 December 1999), pp. 107–23; 'Wine appreciation: playing the rating game', *The Economist* (18 September 1999), pp. 130–2; 'Spirits: grapes of wrath', *The Economist* (3 April 1999), p. 98; John Apthorp, 'Lord of the wines', *EuroBusiness* (August 2000), pp. 76–7; Giles MacDonogh, 'French take to terrier in battle with brands', *Financial Times Survey: World Wine Industry* (15 December 2000), p. I; Stephen Brook, 'The long road from Hirondelle to here', *Financial Times Survey: World Wine Industry* (15 December 2000), p. IV.

internet exercises

Internet exercises for this chapter can be found on the student site of the myPHLIP Web Site at www.booksites.net/kotler.

chapter six

Consumer buyer behaviour

Chapter objectives *After reading this chapter, you should be able to:*

◆ Define the consumer market and construct a simple model of consumer buying behaviour.

◆ Tell how culture, subculture and social class influence consumer buying behaviour.

◆ Describe how consumers' personal characteristics and primary psychological factors affect their buying decisions.

◆ Discuss how consumer decision making varies with the type of buying decision.

◆ Explain the stages of the buyer decision and adoption processes.

introduction

EFFEM's success with Sheba (see preview case on page 190) shows how consumer buying behaviour has many unexpected dimensions. Since the human mind contains as many interacting neurones as there are leaves in the Amazon jungle, it is not surprising that buying behaviour is not simple. Complicated it is, but understanding buyer behaviour is central to marketing management. Just as marketing ends with consumption, so marketing management must begin with understanding customers.

This chapter explores the dynamics of consumer behaviour and the consumer market. **Consumer buying behaviour** refers to the buying behaviour of final consumers – individuals and households that buy goods and services for personal consumption. All of these final consumers combined make up the **consumer market**. The world consumer market consists of about 5.5 billion people, but the billion people living in North America, Western Europe and Japan make up 70 per cent of the world's spending power.[1] Even within these wealthy consumer markets, consumers vary tremendously in age, income, education level and tastes. They also buy an incredible variety of goods and services. How these diverse consumers make their choices among various products embraces a fascinating array of factors.

Consumer buying behaviour
The buying behaviour of final consumers – individuals and households who buy goods and services for personal consumption.

Consumer market
All the individuals and households who buy or acquire goods and services for personal consumption.

preview case

Sheba: the pets' St Valentine's Day

PEDRO QUELHAS BRITO*

Several years of growth averaging 22 per cent year on year has attracted more than 60 new brands from both local and multinational companies to Portugal's €350 million petfood market. EFFEM-Portugal, whose brands include Sheba, Whiskas and Pedigree Pal, has over half of the pet food market but not all its brands were doing well.

EFFEM had played an important role in developing the market. Much of its success came from understanding the behaviour of both pets and their owners. For example, cats are resolved animals. They eat what they like and leave what they dislike. A cat is selective and sensitive regarding its nutritional needs and taste. If given food it dislikes, a cat seeks an alternative. Dogs are different. A hungry dog will eat almost anything, and eats it quickly. For cat food the main concern is to give pleasure and to provide variety. For dogs it is volume and ease of consumption.

Sheba is EFFEM's super-premium brand for cats. With its exceptional quality and its high price, it aims to delight the most discerning cats and is particularly appropriate for special occasions. But Sheba was in trouble. After initial advertising and sales promotional support during its launch, it had been left to fend for itself in the increasingly competitive pet food market. After several years of trading, Sheba's market position and even its commercial existence were threatened by the absence of marketing support and the entrance of new competitors into its market niche. Only 9 per cent of the total market had ever bought a can of Sheba at least once. Sheba's low market share of just 2 per cent justified little promotional expenditure, but for Sheba it was fight back or die.

EFFEM's answer was a two-stage point of sale promotion, with each stage costing as little as a 30-second prime-time TV commercial. Stage one was during the run-up to Christmas. In-store demonstrators approached consumers and asked them if they owned a cat. If customers answered 'yes', they were offered a greetings card and a 100-gram can of Sheba. In this way both owners and pets received a gift. This sampling raised customers' brand awareness and knowledge of Sheba. Besides giving information, the card encouraged the pet's owners to show their love for their cat by giving it Sheba because 'it deserves it'. The card and its message were designed to generate favourable feelings. After all, it was Christmas time and this 'Santa Claws' gave away 12,000 cans of very special Sheba.

The second stage of the campaign repeated the Christmas promotion, but with St Valentine's Day as the theme. The Valentine's card showed two cats, probably lovers, with the messages: 'Because today is a special day, Sheba has a gift for your cat' and 'Let it know how you love [your cat]'. During the campaign 11,900 cans were given to customers at the point of sale. The Valentine's card also doubled as a cash-back coupon with a face value of €0.50. The refund and the emotional appeal of the message helped customers to confirm their preference for Sheba while showing their love for their cat.

The promotions reversed Sheba's sales decline. The impact on brand awareness/knowledge and repeat purchase was evident and the percentage of consumers who had ever tried Sheba increased to 22 per cent.

Questions

1. Is Sheba based on the tastes of cats or their owners?

2. Does the consumer awareness and knowledge achieved account for the success of the Sheba campaign? If not, what does account for the success?

3. Given that Sheba's sales promotion campaign was so much more successful than conventional advertising, why is it not used more often?

***

* Universidade do Porto, Portugal.

models of consumer behaviour

In earlier times, marketers could understand consumers well through the daily experience of selling to them. But as firms and markets have grown in size, many marketing decision makers have lost direct contact with their customers and must now turn

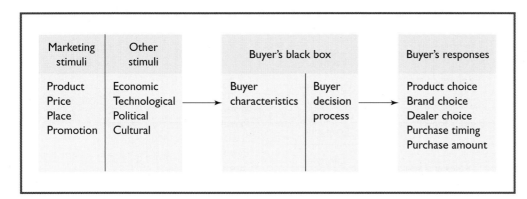

Figure 6.1

Model of buying behaviour

to consumer research. They spend more money than ever to study consumers, trying to learn more about consumer behaviour. Who buys? How do they buy? When do they buy? Where do they buy? Why do they buy?

The central question for marketers is: how do consumers respond to various marketing stimuli that the company might use? The company that really understands how consumers will respond to different product features, prices and advertising appeals has a great advantage over its competitors. Therefore, companies and academics have researched heavily the relationship between marketing stimuli and consumer response. Their starting point is the stimulus–response model of buyer behaviour shown in Figure 6.1. This shows that marketing and other stimuli enter the consumer's 'black box' and produce certain responses. Marketers must figure out what is in the buyer's black box.[2]

Marketing stimuli consist of the four Ps: product, price, place and promotion. Other stimuli include significant forces and events in the buyer's environment: economic, technological, political and cultural. All these stimuli enter the buyer's black box, where they are turned into a set of observable buyer responses (shown on the right-hand side of Figure 6.1): product choice, brand choice, dealer choice, purchase timing and purchase amount.

The marketer wants to understand how the stimuli are changed into responses inside the consumer's black box, which has two parts. First, the buyer's characteristics influence how he or she perceives and reacts to the stimuli. Second, the buyer's decision process itself affects the buyer's behaviour. This chapter first looks at buyer characteristics as they affect buying behaviour, and then examines the buyer decision process. We will never know what exactly is in the black box or be able perfectly to predict consumer behaviour, but the models can help us understand consumers, help us to ask the right questions, and teach us how to influence them.[3]

characteristics affecting consumer behaviour

Consumer purchases are influenced strongly by cultural, social, personal and psychological characteristics, as shown in Figure 6.2. For the most part, marketers cannot control such factors, but they must take them into account. We illustrate these characteristics for the case of a hypothetical customer, Anna Flores. Anna is a married graduate who works as a brand manager in a leading consumer packaged-goods company. She wants to buy a digital camera to take on holiday. Many characteristics in her background will affect the way she evaluates cameras and chooses a brand.

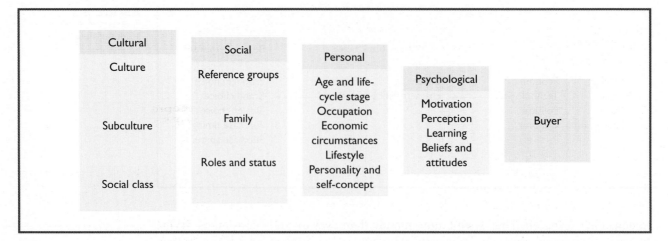

Figure 6.2

Factors influencing behaviour

cultural factors

Cultural factors exert the broadest and deepest influence on consumer behaviour. The marketer needs to understand the role played by the buyer's culture, subculture and social class.

■ Culture

Culture

The set of basic values, perceptions, wants and behaviours learned by a member of society from family and other important institutions.

Culture is the most basic cause of a person's wants and behaviour. Human behaviour is largely learned. Growing up in a society, a child learns basic values, perceptions, wants and behaviours from the family and other important institutions. Like most western people, in her childhood Anna observed and learned values about achievement and success, activity and involvement, efficiency and practicality, progress, material comfort, individualism, freedom, humanitarianism, youthfulness, and fitness and health. Sometimes we take these values for granted, but they are not cultural universals.

> A trade delegation trying to market in Taiwan found this out the hard way. Seeking more foreign trade, they arrived in Taiwan bearing gifts of green baseball caps. It turned out that the trip was scheduled a month before Taiwan elections, and that green was the colour of the political opposition party. Worse yet, the visitors learned after the fact that according to Taiwan culture, a man wears green to signify that his wife has been unfaithful. The head of the community delegation later noted: 'I don't know whatever happened to those green hats, but the trip gave us an understanding of the extreme differences in our cultures.'[4]

Marketers are always trying to spot *cultural shifts* in order to imagine new products that might be wanted. For example, the cultural shift towards greater concern about health and fitness has created a huge industry for exercise equipment and clothing, lower-calorie and more natural foods, and health and fitness services. The switch from pin-stripe suits to casual wear has caused the plummeting sales and share prices of retailers, such as Austin Reed and Moss Bros, whose names are synonymous with formal wear. The increased desire for leisure time has resulted in more demand for convenience products and services, such as microwave ovens and fast food. While consumers the world over are increasingly concerned about healthy eating, they are also tiring of the shopping and chopping needed to prepare family meals. Futurologists are now predicting that cooking will become rare in most homes and that houses without kitchens will be as common as houses without open fires. While many consumers express concerns about food additives and genetically modified products, one of the fastest-growing markets is for functional foods that scientifically benefit health. For example, Flora Pro.activ is a margarine-like spread that is expensive but 'can dramatically reduce cholesterol to help maintain a healthy heart'.[5] Concern for the environment is influencing consumer behaviour both through legislation and through demand for less wasteful goods (see Marketing Highlight 6.1).[6]

■ Subculture

Each culture contains smaller **subcultures** or groups of people with shared value systems based on common life experiences and situations. Subcultures include nationalities, religions, racial groups and geographic regions. Many subcultures make up important market segments and marketers often design products and marketing programmes tailored to their needs. The huge US market of 260 million people has Hispanic (approaching 40 million) and black (over 30 million) subcultures that are bigger than most national markets. Mass marketers often neglect these subcultures, so these can provide market opportunities to enterprising small businesses.

Subculture
A group of people with shared value systems based on common life experiences and situations.

> An entrepreneur in the ex-soviet republic of Kirgizstan saw one such opportunity. He reasoned that the descendants of the ethnic Germans that Stalin transported from the Volga to Kazakhstan and Kirgizstan would buy locally made German beer. He imported the equipment, hops and barley and made beer that conformed to Germany's exacting standards. Selling for much less than imported beers, his Steinbrau now sells in 40 restaurants.

In all developed economies the greying population is growing rapidly. Marketers often have a poor understanding of these over-55s who will be a huge market force in the next millennium. Like all other people, Anna Flores' buying behaviour will be influenced by her subculture identification. It will affect her food preferences, clothing choices, recreation activities and career goals. Subcultures attach different meanings to picture taking and this could affect both Anna's interest in cameras and the brand she buys.[7]

■ Social class

Almost every society has some form of social class structure. **Social classes** are society's relatively permanent and ordered divisions whose members share similar values, interests and behaviours. The registrar-general's six social classes have been widely used since the turn of the twentieth century, although all big countries have their own system. From spring 2001 Britain's Office of National Statistics will adopt a new National Statistics Socio-Economic Classification (NS-SEC) to reflect the social changes of the last century (see Table 6.1). The scheme divides people according to their position in the labour market. Those at the bottom make a short-term exchange of cash for labour while those at the top have long-term contracts and are rewarded by the prospect of career advancement and perks as well as a salary. Although not derived using income, the scale is a good predictor of both income and health except for the self-employed class four who are as healthy, but not as wealthy, as classes one and two. Currently there are a number of projects funded by the European Commission that aim to improve the quality of socio-economic and other statistics across Europe.[8]

Social classes
Relatively permanent and ordered divisions in a society whose members share similar values, interests and behaviours.

Not only do class systems differ in various parts of the world: the relative sizes of the classes vary with the relative prosperity of countries. The 'diamond'-shaped classification (few people at the top and bottom with most in the middle) is typical of developed countries, although the Japanese and Scandinavian scales are flatter. In less developed countries, such as in Latin America and Africa, the structure is 'pyramid'

marketing highlight 6.1

The junk fairy: making the market work

Getting rid of garbage in Germany can take a bit of getting used to. When first faced with the need to dump an item there are often four bins, each with its own role. Green for vegetable matter, yellow for packaging, white and blue. It is all part of the country's drive to reduce waste – even new BMWs are recyclable!

All across Europe land-fill sites are getting full and no one wants new ones near where they live. Burning waste pollutes; sorting it costs. Germany's multi-bin system is part of a policy of making polluters pay. A Packaging Ordinance (*Verpackungsordnung*) makes industry responsible for the collecting, sorting and ultimate recycling of packaging waste. The legislation deals with three kinds of packaging: *primary packaging*: the container that holds the product, like a perfume bottle; *secondary packaging*: outer material whose main function is display, like the box around the perfume bottle; *transport packaging*: the carton or crate used to ship the perfume to stores. All three types must be taken back by retailers and returned to manufacturers.

The industry's solution was the Dual System (DSD), a non-profit company that collects waste directly from consumers in addition to the country's municipal collection systems. Licensing fees for the now widely used green dot funds DSD: a green arrow emblem indicating that a package is collectible by DSD. Now, rather than tossing their packaging out with the municipal rubbish, for which they must pay a fee, consumers can take it to a nearby yellow DSD bin to be collected for free.

Under the DSD system stores are no longer required to take back mounds of primary sales packaging. However, to be eligible as DSD rubbish, a sales package must have the green dot so retailers are reluctant to carry products without it. Further, there is a growing preference among German consumers for recyclable packaging materials, and for less packaging in general. Thus, the Packaging Ordinance influences how companies package their products for the German market.

The ordinance puts the 'polluter pays' principle to work by creating incentives; Germany has no ban on specific packaging materials but sets market mechanisms in motion. If a packaging material is costly to recycle, the price of using it will rise and companies will switch to something else. Thus, the ordinance stimulates companies to find ways to use less packaging. Colgate, for example, designed a toothpaste tube that stands on its head on store shelves without a box.

The major problem with recycling programmes is the lack of a market for recycled material. Notes one packaging expert: 'There seems to be widespread belief in the trash fairy, who comes overnight and turns garbage into gold for free.' In fact much of the packaging collected is not being recycled, but is piling up in warehouses or exported. There is a market in Europe for recycled white or green glass but only Argentina seams to want brown glass. When German plastics turned up in French dumps and incinerators, it caused a Europe-wide scandal.

During the first three years under the new system, total household waste production fell by more than 10 per cent, while recycling quantities increased by 90 per cent. Germany collects, sorts and recycles 60 per cent of its post-consumer plastic-packaging waste, well ahead of the 35 per cent target. Producers and retailers are now working together to help solve environmental problems. The EU is now working on a directive that would set minimum standards for recycling in all of its member states.

However, maybe there are both high- and low-tech trash fairies. In many parts of Europe car boot sales have become a part of life. Rather than dumping everything, families periodically load the back of their car and prove that, if the price is right, there is a market for almost anything. Some car boot sellers have become highly proficient at spotting bargains early in the day that they can sell off later in the day or sell to antique dealers.

Charity shops, from Age Concern to Zoe's Place Baby Hospice, allow the trash fairy to benefit almost everyone. The more wealthy 'feel good' for donating their old clothes and other bits and bobs, astute buyers get bargain 'nearly new items', the charities benefit, jobs are created and underused retail space is filled.

The Internet provides the final trash fairy. SalvageSale.com is an online auction for 'damaged, heavily discounted, distressed or sub-specification materials' (junk) or 'finished goods in commercial quantities' (loads of junk). SalvageSale.com was set up to help insurance companies to sell off damaged stock but now sells an amazing jumble of stuff. On one day it included a lot of seven diesel-powered locomotives, a diving bell, a Russian reefer vessel (?), 429 cartons of canned olives and, the best bargain of all, 90,000 lbs of rubber extrusions.

SOURCE: Adapted from Marilyn Stern, 'Is this the ultimate in recycling?', *Across the Board* (May 1993), pp. 28–31. See also Peter Sibbald, 'Manufacturing for reuse', *Fortune* (6 February 1995), pp. 102–12; 'Plastics waste: Germany beats recycling targets', *Chemical Week* (5 June 1996), p. 22; 'Junk online', *The Economist* (22 July 2000), p. 105; http://www.salvagesale.com; http://www.charityshops.org.uk; http://www.oxfam.org

Table 6.1

National statistics –
socioeconomic
classification

CLASSIFICATION	MEMBERSHIP
1	Higher managerial and professional occupations
1.1	Employers and managers in large organisations (senior private and public sector employees)
1.2	Higher professionals (partners in law firms etc.)
2	Lower managerial and professional occupations (middle managers and professionally qualified people)
3	Intermediate occupations (secretaries, policemen, etc.)
4	Small employers and sole traders
5	Lower supervisory, craft and related occupations (skilled manual workers)
6	Semi-routine occupations (shop assistants, etc.)
7	Routine occupations (semi-skilled or unskilled manual workers)

SOURCE: Office of National Statistics. Socioeconomic classification (ONS). Crown copyright material is reproduced under class Licence Number C01W0000039 with the permission of the Controller of HMSO.

shaped with a concentration of poor people at the base. As countries develop, their class structure moves towards the diamond shape, although there is evidence that the gap between the richest and poorest in the English-speaking countries is now widening.

Some class systems have a greater influence on buying behaviour than others. In most western countries 'lower' classes may exhibit upward mobility, showing buying behaviour similar to that of the 'upper' classes. But in other cultures, where a caste system gives people a distinctive role, buying behaviour is more firmly linked to social class. Upper classes in almost all societies are often more similar to each other than they are to the rest of their own society. When selecting products and services, including food, clothing, household items and personal-care products, they make choices that are less culture-bound than those of the lower classes. This tendency accounts for the strength of global luxury brands such as Mercedes, Rolex, Versace and Remy Martin. Generally, the lower social classes are more culture-bound, although young people of all classes are less so and account for the global youth brands like Nike, Coca-Cola and Swatch.[9]

Anna Flores' occupation puts her in NS-SEC group 2 (lower managerial and professional occupations) although she has set her sights on achieving a 'higher managerial occupation'. Coming from a higher social background, her family and friends probably own expensive cameras and she might have dabbled in photography.

social factors

A consumer's behaviour is also influenced by social factors, such as the consumer's small groups, family, and social roles and status. Because these social factors can strongly affect consumer responses, companies must take them into account when designing their marketing strategies.

■ Groups

Groups influence a person's behaviour. Groups that have a direct influence and to which a person belongs are called **membership groups**. Some are *primary groups* with

Membership groups
Groups that have a direct influence on a person's behaviour and to which a person belongs.

whom there is regular but informal interaction – such as family, friends, neighbours and fellow workers. Some are *secondary groups*, which are more formal and have less regular interaction. These include organisations like religious groups, professional associations and trade unions.

Reference groups are groups that serve as direct (face-to-face) or indirect points of comparison or reference in forming a person's attitudes or behaviour. Reference groups to which they do not belong often influence people. For example, an **aspirational group** is one to which the individual wishes to belong, as when a teenage football fan follows David Beckham or a young girl idolises Britney Spears. They identify with them, although there is no face-to-face contact. Today's parents may be relieved that the modern pop 'heroes' are more agreeable than the rebels, acid freaks and punks that they followed.[10]

Marketers try to identify the reference groups of their target markets. Reference groups influence a person in at least three ways. They expose the person to new behaviours and lifestyles. They influence the person's attitudes and self-concept because he or she wants to 'fit in'. They also create pressures to conform that may affect the person's product and brand choices.

The importance of group influence varies across products and brands, but it tends to be strongest for conspicuous purchases.[11] A product or brand can be conspicuous for one of two reasons. First, it may be noticeable because the buyer is one of the few people who own it – luxuries, such as a vintage Wurlitzer juke box or a Brietling Chronomat GT sports watch, are more conspicuous than necessities because fewer people own the luxuries. Second, a product such as Red Bull or Perrier can be conspicuous because the buyer consumes it in public where others can see it. Figure 6.3 shows how group influence might affect product and brand choices for four types of product – public luxuries, private luxuries, public necessities and private necessities.

A person considering the purchase of a public luxury, such as a yacht, will generally be influenced strongly by others. Many people will notice the yacht because few people own one. If interested, they will notice the brand because the boat is used in public. Thus both the product and the brand will be conspicuous and the opinions of others can strongly influence decisions about whether to own a boat and what brand to buy. At the other extreme, group influences do not much affect decisions about private necessities because other people will notice neither the product nor the brand.

Reference groups
Groups that have a direct (face-to-face) or indirect influence on the person's attitudes or behaviour.

Aspirational group
A group to which an individual wishes to belong.

Figure 6.3

Extent of group influence on product and brand choice

Source: Adapted from William O. Bearden and Michael J. Etzel, 'Reference group influence on product and brand purchase decisions', *Journal of Consumer Research* (September 1982), p.185. © Journal of Consumer Research Inc., 1982. All rights reserved.

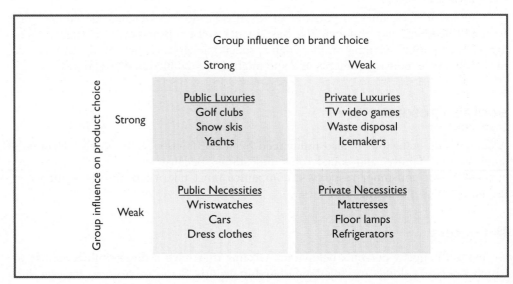

■ Family

Family members can strongly influence buyer behaviour. We can distinguish between two families in the buyer's life. The buyer's parents make up the *family of orientation*. Parents provide a person with an orientation towards religion, politics and economics, and a sense of personal ambition, self-worth and love. Even if the buyer no longer interacts very much with his or her parents, the latter can still significantly influence the buyer's behaviour. In countries where parents continue to live with their children, their influence can be crucial.

Procter & Gamble came a cropper in the European market after their €40 million launch of their new Charmin toilet roll. The company found the product's wet strength was wrong so it blocked European drains. Not because of the design of European toilets but because of a mode of consumer behaviour that must be learned in the family – how they use the toilet paper. Europeans fold their toilet paper while Americans scrunch it. 'This leads to different dynamics in the product', says P&G; 'folding paper means you need more strength.'

But even Europeans are not consistent. The British pay more than twice as much as Americans, French and Germans for their toilet rolls. Why? According to Kimberly-Clark the British demand a Rolls-Royce of toilet papers with a softer, more luxurious texture, more sheets per roll, 2 mm wider and 14 mm longer than other countries. The island race is also sensitive to colour, choosing from ranges that include warm pink, breeze blue and meadow green. The reason for this is their desire that the colour of the tissue matches their bathrooms.[12]

The *family of procreation* – the buyer's spouse and children – has a more direct influence on everyday buying behaviour. This family is the most important consumer buying organisation in society and it has been researched extensively. Marketers are interested in the roles and relative influence of the husband, wife and children on the purchase of a large variety of products and services.

Husband–wife involvement varies widely by product category and by stage in the buying process. Buying roles change with evolving consumer lifestyles. Almost everywhere in the world, the wife is traditionally the main purchasing agent for the family, especially in the areas of food, household products and clothing. But with over 60 per cent of women holding jobs outside the home in developed countries and the willingness of some husbands to do more of the family's purchasing, all this is changing. For example, in the US women now buy about 45 per cent of all cars and men account for about 40 per cent of expenditure on food shopping.[13] Such roles vary widely among different countries and social classes. As always, marketers must research specific patterns in their target markets.

In the case of expensive products and services, husbands and wives more often make joint decisions. Anna Flores' husband may play an *influencer role* in her camera-buying decision. He may have an opinion about her buying a camera and about the kind of camera to buy. At the same time, she will be the primary decider, purchaser and user.

Consumers' buying roles Group members can influence purchases in many ways. For example, men normally choose their own newspaper and women choose their own tights. For other products, however, the **decision-making unit** is more complicated with people playing one or more roles:

◆ **Initiator.** The person who first suggests or thinks of the idea of buying a particular product or service. This could be a parent or friends who would like to see a visual record of Anna's holiday.

Decision-making unit (DMU)
All the individuals who participate in, and influence, the consumer buying-decision process.

Initiator
The person who first suggests or thinks of the idea of buying a particular product or service.

In the purchase of a branded watch for an adult male, the initiator might be his son, the influencers his friends, the decider himself and the buyer his wife.

SOURCE: Reproduced courtesy of Sekonda

A LOT MORE WATCH   FOR YOUR MONEY

A SELECTION OF MEN'S WATCHES BY SEKONDA. PART OF THE EXTENSIVE RANGE AVAILABLE FROM H. SAMUEL AND OTHER LEADING JEWELLERS. FOR FURTHER DETAILS PLEASE CALL 0116 249 4007. WWW.SEKONDA.CO.UK. SPONSORS OF THE SEKONDA ICE HOCKEY SUPERLEAGUE

SEKONDA

Influencer
A person whose view or advice influences buying decisions.

Decider
The person who ultimately makes a buying decision or any part of it – whether to buy, what to buy, how to buy, or where to buy.

Buyer
The person who makes an actual purchase.

User
The person who consumes or uses a product or service.

Role
The activities a person is expected to perform according to the people around him or her.

Status
The general esteem given to a role by society.

◆ **Influencer**. A person whose view or advice influences the buying decisions, perhaps a friend who is a camera enthusiast or a salesperson.

◆ **Decider**. The person who ultimately makes a buying decision or any part of it – whether to buy, what to buy, how to buy or where to buy.

◆ **Buyer**. The person who makes an actual purchase. Once the buying decision is made, someone else could make the purchase for the decider.

◆ **User**. The person who consumes or uses a product or service. Once bought, other members of her family could use Anna's camera.

■ Roles and status

A person belongs to many groups – family, clubs, organisations. The person's position in each group can be defined in terms of both *role* and *status*. With her parents, Anna Flores plays the role of daughter; in her family, she plays the role of wife; in her company, she plays the role of brand manager. A **role** consists of the activities that people are expected to perform according to the persons around them. Each of Anna's roles will influence some of her buying behaviour.

Each role carries a **status** reflecting the general esteem given to it by society. People often choose products that show their status in society. For example, the role of brand manager has more status in our society than the role of daughter. As a brand manager, Anna will buy the kind of clothing that reflects her role and status.

personal factors

A buyer's decisions are also influenced by personal characteristics such as the buyer's age and life-cycle stage, occupation, economic situation, lifestyle, and personality and self-concept.

Table 6.2

Family life-cycle stages

YOUNG	MIDDLE-AGED	OLDER
Single	Single	Older married
Married without children	Married without children	Older unmarried
Married with children	Married with children	
Infant children	Young children	
Young children	Adolescent children	
Adolescent children	Married without dependent children	
Divorced with children	Divorced without children	
	Divorced with children	
	Young children	
	Adolescent children	
	Divorced without dependent children	

SOURCES: Adapted from Patrick E. Murphy and William A. Staples, 'A modernized family life cycle', *Journal of Consumer Research* (June 1979), p. 16; © Journal of Consumer Research, Inc., 1979. See also Janet Wagner and Sherman Hanna, 'The effectiveness of family life cycle variables in consumer expenditure research', *Journal of Consumer Research* (December 1983), pp. 281–91.

■ Age and life-cycle stage

People change the goods and services they buy over their lifetimes. Tastes in food, clothes, furniture and recreation are often age related. Buying is also shaped by the **family life cycle** – the stages through which families might pass as they mature over time. Table 6.2 lists the stages of the family life cycle. Although based on the transient love and marriage model of life,[14] marketers often define their target markets in terms of life-cycle stage and develop appropriate products and marketing plans for each stage. For example, Mark Warner offers family-oriented skiing and water sports holidays with an emphasis on kids' clubs and 'no kids' holidays for couples without children.

Family life cycle
The stages through which families might pass as they mature over time.

Although life-cycle stages remain the same, shifting lifestyles are causing the decline of some products and growth in others. One product that has almost disappeared in recent years is the baby pram, the one-time status symbol of all mums. Besides there being fewer families with children, many mothers now work, so have less time for strolling the pram, and are more likely to travel by car than on foot. Touring caravans is another product class in decline as families with children become fewer, while single- and double-income, no-kids families spend their money on more exotic holidays. While some markets decline, others grow with changing lifestyles.

> The Ally McBeal generation has cultivated numerous Internet services that try to fit their unsettled relationships round their careers: ss.com to help singles meet, secretadmirer.com to see if you have struck and don't know it, match.com to find that perfect match, cupidnet.com to see if you are compatible, ask-a-chick.com for guys to find out where they are getting it wrong, breakupgirl.com to help pick up the pieces and theknot.com or nearlywed.com to close the deal. As the market grows, it is segmenting. Just Lunch focuses on pre-screened lunch dates, goodgenes.com for graduates from top universities, jdate.com for Jewish singles and singleswithscruples.com for 'people with morals and a sense of humour'.[15]

Psychological life-cycle stages have also been identified.[16] Adults experience certain passages or transformations as they go through life. Thus Anna Flores may move

Eastpak use a strong image to communicate that it is a product to have.

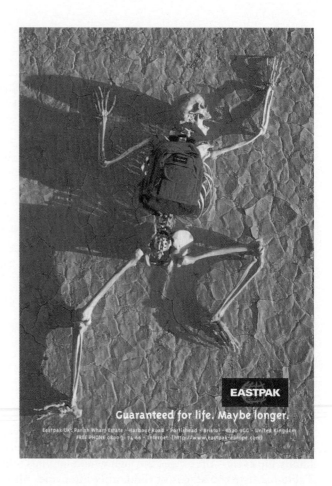

from being a satisfied brand manager and wife to being an unsatisfied person search-ing for a new way to fulfil herself. In fact, such a change may have stimulated her strong interest in photography. The main stimuli to people taking photographs are holidays, ceremonies marking the progression through the life cycle (weddings, graduations and so on) and having children to take photographs of. Marketers must pay attention to the changing buying interests that might be associated with these adult passages.

■ Occupation

A person's occupation affects the goods and services bought. Blue-collar workers tend to buy more work clothes, whereas office workers buy more smart clothes. Marketers try to identify the occupational groups that have an above-average interest in their products and services. A company can even specialise in making products needed by a given occupational group. Thus computer software companies will design different products for brand managers, accountants, engineers, lawyers and doctors.

■ Economic circumstances

A person's economic situation will affect product choice. Anna Flores can consider buying a professional €5,000 Nikon D1 digital camera if she has enough enthusiasm, disposable income, savings or borrowing power. Marketers of income-sensitive goods closely watch trends in personal income, savings and interest rates. If economic indicators point to a recession, marketers can take steps to redesign, reposition and reprice their products.

Table 6.3

Lifestyle dimensions

ACTIVITIES	INTERESTS	OPINIONS	DEMOGRAPHICS
Work	Family	Themselves	Age
Hobbies	Home	Social issues	Education
Social events	Job	Politics	Income
Vacation	Community	Business	Occupation
Entertainment	Recreation	Economics	Family size
Club membership	Fashion	Education	Dwelling
Community	Food	Products	Geography
Shopping	Media	Future	City size
Sports	Achievements	Culture	Stage in life cycle

SOURCE: Joseph T. Plummer, 'The concept and application of lifestyle segmentation', reprinted with permission from *Journal of Marketing* published by the American Marketing Association (January 1974), p. 34.

■ Lifestyle

People coming from the same subculture, social class and occupation may have quite different lifestyles. **Lifestyle** is a person's pattern of living as expressed in his or her activities, interests and opinions. Lifestyle captures something more than the person's social class or personality. It profiles a person's whole pattern of acting and interacting in the world. The technique of measuring lifestyles is known as **psychographics**. It involves measuring the primary dimensions shown in Table 6.3. The first three are known as the *AIO dimensions* (activities, interests, opinions). Several research firms have developed lifestyle classifications. The most widely used is the SRI *Values and Lifestyles (VALS)* typology. The original VALS typology classifies consumers into nine lifestyle groups according to whether they were inner directed (for example, 'experientials'); outer directed ('achievers', 'belongers'); or need driven ('survivors'). Using this VALS classification, a bank found that the businessmen they were targeting consisted mainly of 'achievers' who were strongly competitive individualists.[17] The bank designed highly successful ads showing men taking part in solo sports such as sailing, jogging and water skiing.[18]

Everyday-Life Research by SINUS GmbH, a German company, identifies 'social milieus' covering France, Germany, Italy and the UK. This study describes the structure of society with five social classes and value orientations:

Lifestyle
A person's pattern of living as expressed in his or her activities, interests and opinions.

Psychographics
The technique of measuring lifestyles and developing lifestyle classifications; it involves measuring the chief AIO dimensions (activities, interests, opinions).

◆ Basic orientation: traditional – *to preserve*.

◆ Basic orientation: materialist – *to have*.

◆ Changing values: hedonism – *to indulge*.

◆ Changing values: postmaterialism – *to be*.

◆ Changing values: postmodernism – *to have, to be and to indulge*.

It distinguishes two types of value: traditional values, emphasising hard work, thrift, religion, honesty, good manners and obedience; and material values concerned with possession and a need for security. From these, SINUS developed a typology of social milieus (see Table 6.4): groups of people who share a common set of values and beliefs about work, private relationships, leisure activities and aesthetics, and a common perception of future plans, wishes and dreams. The size and exact nature of these milieus vary between the countries studied, but there are broad international comparisons.

MILIEU	GERMANY	FRANCE	ITALY	UK	DESCRIPTION
Upper conservative	Konservatives-gehobenes	Les Héritiers	Neoconservatori	Upper class	Traditional upper-middle-class conservatives
Traditional mainstream	Floresburgerliches	Les conservateurs installés	Piccola borghesia	Traditional middle class	*Petit bourgeois* group mainly oriented to preserving the status quo
Traditional working class	Traditionsloses Arbeitermilieu	Les laborieux traditionnels	Cultura operaia	Traditional working class	Traditional blue-collar worker
Modern mainstream	Aufstiegsorientiertes	Les nouveaux ambitieux	Rampanti, plus crisaldi	Social climbers, plus progressive working class	Social climber and achievement-oriented white- and blue-collar workers
Trendsetter	Technokratisch-liberales	Les managers moderns	Borghesia illuminata	Progressive middle class	Technocratic-liberals with a postmaterial orientation
Avant-garde	Hedonistisches	Les post-modernistes	Edonisti	'Thatcher's children'	Mainly young pleasure seekers
Sociocritical	Alternatives	Les néo-moralistes	Critica sociale	Socially centred	Pursuing an alternative lifestyle
Under-priveleged	Traditionsloses Arbeitermilieu	Les oubliés, plus les rebelles	Sotto-proletariato urbano	Poor	Uprooted blue-collar workers and destitute

Table 6.4

Typology of social milieus

Knowing the social milieu of a person can provide information about his or her everyday life, such as work likes and dislikes, which helps in product development and advertising. The study finds that the upmarket segments share a similar structure in all four countries; and it identifies trend-setting milieus in each country, containing heavy consumers with comparable attitudinal and sociodemographic characteristics. Important values shared by all these consumers include: tolerance, open-mindedness, an outward-looking approach; career and success, education and culture, a high standard of living, hedonistic luxury consumption, individualism and Europe.

The Anticipating Change in Europe (ACE) study, by the RISC research agency of Paris, investigated social changes in 12 European countries, the United States, Canada and Japan. The objective was to try to understand how social changes influence market trends. RISC describes people using sociodemographic characteristics, socio-cultural profile, activities (sports, leisure, culture), behaviour towards the media (press, radio, television), political inclinations and mood. Using these dimensions, RISC developed six Eurotypes:

1. *The traditionalist* (18 per cent of the European population) is influenced by the culture, socio-economic history and unique situation of his or her country, with a profile reflecting deep-rooted attitudes specific to that country. Consequently, this is the least homogeneous group across countries.

2. *The homebody* (14 per cent) is driven by a strong attachment to his or her roots and childhood environment. Less preoccupied with economic security than the traditionalist, the homebody needs to feel in touch with the social environment. The homebody seeks warm relationships and has difficulty coping with violence in society.

3. *The rationalist* (23 per cent) has an ability to cope with unforeseeable and complex situations, and a readiness to take risks and start new endeavours. Personal fulfilment is more about self-expression than financial reward. The rationalist believes that science and technology will help resolve the challenges facing humanity.

4. *The pleasurist* (17 per cent) emphasises sensual and emotional experiences, preferring non-hierarchically structured groups built around self-reliance and self-regulation and not around leaders or formal decision-making processes.

5. *The striver* (15 per cent) holds the attitudes, beliefs and values that underlie the dynamics of social change. The striver believes in autonomous behaviour and wants to shape his or her life and to exploit mental, physical, sensual and emotional possibilities to the full.

6. *The trend-setter* (13 per cent) favours non-hierarchical social structures and enjoys spontaneity rather than formal procedures. Trend-setters see no need to prove their abilities. Even more individualistic than strivers, they exemplify the flexible response to a rapidly changing environment.

These studies do suggest that there are European lifestyles although, as with social class, there is greater similarity between wealthy Europeans than between poor ones. For this reason, luxury brands and their advertising are often more standardised internationally than other products.[19]

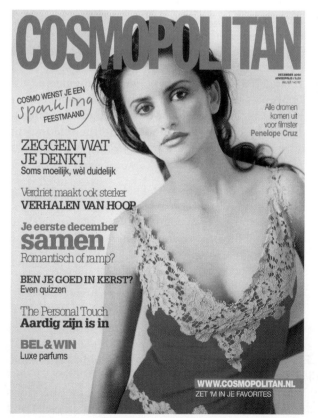

Magazines like Cosmopolitan *are an example of a product whose target market is segmented according to lifestyle criteria.*

SOURCE: *Cosmopolitan* (Netherlands) November 2000, VNU Tijdschriften

Lifestyle classifications need not be universal – they can vary significantly from country to country. McCann-Erickson, for example, found the following British lifestyles: *Avant Guardians* (interested in change); *Pontificators* (traditionalists, very British); *Chameleons* (follow the crowd); and *Sleepwalkers* (contented underachievers). Contrast this with Survey Research Malaysia's seven categories from their developing country: *Upper Echelons* (driven by status and desire to stand out in society); *Not Quite Theres* (ambition for self and family); *Rebel Hangouts* (want to look off mainstream); *Sleepwalkers* (want to get through the day); *Inconspicuous* (want to blend in); *Kampung Trendsetters* (ambitious, city-influenced village dwellers); and *Rural Traditionalists* (abide by traditional rules).[20] Finally, advertising agency D'Arcy, Masius, Benton & Bowles identified five categories of Russian consumer: *Kuptsi* (merchants), *Cossacks*, *Students*, *Business Executives* and *Russian Souls*. Cossacks are characterised as ambitious, independent and status seeking, Russian Souls as passive, fearful of choices and hopeful. Thus, a typical Cossack might drive a BMW, smoke Dunhill cigarettes and drink Remy Martin Cognac, whereas a Russian Soul would drive a Lada, smoke Marlboros and drink Smirnoff Vodka.[21]

The lifestyle concept, when used carefully, can help the marketer understand changing consumer values and how they affect buying behaviour. Anna Flores, for example, can choose to live the role of a capable homemaker, a career woman or a free spirit – or all three. She plays several roles, and the way she blends them expresses her lifestyle. If she ever became a professional photographer, this would change her lifestyle, in turn changing what and how she buys.

■ Personality and self-concept

Personality
A person's distinguishing psychological characteristics that lead to relatively consistent and lasting responses to his or her own environment.

Each person's distinct personality influences his or her buying behaviour. **Personality** refers to the unique psychological characteristics that lead to relatively consistent and lasting responses to one's own environment. Personality is usually described in terms of traits such as self-confidence, dominance, sociability, autonomy, defensiveness, adaptability and aggressiveness.[22] Personality can be useful in analysing consumer behaviour for certain product or brand choices. For example, coffee makers have discovered that heavy coffee drinkers tend to be high on sociability. Thus Nescafé ads show people together over a cup of coffee.

Self-concept
Self-image, or the complex mental pictures that people have of themselves.

Many marketers use a concept related to personality – a person's **self-concept** (also called *self-image*). The basic self-concept premise is that people's possessions contribute to and reflect their identities: that is, 'we are what we have'. Thus, in order to understand consumer behaviour, the marketer must first understand the relationship between consumer self-concept and possessions. For example, people buy books to support their self-images:

> People have the mistaken notion that the thing you do with books is read them. Wrong . . . People buy books for what the purchase says about them – their taste, their cultivation, their trendiness. Their aim . . . is to connect themselves, or those to whom they give the books as gifts, with all the other refined owners of Edgar Allen Poe collections or sensitive owners of Virginia Woolf collections. . . . [The result is that] you can sell books as consumer products, with seductive displays, flashy posters, an emphasis on the glamour of the book, and the fashionableness of the bestseller and the trendy author.[23]

Anna Flores may see herself as outgoing, fun and active. Therefore, she will favour a camera that projects the same qualities. In that case the super-compact and stylish Canon Digital IXUS could attract her. 'Everybody smile and say "aaahhhh". The smallest, cutest digicam we've ever fallen for.'[24]

Really, it is not that simple. What if Anna's *actual self-concept* (how she views herself) differs from her *ideal self-concept* (how she would like to view herself) and from her *others self-concept* (how she thinks others sees her)? Which self will she try to satisfy when she buys a camera? Because this is unclear, self-concept theory has met with mixed success in predicting consumer responses to brand images.

psychological factors

A person's buying choices are further influenced by four important psychological factors: motivation, perception, learning, and beliefs and attitudes.

■ Motivation

We know that Anna Flores became interested in buying a camera. Why? What is she *really* seeking? What *needs* is she trying to satisfy?

A person has many needs at any given time. Some are *biological*, arising from states of tension such as hunger, thirst or discomfort. Others are *psychological*, arising from the need for recognition, esteem or belonging. Most of these needs will not be strong enough to motivate the person to act at a given point in time. A need becomes a *motive* when it is aroused to a sufficient level of intensity. A **motive** (or *drive*) is a need that is sufficiently pressing to direct the person to seek satisfaction. Psychologists have developed theories of human motivation. Two of the most popular – the theories of Sigmund Freud and Abraham Maslow – have quite different meanings for consumer analysis and marketing.

Motive (drive)
A need that is sufficiently pressing to direct the person to seek satisfaction of the need.

Freud's theory of motivation   Freud assumes that people are largely unconscious of the real psychological forces shaping their behaviour. He sees the person as growing up and repressing many urges. These urges are never eliminated or under perfect control; they emerge in dreams, in slips of the tongue, in neurotic and obsessive behaviour or ultimately in psychoses.

Thus Freud suggests that a person does not fully understand his or her motivation. If Anna Flores wants to purchase an expensive camera, she may describe her motive as wanting a hobby or career. At a deeper level, she may be purchasing the camera to impress others with her creative talent. At a still deeper level, she may be buying the camera to feel young and independent again.

Motivation researchers collect in-depth information from small samples of consumers to uncover the deeper motives for their product choices. They use non-directive depth interviews and various 'projective techniques' to throw the ego off guard – techniques such as word association, sentence completion, picture interpretation and role playing.

Motivation researchers have reached some interesting and sometimes odd conclusions about what may be in the buyer's mind regarding certain purchases. For example, one classic study concluded that consumers resist prunes because they are wrinkled-looking and remind people of sickness and old age. Despite its sometimes unusual conclusions, motivation research remains a useful tool for marketers seeking a deeper understanding of consumer behaviour (see Marketing Highlight 6.2).[25]

Maslow's theory of motivation   Abraham Maslow sought to explain why people are driven by particular needs at particular times.[26] Why does one person spend much time and energy on personal safety and another on gaining the esteem of others? Maslow's answer is that human needs are arranged in a hierarchy, from the most pressing to the least pressing. Maslow's hierarchy of needs is shown in Figure 6.4. In order of importance, they are (1) *physiological* needs, (2) *safety* needs, (3) *social* needs, (4) *esteem* needs, (5) *cognitive* needs, (6) *aesthetic* needs and (7) *self-actualisation* needs. A person tries to satisfy the most important need first. When that important need

marketing highlight 6.2

'Touchy-feely' research into consumer motivations

The term *motivation research* refers to qualitative research designed to probe consumers' hidden, subconscious motivations. Because consumers often don't know or can't describe just why they act as they do, motivation researchers use a variety of projective techniques to uncover underlying emotions and attitudes. The techniques range from sentence completion, word association and inkblot or cartoon interpretation tests, to having consumers describe typical brand users or form daydreams and fantasies about brands or buying situations. Some of these techniques verge on the bizarre. One writer offers the following tongue-in-cheek summary of a motivation research session:

> Good morning, ladies and gentlemen. We've called you here today for a little consumer research. Now, lie down on the couch, toss your inhibitions out the window and let's try a little free association. First, think about brands as if they were your *friends* . . . think of your shampoo as an animal. Go on, don't be shy. Would it be a panda or a lion? A snake or a woolly worm? . . . Draw a picture of a typical cake-mix user. Would she wear an apron or a negligée? A business suit or a can-can dress?

Such projective techniques seem dotty, but more and more marketers are turning to these touchy-feely, motivation research approaches to help them probe consumer psyches and develop better marketing strategies.

Many advertising agencies employ teams of psychologists, anthropologists and other social scientists to carry out their motivation research: 'We believe people make choices on a basic primitive level . . . we use the probe to get down to the unconscious.' The agency routinely conducts one-on-one, therapy-like interviews to delve into the inner workings of consumers. Another agency asks consumers to describe their favourite brands as animals or cars (say, Saab versus BMW) in order to assess the prestige associated with various brands.

In an effort to understand the teenage consumer market better, ad agency BSB Worldwide videotaped teenagers' rooms in 25 countries. It found surprising similarities across countries and cultures:

> From the steamy playgrounds of Los Angeles to the stately boulevards of Singapore, kids show amazing similarities in taste, language, and attitude. . . . From the gear and posters on display, it's hard to tell whether the rooms are in Los Angeles, Mexico City, or Tokyo. Basketballs sit alongside soccer balls. Closets overflow with staples from an international, unisex uniform: baggy Levi's or Diesel jeans and rugged shoes from Timberland or Doc Martens.

Similarly, researchers at Sega of America's ad agency have learned a lot about video game buying behaviour by hanging around with 150 kids in their bedrooms and by shopping with them. Above all else, they learned, do everything fast. As a result, in Sega's most recent 15–second commercials, some images fly by so quickly that adults cannot recall seeing them, even after repeated showings. The kids, weaned on MTV, recollect them keenly.

Some marketers dismiss such motivation research as mumbo jumbo. And these approaches do present some problems. They use small samples and researcher interpretations of results are often highly subjective, sometimes leading to rather exotic explanations of otherwise ordinary buying behaviour. However, others believe strongly that these approaches can provide interesting nuggets of insight into the relationships between consumers and the brands they buy. To marketers who use them, motivation research techniques provide a flexible and varied means of gaining insights into deeply held and often mysterious motivations behind consumer buying behaviour.

Sources: Excerpts from Annetta Miller and Dody Tsiantar, 'Psyching out consumers', *Newsweek* (27 February 1989), pp. 46–7; G. De Groot, 'Deep, dangerous or just plain dotty?', ESOMAR Seminar on Qualitative Methods of Research, Amsterdam, 1986; Shawn Tully, 'Teens: The most global market of all', *Fortune* (6 May 1994), pp. 90–7; and Tobi Elkin, 'Product pampering', *Brandweek* (16 June 1997), pp. 38–40. Also see 'They understand your kids', *Fortune* (special issue, Autumn/Winter 1993), pp. 29–30; Cyndee Miller, 'Sometimes a researcher has no alternative but to hang out in a bar', *Marketing News* (3 January 1994), pp. 16, 26; Ronald B. Lieber, 'Storytelling: A new way to get close to your customer', *Fortune* (3 February 1997), pp. 102–8; Jerry W. Thomas, 'Finding unspoken reasons for consumers' choices', *Marketing News* (8 June 1998), pp. 10–11; and Michele Marchetti, 'Marketing's weird science', *Sales & Marketing Management* (May 1999), p. 87; Anne Wrangham, 'A question of quality', *Marketing Business* (May 1998), pp. 19–22; Peter Law, 'Warts'n'all', *Marketing Business* (June 1999), pp. 59–61.

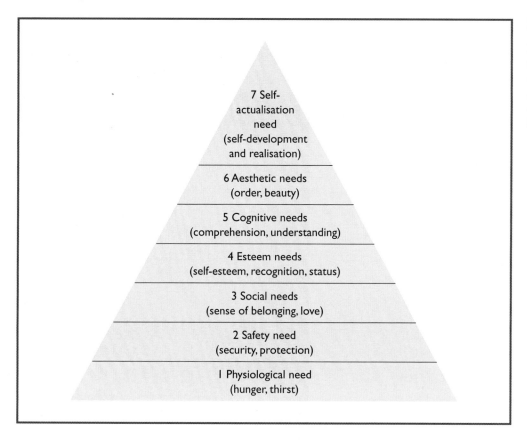

Figure 6.4

Maslow's hierarchy of needs

SOURCE: Adapted from Abraham H. Maslow, *Motivation and personality*, 2nd edn, 1970 (Prentice Hall, Inc.)

is satisfied, it will stop being a motivator and the person will then try to satisfy the next most important need. For example, a starving man (need 1) will not take an interest in the latest happenings in the art world (need 6), or in how he is seen or esteemed by others (need 3 or 4), or even in whether he is breathing clean air (need 2). But as each important need is satisfied, the next most important need will come into play:

> The wine market shows how the different levels of the need hierarchy can be at play at the same time. Buyers of premium wines are seeking self-esteem and self-actualisation. They may achieve this by showing their knowledge by buying 1986 Chateaux Ausone from a specialist wine merchant. Wine buying makes many other people anxious, particularly if it is a gift. They buy the product to fill a social need but are unable to gauge quality. To be safe they buy from a reputable store (Oddbins) or a brand legitimised by advertising (Le Piat d'Or).[27]

Maslow's hierarchy is not universal for all cultures. As the heroes of Hollywood movies amply show, Anglo-Saxon culture values self-actualisation and individuality above all else, but that is not universally so. In Japan and German-speaking countries, people are most highly motivated by a need for order (aesthetic needs) and belonging (esteem needs), while in France, Spain, Portugal and other Latin and Asian countries, people are most motivated by the need for security and belonging.[28]

What light does Maslow's theory throw on Anna Flores' interest in buying a camera? We can guess that Anna has satisfied her physiological, safety and social needs; they do not motivate her interest in cameras. Her camera interest might come from an aesthetic need and esteem needs. Or it might come from a need for self-actualisation or cognition – she might want to be a creative person and express herself through photography or explore her potential.

Selective attention: Because most ads are ignored by consumers, marketers must work hard to develop attention-getting ads. This is the aim of Boots with this ad for Inspiral Condoms.

SOURCE: Boots/Inspiral Condoms/Rockland Corporation. *Agency:* Big Fish design solutions, designed by Paul Lebeter.

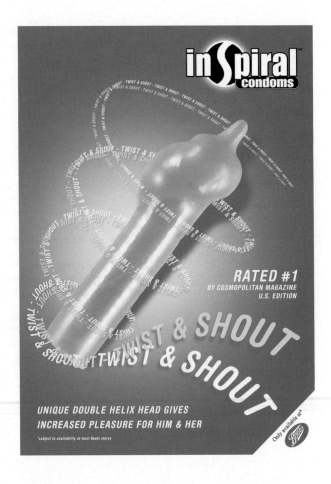

■ Perception

A motivated person is ready to act. How the person acts is influenced by his or her perception of the situation. Two people with the same motivation and in the same situation may act quite differently because they perceive the situation differently. Anna Flores might consider a fast-talking camera salesperson loud and false. Another camera buyer might consider the same salesperson intelligent and helpful.

Why do people perceive the same situation differently? All of us learn by the flow of information through our five senses: sight, hearing, smell, touch and taste. However, each of us receives, organises and interprets this sensory information in an individual way. Thus **perception** is the process by which people select, organise and interpret information to form a meaningful picture of the world. People can form different perceptions of the same stimulus because of three perceptual processes: selective attention, selective distortion and selective retention.

Perception
The process by which people select, organise and interpret information to form a meaningful picture of the world.

Selective attention   People are exposed to a great number of stimuli every day. For example, the average person may be exposed to more than 1,500 ads a day. It is impossible for a person to pay attention to all these stimuli and some studies show people remembering only three or four.[29] **Selective attention** – the tendency for people to screen out most of the information to which they are exposed – means that marketers have to work especially hard to attract the consumer's attention. Their message will be lost on most people who are not in the market for the product. Moreover, even people who are in the market may not notice the message unless it stands out from the surrounding sea of other ads.

Selective attention
The tendency of people to screen out most of the information to which they are exposed.

Selective distortion   Even noted stimuli do not always come across in the intended way. Each person fits incoming information into an existing mind-set. **Selective distortion** describes the tendency of people to adapt information to personal meanings. Anna Flores may hear the salesperson mention some good and bad points about a competing camera brand. Because she already has a strong leaning towards Fuji, Kodak or Agfa, she is likely to distort those points in order to conclude that one camera is better than the others. People tend to interpret information in a way that will support what they already believe. Selective distortion means that marketers must try to understand the mind-sets of consumers and how these will affect interpretations of advertising and sales information:

> Cathay Pacific, the Hong Kong-based airline, found out that although Caucasians saw Cathay as an Asian airline, Asians perceived the airline as being well managed and safe, but not Asian. Seeing their future in Asia where 80 per cent of their passengers came from, Cathay wants to change their view. Peter Sutch, Cathay's chairman, explains their new livery: 'We wanted something Asian in appearance: we wanted a quality look with an Asian flavour.' The airline now offers a wide range of Asian meals and communicates in many Asian languages. In-flight information is now in Japanese, Korean, Mandarin and Cantonese as well as English.[30]

Selective retention   People will also forget much of what they learn. They tend to retain information that supports their attitudes and beliefs. Because of **selective retention**, Anna is likely to remember good points made about the Fuji and forget good points made about competing cameras. She may remember Fuji's good points because she 'rehearses' them more whenever she thinks about choosing a camera.

Because of selective exposure, distortion and retention, marketers have to work hard to get their messages through. This fact explains why marketers use so much drama and repetition in sending messages to their market. Although some consumers are worried that they will be affected by marketing messages without even knowing it, most marketers worry about whether their offers will be perceived at all.[31]

■ Learning

When people act, they learn. **Learning** describes changes in an individual's behaviour arising from experience. Learning theorists say that most human behaviour is learned. Learning occurs through the interplay of *drives*, *stimuli*, *cues*, *responses* and *reinforcement*.

We saw that Anna Flores has a drive for self-actualisation. A *drive* is a strong internal stimulus that calls for action. Her drive becomes a motive when it is directed towards a particular *stimulus object* – in this case, a camera. Anna's response to the idea of buying a camera is conditioned by the surrounding cues. *Cues* are minor stimuli that determine when, where and how the person responds. Seeing cameras in a shop window, hearing a special sale price, and her husband's support are all cues that can influence Anna's *response* to her interest in buying a camera.

Suppose Anna buys the Canon IXUS. If the experience is rewarding, she will probably use the camera more and more. Her response to cameras will be *reinforced*. Then the next time she shops for a camera, binoculars or some similar product, the probability is greater that she will buy a Canon product. We say that she *generalises* her response to similar stimuli.

The reverse of generalisation is *discrimination*. When Anna examines binoculars made by Olympus, she sees that they are lighter and more compact than Nikon's binoculars. Discrimination means that she has learned to recognise differences in sets of products and can adjust her response accordingly.

The practical significance of learning theory for marketers is that they can build up demand for a product by associating it with strong drives, using motivating cues and

Selective distortion
The tendency of people to adapt information to personal meanings.

Selective retention
The tendency of people to retain only part of the information to which they are exposed, usually information that supports their attitudes or beliefs.

Learning
Changes in an individual's behaviour arising from experience.

providing positive reinforcement. A new company can enter the market by appealing to the same drives that competitors appeal to and by providing similar cues, because buyers are more likely to transfer loyalty to similar brands than to dissimilar ones (generalisation). Or a new company may design its brand to appeal to a different set of drives and offer strong cue inducements to switch brands (discrimination).

■ Beliefs and attitudes

Belief
A descriptive thought that a person holds about something.

Through doing and learning, people acquire their beliefs and attitudes. These, in turn, influence their buying behaviour. A **belief** is a descriptive thought that a person has about something. Anna Flores may believe that an Agfa camera takes great pictures, stands up well under hard use and is good value. These beliefs may be based on real knowledge, opinion or faith, and may or may not carry an emotional charge. For example, Anna Flores' belief that an Agfa camera is heavy may or may not matter to her decision.

Marketers are interested in the beliefs that people formulate about specific products and services, because these beliefs make up product and brand images that affect buying behaviour. If some of the beliefs are wrong and prevent purchase, the marketer will want to launch a campaign to correct them.

Attitude
A person's consistently favourable or unfavourable evaluations, feelings and tendencies towards an object or idea.

People have attitudes regarding religion, politics, clothes, music, food and almost everything else. An **attitude** describes a person's relatively consistent evaluations, feelings and tendencies towards an object or idea. Attitudes put people into a frame of mind of liking or disliking things, of moving towards or away from them. Thus Anna Flores may hold such attitudes as 'Buy the best', 'The Japanese make the best products in the world' and 'Creativity and self-expression are among the most important things in life'. If so, the Canon camera would fit well into Anna's existing attitudes.

Attitudes are difficult to change. A person's attitudes fit into a pattern and to change one attitude may require difficult adjustments in many others. Thus a com-

Attitudes are hard to change, but it can be done. Honda's classic 'You meet the nicest people on a Honda' campaign changed people's attitudes about who rides motorcycles.

SOURCE: Reprinted with permission of America Honda Motor Co., Inc.

pany should usually try to fit its products into existing attitudes rather than try to change attitudes. Of course, there are exceptions in which the great cost of trying to change attitudes may pay off. For example:

> In the late 1950s, Honda entered the US motorcycle market facing a major decision. It could either sell its motorcycles to the small but already established motorcycle market or try to increase the size of this market by attracting new types of consumer. Increasing the size of the market would be more difficult and expensive because many people had negative attitudes toward motorcycles. They associated motorcycles with black leather jackets, switchblades and outlaws. Despite these adverse attitudes, Honda took the second course of action. It launched a major campaign to position motorcycles as good clean fun. Its theme 'You meet the nicest people on a Honda' worked well and many people adopted a new attitude toward motorcycles. In the 1990s, however, Honda faces a similar problem. With the ageing of the baby boomers, the market has once again shifted toward only hard-core motorcycling enthusiasts. So Honda has again set out to change consumer attitudes. Its 'Come Ride With Us' campaign aims to re-establish the wholesomeness of motorcycling and to position it as fun and exciting for everyone.[32]

consumer decision process

The consumer's choice results from the complex interplay of cultural, social, personal and psychological factors. Although the marketer cannot influence many of these factors, they can be useful in identifying interested buyers and in shaping products and appeals to serve their needs better. Marketers have to be extremely careful in analysing consumer behaviour. Consumers often turn down what appears to be a winning offer. Polaroid found this out when it lost millions on its Polarvision instant home movie system; Ford when it launched the Edsel; RCA on its Selecta-Vision and Philips on its LaserVision video-disc player; Sony with DAT tapes; and Bristol with its trio of the Brabazon, Britannia and Concorde airliners. So far we have looked at the cultural, social, personal and psychological influences that affect buyers. Now we look at how consumers make buying decisions: first, the types of decision that consumers face; then the main steps in the buyer decision process; and finally, the processes by which consumers learn about and buy new products.

types of buying decision behaviour

Consumer decision making varies with the type of buying decision. Consumer buying behaviour differs greatly for a tube of toothpaste, a tennis racket, an expensive camera and a new car. More complex decisions usually involve more buying participants and more buyer deliberation. Figure 6.5 shows types of consumer buying behaviour based on the degree of buyer involvement and the degree of differences among brands.[33]

complex buying behaviour

Consumers undertake **complex buying behaviour** when they are highly involved in a purchase and perceive significant differences among brands, or when the product is

Complex buying behaviour
Consumer buying behaviour in situations characterised by high consumer involvement in a purchase and significant perceived differences among brands.

Figure 6.5

Four types of buying behaviour

SOURCE: Adapted from Henry Assael, *Consumer Behaviour and Marketing Action* 6th edition, p. 67. (Boston, MA: Kent Publishing Company, 1987) © Wadsworth Inc. 1987. Reprinted by permission of Kent Publishing Company, a division of Wadsworth Inc.

	High involvement	Low involvement
Significant differences between brands	Complex buying behaviour	Variety-seeking buying behaviour
Few differences between brands	Dissonance-reducing buying behaviour	Habitual buying behaviour

The purchase of a laptop involves complex buying behaviour. Ads promoting this kind of item should contain long explicative copy to make the customer more comfortable about the product.

SOURCE: Packard Bell. *Agency*: Fred Fisher Associates

expensive, risky, purchased infrequently and highly self-expressive. Typically, the consumer has much to learn about the product category. For example, a personal computer buyer may not know what attributes to consider. Many product features carry no real meaning: an 'Intel 200MHz Pentium II Pro', 'SVGA display', '16Mb Sync DRAM, 256 Kb Cache' or even a '16X Max CD-ROM with 33.6 BPS fax/data (upgradeable to 56K)'.

This buyer will pass through a learning process, first developing beliefs about the product, then developing attitudes, and then making a thoughtful purchase choice. Marketers of high-involvement products must understand the information-gathering and evaluation behaviour of high-involvement consumers. They need to help buyers learn about product-class attributes and their relative importance and about what the company's brand offers on the important attributes. Marketers need to differentiate their brand's features, perhaps by describing the brand's benefits using print media with long copy. They must motivate store salespeople and the buyer's acquaintances to influence the final brand choice. Recognising this problem, Dixons, the electrical retailers, is setting up the Link chain of stores dedicated to helping baffled buyers on to the information superhighway and multimedia.[34]

dissonance-reducing buying behaviour

Dissonance-reducing buying behaviour occurs when consumers are highly involved with an expensive, infrequent or risky purchase, but see little difference among brands. For example, consumers buying carpeting may face a high-involvement decision because carpeting is expensive and self-expressive. Yet buyers may consider most carpet brands in a given price range to be the same. In this case, because perceived brand differences are not large, buyers may shop around to learn what is available, but buy relatively quickly. They may respond primarily to a good price or to purchase convenience. After the purchase, consumers might experience post-purchase dissonance (after-sales discomfort) when they notice certain disadvantages of the purchased carpet brand or hear favourable things about brands not purchased. To counter such dissonance, the marketer's after-sale communications should provide evidence and support to help consumers feel good both before and after their brand choices.[35]

Dissonance-reducing buying behaviour *Consumer buying behaviour in situations characterised by high involvement but few perceived differences among brands.*

habitual buying behaviour

Habitual buying behaviour occurs under conditions of low consumer involvement and little significant brand difference. For example, take salt. Consumers have little involvement in this product category – they simply go to the store and reach for a brand. If they keep reaching for the same brand, it is out of habit rather than strong brand loyalty. Consumers appear to have low involvement with most low-cost, frequently purchased products.

Habitual buying behaviour *Consumer buying behaviour in situations characterised by low consumer involvement and few significant perceived brand differences.*

Consumers do not search extensively for information about the brands, evaluate brand characteristics and make weighty decisions about which brands to buy. Instead, they passively receive information as they watch television or read magazines. Ad repetition creates *brand familiarity* rather than *brand conviction*. Consumers do not form strong attitudes towards a brand; they select the brand because it is familiar and may not evaluate the choice even after purchase.

Because buyers are not highly committed to any brands, marketers of low-involvement products with few brand differences often use price and sales promotions to stimulate product trial. Gaining distribution and attention at the point of sale is critical. In advertising for a low-involvement product, ad copy should stress only a few key points. Visual symbols and imagery are important because they can be remembered easily and associated with the brand. Ad campaigns should include high repetition of short-duration messages. Television is usually more effective than print media because it is a low-involvement medium suitable for passive learning. Advertising planning should be based on classical conditioning theory, in which buyers learn to identify a certain product by a symbol repeatedly attached to it.

Products can be linked to some involving personal situation. Nestlé did this in a recent series of ads for Gold Blend coffee, each consisting of a new soap-opera-like episode featuring the evolving romantic relationship between neighbours, Sharon and Tony. Nestlé's success in doing this contrasts with the tea market in the United Kingdom where, although it is the national drink, sales promotions dominate sales.

Marketers can convert low-involvement products into higher-involvement ones by linking them to involving situations. Here Nestlé creates involvement with soap-opera-like ads featuring the romantic relationship between two neighbours, Tony and Sharon.
SOURCE: Nestlé UK Ltd

variety-seeking buying behaviour

Variety-seeking buying behaviour
Consumer buying behaviour in situations characterised by low consumer involvement, but significant perceived brand differences.

Consumers undertake **variety-seeking buying behaviour** in situations characterised by low consumer involvement, but significant perceived brand differences. In such cases, consumers often do a lot of brand switching. For example, when purchasing biscuits, a consumer may hold some beliefs, choose a biscuit without much evaluation, then evaluate that brand during consumption. But the next time, the consumer might pick another brand out of boredom or simply to try something different. Brand switching occurs for the sake of variety rather than because of dissatisfaction.

In such product categories, the marketing strategy may differ for the market leader and minor brands. The market leader will try to encourage habitual buying behaviour by dominating shelf space, avoiding out-of-stock conditions and running frequent reminder advertising. Challenger firms will encourage variety seeking by offering lower prices, deals, coupons, free samples and advertising that presents reasons for trying something new.

the buyer decision process

Most large companies research consumer buying decisions in great detail to answer questions about what consumers buy, where they buy, how and how much they buy, when they buy and why they buy. Marketers can study consumer purchases to find answers to questions about what they buy, where and how much. But learning about the *whys* of consumer buying behaviour and the buying decision process is not so easy – the answers are often locked within the consumer's head.

We will examine the stages that buyers pass through to reach a buying decision. We will use the model in Figure 6.6, which shows the consumer as passing through five stages: *need recognition, information search, evaluation of alternatives, purchase decision* and *postpurchase behaviour*. Clearly the buying process starts long before actual purchase and continues long after. This encourages the marketer to focus on the entire buying process rather than just the purchase decision.

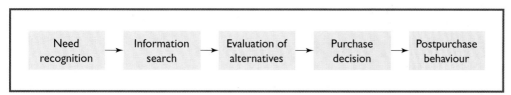

Figure 6.6

Buyer decision process

This model implies that consumers pass through all five stages with every purchase. But in more routine purchases, consumers often skip or reverse some of these stages. A woman buying her regular brand of toothpaste would recognise the need and go right to the purchase decision, skipping information search and evaluation. However, we use the model in Figure 6.6 because it shows all the considerations that arise when a consumer faces a new and complex purchase situation.

To illustrate this model, we return to Anna Flores and try to understand how she became interested in buying a camera and the stages she went through to make the final choice.

need recognition

The buying process starts with **need recognition** – the buyer recognising a problem or need. The buyer senses a difference between his or her *actual* state and some *desired* state. The need can be triggered by *internal stimuli* when one of the person's normal needs – hunger, thirst, sex – rises to a level high enough to become a drive. From previous experience, the person has learnt how to cope with this drive and is motivated towards objects that he or she knows will satisfy it.

A need can also be triggered by *external stimuli*. Anna passes a bakery and the smell of freshly baked bread stimulates her hunger; she admires a neighbour's new car; or she watches a television commercial for a Caribbean vacation. At this stage, the marketer needs to determine the factors and situations that usually trigger consumer need recognition. The marketer should research consumers to find out what kinds of need or problem arise, what brought them about and how they led the consumer to this particular product. Anna might answer that she felt she needed a camera after friends showed her the photographs they took on holiday. By gathering such information, the marketer can identify the stimuli that most often trigger interest in the product and can develop marketing programmes that involve these stimuli.

Compared with other animals, human beings are most conscious of visual stimulus. However, psychologists and marketers are beginning to recognise that smell is an important stimulus that often operates unconsciously. Marketing Highlight 6.3 examines this frontier where science is working hand in hand with science.

Need recognition
The first stage of the buyer decision process in which the consumer recognises a problem or need.

information search

An aroused consumer may or may not search for more information. If the consumer's drive is strong and a satisfying product is near at hand, the consumer is likely to buy it then. If not, the consumer may simply store the need in memory or undertake an **information search** related to the need.

At one level, the consumer may simply enter *heightened attention*. Here Anna becomes more receptive to information about cameras. She pays attention to camera ads, cameras used by friends and camera conversations. Or Anna may go into *active information search*, in which she looks for reading material, phones friends and gathers information in other ways. The amount of searching she does will depend upon

Information search
The stage of the buyer decision process in which the consumer is aroused to search for more information; the consumer may simply have heightened attention or may go into active information search.

marketing highlight 6.3

Pong: the final marketing frontier

Rolls-Royce Cars hit the headlines recently when it was revealed that they had developed an essence of new spray to use on their luxurious upholstery after they found out their cars did not smell new enough. Other sellers use similar tricks. There are few people selling houses who have not recognised the trick of percolating coffee when the house is viewed and few stores that have not used the attractive smell of fresh bread. Philosophers from Aristotle to Kant have ranked base smell below the noble senses of seeing, hearing and touching. Yet fragrances are one of the pillars of luxury marketing, with exclusive brands being adored by the initiated. Creed is one of the most classic of fragrances, used by Prince Charles, Robert Redford and Quincy Jones; Acqua di Parma was adored by Cary Grant, David Niven, Audrey Hepburn and Eva Gardner. Is this obsession an indulgence or does it reflect an insight that few have achieved?

Freud proposes an answer. Smell, he says, is a base sense but one that people have evolved to reject intellectually because of its power. Walking on two legs has taken 1,000 different types of smell receptors in our nose away from the centres of odour that obsess four-legged creatures. With taste, smell was one of the first senses to evolve – it is how amoebas find food. Old it may be, but neglected it is not. One per cent of our 100,000 genes relate to our smell receptors in the nose while only three genes control colour vision. Our smell receptors are also well connected. From the nose they first go to the limbic system – a part of the brain that drives mood, sexual urges and fear. Signals then travel to the hippocampus, which controls memories. Only then do the signals travel to the frontal lobes of the brain involved in conscious thought. Our 1,000 smell receptors are always working busily but subliminally.

One example of this subliminal effect is a range of 'odourless' steroids produced by men and women. These can directly affect mood. Unfortunately, while the masculine version cheers up women, the female one irritates men. There is more. A granny smell, taken from the armpits of menopausal women, makes people happy while a mummy smell, taken from new mums, can cure depression. Smell also influences perception. Men's regard for how attractive women smell without seeing them corresponds strongly to their perception of their visual attractiveness, while the smell of teenage men makes people angry.

Researchers have shown that how people respond to smell can be driven by evolutionary logic. Although women have a stronger sense of smell than men do, they are not so good at identifying attractive guys by smell alone. Instead they are attracted to the smell of men whose immune system least overlaps with theirs and are therefore partners most likely to sire healthy offspring. This handy sensitivity increases when women are ovulating but is, unfortunately, messed up by taking contraceptive pills.

Science is also coming to the help of removing smells that no one finds attractive, body odour (BO). We now know that this is caused by Corynebacteria (Coryn), a group of some of the 7,000 bacteria that inhabit all skin. All the bacteria live off the skin's natural fat-laden secretion but, unfortunately for some, they attract Coryn which is a messy eater that leaves half-digested waste. Quest International, one of the world's largest fragrance houses, is now working on long-active deodorants that attack Coryn rather than clogging up the sweat glands like most of the €1.5 billion worth of deodorants do.

The understanding of the science of odour is now moving out of the realm of the alchemy of exotic fragrances. Aromatic engineering is a rapidly growing business based on pumping designer smells into offices and stores to make customers feel happier and spend more money. Rolls-Royce was early into using odour to make their cars more desirable. Other researchers are working on odours that will automatically change a driver's mood to reduce road rage. What other odour could be used in cars? There is growing evidence that humans have a veromonal nasal organ, a sensor that picks up the pheromones that drive animals sex crazy. However, there is little sign that the ultimate aphrodisiac will ever exist.

SOURCES: Jerome Burne, 'Why smell gets up your nose', *Financial Times* (8 April 2000), p. 11; Nick Foulkes, 'Have you seen this bottle?', *How to Spend It, Financial Times* (8 April 2000), pp. 31–2; 'Making sense of scents', *The Economist* (13 March 1999), p. 137; 'The sweet smell of success', *The Economist* (25 March 2000), p. 118.

the strength of her drive, the amount of information she starts with, the ease of obtaining more information, the value she places on additional information and the satisfaction she gets from searching. Normally the amount of consumer search activity increases as the consumer moves from decisions that involve limited problem solving to those that involve extensive problem solving.

The consumer can obtain information from any of several sources:

+ *Personal sources*: family, friends, neighbours, acquaintances.
+ *Commercial sources*: advertising, salespeople, the Internet, packaging, displays.
+ *Public sources*: mass media, consumer-rating organisations.
+ *Experiential sources*: handling, examining, using the product.

The relative influence of these information sources varies with the product and the buyer. Generally, the consumer receives the most information about a product from commercial sources – those controlled by the marketer. The most effective sources, however, tend to be personal. Personal sources appear to be even more important in influencing the purchase of services.[36] Commercial sources normally *inform* the buyer, but personal sources *legitimise* or *evaluate* products for the buyer. For example, doctors normally learn of new drugs from commercial sources, but turn to other doctors for evaluative information.

As more information is obtained, the consumer's awareness and knowledge of the available brands and features increases. In her information search, Anna learnt about the many camera brands available. The information also helped her drop certain brands from consideration. A company must design its marketing mix to make prospects aware of and knowledgeable about its brand. If it fails to do this, the company has lost its opportunity to sell to the customer. The company must also learn which other brands customers consider so that it knows its competition and can plan its own appeals.

The marketer should identify consumers' sources of information and the importance of each source. Consumers should be asked how they first heard about the brand, what information they received and the importance they place on different information sources.

evaluation of alternatives

We have seen how the consumer uses information to arrive at a set of final brand choices. How does the consumer choose among the alternative brands? The marketer needs to know about **alternative evaluation** – that is, how the consumer processes information to arrive at brand choices. Unfortunately, consumers do not use a simple and single evaluation process in all buying situations. Instead, several evaluation processes are at work.

Certain basic concepts help explain consumer evaluation processes. First, we assume that each consumer is trying to satisfy some need and is looking for certain *benefits* that can be acquired by buying a product or service. Further, each consumer sees a product as a bundle of *product attributes* with varying capacities for delivering these benefits and satisfying the need. For cameras, product attributes might include picture quality, ease of use, camera size, price and other features. Consumers will vary as to which of these attributes they consider relevant and will pay the most attention to those attributes connected with their needs.

Second, the consumer will attach different *degrees of importance* to each attribute. A distinction can be drawn between the importance of an attribute and its salience. *Salient attributes* are those that come to a consumer's mind when he or she

Alternative evaluation
The stage of the buyer decision process in which the consumer uses information to evaluate alternative brands in the choice set.

is asked to think of a product's characteristics. But these are not necessarily the most important attributes to the consumer. Some of them may be salient because the consumer has just seen an advertisement mentioning them or has had a problem with them, making these attributes 'top-of-the-mind'. There may also be other attributes that the consumer forgot, but whose importance would be recognised if they were mentioned. Marketers should be more concerned with attribute importance than attribute salience.

Third, the consumer is likely to develop a set of *brand beliefs* about where each brand stands on each attribute. The set of beliefs held about a particular brand is known as the **brand image**. The consumer's beliefs may vary from true attributes based on his or her experience and the effect of selective perception, selective distortion and selective retention.

Fourth, the consumer is assumed to have a *utility function* for each attribute. The utility function shows how the consumer expects total product satisfaction to vary with different levels of different attributes. For example, Anna may expect her satisfaction from a digital camera to increase with better picture quality; to peak with a medium-weight camera as opposed to a very light or very heavy one and to be a compact. If we combine the attribute levels at which her utilities are highest, they make up Anna's ideal camera. The camera would also be her preferred camera if it were available and affordable.

Fifth, the consumer arrives at attitudes towards the different brands through some *evaluation procedure*. Consumers have been found to use one or more of several evaluation procedures, depending on the consumer and the buying decision.

In Anna's camera-buying situation, suppose she has narrowed her choice set to four cameras: Agfa ePhoto 1280, Ricoh RDC-300Z, Canon Powershot 350 and the amazingly inexpensive Mustek VDC-100. In addition, let us say she is interested primarily in four attributes – picture quality, ease of use, camera size and price. Table 6.5 shows how she believes each brand rates on each attribute.[37] Anna believes the Agfa will give her picture quality of 10 on a 10-point scale; is not so easy to use, 6; is of medium size, 6; and is expensive, 3. Similarly, she has beliefs about how the other cameras rate on these attributes. The marketer would like to be able to predict which camera Anna will buy.

Clearly, if one camera rated best on all the attributes, we could predict that Anna would choose it. But the brands vary in appeal. Some buyers will base their buying decision on only one attribute and their choices are easy to predict. If Anna wants low price above everything, she should buy the Mustek, whereas if she wants the camera that is easiest to use, she could buy either the Ricoh or the Canon.

Most buyers consider several attributes, but assign different importance to each. If we knew the importance weights that Anna assigns to the four attributes, we could predict her camera choice more reliably. Suppose Anna assigns 40 per cent of the

Brand image

The set of beliefs that consumers hold about a particular brand.

Table 6.5

A consumer's brand beliefs about cameras

Camera	Picture quality	Ease of use	Camera size	Price
Agfa	10	6	6	3
Ricoh	6	8	6	6
Canon	8	7	8	6
Mustek	4	6	8	9

importance to the camera's picture quality, 30 per cent to ease of use, 20 per cent to its size and 10 per cent to its price. To find Anna's perceived value for each camera, we can multiply her importance weights by her beliefs about each camera. This gives us the following perceived values:

$$
\begin{aligned}
\text{Agfa} &= 0.4(10) + 0.3(6) + 0.2(6) + 0.1(3) = 7.3 \\
\text{Ricoh} &= 0.4(6) \ \ + 0.3(8) + 0.2(6) + 0.1(6) = 6.6 \\
\text{Canon} &= 0.4(8) \ \ + 0.3(7) + 0.2(8) + 0.1(6) = 7.5 \\
\text{Mustek} &= 0.4(4) \ \ + 0.3(6) + 0.2(8) + 0.1(9) = 5.9
\end{aligned}
$$

We would predict that Anna favours the Canon.

This model is called the *expectancy value model* of consumer choice.[38] This is one of several possible models describing how consumers go about evaluating alternatives. Consumers might evaluate a set of alternatives in other ways. For example, Anna might decide that she should consider only cameras that satisfy a set of minimum attribute levels. She might decide that a camera must have a TV connector. In this case, we would choose the Agfa because it is the only one with that facility. This is called the *conjunctive model* of consumer choice. Or she might decide that she would settle for a camera that had a picture quality greater than 7 *or* ease of use greater than 9. In this case, the Agfa, Ricoh or Canon would do, since they all meet at least one of the requirements. This is called the *disjunctive model* of consumer choice.

How consumers go about evaluating purchase alternatives depends on the individual consumer and the specific buying situation. In some cases, consumers use careful calculations and logical thinking. At other times, the same consumers do little

Evaluating alternatives: In some cases, consumers use careful calculations; in others they do little or no evaluating. In the small print, this Nikon ad emphasises its serious camera technology, compact size, three picture-taking formats, and interchangeable zoom lenses – 'The technology of a serious camera. The spontaneity of a point-and-shoot.'

SOURCE: Nikon Inc.

or no evaluating; instead they buy on impulse and rely on intuition. Sometimes consumers make buying decisions on their own; sometimes they turn to friends, consumer guides or salespeople for buying advice.

Marketers should study buyers to find out how they actually evaluate brand alternatives. If they know what evaluative processes go on, marketers can take steps to influence the buyer's decision. Suppose Anna is now inclined to buy an Agfa because of its picture quality. What strategies might another camera maker, say Canon, use to influence people like Anna? There are several. Canon could modify its camera to produce a version that has fewer features, but is lighter and cheaper. It could try to change buyers' beliefs about how its camera rates on key attributes, especially if consumers currently underestimate the camera's qualities. It could try to change buyers' beliefs about Agfa and other competitors. Finally, it could try to change the list of attributes that buyers consider or the importance attached to these attributes. For example, it might advertise that to be really useful a camera needs to be small and easy to use. What is the point in having a super-accurate camera if it takes too long to set up and is too awkward to carry around?

purchase decision

Purchase decision

The stage of the buyer decision process in which the consumer actually buys the product.

In the evaluation stage, the consumer ranks brands and forms purchase intentions. Generally, the consumer's **purchase decision** will be to buy the most preferred brand, but two factors, shown in Figure 6.7, can come between the purchase *intention* and the purchase *decision*. The first factor is the *attitudes of others*. For example, if Anna Flores' husband feels strongly that Anna should buy the lowest-priced camera, then the chance of Anna buying a more expensive camera is reduced. Alternatively, his love of gadgets may attract him to the Agfa. How much another person's attitudes will affect Anna's choices depends both on the strength of the other person's attitudes towards her buying decision and on Anna's motivation to comply with that person's wishes.

Purchase intention is also influenced by *unexpected situational factors*. The consumer may form a purchase intention based on factors such as expected family income, expected price and expected benefits from the product. When the consumer is about to act, unexpected situational factors may arise to change the purchase intention. Anna may lose her job, some other purchase may become more urgent or a friend may report being disappointed in her preferred camera. Thus preferences and even purchase intentions do not always result in actual purchase choice. They may direct purchase behaviour, but may not fully determine the outcome.

A consumer's decision to change, postpone or avoid a purchase decision is influenced heavily by *perceived risk*. Many purchases involve some risk taking.[39] Anxiety results when consumers cannot be certain about the purchase outcome. The amount of perceived risk varies with the amount of money at stake, the amount of

Figure 6.7

Steps between evaluation of alternatives and a purchase decision

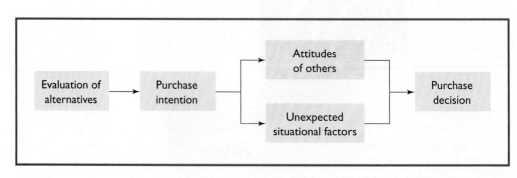

purchase uncertainty and the amount of consumer self-confidence. A consumer takes certain actions to reduce risk, such as avoiding purchase decisions, gathering more information and looking for national brand names and products with warranties. The marketer must understand the factors that provoke feelings of risk in consumers and must provide information and support that will reduce the perceived risk.

postpurchase behaviour

The marketer's job does not end when the product is bought. After purchasing the product, the consumer will be satisfied or dissatisfied and will engage in **postpurchase behaviour** of interest to the marketer. What determines whether the buyer is satisfied or dissatisfied with a purchase? The answer lies in the relationship between the *consumer's expectations* and the product's *perceived performance*. If the product falls short of expectations, the consumer is disappointed; if it meets expectations, the consumer is satisfied; if it exceeds expectations, the consumer is delighted.

Postpurchase behaviour
The stage of the buyer decision process in which consumers take further action after purchase based on their satisfaction or dissatisfaction.

Consumers base their expectations on messages they receive from sellers, friends and other information sources. If the seller exaggerates the product's performance, consumer expectations will not be met – a situation that leads to dissatisfaction. The larger the gap between expectations and performance, the greater the consumer's dissatisfaction. This fact suggests that the seller should make product claims that represent faithfully the product's performance so that buyers are satisfied.

Motoring organisations regularly give pessimistic quotes about how long they will take to reach a customer whose car breaks down. If they say they will be 30 minutes and get there in 20, the customer is impressed. If, however, they get there in 20 minutes after promising 10, the customer is not so happy.

Almost all large purchases result in **cognitive dissonance** or discomfort caused by postpurchase conflict. Consumers are satisfied with the benefits of the chosen brand and glad to avoid the drawbacks of the brands not purchased. On the other hand, every purchase involves compromise. Consumers feel uneasy about acquiring the drawbacks of the chosen brand and about losing the benefits of the brands not purchased. Thus consumers feel at least some postpurchase dissonance for every purchase.

Cognitive dissonance
Buyer discomfort caused by postpurchase conflict.

American consumers are having a love affair with luxurious four ton, seven litre engined Sports Utility Vehicles (SUV). Their popularity has propelled the light trucks sector to 48 per cent of vehicles sold in the US. These no-compromise vehicles have the fuel consumption of a bus. According to Jac Nasser, Ford's chief executive: 'They're practical and promise something few other vehicles offer: the just-in-case factor. Just in case you want to buy a dinghy or a tree, you can do it.' SUVs can do it all but some customers are not happy with their purchases. Many have to rebuild their garages in order to house them and they do not fit some parking lots and cannot get into multi-storey car parks. Drivers also neglect to read the instruction behind the sun visor of their Ford Excursion: 'Avoid unnecessary sharp turns or other abrupt manoeuvres'.[40]

Why is it so important to satisfy the customer? Such satisfaction is important because a company's sales come from two basic groups – *new customers* and *repeat customers*. It usually costs more to attract new customers than to retain current ones. Keeping current customers is therefore often more critical than attracting new ones, and the best way to do this is to make current customers happy. A satisfied customer buys a product again, talks favourably to others about the product, pays less attention to competing brands and advertising, and buys other products from the company. Many marketers go beyond merely *meeting* the expectations of customers – they aim to *delight* the customer. A delighted customer is even more likely to purchase again and to talk favourably about the product and company.

A dissatisfied consumer responds differently. Whereas, on average, a satisfied customer tells three people about a good product experience, a dissatisfied customer gripes to 11 people. In fact, one study showed that 13 per cent of the people who had a problem with an organisation complained about that company to more than 20 people.[41] Clearly, bad word-of-mouth travels farther and faster than good word-of-mouth and can quickly damage consumer attitudes about a company and its products.

Therefore, a company would be wise to measure customer satisfaction regularly. It cannot simply rely on dissatisfied customers to volunteer their complaints when they are dissatisfied. In fact, 96 per cent of unhappy customers never tell the company about their problem. Companies should set up suggestion systems to *encourage* customers to complain. In this way, the company can learn how well it is doing and how it can improve. The 3M Company claims that over two-thirds of its new-product ideas come from listening to customer complaints. But listening is not enough – the company must also respond constructively to the complaints it receives.

Thus, in general, dissatisfied consumers may try to reduce their dissonance by taking any of several actions. In the case of Anna – a Canon digital camera purchaser – she may return the camera, or look at Canon ads that tell of the camera's benefits, or talk with friends who will tell her how much they like her new camera. She may even avoid reading about cameras in case she finds a better deal than she got.

Beyond seeking out and responding to complaints, marketers can take additional steps to reduce consumer postpurchase dissatisfaction and to help customers feel good about their purchases. For example, Toyota writes or phones new car owners with congratulations on having selected a fine car. It places ads showing satisfied owners talking about their new cars ('I love what you do for me, Toyota!'). Toyota also obtains customer suggestions for improvements and lists the locations of available services.

Understanding the consumer's needs and buying process is the foundation of successful marketing. By understanding how buyers go through need recognition, information search, evaluation of alternatives, the purchase decision and postpurchase behaviour, the marketer can pick up many clues as to how to meet the buyer's needs. By understanding the various participants in the buying process and the strongest influences on their buying behaviour, the marketer can develop an effective programme to support an attractive offer to the target market.

New product
A good, service or idea that is perceived by some potential customers as new.

Adoption process
The mental process through which an individual passes from first hearing about an innovation to final adoption.

Adoption
The decision by an individual to become a regular user of the product.

the buyer decision process for new products

We have looked at the stages that buyers go through in trying to satisfy a need. Buyers may pass quickly or slowly through these stages and some of the stages may even be reversed. Much depends on the nature of the buyer, the product and the buying situation.

We now look at how buyers approach the purchase of new products. A **new product** is a good, service or idea that is perceived by some potential customers as new. It may have been around for a while, but our interest is in how consumers learn about products for the first time and make decisions on whether to adopt them. We define the **adoption process** as 'the mental process through which an individual passes from first learning about an innovation to final adoption',[42] and **adoption** as the decision by an individual to become a regular user of the product.

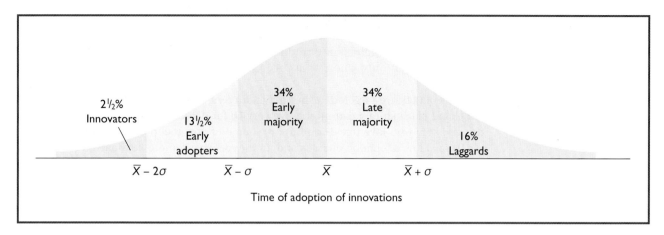

Figure 6.8

Adopter categorisation on the basis of relative time of adoption of innovations

SOURCE: Reprinted with permission of The Free Press, a Division of Simon & Schuster, Inc., from *Diffusion of Innovations*, Fourth Edition by Everett M. Rogers. Copyright © 1995 by Everett M. Rogers. Copyright © 1962, 1971, 1983 by The Free Press.

stages in the adoption process

Consumers go through five stages in the process of adopting a new product:

1. *Awareness*. The consumer becomes aware of the new product, but lacks information about it.
2. *Interest*. The consumer seeks information about the new product.
3. *Evaluation*. The consumer considers whether trying the new product makes sense.
4. *Trial*. The consumer tries the new product on a small scale to improve his or her estimate of its value.
5. *Adoption*. The consumer decides to make full and regular use of the new product.

This model suggests that the new-product marketer should think about how to help consumers move through these stages. Denon, a leading manufacturer of home cinema/ surround-sound equipment, may discover that many consumers in the interest stage do not move to the trial stage because of uncertainty and the large investment. If these same consumers would be willing to use a surround-sound system on a trial basis for a small fee, the manufacturer should consider offering a trial-use plan with an option to buy.

individual differences in innovativeness

People differ greatly in their readiness to try new products. In each product area, there are 'consumption pioneers' and early adopters. Other individuals adopt new products much later. This has led to a classification of people into the adopter categories shown in Figure 6.8.

After a slow start, an increasing number of people adopt the new product. The number of adopters reaches a peak and then drops off as fewer non-adopters remain. Innovators are defined as the first 2.5 per cent of the buyers to adopt a new idea (those beyond two standard deviations from mean adoption time); the early adopters are the next 13.5 per cent (between one and two standard deviations); and so forth.

The five adopter groups have differing values. *Innovators* are adventurous: they try new ideas at some risk. *Early adopters* are guided by respect: they are opinion leaders in their community and adopt new ideas early but carefully. The *early majority* is deliberate: although they are rarely leaders, they adopt new ideas before the average person. The *late majority* is sceptical: they adopt an innovation only after most people have tried it. Finally, *laggards* are tradition-bound: they are suspicious of changes and adopt the innovation only when it has become something of a tradition itself.

> Not all products are targeted at the *early adopters.* Open, owned by BT, BSkyB, HSBC and Matsushita, is an interactive service for digital television aimed at the *late majority* who love television but are scared of new technologies. Using existing televisions, low telephone charges and an inexpensive remote keyboard, Open has lower 'emotional' and financial barriers than Internet adoption. Using their old couch facing their familiar old TV, users can access banking services, shop, gamble or send email.[43]

This adopter classification suggests that an innovating firm should research the characteristics of innovators and early adopters and should direct marketing efforts to them. For example, home computer innovators have been found to be middle-aged and higher in income and education than non-innovators and they tend to be opinion leaders. They also tend to be more rational, more introverted and less social. In general, innovators tend to be relatively younger, better educated and higher in income than later adopters and non-adopters. They are more receptive to unfamiliar things, rely more on their own values and judgement, and are more willing to take risks. They are less brand loyal and more likely to take advantage of special promotions such as discounts, coupons and samples.[44]

Opinion leaders
People within a reference group who, because of special skills, knowledge, personality or other characteristics, exert influence on others.

Manufacturers of products and brands subject to strong group influence must find out how to reach the opinion leaders in the relevant reference groups. **Opinion leaders** are people within a reference group who, because of special skills, knowledge, personality or other characteristics, exert influence on others. Opinion leaders are found in all strata of society and one person may be an opinion leader in certain product areas and an opinion follower in others. Marketers try to identify the personal characteristics of opinion leaders for the products, determine what media they use and direct messages at them. In some cases, marketers try to identify opinion leaders for their products and direct marketing efforts towards them. This often occurs in the music industry, where clubs and radio DJs are influential. In other cases, advertisements can simulate opinion leadership, showing informal discussions between people and thereby reducing the need for consumers to seek advice from others. For example, in an ad for Herrera for Men cologne, two women discuss the question: 'Did you ever notice how good he smells?' The reason? 'He wears the most wonderful cologne.'[45]

If Anna Flores buys a camera, both the product and the brand will be visible to others whom she respects. Her decision to buy the camera and her brand choice may therefore be influenced strongly by opinion leaders, such as friends who belong to a photography club.

role of personal influence

Personal influence
The effect of statements made by one person on another's attitude or probability of purchase.

Personal influence plays a distinctive role in the adoption of new products. **Personal influence** describes the effect of statements made by one person on another's attitude or probability of purchase. Consumers consult each other for opinions about new products and brands, and the advice of others can strongly influence buying behaviour.

Personal influence is more important in some situations and for some individuals than for others. Personal influence is more important in the evaluation stage of the adoption process than in the other stages; it has more influence on later adopters than on early adopters; and it is more important in risky buying situations than in safe situations.

influence of product characteristics
on rate of adoption

The characteristics of the new product affect its rate of adoption. Some products catch on almost overnight (Pokémon), whereas others take a long time to gain acceptance (digital TV). Five characteristics are especially important in influencing an innovation's rate of adoption. For example, consider the characteristics of the MiniDisc in relation to the rate of adoption:

✦ *Relative advantage*: the degree to which the innovation appears superior to existing products. The greater the perceived relative advantage of using a MiniDisc over a cassette – say, it does not tangle or lose quality – the sooner MiniDiscs will be adopted.

✦ *Compatibility*: the degree to which the innovation fits the values and experiences of potential consumers. MiniDiscs, for example, are highly compatible with an active lifestyle.

✦ *Complexity*: the degree to which the innovation is difficult to understand or use. CDs have already introduced customers to the benefits of digital recordings, so the idea no longer seems complex.

✦ *Divisibility*: the degree to which the innovation may be tried on a limited basis. MiniDiscs have a problem here. They require a big investment if people are to replace their in-home, in-car and on-street music systems. And what if the technology changes again?

✦ *Communicability*: the degree to which the results of using the innovation can be observed or described to others. The benefits of MiniDiscs are easy to demonstrate on a hi-fi system, but are the differences big enough to show in a car or Walkman?

Other characteristics influence the rate of adoption, such as initial and ongoing costs, risk and uncertainty, social approval and the efforts of opinion leaders. The new-product marketer has to research all these factors when developing the new product and its marketing programme.

consumer behaviour across international borders

Understanding consumer behaviour is difficult enough for companies marketing in a single country. For companies operating in many countries, however, understanding and serving the needs of consumers is daunting. Although consumers in different countries may have some things in common, their values, attitudes and behaviours often vary greatly. International marketers must understand such differences and adjust their products and marketing programmes accordingly.

Sometimes the differences are obvious. For example, in the UK, where most people eat cereal regularly for breakfast, Kellogg focuses its marketing on persuading consumers to select a Kellogg's brand rather than a competitor's brand. In France, however, where most people prefer croissants and coffee or no breakfast at all, Kellogg's advertising simply attempts to convince people that they should eat cereal for breakfast. Its packaging includes step-by-step instructions on how to prepare cereal. In India, where many consumers eat heavy, fried breakfasts and 22 per cent of consumers skip the meal altogether, Kellogg's advertising attempts to convince buyers to switch to a lighter, more nutritious breakfast diet.[46]

Often, differences across international markets are subtler. They may result from physical differences in consumers and their environments. For example, Remington makes smaller electric shavers to fit the smaller hands of Japanese consumers; and battery-powered shavers for the British market, where some bathrooms have no electrical outlets. Other differences result from varying customs. Consider the following examples:

✦ Shaking your head from side to side means 'no' in most countries but 'yes' in Bulgaria and Sri Lanka.

✦ In South America, southern Europe and many Arab countries, touching another person is a sign of warmth and friendship. In the Orient, it is considered an invasion of privacy.

✦ In Norway or Malaysia, it's rude to leave something on your plate when eating; in Egypt, it's rude *not* to leave something on your plate.

✦ A door-to-door salesperson might find it tough going in Italy, where it is improper for a man to call on a woman if she is home alone.[47]

Failing to understand such differences in customs and behaviours from one country to another can spell disaster for a marketer's international products and programmes.

Marketers must decide on the degree to which they will adapt their products and marketing programmes to meet the unique cultures and needs of consumers in various markets. On the one hand, they want to standardise their offerings in order to simplify operations and take advantage of cost economies. On the other hand, adapting marketing efforts within each country results in products and programmes that better satisfy the needs of local consumers. The question of whether to adapt or standardise the marketing mix across international markets has created a lively debate in recent years.

summary

Markets have to be understood before marketing strategies can be developed. The consumer market buys goods and services for personal consumption. Consumers vary tremendously in age, income, education, tastes and other factors. Marketers must understand how consumers transform marketing and other inputs into buying responses. *Consumer behaviour* is influenced by the buyer's characteristics and by the buyer's decision process. *Buyer characteristics* include four main factors: cultural, social, personal and psychological.

Culture is the most basic determinant of a person's wants and behaviour. It includes the basic values, perceptions, preferences and behaviours that a person learns from family and other key institutions. Marketers try to track cultural shifts that might suggest new ways to serve customers. *Social classes* are subcultures whose members have similar social prestige based on occupation, income, education, wealth and other variables. People with different cultural, subculture and social class characteristics have different product and brand preferences.

Social factors also influence a buyer's behaviour. A person's *reference groups* – family, friends, social organisations, professional associations – strongly affect product and brand choices. The person's position within each group can be defined in terms of *role and status*. A buyer chooses products and brands that reflect his or her role and status.

The buyer's age, life-cycle stage, occupation, economic circumstances, lifestyle, personality and other *personal characteristics* and *psychological factors* influence his or her buying decisions. Young consumers have different needs and wants from older consumers; the needs of young married couples differ from those of retired people; consumers with higher incomes buy differently from those who have less to spend.

Before planning its marketing strategy, a company needs to understand its consumers and the decision processes they go through. The number of buying participants and the amount of buying effort increase with the complexity of the buying situation. There are four types of *buying decision behaviour*: *complex buying behaviour*, *dissonance-reducing buying behaviour*, *habitual buying behaviour* and *variety-seeking buying behaviour*.

In buying something, the buyer goes through a decision process consisting of *need recognition*, *information search*, *evaluation of alternatives*, *purchase decision* and *postpurchase behaviour*. The marketer's job is to understand the buyers' behaviour at each stage and the influences that are operating. This allows the marketer to develop a significant and effective marketing programme for the target market. With regard to new products, consumers respond at different rates, depending on the consumer's characteristics and the product's characteristics. Manufacturers try to bring their new products to the attention of potential early adopters, particularly those with opinion leader characteristics.

A person's buying behaviour is the result of the complex interplay of all these cultural, social, personal and psychological factors. Although marketers cannot control many of these factors, they are useful in identifying and understanding the consumers that marketers are trying to influence.

discussing the issues

1. Thinking about the purchase of an audio hi-fi system, indicate the extent to which cultural, social, personal and psychological factors affect how a buyer evaluates hi-fi products and chooses a brand.

2. Describe and contrast any differences in the buying behaviour of consumers for the following products: a CD; a notebook computer; a pair of trainers; and a breakfast cereal.

3. Why might a detailed understanding of the model of the consumer buying decision process help marketers develop more effective marketing strategies to capture and retain customers? How universal is the model? How useful is it?

4. In designing the advertising for a soft drink, which would you find more helpful: information about

consumer demographics or about consumer lifestyles? Give examples of how you would use each type of information.

5. Take, for example, a new method of contraception, which is being 'sold' to young males. It is a controversial, albeit innovative concept. Your firm is the pioneer in launching this device. What are the main factors your firm must research when developing a marketing programme for this product?

6. It has been said that consumers' buying behaviour is shaped more by perception than by reality. Do you agree with this comment? Why or why not?

applying the concepts

1. Different types of product can fulfil different functional and psychological needs.

   ✦ List five luxury products or services that are very interesting or important to you. Some possibilities are cars, clothing, sports equipment, cosmetics, club membership. List five other

   necessities that you use which have little interest for you, such as pens, laundry detergent or petrol.

   ✦ Make a list of words that describe how you feel about each of the products/services listed. Are there differences between the types of word you used for luxuries and necessities? What does this tell you about the different psychological needs these products fulfil?

2. Different groups may have different types of effect on consumers.

   ◆ Consider an item you bought which is typical of what your peers (a key reference group) buy, such as a compact disc, a mountain bike or a brand of trainer. Were you conscious that your friends owned something similar when you made the purchase? Did this make you want the item more or less? Why or why not?

   ◆ Now, think of brands that you currently use which your parents also use. Examples may include soap, shaving cream or margarine. Did you think through these purchases as carefully as those influenced by your peers or were these

purchases simply the result of following old habits?

3. SRI Consulting, through the Business Intelligence Center online, features the Values and Lifestyles Program (VALS). Visit SRI at sri.com and follow links to the VALS questionnaire.

   ◆ Take the survey to determine your type and then read all about your type. Why or why not does it describe you well?

   ◆ What four products have high indexes for your type? Do you buy these products?

   ◆ Compare the nine Japan-VALS segments with the US VALS. How similar are they and are they likely to explain the European consumer?

   ◆ Other than product design, how can marketers use information from Japan-VALS?

references

1. *World Bank Atlas* (1994); *Microsoft Bookshelf* (1998).

2. Several models of the consumer buying process have been developed by marketing scholars. The most prominent models are those of John A. Howard and Jagdish N. Sheth, *The Theory of Buyer Behaviour* (New York: Wiley, 1969); Francesco M. Nicosia, *Consumer Decision Processes* (Englewood Cliffs, NJ: Prentice Hall, 1966); James F. Engel, Roger D. Blackwell and Paul W. Miniard, *Consumer Behaviour*, 5th edn (New York: Holt, Rinehart & Winston, 1986); James R. Bettman, *An Information Processing Theory of Consumer Choice* (Reading, MA: Addison-Wesley, 1979). For a summary, see Leon G. Schiffman and Leslie Lazar Kanuk, *Consumer Behaviour*, 4th edn (Englewood Cliffs, NJ: Prentice Hall, 1991), Ch. 20.

3. For an insight into this problem see Rik Pieters, 'A control view on the behaviour of consumers: turning the triangle', *European Journal of Marketing*, **27**, 8 (1993), pp. 17–27.

4. For this and other examples of the effects of culture in international marketing, see Philip R. Cateora, *International Marketing,* 8th edn (Homewood, IL: Irwin, 1993), Ch. 4; Sak Onkvisit and John J. Shaw, *International Marketing: Analysis and strategy*, 3rd edn (Upper Saddle River, NJ: Prentice Hall, 1997), Ch. 6.

5. Brian J. Ford, *The Future of Eating* (Thames & Hudson, 2000); Andrew Ward, 'Austin Reed reveals takeover talks as sales suffer 5% fall', *Financial Times* (7 April 2000), p. 23; *The Economist*, 'Blech' (15 January 2000), p. 87.

6. Richard Tomkin, 'Quaker buys "new age" drinks', *Financial Times* (3 November 1994), p. 25; Sara McConnell, 'Banks put their future on the line', *The Times* (9 October 1994), p. 29; Ralph Atkins, 'Families choose direct insurers', *Financial Times* (8–9 October 1994), p. 5.

7. Gerrit Antonides and W. Fred van Raaij, *Consumer Behaviour: a European perspective* (Chichester: Wiley, 1998); 'Mein Herr of Kirgizstan', *The Economist* (15 January 2000), p. 72; 'Ageing workers: a full life', *The Economist* (4 September 1999), pp. 89–91; 'European pensions: Dear Prudence', *The Economist* (11 December 1999), p. 108.

8. Details of NS-SEC and the European initiatives can be found at http://www.statistics.gov.uk. An introduction to the new scheme is in 'Classification', *The Economist* (3 June 2000), p. 31 and Mark Henderson, 'Class tightens its grip on Britain', *The Times* (15 December 1997), p. 7.

9. For a broad discussion of international social class, see Edward W. Candid and Marye Tharp Higler, *Marketing in the International Environment* (Hemel Hempstead: Prentice Hall, 1988), and 'Rich man, poor man', *The Economist* (24 July 1993), p. 73; 'Slicing the cake' and 'For richer, for poorer', *The Economist* (5 November 1994), pp. 13–14 and 19–21 respectively; P. M. Chisnall, 'Constructing classes: towards a new social classification for the UK', *Market Research Society*, **41**, 1 (1999), pp. 97–8.

10. For a look at the cultural twists and turns over recent generations, see Peter Everett, *You'll Never Want to be 16 Again* (London: BBC Publications, 1994) or

Bevis Hillier, *The Style of the Century* (London: Herbert, 1993).

11. William O. Bearden and Michael J. Etzel, 'Reference group influence on product and brand purchase decisions', *Journal of Consumer Research* (September 1982), p. 185; K. Hogg, M. Bruce and Alexander J. Hill, 'Fashion brand preferences among young consumers', *International Journal of Retail & Distribution Management*, **26**, 8 (1998), pp. 293–300.

12. Sheila Jones, 'Procter & Gamble's bottom line is challenged', *Financial Times* (11 May 2000), p. 1; 'Going soft', *The Economist* (4 March 2000), p. 34.

13. Debra Goldman, 'Spotlight men', *Adweek* (13 August 1990), pp. M1–M6; Dennis Rodkin, 'A manly sport: building loyalty', *Advertising Age* (15 April 1991), pp. S1, S12; Nancy Ten Kate, 'Who buys the pants in the family?', *American Demographics* (January 1992), p. 12; Laura Zinn, 'Real men buy paper towels, too', *Business Week* (9 November 1992), pp. 75–6; 'The war between the sexes', *The Economist* (5 March 1994), pp. 96–7; R. R. Dholakia, 'Going shopping: key determinants of shopping behaviours and motivations', *International Journal of Retail & Distribution Management*, **27**, 4 (1999), pp. 154–65.

14. 'Anti-nuclear reaction', *The Economist* (31 December 1999), pp. 65–6; 'What a lot of sterEUtypes', *The Economist* (23 October 1999), p. 65.

15. John Williams, 'Rolls-Royce of prams is overtaken', *Financial Times* (15 May 1999), p. 7; 'Professional heartache: glintineye.com', *The Economist* (26 August 2000), p. 48; Angus J. Kennedy, *The Internet: the Rough Guide* (London: Rough Guides, 1999).

16. See Lawrence Lepisto, 'A life span perspective of consumer behavior', in Elizabeth Hirshman and Morris Holbrook, *Advances in Consumer Research*, vol. 12 (Provo, UT: Association for Consumer Research, 1985), p. 47.

17. Kim Foltz, 'Wizards of marketing', *Newsweek* (22 July 1985), p. 44.

18. For more on VALS and on psychographics in general, see William D. Wells, 'Psychographics: a critical review', *Journal of Marketing Research* (May 1975), pp. 196–213; Arnold Mitchell, *The Nine American Lifestyles* (New York: Macmillan, 1983); Rebecca Pirto, 'Measuring minds in the 1990s', *American Demographics* (December 1990), pp. 35–9; 'VALS the second time', *American Demographics* (July 1991), p. 6. For more reading on the pros and cons of using VALS and other lifestyle approaches, see Lynn R. Kahle, Sharon E. Beatty and Pamela Homer, 'Alternative measurement approaches to consumer values: the list of values (LOV) and values and life

styles (VALS)', *Journal of Consumer Research* (December 1986), pp. 405–9; Mark Landler, 'The bloodbath in market research', *Business Week* (11 February 1991), pp. 72–4.

19. Taken from RISC SA, *ACE* (Lyon: RISC SA, 1989); CCA, *CCA Euro-styles* (Paris: CCA, 1989); Norbert Homma and Jorg Uelzhoffer, 'The internationalisation of everyday-life and milieus', ESOMAR Conference on America, Japan and EC'92: The Prospects for Marketing, Advertising and Research, Venice, 18–20 June 1990; Marieke de Mooij, *Advertising Worldwide: Concepts, theories and practice of international and global advertising* (Hemel Hempstead: Prentice Hall, 1994).

20. Based on details in Marieke de Mooij, *Advertising Worldwide* (Hemel Hempstead: Prentice Hall, 1994), who obtained his information from Eugine Wong of Survey Research Malaysia.

21. Stuart Elliot, 'Sampling tastes of a changing Russia', *The New York Times* (1 April 1992), pp. D1, D19.

22. See Harold H. Kassarjian and Mary Jane Sheffet, 'Personality in consumer behaviour: an update', in Harold H. Kassarjian and Thomas S. Robertson (eds) *Perspectives in Consumer Behaviour* (Glenview, IL: Scott Foresman, 1981), pp. 160–80; Joseph T. Plummer, 'How personality can make a difference', *Marketing News* (March–April 1984), pp. 17–20.

23. Myron Magnet, 'Let's go for growth', *Fortune* (7 March 1994), p. 70.

24. Quote from *Stuff* (September 2000), a magazine for people who lust for hot gadgets.

25. See Annetta Miller and Dody Tsiantar, 'Psyching out consumers', *Newsweek* (27 February 1989), pp. 46–7; Rebecca Piirto, 'Words that sell', *American Demographics* (January 1992), p. 6.

26. Abraham H. Maslow, *Motivation and Personality*, 2nd edn (New York: Harper & Row, 1970), pp. 80–106; E. Wooldridge, 'Time to stand Maslow's hierarchy on its head?', *People Management*, **1**, 25 (1995), pp. 17–19.

27. Robert L. Gluckman, 'A consumer approach to branded wines', *European Journal of Marketing*, **24**, 4 (1990), pp. 27–46.

28. S. J. Vittel, S. L. Nwachukwu and J. H. Barnes, 'The effects of culture on ethical decision-making: an application of Hofstede's typology', *Journal of Business Ethics*, **12**, 10 (1993), pp. 753–60; G. Hofstede, 'Cultural constraints in management theories', *International Review of Strategic Management*, **5** (1994), pp. 27–49; M. Sondergaard, 'Hofstede's consequences: a study of reviews, citations and replications', *Organization Studies*, **15**, 3 (1994), pp. 447–56.

29. John Fiske, *Understanding Popular Culture* (London: Routledge, 1989).

30. Simon Holberton, 'Cathay Pacific puts its future in Hong Kong', *Financial Times* (3 November 1994), p. 32.

31. For a discussion of subliminal perception, see Timothy Moore, 'What you see is what you get', *Journal of Marketing* (Spring 1982); Walter Weir, 'Another look at subliminal "facts"', *Advertising Age* (15 October 1984), p. 46.

32. See 'Honda hopes to win new riders by emphasizing "fun" of cycles', *Marketing News* (28 August 1989), p. 6.

33. Henry Assael, *Consumer Behaviour and Marketing Action* (Boston, MA: Kent Publishing, 1987), Ch. 4. An earlier classification of three types of consumer buying behaviour – routine response behaviour, limited problem solving and extensive problem solving – can be found in John A. Howard and Jagdish Sheth, *The Theory of Consumer Behaviour* (New York: Wiley, 1969), pp. 27–8. Gordon R. Foxall proposes a more sophisticated Behavioural Perspective Model (BPM) in 'A behavioural perspective on purchasing and consumption' and 'Consumer behaviour as an evolutionary process', *European Journal of Marketing*, **27**, 8 (1993), pp. 7–16 and 46–57 respectively; see also John A. Howard, *Consumer Behaviour in Marketing Strategy* (Englewood Cliffs, NJ: Prentice Hall, 1989).

34. Tom Stevenson, 'Dixons opens shops for baffled buyers', *Independent* (17 October 1994), p. 28.

35. V. W. Mitchell and Pari Boustani, 'A preliminary investigation into pre- and post-purchase risk perception and reduction', *European Journal of Marketing*, **28**, 1 (1990), pp. 56–71.

36. Keith B. Murray, 'A test of services marketing theory: consumer information acquisition theory', *Journal of Marketing* (January 1991), pp. 10–25; W. G. Mangold, F. Miller and G. R. Brockway, 'Word-of-mouth communication in the service marketplace', *Journal of Services Marketing*, **13**, 1 (1999), pp. 73–89.

37. The ratings are based on those given in 'Product test: compact cameras', *Which?* (November 1994), pp. 21–6.

38. This was developed by Martin Fishbein. See Martin Fishbein and Icek Ajzen, *Belief, Attitude, Intention, and Behaviour* (Reading, MA: Addison-Wesley, 1975). For a critical review of this model, see Paul W. Miniard and Joel B. Cohen, 'An examination of the Fishbein–Ajzen behavioral intentions model's concepts and measures', *Journal of Experimental*

Social Psychology (May 1981), pp. 309–99; R. Y.-K. Chan and L. Lau, 'A test of Fishbein–Ajzen behavioural intentions model under Chinese cultural settings: are there any differences between PRC and Hong Kong consumers?', *Journal of Marketing Practice: Applied Marketing Science*, **4**, 3 (1998), pp. 85–101.

39. V.-W. Mitchell and Pari Boustani, 'A preliminary investigation into pre- and post-purchase risk perception and reduction', *European Journal of Marketing*, **28**, 1 (1994), pp. 56–71; V.-W. Mitchell, 'Segmenting purchasers of organisational professional services: a risk-based approach', *Journal of Services Marketing*, **12**, 2 (1998), pp. 83–97.

40. See Leon Festinger, *A Theory of Cognitive Dissonance* (Stanford, CA: Stanford University Press, 1957); Schiffman and Kanuk, *Consumer Behaviour*, op. cit., pp. 304–5; Tim Burton, 'Cars so big they don't fit the garage', *Financial Times* (16 January 2000), p. 7.

41. See Karl Albrect and Ron Zemke, *Service America!* (Homewood, IL: Dow-Jones Irwin, 1985), pp. 6–7; Frank Rose, 'Now quality means service too', *Fortune* (22 April 1991), pp. 97–108.

42. The following discussion draws heavily from Everett M. Rogers, *Diffusion of Innovations*, 4th edn (New York: Free Press, 1995); see also Hubert Gatignon and Thomas S. Robertson, 'A propositional inventory for new diffusion research', *Journal of Consumer Research* (March 1985), pp. 849–67; G. Antonides, H. B. Amesz and I. C. Hulscher, 'Adoption of payment systems in ten countries – a case study of diffusion of innovations', *European Journal of Marketing*, **33**, 11/12 (1999), pp. 1123–35.

43. 'Open for couch potatoes', *The Economist* (8 January 2000); David Murphy, 'Tomorrow's window of opportunity', *Marketing Business* (June 1999), pp. 43–5; *Sky: the magazine for sky digital customers* (September 2000); P. Butler and J. Peppard, 'Consumer purchasing on the internet: processes and prospects', *European Management Journal*, **16**, 5 (1998), pp. 600–10.

44. See Schiffman and Kanuk, *Consumer Behaviour*, op. cit., Ch. 18.

45. For these and other examples, see ibid.

46. Mir Maqbool Alam Khan, 'Kellogg reports brisk cereal sales in India', *Advertising Age* (14 November 1994), p. 60.

47. For these and other examples, see William J. Stanton, Michael J. Etzel and Bruce J. Walker, *Fundamentals of Marketing* (New York: McGraw-Hill, 1991), p. 536.

case 6

Aibo: looking for a charged-up spot?

FOR SALE: Puppy. Never needs to go outside, doesn't soil carpets, doesn't chew on furniture or slippers, doesn't eat. Can be turned off and put in the closet when you're on vacation. Contact – www.world.sony.com/robot/get/meet/html.

From the company that gave us the virtual pet comes the robopet – a puppy named Aibo, an entertainment robot. This is no simple animal or machine. Even the name has many possible meanings. Perhaps it stands for 'artificial intelligence robot'. Perhaps it refers to Aibo's camera eyes, which make it an 'eye bot', or maybe it's just Japanese for companion or pal.

What can you do with Aibo? Well, you can play with it. Aibo has a favourite toy, a pink ball, which it will chase down, pick up in its mouth, and return to you just like any real dog would. If you praise Aibo, its tail wags, its eyes light up green, and it plays a happy melody. It's not exactly like a real dog, but close in the sense that Aibo responds visibly to your love and affection.

Aibo can respond to praise and can learn. When you praise Aibo's behaviours, they become stronger and are more likely to be repeated. When scolded, Aibo is sometimes sad and plays a doleful melody. Other times, it responds to scolding by getting agitated and playing an angry melody while its eyes turn red. Although Aibo's responses may be different from a real dog's responses, they do represent the same emotions. Like a real dog, Aibo lets you know that it wants to play by jumping around. In addition to anger, sadness and playfulness, Aibo can show joy (eyes turn green and it plays a happy melody), surprise (eyes light up and it plays a surprised melody and gives a start), discontent (its eyes turn angry red and it moves away), and fear (when it encounters a big hole or rolls onto its back and can't get up, it plays a scared melody).

Voice commands such as 'stay', 'sit', or 'heel' won't work with Aibo because the puppy has no voice-response mechanism. Instead you give it commands through a sound controller. Aibo responds only to perfect tones, so the sound controller contains combinations of preset commands in perfect tones. If Aibo is in a bad mood, it will simply ignore you. When it is in a happy mood, it will perform tricks. Like most temperamental pets, Aibo will play or do tricks only if you're good to it.

When it's time to quit playing, you press the off or the pause button and Aibo lies down and goes to sleep. When not active, Aibo stays in its station, which serves as a battery charger. The robotic puppy comes with two lithium batteries so that one can be charged while the other is in use. A full charge lasts through about 1.5 hours of action.

Aibo comes in three colours (grey, metallic black and silver grey); has stereo microphones for ears; can recognise colours and shapes; and emits a variety of bleeps and chirps. A sensor in its head can distinguish between an amiable pat and a reproachful slap. You can set Aibo to Performance Mode, in which it does tricks, or to Game Mode, in which you control its movements. By making Aibo run and kick, you can even play robot soccer.

Ready to buy an Aibo? You won't find one for sale in any store. It is available only on the Internet at www.world.sony.com/robot/get/meet/html. It's also a little pricey – 250,000 Japanese yen (€2,500). Is anyone willing to pay such a stiff price? In June 1999 Sony offered 5,000 Aibos in Japan and the US and all sold out in only 20 minutes. When Sony offered another 10,000 in November 1999, it received more than 130,000 orders. Facing this greater than anticipated demand, Sony drew lots and selected winners in Japan, the United States and Europe. There appear to be lots of robot-dog's best friends out there!

One of the appealing features of Aibo is its open architecture. Based on experiences with its PlayStation video-game business, Sony decided not to develop everything in-house. Instead, it has invited other developers to create new programs for Aibo. This has resulted in the rapid development of additional memory sticks (programs) that allow you to teach Aibo new tricks or movements.

What kinds of new behaviours could you teach Aibo? How about a hip-shaking dog that sings Elvis songs like – you guessed it – 'You Ain't Nothing but a Hound Dog'. Or how about a dog that really hates cats? Aibo could be programmed to recognise cats and react fiercely to them. In fact, two companies have created computerised cats, so we might soon have good old-fashioned dog and cat fights, but without the blood, gore, or veterinarian bills.

To test consumer reaction to their furless, high-tech critters before offering them for sale, Sony demonstrated Aibos at several trade shows. Uniform reaction to the pet was 'That is so cute!' One enthusiastic consumer commented, 'I love little robots. For me, it would be great. I'm single and I don't have time to keep a dog.' Another said, 'This is the coolest thing I've seen all day.' Numerous journalists privileged enough to play with Aibos found them to be lots of fun – even if they can't do anything useful.

Although Aibo isn't likely to fetch your newspaper, bring you your shoes, or scare away burglars, this little puppy does have much promise from a marketing point of view. Sony hopes to create a whole new industry of entertainment robots, an industry that Sony management believe could be larger than the personal computer market.

These robots usher in the new era of digital creatures. Sure, there are robot fanatics who already gather for the annual Robocup – the World Cup for robots (www.robocup.org), robot sumo wrestling competitions in Japan or Robot Wars: the Helsinki Model Expo (www.model-expo.com/robowars). But those robots appeal only to consumers with specific and sometimes narrow interests. The new Aibo-like entertainment robots have broader appeal. More importantly, they may make people more comfortable with the idea of interacting with humanoid-like machines. Once that happens, robots could become nurses, maids or bodyguards. They might even become partners who will play with and talk to us. There's more than a little bit of *Star Wars'* R2D2 in all this. Back in the eighties, however, R2D2 and his companions seemed a long way off. Now, Aibo and other animal-bots appear to be bringing us into that *Star Wars* world much sooner than we thought.

For those not able to afford an Aibo, there is Wee Bot (http://www.sharperimage.com), which comes in families of adults and children. Wee Bots have big, bright, expressive eyes that move and an extraterrestrial language of beeps, burps, chirps, snores, coos, chortles, giggles, yips, snorts, purrs and moans. What triggers these reactions? Your stroking, scratching and tickling. They express happiness when petted, grouchiness when sleepy and impatience when bored. They respond to commands from a silent wireless 'translator' that converts your wishes into a language the robopet understands. The children, called PeeWee Bots, have their own routines and respond to beamed voice messages from the nearest grown-up Wee Bot. They like exercise and naps, and they eat by making slurping and gulping noises. When happy, they behave. When they are not happy, you need 'special modes' to keep them in line.

Wee Bots don't look like any creature we're used to. They have round bodies, and the adults come in two models: Twirple, which has a purple body and green eyes, or Ziggle, which has an orange body and green eyes. Best of all, they don't cost too much. An adult Wee Bot is €40, a PeeWee Bot is €30, and a whole family (grown up Twirple and babies Bop and Zop) is €100. Just wait until Disney gets in on the act. A Winnie the Pooh bear would be fine, with his very little brain easy to simulate. But how about living with petbots of real character: depressive Eeyore or manic Tigger?

Questions

1. How might personal factors affect the purchase of an Aibo? A Wee Bot?

2. What cultural and social-class factors might affect the decision to buy an Aibo or a Wee Bot?

3. How might reference groups affect a consumer's interest in robot pets or robots in general?

4. What motives or needs is an individual likely to be satisfying in purchasing a pet robot?

5. Why, do you think, did Sony choose to sell Aibos only over the Internet? How might this affect a consumer's buying decision process? Was this a wise decision?

6. How could Internet-only selling affect the rate of diffusion of Aibos? In creating its new industry, what could Sony do to speed the diffusion of entertainment robots?

SOURCES: Neil Gross and Irene Kunii, 'Man's best friend – and no scooper needed', *Business Week* (20 July 1998), p. 531; Irene Kunii, 'This cute little pet is a robot', *Business Week* (24 May 1999), pp. 56–7; Peter Landers, 'At last, a dog that barks, wags its tail, and never has to go out', *Wall Street Journal* (12 May 1999), p. B1; Ginny Parker, 'In Japan, robots are not just for factories anymore', *Greensboro News and Record* (2 November 1999), pp. B6 and B7; 'Robots', *The Economist* (5 June 1999), p. 78; Richard Shaffer, 'Can't anyone make a decent robot?', *Fortune* (19 July 1999), pp. 120–1; 'Sony launches special edition "Aibo" entertainment robot', Sony press release (26 October 1999); 'Sony's Aibo robot dogs draw 130,000 orders in Japan alone', *AsiaPulse News* (15 November 1999), p. 100; A. A. Milne, *Winnie the Pooh Collection* (Greenford, Middlesex: Aura, 1998).

internet exercises

Internet exercises for this chapter can be found on the student site of the MYPHLIP Web Site at www.booksites.net/kotler.

chapter seven

Business-to-business marketing

Chapter objectives   *After reading this chapter, you should be able to:*

- ✦ Explain how business markets differ from consumer markets.

- ✦ Identify the main factors that influence business buyer behaviour.

- ✦ List and define the steps in the business buying decision process.

- ✦ Explain how institutional and government buyers make their buying decisions.

introduction

In some ways, selling business jets to business buyers (see the preview case on page 234) is like selling kitchen appliances to families. Busjet makers ask the same questions as consumer marketers: Who are the buyers and what are their needs? How do buyers make their buying decisions and what factors influence these decisions? What marketing programme will be most effective? But the answers to these questions are usually different in the case of the business buyer. Thus the jet makers face many of the same challenges as consumer marketers – and some additional ones.

In one way or another, most large companies sell to other organisations. Companies such as ABB Asea Brown Boveri (engineering), Norsk Hydro, Akzo Nobel (chemicals) and Arbed (steel) sell *most* of their products to other businesses. Even large consumer-products companies, which make products used by final consumers, must first sell their products to other businesses. For example, Allied Domecq makes many consumer products – La Ina sherry, Presidente brandy, Tetley tea and others. To sell these products to consumers, Allied Domecq must first sell them to wholesalers and retailers that serve the consumer market. Allied Domecq also sells food ingredients directly to other businesses through its Margetts Food and DCA Food Industries subsidiaries.

The **business market** consists of all the organisations that buy goods and services to use in the production of other products and services that are sold, rented or supplied to others. It also includes retailing and wholesaling firms that acquire goods for the purpose of reselling or renting them to others at a profit. The **business buying process** is the decision-making process by which business buyers establish the need for purchased products and services, and identify, evaluate and choose among alternative brands and suppliers.[1] Companies that sell to other business organisations must do their best to understand business markets and business buyer behaviour.

Business market
All the organisations that buy goods and services to use in the production of other products and services, or for the purpose of reselling or renting them to others at a profit.

Business buying process
The decision-making process by which business buyers establish the need for purchased products and services, and identify, evaluate and choose among alternative brands and suppliers.

Business jets: executive toy or a smart investment?

'The jet set' used to refer to the rich and famous who could afford the cost of early jet travel. Now almost everybody flies. Busjet travel retains that exclusive status that 'the jet set' once had as the transport of super-celebrities like Mika Hakkinen, Bill Gates and Madonna, but not for long. Busjet travel is becoming the norm. Sales of busjets, from the 'entry level' €4m Cessna CJ1 to the €41m Airbus A319 corporate jetliner, are booming, with order books full three years ahead.

Once looked upon as an executive indulgence, the busjets have become a logical capital investment:

◆ Busjet travel is down in cost. Typical running cost of the medium-sized, 8–19-seat Dassault Falcon 900EX jet is €1,500 per flying hour based on 1,000 hours per year utilisation. With four passengers the cost is less than €400 each, about the same as a business class fare. Eight people flying brings the cost to that of economy fares; with 16 seats occupied, down to bucket shop prices.

◆ Busjets make better use of a firm's most valuable and perishable resource – executive time. As Richard Gaona of Airbus says: 'It's not the speed of the individual aircraft that counts, but the speed at which you can get to where the business is ahead of the competition.'

◆ Security of flyers and information exist on a busjet in a way it does not in a first-class lounge or cabin. A busjet is a mobile boardroom as well as a mobile office.

◆ At the top end of the range an A319 or Boeing BBJ is a mobile hotel that enables the likes of Boeing's Phil Condit to take in New York, Paris, Moscow, Beijing and Tokyo in four days out of his office.

Recognising organisations that can afford to own and operate a business jet is easy. The difficulty is in reaching key decision makers for jet purchases, understanding their motivations and decision processes, analysing what is important to them, and designing marketing approaches.

There are *rational* and *subjective* factors. A company buying a busjet will evaluate the aircraft on quality and performance, prices, operating costs and service. But having a superior product isn't enough: marketers must also consider *human factors* that affect choice. According to Gulfstream, a leading American supplier of business jets: 'The purchase process may be initiated by the chief executive officer (CEO), a board member wishing to increase efficiency or security, the company's chief pilot, or through vendor efforts like advertising or a sales visit. The CEO will be central in deciding whether to buy the jet, but he or she will be heavily influenced by the company's pilot, financial officer and perhaps by the board itself.'

Each party in the buying process has subtle roles and needs. The salesperson who tries to impress both the CEO with depreciation schedules and the chief pilot with runway statistics will almost certainly not sell a plane if he or she overlooks the psychological and emotional components of the buying decision. 'For the chief executive', observes one salesperson, 'you need all the numbers for support, but if you can't find the kid inside the CEO and excite him or her with the raw beauty of the new plane, you'll never sell the equipment. If you sell the excitement, you sell the jet.'

The chief pilot often has veto power over purchase decisions and may be able to stop the purchase of a certain brand of jet by simply expressing a negative opinion. In this sense, the pilot not only influences the decision but also serves as a 'gatekeeper'. Though the corporate legal staff will handle the purchase agreement and the purchasing department will acquire the jet, they usually have little to say about whether or how the plane will be obtained and which type to select. The users of the jet – management of the buying company, important customers and others – may have an indirect role in choosing the equipment.

The involvement of many people in the purchase decision creates a group dynamic that the selling company must factor into its sales planning. Who makes up the buying group? How will the parties interact? Who will dominate and who submit? What priorities do the individuals have?

Where is the market going? The answer is bigger and faster. The fastest is the Bombardier Global Express (Gex) BD-700 business jet, capable of carrying eight passengers non-stop from Brussels to Buenos Aires. Cruising close to the speed of sound, it knocks an hour off shorter routes like Berlin–Los Angeles. The next stop? Gulfstream and Dassault are considering an SSBJ (supersonic busjet). If a €40m-plus busjet is selling, why not a €55m SSBJ?[2]

Questions

1. What do you think are the reasons for businesses buying executive jets?

2. Is it correct to say that, unlike people in consumer markets, business buyers are rational?

3. Who are the critical people to influence when selling busjets?

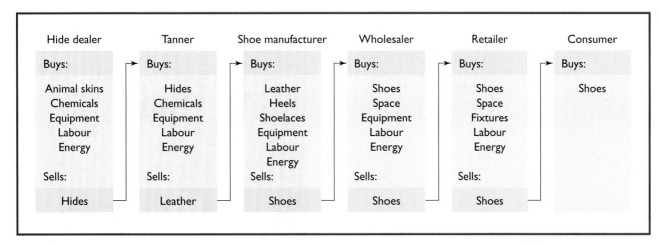

Figure 7.1

Business transactions involved in producing and distributing a pair of shoes

business markets

The business to business market is *huge*: most businesses just sell to other businesses, and sales to businesses far outstrip those to consumers. The reason for this is the number of times that parts of a consumer product are bought, processed and resold before reaching the final consumer. For example, Figure 7.1 shows the large number of business transactions needed to produce and sell a simple pair of shoes. Hide dealers sell to tanners, who sell leather to shoe manufacturers, who sell shoes to wholesalers, who in turn sell shoes to retailers, who finally sell the shoes to consumers. Each party in the chain also buys many other related goods and services. This example shows why there is more business buying than consumer buying – many sets of *business* purchases were made for only one set of *consumer* purchases.

Although the media have given a lot of attention to the booms and busts of business-to-consumer (B2C) dotcom companies, the e-commerce revolution is really business to business (B2B). IDC forecast that B2B e-commerce will be worth €360 bn by 2001 (up from €12 bn in 1997) compared with a forecast of €88 bn for B2C. And, even while the leading B2C company Amazon.com is haemorrhaging cash, B2B e-commerce has become an established part of doing business practice.[3]

characteristics of business markets

In some ways, business markets are similar to consumer markets. Both involve people who assume buying roles and make purchase decisions to satisfy needs. However, business markets do differ. The main differences are in market structure and demand, the nature of the buying unit, and the types of decision and the decision process involved.

■ Market structure and demand

The business marketer normally deals with *far fewer but far larger buyers* than the consumer marketer does. For example, when Michelin sells replacement tyres to final consumers, its potential market includes the owners of cars currently in use. But Michelin's fate in the business market depends on getting orders from a few large car makers. These sales of original equipment are doubly important, since many people

TENCEL® sells fibre to the people who sell fabrics, to the people who sell garments, to the retailers who sell them to consumers. Advertising TENCEL® to consumers pulls the fibre through the chain.

SOURCE: TENCEL®

TENCEL® Sexy, modern, natural, comfort
from an environmentally friendly fibre.

TENCEL®
the natural feeling
www.tencel.com

replace their tyres with the brand already on the car. Even in large business markets, a few buyers normally account for most of the purchasing.

Business markets are also more *geographically concentrated*: international financial services in London, petrochemicals and synthetic fibres around Rotterdam and Amsterdam and the movie industry in Hollywood. Further, business demand is **derived demand** – it ultimately derives from the demand for consumer goods. Fokker hopes to sell Glare (GLAss fibre REinforced aluminium) to Airbus for their super jumbo A380 whose demand is forecast because the consumers' demand for air travel is growing and so airlines want more capacity. If consumer demand for air travel drops, so will the demand for the A380, Glare, Rolls-Royce Trent 900 engine and all the other products used to make the aircraft.[4]

> In late 1997 Ron Woodard, of Boeing, half-jokingly asked airlines to decrease their orders to ease Boeing's over-stretched production. In January 1998 he got more than he asked for. Following the economic troubles in south-east Asia and the resultant decline in local air travel, airlines all over the region were renegotiating orders. Philippine Airlines said it planned to cancel four 747-400 jets; Malaysian Airlines System wants to delay the delivery of 20 aircraft up to five years; Garuda Indonesia left Boeing stranded with jets it ordered but could not afford and stopped lease payments on six new Airbus A330s. More trouble is on the way as Korean Air's value drops to less than three of its fleet of 45 747s.[5]

Many business markets have **inelastic demand**: that is, total demand for many business products is not affected much by price changes, especially in the short run. A drop in the price of concrete will not cause builders to buy much more concrete unless it results in lower construction prices, which, in turn, will increase consumer demand for bridges, factories, runways or offices.[6]

Derived demand
Business demand that ultimately comes from (derives from) the demand for consumer goods.

Inelastic demand
Total demand for a product that is not much affected by price changes, especially in the short run.

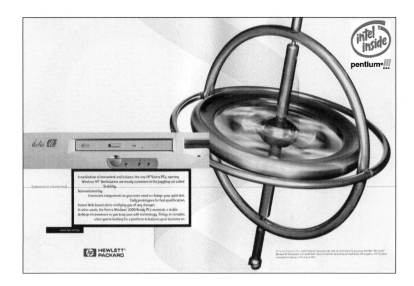

Derived demand: Intel's long-running 'Intel Inside' logo advertising campaign boosts demand for Intel chips and for the PCs containing them. Now, HP and most other computer makers feature the logo in ads like this one.

SOURCE: Copyright 2001 Hewlett-Packard Company

Finally, business markets have more *fluctuating demand*. The demand for many business goods and services tends to change more – and more quickly – than the demand for consumer goods and services does. A small percentage increase in consumer demand can cause large increases in business demand. Sometimes a rise of only 10 per cent in consumer demand can cause as much as a 200 per cent rise in business demand during the next period.

■ Nature of the buying unit

Compared with consumer purchases, a business purchase usually involves *more buyers* and a *more professional purchasing effort*. Often, business buying is done by trained purchasing agents, who spend their working lives learning how to buy well. The more complex the purchase, the more likely that several people will participate in the decision-making process. Buying committees made up of technical experts and top management are common in the buying of primary goods. Therefore, business marketers must have well-trained salespeople to deal with well-trained buyers.

■ Types of decision and the decision process

Business buyers usually face *more complex* buying decisions than do consumer buyers. Purchases often involve large sums of money, complex technical and economic considerations, and interactions among many people at many levels of the buyer's organisation. Because the purchases are more complex, business buyers may take longer to make their decisions. For example, the purchase of a large computer system might take many months or more than a year to complete and could involve millions of pounds, thousands of technical details and dozens of people ranging from top management to lower-level users.

The business buying process tends to be *more formalised* than the consumer buying process. Large business purchases usually call for detailed product specifications, written purchase orders, careful supplier searches and formal approval. The buying firm might even prepare policy manuals that detail the purchase process.

Finally, in the business buying process, buyer and seller are often much *more dependent* on each other. Consumer marketers are usually at a distance from their customers. In contrast, business marketers may roll up their sleeves and work closely with their customers during all stages of the buying process – from helping customers

Business marketers often roll up their sleeves and work closely with their customers throughout the buying and consuming process. In this award-winning business-to-business ad, Fujitsu promises more than just high-tech products: 'Our technology helps keep you moving upward. And our people won't let you down.'

Source: © Fujitsu Ltd

define problems, to finding solutions, to supporting after-sales operations. For instance, 60 per cent of the money needed to develop Bombardier's Gex business jet came from suppliers and risk-sharing partners, including engine suppliers BMW/Rolls-Royce. They customise their offerings to meet individual customer needs. In the short run, orders go to suppliers that meet buyers' immediate product and service needs. However, business marketers must also build close *long-run* relationships with customers. In the long run, business marketers keep a customer's orders by meeting current needs *and* thinking ahead to meet the customer's future needs.

Volkswagen is breaking new ground at its Skoda factory by having suppliers' operations directly inside the car plant. Lucas, Johnson Controls and Pelzer are producing rear axles, seats and carpets in the Czech factory. This is one step ahead of Japanese manufacturers, which often have suppliers nearby.[7]

■ Other characteristics of business markets

Direct purchasing Business buyers often buy directly from producers rather than through intermediaries, especially for items that are technically complex or expensive. Airlines buy aircraft directly from Boeing or Airbus, Kroger buys packaged goods directly from Procter & Gamble and universities buy computers directly from IBM, Dell and so on. This process is increasing rapidly with the rapid growth of B2B exchanges introduced in Marketing Highlight 7.1.

Reciprocity Business buyers often practise *reciprocity*, selecting suppliers that also buy from them. For example, a paper company might buy needed chemicals from a chemical company that in turn buys the company's paper.

> Shaken by European Airbus's success in the airliner market, market leader Boeing has started a worldwide review of its purchasing policies. They intend to match aircraft parts contracts to countries that buy Boeings. With an apparent eye on the Canadian government's purchase of search-and-rescue helicopters and Canadian Airlines International's 737 replacements, Boeing warned: 'Our Canadian business placement must understandably be market based, as it is elsewhere.'[8]

Leasing Business buyers are increasingly leasing equipment instead of buying it outright. Everything from printing presses to power plants, business jets to hay balers,

marketing highlight 7.1

The B2B Internet bazaar

General Electric is among the pioneers in Internet purchasing. In early 1995, GE's Information Services division (GEIS) launched a website that allowed buyers in GE's divisions to purchase industrial products electronically. This website let GE buyers zap out requests for bids to thousands of suppliers, who could then respond over the Internet. Such electronic purchasing has saved GE money, time, and piles of paperwork. *Forbes* gives an account of how it works:

> Last month the machinery at a GE Lighting factory broke down . . . [so they] needed custom replacement parts, fast. In the past GE would have asked for bids from just four domestic suppliers. There was just too much hassle getting the paperwork and production-line blueprints together and sent out to [a long list of] suppliers. But this time they posted the specifications and 'requests for quotes' on GE's Web site – and drew seven other bidders. The winner was a Hungarian [vendor] . . . that would not [even] have been contacted in the days of paper purchasing forms. The Hungarian firm's replacement parts arrived quicker, and GE Lighting paid just $320,000 (€385,000), a 20 per cent savings.

Within little more than a year, GEIS's Internet purchasing system had logged more than $350 million worth of purchases by GE divisions, at a 10–15 per cent savings in costs and a five-day reduction in average order time. In 1997, GE purchased $1 billion worth of materials via the Net and by the end of 2000 expected to be buying $5 billion worth, at 20 per cent savings over the old way.

Based on its own success, GE opened its online procurement services to other companies who pay for access to their Trading Process Network (TPN) (www.tpn.geis.com), an online service that lets member buyers prepare bids, select suppliers, and post orders to its website. Users can select items they wish to buy and use a purchasing card for payment. Once the order is placed, TPN sends a purchase order to a selected supplier or asks for bids from several qualified suppliers. Users of the TPN service have experienced up to a 50 per cent reduction in order cycle times, 30 per cent reduction in procurement costs, and 20 per cent reduction in material costs.

Internet bazaars like GE's TPN promise many benefits:

◆ *Shave transaction costs* for both buyers and suppliers. A Web-powered purchasing program eliminates the paperwork associated with traditional requisition and ordering procedures. At National Semiconductor, the $75 to $250 cost of processing each paper-based requisition has been cut to just $3 per electronic order.

◆ *Reduce time between order and delivery*: Time savings are particularly dramatic for companies with many overseas suppliers. Adaptec, a leading supplier of computer storage, used an extranet to tie all of its Taiwanese chip suppliers together in a kind of virtual family. Now messages from Adaptec flow in seconds from its headquarters to its Asian partners, and Adaptec has reduced the time between the order and delivery of its chips from as long as 16 weeks to just 55 days – the same turnaround time for companies that build their own chips.

◆ *Create more efficient purchasing systems*: One key motivation for GE's massive move to online purchasing has been a desire to get rid of overlapping purchasing systems across its many divisions.

◆ *Forge more intimate relationships* between partners and buyers. Robert Mondavi Corporation puts satellite images of its vineyards out over its extranet so that its independent growers can pinpoint potential vineyard problems and improve the grapes Mondavi purchases from them.

◆ *Level the playing field* between large and small suppliers. By using Internet technology to establish secure, standing information links between companies, extranets have helped firms do business with smaller suppliers. Currently, most large manufacturers use EDI to order supplies, because it provides a secure means of coding and exchanging standardised business forms. However, EDI is an expensive system; it can cost as much as $50,000 to add a single trading partner to an EDI network, compared to $1,000 for a company to join GE's Trading Process Network. Moving business-to-business commerce onto the Web also levels the playing field between local and foreign suppliers, because purchasers can source materials from suppliers all over the globe for no additional transaction cost.

Thus, the Internet promises to change greatly the face of business buying and hence the face of business-to-business marketing. As one expert suggests, 'Internet presence is becoming as common as business cards and faxes.' To stay in the game, business-to-business marketers will need a well-thought-out Internet marketing strategy to support their other business marketing efforts.

Sources: Extracts from Scott Woolley, 'Double click for resin', *Forbes* (10 March 1997), p. 132. Also see Dana Blankenhorn, 'GE's e-commerce network opens up to other marketers', *Advertising Age's Business Marketing* (May 1997), pp. M4, M11; 'Consolidated Edison of New York selects GE's Trading Process Network to facilitate Internet sourcing', press release, www.tpn.geis.com (10 February 1998); Robert D. Hof, 'The "click here" economy', *Business Week* (22 June 1998), pp. 122–8; John Evan Frook, 'Buying behemoth – by shifting $5b in spending to extranets, GE could ignite a development frenzy', *Internetweek* (17 August 1998), p. 1; Richard Waugh and Scott Elliff, 'Using the Internet to achieve purchasing improvements at General Electric', *Hospital Materiel Management Quarterly* (November 1998), pp. 81–3; and James Carbone, 'Internet buying on the rise', *Purchasing* (25 March 1999), pp. 51–6; see Robert Yoegel, 'The evolution of B-to-B selling on the 'Net', *Target Marketing* (August 1998), p. 34; Andy Reinhardt in San Mateo, 'Extranets: Log on, link up, save big', *Business Week* (22 June 1998), p. 134; 'To byte the hand that feeds', *The Economist* (17 January 1998), pp. 61–2; John Jesitus, 'Procuring an edge', *Industry Week* (23 June 1997), pp. 56–62; Ken Brack, 'Source of the future', *Industrial Distribution* (October 1998), pp. 76–80.

and office copiers to off-shore drilling rigs. The biggest buyers of airliners, business jets and cars are leasing companies. Some universities have started leasing student halls of residences to release money for investment elsewhere. In this case they are leasing the facilities they once owned, a strategy often used by large corporations.

The lessee can gain a number of advantages, such as having more available capital, getting the seller's latest products, receiving better servicing and gaining some tax advantages. The lessor often ends up with a larger net income and the chance to sell to customers that might not have been able to afford outright purchase.

a model of business buyer behaviour

At the most basic level, marketers want to know how business buyers will respond to various marketing stimuli. Figure 7.2 shows a model of business buyer behaviour. In this model, marketing and other stimuli affect the buying organisation and produce certain buyer responses. As with consumer buying, the marketing stimuli for business buying consist of the four Ps: product, price, place and promotion. Other stimuli include influential forces in the environment: economic, technological, political, cultural and competitive. These stimuli enter the organisation and are turned into buyer responses: product or service choice; supplier choice; order quantities; and delivery, service and payment terms. In order to design good marketing-mix strategies, the marketer must understand what happens within the organisation to turn stimuli into purchase responses.

Within the organisation, buying activity consists of two main parts: the buying centre, made up of all the people involved in the buying decision, and the buying decision process. Figure 7.2 shows that the buying centre and the buying decision process are influenced by internal organisational, interpersonal and individual factors as well as by external environmental factors.

business buyer behaviour

The model in Figure 7.2 suggests four questions about business buyer behaviour: What buying decisions do business buyers make? Who participates in the buying process?

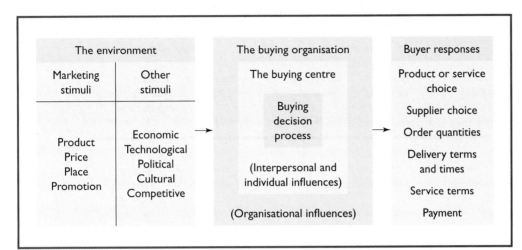

Figure 7.2

A model of business buyer behaviour

What are the strongest influences on buyers? How do business buyers make their buying decisions?

what buying decisions do business buyers make?

The business buyer faces a whole set of decisions in making a purchase. The number of decisions depends on the type of buying situation.

■ Main types of buying situation

There are three main types of buying situation.[9] At one extreme is the *straight rebuy*, which is a fairly routine decision. At the other extreme is the *new task*, which may call for thorough research. In the middle is the *modified rebuy*, which requires some research. (For examples, see Figure 7.3.)

Straight rebuy   In a **straight rebuy**, the buyer reorders something without any modifications. It is usually handled on a routine basis by the purchasing department. It is estimated that 90 per cent of these routine B2B transaction will be by e-commerce within a few years.[10] Based on past buying satisfaction, the buyer simply chooses from the various suppliers on its list. 'In' suppliers try to maintain product and service quality. They often propose automatic reordering systems so that the purchase agent will save reordering time. The 'out' suppliers try to offer something new or exploit dissatisfaction so that the buyer will consider them. 'Out' suppliers try to get their foot in the door with a small order and then enlarge their purchase share over time.

Straight rebuy
A business buying situation in which the buyer routinely reorders something without any modifications.

Modified rebuy   In a **modified rebuy**, the buyer wants to modify product specifications, prices, terms or suppliers. The modified rebuy usually involves more decision participants than the straight rebuy. The 'in' suppliers may become nervous and feel pressured to put their best foot forward to protect an account. 'Out' suppliers may see the modified rebuy situation as an opportunity to make a better offer and gain new business.

Modified rebuy
A business buying situation in which the buyer wants to modify product specifications, prices, terms or suppliers.

New task   A company buying a product or service for the first time faces a **new task** situation. In such cases, the greater the cost or risk, the larger will be the number of decision participants and the greater their efforts to collect information. The new-task situation is the marketer's greatest opportunity and challenge. The marketer not only tries to reach as many key buying influences as possible, but also provides help and information.

New task
A business buying situation in which the buyer purchases a product or service for the first time.

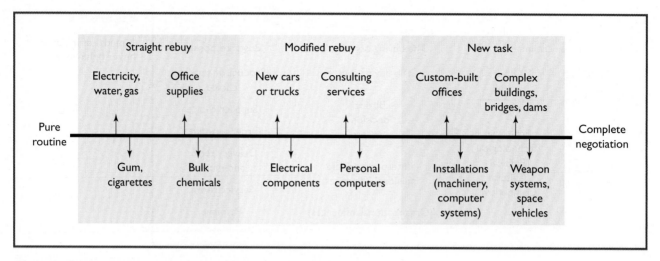

Figure 7.3

Three types of business buying situation

SOURCE: Ben M. Enis, *Marketing Principles*, 3rd edn (1980). © 1980 Scott, Foresman & Co.

■ Specific buying decisions

The buyer makes the fewest decisions in the straight rebuy and the most in the new-task decision. In the new-task situation, the buyer must decide on product specifications, suppliers, price limits, payment terms, order quantities, delivery times and service terms. The order of these decisions varies with each situation and different decision participants influence each choice.

■ Systems buying and selling

Systems buying
Buying a packaged solution to a problem and without all the separate decisions involved.

Many business buyers prefer to buy a packaged solution to a problem from a single seller. Called **systems buying**, this practice began with government buying of powerful weapons and communication systems. Instead of buying and putting all the components together, the government asked for bids from suppliers that would supply the components *and* assemble the package or system.

> Finding its market share squeezed by Airbus in selling airliners, Boeing aims to increase its business by offering a whole network of support services to airlines. Airlines spend over €460bn on support services that Boeing thinks they could provide – that is more than the annual sales of both Boeing and Airbus airliners. Boeing says it has learned this business from its defence division that gets a fifth of its revenue from US Air Force services, such as running bases.
>
> Intershop is an outstandingly successful company, based in old East Germany. It is world market leader in software design and licensing for more than 20,000 companies who sell over the Internet. When companies face the need to set up an e-commerce operation, Intershop provides a range of services that they need.[11]

Sellers have increasingly recognised that buyers like this method and have adopted systems selling as a marketing tool. Systems selling is a two-step process. First, the supplier sells a group of interlocking products: for example, the supplier sells not only glue, but also applicators and dryers. Second, the supplier sells a system of production, inventory control, distribution and other services to meet the buyer's need for a smooth-running operation.

Systems selling is a key business marketing strategy for winning and holding accounts. The contract often goes to the firm that provides the most complete system meeting the customer's needs. Consider the following:

The Indonesian government requested bids to build a cement factory near Jakarta. A Western firm's proposal included choosing the site, designing the cement factory, hiring the construction crews, assembling the materials and equipment and turning the finished factory over to the Indonesian government. A Japanese firm's proposal included all of these services, plus hiring and training workers to run the factory, exporting the cement through their trading companies and using the cement to build some needed roads and new office buildings in Jakarta. Although the Japanese firm's proposal cost more, it won the contract. Clearly the Japanese viewed the problem not as one of just building a cement factory (the narrow view of systems selling) but of running it in a way that would contribute to the country's economy. They took the broadest view of the customers' needs. This is true systems selling.

who participates in the business buying process?

Who buys the goods and services needed by business oganisations? The decision-making unit of a buying organisation is called its **buying centre**, defined as all the individuals and units that participate in the business decision-making process.[12]

The buying centre includes all members of the organisation who play any of five roles in the purchase decision process.[13]

1. **Users**. Members of the organisation who will use the product or service. In many cases, users initiate the buying proposal and help define product specifications.
2. **Influencers**. People who affect the buying decision. They often help define specifications and also provide information for evaluating alternatives. Technical personnel are particularly important influencers.
3. **Buyers**. People with formal authority to select the supplier and arrange terms of purchase. Buyers may help shape product specifications, but they play their most important role in selecting vendors and in negotiating. In more complex purchases, buyers might include high-level officers participating in the negotiations.
4. **Deciders**. People who have formal or informal power to select or approve the final suppliers. In routine buying, the buyers are often the deciders or at least the approvers.
5. **Gatekeepers**. People who control the flow of information to others. For example, purchasing agents often have authority to prevent salespersons from seeing users or deciders. Other gatekeepers include technical personnel and even personal secretaries.

The buying centre is not a fixed and formally identified unit within the buying organisation. It is a set of buying roles assumed by different people for different purchases. Within the organisation, the size and make-up of the buying centre will vary for different products and for different buying situations. For some routine purchases, one person – say a purchasing agent – may assume all the buying centre roles and serve as the only person involved in the buying decision. For more complex purchases, the buying centre may include 20 or 30 people from different levels and departments in the organisation. One survey found that the average number of people involved in a buying decision ranges from about three (for services and items used in day-to-day operations) to almost five (for such high-ticket purchases as construction work and machinery). Another survey detected a trend towards team-based buying – 87 per cent of surveyed purchasing executives expected teams of people from different functions to be making buying decisions in 2000.[14]

Buying centre
All the individuals and units that participate in the business buying-decision process.

Users
Members of the organisation who will use the product or service; users often initiate the buying proposal and help define product specifications.

Influencer
A person whose views or advice carries some weight in making a final buying decision; they often help define specifications and also provide information for evaluating alternatives.

Buyer
The person who makes an actual purchase.

Deciders
People in the organisation's buying centre who have formal or informal powers to select or approve the final suppliers.

Gatekeepers
People in the organisation's buying centre who control the flow of information to others.

Business marketers working in global markets may face even greater levels of buying centre influence. A study comparing the buying decision processes in the United States, Sweden, France and Southeast Asia found that US buyers may be lone eagles compared with their counterparts in some other countries. Sweden had the highest team buying effort, whereas the United States had the lowest, even though the Swedish and US firms had very similar demographics. In making purchasing decisions, Swedish firms depended on technical staff, both their own and suppliers', much more than did the firms in other countries.[15]

The buying centre usually includes some obvious participants who are involved formally in the buying decision. For example, the decision to buy a corporate jet will probably involve the company's chief pilot, a purchasing agent, some legal staff, a member of top management and others formally charged with the buying decision. It may also involve less obvious, informal participants, some of whom may actually make or strongly affect the buying decision. Sometimes, even the people in the buying centre are not aware of all the buying participants. For example, the decision about which corporate jet to buy may actually be made by a corporate board member who has an interest in flying and knows a lot about aircraft. This board member may work behind the scenes to sway the decision. Many business buying decisions result from the complex interactions of ever-changing buying-centre participants.

The division of roles within the buying centre can cause a conflict of interest. Frequent flyer programmes succeed because a flyer or their secretary books a flight and accumulates frequent flyer points while the company pays. Corporate hospitality uses similar mechanisms to influence demand. Typical examples could include offering an important decider hospitality including a few drinks and tickets for a Wimbledon final (cost €3,000), a meeting at the Sydney Olympics (€5,000) or a few days' fishing in Norway (€15,000). To some companies spending €15,000 on entertaining is 'peanuts' compared with the potential return. Unsurprisingly, many companies and tax authorities are investigating or banning such benefits.[16]

what are the main influences on business buyers?

Business buyers are subject to many influences when they make their buying decisions. Some marketers assume that the major influences are economic. They think buyers will favour the supplier who offers the lowest price or the best product or the most service. They concentrate on offering strong economic benefits to buyers. However, business buyers actually respond to both economic and personal factors. Far from being cold, calculating and impersonal, business buyers are human and social as well. They react to both reason and emotion.

Today, most business-to-business marketers recognise that emotion plays an important role in business buying decisions. For example, you might expect that an advertisement promoting large trucks to corporate truck fleet buyers would stress objective technical, performance and economic factors. However, a recent ad for Volvo heavy-duty trucks shows two drivers arm wrestling and claims, 'It solves all your fleet problems. Except who gets to drive.' It turns out that the type of truck a fleet provides can help it to attract qualified drivers. The Volvo ad stresses the raw beauty of the truck and its comfort and roominess, features that make it more appealing to drivers. The ad concludes that Volvo trucks are 'built to make fleets more profitable and drivers a lot more possessive'.

When suppliers' offers are very similar, business buyers have little basis for strictly rational choice. Because they can meet organisational goals with any supplier, buyers can allow personal factors to play a larger role in their decisions. However, when competing products differ greatly, business buyers are more accountable for their choice

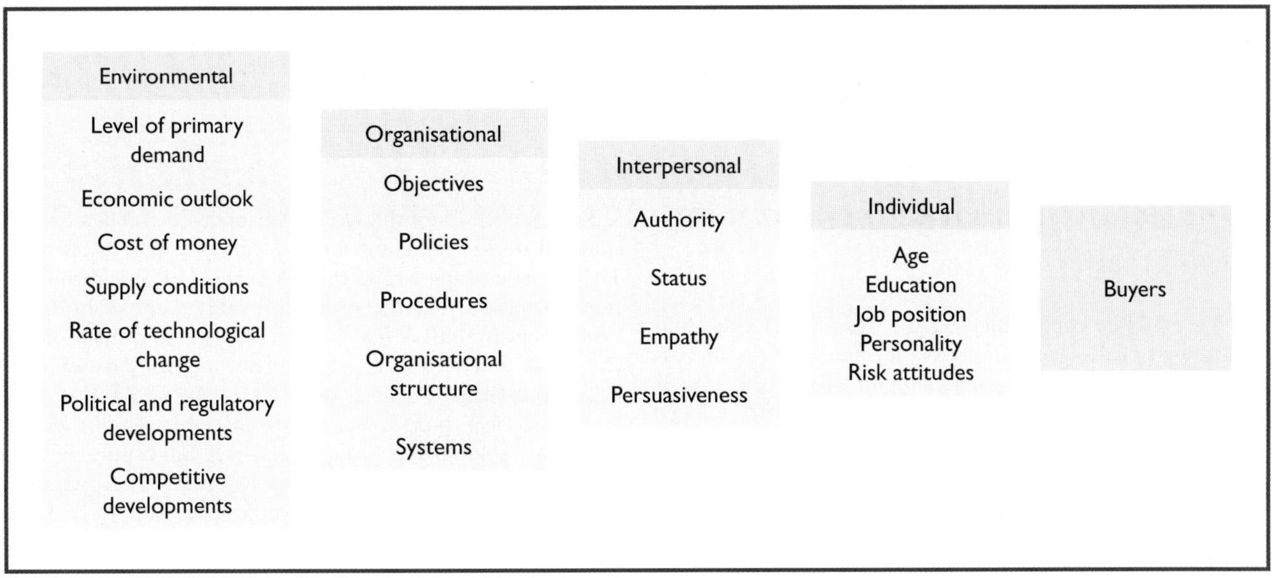

Figure 7.4

The main influences
on business buying
behaviour

and tend to pay more attention to economic factors. Figure 7.4 lists various groups
of influences on business buyers – environmental, organisational, interpersonal, and
individual.[17]

■ Environmental factors

Business buyers are influenced heavily by factors in the current and expected *economic environment*, such as the level of primary demand, the economic outlook, and
the cost of money. As economic uncertainty rises, business buyers cut back on new
investments and attempt to reduce their inventories.

An increasingly important environmental factor is shortages in key materials.
Many companies now are more willing to buy and hold larger inventories of scarce
materials to ensure adequate supply. Business buyers also are affected by technological, political and competitive developments in the environment. Culture and customs
can strongly influence business buyer reactions to the marketer's behaviour and
strategies, especially in the international marketing environment (see Marketing
Highlight 7.2). The business marketer must watch these factors, determine how they
will affect the buyer, and try to turn these challenges into opportunities.

■ Organisational factors

Each buying organisation has its own objectives, policies, procedures, structure and
systems. The business marketer must know these *organisational factors* as thoroughly
as possible. Questions such as these arise: How many people are involved in the
buying decision? Who are they? What are their evaluative criteria? What are the
company's policies and limits on its buyers?

Upgraded purchasing Buying departments have often occupied a low position in
the management hierarchy, even though they often manage more than half of the company's costs. In some industries, such as telecommunications, manufacturers buy in
items approaching 80 per cent of total cost. With good reason, many companies are
upgrading their purchasing activities. Some companies have combined several functions – such as purchasing, inventory control, production scheduling and traffic – into
a high-level function called *strategic materials management*. Buying departments in

marketing highlight 7.2

International marketing manners: when in Rome . . .

Consolidated Amalgamation, Inc., thinks it's time that the rest of the world enjoyed the same fine products it has offered American consumers for two generations. It dispatches vice-president Harry E. Slicksmile to Europe to explore the territory. Mr Slicksmile stops first in London, where he makes short work of some bankers – he rings them up on the phone. He handles Parisians with similar ease: after securing a table at La Tour d'Argent, he greets his luncheon guest, the director of an industrial engineering firm, with the words, 'Just call me Harry, Jacques.'

In Germany, Mr Slicksmile is a powerhouse. Whisking through a lavish, state-of-the-art marketing presentation, complete with the flip charts and audiovisuals, he shows them that this Georgia boy *knows* how to make a buck. Heading on to Milan, Harry strikes up a conversation with the Japanese businessman sitting next to him on the plane. He flips his card on to the guy's tray and, when the two say goodbye, shakes hands warmly and clasps the man's right arm. Later, for his appointment with the owner of an Italian packaging-design firm, our hero wears his comfy corduroy sport coat, khaki pants and Topsiders. Everybody knows Italians are zany and laid back, right?

In order to succeed in global markets, companies must help their managers to understand the needs, customs and cultures of international business buyers.

Wrong. Six months later, Consolidated Amalgamation has nothing to show for the trip but a pile of bills. There was nothing wrong with Consolidated Amalgamation's products, but the orders probably went to firms whose representative had not antagonised and insulted people as much as Harry did. In Europe, they weren't wild about Harry.

This case has been exaggerated for emphasis. People are seldom such dolts as Harry E. Slicksmile, but success in international business has a lot to do with knowing the territory and its people. Poor Harry tried, all right, but in all the wrong ways. The British do not, as a rule, make deals over the phone as much as Americans do. It's not so much a 'cultural' difference as a difference in approach. A proper Frenchman neither likes instant familiarity – questions about family, church or alma mater – nor refers to strangers by their first names.

Harry's flashy presentation was probably also a flop with the Germans, who dislike overstatement and ostentation. According to one German expert, German businesspeople have become accustomed to dealing with Americans. Although differences in body language and customs remain, the past 20 years have softened them. However, calling secretaries by their first names would still be considered rude in Germany: 'They have a right to be called by their surname. You'd certainly ask for – and get – permission first.' In Germany people address each other formally and correctly: for example, someone with two doctorates (which is quite common) must be referred to as 'Herr Doktor Doktor'.

When Harry Slicksmile grabbed his new Japanese acquaintance by the arm, the executive probably considered him disrespectful and presumptuous. The Japanese, like many others in Asia, have a 'no-contact culture' in which even shaking hands is a strange experience. Harry made matters worse by tossing his business card. Japanese people revere the business card as an extension of self and as an indicator of rank. They do not *hand* it to people; they *present* it – with both hands.

Hapless Harry's last gaffe was assuming that Italians are like Hollywood's stereotypes of them. The flair for design and style that has characterised Italian culture for centuries is embodied in the businesspeople of Milan and Rome. They dress beautifully and admire flair, but they blanch at garishness or impropriety in others' attire.

In order to compete successfully in global markets, or even to deal effectively with international firms in their home markets, companies must help their managers to understand the needs, customs and cultures of international business buyers. Here are a few more rules of social and business etiquette that managers should understand when doing business in another country.

France	Dress conservatively, except in the south where more casual clothes are worn. Do not refer to people by their first names – the French are formal with strangers.
Germany	Be especially punctual. A businessperson invited to someone's home should present flowers, preferably unwrapped, to the hostess. During introductions, greet women first and wait until, or if, they extend their hands before extending yours.
Indonesia	Learn how to sing at least one song. At the end of formal gatherings people often take turns in singing unaccompanied.
Italy	Whether you dress conservatively or go native in a Giorgio Armani suit, keep in mind that Italian business people are style conscious. Make appointments well in advance. Prepare for and be patient with Italian bureaucracies.
Japan	Don't imitate Japanese bowing customs unless you understand them thoroughly – who bows to whom, how many times and when. It's a complicated ritual.
Saudi Arabia	Although men will kiss each other in greeting, they will never kiss a woman in public. An American woman should wait for a man to extend his hand before offering hers. If a Saudi offers refreshment, accept – it is an insult to decline it.
United Kingdom	Toasts are often given at formal dinners. If the host honours you with a toast, be prepared to reciprocate. Business entertaining is done more often at lunch than at dinner.
United States	Expect to be asked to meet and work at any time, over breakfast, lunch and dinner. Do not be taken in by street attire; American managers' dress code at work is very formal and conservative.

Don't panic. Most businesspeople you are likely to meet are used to dealing with overseas guests and are used to forgiving their failings. There is, however, a big gap between being forgiven for social transgressions and getting the best deal.

SOURCES: Adapted from Susan Harte, 'When in Rome, you should learn to do what the Romans do', *The Atlanta Journal-Constitution* (22 January 1990), pp. D1, D6; see also Lufthansa's Business Travel Guide/Europe; Sergey Frank, 'Global negotiating', *Sales and Marketing Management* (May 1992), pp. 64–9; Malcolm Wheatley, 'Going, going, gone', *Business Life* (October 1994), pp. 65–8; Cynthia Kemper, 'Global sales success depends on cultural insight', *World Trade* (May 1998), pp. S2–S4; Ann Marie Sabath, *International Business Etiquette Europe: What you need to know to conduct business abroad with charm and savvy* (Career Press, 1999); and Wayne A. Conway, Joseph J. Douress and Terri Morrison, *Dun & Bradstreet's Guide to Doing Business Around the World, Revised* (Upper Saddle River, NJ: Prentice Hall, 1999).

many multinational companies have responsibility for buying materials and services around the world. Many companies are offering higher compensation in order to attract top talent in the buying area. This means that business marketers must also upgrade their salespeople to match the quality of today's business buyers.[18]

Centralised purchasing In companies consisting of many divisions with differing needs, much of the purchasing is carried out at the division level. Recently, however, some large companies have tried to centralise purchasing. Headquarters identifies materials purchased by several divisions and buys them centrally. Centralised purchasing gives the companies more purchasing clout, which can produce substantial savings.

For the business marketer, this development means dealing with fewer, higher-level buyers. Instead of using regional sales forces to sell a large buyer's separate plants, the seller may use a *national account sales force* to service the buyer. For example, at Xerox, over 250 national account managers each handle one to five large national accounts with many scattered locations. The national account managers coordinate the efforts of an entire Xerox team – specialists, analysts, salespeople for individual products – to sell and service important national customers.[19] National account selling is challenging and demands both a high-level sales force and sophisticated marketing effort.

Long-term contracts   Business buyers are increasingly seeking long-term contracts with suppliers. For example, GM wants to buy from fewer suppliers which are willing to locate close to its plants and produce high-quality components. Business marketers are also beginning to offer *electronic order interchange* systems to their customers. When using such systems, the seller places terminals hooked to the seller's computers in customers' offices. Then the customer can order needed items instantly by entering orders directly into the computer. The orders are transmitted automatically to the supplier.

Although buyers are seeking closer relations with suppliers, businesses do not always have each other's interests at heart. In all relationships there is a tension between the comfort of loyalty and the freedom to shop around. Economic and technological changes can make long-term business-to-business relationships inherently unstable.[20] The result is serial monogamy as firms switch between medium-term relationships.

Just-in-time production systems   The emergence of *just-in-time (JIT) production systems* has had a considerable impact on business purchasing policies. JIT, in particular, has produced notable changes in business marketing. JIT means that production materials arrive fit for use at the customer's factory exactly when needed for production, rather than being stored in the customer's inventory until used. The goal of JIT is zero inventory with 100 per cent quality. It calls for coordination between the production schedules of supplier and customer, so that neither has to carry much inventory. Effective use of JIT reduces inventory and lead times and increases quality, productivity and adaptability to change.

> Leyland Trucks practises JIT across the whole value chain, and consequently only needs to start production after it has orders. These practices greatly affect how business marketers sell to and service their customers. Since JIT involves frequent delivery, many business marketers have set up locations closer to their large JIT customers. Closer locations enable them to deliver smaller shipments more efficiently and reliably. Many firms have set up plants close to Nissan's car plant in the north of England and VW now has suppliers producing inside its Czech Skoda plant. Thus JIT means that a business marketer may have to make large commitments to important customers. The Biofoam case at the end of this chapter shows a packaging company becoming an on-site supplier to its customers.[21]

Purchasing performance evaluation   Some companies are setting up incentive systems to reward purchasing managers for especially good purchasing performance, in much the same way that salespeople receive bonuses for especially good selling performance. These systems should lead purchasing managers to increase their pressure on sellers for the best terms.

■ Interpersonal factors

The buying centre usually includes many participants who influence each other. The business marketer often finds it difficult to determine what kinds of *interpersonal factors* and group dynamics enter into the buying process. As one writer notes: 'Managers do not wear tags that say "decision maker" or "unimportant person". The powerful are often invisible, at least to vendor representatives.'[22] Nor does the buying-centre participant with the highest rank always have the most influence. Participants may have influence in the buying decision because they control rewards and punishments, are well liked, have special expertise, or have a special relationship with other important participants. Interpersonal factors are often very subtle. Whenever possible, business marketers must try to understand these factors and design strategies that take them into account.

■ Individual factors

Each participant in the business buying-decision process brings in personal motives, perceptions and preferences. These individual factors are affected by personal characteristics such as age, income, education, professional identification, personality and attitudes towards risk. Also, buyers have different buying styles. Some may be technical types who make in-depth analyses of competitive proposals before choosing a supplier. Other buyers may be intuitive negotiators who are adept at pitting the sellers against one another for the best deal.

> Secretaries and personal assistants are an important target for DHL, the express courier; they may be told by their boss to send a package but have the discretion to choose the courier. To contact them it advertises in *Executive PA* and other secretarial-type publications and 'always attends the Secretaries Show'. In contrast UPS, which has a bias towards small business-to-business parcels, finds that most decisions are made by traffic, distribution and logistics managers. To contact them it schedules its TV advertising around sports events, prime-time films and documentaries.[23]

how do business buyers make their buying decisions?

Table 7.1 lists the eight stages of the business buying process.[24] Buyers who face a new-task buying situation usually go through all stages of the buying process. Buyers making modified or straight rebuys may skip some of the stages. We will examine these steps for the typical new-task buying situation.

■ Problem recognition

The buying process begins when someone in the company recognises a problem or a need that can be met by acquiring a specific good or a service. **Problem recognition** can result from internal or external stimuli. Internally, the company may decide to launch a new product that requires new production equipment and materials. Or a machine may break down and need new parts. Perhaps a purchasing manager is unhappy with a current supplier's product quality, service or prices. Externally, the

Problem recognition
The first stage of the business buying process in which someone in the company recognises a problem or need that can be met by acquiring a good or a service.

Table 7.1

Key stages of the business buying process in relation to important buying situations

| | BUYING SITUATIONS | | |
STAGES OF THE BUYING PROCESS	NEW TASK	MODIFIED REBUY	STRAIGHT REBUY
Problem recognition	Yes	Maybe	No
General need description	Yes	Maybe	No
Product specification	Yes	Yes	Yes
Supplier search	Yes	Maybe	No
Proposal solicitation	Yes	Maybe	No
Supplier selection	Yes	Maybe	No
Order-routine specification	Yes	Maybe	No
Performance review	Yes	Yes	Yes

SOURCE: Adapted from Patrick J. Robinson, Charles W. Faris and Yoram Wind, *Industrial Buying and Creative Marketing* (Boston: Allyn & Bacon, 1967), p. 14.

buyer may get some new ideas at a trade show, see an ad or receive a call from a salesperson who offers a better product or a lower price.

■ General need description

General need description
The stage in the business buying process in which the company describes the general characteristics and quantity of a needed item.

Having recognised a need, the buyer next prepares a **general need description** that describes the characteristics and quantity of the needed item. For standard items, this process presents few problems. For complex items, however, the buyer may have to work with others – engineers, users, consultants – to define the item. The team may want to rank the importance of reliability, durability, price and other attributes desired in the item. In this phase, the alert business marketer can help the buyers define their needs and provide information about the value of different product characteristics. For Fokker to sell Glare, its new aerospace material, for use in the A380 superjumbo it will have to work with Airbus Industries designers to influence the aircraft's design and the sort of material they specify. Increasingly, new products are designed in conjunction with suppliers whose input influences the product specification.

■ Product specification

Product specification
The stage of the business buying process in which the buying organisation decides on and specifies the best technical product characteristics for a needed item.

The buying organisation next develops the item's technical **product specifications**, often with the help of a value analysis engineering team. **Value analysis** is an approach to cost reduction in which components are studied carefully to determine if they can be redesigned, standardised or made by less costly methods of production. The team decides on the best characteristics and specifies them accordingly. Sellers, too, can use value analysis as a tool to help secure a new account. By showing buyers a better way to make an object, outside sellers can turn straight rebuy situations into new-task situations that give them a chance to obtain new business.

Value analysis
An approach to cost reduction in which components are studied carefully to determine if they can be redesigned, standardised or made by less costly methods of production.

■ Supplier search

Supplier search
The stage of the business buying process in which the buyer tries to find the best vendors.

The buyer now conducts a **supplier search** to find the best vendors. The buyer can compile a small list of qualified suppliers by reviewing trade directories, doing a computer search or phoning other companies for recommendations. Today, more and more companies are turning to the Internet to find suppliers. For marketers, this has levelled the playing field – smaller suppliers have the same advantages as larger ones and can be listed in the same online catalogues for a nominal fee:

> Worldwide Internet Solutions Network, better known as WIZnet (www.wiznet.net), has built an 'interactive virtual library of business-to-business catalogs' that is global in coverage. At last report, its database included complete specifications for more than 10 million products and services from 45,000 manufacturers, distributors, and industrial service providers. For purchasing managers, who routinely receive stacks of mail each day, much of it catalogues, this kind of one-stop shopping will be an incredible time-saver (and price saver, because it allows easier comparison shopping). When told by a management consultant, 'Do a search for 3.5-inch (9 cm) platinum ball valves available from a local source', WIZnet found six local sources for buying the exact product in about 15 seconds. More than just electric Yellow Pages, such as the Thomas Register or Industry.net, WIZnet includes all specifications for the products right in the system and offers secure e-mail to communicate directly with vendors to ask for requests for bids or to place an order. More than 10,000 product specs are added to WIZnet per week, and its database includes catalogues from across the globe.[25]

The newer the buying task, and the more complex and costly the item, the greater the amount of time the buyer will spend searching for suppliers. The supplier's task is to get listed in major directories and build a good reputation in the marketplace. Salespeople should watch for companies in the process of searching for suppliers and make certain that their firm is considered.

Many business buyers go to extremes in searching for and qualifying suppliers. Consider the hurdles that Xerox has set up in its qualifying suppliers:

> Xerox qualifies only suppliers who meet ISO 9000 international quality standards (see Chapter 11). But to win the company's top award – certification status – a supplier must first complete the Xerox Multinational Supplier Quality Survey. The survey requires the supplier to issue a quality assurance manual, adhere to continuous improvement principles, and demonstrate effective systems implementation. Once a supplier has been qualified, it must participate in Xerox's Continuous Supplier Involvement process, in which the two companies work together to create specifications for quality, cost, delivery times, and process capability. The final step towards certification requires a supplier to undergo additional quality training and an evaluation based on the same criteria as the Malcolm Baldrige National Quality Award. Not surprisingly, only 176 suppliers worldwide have achieved the 95 per cent rating required for certification as a Xerox supplier.[26]

■ Proposal solicitation

In the **proposal solicitation** stage of the business buying process, the buyer invites qualified suppliers to submit proposals. In response, some suppliers will send only a catalogue or a salesperson. However, when the item is complex or expensive, the buyer will usually require detailed written proposals or formal presentations from each potential supplier.

Business marketers must be skilled in researching, writing and presenting proposals in response to buyer proposal solicitations. Proposals should be marketing documents, not just technical documents. Presentations should inspire confidence and should make the marketer's company stand out from the competition.

Proposal solicitation
The stage of the business buying process in which the buyer invites qualified suppliers to submit proposals.

■ Supplier selection

The members of the buying centre now review the proposals and select a supplier or suppliers. During **supplier selection**, the buying centre will often draw up a list of the desired supplier attributes and their relative importance. In one survey, purchasing executives listed the following attributes as most important in influencing the relationship between supplier and customer: quality products and services, on-time delivery, ethical corporate behaviour, honest communication and competitive prices. Other important factors include repair and servicing capabilities, technical aid and advice, geographic location, performance history and reputation. The members of the buying centre will rate suppliers against these attributes and identify the best suppliers.[27]

As part of the buyer selection process, buying centres must decide how many suppliers to use. Companies once preferred a large supplier base to ensure adequate supplies and to obtain price concessions. These companies would insist on annual negotiations for contract renewal and would often shift the amount of business they gave to each supplier from year to year. Increasingly, however, companies are reducing the number of suppliers. Many have cut the number of suppliers by 20 to 80 per cent. These companies expect their preferred suppliers to work closely with them during product development and they value their suppliers' suggestions.

Supplier selection
The stage of the business buying process in which the buyer reviews proposals and selects a supplier or suppliers.

To better select the most appropriate supplier, companies like SAS offer solutions that increase the level of information about them and improve supplier-relationship management.

SOURCE: SAS. *Agency:* Mason Zimbler

There is even a trend towards single sourcing, using one supplier for a class of goods over a long period. Using one source can not only translate into more consistent product performance, but also operations can configure themselves for one particular raw material or component rather than changing processes to accommodate different suppliers. Many companies, however, are still reluctant to use single sourcing. They fear that they may become too dependent on the single supplier or that the single-source supplier may become too comfortable in the relationship and lose its competitive edge. Some marketers have developed programmes that address these concerns.

■ Order-routine specification

Order-routine specification
The stage of the business buying process in which the buyer writes the final order with the chosen supplier(s), listing the technical specifications, quantity needed, expected time of delivery, return policies and warranties.

The buyer now prepares an **order-routine specification**. It includes the final order with the chosen supplier or suppliers and lists items such as technical specifications, quantity needed, expected time of delivery, return policies and warranties. In the case of maintenance, repair and operating items, buyers are increasingly using *blanket contracts* rather than periodic purchase orders. A blanket contract creates a long-term relationship in which the supplier promises to resupply the buyer as needed at agreed prices for a set time period. The seller holds the stock and the buyer's computer automatically prints out an order to the seller when stock is needed. A blanket order eliminates the expensive process of renegotiating a purchase each time stock is required. It also allows buyers to write more, but smaller, purchase orders, resulting in lower inventory levels and carrying costs.

Blanket contracting leads to more single-source buying and to buying more items from that source. This practice locks the supplier in tighter with the buyer and makes it difficult for other suppliers to break in unless the buyer becomes dissatisfied with prices or service.

■ Performance review

In this stage, the buyer reviews supplier performance. The buyer may contact users and ask them to rate their satisfaction. The **performance review** may lead the buyer to continue, modify or drop the arrangement. The seller's job is to monitor the same factors used by the buyer to make sure that the seller is giving the expected satisfaction.

We have described the stages that would typically occur in a new-task buying situation. The eight-stage model provides a simple view of the business buying-decision process. The actual process is usually much more complex. In the modified rebuy or straight rebuy situation, some of these stages would be compressed or bypassed. Each organisation buys in its own way and each buying situation has unique requirements. Different buying-centre participants may be involved at different stages of the process. Although certain buying-process steps usually do occur, buyers do not always follow them in the same order and they may add other steps. Often, buyers will repeat certain stages of the process.

Performance review
The stage of the business buying process in which the buyer rates its satisfaction with suppliers, deciding whether to continue, modify or drop them.

business buying on the internet

During the past few years, incredible advances in information technology have changed the face of the business-to-business marketing process. **Electronic data interchange** (EDI) links are particularly common in the food and auto industries. These systems give buyers access to lower purchasing costs, and hasten order processing and delivery. In turn, business marketers are connecting with customers to share marketing information, sell products and services, provide customer support services and maintain ongoing customer relationships. The bespoked EDI systems are now giving way to more flexible and less expensive Internet exchanges whose growth is explosive. While Mitsushita uses its EDI only for ordering its parts, its new Internet-based system will include price negotiations, delivery and payments. The company estimates that the system will allow it to save up to ¥40bn (€400m) on the supplies it has to hold in stock.[28]

Electronic Data Interchange (EDI)
Custom-built systems that link the computer systems of major buyers to their suppliers to enable them to coordinate their activities more closely.

In the **Internet exchanges**, buyers post their requirements on the Internet to reach numerous potential suppliers quickly and efficiently. This can be used for both routine and complex products. Japanese Airlines uses the Internet to post orders for in-flight materials, such as plastic cups. Its website carries technical specifications and drawings to show what the company wants, including the airline's logo.[29]

So far, most of the products bought by businesses through Internet or EDI connections are routine MRO materials – maintenance, repair and operations. National Semiconductor has automated almost all of the company's 3,500 monthly requisitions to buy materials ranging from the sterile booties worn in its fabrication plants to state-of-the-art software. The total value of MRO materials pales in comparison to the amount spent for items like airplane parts, computer systems and steel tubing. Yet, MRO materials make up 80 per cent of all business orders, and the transaction costs for order processing are high. Thus, companies have much to gain by streamlining the MRO buying process on the Web (see Marketing Highlight 7.1).

Internet exchanges
Web-based bazaars, often shared by buyers, where suppliers bid against requirements posted on the Internet.

General Electric, the pioneer of Internet buying, plans to be buying *all* of its general operating and industrial supplies online by 2003. Set up in the mid-1990s, its Trading Process Network is a vast Internet bazaar open to its subscribing companies. Other, industry-specific Internet bazaars are taking off and precipitating cross-industry collaboration on a scale once unimaginable:[30]

+ Covisint for car components is a joint venture between Ford, General Motors, DaimlerChrysler and Renault/Nissan.
+ Orbitz is a travel service owned by five major airlines. It promises to 'Remove the barriers between you and your journey'.
+ Chemdex for the exchange of chemicals.
+ Paperex for pulp and paper products.

Not all companies or government agencies are happy with Internet exchanges. The European Commission and the American Federal Trade Commission are worried that EDI reduces competition by tying together buyers and suppliers through expensive IT systems. In contrast, Toyota and Honda are reluctant to participate in the open auction-based Covisint because 'Our parts are not purchased through a bidding process. We buy them by building a relationship with our suppliers over time.' They are also concerned about security: 'The other companies are our rivals, and we are competing on parts.' The concerns are not only Japanese. VW do not want to be a junior partner in the site: 'GM is all about driving cost down, whereas Volkswagen sees an advantage in improving response times and increasing its responsiveness to customers.' Some suppliers are also scared about being locked out as Covisint searches for big, low-cost partners.[31]

institutional and government markets

So far, our discussion of organisational buying has focused largely on the buying behaviour of business buyers. Much of this discussion also applies to the buying practices of institutional and government organisations. However, these two non-business markets have additional characteristics and needs. Thus, in this final section, we will address the special features of institutional and government markets.

institutional markets

Institutional market
Schools, hospitals, nursing homes, prisons and other institutions that provide goods and services to people in their care.

The **institutional market** consists of schools, hospitals, nursing homes, prisons and other institutions that provide goods and services to people in their care. Institutions differ from one another in their sponsors and in their objectives. For example, in the United Kingdom, BUPA hospitals are operated for profit and are predominantly used by people with private medical insurance. National Health Service trust hospitals provide health care as part of the welfare state, while charities, such as the Terrence Higgins Trust and many small hospices, run centres for the terminally ill.

Low budgets and captive patrons characterise many institutional markets. For example, many campus-based students have little choice but to eat whatever food the university supplies. A catering organisation decides on the quality of food to buy for students. The buying objective is not profit because the food is provided as a part of a total service package. Nor is strict cost minimisation the goal – students receiving poor-quality food will complain to others and damage the college's reputation. Thus the university purchasing agent must search for institutional food vendors whose quality meets or exceeds a certain minimum standard and whose prices are low.

Many marketers set up separate divisions to meet the special characteristics and needs of institutional buyers. For example, Heinz produces, packages and prices its ketchup and other products differently to serve better the requirements of hospitals, colleges and other institutional markets.

government markets

The **government market** offers large opportunities for many companies. Government buying and business buying are similar in many ways. But there are also differences that must be understood by companies wishing to sell products and services to governments. To succeed in the government market, sellers must locate key decision makers, identify the factors that affect buyer behaviour and understand the buying decision process.

Government buying organisations are found at national and local levels. The national level is the largest and its buying units operate in both the civilian and military sectors. Various government departments, administrations, agencies, boards, commissions, executive offices and other units carry out buying. Sometimes, the *central buying operation* helps to centralise the buying of commonly used items in the civilian section (for example, office furniture and equipment, vehicles, fuels) and in standardising buying procedures for the other agencies. Defence ministries usually carry out the buying of military equipment for the armed forces.

Government market
Governmental units – national and local – that purchase or rent goods and services for carrying out the main functions of government.

■ Strong influences on government buyers

Like consumer and business buyers, government buyers are affected by environmental, organisational, interpersonal and individual factors. One unique thing about government buying is that it is carefully watched by outside publics, ranging from elected representatives to a variety of private groups interested in how the government spends taxpayers' money. Because their spending decisions are subject to public review, government organisations are buried in paperwork. Elaborate forms must be filled in and signed before purchases are approved. The level of bureaucracy and political sensitivities are high and marketers must cut through this red tape. Ways of dealing with governments vary greatly from country to country, and knowledge of local practices is critical to achieving sales successes (see Marketing Highlight 7.3).

Non-economic criteria also play a growing role in government buying. Government buyers are asked to favour depressed business firms and areas, small business firms, and business firms that avoid race, sex or age discrimination. Politicians will fight to have large contracts awarded to firms in their area or for their constituency to be the site of big construction projects. EuroDisney is an extreme case, as are Britain's Nimrod AWAC aircraft and Japan's ¥800bn (€8bn) G8 summit meeting in remote Kyushu-Okinawa. Sellers need to keep these factors in mind when seeking government business.

Government organisations typically require suppliers to submit bids and they normally award contracts to the lowest bidders. In some cases, however, government buyers make allowances for superior quality or for a firm's reputation for completing contracts on time. Governments will also buy on a negotiated contract basis for complex projects that involve substantial R&D costs and risks or when there is little effective competition. Governments tend to favour domestic suppliers over foreign suppliers, which is a repeated complaint of multinational businesses. Each country tends to favour its own nationals, even when non-domestic firms make superior offers. The European Economic Commission is trying to reduce such biases.

■ How do government buyers make their buying decisions?

Government buying practices often seem complex and frustrating to suppliers, who have voiced many complaints about government purchasing procedures. These include too much paperwork and bureaucracy, needless regulations, emphasis on low bid prices, decision-making delays, frequent shifts in buying personnel and too many policy changes. Yet, despite such obstacles, selling to the government can often be

marketing highlight 7.3

Political graft: wheeze or sleaze?

President Bill Clinton's chef de cabinet was forced to resign for using a government helicopter to take him to a game of golf. He was ordered to reimburse the Treasury for the cost of his jaunt, $13,129.66 (€14,752).

The same year in Paris new Members of the European Parliament were invited to a briefing on the many perks attached to their new status. The subject excited Jean-François Hory. From his place in the front row he turned in his seat, fixed a knowing eye on his new colleagues and addressed them in the manner of an old hand talking down to university freshmen: 'One thing you need to know about travel allowances – they'll want to know your address. If you have one or more second homes, make sure you list the one furthest from Brussels.' Obviously, a return flight from Marseilles to Brussels is worth more than the tram fare from Loos-lès-Lille to Brussels.

Political corruption used to be a thing other countries did, but no more. In the United States, United Kingdom, France, Spain, Italy, Japan and elsewhere, accusations of political corruption involving businesses have shaken the countries' leaders. The problem runs deep. In 1999 Paul van Buitenen's 'whistle blowing' precipitated the resignation of all of the EU's commissioners. Eurofraud is estimated to cost EU taxpayers over €10 billion per year. Sometimes the fiddles are minor, like exaggerating expense claims on Eurojaunts, but often they are not. Antonio Quatraro leapt to his death from a Brussels window. He was a European Commission official responsible for authorising subsidies. A fraud was discovered where he allegedly received backhanders for rigging the auction of Greek-grown tobacco to benefit Italian traders.

The auction rigging would be illegal anywhere, but often what is common practice in one country will bring a senior politician down in another. All governments have codes of practice, but as Table 1 shows, they are not consistent. There are also different cultural traditions about obeying rules. In Britain a Treasury minister had to fight for his political life and was eventually jailed following accusations that a controversial Arab businessman had paid for a weekend that the minister had had at the Paris Ritz Hotel. The bill was less than €600 and in most other European countries he would not have had to declare such a gift. One Swedish cabinet minister resigned after it was disclosed that she had bought a small toy using an official credit card. Meanwhile, Edith Cresson, the former French Prime Minister at the centre of the storm that ended in the resignation of the European Commissioners, had difficulty seeing why she should go.

In Japan the attitude towards political corruption is changing slowly. Kiichi Miyazawa resigned as finance minister after being caught up in the Recruit scandal. Recruit, an employment agency, had secretly given large tranches of its own shares to politicians, including cabinet ministers, in exchange for political favours. But two years later Mr Miyazawa was sufficiently 'rehabilitated' to become prime minister. This follows the 'traditional' pattern for Japanese politicians caught taking bribes or o-shoku, 'defiling one's job'. O-shoku carries no moral overtones about wrongdoing, it just means that through carelessness the publicity has dishonoured the politician's honoured position. The usual line of defence in the Diet is that the politicians knew nothing, since their aides took the money. In that way the politician does

COUNTRY	COMPULSORY REGISTER OF INTERESTS	REGISTER OPEN TO THE PUBLIC?	REGISTER OF INCOME/SHARES DETAILS?	MPs DECLARE INTEREST IN DEBATE?	MUST DECLARE FREE RITZ WEEKEND?
France	Assets	No	No	No	No
Germany	Yes	Yes	No	No	No
Italy	Income	Yes	Yes	No	No
Spain	Yes	No	No	No	No
United Kingdom	Yes	Yes	No	Yes	Yes
United States	Yes	Yes	Yes	No	Yes[a]

NOTE: [a]Gifts over $280 not acceptable.

Table 1 Government codes of practice in various countries

not lose face, junior aides are not worth prosecuting and everyone is happy.

The mood changed after the Sagawa scandal. Shin Kanemaru needed money to split the ruling LDP and start one of his own. He needed a lot of cash and most of it came from Sagawa Kyubin, a trucking company that wanted political favour in order to expand its business. Gold bars and bonds were found in Mr Kanemaru's home and office. He was found guilty of not reporting ¥250m (€2.5m) in 'political donations', but fined less than ¥100,000. After this, a new term entered the Japanese political vocabulary, *seiji fuhai* or 'politics rotten to the point of disintegration'. Helmut Kohl's misdeeds seem small indeed, compared with these.

The scale of curruption that has destoyed the careers of many European politicians is small beer compared with the 'dash' that lubricates trade in most of the developing world. When selling to governments, marketers face a great dilemma. Should they follow St Ambrose's advice to St Augustine: 'When you are at Rome live in the Roman style; when you are elsewhere live as they live elsewhere'? Or should they behave like a saint?

SOURCES: The leading quotation is from 'An open letter to those unnerved by the little judges', by MEP Thierry Jean-Pierre; other sources are Terry McCarthy, 'It's not graft, just duty and obligation', *Independent* (27 October 1994), p. 16; 'Hands up all those hit by sleaze', *The Economist* (29 October 1994), pp. 49–51; 'The sour taste of gravy', *The Economist* (5 November 1994), p. 50; 'Is Europe corrupt?', *The Economist* (29 January 2000), pp. 49–55; 'The honeycomb of corruption', *The Economist: China Survey* (8 April 2000), pp. 10–12; Alix Christie and Julie Read, 'Fraud crusader gears up for a fight', *The European* (11–17 November 1994), p. 11; John McBeth, 'Ground zero', *Far Eastern Economic Review* (22 January 1998), pp. 14–17; Paul van Buitenen, 'Corruption at the heart of Europe', *The Times* (14 March 2000), pp. 10–11.

mastered in a short time. The government is generally helpful in providing information about its buying needs and procedures, and is often as eager to attract new suppliers as the suppliers are to find customers.

When the mighty US Fleet edged its way up the Gulf during Desert Storm, five little plastic boats led it. The little Royal Navy Hunt Class MCMVs (Mine Counter-Measure Vessels) were in a league of their own at the dangerous job of clearing a path for the main fleet. They were made by Vosper Thornycroft, a small British company which is a master at selling to governments around the world. While the world's leading defence contractors seek alliances and mergers to meet the 'peace dividend's' reduced demand, Vosper has an order book worth £600 million and 14 vessels under construction, 95 per cent of them for export. Part of its strength is Vosper's dominance in the niche for glass-reinforced plastic (GRP) mine hunters, corvettes and patrol craft. Just the sort of ships that small navies want.

Vosper's strength extends beyond the vessels. With its vessels it offers a maritime training and support service where it has pioneered computer-based learning. Many clients come from the Middle East and travel with their families, so Vosper has built an Arabic school for 70 pupils next to the maritime training centre. It now does training for other firms selling to the Middle East, so strengthening its position in the region. Others of Vosper's activities get it closely involved in its customers' operations. The company has a three-year contract for the Ministry of Defence's Record Data Centre and has a five-year contract to operate maritime services craft for the Royal Air Force.[32]

Many companies that sell to the government are not so marketing oriented as Vosper Thornycroft, for a number of reasons. Total government spending is determined by elected officials rather than by any marketing effort to develop this market. Government buying has emphasised price, making suppliers invest their effort in technology to bring costs down. When the product's characteristics are specified carefully, product differentiation is not a marketing factor. Nor do advertising or personal selling matter much in winning bids on an open-bid basis.

More companies now have separate marketing departments for government marketing efforts. British Aerospace, Eastman Kodak and Goodyear are examples. These companies want to coordinate bids and prepare them more scientifically, to propose projects to meet government needs rather than just respond to government requests, to gather competitive intelligence, and to prepare stronger communications to describe the company's competence.

summary

The business market is vast. In many ways, business markets are like consumer markets, but business markets usually have fewer, larger buyers who are more geographically concentrated. Business demand is *derived*, largely *inelastic* and more *fluctuating*. More buyers are usually involved in the business buying decision and business buyers are better trained and more professional than are consumer buyers. In general, business purchasing decisions are more complex and the buying process is more formal than consumer buying.

The *business market* includes firms that buy goods and services in order to produce products and services to sell to others. It also includes retailing and wholesaling firms that buy goods in order to resell them at a profit. Business buyers make decisions that vary with the three types of buying situation: *straight rebuys*, *modified rebuys* and *new tasks*. The decision-making unit of a buying organisation – the *buying centre* – may consist of many people playing many roles. The business marketer needs to know the following: Who are the main participants? In what decisions do they exercise influence? What is their relative degree of influence? And what evaluation criteria does each decision participant use? The business marketer also needs to understand the primary environmental, interpersonal and individual influences on the buying process. The business buying-decision process itself consists of eight stages: *problem recognition*, *general needs description*, *product specification*, *supplier search*, *proposal solicitation*, *supplier selection*, *order-routine specification* and *performance review*. As business buyers become more sophisticated, business marketers must keep in step by upgrading their marketing accordingly.

The *institutional market* consists of schools, hospitals, prisons and other institutions that provide goods and services to people in their care. Low budgets and captive patrons characterise these markets. The *government market* is also vast. Government buyers purchase products and services for defence, education, public welfare and other public needs. Government buying practices are highly specialised and specified, with open bidding or negotiated contracts characterising most of the buying. Government buyers operate under the watchful eye of politicians and many private watchdog groups. Hence, they tend to require more forms and signatures and to respond more slowly in placing orders.

discussing the issues

1. Identify the ways in which the fashion clothing market differs from the military uniform market.

2. Which of the main types of buying situation are represented by the following individual circumstances?

   ✦ BMW's purchase of computers that go in cars and adjust engine performance to changing driving conditions.

   ✦ Volkswagen's purchase of spark plugs for its line of Jettas.

   ✦ Honda's purchase of light bulbs for a new Legend model.

3. How would a marketer of office equipment identify the buying centre for a law firm's purchase of dictation equipment for each of its partners?

4. Discuss the principal environmental factors that would affect the purchase of radar speed detectors by national and local police forces.

5. Industrial products companies have advertised products to the general public that consumers are not able to buy. How does this strategy help a company sell products to resellers?

6. Assume you are selling a fleet of fork-lift trucks to be used by a large distribution and warehousing firm. The drivers of the fork-lift trucks need the latest technology that provides comfort, makes driving easy and improves manoeuvrability. This means more expensive trucks that are more profitable for you. The fleet buyer, however, wants to buy established (not necessarily latest) technology that gives the highest productivity. Who might be in the buying centre? How might you meet the varying needs of these participants?

applying the concepts

1. Take your college/university as an example of a business customer for books and other educational materials. Imagine that you are a representative from a publisher who intends to establish sales to the college/university. How might you use the model of business buyer behaviour to help you develop a strategy for marketing effectively to this customer? How useful is the model? What (if any) are the limitations? Are there different levels of customers in this situation (e.g. the library as a buying centre; course team members who agree on the textbooks to recommend for student adoption and library stocks; the individual tutor who chooses recommended textbooks and requests the library to stock; or the college/university bookshop)? How might you deal with these different levels of customer?

2. Make a list of the key factors that a local government institution or agency might consider when deciding to purchase new coffee-making machines for users in its offices. Remembering how government buyers make their buying decisions, suggest a scenario that you, as a potential supplier, would use to sell to this institutional buyer.

references

1. This definition is adapted from Frederick E. Webster, Jr and Yoram Wind, *Organizational Buying Behavior* (Englewood Cliffs, NJ: Prentice Hall, 1972), p. 2; also see K. Thompson, H. Mitchell and S. Knox, 'Organisational buying behaviour in changing times', *European Management Journal*, **16**, 6 (1998), pp. 698–705.

2. Oliver Sutton, 'Buzjet business still buzzing', *Interavia* (September 1999), pp. 30–3; Richard Lofthouse, 'Business jet is business sense', *Interavia* (September 1999), pp. 121–4 and 'If you need to know the price . . .', *Interavia* (September 1999), pp. 127–30; Kevin Cahill, 'Master of the private skies', *Interavia* (September 1999), pp. 138–9;

'Bombadier catches up with itself', *Interavia* (September 1999), pp. 147–8; 'When security is the issue', *Interavia* (September 1999), p. 154; *EuroBusiness* (August 2000); Oliver Sutton, 'It's good to be in small engines', *Interavia* (March 2000), pp. 32–5; Kevin Done, 'Business jets "hold key to supersonic travel"', *Financial Times* (28 July 2000), p. 8; Chuck Hawkins, 'Can a new bird get Gulfstream flying?', *Business Week* (15 February 1993), pp. 114–16; Penny Hughes, 'The $600 million gamble', *BusinessAge* (November 1994), p. 30B; Ian Verchère, 'Long-haul luxury from Bombardier', *The European* (4–10 November 1994), p. 30.

3. Dave Murphy, 'Tomorrow's window of opportunity', *Marketing Business* (June 1999), pp. 43–5; 'E-commerce: the A to Z of B2B', *The Economist* (1 April 2000), pp. 71–4; 'Could B2B B4U', *The Economist* (27 May 2000), p. 113.

4. Hans Heerkens, 'Glaring prospect?', *Interavia* (February 2000), p. 17; 'Airbus Industrie: target the 21st century', *Interavia* (March 1999), pp. 13–53; Arthur Leathly, 'Superjumbo brings revolution to the air', *The Times* (14 March 2000), p. 11.

5. 'That sinking feeling', *The Economist* (17 January 1998), pp. 71–2; Sheila McNutty, 'Malaysia seeks Boeing delay', *Financial Times* (19 January 1988); John Ridding and Michael Skapinker, 'Aircraft makers' confidence dented', *Financial Times* (20 January 1998); Alkman Grantisas, 'Scant shelter', *Far Eastern Economic Review* (22 January 1998), pp. 54–5.

6. This understanding is the foundation of the global strategy of Blue Circle, a leading cement company: Roger Trapp, 'Circling the world', *The Independent – Business Review* (9 June 1999), p. 3; cement.bluecircle.co.uk

7. See Lawrence A. Crosby, Kenneth R. Evans and Deborah Cowles, 'Relationship quality and services selling: an interpersonal influence perspective', *Journal of Marketing* (July 1990), pp. 68–81; Barry J. Farber and Joyce Wycoff, 'Relationships: six steps to success', *Sales and Marketing Management* (April 1992), pp. 50–8; Kevin Done, 'Harmony under the bonnet', *Financial Times* (8 November 1994), p. 17; K. Blois, 'A trust interpretation of business to business relationships: A case-based discussion', *Management Decision*, 36, 5 (1998), 9 pp.; M. A. Zideldin, 'Towards an ecological collaborative relationship management: A "co-operative" perspective', *European Journal of Marketing*, 32, 11/12 (1998), 22 pp.; K. J. Blois, 'Trust in business to business relationships: an evaluation of its status', *Journal of Management Studies*, 36, 2 (1999), pp. 197–215.

8. Bernard Simon and Paul Betts, 'Boeing may tie component deals to aircraft sales', *Financial Times* (8 November 1994), p. 1.

9. Patrick J. Robinson, Charles W. Faris and Yoram Wind, *Industrial Buying Behavior and Creative Marketing* (Boston: Allyn & Bacon, 1967). See also Erin Anderson, Weyien Chu and Barton Weitz, 'Industrial purchasing: an empirical exploration of the buyclass framework', *Journal of Marketing* (July 1987), pp. 71–86; K. Thompson, H. Mitchell and S. Knox, 'Organisational buying behaviour in changing times', *European Management Journal*, 16, 6 (1998), pp. 698–705.

10. Dave Murphy, 'Tomorrow's window of opportunity', *Business Marketing* (June 2000), pp. 43–5.

11. Cait Murphy, 'Will the future belong to Germany?', *Fortune* (2 August 2000), pp. 63–70; 'Aircraft manufacturer: a new kind of Boeing', *The Economist* (22 January 2000), pp. 78–9; For more on systems selling, see Robert R. Reeder, Edward G. Brierty and Betty H. Reeder, *Industrial Marketing: Analysis, planning and control* (Englewood Cliffs, NJ: Prentice Hall, 1991), pp. 264–7.

12. Webster and Wind, *Organizational Buying Behavior*, op.cit., p. 6; P. L. Dawes, G. R. Dowling and P. G. Patterson, 'Factors affecting the structure of buying centers for the purchase of professional business advisory services', *International Journal of Research in Marketing*, 9, 3 (1992), pp. 269–79; E. J. Wilson and A. G. Woodside, 'A two-step model of influence in group purchasing decisions', *International Journal of Physical Distribution & Logistics Management*, 24, 5 (1994), pp. 34–44; M. Farrel and B. Schroder, 'Power and influence in the buying centre', *European Journal of Marketing*, 33, 11/12 (1999), 8 pp.

13. Webster and Wind, *Organizational Buying Behavior*, op.cit., pp. 78–80.

14. For results of both surveys, see 'I think you have a great product, but it's not my decision', *American Salesman* (April 1994), pp. 11–13; and Tim Minahan, 'OEM buying survey – part 2: Buyers get new roles but keep old tasks', *Purchasing* (16 July 1998), pp. 208–9. For more on influence strategies within buying centres, see R. Venkatesh, Ajay K. Kohli and Gerald Zaltman, 'Influence strategies in buying centers', *Journal of Marketing* (October 1995), pp. 71–82; John Monoky, 'Who does the buying?', *Industrial Distribution* (October 1995), p. 48; David I. Gilliland and Wesley J. Johnson, 'Toward a model of business-to-business marketing communications effects', *Industrial Marketing Management* (January 1997), pp. 15–29; and Philip L. Dawes, Don Y. Lee and Grahame R. Dowling, 'Information control and influence in emergent buying centers', *Journal of Marketing* (July 1998), pp. 55–68.

15. Melvin R. Matson and Esmail Salshi-Sangari, 'Decision making in purchases of equipment and materials: a four-country comparison', *International Journal of*

Physical Distribution & Logistics Management, **23**, 8 (1993), pp. 16–30.

16. 'The price of success: losing the lustre', *EuroBusiness* (May 2000), pp. 110–12; 'Corporate hospitality: nice one', *The Economist* (10 June 2000), p. 39.

17. Webster and Wind, *Organizational Buying Behavior*, op.cit., pp. 33–7. Also R. G. Kauffman, 'Influences on organizational buying choice processes: future research directions', *Journal of Business & Industrial Marketing*, **11**, 3/4 (1996), 11 pp.

18. Peter W. Turnbull, 'Organisational buying behaviour', in Michael J. Baker (ed.), *The Marketing Book* (London: Heinemann, 1994), pp. 147–64.

19. Thayer C. Taylor, 'Xerox's sales force learns a new game', *Sales and Marketing Management* (1 July 1985), pp. 48–51.

20. Keith Blois, 'Are business-to-business relationships inherently unstable?', *Journal of Marketing Management*, **13**, 5 (1997), pp. 367–79.

21. Michiyo Nakamoto, 'Building networks', *Financial Times* (13 November 1992), p. 8; Richard Gourlay, 'From fat to lean enterprises', *Financial Times* (8 November 1994), p. 11; Carlos Cordon, 'Doing justice to just in time', *Financial Times* (9 November 1994), p. 14.

22. Ajay Kohli, 'Determinants of influence in organizational buying: a contingency approach', *Journal of Marketing* (July 1989), pp. 50–65.

23. Malcolm Brown, 'Signed, sealed, delivered', *Marketing Business* (June 1992), pp. 30–2.

24. Robinson, Faris and Wind, *Industrial Buying Behavior*, op.cit., p. 14.

25. 'Buying globally made easier', *Industry Week* (2 February 1998), pp. 63–4; and information accessed from John H. Sheridan, online at www.wiznet.net, September 1999.

26. 'Xerox multinational supplier quality survey', *Purchasing* (January 1995), p. 112.

27. See 'What buyers really want', *Sales & Marketing Management* (October 1989), p. 30; 'Purchasing managers sound off', *Sales & Marketing Management* (February 1995), pp. 84–5; Thomas Y. Choi and Janet L. Hartley, 'An exploration of supplier selection practices across the supply chain', *Journal of Operations Management* (November 1996), pp. 333–43; Douglas M. Lambert, Ronald J. Adams and Margaret A. Emmelhainz, 'Supplier selection criteria in the healthcare industry: a comparison of importance and performance', *International Journal of Purchasing and Materials Management* (Winter 1997), pp. 16–22; and Craig M. Gustin, Patricia J. Daugherty and Alexander E. Ellinger, 'Supplier selection decisions in systems/software', *International Journal of Purchasing and Materials Management* (Fall 1997), pp. 41–6.

28. 'You'll never walk alone' in 'The net imperative: a survey of business and the internet', *The Economist* (26 June 1999), pp. 9–17; 'Business-to-business in Japan: no room in the nest', *The Economist* (15 April 2000), pp. 91–2.

29. 'To byte the hand that feeds', *The Economist* (17 January 1998), pp. 75–6; 'A market for monopoly', *The Economist* (17 June 2000), pp. 85–6.

30. Stuart Derrick, 'Market forces', *e.business* (July 2000), pp. 15–16; 'The net imperative: a survey of business and the internet', *The Economist* (26 June 1999), pp. 1–44.

31. Alexander Harney, 'Toyota set to join online trade exchange' and 'Up close but impersonal', *Financial Times* (10 March 2000), p. 33; 'A market for monopoly', *The Economist* (17 June 2000), pp. 85–6; Stuart Derrick, 'Market forces', *e.business* (July 2000), pp. 15–16.

32. General H. Norman Schwartzkopf, *It Doesn't Take a Hero* (London: Bantam, 1992); General Sir Peter de la Billière, *Storm Command* (London: HarperCollins, 1992); Andrew Bolgar, 'Diversifying out of lumpiness', *Financial Times* (2 November 1994), p. 26.

case 7

Biofoam: just peanuts?

Like diamonds, polystyrene peanuts are forever – their volume is growing at a rate of at least 20 million kg annually. Since their introduction in 1970, they have become one of the most popular forms of packaging material. They are lightweight, inexpensive and resilient. They conform to any shape, protect superbly, resist shifting in transit, leave no dusty residue on the goods they protect and are indestructible. That's the problem. Nearly every one of those peanuts used since 1970 is still with us – blowing in the wind or taking up space in a landfill. Worse yet, they will be with us for another 500 years. They're wonderful but not environmentally sound.

The small firm Biofoam thinks it has solved this problem. It sells a peanut made from grain sorghum, a grain now used for animal feed. To make these sorghum peanuts, the company strips the grain of its nutritional value, presses it into pellets, and conveys it through a giant popper. The process creates a product that looks like tan cheese doodles, not so surprising given that the inventors started out to make a snack food. But no one wanted to eat these objects, so the inventors had to find other uses for them. According to Ed Alfke, Biofoam's CEO, the sorghum peanuts do just as good a job as the best foam peanuts and they don't cost any more. Moreover, they hold no electrostatic charge, so they won't cling to nylons or other synthetic fibres (such as your carpet or clothes). Better yet, they are 'absolutely, frighteningly natural', says Tom Schmiegel, a veteran of the plastics industry.

To dispose of a Biofoam peanut, you can: (a) put it in your trash can, (b) throw it on your front lawn as bird food, (c) compost it, (d) put it in your dog's or cat's bowl, (e) set it out with salsa at your next party, or (f) wash it down your drain. The peanut dissolves in water and has some – although limited – nutritional value. Alfke bought into the company because of its environmentally positive stance. He is convinced that green companies will profit from a global regulatory climate that's increasingly hostile to polluters. 'The writing is on the wall for companies that are not environmentally friendly', he says.

Biofoam initially targeted retailers who wanted to send an environmentally friendly message, helped along by the inclusion of a Biofoam pamphlet explaining the advantages of the Biofoam peanut. It targeted the heaviest users of Styrofoam peanuts who consume up to 20 truckloads of loose fill a *day*. To date, Biofoam has signed two major accounts – the Fuller Brush Company and computer reseller MicroAge.

Eventually, Biofoam will have to expand beyond environmentally sensitive firms into a broader market. To convince potential users to use Biofoam peanuts, Alfke has come up with a seemingly no-brainer option: to be environmentally responsible without having to pay more or sacrifice convenience. He is willing to install machines on the customer's premises to produce peanuts in-house – an arrangement that would give Biofoam rent-free production sites. He'll even provide an employee to operate the machinery. Although this strategy might sound unusual, it has been used by other companies such as Xerox to sell copiers and Tetra Pak to sell juice boxes and milk cartons.

The in-house arrangement has benefits for the customer as well as for Biofoam. Users receive immediate, reliable, just-in-time delivery combined with on-site service and a five-year price guarantee with no intermediaries involved. With Biofoam on-site, users never run out of packaging, and they avoid the expense of stockpiling materials. Lower production costs make Biofoam's product price competitive with that of polystyrene. For Biofoam, the arrangement provides a rent-free network of regional manufacturing facilities and an intimacy with each customer. Because the host company will only consume about one-third of the output, Biofoam plans to sell the excess to smaller firms in the host's area.

However, this in-house production arrangement has disadvantages. From the host's perspective, the machinery takes up 140 m² of floor space that could be used to produce something else. Furthermore, some of the output of that 140 m² goes to other firms, benefiting Biofoam but doing nothing for the host. Furthermore, the host has a non-employee working in its plant. The peanut-making machinery is also intrusive. It consists of three machines – an extruder, a conditioning chamber and a deduster – joined by ducts and conveyor belts. The machines make lots of noise (like a giant air conditioner), making conversation in the vicinity impossible. The process creates a smell, rather like the inside of an old barn, and produces heat, a potential problem. Thus, on closer inspection, the in-house arrangement is not entirely desirable. Without this arrangement, however, costs rise considerably. If it had to ship the peanuts to users, Biofoam would have to raise the price 10 to 20 per cent.

Biofoam's competition, the polystyrene loose-fill industry, is a fragmented patchwork of diverse companies. It includes oil companies, chemical producers, fill manufacturers and regional distributors – all of which would suffer from Biofoam's success. The industry is much more rough-and-tumble than CEO Alfke anticipated. So far, Biofoam has a microscopic market share. The company's 1995 sales totalled only €3 million – not much in an industry with potential sales of €200 to €600 million a year. But the €3 million represented a five-fold increase over the previous year. Alfke now projects sales of €90 million in 2000, with 30 per cent pre-tax profits. These projections include sales of products other than sorghum peanuts. Alfke plans to add injectible Biofoam and stiff Biofoam packaging materials. Other promising applications have been suggested, such as using Biofoam to absorb oil spills or in medicinal applications, but Alfke doesn't want to talk about those. For now, 'It's important that we try to stay focused', he claims.

Can Alfke reach his ambitious goals? Many industry observers say no. Environmental claims, say these observers, don't have the impact that they used to have. 'That was something we worried about three years ago', said a purchasing agent. Biofoam's sales representatives are finding the market less environmentally concerned. Others, however, are more optimistic. For example, although she agrees that the novelty of environmentally responsible packaging has worn off, Nancy Pfund, general partner of Hambrecht and Quist's Environmental Technology Fund, thinks that many firms are still interested in environmentally friendly packaging. She notes that companies have 'internalised a lot of environmental procedures without making a lot of noise about it. You also have younger people who grew up learning about the environment in school now entering the consumer market. That's a very strong trend.' Such consumers will demand more responsible packaging.

Are companies that use Biofoam happy with it? Well, some yes, some no. On the positive side is MicroAge Computer. According to Mark Iaquinto, facilities manager, MicroAge had been searching for an acceptable alternative to polystyrene. Now that it's found Biofoam, he's convinced it can stop searching. On the negative side, Norbert Schneider, president of Fuller Brush Company, has concerns about the way the product crumbles in boxes filled with sharp-pointed brushes. Alfke says that Biofoam is working on a solution, but if it doesn't find one soon, Fuller Brush may change packaging suppliers.

Other firms have entered the market with biodegradable, water-soluble foams. Made from corn-starch-based thermoplastics, the products can be rinsed down the drain after use. They can be used in loose-fill packaging applications or moulded in place into shaped packaging. They compare favourably with traditional packaging materials for cost and performance.

So, facing a stiffly competitive industry, new competitors and a softening of environmental concerns, Biofoam will find the going hard. But none of this dents Alfke's enthusiasm. Alfke was a multimillionaire before age 40. 'I've seen a lot of deals', he claims, 'and I've never, *ever* seen a deal as good as this one.' As an experienced businessman, no doubt he *has* seen a lot of deals. He really believes in this one, but is he right?

Questions

1. Outline Biofoam's current marketing strategy.
2. Which elements of the marketing mix are most important for Biofoam to focus on?
3. What is the nature of demand in the loose-fill packaging industry? What factors shape that demand?
4. If you were a buyer of packaging materials, would you agree to Biofoam's offer of machines inside your plant? If not, how could Biofoam overcome your objections?
5. What environmental and organisational factors are likely to affect the loose-fill packaging industry? How will these factors affect Biofoam?
6. Is Alfke right? Is this a good deal? Would you have bought into the firm? Why or why not?

SOURCES: 'The latest trends in . . . protective packaging', *Modern Materials Handling* (October 1996), pp. P8–P12; 'What the experts say', *Inc.* (October 1996), pp. 54–5; Robert D. Leaversuch, 'Water-soluble foams offer cost-effective protection', *Modern Plastics* (April 1997), pp. 32–5; David Whitford, 'The snack food that's packing America', *Inc.* (October 1996), pp. 51–5.

internet exercises

Internet exercises for this chapter can be found on the student site of the myPHLIP Web Site at www.booksites.net/kotler.

chapter eight

Market information and marketing research

Chapter objectives *After reading this chapter, you should be able to:*

- Explain the importance of information to the company.

- Define the marketing information system and discuss its parts.

- Describe the four steps in the marketing research process.

- Compare the advantages and disadvantages of various methods of collecting information.

- Discuss the main methods for estimating current market demand.

- Explain specific techniques that companies use to forecast future demand.

introduction

To carry out marketing analysis, planning, implementation and control, managers need information. As Uganda's President Museveni realised (see preview case opposite), you need information in order to act effectively. Information is not just an input for making better decisions, but also a marketing asset that gives competitive advantage of strategic importance. Competitors can copy each other's equipment, products and procedures, but they cannot duplicate the company's information and intellectual capital. Some companies have recently indicated this by appointing vice presidents of knowledge, learning, or intellectual capital.

All companies started off small and knew their customers first-hand. Managers picked up marketing information by being around people, observing them and asking questions. However, with growth they need more and better information. When they become national or international in scope, they need more information on larger, more distant markets. As incomes increase and buyers become more selective, sellers need better information about how buyers respond to different products and appeals. As sellers use more complex marketing approaches and face more competition, they need information on the effectiveness of their marketing tools. Finally, in today's rapidly changing environments, managers need up-to-date information to make timely decisions.

preview case

Market researching AIDS in Africa: when a little can achieve the unimaginable

AIDS (acquired immune deficiency syndrome) shook the Western world. It caused a backward shift in the sexual revolution born in the 1960s. In developed countries the threatened AIDS epidemic is contained, although it is far from eradicated. The acceptance of the link between AIDS and HIV (human immune-deficiency virus) and of the fact that HIV is mainly transmitted through unprotected sex and drug abuse is well accepted, and has changed people's behaviour. Huge public awareness and scare campaigns accounted for a lot of the success. Also, in rich countries, new and expensive drugs can keep HIV carriers alive and healthy.

The situation in sub-Saharan Africa could not be more different. While the World Health Organisation estimates that there are fewer than two million people in the whole of North America, Europe and Central Asia with HIV/AIDS, in sub-Saharan Africa it is 25 million and growing. Many of the sufferers are innocents. Mother-to-child infections have grown from 100,000 to 800,000 between 1986 and 2000: 250,000 from breast-feeding and the rest before or at delivery. In worst-hit Botswana, Namibia, Swaziland and Zimbabwe, between 20 and 25 per cent of the sexually active population are infected. South Africa's isolation once protected it from the epidemic, but no more. It now has more HIV/AIDS sufferers than any other country in the world and up to a third of sexually active males are HIV-positive. Worse is yet to come. HIV/AIDS is hitting the most economically active members of the population. Without AIDS, Botswana's population of 40–49-year-olds would have been 300,000 in 2020. With AIDS it is expected to slump to fewer than 60,000!

Can the catastrophe be stopped? There is hope for drug donations from rich countries and the International AIDS Vaccine Initiative gives some hope. But among the gloom there are some successes. Being away from the epicentre of the epidemic, Senegal has remained largely AIDS free as a result of vigorous and unambiguous education programmes.

Uganda is close to the epicentre but has turned the tide. President Yoweri Museveni acted on the threat as soon as he came to power. Uganda is a poor country but the President's first act was to commission a series of inexpensive surveys (about €25,000 each) into the sexual behaviour of the population. These, and other studies, uncovered important reasons why AIDS is spreading:

- ✦ Sex is fun and an inexpensive recreation.
- ✦ Condoms make it less so: 'Would you eat a sweet with a wrapper on it?'
- ✦ Some men snip the ends of condoms they are about to use.
- ✦ The discussion of sex is often taboo.
- ✦ Myths abound: Regular infusions of sperm make women grow up beautiful and men can get rid of HIV infection by passing it on to a virgin.
- ✦ Wives who ask their husbands to use a condom are in danger of being beaten up.
- ✦ Drinking local beers is another form of inexpensive entertainment but the inebriated are prone to unsafe sex.

Realising the scale of the problem and the shortage of funds, the President freed dozens of non-government organisations (NGOs) to educate people about unsafe sex. The NGOs used material and approaches that many other African countries found unacceptable, but within a five-year period the HIV-infected women in urban antenatal clinics fell from 30 to 15 per cent.

Meanwhile, in other countries where HIV is rampant governments are in denial and little is being done. In Durban Thabo Mbeki, South Africa's president, opened the world's AIDS conference by saying that scientists in South Africa were divided as to the cause of AIDS and that he had appointed a commission to look into the [non-existent] division.[1]

Questions

1. What research would you commission to gather an understanding of the behaviour leading to the spread of HIV/AIDS?

2. Is it safe to rely on 'inexpensive research' to guide campaigns as critical as those against AIDS?

3. What are the dangers and benefits of freeing a range of NGOs to drive for a social good rather than a single, well coordinated campaign?

The need for more and better information has been met by an explosion of information technologies. The past 30 years have witnessed the emergence of small but powerful computers, fax machines, CD-ROM drives, videoconferencing, the Internet and a host of other advances that have revolutionised information handling. In fact, today's managers often receive too much information. For example, one study found that with all the companies offering data, and with all the information now available through supermarket scanners, a packaged-goods brand manager is bombarded with 1 million to 1 *billion* new numbers each week. Another study found that, on average, office workers spend 60 per cent of their time processing documents; a typical manager reads about a million words a week. The typical business Internet user receives 25 e-mails a day; 15 per cent of users receive between 50 and 100 e-mails per day. Thus, the running out of information is not a problem but seeing through the 'data smog' is.[2]

Despite this data glut, marketers frequently complain that they lack enough information of the *right* kind. For example, a recent survey of managers found that although half the respondents said they couldn't cope with the volume of information coming at them, two-thirds wanted even more. The researcher concluded that, 'despite the volume, they're still not getting what they want.'[3] Thus, most marketing managers don't need *more* information; they need *better* information. Companies have greater capacity to provide managers with good information, but often have not made good use of it. Many companies are now studying their managers' information needs and designing information systems to meet those needs.

Marketing information system (MIS)
People, equipment and procedures to gather, sort, analyse, evaluate and distribute needed, timely and accurate information to marketing decision makers.

the marketing information system

A **marketing information system (MIS)** consists of people, equipment and procedures to gather, sort, analyse, evaluate and distribute needed, timely and accurate information to marketing decision makers. Figure 8.1 illustrates the marketing information system concept. The MIS begins and ends with marketing managers. First, it interacts

Figure 8.1

The marketing information system

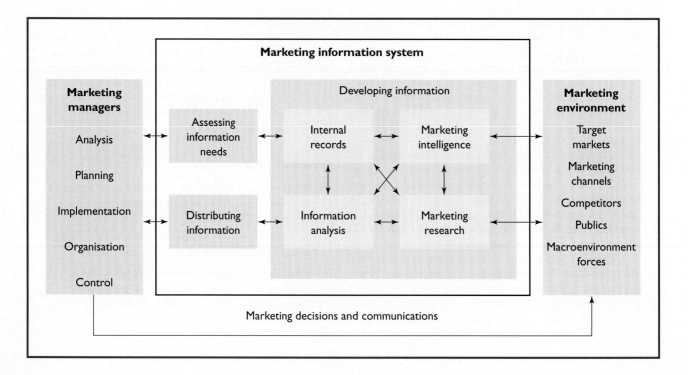

with these managers to assess their information needs. Next, it develops the needed information from internal company records, marketing intelligence activities and the marketing research process. Information analysis processes the information to make it more useful. Finally, the MIS distributes information to managers in the right form at the right time to help them in marketing planning, implementation and control.

developing information

The information needed by marketing managers comes from *internal company records*, *marketing intelligence* and *marketing research*. The information analysis system then processes this information to make it more useful for managers.

internal records

Most marketing managers use internal records and reports regularly, especially for making day-to-day planning, implementation and control decisions. **Internal records information** consists of information gathered from sources within the company to evaluate marketing performance and to detect marketing problems and opportunities. The company's accounting department prepares financial statements and keeps detailed records of sales, orders, costs and cash flows. Manufacturing reports on production schedules, shipments and inventories. The sales force reports on reseller reactions and competitor activities. The customer service department provides information on customer satisfaction or service problems. Research studies done for one department may provide useful information for several others. Managers can use information gathered from these and other sources within the company to evaluate performance and to detect problems and opportunities.

Here are examples of how companies use internal records information in making better marketing decisions:[4]

> *Office World* offers shoppers a free membership card when they make their first purchase at their store. The card entitles shoppers to discounts on selected items, but also provides valuable information to the chain. Since Office World encourages customers to use their card with each purchase, it can track what customers buy, where and when. Using this information, it can track the effectiveness of promotions, trace customers who have defected to other stores and keep in touch with them if they relocate.

> *Istel* is a cross-fertilization scheme set up by AT & T in Europe. The system helps retailers share information about customers. Under the programme customers join the Istel club, which gives them discounts when buying a range of products from member stores. AT & T estimates that its card will save the average customer €100 a year. The retailers then use the information to build databases and to target incentives to valuable customers. 'The grocer may like to know who is a high spender in the scheme but is not shopping with them', says Ruth Kemp of Istel. 'Then they can offer incentives to use their store.'

Information from internal records is usually quicker and cheaper to get than information from other sources, but it also presents some problems. Because internal information was intended for other purposes, it may be incomplete or in the wrong form for making marketing decisions. For example, accounting department sales and cost data used for preparing financial statements need adapting for use in evaluating

Internal records information
Information gathered from sources within the company to evaluate marketing performances and to detect marketing problems and opportunities.

product, sales force or channel performance. In addition, the many different areas of a large company produce great amounts of information, and keeping track of it all is difficult. The marketing information system must gather, organise, process and index this mountain of information so that managers can find it easily and get it quickly.

marketing intelligence

Marketing intelligence

Everyday information about developments in the marketing environment that helps managers prepare and adjust marketing plans.

Marketing intelligence is everyday information about developments in the marketing environment that helps managers prepare and adjust marketing plans. The marketing intelligence system determines the intelligence needed, collects it by searching the environment and delivers it to marketing managers who need it.

Marketing intelligence comes from many sources. Much intelligence is from the company's personnel – executives, engineers and scientists, purchasing agents and the sales force. But company people are often busy and fail to pass on important information. The company must 'sell' its people on their importance as intelligence gatherers, train them to spot new developments and urge them to report intelligence back to the company.

The company must also persuade suppliers, resellers and customers to pass along important intelligence. Some information on competitors comes from what they say about themselves in annual reports, speeches, press releases and advertisements. The company can also learn about competitors from what others say about them in business publications and at trade shows. Or the company can watch what competitors do – buying and analysing competitors' products, monitoring their sales and checking for new patents.

Companies also buy intelligence information from outside suppliers. Dun & Bradstreet is the world's largest research company with branches in 40 countries and a turnover of €1.5 billion. Its largest subsidiary is Nielsen, which sells data on brand shares, retail prices and percentages of stores stocking different brands. Its Info*Act Workstation offers companies the chance to analyse data from three sources on the PCs: Retail Index, which monitors consumer sales and in-store conditions; Key Account Scantrack, a weekly analysis of sales, price elasticity and promotional effectiveness; and Homescan, a new consumer panel. Alliances between marketing research companies allow access to pan-European research. Leading European market research agencies all do more than half their work outside their own country. Among these are The Kanter Group and Taylor Nelson Sofres plc (UK), Nielson Media Research (The Netherlands), GfK and Sample Institut (Germany), Ipos Group SA (France) and Sifo Research (Sweden).[5]

competitor intelligence

Competitor intelligence

Information gathered that informs on what the competition is doing or is about to do.

Marketing intelligence can work not only for, but also against a company. Companies must sometimes take steps to protect themselves from the snooping of competitors. For example, Kellogg's had treated the public to tours of its plants since 1906, but recently closed its newly upgraded plant to outsiders to prevent competitors from getting intelligence on its high-tech equipment. In Japan corporate intelligence is part of the industrial culture. Everyone from assembly-line workers to top executives considers it their duty to filter intelligence about the competition back to management. In its Bangkok offices one European organisation has a huge poster outside its lavatory saying: 'Wash and hush up! You never know who's listening! Keep our secrets secret.'[6]

Some companies set up an office to collect and circulate marketing intelligence. The staff scan relevant publications, summarise important news and send news bulletins to marketing managers. They develop a file of intelligence information and help managers evaluate new information. These services greatly improve the quality of information available to marketing managers. The methods used to gather competitive information range from the ridiculous to the illegal. Managers routinely shred documents because wastepaper baskets can be an information source. Other firms have uncovered more sinister devices such as Spycatcher's TPR recording system that 'automatically interrogates telephones and faxes. Also a range of tiny microphones.'[7]

European firms lag behind their Japanese and American competitors in gathering competitive intelligence. In Japanese companies it is a long-established practice, for, as Mitsui's corporate motto says: 'Information is the life blood of the company.' In the US, competitive intelligence gathering has grown dramatically as more and more companies need to know what their competitors are doing. Sometimes, when the stakes are high, methods become questionable.

Recently Oracle, Microsoft's arch rival, admitted hiring Investigation Group International (IGI) to 'dig into the deals of organisations sympathetic to Microsoft'. Their investigation backfired after an IGI detective tried to bribe a caretaker to give him access to the rubbish bins of the Association of Competitive Technology.

The techniques they use to collect intelligence fall into four main groups:

Getting information from published materials and public documents
Keeping track of seemingly meaningless published information can provide competitor intelligence. For instance, the types of people sought in help-wanted ads can indicate something about a competitor's new strategies and products. Government agencies are another good source. Although it is often illegal for a company to photograph a competitor's plant from the air, aerial photos often are on file with geological survey or environmental protection agencies. These are public documents, available for a nominal fee. According to Leonard Fuld, founder of FCI: 'in some countries the government is a rare font of information. France has the Minitel, in the US we have an opus of information databases and networks.'

Competitors themselves may reveal information through their annual reports, business publications, trade show exhibits, press releases, advertisements, and Web pages. The Internet is proving to be a vast new source of competitor-supplied information. Most companies now place volumes of information on their websites, providing details to attract customers, partners, suppliers or franchisees, and that same information is available to competitors at the click of a mouse button. Press releases that never made it into the press are posted on websites, letting firms keep abreast of competitors' new products and organisational changes. Help wanted ads posted on the Web quickly reveal competitors' expansion priorities.

And it's not only company-sponsored websites that hold rich competitor intelligence booty. Researchers can also glean valuable nuggets of information from trade association websites.

> Gay Owen, controller of Stone Container's specialty-packaging division, visited a trade association Web site and noticed that a rival had won an award for a new process using ultra-violet resistant lacquers. The site revealed the machines' configuration and run rate, which Stone's engineers used to figure out how to replicate the process.[8]

Using Internet search engines, such as Yahoo! or Infoseek, marketers can search specific competitor names, events or trends and see what turns up. There are thousands of online databases. Companies can subscribe to any of more than 3,000 online databases and information search services such as Dialog, DataStar, Lexis-Nexis, Dow Jones News Retrieval, UMI ProQuest, and Dun & Bradstreet's Online Access. Using such databases, companies can conduct complex information searches in a flash from the comfort of their keyboards.

Protection against snooping competitors: The increasing importance of security on the Internet has led to the creation of companies like Infineon, which promotes its concerns about the issue and offers solutions 'to make the Internet and IT communications a more secure place'.

Source: Infineon. *Agency:* J. Walter Thompson

Company Sleuth (www.companysleuth.com) provides users with a steady stream of intelligence data gleaned from the Internet. It searches the Web and gives users daily e-mail reports detailing the business activities, financial moves and Internet dealings of competitors, prospects and clients, often before the information is officially reported. 'In today's information age, companies are leaving a paper trail of information online', says Joshua Kopelman, executive vice president of Infonautics, the company that offers the service. 'Company Sleuth uncovers hard-to-find and seemingly hidden business news and information for users so they don't have to simply rely on old news or intuition when making investment and business decisions.'[9]

Getting information by observing competitors or analysing products
Companies can get to know competitors better by buying their products or examining other physical evidence. An increasingly important form of competitive intelligence is benchmarking, taking apart competitors' products and imitating or improving upon their best features. Benchmarking has helped JCB keep ahead in earth-moving equipment. The company takes apart its international competitors' products, dissecting and examining them in detail. JCB also probed the manufacturing operations, the types of machine tools used, their speeds, manning levels, labour costs, quality control and testing procedures, and raw material. It built up a profile of all its main competitors' operations and performance ratios against which to benchmark. In this way, the company knew the extent to which competitors could vary their prices, what their strengths and weaknesses were, and how JCB could exploit these data to its advantage.

Bloomberg have accused market-leading Reuters of taking snooping too far by hiring Cyberspace Research Associates (CRA) to steal information on Bloomberg's €1,800 a month desktop device that sits on the desk of many city traders. According to

Bloomberg's, with CRA's help, Reuters obtained and cloned Bloomberg's software to speed development of their Reuters 3000, €2,200 per month, 'Bloomberg killer'.[10]

Getting information from people who do business with competitors   Key customers can keep the company informed about competitors and their products:

> Gillette told a large account the date on which it planned to begin selling its new Good News disposable razor. The distributor promptly called Bic and told it about the impending product launch. Bic put on a crash programme and was able to start selling its razor shortly after Gillette did.

Intelligence can also be gathered by infiltrating customers' business operations:

> Companies may provide their engineers free of charge to customers . . . The close, cooperative relationship that the engineers on loan cultivate with the customers' design staff often enables them to learn what new products competitors are pitching.

Getting information from recruits and competitors' employees   Companies can obtain intelligence through job interviews or from conversations with competitors' employees. Approaches sometimes recommended include:

✦ When interviewing people for jobs, pay special attention to those who have worked for competitors, even temporarily.

✦ Send engineers to conferences and trade shows to question competitors' technical people.

✦ Advertise and hold interviews for jobs that don't exist in order to entice competitors' employees to spill the beans.

✦ Telephone competitors' employees and ask direct and indirect questions. 'The rule of thumb' says Jonathan Lax, founder of TMA, 'is to target employees a level below where you think you should start, because that person often knows just as much as his or her senior, and they are not as frequently asked or wary.' Secretaries, receptionists and switchboard operators regularly give away information inadvertently.

■ Why is Europe different?

Niame Fine, founder of Protec Data, believes there are differences between US and European companies. Language and cultural blocks limit cross-border intelligence gathering. Approaching competitors' employees is a subtle business and people are often put on their guard if approached by someone from a different country. She also says Europeans have greater loyalty than their job-hopping American counterparts. However, some European companies are now being accused of beating the Americans at their own game. When Spanish-born José Ignacio Lopez de Arriotua defected from General Motors to Volkswagen to be its new purchasing and production chief, he took seven GM executives with him. Meanwhile Swedish ball-bearing company, SKF, had their production plans passed on to a competitor by a disgruntled employee.

   Although most of these techniques are legal and some are considered to be shrewdly competitive, many involve questionable ethics. The company should take advantage of publicly available information, but avoid practices that might be considered illegal or unethical. A company does not have to break the law or accepted codes of ethics to get good intelligence. So far many European businesses 'do as they would be done by' and linger at the ethical end of the spectrum of competitive intelligence. However, the European picture is not uniform. Paul Carratu, of Carratu International, put France and Italy alongside the US in their use of industrial espionage. For companies still playing catch-up in the spying game, www.fuld.com provides a Competitive Intelligence Guide offering sleuthing tips.[11]

marketing research

Managers cannot always wait for information to arrive in bits and pieces from the marketing intelligence system. They often require formal studies of specific situations. For example, Apple Computer wants to know how many and what kinds of people or companies will buy its new ultralight personal computer. Or a Dutch pet product firm needs to know the potential market for slimming tablets for dogs. What percentage of dogs are overweight, do their owners worry about it, and will they give the pill to their podgy pooches?[12] In these situations, the marketing intelligence system will not provide the detailed information needed. Because managers normally do not have the skills or time to obtain the information on their own, they need formal marketing research.

Marketing research
The function that links the consumer, customer and public to the marketer through information – information used to identify and define marketing opportunities and problems; to generate, refine and evaluate marketing actions; to monitor marketing performance; and to improve understanding of the marketing process.

Marketing research is the function linking the consumer, customer and public to the marketer through information – information used: to identify and define marketing opportunities and problems; to generate, refine and evaluate marketing actions; to monitor marketing performance; and to improve understanding of the marketing process.[13] Marketing researchers specify the information needed to address marketing issues, design the method for collecting information, manage and implement the data collection process, analyse the results and communicate the findings and their implications.

Marketing researchers engage in a wide variety of activities, ranging from analyses of market potential and market shares to studies of customer satisfaction and purchase intentions. Every marketer needs research. A company can conduct marketing research in its research department or have some or all of it done outside. Although most large companies have their own marketing research departments, they often use outside firms to do special research tasks or special studies. A company with no research department will have to buy the services of research firms.

Many people think of marketing research as a lengthy, formal process carried out by large marketing companies. But many small businesses and non-profit organisations also use marketing research. Almost any organisation can find informal, low-cost alternatives to the formal and complex marketing research techniques used by research experts in large firms.

the marketing research process

The marketing research process (see Figure 8.2) consists of four steps: defining the problem and research objectives; developing the research plan; implementing the research plan; and interpreting and reporting the findings.

Figure 8.2

The marketing research process

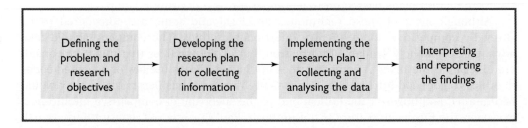

■ Defining the problem and research objectives

The marketing manager and the researcher must work closely together to define the problem carefully and must agree on the research objectives. The manager understands the decision for which information is needed; the researcher understands marketing research and how to obtain the information.

Managers must know enough about marketing research to help in the planning and in the interpretation of research results. If they know little about marketing research, they may obtain the wrong information, accept wrong conclusions, or ask for information that costs too much. Experienced marketing researchers who understand the manager's problem also need involvement at this stage. The researcher must be able to help the manager define the problem and to suggest ways that research can help the manager make better decisions.

Defining the problem and research objectives is often the hardest step in the research process. The manager may know that something is wrong, without knowing the specific causes. For example, managers of a discount retail store chain hastily decided that poor advertising caused falling sales, so they ordered research to test the company's advertising. It puzzled the managers when the research showed that current advertising was reaching the right people with the right message. It turned out that the chain stores were not delivering what the advertising promised. Careful problem definition would have avoided the cost and delay of doing advertising research. It would have suggested research on the real problem of consumer reactions to the products, service and prices offered in the chain's stores.

After the problem has been defined carefully, the manager and researcher must set the research objectives. A marketing research project might have one of three types of objective. The objective of **exploratory research** is to gather preliminary information that will help define the problem and suggest hypotheses. The objective of **descriptive research** is to describe things such as the market potential for a product or the demographics and attitudes of consumers who buy the product. The objective of **causal research** is to test hypotheses about cause-and-effect relationships. For example, would a 10 per cent cut in CD prices increase sales sufficiently to offset the lost margin? Managers often start with exploratory research and later follow with descriptive or causal research.

The statement of the problem and research objectives guides the entire research process. The manager and researcher should put the statement in writing to be certain that they agree on the purpose and expected results of the research.

Exploratory research
Marketing research to gather preliminary information that will help to better define problems and suggest hypotheses.

Descriptive research
Marketing research to better describe marketing problems, situations or markets, such as the market potential for a product or the demographics and attitudes of consumers.

Causal research
Marketing research to test hypotheses about cause-and-effect relationships.

■ Developing the research plan

The second step of the marketing research process calls for determining the information needed, developing a plan for gathering it efficiently and presenting the plan to marketing management. The plan outlines sources of existing data and explains the specific research approaches, contact methods, sampling plans and instruments that researchers will use to gather new data.

Determining information needs Research objectives need translating into specific information needs.

Bolswessanen, the Dutch food and drinks company, decides to conduct research to find out how consumers would react to a new breakfast cereal aimed at the adult market. Across Europe young health-conscious people are abandoning croissants in France, rolls in Belgium and lonely espresso in Italy. Since Nestlé and General Mills set up Cereal Partners Worldwide as a joint venture, they have been very active in the market and the project has started to develop. The European breakfast cereal market has been growing fast, but own labels dominate the adult sector.[14] Can Bolswessanen successfully compete with Kellogg's, the market leader, and the aggressive new competitor, Cereal Partners Worldwide? The company's research might call for the following specific information:

1. The demographic, economic and lifestyle characteristics of current breakfast cereal users. (How do social and demographic trends affect the breakfast cereal market?)
2. Consumer-usage patterns for cereals: how much do they eat, where and when? (Will all the family eat the cereal or does each family member have their favourite?)
3. Retailer reactions to the new product. (Failure to get retailer support could hurt its sales.)
4. Consumer attitudes towards the new product. (Will consumers switch from own brands and is the product attractive enough to compete with Kellogg's?)
5. Forecasts of sales of the new product. (Will the new packaging increase Bolswessanen's profits?)

Bolswessanen's managers will need this and many other types of information to decide whether to introduce the new product.

Secondary data
Information that already exists somewhere, having been collected for another purpose.

Primary data
Information collected for the specific purpose at hand.

Gathering secondary information   **Secondary data** is information that already exists somewhere, having been collected for another purpose. **Primary data** consists of information collected for the specific purpose at hand.

Researchers usually start by gathering secondary data. The company's internal database provides a good starting point. However, the company can also tap a wide assortment of external information sources, ranging from company, public and university libraries to government and business publications.

Commercial data sources   Companies can buy secondary data reports from outside suppliers. For example, Nielsen Media Research sells data on brand shares, retail prices, and percentages of stores stocking different brands. Taylor Nelson Sofres offers TV Audience Measurement using a range of detection techniques to measure cable, satellite, digital and terrestrial TV viewing. Europanel GfK monitors purchases and consumption of over 70,000 households in 23 European countries.[15] These and other firms supply high-quality data to suit a wide variety of marketing information needs.

Online databases and Internet data sources   Using commercial *online databases*, marketing researchers can conduct their own searches of secondary data sources. A recent survey of marketing researchers found that 81 per cent use such online services for conducting research.[16] A readily available online database exists to fill almost any marketing information need. General database services such as CompuServe, Dialog and Lexis-Nexis put an incredible wealth of information at the keyboards of marketing decision makers. For example, a company doing business in Germany can check out CompuServe's German Company Library of financial and product information on over 48,000 German-owned firms. Just about any information a marketer might need is available from online databases.[17]

Advantages and disadvantages of secondary data   Secondary data can usually be obtained more quickly and at a lower cost than primary data. For example, an Internet or online database search might provide all the information Danone needs on yoghurt usage, quickly and at almost no cost. A study to collect primary information might take weeks or months and cost tens of thousands of euros. Also, secondary sources sometimes can provide data an individual company cannot collect on its own – information that either is not directly available or would be too expensive to collect.

Table 8.1

Planning primary data collection

Research approaches	Contact methods	Sampling plan	Research instruments
Observation Survey Experiment	Mail Telephone Personal Internet	Sampling unit Sample size Sampling procedure	Questionnaire Mechanical instruments

For example, it would be too expensive for Danone to conduct a continuing audit to find out about the market shares, prices and displays of competitors' brands. But it can use the Access Panel service of Ipsos which provides this information on 115,000 households across five European countries.

Secondary data can also present problems. The needed information may not exist – researchers can rarely obtain all the data they need from secondary sources. For example, Deanne will not find existing information about consumer reactions to new packaging that it has not yet placed on the market. Even when data can be found, it might not be very usable. The researcher must evaluate secondary information carefully to make certain it is *relevant* (fits research project needs), *accurate* (reliably collected and reported), *current* (up to date enough for current decisions), and *impartial* (objectively collected and reported).

Secondary data provides a good starting point for research and often helps to define problems and research objectives. In most cases, however, the company must also collect primary data.

Planning primary data collection   Good decisions require good data. Just as researchers must carefully evaluate the quality of secondary information they obtain, they must also take great care in collecting primary data to ensure that they provide marketing decision makers with relevant, accurate, current and unbiased information. This could be **qualitative research** that measures a small sample of customers' views, or **quantitative research** that provides statistics from a large sample of consumers. Table 8.1 shows that designing a plan for primary data collection calls for a number of decisions on research approaches, contact methods, sampling plan and research instruments.

Research approaches   **Observational research** is the gathering of primary data by observing relevant people, actions and situations. For example:

✦ A food-products manufacturer sends researchers into supermarkets to find out the prices of competing brands or how much shelf space and display support retailers give its brands.

✦ A bank evaluates possible new branch locations by checking traffic patterns, neighbourhood conditions and the locations of competing branches.

✦ A maker of personal-care products pre-tests its ads by showing them to people and measuring eye movements, pulse rates and other physical reactions.

✦ A department store chain sends observers who pose as customers into its stores to check on store conditions and customer service.

✦ A museum checks the popularity of various exhibits by noting the amount of floor wear around them.

Qualitative research
Exploratory research used to uncover consumers' motivations, attitudes and behaviour. Focus-group interviewing, elicitation interviews and repertory grid techniques are typical methods used in this type of research.

Quantitative research
Research which involves data collection by mail or personal interviews from a sufficient volume of customers to allow statistical analysis.

Observational research
The gathering of primary data by observing relevant people, actions and situations.

Several companies sell information collected through *mechanical observation*. For example, Nielsen and TNS attach 'people meters' to television sets in selected homes to record who watches what programmes. They provide summaries of the size and demographic make-up of audiences for different television programmes. The television networks use these ratings to judge programme popularity and to set charges for advertising time. Advertisers use the ratings when selecting programmes for their commercials. *Checkout scanners* in retail stores also provide mechanical observation data. These laser scanners record consumer purchases in detail. Consumer products companies and retailers use scanner information to assess and improve product sales and store performance.[18] Some marketing research firms now offer **single-source data systems** that electronically monitor both consumers' purchases and consumers' exposure to various marketing activities to evaluate better the link between the two.[19]

Observational research can obtain information that people are unwilling or unable to provide. In some cases, observation is the only way to obtain the needed information. In contrast, some things are simply not observable, such as feelings, attitudes and motives or private behaviour. Long-term or infrequent behaviour is also difficult to observe. Because of these limitations, researchers often use observation along with other data collection methods.

Survey research is the approach best suited for gathering *descriptive* information. A company that wants to know about people's knowledge, attitudes, preferences or buying behaviour can often find out by asking them directly. Survey research is structured or unstructured. *Structured* surveys use formal lists of questions asked of all respondents in the same way. *Unstructured* surveys let the interviewer probe respondents and guide the interview according to their answers.

Survey research may be direct or indirect. In the *direct* approach, the researcher asks direct questions about behaviour or thoughts: for example, 'Why don't you buy clothes at Gap?' In contrast, the researcher might use the *indirect* approach by asking, 'What kinds of people buy clothes at Gap?' From the response to this indirect question, the researcher may be able to discover why the consumer avoids Gap clothing and why it attracts others. It may suggest reasons the consumer is not conscious of.

Survey research is the most widely used method for primary data collection and it is often the only method used in a research study. The principal advantage of survey research is its flexibility. It can obtain many different kinds of information in many different marketing situations. Depending on the survey design, it may also provide information more quickly and at lower cost than observational or experimental research.

However, survey research also presents some problems. Sometimes people are unable to answer survey questions because they do not remember, or never thought about, what they did and why they did it. Or people may be unwilling to respond to unknown interviewers or about things they consider private. Respondents may answer survey questions even when they do not know the answer, simply in order to appear smarter or more informed than they are. Or they may try to help the interviewer by giving pleasing answers. Finally, busy people may not take the time, or they might resent the intrusion into their privacy. Careful survey design can help to minimise these problems.

Experimental research gathers *causal* information. Experiments involve selecting matched groups of subjects, giving them different treatments, controlling unrelated factors and checking for differences in group responses. Thus experimental research tries to explain cause-and-effect relationships. Observation and surveys can collect information in experimental research.

Before extending their product range to include fragrances, researchers at Virgin Megastores might use experiments to answer questions such as the following:

Single-source data systems
Electronic monitoring systems that link consumers' exposure to television advertising and promotion (measured using television meters) with what they buy in stores (measured using store checkout scanners).

Survey research
The gathering of primary data by asking people questions about their knowledge, attitudes, preferences and buying behaviour.

Experimental research
The gathering of primary data by selecting matched groups of subjects, giving them different treatments, controlling related factors and checking for differences in group responses.

Table 8.2

Strengths and weaknesses of the four contact methods

	Mail	Telephone	Personal	Internet
Flexibility	Poor	Good	Excellent	Fair
Quantity of data that can be collected	Good	Fair	Excellent	Good
Control of interviewer effects	Excellent	Fair	Poor	Excellent
Control of sample	Fair	Excellent	Fair	Fair
Speed of data collection	Poor	Excellent	Good	Excellent
Response rate	Poor	Good	Good	Poor
Cost	Good	Fair	Poor	Excellent
Sample frame	Good	Excellent	Fair	Poor

Source: Adapted with permission of Macmillan Publishing Company from *Marketing Research: Measurement and method*, 6th edn, by Donald S. Tull and Del I. Hawkins. Copyright © 1993 by Macmillan Publishing Company.

✦ How much will the fragrances increase Virgin's sales?

✦ How will the fragrances affect the sales of other menu items?

✦ Which advertising approach would have the greatest effect on sales of their fragrances?

✦ How would different prices affect the sales of the product?

✦ How will the product affect the stores' overall image?

For example, to test the effects of two prices, Virgin could set up a simple experiment. It could introduce fragrances at one price in one city and at another price in another city. If the cities are similar and if all other marketing efforts for the fragrances are the same, then differences in the price charged could explain the sales in the two cities. More complex experimental designs could include other variables and other locations.

Contact methods   Mail, telephone, personal interviews and the Internet, a recent development, can collect data. Table 8.2 shows the strengths and weaknesses of each of these contact methods.

Postal questionnaires have many advantages. They can collect large amounts of information at a low cost per respondent. Respondents may give more honest answers to more personal questions on a postal questionnaire than to an unknown interviewer in person or over the phone, since there is no interviewer to bias the respondent's answers.

However, postal questionnaires also have disadvantages. They are not very flexible: they require simple and clearly worded questions; all respondents answer the same questions in a fixed order; and the researcher cannot adapt the questionnaire based on earlier answers. Mail surveys usually take longer to complete and the response rate – the number of people returning completed questionnaires – is often very low. Finally, the researcher often has little control over the postal questionnaire sample. Even with a good mailing list, it is often hard to control *who* at the mailing address fills out the questionnaire.[20]

Telephone interviewing is the best method for gathering information quickly and it provides greater flexibility than postal questionnaires. Interviewers can explain questions that are not understood. Depending on the respondent's answers, they can skip some questions or probe further on others. Telephone interviewing also allows greater sample control. Interviewers can ask to speak to respondents with the desired characteristics, or even by name. Response rates tend to be higher than with postal questionnaires.[21]

However, telephone interviewing also has drawbacks. The cost per respondent is higher than with postal questionnaires and people may not want to discuss personal questions with an interviewer. Using interviewers increases flexibility, but also introduces interviewer bias. The way interviewers talk, small differences in how they ask questions and other differences may affect respondents' answers. Finally, different interviewers may interpret and record responses differently, and under time pressure some interviewers might even cheat by recording answers without asking questions.

Personal interviewing takes two forms – individual and group interviewing. *Individual interviewing* involves talking with people in their homes or offices, in the street, or in shopping malls. The interviewer must gain their cooperation and the time involved can range from a few minutes to several hours. Sometimes people get a small payment in return for their time. *Group interviewing* consists of inviting six to ten people to gather for a few hours with a trained moderator to talk about a product, service or organisation. The moderator needs objectivity, knowledge of the subject and industry, and some understanding of group and consumer behaviour. The participants are normally paid a small sum for attending. The meeting is usually in a pleasant place and refreshments are served to foster an informal setting. The moderator starts with broad questions before moving to more specific issues, and encourages easy-going discussion, hoping that group interactions will bring out actual feelings and thoughts. At the same time, the moderator 'focuses' the discussion – hence the name **focus group** interviewing. The comments are recorded by written notes or on videotapes for study later. Focus group interviewing has become one of the key marketing research tools for gaining insight into consumer thoughts and feelings.[22]

Focus group
A small sample of typical consumers under the direction of a group leader who elicits their reaction to a stimulus such as an ad or product concept.

Personal interviewing is quite flexible and can collect large amounts of information. Trained interviewers can hold a respondent's attention for a long time and can explain difficult questions. They can guide interviews, explore issues and probe, as the situation requires. Personal interviews can utilise any type of questionnaire. Interviewers can show subjects actual products, advertisements or packages, and observe reactions and behaviour. In most cases, personal interviews can be conducted fairly quickly.

The main drawbacks of personal interviewing are costs and sampling problems. Personal interviews may cost three to four times as much as telephone interviews. Group interview studies usually employ small sample sizes to keep time and costs down, and it may be hard to generalise from the results. Because interviewers have more freedom in personal interviews, the problem of interviewer bias is greater.

Which contact method is best depends on what information the researcher wants and on the number and types of respondents needed. Advances in computers and communications have had an impact on methods of obtaining information. For example, most research firms now do Computer Assisted Telephone Interviewing (CATI). Professional interviewers call respondents, often using phone numbers drawn at random. When the respondent answers, the interviewer reads a set of questions from a video screen and types the respondent's answers directly into the computer. Although this procedure requires a large investment in computer equipment and interviewer training, it eliminates data editing and coding, reduces errors and saves time. Other research firms set up terminals in shopping centres – respondents sit down at a terminal, read questions from a screen and type their answers into the computer.[23]

Internet data collection is still in its infancy. But as the use of the World Wide Web and online services widens, online research is becoming a quick, easy and inexpensive method.[24] Online researchers recognise that Web surfers are not representative of the population. Online users tend to be better educated, more affluent and younger than the average consumer, and a higher proportion are male. These are important

marketing highlight 8.1

Marketing research on the Internet

Performing marketing research on the Net is in its infancy but is a quick, easy and inexpensive way to tap into Web users' opinions. Web users are not representative of the population. They are highly important consumers and some of the hardest to reach when conducting research. 'It's very solid for reaching hard-to-get segments', says Paul Jacobson of Greenfield Online. 'Doctors, lawyers, professionals – people you might have difficulty reaching because they are not interested in taking part in surveys. It's also a good medium for reaching working mothers and others who lead busy lives. They can do it in their own space and at their own convenience.'

The Internet is also a good medium for bringing together geographically dispersed people, especially those in higher income groups. For example, one virtual focus group convened by NFO Interactive to discuss the airline industry was made up of high income individuals: 'You just can't get these kinds of people to come into your office but we can get them online.'

Online research can offer two advantages over traditional surveys and focus groups: speed and cost-effectiveness.

Online researchers routinely field quantitative studies and fill response quotas in a few days. Online focus groups require advance scheduling, but results are practically instantaneous.

Research on the Internet is also relatively inexpensive. Participants can gather focus groups from anywhere in the world, removing travel and facility costs. Internet surveys also eliminate most of the postage, phone, labour and printing costs of other survey approaches. Moreover, sample size has little influence on costs. On the Web there is not a huge difference between a 10 and 10,000 sample. 'The cost can be anywhere from 10 per cent to 80 per cent less, especially when you talk about a big sample', says Tod Johnson, head of NPD Group.

However, using the Internet to conduct marketing research does have some drawbacks. A cartoon shows two dogs seated at a computer: 'On the Internet, nobody knows you are a dog', one says to the other. 'If you can't see a person with whom you are communicating, how do you know who they really are?' he says. Also, trying to draw conclusions from a 'self-selected' sample of online users, those who clicked through to a questionnaire or accidentally landed in a chat room can be troublesome.

To overcome sample and response problems, firms that offer online services construct panels of qualified Web regulars to respond to surveys and participate in online focus groups. Research Connections, for example, recruits by telephone and, if necessary, helps new users connect to the Internet.

Even when using qualified respondents, focus group responses can lose something in the translation. Eye contact and body language are two direct, personal interactions of traditional focus group research that are lost in the online world. And while researchers can offer seasoned moderators, the Internet format – running, typed commentary and online 'emoticons' (punctuation marks that express emotion, such as :-) to signify happiness) – greatly restricts respondent expressiveness. Similarly, technology limits researchers' capability to show visual cues to research subjects.

But just as it hinders the two-way assessment of visual cues, Web research can actually permit some participants the anonymity necessary to elicit an unguarded response. 'There are reduced social effects online', Jacobson says. 'People are much more honest in this medium.' Another experienced online researcher agrees. When the subject is personal or sensitive, he suggests, online definitely has advantages. 'People hiding behind a keyboard get pretty brave.'

Some researchers are wildly optimistic about the prospects for marketing research on the Internet. One expert predicts that in the next few years, 50 per cent of all research will be done on the Internet: 'Ten years from now, national telephone surveys will be the subject of research methodology folklore.'

Source: Portions adapted from Ian P. Murphy, 'Interactive research', *Marketing News* (20 January 1997), pp. 1, 17. 'NFO executive sees most research going to Internet', *Advertising Age* (19 May 1997), p. 50; Kate Maddox, 'Virtual panels add real insight for marketers', *Advertising Age* (29 June 1998), pp. 34, 40; 'Online or off target?', *American Demographics* (November 1998), pp. 20–1.

consumers to companies offering products and services online. They are also some of the hardest to reach when conducting a research study. Online surveys and chat sessions (or online focus groups) often prove effective in reaching elusive groups, such as teen, single, affluent and well-educated audiences. To provide access to this community the NOP Research Group has established a partnership with Internet Exchange, Europe's leading Internet café chain, to form global network of sites.

When appropriate, online research offers marketers two distinct advantages over traditional surveys and focus groups: speed and cost-effectiveness. Online researchers can field quantitative studies and fill response quotas in only a matter of days. Online focus groups require some advance scheduling, but results are practically instantaneous. Research on the Internet is also relatively inexpensive. Participants can dial in for a focus group from anywhere in the world, eliminating travel, lodging and facility costs, making online chats cheaper than traditional focus groups. And for surveys, the Internet eliminates most of the postage, phone, labour and printing costs associated with other survey approaches. There is also no difference in the speed and cost of conducting an international survey rather than a domestic one.

Using the Internet to conduct marketing research does have some drawbacks. The method shares a problem with postal surveys: knowing who's in the sample. Trying to draw conclusions from a 'self-selected' sample of online users, those who clicked through to a questionnaire or accidentally landed in a chat room can be troublesome. Online research is not right for every company or product. For example, mass marketers who need to survey a representative cross-section of the population will find online research methodologies less useful, since most low-income consumers do not have online access.

Eye contact and body language are two direct, personal interactions of traditional focus-group research that are lost online. To overcome such sample and response problems, NPD and many other firms that offer online services construct panels of qualified Web regulars to respond to surveys and participate in online focus groups. NPD's panel consists of 15,000 consumers recruited online and verified by telephone; Greenfield Online picks users from its own database, then calls them periodically to verify that they are who they say they are. Another online research firm, Research Connections, recruits in advance by telephone, taking time to help new users connect to the Internet, if necessary.

Some researchers are wildly optimistic about the prospects for market research on the Internet. Marketing Highlight 8.1 gives an insight into some recent development in market research on the internet.

There is no one best contact method to use. The one chosen depends on the information needs, cost, speed and other issues. Table 8.3 shows quantitative data collection methods used across Europe. Rational reasons may account for only part of the variation shown. Face-to-face interview figures are particularly high in southern Europe and the United Kingdom. The low penetration of telephones in some of these countries may be an influence, but it may also reflect cultures who like socialising. For example, Ireland's high use of group discussions in qualitative research may reflect that land's love of conversation. The Scandinavians' use of telephone interviews is partly explained by their being large countries with small populations. In some countries, postal surveys do not work because of low literacy, but another reason is the unwillingness of people to respond. Research agencies and managers also have preferred methods, so they will also exert some personal influence on the choice of method. The relatively low use of the Internet in Europe means that Internet data collection in Europe will lag behind the United States. In addition, the large differences in penetration of the Internet across Europe mean that its use will not be uniform.

Sample
A segment of the population selected for market research to represent the population as a whole.

Sampling plans Marketing researchers usually draw conclusions about large groups of consumers by studying a small sample of the total consumer population. A **sample**

Base: Total Research Turnover	Mail %	Telephone %		On-line %	Face-to-face			Myst. shop %	Other
		CATI	Other		Hall/ Street	CAPI	Other % home		
Austria	3	9	4	1	4	5	10	0	0
Belgium	0	17	2	2	10	4	5	0	3
Denmark	8	14	2	0	3	2	3	0	0
Finland	12	27	1	1	3	6	2	3	0
France	2	10		0	6	15		0	6
Greece	2	5	1	0	7	3	19	3	4
Ireland	1	13	1	0	2	0	19	1	0
Italy	1	14	4	0	7	3	16	1	3
Luxembourg	0	26	0	0	2	5	27	2	15
Norway	10	39		0		14		0	0
Portugal	2	15	2	1	3	0	10	2	0
Spain	2	12	2	0	10	3	21	1	2
Sweden	16	33	2	3	5	–	3	0	0
Switzerland	5	0	30	0	14	–	–	1	1
U.K.	5	6	4	0	6	3	16	1	2

SOURCE: Trade associations and estimates. Average figures are weighted averages for Europe only, and are thus comparable with previous reports. Permission for using this material has been granted by ESOMAR (European Society for Opinion and Marketing Research), Amsterdam, The Netherlands. Adapted from http://www.esomar.nl/press/industryreport01.htm.

Table 8.3

Expenditure on ad hoc quantitative research 1999

is a segment of the population selected to represent the population as a whole. Ideally, the sample should be representative, so that the researcher can make accurate estimates of the thoughts and behaviours of the larger population.

Designing the sample calls for three decisions. First, *who* is to be surveyed (what *sampling unit*)? The answer to this question is not always obvious. For example, to study the decision-making process for a family car purchase, should the researcher interview the husband, wife, other family members or all of these? The responses obtained from different family members vary, so the researcher must determine the information needed and from whom.[25]

Second, *how many* people are to be surveyed (what *sample size*)? Large samples give more reliable results than small samples. However, it is not necessary to sample the entire target market or even a large portion to get reliable results. If well chosen, samples of less than 1 per cent of a population can often give good reliability.

Third, *how* are the people in the sample *to be chosen* (what *sampling procedure*)? Table 8.4 describes different kinds of sample. Using *probability samples*, each population member has a known chance of being included in the sample, and researchers can calculate confidence limits for sampling error. But when probability sampling costs too much or takes too long, marketing researchers often take *non-probability samples*, even though their sampling error is not measurable. These varied ways of drawing samples have different costs and time limitations, as well as different accuracy and statistical properties. Which method is best depends on the needs of the research project.

Research instruments   In collecting primary data, marketing researchers have a choice of two main research instruments: the *questionnaire* and *mechanical devices*.

Table 8.4

Types of sampling

Probability sample	
Simple random sample	Every member of the population has a known and equal chance of selection.
Stratified random sample	The population is divided into mutually exclusive groups (such as age groups), and random samples are drawn from each group.
Cluster (area) sample	The population is divided into mutually exclusive groups (such as blocks), and the researcher draws a sample of the groups to interview.
Non-probability sample	
Convenience sample	The researcher selects the easiest population members from which to obtain information.
Judgement sample	The researcher uses his or her judgement to select population members who are good prospects for accurate information.
Quota sample	The researcher finds and interviews a prescribed number of people in each of several categories.

The *questionnaire* is by far the most common instrument. Broadly speaking, a questionnaire consists of a set of questions presented to a respondent for his or her answers. The questionnaire is very flexible – there are many ways to ask questions. Questionnaires need to be developed carefully and tested before their large-scale use. A carelessly prepared questionnaire usually contains several errors (see Table 8.5).

In preparing a questionnaire, the marketing researcher must decide what questions to ask, the form of the questions, the wording of the questions and the ordering of the questions. Questionnaires frequently leave out questions that need answering, but include questions that cannot be answered, will not be answered, or need not be answered. Each question should be checked to see that it contributes to the research objectives.

The *form* of the question can influence the response. Marketing researchers distinguish between closed-end and open-end questions. **Closed-end questions** include all the possible answers, and subjects make choices among them. Part A of Table 8.6 shows the most common forms of closed-end questions as they might appear in an SAS survey of airline users. **Open-end questions** allow respondents to answer in their own words. The most common forms are shown in part B of Table 8.6. Open-end questions often reveal more than closed-end questions because respondents are not limited in their answers. Open-end questions are especially useful in exploratory research in which the researcher is trying to find out *what* people think, but not measuring *how many* people think in a certain way. Closed-end questions, on the other hand, provide answers that are easier to interpret and tabulate.

Closed-end questions
Questions that include all the possible answers and allow subjects to make choices among them.

Open-end questions
Questions that allow respondents to answer in their own words.

Researchers should also use care in the *wording* of questions. They should use simple, direct, unbiased wording. The questions should be pre-tested before use. The *ordering* of questions is also important. The first question should create interest if possible. Ask difficult or personal questions last, so that respondents do not become defensive. The questions should be in a logical order.

Although questionnaires are the most common research instrument, *mechanical instruments* are also used. We discussed two mechanical instruments – people meters and supermarket scanners – earlier in the chapter. Another group of mechanical

Table 8.5

A 'questionable questionnaire'

Suppose that an adventure holiday director had prepared the following questionnaire to use in interviewing the parents of prospective campers. How would you assess each question?

1. What is your income to the nearest hundred pounds?
   People don't usually know their income to the nearest hundred pounds nor do they want to reveal their income that closely. Moreover, a researcher should never open a questionnaire with such a personal question.

2. Are you a strong or a weak supporter of overnight camping for your children?
   What do 'strong' and 'weak' mean?

3. Do your children behave themselves well on adventure holidays?
   Yes ( ) No ( )
   'Behave' is a relative term. Furthermore, are 'yes' and 'no' the best response options for this question? Besides, will people want to answer this? Why ask the question in the first place?

4. How many adventure holiday operators mailed literature to you last April? This April?
   Who can remember this?

5. What are the most salient and determinant attributes in your evaluation of adventure holidays?
   What are 'salient' and 'determinant' attributes? Don't use big words on me!

6. Do you think it is right to deprive your child of the opportunity to grow into a mature person through the experience of adventure holidays?
   A loaded question. Given the bias, how can any parent answer 'yes'?

devices measures subjects' physical responses. For example, a galvanometer (lie detector) measures the strength of interest or emotions aroused by a subject's exposure to different stimuli: for instance, an ad or picture. The galvanometer detects the minute degree of sweating that accompanies emotional arousal. The tachistoscope flashes an ad to a subject at an exposure range from less than one-hundredth of a second to several seconds. After each exposure, the respondents describe everything they recall. Eye cameras study respondents' eye movements to determine at what points their eyes focus first and how long they linger on a given item.[26]

■ Presenting the research plan

At this stage, the marketing researcher should summarise the plan in a *written proposal*. A written proposal is especially important when the research project is large and complex, or when an outside firm carries it out. The proposal should cover the management problems addressed and the research objectives, the information obtained, the sources of secondary information or methods for collecting primary data, and the way the results will help management decision making. The proposal should also include research costs. A written research plan or proposal makes sure that the marketing manager and researchers have considered all the important aspects of the research and that they agree on why and how to do the research.

■ Implementing the research plan

The researcher next puts the marketing research plan into action. This involves collecting, processing and analysing the information. Data collection can be by the

A. CLOSED-END QUESTIONS

NAME	DESCRIPTION
Dichotomous	A question offering two answer choices.
Multiple choice	A question offering three or more choices.
Likert scale	A statement with which the respondent shows the amount of agreement or disagreement.
Semantic differential	A scale is inscribed between two bipolar words, and the respondent selects the point that represents the direction and intensity of his or her feelings.
Importance scale	A scale that rates the importance of some attribute from 'not at all important' to 'extremely important'.
Rating scale	A scale that rates some attribute from 'poor' to 'excellent'.
Intention-to-buy scale	A scale that describes the respondent's intentions to buy.

B. OPEN-END QUESTIONS

NAME	DESCRIPTION
Completely unstructured	A question that respondents can answer in an almost unlimited number of ways.
Word association	Words are presented, one at a time, and respondents mention the first word that comes to mind.
Sentence completion	Incomplete sentences are presented, one at a time, and respondents complete the sentence.
Story completion	An incomplete story is presented, and respondents are asked to complete it.
Picture completion	A picture of two characters is presented, with one making a statement. Respondents are asked to identify with the other and fill in the empty balloon.
Thematic Apperception Tests (TAT)	A picture is presented, and respondents are asked to make up a story about what they think is happening or may happen in the picture.

Table 8.6 Types of question

EXAMPLE

'In arranging this trip, did you personally phone SAS?' Yes ☐ No ☐

'With whom are you travelling on this flight?'

No one ☐   Children only ☐

Spouse ☐   Business associates/friends/relatives ☐

Spouse and children ☐   An organised tour group ☐

'Small airlines generally give better service than large ones.'

Strongly disagree	Disagree	Neither agree nor disagree	Agree	Strongly agree
1 ☐	2 ☐	3 ☐	4 ☐	5 ☐

SAS Airlines

Large ___×___ : ____ : ____ : ____ : ____ : ____ Small

Experienced ____ : ____ : ____ : ____ : ___×___ : ____ Inexperienced

Modern ____ : ____ : ____ : ___×___ : ____ : ____ Old-fashioned

'Airline food service to me is'

Extremely important	Very important	Somewhat important	Not very important	Not at all important
1 _____	2 _____	3 _____	4 _____	5 _____

'SAS's food service is'

Excellent	Very good	Good	Fair	Poor
1 _____	2 _____	3 _____	4 _____	5 _____

'If in-flight telephone service were available on a long flight, I would'

Definitely buy	Probably buy	Not certain	Probably not buy	Definitely not buy
1 _____	2 _____	3 _____	4 _____	5 _____

EXAMPLE

'What is your opinion of SAS?'_____

'What is the first word that comes to your mind when you hear the following?'

Airline _____

Delta _____

Travel _____

'When I choose an airline, the most important consideration in my decision is _____.'

'I flew SAS a few days ago. I noticed that the exterior and interior of the plane had very bright colours. This aroused in me the following thoughts and feelings.' Now complete the story.

Fill in the empty balloon.

Make up a story about what you see.

Eye cameras determine
where eyes land and
how long they linger on
a given item.

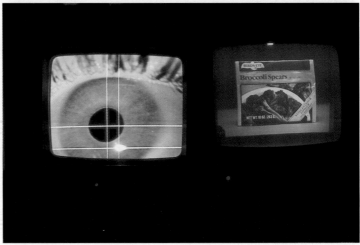

company's marketing research staff or, more usually, by outside firms. The company keeps more control over the collection process and data quality by using its staff. However, outside firms that specialise in data collection can often do the job more quickly and at lower cost.

The data collection phase of the marketing research process is generally the most expensive and the most subject to error. The researcher should watch fieldwork closely to make sure that the plan is implemented correctly and to guard against problems with contacting respondents, with respondents who refuse to cooperate or who give biased or dishonest answers, and with interviewers who make mistakes or take short cuts.

Researchers must process and analyse the collected data to isolate important information and findings. They need to check data from questionnaires for accuracy and completeness, and code it for computer analysis. The researchers then tabulate the results and compute averages and other statistical measures.

■ Interpreting and reporting the findings

The researcher must now interpret the findings, draw conclusions and report them to management. The researcher should not try to overwhelm managers with numbers and fancy statistical techniques. Rather, the researcher should present important findings that are useful in the important decisions faced by management.

However, interpretation should not be by the researchers alone. They are often experts in research design and statistics, but the marketing manager knows more about the problem and the decisions needed. In many cases, findings can be interpreted in different ways and discussions between researchers and managers will help point to the best interpretations. The manager will also want to check that the research project was conducted properly and that all the necessary analysis was completed. Or, after seeing the findings, the manager may have additional questions that can be answered from the data. Finally, the manager is the one who must ultimately decide what action the research suggests. The researchers may even make the data directly available to marketing managers so that they can perform new analyses and test new relationships on their own.

Interpretation is an important phase of the marketing process. The best research is meaningless if the manager blindly accepts wrong interpretations from the researcher. Similarly, managers may have biased interpretations – they tend to accept research results that show what they expected and to reject those that they did not expect or hope for. Thus managers and researchers must work together closely when interpreting research results and both share responsibility for the research process and resulting decisions.[27]

demand estimation

When a company finds an attractive market, it must estimate that market's current size and future potential carefully. The company can lose a considerable amount of profit by overestimating or underestimating the market.

Demand is measured and forecast on many levels. Figure 8.3 shows 90 types of demand measurement! Demand might be measured for six different *product levels* (product item, product form, product line, company sales, industry sales and total sales); five different *space levels* (customer, territory, country, region, world); and three different *time levels* (short range, medium range and long range).

Each demand measure serves a specific purpose. A company might forecast short-run total demand for a product as a basis for ordering raw materials, planning production and borrowing cash. Or it might forecast long-run regional demand for a big product line as a basis for designing a market expansion strategy.

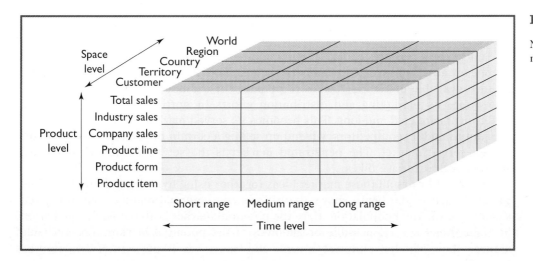

Figure 8.3

Ninety types of demand measurement (6 × 5 × 3)

defining the market

Market demand measurement calls for a clear understanding of the market involved. The term *market* has acquired many meanings over the years. In its original meaning, a market is a physical place where buyers and sellers gather to exchange goods and services. Medieval towns had market squares where sellers brought their goods and buyers shopped for goods. Markets still dominate retailing in the Third World and remain in many towns, but most of today's buying and selling occurs in shopping areas.

To an economist, a market describes all the buyers and sellers who transact over some good or service. Thus the soft-drink market consists of sellers such as Coca-Cola, Pepsi-Cola, Tango and Lilt and all the consumers who buy soft drinks. The economist's interest is the structure, conduct and performance of each market.

To a marketer, a **market** is the set of all actual and potential buyers of a product or service. A market is the set of buyers and an **industry** is the set of sellers. The size of a market hinges on the number of buyers who might exist for a particular market offer. Potential buyers for something have three characteristics: *interest, income* and *access.*

Consider the consumer market for Finnish Tunturi exercise cycles. To assess its market, Tunturi must first estimate the number of consumers who have a potential interest in owning an exercise bike. To do this, the company could contact a random sample of consumers and ask the following question: 'Do you have an interest in buying and owning an exercise bike?' If one person out of ten says yes, Tunturi can assume that 10 per cent of the total number of consumers would constitute the potential market for exercise bikes. The **potential market** is the set of consumers who profess some level of interest in a particular product or service.

Consumer interest alone is not enough to define the exercise bike market. Potential consumers must have enough income to afford the product. They must be able to answer yes to the following question: 'Would you pay €500 for an exercise bike?'. The higher the price, the lower the number of people who can answer yes to this question. Thus market size depends on both interest and income.

Access barriers further reduce exercise bike market size. If Tunturi has no distributors for its products in some areas, potential consumers in those areas are not available as customers. The **available market** is the set of consumers who have interest, income and access to a particular product or service.

Tunturi might restrict sales to certain groups. Excessive repetitive exercise can damage young children, so sales of exercise bikes to anyone under 12 years of age may be discouraged. The remaining adults make up the **qualified available market** – the set of consumers who have interest, income, access and qualifications for the product or service.

Tunturi now has the choice of going after the whole qualified available market or concentrating on selected segments. Tunturi's **served market** is the part of the qualified available market it decides to pursue. For example, Tunturi may decide to concentrate its marketing and distribution efforts in northern Europe, where the winter nights are cold and long. This becomes its served market.

Tunturi and its competitors will end up selling a certain number of exercise bikes in their served market. The **penetrated market** is the set of consumers who have already bought exercise bikes.

Figure 8.4 brings all these market ideas together using hypothetical numbers. The bar on the left of the figure shows the ratio of the potential market – all interested persons – to the total population. Here the potential market is 10 per cent. The bar on the right shows several possible breakdowns of the potential market. The available market – those who have interest, income and access – is 40 per cent of the potential

---

Market
The set of all actual and potential buyers of a product or service.

Industry
A group of firms which offer a product or class of products that are close substitutes for each other. The set of all sellers of a product or service.

Potential market
The set of consumers who profess some level of interest in a particular product or service.

Available market
The set of consumers who have interest, income and access to a particular product or service.

Qualified available market
The set of consumers who have interest, income, access and qualifications for a particular product or service.

Served market (target market)
The part of the qualified available market that the company decides to pursue.

Penetrated market
The set of consumers who have already bought a particular product or service.

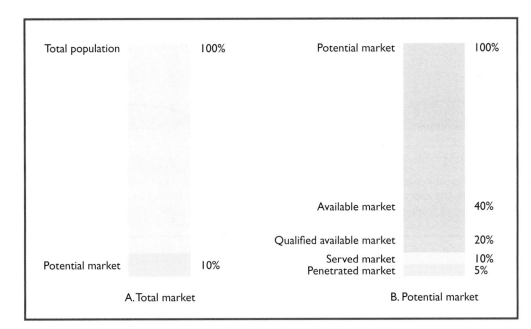

Figure 8.4

Levels of market
definition

market. The qualified available market – those who can meet the legal requirements –
is 50 per cent of the available market (or 20 per cent of the potential market). Tunturi
concentrates its efforts on 50 per cent of the qualified available market – the served
market, which is 10 per cent of the potential market. Finally, Tunturi and its competitors have already penetrated 50 per cent of the served market (or 5 per cent of the
potential market).

These market definitions are a useful tool for marketing planning. If Tunturi is
unsatisfied with current sales, it can take a number of actions. It can expand to other
available markets in Europe or elsewhere. It can lower its price to expand the size of
the potential market. It can try to attract a larger percentage of buyers from its served
market through stronger promotion or distribution efforts to current target consumers.
Or it can try to expand the potential market by increasing its advertising to convert
non-interested consumers into interested consumers. Concern over heart disease
means that many middle-aged people who have avoided exercise for years are being
encouraged to do more. Perhaps Tunturi can work through the health industry to
attract these.

measuring current market demand

Marketers need to estimate three aspects of current market demand: total market
demand; area market demand; and actual sales and market shares.

estimating total market demand

The **total market demand** for a product or service is the total volume that would be
bought by a defined consumer group in a defined geographic area in a defined time
period in a defined marketing environment under a defined level and mix of industry
marketing effort.

Total market demand
*The total volume of a
product or service that
would be bought by a
defined consumer group
in a defined geographic
area in a defined time
period in a defined
marketing environment
under a defined level
and mix of industry
marketing effort.*

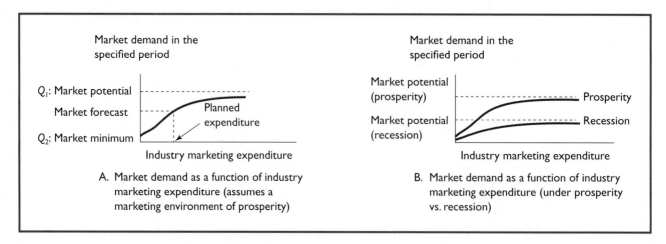

Figure 8.5

Market demand

Total market demand is not a fixed number, but a function of the stated conditions. One of these conditions, for example, is the level and mix of industry marketing effort. Another is the state of the environment. Part A of Figure 8.5 shows the relationship between total market demand and these conditions. The horizontal axis shows different possible levels of industry marketing expenditure in a given period. The vertical axis shows the resulting demand level. The curve represents the estimated level of market demand for varying levels of industry marketing expenditure. Some base sales (called the *market minimum*) would take place without any marketing expenditure. Greater marketing expenditures would yield higher levels of demand, first at an increasing rate and then at a decreasing rate. Marketing expenditures above a certain level would not cause much more demand, suggesting an upper limit to market demand called the *market potential*. The industry market forecast shows the level of market demand corresponding to the planned level of industry marketing expenditure in the given environment.[28]

The distance between the market minimum and the market potential shows the overall sensitivity of demand to marketing efforts. We can think of two extreme types of market: the *expandable* and the *non-expandable*. An expandable market, such as the market for DVD players, is one whose size depends upon the level of industry marketing expenditures. For Figure 8.5A, in an expandable market, the distance between Q_1 and Q_2 would be fairly large. In a non-expandable market, such as that for opera, marketing expenditures generate little demand; the distance between Q_1 and Q_2 would be fairly small. Organisations selling in a non-expandable market can take **primary demand** – total demand for all brands of a given product or service – as given. They concentrate their marketing resources on building **selective demand** – demand for *their* brand of the product or service.

Given a different marketing environment, we must estimate a new market demand curve. For example, the market for exercise bikes is stronger during prosperity than during recession. Figure 8.5B shows the relationship of market demand to the environment. A given level of marketing expenditure will always result in more demand during prosperity than it would during a recession. The main point is that marketers should carefully define the situation for which they are estimating market demand.

Companies have developed various practical methods for estimating total market demand. We will illustrate two here. Suppose Dutch-owned Polygram wants to estimate the total annual sales of recorded compact discs. A common way to estimate total market demand is as follows:

Primary demand
The level of total demand for all brands of a given product or service – for example, the total demand for motor cycles.

Selective demand
The demand for a given brand of a product or service.

where
$$Q = n \times q \times p$$

Q = total market demand;
n = number of buyers in the market;
q = quantity purchased by an average buyer per year; and
p = price of an average unit.

Thus, if there are 10 million buyers of CDs each year and the average buyer buys six discs a year and the average price is €20, then the total market demand for cassette tapes is €1,200 million (= 10,000,000 × 6 × €20).

A variation on the preceding equation is the *chain ratio method*. Using this method, the analyst multiplies a base number by a chain of adjusting percentages. For example, the United Kingdom has no national service, so the British Army needs to attract 20,000 new male recruits each year. There is a problem here, since the Army is already under strength and the population of 16- to 19-year-olds is declining. The marketing question is whether this is a reasonable target in relation to the market potential. The Army estimates market potential using the following method:

Total number of male secondary-school leavers	1,200,000
Percentage who are militarily qualified (no physical, emotional, or mental handicaps)	× 0.50
Percentage of those qualified who are potentially interested in military service	× 0.05
Percentage of those qualified and interested in military service who consider the Army the preferred service	× 0.60

This chain of numbers shows a market potential of 18,000 recruits. Since this is less than the target number of recruits sought, the Army needs to do a better job of marketing itself. They responded by doing motivational research that showed existing advertising did not attract the target age group, although a military career did give them what they wanted. A new campaign therefore aimed to increase the attractiveness of a military career to both men and women.[29]

estimating actual sales and market shares

Besides estimating total and area demand, a company will want to know the actual industry sales in its market. Thus it must identify its competitors and estimate their sales.

The industry's trade association will often collect and publish total industry sales, although not listing individual company sales separately. In this way, each company can evaluate its performance against the industry as a whole. Suppose the company's sales are increasing at a rate of 5 per cent a year and industry sales are increasing at 10 per cent. This company is losing its relative standing in the industry.

Another way to estimate sales is to buy reports from marketing research firms that audit total sales and brand sales. For example, Nielsen and other marketing research firms use scanner data to audit the retail sales of various product categories in supermarkets and pharmacies, and sell this information to interested companies. A company can obtain data on total product category sales as well as brand sales. It can compare its performance with that of the total industry or any particular competitor to see whether it is gaining or losing in its relative standing.[30]

forecasting future demand

Forecasting

The art of estimating future demand by anticipating what buyers are likely to do under a given set of conditions.

Having looked at ways to estimate current demand, we now examine ways to forecast future market demand. **Forecasting** is the art of estimating future demand by anticipating what buyers are likely to do under a given set of conditions. Very few products or services lend themselves to easy forecasting. Those that do generally involve a product with steady sales, or sales growth in a stable competitive situation. But most markets do not have stable total and company demand, so good forecasting becomes a key factor in company success. Poor forecasting can lead to excessively large inventories, costly price markdowns, or lost sales due to being out of stock. The more unstable the demand, the more the company needs accurate forecasts and elaborate forecasting procedures.

> Huge investments ride on the back of forecasts. Current forecasts show a huge growth in the European satellite navigation (Sat-Nav) market for private automobiles from €110 million in 2000 to over €500 million in 2004. The rest of the Sat-Nav market (recreational marine craft, agriculture, etc.) is also expected to be €500 million. That will need a minimum 21, 4 tonne satellites in medium Earth orbit (20,000 km altitude) with three additional geostationary relay satellites in higher orbit. Total minimum cost: €1.6 billion. On the back of this the European Space Agency have to forecast how much of the market for launching the satellites they can grab and launch successfully. So far their Ariane 5 launcher has not been entirely successful but has produced some spectacular fireworks.[31]

Companies commonly use a three-stage procedure to arrive at a sales forecast. First they make an *environmental forecast* (will the European politico-economy support a Sat-Nav system?), followed by an *industry forecast* (will the total Sat-Nav demand be €1 billion by 2004?) and a *company sales forecast* (what share of the Sat-Nav launch business can the European Space Agency get?). The environmental forecast calls for projecting inflation, unemployment, interest rates, consumer spending and saving, business investment, government expenditures, net exports and other environmental events important to the company. The result is a forecast of gross national product, which is used along with other indicators to forecast industry sales. Then the company prepares its sales forecast assuming a certain share of industry sales.

Companies use several specific techniques to forecast their sales. Table 8.7 lists some of these techniques.[32] All forecasts build on one of three information bases: what people say, what people do, or what people have done. The first basis – *what people say* – involves surveying the opinions of buyers or those close to them, such as salespeople or outside experts. It includes three methods: surveys of buyer intentions, composites of sales force opinions and expert opinion. Building a forecast on *what people do* involves another method, that of putting the product into a test market to assess buyer response. The final basis – *what people have done* – involves analysing records of past buying behaviour or using time-series analysis or statistical demand analysis.

buyers' intentions

One way to forecast what buyers will do is to ask them directly. This suggests that the forecaster should survey buyers. Surveys are especially valuable if the buyers have clearly formed intentions, will carry them out and can describe them to interviewers. A typical intention to buy survey would ask:

Table 8.7

Common sales
forecasting techniques

BASED ON:	METHODS
What people say	Surveys of buyers' intentions
	Composite sales force opinions
	Expert opinion
What people do	Test markets
What people have done	Time-series analysis
	Leading indicators
	Statistical demand analysis

Do you intend to buy a car within the next six months?

0.0	0.1	0.2	0.3	0.4	0.5	0.6	0.7	0.8	0.9	1.0
No chance		Slight chance		Fair chance		Good chance		Strong chance		For certain

This is a *purchase probability scale*. In addition, the various surveys ask about the consumer's present and future personal finances and their expectations about the economy. Consumer durable goods companies subscribe to these indices to help them anticipate significant shifts in consumer buying intentions, so that they can adjust their production and marketing plans accordingly. For *business buying*, various agencies carry out intention surveys about plant, equipment and materials purchases. These measures need adjusting when conducted across nations and cultures. Overestimation of intention to buy is higher in southern Europe than it is in northern Europe and the United States. In Asia, the Japanese tend to make fewer overstatements than the Chinese.[33]

composite of sales force opinions

When buyer interviewing is impractical, the company may base its sales forecasts on information provided by the sales force. The company typically asks its salespeople to estimate sales by product for their individual territories. It then adds up the individual estimates to arrive at an overall sales forecast.

Few companies use their sales force's estimates without some adjustments. Salespeople are biased observers. They may be naturally pessimistic or optimistic, or they may go to one extreme or another because of recent sales setbacks or successes. Furthermore, they are often unaware of larger economic developments and do not always know how their company's marketing plans will affect future sales in their territories. They may understate demand so that the company will set a low sales quota. They may not have the time to prepare careful estimates or may not consider it worthwhile.

Accepting these biases, a number of benefits can be gained by involving the sales force in forecasting. Salespeople may have better insights into developing trends than any other group. After participating in the forecasting process, the salespeople may have greater confidence in their quotas and more incentive to achieve them. Also, such grass roots' forecasting provides estimates broken down by product, territory, customer and salesperson.[34]

expert opinion

Companies can also obtain forecasts by turning to experts. Experts include dealers, distributors, suppliers, marketing consultants and trade associations. Thus motor vehicle companies survey their dealers periodically for their forecasts of short-term demand. Dealer estimates, however, are subject to the same strengths and weaknesses as sales force estimates.

Many companies buy economic and industry forecasts. These forecasting specialists are in a better position than the company to prepare economic forecasts because they have more data available and more forecasting expertise.

Occasionally companies will invite a special group of experts to prepare a forecast. They may exchange views and come up with a group estimate (group discussion method). Or they may supply their estimates individually, with the company analyst combining them into a single estimate (pooling of individual estimates). Or they may supply individual estimates and assumptions reviewed by a company analyst, revised and followed by further rounds of estimation (Delphi method).[35]

Experts can provide good insights upon which to base forecasts, but they can also be wrong (see Marketing Highlight 8.2). Where possible, the company should back up experts' opinions with estimates obtained using other methods.

test-market method

Where buyers do not plan their purchases carefully or where experts are not available or reliable, the company may want to conduct a direct test market. This is especially useful in forecasting new-product sales or established-product sales in a new distribution channel or territory. Test marketing is discussed in Chapter 14.

marketing highlight 8.2

Sometimes 'expert opinion' isn't all it should be

Before you rely too heavily on expert opinion, you might be interested in learning how some past 'experts' did with their predictions.

Technology:

◆ 'Everything that can be invented has been invented' (Director of the US Patent Office, 1899).

◆ 'Rail travel at high speed is not possible, because passengers, unable to breathe, would die of asphyxia' (Dr Dioysy Larder in 1828 – the year Stephenson's *Rocket* commenced service).

◆ 'No large steamship will ever cross the Atlantic, since it would require more coal than it could carry' (Dr Larder again, this time in 1859). Two years later the *Great Eastern* crossed the Atlantic.

◆ 'Flight by machines heavier than air is unpractical and insignificant, if not impossible' (Simon Newcombe, 1901). Eighteen months later the Wright brothers flew.

◆ 'Airplanes are interesting toys, but of no military value' (France's Marshal Foch, 1911).

◆ 'The energy produced by the breaking down of the atom is a very poor kind of thing. Anyone who expects a source of power from the transformation is talking moonshine' (Ernest Rutherford, 1919, after *he* had split the first atom).

◆ 'I think there's a world market for about five computers' (Thomas J. Watson, IBM Chairman, 1943).

SOURCE: NOP Research Group Ltd

◆ 'By 1980, all power (electric, atomic, solar) is likely to be virtually costless' (Henry Luce, founder and publisher of *Time*, *Life* and *Fortune*, 1956).

◆ 'With over 50 foreign cars already on sale here, the Japanese auto industry isn't likely to carve out a big slice of the US market for itself' (*Business Week*, 1958).

Entertainment:

◆ 'If Beethoven's Seventh Symphony is not by some means abridged, it will soon fall into disuse' (Philip Hale, nineteenth-century music critic).

◆ 'Can't act, can't sing, slightly bald. Can dance a little' (comments after Fred Astaire's first movie audition).

◆ 'Who the hell wants to hear actors talk?' (Harry Warner, founder of Warner Bros).

◆ 'TV won't be able to hold on to any market it captures after the first six months' (Daryl F. Zanuck, head of 20th Century Fox, 1946).

◆ '[He] is unspeakably untalented' (John Crosby of Elvis Presley, syndicated TV critic, 1954).

◆ In 1965 Clint Eastwood was deemed 'insufficiently promising' and therefore dropped by the Universal Pictures talent school.

◆ 'We don't like their sound. Groups of guitars are on the way out' (Decca Recording Company, 1962, when turning down the Beatles). Pye, Columbia and HMV also rejected the Beatles before their signing with EMI.

◆ 'Unsinkable' (claim made by the *Titanic*'s builders, Harland and Wolff, in 1912, for the ship that cost $7.5 million to build).

◆ 'James Cameron has spent $200 million on a movie and it's a dog. He's finally had it!' (Quote repeated by film critic Adam Smith, referring to the blockbuster film *Titanic*).

Environment:

◆ 'Since populations tend to increase geometrically [1, 2, 4, 8 . . .] and food supply arithmetically [1, 2, 3, 4 . . .], the starvation of Great Britain is inevitable and imminent' (Thomas Robert Malthus, 1798).

◆ 'Population will soon outstrip food production' (Lester Brown of the Worldwatch Institute, 1973).

◆ 'Population will increase faster than world food production, so food prices will rise between 35% and 115% by 2000' (*Global 2000*, report to the President of the United States).

◆ 'We could use up all of the proven reserves of oil in the entire world by the end of the next decade' (Club of Rome, 1972). They also made similar predictions for the reserves of aluminium, copper, lead, natural gas, silver, tin and zinc.

The results so far: known oil reserves are over 1,000 billion barrels, supplies have pushed metals, mineral and food prices down 40 per cent since 1960, and calories consumed per capita in the Third World are 27 per cent higher than in the 1960s!

SOURCES: Patrick McGilligan, *Clint: The Life and Legend* (HarperCollins, London, 1999); 'Sometimes expert opinion isn't all it should be', *Go* (September–October 1985), p. 2; Terry Coleman, *The Liners* (Harmondsworth: Penguin, 1976); Stephen Pile, *The Book of Heroic Failures* (London: Futura, 1980); Charles Gillett, *The Sound of the City: The rise of rock and roll* (London: Souvenir, 1983); 'Environmental scares: plenty of gloom', *The Economist* (20 December 1997); William A. Sherien, *The Fortune Seller: The Big Business of Buying and Selling Predictions* (John Wiley, 1998); 'We woz wrong', *The Economist* (18 December 1999, pp. 61–2); *Encarta: Multimedia encyclopaedia* (Microsoft, 2000).

Time-series analysis
Breaking down past sales into their trend, cycle, season and erratic components, then recombining these components to produce a sales forecast.

Trend
The long-term, underlying pattern of sales growth or decline resulting from basic changes in population, capital formation and technology.

Cycle
The medium-term wavelike movement of sales resulting from changes in general economic and competitive activity.

Seasonality
The recurrent consistent pattern of sales movements within the year.

Leading indicators
Time series that change in the same direction but in advance of company sales.

Statistical demand analysis
A set of statistical procedures used to discover the most important real factors affecting sales and their relative influence; the most commonly analysed factors are prices, income, population and promotion.

time-series analysis

Many firms base their forecasts on past sales. They assume that statistical analysis can uncover the causes of past sales. Then analysts can use the causal relations to predict future sales. **Time-series analysis** consists of breaking down the original sales into four components – trend, cycle, season and erratic components – then recombining these components to produce the sales forecast.

Trend is the long-term, underlying pattern of growth or decline in sales resulting from basic changes in population, capital formation and technology. It is found by fitting a straight or curved line through past sales. **Cycle** captures the medium-term, wavelike movement of sales resulting from changes in general economic and competitive activity. The cyclical component can be useful for medium-range forecasting. Cyclical swings, however, are difficult to predict because they do not occur on a regular basis. **Seasonality** refers to a consistent pattern of sales movements within the year. The term *season* describes any recurrent hourly, weekly, monthly or quarterly sales pattern. The seasonal component may relate to weather factors, holidays and trade customs. The seasonal pattern provides a norm for forecasting short-range sales. Finally, *erratic events* include fads, strikes, snow storms, earthquakes, riots, fires and other disturbances. These components, by definition, are unpredictable and should be removed from past data to see the more normal behaviour of sales.

Suppose the Dutch insurance company ING sells 12,000 new life insurance policies this year and wants to predict next year's December sales. The long-term trend shows a 5 per cent sales growth rate per year. This information alone suggests sales next year of 12,600 (= 12,000 × 1.05). However, a business recession is expected next year, which will probably result in total sales achieving only 90 per cent of the expected trend-adjusted sales. Sales next year are therefore more likely to be 11,340 (= 12,600 × 0.90). If sales were the same each month, monthly sales would be 945 (= 11,340/12). However, December is an above-average month for insurance policy sales, with a seasonal index standing at 1.30. Therefore December sales may be as high as 1,228.5 (= 945 × 1.3). The company expects no erratic events, such as strikes or new insurance regulations. Thus it estimates new policy sales next December at 1,228.5 policies.

leading indicators

Many companies try to forecast their sales by finding one or more **leading indicators**: that is, other time series that change in the same direction but ahead of company sales. For example, a plumbing supply company might find that its sales lag behind the housing starts index by about four months. An index of housing starts would then be a useful leading indicator.

statistical demand analysis

Time-series analysis treats past and future sales as a function of time, rather than as a function of any real demand factors. But many real factors affect the sales of any product. **Statistical demand analysis** is a set of statistical procedures used to discover the most important real factors affecting sales and their relative influence. The factors most commonly analysed are prices, income, population and promotion.

Statistical demand analysis consists of expressing sales (Q) as a dependent variable and trying to explain sales as a function of a number of independent demand variables $X_1, X_2 \ldots X_n$. That is:

$$Q = f(X_1, X_2 \ldots X_n)$$

Using multiple-regression analysis, various equations can be fitted to the data to find the best predicting factors and equation.

For example, the South of Scotland Electricity Board developed an equation that predicted the annual sales of washing machines (Q) to be:[36]

$$Q = 210{,}739 - 703P + 69H + 20Y$$

where

P = average installed price;
H = new single-family homes connected to utilities; and
Y = per capita income.

Thus in a year when an average installed price is £387 (€635), there are 5,000 new connected homes and the average per capita income is £4,800, from the equation we would predict the actual sales of washing machines to be 379,678 units:

$$Q = 210{,}739 - 703(387) + 69(5{,}000) + 20(4{,}800)$$

The equation was found to be 95 per cent accurate. If the equation predicted as well as this for other regions, it would serve as a useful forecasting tool. Marketing management would predict next year's per capita income, new homes and prices, and use them to make forecasts.

Statistical demand analysis can be very complex and the marketer must take care in designing, conducting and interpreting such analysis. Yet constantly improving computer technology has made statistical demand analysis an increasingly popular approach to forecasting.

information analysis

Information gathered by the company's marketing information systems often requires more analysis, and sometimes managers may need more help in applying it to marketing problems and decisions. This help may include advanced statistical analysis to learn more about both the relationships within a set of data and their statistical reliability (Chapters 9 and 10 show these factors used in segmentation and positioning research). Such analysis allows managers to go beyond means and standard deviations in the data. In an examination of consumer non-durable goods in the Netherlands, regression analysis gave a model that forecast a brand's market share (B_t) based upon predicted marketing activity:[37]

$$B_t = -7.85 - 1.45P_t + 0.08A_{t-1} + 1.23D_t$$

where

P_t = relative price of brand;
A_{t-1} = advertising share in the previous period; and
D_t = effective store distribution.

This, and models like it, can help answer marketing questions such as:

+ What are the chief variables affecting my sales and how important is each one?
+ If I raised my price 10 per cent and increased my advertising expenditures 20 per cent, what would happen to sales?
+ How much should I spend on advertising?
+ What are the best predictors of which consumers are likely to buy my brand versus my competitor's brand?
+ What are the best variables for segmenting my market and how many segments exist?

Information analysis might also involve a collection of mathematical models that will help marketers make better decisions. Each model represents some real system, process or outcome. These models can help answer the questions of *what if?* and *which is best?* During the past 20 years, marketing scientists have developed numerous models to help marketing managers make better marketing-mix decisions, design sales territories and sales-call plans, select sites for retail outlets, develop optimal advertising mixes and forecast new-product sales.[38]

distributing information

Marketing information has no value until managers use it to make better marketing decisions. The information gathered through marketing intelligence and marketing research must be distributed to the right marketing managers at the right time. Most companies have centralised marketing information systems that provide managers with regular performance reports, intelligence updates, and reports on the results of studies. Managers need these routine reports for making regular planning, implementation and control decisions. But marketing managers may also need non-routine information for special situations and on-the-spot decisions. For example, a sales manager having trouble with a large customer may want a summary of the account's sales and profitability over the past year. Or a retail store manager who has run out of a best-selling product may want to know the current inventory levels in the chain's other stores.

Developments in information technology have caused a revolution in information distribution. With recent advances in computers, software and telecommunications, most companies have decentralised their marketing information systems. In most companies today, marketing managers have direct access to the information network, at any time and from virtually any location.

While working at a home office, in a hotel room, on an aeroplane – any place where they can turn on a laptop computer and phone in – today's managers can obtain information from company databases or outside information services, analyse the information using statistical packages and models, prepare reports using word processing and presentation software, and communicate with others in the network through electronic communications. Such systems offer exciting prospects. They allow managers to get the information they need directly and quickly and to tailor it to their own needs.

international studies

The globalisation of business is extending the task facing managers. Now managers have to manage campaigns across countries and within different countries. International marketing researchers follow the same steps as domestic researchers, from defining the research problem and developing a research plan to interpreting and reporting the results. However, these researchers often face more and different problems. Whereas domestic researchers deal with fairly homogeneous markets within a single country, international researchers deal with markets in many different countries. These different markets often vary dramatically in their levels of economic development, cultures and customs, and buying patterns. Even gathering basic secondary information in many countries is difficult, and primary information can present even more problems. Despite the EU's increased integration and expansion, information gathering across the EU is far from integrated (see Marketing Highlight 8.3).

marketing highlight 8.3

European research

Europe cannot yet be researched as one market. The EU is getting closer, but huge differences remain. The market research industry is fairly standard across the EU, with most services available everywhere. However, many large agencies, including IRI, GfK and Video Research, cover only a few countries so use local agencies when conducting international studies. Agencies are now forming alliances in order to ease cross-border research. For example, Euroline is a one-stop-shop telephone interviewing consortium set up by agencies in France, Germany, Italy, Spain and the UK. This will allow one questionnaire to be written, transmitted to other countries, translated, then hopefully checked carefully.

There is a huge disparity of incomes and consumption within the EU: Denmark, Germany and Luxembourg have a gross domestic product per capita more than four times that of Portugal. Differences in wealth account for only a small part of the variation in consumption and consumer behaviour. Some differences, like eating habits, are rooted in the different languages, cultural traditions and cuisine of the EU but there are also big differences in the consumption of modern industrial goods. Italy is Europe's least wired developed country and is falling further behind fast: Datamonitor forecasts the growth in Italian households with online PCs growing only 13 per cent during 1998–2003 while the forecast for Greece is 81 per cent. For young and old the contrasts are stark. In Denmark almost 60 per cent of people continue in education until they are over twenty years old while in Portugal over 50 per cent of the population complete their education before they are fourteen. The pension assets are over €160,000 for each Dutch and British pensioner while the comparable figure for France and Germany is less than €10,000.

Competition and distribution also vary. European markets retain locally dominant companies and unique competitive structures. The big multinationals now operate in most markets, but their strength in each market varies. A few large retailers dominate UK retailing while Italy retains numerous mama and papa stores. Europe has many large retail chains, such as Germany's Tengelmann, France's Leclerc and Dutch Ahold, but most of these are little known outside their home country.

Differences still exist in the most basic research measures. In Germany, adulthood ranges from 18 upwards, but in other countries it is as low as 12 years, thus eliminating the teenage market. Social class scales also differ. The traditional British scale has ten components (e.g. age, income, occupation) while Germany uses a scale depending upon three components: income, profession and education. In France, the scale depends upon where as well as what is done: for example, working in public or private sectors. The European Society for Opinion and Marketing Research (ESOMAR) set up working parties to harmonise European socio-demographics. The questions cover age, education, employment, economic standing, etc. Their ESOMAR European Social Grade system (Table 1) is freely available on the Internet and provides a great opportunity for harmonising Trans-European studies.

SOURCES: H. A. Bijmolt, R. T. Framback and T. M. M. Verhallan, 'Strategic marketing research', *Journal of Marketing Management*, **12**, 1/3 (1996), pp. 83–92; *European Market Pocket Book: 2000* (Henley-on-Thames, UK: NTC Publications, 2000); *The World in 2000* (The Economist Publications, London, 2000); Harmonisation of Socio-Demographics: The Development of the ESOMAR European Social Grade (ESOMAR, Amsterdam, 1997). See also a series of journal articles reviewing consumers in different European countries, starting with Peter S. H. Leeflang and W. Fred van Raaij, 'The changing consumer in the Netherlands: recent changes in environmental variables and their consequences for future consumption and marketing', *International Journal of Research in Marketing*, **12**, 5 (1995), pp. 345–63.

GRADE	COUNTRY B	DK	D	E	F	GR	IRL	I	L	NL	P	UK
AB	15	28	22	11	20	13	12	17	23	25	8	19
C1	20	32	20	17	17	13	12	11	18	23	6	12
C2	30	16	30	28	28	21	21	21	23	24	10	17
DE	30	20	24	43	35	53	49	51	32	22	69	41

Non-categorised residuals mean the populations do not sum to 100%.

Table 1 ESOMAR percentage social grades for 12 EU countries

In many foreign markets, the international researcher has a difficult time finding good *secondary data*. Whereas many marketing researchers can obtain reliable secondary data on their domestic market, many countries have almost no research services at all. Some international market research firms operate in several large economies, but most countries are not covered by any. Thus, even when secondary information is available, it must usually be obtained from many different sources on a country-by-country basis, making the information difficult to combine or compare.

Because of the scarcity of good secondary data, international researchers must often collect their own primary data. Here again, researchers face problems not encountered domestically. For example, they may find it difficult simply to develop appropriate samples. Whereas researchers in developed countries can use current telephone directories, census data and any of several sources of socio-economic data to construct samples, such information is lacking or unreliable in many countries. Reaching respondents is often not so easy in other parts of the world. In some countries, very few people have private telephones. In other countries, the postal system is notoriously unreliable. In Brazil, for instance, an estimated 30 per cent of the mail is never delivered. In many developing countries, poor roads and transportation systems make certain areas hard to reach, and personal interviews difficult and expensive.[39]

Differences in cultures from country to country cause additional problems for international researchers. Language is the most obvious culprit. For example, questionnaires must be prepared in one language and then translated into the languages of each country researched. Responses must then be translated back into the original language for analysis and interpretation. This adds to research costs and increases the risks of error:

> Translating a questionnaire from one language to another is far from easy. . . . Many points are [lost], because many idioms, phrases and statements mean different things in different cultures. A Danish executive observed: 'Check this out by having a different translator put back into English what you've translated from the English. You'll get the shock of your life. I remember [an example in which] "out of sight, out of mind" had become "invisible things are insane"'.[40]

Buying roles and consumer decision processes vary greatly from country to country, further complicating international marketing research. Consumers in different countries also vary in their attitudes towards marketing research. People in one country may be very willing to respond, while in other countries non-response can be a difficult problem. For example, custom in some Islamic countries prohibits people from talking with strangers – a researcher simply may not be allowed to speak by phone with women about brand attitudes or buying behaviour. In certain cultures, research questions are often considered too personal. For example, in many Latin American countries, people may feel too embarrassed to talk with researchers about their choice of shampoo, deodorant or other personal-care products. Even when respondents are *willing* to respond, they may not be *able* to because of high functional illiteracy rates. And middle-class people in developing countries often make false claims in order to appear well off. For example, in a study of tea consumption in India, over 70 per cent of middle-income respondents claimed that they used one of several national brands. However, the researchers had good reason to doubt these results – more than 60 per cent of the tea sold in India is unbranded generic tea.

Despite these problems, the recent growth of international marketing has resulted in a rapid increase in the use of international marketing research. Global companies have little choice but to conduct such research. Although the costs and problems associated with international research may be high, the costs of not doing it – in terms of

missed opportunities and mistakes – might be even higher. Once recognised, many of the problems associated with international marketing research can be overcome or avoided.

marketing research in small businesses and non-profit organisations

Many of the marketing research techniques discussed in this chapter also can be used by smaller organisations in a less formal manner and at little or no expense. Managers of small businesses and non-profit organisations can obtain good marketing information simply by *observing* things around them. For example, retailers can evaluate new locations by observing vehicle and pedestrian traffic. They can monitor competitor advertising by collecting ads from local media. They can evaluate their customer mix by recording how many and what kinds of customers shop in the store at different times. In addition, many small business managers routinely visit their rivals and socialise with competitors to gain insights.

Managers can conduct informal *surveys* using small convenience samples. The director of an art museum can learn what patrons think about new exhibits by conducting informal focus groups – inviting small groups to lunch and having discussions on topics of interest. Retail salespeople can talk with customers visiting the store; hospital officials can interview patients. Restaurant managers might make random phone calls during slack hours to interview consumers about where they eat out and what they think of various restaurants in the area.

Managers also can conduct their own simple *experiments*. For example, by changing the themes in regular fund-raising mailings and watching the results, a non-profit manager can find out much about which marketing strategies work best. By varying newspaper advertisements, a store manager can learn the effects of things such as ad size and position, price coupons, and media used.

Small organisations can obtain most of the secondary data available to large businesses. In addition, many associations, local media, chambers of commerce and government agencies provide special help to small organisations. Local newspapers often provide information on local shoppers and their buying patterns. Finally, small businesses can collect a considerable amount of information at very little cost on the Internet. They can scour competitor and customer websites and use Internet search engines to research specific companies and issues.

In summary, secondary data collection, observation, surveys and experiments can all be used effectively by small organisations with small budgets. Although these informal research methods are less complex and less costly, they still must be conducted carefully. Managers must think carefully about the objectives of the research, formulate questions in advance, recognise the biases introduced by smaller samples and less skilled researchers, and conduct the research systematically.[41]

market research ethics

Increasing consumer resentment has become a major problem for the research industry. This resentment has led to lower survey response rates in recent years – one study found that 38 per cent of consumers now refuse to be interviewed in an average survey, up dramatically from a decade before. Another study found that 59 per cent of consumers had refused to give information to a company because they thought it was not really needed or too personal, up from 42 per cent just five years earlier.[42] There are a number of reasons why this resistance to marketing research is rising and much is to do with how market research has been used and abused.

intrusions on consumer privacy

Some consumers fear that researchers might use sophisticated techniques to probe our deepest feelings and then use this knowledge to manipulate our buying. Others may have been taken in by previous 'research surveys' that actually turned out to be attempts to sell them something. Other consumers confuse legitimate marketing research studies with telemarketing or database development efforts and say 'no' before the interviewer can even begin. Most, however, simply resent the intrusion. They dislike mail or telephone surveys that are too long or too personal or that interrupt them at inconvenient times.

misuse of research findings

Research studies can be powerful persuasion tools; companies often use study results as claims in their advertising and promotion. Today, however, many research studies appear to be little more than a search for a sales lead. In fact, in some cases, the research surveys appear to have been designed just to produce the intended effect. Few advertisers openly rig their research designs or blatantly misrepresent the findings; most abuses tend to be subtle 'stretches'. Consider the following examples:[43]

> A study by DaimlerChrysler contends that Americans overwhelmingly prefer Chrysler to Toyota after test-driving both. However, the study included just 100 people in each of two tests. More importantly, none of the people surveyed owned a foreign car, so they appear to be favourably predisposed to US cars.

> A poll sponsored by the disposable diaper industry asked: 'It is estimated that disposable diapers account for less than 2 percent of the content of landfills. In contrast, beverage containers, third-class mail, and yard waste are estimated to account for about 21 percent landfill content. Given this, in your opinion, would it be fair to ban disposable diapers?' Again, not surprisingly, 84 percent said no.

In some cases, so-called independent research studies are paid for by companies with an interest in the outcome. For example, four studies compare the environmental effects of using disposable diapers to those of using cloth diapers. The two studies sponsored by the cloth diaper industry conclude that cloth diapers are more environmentally friendly while the other two studies, sponsored by the paper diaper industry, conclude just the opposite. Yet both appear to be correct *given* the underlying assumptions used.

To counter the misuse of marketing research the industry has developed broad standards, such as ESOMAR's International Code of Marketing and Social Research Practice (www.esomar.nl/codes_3). This code outlines researchers' responsibilities to respondents and to the general public. For example, it says that researchers should make their names and addresses available to participants, and it bans companies from representing activities like database compilation or sales and promotional pitches as research. However, many of the pseudo-research practices that damage the reputation of legitimate marketing research are conducted by sales organisations that are not committed to the market research profession.

summary

A well-designed *marketing information system* (MIS) begins and ends with the user. The MIS first *assesses information needs* by interviewing marketing managers and surveying their decision environment to determine what information is desired, needed and feasible to offer. The MIS next *develops information* and helps managers to use it more effectively. *Internal records* provide information on sales, costs, inventories, cash flows and accounts receivable and payable. Such data are quick and cheap, but must often be adapted for marketing decisions. The *marketing intelligence system* supplies marketing executives with everyday information about developments in the external marketing environment. Intelligence can be from company employees, customers, suppliers and resellers; or by monitoring published reports, conferences, advertisements, competitor actions and other activities in the environment.

Marketing research involves collecting information relevant to a specific marketing problem facing the organisation. Marketing research involves a four-step process. The first step consists of *defining the problem and setting the research objectives*. The objectives may be *exploratory*, *descriptive* or *causal*. The second step consists of developing the *research plan* for collecting data from primary and secondary sources. *Primary data collection* calls for choosing a *research approach* (observation, survey, experiment); choosing a *contact method* (mail, telephone, personal); designing a *sampling plan* (whom to survey, how many to survey and how to choose them) and developing *research instruments* (questionnaire, mechanical). The third step consists of *implementing the marketing research plan* by collecting, processing and analysing the information. The fourth step consists of *interpreting and reporting the findings*. Further information analysis helps marketing managers to apply the information, and provides advanced statistical procedures and models to develop more rigorous findings from the information.

Finally, the marketing information system distributes information gathered from internal sources, marketing intelligence and marketing research to the right managers at the right times. More and more companies are decentralising their information systems through networks that allow managers to have direct access to information. To carry out their responsibilities, marketing managers need measures of current and future market size. We define a *market* as the set of actual and potential consumers of a market offer. Consumers in the market have *interest*, *income* and *access* to the market offer. The marketer has to distinguish various levels of the market, such as the *potential market*, *available market*, *qualified available market*, *served market* and *penetrated market*.

One task is to *estimate current demand*. Marketers can estimate total demand through the chain ratio method, which involves multiplying a base number by successive percentages. For *estimating future demand*, the company can use one or a combination of seven possible forecasting methods, based on what consumers say (*buyers' intentions surveys*, *composite of sales force opinions*, *expert opinion*); what consumers do (*market tests*); or what consumers have done (*time-series analysis*, *leading indicators* and *statistical demand analysis*). The best method to use depends on the purpose of the forecast, the type of product and the availability and reliability of data.

discussing the issues

1. You are a marketing research supplier, designing and conducting studies for a variety of companies. What is the most important thing you may do to ensure your clients will get their money's worth from your services?

2. Companies often face rapidly changing environments. Can market research information go stale? What issues does a manager face in using these research results?

3. What type of research would be appropriate in the following situations and why?

   ✦ Nestlé wants to investigate the impact of children on their parents' decisions to buy breakfast foods.

   ✦ A college or university bookshop wants to get some insights into how students feel about the shop's merchandise, prices and service.

   ✦ L'Oréal wants to determine whether a new line of deodorants for teenagers will be profitable.

   ✦ Gap is considering where to locate a new store in a fast-growing suburb.

   ✦ Nintendo intends to develop a new range of multimedia products for older children and adults, and wants to test the feasibility of the idea.

4. In market measurement and forecasting, which is the more serious problem: overestimating demand or underestimating it? Give your reasons.

5. What leading indicators might help you predict sales of people carriers? mobile phones? baby foods? Describe a general procedure for finding leading indicators of product sales.

applying the concepts

1. People often make their own judgements about the potential for new products. You may hear someone say a new product will 'never sell' or that it will 'sell like hot cakes'. Recall some recent new products or services that you saw or heard about, and about which you made an informal prediction. What attracted your attention enough to get you to comment on the future of the products or services? What was your forecast? Were you correct?

2. Obtain ESOMAR's recommended questionnaire for European Social Grades from http://www.esomar.nl and, if you are a graduate student with work experience, complete it for yourself or, if you are not, complete it for one of your parents. Work out the distribution of your class's ESOMAR Social Grade, MIE (main income earner classification), terminal age of MEI and Economic Status Scale based on ownership level of selected durables. Compare your findings with the European statistics given in Tables 1 to 4 on the ESOMAR European Social Grades website and analyse the difference between your class's distribution, that of your own country and the EU12.

references

1. 'AIDS in third world: a global disaster', *The Economist* (2 January 1999), pp. 50–2; 'A turning point for AIDS?', *The Economist* (15 July 2000), pp. 117–19 and also the web sites 'AIDS in Africa' time.com/time/europe/photoessays/aids/; 'AIDS in AFRICA' ccisd.org/sidafrique/a_index.html; 'AIDS: Africa in Peril' cnn.com/SPECIALS/2000/aids and 'AIDS in Africa: distinguishing fact and fiction' virusmyth.com/aids/data/epafrica.htm

2. Joseph M. Winski, 'Gentle rain turns into torrent', *Advertising Age* (3 June 1991), p. 34; David Shenk, *Data Smog: Surviving the Information Glut* (San Francisco: HarperSanFrancisco, 1997); Nancy Doucette, 'Relieving information overload', *Rough Notes* (February 1998), pp. 26–7; and Diane Trommer, 'Information overload – study finds intranet users overwhelmed with data', *Electronic Buyers' News* (20 April 1998), p. 98.

3. Alice LaPlante, 'Still drowning!', *Computer World* (10 March 1997), pp. 69–70.

4. Jeffrey Rotfeder and Jim Bartimo, 'How software is making food sales a piece of cake', *Business Week* (2 July 1990), pp. 54–5; Victoria Griffith, 'Smart selling to big spenders', *Financial Times* (1 July 1994), p. 16.

5. American Marketing Association, *Honomichl Global Top 25* (Chicago, IL, 14 August 2000).

6. Ibid., p. 46; Leonard M. Fuld, 'Competitor intelligence: can you plug the leaks?', *Security Management* (August 1989), pp. 85–7; Kate Button, 'Spies like us', *Marketing Business* (March 1994), pp. 7–9.

7. See Howard Schlossberg, 'Competitive intelligence pros seek formal role in marketing', *Marketing News* (5 March 1990), pp. 2, 28; Gary B. Roush, 'A program for sharing corporate intelligence', *Journal of Business Strategy* (January–February 1991), pp. 4–7; Michele Galen, 'These guys aren't spooks: they're "competitive analysts"', *Business Week* (14 October 1991), p. 97.

8. 'Spy/Counterspy', *Context* (Summer 1998), pp. 20–1.

9. 'Company sleuth uncovers business info for free', *Link-Up* (January–February 1999), pp. 1, 8.

10. Simon Reeve, Nicholas Moss and Dusko Doder, 'Reutergate', *The European* (9–15 January 1998), pp. 20–2.

11. Peter Marsh, 'Is there a spy in your boardroom?', *Financial Times* (18 October 1994), p. 35; Richard Rivlin, 'Suspicion', *The Business FT Weekend Magazine* (27 May 2000), pp. 32–6.

12. Isabel Conway, 'Now there's a slimming pill for podgy pooches', *The European – élan* (30 September–6 October 1994), p. 5.

13. The American Marketing Association officially adopted this definition in 1987.

14. Peggy Hollinger, 'Europe reaches for the cereals', *Financial Times* (4 October 1994), p. 21.

15. American Marketing Association, *Honomichl Global Top 25* (Chicago, IL, 14 August 2000).

16. 'Researching Researchers', *Marketing Tools*, September 1996, pp. 35–6.

17. See Marydee Ojala, 'The daze of future business research', *Online* (January–February 1998), pp. 78–80; and Guy Kawasaki, 'Get your facts here', *Forbes* (23 March 1998), p. 156.

18. See Rebecca Pirate, 'Do not adjust your set', *American Demographics* (March 1993), p. 6; Zachary Schiller, 'Thanks to the checkout scanner, marketing is losing some of its mystery', *Business Week* (28 August 1989), p. 57; Lynn G. Coleman, 'IRI, Nielsen slug it out in the scanning wars', *Marketing News* (2 September 1991), pp. 1, 47; Philip Kleinman, 'Electronics the tool in interviewer's armoury', *Financial Times* (30 March 1990), p. 16.

19. Mikael Hernant and Per-Göran Persson, 'A study of consumers' usage of sales promotions introducing a new type of single source data', in Josée Bloemer, Jos Lemmink and Hans Kasper, *European Marketing Academy Proceedings* (Maastricht, 1994), pp. 335–53.

20. Considerable research has been conducted on how best to increase the response rate of postal interviews. For a review see David Jobber, 'An examination of the effects of questionnaire factors on response to an industrial mail survey', *International Journal of Research in Marketing*, 6, 2 (1989), pp. 129–40; David Jobber and John Saunders, 'A note on the applicability of the Bruvold–Comer model of mail survey response rates to commercial populations', *Journal of Business Research*, **26**, 3 (1993), pp. 223–36.

21. Jacob Hornik and Tamar Zaig, 'Increasing compliance in costly telephone interviews: a test of four inducement techniques', *International Journal of Research in Marketing*, 8, 2 (1991), pp. 147–53.

22. See Thomas L. Greenbaum, 'Focus group spurt predicted for the '90s', *Marketing News* (8 January 1990), pp. 21, 22; *Marketing News*, special issue on focus groups (27 May 1991).

23. Selwyn Feinstein, 'Computers replacing interviewers for personnel and marketing tasks', *Wall Street Journal* (9 October 1986), p. 35; Diane Crispell, 'People talk, computers listen', *American Demographics* (October 1989), p. 8; Helen Slingsby, 'A high street revolution', *Financial Times* (30 March 1990), p. 17.

24. 'Researching researchers', *Marketing Tools* (September 1996), pp. 35–6.

25. For an international review of response differences, see Robert A. Peterson, Dana L. Alden, Mustafa O. Attir and Alain J. P. Jolibert, 'Husband–wife report disagreement: a cross-national investigation', *International Journal of Research in Marketing*, **5**, 2 (1988), pp. 125–36.

26. For more on mechanical measures, see Michael J. McCarthy, 'Mind probe', *Wall Street Journal* (22 March 1991), p. B3.

27. For an interesting discussion of the importance of the relationship between market researchers and research users, see Christine Moorman, Gerald Zaltman and Rohit Deshpande, 'Relationships between providers and users of market research: the dynamics of trust within and between organizations', *Journal of Marketing Research* (August 1992), pp. 314–28; Christine Moorman, Rohit Deshpande and Gerald Zaltman, 'Factors affecting trust in market research relationships', *Journal of Marketing* (January 1993), pp. 81–101.

28. For further discussion, see Gary L. Lilien, Philip Kotler and K. Sridhar Moorthy, *Marketing Models* (Englewood Cliffs, NJ: Prentice Hall, 1992).

29. For more on forecasting total market demand, see F. William Barnett, 'Four steps to forecast total market demand', *Harvard Business Review* (July–August 1988), pp. 28–34; David Churchill, 'Marilyn's bait for the boys', *Financial Times* (30 March 1994), p. 17.

30. For a more comprehensive discussion of measuring market demand, see Philip Kotler, *Marketing Management: Analysis, planning, implementation and control*, 8th edn (Englewood Cliffs, NJ: Prentice Hall, 1994), Ch. 10.

31. Chris Bullock, 'Europe looks beyond Ariane 5', *Interavia* (April 1999), pp. 42–7; and 'Keeping Europe in the Sat-Nav race', *Interavia* (March 1999), pp. 62–3.

32. For a listing and analysis of these and other forecasting techniques, see David M. Georgoff and Robert G. Murdick, 'Manager's guide to forecasting', *Harvard Business Review* (January–February 1986), pp. 110–20; Donald S. Tull and Del I. Hawkins, *Marketing Research: Measurement and method* (New York: Macmillan, 1993), Ch. 21.

33. Lynn Y. S. Lin, 'Comparison of survey responses among Asian, European and American consumers and their interpretations', ESOMAR Conference, Venice (18–20 June 1990), pp. 120–32.

34. For more on the sales force composite method, see Tull and Hawkins, *Marketing Research*, op. cit., pp. 705–6.

35. See Kip D. Cassino, 'Delphi method: a practical "crystal ball" for researchers', *Marketing News* (6 January 1984), sect. 2, pp. 10–11.

36. From Luiz Moutinho, *Problems in Marketing* (London: Chapman, 1991).

37. Karel Jan Alsem, Peter S. H. Leeflang and Jan C. Reuyl, 'The forecasting accuracy of market share models using predicted values of competitive marketing behaviour', *International Journal of Research in Marketing*, 6, 3 (1989), pp. 183–98.

38. For more on statistical analysis, consult a standard text, such as Tull and Hawkins, *Marketing Research*,

op. cit. For a review of marketing models, see Lilien *et al.*, *Marketing Models*, op. cit.

39. Many of the examples in this section, along with others, are found in Subhash C. Jain, *International Marketing Management*, 3rd edn (Boston, MA: PWS-Kent Publishing, 1990), pp. 33–49; see also Vern Terpstra and Ravi Sarathy, *International Marketing* (Chicago, IL: Dryden Press, 1991), pp. 208–13.

40. Jain, *International Marketing Management*, op. cit., p. 338.

41. See Nancy Levenburg and Tom Dandridge, 'Can't afford research? Try miniresearch', *Marketing News* (31 March 1997), p. 19; and Nancy Levenburg,

'Research resources exist for small businesses', *Marketing News* (4 January 1999), p. 19.

42. 'MRA study shows refusal rates are highest at start of process', *Marketing News* (16 August 1993), p. A15; 'Private eyes', *Marketing Tools* (January–February 1996), pp. 31–2. See also John Hagel III and Jeffrey F. Rayport, 'The coming battle for consumer information', *Harvard Business Review* (January–February 1997), pp. 53–65.

43. See Cynthia Crossen, 'Studies galore support products and positions, but are they reliable?', *Wall Street Journal* (14 November 1991), pp. A1, A9. Also see Betsy Spethmann, 'Cautions consumers have surveyers wary', *Advertising Age* (10 June 1991), p. 34.

case 8

Judy Greene Pottery*

ANN M. TORRES**

Doing something harder is what Judy Greene has done and continues to do. In fact, Paul, Judy's husband and business partner, likens Judy to the blade on an ice-breaker ship. 'Judy has to continually break the ice in developing new ideas. Judy never looks back; she is always looking ahead. Like most artists, her *next* piece is the most important.'[1]

Judy is a prominent contemporary potter whose company, *Judy Greene Pottery*, is noted for the quality and design of its output as well as the entrepreneurial qualities of its director. Judy Greene is engaged not only in developing products and designs, but also in managing the manufacturing and retail operations of the firm. Judy's business has been successful, experiencing phenomenal growth rates over the last ten years. Her main concern is to ensure its future prosperity.

Judy Greene Pottery

When aged 31, Judy left the Irish pottery company *Potaireacht Cléire* in 1981 to start her own business. She had no business plan, no capital and no time to take business-training classes. So, she put key figures on a sheet of paper and went to see the bank manager. An overdraft of €19,000 was approved. By 1998, sales turnover had reached €1,000,000. Judy's aim was to achieve €1,250,000+ in sales by 2000 and an additional 25 per cent by 2005.

Judy attributes her success, in those years, to having her workshop on the retail site allowing for close, consistent contact with customers. In fact, customers were vital in providing feedback for testing new product ideas. Judy noted that, 'if it worked it sold. The customers walking through the workshop were like having a marketing department walking through the door every day.'[2] Judy contemplated what to do next. Her handmade pottery has been extraordinarily successful and she wishes to focus on developing future strategies to ensure continued prosperity.

Irish market for giftware and crafts

The Irish crafts/gift market had an estimated annual turnover of €127 million. Handcrafted pottery accounted for approximately 9 per cent of that market giving a per capita expenditure on pottery of less than €2.50. Pottery made in a studio environment (i.e. handcrafted) has 70 per cent of the Irish market, and is usually found at the upper price band for tableware and gift items[3] and is not as price sensitive as other product categories. The craft/gift industry had been a growth market for many years. However, there are signs that growth is beginning to slow.

There are several trends which relate to the Irish craft/gift industry overall:

✦ The young and more travelled customers are moving away from traditional and safe gifts.

✦ The influence from the tourist industry continues to be strong.

✦ The healthy economic climate provides a good foundation for opportunities not only for established firms, but also for new entrants.

Customer profiles

Judy's current customers are mostly female, 25 to 45 years of age and older, coming from mostly middle and upper middle incomes. Many of the younger customers (i.e. mid-twenties to mid-thirties) are newly married couples and/or new homeowners. Exhibit 8.1 gives customer segments. Tourists buy in the retail shop and ship their purchases home, perhaps purchasing again later through mail order. Most of these tourist/mail-order sales are made to customers from the US (90%); smaller proportions are made to tourists from the UK (5%), and other countries (5%). Export sales are made through individual retailers who have sought out *Judy Greene* products or through supplying specialist consumer catalogues. The majority of sales are made to retailers in the US (55%); and smaller proportions are made to retailers from Canada (15%), France (10%), UK (10%) and other countries (10%).

---

* Based on Ann M. Torres' longer and excellent prize winning comprehensive case 'Judy Greene Pottery: Marketing Irish Handcrafted Products', 1999.

** National University of Ireland, Galway.

[1] Personal interview with Paul Fox, 25 August 1998.

[2] Personal interview with Judy Greene, 20 February 1998.

[3] *Market Opportunities – Giftware Market Republic of Ireland*, An Bord Tráchtála, based on estimates given in 1994 and calculated for 1998, pp. 6–7.

EXHIBIT 8.1 CUSTOMER SEGMENTATION FOR *JUDY GREENE POTTERY* FOR 1998		
MARKET SEGMENT	OCT.–MARCH	APRIL–SEPT.
Domestic	90%	80%
Export	2%	5%
Tourist	4%	10%
Mail-order	4%	5%
Total	**100%**	**100%**

EXHIBIT 8.2 VISITORS TO GALWAY CITY FOR 1996	
COUNTRY	PERCENTAGE
Ireland & N. Ireland (i.e. other than Galway)	42%
United Kingdom	17%
United States of America	15%
Germany	8%
France	7%
Other Europe	7%
Rest of World	4%
Total	**100%**

SOURCE: *Galway Chamber of Commerce.*

Customer trends

Customer trends are changing and their tastes appear to be moving slowly away from pottery back to china, porcelain and cut glass. Most important for Judy is to identify and stay ahead of the trends. To identify trends, Judy 'devours' interior design magazines and travels abroad to Europe and the United States to see what is popular and selling there. 'Typically what is selling in Frankfurt now, will be in Ireland in 2 years time.'[4] For this reason, she finds that the timing of new products and designs is crucial. In fact, the idea for one of her best selling products, oil burners, was developed as a direct result of a trip to a ceramics fair in Munich, five years ago. While in Germany, she went to numerous chemist shops to examine the design, function and safety features of various kinds of oil burners. It was one of the most cost-efficient ways to do her R&D work. Thus, when she returned to Galway she wasted little time and resources in developing her final product.

Judy readily admits that reading interior design magazines and examining other markets is no guarantee of success in the Irish market, as design and colour trends may not suit Irish tastes. However, identifying the potential trends and then customising them for the consumers in the home market affords a better chance of success. Judy also relies quite heavily on customer feedback. The retailers and customers who buy *Judy Greene Pottery* are always looking for new designs, so Judy has to stay fresh and respond to their feedback. Judy is aware that she needs to capitalise on ideas for new lines to 'stay fresh' in a highly competitive market. Yet, at the same time, she is also knows it is important to stay true to her own style. Balancing these two concerns is challenging while trying to satisfy customer demand.

With respect to design preferences, 10 years ago when Judy started, flowers and flowery designs were 'in'. Now she has to consider what the upcoming generations want, as they will be the customers of the future. The younger age groups are more interested in simpler, more classical lines of design. Judy believes that 'younger customers are looking for something Irish, but not hackneyed symbols of shamrocks and shillelaghs'. In response, Judy introduced her *Connemara Collection* to appeal to the younger markets.

Furthermore, Galway being a tourist town, there are the tastes of visitors to consider. Judy has noticed that the English tourists love the flowery designs and will buy everything in the shop. German visitors prefer the simpler designs and buy the larger, exclusive, unique and one-of-a-kind pottery pieces. The American visitors will be one of two types: either ones that buy 'seconds' from the bargain baskets; or ones who buy entire dinner sets, because they like the design and consider money to be no object. Finally, the French and Italian tourists do not buy a lot of pottery and prefer to purchase items in *Design Concourse Ireland*.

As a member of the Galway Chamber of Commerce, Judy does have access to a research report, *Galway Tourism 1997*. According to this report, there were 920,000 visitors to Galway City in 1996 (see Exhibit 8.2) spending an average of €21.34 on gifts.

Focus group research

Although Judy believed she had a good understanding of her loyal customers, she thought it worthwhile to investigate various other (potential) customer segments. Her objectives in pursuing this research were to learn more about:

✦ where people got their ideas for fashion, interior design and home furnishings;

✦ their general perceptions of porcelain, china, and pottery;

✦ what brands of pottery they knew, liked, and bought (i.e. for themselves or a gift);

✦ their buying patterns and criteria when buying pottery.

---

[4] Personal interview with Judy Greene, 10 August 1998.

Exhibit 8.3 Summary of customer profiles

FOCUS GROUPS:	Young Graduates	Professionals	Homemakers	Loyal Customers
Customer segment	Future customers	High disposable income customers	Mature customers	Core customer base
Description of personal style	'Classical casuals'	'Practical minimalist'	'Functional traditionalist'	'Timeless modernist'
Purchase motivations	Brand, style and current trends	Convenience, practicality, functionality and value	Function, personal taste and habit (not by brand and fashion)	Quality, function, consistent with own styles – i.e. timeless, smart, won't date
Perception of current fashion	Retro, 1950s style, tailored, classical casual	Space, efficiency, functionality, bright, airy, timeless, simplistic, minimalist	Natural, wood and earth tones, changes slowly over time	Country style, spacious, airy, more for younger people
Pottery preferred (i.e. with respect to style, design, colour etc.)	Simpler, less fussy designs, in bold colours and shapes – like a lot of variety	Clean, simple lines, in white, natural and terracotta tones	Traditional (terracotta) designs and lines in muted colours	Classical lines with a modern twist, but timeless
Q1: Where do you get ideas for fashion, interior design and home furnishings?	Magazines, peers, shop windows, self, 'what I like'	Magazines, peers, friends, i.e. what others did in their homes	Magazines, out of own head, friends and relatives	Irish magazines, visit the shops, own style
Q2: How do you describe your own style and that of your surroundings (i.e. home or accommodation)	Own style is casual, easy to maintain, comfortable; style, brand and quality conscious, very fashion conscious, very aware of trends	Practical, comfortable, focused, minimalist, simple, convenient, consistent	Casual, functional, individualistic, not overly concerned about fashion	Classical, good quality, elegant, independent thinkers, smart styles, not too trendy or dated, old-style with a modern twist
Q3: Words you associate with china and porcelain?	Formal, dainty, dust-collectors, old-fashioned, out of date	Too outdated, costly, expensive, fussy, delicate, irritating	Dainty, impractical, unused, flowery, expensive, not for everyday use	Delicate, lovely, pretty, formal dining room, formal, never used
Q4: Words you associate with pottery?	Earthy, natural, raw/unaffected, in fashion	Functional, chunky, durable, heavy	Chunky, practical, functional, old-fashioned	Warm, earthy, comforting, casual, intimate
Q5: What are important factors when buying pottery?	Colour, shape, design, texture, depends on occasion	Occasion (gift) recipient's taste and preferences, look and design, function, and price	Practicality, functional, shape, colour, simplicity, design, style	Shape, colour, functionality
Q6: What brands of pottery are you most familiar with (i.e. name recognition)?	Stephen Pearce, Judy Greene, and to lesser extent Nicholas Mosse, Michael Kennedy	Stephen Pearce, Judy Greene and to a lesser extent Nicholas Mosse	Stephen Pearce, Judy Greene and Nicholas Mosse	Stephen Pearce, Jack O'Patsy, Judy Greene, Louis Mulcahy and Nicholas Mosse
Q7: How important is the brand (name) in general and when purchasing pottery?	Very brand and style conscious	Brand not a big issue – more emphasis on function, convenience, comfort and price–value relationship	Brand name is not important	Appreciate value of brand, but brand name is more important for gifts
Q8: How important is price when purchasing pottery?	Brand carries (a lot) more importance, but they also look at price carefully	Value conscious more than price conscious	Price is not very important	Price is not at all important
Q9: How important is in-store service?	Very important	Convenience is very important	Important part of the purchase experience	Extremely important

Judy was interested in qualitative information that explained why people think or feel the way they do and so hired a market research firm to organise and facilitate focus group interviews. The researchers identified four customer types.

Young Graduates – future customers The average age of participants in this focus group was 23 years. All participants had finished their undergraduate studies. At the time of the interviews, they were in the process of postgraduate studies, or in their first job. None of them owned their own home, and they were living either in the family home or in rented accommodation.

The *Young Graduates* described themselves as being very style and fashion conscious. They were very aware of current fashion trends. In addition, many of them liked to buy branded products and perceived that a good brand name added value to their purchases. Most of their influences came from magazines, shop windows or their peers. However, they also had a clear idea of what they liked and the designs and styles they preferred.

Professionals – higher disposable income customers
The average age of participants in this focus group was 36 years. All participants were homeowners and professional women in a full-time job. The majority of these women were married and had families (i.e. children).

The *Professionals* viewed themselves as very practical individuals who preferred comfort, convenience and simplicity in their surroundings and clothing. Terms such as 'very convenient, no thought involved, easy to manage and maintain, comfortable and practical' were mentioned frequently as important factors for purchases to suit their lifestyle. Many of the *Professionals* expressed that they led busy, hectic lives and sought purchases that made their lives easier.

Homemakers – mature customers The average age of participants in this focus group was 50 years and they had had their home for a number of years. Many of the women identified themselves as homemakers, although many of them work outside the home, or did so at one time. All the women were married and the majority had families (i.e. children).

The *Homemakers* felt that words such as 'casual, functional, traditional and classical' most accurately described themselves and their preferred surroundings. Influences on their choice of style came from themselves and from magazines, as well as from their friends and relatives. However, they did not believe they were influenced by trends in fashion. Essentially, they had

developed their own style and preferred to 'stick with it'.

Loyal Customers – core customer base The fourth focus group was composed of loyal Judy Greene customers. As this was the only criterion, participants' profiles were more diverse than in the other focus groups. The women ranged in age from 35 to 67 years. All the women had their own home. Most of them were married and many of them had children. Half of the participants were professional women in full-time positions, and ranged in age from 37 to 54 years, while the other half identified themselves as homemakers, and ranged in age from 35 to 67 years.

The *Loyal Customers* perceived themselves to be independent thinkers. They did not believe they were heavily influenced by trends in fashion and interior design. In general, they favoured clothing and home furnishings that were 'classical, elegant, and of good quality'. Although they appreciated classical styling, they did not view themselves as traditional. Consequently, they clarified that they preferred 'an old style with a modern twist, and a mix of antique and modern furnishings'. Essentially, they liked 'things that won't date, that are smart, but not too trendy'. Many of these women expressed an opinion that 'fashion was for younger people'. Essentially, they felt they were at a stage in their lives where their identities were established and they were comfortable with themselves.

As a whole, the groups preferred pottery to china and porcelain. Still, each group did have distinct characteristics in terms of motivation for purchase, importance of branding, purchase criteria, and preferences for style, design, colour etc. Exhibit 8.3 summarises the participants' responses from the focus group interviews.

Questions

1. Classify the types of marketing research used by Judy Greene over her firm's evolution.

2. What market research would you suggest that Judy Greene should have done before starting up her business?

3. To what extent did the qualitative research reported fulfil Judy Greene's research objectives?

4. Based on the research conducted so far, what recommendations would you make to Judy Greene concerning the way ahead for her company?

5. What further research would you recommend she does?

internet exercises

Internet exercises for this chapter can be found on the student site of the MYPHLIP Web Site at www.booksites.net/kotler.

part three

Core strategy

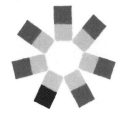

'The meek shall inherit the earth, but they'll not increase market share.'

WILLIAM G. MCGOWAN

part introduction

PART THREE OF *PRINCIPLES OF MARKETING* covers core strategy, the centre of the marketing process.

Within core strategy, marketing knowledge is made into the strategies that guide marketing action. Businesses mostly succeed by concentrating on a group of customers they can serve better than anyone else. Chapter 9 explains how markets can be broken down into customer segments and how to choose the ones to target. Chapter 10 then looks at ways to address the target segments by creating mental associations that attract customers to the product or services.

A Levi ad once claimed that 'quality never goes out of style'. That has become a byword for much of modern marketing, as marketers try to escape from making single transactions with customers to establishing relationships that both enjoy. Chapter 11 returns to marketing's central belief in customer satisfaction to see how quality, value and service can help.

Increasingly, it is not enough for marketers to look at customers; they must also look at what their competitors are doing and respond to them. Chapter 12 shows that success in marketing does not mean direct confrontation with competitors. It is often best to find new ways to please customers that build upon a business's unique strengths.

chapter nine

Market segmentation and targeting: satisfying human needs

Chapter objectives *After reading this chapter, you should be able to:*

- Define market segmentation and market targeting.

- List and discuss the primary bases for segmenting consumer and business markets.

- Explain how companies identify attractive market segments and choose a market-coverage strategy.

introduction

Target marketing
Directing a company's effort towards serving one or more groups of customers sharing common needs or characteristics.

Market segmentation
Dividing a market into distinct groups of buyers with different needs, characteristics or behaviour, who might require separate products or marketing mixes.

Market targeting
The process of evaluating each market segment's attractiveness and selecting one or more segments to enter.

Organisations that sell to consumer and business markets recognise that they cannot appeal to all buyers in those markets or at least not to all buyers in the same way. Buyers are too numerous, too widely scattered and too varied in their needs and buying practices. Companies vary widely in their abilities to serve different segments of the market. Rather than trying to compete in an entire market, sometimes against superior competitors, each company must identify the parts of the market that it can serve best. Segmentation is thus a compromise between mass marketing, which assumes everyone can be treated the same, and the assumption that each person needs a dedicated marketing effort.

Few companies now use mass marketing. Instead, they practise **target marketing** – identifying market segments, selecting one or more of them, and developing products and marketing mixes tailored to each. In this way, sellers can develop the right product for each target market and adjust their prices, distribution channels and advertising to reach the target market efficiently. Instead of scattering their marketing efforts (the 'shotgun' approach), they can focus on the buyers who have greater purchase interest (the 'rifle' approach).

Figure 9.1 shows the major steps in target marketing. **Market segmentation** means dividing a market into distinct groups of buyers with different needs, characteristics or behaviours, who might require separate products or marketing mixes. The company identifies different ways to segment the market and develops profiles of the resulting market segments. **Market targeting** involves evaluating each market segment's

preview case

Procter & Gamble: how many is too many?

Procter & Gamble is the market leader in the US and the European detergent markets. Its laundry detergents alone include Ariel, Bold, Cheer, Dash Tide, Dreft, Era, Gain, Ivory Snow and Oxydol. Besides its many detergents Procter & Gamble sells eight brands of hand soap (Zest, Coast, Ivory, Safeguard, Camay, Oil of Olay, Kirk's and Lava); six shampoos (Prell, Head & Shoulders, Ivory, Pert, Pantene and Vidal Sassoon); four brands each of liquid dish-washing detergents (Joy, Ivory, Dawn and Liquid Cascade), toothpaste (Crest, Gleam, Complete and Denquel), coffee (Folger's, High Point, Butternut and Maryland Club) and toilet tissue (Charmin, White Cloud, Banner and Summit); three brands of floor cleaner (Spic & Span, Top Job and Mr Clean); and two brands each of deodorant (Secret and Sure), cooking oil (Crisco and Puritan), fabric softener (Downy and Bounce) and disposable nappies (Pampers and Luvs). Moreover, many of the brands are offered in several sizes and formulations (for example, you can buy large or small packages of powdered or liquid Tide in any of three forms – regular, unscented or with bleach).

These P&G brands compete with one another on the same supermarket shelves. Why would P&G introduce several brands in one category instead of concentrating its resources on a single leading brand? The answer lies in different people wanting different *mixes of benefits* from the products they buy. Take laundry detergents as an example. People use laundry detergents to get their clothes clean. They also want other things from their detergents – such as economy, bleaching powder, fabric softening, fresh smell, strength or mildness and suds. We all want *some* of every one of these benefits from our detergent, but we may have different *priorities* for each benefit. To some people, cleaning and bleaching power are most important; to others, fabric softening matters most; still others want a mild, fresh-scented detergent. Thus there are groups – or segments – of laundry detergent buyers and each segment seeks a special combination of benefits.

Procter & Gamble has identified at least nine important laundry detergent segments, along with numerous subsegments, and has developed a different brand designed to meet the special needs of each. P&G's brands aim at different segments, for example:

♦ *Tide* is 'so powerful, it cleans down to the fibre'. It's the all-purpose family detergent for extra-tough laundry jobs. 'Tide's in, dirt's out.' *Tide with Bleach* is 'so powerful, it whitens down to the fibre'.

♦ *Oxydol* contains bleach. It 'makes your white clothes really white and your coloured clothes really bright. So don't reach for the bleach – grab a box of Ox!'

♦ *Bold* is the detergent with fabric softener. It 'cleans, softens and controls static'. Bold liquid adds 'the fresh fabric softener scent'.

♦ *Dash* is P&G's value entry. It 'attacks tough dirt', but 'Dash does it for a great low price'.

♦ *Era Plus* has 'built-in stain removers'. It 'gets tough stains out and does a great job on your whole wash too'.

By segmenting the market and having several detergent brands, P&G has an attractive offering for customers in all important preference groups. All its brands combined hold a market share much greater than any single brand could obtain.[1]

Questions

1. What are the costs and benefits to P&G and customers of spreading its marketing effort across so many brands rather than concentrating on one?

2. If you were in competition with P&G, would you match it brand for brand, concentrate on fewer segments or try to find new ones?

3. Suggest alternative segments for P&G to enter and suggest how the brands for that segment should be promoted.

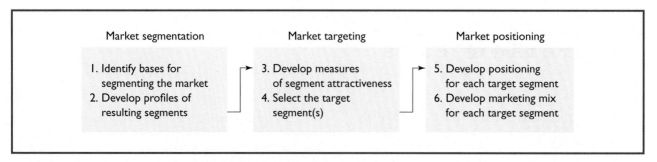

Figure 9.1

Six steps in market segmentation, targeting and positioning

attractiveness and selecting one or more of the market segments to enter. **Market positioning** is setting the competitive positioning for the product and creating a detailed marketing mix. We discuss each of these steps in turn.

Market positioning
Arranging for a product to occupy a clear, distinctive and desirable place relative to competing products in the minds of target consumers. Formulating competitive positioning for a product and a detailed marketing mix.

market segmentation

Markets consist of buyers, and buyers differ in one or more ways. They may differ in their wants, resources, locations, buying attitudes and buying practices. Through market segmentation, companies divide large, heterogeneous markets into smaller segments that can be reached more efficiently with products and services that match their unique needs. In this section, we discuss seven important segmentation topics: levels of market segmentation, segmenting consumer markets, segmenting business markets, segmenting international markets, multivariate segmentation, developing market segments and requirements for effective segmentation.

levels of market segmentation

Because buyers have unique needs and wants, each buyer is potentially a separate market. Ideally, then, a seller might design a separate marketing programme for each buyer. However, although some companies attempt to serve buyers individually, many others face larger numbers of smaller buyers and do not find complete segmentation worthwhile. Instead, they look for broader classes of buyers who differ in their product needs or buying responses. Thus, market segmentation can be carried out at many different levels. Companies can practise no segmentation (mass marketing), complete segmentation (micromarketing) or something in between (segment marketing or niche marketing).

■ Mass marketing

Mass marketing
Using almost the same product, promotion and distribution for all consumers.

Companies have not always practised target marketing. In fact, for most of the twentieth century, major consumer-products companies held fast to **mass marketing** – mass producing, mass distributing and mass promoting about the same product in about the same way to all consumers. Henry Ford epitomised this marketing strategy when he offered the Model T Ford to all buyers; they could have the car 'in any colour as long as it is black'. That cost Ford the world market leadership that it has never regained.

The traditional argument for mass marketing is that it creates the largest potential market, which leads to the lowest costs, which in turn can translate into either lower prices or higher margins. However, many factors now make mass marketing more difficult. For example, the world's mass markets have slowly splintered into a profusion of smaller segments – from those living near the Arctic to the tropics; from the grey market to the gay market. It is increasingly hard to create a single product or programme that appeals to all of these diverse groups. The proliferation of advertising media and distribution channels has also made it difficult to practise 'one size fits all' marketing:

> American and British stars' dominance of pop music is declining as the world's teenagers increasingly buy more local music. One reason is the fragmentation of America's own pop market into rap, hip-hop, grunge, new country, etc. that appeals to distinct US markets. According to EMI's Rupert Perry: 'Trying to sell the Europeans some of that is like selling to somebody in LA a yodelling band from Munich.' The low-cost technology of modern recording that has driven the American fragmentation is also allowing local European acts to record and gain media attention. The result is Euro pop stars such as Polygram's Andrea Bocelli, a blind Italian tenor, and MCA's Swedish pop sensation, Aqua.

Not surprisingly, many companies are retreating from mass marketing and turning to segmented marketing.

■ Segmenting markets

A company that practises **segment marketing** recognises that buyers differ in their needs, perceptions and buying behaviours. The company tries to isolate broad segments that make up a market and adapts its offers to match more closely the needs of one or more segments. Thus, BMW has designed specific models for different income and age groups. In fact, it sells models for segments with varied *combinations* of age and income: for instance, the short wheelbase 3 series for young urban drivers. Hilton markets to a variety of segments – business travellers, families and others – with packages adapted to their varying needs.

Segment marketing
Adapting a company's offerings so they more closely match the needs of one or more segments.

Segment marketing offers several benefits over mass marketing. The company can market more efficiently, targeting its products or services, channels and communications programmes towards only consumers that it can serve best. The company can also market more effectively by fine-tuning its products, prices and programmes to the needs of carefully defined segments. And the company may face fewer competitors if fewer competitors are focusing on this market segment.

■ Niche marketing

Market segments are normally large identifiable groups within a market – for example, luxury car buyers, performance car buyers, utility car buyers and economy car buyers. **Niche marketing** focuses on subgroups within these segments. A *niche* is a more narrowly defined group, usually identified by dividing a segment into subsegments or by defining a group with a distinctive set of traits who may seek a special combination of benefits. For example, the utility vehicles segment might include light trucks and off-the-road vehicles. And the off-the-road vehicle subsegment might be further divided into the utilitarian segment (Land Rover and Mercedes G-Wagen), light sports utility vehicles (Suzuki Vitara and Land Rover Freelander) and luxury sports utility vehicles (Range Rover and Mitsubishi Shogun) niches.

Niche marketing
Adapting a company's offerings to more closely match the needs of one or more subsegments where there is often little competition.

Whereas segments are fairly large and normally attract several competitors, niches are smaller and normally attract only one or a few competitors. Niche marketers have to understand their niches' needs so well that their customers willingly pay a price premium. For example, Ferrari gets a high price for its cars because its loyal buyers feel that no other automobile comes close to offering the product–service–membership benefits that Ferrari does.

Niching offers smaller companies an opportunity to compete by focusing their limited resources on serving niches that may be unimportant to, or overlooked by, larger competitors. For example, Mark Warner succeeds by selling to distinct holiday niches: all-inclusive family water sports holidays in southern Europe to northern Europeans, and no-kids holidays for older people who want some peace and quiet. However, large companies also practise niche marketing. For example, American Express offers not only its traditional green cards but also gold cards, corporate cards and even platinum cards aimed at a niche consisting of the top-spending 1 per cent of its 36 million cardholders.[2] And Nike makes athletic gear for basketball, running and soccer, but also for smaller niches such as biking and street hockey.

In many markets today, niches are the norm. As an advertising agency executive observed: 'There will be no market for products that everybody likes a little, only for products that somebody likes a lot.'[3] Other experts assert that companies will have to 'niche or be niched'.[4]

■ Micromarketing

Micromarketing
A form of target marketing in which companies tailor their marketing programmes to the needs and wants of narrowly defined geographic, demographic, psychographic or behavioural segments.

Segment and niche marketers tailor their offers and marketing programmes to meet the needs of various market segments. At the same time, however, they do not customise their offers to each individual customer. Thus, segment marketing and niche marketing fall between the extremes of mass marketing and micromarketing. **Micromarketing** is the practice of tailoring products and marketing programmes to suit the tastes of specific individuals and locations. Micromarketing includes *local marketing* and *individual marketing*.

Local marketing   Local marketing involves tailoring brands and promotions to the needs and wants of local customer groups – cities, neighbourhoods and even specific stores. Thus, IKEA customises each store's merchandise and promotions to match its local clientele. C&A's difficulties, which are forcing it to pull out of some European markets, have been blamed upon the centralisation of their buying in Brussels.

Local marketing has some drawbacks. It can drive up manufacturing and marketing costs by reducing economies of scale. It can also create logistical problems as companies try to meet the varied requirements of different regional and local markets. And a brand's overall image may be diluted if the product and message vary in different localities. Still, as companies face increasingly fragmented markets, and as new supporting technologies develop, the advantages of local marketing often outweigh the drawbacks.

> Having few top US or UK artists in their stable, Bertelsmann Music Group (BMG) has led the pop music industry in signing local European acts. Their early lead is paying off in an otherwise lacklustre industry, although everyone's profits are down. 'It is better for a record company to sell 10m copies of one album than 1m copies of ten', explains Deutsche Morgan Grenfell's Tom Hall. It takes an awful lot of Aquas to match a Michael Jackson!

Local marketing helps a company to market more effectively in the face of pronounced regional and local differences in community demographics and lifestyles. It also meets the needs of the company's 'first-line customers' – retailers – who prefer more fine-tuned product assortments for their neighbourhoods. It maintains local variety and colour, but at a cost.

Individual marketing
Tailoring products and marketing programmes to the needs and preferences of individual customers.

Individual marketing   In the extreme, micromarketing becomes **individual marketing** – tailoring products and marketing programmes to the needs and preferences of individual customers. Individual marketing has also been labelled 'markets-of-one marketing', 'customised marketing' and 'one-to-one marketing' (see Marketing Highlight 9.1).[5] The prevalence of mass marketing has obscured the fact that for centuries

marketing highlight 9.1

If it will digitise, it will customise

You walk into a booth that bathes your body in patterns of white light and captures your exact three-dimensional form. The resulting digitised data are imprinted on a credit card, which you then use to order customised clothing. No, this is not a scene from *Star Wars*; it is how you will be able to buy clothing very soon. A consortium of over 100 apparel companies is developing body-scanning technology to make mass customisation the norm.

Although body-scanning technology is still to come, many companies are already using existing technologies to tailor their products to individual customers. Here are just a few examples:

◆ *Levi-Strauss*. In Levi's Personal Pair programme for women, a sales clerk takes a customer's measurements and enters them into a computer. Two days later, the customer receives jeans cut to her specific needs. Additional jeans can be ordered at any time without visiting the store. Levi is now launching Original Spin, offering more style options and men's jeans. Whereas a fully stocked Levi's store carries 130 ready-to-wear pairs of jeans for a given waist and inseam, with Original Spin it will jump to 750.

◆ *www.barbie.com* enables you to make your own Special Friend of Barbie choosing skin tone, eye colour, hairdo and hair colour, clothes, accessories and name. There is also a questionnaire for detailing your doll's likes and dislikes. When Barbie's Special Friend arrives in the mail, the doll's name is on the packaging along with a computer-generated paragraph about her personality.

◆ *Make your own CD*. Several Web companies offer the chance to customise a CD. Simply run through their catalogue, sample tracks, submit your list and your CD is in the mail. Customisers include Cductive.com, cdj.co.uk, razercuts.co.uk and supersonicboom.com.

◆ *Paris Miki*. At this Tokyo eyeglass store, software allows technicians to design lenses and frames that conform to the shape of the customer's face. Using a monitor, styles are superimposed on a scanned image of the person's face. The customer then chooses a style, the glasses are made up and the person walks out with their customised glasses.

◆ *Idtown.com* is a Hong Kong-based website that can sell you any of an almost infinite variety of designs of watches assembled from standard parts and costing the same as off-the-shelf designs.

Although consumer goods are now being marketed one-to-one, business-to-business marketers have been providing customers with tailor-made goods for some time. Often they can supply products and services cheaper and quicker than it used to take to make standardised ones. Particularly for small companies, mass customisation provides a way to stand out against larger competitors. *ChemStation* was a pioneer of this way of doing business.

ChemStation, a small industrial-detergent company, offers its industrial customers individually concocted soap formulas. What cleans a car won't work to clean an aircraft or equipment in a mineshaft. Information collected by ChemStation about a specific customer's cleaning needs is fed into their Tank Management System (TMS) database. Next, they develop a special 'detergent recipe' for the customer, assign it a number, and enter the formula into the TMS. Then, plant workers enter the customer's recipe number into a machine, which mixes up a batch of the special brew. ChemStation then delivers the mixture to a tank installed at the customer's site. The company monitors usage and automatically refills the tank when supplies run low. The customisation system gives customers what they need and reduces costs, resulting in higher margins. Mass customisation also helps ChemStation to lock out competitors. No one – not even the customer – knows what goes into each formula, making it hard for a customer to switch suppliers.

Three trends are behind the growth in one-to-one marketing. The first is the ever-increasing emphasis on customer value and satisfaction. The second is data warehouses allowing companies to store trillions of bytes of customer information. Computer-controlled factory equipment and industrial robots can now quickly readjust assembly lines. Finally, the Internet ties it all together and makes it easy for a company to interact with customers, learn about their preferences and respond. True marketing: giving customers what they want, rather than what the company can produce.

SOURCES: See Erick Schonfeld, 'The customized, digitized, have-it-your-way economy', *Fortune* (28 September 1998), pp. 115–24; Luisa Kroll, 'Digital demin', *Forbes* (28 December 1998), pp. 102–3; Jim Barlow, 'Individualizing mass production', *Houston Chronicle* (13 April 1997), p. E1; Marc Ballon, 'Sale of modern music keyed to customization', *Inc* (May 1998), pp. 23, 25; Robert D. Hof, 'Now it's your Web', *Business Week* (5 October 1998), pp. 164–76; Don Peppers, Martha Rogers and Bob Dorf, 'Is your company ready for one-to-one marketing?', *Harvard Business Review* (January–February 1999), pp. 151–60; Angus Kennedy, *The Internet: The Rough Guide* (2000); and 'All yours' *The Economist* (1 April 2000), pp. 65–6.

consumers were served as individuals: the tailor custom-made the suit, the cobbler designed shoes for the individual, the cabinetmaker made furniture to order.

Customers can still enjoy such 'customised marketing'. Vick Nagle's Constant Tailoring still visits 'gentleman customers' to measure, try and complete tailored clothes made of only the best fabric. Ashby Pine works out of a small workshop-cum-display area in Ashby de la Zouch making made-to-measure furniture. Both owners love their materials and craftsmanship. Ashby Pine has clear objectives: 'We have managed our business down to the level of having a few good customers who we enjoy working with.'

New technologies are permitting many larger companies to return to customised marketing. More powerful computers, detailed databases, robotic production, and immediate and interactive communication media such as e-mail, fax and the Internet – all have combined to foster 'mass customisation'.[6] **Mass customisation** is the ability to prepare on a mass basis individually designed products and communications to meet each customer's requirements.

Mass customisation
Preparing individually designed products and communication on a large scale.

Consumer marketers are now providing custom-made products in areas ranging from hotel stays and furniture to clothing and bicycles. For example, Suited for Sun, a swimwear manufacturer, uses a computer/camera system in retail stores to design custom-tailored swimsuits for women. The customer puts on an 'off the rack' garment, and the system's digital camera captures her image on the computer screen. The shop assistant applies a stylus to the screen to create a garment with perfect fit. The customer can select from more than 150 patterns and styles, which are re-imaged over her body on the computer screen until she finds the one that she likes best. The system then transmits the measurements to the factory, and the one-of-a-kind bathing suit is mailed to the delighted customer in a matter of days.

TiVo is one of a new generation of products that does the thinking for the customer. It is a digital personal video recorder that can store up to 40 hours of programmes as well as being able to record and play back at the same time. More than that, the box learns the programmes its owner likes and sorts out its own recording schedule (the information is also passed back to the programme makers). When wanting to view, the owner is presented with recording customised to fit their tastes.[7]

The move towards individual marketing mirrors the trend in consumer *self-marketing*. Increasingly, individual customers are taking more responsibility for determining which products and brands to buy. Consider two business buyers with two different purchasing styles. The first sees several salespeople, each trying to persuade him to buy their product. The second sees no salespeople but rather logs on to the Internet; searches for information on and evaluations of available products; interacts electronically with various suppliers, users and product analysts; and then makes up her own mind about the best offer. The second purchasing agent has taken more responsibility for the buying process, and the marketer has had less influence over her buying decision.

Ageing rock band Marillion established a dialogue with their fans prior to completing their as yet unnamed album set for April 2001 release by EMI. While still recording in their Racket Club Studio, they e-mailed 30,000 fans on their data base. Fans pre-ordering the album will receive an extra CD and additional artwork in which they will be named. Within two weeks of e-mailing they had 5,500 orders, some offering tremendous support to the band: 'I only want one [CD] but I'm sending 500 quid (€820) because I want to be part of it.' The pre-ordering made the fans happy, and enabled Marillion to cut a good deal with EMI since the record company was guaranteed a hit.[8]

As the trend towards more interactive dialogue and less advertising monologue continues, self-marketing will grow in importance. As more buyers look up consumer reports, join Internet product-discussion forums and place orders, marketers will have to influence the buying process in new ways. They will need to involve customers more in all phases of the product-development and buying process, increasing opportunities for buyers to practise self-marketing.

segmenting consumer markets

There is no single way to segment a market. A marketer has to try different segmentation variables, alone and in combination, to find the best way to view the market structure. Table 9.1 outlines the major variables used in segmenting consumer markets. Here we look at the major *geographic, demographic, psychographic* and *behavioural variables*.

■ Geographic segmentation

Geographic segmentation calls for dividing the market into different geographical units, such as nations, states, regions, counties, cities or neighbourhoods. A company may decide to operate in one or a few geographical areas, or to operate in all areas but pay attention to geographical differences in needs and wants.

Geographic segmentation
Dividing a market into different geographical units such as nations, states, regions, counties, cities or neighbourhoods.

International lifestyles are emerging, but there are counter forces that continue to shape markets. Cross-cultural research has defined five 'mentality fields' for cars in Europe.[9] These show how much language demarcates common cultures and ways of life:

1. The north (Scandinavia).
2. The north-west (the United Kingdom, Iceland and parts of Norway, Belgium and Holland).
3. The centre (German mentality field extending to Switzerland and parts of Eastern Europe).
4. The west (the French-speaking area, including parts of Switzerland and Belgium).
5. The south (the Mediterranean, covering Spanish, Portuguese, Italian and Greek languages).

Self-expression is important to car buyers in all the geographical regions, but the similarity ends there. The western groups seek quality and practicality, the south want value for money, while the north-western group sees their car in very personal terms. The differences influence the cars they buy and how they are equipped. Although all developed nations worry about the environment, they do so in different ways. In Italy, France and the UK, motorists do not see their car as a source of pollution, while in Germany, demand for environmentally friendly cars is growing fast.

Pargasa, the large Swiss investment group, concentrates on francophone Europe. It has ten core holdings including French Paribas, Swiss Orior and Belgium's Petrofina, but these and other holdings are all concentrated in France and the French-speaking parts of Belgium and Switzerland. According to Aimery Langois-Meurinne, the group's chief executive, it would like to extend its core holdings to much more than ten. Geographically it is pulling in its wings from the United Kingdom and the United States, but it wants to expand closer to home. 'We are trying to understand Germany and German-speaking Switzerland', he says, 'but we are starting from a low base.'[10]

VARIABLE	TYPICAL BREAKDOWNS
Geographic	
Region	In the USA these are Pacific, Mountain, West North Central, West South Central, East North Central, East South Central, South Atlantic, Middle Atlantic, New England. Each country has its own variation on this.
County size	A, B, C, D.
City size	Under 5,000; 5,000–20,000; 20,000–50,000; 50,000–100,000; 100,000–250,000; 250,000–500,000; 500,000–1,000,000; 1,000,000–4,000,000; 4,000,000 and over.
Density	Urban, suburban, rural.
Climate	Tropical, sub-tropical, arctic, etc.
Demographic	
Age	Under 6, 6–11, 12–19, 20–34, 35–49, 50–64, 65+.
Gender	Male, female.
Family size	1–2, 3–4, 5+.
Family life cycle	Young, single; young, married, no children; young, married, youngest child under 6; young, married, youngest child 6 or over; older, married with children; older, married, no children under 18; older, single; other.
Income	Under €10,000; 10,000–15,000; 15,000–20,000; 20,000–30,000; 30,000–50,000; 50,000–75,000; 75,000–100,000; 100,000 and over.
Occupation	Professional and technical; managers, officials and proprietors; clerical, sales; craftsmen, foremen; operatives; farmers; retired; students; homemakers; unemployed.
Education	Grade school or less; some high school; high school graduate; university; postgraduate; professional.
Religion	Catholic, Protestant, Jewish, Islamic, etc.
Race	White, Black, Asian, Hispanic and others.
Nationality	American, British, French, German, Scandinavian, Italian, Latin American, Middle Eastern, Japanese and others.
Psychographic	
Social class	Lower lowers, upper lowers, working class, middle class, upper middles, lower uppers, upper uppers.
Lifestyle	Achievers, believers, strivers.
Personality	Compulsive, gregarious, authoritarian, ambitious.
Behavioural	
Purchase occasion	Regular occasion, special occasion.
Benefits sought	Quality, service, economy.
User status	Non-user, ex-user, potential user, first-time user, regular user.
Usage rate	Light user, medium user, heavy user.
Loyalty status	None, medium, strong, absolute.
Readiness state	Unaware, aware, informed, interested, desirous, intending to buy.
Attitude towards product	Enthusiastic, positive, indifferent, negative, hostile.

Table 9.1

Market segmentation variables for consumer markets

Climatic differences lead to different lifestyles and eating habits. In countries with warm climates, social life takes place outdoors and furniture is less important than in Nordic countries. Not noticing the different sizes of kitchens has caused many marketing mistakes. Philips started making profits in the Japanese market only after it made small coffee makers to fit the cramped conditions there. In Spain, Coca-Cola withdrew its two-litre bottle after finding it did not fit local refrigerators.[11]

Many companies today have regional marketing programmes within national boundaries – localising their products, advertising, promotion and sales efforts to fit the needs of individual regions, cities and even neighbourhoods. Others are seeking to cultivate yet untapped territory. For example, IKEA expanded globally using its large blue-and-yellow stores and dedicated out-of-town sites. IKEA was part of a trend towards out-of-town shopping. Its stores attracted customers from great distances, so that countries were served by a handful of stores. IKEA changed its strategy when acquiring the Habitat furniture chain from Storehouse in the early 1990s. The small stores gave it access to passing trade and new customer segments who are less willing to travel. The Habitat chain also serves small towns. In making this significant shift, IKEA is also following the European trend towards town-centre malls. Having seen American urban decay, European politicians are resisting out-of-town developments.

■ Demographic segmentation

Demographic segmentation consists of dividing the market into groups based on variables such as age, gender, sexual orientation, family size, family life cycle, income, occupation, education, religion, ethnic community and nationality. Demographic factors are the most popular bases for segmenting customer groups. One reason is that consumer needs, wants and usage rates often vary closely with demographic variables. Another is that demographic variables are easier to measure than most other types of variable. Even when market segments are first defined using other bases – such as personality or behaviour – their demographics need knowing to assess the size of the target market and to reach it efficiently.

Demographic segmentation
Dividing the market into groups based on demographic variables such as age, sex, family size, family life cycle, income, occupation, education, religion, race and nationality.

Age Consumer needs and wants change with age. Some companies use age and **life-cycle segmentation**, offering different products or using different marketing approaches for different age and life-cycle groups. For example, Life Stage vitamins come in four versions, each designed for the special needs of specific age segments: chewable Children's Formula for children from 4 to 12 years old; Teen's Formula for teenagers; and two adult versions (Men's Formula and Women's Formula). Johnson & Johnson developed Affinity Shampoo to help women over 40 overcome age-related hair changes. McDonald's targets children, teens, adults and senior citizens with different ads and media. Its ads to teens feature dance-beat music, adventure and fast-paced cutting from scene to scene; ads to senior citizens are softer and more sentimental.

Life-cycle segmentation
Offering products or marketing approaches that recognise the consumer's changing needs at different stages of their life.

LEGO's range shows the limits of age-based segmentation. For babies there are Duplo rattles (0 to 3 months), then there are round-edged activity toys made of two or three pieces (3 to 18 months). All these have the familiar LEGO lugs so that they will fit on to LEGO products. Next come Duplo construction kits or toys (2 to 5 years). Duplo bricks look like LEGO bricks, but are twice the size so that young children can manipulate but not swallow them. Duplo kits start simple, but there are more complex ones – like train sets or zoo sets – that are suitable for children with increasing sophistication. By the age of 3, children have developed the manipulative skills that allow them to progress to LEGO Basic. This is targeted at 3- to 12-year-olds. The progression is made easy by the small LEGO bricks fitting to Duplo ones.

Age-based segmentation works until children are 5 years old when fewer and fewer girls buy LEGO and boys' interests diversify. In comes LEGO Pirates (6–12 years), Railways (6–12), Technic (7–12), Model Team (9–12) and so on. Lego's product for the new millennium is Mindstorm, intelligent LEGO bricks. The result of a ten-year, DKr100 million (€13.4m) project, the bricks are programmed via an infrared transmitter connected to a PC. According to Lego's Tormod Askildsen: 'It can be used to make all kinds of devices', such as an intruder alarm set up to empty Ping-Pong balls on an unsuspecting parent visiting a child's room. LEGO has great faith in Mindstorm's ability to enliven stagnant toy sales and woo children away from the virtual world of computer games.[12]

Marketers are continually trying to stretch the age envelope. Teletubbies and Rugrats are movies aimed at kids still wearing nappies. Both based on intensive market research, the movies project diametrically opposed views of life. They do, however, share one feature that has always been a feature of teen fads: parents don't like them.

At the other end of childhood Sega and Sony are trying to extend computer gaming technology into business markets. Sega, which has typically focused on the teen market, is now targeting older customers. According to a Sega licensing executive, Sega's core market of 10- to 18-year-olds 'sit in their bedrooms playing games for hours'. Then, however, 'they turn 18 and discover girls . . . and the computer gets locked away'. To retain these young customers as they move into new life-cycle stages, Sega is launching a range of products for adults under its Sega Sports brand, including clothing, shoes, watches, and sports equipment such as footballs and basketballs.[13]

Ethnic segmentation

Offering products or marketing approaches that recognise the special strengths or needs of an ethnic community.

Ethnic segmentation   The multi-ethnic communities within Europe define market segments for all manner of goods: clothes, music, cosmetics and many others. The communities also nurture businesses that appear beyond their own ethnic boundaries. The Halal Food Authority (HFA) runs a system designed to overcome the widespread abuse of the Islamic system of ritual slaughter. The Authority's chairman, Muhammad Ghayasuddin, estimates that more than 80 per cent of the meat being sold as halal is in reality haram (forbidden meat). HFA's inspection scheme increases the cost of meat but, as Zahid Qureshi, an operator of a halal meat shop says: 'I'd rather have less meat to sell, and fewer customers, but at least be selling genuine halal.'

Gulam Kaderbhoy Noon has expanded his ethnic foods business to a wider community. In just over ten years he has made his Noon Products Europe's largest Indian ready-made meals business. Among his early inventions was Bombay Mix, a spicy nuts and nibbles snack food. He sells 3 million meals a month, many of which are the own-brands of leading grocers. He insists on authentic recipes, methods and ingredients rather than flavourings. Turmeric grows all over India, he explains, '[but] there's one area with a reputation for the very best, and that's the turmeric I want. It's such a small thing in terms of cost, but it's the pains you go to that counts. All good food is in its ingredients.'[14]

Life-cycle stage   Life-cycle stage is important in recreation markets. In the holiday market, for instance, Club 18–30 aims at young singles seeking the four Ss: sun, sand, sea and sex. This boisterous segment does not mix well with the families that the Club Mediterranean caters for. Children's activities and all-day child care are an important part of the latter's provision. Saga Holidays caters for older people. Its prices are kept low by travelling off-peak. Saga also provides insurance for older people and aims to set up and run radio stations for them. Given the ageing population in Europe and other developed economies, Saga looks set to grow.[15]

Gender segmentation

Dividing a market into different groups based on sex.

Gender   Gender segmentation is usual in clothing, hairdressing, cosmetics and magazines. Recently, marketers have noticed other opportunities for gender segmentation. For example, both men and women use most deodorant brands. Procter & Gamble, however, developed Secret as the brand specially formulated for a woman's chemistry, and then packaged and advertised the product to reinforce the female image. In contrast, Gillette's association with shaving makes its deodorant male oriented.

The car industry has also begun to use gender segmentation extensively. Women are a growing part of the car market. 'Selling to women should be no different than selling to men', notes one analyst. 'But there are subtleties that make a difference.'[16] Women have different frames, less upper-body strength and greater safety concerns. To address these issues, car makers are redesigning their cars with bonnets and boots that are easier to open, power steering in small cars, seats and seat belts that fit women better. They have also increased their emphasis on safety, highlighting features such as airbags and remote door locks. In their advertising, some manufacturers target women directly. Indeed, much TV advertising of small cars is now aimed at women, pioneered by Volkswagen: an angry, smartly dressed woman leaves a town house – she throws away a ring, discards a fur coat but, after hesitating, keeps the keys to the Volkswagen Golf. Volkswagen now devotes 30 per cent of its television advertising budget to advertisements for women. Large advertising spreads are designed especially for women consumers in such magazines as *Cosmopolitan* and *Vogue*.

A growing number of websites also target women. For example, the Girls On Network (www.girlson.com) appeals to 18- to 34-year-old women with hip, 20-something-style film, television and book reviews and features. After only two years, this site has 100,000 members and averages 5 million page views per month. Handbag.com aims to be wider in its appeal, providing a service for those less familiar with the web. Handbag.com promotes itself as 'The Ultimate Accessory – a lifeline for most women. Somewhere to keep everything you need to see you through the day.'

With women now representing 45 per cent of web users – up from 10 per cent five years ago – there is an increasing number of portals dedicated to women. Examples are Charlottestreet.com and Freeserve's Icircle. IPC, publishers of *Marie Claire* and many other magazines, have launched Beme.com. 'The channels on the site are very mood based', according to editor Claire Simmonds. The look of the site betrays its origin in the home of many classy women's magazines. Besides being easy to navigate, the site is stylish, easy on the eyes and only contains ads carefully vetted to fit its ambience.[17]

Income **Income segmentation** is often used for products and services such as cars, boats, clothing, cosmetics and travel. Many companies target affluent consumers with luxury goods and convenience services. The brands behind the French LVMH group's initials betray its focus on affluent consumers: Louis Vuitton luggage, Moët & Chandon champagne and Hennessy cognac. The group's links with the UK's Guinness, which owns Johnnie Walker Red and Black Labels as well as Guinness, mean it has an interest in five out of Europe's top ten brands. Not surprisingly, LVMH is growing fast and appears recession-proof. The company's brands are growing and it is seeking other luxury brands. Besides its *haute couture* activities, LVMH owns Parfums Christian Dior, has taken control of Guerlain, the French fragrance house, and is stalking Van Clef & Arpels, the Paris-based jeweller.[18]

> **Income segmentation**
> *Dividing a market into different income groups.*

However, not all companies grow by retaining their focus on the top-income segment. Foreign and long-haul travel was once for the wealthy, but the travel market is now a mass industry. P&O aims to do the same with cruises. Once the preserve of the rich and retired, P&O Cruises are entering the mass market. The mass-market tour operator Airtours is also entering the cruise market and aiming even further down market. It will sail the Mediterranean and the Canary Islands with a ship bought from Closter Cruise of Norway. P&O's marketing director welcomes Airtours' market entry: 'What Airtours are good at is talking to a slightly younger, more down-market group of customers. They will put cruising in people's minds.' Airtours' managing director pledged to 'revolutionise the market . . . You've seen nothing yet. This is a different end of the market to where cruising has been before.'[19]

Established retailers, following the wheel of retailing and developing more sophisticated stores with added values, have allowed new entrants to succeed by targeting less affluent market segments. KwikSave, Lidl and Aldi have taken advantage of this opportunity with a lean organisation, narrow product ranges, economically located stores and a no-frills operation that keeps prices down.

■ Geodemographics

Geodemographics is an increasingly used segmentation method. Originally developed by the CACI Market Analysis Group as ACORN (A Classification Of Residential

> **Geodemographics**
> *The study of the relationship between geographical location and demographics.*

marketing highlight 9.2

ACORN and related classificatory systems

As a direct challenge to the socioeconomic classification system, the ACORN (A Classification Of Residential Neighbourhoods) system was developed by the CACI Market Analysis Group. The system is based on population census data and classifies residential neighbourhoods into 54 types within 17 groups and 6 main categories. The groupings were derived through a clustering of responses to census data required by law on a regular basis. The groupings reflect neighbourhoods with similar characteristics. (Table 1 shows how the main categories break down into increasingly small subgroups and types.)

Early uses of ACORN were by local authorities to isolate areas of inner-city deprivation (the idea came from a sociologist working for local authorities), but it was soon seen to have direct marketing relevance, particularly because the database enabled postcodes to be ascribed to each ACORN type. Hence its use particularly in direct mail marketing.

CACI's own research links the neighbourhood groups to demographics and buyer behaviour, together with the ability to target households. The system, therefore, provides a direct link between off-the-peg segmentation and individuals, unlike earlier methods that only provided indirect means of contacting the demographic or personality segments identified. Geodemographics are now a well-established marketing tool with many types of application from retail location to direct mailing, from town planning to social services. The following are examples:

Category	Name	%
ACORN categories		
A	Thriving	20
B	Expanding	12
C	Rising	8
D	Settling	24
E	Aspiring	14
F	Striving	23
ACORN category A groups		
1	Wealthy achievers, suburban areas	15
2	Affluent greys, rural communities	2
3	Prosperous pensioners, retirement areas	2
ACORN group 1 types		
1.1	Wealthy suburbs, large detached houses	3
1.2	Villages with wealthy commuters	3
1.3	Mature, affluent home-owning areas	3
1.4	Affluent suburbs, older families	4
1.5	Mature, well-off suburbs	3

SOURCE: © CACI Ltd., 2001. All rights reserved.

Table 1 A Classification Of Residential Neighbourhoods (ACORN)

Ikea's catalogue targeting Many companies now use geodemographic segmentation to help their decision making. IKEA, the Swedish furniture retailer, uses it to analyse its customer base. The store provides a vast range of stylish and original furniture, fittings and fabrics at affordable prices, a simple and effective formula that has worked throughout the world. The company retails from large out-of-town stores and sells furniture in easy-to-assemble kit format, passing on the cost savings it gains from this to the customer.

A key element in Ikea's success is its catalogue: produced once a year, it features a broad selection of products. The company's local catalogue distribution around each of its stores represents a large promotional investment. Geodemographic analysis of its store catchment areas helps IKEA define its local distribution plans for the catalogue and to evaluate how effective the previous distribution has been. To do this, IKEA analysed its customer data to see where customers were coming from, and also their level of expenditure before and after the distribution. This helped IKEA predict likely return on its investment in the next catalogue distribution. The analysis also looked at the size and frequency of purchase, and the distance its customers live from each store. Using this information combined with its ACORN classification types has allowed IKEA to improve understanding of the relationship between each of these elements. In addition to determining the postcode sectors that offer best potential for catalogue distribution, this information will help IKEA across its marketing mix to assess other promotional opportunities.

Macmillan Cancer Relief mailing Macmillan Cancer Relief is a charity specialising in attracting funds for cancer relief. It uses CACI's direct marketing services for targeted mailing campaigns aimed at committed givers. Macmillan Cancer Relief, for example, targets high-earning individuals using Investor*ACORN. In addition, the charity uses the CACI-profiled Macmillan Cancer Relief database of committed givers to identify new individuals with similar characteristics to existing givers. This has then been combined with the Electoral Roll for Macmillan Cancer Relief's targeted mail campaigns.

SOURCES: *ACORN User Guide* (London: CACI Information Services, 1993); Mark Mulcahey, 'CACI's customer analysis helping IKEA define their target markets', *Marketing Systems*, **9**, 1 (1994), p. 11; Julie Randall, 'CACI working with Ideal Standard to identify their optimum dealership areas', *Marketing Systems*, **9**, 1 (1994), p. 12; V.-W. Mitchell and Peter J. McGoldrick, 'The role of geodemographics in segmenting and targeting consumer markets: a Delphi study', *European Journal of Marketing*, **28**, 5 (1994), pp. 54–72; also www.caci.co.uk that contains details of these and other cases including www.UpMyStreet.com, an example of geodemographic classification.

Table 9.2

CCN EuroMOSAIC
households across
Europe (%)

Category	Name	B	D	IRL	I	NL	N	E	S	GB
E01	Elite suburbs	8	16	6	4	5	18	1	8	12
E02	Service (sector) communities	22	20	29	12	14	7	17	18	16
E03	Luxury flats	9	7	2	5	8	8	7	3	5
E04	Low-income inner city	5	9	10	8	11	10	1	8	9
E05	High-rise social housing	...	3	...	8	11	4	1	7	5
E06	Industrial communities	12	13	5	19	14	10	18	12	19
E07	Dynamic families	17	8	10	13	14	15	5	9	14
E08	Lower-income families	9	4	12	8	6	7	7	7	8
E09	Rural/agricultural	14	14	21	17	13	17	23	19	6
E10	Vacation/retirement	4	6	4	5	4	3	19	9	6

Neighbourhoods), it uses 40 variables from population census data to group residential areas. Marketing Highlight 9.2 shows ACORN in use.

Geodemographics is developing fast. Databases are now available in all the large economies. ACORN has been joined by PIN (Pinpoint Identified Neighbourhoods), Mosaic and Super Profile. Linking them to consumer panel databases is increasing the power of basic geodemographic databases. This allows trends to be tracked: for example, over a four-year period, 28 per cent more people living in 'less well-off public housing' took package holidays.[20] CCN Marketing has since extended this process to cover the EU using its EuroMOSAIC (Table 9.2).

■ Psychographic segmentation

Psychographic segmentation divides buyers into groups based on social class, lifestyle or personality characteristics. People in the same demographic group can have very different psychographic make-ups.

**Psychographic
segmentation**
*Dividing a market into
different groups based
on social class, lifestyle
or personality
characteristics.*

Social class   In Chapter 6, we described social classes and showed how they affect preferences in cars, clothes, home furnishings, leisure activities, reading habits and retailers. Many companies design products or services for specific social classes, building in features that appeal to them. In the UK, Butlin's holiday camps cater for working-class families. They cater for the whole family, but prominent attractions are variety shows, bingo, slot machines, discos, dancing and organised entertainment. The camps are very busy and the emphasis is upon fun. Much of the accommodation is basic, regimented, crowded and self-catering. Less industrial are the Gran Dorado and Center Parcs chains. Gran Dorado, a middle-class family resort village, has the appearance of a small suburban community of cottages but with too many cars. In contrast, Center Parcs has a carless woodlands layout with an emphasis on the outdoors and relaxation. Further up-market is Club Med whose ski and sea resorts have an emphasis on exotic locations and good food as well as activities.[21]

Lifestyle   As discussed in Chapter 6, people's interest in goods is affected by their lifestyles. Reciprocally, the goods they buy express their lifestyles. Marketers are increasingly segmenting their markets by consumer lifestyles. For example, General Foods used lifestyle analysis in its successful repositioning of Sanka decaffeinated coffee. For years, Sanka's staid, older image limited the product's market. To turn this situation around, General Foods launched an advertising campaign that positioned Sanka as an ideal drink for today's healthy, active lifestyles. The campaign targeted achievers of all ages, using a classic achiever appeal that Sanka 'Lets you be your best'. Advertising showed people in adventurous lifestyles, such as kayaking through rapids.[22]

Lifestyle segments are either off-the-shelf methods from agencies or customised methods for individual companies. Many companies opt for off-the-shelf methods because of their familiarity and the high cost and complexity of developing their own. The ad agency Young and Rubican's Cross-Cultural Consumer Characterisation (4Cs) is a typical off-the-shelf method. It has three main segments:

✦ *The constrained.* People whose expenditure is limited by income. It includes the *resigned poor* who have accepted their poverty and the more ambitious *struggling poor*.

✦ *The middle majority.* This segment contains *mainstreams* – the largest group of all – *aspirers* and *succeeders*.

✦ *The innovators.* A segment consisting of *transitionals* and *reformers*.

The *succeeders* are a successful group of people who like to feel in control. By showing travellers – having lost their traveller's cheques and had them quickly returned – in complete control of the situation, American Express advertising would appeal to this segment. They would be equally attracted to the ability to customise their Mercedes car. In contrast, *mainstreams* need security. They will buy well-known, safe major brands and avoid risk. Highly educated *reformers* would have none of that. They would trust their own judgement and try new ideas. These people are at the forefront of many new trends, such as ecologically friendly products and new tourist destinations.

Lifestyle segments can be superimposed on other segmentation methods. For instance, Third Age Research recognises the different lifestyles of older people. It identifies *explorers* who like to take up new activities, the *organisers*, the *apathetic*, the *comfortable*, the *fearful*, the *poor me*, the *social lion* and the *status quo*.

Based on a study of over 2,000 respondents and 30,000 'snacking occasions', Nestlé developed its own lifestyle segments of the snacking market. Two major segments it identified were the very different *depressive chocolate lovers* and *energetic males*. The *depressive chocolate lovers* are predominantly young women who buy fast food and eat chocolate. They eat chocolate at any time, but particularly when depressed, to unwind or when bored in the evening at home. For these people taste is important, so they buy expensive products, like boxed chocolates, for themselves. Terry's Chocolate Orange, All Gold, Cadbury's Milk Flake and Black Magic appeal to them. In contrast, *energetic males* are young and disproportionately middle income lads. They live at a fast pace, work hard, eat fast food and are reckless shoppers. Work tires them, but they exercise regularly and like lively places. They also eat chocolate in a hurry in the evening, at lunch or at mid-morning or afternoon breaks. Boxed chocolates are not for them, but they get their energy fix from countlines like Mars and Snickers.

Being multidimensional, lifestyle segments provide a rich picture of consumers. The *depressive chocolate lovers* and *energetic males* may be the same age and social class, but the lifestyle segments start to tell us about the people and what appeals to them. An ad for the *energetic males* needs to be lively, social and fast – the product grabbed firmly and eaten. Hofmeister used such a campaign showing George the Bear on a night out with the lads to revitalise the sales and image of its lager. In contrast, Cadbury's adverts show a quiet, solitary woman anticipating and indulging herself with a Milk Flake.

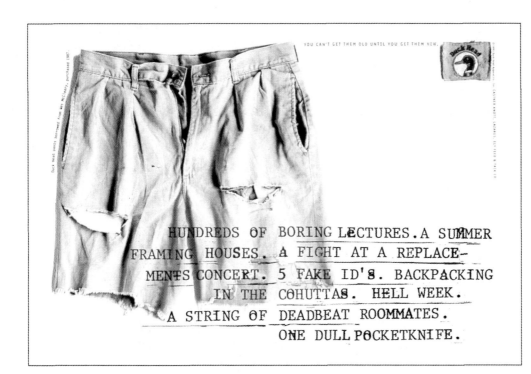

YOU CAN'T GET THEM OLD UNTIL YOU GET THEM NEW.

HUNDREDS OF BORING LECTURES. A SUMMER
FRAMING HOUSES. A FIGHT AT A REPLACE-
MENTS CONCERT. 5 FAKE ID'S. BACKPACKING
IN THE COHUTTAS. HELL WEEK.
A STRING OF DEADBEAT ROOMMATES.
ONE DULL POCKETKNIFE.

Lifestyle segmentation: Duck Head targets a casual student lifestyle, claiming, 'You can't get them old until you get them new.'

SOURCE: Duck Head Apparel Co.

Personality Marketers have also used personality variables to segment markets, giving their products personalities that correspond to consumer personalities. Successful market segmentation strategies based on personality work for products such as cosmetics, cigarettes, insurance and alcohol.[23] Honda's marketing campaign for its motor scooters provides another good example of personality segmentation:

> Honda *appears* to target its motor scooters at the hip and trendy 16- to 22-year-old age group, but the company's ads aim at a much broader personality group. One ad, for example, shows a delighted child bouncing up and down on his bed while the announcer says, 'You've been trying to get there all your life.' The ad reminds viewers of the euphoric feelings they got when they broke away from authority and did things their parents told them not to do. And it suggests that they can feel that way again by riding a Honda scooter. So even though Honda seems to be targeting young consumers, the ads appeal to trendsetters and independent personalities in all age groups. In fact, over half of Honda's scooter sales are to young professionals and older buyers – 15 per cent are purchased by the over-50 group. Thus, Honda is appealing to the rebellious, independent kid in all of us.[24]

■ Behavioural segmentation

Behavioural segmentation divides buyers into groups based on their knowledge, attitudes, uses or responses to a product. Many marketers believe that behaviour variables are the best starting point for building market segments.

Occasions Buyers can be grouped according to occasions when they get the idea to buy, make their purchase or use the purchased item. **Occasion segmentation** can help firms build up product usage. For example, most people drink orange juice at breakfast, but orange growers have promoted drinking orange juice as a cool and refreshing drink at other times of the day. Mother's Day and Father's Day are promoted to increase the sale of confectionery, flowers, cards and other gifts. The turkey farmer

Behavioural segmentation
Dividing a market into groups based on consumer knowledge, attitude, use or response to a product.

Occasion segmentation
Dividing the market into groups according to occasions when buyers get the idea to buy, actually make their purchase, or use the purchased item.

Benefit segments	Demographics	Behaviour	Psychographics	Favoured brands
Economy (low price)	Men	Heavy users	High autonomy, value oriented	Brands on sale
Medicinal (decay prevention)	Large families	Heavy users	Hypochondriacal, conservative	Crest
Cosmetic (bright teeth)	Teens, young adults	Smokers	High sociability, active	Aqua-Fresh, Ultra Brite
Taste (good tasting)	Children	Spearmint lovers	High self-involvement, hedonistic	Colgate, Aim

Sources: Adapted from Russell J. Haley, 'Benefit segmentation: a decision-oriented research tool', *Journal of Marketing* (July 1968), pp. 30–5; see also Haley, 'Benefit segmentation: backwards and forwards', *Journal of Advertising Research* (February–March 1984), pp. 19–25; and Haley, 'Benefit segmentation – 20 years later', *Journal of Consumer Marketing*, **1** (1984), pp. 5–14.

Table 9.3

Benefit segmentation of the toothpaste market

Bernard Matthews fought the seasonality in the turkey market. In some European countries the American bird was as synonymous with Christmas as Santa Claus. He had a problem. In most families, Christmas dinner was the only meal big enough to justify buying such a big bird. His answer was to repackage the meat as turkey steaks, sausages and burgers, and promote them for year-round use. His reformulated turkey is so successful that he is now reformulating New Zealand lamb.

Kodak uses occasion segmentation in designing and marketing its single-use cameras, consisting of a roll of film with an inexpensive case and lens sold in a single, sealed unit. The customer simply snaps off the roll of pictures and returns the film, camera and all, to be processed. By mixing lenses, film speeds and accessories, Kodak has developed special versions of the camera for just about any picture-taking occasion, from underwater photography to taking baby pictures:

> Standing on the edge of the Grand Canyon? [Single-use cameras] can take panoramic, wide-angle shots. Snorkelling? Focus on that flounder with a [different single-use camera]. Sports fans are another target: Kodak now markets a telephoto version with ultra fast . . . film for the stadium set. . . . Planners are looking at a model equipped with a short focal-length lens and fast film requiring less light . . . they figure parents would like . . . to take snapshots of their babies without the disturbing flash. . . . In one Japanese catalogue aimed at young women, Kodak sells a package of five pastel-coloured cameras . . . including a version with a fish-eye lens to create a rosy, romantic glow.[25]

Polaroid shows different uses for its instant camera. Originally promoted as capturing happy family events, the product is now shown in other uses – to photograph a damaged car, an antique seen in a shop or a possible house purchase.

Benefits sought A powerful form of segmentation is to group buyers according to the different *benefits* that they seek from the product. **Benefit segmentation** requires finding the main benefits people look for in the product class, the kinds of people who look for each benefit and the major brands that deliver each benefit. One of the best examples of benefit segmentation was for the toothpaste market (see Table 9.3). Research found four benefit segments: economic, medicinal, cosmetic and taste. Each benefit group had special demographic, behavioural and psychographic characteristics. For example, the people seeking to prevent decay tended to have large families,

Benefit segmentation
Dividing the market into groups according to the different benefits that consumers seek from the product.

were heavy toothpaste users and were conservative. Each segment also favoured certain brands. Most current brands appeal to one of these segments. For example, Crest tartar-control toothpaste stresses protection and appeals to the family segment; Aim looks and tastes good and appeals to children.

> Colgate-Palmolive used benefit segmentation to reposition its Irish Spring soap. Research showed three deodorant soap benefit segments: men who prefer lightly scented deodorant soap; women who want a mildly scented, gentle soap; and a mixed, mostly male segment that wanted a strongly scented, refreshing soap. The original Irish Spring did well with the last segment, but Colgate wanted to target the larger middle segment. Thus it reformulated the soap and changed its advertising to give the product more of a family appeal.[26]

In short, companies can use benefit segmentation to clarify why people should buy their product, define the brand's chief attributes and clarify how it contrasts with competing brands. They can also search for new benefits and launch brands that deliver them.

User status Some markets segment into non-users, ex-users, potential users, first-time users and regular users of a product. Potential users and regular users may require different kinds of marketing appeal. For example, one study found that blood donors are low in self-esteem, low risk takers and more highly concerned about their health; non-donors tend to be the opposite on all three dimensions. This suggests that social agencies should use different marketing approaches for keeping current donors and attracting new ones.

A company's market position will also influence its focus. Market share leaders will aim to attract potential users, whereas smaller firms will focus on attracting current users away from the market leader. Golden Wonder concentrated on regular users to give it a dominant market share with its Pot Noodle and Pot Rice. It was first on the market with its dehydrated snack meals in pots, but new entrants took sales from it. It gained 80 per cent market share by making its brand more appealing to existing users. Kellogg's took a different approach with its Bran Flakes breakfast cereal. Rather than keeping to the original health conscious users, it aimed at non-users by promoting the superior flavour of the product.[27]

Usage rate Some markets also segment into light, medium and heavy-user groups. Heavy users are often a small percentage of the market, but account for a high percentage of total buying. For example, the owner of a pub in a mining town knows that 41 per cent of the adult population of the village buy beer. However, the heavy users accounted for 87 per cent of the beer consumed – almost seven times as much as the light users. Clearly, the owner would prefer to attract heavy users to his pub rather than light users.

Airlines' frequent flyer programmes are aimed at heavy users who, because they are business travellers, also buy expensive tickets. British Airways Executive Club blue card members get free AirMiles each time they travel and other priority benefits when booking and checking in. As usage mounts, Club members are upgraded to silver and gold cards, each giving extra benefits and services. Almost all airlines offer similar incentives, but since benefits mount with usage, it pays the frequent flyer to be loyal. Some operators share their schemes to provide wider benefits to the regular traveller.

Several converging new technologies have young people as heavy users. Once stereotyped as heavy users of clothes and pop music, today's young are leading the market in computer games, use of the Internet and mobile phones. The convergence has not been lost on marketers. The latest generation of computer games machines enable Internet access as well as having the ability to play CD music and DVD movies

– all media highly used by the young. Although the original use of mobile phones trickled down from wealthy professionals to mass use, the young are now the heaviest using and most innovative group. Following this trend, new generation WAP (Wireless Application Protocol) mobile phones that give rapid access to the Internet are being aimed at the heavy user, youth market.[28]

Loyalty status   Many firms are now trying to segment their markets by loyalty and are using loyalty schemes to do it. They assume that some consumers are completely loyal – they buy one brand all the time. Others are somewhat loyal – they are loyal to two or three brands of a given product, or favour one brand while sometimes buying others. Still other buyers show no loyalty to any brand. They either want something different each time they buy or always buy a brand on sale. In most cases, marketers split buyers into groups according to their loyalty to their product or service, then focus on the profitable loyal customers.

Loyalty schemes go beyond the continuity programmes that have been used for decades. They seek to build a relationship between the buyer and the brand. In Australia members of Unilever's Omomatic Club – for people with front-loading washing machines – get newsletters, brochures, samples and gift catalogues. 'Front loaders' are rare in Australia, so the club keeps Unilever in touch with a micromarket that its Omomatic detergent is made for. Nestlé's Casa Buitoni Club is for people interested in an Italian lifestyle and cooking. The pasta market is fragmented and penetrated by retailers' own brands, so the club aims to build loyalty and Buitoni's brand heritage of focusing on enthusiasts. The Swatch's Club was formed after Swatch studied the market for cult objects. Members are helped to build up their Swatch collection and offered special editions.

The effectiveness of loyalty schemes and segmentation by loyalty is limited by how people buy. Loyal customers are few and very hard to find in most markets. Most customers are promiscuous and polygamous in their relationship with brands. Those with favoured brands will promiscuously try alternatives occasionally, and most customers choose from a repertoire of favourites. But even the polygamous brand users change their repertoires and make opportunistic purchases. There is also a limit to the attention customers devote to some brands, plus the low cost of switching from one brand to another. In many markets, attempts to build brand loyalty will, like most sales promotions, last only as long as the campaign. There is also a danger of loyalty being displaced from the brand to the loyalty scheme – the air miles acquired becoming more important than the airline flown.[29]

Buyer-readiness stages
The stages that consumers normally pass through on their way to purchase, including awareness, knowledge, liking, preference, conviction and purchase.

Buyer-readiness stage   A market consists of people in different **buyer-readiness stages** of readiness to buy a product. Some people are unaware of the product; some are aware; some are informed; some are interested; some want the product; and some intend to buy. The relative numbers at each stage make a big difference in designing the marketing programme. Car dealers use their databases to increase customer care and to estimate when customers are ready to buy. Guarantees lock customers into having the first few services from a dealer, but after that, the dealer can estimate when services are needed. Close to the due date the customer is sent a reminder or rung to arrange for a service. Some time later the dealer can estimate that the customer is getting ready to buy a new car and can then send out details of new models or deals. Indiscriminate mailing that does not take into account the buyer-readiness stage can damage relationships. By sending unwanted brochures the dealer becomes a source of junk mail. Even worse, recent customers' satisfaction reduces if they are told about a better deal or replacement model soon after their purchase.

Attitude towards product   People in a market can be enthusiastic, positive, indifferent, negative or hostile about a product. Door-to-door workers in a political campaign use a given voter's attitude to determine how much time to spend with that voter. They thank enthusiastic voters and remind them to vote; they spend little or no time trying to change the attitudes of negative and hostile voters. They reinforce those who are positive and try to win the votes of those who are indifferent. In such marketing situations, attitudes can be effective segmentation variables.

The world charity Oxfam needs to keep donations up and costs down. Segmentation helps it do this. It values all donors, but treat segments differently. A lot of its income is from *committed givers* who donate regularly, but want low involvement with the charity. They get *Oxfam News*, special appeals and gift catalogues. *Oxfam Project Partners* want and get much more contact with Oxfam. These are further segmented by their choice of project, on which they get regular feedback. Through this scheme, Oxfam, like Action Aid, develops a relationship between the giver and the final recipient. *Leading donors* receive special customer care and information about how their money was spent. Many donors can give little time to Oxfam, but other groups enjoy working in the charity's shops or are enthusiastic *lottery ticket vendors*.[30]

segmenting business markets

Consumer and business marketers use many of the same variables to segment their markets. Business buyers segment geographically or by benefits sought, user status, usage rate, loyalty status, readiness state and attitudes. Yet business marketers also use some additional variables which, as Table 9.4 shows, include business customer *demographics* (industry, company size); *operating characteristics*; *buying approaches*; *situational factors*; and *personal characteristics*.[31]

The table lists important questions that business marketers should ask in determining which customers they want to serve. By going after segments instead of the whole market, companies have a much better chance to deliver value to consumers and to receive maximum rewards for close attention to consumer needs. Thus Pirelli and other tyre companies should decide which *industries* they want to serve. Manufacturers buying tyres vary in their needs. Makers of luxury and high-performance cars want higher-grade tyres than makers of economy models. In addition, the tyres needed by aircraft manufacturers must meet much higher safety standards than tyres needed by farm tractor manufacturers.

Within the chosen industry, a company can further segment by *customer size* or *geographic location*. The company might set up separate systems for dealing with larger or multiple-location customers. For example, Steelcase, a big producer of office furniture, first segments customers into ten industries, including banking, insurance and electronics. Next, company salespeople work with independent Steelcase dealers to handle smaller, local or regional Steelcase customers in each segment. Many national, multiple-location customers, such as Shell or Philips, have special needs that may reach beyond the scope of individual dealers. So Steelcase uses national accounts managers to help its dealer networks handle its national accounts.

Within a given target industry and customer size, the company can segment by *purchase approaches and criteria*. For example, government, university and industrial laboratories typically differ in their purchase criteria for scientific instruments. Government labs need low prices (because they have difficulty in getting funds to buy instruments) and service contracts (because they can easily get money to maintain instruments). University labs want equipment that needs little regular service because they do not have service people on their payrolls. Industrial labs need highly reliable equipment because they cannot afford downtime.

Table 9.4 focuses on business buyer *characteristics*. However, as in consumer segmentation, many marketers believe that *buying behaviour* and *benefits* provide

Table 9.4

Primary segmentation
variables for business
markets

Demographics

Industry. Which industries that buy this product should we focus on?

Company size. What size companies should we focus on?

Location. What geographical areas should we focus on?

Operating variables

Technology. What customer technologies should we focus on?

User/non-user status. Should we focus on heavy, medium or light users, or non-users?

Customer capabilities. Should we focus on customers needing many services or few services?

Purchasing approaches

Purchasing function organisations. Should we focus on companies with highly centralised or decentralised purchasing organisations?

Power structure. Should we focus on companies that are engineering dominated, financially dominated or marketing dominated?

Nature of existing relationships. Should we focus on companies with which we already have strong relationships or simply go after the most desirable companies?

General purchase policies. Should we focus on companies that prefer leasing? Service contracts? Systems purchases? Sealed bidding?

Purchasing criteria. Should we focus on companies that are seeking quality? Service? Price?

Situational factors

Urgency. Should we focus on companies that need quick delivery or service?

Specific application. Should we focus on certain applications of our product rather than all applications?

Size of order. Should we focus on large or small orders?

Personal characteristics

Buyer–seller similarity. Should we focus on companies whose people and values are similar to ours?

Attitudes towards risk. Should we focus on risk-taking or risk-avoiding customers?

Loyalty. Should we focus on companies that show high loyalty to their suppliers?

Sources: Adapted from Thomas V. Bonoma and Benson P. Shapiro, *Segmenting the Industrial Market* (Lexington, MA: Lexington Books, 1983); see also John Berrigan and Carl Finkbeiner, *Segmentation Marketing: New methods for capturing business* (New York: Harper Business, 1992).

---

the best basis for segmenting business markets. For example, a recent study of the customers of Signode Corporation's industrial packaging division revealed four segments, each seeking a different mix of price and service benefits:

1. *Programmed buyers.* These buyers view Signode's products as not very important to their operations. They buy the products as a routine purchase, usually pay full price and accept below-average service. Clearly this is a highly profitable segment for Signode.

2. *Relationship buyers.* These buyers regard Signode's packaging products as moderately important and are knowledgeable about competitors' offerings. They prefer to buy from Signode as long as its price is reasonably competitive. They receive a small discount and a modest amount of service. This segment is Signode's second most profitable.

3. *Transaction buyers*. These buyers see Signode's products as very important to their operations. They are price and service sensitive. They receive about a 10 per cent discount and above-average service. They are knowledgeable about competitors' offerings and are ready to switch for a better price, even if it means losing some service.

4. *Bargain hunters*. These buyers see Signode's products as very important and demand the deepest discount and the highest service. They know the alternative suppliers, bargain hard and are ready to switch at the slightest dissatisfaction. Signode needs these buyers for volume purposes, but they are not very profitable.[32]

This segmentation scheme has helped Signode to do a better job of designing marketing strategies that take into account each segment's unique reactions to varying levels of price and service.[33]

segmenting international markets

Few companies have either the resources or the will to operate in all, or even most, of the more than 170 countries that dot the globe. Although some large companies, such as Unilever or Sony, sell products in more than 100 countries, most international firms focus on a smaller set. Operating in many countries presents new challenges.[34] The different countries of the world, even those that are close together, can vary dramatically in their economic, cultural and political make-up. Thus, just as they do within their domestic markets, international firms need to group their world markets into segments with distinct buying needs and behaviours.

Companies can segment international markets using one or a combination of several variables. They can segment by *geographic location*, grouping countries by regions such as western Europe, the Pacific Rim, the Middle East or Africa. Countries in many regions have already organised geographically into market groups or 'free-trade zones', such as the European Union, the Association of South-East Asian Nations and the North American Free Trade Association. These associations reduce trade barriers between member countries, creating larger and more homogeneous markets.

Geographic segmentation assumes that nations close to one another will have many common traits and behaviours. Although this is often the case, there are many exceptions. For example, although the United States and Canada have much in common, both differ culturally and economically from neighbouring Mexico. Even within a region, consumers can differ widely:

> Many marketers think everything between the Rio Grande and Tierra del Fuego at the southern tip of South America is the same, including the 400 million inhabitants. They are wrong. The Dominican Republic is no more like Argentina than Sicily is like Sweden. Many Latin Americans do not speak Spanish, including 140 million Portuguese-speaking Brazilians and the millions in other countries who speak a variety of Indian dialects.[35]

Some world markets segment on *economic factors*. For example, countries might group by population income levels or by their overall level of economic development. Some countries, such as the so-called Group of Eight – the United States, the United Kingdom, France, Germany, Japan, Canada, Italy and Russia – have established highly industrialised economies. Other countries have newly industrialised or developing economies (Singapore, Malaysia, Taiwan, South Korea, Brazil, Mexico and now China). Still others are less developed (India, sub-Saharan Africa). A company's economic structure shapes its population's product and service needs and, therefore, the marketing opportunities it offers.

Political and legal factors such as the type and stability of government, receptivity towards foreign firms, monetary regulations and the amount of bureaucracy can segment countries. These factors can play a crucial role in a company's choice of which countries to enter and how. *Cultural factors* can also segment markets. International markets can group according to common languages, religions, values and attitudes, customs and behavioural patterns.

Segmenting international markets by geographic, economic, political, cultural and other factors assumes that segments should consist of clusters and countries. However, many companies use a different approach, called *intermarket segmentation*. Using this approach, they form segments of consumers who have similar needs and buying behaviour even though they are from different countries. For example, BMW, Mercedes-Benz, Saab and Volvo target the world's well-to-do, regardless of their country. Similarly, an agricultural chemical manufacturer might focus on small farmers in a variety of developing countries:

> These [small farmers], whether from Pakistan or Indonesia or Kenya or Mexico, appear to represent common needs and behaviour. Most of them till the land using bullock carts and have little cash to buy agricultural inputs. They lack the education . . . to appreciate fully the value of using fertiliser and depend on government help for such things as seeds, pesticides and fertiliser. They acquire farming needs from local suppliers and count on word-of-mouth to learn and accept new things and ideas. Thus, even though these farmers are continents apart and even though they speak different languages and have different cultural backgrounds, they may represent a homogeneous market segment.[36]

multivariate segmentation

Most of the time companies integrate ways of segmenting markets. We have already mentioned how Lego segments by age until children develop different interests, and how Third Age Research first focuses on older people, then forms lifestyle segments. There are several ways of combining segments.

■ Simple multivariate segmentation

Many companies segment markets by combining two or more demographic variables. Consider the market for deodorant soaps. Many different kinds of consumer use the top-selling deodorant soap brands, but gender and age are the most useful variables in distinguishing the users of one brand from those of another. In the United States, men and women differ in their deodorant soap preferences. Top men's brands include Dial, Safeguard and Irish Spring – these brands account for over 30 per cent of the men's soap market. Women, in contrast, prefer Dial, Zest and Coast, which account for 23 per cent of the women's soap market. The leading deodorant soaps also appeal differently to different age segments. For example, Dial appeals more to men aged 45 to 68 than to younger men. Women aged 35 to 44, however, are more likely than the average woman to use Dial. Coast appeals much more to younger men and women than to older people – men and women aged 18 to 24 are about a third more likely than the average to use Coast.[37]

■ Advanced multivariate segmentation

In multivariate segmentation, segments are formed using a number of variables simultaneously. We have already introduced some of these – for example, geodemographic segmentation based on census data, and lifestyle segments based on psychographic variables. Marketing Highlight 9.3 tells how this is done. Since multivariate segments are composed of several dimensions, they provide a much fuller picture of the consumer.

marketing highlight 9.3

Clustering customers

Cluster analysis starts with details of more than 200 individuals and builds them up into clusters that are similar. The measures can be demographic (as used in geodemographic segmentation), psychographic (as in lifestyle segmentation) or both. Usually all the data gathered are on a set of uniform scales (say 1 to 7), used to represent demographic attitude, or other dimensions.

1. Cluster analysis first looks at all the individuals and determines which two are most alike. Measures describe how alike the individuals are.

2. It then joins the most alike pair into a cluster that thus becomes a composite individual.

3. Cluster analysis then looks for the next most alike pair and joins them. This could involve the composite cluster joining with one other individual.

4. The process continues until measurements show that the individuals or clusters to be joined are *not* alike.

A dendrogram shows the individual clusters and how easy it is to join them. In Figure 1 the cluster containing 1, 2, 3 and 10 forms early and so do the clusters containing 4, 7 and 9, and 5, 6 and 8. These three clusters could become segments, since they each include objects that look alike. If we try to force the three clus-

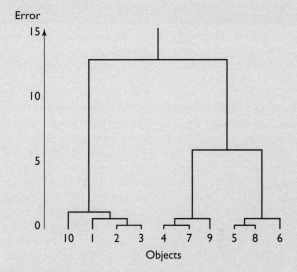

Figure 1 Dedrogram showing cluster formation

ters to make two, there is a jump in 'error' as clusters 4, 7 and 9, and 5, 6 and 8 combine. The big jump suggests there are three natural segments. The individuals in the cluster are not exactly alike, but they may be close enough to be treated as segments.

Cluster analysis identified three benefit segments from 199 meat eaters in the Netherlands (Table 1). Cluster analysis of the discriminating variables gave the segments. The descriptive variables were not used to

	RURAL FAT MAN	URBAN QUALITY SEEKER	ROUNDED MEAT EATER
Cluster size (%)	35	41	24
Discriminating variables			
Quality	1.88	2.20	1.42
Fatness	0.03	0.88	0.63
Exclusiveness	0.92	0.53	0.23
Convenience	0.55	0.59	0.45
Descriptive variables			
Preferences			
Sirloin steak	2.70	6.94	7.52
Pork belly steaks	7.81	4.17	5.56
Brisket beef steaks	6.16	4.93	5.69
Demographics			
Region	East	North	West
Residence	Rural	Urban	–
Gender	Male	Female	–

Table 1 The use of cluster analysis: three benefit segments identified among meat eaters

find the clusters, but they show cluster differences and help target them.

The segments can help market meat products in the Netherlands. None of the segments like fatty meats, but the 'rural fat man' is not worried about fat, likes cheap cuts and is not looking for exclusivity. The 'urban quality seeker' is different. She wants quality, exclusiveness and no fat. She tends to live in northern towns and prefers steak to other cuts of meat.

Although cluster analysis is a simple process, a user has to answer several questions before using it. One question is: What is alike? A Porsche and a Skoda may be alike in size, but most people's attitude towards them is quite different. Another question is: What do you do when individuals join to make a new cluster? Do you take the average of them? These and other technical questions need answering by anyone using cluster analysis. Neglect these issues and GIGO (Garbage In, Garbage Out) rules. Cluster analysis is a powerful method that can produce convincing-looking segments from random data. It also produces different results depending upon how the above questions are answered. The rules for its use are, therefore, test, test and re-test:

1. Use well-proven methods.
2. See if the clusters are 'natural' by re-creating them using different measures of alikeness.
3. Use some other data to see if the same clusters emerge from them.
4. Test the clusters practically to see if they do behave differently. This can sometimes be done using old data. Recently a bank was able to validate its segments by showing how they had responded differently to past sales promotions.

Sources: John Saunders, 'Cluster analysis', *Journal of Marketing Management*, **10**, 1–3 (1994), pp. 13–28; Michel Wedel and Cor Kistemaker, 'Consumer benefit segmentation using clusterwise linear regression', *International Journal of Research in Marketing*, **6**, 1 (1989), pp. 45–59; Dick R. Wittink, Marco Vriens and Wim Burhenne, 'Commercial use of conjoint analysis in Europe: results and critical reflection', *International Journal of Research in Marketing*, **11**, 1 (1994), pp. 73–84.

A multinational drug company used to segment its market geographically until it found that its sales budgets were limited by legislation. That meant that it had to use its detailers (ethical drug salespeople) more carefully. It developed its multivariate segments using the prescribing habits of doctors for numerous drugs. It identified nine segments of doctors with clear marketing implications. Among them were:

✦ *Initiators* who prescribed a wide range of drugs in large volumes, but were also eager to try new ones. They were opinion leaders and researchers, but did not have time to see detailers. This group is hard for detailers to see, but critical to the success of new products. They were recognised as 'thought leaders' and had special, research-based promotions and programmes designed for them.

✦ *Kinderschrecks* have quite high prescription rates and were willing to see detailers, but had few children patients. They are an accessible and attractive target, but not for children or postnatal products.

✦ *Thrifty housewives* were often married women with children who did not run their medical practice full time. They had few patients, prescribed very few drugs and were usually unavailable to detailers. This segment was not attractive.

This allowed the drug company to select target markets for campaigns and help detailers when selling to them.[38]

■ Multistage segmentation

It is often necessary to segment a market first one way and then another. For example, most multinationals segment their markets first regionally or nationally (macrosegmentation) and then by another means inside each area (microsegmentation). This can reflect the changing needs of geographical areas or the autonomy that is given to local managers to run their businesses. Often the macrosegmentation is demographic while microsegmentation is psychographic or behavioural. A Swedish study of an industrial market shows a clear split.[39] At the macro level, the most commonly used methods are geographical, firm size, organisation (how customer firms are structured), age of firm and age of the chief executive. At the micro level there is more variety: firms' goals, market niches, competition, competitive advantage, expansion plans, personal needs, type of work done, customer type and size of customers.

At times, segmentation may reach to three or more levels. In industrial markets, for instance, a third level could be the individuals within a buying centre – the likely user of a machine tool being approached in a different way to the financial director who would have to pay for it.

developing market segments

Segmenting markets is a research-based exercise with several stages. These apply irrespective of whether the method used is simple demographics or complex and multivariate.

1. *Qualitative research.* Exploratory research techniques find the motivations, attitude and behaviour of customers. Typical methods are focus-group interviewing, elicitation interviews or repertory grid techniques. At the same time, the researcher can find out the customers' view of competitive products. It is easy for a maker to define the competition in terms of those making similar products, whereas the customers take a broader view. Once brewers realised that people sometimes drank mineral water or soft drinks instead of beer, they knew the structure of their market was changing.

2. *Quantitative research.* Quantitative research identifies the important dimensions describing the market. Data are gathered by mail or personal interviews from enough customers to allow analysis. The sample size will depend upon the level of accuracy needed, the limits of the statistical techniques to be used and the need for sufficient information on each segment. The usual minimum is 100 interviews per segment; if, therefore, there are three or four unequal segments, several hundred completed questionnaires will do. These are used to produce a structured questionnaire measuring:

    (a) attributes and their importance ratings;

    (b) brand awareness and brand ratings;

    (c) product-usage patterns;

    (d) attitude towards the product category; and

    (e) demographics, psychology and media habits.

3. *Analysis.* The data collected depend on the sort of analysis to be used. The most common process is the use of *factor analysis* to remove highly correlated variables, then *cluster analysis* to find the segments. Other techniques are available. Practitioners often use *Automatic Interaction Detection* (AID), and *conjoint analysis* is growing in popularity.

4. *Validation.* It is important to check if the segments are real or have occurred by chance. *Cluster analysis* has an ability to extract interesting-looking clusters from random data, so this stage is critical. Validation can be by analysing the statistics from the analysis, replicating the results using new data, or experimenting with the segments.

5. *Profiling.* Each cluster is profiled to show its distinguishing attitudes, behaviour, demographics and so forth. Usually the clusters get a descriptive name. We saw some of these earlier: *thrifty housewives* and *initiators* among doctors, *organisers* and *explorers* among older people, or the *energetic male* and *depressive chocolate eater*.

requirements for effective segmentation

Clearly there are many ways to segment a market, but not all segmentations are effective. Indeed, there is quite a gap between the sophisticated approaches to segmentation that are sometimes suggested and what is actually used by practitioners.[40] For example, buyers of table salt may divide into blond and brunette customers, but hair colour obviously does not affect the purchase of salt. Furthermore, if all salt buyers bought the same amount each month, believed all salt is the same and wanted to pay the same price, the company would not benefit from segmenting this market.

To be useful, market segments must have the following characteristics:

Measurability
The degree to which the size, purchasing power and profits of a market segment can be measured.

✦ **Measurability**. The size, buying power and profiles of the segments need measuring. Certain segmentation variables are difficult to measure. For example, there are 30 million left-handed people in Europe – almost equalling the entire population of Canada – yet few firms target them. The crucial problem may be that the segment is hard to identify and measure.

In contrast, the one-time repressed gay market is becoming increasingly important. Some companies, such as Massow Financial Services or the travel agents Sensations and D Tours, are specialising in the gay market. Others, such as the British Tourist Authority, KLM, Royal Shakespeare Company and Absolut Vodka, have products and campaigns tailored to the community. Estimates put the gay market between 6 and 20 per cent of the population and Mintel's Pat Neviani-Aston admits that reliable estimates are few because of people's residual unwillingness to reveal their true sexuality.

Accessibility
The degree to which a market segment can be reached and served.

✦ **Accessibility**. Can market segments be effectively reached and served? Some mainstream campaigns – including those for Guinness in the UK, IKEA in Scandinavia and P&G's Lenor in Germany – have used gay themes. However, word of mouth is very important in the often tightly knit gay community. To this can be added the gay media, such as *Blue Magazine*, and gay venues.

Substantiality
The degree to which a market segment is sufficiently large or profitable.

✦ **Substantiality**. The market segments are large or profitable enough to serve. This is certainly true of the gay market, described by the *Wall Street Journal* as 'the most profitable market in the country'. The gay community shares many of the features of young heterosexuals that makes it very attractive, explains Pat Neviani-Aston: 'dual income, no kids, fairly affluent, higher than average number of holidays, into fashion, cultural events, theatre, good restaurants and hotels'.

Actionability
The degree to which effective programmes can be designed for attracting and serving a given market segment.

✦ **Actionability**. Effective programmes need to attract and serve the segments. There are many cases of this being possible within the gay community. Both Absolut Vodka and Bacardi have strong campaigns built around the gay scene. Both British Airways and the British Tourist Authority have partnered with IGLTA (International Gay and Lesbian Travel Association) to attract US gay customers. British Airways also supports the Rainbow Card, a Visa card co-founded with Martina Navratilova.[41]

market targeting

Marketing segmentation reveals the firm's market-segment opportunities. The firm now has to evaluate the various segments and decide how many and which ones to target. At this point we will look at how companies evaluate and select target segments.

PURE SMIRNOFF. THE DIFFERENCE IS CLEAR.

This Smirnoff vodka ad leaves its target market in little doubt.

evaluating market segments

In evaluating different market segments, a firm must look at two dimensions: segment attractiveness and company fit.

■ Segment attractiveness

The company must first collect and analyse data on current sales value, projected sales-growth rates and expected profit margins for the various segments.[42] Segments with the right size and growth characteristics are interesting. But 'right size and growth' are relative matters. Some companies will want to target segments with large current sales, a high growth rate and a high profit margin. However, the largest, fastest-growing segments are not always the most attractive ones for every company. Smaller companies may find that they lack the skills and resources needed to serve the larger segments, or that these segments are too competitive. Such companies may select segments that are smaller and less attractive, in an absolute sense, but that are potentially more profitable for them.

A segment might have desirable size and growth and still not be attractive from a profitability point of view. The company must examine several significant structural factors that affect long-run segment attractiveness. For example, the company should assess current and potential *competitors*. A segment is less attractive if it already contains many strong and aggressive competitors. The relative *power of buyers* also affects segment attractiveness. If the buyers in a segment possess strong or increasing bargaining power relative to sellers, they will try to force prices down, demand more quality or services, and set competitors against one another. All these actions will reduce the sellers' profitability. Finally, segment attractiveness depends on the relative *power of suppliers*. A segment is less attractive if the suppliers of raw materials, equipment, labour and services in the segment are powerful enough to raise prices or reduce the quality or quantity of ordered goods and services. Suppliers tend to be powerful when they are large and concentrated, when few substitutes exist, or when the supplied product is an important input.

■ Business strengths

Even if a segment has the right size and growth and is structurally attractive, the company must consider its objectives and resources for that segment. It is best to discard some attractive segments quickly because they do not mesh with the company's *long-run objectives*. Although such segments might be tempting in themselves, they might divert the company's attention and energies away from its main goals. They might be a poor choice from an environmental, political or social-responsibility viewpoint. For example, in recent years, several companies and industries have been criticised for unfairly targeting vulnerable segments – children, the aged, low-income minorities and others – with questionable products or tactics.

Even powerful companies find it hard making headway in markets where they start weak. RTZ is the world's largest mineral extraction company, but when it moved into bulk chemicals and petroleum, it found it could not compete. Before moving into a segment, a firm should consider its current position in that market. A low *market share* indicates weakness. Has the firm the energy, will or resources to build it up to economical levels? A firm's *growing market share* suggests strength, while, conversely, a declining market share suggests a weakness that entering new segments may not help. If a segment uses a firm's *marketing assets*, then it fits the company's strengths. If not, the segment could be costly to develop. This accounts for Whitbread selling off its 'unbranded' pub chains that it sees as low-margin activities that lack the brand-building potential of Marriot hotels, Brewers Fayre restaurants and David Lloyd sports clubs.[43]

Mars' excursion into the iced confectionery market proved difficult. The European iced confectionery market is growing, Mars has the technology and brands that stretched well into ice-cream, but it did not have freezers in shops. Freezers are usually owned by Unilever's Walls or Nestlé's Lyons Maid, both experts in frozen food, who had no reason to let Mars in. However, Mars' *unique products* and *valued reputation* allowed it to gain market share against established competitors.

Non-marketing dimensions influence the ability of a company to succeed in a segment. Has it *low costs*, or has it *underutilised capacity*? Also, does the segment fit the firm's *technology strengths*? DaimlerChrysler has bought high-technology businesses because it believes it will gain from them information and skills it could use in its core car and truck activities. Final considerations are the resources that the firm can bring to the market. These include appropriate *marketing skills*, *general management strengths* and the chance for *forward or backward integration* into the firm's other activities.

■ Selecting market segments

Royal Dutch/Shell's directional policy matrix plots market attractiveness of segments against business strengths. We introduced the method, along with GE's matrix, in Chapter 3. Originally developed as a way of balancing business portfolios, it is also well suited to decision making about which markets to target.[44] Figure 9.2 shows an application by an Austrian industrial engineering and construction company.[45]

Figure 9.2

Portfolio of customer segments

Source: Angelika Dreher, Angelika Ritter and Hans Mühlbacher, 'Systematic positioning: a new approach and its application', in *European Marketing Academy Proceedings*, Aarhus, Denmark, 26–9 May 1992, p. 324.

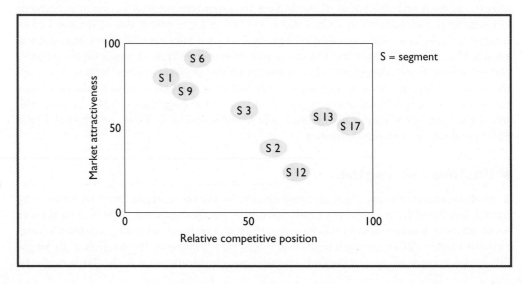

When a segment fits the company's strengths, the company must then decide whether it has the skills and resources needed to succeed in that segment. Each segment has certain success requirements. If the company lacks and cannot readily obtain the strengths needed to compete successfully in a segment, it should not enter the segment. Even if the company possesses the *required* strengths, it needs to employ skills and resources *superior* to those of the competition to really win in a market segment. The company should enter segments only where it can offer superior value and gain advantages over competitors. The company in Figure 9.2 is not very strong in any of the most attractive segments. Segments 13 and 17 look most appealing because they are moderately attractive and fit the firm's strengths. Segment 3 is similar, but the firm needs to build its strengths if it is to compete there. Segments 1, 6 and 9 are attractive, but do not fit the firm's strengths. The firm has to develop new strengths if it is to compete in them. Without the investment the segments are not worth entering, so the firm has to consider the investment needed to enter more than one. Although the firm's strengths are suitable for segments 2 and 12, they are not attractive.

segment strategy

After evaluating different segments, the company must now decide which and how many segments to serve. This is the problem of *target-market selection*. A **target market** consists of a set of buyers who share common needs or characteristics that the company decides to serve. Figure 9.3 shows that the firm can adopt one of three market-coverage strategies: undifferentiated marketing, differentiated marketing and concentrated marketing.

Target market
A set of buyers sharing common needs or characteristics that the company decides to serve.

■ Undifferentiated marketing

Using an **undifferentiated marketing** strategy, a firm might decide to ignore market segment differences and go after the whole market with one offer. This can be because there are weak segment differences or through the belief that the product's appeal transcends segments. The offer will focus on what is *common* in the needs of consumers rather than on what is *different*. The company designs a product and a marketing programme that appeal to the largest number of buyers. It relies on quality, mass distribution and mass advertising to give the product a superior image in people's minds. Advertising and promotions have to avoid alienating segments, and so are often based on product features, like 'Polo, the mint with the hole', or associated with a personality of broad appeal, like Esso's tiger.

Undifferentiated marketing
A market-coverage strategy in which a firm decides to ignore market segment differences and go after the whole market with one offer.

Undifferentiated marketing provides cost economies. The narrow product line keeps down production, inventory and transportation costs. The undifferentiated advertising programme keeps down advertising costs. The absence of segment marketing research and planning lowers the costs of market research and product management.

Most modern marketers, however, have strong doubts about this strategy. Difficulties arise in developing a product or brand that will satisfy all consumers. Firms using undifferentiated marketing typically develop an offer aimed at the largest segments in the market. When several firms do this, there is heavy competition in the largest segments and neglected customers in the smaller ones. The result is that the larger segments may be less profitable because they attract heavy competition. Recognition of this problem has led to firms addressing smaller market segments. Another problem is erosion of the mass market as competitors develop new appeals or segments. For example, Polo mints have faced attacks from competitors aiming at different benefit segments: Extra Strong mints for people who want a strong taste and Clorets as breath fresheners. At the same time, Polo faces direct competition from similarly packaged Trebor Mints in Europe and Duplex in south-east Asia.

Figure 9.3

Three alternative
market-coverage
strategies

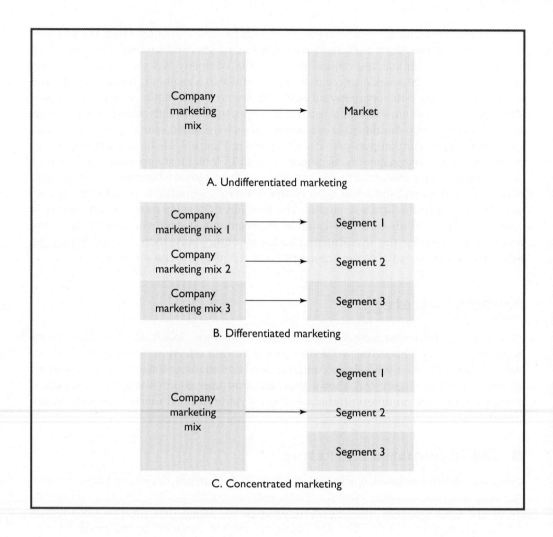

A. Undifferentiated marketing

B. Differentiated marketing

C. Concentrated marketing

■ Differentiated marketing

**Differentiated
marketing**
*A market-coverage
strategy in which a firm
decides to target several
market segments and
designs separate offers
for each.*

Using a **differentiated marketing** strategy, a firm decides to target several market segments and designs separate offers for each. General Motors tries to produce a car for every 'purse, purpose and personality'. By offering product and marketing variations, it hopes for higher sales and a stronger position within each market segment. GM hopes that a stronger position in several segments will strengthen consumers' overall identification of the company with the product category. It also hopes for greater repeat buying because the firm's offer better matches the customer's desire.

Originally Martini products were not marketed separately. Advertising concentrated on the Martini brand and its exciting international lifestyle: 'anytime, anyplace, anywhere'. That changed to having the main Martini brands aimed at clearly defined target markets:

✦ Martini Rosso, the most popular variety, is aimed at a broad sector of the market. Its ads show it being enjoyed by an attractive young couple with 'Our martini is Rosso' or by a small chic group relaxing in elegant surroundings: 'The bitter sweet sensation'.

✦ Martini Bianco is targeted at people in their twenties who like light alcoholic drinks. It is shown being casually drunk with ice by a sporty, boisterous set, out of doors: 'The sunny side of life'.

✦ Martini Extra Dry is for the sophisticated drinker. The advertising focuses on the bottle and the product in an atmosphere of quiet sophistication.[46]

Differentiated marketing typically creates more total sales than does undifferentiated marketing. KLM could fill all the seats on its New York flights charging APEX fares, but its own income and the number of flyers are increased by segmenting the market. In the main cabin or on the upper deck of each Boeing 747-400 taking off from Schiphol Airport, there will be about 300 economy passengers. Some of these, holding restricted APEX tickets costing about €500, will be sitting next to people who have paid over €1,000 for the same flight. They may have booked late or have an open ticket. Forward of them will be about 80 Flying Dutchmen, KLM business-class passengers whose companies paid €3,000 for each seat. In the extreme nose could be about 20 first-class passengers at over €5,000 each. The flight could not operate if everyone paid APEX fares because the Boeing would be full before the airline had covered the operating cost. If only full economy fares were charged, many passengers could not afford to fly, so an economy-class 747-400 could not be justified. Also, some first-class passengers would be deterred from travelling with the crowd. First-class passengers demand big seats, and their catering alone costs over €100 each, but they help maximise the revenue of the airline and the number of people flying.

■ Concentrated marketing

A third market-coverage strategy, **concentrated marketing**, is especially appealing when company resources are limited. Instead of going after a small share of a large market, the firm goes after a large share of one or a few submarkets. For example, Oshkosh Trucks is the world's largest producer of airport rescue trucks and front-loading concrete mixers. Mills & Boon, which has grown to be one of the world's most successful publishers, targets its inexpensive romantic novels at women in search of romance. The company has researched and knows its market:

Concentrated marketing
A market-coverage strategy in which a firm goes after a large share of one or a few submarkets.

✦ Having the word 'wedding' in a book title guarantees higher sales.

✦ The heroine is often plain, not gorgeous, to promote reader identification: 'no oil painting in the way of looks'; kind and polite and pleasant and unobtrusive. And best of all, homely.

✦ The best settings for the story are a hospital or an aircraft (lots of chance for life or death action); doctors and pilots are the best heroes.

✦ The novels always end happily.[47]

Like Mills & Boon, through concentrated marketing, a firm can achieve a strong market position in the segments (or niches) it serves because of its greater knowledge of the segments and its special reputation. It also enjoys many operating economies because of specialisation in production, distribution and promotion. A firm can earn a high rate of return on its investment from well-chosen segments.

At the same time, concentrated marketing can involve higher than normal risks. A particular market segment can turn sour. For example, when the 1980s boom ended, people stopped buying expensive sports cars and Porsche's earnings went deeply into the red. Another risk is larger competitors entering the segment. High margins, the glamour and lack of competition in the sports car market has attracted Mazda, Toyota and Honda as powerful competitors in that market. Fashion changes can also damage the niche's credibility. The yuppies who made Porsche's fortunes in the 1980s are over the recession, but have grown up and now have kids and a different lifestyle. Big, chunky, luxuriously appointed 4 × 4 land cruisers or people carriers are what they want now.

■ Choosing a market-coverage strategy

Many factors need considering when choosing a market-coverage strategy. The best strategy depends on *company resources*. Concentrated marketing makes sense for a firm with limited resources. The best strategy also depends on the degree of *product variability*. Undifferentiated marketing is suitable for uniform products such as grapefruit or steel. Products that can vary in design, such as cameras and cars, require differentiation or concentration. Consider the *product's stage in the life cycle*. When a firm introduces a new product, it is practical to launch only one version, and undifferentiated marketing or concentrated marketing therefore makes the most sense. In the mature stage of the product life cycle, however, differentiated marketing begins to make more sense. Another factor is *market variability*. Undifferentiated marketing is appropriate when buyers have the same tastes, buy the same amounts and react in the same way to marketing efforts. Finally, *competitors' marketing strategies* are important. When competitors use segmentation, undifferentiated marketing can be suicidal. Conversely, when competitors use undifferentiated marketing, a firm can gain by using differentiated or concentrated marketing.

summary

Sellers can take three approaches to a market. *Mass marketing* is the decision to mass-produce and mass-distribute one product and attempt to attract all kinds of buyers. *Target marketing* is the decision to identify the different groups that make up a market and to develop products and marketing mixes for selected target markets. Sellers today are moving away from mass marketing and product differentiation towards target marketing because this approach is more helpful in spotting market opportunities and developing more effective products and marketing mixes.

The key steps in target marketing are market segmentation, market targeting and market positioning. *Market segmentation* is the act of dividing a market into distinct groups of buyers who might merit separate products or marketing mixes. The marketer tries different variables to see which give the best segmentation opportunities. For consumer marketing, the chief segmentation variables are geographic, demographic, psychographic and behavioural. Business markets segment by business consumer demographics, operating characteristics, buying approaches and personal characteristics. The effectiveness of segmentation analysis depends on finding segments that are *measurable, accessible, substantial* and *actionable*.

Next, the seller has to target the best market segments. The company first evaluates each segment's size and growth characteristics, structural attractiveness and compatibility with company resources and objectives. It then chooses one of three market-coverage strategies. The seller can ignore segment differences (*undifferentiated marketing*), develop different market offers for several segments (*differentiated marketing*), or go after one or a few market segments (*concentrated marketing*). Much depends on company resources, product variability, product life-cycle stage and competitive marketing strategies.

discussing the issues

1. What are the benefits of mass marketing versus market segmentation for a business? Discuss in relation to examples of product and service providers.

2. What variables are used for segmenting the market for: (a) casual clothing; (b) night clubs; (c) holidays?

3. The European Union, with its 15 member states, is now viewed as an attractive and distinctive geographic market segment. Do you agree with this view? To what extent can businesses market in the same way to different consumers in member states? What does this imply about market segmentation?

4. What are the merits and limitations of differentiated, undifferentiated and concentrated marketing? Give examples of product or service providers that have pursued these market coverage strategies. How successful were these strategies?

5. Financial services providers are looking to segment their markets in the face of greater competition and ever more demanding customers. Would segmentation work for financial services? Show how financial services providers might go about segmenting their markets and implementing selected targeting strategies.

applying the concepts

1. Alldays, a convenience store, has located two appropriate properties: one in Appleby Magna (postcode DE12 7AQ) and the other in nearby Measham (postcode DE12 7HR). Visit www.upmystreet.com to view the ACORN geodemographics of the two locations and suggest how Alldays' merchandise and promotions should be adjusted to meet the needs of the alternative communities.

2. Being a very large cinema complex, the 30-screen Warner Village Star City has moved away from the mass marketing of most cinemas. Visit www.warnervillage.co.uk to identify the methods used to segment the market and determine how the segments are catered for. How should Star City's retailing and catering be designed to meet the needs and expectations of the diverse segments?

references

1. See Kerri Walsh, 'Soaps and detergents', *Chemical Week* (28 January 1998), pp. 27–9; Christine Bittar, 'P&G sets anti-fade plan for ailing powder detergents: new SKUs', *Brandweek* (22 March 1999), p. 4; and information accessed online from www.pg.com and www.tide.com.

2. Edward Baig, 'Platinum cards: move over AmEx', *Business Week* (19 August 1996), p. 84.

3. Laurel Cutler, quoted in 'Stars of the 1980s cast their light', *Fortune* (3 July 1989), p. 76.

4. Robert E. Linneman and John L. Stanton, Jr, *Making Niche Marketing Work: How to grow bigger by acting smaller* (New York: McGraw-Hill, 1991); Tevfik Dalgic and Maarten Leeuw, 'Niche marketing revisited: Concept, applications and some European cases', *European Journal of Marketing*, **28**, 4 (1994), pp. 39–55.

5. See Don Peppers and Martha Rogers, *The One-to-One Future: Building relationships one customer at a time* (New York: Currency/Doubleday, 1993).

6. See *Harvard Business Review* (March–April 1995), pp. 103–14; Christopher W. Hart, 'Made to order', *Marketing Management* (Summer 1996), pp. 11–22; James H. Gilmore and B. Joseph Pine II, 'The four faces of customization', *Harvard Business Review* (January–February 1997), pp. 91–101; Brian Fitzgerald, 'Mass customization – at a profit', *World Class Design to Manufacture*, **2**, 1 (1995), pp. 43–6; Christoper W. L. Hart, 'Mass customization: conceptual underpinnings, opportunities and limits', *International Journal of Service Industry Management*, **6**, 2 (1995), pp. 36–45.

7. Fiona Harvey, 'Watching me, watching you', *FT Creative Business* (10 October 2000); Christopher

Parker, 'US tunes into TV with a brain', *FT Creative Business* (10 October 2000), pp. 6–7.

8. Paul Sexton, 'We want to be Marillionaires', *FT Creative Business* (10 October 2000), p. 14.

9. Jocken Pläcking, *Marketing-Kommunikation im Autobilmarkt Europa* (Stuttgart: Motor-Presse, 1990).

10. Ian Rogers, 'Pergesa emerges from the gloom under a new guise', *Financial Times* (3 August 1994), p. 21.

11. Marieke De Mooij, *Advertising Worldwide: Concepts, theories and practical multinational and global advertising*, 2nd edn (London: Prentice Hall, 1994).

12. David Blackwell, 'Intelligent as a brick', *Financial Times* (27 January 1998), p. 18; Claire Irvin, *Marketing Business* (September 1999), pp. 36–9.

13. 'Diaper movies: Tommy and Dill', *The Economist* (3 April 1999), p. 99; 'Serious games', *The Economist* (8 July 2000), pp. 129–30; 'Sega to target adults with brand extensions', *Marketing Week* (12 March 1998), p. 9.

14. Alison Maitland, 'Halal meat row divides community', *Financial Times* (27 July 1994), p. 6; Adam Barnes, 'Nawab of cash and curry', *Business FT Weekend Magazine* (30 September 2000), pp. 26–9.

15. 'Can Europe compete? Ageing Europe', *Financial Times* (8 March 1994), p. 14; Rajshekhar G. Javalgi and Paul Dion, 'A life cycle segmentation approach to marketing financial products and services', *The Service Industries Journal*, **19**, 3 (1999), pp. 74–96.

16. See Pat Anderson, 'Car advertisers target women behind the wheel', *Campaign* (8 July 1994), p. 13; Barbara Beck, 'Women and work: Your money or your time', *The Economist* (18 July 1998), p. S8.

17. 'A focus on women at iVillage.com', *New York Times* (3 August 1998), p. D6; Helene Stapinski, 'Online markets: You go, girls', *Sales & Marketing Management* (January 1999), pp. 47–8; Sarah Bridges, 'World wide women', *e.business* (April 2000), p. 78; and information accessed online at www.handbag.com and www.girlson.com.

18. Alice Rawsthorn, 'LVMH see strong profits growth', *Financial Times* (18–19 June 1994), p. 11; 'LVMH and Guinness: rearranging their affairs', *EuroBusiness* (February 1994), p. 6; David Short, 'Nescafé still strongest brew on top shelf', *The European* (22–8 July 1994), p. 22; Ian Harding, 'Take-overs fail to slake Arnault's thirst for a fight', *The European* (5–11 August 1994), p. 32.

19. Michael Skapinker, 'Cruise industry charts mass-market course', *Financial Times* (10 June 1994), p. 11.

20. See Graham J. Hooley, John Saunders and Nigel Piercy, *Marketing Strategy and Competitive Positioning* (London: Prentice Hall, 1998).

21. For an insight on the differences between these leisure parks, visit their websites: centerparcs.com, clubmed.com and gandorado.nl.

22. 'Lifestyle push', *Marketing Week*, **22**, 35 (1999), pp. 71–3; 'Levi's makeover lacks real design', *Marketing Week* (30 September 1999); Orsay Kucukemiroglu, 'Market segmentation by using consumer lifestyle dimensions and ethnocentrism: an empirical study', *European Journal of Marketing*, **33**, 5/6 (1999), pp. 470–87.

23. For a detailed discussion of personality and buyer behaviour, see Leon G. Schiffman and Leslie Lazar Kanuk, *Consumer Behavior*, 4th edn (Englewood Cliffs, NJ: Prentice Hall, 1991), Ch. 4; also Paul J. Albanese, 'Personality and consumer behaviour: an operational approach', *European Journal of Marketing*, **27**, 8 (1993), pp. 28–36.

24. See Laurie Freeman and Cleveland Horton, 'Spree: Honda's scooters ride the cutting edge', *Advertising Age* (5 September 1985), pp. 3, 35.

25. Mark Maremont, 'The hottest thing since the flashbulb', *Business Week* (7 September 1992).

26. See Schiffman and Kanuk, *Consumer Behavior*, op. cit., p. 48, and for a recent sophisticated example see Günther Botschen, Eva M. Thelen and Rik Pieters, 'Using means–end structures for benefit segmentation: An application to services', *European Journal of Marketing*, **33**, 1/2 (1999), pp. 38–58.

27. Jeremy Elliott, 'Breaking the bran barrier – Kellogg's Bran Flakes', in Charles Channon (ed.), *20 Advertising Histories* (London: Cassell, 1989), pp. 1–15; Terry Bullen, 'Golden Wonder: a potted success', in ibid., pp. 178–98.

28. Kim Benjamin, 'Moving with the Internet', *e.business* (April 2000), pp. 18–20; 'Waves of the future', *The Economist* (8 July 2000), pp. 107–9; 'Playing with the big boys', *The Economist* (15 May 1999), pp. 97–8; Sarah Bridges, 'The net generation', *e.business* (May 2000), p. 19; Loraine Wolf, 'Yoof!', *Marketing Means Business for the CEO*, Chartered Institute of Marketing (1999), pp. 44–8; Mark Elliott, 'Net benefits', *Marketing Business* (April 2000), pp. 21–4.

29. For a comprehensive discussion of loyalty schemes, see Mark Uncles, 'Do you or your customers need a loyalty scheme?', *Journal of Targeting, Measurement and Analysis for Marketing*, **2**, 4 (1994), pp. 335–50; see also F. F. Reichheld, 'Loyalty-based management', *Harvard Business Review* (March–April 1993), pp. 64–73; Andrew S. C. Ehrenberg, 'Locking them in forever', *Admap*, **28**, 11 (1992), p. 14.

30. Martin Howard, 'The practicalities of developing better analysis and segmentation techniques for fine focusing and improving targeting', Institute for International Research, Conference on Advanced

Customer Profiling, Segmentation and Analysis, London, 10 February 1994.

31. See D. Sudharshan and Frederick Winter, 'Strategic segmentation of industrial markets', *Journal of Business & Industrial Marketing*, **13**, 1 (1998), pp. 8–21; V.-W. Mitchell, 'Segmenting purchasers of organisational professional services: a risk-based approach', *Journal of Services Marketing*, **12**, 2 (1998), pp. 83–97; Bill Merrilees, Rohan Bentley and Ross Cameron, 'Business service market segmentation: the case of electrical and mechanical building maintenance services', *Journal of Business & Industrial Marketing*, **14**, 2 (1999), pp. 151–63.

32. V. Kasturi Rangan, Rowland T. Moriarty and Gordon S. Swartz, 'Segmenting customers in mature industrial markets', *Journal of Marketing* (October 1992), pp. 72–82.

33. For another interesting approach to segmenting the business market, see John Berrigan and Carl Finkbeiner, *Segmentation Marketing: New methods for capturing business* (New York: Harper Business, 1992).

34. P. G. Walters, 'Global market segmentation and challenges', *Journal of Marketing Management*, **13**, 1–3 (1997), pp. 163–80; Carl R. Frear, Mary S. Alguire and Lynn E. Metcalf, 'Country segmentation on the basis of international purchasing patterns', *Journal of Business & Industrial Marketing*, **10**, 2 (1995), pp. 59–68.

35. Marlene L. Rossman, 'Understanding five nations of Latin America', *Marketing News* (11 October 1985), p. 10; as quoted in Subhash C. Jain, *International Marketing Management*, 3rd edn (Boston, MA: PWS–Kent Publishing, 1990), p. 366; also see Carl R. Frear, Mary S. Alguire and Lynn E. Metcalf, 'Country segmentation on the basis of international purchasing patterns', *Journal of Business & Industrial Marketing*, **10**, 2 (1995), pp. 59–68.

36. Subhash C. Jain, *International Marketing Management*, 3rd edn (Boston, MA: PWS–Kent Publishing, 1990), p. 366.

37. Thomas Exter, 'Deodorant demographics', *American Demographics* (December 1987), p. 39.

38. Taken from Jens Maier and John Saunders, 'The implementation of segmentation in sales management', *Journal of Personal Selling and Sales Management*, **10**, 1 (1990), pp. 39–48.

39. Gert-Olof Boström and Timothy L. Wilson, 'Market segmentation in professional services – case of CAD adoption amongst architectural firms', European Marketing Academy Proceedings, Barcelona, Spain,

25–8 May 1993, pp. 249–60; Carl R. Frear, Mary S. Alguire and Lynn E. Metcalf, 'Country segmentation on the basis of international purchasing patterns', *Journal of Business & Industrial Marketing*, **10**, 2 (1995), pp. 59–68.

40. Mark Jenkins and Malcolm MacDonald, 'Market segmentation: organisational archetypes and research agendas', *European Journal of Marketing*, **31**, 1 (1997), pp. 17–32; Francisco J. Sarabia, 'Model for market segments: evaluation and selection', *European Journal of Marketing*, **30**, 1 (1996), pp. 58–74; Erwin Danneels, 'Market segmentation: normative model versus business reality: an explanatory study of the apparel market in Belgium', *European Journal of Marketing*, **30**, 12 (1996), pp. 39–49.

41. Robert Dwek, 'Pursuing the Pink', *Marketing Business* (May 1999), pp. 12–15; 'Much more than a good night out', *The Economist* (30 October 1999), p. 37.

42. For an example of how customer profitability can be used to determine target segments in the Scandinavian banking industry, see K. Storbacka, 'Segmentation based on customer profitability – retrospective analysis of retail banking customer bases', *Journal of Marketing Management*, **13**, 5 (1997), pp. 479–93.

43. John Thornhill and Lina Saigol, 'Future Whitbread butterfly emerges from its chrysalis', *Financial Times* (20 October 2000), p. 26.

44. The methods are introduced in S. J. Q. Robinson, R. E. Hitchins and D. P. Wade, 'The directional policy matrix: tool for strategic planning', *Long Range Planning*, **11**, 3 (1978), pp. 8–15; Yoram Wind and Vejay Mahajan, 'Designing product and business portfolios', *Harvard Business Review* (January–February 1981), pp. 155–65. They are reviewed in Robin Wensley, 'Strategic marketing: boxes, betas or basics', *Journal of Marketing*, **45**, 3 (Summer 1981), pp. 173–82.

45. Angelika Dreher, Angelika Ritter and Hans Mühlbacher, 'Systematic positioning: a new approach and its application', European Marketing Academy Proceedings, Aarhus, Denmark, 26–9 May 1992, pp. 313–29.

46. Rein Rijkens, *European Advertising Strategies* (London: Cassell, 1992), pp. 121–32.

47. Joseph McAleer, 'A saga of romance, big business and unrequited lust', *The Times* (29 October 1999), pp. 37–8; John Walsh and Jojo Moyes, 'Swoon! Mills & Boon make eyes at male reader' (28 September 2000), p. 1.

case 9

Coffee-Mate

Greg, category manager for coffee creamers, was evaluating his ad agency's proposal for Coffee-mate (Exhibit 9.1). The £25 million (€42 million) a year coffee creamer market was small with a household penetration of only 18 per cent. Despite the growth of private labels to take 37 per cent of the market, Coffee-Mate's £1.5 million advertising budget had enabled it to hold a 55 per cent market share and squeeze both private label and other brands (Complement, Kenco and Compleat). However, budgets were being squeezed so unless the advertising campaign could show some sales gain, there was a danger that the category could be milked to provide income to invest in food products with more growth potential.

Competition in the coffee creamer market

The coffee creamer market is distinct from the declining £43 million instant dry milk market (Marvel, St Ivel Five Pints and Pint Size). Dried or powdered milk had been associated with slimming (e.g. Marvel adopted this positioning). Dried or powdered milk is not a direct substitute for coffee creamers because of its poor mixing qualities. It is used as a whitener in tea or coffee only in 'emergencies' when the household has run out of milk.

The coffee creamer market is undergoing a change in parallel with consumers' developing tastes for skimmed and semi-skimmed milk in their coffee. Milk is the most popular whitener for coffee. Although cream is thought to be the best whitener, consumers perceive cream as reserved, ritualistic and appropriate for special occasions but not for daily use.

Powdered or dried milk is a distress product, creamers are regarded as an indulgence, although non-users did not see creamers as anything like a substitute for cream and were generally suspicious of the product.

Coffee-Mate is a blend of dried glucose and vegetable fat, but cannot be legally defined as non-dairy, since it also contains milk derivatives. Recent improvements to the product include the relaunch of Coffee-Mate 100 g and 200 g in straight-sided glass jars with paper labels, and a 'Nidoll-contoured' jar with shrink-wrapped label. Packs of 500 g and 1 kg are available in cartons with an inner bag. When Coffee-Mate Lite, a low-fat alternative to Coffee-Mate, was introduced, cannibalisation of volume was minimal. The volume generated by Lite is a key feature in the development of the brand, which has experienced a 10 per cent growth in sales volume in the first three years following Lite's launch.

Coffee-Mate consumer

The average Coffee-Mate consumer buys 1.5 kg annually. There is no *strong* demographic bias among coffee creamer buyers although there is a slight skew towards 45–64-year-olds, two-person households and households without children. Heavy buyers of Coffee-Mate have a slight bias towards lower social class, aged 45+,

EXHIBIT 9.1 PROPOSED TV AD TO BOOST SALES

VISION	SOUND
Jane and John, an affluent thirty-something couple, are entertaining two other similar couples.	Soft soul music playing throughout.
They are ending their meal by drinking coffee out of fine china cups and eating After Eights.	John (to one of the other guests): 'Do you want another cup?' Guest 1: 'Yes, please.' Guest 2: 'Me, too! With cream!'
Jane looks, alarmed, at John. John glances at the empty cream jug.	Jane (thinking quickly): 'I'll make it!'
Jane rushes into kitchen and frantically looks for cream (there is none) and milk (all gone).	
Jane pauses, smiles, then gets out the Coffee-Mate. Jane pours the coffee and adds the Coffee-Mate. Jane returns with coffee. Guest sips the coffee containing Coffee-Mate.	Guest 1: 'Lovely, even better than the last one!' Guest 2: 'Yes, how do you do it?'
John smiles quizzically (and admiringly) at Jane. Jane leans back in her chair, smiling knowingly.	Voice: 'Coffee-Mate, never be without it!'

EXHIBIT 9.2 REASONS FOR LAPSING AND REJECTION
(NUMBER OF RESPONDENTS)

SPONTANEOUS RESPONSE	LAPSING	REJECTION
Don't drink coffee	11	22
Drink black coffee	5	6
Prefer milk	50	33
Prefer skimmed milk	5	3
Don't like them	10	18
Leaves coffee too hot	2	1
No need to use them	5	5
Don't think to buy them	1	4
Doesn't mix	4	1
Prefer pure things	4	3
Fattening	2	2
Too rich/creamy	1	2
Other	5	3
Don't know	4	9

EXHIBIT 9.3 CONSUMPTION BY INCOME GROUP
(PER PERSON/WEEK)

WEEKLY INCOME (£)	WEEKLY EXPENDITURE (£)
645+	0.25
475–644	0.19
250–474	0.20
125–249	0.18
0–124	0.17
125+ (no earners)	0.32
0–125 (no earners)	0.19
Old-age pensioners	18.64

SOURCE: National Food Survey. Crown copyright material is reproduced under Class Licence Number C01W0000039 with the permission of the Controller of HMSO.

2–3-person households with children. Coffee-Mate Lite users have a slight bias towards 45–64-year-olds, full-time working housewives and households without children.

AGB Superpanel data suggest that buyers of Coffee-Mate use all brands and types of coffee. The creamer market has a low interest level since it is not a weekly shopping item. Reasons given for lapsed usage were similar to non-users (Exhibit 9.2).

Because Coffee-Mate and Coffee-Mate Lite are 'consumed' with coffee, popularity and demand will also be affected by the annual coffee consumption, which is static at a low 3 kg per head in the UK (about 1.5 cups per day). The figure for Italy, France and Germany is 5 kg and 11–13 kg in the Benelux region and Scandinavia. The National Food Survey suggests that the higher a household's income, the more it spends on coffee (Exhibit 9.3). Childless households are the most intense coffee drinkers (Exhibit 9.4).

EXHIBIT 9.4 CONSUMPTION BY HOUSEHOLD SIZE
(PER PERSON/WEEK)

ADULTS IN HOUSEHOLD	CHILDREN IN HOUSEHOLD	WEEKLY EXPENDITURE (£)
1	0	0.27
1	1+	0.15
2	0	0.25
2	1	0.18
2	2	0.15
2	3	0.15
2	4+	0.11
3	0	0.23
3+	1–2	0.16
3+	3+	0.12
4+	0	0.25

SOURCE: National Food Survey. Crown copyright material is reproduced under Class Licence Number C01W0000039 with the permission of the Controller of HMSO.

Dried milk

The image of powdered milk is as a distress product where the *brand* is *bought*, but the *product* is *tolerated*: 'You tend to buy powdered milk thinking that you will need it when you run out, and occasionally you do.' 'Powdered milk is useful if you run out of real milk. You can make it up and use it just like the real thing, but it doesn't taste too good. You have to be a bit desperate to want to use it.'

Other negatives attach to dry milk. Respondents considered it to be inconvenient to prepare. Frequently its performance is seen as disappointing: it is 'lumpy', resulting in 'bits' floating on the top of their coffee. The product also tends to 'congeal' when spooned into tea or coffee. When made up and poured, the product's poor taste qualities are apparent: 'We have had it in our Cornflakes when we've run out, but quite honestly, it tastes so disgusting that in the future I don't think I'd bother.' 'It's all right for baking, but if you want to use it like real milk, it's not really advisable.'

Whiteners/coffee creamers

Coffee creamers have a more polarised image across users and non-users. *Loyal* or *confirmed creamer users* regard creamer as almost a treat. These hedonistic and indulgent properties are sometimes enhanced by the brand (e.g. Coffee-Mate) being perceived as having relaxing or comforting benefits: 'Creamers are a little bit of an indulgence. They make coffee taste so much better. They add something to it which improves the taste.' 'First thing in the morning I tend to have coffee with semi-skimmed milk, but towards 11 o'clock I want something which is more relaxing, more substantial, so I have coffee with Coffee-Mate. It seems to be comforting.'

Creamers' taste is a motivating force behind usage. Loyal users appreciate the thicker, creamier taste. Creamers are considered to supplement the taste of coffee, to complement and improve its flavour. For Coffee-Mate, the perceptions are extremely positive. Users enjoy its sweet delivery, stating that they need not add sugar to it. Fans feel that it does produce a creamy cup of coffee whether or not it is added to instant or freshly brewed 'real' coffee: 'Coffee without Coffee-Mate, just made with milk, tastes like it's got something missing.' 'Coffee-Mate kind of lifts the flavour. It makes a richer, better-tasting cup of coffee, whether it be an instant or a real one.'

Non-users' perceptions of coffee creamers are tainted by their negative attitudes towards dried milk. Creamers are something you have put by for an emergency: 'If someone gave me a cup of coffee with creamer in it, I would think they were doing it because they had run out of milk. I wouldn't have thought it was because they like the taste of it. Surely nobody could like the taste.'

Thus, in marked contrast to the users, non-users describe creamers as changing the taste of coffee, masking its pure taste rather than enhancing it. They also criticised its high sugar content, which the consumers feel delivers a flavour that is unacceptably sweet. They perceive it to be a poor alternative to cream: 'You can always tell when someone's used creamers, it just tastes powdery. It doesn't taste like cream, it has a taste all of its own.' 'Whiteners taste nothing like cream. They taste powdery. You always know when they're there.'

Lapsed users still see creamers as a bit of an indulgence and a treat. However, they feel an element of guilt in using the product: 'I like coffee creamers – I like the taste. But I stopped using them because I felt I was putting on too much weight and I needed to cut down. I just think there is too much in there, it's just glucose syrup and vegetable fat.' 'My husband had to go on a low-cholesterol diet and I figured that there was just too much fat in the coffee creamers. We've become accustomed now to drinking it black, or with very little skimmed milk.'

Health concerns are having an impact upon milk consumption. This change has been prompted by consumers' concern over health in general, and their level of fat intake in particular. Some consumers found it difficult to wean themselves and their families off milk, initially, and then semi-skimmed milk, in favour of the fully skimmed variety. However, many are persistent in adopting an overall preventative health maintenance regime as well as controlling their weight. So, while a few retained the notion that a cup of real coffee made with cream was the ideal, many others considered their ideal to be coffee drunk with just a dash of milk or black.

Coffee-Mate is in danger of being redundant since it is perceived to be too close to cream in its taste and texture while its creamy association is increasingly deemed unhealthy. Coffee-Mate Lite may redeem the situation by offering the same benefits of creamy and rich taste without causing injury to health and weight.

Consumer analyses

TGI User Surveys covering instant/ground coffee and powdered milk/coffee creamer markets yielded five potential consumer groups for Coffee-Mate.

'Sharon and Tracy' – experimentalists (sample proportion: 15.4 per cent)

They like to enjoy themselves and try new things. They enjoy spending money happily and seem to be very materialistic and status conscious. They go out frequently and are uninterested in political or environmental issues. Although they are heavy users of instant coffee, they are low-level users of ground coffee. They claim to use Nescafé granules and Maxwell House powder most often. They are below-average users of the category and average users of Coffee-Mate, but heavy users of cream.

They are younger (15–44 years) with a mid- to down-market bias (C2D) and children. They are of middle income (£15,000 up to £30,000), but live in state-owned property, in underprivileged areas.

They read many 'low brow' newspapers and the 'mums' magazines such as *Bella*, *Chat* and *Woman*. They are heavy users of commercial terrestrial TV, breakfast programmes, satellite TV and are heavy listeners to pop radio channels. They cannot resist buying magazines and read papers for entertainment rather than for news.

They spend average to high amounts on the main grocery shop. They love shopping for anything, be it food, clothes, kitchen gadgets or whatever. They like to keep up with fashion and believe they are stylish, and feel it is important to try to keep looking young. They will try anything new. They will respond to seeing new things in advertising or in the store.

They are very gregarious and socialise often (heavy users of pubs, wine bars and restaurants). They like to enjoy life and not worry about the future. They holiday abroad (eat, drink and lie in the sun) and like to treat themselves. They tend to spend money without thinking, spend more with their credit card and are no good at saving their money. They feel that it is important for people to think they are doing well. They buy cars for their looks and believe that brands are better than own labels.

They are not really using Coffee-Mate as much as one would have expected.

'Eileen and Mary' – cost constrained, older, conservative (23.6 per cent)

Very price aware, they budget when shopping and look for lowest prices. They are very traditional in their habits (don't like foreign food or foreign holidays). They worry about food ('food is not safe nowadays'), feel safe using products recommended by experts and think fast food is junk. They think it is worth paying more for organic fruit and vegetables and environmentally friendly products, but don't do much about it, perhaps because they can't afford to.

They are light users of instant coffee, using Maxwell House brands most often. They are average users of dried milk but are not really users of Coffee-Mate and never use cream. They are older (55+) and down-market (C2DE). They are not working or are retired in one- or two-person households; hence fewer of this type have children at home. They live in multi-ethnic areas, council areas and underprivileged areas on a low household income (£5,000–11,000).

They read the tabloid press and *Bella* and *Chat*. They are also heavy users of terrestrial commercial ITV and listen to commercial pop radio stations.

Their expenditure on grocery shopping is low and they tend to shop daily at small grocers. They enjoy shopping, but always look for the lowest prices, decide what they want before they go shopping and budget for every penny. They frequently enter competitions, find saving difficult, save for items they want and like to pay cash.

They are very conservative. They like routine, dislike untidiness, would buy British if they could, have a roast on Sundays and prefer brands to own label. They believe job security is more important than money, would rather have a boring job than no job, and prefer to do rather than take responsibility. Due to both their age and financial constraints, they socialise rarely. Most of this group never entertain friends to a meal, never go to a pub, a wine bar or a restaurant.

'Sarah and Anna' – affluent, young foodies (24.4 per cent)

Unencumbered by children and well off, they love both travelling and food (many claim to be vegetarian). They do not have to budget and can afford to treat themselves to perfume and foreign holidays, preferably more than once a year. They are not interested in additional channels on satellite TV and tend to be light users of all media.

They are heavy users of coffee and ground coffee. They buy decaffeinated, Gold Blend, Alta Rica and Cap Colombie. They are above-average users of creamers, claim to buy Coffee-Mate and Marvel most often, and also use cream.

Aged 35–54, predominantly ABC1, they earn above-average incomes and work full time. They live in areas of affluent minorities, young married suburbs and metro singles, in one- or two-person households.

They read quality newspapers, are light users of commercial radio but they do listen to the radio (usually the BBC) in the car.

They have a high expenditure on their main grocery shop (£71+) but shop infrequently at a large grocery supermarket. They really enjoy cooking and food, read recipes in magazines and like to try out new foods. Their tastes will be varied as they also enjoy travelling abroad on holiday, where they avoid the package trips and like to do as much as possible.

They entertain frequently and invite friends for meals. They also use pubs and wine bars, though not as much as 'Sharon and Tracy', and they are heavy users of restaurants.

They are health conscious (well, they can afford to be) and claim to include fibre in their diet, eat whole-meal bread, have less fat in their diet and eat fewer sweets and cakes. They are prepared to pay more for food without additives and for environmentally friendly products. They also exercise.

They can afford to treat themselves and prefer to buy one good thing rather than many cheap ones. They also like to keep up with technology and want to stand out from the crowd. In their fortunate position they enjoy life and don't worry about the future.

They claim never to buy any product tested on animals, use recycling banks and disapprove of aerosols more than the population at large. They make use of credit cards, especially for business, like to be well insured and consult professional advisers.

'Dawn and Lisa' – cost constrained, young families (13.9 per cent)

This group is severely constrained by their low incomes. But unlike the previous group, they are often young, working part-time or are unemployed or students. They are also not remotely concerned about health or the environment. Many left school before the age of 16.

They are heavy users of instant coffee but do not use ground coffee. They buy Nescafé granules and Maxwell House powder. They are below-average users of creamers and never use cream.

This group is biased towards the 15–34 age group and is down-market (C2DE) with low incomes (£5,000–11,000). They tend to live in state housing in fading industrial areas. They have young families and there is a slightly greater bias to larger families than in other groups.

They read the tabloid press, *Bella* and *Chat*, and they are heavy viewers of commercial terrestrial and satellite TV, and heavy listeners to independent radio.

Their expenditure on the main grocery shop is low and they shop daily or once a week at discount grocery stores. They always look for the lowest price, watch what they spend, budget for every penny and look out for special offers. They want to save but find it difficult.

As a result of their difficult financial circumstances, they rarely use wine bars, pubs or restaurants. They claim to enjoy going to the pub, but cannot afford to these days. Similarly, when they can afford a holiday, they prefer to do so in the UK.

They have little time or money to worry about the environment or health issues, and claim that health food is bought by fanatics. They believe that frozen food is as nutritious as fresh foods. They tend to buy own label, presumably because it is cheaper rather than because they believe own-label goods are better than branded goods.

'Dorothy and Amy' – affluent (22.7 per cent)

This group does not have to be price conscious. They are older, sometimes retired or working part-time, and are well off. Often they own their house outright. They are, however, fairly traditional. They are not interested in travelling abroad, they are not health conscious and they are not media aware.

They are the people most likely to be buying Coffee-Mate. They buy instant coffee to the same degree as the rest of the population and are light users of ground coffee. But they use creamers as well as cream.

Dorothy and Amy are older (55+) and are up-market (AB and C1). They still have a reasonable household income despite being retired (£25,000+) and their children have left home. They are clearly a group who have disposable income and are not worried about budgeting. They are to be found in affluent minorities, older suburbs and young married suburbs.

They are readers of quality press, light viewers of ITV and never listen to commercial radio. They are not media aware, claiming to watch little TV and not to notice posters, and do not expect ads to entertain.

Their expenditure on the main grocery shop is above average. They do not enjoy shopping as much as other groups, are not price conscious but are prudent with money (consider themselves good at saving). They do not want to try new things, are not keen to keep up with the latest fashion and are not concerned with their appearance. They buy foreign goods if possible, will pay extra for quality goods, but are not really indulgent.

This is a group whose attitudes tend to lag. They get a great deal of pleasure from gardening and others often ask their advice on the matter. As a group they are happy with their standard of living. They do not often go to pubs, wine bars or restaurants, but they do have people home for meals.

Questions

1. What are the main benefits of Coffee-Mate and what is limiting its sales?

2. How would the promotion of Coffee-Mate change with the benefits promoted and the competition targeted?

3. Should Coffee-Mate be mass marketed, aimed at one segment or aimed at multiple segments?

4. Evaluate the segments from TGI's user survey for target attractiveness and their fit to Coffee-Mate's strengths. Which of the segments would you target and why?

5. Evaluate the proposed ad for the target market and benefits promoted. Will the ad help propel Coffee-Mate's further growth? Create an alternative ad for your chosen target market.

Sources: Economist Intelligence Unit, *Retail Business*, no. 418 (December 1992); British Market Research Bureaux, *Instant Powdered Milk and Coffee Creamers* (1992); company sources.

internet exercises

Internet exercises for this chapter can be found on the student site of the MYPHLIP Web Site at www.booksites.net/kotler.

chapter ten

Positioning

Chapter objectives *After reading this chapter, you should be able to:*

+ Define differentiation and market positioning.

+ Explain why companies seek to differentiate their markets and use positioning strategies.

+ List and discuss the principal ways in which companies can differentiate their products.

+ Explain how companies can position their products for maximum competitive advantage in the marketplace.

introduction

Core strategy is at the hub of marketing. It is where company strengths meet market opportunities. It has two parts: first, the identification of a group of customers for whom the firm has a differential advantage; and second, positioning its offerings in the customer's mind. As can be seen from the preview case overleaf, this is what Castrol did. While the big oil companies saw the lubricant market as mature, Castrol identified target markets and built strengths in them. Its motor racing experience, knowledge of high-performance oils and brand name are competitive advantages in the motor enthusiast market. In the US, its support of Grand Prix and Indy car racing helped position Castrol Syntec as a high-performance product. In developing countries, its early investments in distribution give Castrol a differential advantage in the emergent markets. There, too, Castrol's association with Grand Prix racing gives the products an exotic international appeal. This chapter first examines how firms can differentiate themselves and then the positioning alternatives.

Core strategy
The identification of a group of customers for whom the firm has a differential advantage, and then positioning itself in that market.

differentiation

Consumers typically choose products and services that give them the greatest value. Thus the key to winning and keeping customers is to understand their needs and buying processes better than competitors do, and to deliver more value. To the extent that a company can position itself as providing superior value to selected target markets,

preview case

Castrol: liquid engineering

The enthusiast

Antoni carefully measured four litres of Syntec into his greatest love, his new Van Dieman Formula Ford racing car. Tomorrow he was racing her for the first time and wanted to do well. Racing the Formula Fords was exciting, but his real dream was to race Formula 1 cars. That is why he had left his home in Barcelona to work for a specialist engineering firm in rural England.

Leaving Spain was hard, but he wanted to be at the heart of the world's motor sports industry. More than three-quarters of the world's purpose-built single-seater cars came from local small firms like Reynard, Ralt and Van Dieman. Few of the 450,000 people watching the Indianapolis 500 race knew that almost all the cars and engines originated in Europe.

Antoni got his Syntec oil from an American friend. He was glad of the gift, since the synthetic motor oil cost four times as much as regular lubricants. In motor racing every little helps and the oil could make the difference between winning and losing.

Syntec

Syntec is Burmah Castrol's 'flagship' product. Targeted at enthusiasts and technically advanced users of motor oil, the product appeared on the US market with a $20 million (€22 million). Despite its high price, Syntec sells well. It will never have a high market share, but it allows Castrol to create gradations in the market at intermediate prices.

Syntec fits Castrol's strategy of having a high price and high marketing expenditure. Sponsorship of rallying, Grand Prix racing and the Indy car series positions Castrol as a quality, high-performance product used by the experts. Its TV advertising shows Castrol GTX as 'liquid engineering' and so encourages motorists to cosset their engines by using a premium-priced product. The campaign helped Castrol increase its share of the US DIY market from 5 to 15 per cent in ten years.

The 'have somes' and 'near haves'

Some of Castrol's greatest successes are in developing countries. The company's positioning in the developing world is not the same as in developed countries. According to Ian Pringle, Castrol's Asia director, 'have somes' are the key to its marketing in Asia. They are the real middle class of Asia who want to buy cars, houses and consumer durables. They treasure and care for their possessions. The segment is growing fast. By a combination of political patronage and technology, the company has captured 71 per cent of the rapidly growing Indian market.

Castrol's marketing also covers the Asian 'near haves', who are likely to buy a motor cycle as their first vehicle. According to Mr Pringle, these groups are important because rapid economic development leads to consumers 'leapfrogging' intermediate technologies: for example, people progressing from having no telephone direct to a cellular phone. Mr Pringle believes that some brand loyalty persists when 'near haves' become 'have somes'. That is why Castrol has made the motorcycle market central to its marketing strategy in Vietnam and Thailand. In Thailand, Castrol concentrated on building distribution and its image among motorcyclists despite government past controls. Then, when the motorcycle population leapt from 1 million to 5 million, it was able to hold on to its leading position.

World coverage

Appropriate targeting and positioning of Castrol lubricants ensures that the company makes profits in markets as different as Vietnam's 'near haves' and the US 'have lots'. By positioning product to fit the market's stage of development, Castrol is profitable in both mature and developing markets.

Mr Tim Stevenson, Castrol's chief executive, says that the company has proved wrong the sceptics who argue that Castrol is a small business liable to be snuffed out by the oil majors. While the world lubricant market has been almost flat over the last ten years, Castrol's profits have grown at 14 per cent annually and sales by an average 6 per cent per year. Some maturity; some snuffing out![1]

Questions

1. How can Castrol's involvement in motor sports help it in markets where few people will ever have a chance to see the sport live, never mind participate in it?

2. Why do you think Burmah Oil concentrates on engine oils rather than the huge market for motor fuel?

3. What personalities could be used to help strengthen people's perception of Castrol?

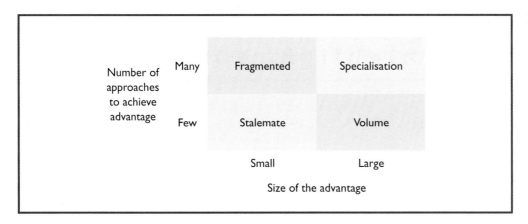

Figure 10.1

The new BCG matrix

either by offering lower prices than competitors do or by providing more benefits to justify higher prices, it gains **competitive advantage**.[2]

Strong positions are not built upon empty promises. If a company positions its product as *offering* the best quality and service, it must then *deliver* the promised quality and service. Positioning therefore begins with *differentiating* the company's marketing offer, so that it will give consumers more value than competitors' offers do. Marketing Highlight 10.1 relates how a German company successfully achieved the US market. It is not just a matter of being different; success comes from being different in a way that customers want.

> Arby's, the fast-food chain, explains how it competes by being different: 'Being different makes you more interesting. Of course it's not always good to be different (you don't want to be the only one standing up in an electrical storm). But in most cases being different is good. Great tasting, lean Roast Beef and 3 fantastic ways. And *no* dull, boring burger!'

Not every company can find many opportunities for differentiating its offer and gaining competitive advantage.[3] In some industries it is harder than others. The Boston Consulting Group explains four types of industry based on the number of competitive advantages and the size of those advantages (see Figure 10.1).

The four industry types are:

1. **Volume industries**, where there are a few large advantages to be had. The airline industry is one of these. A company can strive for low costs or differentiate by service quality, but can win 'big' on both bases. In these industries, profitability is correlated with company size and market share. As a result, most minor airlines lose money while the main players try to form global alliances to build share. In this case almost all the industry leaders, VW, Hoechst, Hitachi, Unilever and Glaxo Wellcome, are large, low-cost operators providing a high-quality service.[4]

2. **Stalemate industries** produce commodities where there are few potential advantages and each is small. Many old industries like steel and bulk chemicals fall into this category. In these industries it is hard to differentiate products or have significantly lower costs. European firms in these sectors often lose money, since they are unable to compete with products from economies with low-cost labour. Even size and modern plant cannot counter high labour costs.

3. **Fragmented industries** offer many opportunities to differentiate, but each opportunity is small. Many service industries are fragmented. Restaurants are an extreme example: Hard Rock Café has a global reputation and long queues, but

Competitive advantage
An advantage over competitors gained by offering consumers greater value, either through lower prices or by providing more benefits that justify higher prices.

Volume industry
An industry characterised by few opportunities to create competitive advantages, but each advantage is huge and gives a high pay-off.

Stalemate industry
An industry that produces commodities and is characterised by a few opportunities to create competitive advantages, with each advantage being small.

Fragmented industry
An industry characterised by many opportunities to create competitive advantages, but each advantage is small.

marketing highlight 10.1

Schott: positioning for success

Positioning came to the help of the German company Schott in marketing Ceran in the US. Ceran, a glass-ceramic material made to cover the cooking surface of electric ranges, seemed to have everything going for it. It was completely non-porous (and thus stain resistant), easy to clean and long-lasting. Also, when one burner was lit, the heat does not spread; it stays confined to the circle directly above the burner. And after ten years, Ceran hobs still looked and performed like new.

Schott anticipated some difficulty in the US markets. It would have to win over American cooker manufacturers, which would then have to promote Ceran to middle markets – dealers, designers, architects and builders. These middle-market customers would, in turn, influence final consumers. Schott set out to sell Ceran to its target of 14 appliance manufacturers. Schott promoted Ceran's impressive technical and engineering attributes. The appliance companies listened politely to the sales pitch, ordered samples and then . . . nothing.

Market research revealed two problems. First, Schott had failed to position Ceran among the manufacturers' customers. The material was still unknown among final consumers, dealers, designers, architects and builders. Second, the company was attempting to position the product on the wrong benefits. When selecting a hob, customers cared more about appearance and cleanability than sophisticated engineering. Their biggest questions were 'How does it look?' and 'How easy is it to use?'.

Based on these findings, Schott repositioned Ceran, shifting emphasis towards the material's inherent beauty and design versatility. An extensive promotion campaign communicated the new position to middle-market and final buyers. Advertising presented the black hob as 'Formalware for your kitchen', as streamlined and elegant as a tuxedo. As a follow-up, to persuade designers to specify Ceran, Schott positioned Ceran as 'More than a rangetop, a means of expression'. To reinforce this beauty and design positioning, ads featured visuals of a geometric grid of a hob with one glowing red burner.

In addition to advertising, a massive public relations effort resulted in substantial coverage in home improvement publications. It also produced a video news release featuring Ceran that was picked up by 150 local TV stations nationwide. To reinforce a weak link in the selling chain, a video helped retail salespeople show customers the benefits of Ceran in their stores.

Ceran is now selling well. All 14 North American appliance makers are buying production quantities of Ceran and use it in several smooth-top models. Schott is the major smooth-top supplier in the US, and smooth tops now account for more than 15 per cent of the electric stove market. At a recent Kitchen & Bath Show, 69 per cent of all range models on display had smooth tops.

SOURCES: Adapted from Nancy Arnott, 'Heating up sales: formalware for your kitchen', *Sales and Marketing Management* (June 1994), pp. 77–8. See also Richard J. Babyak, 'Tabletop cooking', *Appliance Manufacturer* (February 1997), pp. 65–7.

---

its overall share of the market is small. Even market leaders, like McDonald's and KFC, have a small share of the market relative to leaders in other industries. In fragmented industries, profitability is not closely related to size. For many years, global Pizza Hut was not profitable, while every large town has restaurateur millionaires who own few eating places. At the same time, many small restaurants fail each year.

Specialised industry
An industry where there are many opportunities for firms to create competitive advantages that are huge or give a high pay-off.

4. **Specialised industries** offer companies many opportunities to differentiate in a way that gives a high pay-off. Pharmaceuticals is a specialised industry. A disproportionately large proportion of the world's most successful companies come from the sector where firms like Novartis, Glaxo Wellcome and Roche are market leaders for particular treatment. Less conspicuous specialised industries are those for scientific instruments and publishing.

Figure 10.2 shows the returns to be had from differentiation using results taken from the Profit Implications of Marketing Strategy (PIMS) study of American and European firms.[5] This study shows that firms with the lowest return on investment

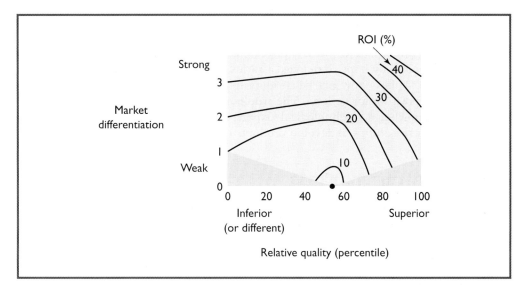

Figure 10.2

How differentiation and
quality drive profitability

SOURCE: SPI's
Quality/Differentiation
Data Base.

(RoI) operate in commodity markets where there is no differentiation on quality or
anything else, such as the coal industry. Where there is room for differentiation, losers
have inferior quality (Aeroflot) and more returns than winners (KLM). The most highly
performing group of companies are 'power companies', which have superior quality in
differentiable markets (BMW, Bertelsmann and Nokia). These are ahead of nichers
(such as local airlines), which score lower on quality and ROI than the 'power companies'. According to PIMS, the 'power companies' often have a high market share,
since quality, share and RoI are interrelated.

Differentiation may be harder in some industries than others, but creative firms
have shown that any market can be differentiated.[6] Few people see the brick market
as exciting, but one brick company found a way of getting a competitive advantage.
Bricks used to be delivered to building sites in a truck that tipped them on to the
ground. In the process many bricks got broken or lost. Workers on the site also had to
spend time stacking the bricks. The brick company's idea was to put the bricks on pal-
lets that were lifted off the truck by a small integral crane. The idea was so successful
that soon all bricks came that way. The firm's next idea was to carry a small off-the-
road fork-lift truck with the bricks, so that it could deliver them to the exact spot
where the site manager wanted them.

Oil is a *stalemate industry*, but Royal Dutch/Shell remains the leading petroleum
retailer by understanding that fuel is a distress purchase that people do not enjoy.
They succeed by making their petrol stations easy to use and paying attention to all
the other reasons people stop on a journey: to find their way, get a snack, make a
phone call or go to a clean toilet.

Differential advantages can be transient. Some companies find many major advantages that are easily copied by competitors and are, therefore, highly perishable. This
is particularly true in financial services, where successful ideas are quickly followed by
competitors. The Bank of Scotland's Direct Line insurance company succeeded by
offering an economic and high-quality personal insurance service through television
advertising and telephone selling. It was so successful that established insurers had to
follow. Zurich Insurance intends to attack the conservative German and Italian insurance markets in the same way. Like many online business-to-consumer companies,
the Internet financial service providers First-e, Egg and Smile have used price, in the
form of high interest on current accounts, to get customers to switch their accounts.
However, so far their growth has not produced profitability. One reason is that a low
price position is easy for others to follow unless a company has huge cost advantages.[7]

The solution for companies facing the erosion of their advantage is to keep identifying new potential advantages and to introduce them one by one to keep competitors off balance. These companies do not expect to gain a single substantial permanent advantage. Instead, they hope to manage a series of advantages that will increase their share over time. This is how market leaders like Microsoft, Intel, Sony and Gillette have held their position for so long. The true competitive advantage of these firms is their market knowledge, technological expertise, creativity and entrepreneurship, which give them the ability to develop products quickly.

differentiating markets

In what specific ways can a company differentiate its offer from those of competitors? A company or market offer can be differentiated along the lines of product, services, personnel or image.

■ Product differentiation

A company can differentiate its physical product. At one extreme, some companies offer highly standardised products that allow little variation: chicken, steel and aspirin. Yet even here, some meaningful differentiation is possible. For example, Perdue claims that its branded chickens are better – fresher and more tender – and gets a 10 per cent price premium based on this differentiation.

Other companies offer products that can be highly differentiated, such as cars, commercial buildings and furniture. Here the company faces an abundance of design parameters.[8] It can offer a variety of standard or optional *features* not provided by competitors. Thus Volvo provides new and better safety features, while Lufthansa offers wider seats to business-class flyers. In the UK, Brewers Fayre pubs are aimed at families. Besides the usual food and drink, most Brewers Fayres have a toddlers' area, a play zone for bigger children and a 'Charlie Chalk Fun Factory – a large self-contained area full of games, toys and adventure equipment'.

Companies can also differentiate their products on *performance*. Whirlpool designs its dishwasher to run more quietly; Unilever formulates Radion to remove odours as well as dirt from washing. *Style* and *design* can also be important differentiating factors. Thus many car buyers pay a premium for Jaguar cars because of their extraordinary look, or Bose speakers because of their compactness, power and professional credibility. Similarly, companies can differentiate their products on such attributes as *innovation, consistency, durability, reliability* or *repairability*.

■ Services differentiation

In addition to differentiating its physical product, the firm can also differentiate the services that accompany the product. Some companies gain competitive advantage through speedy, reliable or careful *delivery*. Harrods, the luxury retailer, delivers to its customers using replica vintage vans – a service particularly popular at Christmas. At the other end of the scale, Domino's Pizza promises delivery in less than 30 minutes or reduces the price.

Installation can also differentiate one company from another. IBM, for example, is known for its quality installation service for its servers. It delivers all pieces of purchased equipment to the site at one time, rather than sending individual components to sit and wait for others to arrive. And when asked to move IBM equipment and install it in another location, IBM often moves competitors' equipment as well. Companies can further distinguish themselves through their *repair services*. Many a car buyer would gladly pay a little more and travel a little further to buy a car from a dealer that provides top-notch repair service.

Some companies differentiate their offers by providing a *customer training* service. For instance, GE not only sells and installs expensive X-ray equipment in hospitals, but also trains the hospital employees who will use the equipment. Other companies offer free or paid *consulting services* – data, information systems and advice services that buyers need. For example, reinsurance company M&G provides information and advice to its customers. It also provides specialist help in developing new products.

Companies can find many other ways to add value through differentiated services. In fact, they can choose from a virtually unlimited number of specific services and benefits through which to differentiate themselves from the competition. Milliken provides one of the best examples of a company that has gained competitive advantage through superior service:

> Milliken sells shop towels to industrial launderers who rent them to factories. These towels are physically similar to competitors' towels. Yet Milliken charges a higher price for its towels and enjoys the leading market share. How can it charge more for essentially a commodity? The answer is that Milliken continuously 'decommoditizes' this product through continuous service enhancement for its launderer customers. Milliken trains its customers' salespeople; supplies prospect leads and sales promotional material to them; supplies on-line computer order entry and freight optimization systems; carries on marketing research for customers; sponsors quality improvement workshops; and lends its salespeople to work with customers on Customer Action Teams. Launderers are more than willing to buy Milliken shop towels and pay a price premium because the extra services improve their profitability.[9]

Speed of service is a competitive advantage used by many firms. Fast food is now common on the world's high streets and malls, along with services like one-hour photo processing and Vision Express's one-hour service for spectacles. These services provide a direct benefit to customers by giving rapid gratification and allowing services to be completed within one shopping trip. Speed also helps sell more expensive goods. Abbey National found that its success in providing large mortgages depended upon how fast it could confirm that it would give a person a home loan. It responded by allowing local managers to make loan decisions rather than processing applications centrally. In the car market Toyota's two-day policy means that it can supply a well-equipped Lexus within two days, while many other luxury car makers expect prospects to wait several weeks for custom-built cars.

The success of courier services like TNT and DHL shows that many people are willing to pay extra for a quick, secure service. A study of the importance of service responsiveness to users of small business-computer-based systems shows how speed is valued:

◆ Eighty-five per cent of users were willing to pay a 10 per cent premium price for same-day service; 60 per cent would pay 20 per cent more; and 40 per cent would pay a 30 per cent premium.

◆ On average, same-day service was worth twice as much as brand name and distributor reputation, and worth four times more than technical features.[10]

■ Personnel differentiation

Companies can gain a strong competitive advantage through hiring and training better people than their competitors do. Singapore Airlines enjoys an excellent reputation largely because of the grace of its flight attendants. McDonald's people are courteous, TGI Fridays is fun, Richer Sounds staff are enthusiastic and knowledgeable and Mark Warner's resort staff are friendly and upbeat.

Service differentiation: KPN Qwest's ad focuses on speed as its main competitive advantage.
Source: KPN Qwest.
Agency: PPGH JWT Colors
Photographer: Jan Willem Scholten

From *Helsinki* ...

... *to Barcelona, in a flash.*

Not so very long ago, business data communication across Europe seemed to take an age. Low bandwidth connections via networks that were originally designed in the 19th century. Now there's a completely new network, designed and built specifically to meet the needs of today's businesses. A network that operates at the speed of light itself to deliver the bandwidth you need to compete in the 21st century. KPNQwest's EuroRings™ fibre-optic network spans Europe and connects to the world, providing a secure, high-bandwidth platform for e-business, IP connections, intranets, extranets or any other corporate data communications requirement. What are you waiting for? *KPNQwest. Business communications @ the speed of light.*

kpn Qwest

Personnel differentiation requires that a company should select its customer-contact people carefully and train them well. These personnel must be competent – they must possess the required skills and knowledge. They need to be courteous, friendly and respectful. They must serve customers with consistency and accuracy. And they must make an effort to understand customers, to communicate clearly with them, and to respond quickly to customer requests and problems.

Personnel differentiation: The Regent Hong Kong's personnel 'welcome you, move you, enrich you and delight you'.

SOURCE: Regent International Hotels

Allied Breweries relates the type of staff they wish to employ to the market segments served. A segmentation study identified four pub segments in the United Kingdom (see Table 10.1) and the managers needed to run them. *Local community pubs* needed a good controller who was mature and experienced. He or she had to be 'one of the crowd', be involved in the local community and be an organiser of pub teams and other events. The personality of the manager is the key to success of *broad-based locals*. They need to maintain a high profile and set the mood of the pub and other staff. *Young persons' circuit pubs* need good organisers who are tolerant but firm. These places are very busy at peak times, so service standards have to be high and efficient. Users of *quality traditional dry pubs* expect attention to detail and high professional standards. Good food is important, so the manager's job is more complicated than for other pubs. The manager may not have a strong personality, but organisational and financial skills are important.

■ Image differentiation

Even when competing offers look the same, buyers may perceive a difference based on company or brand images. Thus companies work to establish *images* that differentiate them from competitors. A company or brand image should convey a singular and distinctive message that communicates the product's main benefits and positioning. Developing a strong and distinctive image calls for creativity and hard work. A company cannot implant an image in the public's mind overnight using only a few advertisements. If 'IBM means service', this image must be supported by everything the company says and does.

Symbols can provide strong company or brand recognition and image differentiation. Companies design signs and logos that provide instant recognition. They associate

	LOCAL COMMUNITY PUB	BROAD-BASED LOCAL	YOUNG PERSONS' CIRCUIT PUB	QUALITY TRADITIONAL DRY PUB
Location	Public housing estates or old terraced housing	Housing estates	Town centre or suburban high street	Prosperous villages or remote country sites
Customer demographics	Generally males of all ages	Men and women aged 18 to 44	Aged 18 to 24. Single-sex groups at lunchtime	Aged 35 plus as couples or with family. Managerial and professional
Customer geography	Local	Work within a mile of the pub	From 5-mile radius	Five miles or over
Pub journey	Walk	Walk or car	Public transport	Car
Consumer behaviour	Price conscious, shop locally, but do not drink at home	Price conscious, like pub games	Fashion-conscious and like background noise	Dislike pub games and background noise
Readership	Popular newspapers	Popular newspapers	Music press	Quality newspapers
Drinks	Thirty per cent standard lager and white spirits	Beer, wine and whisky	Standard lagers plus some premium lagers and spirits	Drinks only 60 per cent of sales
Food	Basic lunchtime sandwiches	A little more than the local community pubs	Little	Appreciate good food

Table 10.1

Allied Breweries pub segments

themselves with objects or characters that symbolise quality or other attributes, such as the Mercedes star, the Johnnie Walker character, the Michelin man or the Lacoste crocodile. The company might build a brand around some famous person, as with perfumes such as Passion (Elizabeth Taylor) and Uninhibited (Cher). Some companies even become associated with colours, such as Kodak (yellow), Benson & Hedges (gold) or Ferrari (red).

The chosen symbols must be communicated through advertising that conveys the company or brand's personality. The ads attempt to establish a story line, a mood, a performance level – something distinctive about the company or brand. The atmosphere of the physical space in which the organisation produces or delivers its products and services can be another powerful image generator. Hyatt hotels has become known for its atrium lobbies, TGI Friday's restaurants for American memorabilia, and Scruffy Murphy's Pubs with Irish memorabilia. Thus a bank that wants to distinguish itself as the 'friendly bank' must choose the right building and interior design – layout, colours, materials and furnishings – to reflect these qualities. A far cry from the majestic edifices that many banks have inherited.

A company can also create an image through the types of event it sponsors. Perrier, the bottled water company, became known by laying out exercise tracks and sponsoring health sports events. Other organisations have identified themselves closely with cultural events, such as orchestral performances and art exhibits. Still other organisations support popular causes. For example, Heinz gives money to hospitals and Quaker gives food to the homeless.

The crocodile gives instant brand recognition for Lacoste. In the same way, there can be a very strong association between certain colours and companies, like blue for Philips.

SOURCES: (left) Lacoste. *Agency:* Pentland Group. (right) Philips Consumer Electronics. *Agency:* Euro RSCG

■ Value positioning

Value positioning offers a range of positioning alternatives based on the value an offering delivers and its price. Consumers typically choose products and services that give them the greatest value. Thus, marketers want to position their brands on the key benefits that they offer relative to competing brands. The full positioning of a brand is called the brand's value proposition – the full mix of benefits upon which the brand is positioned. It is the answer to the customer's question 'Why should I buy your brand?'. Volvo's value proposition hinges on safety but also includes reliability, roominess and styling, all for a price that is higher than average but seems fair for this mix of benefits.

Figure 10.3 shows possible value propositions upon which a company might position its products. In the figure, the five green cells represent winning value propositions – positioning that gives the company competitive advantage. The red cells, however, represent losing value propositions, and the centre cell represents at best a marginal proposition. In the following sections, we discuss the five winning value propositions companies can use to position their products: more for more, more for the same, the same for less, less for much less, and more for less.[11]

More for more 'More for more' positioning involves providing the most upscale product or service and charging a higher price to cover the higher costs. Ritz-Carlton Hotels, Mont Blanc writing instruments, Mercedes-Benz automobiles or Tod's 133 stud

Value positioning
A range of positioning alternatives based on the value an offering delivers and its price.

A brand's value proposition:
Carlsberg advertises the value of
its offering by claiming that it is
'probably the best in the world'.

Source: Carlsberg Breweries AS.
Agency: Publicis Törma Finland for
Carlsberg Norway, 1999

Figure 10.3

Value positions

		Price		
		Less	Same	More
Benefits	More	More for Less	More for the Same	More for More
	Same	The Same for Less	Me too	
	Less	Less for much Less		

driving shoes[12] – each claims superior quality, craftsmanship, durability, performance
or style and charges a price to match. Not only is the marketing offer high in quality,
it also offers prestige to the buyer. It symbolises status and a lofty lifestyle. Often, the
price difference exceeds the actual increment in quality.

More for more *value proposition:*
Häagen-Dazs produces and
commercialises super premium
ice-cream at unusually high prices.
SOURCE: Pillsbury UK Limited.
Agency: Euros

Sellers offering 'only the best' can be found in every product and service category, from hotels, restaurants, food and fashion to cars and kitchen appliances. Consumers are sometimes surprised, even delighted, when a new competitor enters a category with an unusually high-priced brand. Starbucks coffee entered as a very expensive brand in a largely commodity category; Häagen-Dazs came in as a super premium ice-cream brand at a price never before charged. In general, companies should be on the lookout for opportunities to introduce a 'much more for much more' brand in any under-developed product or service category. For example, the €400 Dualit Toaster, a hand-assembled appliance, keeps toast warm for 10 minutes.[13]

Yet 'more for more' brands can be vulnerable. They often invite imitators who claim the same quality but at a lower price. Luxury goods that sell well during good times may be at risk during economic downturns when buyers become more cautious in their spending.

More for the same   Companies can attack a competitor's more for more positioning by introducing a brand offering comparable quality but at a lower price. For example, Toyota introduced its Lexus line with a 'more for the same' value proposition. In the US the headline read: 'Perhaps the first time in history that trading a $72,000 (€81,000) car for a $36,000 car could be considered trading up.' It communicated the high quality of its new Lexus through rave reviews in car magazines, through a widely distributed videotape showing side-by-side comparisons of Lexus and Mercedes-Benz automobiles, and through surveys showing that Lexus dealers were providing customers with better sales and service experiences than were Mercedes dealerships. Many Mercedes-Benz owners switched to Lexus, and the Lexus repurchase rate has been 60 per cent, twice the industry average. Their new C-series shows Mercedes fighting back. Not only is the line model stylish and much more sporty than its predecessor, it comes as well equipped. The only equipment available on the Mercedes top of the range S-class that is not on the C-class standard options list are the S-class's air suspension and fan-cooled driver's seats![14]

The same for less   Offering 'the same for less' can be a powerful value proposition – everyone likes a good deal. For example, Amazon.com sells the same book titles as its brick-and-mortar competitors but at lower prices. Discounts stores such as Matalan and Aldi use this positioning. They don't claim to offer different or better products. Instead, they offer many of the same brands as other stores but at deep discounts based on superior purchasing power and lower-cost operations.

Other companies develop imitative but lower-priced brands in an effort to lure customers away from the market leader. For example, Advanced Micro Devices (AMD) and Cyrix make less expensive versions of Intel's market-leading microprocessor chips. Many personal computer companies make 'IBM clones' and claim to offer the same performance at lower prices.

Less for much less   A market almost always exists for products that offer less and therefore cost less. Few people need, want or can afford 'the very best' in everything they buy. In many cases, consumers will gladly settle for less than optimal performance or give up some of the bells and whistles in exchange for a lower price. For example, many travellers seeking lodgings prefer not to pay for what they consider unnecessary extras, such as a pool, cable television, attached restaurant, or mints on the pillow. Motel chains such as Motel 6 suspend some of these amenities and charge less accordingly.

'Less for much less' positioning involves meeting consumers' lower performance or quality requirements at a much lower price. In Europe low-cost airlines, such as EasyJet, Go, Virgin Express and Ryanair, are proliferating where deregulation allows. It is wrong to think that less for less positioning is for people with less money to spend. Many users are business people whose companies are keen to reduce travel budgets. The most regular users are people working away who use budget airlines to get home more often or people owning villas who visit their summer home for short breaks as well as long holidays. Other heavy users are shoppers travelling to global retail centres, such as Paris, London, New York or Chicago, and golfers flying off for a game in Scotland or Spain.[15]

More for less   Of course, the winning value proposition would be to offer 'more for less'. Many companies claim to do this. For example, Dell Computer claims to have better products *and* lower prices for a given level of performance. Procter & Gamble claims that its laundry detergents provide the best cleaning *and* everyday low prices. In the short run, some companies can actually achieve such lofty positions.

Yet in the long run, companies will find it very difficult to sustain such best-of-both positioning. Offering more usually costs more, making it difficult to deliver on the 'for less' promise. Companies that try to deliver both may lose out to more focused competitors.

All said, each brand must adopt a positioning strategy designed to serve the needs and wants of its target markets. 'More for more' will draw one target market, 'less for much less' will draw another, and so on. Thus, in any market, there is usually room for many different companies, each successfully occupying different positions.

The important thing is that each company must develop its own winning positioning strategy, one that makes it special to its target consumers. Offering only 'the same for the same' provides no competitive advantage, leaving the firm in the middle of the pack. Companies offering one of the three losing value propositions – 'the same for more', 'less for more', and 'less for the same' – will inevitably fail. Here, customers soon realise that they've been underserved, tell others, and abandon the brand.

product positioning

A **product's position** is the way the product is *defined by consumers* on important attributes – the place the product occupies in consumers' minds relative to competing products. Thus Tide is positioned as a powerful, all-purpose family detergent, Radion removes odours, and Fairy is gentle. Skoda and Subaru are positioned on economy.

Product position
*The way the product is
defined by consumers
on important attributes
– the place the product
occupies in consumers'
minds relative to
competing products.*

> One-time BMW manager Wolfgang Reitzle says he has the best job in the world. He runs Premier Auto Group, Ford's luxury car arm, from his office in a Georgian town house in Berkeley Square, London. Although all his brands are made by Ford, he aims to grow all his brands by positioning that keeps them separate and clear in the customer's mind: 'You try to keep a certain image or profile that makes customers not only buy a car, but join a club.'
>
> The product positions of all the range are not yet sorted. Jaguar is 'The art of performance', Volvo is 'For life', Lincoln is 'American luxury' and Range Rover 'The best 4 × 4 by far'. Still to be determined is the product position of the low volume, expensive but mouth-watering Aston Martin. His desire is to increase its 651 per year current sales by five-fold in five years. And without referring to 007, Goldfinger and ejector seats?

A firm's *competitive advantage* and its *product's position* can be quite different. A competitive advantage is the strength of a company, while a product's position is a prospect's perception of a product. A competitive advantage, like low costs or high quality, could influence a product's position, but in many cases it is not central to it. One of Ford's competitive advantages is the ability of Jaguar to share engineering with Lincoln/Mercury although the products are far apart in the customer's minds.[16]

Consumers are overloaded with information about products and services. They cannot re-evaluate products every time they make a buying decision. To simplify buying decision making, consumers organise products into categories – that is, they 'position' products, services and companies in their minds. A product's position is the complex set of perceptions, impressions and feelings that consumers hold for the product compared with competing products. Consumers position products with or without the help of marketers. But marketers do not want to leave their products' positions to chance. They *plan* positions that will give their products the greatest advantage in selected target markets, and they *design* marketing mixes to create these planned positions.

Positioning was popularised by advertising executives Al Ries and Jack Trout.[17] They saw it as a creative exercise done with an existing product:

> Positioning starts with a product, a piece of merchandise, a service, a company, an institution or even a person . . . But positioning is not about what you do to a product. Positioning is what you do to the mind of the prospect. That is, you position products in the mind of the prospect.

They argue that current products generally have a position in the minds of consumers. Thus Rolex is thought of as the world's top watch, Coca-Cola as the world's largest soft-drink company, Porsche as one of the world's best sports cars, and so on. These brands own those positions and it would be hard for a competitor to steal them.

Ries and Trout show how familiar brands can acquire some distinctiveness in an 'overcommunicated society', where there is so much advertising that consumers screen out most of the messages. A consumer can only know about seven soft drinks, even though there are many more on the market. Even then, the mind often knows them in the form of a *product ladder*, such as Coke > Pepsi > Fanta or Hertz > Avis > Budget. In such a ladder, the second firm usually has half the business of the first firm, and the third firm enjoys half the business of the second firm. Furthermore, the top firm is remembered best.

People tend to remember *no. 1*. For example, when asked, 'Who was the first person successfully to fly the Atlantic Ocean?', people usually answer, 'Charles Lindbergh'. When asked, 'Who was the second person to do it?', they draw a blank. That is why companies fight for the no. 1 position. In reality, the first people to fly the Atlantic were Alcock and Brown, but Charles Lindbergh won the publicity battle.

Ries and Trout point out that the 'size' position can be held by only one brand. What counts is to achieve a no. 1 position along some valued attribute, not necessarily 'size'. Thus 7-Up is the no. 1 'Uncola', Porsche is the no. 1 small sports car and Foster's is Australia's top-selling lager. In the United States, Heineken is 'the' imported beer because it was the first heavily promoted imported beer. The marketer should identify an important attribute or benefit that can convincingly be won by the brand. In that way brands hook the mind in spite of the incessant advertising bombardment reaching consumers.

According to Ries and Trout, there are three positioning alternatives:

1. The first strategy they suggest is to strengthen a brand's *current position* in the mind of consumers. Thus Avis took its second position in the car rental business and made a strong point about it: 'We're number two. We try harder.' This was believable to the consumer. 7-Up capitalised on *not* being a cola soft drink by advertising itself as the Uncola.

2. Their second strategy is to search for a new *unoccupied position* that is valued by enough consumers and grab it: 'Cherchez le creneau', 'Look for the hole'. Find a hole in the market and fill it, they say. Vidal Sassoon's Wash & Go was based on recognising that the fashion for exercise meant that people washed their hair frequently, quickly and away from home. By combining a shampoo and hair conditioner in one the company was able to fill a latent market need. Similarly, after recognising that many housewives wanted a strong washing powder to treat smelly clothes, Unilever successfully launched Radion.

   > Across Europe new 'newspapers' have filled a down-market gap left by the traditional press. In Britain the *Sunday Sport* started as a weekly paper reporting on sensationalist stories – 'Double decker bus found in iceberg' – sport and sex, but has now grown into a daily paper. In France the new *Infos du Monde* reached sales of 240,000 a week after just two months. 'Our readers don't want "dirty" news', says *Infos*. It instead seeks the bizarre in ordinary life; fairground freaks are popular – 'Four-legged woman from Cannes looks for love'. Another sensationalist publication is the German-owned *Voici*, a glossy scandal sheet full of show-biz personalities. *Infos* has sent some of its staff to the United States to learn from their *Weekly World News*, a magazine specializing in blood, sex and gore. Some newspaper vendors are embarrassed about the newspapers and the established press sees the new publications as distasteful. They also worry about the disturbing misinformation they monger. But, as a Gare du Nord news kiosk seller says: 'If people lead such dull and boring lives that their day is brightened by reading about a man with an axe stuck in his head, what's wrong with that?'[18]

3. Their third strategy is to *deposition* or *reposition* the competition. Most US buyers of dinnerware thought that Lenox china and Royal Doulton both came from Europe. Royal Doulton countered with ads showing that Lenox china is from New Jersey, but theirs came from England. In a similar vein, Stolichnaya

vodka attacked Smirnoff and Wolfschmidt vodka by pointing out that these brands were made locally, but 'Stolichnaya is different. Similarly, it is Russian.' Guinness, the world's leading stout, has strong Irish associations. However, the focus on individuality in its Rutger Hauer 'Pure Genius' campaign has allowed Murphy's and Beamish to attack Guinness's Irish heritage. A final example is Kaliber no-alcohol beer, drunk by people who want a good time or, as Billy Connolly says in its ads posted next to those for Wonderbra, 'Hello girls!'.

Ries and Trout essentially deal with the psychology of positioning – or repositioning – a current brand in the consumer's mind. They acknowledge that the positioning strategy might call for changes in the product's name, price and packaging, but these are 'cosmetic changes done for the purpose of securing a worthwhile position – in the prospect's mind'.

perceptual mapping

Perceptual maps are a valuable aid to product positioning. These maps use *multidimensional scaling* of perceptions and preferences that portray psychological distance between products and segments, using many dimensions. They contrast with conventional maps that use two dimensions to show the physical distance between objects. Physical and psychological maps of the same items can be quite different. Disneyland in California and Disney's Magic Kingdom in Florida are thousands of kilometres apart physically, but psychologically close together.

In their simplest form, perceptual maps use two dimensions. For example, Figure 10.4 shows the average *value for money* and *accessibility* rating of European holiday destinations.[19] The perceptual map shows that France, Germany and the Netherlands, which are physically close together, are also psychologically close holiday destinations using these two criteria. In contrast, Spain and the United Kingdom are psychologically close together, but are physically distant. France is Europe's most popular holiday destination and this map partly shows why: it offers the best value for money among the accessible nations. The lack of destinations in the high *value for money* and easy *access* quadrant suggests a *cherchez le creneau* positioning opportunity for new destinations. Hungary and the Czech Republic could fill the hole in the market.

Of course, holidaymakers have a more complicated view of destinations than the two-dimensional map suggests. And if the map had other dimensions, it would change: for instance, adding weather would certainly separate Spain and the United Kingdom. Multidimensional scaling produces maps that show many dimensions at the same time

Perceptual maps
A product positioning tool that uses multidimensional scaling of consumers' perceptions and preferences to portray the psychological distance between products and segments.

Figure 10.4

Two-dimensional perceptual maps of European tourist destinations

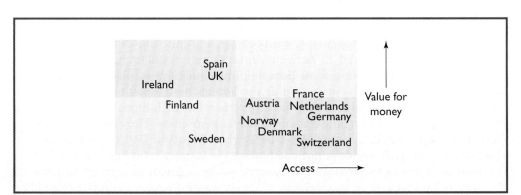

This award-winning campaign attracted immense attention without offending women. Sales of Wonderbra were reported to have more than doubled as a result.

SOURCE: Playtex

This poster ad promotes a distinct advantage of no-alcohol beer when meeting the girl in the Wonderbra.

SOURCE: © Guinness Ltd.

(Figure 10.5). To read these maps, trace back the individual dimensions one at a time. For example, the perception is that Switzerland has *good facilities*; Germany and Sweden quite good ones; Denmark, the Netherlands and Norway average ones; and the United Kingdom, Spain and Ireland *poor facilities*. Finland has an extreme position on the map. Prospective travellers see its people as *friendly and hospitable*, while the country is a *unique and different* place with *wild areas, beautiful scenery* and *peace and quiet*. More negatively, travellers do not perceive Finland as *accessible*, or as a place for *entertainment*, or as a *cultural experience*.

The perceptual map shows how holidaymakers segment, as well as the possible destinations. A, the largest segment, wants cheap, sunshine holidays and liked Spain. Segment C, who represented 15 per cent of the sample population, are a natural target market for Finland. They want peaceful, quiet holidays in places with beautiful scenery. Norway is already successful at marketing these 'back to nature' ideals as 'natural tourism'.[20] The target group mainly consists of high-income couples or families with one child who organise their holidays themselves. They are mainly Dutch, German or Scandinavian, but half have never visited Finland. To attract this segment the Finnish Tourist Board does not need massively to reposition Finland as a holiday destination. It needs to promote the country as the segment sees it, while reducing the perception that it is an *inaccessible* place. Promoting luxury car ferries that allow

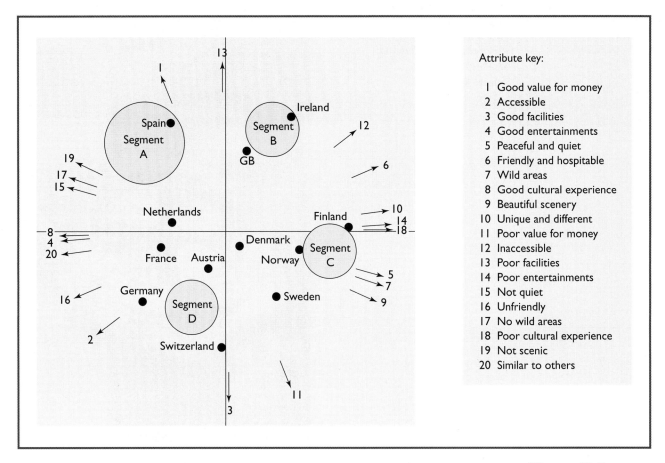

Figure 10.5

Internal property-fitting analysis using PREFMAP

SOURCE: G. Hooley, 'The Finnish Tourist Board', in Peter Doyle and Norman Hart (eds), *Case Studies in International Marketing* (Heinemann, 1982), p. 68. Reprinted with permission of Heinemann Educational Publishers.

travellers to start their holiday with a relaxing cruise across the Baltic Sea would be one way of doing this. Strangely, Barbados has a similar positioning problem to Finland as a holiday destination. Europeans perceive the Caribbean island as a millionaire's playground that is a long way away. In response, Barbados tries to reposition itself by promoting 'Barbados. It's closer than you think . . . A sunshine holiday there can cost as little as one of Europe's premier resorts.'[21]

positioning strategies

Marketers can follow several positioning strategies. These strategies use associations to change consumers' perception of products.

Product attributes position many technical products. The positioning of Ericsson's R380 mobile communicators is based on the touch screen access it gives e-mail, WAP and organiser, while much of BMW's advertising promotes individual *technical items* like fresh air filters. In the exclusive watch market Breitling, Baume & Mercier and Audemars Piguet's positioning are on their mechanical movements. Some of their designs leave the mechanisms exposed and one ad argues 'Since 1735 there has never been a quartz Blancpain. And there never will be.'

Benefits offered or the needs they fill position many products – Crest toothpaste reduces cavities, Aim tastes good and Macleans Sensitive relieves the pain of sensitive teeth. In the confectionery industry, Italian Baci and Ferrero Rocher are gifts, while Mars and Snickers bars satisfy hunger.

Positioning strategies: Breitling has chosen to position its watches on the attributes of precision and reliability.

SOURCE: Breitling SA

Huhtamaki is Finland's largest industrial company but LEAF, its confectionery division, is only tenth in size worldwide. It developed competitive advantage in 'functional chewing and bubble gums'. Its Xylitol Jenkki Xylifresh, probably 'the world's most researched chewing gum', has been used as a reference standard by medical schools measuring dental hygiene. LEAF's other functional gums include BenBits ExtraFresh and Fresh 4 Ever breath fresheners, and vitamin-enriched E.Z.C. Its sugar-based confectionery includes vitamin-enriched +Energi and Läkerol throat soother.

Usage occasions position many products. Mentadent Night Action toothpaste, for instance, is for evening use. In the summer, Gatorade is positioned as a drink for replacing athletes' body fluids; in the winter, it can be positioned as the drink to use when the doctor recommends plenty of liquids. KitKat and After Eight mints sell alongside Snickers and Ferrero Rocher, but the positioning is on usage occasion. Internationally, KitKat means 'Have a break', while After Eight is an after-dinner mint to share.

Red Bull, a soft drink made by a small Austrian company, is a huge success across Europe. According to its sales director: 'We don't want to be compared with the soft drink market. Of course, Red Bull has quite a key position in the market, but it is mainly a sports drink.' Red Bull's origin is in the huge Japanese market for energy drinks. Each can has 80 milligrams of caffeine, a third more than the equivalent amount of Coca-Cola. This has made the drink popular with teetotaller young ravers who can consume several cans a night.[22]

Users help position products. Johnson & Johnson improved the market share for its baby shampoo from 3 per cent to 14 per cent by repositioning the product towards a new *user category* of adults who wash their hair frequently and need a gentle shampoo. Often products are positioned by associating them with their *user class*. Nescafé Gold Blend increased sales dramatically after showing a series of ads romancing thirty somethings, as did Tango soft drinks as a result of the youthful 'You've been Tangoed' campaign.

Activities are often used to sell expensive products. The Geneva-based SMH group positions its watches using sports. Thus Rado has come to specialise in tennis, Omega in sailing and aerospace, 'the first and only watch on the moon', and Longines in skiing and aviation.[23] This positioning activity goes beyond advertising and promotions. Rolex positions its watches using adventurers and backs this with its Sfr450,000 (€298,000) Awards for Enterprise. Over 30 people are Rolex Laureate for their original and creative schemes. The take-off of TAG Heuer as a brand traces back to Steve McQueen wearing a Heuer chronograph and driving the then mythical Heuer-sponsored sports car in the movie *Le Mans*. Since then, TAG Heuer has grown to be Formula 1's official time keeper as it stuck determinedly to its motor sports positioning.[24]

Personalities often help positioning. Prestigious brands are often positioned using successful personalities who can add to a product's character. American Express runs ads showing caricatures of famous businesspeople who are also users; Jameson Irish Whiskey uses sportsmen in its positioning; and Hugo Boss identifies successful people as models in its 'Men at Work' campaign.[25]

Nike started 1990 as the third-place sports shoe after Reebok and Adidas but grew to no. 1 with 32 per cent market share by associating its products with the basketball star Michael Jordan, Tiger Woods and other famous sports personalities. After losing market leadership to Nike, Reebok aped Nike's position by spending $400 million on sports sponsorship against Nike's $1 billion. It failed. With a market share down to 15 per cent in 1998, Reebok backed off sports sponsorship. 'We don't want to compete head-on with Nike any more. They'll do their thing and we'll do ours', said Reebok's Paul Fireman. 'Getting stars to endorse products has been a priority for the past three years, and hasn't given us much of a payback.' Reebok will concentrate on older consumers, who are less susceptible to fashion and star endorsements. It will back away from Nike's dominant position in basketball and cross-training shoes to focus on its traditional strengths in running and walking. 'We're the tortoise, not the hare', explained Fireman.[26]

Origin positions product by association with its place of manufacture. Much of Perrier's success depended on the sophistication its French origin gave to it. Similarly, Audi's 'Vorsprung durch Technik' positioned its cars as German or Renault's 'Créateur d'automobiles' as French. Drinks are often positioned using origin. Foster's and Castlemaine XXXX lagers' positioning uses their Australian heritage, plus masculine humour to reinforce their character. Marketing Highlight 10.2 shows how a leading European company has positioned a whole range of its beers using *origin*.

Other brands can help position products. Clinique's advertising for its 'skin supplies for men' prominently features a Rolex watch. Where firms have traditionally crafted products, such as Wilkinson Sword or Holland & Holland shotguns, these lend glamour to more recent products – in these instances, shaving products and men's clothing respectively. After Volkswagen bought the Czech Skoda company, it used the Volkswagen name to transfer some of its strong reputation to Skoda. 'Volkswagen were so impressed, they bought the company' ran one press ad. The responsible ad agency, GGK, explains: 'The Volkswagen connection hit the spot. People immediately latched on to it. It allowed susceptible people [who might be persuaded to buy a Skoda] a route into the brand.' Dealers reported an instant 50 per cent sales increase. With VW engineering and Skoda 'more for less' positioning sales and customer loyalty have

marketing highlight 10.2

The place is the thing

Towns have long used famous characters to position the locations and give them a theme. Often these have some historical association, having been born, lived or died there. Some of Europe's more conspicuous cases are Mozart's Salzburg, Wagner's Bayreuth and Shakespeare's Stratford-upon-Avon. Other towns have positioned themselves with mythical or literary characters, such as Nottingham's Robin Hood (whose enemy supposedly lived there) or Ashby-de-la-Zouch's Ivanhoe (who fought the Black Knight at Ashby Castle). Such associations are sometimes used to market unexpected locations. After the Oscar-winning successes of *Shakespeare in Love*, Hackney, a run-down part of London, built on its associations with Shakespeare through its links with Babage, Shakespeare's mentor.

Besides using people to position places, places are often used to position portfolios of products. Belgian Interbrew is Europe's largest brewer. It retains its hold on the European market by trading on the geographical heritage of its products. The company certainly has plenty of heritage to trade on. First trading in Belgium as Den Hoorn in 1366, it changed its name to Artois

400 years later. Stella Artois remains Belgium's favoured tipple; elsewhere it is marketed as being 'reassuringly expensive'. Another one of Interbrew's brands, Bass, can probably lay claim to the best product placement of all time, having a prominent position in Manet's *A Bar at the Folies Bergère*. Other beers it promotes are Boddingtons, 'the cream of Manchester', Newcastle Brown and Caffrey's Irish beer.

Whitbread, once owner of many of Interbrew's drinks, positions its restaurant chains geographically. Their Pizza Hut and TGI Friday are both positioned as American although the Hut is for families and the TGI is for twenty-somethings. Café Rouge is French, Costa Coffee continental, Brewers Fayre 'Olde Englande' and Beefeaters British and carnivore.

SOURCES: Michelin Green Guides to Austria, Germany and Great Britain; Alison Smith, 'Whitbread to shake up restaurants', *Financial Times* (1 November 2000), p. 27; Dan Bilefsky, 'Interbrew offer set to raise €3.3bn', *Financial Times* (9 November 2000), p. 33; Mike Levy, 'Marketing Cinderellas', *Marketing Business* (July/August 2000), pp. 26–7.

Positioning strategies: The 'Norwegian footwear' slogan used by Viking is an example of a positioning strategy based on origin.
SOURCE: Mann (Norway) October 2000

The Ruhr's advertising positions it against the competition at the heart of Europe. This is a visual of a former compaign of the Ruhr. It ended in 1995/96.

SOURCE: Copyright Kommünalverband Rührgebeit

continued to grow. Ads still play on Skoda's past reputation but its Fabia 1.4 became the *What Car?* Car of the Year 2000. In 2002 its V8 engined B-plus project will project the company into the executive car market.[27]

Competitors provide two positioning alternatives. A product can be positioned directly *against a competitor*. For example, in ads for their personal computers, Compaq and Dell directly compared their products with IBM personal computers. The direct-selling computer company dan compares its performance with all other suppliers: '1st in repurchase intention, 1st in repair satisfaction', and so on. In its famous 'We're number two, so we try harder' campaign, Avis successfully positioned itself against the larger Hertz. A product may also be positioned *away from competitors* – 7-Up became the no. 3 soft drink when it was positioned as the 'Uncola', the fresh and thirst-quenching alternative to Coke and Pepsi. River Island Expeditions positions its holidays, its adventures for travellers, away from package holidays and the tourists who go on them. It says: 'The traveller is active; he goes strenuously in search of people, of adventure, of experience. The tourist is passive; expects interesting things to happen to him. He goes "sight-seeing" (Daniel J. Boorstin, 1962).'

Product class membership is the final means of positioning. For example, Van Den Bergh's I Can't Believe It's Not Butter is clearly positioned against butter, while other yellow fats are promoted as cooking oils. Camay hand soap is positioned with bath oils rather than with soap.

Marketers often use a *combination* of these positioning strategies. Johnson & Johnson's Affinity shampoo is positioned as a hair conditioner for women over 40 (product class *and* user). And in its Christmas campaigns, Martell cognac and Glenlivet malt whisky both neglect the lucrative 18- to 35-year olds to concentrate on the over-35s (*usage situation* and *user*).

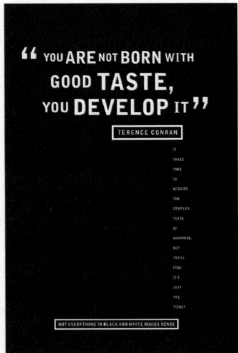

choosing and implementing a position strategy

Some firms find it easy to choose their positioning strategy. For example, a firm well known for quality in certain segments will go for this position in a new segment if there are enough buyers seeking quality. In many cases, two or more firms will go after the same position: for instance, British Airways and Lufthansa in the European business market. Then, each will have to find other ways to set itself apart, such as Lufthansa's promise of reliability and wider seats, and BA's lie-flat seats and executive lounges. Each firm must differentiate its offer by building a unique bundle of competitive advantages that appeal to a substantial group within the segment.

Having identified a set of possible competitive advantages upon which to build a position, the next stages are to select the right competitive advantages and effectively communicate the chosen position to the market.

selecting the right competitive advantages

Suppose a company is fortunate enough to have several potential competitive advantages. It must now choose the ones upon which it will build its positioning strategy. It must decide *how many* differences to promote and *which ones*.

■ How many differences to promote?

Many marketers think that companies should aggressively promote only one benefit to the target market. Ad man Rosser Reeves, for example, said a company should develop a **unique selling proposition (USP)** for each brand and stick to it. Each brand should pick an attribute and tout itself as 'no. 1' on that attribute. Buyers tend to remember 'no. 1' better, especially in an over-communicated society. Thus Crest toothpaste consistently promotes its anti-cavity protection, and Mercedes promotes its great automotive engineering. What are some of the 'no. 1' positions to promote? The most significant ones are 'best quality', 'best service', 'lowest price', 'best value' and 'most advanced technology'. A company that hammers away at one of these positions and consistently achieves it will probably become best known and remembered for it.

The difficulty of keeping functional superiority has made firms focus on having a unique **emotional selling proposition (ESP)** instead of a USP. The product may be similar to competitors' products, but it has unique associations for consumers. Leading names like Rolls-Royce, Ferrari and Rolex have done this. Other cars outperform Ferrari on the road and track, but 'the red car with the prancing horse' is the world's no. 1 sports car. Many Formula One racing drivers still dream of racing a Ferrari and Ferrari pay the 'world's best driver' €40 million a year to make sure he can keep winning for them.[28]

Other marketers think that companies should position themselves on more than one differentiating factor. This may be necessary if two or more firms are claiming to be best on the same attribute. Steelcase, an office furniture systems company, differentiates itself from competitors on two benefits: best on-time delivery and best installation support. Volvo positions its automobiles as 'safest' and 'most durable'. Fortunately, these benefits are compatible – a very safe car is also very durable.

Today, in a time when the mass market is fragmenting into many small segments, companies are trying to broaden their positioning strategies to appeal to more segments. For example, Beecham promotes its Aquafresh toothpaste as offering three benefits: 'anti-cavity protection', 'better breath' and 'whiter teeth'. Clearly, many people want all three benefits, and the challenge is to convince them that the brand delivers all three. Beecham's solution was to create toothpaste that squeezed out of the tube in three colours, thus visually confirming the three benefits. In doing this, Beecham attracted three segments instead of one.

However, as companies increase the number of claims for their brands, they risk disbelief and a loss of clear positioning. Usually, a company needs to avoid three serious positioning errors. The first is **underpositioning** – that is, failing to position the company at all. Some companies discover that buyers have only a vague idea of the brand, or that they do not really know anything special about it. This has occurred with dark spirits – whisky and brandy – where young drinkers have drifted away from them. United Distillers and Hiram Walker aim to reverse this trend with their Bell's and Teacher's brands by targeting 25- to 35-year-old men. There is much focus on extending the use of both brands as a mixer. This is an anathema to many whisky drinkers, but United Distillers has successfully promoted it as a mixer in both Spain and Greece.[29] The second positioning error is **overpositioning** – that is, giving buyers too narrow a picture of the company. Thus a consumer might think that the Steuben glass company makes only fine art glass costing €1,000+ and up, when it also makes affordable fine glass starting at around €50.

Finally, companies must avoid **confused positioning** – that is, leaving buyers with a confused image of the company. For example, Burger King has struggled without success for years to establish a profitable and consistent position. Since 1986, it has undertaken five separate advertising campaigns, with themes ranging from 'Herb the nerd doesn't eat here' and 'This is a Burger King town', to 'The right food for the right times' and 'Sometimes you've got to break the rules'. This barrage of positioning statements has left consumers confused and Burger King with poor sales and profits.[30]

Implausible positioning occurs when the positioning strategy stretches the perception of the buyers too far. Toyota recognised this when it created the Lexus brand rather than try to stretch its highly respected name into the luxury car market. When TiVo personal video recorders were first launched in the US priced from $300 (€337)

Unique selling proposition (USP)
The unique product benefit that a firm aggressively promotes in a consistent manner to its target market. The benefit usually reflects functional superiority: best quality, best services, lowest price, most advanced technology.

Emotional selling proposition (ESP)
A non-functional attribute that has unique associations for consumers.

Underpositioning
A positioning error referring to failure to position a company, its product or brand.

Overpositioning
A positioning error referring to too narrow a picture of the company, its product or a brand being communicated to target customers.

Confused positioning
A positioning error that leaves consumers with a confused image of the company, its product or a brand.

Implausible positioning
Making claims that stretch the perception of the buyers too far to be believed.

marketing highlight 10.3

When positions collide

Some positions, just like some segments, do not mix. Not only differing in their tastes, but positively disliking one another. Marketers can sometimes use this alienation profitably. When the marketers of 'ever so nice' Smarties children's confectionery recognised that growing 'pest power' meant that they had to attract children rather than parents, they did it with a vengeance. Not only did Smarties TV advertising become exciting for children, but the company also tapped into playground cults. The first was 'cool dood' sunglasses, then came the 'gruesome greenies' pouch and the 'zapper', a pocket-sized machine that made noises guaranteed to annoy parents and teachers. Ironically, from the same stable comes the Milky Bar Kid – a squeaky clean nice boy dressed in white whom many parents love but who is far from appealing to streetwise kids. The Milky Bar Kid works because it is aimed at parents who buy white chocolate Milky Bar products for their very young children.

Sometimes, trying to appeal directly to the tastes of children can backfire. Healthy children's cereal Weetabix had to withdraw a campaign showing its cereal bars dressed as skin-heads who came too close to looking like football hooligans. Lego faced a similar backlash when it promoted its educational toys using an unsavoury Lego character driving a Lego car recklessly. Some parents thought it looked too much like joy-riding.

This alienation positioning has been used by a succession of pop musicians. Often their positioning is by behaviour. It is hard to imagine that part of the appeal of the classic 1960s rock bands The Who and the Rolling Stones was their noisy music as well as their wrecking of their instruments and hotel rooms. Even the Beatles were 'mop heads' until the Stones out-alienated them. They followed in the tradition set by such objectionable creatures as Elvis Presley and Cliff Richard. Each generation discovers alienation positions, although few went so far as punk bands such as the Sex Pistols.

Sometimes the excitement, youth and energy make these outsiders attractive to people trying to position themselves. In the 'swinging sixties', the then British prime minister, Harold Wilson, held parties at 10 Downing Street where he could be photographed alongside pop personalities. Probably the saddest case of this pop positioning was Richard Nixon being photographed with Elvis as part of an anti-drugs campaign. Pop positioning was too good a trick for Britain's New Labour to miss. Soon after gaining power, Tony Blair was photographed with Oasis's Noel Gallagher at a 10 Downing Street pop party. It became one pop position too far at the 1998 Brit music industry awards. While the music industry was helping pop position New Labour, anarchist pop group Chumbawamba exploited alienation positioning by pouring a bucket of water over John Prescott, deputy prime minister. It is dangerous when positions collide.

SOURCES: David Murray, 'What the audience really wants', *Financial Times* (29 December 1997), p. 7; Alice Rawsthorn, 'Ministers may launch fashion policy collection', *Financial Times* (17 February 1998), p. 12.

to $600, customers did not buy. The reason was that people did not believe what the ad showed. It contained a man watching a live game on TV, pausing the game to get a drink, then restarting the 'live' game where he left off. Since TiVo's can digitally record and play back at the same time, the benefit the ad shows is real but people could not believe the claim. TiVo is soon to be relauched at a lower price and promoting the machines' more believable long recording time per disc (40 hours) and digital quality. Some market positions, while attracting one group of customers, can alienate others and so backfire, as Marketing Highlight 10.3 tells.

■ Which differences to promote?

Not all brand differences are meaningful or worthwhile. Not every difference makes a good differentiator. Each difference has the potential to create company costs as well as customer benefits. Therefore, the company must carefully select the ways in which it will distinguish itself from competitors. A difference is worth establishing insofar as it satisfies the following criteria:

COMPETITIVE ADVANTAGE	COMPANY STANDING (1–10)	COMPETITOR STANDING (1–10)	IMPORTANCE OF IMPROVING STANDING (H-M-L)	AFFORDABILITY AND SPEED (H-M-L)	COMPETITOR'S ABILITY TO IMPROVE STANDING (H-M-L)	RECOMMENDED ACTION
Technology	8	8	L	L	M	Hold
Cost	6	8	H	M	M	Watch
Quality	8	6	L	L	H	Watch
Service	4	3	H	H	L	Invest

Table 10.2

Finding competitive advantage

+ *Important.* The difference delivers a highly valued benefit to target buyers.

+ *Distinctive.* Competitors do not offer the difference, or the company can offer it in a more distinctive way.

+ *Superior.* The difference is superior to other ways by which customers might obtain the same benefit.

+ *Communicable.* The difference is communicable and visible to buyers.

+ *Pre-emptive.* Competitors cannot easily copy the difference.

+ *Affordable.* Buyers can afford to pay for the difference.

+ *Profitable.* The company can introduce the difference profitably.

Many companies have introduced differentiations that failed one or more of these tests. The Westin Stamford hotel in Singapore advertises that it is the world's tallest hotel, a distinction that is not important to many tourists – the fact scared many. AT&T's original picturevision phones failed, partly because the public did not think that seeing the other person was worth the phone's high cost. Philips Laservision failed too. Although the laser disks gave excellent picture quality, there were few disks available and the machines could not record. These drawbacks meant that consumers saw Laservision as offering no advantage over videotape machines.

Some competitive advantages are too slight, too costly to develop, or too inconsistent with the company's profile. Suppose that a company is designing its positioning strategy and has narrowed its list of possible competitive advantages to four. The company needs a framework for selecting the one advantage that makes the most sense to develop. Table 10.2 shows a systematic way of evaluating several potential competitive advantages and choosing the right one.

In the table, the company compares its standing on four attributes – technology, cost, quality and service – to the standing of its chief competitor. Let's assume that both companies stand at 8 on technology (1 = low score, 10 = high score), which means that they both have good technology. The company questions whether it can gain much by improving its technology further, especially given the high cost of new technology. The competitor has a better standing on cost (8 instead of 6), and this can hurt the company if the market gets more price sensitive. The company offers higher quality than its competitor (8 instead of 6). Finally, both companies offer below-average service (4 and 3).

At first glance, it appears that the company should go after cost or service to improve its market appeal over the competitor. However, it must consider other factors. First, how important are improvements in each of these attributes to the target customers? The fourth column shows that both cost and service improvements would be highly important to customers. Next, can the company afford to make the improvements? If so, how fast can it complete them? The fifth column shows that the company could improve service quickly and affordably. But if the firm decided to do this, would the competitor be able to improve its service also? The sixth column shows that the competitor's ability to improve service is low, perhaps because the competitor does not believe in service or has limited funds. The final column then shows the appropriate actions to take on each attribute. It makes the most sense for the company to invest in improving its service. Service is important to customers; the company can afford to improve its service and can do it fast, and the competitor will probably not be able to catch up.

communicating and delivering the chosen position

Once it has chosen a position, the company must take strong steps to deliver and communicate the desired position to target consumers. All the company's marketing-mix efforts must support the positioning strategy. Positioning the company calls for concrete action – it is not just talk. If the company decides to build a position on better quality and service, it must first *deliver* that position. Designing the marketing mix – product, price, place and promotion – involves working out the tactical details of the positioning strategy. Thus a firm that seizes upon a 'high-quality position' knows that it must produce high-quality products, charge a high price, distribute through high-quality dealers and advertise in high-quality media. It must hire and train more service people, find retailers that have a good reputation for service, and develop sales and advertising messages that broadcast its superior service. This is the only way to build a consistent and believable high-quality, high-service position.

Calvin Klein Cosmetics has noticed a shift in the fragrance market. Shiseido launched a classic fragrance by Jean-Paul Gaultier, *enfant terrible* of French

Unilever positioned its best-selling Lever 2000 soap on three benefits in one: cleansing, deodorising, and moisturising benefits. It's good 'for all your 2000 parts.'
SOURCE: Unilever plc

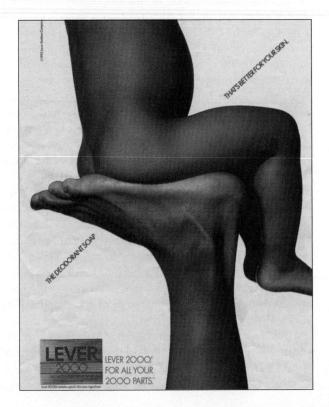

fashion, that broke industry rules with its punky advertising and packaging – a bottle in the shape of a woman's torso encased in an aluminium can. L'Oréal responded with Eden, a new Cacharel fragrance for ecologically concerned consumers.

Calvin Klein's response is *cK one*, a 'shared fragrance for young consumers who, he believes, are ready to buy a scent created for both sexes'. The designer's other fragrances, Obsession, Eternity and Escape, are for women only. The positioning of *cK one* is radical and covers the whole marketing mix. The range includes youth-oriented products, such as massage oil. The bottles and display material are by Fabien Baron, designer of advertising campaigns for other Calvin Klein products as well as Valentino, Burberry's and Giorgio Armani. He also collaborated with Madonna in the production of her *Sex* book. He says Calvin's response to the bottle was 'Boom! Yeah! Right on.' It is a frosted glass flask with aluminium top and recycled paper packaging.

The rest of the marketing mix backs *cK one*'s radical positioning. Prices are low – about 70 per cent of Obsession's – and it will sell in novel distribution outlets, notably Tower Records. To ensure that the multi-million dollar launch is a success, Calvin Klein's corporation will send 12,000 gorgeous members of both sexes to stores to splash it on shoppers.[31]

Companies often find it easier to come up with a good positioning strategy than to implement it. Establishing a position or changing one usually takes a long time. In contrast, positions that have taken years to build can quickly disappear. Once a company has built the desired position, it must take care to maintain the position through consistent performance and communication. It must closely monitor and adapt the position over time to match changes in consumer needs and competitors' strategies. This is how world-leading brands such as Coca-Cola, Nescafé, Snickers, BMW, Rolex, Estée Lauder, Johnnie Walker and Chanel have remained pre-eminent for so long. The company should avoid abrupt changes that might confuse consumers. Coca-Cola forgot this when it introduced its disastrous new Coke, Marlboro's price cuts made the brand fall from being the most highly valued brand to out of the top ten, and Unilever's hasty introduction of the Persil/Omo Power benefited Procter & Gamble. Violent changes rarely succeed – a product's position should evolve as it adapts to the changing market environment.

summary

The *core strategy* of a company shows how it will address the markets it has targeted. By *differentiation* it develops the strengths of the company, so that they meet the target markets' needs; then, by market positioning, it manages the way consumers view the company and its products.

Differentiation helps a firm compete profitably. It gives it a *competitive advantage*. If a firm does not differentiate, it will be like 'all the rest' and be forced to compete on price. Differentiation is harder in some industries than others, but it is rare that a creative marketer cannot differentiate a market in some way.

Value-based position offers a range general positioning alternative based on the value delivered for its price. Several potentially successful strategies range from *more for more*, where customers are offered great products or service at a higher price, to *less for less* which offers basic services at discount prices. Combinations of price and value that are the same as those already in the market are unlikely to succeed, as are offerings that deliver less value to customers.

There are four main ways to differentiate: *product differentiation, service differentiation, personnel differentiation* and *image differentiation*. The ease of following new technological innovations means that the product is becoming an increasingly difficult way to differentiate. Now service and image are the main ways people distinguish between products. As systems and methods become more common, personnel differentiation becomes more important. The firm is its people and they are usually what the customer is most sensitive to.

A firm's functional strengths give it its competitive advantage. Market positioning is about managing customers' view of the company and its products. It is about perception. *Perceptual maps* are a way of revealing how customers see markets. They show which products customers see as alike and those that are not. They can also show segments and the dimensions that customers use to split up the market.

There are several positioning strategies for shifting and holding customers' perceptions. Positioning works by associating products with product attributes or other stimuli. Successful firms usually maintain a clear differential advantage and do not make violent changes to their market positions.

discussing the issues

1. In marketing products and services, 'being different is good', so the pros say. Why should firms differentiate their product or service offerings? What are the specific ways in which a producer of goods or services differentiates its offer from those of competitors? Discuss, using specific examples.

2. What roles do product attributes and perceptions of attributes play in positioning a product? Can an attribute held by several competing brands be used in a successful positioning strategy?

3. Famous personalities are often used in advertising products. Think of examples you know and work out what values the personality brings to the brand.

4. Think of well-known beer or lager brands. How well are these positioned in relation to one another? Do manufacturers clarify or confuse the positioning themes? Are the differences they promote meaningful or worthwhile?

5. Is positioning helpful to not-for-profit organisations? If so, how should a charity select and implement a positioning strategy? If not, why?

applying the concepts

1. By looking at advertising and at products themselves, we can often see how marketers are attempting to position their products and what target market they hope to reach.

   ✦ Define the positionings of and target markets for Coca-Cola, Pepsi Cola, Red Bull, Tango and 7-Up.

   ✦ Define the positionings of and target markets for KitKat, Lion Bar, Snickers, Aero, Mars Bars and Twix.

   ✦ Do you think that the soft drinks and confectionery industries achieve distinctive positionings and target markets? Are some more clearly defined than others?

2. As the Internet develops, lifestyle magazines (*the net*) and websites (*hot-toast.com* and *handbag.com*) are growing in importance compared to nerd (*Internet Works*) or rooky (*Internet Made Easy*) magazines or websites. Examine some of these lifestyle offerings to determine what mechanisms, such as style, personalities and services, they use to position themselves differently from more utilitarian options.[32]

references

1. Based on John Griffiths, 'The pace hots up', *Financial Times* (26 January 1990), p. I; Andrew Bolger, 'Growth by successful targeting', *Financial Times* (21 June 1994), p. 12; Shiraz Sidhva, 'Carmakers drive deep into India', *Financial Times* (20 July 1994), p. 28; David Done, 'Benetton Grand Prix team changes gear', *Financial Times* (24 August 1994), p. 2; Meg Carter, 'Wheels of fortune', *Marketing Week* (26 August 1994), pp. 28–30; Anil Bhoyrul, 'Devil take the hindmost', *Business Age*, **4**, 49 (1994), pp. 20–3; John Griffiths, 'Steering into a commanding lead', *Financial Times* (15 January 1998), p. 25.

2. For a discussion of the concepts of differentiation and competitive advantage, and methods for assessing them, see Michael Porter, *Competitive Advantage* (New York: Free Press, 1985), Ch. 2; George S. Day and Robin Wensley, 'Assessing advantage: a framework for diagnosing competitive superiority', *Journal of Marketing* (April 1988), pp. 1–20; Philip Kotler, *Marketing Management*, 7th edn (Englewood Cliffs, NJ: Prentice Hall, 1991), Ch. 11; Grahan Hooley and John Saunders, *Competitive Positioning: The key to market success* (Hemel Hempstead: Prentice Hall, 1993).

3. For an interesting discussion of finding ways to differentiate marketing offers, see Ian C. MacMillan and Rita Gunther McGrath, 'Discovering new points of differentiation', *Harvard Business Review* (July–August 1997), pp. 133–45.

4. 'Global business outlook', *Financial Times Survey* (13 January 1998).

5. For a review of this and other results, see Robert D. Buzzell and Bradley T. Gale, *The PIMS Principle: Linking strategy to performance* (New York: Free Press, 1987).

6. Theodore Levitt, 'Making success through differentiation – of anything', *Harvard Business Review* (January–February 1980).

7. 'Western Europe's insurance tangle', *The Economist* (18 June 1994), pp. 115–16; 'e.Business Report', *e.business* (February 2000), 30–47.

8. See David A. Garvin, 'Competing on the eight dimensions of quality', *Harvard Business Review* (November–December 1987), pp. 101–9.

9. See Tom Peters, *Thriving on Chaos* (New York: Knopf, 1987), pp. 56–7.

10. For details of this and other examples, see George Stalker and Thomas M. Hout, *Competing Against Time* (London: Collier Macmillan, 1990).

11. See Philip Kotler, *Kotler on Marketing* (Upper Saddle River, NJ: Prentice Hall, 1999), pp. 59–63.

12. Bettina von Hase, 'This shoe walks', *Business FT Weekend Magazine* (4 November 2000), 30–4.

13. Mercedes M. Cardona and Jack Neff, 'Everything's at a premium', *Advertising Age* (2 August 1999), pp. 12, 15.

14. Michael Harvey, 'As sport as you want to be', *Weekend FT* (28–29 October 2000), p. XVII.

15. Gillian O'Conner, 'Business opts for no-frills flights', *Financial Times* (13 March 2000), p. 3; Kevin Done, 'EasyJet orders 17 aircraft in expansion drive', *Financial Times* (30 March 2000), p. 26; Kenin Done, 'Web prompts "huge" savings for Ryanair', *Financial Times* (8 November 2000), p. 34; David Humphries, 'Niche airports for high-flyers', *How To Spend It* (4–5 November 2000), pp. 8–10.

16. Jane Tawbase, 'Jaguar's new dream is a reality', *EuroBusiness* (June 2000), pp. 72–3; Jane Tawbase, 'Filling the garages of families', *EuroBusiness* (July 2000), pp. 70–4; 'Her luxury', *The Economist* (4 November 2000), p. 124.

17. Positioning was introduced in the seminal work by Al Ries and Jack Trout, *Positioning: The battle for your mind* (New York: McGraw-Hill, 1981); see also Al Ries and Jack Trout, *Marketing Warfare* (New York: McGraw-Hill, 1986). Al Ries develops his ideas in 'The mind is the ultimate battlefield', *Journal of Business Strategy* (July–August 1988), pp. 4–7.

18. Julie Street, 'Success crowns crash course in sensationalism', *The European – élan* (10–16 June 1994), p. 5.

19. These figures and others relating to European tourist destinations are based on a study by A. Haahti, Helsinki School of Economics, R. R. van den Heuvel, Groningen University and G. J. Hooley of Aston University. The results are disguised for the purpose of confidentiality. A case study called 'Finnish Tourist Board' by Graham Hooley appears in Peter Doyle and Norman Hart (eds), *Case Studies in International Marketing* (London: Heinemann, 1982), pp. 61–86.

20. Leiv Gunner Lie, 'Norway cashes in on the magic of the mountains', *The European* (10–16 June 1994), p. 20.

21. For more on the practicalities of perceptual maps see Graham Hooley, John Saunders and Nigel Piercy, *Marketing Strategy and Competitive Positioning* (Hemel Hempstead: Prentice Hall, 1998).

22. David Short, 'Red Bull set to lock horns with multinationals', *The European* (19–25 August 1994).

23. Susan Jacquet, 'Ethics and responsibility', *Swiss Quality Timing* (Spring 1994), pp. 40–1.

24. Birna Helgadottir, 'Time has come to realise your dreams', *The European – élan* (16–22 September 1994), p. 6; Tom Rubython, 'Turnaround artist' *EuroBusiness* (April 2000), pp. 38–42.

25. Mike Baldwin, 'Nice car, shame about the driver', *Today* (20 September 1994), p. 7.

26. Victoria Griffith, 'Reebok backs off in sponsorship battle', *Financial Times* (15 January 1998), p. 36.

27. Diane Summers, 'Skoda's sales drive is no joke', *Financial Times* (12 May 1994), p. 11; Stephen Bayley, 'Freedom and its discontents', *The European Magazine* (6–12 March 1997), pp. 14–17; Paul Mungo, 'Wipe the smile off', *Business Financial Times Weekend Magazine* (29 April 2000), pp. 20–2, 40.

28. Catherine Monk, 'No more red', *EuroBusiness* (April 2000), pp. 68–74; Catherine Monk, 'Ordering up a world champion', *EuroBusiness* (April 2000), pp. 146–8.

29. Ros Snowden, 'Spirit of adventure', *Marketing Week* (15 August 1994), pp. 32–5.

30. Mark Landler and Gail DeGeorge, 'Tempers are sizzling over Burger King's new ads', *Business Week* (12 February 1990), p. 33; Philip Stelly, Jr, 'Burger King rule breaker', *Adweek* (9 November 1990), pp. 24, 26.

31. Alice Rawsthorn, 'A nose for innovation', *Financial Times* (4 August 1994), p. 11; Bronwyn Cosgrove, 'Fabulous Fabien's pure object of desire', *The European – élan* (23–9 September 1994), pp. 14–15.

32. Virginia Mathews, 'Net mags defy sceptics', *The Times* (30 June 2000), p. 31; Mark Effiot, 'Net benefits', *Marketing Business* (April 2000), pp. 26–7.

case 10

SoBe's herbal hedonism*

There are not many companies where the top executives rejoice in comic book names and that include promotional love buses and armoured trucks among the few assets on their balance sheets. SoBe, the 'New Age' US beverage group run by the 'Lizard King' and the 'Manatee', is one.

Founded in 1995, SoBe prides itself on being a 'virtual' brand company that does things differently. But the financial results it produces would impress even the most buttoned-down Wall Street banker. Over the past five years SoBe has lifted its revenues from $2.4m (€2.7m) to an estimated $225m this year and it has plans to expand overseas. In April 2000 it entered the EU and it is now selling its drinks through Sainsbury's, the UK's second largest grocery chain.

SoBe says its success is due to its ability to promote fashionable, herb-based teas and juices for the youth market. But its eye-catching growth is creating challenges: it may be easy to create a buzz about a new brand but the trick is to sustain it. The question now is whether SoBe can enter the mainstream drinks market without losing its alternative image. Will a mooted deal with Coca-Cola, the multinational soft drinks group, kill SoBe's iconoclastic appeal?

The company's founders, Lizard King and Manatee, are both drinks industry veterans with decades of experience gained from working for Pepsi Cola and the Stroh beer company. The two executives were convinced there was a niche for a different kind of New Age drink that would appeal to young partygoers. They were determined to build their brand from the grassroots to maximise its youth appeal.

'Kids are fickle and hard to reach. These are people you can turn on or turn off in a heartbeat. You have to stay fresh and new', says Manatee. 'We are building this brand up and down the street and can conceive of a product and put it into the market within two and a half months.'

In order to project an image of healthy hedonism, SoBe added herbs and nutrients such as ginseng, ginkgo and guarana to its teas and juices. 'The only trouble is that herbs taste like shit', says Lizard Communicator, vice-president of corporate communications. So the company consulted a flavour laboratory in Heidelberg, Germany, to come up with sweet-tasting products. SoBe then packaged its drinks in chunky, clear glass bottles labelling them with two lizards, which were supposed to represent the yin and yang of life. SoBe branded its drinks by characteristics – Power, Wisdom and Drive – rather than flavours. Its latest product is called Adrenaline Rush.

The company has also concentrated on grassroots marketing, selling its drinks through what it calls the 'single-serve, cold channel' in local supermarkets, petrol stations and delicatessens. To attract young sports fanatics, SoBe has also set up fridges in bike and snowboard shops and sends its love buses and armoured cars out to extreme sports events, where they distribute 'lizard gear' such as T-shirts, keyrings and belts and hand out free samples of the drinks. The brand is also promoted by Team Lizard, a group of athletes sponsored by SoBe, including Biker Sherlock, the downhill skateboarder and street luger, and John Daly, the long-hitting golf champion.

SoBe has encouraged customer feedback by setting up a toll-free telephone line where consumers can tell the Lizard King what they think of the latest products. They can also post their comments on SoBe's interactive website, which receives more than 2m hits a month. This summer SoBe launched a $9m radio advertising campaign incorporating some of these personal customer testimonials. So far SoBe has shied away from mainstream television advertising. 'We have not yet found a creative story that would bring in more customers than it would lose', says Manatee. 'A lot of kids are simply wallpapering Coke and Pepsi ads because they are not doing anything different.'

However, SoBe is not alone in the New Age drinks market: competition is increasingly fierce as the traditional soft-drinks market turns flat. For the past 28 years Snapple has sold similar drinks, with varying degrees of success. But the company has just been bought for $1.45bn by Cadbury Schweppes, the UK drinks group, which promises to add financial and managerial muscle to the market-leading Snapple brand.

'I think it was a great strategic move by Cadbury and enhances their distribution system', says Manatee. 'It has also helped legitimise the New Age category (of drinks) and has spruced up Coke's and Pepsi's awareness of it.' SoBe is itself aiming to clinch a deal with Coca-Cola, which is interested in buying a 20 per cent stake in the company. With an assumed market value of

---

* Reproduced with minor modifications from John Thornhill, 'Herbal hedonism with Coke's fizz', *Financial Times* (27 October 2000), p. 17.

about 250m dollars, it is easy to see why SoBe's founders are keen to cash in some of their chips.

Manatee argues that SoBe can benefit greatly from Coca-Cola's distribution network and multinational scale. 'We think that with the right partners and the right brand mix we can continue to grow this brand. We want to remain a separate entity but be able to benefit from Coca-Cola's assistance and distribution', he says. 'If the partnership is managed correctly it can be beneficial to both sides.'

Manatee acknowledges the risk that SoBe could lose some of its wacky image if it goes ahead with the Coca-Cola deal but believes the company's youthful workforce will keep it honest. 'There are risks that the edges will be filed off. But we intend to remain outside the box', he says.

It is an open question how SoBe's customers will react to the company's becoming a more traditional corporate entity. The company believes that they will remain loyal just as long as SoBe keeps producing the goods. However, even Lizard Communicator admits: 'Mainstream is a word that scares us.'

Questions

1. How does SoBe's position in the marketplace differ from that of conventional soft drinks?

2. What mechanisms and associations does SoBe use to position itself in the customer's mind?

3. Does the use of the names Lizard King, Manatee and Lizard Communicator have any real value in helping SoBe's performance?

4. Will SoBe's customers remain loyal 'just as long as SeBe keeps producing the goods' and what are 'the goods'?

5. When 'New Age' drinks company Snapple was taken over by a 'traditional corporate entity' its sales and profits slumped badly. Why?

6. What does SoBe need to do to ensure that the same does not happen because of its association with Coke?

internet exercises

Internet exercises for this chapter can be found on the student site of the MYPHLIP Web Site at www.booksites.net/kotler.

chapter eleven

Building customer relationships: customer satisfaction, quality, value and service

Chapter objectives   _After reading this chapter, you should be able to:_

✦ Define _customer value_ and discuss its importance in creating and measuring customer satisfaction and company profitability.

✦ Discuss the concepts of _value chains_ and _value delivery systems_ and explain how companies go about producing and delivering customer value.

✦ Define quality and explain the importance of total quality marketing in building value-laden, profitable relationships with customers.

✦ Explain the importance of retaining current customers as well as attracting new ones.

✦ Discuss customer relationship marketing and the main steps in establishing a customer relationship programme.

introduction

Today's companies face tough competition and things will only get harder. In previous chapters, we argued that to succeed in today's fiercely competitive markets, companies have to move from a _product and selling philosophy_ to a _customer and marketing philosophy_. This chapter tells in more detail how companies can win doing a better job of _meeting and satisfying consumer and customer needs_. In launching 'seriously' vodka (see preview case overleaf), Facile is going beyond promoting and selling the product to establishing a relationship with bar staff that allows them to influence and share in the long-term success of the drink.

At one time, there was little need for such concerns for customer relationships or satisfaction. In sellers' markets – characterised by shortages and near-monopolies – companies did not make special efforts to please customers. In eastern Europe, for

preview case

Facile's seriously rich barmen

Philip Diklev is a gangling, punctilious Swedish wine waiter with a goatee beard and a three-piece suit and an ambition to revolutionise the global spirits business. 'There is an enormous waste in the industry', he grimaces, as if sampling a corked Beaujolais. 'We are trying to do everything differently.'

Mr Diklev is the executive chairman of Facile, a start-up Swedish drinks company floated on the Stockholm stock market in April [2000]. Today the company launched an innovative scheme in London to market its vodka, which trades under the brand name 'seriously' (with a lower-case s). 'We have the enormous advantage of being able to start from scratch. But our intention is to be one of the vodka brand leaders in the world', he says.

Facile is betting its business on the belief that it is the bar owners in the UK's 112,000 licensed outlets who make or break a new brand. It has set up a novel option scheme that will give the bar owners equity in the Drinks Company in proportion to the number of bottles they sell. The options, which are exercisable in five years' time, could eventually give bar owners up to 16.7 per cent of the company's entire equity.

'Bar owners will become our biggest shareholders', Mr Diklev says. 'We are paying them a lot of money in the faith that they are brand builders. We are paying them for the job that they have done in the past and never been paid for.'

Facile's thinking is based on research showing that 43 per cent do not know what they are going to drink when they approach the bar. This gives the bar owners enormous influence on purchasing decision. Facile hopes that bar owners recommending the vodka create a 'buzz' around the brand before it is launched in retail outlets next April [2001].

Other drinks companies are aware of the importance of opinion formers and have been seducing bar owners for years by paying for refurbishments or providing free refrigerators. But Facile is perhaps the first company to give such a direct financial incentive in the brand's success.

Rita Clifton, chief executive officer of Interbrand, the brand consultancy, says this options scheme is potentially interesting for several reasons. First, it is a relatively cheap and risk-free way for a small company to launch a brand, because it relies on deferred incentives rather than up-front payments. Second, it conforms to textbook models of 'warm' ownership, which suggest that the best shareholders are those who have a direct and sympathetic involvement with its brand.

'When you are launching a new brand you cannot boil the ocean. Therefore the choice of the bar owner to spread your message is a very good one. Viral marketing or word-of-mouth advertising can get a brand off to a fast and authentic start', says Ms Clifton.

However, the giant multinational drink companies still adhere to the faith that you have to create mass appeal among your customers if you are ever to create a truly successful brand.

'You have to come up with the right consumer proposition', says Paul Walsh, chief executive of Diageo, the British drinks group, which markets Smirnoff vodka. 'If the consumer does not like what you are offering all incentives to the bar staff will come to nothing. I am a firm believer in pull marketing.'

Facile spent more than three years developing its seriously vodka and claims its unique non-bitter taste has proved extremely popular in blind tasting. The company is also trying to create a 'pull' element to its marketing by spending £4m [€6.67m] on a quirky – but relatively conventional – advertising campaign.

Mr Diklev says that, if successful, Facile could extend its options scheme to other spirits and to other markets. 'London has been the centre of the spirits world for 200 years and the UK is an amazingly trend-setting market. If it works here then it will be understood in every other part of the world', he says.

Questions

1. How does Facile's launch strategy differ from that preferred by Diageo?

2. Is Facile correct in choosing to establish a relationship with bar staff rather than customers?

3. Is Facile correct in thinking that: 'If it works here [the UK] then it will be understood in every other part of the world'? Why or why not?

Source: Initially published in 'Trying to make selling spirits seriously easy', John Thornhill, *Financial Times* (11 Sept. 2000).

example, millions of would-be consumers used to stand sullenly in line for hours only to receive poorly made clothes, toiletries, appliances and other products at high prices. Producers and retailers showed little concern for customer satisfaction with goods and services. Sellers paid relatively little heed to marketing theory and practice.

In buyers' markets, in contrast, customers can choose from a wide array of goods and services. In these markets, if sellers fail to deliver acceptable product and service quality, they will quickly lose customers to competitors. Also, what is acceptable today may not be acceptable to tomorrow's ever-more-demanding consumers. Consumers are becoming more educated and demanding, and their quality expectations have been raised by the practices of superior manufacturers and retailers. The decline of many traditional western industries in recent years – cars, cameras, shipping, machine tools, consumer electronics – offers dramatic evidence that firms offering only average quality lose their consumer franchises when attacked by superior competitors.

satisfying customer needs

To succeed or simply to survive, companies need a new philosophy. To win in today's marketplace, companies must be **customer-centred** – they must deliver superior value to their target customers. They must become adept in *building customer relationships*, not just *building products*. They must be skilful in *market engineering*, not just *product engineering*. The views of the chief executive of GEC Industries, George Simpson, were honed at Rover where the corporate culture had to shift to the notion that customers need to like the cars they buy. There was, he says, 'a bit of a tendency to have technology for technology's sake'.[1]

Too often, marketing is ignored in the boardroom of companies with the view that the job of obtaining customers is the job of the marketing or sales department.

> A survey conducted by Taylor Nelson Sofres showed that 57 per cent of companies with over €1m turnover had no board level marketing director. Half of the companies studied conducted no regular usage or attitude studies and 44 per cent admitted that the customer is rarely, if ever, represented in the boardroom.[2]

In contrast, winning companies have come to realise that marketing cannot do this job alone. Although marketing plays a leading role, it is only a partner in attracting and keeping customers. The world's best marketing department cannot successfully sell poorly made products that fail to meet consumer needs. The marketing department can be effective only in companies in which all departments and employees have teamed up to form a competitively superior *customer value-delivery system*.

Consider McDonald's. People do not swarm to the world's 11,000 McDonald's restaurants only because they love the chain's hamburgers. Many other restaurants make better-tasting hamburgers. Consumers flock to the McDonald's *system*, not just to its food products. Throughout the world, McDonald's finely tuned system delivers a high standard of what the company calls QSCV – Quality, Service, Cleanliness and Value. The system consists of many components, both internal and external. McDonald's is effective only to the extent that it successfully partners its employees, franchisees, suppliers and others in jointly delivering exceptionally high customer value.

This chapter discusses the philosophy of customer-value-creating marketing and the customer-focused firm. It addresses several important questions: What is customer value and customer satisfaction? How do leading companies organise to create and deliver high value and satisfaction? How can companies keep current customers as well as get new ones? How can companies practise total quality marketing?

Customer-centred company
A company that focuses on customer developments in designing its marketing strategies and on delivering superior value to its target customers.

Triumph communicates specific benefits that target consumers.

SOURCE: Triumph International Ltd

defining customer value and satisfaction

Forty years ago, Peter Drucker observed that a company's first task is 'to create customers'. However, creating customers can be a difficult task. Today's customers face a vast array of product and brand choices, prices and suppliers. The company must answer a key question: How do customers make their choices?

The answer is that customers choose the marketing offer that gives them the most value. Customers are value-maximisers, within the bounds of search costs and limited knowledge, mobility and income. They form expectations of value and act upon them. Then they compare the actual value they receive in consuming the product to the value expected, and this affects their satisfaction and repurchase behaviour. We will now examine the concepts of customer value and customer satisfaction more carefully.

customer value

Customer delivered value

The difference between total customer value and total customer cost of a marketing offer – 'profit' to the customer.

Consumers buy from the firm that they believe offers the highest **customer delivered value** – the difference between *total customer value* and *total customer cost* (see Figure 11.1). For example, suppose that an Irish farmer wants to buy a tractor. He can either buy the equipment from his usual supplier, Massey-Ferguson, or a cheaper east European product. The salespeople for the two companies carefully describe their respective offers to the farmer.

The farmer evaluates the two competing tractors and judges that Massey-Ferguson's tractor provides higher reliability, durability and performance. He also decides that Massey-Ferguson has better accompanying service – delivery, training

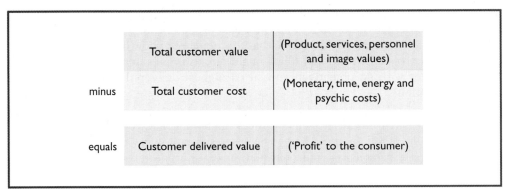

Figure 11.1

Customer delivered value

and maintenance – and views Massey-Ferguson personnel as more knowledgeable and responsive. Finally, the farmer places higher value on Massey-Ferguson's reputation. He adds all the values from these four sources – *product, services, personnel* and *image* – and decides that Massey-Ferguson offers more **total customer value** than does the east European tractor.

Does the farmer buy the Massey-Ferguson tractor? Not necessarily. He will also examine the **total customer cost** of buying the Massey-Ferguson tractor versus the east European tractor product. First, he will compare the prices he must pay for each of the competitors' products. The Massey-Ferguson tractor costs a lot more than the east European tractor does, so the higher price might offset the higher total customer value. Moreover, total customer cost consists of more than just monetary costs. As Adam Smith observed more than two centuries ago: 'The real price of anything is the toil and trouble of acquiring it.' Total customer cost also includes the buyer's anticipated time, energy and psychic costs. The farmer will evaluate these costs along with monetary costs to form a complete estimate of his costs.

The farmer compares total customer value to total customer cost and determines the total delivered value associated with Massey-Ferguson's tractor. In the same way, he assesses the total delivered value for the east European tractor. The farmer then will buy from the competitor that offers the highest delivered value.

How can Massey-Ferguson use this concept of buyer decision making to help it succeed in selling its tractor to this buyer? Massey-Ferguson can improve its offer in three ways. First, it can increase total customer value by improving product, services, personnel or image benefits. Second, it can reduce the buyer's non-monetary costs by lessening the buyer's time, energy and psychic costs. Third, it can reduce the buyer's monetary costs by lowering its price, providing easier terms of sale or, in the longer term, lowering its tractor's operating or maintenance costs.

Suppose Massey-Ferguson carries out a *customer value assessment* and concludes that buyers see Massey-Ferguson's offer as worth €20,000. Further suppose that it costs Massey-Ferguson €14,000 to produce the tractor. This means that Massey-Ferguson's offer potentially generates €6,000 (€20,000 – €14,000) of *total added value*. Massey-Ferguson needs to price its tractor between €14,000 and €20,000. If it charges less than €14,000, it won't cover its costs. If it charges more than €20,000, the price will exceed the total customer value. The price Massey-Ferguson charges will determine how much of the total added value will be delivered to the buyer and how much will flow to Massey-Ferguson. For example, if Massey-Ferguson charges €16,000, it will grant €4,000 of total added value to the customer and keep €2,000 for itself as profit. If Massey-Ferguson charges €19,000, it will grant only €1,000 of total added value to the customer and keep €5,000 for itself as profit. Naturally, the lower Massey-Ferguson's price, the higher the delivered value of its offer will be and, therefore, the higher the customer's incentive to purchase from Massey-Ferguson. Delivered value should be

Total customer value
The total of the entire product, services, personnel and image values that a buyer receives from a marketing offer.

Total customer cost
The total of all the monetary, time, energy and psychic costs associated with a marketing offer.

viewed as 'profit to the customer'. Given that Massey-Ferguson wants to win the sale, it must offer more delivered value than the east European tractor does.[3]

Some marketers might rightly argue that this concept of how buyers choose among product alternatives is too rational. They might cite examples in which buyers did not choose the offer with an objectively measured highest delivered value. Consider the following situation:

> The Massey-Ferguson salesperson convinces the farmer that, considering the benefits relative to the purchase price, Massey-Ferguson's tractor offers a higher delivered value. The salesperson also points out that the east European tractor uses more fuel and requires more frequent repairs. Still, the farmer decides to buy the east European tractor.

How can we explain this appearance of non-value-maximising behaviour? There are many possible explanations. For example, perhaps the farmer has a long-term friendship with the east European tractor salesperson. Or the farmer might have a policy of buying at the lowest price. Or perhaps the farmer is short of cash, and therefore chooses the cheaper east European tractor, even though the Massey-Ferguson machine will perform better and be less expensive to operate in the long run.

Clearly, buyers operate under various constraints and sometimes make choices that give more weight to their personal benefit than to company benefit. However, the customer delivered value framework applies to many situations and yields rich insights. The framework suggests that sellers must first assess the total customer value and total customer cost associated with their own and competing marketing offers to determine how their own offers measure up in terms of customer delivered value. If a seller finds that competitors deliver greater value, it has two alternatives. It can try to increase customer value by strengthening or augmenting the product, services, personnel or image benefits of the offer. Or it can decrease total customer cost by reducing its price, simplifying the ordering and delivery process, or absorbing some buyer risk by offering a warranty.[4]

customer satisfaction

Consumers form judgements about the value of marketing offers and make their buying decisions based upon these judgements. *Customer satisfaction* with a purchase depends upon the product's performance relative to a buyer's expectations. A customer might experience various degrees of satisfaction. If the product's performance falls short of expectations, the customer is dissatisfied. If performance matches expectations, the customer is satisfied. If performance exceeds expectations, the customer is highly satisfied or delighted.

But how do buyers form their expectations? Expectations are based on the customer's past buying experiences, the opinions of friends and associates, and marketer and competitor information and promises. Marketers must be careful to set the right level of expectations. If they set expectations too low, they may satisfy those who buy, but fail to attract enough buyers. In contrast, if they raise expectations too high, buyers are likely to be disappointed. For example, Holiday Inn ran a campaign a few years ago called 'No Surprises', which promised consistently trouble-free accommodation and service. However, Holiday Inn guests still encountered a host of problems and the expectations created by the campaign only made customers more dissatisfied. Holiday Inn had to withdraw the campaign.

Still, some of today's most successful companies are raising expectations – and delivering performance to match. These companies embrace *total customer satisfaction*. For example, Honda claims, 'One reason our customers are so satisfied is that we aren't' or, as dan Technology puts it, 'We value your business. We want you to buy from us again.' These companies aim high because they know that customers who are *only* satisfied will still find it easy to switch suppliers when a better offer comes along. In one consumer packaged-goods category, 44 per cent of consumers reporting satisfaction later switched brands. In contrast, customers who are *highly satisfied* are much less ready to switch. One study showed that 75 per cent of Toyota buyers were highly satisfied and about 75 per cent said they intended to buy a Toyota again. Thus *customer delight* creates an emotional affinity for a product or service, not just a rational preference, and this creates high customer loyalty.

Today's winning companies track their customers' expectations, perceived company performance and customer satisfaction. They track this for their competitors as well. Consider the following:

> A company was pleased to find that 80 per cent of its customers said they were satisfied with its new product. However, the product seemed to sell poorly on store shelves next to the leading competitor's product. Company researchers soon learned that the competitor's product attained a 90 per cent customer satisfaction score. Company management was further dismayed when it learned that this competitor was aiming for a 95 per cent satisfaction score.

For customer-centred companies, customer satisfaction is both a goal and an essential factor in company success. Companies that achieve high customer satisfaction ratings make sure that their target market knows it. These companies realise that highly satisfied customers produce several benefits for the company. They are less price sensitive and they remain customers for a longer period. They buy additional products over time as the company introduces related products or improvements. And they talk favourably to others about the company and its products.

> Food on US domestic flights shows alternative interpretations of customer satisfaction. In a battle to keep prices down airlines have squeezed the average cost of an in-flight meal from $5.62 (€6.35) in 1992 to $4.13. On short-haul economy flights the cost gets as low as $3 for food and beverage. Even on Concorde, food accounts for only €53 of a €6,600 transatlantic ticket. Low air pressure does reduce people's taste sensitivity but how low can limp lettuce go? Bucking convention Midwest Express Airline (MEA) invested in food. Their trick was to spend €10 a meal on food. That covers free champagne and wine, and cookies baked in flight all served on china plates. Attendants work 'as though they were serving in a fine restaurant'. This focus on delivering customer value has helped make MEA one of the world's best performing airlines and the only US carrier in the top ten for service.[5]

Although the customer-centred firm seeks to deliver high customer satisfaction relative to competitors, it does not attempt to *maximise* customer satisfaction. Even MEA does not offer the best champagne. A company can always increase customer satisfaction by lowering its price or increasing its services, but this may result in lower profits. In addition to customers, the company has many stakeholders, including employees, dealers, suppliers and stockholders. Spending more to increase customer satisfaction might divert funds from increasing the satisfaction of these other 'partners'. Thus the purpose of marketing is to generate customer value profitably. Ultimately, the company must deliver a high level of customer satisfaction, while at the same time delivering at least acceptable levels of satisfaction to the firm's other stakeholders. This requires a very delicate balance: the marketer must continue to generate more customer value and satisfaction, but not 'give away the house'.[6] Many of the world's most successful companies build their strategies on customer satisfaction, but as Marketing Highlight 11.1 shows, you do not have to be big to succeed.

marketing highlight 11.1

Cold turkey has got me on the run

'Oh dear! Am I in trouble now.' It was a week before Christmas as the recalcitrant academic trudged up and down Castle Street trying to buy a goose for Christmas dinner. Long before Charles Dickens' time, when Scrooge sent 'the prize Turkey . . . the big one' to Bob Cratchit's house, goose was the traditional English Christmas fayre. Introduced to Europe from America in the sixteenth century, turkey had displaced goose in all of Castle Street's butchers. Sick of having cold turkey salad, turkey sandwiches and that dreadful turkey curry for days after Christmas, the academic's family had decided to have goose 'for a change'. His job was to get one, but he had left it too late.

Butcher after butcher came out with the worn-out lines, 'You should have ordered one weeks ago', 'We can't get them anywhere' or 'There's no call for them these days.' Even, 'A goose? They're so greasy. How about a nice fat turkey? It'll last you for days.' SCREAM!

Defeated, he slumped into his car to drive home. It was dark and on the way through a village he saw the lights of a small shop he had not noticed before – a small independent butcher, well stocked, brightly lit and full of customers. 'Funny,' he thought, 'there aren't many of those these days. Still, let's have one last try.'

On joining the festive throng inside, he noticed a sign on the wall. It read:

The Ten Commandments of good business

1. The customer is the most important person in my business.

2. The customer is not dependent on us; we are dependent on him.

3. A customer is not an interruption of our work; he is the purpose of it.

4. A customer does us a favour when he calls; we are not doing him a favour by serving him.

5. The customer is part of our business, not an outsider.

6. The customer is not a cold statistic; he is a flesh and blood human being with feelings and emotions like ours.

7. The customer is not someone to argue or match wits with.

8. The customer brings us his wants; it is our job to fill those wants.

9. The customer is deserving of the most courteous and attentive treatment we can give him.

10. The customer is the lifeblood of this, and every other, business.

'Merry Christmas, what can I do for you?' asked the butcher.

'Have you a goose?' the academic asked timidly.

'I haven't got any in, but I'll get one for you. What size do you want?'

Later on, at a local inn, the talk turned to food. 'Have you come across that great butcher in the next village?'

'Great butcher? Come off it. A butcher's a butcher's a butcher!'

'Not this one, he will do anything for you. Nice guy, too.'

Lesson: You do not have to be big to be great.

SOURCES: Charles Dickens, *A Christmas Carol* (London: Hazell, Watson & Viney, 1843); John Lennon, *Cold Turkey* (London: Apple, 1969).

tracking customer satisfaction

Successful organisations are aggressive in tracking both customer satisfaction and dissatisfaction. Several methods are used.

Complaint and suggestion systems A customer-centred organisation makes it easy for customers to make suggestions or complaints. Hospitals place suggestion boxes in the corridors, supply comment cards to existing patients and employ patient advocates to solicit grievances. Some customer-centred companies may set up free customer hot-lines to make it easy for customers to enquire, suggest or complain. Virgin Trains immediately hand out customer complaint forms as soon as there is any reason for passengers to complain, such as a train being delayed.

Successful companies try very hard. All visitors to Richer Sounds shops get a card showing the shop's team and saying: 'We're listening.' It's a Freepost letter addressed to Julian Richer, the owner of the chain. Inside it reads:

Thank you for your support and making us the UK's most successful hi-fi retailer. In order to maintain No. 1 position, we need to know where we've gone wrong. Suggestions or comments regarding customer service, however small, are gratefully received. Every one has Mr Richer's personal attention . . . Please, please, please let us know, as we really do care!

Customer satisfaction surveys   Complaint and suggestion systems may not give the company a full picture of customer satisfaction. One out of every four purchases results in consumer dissatisfaction, but less than 5 per cent of dissatisfied customers complain. Rather than complain, most customers simply switch suppliers. As a result, the company needlessly loses customers.

Responsive companies take direct measures of customer satisfaction by conducting regular surveys. They send questionnaires or make telephone calls to a sample of recent customers to find out how they feel about various aspects of the company's performance.

Magazines and consumers' associations often conduct independent surveys. These are invaluable since companies can easily be deluded by their own results. For instance, a conference centre may be happy that 85 per cent of its customers say its service is good, but what if 95 per cent of the customers also rate a competitor as excellent?

Bozell Worldwide's Quality Poll gives a league table and shows how biased local perceptions can be. Gallup conducted a study that asked 20,000 people in 20 countries to rate the quality of manufactured goods from 12 countries. All countries rated themselves higher than other people did. The French put French goods on top, while the Japanese gave themselves twice the rating (76 per cent) that the full sample did (38.5). All other countries were optimistic too: Germans gave themselves 49 per cent against the full sample's 36 per cent and the United Kingdom 39 per cent against 22 per cent.

Ghost shopping   This involves researchers posing as buyers. These 'ghost shoppers' can even present specific problems in order to test whether the company's personnel handle difficult situations well. For example, ghost shoppers can complain about a restaurant's food to see how the restaurant handles this complaint. Research International's Mystery Shopper surveys can measure many dimensions of customer performance. By telephoning it can measure a firm's telephone technique: how many rings it takes to answer, the sort of voice and tone and, if transferred, how many leaps it took before being correctly connected.

Managers themselves should leave their offices from time to time and experience first-hand the treatment they receive as 'customers'. As an alternative, managers can phone their companies with different questions and complaints to see how the call is handled.

Lost customer analysis   Companies should contact customers who have stopped buying or who have switched to a competitor, to learn why this happened. Not only should the company conduct such *exit interviews*, it should also monitor the *customer loss rate*. A rising loss rate indicates that the company is failing to satisfy its customers.[7]

delivering customer value and satisfaction

Customer value and satisfaction are important ingredients in the marketer's formula for success. But what does it take to produce and deliver customer value? To answer this, we will examine the concepts of a *value chain* and *value delivery system*.

value chain

Value chain
A major tool for identifying ways to create more customer value.

Michael Porter proposed the **value chain** as the main tool for identifying ways to create more customer value (see Figure 11.2).[8] Every firm consists of a collection of activities performed to design, produce, market, deliver and support the firm's products. The value chain breaks the firm into nine value-creating activities in an effort to understand the behaviour of costs in the specific business and the potential sources of competitive differentiation. The nine value-creating activities include five primary activities and four support activities.

The primary activities involve the sequence of bringing materials into the business (inbound logistics), operating on them (operations), sending them out (outbound logistics), marketing them (marketing and sales) and servicing them (service). For a long time, firms have focused on the product as the primary means of adding value, but customer satisfaction also depends upon the other stages of the value chain.[9] The support activities occur within each of these primary activities. For example, procurement involves obtaining the various inputs for each primary activity – only the purchasing department does a fraction of procurement. Technology development and human resource management also occur in all departments. The firm's infrastructure covers the overhead of general management, planning, finance, accounting and legal and government affairs borne by all the primary and support activities.

Under the value-chain concept, the firm should examine its costs and performance in each value-creating activity to look for improvements. It should also estimate its competitors' costs and performances as benchmarks. To the extent that the firm can perform certain activities better than its competitors, it can achieve a competitive advantage.

The firm's success depends not only on how well each department performs its work, but also on how well the activities of various departments are coordinated. Too often, individual departments maximise their own interests rather than those of the

Figure 11.2

The generic value chain

SOURCE: Reprinted with permission of The Free Press, a Division of Simon & Schuster, Inc., from *Competitive Advantage: Creating and Sustaining Superior Performance* by Michael E. Porter. Copyright © 1985, 1998 Michael E. Porter.

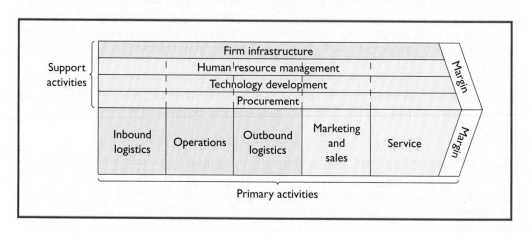

Value chain: this ad states the competitive advantage that HSBC derives from understanding each stage of the industry value chain. Credit: Designed by KBW Ltd for HSBC.

SOURCE: HSBC Investment Bank plc. *Agency*: KBW Ltd

Sheer Power

The sparrowhawk has a commanding presence through its power, agility and exceptional vision.

Our Investment Banking and Markets business has formidable strength in managing acquisitions and equity raising in the energy and utilities sectors. Our specialist knowledge covers the full range of industry activity from oil exploration through to transmission and distribution of gas and electricity.

Our detailed understanding of each stage of this industry value chain is the foundation of our execution strength in a fast changing global environment.

ak enerji	Joint global co-ordinator and sole international bookrunner for the US$119 million initial public offering for ak enerji, an independent Turkish power generating company
Endesa	Adviser on the Eur400 million pending acquisition of NRE and GRE, electricity and gas distributors for Eindhoven, Netherlands
LG-Caltex Oil and Texaco	Adviser to LG-Caltex Oil and Texaco on the US$690 million acquisition of two CHP plants from Korea Electric Power
National Grid	Global co-ordinator for £1.2 billion offering of Energis shares and EPICs
Russian Federal Property Fund	Adviser to the Russian government on the US$440 million sale of a 9% equity stake in Lukoil
ScottishPower	Broking adviser to ScottishPower on the US$7.5 billion acquisition of PacifiCorp

www.ib.hsbc.com

HSBC

YOUR WORLD OF FINANCIAL SERVICES

whole company and the customer. For example, a credit department might attempt to reduce bad debts by taking a long time to check the credit of prospective customers: meanwhile, salespeople get frustrated and customers wait. A distribution department might decide to save money by shipping goods by rail; again the customer waits. In each case, individual departments have erected walls that impede the delivery of quality customer service.

To overcome this problem, companies should place more emphasis on the smooth management of *core business processes*, most of which involve inputs and cooperation from many functional departments. These core business processes include the following:

- *Product development process.* All the activities involved in identifying, researching and developing new products with speed, high quality and reasonable cost.

- *Inventory management process.* All the activities involved in developing and managing the right inventory levels of raw materials, semi-finished materials and finished goods, so that adequate supplies are available while the costs of high overstocks are avoided.

> ✦ *Order-to-payment process*. All the activities involved in receiving orders, approving them, shipping the goods on time and collecting payment.
>
> ✦ *Customer service process*. All the activities involved in making it easy for customers to reach the right parties within the company to obtain service, answers and resolutions of problems.

Successful companies develop superior capabilities in managing these and other core processes. In turn, mastering core business processes gives these companies a substantial competitive edge.[10]

Many Internet companies have fallen at the final, *customer service*, stage of the value chain. The fear of a faceless company is real among customers, especially in France and Italy, yet a recent survey found that only one-fifth of websites had human contact available through them. Across Europe only a minority of Internet users are willing to make a purchase without some personal contact, even from a well-known company. This reliance on a single, impersonal link with customers is said to account for the slow uptake of Internet shopping in Europe and, according to Datamonitor, is likely to cost European companies €150 billion by 2004.[11]

In its search for competitive advantage, the firm needs to look beyond its own value chain, into the value chains of its suppliers, distributors and, ultimately, customers. More companies today are 'partnering' with the other members of the supply chain to improve the performance of the **customer value delivery system**. For example:

Customer value delivery system
The system made up of the value chains of the company and its suppliers, distributors and ultimately customers, who work together to deliver value to customers.

One of Levi's biggest retailers is Sears. Every night, Levi's learns the sizes and styles of its blue jeans that sold through Sears and other large outlets. Levi's then electronically orders more fabric from the Milliken Company, its fabric supplier. In turn, Milliken relays an order for more fibre to DuPont, the fibre supplier. In

Atlas Commerce offers the opportunity of increased collaboration in the management of supply chains.
Source: Atlas Commerce

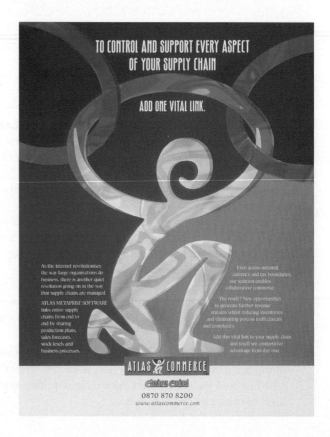

this way, the partners in the supply chain use the most current sales information to manufacture what is selling, rather than to manufacture based on potentially inaccurate sales forecasts. This is known as a *quick response* system, in which goods are pulled by demand, rather than pushed by supply.

As companies struggle to become more competitive, they are turning, ironically, to greater cooperation. Companies used to view their suppliers and distributors as cost centres and, in some cases, as adversaries. Today, however, they are selecting partners carefully and working out mutually profitable strategies. Increasingly in today's marketplace, competition no longer takes place between individual competitors. Rather, it takes place between the entire value delivery systems created by these competitors.

Therefore, marketing can no longer be thought of as only a selling department. That view of marketing would give it responsibility only for formulating a promotion-oriented marketing mix, without much to say about product features, costs and other important elements. Under the new view, marketing is responsible for *designing and managing a superior value delivery system to reach target customer segments*. Today's marketing managers must think not only about selling today's products, but also about how to stimulate the development of improved products, how to work actively with other departments in managing core business processes and how to build better external partnerships.[12]

total quality management

Customer satisfaction and company profitability are linked closely to product and service quality delivered through the whole value chain. Higher levels of quality result in greater customer satisfaction, while at the same time supporting higher prices and often lower costs. Therefore, *quality improvement programmes* normally increase profitability. The Profit Impact of Marketing Strategies studies show similarly high correlation between relative product quality and profitability for Europe and the US (see Figure 11.3).[13]

The task of improving product and service quality should be a company's top priority. Most customers will no longer tolerate poor or average quality. Companies today have no choice but to adopt total quality management if they want to stay in the race, let alone be profitable. According to GE's chairman, John F. Welch, Jr: 'Quality is our best assurance of customer allegiance, our strongest defense against foreign competition and the only path to sustained growth and earnings.'[14]

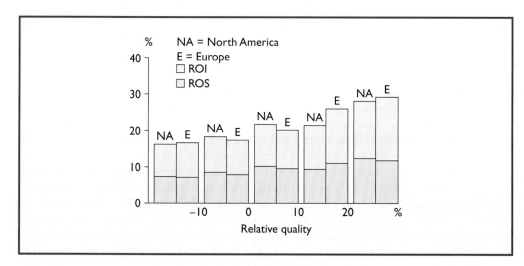

Figure 11.3

Relative quality boosts rate of return

SOURCE: Bob Luchs, 'Quality as a strategic weapon: measuring relative quality, value and market differentiation', *European Business Journal*, **2**, 4 (1990), p. 39.

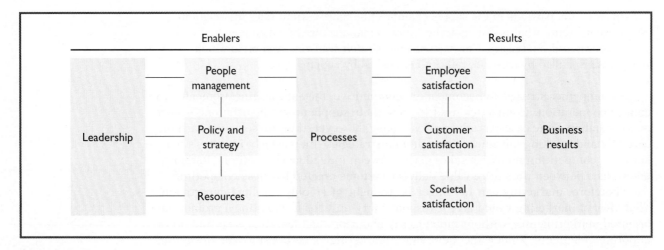

Figure 11.4

European Foundation for Quality Management's model of business excellence

Quality
The totality of features and characteristics of a product or service that bear on its ability to satisfy stated or implied needs.

Total quality management (TQM)
Programmes designed to constantly improve the quality of products, services, and marketing processes.

Quality has been variously defined as 'fitness for use', 'conformance to requirements' and 'freedom from variation'.[15] The American Society for Quality Control defines **quality** as the totality of features and characteristics of a product or service that bear on its ability to satisfy stated or implied needs. This is a customer-centred definition of quality. It suggests that a company has 'delivered quality' whenever its product and service meets or exceeds customers' needs, requirements and expectations.

It is important to distinguish between performance quality and conformance quality. *Performance quality* refers to the *level* at which a product performs its functions. Compare Skoda and Mercedes. A Mercedes provides higher performance quality than a Skoda: it has a smoother ride, handles better and lasts longer. It is more expensive and sells to a market with higher means and requirements. *Conformance quality* refers to freedom from defects and the *consistency* with which a product delivers a specified level of performance. Both a Mercedes and a Skoda could offer equivalent conformance quality to their respective markets, since each consistently delivers what its market expects. A €100,000 car that meets all of its requirements is a quality car; so is a €10,000 car that meets all of its requirements. However, if the Mercedes handles badly or if the Skoda gives poor fuel efficiency, then both cars have failed to deliver quality, and customer satisfaction suffers accordingly.

In the European Foundation for Quality Management's excellence model (Figure 11.4) marketing shares the responsibility for striving for the highest quality of a company, product or service. Marketing's commitment to the whole process needs to be particularly strong because of the central role of customer satisfaction to both marketing and **total quality management (TQM)**. Within a quality-centre company, marketing management has two types of responsibility. First, marketing management participates in formulating the *strategies and policies* that direct *resources* and strive for quality excellence. Secondly, marketing has to deliver marketing quality alongside product quality. It must perform each marketing activity to consistently high standards: marketing research, sales training, advertising, customer services and others. Much damage can be done to customer satisfaction with an excellent product if it is oversold or is 'supported' by advertising that builds unrealistic expectations.

Within quality programmes, marketing has several roles. Firstly, marketing has responsibility for correctly identifying customers' needs and wants, and for communicating them correctly to aid product design and to schedule production. Secondly, marketing has to ensure that customers' orders are filled correctly and on time, and must check to see that customers receive proper instruction, training and technical assistance in the use of their product. Thirdly, marketers must stay in touch with customers after the sale, to make sure that they remain satisfied. Finally, marketers must gather and convey customers' ideas for product and service improvement back to the company.

TQM has played an important role in educating businesses that quality is more than products and services being well produced, but is about what marketing has been saying all the time: *customer satisfaction*. At the same time, TQM extends marketing's view to realise that the acquisition, retention and satisfaction of good employees is central to the acquisition, retention and satisfaction of customers.[16]

Total quality is the key to creating customer value and satisfaction. Total quality is everyone's job, just as marketing is everyone's job:

> Marketers who don't learn the language of quality improvement, manufacturing and operations will become as obsolete as buggy whips. The days of functional marketing are gone. We can no longer afford to think of ourselves as market researchers, advertising people, direct marketers, marketing strategists – we have to think of ourselves as customer satisfiers – customer advocates focused on whole processes.[17]

Marketers must spend time and effort not only to improve external marketing, but also to improve internal marketing. Marketers must be the customer's watchdog or guardian, complaining loudly for the customer when the product or the service is not right. Marketers must constantly uphold the standard of 'giving the customer the best solution'.

customer value

There is no limit to how much a company could spend to improve quality, or in other marketing efforts, to obtain and retain customers. This rises the critical question, how much is a customer worth? Companies are increasingly realising that the answer is: a great deal. Recent acquisitions in the Internet and telecommunications industry suggest values approaching €10,000. Marketing Highlight 11.2 gives some insight into these valuations.

Internet companies are willing to pay a high price for prospective customers because they hope to turn them into *profitable customers*. We define a **profitable customer** as a person, household or company whose revenues over time exceed, by an acceptable amount, the company's costs of attracting, selling and servicing that customer. Note that the definition emphasises lifetime revenues and costs, not profit from a single transaction. Here are some dramatic illustrations of **customer lifetime value**:

> Tom Peters, noted author of several books on managerial excellence, runs a business that spends $1,500 a month on Federal Express service. His company spends this amount 12 months a year and expects to remain in business for at least another 10 years. Therefore, he expects to spend more than $180,000 on future Federal Express service. If Federal Express makes a 10 per cent profit margin, Peters' lifetime business will contribute $18,000 to Federal Express's profits. Federal Express risks all of this profit if Peters receives poor service from a Federal Express driver or if a competitor offers better service.

Few companies actively measure individual customer value and profitability. For example, banks claim that this is hard to do because customers use different banking services and transactions are logged in different departments. However, banks that have managed to link customer transactions and measure customer profitability have been appalled by how many unprofitable customers they find. Some banks report

Profitable customer
A person, household or company whose revenues over time exceed, by an acceptable amount, the company's costs of attracting, selling and servicing that customer.

Customer lifetime value
The amount by which revenues from a given customer over time will exceed the company's costs of attracting, selling and servicing that customer.

marketing highlight 11.2

Buying customers

The scramble of Internet providers and telecommunications companies for customers has been likened to a madhouse. The Internet service provider (ISP) Freeserve is an example. As the name implies, Freeserve provides free Internet service for its customers whose activities, on average, contribute an income of €13 a year to the company, with whom they have no contract. Despite this, the market value of Freeserve indicates that each of their customers is worth €4,375. Table 1 gives the valuation of some other leading companies based on dividing their market capitalisation by their number of subscribers.

Are the prices lunatic? Cliff Stanford, founder of ISP Demon International, thinks not. In 1998 he made €100m selling his share in Demon International to Scottish Power for €535 per customer. The customers are now valued at €6,000 each. The high valuations are because the companies are foregoing current income in search of a customer base that will drive them to market leadership when IPS, telecoms and TV converge.

'Dominance is everything', says Mr Stanford. 'It's not the number of subscribers you have, it's the number you have compared to everybody else. We honestly don't know what the Internet is going to be in a year, or two years' time, so what people are doing is competing for dominance when we do.'

Sources: Charles Orton-Jones, 'Just how much is a customer worth?', *EuroBusiness* (February 2000), pp. 28–9; Andrew Lorenz, 'Target Germany', *The Sunday Times* (21 November 1999); Christopher Price, 'Upward Mobility', *Marketing Business* (March 1999), pp. 36–9; 'A mobile merry-go-round', *The Economist* (23 October 1999), pp. 113–14.

Company	Nationality	Sector	Subscribers (m)	Annual revenue/ customer (€)	Market value/ customer (€)
AOL	US	Internet	21	276	9,523
Orange	UK	Telecom	3.4	625	9,412
Mannesmann	Germany	Telecom	21	365	6,095
Vodaphone Airtouch	UK/US	Telecom	31.5	605	4,889
On digital	UK	TV	0.5	627	4,800
One2one	UK/Germany	Telecom	3.2	–	4,525
Freeserve	UK	Internet	1.6	13	4,375
BSkyB	UK	TV	8	191	3,375
Kirch Pay TV	Germany	TV	2	300	3,000
Cablecom	Switzerland	Cable	1.4	276	2,753
Cellnet	Europe	Telecom	5.5	611	2,327
Canal Plus	France	TV	12.8	203	1,148

Table 1

losing money on over 45 per cent of their retail customers. It is not surprising that many banks now charge fees for services that they once supplied free.

Although financially defendable, the logical conclusion of focussing on only profitable customers can be socially unacceptable. When already highly profitable British banks started closing unprofitable branches and charging for the customers of other banks using their ATM (Automatic Teller Machines) there was a public and political outcry. The policy was leaving many poor people 'unbanked' and rural communities neglected. The result was a public relations disaster for Barclays whose economies coincided with big bonus payments to its top managers and an expensive advertising campaign boasting of its size.[18]

customer retention

In the past, many companies took their customers for granted. Customers often did not have many alternative suppliers, or the other suppliers were just as poor in quality and service, or the market was growing so fast that the company did not worry about fully satisfying its customers. A company could lose 100 customers a week, but gain another 100 customers and consider its sales to be satisfactory. Such a company, operating on a 'leaky bucket' theory of business, believes that there will always be enough customers to replace the defecting ones. However, this high *customer churn* involves higher costs than if a company retained all 100 customers and acquired no new ones.

Companies must pay close attention to their customer defection rate and undertake steps to reduce it. First, the company must define and measure its retention rate. For a magazine, it would be the renewal rate; for a consumer packaged-goods firm, it would be the repurchase rate. Next, the company must identify the causes of customer defection and determine which of these can be reduced or eliminated. Not much can be done about customers who leave the region or about business customers who go out of business. But much can be done about customers who leave because of shoddy products, poor service or prices that are too high. The company needs to prepare a frequency distribution showing the percentage of customers who defect for different reasons.

A satisfaction study can show how a company has been misplacing its effort.

> A satisfaction benchmarking study for a restaurant showed that customers rated highly the restaurant's *décor* and the *size of the portions* served. However, the customers did not rate the two criteria as important. In contrast customers thought that the *quality of food* and *cleanliness of toilets* were very important but dimensions on which the restaurant performed poorly. On other dimensions that the customers thought important, the restaurant did fine: *overall cleanliness, speed of service* and *helpfulness of staff*. The benchmarking study clearly showed how the restaurant could improve customer satisfaction and, maybe, cut costs by reducing portions.

It is well known in service industries, where de-skilled McJobs abound, that employee satisfaction and retention precede customer satisfaction and retention. The relationship is also strong in rapid growth industries where the poaching of staff drives up wages and in many markets where making sales depends on the continuity of long-term relationships with key accounts. The SAS Institute, the world's largest software company, sees a close relationship between its performance and labour turnover. Its employee-oriented management keeps annual labour turnover at 4 per cent compared with an industry average of 20 per cent. SAS's methods go beyond the €65,000 of M&Ms it doles out to its 7,500 employees each year. The company keeps working hours down, has free health care on 'campus', plus gyms, tennis courts, theatres and other benefits. Employees sing the praises of the company and keep customers well satisfied – 98 per cent of them renew their licences on SAS software each year![19]

By reducing customer defections by only 5 per cent, companies can improve profits by anywhere from 25 to 85 per cent.[20] Unfortunately, classic marketing theory and practice centres on the art of attracting new customers rather than retaining existing ones. The emphasis has been on creating *transactions* rather than *relationships*. Discussion has focused on *pre-sale activity* and *sale activity* rather than on *post-sale activity*. Today, however, more companies recognise the importance of retaining current customers by forming relationships with them.

relationship marketing

Relationship marketing
The process of creating, maintaining and enhancing strong, value-laden relationships with customers and other stakeholders.

Relationship marketing involves creating, maintaining and enhancing strong relationships with customers and other stakeholders. Increasingly, marketing is moving away from a focus on individual transactions and towards a focus on building value-laden relationships and marketing networks. Relationship marketing is oriented more towards the long term. The goal is to deliver long-term value to customers and the measure of success is long-term customer satisfaction. Relationship marketing requires that all of the company's departments work together with marketing as a team to serve the customer. It involves building relationships at many levels – economic, social, technical and legal – resulting in high customer loyalty.

We can distinguish five different levels or relationships that can be formed with customers who have purchased a company's product, such as a car or a piece of equipment:

✦ *Basic*. The company salesperson sells the product, but does not follow up in any way.

✦ *Reactive*. The salesperson sells the product and encourages the customer to call whenever he or she has any questions or problems.

✦ *Accountable*. The salesperson phones the customer a short time after the sale to check whether the product is meeting the customer's expectations. The salesperson also solicits from the customer any product improvement suggestions and any specific disappointments. This information helps the company continuously to improve its offering.

✦ *Proactive*. The salesperson or others in the company phone the customer from time to time with suggestions about improved product use or helpful new products.

✦ *Partnership*. The company works continuously with the customer and with other customers to discover ways to deliver better value.

Figure 11.5 shows that a company's relationship marketing strategy will depend on how many customers it has and their profitability. For example, companies with many low-margin customers will practise *basic* marketing. Thus Heineken will not phone all of its drinkers to express its appreciation for their business. At best, Heineken will be reactive by setting up a customer information service. At the other extreme, in

Figure 11.5

Relationship levels as a function of profit margin and number of customers

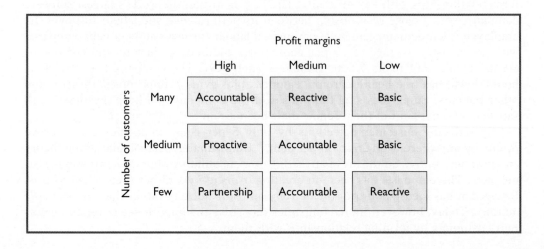

markets with few customers and high margins, most sellers will move towards part-nership marketing. In exploring the Airbus A340–500 and A340–600, a very large commercial transport, Airbus Industries will work closely with the aero-engine manu-facturers as well as with Lufthansa, Virgin Atlantic, Air Canada and Taiwan's Era Air, who have shown interest in buying the aircraft. For these businesses, the emphasis has to be on *network marketing*, where the interdependence of firms means they are part of an interdependent network. Marketing Highlight 11.3 explores this approach.

What specific marketing tools can a company use to develop stronger customer bond-ing and satisfaction? It can adopt any of three customer value-building approaches.[21] The first relies primarily on adding *financial benefits* to the customer relationship. For example, airlines offer frequent-flyer programmes, hotels give room upgrades to their frequent guests, and supermarkets give patronage refunds.

Although these reward programmes and other financial incentives build customer preference, they can be easily imitated by competitors and thus may fail to differenti-ate the company's offer permanently. The second approach is to add *social benefits* as well as financial benefits. Here company personnel work to increase their social bonds with customers by learning individual customers' needs and wants, and then indi-vidualising and personalising their products and services.

The third approach to building strong customer relationships is to add *structural ties* as well as financial and social benefits. For example, a business marketer might supply customers with special equipment or computer linkages that help them man-age their orders, payroll or inventory. An investment banker, J.P. Morgan, provides its RiskMetrics financial risk measurement system free of charge to its customers. It has two reasons for doing so. First, says the company, it will promote greater transparency to risk and so help identify problems. Second, J.P. Morgan must also be hoping that the association of its name with a widely accepted benchmarking system will yield long-term commercial advantages, partly through strengthening ties with existing cus-tomers. There are clear customer needs here. In the 12 months prior to RiskMetrics' release, estimated derivatives losses by firms, including Metallgesellschaft and Kashima Oil, approached €20 billion.[22]

The main steps in establishing a relationship-marketing programme in a company are:

+ *Identify the key customers meriting relationship management.* Choose the largest or best customers and designate them for relationship management. Other customers can be added that show exceptional growth or pioneer new industry developments.

+ *Assign a skilled relationship manager to each key customer.* The salesperson currently servicing the customer should receive training in relationship management or be replaced by someone more skilled in relationship management. The relationship manager should have characteristics that match or appeal to the customer.

+ *Develop a clear job description for relationship managers.* Describe their reporting relationships, objectives, responsibilities and evaluation criteria. Make the relationship manager the focal point for all dealings with and about the client. Give each relationship manager only one or a few relationships to manage.

+ *Have each relationship manager develop annual and long-range customer relationship plans.* These plans should state objectives, strategies, specific actions and required resources.

+ *Appoint an overall manager to supervise the relationship managers.* This person will develop job descriptions, evaluation criteria and resource support to increase relationship manager effectiveness.

marketing highlight 11.3

Network marketing: We are not alone . . .

Most companies do not sell to final consumers, but provide products and services to other businesses to which they have to be closely allied. For example, Messier Dowty, makers of landing gear for aircraft, cannot design or market its products in isolation since its landing gear is only of any use if 'designed into' an aircraft. The company, therefore, is part of a *network* including airforces as well as the supplier of tyres for its landing gear. Messier Dowty itself is the result of another network, since it is an Anglo-French joint venture between the TI group and Snecma.

Originating from Scandinavian research, network marketing accepts the influence of a web of interdependencies between firms. Relationship marketing has a clear focus on a business managing the relationship life cycle with its customers, while network marketing recognises interdependencies and a wider range of stakeholders. Table 1 compares both network and relationship marketing with the traditional marketing based on discrete transactions. It shows that transaction and relationship marketing are similar in that they are both 'done by the seller to the buyer'. In contrast, network marketing is only prescriptive in emphasising the importance of networks in understanding how firms behave rather than telling of a winning strategy. The alternative use of the term 'markets-as-networks' in place of network marketing gives a better impression of its passive role.

Interest in markets-as-networks grew out of the general trend in business for firms to emphasise 'partnership' and 'strategic alliances'. This trend goes beyond marketing to include buying, distribution, R&D and manufacturing. Long before relationship marketing was recognised, leading businesses had developed 'relationship buying', where Japanese companies in particular established very close links with a few preferred suppliers. Many leading companies, including retailers, have now adopted this approach to the extent that the buyer dictates the R&D and product, as well as the sales and marketing of the seller.

When firms and people find relatively simple two-way networks very complicated, it is not surprising that multimember networks are hard to manage. In high-spending sectors, such as defence and aerospace, Europe's national competitors are failing against the rapidly integrating US industry as reflected in the Boeing-MacDonnell Douglas combine. Airbus hopes to compete with Boeing's 777 and smaller 747 with its Airbus A340-600, but for it to do so the owners of Airbus have to agree. That means obtaining the agreement of Britain's BAe, France's Aerospatiale, Germany's DASA and Spain's Casa, as well as the governments which will have to pay one-third of the development costs. Because of the UK government's reluctance to provide $120 million, BAe is talking to manufacturers in Italy, China, Taiwan, Malaysia and North America, in the hope that their governments will be more generous. As a result of this confusion, European politicians have called for a swift restructuring of Airbus. Some network! No wonder the Eurofighter is struggling to stay in the air!

SOURCES: Andrew Edgecliffe-Johnson, 'TI and French Aerospace link up', *Financial Times* (11 December 1996), p. 23; Roderick J. Bridie, Nicole E. Coviello, Richard W. Brohner and Victoria Little, 'Towards a paradigm shift in marketing? An examination of current marketing practices', *Journal of Marketing Management*, **13**, 5 (1997), pp. 383–406; Lars-Gunnar Mattson, 'Relationship marketing' and 'The markets-as-networks approach – a comparative analysis of two evolving streams of research', *Journal of Marketing Management*, **13**, 5 (1997), pp. 447–61; Michael Shapirho, 'Go-ahead expected with new airbus', *Financial Times* (6–7 December 1997), p. 2; 'Farewell to arms', *The Economist* (22 November 1997), Web pages; Adam Jones, 'Aerospace industry consolidation cleared for take-off in Europe', *The Times* (10 December 1997), p. 29.

	TRANSACTIONAL MARKETING	RELATIONSHIP MARKETING	NETWORK MARKETING
Focus	Profitable transactions	Profitable relationships	Links between organisations
Players	Buyers and sellers in an open market	Buyers and sellers in a relationship	Seller, buyer and other organisations
Communications	Firm to market	Individual to individual	Organisation at many levels
Communications style	Arm's length	Interpersonal	Multipersonal
Duration	Discrete	Life cycle	Continuous but of varying intensity
Formality	Formal	Managed	Interactive
Power	Active seller	Seller manages	Reciprocal relationships

Table 1 Comparison of transactional, relationship and network marketing

Volvo's Oncore and Care programmes recognise that the company has multiple relationships with its customers and ensure systematic approaches and consistent treatment across them:[23]

	Corporate clients	Drivers (corporate clients' employees)	Dealers
Volvo	Relationships govern Volvo's inclusion on entitlement list (the make of employee's company cars)	Volvo maintains a direct marketing relationship with all drivers of its cars	Volvo works hard with all its dealer network to maintain and improve its standards
Dealers	Local dealers usually deliver and service the cars	Dealers are the front line of meeting the drivers' expectations	
Drivers	Agreements reached affect which models are available to clients' employees		

When it has properly implemented relationship management, the organisation begins to focus on managing its customers as well as its products. At the same time, although many companies are moving strongly towards relationship marketing, it is not effective in all situations:

> When it comes to relationship marketing . . . you don't want a relationship with every customer. . . . In fact, there are some bad customers. [The objective is to] figure out which customers are worth cultivating because you can meet their needs more effectively than anyone else can.[24]

In the end, companies must judge which segments and which specific customers will be profitable.

customer relationship management

Customer Relationship Management (CRM) systems are IT-based applications that integrate a company's information about customers with the knowledge of how to use that information. Their occurrence marks the meeting of the technology that has enabled the Internet with the humanity of relationship marketing.

CRM systems are based on the basic marketing belief that an organisation that knows its customers and how to treat them has an advantage in the market. The aim is to treat all customers like individuals. Its components may include data warehouses that store all a company's information, customer service systems, call centres, e-commerce, Web marketing, operations systems (that handle order entry, invoicing, payments, point of sale, inventory systems, etc.) and sales systems (mobile sales communications, appointment making, routing, etc.). In practice, CRM systems range from automated customer-contact systems to the company-wide pooling of customer information.

The implementation of CRM needs the close cooperation between suppliers of one of the many CRM systems on offer, such as Visual Elk, Avenue and Relationship Organiser, and the user.

Customer Relationship Management (CRM) systems
IT-based applications that integrate a company's information about customers with the knowledge of how to use that information.

Blockbuster Video, a MicroStrategy customer, provides one example of an application of CRM. The system mines Blockbuster's databases, identifying the films people like by segment, theme or age group. It then prompts personalised phone calls or e-mails to customers offering to reserve a film it infers they will like.

According to MicroStrategy, 'The critical component is that it is based on conditions that the customer controls . . . The customer can turn it off, the customer sets the thresholds and triggers and sets the rules. From the company's perspective, they are not just 'spamming' people who have signalled no interest.'

CRM systems are capital investments that integrate strategy, marketing and IT. As such, they cut across traditional organisational structures and force the integration of activities. Implementing CRM systems is no small task, and one that risks doing harm if done badly. 'There is no doubt that CRM can be a major factor in achieving competitive advantage', according to Malcolm McDonald, but 'get CRM wrong and customers leave, never to return.'[25]

when to use relationship marketing

Relationship marketing is not effective in all situations, although CRM systems are reducing the value threshold at which it becomes appropriate. Transaction marketing, which focuses on one sales transaction at a time, is more appropriate than relationship marketing for customers who have short time horizons and can switch from one supplier to another with little effort or investment. This situation often occurs in 'commodity' markets, such as steel, where various suppliers offer largely undifferentiated products. A customer buying steel can buy from any of several steel suppliers and choose the one offering the best terms on a purchase-by-purchase basis. The fact that one steel supplier works at developing a longer-term relationship with a buyer does not automatically earn it the next sale; its price and other terms still have to be competitive. Global e-procurement systems, like the motor industry's Covisint and aerospace's Exostar, where buyers flag their requirements on the Internet, are tightening profit margins and breaking down close relationships between buyers and suppliers. For example, by using Internet auctions and exchanges BAe aims to decrease its purchasing bill by 5 per cent and its number of suppliers from 14,000 to 2,000 by 2002.[26]

In contrast, relationship marketing can pay off handsomely with customers that have long time horizons and high switching costs, such as buyers of office automation systems. It can also be part of an e-procurement system, such as Covisint, that will involve suppliers in new product development. When buying complex systems, buyers usually research competing suppliers carefully and choose one from whom they can expect state-of-the-art technology and good long-term service. Both the customer and the supplier invest a lot of money and time in building the relationship. The customer would find it costly and risky to switch to another supplier and the seller would find that losing this customer would be a considerable loss. Thus each seeks to develop a solid long-term working relationship with the other. It is with such customers that relationship marketing has the greatest pay-off.

In these situations, the 'in-supplier' and 'out-supplier' face very different challenges. The in-supplier tries to make switching difficult for the customer. It develops product systems that are incompatible with those of competing suppliers and installs its own ordering systems which simplify inventory management and delivery. It works to become the customer's indispensable partner. Out-suppliers, in contrast, try to make it easy and less costly to switch suppliers. They design product systems that are compatible with the customer's system, that are easy to install and learn, that save the customer a lot of money, and that promise to improve through time.

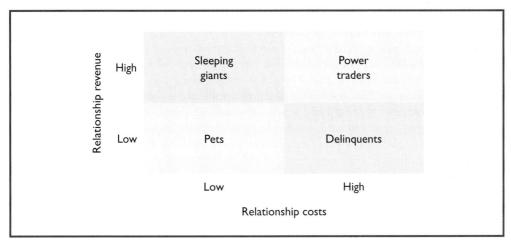

Figure 11.6

Comparing customer
relationship revenues
with relationship costs

The appropriateness of transaction versus relationship marketing depends on the type of industry and the wishes of the particular customer. Some customers value a high-service supplier and will stay with that supplier for a long time. Other customers want to cut their costs and will switch suppliers readily to obtain lower costs.

Thus relationship marketing is not the best approach in all situations. For it to be worthwhile, relationship revenue needs to exceed relationship costs. Figure 11.6 suggests that some customers are very profitable *sleeping giants*, which generate significant revenue and are profitable but relatively undemanding. Much of the relationship marketing activity is taken up by the *power traders*, which provide significant revenue but are demanding. These are as profitable as the *pets*, which provide little revenue but have appropriately small relationship costs. Transaction marketing is probably adequate for these. The most difficult group is the *delinquents*, which provide little revenue but are demanding. What can a company do about these? One option is to shift the *delinquent* customers to products that are likely to be less difficult to operate or less complicated. Vodaphone's *Pay as you Talk* phone service does this by providing contracts to less well-off customers who prepay for the phone's use. Banks' high charges on unnegotiated overdrafts are a way of doing this. If these actions cause the unprofitable customer to defect, so be it. In fact, the company might benefit by *encouraging* these unprofitable customers to switch to competition.[27]

summary

Today's customers face a growing range of choices in the products and services they can buy. They base their choices on their perceptions of *quality, value* and *service*. Companies need to understand the determinants of *customer value* and *satisfaction*. *Customer delivered value* is the difference between *total customer value* and *total customer cost*. Customers will normally choose the offer that maximises their delivered value.

Customer satisfaction is the outcome felt by buyers who have experienced a company performance that has fulfilled expectations. Customers are satisfied when their expectations are met and delighted when their expectations are exceeded. Satisfied customers remain loyal longer, buy more, are less price sensitive and talk favourably about the company. To be known, customer satisfaction has to be measured and there are several established ways of doing this.

To create customer satisfaction, companies must manage their own *value chains* and the entire *value delivery system* in a customer-centred way. The company's goal is not only to get customers, but, even more importantly, to retain customers. *Total quality management* has become a leading approach to providing customer satisfaction and company profitability across the whole value chain. Delivering quality requires total management and employee commitment as well as measurement and reward systems. Marketers play an especially critical role in their company's drive towards higher quality.

Customer relationship marketing provides the key to retaining customers and involves building financial and social benefits as well as structural ties to customers. *Customer relationship marketing* systems integrate strategy, IT and relationship marketing to deliver value to customers and treat them individually. Companies must decide the level at which they want to build relationships with different market segments and individual customers, from such levels as basic, reactive, accountable and proactive to full partnership. Which is best depends on a customer's lifetime value relative to the costs required to attract and retain that customer.

discussing the issues

1. Describe a situation in which you became a 'lost customer'. Did you drop the purchase because of poor product quality, poor service quality or both? What should the firm do to 'recapture' lost customers?

2. Recall a purchase experience in which the sales assistant or some other representative of an organisation went beyond the normal effort and 'gave his/her all' to produce the utmost in service quality. What impact did the noticeable effort have on the purchase outcome?

3. Total quality management is an important approach to providing customer satisfaction and company profits. How might total quality be managed for the following product and service offerings:

(a) a packaged food product; (b) a restaurant meal; (c) a public utility (such as power supply or garbage collection); (d) a family holiday; (e) a university education?

4. Recall incidents when you have purchased, or tried to purchase similar items through two or more of the Internet direct marketing call centres or bricks-and-mortar stores. How does the meaning of service quality differ across the three channels and how did they compare in operation?

5. Thinking of the operation of a not-for-profit organisation, such as a charity, propose some ways in which relationship marketing could help them collect money from donors.

applying the concepts

1. Write a letter of complaint to a firm about one of its products or services. What was the firm's response? Did you receive a refund or replacement product, a response letter or no reply at all? How does the type of response affect your attitude towards the company?

2. Determine two or three relatively obscure subjects on which you could need to purchase a book, for

example house prices, the history of puppetry or Portuguese cooking. Then visit several Web book retailers and compare the quality of their service and the mechanisms they use to build relationships into their service (sites could include amazon.com, amazon.co.uk, bol.com, bn.com, waterstones.com). Compare the best with a search at a local bricks-and-mortar bookstore.

references

1. Paul Cheeseright, 'Simpson aims to accelerate Lucas', *Financial Times* (11 October 1994), p. 21.

2. Mike Sommers, 'Getting the customer into the board room', *Marketing Business* (May 1999), pp. 28–31.

3. For more on measuring customer delivered value, and on 'value/price ratios', see Alan Mitchell, 'Value focused strategy is key to brand growth', *Marketing Week*, **22**, 13 (1999), pp. 36–7 and Kenneth N. Thompson, Barbara J. Coe and John R. Lewis, 'Gauging the value of suppliers' products: Buyer-side applications of economic value pricing models', *Journal of Business & Industrial Marketing*, **9**, 2 (1994), pp. 29–40.

4. For an interesting discussion of value and value strategies, see Michael Treacy and Fred Wiersema, 'Customer intimacy and other value disciplines', *Harvard Business Review* (January–February 1993), pp. 84–93; Albert Caruana and Pierre R. Berthon, 'Service quality and satisfaction – the moderating role of value', *European Journal of Marketing*, **34**, 11/12 (2000), pp. 1338–53; Shirley Daniels, 'Customer value management', *Work Study*, **49**, 2 (2000), pp. 67–70 and Annika Ravald and Christian Grönroos, 'The value concept and relationship marketing', *European Journal of Marketing*, **30**, 2 (1996), pp. 19–30.

5. *The Economist*, 'Customers and suppliers: a pressurised environment' (13 March 1999), pp. 111–2.

6. Thomas E. Caruso, 'Got a marketing topic? Kotler has an opinion', *Marketing News* (8 June 1992), p. 21. Also see Jeremy Hope, 'Customers: strategic, loyal and profitable?', *Management Accounting*, **76**, 9 (1998), pp. 20–2; Antonella Carù and Antonella Cugini, 'Profitability and customer satisfaction in services: An integrated perspective between marketing and cost management analysis', *International Journal of Service Industry Management*, **10**, 2 (1999), pp. 132–57.

7. Tor Wallin Anfreassen, 'Antecedents to satisfaction with service recovery', *European Journal of Marketing*, **34**, 1/2 (2000), pp. 156–75; Kate Stewart, 'The customer exit process – A review and research agenda', *Journal of Marketing Management*, **14**, 4 (1998), pp. 235–50.

8. Michael E. Porter, *Competitive Advantage: Creating and sustaining superior performance* (New York: Free Press, 1985); David Walters, 'Implementing value strategy through the value chain', *Management Decision*, **38**, 3 (2000), pp. 160–78.

9. For an analysis of the relative contribution of the product, sales service and after-sales service, see José M. M. Bloemer and Jos G. A. M. Lemmink, 'The importance of customer satisfaction in explaining brand and dealer loyalty', *Journal of Marketing Management*, **8**, 4 (1992), pp. 351–64.

10. See George Stalk, Philip Evans and Laurence E. Shulman, 'Competing capabilities: the new rules of corporate strategy', *Harvard Business Review* (March–April 1992), pp. 57–69; Benson P. Shapiro, V. Kasturi Rangan and John J. Sviokla, 'Staple yourself to an order', *Harvard Business Review* (July–August 1992), pp. 113–22.

11. Stuart Derrick, 'Saving face', *e.business* (June 2000), pp. 19–20; Stuart Derrick, 'Moving target', *e.business* (July 2000), p. 69; *Fletcher Research,* 'Multichannel strategies: call centre and web integration' (2000).

12. For more discussion, see Shirley Daniels, 'Customer value management', *Work Study*, **49**, 2 (2000), pp. 67–70, Douglas Brownlie, Mike Saren, Robin Wensley and Richard Whittington, 'Rethinking marketing: towards critical marketing accountings', *European Journal of Marketing*, **34**, 1/2 (2000). pp. 223–6.

13. 'Business and Community Annual Report (1997)', *Financial Times* (4 December 1997), p. 5.

14. Specifically, Bob Luchs, 'Quality as a strategic weapon: measuring relative quality, value, and market differentiation', *European Business Journal*, **2**, 4 (1990), pp. 34–47; and generally Robert D. Buzzell and Bradley T. Gale, *The PIMS Principles: Linking strategy to performance* (New York: Free Press, 1987), Ch. 6.

15. Ziaul Huq and Justin D. Stolen, 'Total quality management contrasts in manufacturing and service industries', *International Journal of Quality & Reliability Management*, **15**, 2 (1998), pp. 138–61; T. Thiagarajan and M. Zairi, 'A review of total quality management in practice: understanding the fundamentals through examples of best practice applications – part III', *The TQM Magazine*, **9**, 6 (1997), pp. 414–17.

16. See Joe Folkman, 'Employee surveys that make a difference', *Journal of Services Marketing*, **14**, 5 (2000), pp. 432–6; G. Ronald Gilbert, 'Measuring internal customer satisfaction', *Managing Service Quality*, **10**, 3 (2000), pp. 178–86 and Zoe S. Dimitriades, 'Total involvement in quality management', *Team Performance Management: An International Journal*, **6**, 7/8 (2000), pp. 117–22.

17. J. Daniel Beckham, 'Expect the unexpected in health care marketing future', *The Academy Bulletin* (July 1992), p. 3.

18. 'British banks in the balance' *The Economist* (18 July 2000), pp. 115–16; Nick Watson, 'UK banks under attack', *EuroBusiness* (May 2000), p. 141; James Mackintosh, 'Barclays in ATM climbdown', *Financial Times* (4 July 2000), p. 1; David Ibison, 'High Street "villain" takes flak for the big four', *Financial Times* (5 April 2000), p. 3.

19. Chartered Institute of Marketing, 'Customer retention' in *Marketing Means Business*, Chartered Institute of Marketing (Moore Hall, Chartered Institute of Marketing, 1999), pp. 84–8; Fiona Harvey, 'Of chocolates and profit sharing', *Financial Times* (26 July 2000), p. 13; 'Workers of the world, stop moaning', *The Guardian* (16 August 2000); Malcolm McDonald, 'Up close and personal', *Marketing Business* (September 1998), pp. 52–5; Peter Bartram, 'Engineered for growth', *Marketing Business* (February 1999), pp. 24–9.

20. Redrick F. Reicheld and W. Earl Sasser, Jr, 'Zero defections: quality comes to service', *Harvard Business Review* (September–October 1990), pp. 301–7; Mike Page, Leyland Pitt and Pierre Berthon, 'Analyzing and reducing customer defections', *Long Range Planning*, **29**, 6 (1996), pp. 821–34.

21. Leonard L. Berry and A. Parasuraman, *Marketing Services: Competing through quality* (New York: Free Press, 1991), pp. 136–42.

22. Richard Lapper, 'J. P. Morgan offers free use of its toolbox', *Financial Times* (11 October 1994), p. 27.

23. Peter Bartram, 'Engineering for growth', *Marketing Business* (February 2000), pp. 24–7.

24. Thomas E. Caruso, 'Kotler: future marketers will focus on customer database to compete globally', *Marketing News* (8 June 1992), p. 21; also see Y. H. Wong, 'Key to key account management: relationship (guanxi) model', *International Marketing Review*, **15**, 3 (1998), pp. 215–31.

25. Malcolm McDonald, 'On the right track', *Marketing Business* (April 2000), pp. 28–9; David Murphy, 'Making CRM work', *Marketing Business* (November 1999), pp. 42–5; 'I want a relationship', *Marketing Business* (e-business: 2000), pp. vi–vii; Mosad Zineldin, 'Total relationship management (TRM) and total quality management (TQM)', *Managerial Auditing Journal*, **15**, 1/2 (2000), pp. 20–8; Mosad Zineldin, 'Exploring the common ground of total relationship management (TRM) and total quality management (TQM)', *Management Decision*, **37**, 9 (1999), pp. 719–30.

26. Kim Benjamin, 'BA's on-line flight path', *e-business* (June 2000), pp. 55–60; Nikki Tait, 'Racing down the electronic highway', *Financial Times: e-procurement* (Winter 2000), pp. 18–19; Geoff Nairn, 'Launching a strike against military costs', *Financial Times: e-procurement* (Winter 2000), pp. 20–1.

27. Lawrence A. Crosby, Kenneth R. Evans and Deborah Cowles, 'Relationship quality and services selling: an interpersonal influence perspective', *Journal of Marketing* (July 1990), pp. 68–81; Barry J. Farber and Joyce Wycoff, 'Relationships: six steps to success', *Sales and Marketing Management* (April 1992), pp. 50–8.

case 11

National Gummi AB

Thomas Helgasson*

National Gummi has problems. For them it is a new problem, but it is close to that being faced by many small to medium-sized companies these days as their major local customers become part of major multinational companies. Years spent building up relationships with them are in danger of being devalued as their customer's HQ is suddenly centred in a new culture oceans away. What is even more worrying is the standardisation of products; the rationalisation of suppliers and the use of alien e-purchasing systems often follow the consolidation of companies into global giants. All this is happening to National Gummi AB whose major customers, Ford and GM, have swallowed Saab and Volvo, respectively.

National Gummi is a small company situated in the south of Sweden. Founded in 1941, it is now managed by the third generation of the founding family. It has 145 employees and a turnover of SKr 175m (€20m). National Gummi's main business is making rubber seals that go round the doors and windows of vehicles. Between them Saab and Volvo account for two-thirds of National Gummi's turnover, so to lose their business would be catastrophic. Through close personal relationships over the last 40 years the two Swedish carmakers have learned to trust National Gummi and recognise that the company that can solve their door and window sealing problems.

The product

Most sealing systems are made of rubber, a material with some drawbacks. Rubber cannot be recycled, it is expensive, complicated to handle in manufacture and is seen by final consumers as being environmentally unfriendly. National Gummi's aim is to change from using rubber to more environmentally friendly Thermo Plastic Elastomers (TPE) that are partly plastic and part rubber. Being a compound, its properties can be changed to fit the needs of doors and windows, while rubber has fixed properties. TPE is also recyclable either as waste material left over from manufacturing or as recovered from a scrapped vehicle, easy and fast to use in production, has lower production costs and is generally more environmentally friendly than rubber. TPE's main disadvantage is that it is less 'elastic' than rubber so does not form an effective seal in some parts of all cars, which means that it will have to be used alongside rubber in car assembly.

National Gummi aims to solve TPE's elasticity problem but expects that everyone else in the industry is trying to do the same thing. Following the tradition of past partnerships, in 1998 National Gummi, Saab and Volvo set up a joint project team to develop better TPE seals. After some discussion, the team was made up of two National Gummi engineers, one engineer from each of Saab and Volvo, a polymer-researcher from IFP Research Ltd and a marketer from Halmstad University. Members of the project team all contributed different skills. The National Gummi engineers knew a lot about seals but had little experience with the rest of car assembly. In contrast, the Saab and Volvo engineers had a limited experience of seals but knew a lot about cars generally. The IFP researcher had expertise in plastics and rubber generally rather than in their use as seals.

It is common for the Swedish carmakers to work with suppliers on new projects. For components such as floor mats or light bulbs there is little reason to involve suppliers until late in product development. However, with a component such as a seal, which will affect both design and assembly, early participation of all parties in design is very important. The engineers do not have it all their own way in design. The carmakers' marketing people will be championing their customers' requirements, while the purchasing department will be fighting to get costs down.

A relationship without marketing

It is very difficult to become a new supplier to either Saab or Volvo. New 'partners' have to fill all technical requirements, have a low price and be someone that the companies can trust. The relationships are important since the quality and value of the final product are only as good as the components. Of course, National Gummi's 40 years of service and numerous long-standing personal friendships with the carmakers' people give National Gummi a great advantage. Saab and Volvo feel that the people at National Gummi are more than just business partners. They are friends with whom they have worked for many years and who have cooperated in solving many business problems. Through long partnership, National Gummi know the needs of Saab and Volvo and how to work with them.

Of course, National Gummi's relationship with the carmakers has changed over the years. One of National Gummi's early advantages was their extreme proximity

* Halmstad University, Sweden

to the car plants. When that was the case it was possible to make a visit and solve design or manufacturing problems within hours. Over the years, Saab and Volvo had become more international with operations all over Europe. In some markets National Gummi had to deal with Saab and Volvo through agents and the business had shifted from one with a single language and culture to a multilingual, multi-cultural entity. IT had started to play a bigger role in routine communications between the carmakers and their suppliers. Meeting the needs of quality management and just-in-time management had also applied pressures, and National Gummi had to establish representation and extra facilities adjacent to car plants. It had become harder and harder for a small independent company to survive in a rapidly changing and increasingly global industry.

Increasingly, communications between National Gummi and the carmakers were electronic: e-mail, telephone, fax and shared software to handle orders and design drawings. However, personal communications remained paramount in maintaining understanding between National Gummi and its customers. Video-conferencing had been used to work with more geographically distant partners and National Gummi knew of several cases of small companies exploiting global markets through the World Wide Web.

The closeness of National Gummi to its customers had allowed the company to develop without the need for conventional marketing skills. Engineers did technical selling and new customers had always found National Gummi rather than the other way round. This worked fine as long as Saab and Volvo remained good partners who respected the profit margins needed by subcontractors. The threat now was the tendency of the industry to seek system solutions rather than components; for example, subcontracting the provision of whole door assemblies, window and door seals included, rather than lots of bits and pieces. These jobs were hard for a small company like National Gummi to tender for and demanded lots of skills that they did not have.

Saab and Volvo were also part of large American companies that put less emphasis on the personal relationships that had been National Gummi's major advantage for so long. Saab and Volvo retained marketing operations in Sweden but these were becoming servants to the global operations, such as Ford's Berkeley Square-based Premier Automobile Group which manages Volvo alongside the Aston Martin, Jaguar, Land Rover, Lincoln and Mercury brands. Covisint, the giant electronic automobile component exchange with its headquarters in Michigan, was also being set up by DaimlerChrysler,

Ford, GM, Nissan and Renault. Expected to have a turnover of $250 billion (€280 billion), the Internet exchange would have at least one office in Europe. One of the aims of establishing Covisint is to squeeze margins out of suppliers to the tune of $1,000 to $4,000 per car in the US where costs are already low.

As a small components company with limited potential for systems solutions or advanced research, National Gummi knew it would have to change in order to survive. Advisers had suggested several alternative ways ahead for National Gummi:

1. To become a sub-subcontractor and supply one of the major subcontractors with components. In this case, National Gummi's customers would become the car manufacturer's prime vendors who supplied door assemblies.

2. To specialise in components that are not a part of a system so are sold separately to carmakers.

3. To increase that part of their activities that does not go to Volvo or Saab by finding new customers or selling more to existing customers. Aside from Saab and Volvo, National Gummi has about 2,000 smaller customers.

4. For National Gummi to be more proactive in trying to find customers instead of waiting for customers to find them.

Questions

1. Why is National Gummi facing the problems it is and what could it have done to avoid them?

2. Since National Gummi survived for so long without any marketing activities, would it have been an unnecessary luxury to develop them until recently?

3. How did National Gummi add value to its service to its past clients and how can it continue to do so? Does the development of electronic exchanges mean that relationships between customers and suppliers are history?

4. Since the close relationships between National Gummi and the Swedish carmakers were the foundation of its past success, does the company's present state suggest a danger in relationship marketing? Does relationship marketing differ from what National Gummi has been doing?

5. Examining the strengths and weaknesses of National Gummi, what strategy would you propose for them?

internet exercises

Internet exercises for this chapter can be found on the student site of the MYPHLIP Web Site at www.booksites.net/kotler.

chapter twelve

Creating competitive advantages

Chapter objectives   *After reading this chapter, you should be able to:*

✦ Explain the importance of developing competitive marketing strategies that position the company against competitors and give it the strongest possible competitive advantage.

✦ Identify the steps that companies go through in analysing competitors.

✦ Discuss the competitive strategies that market leaders use to expand the market

and to protect and expand their market shares.

✦ Describe the strategies that market challengers and followers use to increase their market shares and profits.

✦ Discuss how market nichers find and develop profitable corners of the market.

introduction

Understanding customers is not enough. As the computer game machines market shows (see preview case overleaf), this is a period of intense competition in local and global markets. Many economies are deregulating and encouraging market forces to operate. The EU is removing trade barriers among European nations and deregulating many previously protected markets. Multinationals are moving aggressively into the south-east Asian markets and competing globally. The result is that companies have no choice but to be 'competitive'. They must start paying as much attention to tracking their competitors as to understanding target customers. Nintendo at first succeeded by being innovative and providing an excellent product that competitors could not match. Their innovativeness revitalised the market, made it grow, made it profitable and large. In doing so they attracted new powerful competitors from other industries, first consumer electronics-based Sony and now super-wealthy Microsoft.

Under the marketing concept, companies gain **competitive advantage** by designing offers that satisfy target-consumer needs better than competitors' offers. They might deliver more customer value by offering consumers lower prices than competitors for similar products and services, or by providing more benefits that justify higher prices. Marketing strategies must consider the strategies of competitors as well as the needs of target consumers. The first step is **competitor analysis**: the process of identifying

Competitive advantage
An advantage over competitors gained by offering consumers greater value, either through lower prices or by providing more benefits that justify higher prices.

Competitor analysis
The process of identifying key competitors; assessing their objectives, strategies, strengths and weaknesses, and reaction patterns; and selecting which competitors to attack or avoid.

417

preview case

PS2 meets the X-box: certainly not all fun and games

In the games machine market life is even more challenging than *Tomb Raider*, more aggressive than *Grand Theft Auto* and more brutal than *Resident Evil*. In the early 1980s, no home could be without a video game console and a dozen cartridges. By 1983 Atari, Mattel and a dozen other companies offered some version of a video game system and industry sales topped €3.6 billion worldwide. Then, by 1985, home video game sales had plummeted to €100 million. Game consoles gathered dust and cartridges, originally priced as high as €40 each, sold for €5. Industry leader Atari was hardest hit. Atari sacked 4,500 employees and sold the subsidiary at a fraction of its 1983 worth. Industry experts blamed the death of the industry on the fickle consumer. Video games, they said, were a passing fad.

However, Nintendo, a 100-year-old toy company from Kyoto, did not agree. In late 1985, on top of the ruins of the video game business, the company introduced its Nintendo Entertainment System (NES). A year later, Nintendo had sold over 1 million NES units. By 1991 Nintendo and its licensees had annual sales of $4 billion in a now revitalised €5 billion video game industry. Nintendo had 80 per cent share of the world market. Forty per cent of Japanese households and about 20 per cent of US and EU households had a NES.

How did Nintendo do it? First, it recognised that video game customers were not so much fickle as bored. The company sent researchers to visit video arcades to find out why alienated home video game fans still spent hours happily pumping arcade machines. The researchers found that Nintendo's *Donkey Kong* and similar games were still mainstays of the arcades, even though home versions were failing. The reason? The arcade games offered better quality, full animation and challenging plots. Home video games, on the other hand, offered only crude quality and simple plots. Despite their exotic names and introductory hype, each new home game was boringly identical to all the others, featuring slow characters that moved through ugly animated scenes to the beat of monotonous, synthesised tones. Kids had outgrown the first-generation home video games.

Nintendo saw the fall of the video game industry as an opportunity. It set out to differentiate itself by offering superior quality – by giving home video games customers a full measure of quality entertainment value for their money. Nintendo designed a basic game system that sold for about €100 yet boasted near arcade-quality graphics. Equally important, it developed innovative and high-quality *Game Paks* to accompany the system. New games constantly appear and mature titles are weeded out to keep the selection fresh and interesting. The games contain consistently high-quality graphics and game plots vary and challenge the user. Colourful, cartoon-like characters move fluidly about cleverly animated screens. The most popular games involved sword-and-sorcery conflicts, or the series of *Super Mario* fantasy worlds, where young heroes battle to save endangered princesses or fight the evil ruler, *Wart*, for peace in the *World of Dreams*.

By differentiating itself through superior products and service, and by building strong relationships with its customers, Nintendo built a seemingly invincible quality position in the video game market. But it soon came under attack. New competitors such as Sony and Sega exploited the opportunities created as Nintendo junkies became bored and sought the next new video thrill. Sony beat Nintendo at its own game – product superiority – when it hit the market with its PlayStation machine, an advanced new system that offered even richer graphics, more lifelike sound and more complex plots. Nintendo countered with the Nintendo 64 and a fresh blast of promotion, but the competition has intensified and, while Nintendos were being discounted, the PlayStation was the Christmas hit toy of 1997.

Meanwhile the computer games world is attacked for being 'violent, destructive, xenophobic, racist and sexist'. Sega Europe has also been attacked for marketing gruesome games such as *Mortal Kombat* and *Murder Death Kill*. The industry has been criticised for cultivating a generation of 'Video Kids' for whom 30 seconds without scoring is boring; moral zombies hooked on worlds where the rules are shot or be shot, consume or be consumed, fight or lose. In Japan, where many of the games come from, consumers are more broad-minded than in most western countries. Nintendo needs to extend its customer range beyond the terminally fickle teenage males. Sega sponsored roadshows with teen magazines, and put girls in its TV ads after complaints from schoolchildren on its 'advisory board' about sexism in advertising. Sega Europe created a new toy division to target 'housewives with children, instead of 14-year-old boys'. The first product was Pico, an electronic learning aid for kids that has taken a 'significant' share of the Japanese high-tech toys market. The €9 million European launch included TV, press and posters with a full below-the-line campaign. Next came an 'electronic learning aid that thinks it's a toy' for three- to seven-year-olds. At the older end of the market more cerebral 'stealth games' are taking hold in Japan. These reward. *Metal Gear Solid* and *Theft* reward silence, concealment and strategy more than bang and blast. Is this new thrust making gaming more civilised? No way.

While Nintendo and Sega chased the new markets, Sony's PlayStation blasted the 1997 Christmas market with the 'arcade feel' of *Ridge Racer* and *Crash Bindicoot* and 'scary, tension building' *Doom*. It is the kids who drive the games market and what they want is power and the latest cult machine. Three years after PlayStation blasted the competition, their €450 PlayStation 2 (PS2) is aimed to do the same again for Christmas 2000. With Internet access, CD and DVD playability the PS2's 128-bit microprocessor has twice the power of Intel's latest Pentium chip. So powerful is the PS2's processor that its export had to be specially licensed by the Japanese government since it has the performance necessary to guide a cruise missile.

However, Sony is not having it all their own way. The lucrative games machines market has attracted Microsoft whose X-box will appear in late 2001. Unlike other games machines, the X-box is intended for use in a living room using the family TV and operating Microsoft's PC products. Nintendo, too, is fighting back and hopes to launch their Game Cube before the X-box. Certainly, not all formats will succeed.

Meanwhile, in the run-up to Christmas 2000 Sony has production problems. It looks like worldwide demand for the PS2 is so high that even those people who have pre-ordered PS2s for Christmas have no guarantee of getting one by 25 December. Sega, whose 1999 Dreamcast sales were lacklustre, is hoping to take advantage of Sony's difficulties by launching an updated Dreamcast with DVD compatibility at the same price as the PS2. 'I'm sure this deal will encourage many more customers to pick up a Dreamcast for Christmas', says Saga Europe's chief executive. 'They will have no problems finding Dreamcasts in stores as retailers are piling them high. Our timing is spot on to take advantage of the Christmas rush.'[1]

Questions

1. Why do you think Microsoft has chosen to challenge market leader Sony in the computer games market?

2. What are the key ingredients for success in the computer games market?

3. Using information from the case, and your own knowledge, compare the competitive strengths and weaknesses of the competitors in the computer game machine market. Who do you think will be the long-term winners and why?

key competitors; assessing their objectives, strengths and weaknesses, strategies and reaction patterns; and selecting which competitors to attack or avoid. The second step is developing **competitive strategies** that strongly position the company against competitors and give the company the strongest possible competitive advantage.

Competitive strategies
Strategies that strongly position the company against competitors and that give the company the strongest possible strategic advantage.

competitor analysis

To plan effective competitive marketing strategies, the company needs to find out all it can about its competitors. It must constantly compare its products, prices, channels and promotion with those of close competitors. In this way the company can find areas of potential competitive advantage and disadvantage. It can launch more effective marketing campaigns against its competitors and prepare stronger defences against competitors' actions.

What do companies need to know about their competitors? They need to know: Who are our competitors? What are their objectives? What are their strategies? What are their strengths and weaknesses? What are their reaction patterns? Figure 12.1 shows the main steps in analysing competitors.

identifying the company's competitors

Normally, it would seem a simple matter for a company to identify its competitors. Coca-Cola knows that Pepsi is its strongest competitor; and Caterpillar knows that it

Figure 12.1

Steps in analysing
competitors

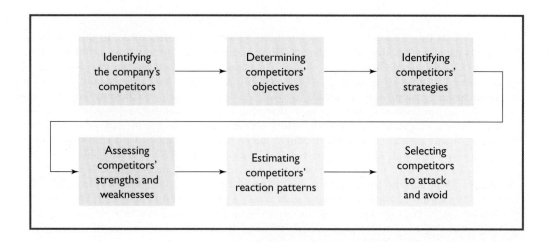

*Under the broadest consideration,
companies that manufacture certain
healthy foods like fish are competing
with the cosmetics industry.*

SOURCE: Unilever/Advertising Archives

competes with Komatsu. At the most obvious level, a company can define its *product
category competition* as other companies offering a similar product and services to
the same customers at similar prices. Thus Volvo might see Mercedes as a foremost
competitor, but not Rolls-Royce Cars or Reliant (makers of the three-wheeled cars that
Mr Bean bullies).

In competing for people's money, however, companies actually face a much wider
range of competitors. More broadly, the company can define its *product competition*
as all firms making the same product or class of products. Volvo could see itself as
competing against all other car manufacturers. Even more broadly, competitors might

include all companies making products that supply the same service. Here Volvo would see itself competing against not only other car manufacturers, but also the makers of trucks, motor cycles or even bicycles. Finally and still more broadly, competitors might include all companies that compete for the same consumer's money. Here Volvo would see itself competing with companies that sell major consumer durables, foreign holidays, new homes or extensive home repairs or alterations.

■ The industry point of view

Many companies identify their competitors from the *industry* point of view. An **industry** is a group of firms that offer a product or class of products that are close substitutes for each other. We talk about the car industry, the oil industry, the pharmaceutical industry or the beverage industry. In a given industry, if the price of one product rises, it causes the demand for another product to rise. In the beverage industry, for example, if the price of coffee rises, this leads people to switch to tea or lemonade or soft drinks. Coffee, tea, lemonade and soft drinks are substitutes, even though they are physically different products. A company must strive to understand the competitive pattern in its industry if it hopes to be an effective 'player' in that industry.

Industry
A group of firms that offer a product or class of products that are close substitutes for each other. The set of all sellers of a product or service.

■ The market point of view

Instead of identifying competitors from the industry point of view, the company can take a *market* point of view. Here it defines its *task competition* as companies that are trying to satisfy the same customer need or serve the same customer group. From an industry point of view, Heineken might see its competition as Beck's, Guinness, Carlsberg and other brewers. From a market point of view, however, the task competition may include all 'thirst quenching' or 'social drinking'. Energy drinks, new age drinks, 'designer' water and many other drinks could satisfy the needs. Similarly, Crayola might define its task competitors as other makers of crayons and children's drawing supplies. Alternatively, from a market point of view, it would include as competitors all firms making recreational products for the children's market. Generally, the market concept of competition opens the company's eyes to a broader set of actual and potential competitors. This leads to better long-run market planning.

The key to identifying competitors is to link industry and market analysis by mapping out product/market segments. Figure 12.2 shows the product/market segments in the toothpaste market by product types and customer age groups. We see that P&G (with several versions of Crest and Gleam) and Colgate-Palmolive (with Colgate) occupy nine of the segments; Lever Brothers (Aim), three; and Beecham (Aqua Fresh) and Topol, two. If Topol wanted to enter other segments, it would need to estimate the market size of each segment, the market shares of the current competitors, and their current capabilities, objectives and strategies. Clearly each product/market segment would pose different competitive problems and opportunities.

Taking a customer-oriented view of the market is critical to avoiding 'competitor myopia' where the immediate competition blinds a company to latent competitors who can completely destroy the old ways of doing business.

Encyclopedia Britannica viewed itself as competing with other publishers of printed encyclopedia sets selling for as much as €2,500 per set. However, it learned a hard lesson when Microsoft Encarta, an encyclopedia on CD-ROM, was introduced and sold for only €60. It seems that parents bought the *Britannica* less for its intellectual content than out of a desire to do what's right for their children. Although less comprehensive than the *Britannica*, Encarta and other CD-ROM encyclopedias served this 'do what's right' purpose well. By the time *Britannica* introduced its own CD-ROM and online versions, its sales plunged by more than 50 per cent. Thus,

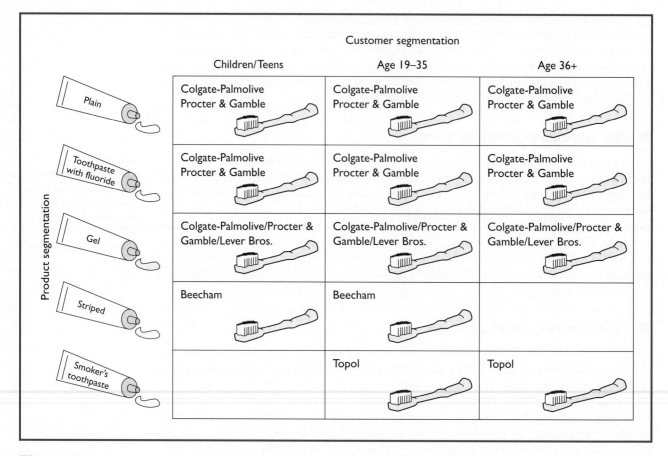

Figure 12.2

Product/market
segments for toothpaste

SOURCE: William A.
Cohen, *Winning on the
Marketing Front* (New
York: Wiley, 1986), p. 63.

Encyclopedia Britannica's real competitor was general databases, in books, on CD-
ROM, websites (studyweb.com) or even news groups (comp.infosystems.interpedia).[2]

determining competitors' objectives

Having identified the main competitors, marketing management now asks: What does
each competitor seek in the marketplace? What drives each competitor's behaviour?

The marketer might at first assume that all competitors would want to maximise
their profits and choose their actions accordingly. However, companies differ in the
emphasis they put on short-term versus long-term profits, and some competitors are
oriented towards 'satisfying' rather than 'maximising' profits. They have profit goals
that satisfy them, even if the strategies could produce more profits.

Marketers must look beyond competitors' profit goals. Each competitor has a mix
of objectives, each with differing importance. The company wants to know the relative
importance that competitors place on current profitability, market share growth, cash
flow, technological leadership, service leadership and other goals. Knowing a competitor's objectives reveals if it is satisfied with its current situation and how it might react
to competitive actions. For example, a company that pursues low-cost leadership will
react much more strongly to a competitor's cost-reducing manufacturing breakthrough
than to the same competitor's advertising increase. A company must also monitor its
competitors' objectives for attacking various product/market segments. If the company
finds that a competitor has discovered a new segment, this might be an opportunity. If
it finds that competitors plan new moves into segments now served by the company,
it will be forewarned and, hopefully, forearmed.

identifying competitors' strategies

The more that one firm's strategy resembles another firm's strategy, the more the firms compete. In most industries, the competitors sort into groups that pursue different strategies. A **strategic group** is a group of firms in an industry following the same or a similar strategy in a given target market. For example, in the major appliance industry, Electrolux, Hotpoint and Zanussi all belong to the same strategic group. Each produces a full line of medium-price appliances supported by good service. Quality-oriented Bosch, country-living Aga and stylish Alessi, on the other hand, belong to a different strategic group. They both produce a narrow line of appliances and charge a premium price.

Some important insights emerge from strategic group identification. For example, if a company enters one of the groups, the members of that group become its key competitors. Thus, if the company enters the first group against Electrolux, Hotpoint and Zanussi, it can succeed only if it develops some strategic advantages over these large competitors.

Although competition is most intense within a strategic group, there is also rivalry among groups. First, some of the strategic groups may appeal to overlapping customer segments. For example, no matter what their strategy, all major appliance manufacturers will go after the apartment and home builders segment. Second, the customers may not see much difference in the offers of different groups – they may see little difference in quality between Electrolux and Bosch. Finally, members of one strategic group might expand into new strategy segments, as Hotpoint has done by extending its washing machine range to approach Bosch's prices.

The company needs to look at all the dimensions that identify strategic groups within the industry. It needs to know each competitor's product quality, features and mix; customer services; pricing policy; distribution coverage; sales force strategy; and advertising and sales promotion programmes. It must study the details of each competitor's R&D, manufacturing, buying, financial and other strategies.

Strategic group
A group of firms in an industry following the same or a similar strategy.

assessing competitors' strengths and weaknesses

Can a company's competitors carry out their strategies and reach their goals? This depends on each competitor's resources and capabilities. Marketers need to identify accurately each competitor's strengths and weaknesses. For example, for a long time the popular music industry had been dominated by American and British acts. Abba signalled a change in the industry structure with an increasing number of bands either being Swedish or recording in Sweden. Marketing Highlight 12.1 looks at this phenomenon and looks for the source of Sweden's competitive strength in popular music.

As a first step, a company gathers key data on each competitor's business over the last few years. It wants to know about competitors' goals, strategies and performance. Admittedly, some of this information will be hard to collect. For example, industrial goods companies find it hard to estimate competitors' market shares because they do not have the same syndicated data services that are available to consumer packaged-goods companies. Still, any information they can find will help them form a better estimate of each competitor's strengths and weaknesses.

Companies normally learn about their competitors' strengths and weaknesses through secondary data, personal experience and hearsay. They can also increase their knowledge by conducting primary marketing research with customers, suppliers and dealers. Recently, a growing number of companies have turned to **benchmarking**, comparing the company's products and processes to those of competitors or leading firms in other industries to find ways of improving quality and performance. Benchmarking has become a powerful tool for increasing a company's competitiveness.

In searching for competitors' weaknesses, the company should try to identify any assumptions they make about their business and the market that are no longer valid.

Benchmarking
The process of comparing the company's products and processes to those of competitors or leading firms in other industries to find ways to improve quality and performance.

marketing highlight 12.1

The swinging Swedes

Why has pop music become one of Sweden's greatest exports and Stockholm one of the hit-making capitals of the world?

Melody makers

'Swedes are very musical people to start with', says Bol Hydena, MD of Nordic MTV. 'Melody-making is important to us and somehow we all seem to be good at it, perhaps because we are exposed to it at such an early age. Most everyone goes to music lessons when they are young. And we all have to sing – the making of song is a national art. According to Holger Jensen, professor of music at Stockholm University, 'Swedes have an almost inborn ability to create easy, nice-sounding melodies.'

State support

At Sweden's secondary schools, any instrument is easily available to anyone who wants to play. Pupils are strongly encouraged to study musical composition. The immediate result is that thousands of bands, from the awful to the superb, play at weekends in front rooms and garages across the country. Another important tradition, dating back to pre-Woodstock days, is that new and established singers and bands can try out their material in so-called people's or folk parks. Abba, notably, were a product of the circuit that has grown up around these free, government-supported, outdoor venues.

Anglophiles

Swedes pride themselves on their ability to speak and sing in English and, because American and British movies are generally subtitled rather than dubbed, they also have a good grasp of American and English idioms. According to one defiant Swedish-language singer, 'on a certain level, we're all American and English wannabes'. There's nothing particularly Swedish about the chart-topping songs that Max Martin and his musicians whip up for Britney Spears and the Backstreet Boys, but some Swedes argue that Martin's ability to imitate Anglo-American pop and add hummable lyrics is itself thoroughly Swedish.

Market economics

Because the domestic Swedish market is so small, real money-making success requires acts to win fans from abroad. In a country where thousands aspire to a music career, to survive for any length of time one needs to be able to create music for the larger, English listening market. As Sanji Tandan, managing director of Warner Brothers Sweden, puts it: 'They've got to be able to make it out there to make it in here.'

Blonde looks

To really, really make it big requires one more crucial factor. As Prof. Jensen slyly observes: 'An interesting feature common to Abba, Roxette, Ace of Base, the Cardigans and others, is the union of male and female – usually with at least one blonde woman.'

SOURCE: Extract from 'Stockholm syndrome', *The Business FT Weekend* (11 November 2000), pp. 18–22.

Some companies believe they produce the best quality in the industry when this is no longer true. Many companies are victims of rules-of-thumb such as 'customers prefer full-line companies', 'the sales force is the only important marketing tool' or 'customers value service more than price'. If a competitor is operating on a significant wrong assumption, the company can take advantage of it.

estimating competitors' reaction patterns

A competitor's objectives, strategies and strengths and weaknesses explain its likely actions, and its reactions to moves such as a price cut, a promotion increase or a new product introduction. In addition, each competitor has a certain philosophy of doing business, a certain internal culture and guiding beliefs. Marketing managers need a deep understanding of a given competitor's mentality if they want to anticipate how that competitor will act or react.

Each competitor reacts differently. Some do not react quickly or strongly to a competitor's move: they may feel that their customers are loyal; they may be slow in noticing the move; they may lack the funds to react. Some competitors react only to certain types of assault and not to others. They might always respond strongly to price cuts in order to signal that these will never succeed. But they might not respond at all to advertising increases, believing these to be less threatening. Other competitors react swiftly and strongly to any assault. As Unilever has found with its Persil/Omo Power, P&G does not let a new detergent come easily into the market. Many firms avoid direct competition with P&G and look for easier prey, knowing that P&G will fight fiercely if challenged. Finally, some competitors show no predictable reaction pattern. They might or might not react on a given occasion and there is no way to foresee what they will do based on their economics, history or anything else.

In some industries, competitors live in relative harmony; in others, they fight constantly. Knowing how key competitors react gives the company clues on how best to attack competitors or how best to defend the company's current positions.[3]

selecting competitors to attack and avoid

Management has already largely determined its main competitors through prior decisions on customer targets, distribution channels and marketing-mix strategy. These decisions define the strategic group to which the company belongs. Management must now decide which competitors to compete against most vigorously. The company can focus its attack on one of several classes of competitors.

■ Strong or weak competitors

Most companies prefer to aim their shots at their weak competitors. This requires fewer resources and less time. Conversely, the firm may gain little. Alternatively, the firm should also compete with strong competitors to sharpen its abilities. Furthermore, even strong competitors have some weaknesses and succeeding against them often provides greater returns.

A useful tool for assessing competitor strengths and weaknesses is **customer value analysis** – asking customers what benefits they value and how they rate the company versus competitors on important attributes. Customer value analysis also points out areas in which the company is vulnerable to competitors' actions.

Customer value analysis
Analysis conducted to determine what benefits target customers value and how they rate the relative value of various competitors' offers.

■ Close or distant competitors

Most companies will compete with those competitors who resemble them the most. Thus, Citroën/Peugeot competes more against Renault than against Porsche. At the same time, the company may want to avoid trying to 'destroy' a close competitor. Here is an example of a questionable 'victory':

> Bausch & Lomb in the late 1970s moved aggressively against other soft contact lens manufacturers with great success. However, this led to competitors selling out to large firms. Johnson & Johnson acquired Vistakon, a small nicher that served the tiny portion of the contact-lens market for people with astigmatism. Backed by J&J's deep pockets, Vistakon proved a formidable opponent. When the small but nimble Vistakon introduced its innovative Acuvue disposable lenses, Bausch & Lomb had to

take some of its own medicine. According to one analyst, 'The speed of the [Acuvue] roll-out and the novelty of [J&J's] big-budget ads left giant Bausch & Lomb . . . seeing stars'. While Bausch & Lomb reeled, Vistakon grew to become market leader in the fast-growing disposable contact-lens market.[4]

In this case, the company's success in hurting a close rival brought in tougher competitors.

■ 'Well-behaved' or 'disruptive' competitors

A company really needs and benefits from competitors. The existence of competitors results in several strategic benefits. Competitors may help increase total demand. They share the costs of market and product development, and help to legitimise new technology. They may serve less attractive segments or lead to more product differentiation. Finally, they may improve bargaining power against labour or regulators.

However, a company may not view all of its competitors as beneficial. An industry often contains 'well-behaved' competitors and 'disruptive' competitors.[5] Well-behaved competitors play by the rules of the industry. They favour a stable and healthy industry, set prices in a reasonable relation to costs, motivate others to lower costs or improve differentiation, and accept a reasonable level of market share and profits. Disruptive competitors, on the other hand, break the rules. They try to buy share rather than earn it, take large risks, invest in overcapacity and generally shake up the industry. For example, British Airways, KLM and United see each other as well-behaved competitors because they play by the rules and attempt to set their fares sensibly. Conversely, they find Air France and Olympic disruptive competitors because they destabilise the airline industry through their overextended networks and dependence on state handouts. A company might be smart to support well-behaved competitors, aiming its attacks at disruptive competitors – as, for instance, in the attempt by several airlines, spearheaded by BA, KLM and SAS, to block the European Commission's approval of a €3 billion package of state aid for Air France.[6]

The implication is that 'well-behaved' companies should try to shape an industry that consists only of well-behaved competitors. Through careful licensing, selective retaliation and coalitions, they can make competitors behave rationally and harmoniously, follow the rules, try to earn share rather than buy it, and differentiate somewhat to compete less directly.

designing the competitive intelligence system

We have described the main types of information that company decision-makers need to know about their competitors. This information needs collecting, interpreting, distributing and using. Although the cost in money and time of gathering competitive intelligence is high, the cost of not gathering it is higher. Yet the company must design its competitive intelligence system in a cost-effective way.

The competitive intelligence system first identifies the vital types of competitive information and the best sources of this information. Then the system continuously collects information from the field (sales force, channels, suppliers, market research firms, trade associations) and from published data (government publications, speeches, articles). Next, the system checks the information for validity and reliability, interprets it and organises it in an appropriate way. Finally, it sends key information to relevant decision-makers and responds to enquiries from managers about competitors.

With this system, company managers will receive timely information about competitors in the form of phone calls, bulletins, newsletters and reports. In addition,

*Boddingtons single-mindedly
focus on the product's attribute,
smoothness – as evidenced by the
creamy head – to differentiate itself.*
Source: BBH, *Photography*: Tif Hunter

managers can contact the system when they need an interpretation of a competitor's
sudden move, or when they require to know a competitor's weaknesses and strengths
or how a competitor will respond to a planned company move.

Smaller companies that cannot afford to set up a formal competitive intelligence
office can assign specific executives to watch specific competitors. Thus a manager
who used to work for a competitor might follow closely all developments connected
with that competitor; he or she would be the 'in-house' expert on that competitor.
Any manager needing to know the thinking of a given competitor could contact the
assigned in-house expert.[7]

competitive strategies

Having identified and evaluated the main competitors, the company must now design
competitive marketing strategies that best position its offer against competitors' offerings.[8] What broad marketing strategies can the company use? Which ones are best for
a particular company or for the company's different divisions and products?

No one strategy is best for all companies. Each company must determine what
makes the most sense, given its position in the industry and its objectives, opportunities and resources. Even within a company, different businesses or products need different strategies. Johnson & Johnson uses one marketing strategy for its leading brands
in stable consumer markets and a different marketing strategy for its new high-tech
healthcare businesses and products. Recognising the difference in the way its business
had to be treated, the ICI chemicals company spun off its biosciences activities as a

separately quoted company, Zeneca.[9] We now look at broad competitive marketing strategies that companies can use.

competitive positions

Firms competing in a given target market will, at any moment, differ in their objectives and resources. Some firms will be large, others small. Some will have great resources, others will be strapped for funds. Some will be old and established, others new and fresh. Some will strive for rapid market share growth, others for long-term profits. And the firms will occupy different competitive positions in the target market.

Michael Porter suggests four basic competitive positioning strategies that companies can follow – three winning strategies and one losing one.[10] The three winning strategies are:

1. *Overall cost leadership*. Here the company works hard to achieve the lowest costs of production and distribution, so that it can price lower than its competitors and win a large market share. After years of stable industrial structures, changes in the economics of the EU and technology have stimulated a rush for mergers and acquisitions as once nationally dominant firms struggle for scale in the enlarged market. The biggest grab of all has been Vodafone AirTouch's acquisition of Mannesmann. Another major consolidation is aerospace where the aim is to use scale and lean production to drive costs down.[11]

   However, big is not always beautiful. In the steel industry small mini-mills, including Nucor and Chaparral Steel, which use electric furnaces to convert scrap metal, are undercutting the large integrated suppliers, while in retailing big stores are struggling against more nimble and more focused competitors. Scale can sometimes help cut costs but, by itself, it is neither a necessary nor a sufficient way of achieving overall cost leadership.

2. *Differentiation*. Here the company concentrates on creating a highly differentiated product line and marketing programme, so that it comes across as the class leader in the industry. Most customers would prefer to own this brand if its price is not too high. Bose follows this strategy with its ultra-small hi-fi speakers, as does Vosper Thornycroft with its plastic warships.

   > Nike is a good example of creative differentiation. Nike has no manufacturing capacity but makes its money by coming up with new ideas and marketing them: 'It's the idea of Air Jordan sneakers, not the shoe, that permits Nike to sell them for more than $100 (€113). It's the sizzle not the fit', says Seth Gordin.

   > In a completely different market, Vosper Thornycroft is thriving despite the peace dividend cutting military spending by unleashing what Seth Gordin calls the 'ideas virus'. They are prototyping Triton, a radically new trimaran warship that is significantly less expensive, faster, more stable and more spacious than conventional weapon systems.[12]

3. *Focus*. Here the company focuses its effort on serving a few market segments well rather than going after the whole market. Many firms in northern Italy excel at this. Among them are Luxottica, the world's leading maker of spectacle frames, pasta makers Barilla and many dynamic small textile firms in the Prato.[13]

Companies that pursue a clear strategy – one of the above – are likely to perform well. The firm that carries out that strategy best will make the most profits. Firms that do not pursue a clear strategy – *middle-of-the-roaders* – do the worst. Olivetti, Philips, and Marks & Spencer all came upon difficult times because they did not stand out as

marketing highlight 12.2

Competitive strategy: don't play in the middle of the road

Being mainstream used to be a blessing for products. Now it is becoming a curse. Today, companies in most industries face slow-growing and fiercely competitive markets. Solid middle-of-the-road names like Marks & Spencer, Olivetti and Holiday Inn are struggling against a lot of new competitors that strike from both above and below. Encircled by rivals offering either more luxurious goods or plain cheaper ones, companies with products in the middle are finding their market shares dwindling. They are striving to break away from the image of being 'just average'. 'Getting stuck in the middle is a terrible fate', notes one advertising agency executive. '[You remain] a mass brand as the market splinters.'

Examples abound of products and services caught in the middle – adequate but not exciting – losing ground to more clearly positioned competitors at both the high and low ends. For example, swanky stores such as Gap and budget outlets such as Aldi and Matalan are prospering, while long-established high street stores flounder. Häagen-Dazs, Ben & Jerry's and other 'super-premium' ice-creams are thriving – as are grocers' own bargain labels – while middle brands such as Crosse & Blackwell are struggling. Travellers want either economy lodging at chains such as Travelodge or to sleep in the lap of luxury; want to fly business class from London Docklands airport or frill-free easyJet. Operations in the 'murky middle' are facing increasing pressure from competitors at both ends of the spectrum. An advertising executive exclaims: 'There's no future for products everyone likes a little.'

If a brand in the middle cannot sell on prestige, it has to compete on value. To make Sealtest stand out against own-brand ice-creams, Kraft borrowed tactics from fancier brands. It recently added a layer of cellophane inside the carton. It also made the package's graphics cleaner and more modern. The idea is to keep the price about in the middle, but to come across as better value. Still, the product remains in that not-cheap, not-expensive limbo – a very tough sell.

For some, it finally gets to the point where the middle market is just not worth it. Marriott tried to string its Bob's Big Boy, Allie's and Wag's coffee shops into a single chain of casual restaurants. It was a vague niche that few consumers wanted. The restaurants were not as cheap or as appealing to children as fast food, nor could they please adults with an attractive dining-out atmosphere. Marriott ended up quitting the restaurant business. 'We were sandwiched in the middle', a Marriott spokesman says.

In the hotel industry, where chains have spread rapidly, companies are trying to escape the middle by extending their reach to cover people needing smaller units or wanting higher-priced ones. Holiday Inn, which no longer has the casual family traveller all to itself, has added a more up-market Holiday Inns Crown Plaza.

To win in the marketplace, a company must gain competitive advantage by offering something that competitors do not. It might offer consumers the best price for a given level of quality or offer a differentiated product one with unique features or higher quality for which consumers are willing to pay a higher price. It might focus on serving the special needs of a specific market segment. Companies in the middle usually end up not being very good at anything. Some big losers finally have to seek protection from creditors in the bankruptcy courts or, like Rover, be dismembered and sold off in bits by a more successful company.

SOURCES: 'Is there room for Volkswagen?', *The Economist* (28 August 1993), p. 55; *The Financial Times – FT500* (10 February 1993); and portions adapted from Kathleen Deveny, 'Middle-price brands come under siege', *Wall Street Journal* (2 April 1990), pp. B1, B7.

the lowest in cost, highest in perceived value or best in serving some market segment. Middle-of-the-roaders try to be good on all strategic counts, but end up being not very good at anything (see Marketing Highlight 12.2).

competitive moves

Businesses maintain their position in the marketplace by making *competitive moves* to attack competitors or defend themselves against competitive threats. These moves

Figure 12.3

Market structure

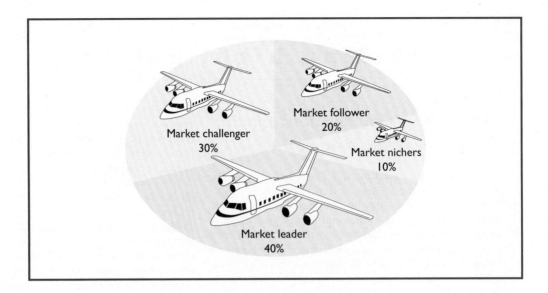

Market leader

The firm in an industry with the largest market share; it usually leads other firms in price changes, new product introductions, distribution coverage and promotion spending.

Market challenger

A runner-up firm in an industry that is fighting hard to increase its market share.

Market follower

A runner-up firm in an industry that wants to hold its share without rocking the boat.

Market nicher

A firm in an industry that serves small segments that the other firms overlook or ignore.

change with the role that firms play in the target market – that of leading, challenging, following or niching. Suppose that an industry contains the firms shown in Figure 12.3. Some 40 per cent of the market is in the hands of the **market leader**, the firm with the largest market share. Another 30 per cent is in the hands of a **market challenger**, a runner-up that is fighting hard to increase its market share. Another 20 per cent is in the hands of a **market follower**, another runner-up that wants to hold its share without rocking the boat. The remaining 10 per cent is in the hands of **market nichers**, firms that serve small segments not being pursued by other firms.

We now look at specific marketing strategies that are available to market leaders, challengers, followers and nichers. In the sections that follow, you should remember that the classifications of competitive positions often apply not to a whole company, but only to its position in a specific industry. For example, large and diversified companies such as P&G, Unilever, Nestlé, Procordia or Société Générale de Belgique – or their individual businesses, divisions or products – might be leaders in some markets and nichers in others. For example, Procter & Gamble leads in dishwashing and laundry detergents, disposable nappies and shampoo, but it is a challenger to Unilever in hand soaps. Companies' competitive strengths also vary geographically. Buying Alpo from Grand Metropolitan in 1994 made Nestlé the challenger in the US pet-foods market behind Ralston Purina's 18 per cent share. However, in the submarket for US canned cat food, Nestlé has a commanding 39 per cent share. By contrast, in the fragmented European pet-foods market, Nestlé Friskies languishes in fourth place behind Mars' Pedigree (47 per cent), Dalgety and Quaker. However, even with that low base, Nestlé's Go Cat is Europe's top-selling dry cat food.[14]

market-leader strategies

Most industries contain an acknowledged market leader. The leader has the largest market share and usually leads the other firms in price changes, new product introductions, distribution coverage and promotion spending. The leader may or may not be admired, but other firms concede its dominance. The leader is a focal point for competitors, a company to challenge, imitate or avoid. Some of the best-known market leaders are Boeing (airliners), Nestlé (food), Microsoft (software), L'Oréal (cosmetics), McDonald's (fast food) and De Beer (diamonds).

THE AIRBUS FAMILY.
NEXT STOP.
SEVENTH HEAVEN.

The A320 is the world's best selling family of passenger jet. The A320 is the most efficient aircraft in its category. The A340 is the most widely distributed aircraft among airlines in its category. Throughout the Airbus family you'll find the same quality of technology and design. When it comes to improving your fleet, we'll stop at nothing.

AIRBUS

Although Boeing is the market leader in airlines, Airbus challenges it by claiming that its 'A320 is the world's best selling family of passenger jet, the most efficient and widely distributed aircraft in its category'.
SOURCE: Airbus. *Agency*: Euro RSCG WNEK Gosper

Manchester United certainly do not win all football championships but they are overpowering leaders as a world sports brand. The club's global membership and merchandising swamps all other. This generates wealth that allows them to buy players at prices that would make other teams wince. In Britain's high spending Premier League MUFC is valued at more than all the other teams together![15]

A leader's life is not easy. It must maintain a constant watch. Other firms keep challenging its strengths or trying to take advantage of its weaknesses. The market leader can easily miss a turn in the market and plunge into second or third place. A product innovation may come along and hurt the leader (as when Nokia's and Ericsson's digital phones took the lead from Motorola's analogue models). The leader might grow arrogant or complacent and misjudge the competition. This has resulted in General Motors and Ford losing sales in Europe; after underestimating revitalised competition from VW and Renault, the US giants concentrated their activities in the US. Other leaders might look old-fashioned against new and peppier rivals (as when Britain's Marks & Spencer lost serious ground to more current or stylish brands like Gap, Lees, Tommy Hilfiger, DKNY and Guess).[16]

Remaining an industry leader demands action on four fronts. First, the firm must find ways to expand total demand. Second, the firm can try to expand its market share further, even if market size remains constant. Third, a company can retain its strength by reducing its costs. Fourth, the firm must protect its current market share through good defensive and offensive actions (Figure 12.4).

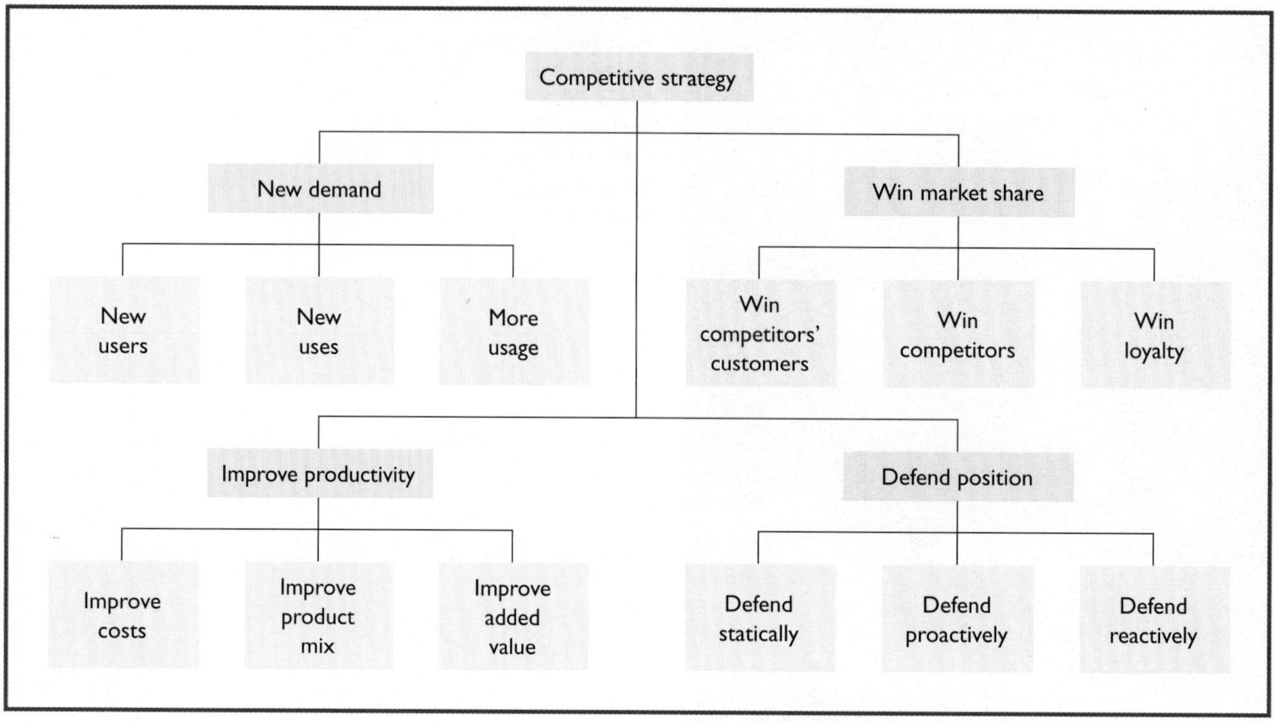

Figure 12.4

Market leader strategies

■ Expanding the total market

The leading firm normally gains the most when the total market expands. If people take more pictures, then as the market leader, Kodak stands to gain the most. If Kodak can persuade more people to take pictures, or to take pictures on more occasions, or to take more pictures on each occasion, it will benefit greatly. Generally, the market leader should look for new users, new uses and more usage of its products.

New users Every product class can attract buyers who are still unaware of the product, or who are resisting it because of its price or its lack of certain features. A seller can usually find new users in many places. For example, L'Oréal might find new fragrance users in its current markets by convincing women who do not use expensive fragrance to try it. Or it might find users in new demographic segments: for instance, men's fragrances are currently a fast-growing market. Or it might expand into new geographic segments, perhaps by selling its fragrances to the new wealthy in eastern Europe.

> In prudish UK, market leader *Ann Summers* is expanding the market by making 'accessible sex shops' mainstream and by appealing to women. Says owner, Jacqueline Gold, '70 per cent of our sales are lingerie. It's the fun element, people, and particularly women, enjoy coming into the store.' Having purchased niche retailer *Knickerbox*, the company aim to have a sex shop on every high street within three years.[17]

New uses The marketer can expand markets by discovering and promoting new uses for the product. DuPont's nylon is an example of new-use expansion. Every time nylon became a mature product, some new use appeared. Nylon was first used as a fibre for parachutes; then for women's stockings; later as a leading material in shirts and blouses; and still later in vehicle tyres, upholstery and carpeting.

More usage   A third market expansion strategy is to persuade people to use the product more often or to use more per occasion. Campbell encourages people to consume more of its soup by running ads using it as an ingredient in recipes in women's magazines. P&G advises users that its Head & Shoulders shampoo is more effective with two applications instead of one per hair wash.

The Michelin Tyre Company found a creative way to increase usage per occasion. It wanted French car owners to drive more miles per year, resulting in more tyre replacement. Michelin began rating French restaurants on a three-star system and publishing them in its Red Guides. It reported that many of the best restaurants were in the south of France, leading many Parisians to take weekend drives south. Michelin also publishes its Green Guide containing maps and graded sights to encourage additional travel.

■ Expanding market share

Market leaders can also grow by increasing their market shares further. In many markets, small market-share increases mean very large sales increases. For example, in the coffee market, a 1 per cent increase in market share is worth about €50 million; in soft drinks about €500 million! No wonder normal competition turns into marketing warfare in such markets. Many studies have found that profitability rises with increasing market share.[18] Businesses with very large relative market shares averaged substantially higher returns on investment. Because of these findings, many companies have sought expanded market shares to improve profitability. General Electric, for example, declared that it wants to be at least no. 1 or 2 in each of its markets or else get out. GE shed its computer, air-conditioning, small appliances and television businesses because it could not achieve a top-dog position in these industries. Nestlé intends to hold its position as the world's leading food company, although France's Danone also has designs on that spot. Both have been acquiring businesses, Nestlé buying Perrier and Rowntree among others, while Danone own Jacobs, Kronenbourg, Amora, Lee & Perrins and HP sauce.[19] There are three main ways by which these firms can further increase their leading position.

Win customers   Winning competitors' customers is rarely easy. Sales promotions and price reductions can produce increased share quickly, but such gains are made at the expense of profitability and disappear once the promotion ends. Exceptions to this are price fights stimulated by market leaders with more resources than competitors. Internet businesses are currently absorbing huge losses as they use low price and high advertising expenditure to buy share in the growing market.

In the long term, market share gains are achieved by investment in quality, innovation or brand building. For instance, Mercedes' new C-Class model has helped the company increase its sales by 23 per cent. Sales were up 40 per cent in western Europe (excluding Germany), 34 per cent in the United States and 30 per cent in Japan. In Germany the 38 per cent growth gave a 2 per cent rise in market share.

Win competitors   Leading mature companies often find it easier to buy competitors rather than win their customers. Sometimes this can launch the company into new sectors, as did BMW's failed purchase of the Rover Group with its small cars and cross-country vehicles or Mercedes' questionable merger with Chrysler. More often it is a dash for firms to achieve scale by acquiring businesses similar to themselves. In the mobile phone market companies are paying huge prices for competitors in takeover battles to gain a dominant position. This is also occurring among European banks who are seeking local dominance of e-banking in the enlarged European market, for example, MeritaNordbanken's (Finnish–Swedish) acquisition of Unidanmark (Danish).[20]

Win loyalty   Loyalty schemes have grown hugely in recent years. At their best these are attempts to build customer relationships based on the long-run customer satisfaction discussed in Chapter 11. In the UK grocery market Tesco challenged and overtook Sainsbury's as the market leader by introducing a hugely popular loyalty scheme while Sainsbury's was resisting the trend. Too often these schemes are sales promotions where the customer's loyalty is to the scheme, not the company using it. To have any lasting effects they must establish customer relationships that go beyond collecting points that are redeemable against a gift. Such schemes are easy to follow and once everyone has one, they impose a cost with little benefit.

Gaining increased market share will improve a company's profitability automatically. Much depends on its strategy for gaining increased market share. We see many high-share companies with low profitability and many low-share companies with high profitability. The cost of buying higher market share may far exceed the returns. Higher shares tend to produce higher profits only when unit costs fall with increased market share, or when the company's premium price covers the cost of supplying higher-quality goods.

In addition, many industries contain one or a few highly profitable large firms, several profitable and more focused firms, and a large number of medium-sized firms with poorer profit performance. For example, BMW holds only a small share of the total car market, but it earns high profits because it is a high-share company in its luxury car segment. It achieved this high share in its served market because it does other things right, such as producing high quality, giving good service and holding down its costs.

■ Improving productivity

Market productivity means squeezing more profits out of the same volume of sales. The size advantage of market leaders can give them lower costs than the competition. Size itself is not sufficient to achieve low costs because this could be achieved by owning unrelated activities that impose extra costs. The lowest costs often occur when a market leader, such as McDonald's, keeps its business simple. The buying and selling of subsidiary businesses often reflects businesses trying to gain strength by simplifying their activities. This explains the sales of Orangina, a soft-drinks business, to Coca-Cola for €760m by the French drinks company Pernod Ricard. By this transaction Coca-Cola gains in efficiency and scale by having more soft drinks to sell globally. With the proceeds from the sale, Pernod Ricard aims to add more wines and spirits brands to its existing range, which includes Wild Turkey, Dubonnet, Havana Club and Jacob's Creek.[21]

Improve costs   To remain competitive, market leaders fight continually to reduce costs. After facing difficulties in the early 1990s, Mercedes used all the classical means of cutting costs:

◆ *Reduce capital cost.* Firms reduce their capital cost by doing less or doing things quickly. Just-in-time (JIT) methods mean firms have less capital tied up in raw materials, work in progress on the shop floor and finished goods. By accelerating its product development Mercedes will increase its market responsiveness and accumulated development costs. It will also reduce capital costs by doing less itself. Component manufacturers will provide more preassembled parts and a joint venture with a Romanian company will make car-interior parts.

◆ *Reduce fixed costs.* Mercedes acknowledges that Japan's manufacturers have an average 35 per cent cost advantage over their German competitors. Japan's lower capital cost and longer working hours explain only 10 per cent of the difference. Mercedes responded by cutting 18,000 jobs to save €3 billion. Forced redundancies are almost unknown in Germany, so the deduction is made by the 'social measures' of the non-replacement of people, early retirement and retraining.

✦ *Reduce variable cost*. The company is sticking to its unconventional production methods where 10–15 'group workers' operate round cradles holding body shells. Meanwhile its new car plant at Rastatt will pioneer methods of 'lean production', logistics, total quality and workforce management. Other plants will adopt the proven methods. Car design will also change. It will be quicker, and future cars will be designed to a target price, rather than making the best car and then pricing it. The lessons will be passed on to Mercedes' suppliers. In future they will work closer to Mercedes' research and development. The aim is to reduce the number of parts fitted at the works. The company is also changing its 'Made in Germany' policy, to produce where labour costs are lower.

Change product mix   The aim here is to sell more high-margin vehicles. Mercedes' current range does not cover luxury off-road vehicles, people-movers or small sports cars – all growth areas commanding premium prices. Moving into these markets will reduce Mercedes' dependence on its 'lower-priced' models. While other tour operators were faced with discounting wars, Airtours profits rose by moving its product mix, moving away from the UK's low-cost package holidays to concentrate on less price-sensitive customers in Canada, California and the Scandinavian countries.

Add value   Mercedes makes and sells cars, but its customers want prestige and transport. Mercedes can add value by offering long-term service contracts, leasing deals or other financial packages that make buying easier and less risky for customers. In the past, Mercedes sold basic models that are poorly equipped by modern standards. Customers then paid extra to have a car custom made for them with the features they wanted. The 'Made in Germany' label that has served the company for so long is no longer enough to command a premium price. The aim is to maintain a price premium by the brand's strength and superior quality across a broad range of products. This contrasts with the Japanese, whose well-equipped luxury Lexus (Toyota), Acura (Honda) and Infiniti (Nissan) brands have tightly targeted small ranges.

■ Defending its position

While trying to expand total market size, the leading firm must also constantly protect its current business against competitor attacks. AXA must constantly guard against ING in the life assurance market; Exxon against Royal Dutch/Shell; Gillette against Bic; Kodak against Fuji; Boeing against Airbus; Nestlé against Unilever.

What can the market leader do to protect its position? First, it must prevent or fix weaknesses that provide opportunities for competitors. It needs to keep its costs down and its prices in line with the value that the customers see in the brand. The leader should 'plug holes' so that competitors do not jump in. The best defence is a good offence and the best response is *continuous innovation*. The leader refuses to be content with the way things are and leads the industry in new products, customer services, distribution effectiveness and cost cutting. It keeps increasing its competitive effectiveness and value to customers. It takes the offensive, sets the pace and exploits competitors' weaknesses.

Increased competition in recent years has sparked management's interest in models of military warfare. Leader companies can protect their market positions with competitive strategies patterned after successful military defence strategies. Figure 12.5 shows six defence strategies that a market leader can use.[22]

Position defence   The most basic defence is a position defence in which a company holds on to its position by building fortifications around its markets. Simply defending

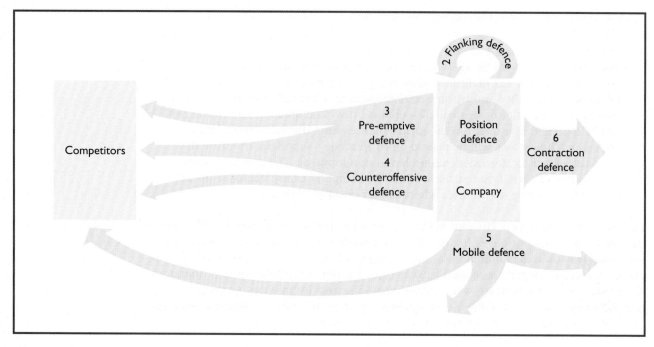

Figure 12.5

Defence strategies

one's current position or products rarely works. Henry Ford tried it with his Model T and brought an enviably healthy Ford Motor Company to the brink of financial ruin. Even lasting brands such as Coca-Cola and Nescafé cannot supply all future growth and profitability for their companies. These brands must be improved and adapted to changing conditions and new brands developed. Coca-Cola today, in spite of being the world leader in soft drinks, is aggressively extending its beverage lines and has diversified into desalinisation equipment and plastics.

Flanking defence When trying to hold its overall position, the market leader should watch its weaker flanks closely. Smart competitors will normally attack the company's weaknesses. Thus the Japanese successfully entered the US small car market because local carmakers left a gaping hole in that submarket. Using a flanking defence, the company carefully checks its flanks and protects the more vulnerable ones. In this way Nestlé's Nescafé and Gold Blend have the support of flanking brands Blend 37, Alta Rica and Cap Colombie. By Unilever acquiring Ben & Jerry's ice-creams and Cadbury Schweppes buying Snapple, the two multinationals are more able to defend their mainstream markets against 'new age' offerings.[23]

Pre-emptive defence The leader can be proactive and launch a pre-emptive defence, striking competitors before they can move against the company. A pre-emptive defence assumes that an ounce of prevention is worth a pound of cure. Thus, when threatened in the mid-1980s by the impending entry of Japanese manufacturers into the US market, Cummins Engine slashed its prices by almost a third to save its no. 1 position in the $2 billion (€1.77 billion) heavy-duty truck engine market. Today, Cummins claims a commanding 50 per cent market share in North America and not a single US-built tractor-trailer truck contains a Japanese engine.[24]

Counteroffensive defence When attacked, despite its flanking or pre-emptive efforts, a market leader may have to be reactive and launch a counteroffensive defence. When Fuji attacked Kodak in the film market, Kodak counterattacked by dramatically increasing its promotion and introducing several innovative new film products. Mars' attack on the ice-cream market, using its brand extensions of Mars Bars, Snickers,

Bounty and so on, created a new product class of ice-confectionery. Unilever's Walls ice-cream division, which is market leader in parts of Europe, had difficulty countering this because it had no confectionery brands to use in that way. It overcame the problem by developing brand extensions of Cadbury's products, a competitor of Mars, which has no ice-cream interests.

Sometimes companies hold off for a while before countering. This may seem a dangerous game of 'wait and see', but there are often good reasons for not jumping in immediately. By waiting, the company can understand more fully the competitor's attack and perhaps find a gap through which to launch a successful counteroffensive.

Mobile defence   In a mobile defence a company is proactive in aggressively defending a current market position. The leader stretches to new markets that can serve as future bases for defence and attack. Through *market broadening*, the company shifts its focus from the current product to the broader underlying consumer need. For example, Armstrong Cork redefined its focus from 'floor covering' to 'decorative room covering' (including walls and ceilings) and expanded into related businesses balanced for growth and defence. *Market diversification* into unrelated industries is the other alternative for generating 'strategic depth'. When the tobacco companies like British American Tobacco (BAT) and Philip Morris faced growing curbs on cigarette smoking, they moved quickly into new consumer products industries.

Contraction defence   Large companies sometimes find they can no longer defend all of their positions, since their resources are spread too thin and competitors are nibbling away on several fronts. So they react with a contracting defence (or strategic withdrawal). The company gives up weaker positions and concentrates its resources on stronger ones. During the 1970s, many companies diversified wildly and spread themselves too thin. In the slow-growth 1980s, ITT, Paribas, Suez, ENI, Quaker, Storehouse and dozens of other companies pruned their portfolios to concentrate resources on products and businesses in their core industries. These companies now serve fewer markets, but serve them much better.

> The British motorcycle industry showed an extreme case of a contracting defence. Norton, Triumph, BSA, etc. once dominated the world motorcycle market. First challenged by the small bikes made by Honda, Yamaha and others, they contracted into making medium-sized (250 cc) to super-bikes. When the Japanese made 250 cc machines, the British market retreated from entry-level machines to concentrate on larger ones. Eventually only Triumph and Norton super-bikes remained as small, out-of-date specialist manufacturers facing the Japanese giants, and they did not last long. A successful contracting defence must be a retreat into a position of strength.

market-challenger strategies

Firms that are second, third or lower in an industry are sometimes very large. Many European market leaders are in this position relative to their major US or Japanese competitors. Table 12.1 shows some of them. These runner-up firms can adopt one of two competitive strategies: they can attack the leader and other competitors in an aggressive bid for more market share (market challengers); or they can play along with competitors and not rock the boat (market followers). We now look at competitive strategies for market challengers.

■ Defining the strategic objective and the competitor

A market challenger must first define its strategic objective. Most market challengers seek to increase their profitability by increasing their market shares. The strategic

SECTOR	WORLD LEADER	REVENUE (€bn)	EUROPEAN LEADER	REVENUE (€bn)	WORLD RANKING
Aerospace	Boeing	63	BAe	13	6
Airlines	AMR	22	BA	17	3
Beverage	Pepsico	25	Diageo	22	2
Chemicals	DuPont	44	Buyer	35	2
Electronics	GE	114	Siemens	75	2
General merchandisers	Wal-Mart	157	Pinault-Printemps	21	7
Metals	Nippon	24	Arbed	13	4
Motors	GM	182	Daimler-Chrysler	175	3
Petroleum	Exxon Mobil	114	Royal Dutch/Shell	106	2
Pharmaceuticals	Merck	30	Novartis	25	3
Telecommunications	Nippon	86	Deutsche Telekom	45	3

SOURCE: The Fortune Global 500, *Fortune* (2 August 1999), pp. F-15–42. © 1999 Time, Inc. All rights reserved.

Table 12.1

European leaders' world ranking

objective chosen depends on who the competitor is. In most cases, the company can choose which competitors it will challenge.

The challenger can attack the market leader – a high-risk but potentially high-gain strategy that makes good sense if the leader is not serving the market well. To succeed with such an attack, a company must have some sustainable competitive advantage over the leader – a cost advantage leading to lower prices or the ability to provide better value at a premium price.

> For a long time Diageo's Burger King has challenged McDonald's in the US home market on taste, but its recent challenges, including an accelerated programme of building new outlets, better value (with 75 per cent more meat than a Big Mac) and direct taste challenges, have got McDonald's reeling. After 'The taste that beat McDonald's fries' came 'Get ready for a taste that beats Big Mac' and Free FryDay promotions. Meanwhile Mac's new Arch Deluxe burger bombed and a sales promotion deal with too many strings alienated customers.[25]

The challenger can avoid the leader and instead attack firms its own size, or smaller local and regional firms. Many of these firms are underfinanced and will not be serving their customers well. Several of the large beer companies grew to their present size not by attacking large competitors, but by gobbling up small local or regional competitors.

Thus the challenger's strategic objective depends on which competitor it chooses to attack. If the company goes after the market leader, its objective may be to wrest a certain market share. Bic knows that it cannot topple Gillette in the razor market – it simply wants a larger share. Or the challenger's goal might be to take over market leadership. Dell entered the personal computer market late, as a challenger, but quickly became the market leader. If the company goes after a small local company, its objective may be to put that company out of business. The important point remains: the company must choose its opponents carefully and have a clearly defined and attainable objective.

■ Choosing an attack strategy

How can the market challenger best attack the chosen competitor and achieve its strategic objectives? Figure 12.6 shows five possible attack strategies.

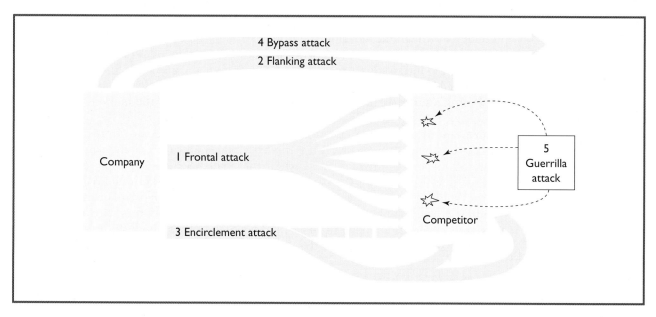

Figure 12.6

Attack strategies

Frontal attack   In a full frontal attack, the challenger matches the competitor's product, advertising, price and distribution efforts. It attacks the competitor's strengths rather than its weaknesses. The outcome depends on who has the greater strength and endurance. Even great size and strength may not be enough to challenge a firmly entrenched and resourceful competitor successfully.

> Unilever has twice the world-wide sales of P&G and five times the sales of Colgate-Palmolive, but its American subsidiary trails P&G by a wide margin in the United States. Unilever launched a full frontal assault against P&G in the detergent market while Unilever's Wisk was already the leading liquid detergent. In quick succession, it added a barrage of new products – Sunlight dishwashing detergent, Snuggle fabric softener, Surf laundry powder – and backed them with aggressive promotion and distribution efforts. P&G spent heavily to defend its brands and held on to most of its business. It counterattacked with Liquid Tide, which came from nowhere in just 17 months to run neck-and-neck with Wisk. Unilever did gain market share, but most of it came from smaller competitors.[26]

If the market challenger has fewer resources than the competitor, a frontal attack makes little sense.

Flanking attack   Rather than attacking head on, the challenger can launch a flanking attack. The competitor often concentrates its resources to protect its strongest positions, but it usually has some weaker flanks. By attacking these weak spots, the challenger can concentrate its strength against the competitor's weakness. Flank attacks make good sense when the company has fewer resources than the competitor.

> When Airbus Industries started making airliners it was up against Boeing, a company that dominates the industry. Lockheed and McDonnell Douglas had once challenged Boeing as plane makers, but Lockheed had withdrawn from the industry and McDonnell Douglas was reduced to making derivatives of its old aircraft. Airbus's first move was to develop the A300 with range and payload performance different from Boeing's established 727, 737 and 747 range. Airbus is now topping the Boeing range with its super-jumbo.

Another flanking strategy is to find gaps that are not being filled by the industry's products, fill them and develop them into strong segments. European and Japanese carmakers do not try to compete with American carmakers by producing large, flashy, gas-guzzling contraptions. Instead they recognised an unserved consumer segment that wanted small, fuel-efficient cars and moved to fill this hole. To their satisfaction and Detroit's surprise, the segment grew to be a large part of the market.

Encirclement attack   An encirclement attack involves attacking from all directions, so that the competitor must protect its front, sides and rear at the same time. The encirclement strategy makes sense when the challenger has superior resources and believes that it can break the competitor's hold on the market quickly. An example is Seiko's attack on the watch market. For several years, Seiko has been gaining distribution in every big watch outlet and overwhelming competitors with its variety of constantly changing models. In most markets Seiko offers about 400 models, but its marketing strength is backed by the 2,300 models it makes and sells worldwide.

Bypass attack   A bypass attack is an indirect strategy. The challenger bypasses the competitor and targets easier markets. The bypass can involve diversifying into unrelated products, moving into new geographic markets or leapfrogging into new technologies to replace existing products. Technological leapfrogging is a bypass strategy used often in high-technology industries. Instead of copying the competitor's product and mounting a costly frontal attack, the challenger patiently develops the next technology. When satisfied with its superiority, it launches an attack where it has an advantage.

> After years of being beaten by the huge American competitors, Pratt & Whitney and General Electric, Rolls-Royce aero engines is now forecast to become market leader with its Trent 500 for new wide body airliners. They are achieving this by having an advanced '3 spool' engine technology that has enabled them to stretch their engines to meet the huge thrust needed by new generation airliners. P&W and GE are holding their position in the current market but are losing ground where the new, bigger engines are needed.[27]

Guerrilla attack   A guerrilla attack is another option available to market challengers, especially smaller or poorly financed ones:

> British Airways is facing Virgin Atlantic run by a much wilier entrepreneur, Richard Branson. He makes guerrilla attacks on his much larger competitors. In these attacks the agile challenger typically makes small, periodic attacks to harass and demoralize the competitor, hoping eventually to establish permanent footholds. It might use selective price cuts, novel products, executive raids, intense promotional outbursts or assorted legal actions. Virgin has been successful so far and taken 22 per cent of the London to New York market. It is also expanding quickly using franchising, an approach new to the airline industry.[28]

Normally, guerrilla actions are by smaller firms against larger ones. The smaller firms need to be aware, however, that continuous guerrilla campaigns can be expensive and must eventually be followed by a stronger attack if the challenger wishes to 'beat' the competitor.

market-follower strategies

Not all runner-up companies will challenge the market leader. The effort to draw away the leader's customers is never taken lightly by the leader. If the challenger's lure is lower prices, improved service or additional product features, the leader can quickly match these to diffuse the attack. The leader probably has more staying power in an all-out battle. A hard fight might leave both firms worse off and this means the challenger must think twice before attacking. Many firms therefore prefer to follow rather than attack the leader.

A follower can gain many advantages. The market leader often bears the huge expenses involved with developing new products and markets, expanding distribution channels, and informing and educating the market. The reward for all this work and risk is normally market leadership. The market follower, on the other hand, can learn from the leader's experience and copy or improve on the leader's products and marketing programmes, usually at a much lower investment. Although the follower will probably not overtake the leader, it can often be as profitable.[29]

In some industries – such as steel, fertilisers and chemicals – opportunities for differentiation are low, service quality is often comparable and price sensitivity runs high. Price wars can erupt at any time. Companies in these industries avoid short-run grabs for market share because the strategy only provokes retaliation. Most firms decide against stealing each other's customers. Instead they present similar offers to buyers, usually by copying the leader. Market shares show a high stability.

This is not to say that market followers are without strategies. A market follower must know how to hold current customers and win a fair share of new ones. Each follower tries to bring distinctive advantages to its target market – location, services, financing. The follower is a primary target of attack by challengers. Therefore, the market follower must keep its manufacturing costs low and its product quality and services high. It must also enter new markets as they appear. Following is not the same as being passive or a carbon copy of the leader. The follower has to define a growth path, but one that does not create competitive retaliation.

The market-follower firms fall into one of three broad types. The *cloner* closely copies the leader's products, distribution, advertising and other marketing moves. It originates nothing – it simply attempts to live off the market leader's investments. IBM's demise started after outsourcing (286 chips from Intel and the MS-DOS operating system from Microsoft) and open architecture allowed low-cost market entrants to copy its PCs.

> Dutch flower growers, who dominate the international flower trade, are facing intense competition from growers in Israel, Kenya and Zimbabwe. They can grow exactly what the Dutch do but, unlike the North Europeans, have no big heating bills, cheap labour and unregulated use of fertilizers. The flood of foreign stems has knocked 40 per cent off rose prices and Dutch growers are increasingly resigned to losing the rose and carnation trade.[30]

The *imitator* copies some things from the leader, but maintains some differentiation with packaging, advertising, pricing and other factors. The leader does not mind the imitator as long as the imitator does not attack aggressively. The imitator may even help the leader avoid the charges of monopoly.

> Today's imitators are often retailers making look-alike own brands. The British Producers and Brand Owners Group (BPOG) was formed in response to own brands aping the market leaders too closely. Sainsbury's highly publicized launch of Classic Cola precipitated BPOG's formation and resulted in the retailer backing off. Other confrontations include Sainsbury's Full Roast (based on Nescafé) and Tesco's Unbelievable low fat spread (close to Van den Bergh's I Can't Believe It's Not Butter).[31]

Finally, the *adapter* builds on the leader's products and marketing programmes, often improving them. The adapter may choose to sell to different markets to avoid direct confrontation with the leader. Many IBM PC lookalikes did this – Amstrad became one of the earliest successful marketers in the PC market when it started selling its ready-for-use machines through conventional electrical goods retailers rather than computer specialists. Now Dell and dan Technologies combine direct selling with excellent customer support. Often the adapter grows into a future challenger, as many Japanese firms have done after adapting and improving products developed elsewhere.

market-nicher strategies

Almost every industry includes firms that specialise in serving market niches. Instead of pursuing the whole market or even large segments of the market, these firms target segments within segments or niches. This is particularly true of smaller firms because of their limited resources. The main point is that firms with low shares of the total market can be highly profitable through clever niching (see Marketing Highlight 12.3).

Highly successful mid-size companies found that, in almost all cases, these companies niched within a larger market rather than going after the whole market.

> In *Hidden Champions*, Herman Simon documents the surprising number of German companies that are barely known but have strong profits and global market shares exceeding 50 per cent in their respective niches. Tetra has 80 per cent of the world tropical fish market; Hohner has 85 per cent of the harmonica market; Bechner makes 50 per cent of the world's umbrellas; and Steiner Optical make 80 per cent of the world's military field glasses.

Why is niching profitable? The main reason is that the market nicher ends up knowing the target customer group so well that it meets their needs better than other firms which casually sell to this niche. As a result, the nicher can charge a substantial mark-up over costs because of the added value. Whereas the mass marketer achieves *high volume*, the nicher achieves *high margins*.

Nichers try to find one or more market niches that are safe and profitable. An ideal market niche is big enough to be profitable and has growth potential. It is one that the firm can serve effectively. Perhaps most importantly, the niche is of little interest to large competitors. The firm can build the skills and customer goodwill to defend itself against an attacking big competitor as the niche grows and becomes more attractive.

> Logitech has become a €500 million global success story by focusing on human interface devices – computer mice, game controllers, keyboards, and others. It makes every variation of computer mouse imaginable. Logitech turns out mice for left- and right-handed people, cordless mice that use radio waves, mice shaped like real mice for children, and 3-D mice that let the user appear to move behind screen objects. This year, the company's 200 millionth mouse will roll off the production line. Breeding computer mice has been so successful that Logitech dominates the world market, with Microsoft as its runner-up.

Externalities
Activities or facilities that are external to an organisation but affect its performance.

Many nichers do not grow so global but thrive in clusters where the proximity on similar neighbours and local services are positive externalities. **Externalities** are activities or facilities that are external to an organisation but affect its performance. Such a cluster is in the English market town of High Wycombe, where the local furniture college and pool of skilled woodworkers support specialist furniture makers. Among the cluster are Teal, who make tables and chairs for hospitals, Hands, makers of integrated office 'pods' of furniture aimed at the high-tech businesses, and Danish Labofa Antocks Lairn, who make restaurant furniture. The most influential cluster of all is California's Silicon Valley, although northern Italy provides the climate in which such

marketing highlight 12.3

Concentrated marketing: two nice niches

Jo Brand is a size-challenged comedienne whose act often includes two themes: her size and her love for cakes. The following two niche companies are for her.

Betty's Café Tea Rooms

There are only four Betty's Café Tea Rooms and one Taylor's Tea Room, but they serve 2 million cups of tea a year. They do not advertise, yet year round people queue for a chance to taste their exquisitely expensive tea, coffee and cakes. Inside, a pianist plays light classical music. The rooms are simple, but rich with the atmosphere of times past. Formally dressed waiters, or waitresses wearing black skirt, starched white blouse and apron, serve. Betty's is proud of its heritage and quietly boasts of the York Betty's being built by the same team of craftsmen as the luxury liner, *Queen Mary*.

The first Betty's was opened in Harrogate in 1919 by a Swiss confectioner. He visited the Yorkshire Dales, liked it, stayed and started Betty's. His timing was as good as his patisserie. Harrogate was booming and Betty's was just about the only place an unchaperoned woman could go. Betty's succeeds because of its unique quality and atmosphere. The pastries range from exotic Amadeus torte to local Yorkshire curd tarts and fat rascals. The bakers and confectioners train at Richemont College, Lucerne.

Betty's is a clever multiple nicher. It has diversified into other businesses close to its original business. Each of its Café Tea Rooms retails expensive gift-oriented confectionery, which suits their location in tourist towns. It also has a mail-order business selling cakes, chocolates and speciality teas and coffees by post. Finally, it markets Yorkshire Tea, a brand sold and positioned nationally as a traditional Yorkshire 'cuppa'.

Dawn French fashions

An outdated study of the contours of 5,000 women links Betty's golden age to Dawn French's fashions. The study's results gave the British Standard Sizes that have pained women for decades. The sizes worked well in the 1950s when food rationing had just ended and people walked a lot, but not now. A recent study of women's contours by J. D. Williams shows that things have changed. For years the company has been selling mail-order clothes to women with a fuller figure who were unable to get suitable clothes from high-street stores. Nigel Green, marketing director of J. D. Williams' Classic Combinations catalogue business, explains:

> Today's woman enjoys a far more self-indulgent lifestyle and is not only taller, but has a noticeably bigger and lower bust, an appreciably larger waist and rib cage, a more rounded tummy, a larger and flatter bottom and far fuller upper arms. And while her hip size may still be 90 cm, the standard British figure [the original size 12] is now more likely to be 95–70–90 than 90–60–90 . . . The old-fashioned dress sizes meant that women . . . had to live with . . . blouses that gape, waistbands that cut and skirts that ride up.

Nigel Green believes these new sizes will give his niche company a unique selling proposition.

Other moves are afoot in the high street. 'Women are no longer prepared to put their lives on hold until they can starve themselves down to size', says Christina Bounce, of Country Casuals Holdings. She continues: 'They are generally feeling happier about their own size, even when it doesn't conform to fashion stereotypes.' D. H. Evans, the Outsize Shop, have long served the outsize market, but the emerging market shows that women no longer feel the need to don masks before entering the premises.

Dawn French's shops, 1647, sell high fashions for the amply proportioned. Few in the trade believe the claim implicit in the shop name that 47 per cent of women are over size 16, but the huge success of the niche retailers shows where the future lies. 'There is correlation between age and increased size and obesity', says Verdict's Clive Vaughan. So, as the middle-aged market grows in number, affluence and girth, the outsize market is a nice niche. But, as Joan Miller of Betty's says, 'If everyone round here decides to get health conscious, we're in real trouble.'

SOURCES: Nicholas Lander, 'British tea and torte', *Financial Times* (4–5 June 1994), p. XI; Virginia Matthews, 'Oversized and over here', *Marketing Week* (23 September 1994), p. 25.

Zumtobel Staff specialises in the lighting design for restaurants and hotels.

SOURCE: Zumtobel Staff and CASH, Public Animation

companies abound. Among them are silk from Como, wool from Biella, gold from Vincenza, Ferrari, Ducati and Alfa Romeo.[32]

The key idea in nichemanship is specialisation. The firm has to specialise along market, customer, product or marketing-mix lines. Here are several specialist roles open to a market nicher:

✦ *End-use specialist*. The firm specialises in serving one type of end-use customer. For example, Reuters provides financial information and news to professionals and Moss Bros' strength is in clothes hire.

✦ *Vertical-level specialist*. The firm specialises at some level of the production–distribution cycle. For example, the Dutch-based Anglo-Italian company EVC is Europe's leading manufacturer of polyvinylchloride (PVC), while Country Homes' niche is as an intermediary between owners of country cottages and people who want to hire them for holidays.

✦ *Customer-size specialist*. The firm concentrates on selling to either small, medium or large customers. Many nichers specialise in serving small customers neglected by the large companies. Fuji gained its initial success in the photocopying market by specialising in small firms neglected by Xerox. Many regional advertising agencies also specialise in serving medium-sized clients.

✦ *Specific-customer specialist*. The firm limits its selling to one or a few large customers. For example, Teal, making tables and chairs for hospitals.

✦ *Geographical specialist*. The firm sells only in a certain locality, region or area of the world. Most retail banks stay within their national boundaries. Two odd exceptions to this rule are the European HSBC and Standard & Charter, whose main interest is south-east Asia.

Fisherman's Friend's unique packaging, advertising and function help it hold its market niche.

Source: Lofthouse of Fleetwood Ltd

✦ *Product or feature specialist.* The firm specialises in producing a certain product, product line or product feature. Examples are Rolls-Royce, the only supplier of tilt-thrust jet engines, or Pear Tree, a maker of tree houses.

✦ *Quality–price specialist.* The firm operates at the low or high end of the market. For example, Hewlett-Packard specialises in the high-quality, high-price end of the hand-calculator market, while Tring International sells very cheap CDs.

✦ *Service specialist.* The firm offers one or more services not available from other firms: for example, NASA's ability to recover and repair satellites.

Niching carries a very significant risk, in that the market niche may dry up or be attacked. Porsche was hit by both of these threats when the demand for luxury cars declined in the early 1990s and Honda, Toyota and Mazda attacked the sports car market. On a different scale, innovation and intense competition between multinationals and social trends eventually killed off Pollards Cornish Ice Cream.[33] Its niche was selling high-fat dairy ice-cream – an estimated 100 calories per cone – to the declining number of tourists in south-west England.

The danger of the disappearing niche is why many companies use **multiple niching**. By developing two or more niches, the company increases its chances of survival. Most of the wealth of successful healthcare companies comes from their each having products in a few niches that they dominate. For instance, Sweden's Gambio concentrates on renal care, cardiovascular surgery, intensive care and anaesthesia, blood compound technology and preventive health services. Belgium's market leading Internet service provider, Belgacom Skynet, has developed multiple niches. Besides Skynet, these include the Business.net portal providing free Internet access for business users, and easy.be with a variety of media content sources.[34]

Multiple niching
Adopting a strategy of having several independent offerings that appeal to several different subsegments of customer.

balancing customer–competitor orientations

We have stressed the importance of a company watching its competitors closely. Whether a company is a market leader, challenger, follower or nicher, it must find the competitive marketing strategy that positions it most effectively against its competitors. It must continually adapt its strategies to the fast-changing competitive environment.

This question now arises: Can the company spend too much time and energy tracking competitors, damaging its customer orientation? The answer is yes! A company can become so competitor-centred that it loses its even more important customer focus. A **competitor-centred company** is one whose moves are based mainly on competitors' actions and reactions. The company spends most of its time tracking competitors' moves and market shares, and trying to find strategies to counter them.

This mode of strategy planning has some pluses and minuses. On the positive side, the company develops a fighter orientation. It trains its marketers to be on constant alert, watching for weaknesses in their position and watching for competitors' weaknesses. On the negative side, the company becomes too reactive. Rather than carrying out its own consistent customer-oriented strategy, it bases its moves on competitors' moves. As a result, it does not move in a planned direction towards a goal. It does not know where it will end up, since so much depends on what the competitors do.

A **customer-centred company**, in contrast, focuses more on customer developments in designing its strategies. Clearly, the customer-centred company is in a better position to identify new opportunities and set a strategy that makes long-run sense. By watching customer needs evolve, it can decide what customer groups and what emerging needs are the most important to serve, given its resources and objectives.

In practice, today's companies must be **market-centred companies**, watching both their customers and their competitors. They must not let competitor-watching blind them to customer focusing. Figure 12.7 shows that companies have moved through four orientations over the years. In the first stage, they were product-oriented, paying little attention to either customers or competitors. In the second stage, they became customer-oriented and started to pay attention to customers. In the third stage, when they started to pay attention to competitors, they became competitor-oriented. Today, companies need to be market-oriented, paying balanced attention to both

Competitor-centred company
A company whose moves are mainly based on competitors' actions and reactions; it spends most of its time tracking competitors' moves and market shares and trying to find strategies to counter them.

Customer-centred company
A company that focuses on customer developments in designing its marketing strategies and on delivering superior value to its target customers.

Market-centred company
A company that pays balanced attention to both customers and competitors in designing its marketing strategies.

Figure 12.7

Evolving company orientations

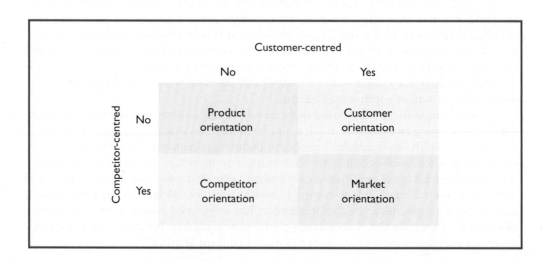

customer and competitors. A market orientation pays big dividends – one recent study found a substantial positive relationship between a company's marketing orientation and its profitability, a relationship that held regardless of type of business or market environment.[35]

summary

To prepare an effective marketing strategy, a company must consider its competitors as well as its actual and potential customers. It must continuously analyse its competitors and develop competitive marketing strategies that effectively position it against competitors and give it the strongest possible *competitive advantage.*

Competitor analysis first involves identifying the company's main competitors, using both an industry and a market-based analysis. The company then gathers information on competitors' objectives, strategies, strengths and weaknesses, and reaction patterns. With this information to hand, it can select competitors to attack or avoid. Competitive intelligence must be collected, interpreted and distributed continuously. Company marketing managers should be able to obtain full and reliable information about any competitor affecting their decisions. The major alternative competitive positions are *cost leadership, differentiation* and *focus.* Many firms fail because they do not follow any of these and so become *stuck in the middle.*

Which *competitive marketing strategy* makes the most sense depends on the company's industry position and its objectives, opportunities and resources. The company's competitive marketing strategy depends on whether it is a market leader, challenger, follower or nicher.

A *market leader* faces three challenges: expanding the total market, protecting market share and expanding market share. The market leader wants to find ways to expand the total market because it will benefit most from any increased sales. To expand market size, the leader looks for *new users* of the product, *new uses* and *more usage.* To protect its existing market share, the market leader has several *defences: position defence, flanking defence, pre-emptive defence, counteroffensive defence, mobile defence* and *contraction defence.* The most sophisticated leaders cover themselves by doing everything right, leaving no openings for competitive attack. Leaders can also try to increase their market shares. This makes sense if profitability increases at higher market-share levels.

A *market challenger* is a firm that aggressively tries to expand its market share by attacking the leader, other runner-up firms or smaller firms in the industry. The challenger can choose from a variety of *attack strategies,* including a *frontal attack, flanking attack, encirclement attack, bypass attack* and *guerrilla attack.*

A *market follower* is a runner-up firm that chooses not to rock the boat, usually out of fear that it stands to lose more than it might gain. The follower is not without a strategy, however, and seeks to use its particular skills to gain market growth. Some followers enjoy a higher rate of return than the leaders in their industry.

A *market nicher* is a smaller firm that serves some part of the market that is not likely to attract the larger firms. Market nichers often become specialists in some end use, vertical level, customer size, specific customer, geographic area, product or product feature, or service.

A competitive orientation is important in today's markets, but companies should not overdo their focus on competitors. Companies are more likely to be hurt by emerging consumer needs and new competitors than by existing competitors. Companies that balance consumer and competitor considerations are practising a true market orientation.

discussing the issues

1. Are the Internet banks being 'well behaved' in undercutting the rates charged by established banks? The established banks do not think so, but is the cost cutting good for the customers?

2. Consider Richard Branson's attempts at taking on market leaders in the airlines (e.g. British Airways on transatlantic routes), soft drinks (e.g. Coca-Cola) and, more recently, financial services (as seen in the launch of Virgin Direct, which will challenge current providers of traditional and direct insurance products). What market-leader strategies would you recommend for the no. 1 competitor in each of these sectors? Why?

3. A local school faces being closed down as demographics and legislation that allows local competition reduce the number of children attending the school. So far the school has survived on a fixed sum given to the school by the government for each child attending. How could the school increase its chances of survival?

4. The goal of the marketing concept is to satisfy customer wants and needs. What is the goal of a competitor-centred strategy? Discuss whether the marketing concept and competitor-centred strategy are in conflict.

5. Does the global reach and discounting on the Internet mean that the time for nichers or followers is past or does the range of the Internet provide more niching opportunities than ever before? Think of cases for and against the alternative arguments.

applying the concepts

1. In the rapidly expanding world of the Internet and personal information and communications devices, AOL's plan is to get inside every information appliance. According to AOL's CEO, 'We want to be as pervasive as the telephone or TV, but even more valuable in people's lives.' To this end, AOL is partnering with a broad range of companies. For example, in addition to its already established relationships with Netscape and Sun Systems, AOL will invest approaching $1 billion in Gateway over two years to help develop and co-market Internet appliances. It will partner with 3Com to put its online services on Palm handheld devices. AOL's instant message service will now be part of all new Motorola smart wireless devices, and AOL has joined with DirecTV and Philips Electronics to preload set-top boxes with AOL features and access. However, all will not be easy. AOL is going up against Microsoft with its deep pockets, and its recent moves have attracted Yahoo! All three competitors plan to spread their services to all manner of information devices early in the twenty-first century. For more information, visit www.aol.com.

   (a) What do you see as the major strengths and weaknesses of AOL? How do those strengths and weaknesses match those of Microsoft and Yahoo!?

   (b) What competitive position does AOL hold in its industry? Does this position change as it partners across industry lines?

   (c) Which of the competitive strategies outlined in the chapter is AOL using? How will competitors respond?

   (d) Propose one additional partnership that you think would make sense for AOL. Explain.

2. Yum, yum, yum. http://shop.deutschepost.de/pralinespost, www.chocexpress.com, www.chocolaterie-stettler.ch, www.prestat.co.uk and www.zchocolat.com are battling it out for the fine chocolates market on the Internet.

   (a) Visit the websites and evaluate what each of the providers is doing to get an upper hand in the market.

   (b) Enumerate the features offered by the websites.

   (c) Evaluate the extent to which they are successfully pursuing a niche strategy.

   (d) State which of the websites you think is providing the best service, giving reasons for your choice.

   (e) Do you think the websites have just extended the competition for luxury chocolates by taking sales from the competition or are they likely to expand the market?

references

1. See Rebecca Fannin, 'Zap?', *Marketing and Media Decisions* (November 1989), pp. 35–40; Raymond Roel, 'The power of Nintendo', *Direct Marketing* (September 1989), pp. 24–9; Stewart Wolpin, 'How Nintendo revived a dying industry', *Marketing Communications* (May 1989), pp. 36–40; Richard Brandt, 'Clash of the Titans', *Business Week* (7 September 1992), p. 34; Mark Jones and Margaret Bennett, 'Game over?', *Marketing Business* (December–January 1993–4), pp. 8–11; Ros Snowden, 'New Sega arm targets mothers', *Marketing Week* (7 October 1994), p. 9; 'Dip into the future, far as cyborg eye can see: and wince', *The Economist* (3 January 1997), pp. 81–3; 'Computing: that's entertainment'; 'Computer games: gently does it', *The Economist* (8 May 1999), pp. 122–3; 'Game wars', *The Economist* (22 April 2000), p. 72; Louise Kehoe, 'Microsoft to take on video game leaders', *Financial Times* (10 March 2000), p. 25; Oliver Edwards, 'X-box is no dog', *EuroBusiness* (May 2000), pp. 35–6; Satham Sanghera, 'Sega moves to increase share of UK market', *Financial Times* (13 October 2000), p. 3.

2. Philip B. Evans and Thomas S. Wurster, 'Strategy and the new economics of information', *Harvard Business Review* (September–October 1997), pp. 70–83; Michael Krantz, 'Click till you drop', *Time* (20 July 1998), pp. 34–9; and Ed Tallent, 'Encyclopedia Britannica Online', *Library Journal* (15 May 1999), pp. 138–9.

3. For discussions of the underlying rules of competitive interaction and reaction, see Peter S. H. Leeflang and Dick R. Wittink, 'Competitive reaction versus consumer response: Do managers overreact?', *International Journal of Research in Marketing*, **13**, 2 (1996), pp. 103–19; C. Carl Pegels and Yong Il Song, 'Competitive inter-firm interactions: determinants of divergence versus convergence', *Management Decision*, **38**, 3 (2000), pp. 194–208; Jos Lemmink and Hans Kasper, 'Competitive reactions to product quality improvements in industrial markets', *European Journal of Marketing*, **28**, 12 (1994), pp. 50–68.

4. See Michael E. Porter, *Competitive Advantage* (New York: Free Press, 1985), pp. 226–7 and Joseph Weber, 'How J & J's foresight made contact lenses pay', *Business Week* (4 May 1992), p. 132.

5. See Porter, *Competitive Advantage*, op.cit., pp. 226–7.

6. Ian Verchère, 'Sabena seeks divorce from Air France', *The European* (7–13 October 1994), p. 1; John Ridding, 'Air France reduces loss to Ffr2.61bn', *Financial Times* (3 October 1994), p. 22.

7. For more discussion, see Howard Schlossberg, 'Competitive intelligence pros seek formal role in marketing', *Marketing News* (5 March 1990), pp. 2, 28; Michele Galen, 'These guys aren't spooks, they're "competitive analysts"', *Business Week* (14 October 1991), p. 97; James W. Taylor, 'Competitive intelligence: a status report on US business practices', *Journal of Marketing Management*, **8**, 2 (1992), pp. 117–26; Peter Marsh, 'Is there a spy in your boardroom?', *Financial Times* (18 October 1994), p. 35; Phillip C. Wright and Géraldine Roy, 'Industrial espionage and competitive intelligence: one you do, one you do not', *Journal of Workplace Learning*, **11**, 2 (1999), pp. 53–9; James Gulliford, 'The challenge of competitor intelligence', *Management Services*, **42**, 1 (1998), pp. 20–2; Peter Bartram, 'The spying game', *Director*, **51**, 9 (1998), pp. 46–50.

8. See Porter, *Competitive Advantage*, op. cit.; Pankaj Ghemawat, 'Sustainable advantage', *Harvard Business Review* (September–October 1986), pp. 53–8; Michael E. Porter, 'From competitive advantage to corporate strategy', *Harvard Business Review* (May–June 1987), pp. 43–59; George S. Day and Robin Wensley, 'Assessing competitive advantage: a framework for diagnosing competitive superiority', *Journal of Marketing* (April 1988), pp. 1–20; Graham Hooley and John Saunders, *Competitive Positioning: The key to marketing success* (Hemel Hempstead: Prentice Hall, 1993).

9. Clive Cookson and Tony Jackson, 'An institution under threat', *Financial Times* (18 May 1991), p. 6; Richard Gourlay, 'Shaping up for a split decision', *Financial Times: FT 500* (10 February 1993), p. 19.

10. Michael E. Porter, *Competitive Strategy: Techniques for analyzing industries and competitors* (New York: Free Press, 1980), Ch. 2. For other strategy types see Stavros P. Kalafatis, Markos H. Tsogas and Charles Blankson, 'Positioning strategies in business markets', *The Journal of Business & Industrial Marketing*, **15**, 6 (2000), pp. 416–37. Harry Vardis and Sandra Vasa-Sideris, 'The PISCESSM Process: guiding clients to creative positioning strategies', *The Journal of Business & Industrial Marketing*, **15**, 2/3 (2000), pp. 163–9.

11. Kevin Done, 'Flurry of deals show pace of consolidation', *Financial Times Survey: Aerospace* (24 July 2000), pp. 1–2; Nick Cook, 'The race is on in lean production', *Interavia* (September 1999), pp. 15–17; Chris Ayers, 'Phone giants play numbers', *The Times* (18 November 1999), p. 41; 'Less mania, more merger', *The Economist* (29 May 1999), pp. 16–17.

12. See Seth Gordon, *Unleashing the idea virus* (Do You Zoom Inc: US), 2000; also Paul Kendall, 'The triple

destroyer', *Daily Mail* (7 October 2000), p. 27; Andrew Ward, 'Vosper set to benefit from new destroyer contract', *Financial Times* (17 May 2000), p. 31; Richard Tomkin, 'In a culture of sameness, what's the big idea?', *Financial Times* (17 November 2000), p. 18.

13. See Italian Institute for Foreign Trade, Spotlighting Italy: focus on clusters, *The Economist* (5 February 2000), promotional supplement.

14. David Blackwell, 'Making a meal of a dog's dinner', *Financial Times* (25 October 1994), p. 21.

15. 'Footballer's roadshow', *The Economist* (8 April 2000), p. 40; www.manutd.com

16. Doug Cameron, 'The wheels come off GM in Europe', *The European* (2–8 February 1998), pp. 20–2; 'Marks and Spencer: black marks', *The Economist* (16 November 1999), p. 106.

17. Anna Minton, 'Changing the knickers of the British high street', *Financial Times* (24 March 2000), p. 30.

18. See Robert D. Buzzell, Bradley T. Gale and Ralph G. M. Sultan, 'Market share – the key to profitability', *Harvard Business Review* (January–February 1975), pp. 97–106; Ben Branch, 'The laws of the marketplace and ROI dynamics', *Financial Management* (Summer 1980), pp. 58–65. Others suggest that the relationship between market share and profits has been exaggerated. See J. Martin Fraering and Michael S. Minor, 'The industry-specific basis of the market share–profitability relationship', *Journal of Consumer Marketing*, **11**, 1 (1994), pp. 27–37; Ann T. Kuzma and William L. Shanklin, 'How medium-market-share companies achieve superior profitability', *Journal of Business & Industrial Marketing*, **7**, 3 (1992); *Journal of Consumer Marketing*, **9**, 1 (1992).

19. Ian Harding, 'BSN provide food for thought', *The European* (25–31 March 1994), p. 28.

20. 'Casting the net', *The Economist* (11 March 2000), p. 122 and Susan Hart, Andrew Smith, Leigh Sparks and Nikolaos Tzokas, 'Are loyalty schemes a manifestation of Relationship Marketing?', *Journal of Marketing Management*, **15**, 6 (1999), pp. 541–62.

21. Richard Tomkins, 'Coca-Cola adds fizz with Orangina buy', *Financial Times* (21 February 1997), p. 21.

22. For more discussion on defence and attack strategies, see Low Sui Pheng, 'Applying the *Thirty-six Chinese Strategies of War* to retail marketing and planning', *Marketing Intelligence & Planning*, **16**, 2 (1998), pp. 124–35. Graham J. Hooley, John A. Saunders and Nigel F. Piercy, *Marketing Strategy & Competitive Positioning* (Hemel Hempstead: Prentice Hall Europe, 1998).

23. Richard Tomkins, 'Cadbury ignores history and buys Snapple', *Financial Times* (19 September 2000), p. 27; 'Unilever: fat and thin', *The Economist* (15 April 2000), p. 85.

24. See Lois Therrien, 'Mr Rust Belt', *Business Week* (17 October 1988), pp. 72–80, 'In the slow lane', *The Economist* (7–13 October 2000), p. 118.

25. Richard Tomkins, 'Burger King fries harder', *Financial Times* (5 January 2000), p. 21.

26. See 'Easy does it', *The Economist* (18–24 November 2000), pp. 122–5.

27. Oliver Sutton, 'Battlespace 2000 in big engines', *Interavia* (September 1999), pp. 12–14.

28. 'Virgin Atlantic: still on course', *The Economist* (22 January 1994), pp. 63–4.

29. See Kamel Mellahi and Michael Johnson, 'Does it pay to be a first mover in e.commerce? The case of Amazon.com', *Management Decision*, **38**, 7 (2000), pp. 445–52; Marvin B. Lieberman and David B. Montgomery, 'First-mover (dis)advantages: Retrospective and link with the resource-based view', *Strategic Management Journal*, **19**, 12 (1998), pp. 1111–25.

30. Michael Griffin, 'Imports cut into Dutch flower power', *Financial Times* (5 August 1994), p. 22.

31. Claire Murphy, 'Brand owners plot fresh assault', *Marketing Week* (3 June 1994), p. 7.

32. 'The complications of clustering', *The Economist* (2 January 1999), pp. 57–8; Peter Marsh, 'Adaptability furnishes key to craftsmen's long survival', *Financial Times* (6 September 2000), p. 7; also see a Spanish cluster in Sacha Vaughan, 'Smuggler's legacy', *Weekend FT* (15–16 January 2000), p. XII.

33. Tim Burt, 'Tourists lose their taste for Pollards Cornish Ice Cream', *Financial Times* (25 October 1994), p. 24.

34. Robert Taylor, 'Gambio: looking forward to a healthy future', *Financial Times: FT500* (10 February 1993), p. 17; Daniel Green, 'Tagamet's US sales fall 76% in quarter', *Financial Times* (19 October 1994), p. 25; Catherine Monk, 'Sprouting in new directions', *EuroBusiness* (July 2000), p. 120.

35. See John C. Narver and Stanley F. Slater, 'The effect of a market orientation on business profitability', *Journal of Marketing* (October 1990), pp. 20–35; Tung-Zong Chang, Rajiv Mehta, Su-Jane Chen, Pia Polsa and Jolanta Mazur, 'The effects of market orientation on effectiveness and efficiency: the case of automotive distribution channels in Finland and Poland', *Journal of Services Marketing*, **13**, 4/5 (1999), pp. 407–18; Tung-Zong Chang and Su-Jane Chen, 'Market orientation, service quality and business profitability: a conceptual model and empirical evidence', *Journal of Services Marketing*, **12**, 4 (1998), pp. 246–64; Wolfgang Fritz, 'Market orientation and corporate success: findings from Germany', *European Journal of Marketing*, **30**, 8 (1996), pp. 59–74.

case 12

The mobile maelstrom

Robert A. van der Zwart and Samual Pronk*

Libertel had been successful in the Dutch mobile phone operator market but the market was hotting up as new technology offered meant that several major strategic choices had to be made. Mobile penetration rates increased from 2 per cent in 1995 to an expected 25–30 per cent in 1999. As the market is changing as it grows, market leader KPN claims that 6 out of 10 new customers now buy a prepaid mobile phone product instead of a mobile subscription contract.

In July 1994, KPN, a former state-owned monopolist, launched 'The Mobile Network' to become the first GSM 900 network in the Netherlands. Libertel, a subsidiary of ING and Vodafone, followed them in September 1995 with their GSM 900 network. For a while the two competitors fought it out alone until the 1998 auction of GSM 1800 frequencies. This allowed Telfort (a joint venture between British Telecom and the Dutch Railways), Dutchtone (an alliance between Rabobank, ABN AMRO and France Télécom), and Ben (an alliance between Belgacom and TeleDanmark) to join the market one after another. Both KPN and Libertel gained GSM 1800 frequencies, but regulatory restrictions inhibit the use of these frequencies until the end of 1999. According to *Het Financieele Dagblad*, €800m were invested in the GSM 1800 licences by four mobile operators, excluding KPN. Of these, Telfort paid €230m in the auction of GSM frequencies. Latecomer Ben, which spent €680m buying licences and operating the network (excluding marketing costs), expects to reach its break-even point by 2003.

The standing and position of each of the competitors is quite different:

+ *KPN* is market leader in wireless communications with 2.2 million customers but expects to lose about 5 per cent market share in 1999. 'We are a Dutch company, we are the biggest and we'd like to keep on being the market leader. We offer the largest variety of subscription contracts. Moreover, we have had experience in the wireless communications market for years.'

+ *Libertel* has a market share of 36 per cent and 1.2 million customers. Since their entrance into the wireless market, call tariffs have dropped by 60 per cent. 'We are the trend setting and the most innovative mobile operator.'

+ *Telfort* has sold 50,000 GSM subscriptions. Telfort wants to attack the market position of Libertel. 'We'd like to keep it simple, so we offer a clear tariff structure. We are also present at many selling points.'

+ *Dutchtone* sells 2,000–3,000 product packages a week, and expects to capture 150,000 customers by the end of 1999. This amounts to a market share of 15–20 per cent. 'We are a new Dutch telecom company – enthusiastic and professional. Our guiding principles are clarity, simplicity, and affordability. No juggling with all kinds of complicated subscriptions and tariff structures, no confusing offers.'

+ *Ben* expects to attract 180,000–230,000 customers by the end of 1999. Within a few years Ben aims for 20 per cent market share in Dutch wireless communications. 'We'd like to meet you in the first place instead of selling you a mobile phone. We'd like to keep it simple and personal. We discuss mobile telephony in common language.'

Although many providers aim to keep things simple, users are faced with a wide range of price options (Table 1). After analysing the pricing of the competitors the consultants PriceWaterhouseCoopers concluded that, to remain price competitive, KPN would have to cut its prices by half. However, they also estimated that, if charging the reduced prices, KPN would face a dramatic €450m loss.

All mobile operators offer both prepaid telephone cards and monthly subscription contracts. Since prepaid (PP) telephone cards do not involve any monthly subscription fee, prepaid cards offer flexibility to customers who desire to be wirelessly connected but who do not wish to suffer from high subscription charges. Moreover, a prepaid card disciplines calling behaviour. Although mobile operators receive calling revenues in advance, prepaid cards have a drawback as they induce unpredictable network traffic.

---

* Robert van der Zwart is an Assistant Professor of Marketing and Samual Pronk is a Research Assistant at the Centre for Supply Chain Management at Nyenrode University, the Netherlands.

Service	Light user (5 min, 20% peak)	Moderate user (65 min, 60% peak)	Heavy user (100 min, 80% peak)
Ben PP	2	34	
Ben Regelnatig		11	20
Ben Vaak		14	14
Dutchtone Consumer	0 (yes, nearly free!)	15	31
Dutchtone PP	2		
Dutchtone Professional		30	36
KPN Allround		42	52
KPN Economy		37	56
KPN Hi	1	32	
KPN PP	3	43	
KPN Premium		37	50
Libertel BelMaar		18	35
Libertel Izi	2	42	
Libertel Personal		43	
Libertel Personal 30		40	60
Libertel Personal 60		36	54
Libertel Pro			57
Libertel Pro 120			51
Telfort 25		19	22
Telfort 50		22	22
Telfort PP	2	33	

Source: PriceWaterhouseCoopers Management consultants 'Prijvergelijkingen mobiel bellen' in Zembla-documentaire "Mobiele miljarden". 1999 February 4th. http://www.omroep.nl/vara/tv/zembla/gsm.html. (1999)

Table 1 Monthly tariff structures (fees and prepaid tariffs in euros)

Mobile operators reveal little about their promotional expenditure. According to Ernst Moeksis, a KPN spokesman, venture teams and marketing consultants are deployed in case competitive rivalries release new information. Nevertheless, there are some indications of promotional efforts. According to BBC, promotional expenses in telecommunications were €340m in 1998. In 1999 mobile communication promotions alone are expected to top €100m. Distribution, via company-owned and other outlets, varies greatly from company to company.

The market

'I wish I could split myself in two persons, so I could be in two places at the same time' is a phrase which expresses such a compressed life rhythm.

(Popcorn and Marigold 1996: 235).

Nokia also acknowledges the compressed life rhythm:

. . . the division between leisure time and work time is blurring. Lifestyle changes are forcing people to rethink how they spend time on the job,

time off the job and the time in between. The perception of the distance travelled to work and personal locations, the accessibility of transportation and the way to spend the time best are changing rapidly. This creates a situation where more and more people are on the move, and the time spent on the move is neither work time nor free time, but mobile time.

This does not imply an unconditional demand for wireless communications from all people. The young are the heaviest users. A Nokia survey revealed that the Dutch average is 38.5 years, 4 years below the European average. According to *HP/De Tijd*, further insight into the demographic profile of Dutch mobile customers is hard to obtain. Since nearly one-third of the Dutch mobile customers use prepaid cards, no registered information on mobile calling behaviour is available. A Nokia market study revealed some demographic profiling, although its main concern is adoption of Value Added Services (VAS) (such as online consulting of a city navigator on your mobile telephone) amongst early adapters in Finland (Table 2).

Whether monetary issues are unlikely to restrain the market or not, Wim Nieuwenhuijse, a consultant

UNDER 18 YEARS OLD	19–25	25–36
Heavy SMS users	Heavy SMS users	Moderate SMS users
Are aware of and have used	Are aware of and have used	Are aware of and have used
Gender doesn't play very big role	Male	Male
Monetary issues unlikely to restrain, parents pay the bill	Monetary issues likely to restrain interest in VAS	Monetary issues don't restrain
Live with parents	Students	Highly educated, working on managerial level or as an expert
Quite familiar with Internet technology	Internet and information technology literate	Internet and information technology literate
All very mobile people, participating actively in sports and outdoor activities		

SOURCE: Nokia Telecommunications Oy 'Wireless Data Evolution White Paper' in *Nokia Wireless Data Library* (April 1998). http://www.forum.nokia.com/download/wp_wdeu.pdf. Feb. 11th 1999. 1998: 12

Table 2 Value Added Service results

of Robert Pino & Company, argues that countries with relatively low cost of ownership experience high penetration rates of mobile customers. Once customers have to pay their own bill (instead of having their employers pay), calling behaviour changes. Thus, mobile calling behaviour can be characterised as price conscious.

Price consciousness also seems to apply to the business segment of the telecommunications market. According to Nokia, the business market can be segmented on the basis of the different business roles:

Although there may be many professionals in a company with different roles, those whose jobs often require working away from the office are the most likely to be the first adopters of wireless data services. . . .

Three main groups emerge:

✦ *Global Nomads* – 40%: front line professionals who travel on business a lot.

✦ *Migrators* – 30%: expert support functions – internal movers, trainers, using the same services as Global Nomads, but adopting them somewhat later . . .

✦ *Settlers* – 30%: less mobile functions – administration, finance. The last group to adopt these services. Office mobility issues are very relevant . . .

As the amount of wireless data products grows and their use becomes widespread, the Global Nomads will be the first mobile professional adopters, with Migrants and Settlers following behind. . . .

Technology

The technological environment of wireless communications is very turbulent. Technology determines what is possible in mobile telephony and five big waves are on the way.

Fixed Mobile Convergence (FMC) FMC provides 'one phone for all situations' and comprises a melting together of both fixed and mobile telephony. FMC is an opportunity to attract potential customers of fixed network operators by offering the equivalent of a fixed service on a mobile phone, for example Home Zone Tariffing (HZT), where mobile calls made via the base station close to the customers' home are cheaper than normal mobile calls.

Fixed line operators can fight back by encouraging their customers to use the fixed phone by connecting DECT (Digital Enhanced Cordless Telecommunications) cordless base stations to existing fixed lines. DECT is an advanced technology that supports wireless telephony at home and in the office and has more capabilities for wireless communication than the existing generation of wireless telephones.

Universal Mobile Telecommunications System (UMTS) UMTS, a third-generation mobile telecommunications system, is an initiative to build further on the European success in GSM telephony. UMTS service provision, including Internet and other flexible and personalised services, goes further than the possibilities offered by the current second-generation systems, such as GSM, and enables combined use of terrestrial and satellite components.

From the user's perspective, UMTS is a mobile carrier of new, innovative services, whereby the emphasis will be placed on the supply of information. Mobile multimedia will be made possible within UMTS thanks to transmission speeds of 144–384 kbit/s up to 2 Mbit/s in areas with a high level of coverage and a limited mobility. In addition:

1. UMTS services are expected also to be accessible though fixed networks. Using a personal identification, every user will have access to his or her own personal network environment from any fixed or mobile telephone. Personal mobility is guaranteed, even if the user is not carrying his or her mobile telephone or is out of range of a mobile network, concepts which are referred to as the Virtual Home Environment (VHE) and Universal Personal Telecommunications (UPT). This is primarily what distinguishes UMTS from OSM.

2. UMTS offers a far broader range of communication, information and entertainment services than has been the case up to now with mobile networks. The development and availability of online content will determine the success of UMTS. Major opportunities are available in the development of services specifically geared towards mobile users by, for example, combining location and route data with online data files.

3. UMTS offers access to communication, information and entertainment services with a video component, enabling audiovisual, broadcasting and telecommunications sectors to supplement one another.

4. There appear to be at least two market developments under way. First, there is a greater user demand for packages of combined services, whereby the same package of services is available on both the mobile network and the fixed network. The user wants accessibility under one number, irrespective of the network though which communication takes place. In addition, there is a demand for more advanced forms of (mobile) communications than speech, such as electronic mail and Internet applications.

Symbian This is a consortium of Nokia, Ericsson, Motorola and Psion who are jointly working on the next generation of wireless, handheld computers. For a long time Psion dominated the market in organisers, but sees its position being threatened by Microsoft's Windows CE operating system. Symbian is working on Epoc, an alternative operating system for handheld computers. It has several advantages over Windows CE. Epoc has a less intensive energy use than Windows CE. Epoc can also be customised to fit the needs of the different Epoc licensees. In contrast, Windows CE has a rigorously defined user environment.

Bluetooth This is an open standard for wireless communications being developed by Ericsson, IBM, Intel, Nokia and Toshiba. It facilitates wireless communication between laptops, printers, scanners, fax machines and mobile telephones by using radio devices that work within a periphery of 10 metres. In creating this standard Ericsson is responsible for developing the radio technology, Toshiba and IBM are jointly specifying the conditions under which Bluetooth technology can be built in mobile equipment, Intel is donating its advanced expertise on software and chips and Nokia is developing software necessary for the radio and handsets.

Satellite Communications (SatComs) SatComs are currently treated as a viable complement to existing terrestrial cellular networks. Employees of multinational companies use SatComs in regions where coverage by a fixed or mobile network is absent or poor. Heavy users of satellite servers could be found in areas such as newsgathering, oil exploration or shipping. High costs, expensive and bulky equipment and annoying delays in voice transmission inhibited mass introduction of satellite services. Nevertheless, organisations such as Iridium, Globalstar and Inmarsat have planned to invest about €40 billion in satellite communications by 2003 as they foresee a growing demand for satellite services in traditional telephony, mobile telephony and broadband Internet traffic.

Should satellite operators be considered a serious competitive threat to terrestrial mobile operators? Views are mixed:

> For cellular companies, the real worry is not that they will he unable to compete with satellite operators, but that they will fail to embrace satellites' capabilities quickly enough. Despite their low call volumes, satellite networks are set to become important additions to terrestrial networks for two reasons. First, by using dual-mode handsets that work on both cellular and satellite networks, wireless companies that enter partnerships with GMPCS operators (GMPCS is a satellite communication standard) will be able to extend their coverage to the whole of the Earth's surface. Those that do not will risk being left behind, especially in the important business segment. As many cellular operators have found, coverage is a key buying factor for customers. Second, satellite calls will be highly profitable. Cellular operators will take a cut on every call customers make when they roam on to a satellite network, just as they do when customers use a GSM network. These calls will be charged at premium rates but incur low marginal costs. In

fact, the margins on roamed calls in the GSM world are so attractive that some operators now derive almost one-fifth of their revenue from roaming. Cellular operators should recognise this and promote the adoption of satellite roaming services in their territories.

(Evans and Rose, 1998: 11)

Questions

1. How would you classify the five competitors in the market concerning their competitive positions?

2. What accounts for the large differences in price in the market?

3. Should KNP cut its prices to stay competitive? If so, how can they remain profitable? If not, suggest an alternative defence.

4. Suggest potential competitive strategies for the challenger and followers in the market.

5. What approach should Libertel take concerning the new technologies in the market and why should it differ from that of Dutchtone?

Sources: J. C. Arnbak, 'Toespraak 8ᵉ jaarcongres Mobiele Communicatie', *Opta Actueel* (16 December 1998); S. Nold, B. G. August, M. Knickrehm and P. J. Roche, 'Winning in Wireless', *The McKinsey Quarterly*, 2 (Spring 1998), pp. 18–31; P. Awde, 'Value-services for fixed networks', *Financial Times* (18 November 1998), FT Telecom p. 10; I. Beijnum, 'Jljitsch GSM-verhaal', *Pagina van Jljitsch van Betinum* (11 February 1999); H. Botman, 'Koopgids voor een GSM-telefoon', *Trouw* (8 February 1999); M. Couzy, 'Voor 80 miljard nieuwe telecomdiensten via satelliet', *Computable on line archief & literatuur* (14 August 1998), p. 25; M. Couzy, 'V&W wil meer aanbod bij opvolger GSM', *Computable on line archief & literatuur* (31 July 1998); A. J. Diepen and K. Gilbert, 'Benchmarkstudie telecommunicatie infrastructuur en diensten', *Rapport aan Hoofddirectie Telecommunicatie en Post* (February 1998) pp. 9–11; A. L. Evans and J. S. Rose, 'The future of satellite communications', *The McKinsey Quarterly* (Spring 1998), pp. 6–17; K. van Gilst, 'Bellen, Bellen, maar geen gehoor', *Adformatie* (24 January 1999), p. 3; M. Houben, 'KPN Telecom moet zich zorgen maken over positie op thuismarkt', *Het Financieele Dagblad* (20 February 1998), p. 13; A. Kantelberg, 'De tienertelefoon', *HP/De Tijd* (4 December 1998), pp. 33–9; J. Libbenga, 'Slimme Telefoon dicteert IT-wereld', *Automatiseringsgids* (4 December 1998), p. 7; W. Nieuwenhuijse, 'Marktturbulentie in mobiel waaiert uit', *Tijdschrift voor Marketing* (February 1998), pp. 46–8; Nokia Telecommunications Oy, 'Wireless Data Evolution White Paper', *Nokia Wireless Data Library* (April 1998); Nokia Telecommunications Oy, 'The demand for value-added services', *Nokia Wireless Data Library* (December 1998); F. Popcorn and L. Marigold, *Clicking* (London: Thorsons, 1996), p. 235; PriceWaterhouseCoopers Management Consultants, 'Prijsvergelijkingen mobiel bellen', *Zembla-documentaire 'Mobiele mi/jarden'*, 1999; Project Group UMTS, 'Consultation document UMTS', *Ministry of Transport, Public Works and Water Management; Telecommunications and Post Department* (16 July 1998); Redactie Economie, 'Nieuwkomer Ben wordt prijsvechter', *Trouw* (3 February 1999); S. Reeve, 'Direct dialling to success', *The European* (9 November 1998) p. 8; H. Schrameyer, 'Rumour around Dutchtone', *Adformatie* (4 January 1998), p. 20; W. Webb, 'Alternative strategies for fixed mobile convergence', *Motorola Cellular Infrastructure Group* (11 February 1999); www.ben.nl, www.dutchtone.nl, www.kpn.com, www.libertel.nl, www.telfort.nl

internet exercises

Internet exercises for this chapter can be found on the student site of the ᴍʏᴘʜʟɪᴘ Web Site at www.booksites.net/kotler.

part four

Product

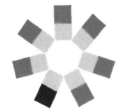

'A hamburger by any other name costs twice as much.'

EVAN ESAR (MODERN MARKETER)

part introduction

Chapter 13

Brands, products, packaging and support services

Chapter 14

New-product development and product life-cycle strategies

Chapter 15

Marketing services

IN PART FOUR WE LOOK at the first component in the marketing mix – the product.

Designing good products that customers want to buy is a challenging task. Customers do not buy mere products. They seek product benefits and are often willing to pay more for a brand that genuinely solves their problems. Chapter 13 explores how marketers can satisfy customer needs by adding value to the basic product; it also shows the complexity arising in product, branding and packaging decisions, and how various forces in the environment pose tough challenges for marketers in the new century.

Markets do not stand still. Companies must adapt their current offerings or create new ones in response to changing customer needs, or to take advantage of new marketing and technological opportunities. Chapter 14 looks at how to develop and commercialise new products. Importantly, after launch, marketing managers must carefully manage the new product over its lifetime to get the best return from their new-product effort.

While Chapters 13 and 14 deal with products, Chapter 15 looks more specifically at intangible products or services. It examines the unique characteristics of services and how organisations adapt their approach when marketing them.

chapter thirteen

Brands, products, packaging and support services

Chapter objectives *After reading this chapter, you should be able to:*

✦ Define the term *product*, including the core, actual and *augmented* product.

✦ Explain the main classifications of consumer and industrial products.

✦ Describe the roles of product branding, packaging, labelling and product support services.

✦ Explain the decisions that companies make when developing product lines and mixes.

✦ List the considerations that marketers face in making international product decisions.

introduction

The preview case opposite shows that, clearly, toiletries and cosmetics are more than just toiletries and cosmetics when L'Oréal sells them. This chapter begins with a deceptively simple question: *What is a product?* After answering this question, we look at ways to classify products in consumer and business markets. Then we discuss the important decisions that marketers make regarding individual products. These decisions go beyond product design and involve *branding*, *packaging*, *labelling* and *product-support services*. Next, we move from decisions about individual products to decisions about building *product lines* and *product mixes*. Finally, we address some complex considerations in international product decisions.

what is a product?

A pair of Adidas trainers, a Volvo truck, a Nokia mobile telephone, a Tony & Guy haircut, an Oasis concert, a Club Med vacation, an online investment service, advice from

preview case

L'Oréal: are you worth it?

L'Oréal sells cosmetics and toiletries to consumers around the world. One market that has certainly been booming lately is that for hair care products. Brands such as Elvive, Lancôme, Helena Rubenstein and Kérastase, part of the L'Oréal stable, are capitalising on this trend. In one sense, L'Oréal's hair care products – shampoo, conditioners, styling agents – are no more than careful mixtures of chemicals with different smells and colours. But L'Oréal knows that when it sells shampoos and conditioners, it sells much more than a bottle of coloured or fragrant soapy fluids – it sells what the fluids can do for the women who use them.

Many hair care products are promoted using alluring chat-up lines: 'Your hair is instantly shinier, stronger, healthier, and getting better and better and . . .' Who would believe that shampoos and conditioners that are designed to rinse away can have any lasting benefits? But women do not see shampoos and conditioners that way. Many things beyond the ingredients add to a shampoo's allure. While hair is dead, it is organic, so will respond to some care and attention. Many consumers believe that their favourite shampoo does more than wash away the grit in their hair; it makes them feel good about themselves.

Thanks to recent scientific breakthroughs, many hair care products can make a difference.

The L'Oréal laboratories in Paris, employing 2,500 employees, dedicate over £180 million a year to R&D. This investment pays. For example, Kérastase, part of the L'Oréal group, developed Ceramide F – a synthetic copy of naturally occurring hair ceramides – which reconstructs the hair's internal structure. Sounds far fetched? But consumers say it works. Kérastase Forcintense revitalises hair that is severely damaged through colouring, overstyling or perming. Other L'Oréal product innovations include colour and conditioning agents –Majirel, Majirouge and Majiblond – for treating fading hair colours due to washing or sunlight and special formulations – Majimèches – for blondes. All these functional benefits enable L'Oréal to promote the brand's superior performance benefits to consumers.

The wash-in, wash-out nature of hair care suggests that product performance alone may be sufficient to satisfy users. Hairstylist Sam McKnight says that it is an emotionally charged marketplace: a bad hair day means an unhappy woman.There is also a limit to what all the scientific breakthroughs in hair care can do for how a woman feels when she has had a hair wash. McKnight argues that scents and colours must be chosen carefully to match women's desires, moods and lifestyles. His new range of products eschew science and concentrate on the smell. Called 'Sexy', they are expensive, exclusive and smell like no other shampoo has ever smelled before.

Additionally, hair care brands have done well because of the advertising spends that have gone in to promote shampooing as a pleasurable pastime rather than an activity akin to doing a load of washing. L'Oréal and rival firms know just how important this is. Brands such as Elvive, Pantene (by Procter & Gamble) and Organics (by Elida/Fabergé/Unilever) have advertising spends that will make a girl's hair curl. L'Oréal's leading brand Elvive also tries to capture the essence of pleasure using advertisements that sound tempting: 'Because I'm worth it', says L'Oréal.

Companies also have to play on the shampoo's name, an important product attribute. Names such as Sexy, Dream Hair Sensational and Frizz-Ease suggest that the shampoos and conditioners will do something more than just wash your hair. L'Oréal must also package its hair care products carefully. To consumers, the bottle and package are the most tangible symbols of the product's image. Bottles must feel comfortable, be easy to handle and help to differentiate the product from other brands on the shelf.

So when a woman buys hair shampoos and conditioners, she buys much, much more than simply soapy fluids. The product's image, its promises, its feel, its name and package, even the company that makes it, all become a part of the *total product*.

Hope in a bottle or just so much hype? The answer: it's up to each of us to decide whether we're worth it.[1]

Questions

1. Distinguish between the core, tangible and augmented product that L'Oréal sells.

2. A hair care product's name is a central product attribute. What are the key branding decisions that L'Oréal's marketing managers have to make?

3. L'Oréal markets its hair care products worldwide. What major considerations does the firm face in determining global product decisions?

Figure 13.1

Three levels of product

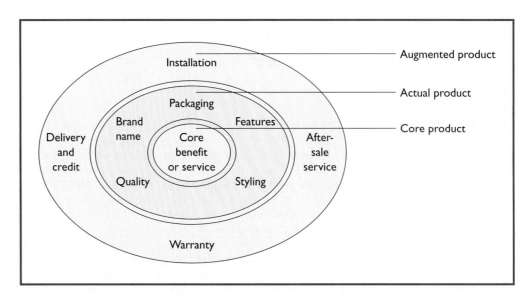

your doctor – all are products. We define a **product** as anything that is offered to a market for attention, acquisition, use or consumption and that might satisfy a want or need. Products include more than just tangible goods. Broadly defined, products include physical objects, services, persons, places, organisations, ideas or mixes of these entities. Thus, throughout this text, we use the term *product* broadly to include any or all of these entities.

Services are products that consist of activities, benefits or satisfactions that are offered for sale that are essentially intangible and do not result in the ownership of anything. Examples are banking, hotel, haircuts, tax preparation and home repairs. Because of the importance of services in the world economy, we give special attention to services marketing which is addressed in greater detail in Chapter 15.

Product planners need to think about the product on three levels. The most basic level is the **core product**, which addresses the question: *What is the buyer really buying?* As Figure 13.1 illustrates, the core product stands at the centre of the total product. It consists of the problem-solving benefits that consumers seek when they buy a product. A woman buying lipstick buys more than lip colour. Charles Revson of Revlon saw this early: 'In the factory, we make cosmetics; in the store, we sell hope.' Theodore Levitt has pointed out that buyers 'do not buy quarter-inch drills; they buy quarter-inch holes'. Thus when designing products, marketers must first define the core of *benefits* that the product will provide to consumers.

The product planner must next build an **actual product** around the core product. Actual products may have as many as five characteristics: a *quality level*, *features*, *styling*, a *brand name* and *packaging*. For example, Sony's cam camcorder is an actual product. Its name, parts, styling, features, packaging and other attributes have all been combined carefully to deliver the core benefit – a convenient, high-quality way to capture important moments.

Finally, the product planner must build an **augmented product** around the core and actual products by offering additional consumer services and benefits. Sony must offer more than a camcorder. It must provide consumers with a complete solution to their picture-taking problems. Thus when consumers buy a Sony camcorder, Sony and its dealers might also give buyers a warranty on parts and workmanship, instructions on how to use the camcorder, quick repair services when needed and a freephone number to call if they have problems or questions. To the consumer, all of these augmentations become an important part of the total product.

Therefore, a product is more than a simple set of tangible features. Consumers tend to see products as complex *bundles of benefits* that satisfy their needs. When developing products, marketers must first identify the *core* consumer needs that the product will satisfy. They must then design the *actual* product and finally find ways to *augment* it in order to create the bundle of benefits that will best satisfy consumers.

Today, most competition takes place at the product augmentation level. Successful companies add benefits to their offers that will not only *satisfy*, but also *delight* the customer. For instance, hotel guests find chocolates on the pillow or a bowl of fruit or a VCR with optional videotapes. However, each augmentation costs the company money, and the marketer has to ask whether customers will pay enough to cover the extra cost. Moreover, augmented benefits soon become *expected* benefits: hotel guests now expect cable television, trays of toiletries and other amenities in their rooms. This means that competitors must search for still more features and benefits to differentiate their offers.

product classifications

Before we examine individual product decisions, let us explain several product-classification schemes. Products can be classified according to their durability and tangibility. **Non-durable products** are goods that are normally consumed quickly and used on one or a few usage occasions, such as beer, soap and food products. **Durable products** are products used over an extended period of time and normally survive for many years. Examples are refrigerators, cars and furniture.

Marketers have also divided products and services into two broad classes based on the types of customer that use them – consumer products and industrial products.

consumer products

Consumer products are those bought by final consumers for personal consumption. Marketers usually classify these goods based on *consumer shopping habits*. Consumer products include *convenience products*, *shopping products*, *speciality products* and *unsought products*. These products differ in the way consumers buy them, so they differ in how they are marketed (see Table 13.1).

Convenience products are consumer goods and services that the consumer usually buys frequently, immediately and with a minimum of comparison and buying effort. Examples are soap, sweets, newspapers and fast food. Convenience goods are usually low priced, and marketers place them in many locations to make them readily available when customers need them. Convenience products can be divided further into *staples*, *impulse goods* and *emergency goods*.

Staples are goods that consumers buy on a regular basis, such as milk, toothpaste or bread. *Impulse goods* are purchased with little planning or search effort, such as chocolate bars and magazines, which are often placed next to checkout counters because shoppers may not otherwise think of buying them. *Emergency products* are purchased when a need is urgent – umbrellas during a rainstorm or boots and shovels during the year's first snowstorm.

Shopping products are less frequently purchased and consumers spend considerable time and effort gathering information and comparing alternative brands carefully on suitability, quality, price and style. Examples of shopping products are furniture, clothing, used cars and major household appliances. Shopping products can be divided into *homogeneous* and *heterogeneous* goods. Shopping products marketers usually distribute their products through fewer outlets but provide deeper sales support to give customers information and advice to help them in their comparison efforts.

Non-durable product
A consumer product that is normally consumed in one or a few uses.

Durable product
A consumer product that is usually used over an extended period of time and that normally survives many uses.

Consumer product
A product bought by final consumers for personal consumption.

Convenience product
A consumer product that the customer usually buys frequently, immediately, and with a minimum of comparison and buying effort.

Shopping product
A consumer product that the customer, in the process of selection and purchase, characteristically compares with others on such bases as suitability, quality, price and style.

MARKETING CONSIDERATION	TYPE OF CONSUMER PRODUCT			
	CONVENIENCE	SHOPPING	SPECIALITY	UNSOUGHT
Customer buying behaviour	Frequent purchase, little planning, little comparison or shopping effort, low customer involvement	Less frequent purchase, much planning and shopping effort, comparison of brands on price, quality, style	Strong brand preference and loyalty, special purchase effort, little comparison of brands, low price sensitivity	Little product awareness, knowledge (or if aware, little or even negative interest)
Price	Low price	Higher price	High price	Varies
Distribution	Widespread distribution, convenient locations	Selective distribution in fewer outlets	Exclusive distribution in only one or a few outlets per market area	Varies
Promotion	Mass promotion by the producer	Advertising and personal selling by both producer and resellers	More carefully targeted promotion by both producer and resellers	Aggressive advertising and personal selling by producer and resellers
Examples	Toothpaste, magazines, laundry detergent	Major appliances, televisions, furniture, clothing	Luxury goods, such as Rolex watches or fine crystal	Life insurance, Red Cross blood donations

Table 13.1

Marketing considerations for consumer products

Speciality product
A consumer product with unique characteristics or brand identification for which a significant group of buyers is willing to make a special purchase effort.

Unsought product
A consumer product that the consumer either does not know about or knows about but does not normally think of buying.

Industrial product
A product bought by individuals and organisations for further processing or for use in conducting a business.

Speciality products are consumer goods with unique characteristics or brand identification for which a significant group of buyers is willing to make a special purchase effort. Examples include specific brands and types of car, high-priced home entertainment systems and photographic equipment, designer clothes, the services of medical or legal specialists and luxury goods. A jukebox, for example, is a speciality good because buyers are usually willing to travel great distances to buy one. Buyers normally do not compare speciality goods. They invest only the time needed to reach dealers carrying the wanted products.

Unsought products are consumer goods that the consumer either does not know about or knows about but does not normally think of buying. Most major new innovations are unsought until the consumer becomes aware of them through advertising. Classic examples of known but unsought goods are life insurance, home security systems and blood donations. By their very nature, unsought goods require a lot of advertising, personal selling and other marketing efforts.

industrial products

Industrial products are those bought for further processing or for use in conducting a business. Thus the distinction between a consumer product and an industrial product is based on the *purpose* for which the product is purchased. If a consumer buys a lawnmower for home use, the lawnmower is a consumer product. If the same consumer buys the same lawnmower for use in a landscaping business, the lawnmower is an industrial product.

There are three groups of industrial product: *materials and parts*, *capital items* and *supplies and services* (see Figure 13.2).

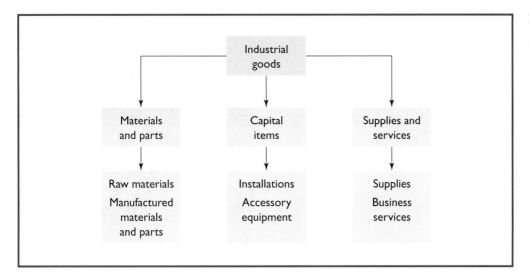

Figure 13.2

Classification of
industrial goods

Materials and parts are industrial goods that become a part of the buyer's product, through further processing or as components. They include raw materials and manufactured materials and parts.

Raw materials consist of farm products (wheat, cotton, livestock, fruits, vegetables) and natural products (fish, timber, crude petroleum, iron ore).

Manufactured materials and parts include component materials (iron, yarn, cement, wires) and component parts (small motors, tyres, castings). Component materials are usually processed further – for example, pig iron is made into steel, and yarn is woven into cloth. Component parts enter the finished product complete with no further change in form, as when Electrolux puts small motors into its vacuum cleaners and Volvo adds tyres to its automobiles. Most manufactured materials and parts are sold directly to industrial users. Price and service are the most significant marketing factors, and branding and advertising tend to be less important.

Capital items are industrial products that help in the buyers' production or operations. They include installations and accessory equipment. *Installations* consist of buildings (factories, offices) and fixed equipment (generators, drill presses, large computer systems, lifts). *Accessory equipment* includes portable factory equipment and tools (hand tools, lift trucks) and office equipment (fax machines, printers, desks). These products do not become part of the finished product. They have a shorter life than installations and simply aid in the production process. Most sellers of accessory equipment use intermediaries because the market is spread out geographically, the buyers are numerous and the orders are small.

Supplies and services are industrial products that do not enter the finished product at all. *Supplies* include operating supplies (lubricants, coal, computer paper, pencils) and repair and maintenance items (paint, nails, brooms). Supplies are the convenience goods of the industrial field because they are usually purchased with a minimum of effort or comparison. *Business services* include maintenance and repair services (window cleaning, computer repair) and business advisory services (legal, management consulting, advertising). Such services are usually supplied under contract.

Materials and parts
Industrial products that enter the manufacturer's product completely, including raw materials and manufactured materials and parts.

Capital items
Industrial goods that partly enter the finished product, including installations and accessory equipment.

Supplies and services
Industrial products that do not enter the finished product at all.

organisations, persons, places and ideas

In addition to tangible products and services, in recent years marketers have broadened the concept of a product to include other 'marketable entities' – namely, organisations, persons, places and ideas.

Capital items: this ad positions Rockwell as a world leader in industrial automation, supplying advanced technology and services to help serve the needs of customers such as Nestlé, Unilever and Compaq.

SOURCE: reprinted with permission of Rockwell Corporation. *Agency:* Chilworth Communications

Organisations often carry out activities to 'sell' the organisation itself. *Organisation marketing* consists of activities undertaken to create, maintain or change the attitudes and behaviour of target consumers toward an organisation. Both profit and non-profit organisations practise organisation marketing. Business firms sponsor public relations or corporate advertising campaigns to polish their images. *Corporate image advertising* is a major tool companies use to market themselves to various publics. For example, IBM wants to establish itself as the company to turn to for 'e-Business Solutions'. Similarly, non-profit organisations, such as churches, colleges, charities, museums and performing arts groups, market their organisations in order to raise funds and attract members or patrons.

People can also be thought of as products. *Person marketing* consists of activities undertaken to create, maintain, or change attitudes or behaviour towards particular people. All kinds of people and organisations practise person marketing. Presidents or prime ministers of nations must be skilful in marketing themselves, their parties and their platforms to get needed votes and programme support. Entertainers and sports figures use marketing to promote their careers and improve their impact and incomes. Professionals such as doctors, lawyers, accountants and architects market themselves in order to build their reputations and increase business. Business leaders use person marketing as a strategic tool to develop their companies' fortunes as well as their own. Businesses, charities, sports teams, fine arts groups, religious groups and other organisations also use person marketing. Creating or associating with well-known personalities often helps these organisations achieve their goals better. Thus, brands such as Coca-Cola, Adidas, Nike and McDonald's have invested millions of euros to link themselves with celebrities.

Place marketing: The Irish Tourist Board has built a flourishing tourism business – 'Awaken to a different world, Ireland!'.

SOURCE: Bord Fáilte – Irish Tourist Board

Place marketing involves activities undertaken to create, maintain or change attitudes or behaviour towards particular places. Thus, cities, states, regions and even entire nations compete to attract tourists, new residents, conventions and company offices and factories. For example, today, it is common to find cities, counties and countries marketing their tourist attractions. Many of these also operate industrial development offices that try to sell companies on the advantages of locating new plants in their locations. For example, Ireland is an outstanding place marketer. The Irish Development Board has attracted over 500 companies to locate their plants in Ireland. At the same time, the Irish Tourist Board has built a flourishing tourism business, and the Irish Export Board has created attractive markets for Irish exports.[2]

Ideas can also be marketed. In one sense, all marketing is the marketing of an idea, whether it be the general idea of brushing your teeth or the specific idea that AquaFresh provides an effective decay prevention. Here, however, we narrow our focus to the marketing of *social ideas*, such as public health campaigns to reduce smoking, alcoholism, drug abuse, child abuse and overeating; environmental campaigns to promote wilderness protection, clean air and conservation; and other campaigns such as education reforms, organ donations, family planning, human rights and racial equality. This area has been called *social marketing*, which includes the creation and implementation of programmes seeking to increase the acceptability of a social idea, cause or practice within targeted groups.

But social marketing involves much more than just advertising. Many public marketing campaigns fail because they assign advertising the primary role and fail to develop and use all the marketing mix tools.[3]

individual product decisions

Let us now look at decisions relating to the development and marketing of individual products. We will focus on decisions about *product attributes*, *branding*, *packaging*, *labelling* and *product-support services*.

product attributes

Developing a product involves defining the benefits that the product will offer. These benefits are communicated and delivered by tangible product attributes, such as *quality*, *features, style* and *design*. Decisions about these attributes are particularly important as they greatly affect consumer reactions to a product. We will now discuss the issues involved in each decision.

■ Product quality

Product quality

The ability of a product to perform its functions; it includes the product's overall durability, reliability, precision, ease of operation and repair, and other valued attributes.

Quality is one of the marketer's major positioning tools. Quality has two dimensions – level and consistency. In developing a product, the marketer must first choose a *quality level* that will support the product's position in the target market. Here, **product quality** stands for the ability of a product to perform its functions. It includes the product's overall durability, reliability, precision, ease of operation and repair, and other valued attributes. Although some of these attributes can be measured objectively, from a marketing point of view, quality should be measured in terms of buyers' perceptions. Companies rarely try to offer the highest possible quality level – few customers want or can afford the high levels of quality offered in products such as a Rolls-Royce, a Sub Zero refrigerator or a Rolex watch. Instead, companies choose a quality level that matches target market needs and the quality levels of competing products.

Beyond quality level, high quality can also mean high levels of quality *consistency*. Here, product quality means *conformance quality* – freedom from defects and *consistency* in delivering a targeted level of performance. In this sense, a Nissan can have just as much quality as a Rolls-Royce. Although a Nissan dose not perform as well as a Rolls, it can consistently deliver the quality that customers pay for and expect.

During the past two decades, a renewed emphasis on quality has spawned a global quality movement. Many firms implemented 'total quality management' (TQM) programmes, efforts to constantly improve product and process quality in every phase of their operations. Recently, however, the total quality movement has attracted criticism. Too many companies view TQM as a magic cure-all and created token total quality programmes that applied quality principles only superficially. Today, companies are taking a 'return on quality' approach, viewing quality as an investment and holding quality efforts accountable for bottom-line results.[4]

Beyond simply reducing product defects, the ultimate goal of total quality is to improve customer satisfaction and value. For example, when Motorola first began its total quality programme in the early 1980s, its goal was to reduce manufacturing defects drastically. Later, however, Motorola's quality concept evolved into one of *customer-defined quality* and *total customer satisfaction*. 'Quality', noted Motorola's vice-president of quality, 'has to do something for the customer. . . . Our definition of a defect is "if the customer doesn't like it, it's a defect."' Similarly, Siemens defines quality this way: 'Quality is when our customers come back and our products don't.'[5] As more and more companies have moved towards such customer-driven definitions of quality, their TQM programmes are evolving into customer satisfaction and customer retention programmes.

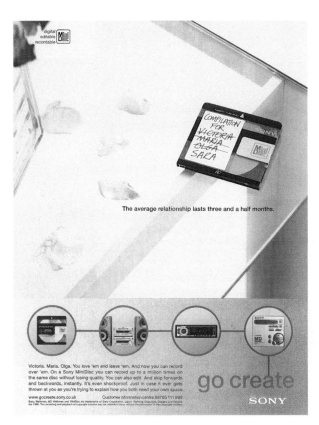

This Sony ad promotes the superior quality of the Mini Disc by claiming that 'you can record up to a million times on the same disc without losing quality'.

SOURCE: Sony/Advertising Archives.
Agency: Saatchi & Saatchi.
Photographer: Jo Magrean

Thus, many companies today have turned customer-driven quality into a potent strategic weapon. They create customer satisfaction and value by consistently and profitably meeting customers' needs and preferences for quality. In fact, quality has now become a competitive necessity – in the twenty-first century, only companies with the best quality will thrive.

■ Product features

A product can be offered with varying features. A 'stripped-down' model, one without any extras, is the starting point. The company can create more features by adding higher-level models. Features are a competitive tool for differentiating the company's product from competitors' products. Being the first producer to introduce a needed and valued new feature is one of the most effective ways to compete.

How can a company identify new features and decide which ones to add to its product? The company should periodically survey buyers who have used the product and ask these questions: How do you like the product? Which specific features of the product do you like most? Which features could we add to improve the product? How much would you pay for each feature? The answers provide the company with a rich list of feature ideas. Each feature should be assessed on the basis of its *customer value* versus its *company cost*. Features that customers value little in relation to costs should be dropped; those that customers value highly in relation to costs should be added.

■ Product style and design

Another way to add customer value is through *product design*. Some companies have reputations for outstanding style and design, such as Black & Decker in cordless appliances and tools, Bose in audio equipment and Braun in shavers and small household

BMW creates competitive advantage by highlighting product attributes.

Source: BMW, (UB)
Photographer: Tif Hunter

appliances. Some companies have integrated style and design with their corporate culture. Consider IKEA, the Swedish home furnishing chain. Its corporate culture is 'småländsk' – thrift is a virtue, no extravagance is allowed. This identity is reflected in IKEA's thrifty (but stylish) designs and the dominance of traditional Scandinavian materials of light wood, linen and cotton textiles. Another company, the carmaker Saab, promotes a design philosophy of simplicity and purity. 'There are few excesses; form follows function. We also believe in fidelity to materials – when it's plastic, we don't try to make it look like wood', says a Saab spokesperson.[6] Many companies, however, lack a 'design touch'. Their product designs function poorly or are dull or common looking. Yet design can be one of the most powerful competitive weapons in a company's marketing arsenal.

Design is a broader concept than style. *Style* simply describes the appearance of a product. A sensational style may grab attention and produce pleasing aesthetics, but it does not necessarily make the product *perform* better. In some cases, it might even result in worse performance. For example, a chair may look great yet be extremely uncomfortable. Unlike style, *design* is more than skin deep – it goes to the very heart of a product. Good design contributes to a product's usefulness as well as to its looks.

As competition intensifies, design will offer one of the most potent tools for differentiating and positioning products of all kinds. That investment in design pays off has certainly been recognised by global companies which have embraced design. Nike, for example, employs 60 designers and releases 500 footwear designs each year. Its shoes are worn by athletes, but are aimed primarily at a youthful market for which high-performance footwear is currently fashionable.[7] The iMac computer, introduced in 1998, combined style and content. In response to the project brief – to design a new computer for consumers that was simple, approachable and affordable, Jonathan Ive, Apple's chief designer, produced the award-winning iMac. The computer's cuteness and distinctive colour single-handedly turned the tide for Apple, making it the fastest-selling computer in Apple's history. Others like Minolta (cameras), Sony (hi-fis), Philips (compact disc players and shavers), Ford (cars) and Swatch (watches) have also profited from their commitment to product design. Differentiating through design

The thrill of surfing.
The agony of choosing a color.

Combining style and content, Apple produced this award-winning iMac computer, with its sleek egg-shaped, single-unit monitor and hard drive in a futuristic translucent casing.

SOURCE: TBWA/Chiat/Day

is also a familiar strategy in premium products such as Rolex watches, Porsche cars and Herman Miller office furniture. These products stand out from the crowd. Good design can attract attention, improve product performance, cut production costs and give the product a strong competitive advantage in the target market.[8]

branding

Perhaps the most distinctive skill of professional marketers is their ability to create, maintain, protect and enhance brands of their products. Consumers view a brand as an important part of a product, and branding can add value to a product. For example, most consumers would perceive a bottle of Chanel perfume as a high-quality, expensive product. But the same perfume in an unmarked bottle would probably be viewed as lower in quality, even if the fragrance were identical.

■ What is a brand?

A **brand** is a name, term, sign, symbol, design or a combination of these, which is used to identify the goods or services of one seller or group of sellers and to differentiate them from those of competitors.[9] Powerful brand names have *consumer franchise* – that is, they command strong consumer loyalty. This means that a sufficient number of customers demand these brands and refuse substitutes, even if the substitutes are offered at somewhat lower prices. Companies that develop brands with a strong consumer franchise are insulated from competitors' promotional strategies. Thus it makes sense for a supplier to invest heavily to create strong national or even global recognition and preference for its brand name.

A brand can deliver up to four levels of meaning:

1. *Attributes.* A brand first brings to mind certain product attributes. For example, Mercedes suggests such attributes as 'well engineered', 'well built', 'durable', 'high prestige', 'fast', 'expensive' and 'high resale value'. The company may use one or more of these attributes in its advertising for the car. For years, Mercedes advertised 'Engineered like no other car in the world'. This provided a positioning platform for other attributes of the car.

2. *Benefits.* Customers do not buy attributes, they buy benefits. Therefore, attributes must be translated into functional and emotional benefits. For example, the

Brand
A name, term, sign, symbol or design, or a combination of these, intended to identify the goods or services of one seller or group of sellers and to differentiate them from those of competitors.

attribute 'durable' could translate into the functional benefit, 'I won't have to buy a new car every few years.' The attribute 'expensive' might translate into the emotional benefit, 'The car makes me feel important and admired.' The attribute 'well built' might translate into the functional and emotional benefit, 'I am safe in the event of an accident.'

3. *Values.* A brand also says something about the buyers' values. Thus Mercedes buyers value high performance, safety and prestige. A brand marketer must identify the specific groups of car buyers whose values coincide with the delivered benefit package.

4. *Personality.* A brand also projects a personality. Motivation researchers sometimes ask, 'If this brand were a person, what kind of person would it be?'. Consumers might visualise a Mercedes automobile as being a wealthy, middle-aged business executive. The brand will attract people whose actual or desired self-images match the brand's image.[10]

All this suggests that a brand is a complex symbol. If a company treats a brand only as a name, it misses the point of branding. The challenge of branding is to develop a deep set of meanings or associations for the brand.

Given the four levels of a brand's meaning, marketers must decide the levels at which they will build the brand's identity. It would be a mistake to promote only the brand's attributes. Remember, buyers are interested not so much in brand attributes as in brand benefits. Moreover, competitors can easily copy attributes. Or the current attributes may later become less valuable to consumers, hurting a brand that is tied too strongly to specific attributes.

Even promoting the brand on one or more of its benefits can be risky. Suppose Mercedes touts its main benefit as 'high performance'. If several competing brands emerge with as high or higher performance, or if car buyers begin placing less importance on performance as compared to other benefits, Mercedes will need the freedom to move into a new benefit positioning.

The most lasting and sustainable meanings of a brand are its core values and personality. They define the brand's essence. Thus Mercedes stands for 'high achievers and success'. The company must build its brand strategy around creating and protecting this brand personality. Although Mercedes has recently yielded to market pressures by introducing lower-price models, this might prove risky. Marketing less expensive models might dilute the personality that Mercedes has built up over the decades.

■ Brand equity

Brands vary in the amount of power and value they have in the marketplace. Some brands are largely unknown to most buyers. Other brands have a high degree of consumer *brand awareness.* Still others enjoy *brand preference* – buyers select them over the others. Finally, some brands command a high degree of *brand loyalty.* A top executive at H.J. Heinz proposes this test of brand loyalty: 'My acid test . . . is whether a [consumer], intending to buy Heinz Ketchup in a store but finding it out of stock, will walk out of the store to buy it elsewhere or switch to an alternative product.'

A powerful brand has high **brand equity.** Brands have higher brand equity to the extent that they have higher brand loyalty, name awareness, perceived quality, strong brand associations and other assets such as patents, trademarks and channel relationships.[11] A brand with strong brand equity is a valuable asset. In fact, it can even be bought or sold for a price. Many companies base their growth strategies on acquiring and building rich *brand portfolios.* For example, Switzerland's Nestlé bought Rowntree (UK), Carnation (US), Stouffer (US), Buitoni-Perugina (Italy) and Perrier (France), making it the world's largest food company controlling many desirable 'brands'.

Brand equity
The value of a brand, based on the extent to which it has high brand loyalty, name awareness, perceived quality, strong brand associations, and other assets such as patents, trademarks and channel relationships.

Measuring the actual equity of a brand name is difficult.[12] Because it is so hard to measure, companies usually do not list brand equity on their balance sheets. Although it is difficult to incorporate brand values in balance sheets, new accounting standards (e.g. the UK Financial Reporting Standard, FRS 10, and its international equivalent, IAS 38), enforced recently, compel firms to put a value on their acquired brands on their balance sheets. Accounting for brands may pose a challenge to marketers in the new millennium, but given the recent mergers and acquisition trend in Europe, assessing how much brands are worth helps management to see the link between the money spent on acquiring a brand and the value created. Brand accounting makes sense as it gets managers to consider how they might manage the acquired brand as an asset that the company has paid, often handsomely, for.[13] For example, Germany's Mannesmann paid nearly £20 billion for the mobile phone brand Orange. Britain's Vodafone AirTouch acquired Mannesmann for $190 billion. Volkswagen snapped up Rolls-Royce Motor Cars Ltd for £479 million. Unilever paid $2.3 billion for SlimFast, a US dietary food company. Nestlé paid £2.5 billion to buy Rowntree. According to one estimate, the brand equity of Marlboro is $47 billion, Coca-Cola $48 billion and IBM $18 billion. Other brands rating among the world's most valuable include Microsoft, Nokia, Intel and McDonald's (see Marketing Highlight 13.1).[14]

High brand equity provides a company with many competitive advantages. A powerful brand enjoys a high level of consumer brand awareness and loyalty, and the company will incur lower marketing costs relative to revenues. Because consumers expect stores to carry the brand, the company has more leverage in bargaining with retailers. Because the brand name carries high credibility, the company can more easily launch line and brand extensions, as when Lever Brothers leveraged its well-known

marketing highlight 13.1

The world's billion-dollar brands

Companies around the world invest large amounts of money each year to create awareness and preference for their top brands. Powerful brand names command strong consumer loyalty and provide competitive advantage in the marketplace. Those that become 'superbrands' achieve instant recognition among the majority of the population, at home and abroad.

What are the world's most valuable brands? Interbrand, a branding consultancy, analyses economic earnings forecasts for the world's best-known brands and translate those forecasts into brand valuations. The brand's economic earning is estimated using publicly available marketing and financial information and is equal to the brand's future operating profits minus a capital and a 35 per cent tax charge. Then Interbrand calculates the proportion of that figure that is attributable to the brand by applying a 'role of branding' index to the earnings figure, based on its own assessment of the role played by brands in different markets. Then, to reflect the amount of risk, it applies a discount

to the earnings. The method of analysis means that private companies' brands where information is unavailable (e.g. Levi's, Lego, Mars) or firms where earnings are not generated in the accepted sense (e.g. Visa, MasterCard, the BBC) are omitted.

In 2000, Interbrand identified the billion-dollar brands – 75 names in total that exceeded the $1 billion (€1.12 billion) threshold. The consultancy puts Coca-Cola and Microsoft as arch rivals in the race to top of the 'billion-dollar brand' league table. Although Coca-Cola still heads the league table, its rapid decline in value (–13 per cent over the year), is remarkable for an icon that once looked invincible!

Interbrand's valuations show that some 'old economy' brands have lost their value as 'new economy' brands have gained. Kodak, Heinz, Xerox, Hertz, Burger King, Johnnie Walker, Guinness and Pampers all showed declines. Interbrand found that many 'new economy' brands showed double digit percentage gains in value, and technology companies currently account for four of the top five brands. Ericsson's value is estimated to have plunged some 47 per cent, reflecting the outstanding

The billion dollar brands

Rank 2000 (1999)	Brand	Country	Brand Value 2000 ($bn)	Brand Value 1999 ($bn)	% Change	Rank 2000 (1999)	Brand	Country	Brand Value 2000 ($bn)	Brand Value 1999 ($bn)	% Change
1 (1)	Coca-Cola	US	72.5	83.8	−13	39 (−)	SAP	Germany	6.1	*	*
2 (2)	Microsoft	US	70.2	56.7	24	40 (43)	Ikea	Sweden	6.0	**	**
3 (3)	IBM	US	53.2	43.8	21	41 (−)	Duracell	US	5.9	*	*
4 (7)	Intel	US	39.0	30.0	30	42 (−)	Philips	Netherlands	5.5	*	*
5 (11)	Nokia	Finland	38.5	20.7	86	43 (−)	Samsung	S. Korea	5.2	*	*
6 (4)	General Electric	US	38.1	33.5	14	44 (−)	Gucci	Italy	5.2	*	*
7 (5)	Ford	US	36.4	33.2	10	45 (33)	Kleenex	US	5.1	4.6	12
8 (6)	Disney	US	33.6	32.8	4	46 (−)	Reuters	UK	4.9	*	*
9 (8)	McDonald's	US	27.9	26.2	6	47 (35)	AOL	US	4.5	4.3	5
10 (9)	AT&T	US	25.5	24.2	6	48 (57)	Amazon.com	US	4.5	1.4	233
11 (10)	Marlboro	US	22.1	21.0	5	49 (39)	Motorola	US	4.4	3.6	22
12 (12)	Mercedes	Germany	21.1	17.8	19	50 (41)	Colgate	US	4.4	3.6	24
13 (14)	Hewlett-Packard	US	20.6	17.1	20	51 (34)	Wrigley's	US	4.3	4.4	−2
14 (−)	Cisco Systems	US	20.0	*	*	52 (44)	Chanel	France	4.1	3.1	32
15 (20)	Toyota	Japan	18.9	12.3	53	53 (40)	Adidas	Germany	3.8	3.6	5
16 (25)	Citibank	US	18.9	**	**	54 (−)	Panasonic	Japan	3.7	*	*
17 (15)	Gillette	US	17.4	15.9	9	55 (50)	Rolex	Switzerland	3.6	2.4	47
18 (18)	Sony	Japan	16.4	14.2	15	56 (42)	Hertz	US	3.4	3.5	−3
19 (19)	American Express	US	16.1	12.6	28	57 (46)	Bacardi	Bermuda	3.2	2.9	10
20 (24)	Honda	Japan	15.2	11.1	37	58 (45)	BP	UK	3.1	3.0	3
21 (−)	Compaq	US	14.6	*	*	59 (48)	Moët & Chandon	France	2.8	2.8	0
22 (13)	Nescafé	Switzerland	13.7	**	**	60 (49)	Shell	UK	2.8	2.7	4
23 (22)	BMW	Germany	13.0	11.3	15	61 (47)	Burger King	UK	2.7	2.8	−4
24 (16)	Kodak	US	11.9	14.8	−20	62 (51)	Smirnoff	UK	2.4	2.3	6
25 (21)	Heinz	US	11.8	11.8	−1	63 (38)	Barbie	US	2.3	**	**
26 (27)	Budweiser	US	10.7	8.5	26	64 (52)	Heineken	Netherlands	2.2	2.2	2
27 (23)	Xerox	US	9.7	11.2	−14	65 (−)	Wall Street Journal	US	2.2	*	*
28 (26)	Dell	US	9.5	9.0	5	66 (54)	Ralph Lauren/Polo	US	1.8	1.6	11
29 (29)	Gap	US	9.3	7.9	18	67 (55)	Johnnie Walker	UK	1.5	1.6	−6
30 (28)	Nike	US	8.0	8.2	−2	68 (58)	Hilton	UK/US	1.5	1.3	12
31 (31)	Volkswagen	Germany	7.8	6.6	19	69 (−)	Jack Daniels	US	1.5	*	*
32 (17)	Ericsson	Sweden	7.8	14.8	−47	70 (−)	Armani	Italy	1.5	*	*
33 (30)	Kellogg's	US	7.4	7.1	4	71 (56)	Pampers	US	1.4	1.4	−2
34 (37)	Louis Vuitton	France	6.9	4.1	69	72 (−)	Starbucks	US	1.3	*	*
35 (32)	Pepsi-Cola	US	6.6	5.9	12	73 (59)	Guinness	UK	1.2	1.3	−3
36 (36)	Apple	US	6.6	4.3	54	74 (−)	Financial Times	UK	1.1	*	*
37 (−)	MTV	US	6.4	*	*	75 (−)	Benetton	Italy	1.0	*	*
38 (53)	Yahoo!	US	6.3	1.8	258						

* new entry ** not comparable due to change in availability of data.
SOURCE: Interbrand/Citibank

Table 1 The world's top 75 brands

performance of Nokia, its biggest rival. Even so, dotcom companies have yet to make much impact because few have global scale or foreseeable earnings, according to the Interbrand study. The only online brands in their league table are AOL, Yahoo! and Amazon.com. The latter two Internet brands showed a remarkable three-digit growth in value. Newcomers include media properties like the Financial Times, Wall Street Journal and MTV, Internet equipment maker Cisco Systems, and German software group SAP.

Nearly all brands that lost value belonged to the food, drink or consumer packaged-goods businesses: many of the lowest gainers include McDonald's, Marlboro, Gillette, Nestlé, Unilever, Diageo and Kellogg's (see Table 1). The results may send some shivers down the spine of these 'old economy' companies. Coca-Cola's 13 per cent slide in value in just one year raises one critical question for every brand manager – 'Just how immortal are brands, even the world's seemingly most powerful brands?'. Time now for brand owners to think how to 'bite back' as the new economy unfolds.

SOURCES: Louella Miles, 'Brands of gold', *Marketing Business* (December/January 2000), pp. 18–21; Richard Tomkins, 'Coca-Cola loses its fizz', *Financial Times* (18 July 2000), p. 17; see also 'Leaders of the pack', *Financial Times* (18 July 2000), p. 17; 'Brands bite back', *The Economist* (21 March 1998), p. 98.

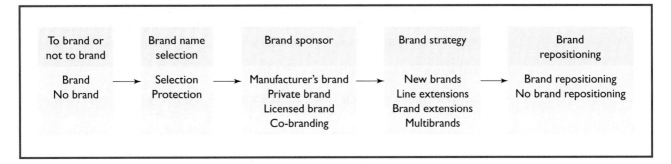

To brand or not to brand	Brand name selection	Brand sponsor	Brand strategy	Brand repositioning
Brand No brand	Selection Protection	Manufacturer's brand Private brand Licensed brand Co-branding	New brands Line extensions Brand extensions Multibrands	Brand repositioning No brand repositioning

Figure 13.3

Major branding decisions

Persil brand to introduce dishwashing detergent. Above all, a powerful brand offers the company some defence against fierce price competition.

Marketers need to manage their brands carefully in order to preserve brand equity. In order to maintain or improve brand awareness, perceived brand quality and usefulness, and positive brand associations over time, they need to work with R&D to provide a constant flow of improved and innovative products to satisfy customers' changing needs. Investment in skilful advertising and excellent trade and consumer service is also necessary. Some companies appoint 'brand equity managers' to guard their brands' images, associations and quality. They work to prevent brand managers from overpromoting brands in order to produce short-term profits at the expense of long-term brand equity.

Some analysts see brands as *the* most enduring asset of a company, outlasting the company's specific products and facilities. Yet, behind every powerful brand stands a set of loyal customers. Therefore, the basic asset underlying brand equity is *customer equity*. This suggests that the proper focus of marketing planning is that of extending *loyal customer lifetime value*, with brand management serving as an essential marketing tool.

Branding poses challenging decisions to the marketer. Figure 13.3 shows the key branding decisions. We will examine each of these in turn.

■ To brand or not to brand

The company must first decide whether it should put a brand name on its product. Branding has become so strong that today hardly anything goes unbranded. Salt is packaged in branded containers, common nuts and bolts are packaged with a distributor's label, and automotive parts – spark plugs, tyres, filters – bear brand names that differ from those of the carmakers. Even fruit and vegetables are branded – Sunkist oranges, Del Monte pineapples and Chiquita bananas.

Some products, however, carry no brands. 'Generic' products are unbranded, plainly packaged, less expensive versions of common products ranging from such items as spaghetti to paper towels and canned peaches. They often bear only black-stencilled labels and offer prices as much as 40 per cent lower than those of main brands. The lower price is made possible by lower-quality ingredients, lower-cost packaging and lower advertising costs.

Despite the limited popularity of generics, the issue of whether or not to brand is very much alive today. This situation highlights some key questions: Why have branding in the first place? Who benefits? How do they benefit? At what cost?

Branding helps buyers in many ways:

✦ Brand names tell the buyer something about product quality. Buyers who always buy the same brand know that they will get the same quality each time they buy.

✦ Brand names also increase the shopper's efficiency. Imagine a buyer going into a supermarket and finding thousands of generic products.

+ Brand names help call consumers' attention to new products that might benefit them. The brand name becomes the basis upon which a whole story can be built about the new product's special qualities.

Branding also gives the supplier several advantages:

+ The brand name makes it easier for the supplier to process orders and track down problems.

+ The supplier's brand name and trademark provide legal protection for unique production features that otherwise might be copied by competitors.

+ Branding enables the supplier to attract a loyal and profitable set of customers.

+ Branding helps the supplier to segment markets. For example, Cadbury can offer Dairy Milk, Milk Tray, Roses, Flake, Fruit and Nut and many other brands, not just one general confectionery product for all consumers.

Branding also adds value to consumers and society:

+ Those who favour branding suggest that it leads to higher and more consistent product quality.

+ Branding also increases innovation by giving producers an incentive to look for new features that can be protected against imitating competitors. Thus, branding results in more product variety and choice for consumers.

+ Branding helps shoppers because it provides much more information about products and where to find them.

■ Brand name selection

Selecting the right name is a crucial part of the marketing process. A good name can add greatly to a product's success. However, finding the best brand name is a difficult task. It begins with a careful review of the product and its benefits, the target market and proposed marketing strategies.

Desirable qualities for a brand name include the following:

1. It should suggest something about the product's benefits and qualities. Examples: Pro-active (a cholesterol-lowering margarine); Oasis (a still fruit drink), Kleenex (tissue paper), Frisp (a light savoury snack), TimeOut (a chocolate biscuit to go with coffee or tea breaks).

2. It should be easy to pronounce, recognise and remember. Short names help. Examples: Dove (soap), Yale (security products), Hula Hoops (potato crisps shaped like the name). But longer ones are sometimes effective. Examples: 'I Can't Believe It's Not Butter' margarine, Better Business Bureau.

3. The brand name should be distinctive. Examples: Shell, Kodak, Virgin.

4. The name should translate easily (and meaningfully) into foreign languages. For example, in Chinese Ferrari is pronounced as 'fa li li', the Chinese symbols for which mean 'magic, weapon, pull, power', which flatter the brand. But accountancy firm Price Waterhouse was reported to have been translated as 'expensive water closet'.

5. It should be capable of registration and legal protection. A brand name cannot be registered if it infringes on existing brand names. Also, brand names that are merely descriptive or suggestive may be unprotectable. For example, the Miller Brewing Company registered the name Lite for its low-calorie beer and invested millions in establishing the name with consumers. But the courts later ruled that the terms *lite* and *light* are generic or common descriptive terms applied to beer and that Miller could not use the Lite name exclusively.[15]

Finding a name for a product designed for worldwide markets is not easy. Companies must avoid the pitfalls inherent in injudicious product naming.

Once chosen, the brand name must be registered with the appropriate Trade Marks Register, giving owners intellectual property rights and preventing competitors from using the same or similar name. Many firms try to build a brand name that will eventually become identified with the product category. Brand names such as Hoover, Kleenex, Levi's, Scotch Tape, Post-it Notes, Formica and Fiberglas have succeeded in this way. However, their very success may threaten the company's rights to the name. Many originally protected brand names, such as cellophane, aspirin, nylon, kerosene, linoleum, yo-yo, trampoline, escalator, thermos and shredded wheat, are now names that any seller can use.[16]

■ Brand sponsor

A manufacturer has four sponsorship options. The product may be launched as a **manufacturer's brand** (or national brand), as when Lever Brothers, Nestlé and IBM sell their output under their own manufacturer's brand names. Or the manufacturer may sell to intermediaries that give it a **private brand** (also called *retailer brand*, *distributor brand* or *store brand*). For example, Cott, a Canadian company, makes store-branded foods and drinks, and supplies to retailers worldwide. Although most manufacturers create their own brand names, others market **licensed brands**. For example, some apparel and accessories sellers pay large fees to put the names or initials of fashion innovators such as Calvin Klein, Pierre Cardin and Gucci on their products. Finally, companies can join forces and **co-brand** a product.

Manufacturers' brands versus private brands   Manufacturers' brands have long dominated the retail scene. In recent times, however, an increasing number of supermarkets, department and discount stores, and appliance dealers have developed their own private brands. These private brands are often hard to establish and costly to stock and promote. However, intermediaries develop private labels because they can be profitable. They can often locate manufacturers with excess capacity that will produce the private label at a low cost, resulting in a higher profit margin for the intermediary. Private brands also give intermediaries exclusive products that cannot be bought from competitors, resulting in higher store traffic and loyalty. An example of a retailer that has a private brand is Marks & Spencer, with its St Michael label. In Sainsbury's supermarkets, the store's own brand of laundry detergents, called Novon, is marketed alongside products produced by P&G and Lever Brothers.

Manufacturer's brand (national brand)
A brand created and owned by the producer of a product or service.

Private brand (middleman, distributor or store brand)
A brand created and owned by a reseller of a product or service.

Licensed brand
A product or service using a brand name offered by the brand owner to the licensee for an agreed fee or royalty.

Co-brand
The practice of using the established brand names of two different companies on the same product.

The competition between manufacturers' and private brands is called the *battle of the brands*. In this battle, intermediaries have many advantages. They control what products they stock, where they go on the shelf and which ones they will feature in local circulars. They even charge manufacturers *slotting fees* – payments demanded by retailers before they will accept new products and find 'slots' for them on the shelves. Intermediaries can give their own store brands better display space and make certain they are better stocked. They price store brands lower than comparable manufacturers' brands, thereby appealing to budget-conscious shoppers, especially in difficult economic times. As store brands improve in quality and as consumers gain confidence in their store chains, store brands are posing a strong challenge to manufacturers' brands (see Marketing Highlight 13.2).

Licensing   Most manufacturers take years and spend millions to create their own brand names. However, some companies license names or symbols previously created by other manufacturers, names of celebrities, and characters from popular movies and books – for a fee, any of these can provide an instant and proven brand name. Apparel and accessories sellers pay large royalties to adorn their products – from blouses to ties, and linens to luggage – with the names or initials of well-known fashion innovators such as Calvin Klein, Gucci, Tommy or Armani.

Sellers of children's products attach an almost endless list of character names to clothing, toys, school supplies, linens, dolls, lunch boxes, cereals and other items. The character names include such classics as Disney's Mickey and Minnie Mouse, Peanuts, Barbie, the Flintstones, Winnie the Pooh and Sesame Street to the more recent Teletubbies, Pokémon and Powerpuff Girls.

Corporate brand licensing

A form of licensing whereby a firm rents a corporate trademark or logo made famous in one product or service category and uses it in a related category.

The fastest-growing licensing category is **corporate brand licensing** – renting a corporate trademark or logo made famous in one category and using it in a related category. Some examples include Cosmopolitan underwear, swimwear and home furnishings, Royal Ascot ties, hats, cashmere socks and jewellery, Porsche sunglasses and accessories.

Name and character licensing has become a big business in recent years. More and more for-profit and non-profit organisations are licensing their names to generate additional revenues and brand recognition. Coca-Cola's licensing programme has met with extraordinary success. It consists of a department overseeing more than 240 licences and at least 10,000 products, ranging from baby clothes and boxer shorts to earrings and even a fishing lure shaped like a tiny Coke can. Even the Vatican engages in licensing: heavenly images from its art collection, architecture, frescoes and manuscripts are now imprinted on such earthy objects as T-shirts, ties, glassware, candles and ornaments.[17]

marketing highlight 13.2

The battle for the brands

Many consumer packaged-goods companies across the world have struggled of late against a background of falling stock prices. Between June 1998 and January 2000, Unilever's £51 billion (€85.6 billion) stockmarket value shrank by almost £20 billion (€33.6 billion). Danone's shares have fallen from a peak of €280 in the summer of 1998 to €214 in February 2000. American food manufacturers, including household names like Heinz, Kellogg's and Campbell Soup, have all suffered too, underperforming the American stockmarket by 30 per cent or more in the past two years.

Not only do these companies have to cope with declining market values, they also face falling prices, stiff competition from private-label products and

Own brands versus manufacturers' brands: witness here the essence of the 'product lookalike' threat confronting brand owners in the UK grocery and packaged goods market.

Source: Marketing Week

difficulties in innovating in overcrowded markets. Until the 1970s, consumer branded-goods manufacturers like Unilever and Procter & Gamble, who owned strong brands, controlled the relationship between themselves and their retailers. Over the 1980s and 1990s, things changed as big multiple retailers such as Sainsbury and Tesco in the UK, Wal-Mart in the US, Carrefour in France, Delhaize in Belgium and other supermarket chains across Europe began to act like manufacturers, putting their own private-labels on the products they sold. They also recognised that consumers were increasingly prepared to buy stores' own-label products if they were offered at an attractive price at no expense to quality. 'Good value for money own-labels' quickly offered retailers profitable alternatives to manufacturers' brands.

Retailers also started to increase their efficiency by investing in checkout scanners, IT and database technologies. These enabled them to know more about what products were moving off the shelves and what their customers wanted than the branded goods manufacturers themselves. These retailers also learnt how to advertise and promote their own labels, just like branded goods manufacturers. Moreover, they learnt how to create stronger store and private brand values through relationship marketing. These events tilted the balance of power firmly in favour of the mighty retail chains.

More recently, retail giants are consolidating. Mergers (e.g. the US Wal-Mart's takeover of Britain's Asda, the merger between Carrefour and Promodés of France) will result in an industry dominated by five to six global groups in the future. The perennial battle between retailers and manufacturers is not quite over. Instead, a new phase has begun. Manufacturers are seemingly fighting back. Some, like Unilever, are busy 'shrinking' to grow. Unilever plans to reduce the number of brands in the Group's portfolio from 1,600 to 400 as part of a strategy to achieve stronger

brand focus. The big brand manufacturers know that they need to achieve a similar scale to maintain their bargaining power with the increasingly large retailers. This means developing or building (or adding through mergers and acquisitions) global brands so strong that retailers cannot afford to ignore them. Unilever's recent purchase of Bestfoods (mostly for its Knorr soups and sauces and Hellmann's salad dressings), Ben & Jerry's Homemade (ice-cream) and SlimFast Foods aims to do just this – grow a stable of global brands.

Manufacturers are also experimenting with ways to bypass retailers. Firms are creating their own channels and outlets. For example, Unilever's Myhome, a home cleaning service, visits people's homes and does the cleaning and laundry, using the company's branded detergents, hence bypassing the retailer. Unilever has opened café-style tea houses called Ch'a. Café Nestlé is a chain of coffee houses opened by Nestlé. Then there is the Internet. Heinz Direct offers to ship cases of Heinz tomato ketchup, baked beans and soups to almost any destination in the world! P&G's Reflect.com, an online beauty care business, allows women to design their own beauty products and order for home delivery.

Although there are obstacles to overcome in operating profitable Web-based business-to-consumer (B2C) retailing services, brand manufacturers, undeterred, continue to experiment. Meanwhile, they know that scale is the name of the game. Web-based alliances are being exploited to gain massive supply-chain efficiencies. For example, some 49 of the world's biggest consumer goods companies have recently invested $250 million (€297.5 million) to create Transora, a global online business-to-business (B2B) marketplace, for coordinating procurement of raw materials, packaging, supplies and services.

In a sense, although retailers have begun to think and act like manufacturers, so too are manufacturers beginning to act like retailers. The battle rages on. Winners will follow one simple rule – success through delivering superior value to target customers. Ultimately, consumer franchise is the name of the game!

Sources: Jeremy Braune, 'The brand bond', *Marketing Business* (October 1999), pp. 46–7; 'Branded goods (1). Shrinking to grow', *The Economist* (26 February 2000), pp. 100–4; Richard Tomkins, 'Manufacturers strike back', *Financial Times* (16 June 2000), p. 16; Laura Mazur, 'Brands', *Marketing Business* (June 1997), p. 31; Alan Mitchell, 'Suppliers face tricky new remit', *Marketing Week* (8 May 1997), pp. 34–5; Cyndee Miller, 'Big brands fight back against private labels', *Marketing News* (16 January 1995), pp. 8–9; Haari Laaksonen, *Own Brands in Food Retailing across Europe* (Oxford: Oxford Institute of Retail Management, 1994).

Figure 13.4

Four brand strategies

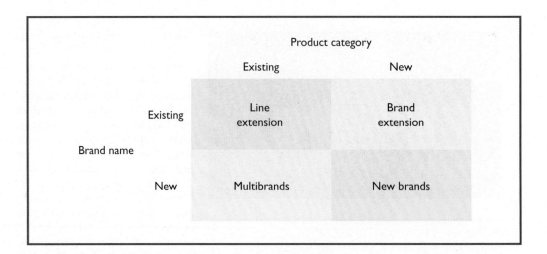

Co-branding   Although companies have been co-branding products for many years, there has been a recent resurgence in co-branded products. Co-branding occurs when two established brand names of different companies are used on the same product or service. Co-branding partners seek to mutually enhance each other's service or product brand through close association. For example, Kellogg's joined forces with ConAgra to co-brand Kellogg's Healthy Choice cereals. In most co-branding situations, one company licenses another company's well-known brand to use in combination with its own.

Co-branding offers many advantages. Because each brand dominates in a different category, the combined brands create broader consumer appeal and greater brand equity. Co-branding also allows companies to enter new markets with minimal risk or investment. For example, by licensing its Healthy Choice brand to Kellogg, ConAgra entered the breakfast segment with a solid product. In return, Kellogg could leverage the broad awareness of the Healthy Choice name in the cereal category.

Co-branding also has its limitations. If a company chooses the wrong partner, or the partner suffers a setback or bad publicity, the company will be tainted by the association. In addition, such relationships usually involve complex legal contracts and licences. Co-branding partners must carefully coordinate their advertising, sales promotion and other marketing efforts. Finally, when co-branding, each partner must trust that the other will take good care of its brand.[18]

■ Brand strategy

A company must define its overall branding strategy, which affects all of its products. This strategy will also guide the branding of new products. A company has four choices when it comes to brand strategy (see Figure 13.4). It can introduce *line extensions* (existing brand names extended to new forms, sizes and flavours of an existing product category), *brand extensions* (existing brand names extended to new product categories), *multibrands* (new brand names introduced in the same product category) or *new brands* (new brand names in new product categories).

Line extension

Using a successful brand name to introduce additional items in a given product category under the same brand name, such as new flavours, forms, colours, added ingredients or package sizes.

Line extensions   Line extensions occur when a company introduces additional items in a given product category under the same brand name, such as new flavours, forms, colours, ingredients or package sizes. Thus, Danone has added several new flavours to its yoghurt line, as well as fat-free and large, family/economy-size varieties.

The vast majority of new-product activity consists of line extensions. A company introduces line extensions in order to meet consumers' desires for variety, utilise excess capacity or simply to command more shelf-space from resellers. Or it might recognise a latent consumer want and try to capitalise on it. However, line extensions involve some risks. The brand name might lose its specific meaning – some marketing strategists call this the 'line-extension trap'.[19] In the past, when consumers asked for a Coke, they received a six-ounce bottle of the classic beverage. Today the vendor has to ask: New, Classic, or Cherry Coke? Regular or diet? Caffeine or caffeine free? Bottle or can?

Heavily extended brands can also cause consumer confusion or frustration. A consumer buying cereal at a supermarket will be confronted by more than 150 brands, up to 30 different brands, flavours and sizes of oatmeal alone. By itself, Quaker offers its original Quaker Oats, several flavours of Quaker instant oatmeal, and several dry cereals such as Oatmeal Squares, Toasted Oatmeal and Toasted Oatmeal-Honey Nut.

Another risk is that many line extensions will not sell enough to cover their development and promotion costs. Or even when they sell enough, the sales may come at the expense of other items in the line. A line extension works best when it takes sales away from competing brands, not when it 'cannibalises' the company's other items.[20]

Brand extensions   A **brand-extension** (or brand-stretching) strategy is any effort to use a successful brand name to launch new or modified products in a new category. Swiss Army Brand sunglasses is a brand extension. Procter & Gamble put its Fairy name on laundry powder and dishwashing detergent with effective results. Swatch spread from watches into telephones. And Honda stretched its company name to cover such different products as its cars, motorcycles, lawnmowers, marine engines and snowmobiles.

> **Brand extension**
> *Using a successful brand name to launch a new or modified product in a new category.*

A brand-extension strategy offers many advantages. First, brand extensions capture greater market share and realise greater advertising efficiency than individual brands.[21] Second, a well-regarded brand name helps the company enter new product categories more easily as it gives a new product instant recognition and faster acceptance. Sony puts its name on most of its new electronic products, creating an instant perception of high quality for each new product. Thus, brand extensions also save the high advertising cost usually required to familiarise consumers with a new brand name.

At the same time, a brand-extension strategy involves some risk. Brand extensions such as Bic pantyhose, Heinz pet food and Cadbury soup met early deaths. In each case, the brand name was not appropriate to the new product, even though it was well made and satisfying. Brand extensions fail if the established brand name is launched into a very different market from the original brand and target customers in the new market did not value the brand's associations. Would you consider buying Chanel galoshes? Or a Pepsi single malt whisky?

A brand name may also lose its special positioning in the consumer's mind through overuse. *Brand dilution* occurs when consumers no longer associate a brand with a specific product or even highly similar products. Business observers, for example, have questioned the 'elasticity' of the Virgin name. Richard Branson has extended the Virgin name, which appears on a huge range of disparate products, ranging from music and entertainment media shops, airlines, mobile phones and Internet services to personal financial services, cosmetics, cola drinks, vodka and bridal wear. They wonder if Virgin may run the risk of overusing the brand's power of quality, innovation, value for money and fun, and its emotional 'take on the big bullies and give you something better' associations.

Transferring an existing brand name to a new customer segment or product group requires great care (see Marketing Highlight 13.3). The best result is one when the extension enhances the core brand and builds the sales of both current and new products. Companies that are tempted to transfer a brand name must research whether the brand's associations fit the new product.[22]

Multibrands   Companies such as Lever Brothers, Mars and Procter & Gamble create individual brand identities for each of their products. Lever's line of laundry detergents – Persil, Surf, Radion, etc. – have distinct labels, with the corporate name hardly featured. Similarly, Procter & Gamble produces at least nine brands of laundry products.

marketing highlight 13.3

From JCB Juniors to Harley-Davidson armchairs: brand extensions are the rage

When BMW bought the Rolls-Royce name – nothing else, just the *name* – for £40 million (€65.6 million), it confirmed what savvy investors have always known: a strong brand name is one of the most valuable assets a company has. Now companies are realising that they should not confine such assets only to products in their own traditional product categories. Instead, more and more companies, from the Fortune 500 to the not-for-profit sector, are extending their names to generate additional brand recognition and revenues. That's why we are suddenly seeing products like Royal Doulton perfume, Coca-Cola Picnic Barbie, JCB outdoor clothing and even Harley-Davidson armchairs and baby clothes.

Most companies have long sold promotional merchandise bearing their names and logos to dealers and distributors. However, companies are making a shift to leverage their brands both to capitalise on brand awareness in current markets and to extend or stretch their brands into new markets. For example, through licensing arrangements, leading earth-moving and construction equipment manufacturers such as JCB, Caterpillar and John Deere, companies with narrow markets, have extended their brand to a wide range of products aimed at generating additional sales among those already hooked on their brands.

JCB has extended its brand's appeal beyond their industrial heritage to fashion-conscious young people, children and DIY enthusiasts. JCB's market research shows that the JCB brand epitomises 'yellow', 'digger' and 'durable', values that existing customers, children and adults associated with the brand. Whereas adults saw the brand as a British one of quality and functionality, kids saw it as big, muddy and 'fun'. Taking these values and associations into account, and through close ongoing partnerships with selected licensees, the company created JCB Works, a line of outdoor and rugged clothing such as combat trousers, fleece and funnel-neck jumpers, footwear and sports equipment. All are designed to reflect urban credibility, strength, integrity and functionality. JCB Juniors comprise a range of reliable and built-to-last toys which emphasise a return to traditional values. The theme for the kids' range is 'dads and lads' and tries to capture the spirit of learning, play and fun. The JCB Sitemaster, the name of the actual JCB digger, comprises a range of DIY quality power tools, outdoor power products and hand tools.

Thus, although a JCB child's overall may seem a strange item for the brand to end up on, like other unlikely products such as Harley-Davidson armchairs and Royal Doulton perfumes, brand extensions are a company's way of reaching out to new targets. In JCB's case, the idea is to extend the relationship with consumers by appealing to them from an early age. In Harley's case, it is to attract women, who make up only 9 per cent of the company's market. Harley also extends to toys, including a Barbie doll dressed in a 'very feminine outfit' to appeal to future generations of Harley purchasers. The ultimate goal is to sell more bikes to buyers who are not part of the core market.

Brand extensions work so long as the extension does not muddy the image of what the brand stands for. Extensions like Disney's spread from cartoon films to publishing, theme parks, hotels and cruises worked because the operations are united by the idea of family entertainment. To a great extent, Richard Branson could stretch his Virgin brand because Virgin stood for his renegade, 'we're on your side' approach rather than a specific product or service.

However, many tobacco companies are having to diversify their brands since the health risks of smoking became known and tobacco sales are declining. There are all sorts of products cigarette brands have ended up in: there are Benson and Hedges cafés, Camel clothing and Dunhill eau de toilette. But what do you make of a Marlboro Hotel, even if it offered non-smoking rooms? Or a Marlboro mobile phone – so you can talk, not smoke, while you drive?

SOURCES: Claire Irvin, 'From crib to consumer', *Marketing Business* (March 2000), pp. 17–19; Richard Tomkins, 'Brands set to light up tobacco company sales', *Financial Times* (7 March 2000), p. 30; Peter Law, 'True grit', *Marketing Business* (June 2000), pp. 35–7; Alison Smith, 'Moving out of the shadows', *Financial Times* (5 June 1998), p. 15.

These manufacturers argue that a **multibrand strategy** – managing a stable of brand names within the same product category – permits finer segmentation of the market, with each brand name suggesting different functions or benefits appealing to different buying motives of different customer segments.

Some companies develop multiple brands, not for individual products, but for different families of products. For example, the Japanese electronics group Matsushita has opted to use **range branding** and developed separate range names for its audio product families – Technics, National, Panasonic and Quasar.

A major drawback of multibranding is that each brand might obtain only a small market share, and none may be very profitable. The company may end up spreading its resources over many brands instead of building a few brands to a highly profitable level. These companies should reduce the number of brands they sell in a given category and set up tighter screening procedures for new brands.

The multibranding approach contrasts with the **corporate branding** strategy. In corporate branding, the firm makes its company name the dominant brand identity across all of its products, as in the case of Mercedes-Benz, Philips and Heinz. The main advantages are economies of scale in marketing investments and wider recognition of the brand name. It also facilitates introduction of new products, especially when the corporate name is well established.

Other companies have used a **company and individual branding** approach to naming their products. This approach focuses on both the corporate and individual brand names. Kellogg's (e.g. Cornflakes, Raisin Bran, Rice Krispies, Coco Pops, etc.), Nestlé (KitKat, Nescafé, Coffee Mate, etc.) and Cadbury's (e.g. Wispa, Flake, Roses, Fruit and Nut, Milk Tray, Wholenut, Dairy Milk) are supporters of this branding strategy.

New brands Firms that favour a multibrand approach are likely to create a new brand to differentiate a new product, whether it is introduced into an existing or a new-product category. However, for some companies, a new brand may be created because it is entering a new-product category for which none of the company's current brands seems appropriate. For example, Toyota established a separate family name – the Lexus – for its new luxury executive cars in order to create a distinctive identity for the latter and to position these well away from the traditional mass-market image of the 'Toyota' brand name. Alternatively, a company may be compelled to differentiate its new product, and a new brand is the best route to signal its identity. Seiko introduced a line of higher-priced watches (Seiko Lasalle) and lower-priced watches (Pulsar), which is used as a *flanker* or *fighter brand* aimed at customers who want a less expensive watch and to protect the flanks of its mainstream Seiko brand.

As with multibranding, offering too many brands can result in a company spreading its resources too thinly. And in some industries, such as consumer-packaged goods, consumers and retailers have become concerned that there are already too many brands, with too few differences between them. Thus, Procter & Gamble, Lever Brothers and other large consumer product marketers are now pursuing *megabrand* strategies – weeding out weaker brands and focusing their marketing dollars only on brands that can achieve the number-one or number-two market-share positions in their categories.

■ Brand repositioning

However well a brand is initially positioned in a market, the company may have to reposition it later. A competitor may launch a brand position next to the company's brand and cut into its market share. Or customer wants may shift, leaving the company's brand with less demand. Marketers should consider repositioning existing brands before introducing new ones in order to build on existing brand recognition and consumer loyalty.

Multibrand strategy
A strategy under which a seller develops two or more brands in the same product category.

Range branding strategy
A brand strategy whereby the firm develops separate product range names for different families of product.

Corporate brand strategy
A brand strategy whereby the firm makes its company name the dominant brand identity across all of its products.

Company and individual brand strategy
A branding approach that focuses on the company name and individual brand name.

In a competitive marketplace for imaging systems, HP Invent repositions itself as better than traditional photography reminding buyers that 'You still say cheese.'

SOURCE: Hewlett Packard.
Agency: Publicis/SF Goodbee

**You still say cheese.
That much is the same.**

Think of it as photography, part 2. No film, no developing, keep only the pictures you want, delete the rest. Print them at home, without a computer, or even cables. Or send them to everyone you know everywhere in the world from your pc right now. Make them, share them, store them, smile.

Digital images from hp. www.hp.com

Repositioning may require changing both the product and its image. For example, Kentucky Fried Chicken changed its menu, adding lower-fat skinless chicken, and non-fried items such as broiled chicken and chicken salad sandwiches to reposition itself towards more health-conscious fast-food consumers. It also changed its name to KFC. A brand can also be repositioned by changing only the product's image. For example, Bulmer, the United Kingdom's leading cider maker, successfully repositioned its mainstream brands, Strongbow and Woodpecker, by giving them a more contemporary lifestyle image, a marked contrast to cider's traditional rustic image. Bulmer spent over £10 million in a series of new advertising appeals to change consumer perceptions of these two brands.

A brand may also be radically repositioned to keep up with changing customer needs and competitive pressures.

In response to rising competition from designer labels and discount retailers, and notwithstanding years of under-investment, M&S was compelled to overhaul its brand. The UK retailer is now fighting back – the M&S brand is being updated to present a smarter image by changing everything, from labels to carrier bags, and van liveries to staff uniforms. The group's St. Michael brand no longer appears as part of the main brand but is relegated to a mark of quality, dubbed the 'St. Michael Promise'. The M&S brand has been updated on all labels, packaging, literature and clothing tags. Stores have been refurbished to present a new, fresh look.

Having looked at branding decisions, we now turn to another important product decision – packaging.

Packaging
The activities of designing and producing the container or wrapper for a product.

packaging decisions

Many products offered to the market have to be packaged. **Packaging** involves designing and producing the container or wrapper for a product. The package may include the product's primary container (the tube holding and protecting Colgate toothpaste);

CUSTER'S LAST STAND

GUNFIGHT AT THE O.K. CORRAL

STATUE OF LIBERTY UNVEILED

NEW YORK SUBWAY OPENS

FORD BUILDS MODEL T

WORLD WAR I ENDS

PROHIBITION

BONNIE AND CLYDE KILLED

MOUNT RUSHMORE COMPLETED

CUBAN MISSILE CRISIS

FIRST MOON LANDING

CLINTON RE-ELECTED

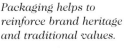

Packaging helps to reinforce brand heritage and traditional values.

Source: Budweiser, Anheuser-Busch Companies Ltd

a secondary package that is thrown away when the product is about to be used (the cardboard box containing the tube of Colgate); and the shipping package necessary to store, identify and ship the product (a corrugated box carrying six dozen tubes of Colgate toothpaste). Labelling, printed information appearing on or with the package, is also part of packaging.

In recent times, many factors, beyond containing and protecting the product, have made packaging an important marketing tool. Increased competition and clutter on retail store shelves means that packages must now perform many sales tasks – from attracting attention, to describing the product, to making the sale. Companies are realising the power of good packaging to create instant consumer recognition of the company or brand. For example, in an average supermarket, which stocks 15,000 to 17,000 items, the typical shopper passes by some 300 items per minute, and 53 per cent of all purchases are made on impulse. In this highly competitive environment, the package may be the seller's last chance to influence buyers. It becomes a 'five-second commercial'. Research shows that a sizeable chunk of buyers can be swayed at the last minute from buying their cat's favourite tin of tuna bites if their eye is caught by a well-designed, competitive brand. Hence, manufacturers must use pack design – shape, graphics and texture – to project their brand values and differentiate them in an overcrowded market. The package can also reinforce the product's positioning. Coca-Cola's familiar bottle speaks volumes about the product inside. According to a packaging expert, people taste Coke differently from a contour bottle versus a generic package.[23] Innovative packaging can give a company an advantage over competitors. For example, Perrier and Grolsch used creative packaging to differentiate the product and have enjoyed good market results.

Developing a good package for a new product requires making many decisions. The first task is to establish the **packaging concept**, which states what the package should *be* or *do* for the product. Should the main functions of the package be to offer product protection, introduce a new dispensing method, communicate certain qualities about the product, the brand or the company, or something else? Decisions, then, must be made on package design that cover specific elements of the package, such as size, shape, materials, colour, text and brand mark. These various elements must work

Packaging concept
What the package should be or do for the product.

together to support the product's position and marketing strategy and be consistent with the product's advertising, pricing and distribution.

In recent years, product safety has also become a major packaging concern. We have all learned to deal with hard-to-open 'childproof' packages. And after the rash of product tampering scares during the 1980s, most drug producers and food makers are now putting their products in tamper-resistant packages. In making packaging decisions, the company also must heed growing environmental concerns and make decisions that serve society's interests as well as immediate customer and company objectives. Shortages of paper, aluminium and other materials suggest that marketers should try to reduce packaging. Many packages end up as broken bottles and crumpled cans littering the streets and countryside. All of this packaging creates a major problem in solid waste disposal, requiring huge amounts of labour and energy.

Fortunately, many companies have gone 'green'. Tetra Pak, a major Swedish multinational, provides an example of the power of innovative packaging that takes environmental concerns into account.

> Tetra Pak invented an 'aseptic' package that enables milk, fruit juice and other
> perishable liquid foods to be distributed without refrigeration. Not only is this
> packaging more environmentally responsible, it also provides economic and
> distribution advantages. Aseptic packaging allows dairies to distribute milk over
> a wider area without investing in refrigerated trucks and facilities. Supermarkets
> can carry Tetra Pak packaged products on ordinary shelves, allowing them to save
> expensive refrigerator space. Tetra's motto is 'the package should save more than it
> cost'. Tetra Pak advertises the benefits of its packaging to consumers directly and
> even initiates recycling programmes to save the environment.

labelling decisions

Labels may range from simple tags attached to products to complex graphics that are part of the package. They perform several functions. At the very least, the label *identifies* the product or brand, such as the name 'Sunkist' stamped on oranges. The label might also *grade* the product, or *describe* several things about the product – who made it, where it was made, when it was made, its contents, how it is to be used and how to use it safely. Finally, the label might *promote* the product through attractive graphics.

There has been a long history of legal concerns about packaging and labels. Labels can mislead customers, fail to describe important ingredients or fail to include needed safety warnings. As a result, many countries have laws to regulate labelling. The EU, for example, has comprehensive European Community legislation, which set mandatory labelling requirements and adherence to packaging standards. For drinks, a new EU directive has been recently enforced which subjects both non-alcoholic and alcoholic beverage to stringent labelling requirements.[24]

Labelling has also been affected in recent times by *unit pricing* (stating the price per unit of standard measure), *open dating* (stating the expected shelf life of the product) and *nutritional labelling* (stating the nutritional values in the product). In the case of the latter, sellers are required to provide detailed nutritional information on food products. In some countries, the use of health-related terms such as *low-fat*, *light* and *high-fibre* is also regulated. As such, sellers must ensure that their labels contain all the required information and comply with national or international (e.g. US, EU) requirements.

product-support services decisions

Customer service is another element of product strategy. A company's offer to the marketplace usually includes some services, which can be a minor or a major part of the total offer. In fact, the offer can range from a pure good on the one hand to a pure service on the other. In Chapter 15, we will discuss services as products in themselves. Here, we address **product-support services** – services that augment actual products. More and more companies are using product-support services as a major tool in gaining competitive advantage.

Product-support services
Services that augment actual products.

Good customer service makes sound business sense. It costs less to keep the goodwill of existing customers than it does to attract new customers or woo back lost customers. A study comparing the performance of businesses that had high and low customer ratings of service quality found that the high-service businesses managed to charge more, grow faster and make more profits.[25] Clearly, marketers need to think about their service strategies.

A company should design its product and support services to meet the needs of target customers. Customers vary in the value they assign to different services. Some consumers want credit and financing services, fast and reliable delivery, or quick installation. Others put more weight on technical information and advice, training in product use, or after-sale service and repair. The first step in deciding which product-support services to offer is to determine both the services that target consumer value and the relative importance of these services.

Determining customers' service needs involves more than simply monitoring complaints that come in over freephone lines or on comment cards. The company should periodically survey its customers to assess the value of current services and to obtain ideas for new ones. Once the company has assessed the value of various services to customers, it must next assess the costs of providing these services. It can then develop a package of services that will both delight customers and yield profits to the company.

Many companies are now using the Internet to provide support services that were not possible before. For example, major international airlines such as American Airlines provide support websites for their frequent flier members. Members can streamline the booking process by creating profiles of their home airports, usual routes and seating and meal preferences for themselves and their families. Beyond using the site to book tickets, members can check the status of their frequent flier accounts and take advantage of special member fares. Moreover, using these profiles, the company can, say, offer discounts on flights to certain holiday destinations for parents whose children's school vacations start in a few weeks.[26]

product decisions and social responsibility

Product decisions have attracted much public attention in recent years. When making such decisions, marketers should consider carefully a number of public policy issues and regulations involving acquiring or dropping products, patent protection, product quality and safety and product warranties.

Regarding the addition of new products, national governments or competition authorities may prevent companies from adding products through acquisitions if the effect threatens to lessen competition. Companies dropping products must be aware that they have legal obligations, written or implied, to their suppliers, dealers and customers who have a stake in the discontinued product. Companies must also obey patent laws when developing new products. A company cannot make its product illegally similar to another company's established product.

In whichever country manufacturers market their products, they must comply with specific laws regarding product quality and safety which serve to protect consumers. For example, various Acts provide for the inspection of sanitary conditions in the meat- and poultry-processing industries. Safety legislation exists to regulate fabrics, chemical substances, automobiles, toys, drugs and poisons.

If consumers have been injured by a product that has been designed defectively, they can sue manufacturers or dealers. Product liability suits can lead to manufacturers paying victims awards that can run into millions of euros. Or, faulty products can cost the company money because of the need to recall and replace faulty merchandise. For example, in September 1999, Intel had to recall and scrap some one million motherboards because of a problem with Intel chips. The recall had cost Intel over $300 million (€357 million).[27] But some product defects can cost customers a great deal of anxiety or pain. Sagami Rubber Industries, a Japanese condom producer, had to withdraw from sale 850,000 multipack packets of its new polyurethane condoms (called Sagami Original) because invisible pinholes were found in the condoms. The recall cost the company $2.3 million, but imagine the misfortune awaiting unsuspecting users of the defective condoms![28]

product line decisions

We have looked at product strategy decisions such as branding, packaging, labelling and services for individual products. But product strategy also calls for building a product line. A **product line** is a group of products that are closely related because they function in a similar manner, are sold to the same customer groups, are marketed through the same types of outlet, or fall within given price ranges. For example, Volvo produces several lines of cars, Philips produces several lines of hi-fi systems and Nike produces several lines of athletic shoes. In formulating product line strategies, marketers face a number of tough decisions.

Product line
A group of products that are closely related because they function in a similar manner, are sold to the same customer groups, are marketed through the same types of outlet, or fall within given price ranges.

product line-length decisions

Product line managers have to decide on product line length – the number of items in the product line. The line is too short if the manager can increase profits by adding items; the line is too long if the manager can increase profits by dropping items. Product line length is influenced by company objectives and resources. Companies that want to be positioned as full-line companies, or that are seeking high market share and market growth, usually carry longer lines. Companies that are keen on high short-term profitability generally carry shorter lines consisting of selected items.

Figure 13.5

Product-line stretching decisions

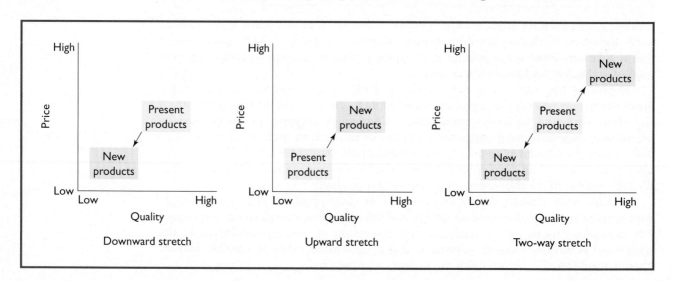

Product line stretching: DaimlerChrysler introduced several smaller, lower-priced models, including smart city-coupé, starting at €8405,64, smart is the innovative brand for the sub-a segment in the DaimlerChrysler group.

SOURCE: MCC
Smart GmbH
www.media.smart.com

Over time, product line managers tend to add new products. The manager may want to use up excess manufacturing capacity, or the sales force and distributors are calling for a more complete product line to satisfy their customers, or the firm needs to add items to the product line to increase sales and profits. However, as the manager adds items, several costs rise: design and engineering costs, inventory carrying costs, manufacturing changeover costs, order-processing costs, transportation costs, and promotional costs to introduce new items. Consequently, the company must plan product line growth carefully. It can systematically increase the length of its product line in two ways: by *stretching* its line and by *filling* its line. **Product line stretching** occurs when a company lengthens its product line beyond its current range. Figure 13.5 shows that the company can stretch its line downwards, upwards or both ways.

Product line stretching
Increasing the product line by lengthening it beyond its current range.

■ Downward stretch

Many companies initially locate at the upper end of the market and later stretch their lines downwards. A company may stretch downwards to plug a market hole that otherwise would attract a new competitor or to respond to a competitor's attack on the upper end. Or it may add low-end products because it finds faster growth taking place in the low-end segments.

Mercedes stretched downwards for all these reasons. Facing a slow-growth luxury car market and attacks by Japanese automakers on its high-end positioning, Mercedes successfully introduced its C-Class cars at €35,000 without harming its ability to sell other Mercedes for €100,000 or more. And in a joint venture with Switzerland's Swatch watchmaker, Mercedes launched the €12,000 Smart microcompact car, an environmentally correct second car. Just 2.3 metres long, and affectionately dubbed the 'Swatchmobile', the Smart is 'designed for two people and a crate of beer'.[29] Similarly, Compaq and IBM had to add less expensive personal computer lines to fend off competition from low-priced 'clones' and to take advantage of faster market growth in the lower end of the computer market.

■ Upward stretch

Companies at the lower end of the market may want to stretch their product lines *upwards*. Sometimes, companies stretch upwards in order to add prestige to their current products. They may be attracted by a faster growth rate or higher margins at the higher end, or they may simply want to position themselves as full-line manufacturers. Thus, Toyota, the leading Japanese auto company, introduced an up-market line – Lexus

– and used an entirely new name rather than its own name. Other companies have included their own names in moving up-market. For example, Gallo introduced Ernest and Julio Gallo Varietals and priced these wines at more than twice the price of its regular wines.[30]

An upward stretch decision can be risky. The higher-end competitors not only are well entrenched, but also may strike back by entering the lower end of the market. Prospective customers may not believe that the newcomer can produce quality products. Finally, the company's salespeople and distributors may lack the talent and training to serve the higher end of the market.

■ Two-way stretch

Companies in the middle range of the market may decide to stretch their lines in both directions. Sony did this to hold off copycat competitors of its Walkman line of personal tape players. Sony introduced its first Walkman in the middle of the market. As imitative competitors moved in with lower-priced models, Sony stretched downwards. At the same time, in order to add lustre to its lower-priced models and to attract more affluent consumers keen to trade up to a better model, Sony stretched the Walkman line upwards. It sells more than 100 models, ranging from a plain playback-only version for €30 to a high-tech, high-quality €550 version that both plays and records. Using this two-way stretch strategy, Sony came to dominate the global personal tape player market.

■ Product line-filling decisions

Product line filling
Increasing the product line by adding more items within the present range of the line.

An alternative to product line stretching is **product line filling** – adding more items within the present range of the line. There are several reasons for product line filling: reaching for extra profits, satisfying dealers, using excess capacity, being the leading full-line company, and plugging holes to keep out competitors. Thus Sony filled its line by adding solar-powered and waterproof Walkmans and an ultralight model that attaches to a sweatband for joggers, cyclists, tennis players and other exercisers. However, line filling is overdone if it results in cannibalisation and customer confusion. The company should, therefore, ensure that new items are *noticeably different* from existing ones.

product-mix decisions

Product mix (product assortment)
The set of all product lines and items that a particular seller offers for sale to buyers.

Some companies may offer, not one, but several lines of products which form a **product mix** or *product assortment*. For example, a cosmetics firm may have four main product lines in its product mix: cosmetics, jewellery, fashions and household items. Each product line may consist of sublines. For example, cosmetics beak down into lipstick, powder, nail varnish, eye-shadows and so on. Each line and subline may have many individual items. For example, eye-shadows contain a string of items, ranging from different colours to alternative application modes (e.g. pencil, roll-on, powder).

A company's product mix has four important dimensions: width, length, depth and consistency. For example, Procter & Gamble markets a fairly wide product mix consisting of many product lines, including paper, food, household cleaning, medicinal, cosmetics and personal care products. Product mix *length* refers to the total number of items the company carries within its product lines. P&G typically carries many brands within each line. For example, it sells eight laundry detergents, six hand soaps, six shampoos and four dishwashing detergents.

Product line *depth* refers to the number of versions offered of each product in the line. Thus, P&G's Crest toothpaste comes in three sizes and two formulations (paste and gel). Finally, the *consistency* of the product mix refers to how closely related the various product lines are in end use, production requirements, distribution channels or some other way. P&G's product lines are consistent insofar as they are consumer products that go through the same distribution channels. The lines are less consistent insofar as they perform different functions for buyers.

These product-mix dimensions provide the handles for defining the company's product strategy. The company can increase its business in four ways:

1. It can add new product lines, thus widening its product mix. In this way, its new lines build on the company's reputation in its other lines.

2. The company can lengthen its existing product lines to become a more full-line company.

3. It can add more product versions of each product and thus deepen its product mix.

4. The company can pursue more product line consistency, or less, depending on whether it wants to have a strong reputation in a single field or in several fields.

Having addressed the key product decisions facing marketers, we now turn to some of the key issues that marketers consider in making international product decisions.

international product decisions

International marketers face special product and packaging challenges. As discussed in Chapter 5, they must decide what products to introduce in which countries, and how much of the product to standardise or adapt for world markets. On the one hand, companies would like to standardise their offerings. Standardisation helps a company to develop a consistent worldwide image. It also lowers manufacturing costs and eliminates duplication of research and development, advertising and product design efforts. On the other hand, consumers around the world differ in their cultures, attitudes and buying behaviours. And markets vary in their economic conditions, competition, legal requirements and physical environments. Companies must usually respond to these differences by adapting their product offerings. Something as simple as an electrical outlet can create big product problems:

> Those who have travelled to Europe know the frustration of electrical plugs, different voltages, and other annoyances of international travel. . . . Philips, the electrical appliance manufacturer, has to produce 12 kinds of irons to serve just its European market. The problem is that Europe still lacks a universal [electrical] standard. The ends of irons bristle with different plugs for different countries. Some have three prongs, others two; prongs protrude straight or angled, round or rectangular, fat, thin, and sometimes sheathed. There are circular plug faces, squares, pentagons and hexagons. Some are perforated and some are notched. One French plug has a niche like a keyhole; British plugs carry fuses.[31]

Packaging also presents new challenges for international marketers. Packaging issues can be subtle. For example, names, labels and colours may not translate easily from one country to another. Consumers in different countries also vary in their packaging preferences. Europeans like efficient, functional, recyclable boxes with understated designs. In contrast, the Japanese often use packages as gifts. Thus in Japan, Lever Brothers packages its Lux soap in stylish gift boxes. Packaging may even have to be tailored to meet the physical characteristics of consumers in various parts of the world. For instance, soft drinks are sold in smaller cans in Japan to fit the smaller Japanese hand better.

Companies may have to adapt their packaging to meet specific regulations regarding package design or label contents. For instance, some countries ban the use of any foreign language on labels; other countries require that labels be printed in two or more languages. Labelling laws vary greatly from country to country. Thus, although product and package standardisation can produce benefits, the international company must usually modify its offerings to the unique needs of specific international markets.

In summary, whether domestic or international, product strategy calls for complex decisions on product line, product mix, branding, packaging and service support strategy. These decisions must be made not only with a full understanding of consumer wants and competitors' strategies, but also with considerable sensitivity to the broader, particularly regulatory, environment affecting product, packaging and labelling.

summary

The concept of a *product* is complex and can be viewed on three levels: the *core product*, the *actual product* and the *augmented product*. Marketers must develop a product strategy that calls for coordinated decisions on product items, product lines and the product mix.

The *core product* is the essential problem-solving benefit that the customer seeks when buying a product. The *actual product* exists around the core and includes the features, styling, design, quality level, brand name and packaging. The *augmented product* is the actual product plus the various services offered with it, such as warranty, free delivery, installation and maintenance.

We defined the product as anything that can be offered to a market for attention, acquisition, use or consumption that might satisfy a need or want. Products include physical objects, services, persons, places, organisations, ideas or mixes of these entities.

There are three basic types of *product classification*. *Durable goods* are used over an extended period of time. *Non-durable goods* are consumed more quickly, usually in a single use or on a few usage occasions. *Services* are activities or benefits offered for sale which are basically intangible and do not result in ownership of anything. Each of these products can be bought by either consumer or industrial customers. *Consumer goods* are sold to the final end-user for personal consumption. They are classified according to consumer shopping habits (convenience, shopping, specialty, and unsought products). *Industrial goods* are bought by individuals or organisations for further processing or use in conducting a business. They are classified according to their cost and the way they enter the production process (materials and parts, capital items and supplies and services).

Marketers develop strategies for items in their product lines by making decisions about the *product attributes*, *branding*, *packaging*, *labelling* and *product-support services*. *Product attributes* deliver tangible benefits such as the product quality, features and design. A *brand* identifies and differentiates goods or services through the use of a name or distinctive design element, resulting in long-term value known as *brand equity*. Branding decisions include whether to brand or not, selecting a brand name, garnering brand sponsorship and determining a brand strategy. *Package* and *labelling* decisions are important as they carry brand equity through appearance and affect product performance with functionality. Packaging provides benefits such as protection, economy, convenience and promotion. Package decisions often include designing labels which identify, describe and possible promote the product. Companies also develop *product support services* that enhance customer service and satisfaction and safeguard against competitors.

Most companies offer a product line rather than a single product. Product strategy therefore requires *product line decisions* that build individual products into a logical portfolio. A product line is a group of products that are closely related because of similar function, customers, channels of distribution or pricing. The number of items it contains is referred to as the *product line length*. To occupy a gap that might be otherwise filled by a competitor, the company can increase its product line length by *stretching upwards* to a higher-priced segment, *downwards* to a lower-priced segment or by *stretching both ways*. Profits can sometimes be increased by *product line filling*, adding more items within the present range of the line. The set of product lines and items within these lines offered to customers make up the *product mix* which can be described according to its *width, length, depth* and *consistency*.

The *width* of a product mix is the number of different types of product line that a company offers. Product-mix *length* is the total number of items that the company carries. *Depth* is the number of versions, such as colours or flavours, offered for each product in a line. *Consistency* measures how closely related different product lines are to one another based on end use, distribution channels or production methods.

Marketers face complex considerations in *international product decisions*, including: a decision about what products to introduce in what countries; whether to *standardise* the product and packaging; and whether to *adapt* it to local conditions.

Overall, developing products and brands is a complex and demanding task. Market-oriented firms create a differential advantage through evaluating the many issues surrounding product decisions and maintaining consistency with broad company objectives. Customer needs and wants invariably lie at the heart of sound product strategies.

discussing the issues

1. What are the core, tangible and augmented products of the educational experience that universities offer?

2. Various classes of consumer products differ in the ways that consumers buy them. As such, they also differ in how they are marketed.

   (a) Select an example of an unsought product and suggest how a marketer might convert this product into a speciality, shopping or convenience product.

   (b) Explain how personal computer manufacturers have been able to convert their speciality products into broader-based shopping products.

3. In recent years, many European and US carmakers have tried to reposition many of their brands. Thinking about examples of such repositioning efforts, describe whether a brand has moved to a high-quality end of the market or moved down-market. How easy is it for carmakers to reposition

their brands? What else could they do to change consumers' perceptions of their cars?

4. Why are many people willing to pay more for branded products than for unbranded products? What does this say about the value of branding?

5. Coca-Cola started with one type of cola drink. Now we find Coke in nearly a dozen varieties. It seems that almost every major brand has been greatly extended, some even past the breaking point. Why do consumer-goods manufacturers extend their brands? What issues do these brand extensions raise for manufacturers, retailers and consumers?

6. Brand name and symbol licensing has become a multi-billion-dollar worldwide business. Compare brand extension by the brand owner with licensing a brand name for use by another company. What are the opportunities and risks of each approach?

applying the concepts

1. Take a packet of Nestlé or Kellogg's breakfast cereal. Note the packaging design and labelling information. Identify the kinds of information found on the package. You will also see instructions for consumers on how to find Kellogg's on the Internet. If possible, visit the company's website, which will offer further opportunity to find out more about the company's products, recipes, and so forth. What are the key conclusions that can be drawn concerning the role that packaging and labelling information play in building the brand's strength and identity, and in projecting brand values and differentiating the brand from competitors' offerings (you may also evaluate a competitor's product – perhaps the grocery store's own-label cereal)?

2. The element of the 'core product' in the automobile industry is transportation. The major problem-solving benefit is how to get from one place to another quickly and safely. However, most automobile manufacturers differentiate their products with additional service benefits. The various service approaches are almost as varied as are the automobile manufacturers themselves. Examine the websites for Fiat (www.fiat.com), Renault (www.renault.com), Mercedes-Benz (www.mercedes.co.uk), Ford (www.ford.com), General Motors (www.gm.com), Honda (www.honda.com), Lexus (www.lexus.com) and Toyota (www.toyota.com). Look beyond the automobiles themselves and closely examine the manufacturers' services and service options.

   (a) What primary services do the various automobile manufacturers offer? Prepare a grid that compares each company to the others.

   (b) What services do the different companies appear to offer in common? What services do the various companies use to differentiate themselves from one another?

   (c) Do any of the sites suggest that a company understands the service–profit chain? Explain.

   (d) Do any of the auto companies employ interactive marketing with respect to the service component? Explain.

   (e) What role does the Internet play in the product/service strategies of the companies in question?

references

1. Carmel Allen, 'Profit and gloss', *How to Spend It, Weekend FT* (October 2000), pp. 63–4; Birna Helgadottir, 'The glamazons are here', *Business FT Weekend Magazine* (29 July 2000), pp. 30–3; William Hall and John Willman, 'Success without a ripple', *Financial Times* (13 March 2000), p. 14.

2. See Philip Kotler, Irving J. Rein and Donald Haider, *Marketing Places: Attracting investment, industry, and tourism to cities, states, and nations* (New York: Free Press, 1993), pp. 202, 273.

3. See V. Rangan Kasturi, Sohel Karim and Sheryl K. Sandberg, 'Do better at doing good', *Harvard Business Review* (May–June 1996), pp. 42–54; Sue Adkins, *Cause Related Marketing: Who cares wins* (London: Butterworth Heinemann, 1999).

4. Valerie A. Zeithaml, Leonard L. Berry and A. Parasuraman, 'The behavioral consequences of service quality', *Journal of Marketing* (April 1996), pp. 31–46; Otis Port, 'The Baldrige's other reward', *Business Week* (10 March 1997), p. 75; and George Thorne, 'TQM connects all segments of marketing', *Advertising Age's Business Marketing* (March 1998), p. 34.

5. Philip Kotler, *Kotler on Marketing* (New York: Free Press, 1999), p. 17.

6. Gunilla Kines, 'A walk on the safe side', *The European Magazine* (24–30 April 1997), p. 12; Maria Werner, 'IKEA's design for thrifty, stylish living', *The European Magazine* (24–30 April 1997), p. 15.

7. Susan Lambert, *Form Follows Function* (London: Victoria and Albert Museum, 1993), p. 57.

8. For more on design, see Christopher Lorenz, *The Design Dimension* (Oxford: Blackwell, 1990); see also Stephen Potter, Robin Roy, Claire H. Capon, Margaret Bruce, Vivien Walsh and Janny Lewis, *The Benefits and Costs of Investment in Design: Using professional design expertise in product, engineering and graphics projects* (Manchester: Open University/UMIST, September 1991).

9. See Peter D. Bennett, *Dictionary of Marketing Terms* (Chicago, IL: American Marketing Association, 1988).

10. Jean-Noel Kapferer, *Strategic Brand Management: New approaches to creating and evaluating brand equity* (London: Kogan Page, 1992), p. 38 ff.

11. David A. Aaker, *Managing Brand Equity* (New York: Free Press, 1991).

12. See T. P. Barwise, C. J. Higson, J. A. Likierman and P. R. Marsh, *Accounting for Brands* (London: Institute of Chartered Accountants in England and Wales, 1990); Peter H. Farquhar, Julia Y. Han and Yuji Ijiri, 'Brands on the balance sheet', *Marketing Management* (Winter 1992), pp. 16–22; Kevin Lane Keller, 'Conceptualising, measuring, and managing customer-based brand equity', *Journal of Marketing* (January 1993), pp. 1–22.

13. Peter Williams, 'Making the most of your assets', *Marketing Business* (March 1999), pp. 30–3.

14. Kurt Badenhausen, 'Most valuable brands', *Financial World* (September/October 1997), pp. 62–3. Also see Terry Lefton and Weston Anson, 'How much is your brand worth?', *Brandweek* (26 January 1996), pp. 43–4 and Kevin Lane Keller, *Strategic Brand Management: Building, measuring and managing brand equity* (Upper Saddle River, NJ: Prentice-Hall, 1997).

15. Thomas M. S. Hemnes, 'How can you find a safe trademark?', *Harvard Business Review* (March–April 1995), p. 44.

16. For a discussion of legal issues surrounding the use of brand names, see Dorothy Cohen, 'Trademark strategy', *Journal of Marketing* (January 1986), pp. 61–74; 'Trademark woes: help is coming', *Sales and Marketing Management* (January 1988), p. 84; Jack Alexander, 'What's in a name? Too much, said the FCC', *Sales and Marketing Management* (January 1989), pp. 75–8.

17. See Richard Tomkins, 'Coke to branch out into clothing', *Financial Times* (18 July 2000), p. 31; Silvia Sansoni, 'Gucci, Armani, and . . . John Paul II?', *Business Week* (13 May 1996), p. 61; Bart A. Lazar, 'Licensing gives known brands new life', *Advertising Age* (16 February 1998), p. 8; and Laura Petrecca, '"Corporate Brands" put licensing in the spotlight', *Advertising Age* (14 June 1999), p. 1.

18. Tom Blackett and Robert Boad, *Co-branding: The science of alliance* (London: Macmillan, 1999).

19. Al Ries and Jack Trout, *Positioning: The battle for your mind* (New York: McGraw-Hill, 1981).

20. For more on line extensions, see Kevin Lane Keller and David A. Aaker, 'The effects of sequential introduction of line extensions', *Journal of Marketing* (February 1992), pp. 35–50; Srinivas K. Reddy, Susan L. Holak and Subodh Bhat, 'To extend or not to extend: success determinants of line extensions', *Journal of Marketing Research* (May 1994), pp. 243–62.

21. Daniel C. Smith and C. Whan Park, 'The effects of brand extensions on market share and advertising efficiency', *Journal of Marketing Research* (August 1992), pp. 296–313. Also, see Julie Liesse, 'Brand extensions take centre stage', *Advertising Age* (8 March 1993), p. 12.

22. Susan M. Broniarczyk and Joseph W. Alba, 'The importance of brand in brand extension', *Journal of Marketing Research* (May 1994), pp. 214–28; Deborah Roedder John, Barbara Loken and Christopher Joiner, 'The negation impact of extensions: can flagship products be diluted?', *Journal of Marketing* (January 1998), pp. 19–32; and Zeynep Gurrhan-Canli and Durairaj Maheswaran, 'The effects of extensions on brand name dilution and enchancement', *Journal of Marketing* (November 1998), pp. 464–73.

23. Joan Holleran, 'Packaging speaks volumes', *Beverage Industry* (February 1998), p. 30.

24. Claire Irvin, 'EU calls time on labelling', *Marketing Business* (July/August 1999), p. 22.

25. Bro Uttal, 'Companies that serve you best', *Fortune* (7 December 1987), pp. 98–116; see also William H. Davidow, 'Customer service: the ultimate marketing weapon', *Business Marketing* (October 1989), pp. 56–64; Barry Farber and Joyce Wycoff, 'Customer service: evolution and revolution', *Sales and Marketing Management* (May 1991), pp. 44–51.

26. Robert D. Hof, 'Now it's your web', *Business Week* (5 October 1998), pp. 164–76.

27. Tom Foremski, 'Intel says that recall could cost it $300m', *Financial Times* (11 May 2000), p. 46.

28. Susanna Voyle, 'Recall of faulty products may help imports', *Financial Times* (16 April 1998), p. 6.

29. John Templeman, 'A Mercedes in every driveway?', *Business Week* (26 August 1996), pp. 38–40 and Sam Pickens and Dagmar Mussey, 'Swatch taps Zurich shop to develop Euro car ads', *Advertising Age* (19 May 1997), p. 32.

30. See David A. Aaker, 'Should you take your brand to where the action is?', *Harvard Business Review* (September–October 1997), pp. 135–43.

31. Philip Cateora, *International Marketing*, 7th edn (Homewood, IL: Irwin, 1990), p. 260.

case 13

Colgate: one squeeze too many?

You probably know about Colgate toothpaste – perhaps you have even used it. But what would you think of Colgate aspirin or Colgate antacid? Would you buy Colgate laxatives or Colgate dandruff shampoo?

That is exactly what Colgate-Palmolive would like to know. Colgate wants to investigate the possibility of entering the over-the-counter (OTC) drugs market. Can it use its Colgate brand name, developed in the oral-care products market, in the OTC healthcare market?

Why does the OTC market interest Colgate? The first reason is market size. The worldwide OTC market annually accounts for over $35 billion in sales. It is the largest non-food consumer products industry, and it is growing at over 6 per cent annually.

Several trends are fuelling this rapid growth. Consumers are more sophisticated than they were and they increasingly seek self-medication rather than seeing a doctor. Companies are also switching many previously prescription-only drugs to OTC drugs. The companies can do this when they can show, based on extensive clinical tests, that the drug is safe for consumers to use without monitoring by a doctor. Moreover, OTC drugs tend to have very long product life cycles. Medical researchers are also discovering new drugs or new uses or benefits of existing drugs. For example, researchers have found that the psyllium fibre used in some OTC natural laxatives is effective in controlling cholesterol.

Beyond the size and growth of the market, Colgate also knows that the OTC market can be extremely profitable. Analysts estimate that the average cost of goods sold for an OTC drug is only 29 per cent, leaving a gross margin of 71 per cent. Advertising and sales promotions are the largest expenditure categories for these products, accounting for an average of 42 per cent of sales. OTC drugs produce on average 11 per cent after-tax profit.

Because of the OTC market's attractiveness, Colgate conducted studies to learn the strength of its brand name with consumers. Colgate believes in the following equation: brand awareness + brand image = brand equity. Its studies found that Colgate was no. 1 in brand awareness, no. 2 in brand image and no. 2 in brand equity among OTC consumers in the US, even though it did not sell OTC products. The Tylenol brand name earned the no. 1 spot in both brand image and brand equity. Similar studies among OTC consumers in major European markets supported Colgate's relatively strong brand equity position. Thus Colgate's research shows that the OTC market is very large, is growing rapidly and is very profitable, and that Colgate has a strong brand equity position with OTC consumers. Most companies would find such a situation very attractive.

Colgate realises that entering the OTC market will not be easy. First, its research suggests that the typical OTC product does not reach the break-even point for four years and does not recover development costs until the seventh year. OTC firms must therefore be correct in their product development decisions or they risk losing a great deal of money.

Second, OTC drugs require a high level of advertising and promotion expenditures: 25 per cent of sales on year-round media alone. A firm must have substantial financial resources to enter this market.

Third, because of the market's attractiveness, entering firms face stiff competition. The market has many competitors and is the least concentrated of any large consumer market. In Europe, no company has more than 3.5 per cent of the market and the top 15 companies account for only 25 per cent market share. Established companies like Bayer, Rhône-Poulenc Rorer, Sanofi, Boots, Boehringer Ingelheim and Warner-Lambert have strong sales forces and marketing organisations. They are strong financially and are willing to take competitors to court if they perceive any violations of laws or regulations. These firms also have strong research and development organisations that spin out new products. As governments squeeze state drug budgets, ethical drug companies have been aggressively working their way into the OTC market. There have been a string of acquisitions, ranging from Roche's purchase of Nicholas Laboratories to SmithKline Beecham's purchase of Stirling Winthrop from Kodak. Merck, America's leading drug company, has teamed up with Johnson & Johnson in the OTC market.

Fourth, because of the high and rising level of fixed costs, such as the costs of advertising and R&D, many smaller firms are leaving the industry or being acquired by larger firms. Many of the world's leading ethical drug companies' industry observers estimate that an OTC firm must have at least several hundred million dollars in sales. It needs this to cover fixed costs and to have the power to match big retailers. So the OTC firms are growing larger and larger, and they are willing to fight aggressively for market share.

Given all these barriers to entry, you might wonder why Colgate would want to pursue OTC products, even if the industry is growing and profitable. Colgate has adopted a strategy that aims to make it the best global consumer products company. It believes that oral-care and OTC products are very similar. Both rely on their ingredients for effectiveness, are highly regulated and use similar marketing channels.

Colgate set up its Colgate Health Care Laboratories to explore product and market development opportunities in the OTC market. Colgate carried out a test market for a line of OTC products developed by its Health Care Laboratories. It test marketed a wide line of OTC products, from a nasal decongestant to a natural fibre laxative, under the brand name Ektra. The predominantly white packages featured the Ektra name with the Colgate name in smaller letters below it.

Following the test market results, Colgate quietly established another test market to test a line of ten OTC healthcare products, all using the Colgate name as the brand name. The line includes aspirin-free pain reliever, ibuprofen, cold tablets, night-time cold medicine, antacid, natural laxative and anti-dandruff shampoo. The test sought to establish how well the Colgate name would compete against established brands in each of the ten OTC product sectors.

Industry observers realise that the new line represents a significant departure from Colgate's traditional, high-visibility household goods and oral-care products. Responding to enquiries, Colgate suggests that: 'The Colgate name is already strong in oral hygiene, now we want to learn whether it can represent health care across the board. We need to expand into more profitable categories.'

Colgate will not talk specifically about its new line. Pharmacists, however, say that Colgate has blitzed the town with coupons and ads. Representatives have given away free tubes of toothpaste with purchases of the new Colgate products and have handed out coupons worth virtually the full price of the new products. If all that promotion was not enough, the manager of one store points out that Colgate has priced its line well below competing brands – as much as 20 per cent below in some cases. The same manager reports that the new products' sales are strong, but also adds: 'With all the promotion they've done, they should be. They're cheaper, and they've got Colgate's name on them.'

Yet even if Colgate's test proves a resounding success, marketing consultants say expanding the new line could prove dangerous and, ultimately, more expensive than Colgate can imagine. 'If you put the Colgate brand name on a bunch of different products, if you do it willy-nilly at the lowest end, you're going to dilute what it stands for – and if you stand for nothing, you're worthless', observes a spokesperson from Lipincott and Margolies, a firm that handles corporate identity projects. Colgate might also end up alienating customers by slapping its name on so many products. If consumers are dissatisfied with one product, they might be dissatisfied with everything across the board.

Moreover, Colgate's new line moves far afield from its familiar turf. Although its new line is selling well, sales might not stay so strong without budget prices and a barrage of advertising and promotion. 'People are looking at it right now as a generic-style product', observes one store manager. 'People are really price conscious, and as long as the price is cheaper, along with a name that you can trust, people are going to buy that over others.'

Al Ries, chairman of Trout & Ries marketing consultants, questions whether any line extensions make sense – not only for Colgate, but also for other strong brand names. He says the reason Colgate has been able to break into the OTC drugs market is that other drugs have expanded and lost their niches. Mr Ries argues that Colgate and the traditional OTC medicine companies are turning their products into generic drugs instead of brands. They are losing 'the power of a narrow focus', he says. 'It reflects stupidity on the part of the traditional over-the-counter marketers. . . . If the traditional medicines maintained their narrow focus, they wouldn't leave room for an outsider such as Colgate.'

If Colgate is too successful, meanwhile, it also risks cannibalising its flagship product. Consultants note that almost all successful line extensions, and many not-so-successful ones, hurt the product from which they took their name. 'If Colgate made themselves to mean over-the-counter medicine, nobody would want to buy Colgate toothpaste', contends Mr Ries.

A Colgate spokesperson argues that Colgate could 'save tens of millions of dollars by not having to introduce a new brand name' for its new products. But in doing so, it might also 'kill the goose that laid the golden egg'. Other marketing consultants believe that Colgate may be able to break into the market, but that it will take much time and money. 'They just don't bring a lot to the OTC party', one consultant indicates.

Although senior management at Colgate says that the company will continue to try to build share in its traditional cleanser and detergent markets, personal care is considered a stronger area. Leveraging a name into new categories can be tricky, requiring patience from sceptical retailers and fickle consumers. 'It isn't so much a question of where you can put the brand name', says one marketing consultant. 'It's what products the consumer will let you put the brand name on.'

Questions

1. What core product is Colgate selling when it sells toothpaste or the other products in its new line?

2. How would you classify these new products?

3. What implications does this classification have for marketing the new line?

4. What brand decisions has Colgate made? What kinds of product line decision? Are these decisions consistent?

5. How would you package the new products and what risks do you see in these packaging decisions?

6. Even if Colgate is successful in extending the brand into a range of OTC product markets in the US, to what extent will the company be able to repeat this success in its European markets?

SOURCES: Sean Brierley, 'Drug dependence', *Marketing Week* (14 November 1994), pp. 32–5; Clive Cookson, 'Roche deal puts fizz in the drug races', *Financial Times* (4 June 1991), p. 19; Paul Abrahams, 'A dose of OTC medicine for growth strategy', *Financial Times* (30 August 1994), p. 19; 'Hoffmann-La Roche: staying calm', *The Economist* (28 September 1991), p. 120; David Pilling, 'Drug group wrestle with seismic shifts in business practices', *Financial Times Survey. Life Sciences and Pharmaceuticals* (6 April 2000), p. I; Colgate Health Care Laboratories also cooperated in the development of this case.

internet exercises

Internet exercises for this chapter can be found on the student site of the MYPHLIP Web Site at www.booksites.net/kotler.

chapter fourteen

New-product development and product life-cycle strategies

Chapter objectives *After reading this chapter, you should be able to:*

✦ Explain how companies find and develop new-product ideas.

✦ List and define the steps in the new-product development process.

✦ Describe the stages of the product life cycle.

✦ Explain how marketing strategy changes during a product's life cycle.

introduction

In competitive markets, the best and strongest firms sustain growth and maintain profitability over the longer term through successfully developing a steady stream of new products or services. Firms must develop new products or services because of the rapid changes in customer tastes, technology and competition. The sheer number of product innovations and extensions launched in European countries in a given year testifies to consumers' voracious appetite for new and improved offerings. Over 1999, there were some 195 new deodorants introduced in these countries; 791 new desserts; 765 men's and women's fragrances; 241 fruit and vegetable products; 1,002 haircare products; 314 vitamins and dietary supplements; 46 toilet, face or kitchen tissues; 796 prepared meals; 236 oral hygiene products; 275 pet foods; 1,611 skincare products; 206 soaps; and 360 innovations using fish![1] Moreover, products have a finite life which is determined by the overall pace of new-product innovation taking place in the product-market as well as by how well the marketing manager manages the brand during all stages of the product life cycle. Introducing new products alone is therefore not sufficient. The firm must also know how to manage the new product as it goes through its life cycle: that is, from its birth, through growth and maturity, to eventual demise as newer products come along that better serve consumer needs.

This product life cycle presents two principal challenges. First, because all products eventually decline, the firm must find new products to replace ageing ones (the

preview case

Elan: parabolic fun makers face a bumpy ride

To the uninitiated, a ski's a ski. But for many ski bums, technology in skis has raised the heights of pleasure, thanks to Elan. Elan, a mid-sized Slovenian company, was founded in 1948 by Yugoslavian soldiers, returning from the war. Now owned by a Croatian Bank, it is the only well-known Yugoslavian brand name to have survived the break-up of the country. Against the shark-toothed wall of the Julian Alps, its factory looks rather nondescript. However, Elan boasts a glittering history. Back in 1977, Ingemar Stenmark, arguably the greatest-ever ski racer, had his skis made there, putting the little Slovenian business on the map. And it was here that the parabolic ski, the most significant innovation in skiing for many decades, was invented.

Elan's big breakthrough came when, in 1988, the company decided to invent the skiing equivalent of the over-sized tennis racquet – a ski that would enable skiers to have more fun on the snow without falling over. This was a shaped ski called SCX (side-cut experimental) which was introduced into the North American market in 1993. The ski was named ski of the year by the trade press and rival firms soon followed with the introduction of their own versions of shaped skis. Today, shaped skis of one form or other account for 70 per cent of ski sales.

There are, however, problems ahead for Elan. Its success in the past lies in its flair for technological innovation. The ski business is, however, changing fast. Becoming more like a fashion than manufacturing business, industry players are churning out new products rapidly. But most of what passes for innovation is gimmicky and marketing. Like fashion houses, ski makers are repackaging their products every autumn, persuading skiers that last season's wonder boards are nothing compared to this year's marvels. A so-called breakthrough is often nothing more than a new colour or a sheen of titanium. Others, more dazzling, claim to have 'piezo-chips', the same technology used by the US Department of Defense to dampen vibration on the wings of fighter planes.

Fast imitation by competitors also presents problems. Unless they are proprietary technology, most new products that take off are soon copied by competitors, particularly the big firms. Moreover, the ski industry is in maturity and has consolidated, resulting in a few big players with resources to out-compete minnows such as Elan. The big companies such as France's Rossignal and Head from Austria can spend more on advertising, million-dollar endorsements of ski racers and product-placement in retail outlets. Their sales are also doing well after a slump in the 1990s. Many are also growing by gobbling up smaller companies.

Some medium-sized manufacturers have survived by diversifying their business as in K2, an American company that now makes sports equipment – roller blades, bicycles, fishing poles and backpacks – as well as skis. Elan has tried diversification, but without much success. For now, small, vulnerable and undercapitalised, Elan strives to survive through innovation. It's latest offering? The short, shaped ski.

Markets do not stand still. When customer wants or technology changes, companies, big or small, must create new products to keep abreast of such changes in the marketplace. While new technology creates new products to fit with customer requirements, management must recognise that it gets tougher as they go on – customer and market needs are continually evolving, and products and marketing methods must follow suit.[2]

Questions

1. Firms survive through product innovation. How do firms identify and develop new-product opportunities?

2. What role does marketing play in new-product development?

3. As the new product ages, how should the firm adapt its marketing strategies in the face of changing tastes, technologies and competition?

problem of *new-product development*). Second, the firm must be good at adapting its marketing strategies in the face of changing customer wants, technologies and competition (the problem of *product life-cycle strategies*). We look initially at the problem of finding and developing new products, and then at the challenge of managing them successfully over their life cycles.

innovation and new-product development

Product innovation encompasses a variety of product development activities – product improvement, development of entirely new ones, and extensions that increase the range or number of lines of product the firm can offer. Product innovations are not to be confused with **inventions**. The latter are new technologies or products which may or may not deliver benefits to customers. An **innovation** is defined as *an idea, service, product or piece of technology that has been developed and marketed to customers who perceive it as novel or new*. Innovation entails a process of identifying, creating and delivering new-product values or benefits that were not offered before in the marketplace.

A firm can obtain new products in two ways. One is through *acquisition* – by buying a whole company, a patent or a licence to produce someone else's product. Many large companies have decided to acquire existing brands rather than to create new ones because of the rising costs of developing and introducing major new products. The other route to obtaining new products is through **new-product development** in the company's own research and development department. By new products we mean original products, product improvements, product modifications and new brands that the firm develops through its own research and development efforts. In this chapter, we concentrate on how businesses create and market new products.

risks and returns in innovation

Innovation can be very risky. New products fail for a number of reasons:

1. New-product development is an expensive affair – it cost Tate & Lyle around £150 million to develop a new sugar substitute; pharmaceutical firms spend an average of £200 million or more to develop a new drug; while developing a super-jumbo jet would cost billions.

2. New-product development takes time. Although companies can dramatically shorten their development time, in many industries, such as pharmaceuticals, biotechnology, aerospace and food, new-product development cycles can be as long as 10–15 years. For example, the new-product launch cycle of consumer product firms such as Gillette may be anything from two to ten years. The uncertainty and unpredictability of market environments further raise the risks of commercialisation.

    Consider the following example. A Swedish start-up firm called Anoto, with the backing from Ericsson, the mobile phone company, has created a high-tech pen that allows users to send hand-written notes and hand-drawn pictures over the Internet and to mobile phones. Slightly fatter than a normal pen, Anoto's pen writes in normal ink, but contains a small camera, radio transmitter, rechargeable battery and ink cartridge. Special paper is used which contains millions of tiny dots that the pen's camera can see, drawing a virtual picture of the writing in its memory and transmitting this picture using radio technology called Bluetooth to a mobile phone. From there, the picture is sent across the Internet to a recipient's e-mail inbox or displayed on the screen of a mobile phone. Bluetooth is backed by computer and communications firms such as Microsoft, IBM, Intel and Nokia. By 2001, when Anoto's pen is introduced, Bluetooth phones will also be on sale. Although all this sounds exciting,

Invention
A new technology or product that may or may not deliver benefits to customers.

Innovation
An idea, service, product or technology that has been developed and marketed to customers who perceive it as novel or new. It is a process of identifying, creating and delivering new-product or service values that did not exist before in the marketplace.

New-product development
The development of original products, product improvements, product modifications and new brands through the firm's own R&D efforts.

analysts point to the risks and uncertainty surrounding the exploitation of new technology. They argue that, while a clever idea, Anoto's pen could well become obsolete, being eclipsed by voice recognition as it takes off in the next 2–3 years.[3]

3. Unexpected delays in development are also a problem. History is littered with grand pioneering engineering projects which have failed to satisfy the original expectations of bankers, investors and politicians. The £10 billion cost of the Channel tunnel, which opened on 6 May 1994, a year later than originally planned, was more than double the £4.8 billion forecast at the start of the project in 1987.

4. New products continue to fail at a disturbing rate. One recent study estimated that new consumer packaged goods (consisting mostly of line extensions) fail at a rate of 80 per cent. Another study suggested that of the tens of thousands of new consumer food, beverage, beauty and healthcare products launched each year, only 40 per cent will be around five years later. Moreover, failure rates for new industrial products may be as high as 30 per cent.[4]

Despite the risks, firms that learn to innovate well become less vulnerable to attacks by new entrants which discover new ways of delivering added values, benefits and solutions to customers' problems.

why do new products fail?

Why do so many new products fail? There are several reasons. Although an idea may be good, the market size may have been overestimated. There just wasn't the demand for the product. Perhaps the actual product was not designed as well as it should have been. It may be a 'me too' product which is no better than products that are already established in the marketplace. Or maybe it was incorrectly positioned in the market, priced too high, or advertised and promoted badly. A high-level executive might push a favourite idea despite poor marketing research findings. Sometimes the costs of product development are higher than budgeted and sometimes competitors fight back harder than expected.

what influences new-product success?

Because so many new products fail, companies are anxious to learn how to improve their odds of new-product success. One way is to identify successful new products and find out what they have in common. Various studies suggest that new-product success depends on developing a *unique superior product*, one offering customers better quality, new features and higher value in use. Another key success factor is a *well-defined product concept* prior to development, in which the company carefully defines and assesses the target market, the product requirements and the benefits before proceeding. New products that are better than existing products at *meeting market needs* and delivering what customers really wanted invariably do well. Other success factors have also been suggested – senior management commitment, relentless commitment to innovation, a smoothly functioning and proficiency in executing the new-product development process.[5] Thus, successful commercialisation of new products requires a company to have a clear understanding of its consumers, markets and competitors and to develop products that deliver superior value to customers.

Successful new-product development may be an even bigger challenge in the future. Keen competition has led to increasing market fragmentation – companies must now aim at smaller market segments rather than the mass market, and this means smaller sales and profits for each product. New products must meet growing social and government constraints, such as consumer safety and environmental standards. The costs of finding, developing and launching new products will increase steadily due to rising manufacturing, media and distribution costs. Many companies that cannot afford the funds needed for new-product development will emphasise product modification and imitation rather than true innovation. Even when a new product is successful, rivals are so quick to copy it that the new product is typically fated to have only a short life.

So, companies face a problem – they must develop new products, but the odds weigh heavily against success. The solution lies in strong *new-product planning* and in setting up a systematic *new-product development process* for finding and growing new products. Top management must ultimately take the lead in setting the company-wide strategy and committing adequate resources to support product innovation.

Successful new-product development requires a company-wide effort. Successful innovative companies not only have a clearly articulated new-product strategy and consistent commitment of resources to new-product development. To ensure effective execution of new-product development, these companies have set up formal and sophisticated organisations for encouraging employees to excel in innovation and facilitating the new-product development process (see Marketing Highlight 14.1). Let us now take a look at the major steps in the new-product development process.

new-product development process

The new-product development process for finding and growing new products consists of nine main steps (see Figure 14.1).

new-product strategy

Effective product innovation is guided by a well-defined *new-product strategy*. The new-product strategy achieves four main goals: first, it gives direction to the new-product team and *focuses team effort*; second, it helps to *integrate* functional or departmental efforts; third, where understood by the new-product team, it allows tasks to be *delegated* to team members, who can be left to operate independently; and fourth, the very act of producing and getting managers to agree on a strategy requires *proactive*, not reactive, management, which increases the likelihood of a more thorough search for innovation opportunities.

Figure 14.1

Steps in new product development

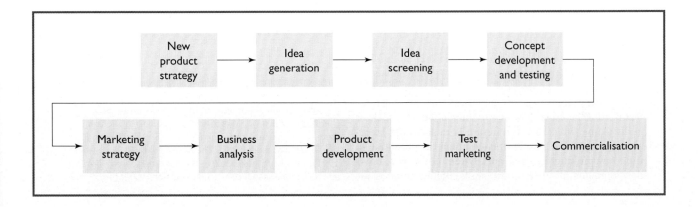

marketing highlight 14.1

3M: championing innovation

The 3M Company markets more than 50,000 products worldwide. These products range from Scotch tapes and Post-It notes to pharmaceuticals and electronic components. 3M views innovation as its path to growth, and new products as its lifeblood. More than 30 per cent of each year's sales come from products that did not exist four years previously. Its legendary emphasis on innovation has consistently made 3M one of the world's most admired companies.

3M's impressive record is due to several factors. The company works hard to create an environment that supports innovation. It invests some 7 per cent of annual group sales in research and development – twice as much as the average company. To develop new products of the future quickly, senior management tolerates informal structures: they seek out and destroy corporate bureaucracy that might interfere with new-product progress.

3M's innovative culture is exemplified by a management that encourages everyone to look for new products. The company's renowned '15 per cent rule' gives all employees space, allowing them to spend up to 15 per cent of their time 'bootlegging' – that is, working on projects of personal interest whether or not those projects directly benefit the company. When a promising idea comes along, 3M forms a venture team made up of the researcher who developed the idea and volunteers from manufacturing, sales, marketing and the legal department. Cross-functional teams, the touchstone of 3M's efforts, facilitate the flow of ideas and technology around the company. The team nurtures the product and protects it from company bureaucracy. Team members stay with the product until it succeeds or fails and then return to their previous jobs. Some teams have tried three or four times before finally making a success of an idea.

3M's management culture encourages the cross-fertilisation of ideas between the 150 businesses that make up the group. Much of this effort to promote serendipity is done through informal interchanges such as routine or chance encounters between colleagues, or networking such as employee-run technical forums or getting technicians to go out and meet customers. Cross-fertilisation is also reinforced by official bodies, such as audit teams, whose main function is to go round laboratory groups and assess the commercial potential of their new-product programmes. Often they come across developments in one lab that can be helpful to another.

The company knows that it must try thousands of new-product ideas to hit one big jackpot. One well-worn slogan at 3M is 'You have to kiss a lot of frogs to find a prince.' This often means making mistakes, but 3M accepts blunders and dead ends as a normal part of creativity and innovation. As it turns out, 'blunders' have turned into some of 3M's most successful products. There is the familiar story about the chemist who accidentally spilled a new chemical on her tennis shoes. Some days later, she noticed that the spots hit by the chemical had not become dirty. The chemical eventually became Scotchgard fabric protector.

And then there's the one about 3M scientist Spencer Silver who developed a superstrong adhesive that didn't stick very well at all. He sent the apparently useless substance on to other 3M researchers to see if they could find something to do with it. Nothing happened for several years. Then Arthur Fry, another 3M scientist and a choir member, found that scraps of paper dabbed with Mr Silver's weak glue stuck nicely to pages marked out in his hymnal and later peeled off without damaging the hymnal. Eureka! Mr Fry's problem of marking places in his hymnal was solved. Thus were born 3M's ubiquitous Post-it notes, a product that now has sales of over $100 million a year!

As a benchmark, the 3M model has attracted many proponents and followers worldwide. At the heart of its philosophy is the recognition of the capacity of the individual to add value through innovation. In order to extract that capacity to innovate among the workforce, management must uphold its commitment to nurturing and sustaining a culture of innovation. 3M acknowledges that there is no room for complacency if it wants to remain a corporate superstar.

SOURCES: Alison Maitland, '3M has succession taped', *Financial Times* (11 May 2000), p. 22; Martin Dickson, 'Back to the future', *Financial Times* (30 May 1994), p. 7; '3M, 60,000 and counting', *The Economist* (30 November 1991), pp. 86–9; Kevin Kelly, '3M running scared? Forget about it', *Business Week* (16 September 1991), pp. 59–62.

Successful innovative companies are placing more emphasis upon the use of definitive strategy statements or a **product innovation charter (PIC)**. The PIC draws managers' attention to the reasons or *rationale* behind the firm's search for innovation opportunities, the *product/market* and *technology* to focus on, the miscellaneous *goals* or *objectives* (market share, cash flow, profitability, etc.) to be achieved, and *guidelines* on the nature or level of innovativeness that will sell the new product.[6] The charter spells out the priority that managers should place on developing breakthrough products, changing existing ones and imitating competitors' products. Given that many or most new-product ideas are likely to be unsuitable for development, senior management has to establish specific criteria for new-product idea selection. Ideas are accepted based on the specific *strategic roles* the new-products are expected to play. A new-product's role might be to help the company maintain its industry position as an innovator, to defend a market-share position, or to get a foothold in a future new market. Or the new product might help the company to take advantage of its special strengths or exploit technology in a new way.

Product innovation charter (PIC)
A new-product strategy statement formalising management's reasons or rationale behind the firm's search for innovation opportunities, the product/market and technology to focus upon, and the goals and objectives to be achieved.

idea generation

The PIC should then direct the search for new-product ideas. **Idea generation** should be proactive and systematic rather than haphazard. This ensures that the company will not only find many ideas, but also ones that are good for its type of business. A company typically has to generate many ideas in order to find a few good ones. A recent survey of product managers found that of 100 proposed new product ideas, 39 begin the product development process, 17 survive the development process, 8 actually reach the marketplace and only 1 eventually reaches its business objectives. For pharmaceuticals companies, it can take some 6,000 to 8,000 starting ideas to produce one commercial success.[7]

Idea generation
The systematic search for new-product ideas.

To obtain a flow of new-product ideas, the company can tap many sources. Chief sources of new-product ideas include internal sources, customers, competitors, distributors and suppliers.

■ Internal sources

The company can find new ideas through its own formal research and development efforts. It can pick the brains of its executives, scientists, engineers, designers, manufacturing and salespeople. Some companies have established 'intrapreneurial' programmes that encourage employees to think up and develop new product ideas (see Marketing Highlight 14.1). Formal or informal suggestion schemes can also be used to tap staff's ideas. Toyota claims that employees submit two million ideas annually – about 35 suggestions per employee – and that more than 85 per cent of these ideas are implemented.

■ Customers

Good new-product ideas also come from watching and listening to customers. The company can analyse customer questions and complaints to find new products that better solve consumer problems. It can conduct surveys or focus groups to learn about consumer needs and wants. Or company engineers or salespeople can meet with or work alongside customers to get suggestions and ideas. For example, companies such as Hewlett-Packard, Sony, Toyota and many other effective innovators are known to have their design engineers talk with final consumers to get ideas for new products.

Customers often create new products on their own, and companies can benefit by finding these products and putting them on the market. About one-third of all the software IBM leases for its computers is developed by outside users.[8]

Customers, however, may not always know their future needs and wants. If Philips had questioned consumers 30 years ago about what new audio technology they wanted, they would never have said a personal stereo – the idea would not have occurred to them. This is one of the reasons why Finnish mobile communications company Nokia employs a team of people around the world whose job is to think ten years ahead and dream up ideas. They have to anticipate future needs before the consumer has even become aware of them. They must also predict the innovations of their rivals, so that the company can be one step ahead. Every so often, the ideas team hold focus groups for ordinary users and ask them what they want from their phones when they are on the move. The users are offered a handful of new ideas and their reactions are videoed. The team always pay attention to the quirky suggestions because there is often a lot of truth in them. The company also consults anthropologists to help unravel consumers' reactions, and these generate leads which give the team something to build on. It was anticipating needs before they exist that brought about Nokia's revolutionary 9000 Communicator, which was the world's first all-in-one mobile communications device – a fax, phone, digital diary, calculator and palm-top computer all rolled into one. It will not be long before Nokia's handset will become a mobile office and multimedia communications device the size of a business card![9]

■ Competitors

Competitors are another good source of new-product ideas. Companies watch competitors' ads and other communications to get clues about their new products. They buy competing new products, take them apart to see how they work, analyse their sales, and decide whether the company should bring out a new product of its own.

■ Distributors, suppliers and others

Resellers are close to the market and can pass along information about consumer problems and new-product possibilities. Suppliers can tell the company about new concepts, techniques and materials that can be used to develop new products. Other idea sources include trade magazines, shows and seminars; government agencies; advertising agencies; marketing research firms; university and commercial laboratories; science parks; and inventors. Companies may also turn to new-product consultants to find new ideas and problem-solutions to serve customer needs better.

> For example, some years ago, Europe's biggest brewer, Heineken of the Netherlands, had to recall millions of bottles of its home-brewed Export beer due to contamination by glass particles. To avoid future such incidents, which are potentially very costly and damaging for the brand and the company, the brewer got its packaging research and development people to investigate potential solutions to the problem. They could not find anything they could buy off the shelf, so turned to the UK's PA Consulting Group, which looked at a variety of solutions, ranging from X-rays and gamma rays to nuclear magnetic resonance and ultrasonic techniques. PA eventually developed a solution inspired by a technique used by pharmaceutical firms to inspect vials. The consultants worked with a UK bottle-handling specialist and image-processing specialists to develop a system for Heineken. The safety innovation, as Heineken called it, underlined the importance of drawing inspiration from external parties to generate novel problem solutions.[10]

The search for new-product ideas should be systematic in order to ensure that many good ideas will surface, not sputter in and die. Top management avoid these problems by installing an idea management system that directs the flow of new ideas to a central point where they can be collected, reviewed and evaluated. The company may set up

'Intrapreneurial' programmes encourage employees to think up and develop new product ideas. 3M's spectacularly successful Post-it notes evolved out of such a programme.

Source: 3M

an idea management system in a number of ways: appoint a respected senior person to be the company's idea manager; create a multidisciplinary idea management committee, consisting of people from R&D, engineering, purchasing, operations, finance, sales and marketing, who meet regularly and evaluate proposed new-product ideas; set up a free-phone number for anyone who want to volunteer new ideas to the idea manager; encourage all of the company's stakeholders – employees, suppliers, distributors, dealer and so forth – to send their ideas to the idea manager; and set up a formal recognition programme to reward those who contribute the best ideas.[11]

The idea manager approach yields two favourable outcomes. First, it helps foster an innovation-oriented company culture. It shows that top management supports, encourages and rewards innovation. Second, it yields a steady stream of ideas from which good ones will emerge. As the system matures, ideas will flow more freely. Importantly, companies that use such a formalised approach to finding new ideas will find that no longer will good ideas wither for the lack of a sounding-board or a senior product advocate.

idea screening

The purpose of idea generation is to create a large number of ideas. The purpose of the succeeding stages is to *reduce* that number. The first idea-reducing stage is

Idea screening

Screening new-product ideas in order to spot good ideas and drop poor ones as soon as possible.

idea screening. The purpose of screening is to spot good ideas and drop poor ones as soon as possible. As product development costs rise greatly in later stages, it is important for the company to go ahead only with those product ideas that will turn into profitable products.

Most companies require their executives to write up new-product ideas on a standard form that can be reviewed by a new-product committee. The write-up describes the product, the target market and the competition, and makes some rough estimates of market size, product price, development time and costs, manufacturing costs and rate of return. The committee then evaluates the idea against a set of general criteria. Typically, the committee asks questions such as these: Is the product truly useful to consumers and society? Is this product good for our particular company? Does it mesh well with the company's objectives and strategies? Do we have the people, skills and resources to make it succeed? Does it deliver more value to customers than competing products? Is it easy to advertise and distribute? Many companies have well-designed systems for rating and screening new-product ideas.

concept development and testing

Product idea

An idea for a possible product that the company can see itself offering to the market.

Attractive ideas must be developed into product concepts. It is important to distinguish between a *product idea*, a *product concept* and a *product image*. A **product idea** is an idea for a possible product that the company can see itself offering to the market. A **product concept** is a detailed version of the idea stated in meaningful consumer terms. A **product image** is the way consumers perceive an actual or potential product.

Product concept

A detailed version of the new-product idea stated in meaningful consumer terms.

■ Concept development

Suppose DaimlerChrysler is getting ready to commercialise its experimental fuel-cell-powered electric car. This car's low-polluting fuel-cell system runs directly off liquid hydrogen. It is highly fuel efficient (75 per cent more efficient than petrol engines) and gives the new car an environmental advantage over standard internal combustion engine cars. DaimlerChrysler is currently road-testing its NECAR 4 (New Electric Car) sub-compact prototype and plans to deliver the first fuel-cell cars to customers in 2004. Based on the tiny Mercedes A-Class, the car accelerates quickly, reaches speeds of 90 miles per hour, and has a 280-mile driving range, giving it a huge edge over battery-powered electric cars which travel only about 80 miles before needing 3–12 hours of recharging.[12]

Product image

The way consumers perceive an actual or potential product.

DaimlerChrysler's task is to develop its fuel-cell powered electric car into alternative product concepts, find out how attractive each is to customers and choose the best one.

Source: Copyright DaimlerChrysler/Liason Agency

DaimlerChrysler's task is to develop this new product into alternative product concepts, find out how attractive each concept is to customers, and choose the best one. To increase the likelihood of concept acceptance, some firms involve the customer (or potential customer) in concept development – customers may, for example, be invited to the DaimlerChrysler's design reviews in the early stages of the new-product process. The following product concepts for the fuel-cell electric car might be created:

♦ *Concept 1.* A moderately priced subcompact designed as a second family car to be used around town. The car is ideal for running errands and visiting friends.

♦ *Concept 2.* A medium-cost sporty compact appealing to young people.

♦ *Concept 3.* An inexpensive subcompact 'green' car appealing to environmentally conscious people who want practical transportation and low pollution.

■ Concept testing

Concept testing calls for testing new-product concepts with a group of target consumers. The concepts may be presented to consumers symbolically or physically. Here, in words, is *Concept 3*:

> An efficient, fun-to-drive, fuel-cell-powered electric subcompact car that seats four. This high-tech wonder runs on hydrogen created from methanol fuel, providing practical and reliable transportation with almost no pollution. It goes up to 120 km per hour and, unlike battery-powered electric cars, never needs recharging. It's priced, fully equipped, at €25,000.

For some concept tests, a word or picture description might be sufficient. However, a more concrete and physical presentation of the concept will increase the reliability of the concept test. Today, marketers are finding innovative ways to make product concepts more real to consumer subjects. For example, some are using virtual reality to test product concepts. Virtual reality programs use computers and sensory devices (such as goggles or gloves) to simulate reality. For example, a designer of kitchen cabinets can use a virtual reality program to help a customer 'see' how his or her kitchen would look and work if remodelled with the company's products. Virtual reality is still in its infancy, but its applications are increasing daily.

After being exposed to the concept, consumers may then be asked to react to it by answering the questions in Table 14.1. The answers will help the company decide

Concept testing
Testing new product concepts with a group of target consumers to find out if the concepts have strong consumer appeal.

Table 14.1

Questions for fuel-cell-powered electric car concept test

1. Do you understand the concept of a fuel-cell-powered electric car?
2. Do you believe the claims about the car's performance?
3. What are the main benefits of the fuel-cell-powered electric car compared with a conventional car?
4. What improvements in the car's features would you suggest?
5. For what uses would you prefer a fuel-cell-powered electric car to a conventional car?
6. What would be a reasonable price to charge for the car?
7. Who would be involved in your decision to buy such a car? Who would drive it?
8. Would you buy such a car? (Definitely, probably, probably not, definitely not)

which concept has the strongest appeal. For example, the last question asks about the consumer's intention to buy. Suppose 10 per cent of the consumers said they 'definitely' would buy and another 5 per cent said 'probably'. The company could project these figures to the population size of this target group to estimate sales volume. Concept testing offers a rough estimate of potential sales, but managers must view this with caution. The estimate is uncertain largely because consumers do not always carry out stated intentions.[13] Potential customers may like the idea of the new product, but might not want to pay for one! It is still important to carry out such tests with product concepts so as to gauge customers' response as well as to identify aspects of the concept that are particularly liked or disliked by potential buyers. Feedback might suggest ways to refine the concept, thereby increasing its appeal to customers.

marketing strategy development

Marketing strategy
The marketing logic by which the business unit hopes to achieve its marketing objectives.

Marketing strategy statement
A statement of the planned strategy for a new product that outlines the intended target market, the planned product positioning, and the sales, market share and profit goals for the first few years.

Suppose DaimlerChrysler finds that Concept 3 for the fuel-cell-powered electric car tests best. The next step is to develop a **marketing strategy** for introducing this car to the market.

The **marketing strategy statement** consists of three parts. The first part describes the target market, the planned product positioning, and the sales, market share and profit goals for the first few years. Thus:

> The target market is younger, well-educated, moderate-to-high income individuals, couples or small families seeking practical, environmentally responsible transportation. The car will be positioned as more economical to operate, more fun to drive and less polluting than today's internal combustion engine cars, and as less restricting than battery-powered electric cars which must be recharged regularly. The company will aim to sell 100,000 cars in the first year, at a loss of not more than €15 million. In the second year, the company will aim for sales of 120,000 cars and a profit of €25 million.

The second part of the marketing strategy statement outlines the product's planned price, distribution and marketing budget for the first year.

> The fuel-cell-powered electric car will be offered in three colours and will have optional air-conditioning and power-drive features. It will sell at a retail price of €20,000 – with 15 per cent off the list price to dealers. Dealers who sell more than 10 cars per month will get an additional discount of 5 per cent on each car sold that month. An advertising budget of €20 million will be split 50–50 between national and local advertising. Advertising will emphasise the car's fun and low emissions. During the first year, €150,000 will be spent on marketing research to find out who is buying the car and to determine their satisfaction levels.

The third part of the marketing strategy statement describes the planned long-run sales, profit goals and marketing mix strategy:

> The company intends to capture a 3 per cent long-run share of the total car market and realise an after-tax return on investment of 15 per cent. To achieve this, product quality will start high and be improved over time. Price will be raised in the second and third years if competition permits. The total advertising budget will be raised each year by about 10 per cent. Marketing research will be reduced to €60,000 per year after the first year.

business analysis

Once management has decided on its product concept and marketing strategy, it can evaluate the business attractiveness of the proposal. **Business analysis** involves a review of the sales, costs and profit projections for a new product to find out whether they satisfy the company's objectives. If they do, the product proceeds to the product development stage.

To estimate sales, the company looks at the sales history of similar products and conducts surveys of market opinion. It then estimates minimum and maximum sales to assess the range of risk. After preparing the sales forecast, management can estimate the expected costs and profits for the product, including marketing, R&D, manufacturing, accounting and finance costs. The company then uses the sales and costs figures to analyse the new product's financial attractiveness.

Business analysis
A review of the sales, costs and profit projections for a new product to find out whether these factors satisfy the company's objectives.

product development

So far, for many new-product concepts, the product may have existed only as a word description, a drawing or perhaps a crude mock-up. If the product concept passes the business test, it moves into **product development**. Here, R&D or engineering develops the product concept into a physical product. The product development step, however, now calls for a large jump in investment. It will show whether the product idea can be turned into a workable product.

The R&D department will develop one or more physical versions of the product concept. R&D hopes to design a prototype that will satisfy and excite consumers and that can be produced quickly and at budgeted costs. Developing a successful prototype can take days, weeks, months or even years. Sometimes product design and development may pose a serious challenge for the firm and companies have to find ways to get round these obstacles.

Consider the experience of Dentronic, a young Swedish company, spun off from the University of Umeå. Dentronic developed a new dental system called Decim, a composite for filling teeth that replaces mercury amalgam, which is a serious health hazard for dentists who have to handle it on a daily basis. Decim is better than other modern alternatives based on polymeric materials as it is longer lasting and has lower toxicity problems. However, the material, based on zirconium dioxide, requires a special combination of software and hardware systems to make up the filling. Unlike amalgam, it cannot be mixed as a paste in the surgery. Instead it involves advanced manufacturing techniques. A cast has to be made of the patient's tooth cavity as the model for CAD/CAM preparation of a corresponding inlay. The cast is captured by a special laser scanner, converted into a three-dimensional drawing, with manual adjustment of the chewing surface. A numerically controlled manufacturing unit automatically machines the inlay to shape, and, after polishing, it is cemented in place in the tooth, giving a perfect fit. Through an innovation network agency, IRC Northern Sweden, Dentronic secured the collaboration of a British software house as well as signed up with French ceramic materials supplier Norton Desmarquet which developed and manufactured exclusively for the company. Thanks to these external partners, Dentronic was able to surmount serious development and production problems which would have stalled the firm's efforts to commercialise its new non-toxic technology. Dentronic launched the Decim system under the brand name Denzir in Sweden in November 1999, followed by rapid international rollouts over 2000.[14]

When the prototypes are ready, the prototypes undergo rigorous functional tests under laboratory and field conditions to make sure that the product performs safely and effectively.

Product development
Developing the product concept into a physical product in order to ensure that the product idea can be turned into a workable product.

The prototype must have the required functional features and also convey the intended psychological characteristics. The fuel-cell-powered electric car, for example, should strike consumers as being well built and safe. Management must learn what makes consumers decide that a car is well built. To some consumers, this means that the car has 'solid-sounding' doors. To others, it means that the car is able to withstand heavy impact in crash tests. Consumer tests are conducted, in which consumers test-drive the car and rate its attributes. For some products, prototyping and product development may involve both the key intermediaries that supply the product or service and the final consumer or end-user.

When designing products, the company should look beyond simply creating products that satisfy consumer needs and wants. Too often, companies design their new products without enough concern for how the designs will be produced. Companies may minimise production problems by adopting an approach towards product development called *design for manufacturability and assembly* (DFMA). Using this approach, companies work to fashion products that are *both* satisfying *and* easy to manufacture. This often results not only in lower costs, but also in higher-quality and more reliable products.

test marketing

Test marketing
The stage of new-product development where the product and marketing programme are tested in more realistic market settings.

If the product passes functional and consumer tests, the next step is **test marketing**, the stage at which the product and marketing programme are introduced into more realistic market settings.

Test marketing gives the marketer experience with marketing the product before going to the great expense of full introduction. It lets the company test the product and its entire marketing programme – positioning strategy, advertising, distribution, pricing, branding and packaging, and budget levels – in real market situations. The company uses test marketing to learn how consumers and dealers will react to handling, using and repurchasing the product. The results can be used to make better sales and profit forecasts. Thus a good test market can provide a wealth of information about the potential success of the product and marketing programme.

The amount of test marketing needed varies with each new product. Test marketing costs can be enormous and test marketing takes time that may allow competitors to gain advantages. When the costs of developing and introducing the product are low or when management is already confident that the new product will succeed, the company may do little or no test marketing. Companies often do not test market simple line extensions, minor modifications of current products or copies of successful competitors' products. However, when the new-product introduction requires a large investment, or when management is not sure of the product or marketing programme, the company may do a lot of test marketing. For example, Lever USA spent two years testing its highly successful Lever 2000 bar soap in Atlanta before introducing it internationally.

The idea of test marketing also applies to new service products. For example, an airline company preparing to introduce a secure, cost-saving system of electronic ticketing may try out the new service first on domestic routes before rolling out the service to international flights. Or it might offer the ticketless system on its busiest routes and restrict the test to its most frequent travellers. The system's effectiveness and customers' acceptance and reactions can then be gauged prior to making the decision to extend the service to cover all of its domestic or global networks.

Whether or not a company decides to test market, and the amount of testing it does, depends on the cost and risk of introducing the product on the one hand, and on the testing costs and time pressures on the other. Although the costs of test marketing can be high, they are often small when compared to the costs of making a major

Lever USA spent two years testing its highly successful Lever 2000 bar soap before introducing it internationally.

SOURCE: Unilever plc

mistake. For example, as illustrated in the 'Unilever: Power?' case at the end of Chapter 4, the Anglo-Dutch company learned a costly lesson when it decided to skip formal test marketing for its new European laundry detergent, Power, and forged ahead with its £200 million Europe-wide launch. The company spent another £70 million on the withdrawal of the defective, clothing-annihilating Power detergent a year after its introduction.

When using test marketing, consumer-products companies usually choose one of three approaches – standard test markets, controlled test markets or simulated test markets.

■ Standard test markets

Using standard test markets, the company finds a small number of representative test cities, conducts a full marketing campaign in these cities and uses store audits, consumer and distributor surveys, and other measures to gauge product performance. It then uses the results to forecast national sales and profits, to discover potential product problems and to fine-tune the marketing programme.

Standard market tests have some drawbacks. They can be costly and may take a long time – some last as long as three years. Moreover, competitors can monitor test-market results or even interfere with them by cutting their prices in test locations, increasing their promotion or even buying up the product being tested. Finally, test markets give competitors a look at the company's new product well before it is introduced nationally. Thus, competitors may have time to develop defensive strategies and may even beat the company's product to the market. For example, prior to its launch in the United Kingdom, Carnation Coffee-Mate, a coffee-whitener, was test marketed over a period of six years. This gave rival firm Cadbury ample warning and the opportunity to develop and introduce its own product – Marvel – to compete head-on with Coffee-Mate.

Despite these disadvantages, standard test markets are still the most widely used approach for major market testing. However, many companies today are shifting towards quicker and cheaper controlled and simulated test marketing methods.

■ Controlled test markets

Several research firms keep controlled panels of stores which have agreed to carry new products for a fee. The company with the new product specifies the number of stores and geographical locations it wants. The research firm delivers the product to the participating stores and controls shelf location, amount of shelf space, displays and point-of-purchase promotions, and pricing according to specified plans. Sales results are tracked to determine the impact of these factors on demand.

Controlled test-marketing systems are particularly well developed in the United States. Systems like Nielsen's Scantrack and Information Resources Inc.'s (IRI) BehaviorScan track individual behaviour from the television set to the checkout counter. IRI, for example, keeps panels of shoppers in carefully selected cities. It uses microcomputers to measure TV viewing in each panel household and can send special commercials to panel member television sets. Panel consumers buy from cooperating stores and show identification cards when making purchases. Detailed electronic-scanner information on each consumer's purchases is fed into a central computer, where it is combined with the consumer's demographic and TV viewing information and reported daily. Thus BehaviorScan can provide store-by-store, week-by-week reports on the sales of new products being tested. And because the scanners record the specific purchases of individual consumers, the system can also provide information on repeat purchases and the ways that different types of consumer are reacting to the new product, its advertising and various other elements of the marketing programme.[15]

Controlled test markets take less time than standard test markets (six months to a year). However, some companies are concerned that the limited number of small cities and panel consumers used by the research services may not be representative of their products' markets or target consumers. And, as in standard test markets, controlled test markets allow competitors to get a look at the company's new product.

■ Simulated test markets

Companies also can test new products in a simulated shopping environment. The company or research firm shows, to a sample of consumers, ads and promotions for a variety of products, including the new product being tested. It gives consumers a small amount of money and invites them to a real or laboratory store, where they may keep the money or use it to buy items. The researchers note how many consumers buy the new product and competing brands. This simulation provides a measure of trial and the commercial's effectiveness against competing commercials. The researchers then ask consumers the reasons for their purchase or non-purchase. Some weeks later, they interview the consumer by phone to determine product attitudes, usage, satisfaction and repurchase intentions. Using sophisticated computer models, the researchers then project national sales from results of the simulated test market. Recently, some marketers have begun to use interesting new high-tech approaches to simulated test market research, such as virtual reality and the Internet (see Marketing Highlight 14.2).

marketing highlight 14.2

Virtual reality test marketing: the future is now

Virtual reality – that's the wave of the future for test-marketing and concept-testing research. So says Gadd International Research. Gadd has developed a research tool called Simul-Shop, a CD-ROM virtual-reality approach that re-creates shopping situations in which researchers can test consumers' reactions to such factors as product positioning, store layouts and package designs. Suppose a breakfast cereal marketer wants to test reactions to a new package design and store-shelf positioning. Using Simul-Shop on a standard desktop PC, test shoppers begin their shopping with a screen showing the outside of a grocery store. They click to enter the virtual store and are guided to the appropriate store section. Once there, they scan the shelf, pick up various cereal packages, rotate them, study the labels, look around to see what is on the shelf behind them. About the only thing they can't do is open the box and taste the cereal. The virtual shopping trip includes full sound and video, along with a guide who directs users through the experience and answers their questions.

Virtual reality testing can take any of several forms. For example, Alternative Realities Corporation (ARC) offers a virtual reality amphitheatre called the VisionDome. The Dome offers 360 by 160 degrees of film projection, allowing as many as 40 people at one time to participate and interact in a virtual reality experience. When conducting research on, say, a car, customers can go into a VisionDome, see that car in three dimensions, look at it from every angle, sit in it and take it out for a test drive. Customers can immerse themselves totally in the product. They can configure that car exactly the way they want it.

Virtual reality as a research tool offers several advantages. One, it is relatively inexpensive. A company can conduct a Simul-Shop study for around €25,000, including initial programming and the actual research on 75–100 people. Such research becomes more accessible to firms that can't afford the full expense of market-testing campaigns or creating actual mock-ups for different product colour, shape or size. Another advantage is flexibility. A virtual reality store can display an almost infinite variety of products, sizes, styles and flavours in response to consumers' desires and needs. The tool can create any number of simulated surroundings, ranging from food store interiors and new car showrooms to farms, or the open road. The technique's interactivity allows marketers and consumers to work together via computer on new product designs and marketing programmes.

Finally, virtual reality has great potential for international marketing research. With virtual reality, researchers can use a single standardised approach to evaluate products and programmes worldwide. For example, a multinational company conducting virtual-shopping studies in North and South America, Europe, Asia and Australia can create virtual stores in each country and region using the appropriate local products, shelf layouts and currencies. Once the stores are online, a product concept can be quickly tested across locations. Research results, revealing markets with the greatest opportunity for a successful launch, can be communicated to headquarters electronically.

Virtual reality research also has its limitations. Simulated shopping situations never quite match the real thing. It is not clear how true test participants' responses are in a simulated experience.

So what's ahead for virtual reality in marketing? Some pioneers are extremely enthusiastic about the technology – they predict that the virtual store may become a major channel for personal and direct interactions with consumers – not just for research, but sales and service as well. The potential for conducting this type of research over the Internet is explosive as virtual stores become a reality on the Web. As one observer notes, 'This is what I read about in science fiction books when I was growing up. It's the thing of the future.' For many marketers, that future is already a virtual reality.

Sources: Quotes and extracts from Raymond R. Burke, 'Virtual shopping: breakthrough in marketing research', *Harvard Business Review* (March–April 1996), pp. 120–31; Tom Dellacave, Jr, 'Curing market research headaches', *Sales and Marketing Management* (July 1996), pp. 84–5; Brian Silverman, 'Get 'em while they're hot', *Sales and Marketing Management* (February 1997), pp. 47–8, 52; Tim Studt, 'VR speeds up car designs', *Research & Development* (March 1998), p. 74; Sara Sellar, 'The perfect trade show rep', *Sales & Marketing Management* (April 1999), p. 11.

Simulated test markets overcome some of the disadvantages of standard and controlled test markets. They usually cost much less, can be run in eight weeks and keep the new product out of competitors' view. Yet, because of their small samples and simulated shopping environments, many marketers do not think that simulated test markets are as accurate or reliable as larger, real-world tests. Still, simulated test markets are used widely, often as 'pre-test' markets. Because they are fast and inexpensive, they can be run to assess quickly a new product or its marketing programme. If the pre-test results are strongly positive, the product might be introduced without further testing. If the results are very poor, the product might be dropped or substantially redesigned and retested. If the results are promising but indefinite, the product and marketing programme can be tested further in controlled or standard test markets.[16]

■ Test marketing new industrial products

Business marketers use different methods for test marketing their new products, such as: product-use tests; trade shows; distributor/dealer display rooms; and standard or controlled test markets.

Product-use tests Here the business marketer selects a small group of potential customers who agree to use the new product for a limited time. The manufacturer's technical people watch how these customers use the product. From this test the manufacturer learns about customer training and servicing requirements. After the test, the marketer asks the customer about purchase intent and other reactions. For some products, product-use tests may involve both the business customer and final or end-user.

Trade shows These shows draw a large number of buyers who view new products in a few concentrated days. The manufacturer sees how buyers react to various product features and terms, and can assess buyer interest and purchase intentions.

Distributor and dealer display rooms The new industrial product may be placed next to other company products and possibly competitors' products in the show rooms. This method yields preference and pricing information in the normal selling atmosphere of the product.

Standard or controlled test markets These are used to measure the potential of new industrial products. The business marketer produces a limited supply of the product which is sold by the salespeople to customers in a limited number of geographical areas. The company gives the product full advertising, sales promotion and other marketing support. Such test markets let the company test the product and its marketing programme in real market situations.

commercialisation

Commercialisation
Introducing a new product into the market.

Test marketing gives management the information needed to make a final decision about whether to launch the new product. If the company goes ahead with **commercialisation** – that is, introducing the new product into the market – it will face high costs. The company will have to build or rent a manufacturing facility. It must have sufficient funds to gear up production to meet demand. Failure to do so can leave an opening in the market for competitors to step in.

For example, London-based electronics company Psion's new Series 5 palmtop organisers, launched in 1997, were so popular that the firm could not meet demand initially, due to problems at one of its component suppliers. The backlog of orders was taking some four months to clear. Potentially, that left a gap in the handheld computer market for American and Japanese rivals, which built similar machines based on an operating system designed by US software giant Microsoft.

Companies may have to spend millions on new-product advertising and sales promotion in the first year of launch. For example, Gillette spent £200 million on the global launch of its new three-blade shaving system, the Mach 3 Sensor Excel. Similarly, Unilever spent nearly £200 million to promote Omo and Persil Power across Europe.

The company launching a new product must make four decisions.

■ When?

The first decision is introduction timing – whether the time is right to introduce the new product. If it will eat into the sales of the company's other products, its introduction may be delayed. If it can be improved further, or if the economy is down, the company may wait until the following year to launch it.

■ Where?

The company must decide where to launch the new product. Should it be in a single location, or region, several regions, the national market or the international market? Few companies have the confidence, capital and capacity to launch new products into full national or international distribution. They will develop a planned market rollout over time. In particular, small companies may enter attractive cities or regions one at a time. Larger companies may quickly introduce new products into several regions or into the national market.

Companies such as Nokia, Unilever, Procter & Gamble and Colgate-Palmolive, with international distribution systems, may introduce new products through global rollouts. Colgate-Palmolive used a 'lead-country' strategy for its Palmolive Options shampoo and conditioner: it was first introduced in Australia, the Philippines, Hong Kong and Mexico, then rapidly rolled out into Europe, Asia, Latin America and Africa. However, international firms are increasingly introducing their new products in swift global assaults.

■ To whom?

Within the rollout markets, the company must target its distribution and promotion to customer groups who represent the best prospects. These prime prospects should have been profiled by the firm in earlier research and test marketing. For instance, Psion's Series 5 palmtop organiser, with a price tag of £500, was targeted at high-income executives. Generally, firms must fine-tune their targeting efforts, starting with the innovators, then looking especially for early adopters, heavy users and opinion leaders. Opinion leaders are particularly important as their endorsement of the new product has a powerful impact upon adoption by other buyers in the marketplace.

■ How?

The company also must develop an *action plan* for introducing the new product into the selected markets. It must spend the marketing budget on the marketing mix and various other activities. For example, Microsoft introduced its Windows 95 operating system for personal computers in a fanfare of publicity. Observers estimated that the company spent some $1 billion, one of the biggest-ever blitzes in advertising. The company paid up to $600,000 to fund 1.5 million copies of the software for *The Times* newspaper in London on the day of the product's launch. The soundtrack to the campaign was the Rolling Stones song, 'Start me up', for which the company had to pay $8 million. The first European markets to get Windows 95 were Benelux, France, Ireland and the United Kingdom, followed immediately by Denmark, Finland, Germany, Norway, Portugal, Spain and Sweden, and then Greece. Distributors the world over wanted to be the first to sell a copy of the software. Thousands queued late at night outside stores for the first copies. The world's first buyer was a business student in New Zealand, 12 hours ahead of the European launch![17]

speeding up new-product development

Many companies have traditionally used a sequential product development approach in which new products are developed in an orderly series of steps shown in Figure 14.1, starting with determining the new product strategy and ending with commercialisation. Under this **sequential product development** approach, one company department works individually to complete its phase of the development process before passing the new product on to the next department, as in a kind of relay race. The sequential process has its merits – it helps bring order and control to risky and complex new-product development projects. But the approach also can be fatally slow. In a sequential process, a bottleneck at one phase can seriously slow or even halt the entire project.

Today, 'speed to market' and reducing new-product development 'cycle time' have become pressing concerns to companies in all industries. One study, for example, found that a six-month delay in introducing a new product cut its lifetime profits by one-third. By contrast, spending 10 per cent over the development budget will reduce profits by only 2 per cent.[18]

In order to get their new products to market more quickly, many companies are dropping the sequential product development method in favour of the faster, more flexible **simultaneous product development** or team-based approach. Under this approach, company departments work closely together, overlapping the steps in the product development process to save time and increase effectiveness. Instead of passing the new product from department to department, the company assembles a team of people from various departments that stays with the new product from start to finish. Simultaneous development is more like a rugby match than a relay race – team members pass the new product back and forth as they move down-field towards the common goal of a speedy and successful new-product launch.

Top management gives the product development team general strategic direction, but on a clear-cut product idea or work plan. It challenges the team with stiff and seemingly contradictory goals – 'turn out carefully planned and superior new products, but do it quickly' – and then gives the team whatever freedom and resources it needs to meet the challenge. The team becomes a driving force that pushes the product forward. The new product team typically consists of people from the marketing, design, manufacturing and legal departments and even the supplier and customer companies.

However, the simultaneous approach has some limitations. Superfast product development can be riskier and more costly than the slower, more orderly sequential approach. And it often creates increased organisational tension and confusion. But in rapidly changing industries, facing increasingly shorter product life cycles, the rewards of fast and flexible product development far exceed the risks. Companies that get new and improved products to the market faster than competitors gain a dramatic competitive edge. They can respond more quickly to emerging consumer tastes and charge higher prices for more advanced designs.[19]

Sequential product development

A new-product development approach in which one company department works individually to complete its stage of the process before passing the new product along to the next department and stage.

Simultaneous product development

An approach to developing new products in which various company departments work closely together, overlapping the steps in the product development process to save time and increase effectiveness.

organisation for innovation

There are various ways in which companies organise for new-product development. The most common forms of organisation include product managers, new-product managers, new-product committees/departments and venture teams.

Many companies assign responsibility for new-product ideas to their product managers. Because these managers are close to the market and competition, they are ideally situated to find and develop new-product opportunities. In practice, however, this system has several faults. Product managers are usually so busy managing their product lines that they give little thought to new products other than brand modifications or extensions. They also lack the specific skills and knowledge needed to evaluate and develop new products.

Some companies have new-product managers who report to group product managers. This position 'professionalises' the new-product function. On the other hand, new-product managers tend to think in terms of product modifications and line extensions limited to their current product and markets.

Most companies have a high-level management committee charged with reviewing and approving new-product proposals. It usually consists of representatives from marketing, manufacturing, finance, engineering and other departments. Its function is not developing or coordinating new products so much as reviewing and approving new-product plans.

Large companies often establish a new-product department headed by a manager who has substantial authority and access to top management. The department's chief responsibilities include generating and screening new ideas, working with the R&D department, and carrying out field testing and commercialisation.

A more free-standing approach involves assigning major new-product development work to venture teams. A venture team is a group brought together from various operating departments and charged with developing a specific product or business. Team members are relieved of their other duties, and given a budget and a time frame. In some cases, this team stays with the product long after it is successfully introduced.

But successful new-product development is not just about having a special organisational *structure* for new-product development. An innovative organisation must have, at its helm, *top management* that gives priority to new products, which are seen as the life-blood of the company. Their *vision* for innovation is clearly communicated to, and its *value shared* by, staff at all levels of the organisation. A clear *strategy* as guiding force, backed by top management support, ensures that teams consistently perform. Top management not only believes wholeheartedly in, but also devotes sufficient resources to, new-product development. A strongly innovative organisation is also committed to its people (*staff*), investing continually in helping them to acquire and maintain the necessary *skills* to meet the challenge of innovation. The organisation must also embrace the *product champions* who, against all the odds, strive to take projects to completion. They, in turn, rely on the *executive champion*, whose authority is invaluable in fighting off the political battles that interfere with new-product progress. Furthermore, information and communication *systems* are designed to facilitate learning and to ensure that information flows quickly to critical individuals responsible for making or implementing new-product development decisions. Real innovation is a risky activity, so firms must foster an *entrepreneurial culture* and *climate* for innovation, with planning, control and reward systems encouraging risk-taking as opposed to its avoidance. Last, but not least, to innovate effectively, firms must build customer-focused, functionally well-integrated organisations. In successful innovative firms, new-product development is seldom left to chance. There may be an element of luck underpinning successful commercialisation of innovations. Luck, unfortunately, is not easy to replicate. The lessons of strategic new-product planning and implementation, however, are.[20]

We have looked at the problem of finding and developing new products. Next, let us examine the problem of managing them over their life cycle.

product life-cycle strategies

After launching the new product, the management challenge lies in making sure that the product enjoys a long and healthy life. The new product is not expected to sell for ever, but the company will seek to recover a decent profit to cover all the effort and risk that went into launching it. Management is aware that each product will have a life cycle, although the exact shape and length is not known in advance.

Figure 14.2 shows a typical **product life cycle (PLC)**, the course that a product's sales and profits take over its lifetime. The product life cycle has five distinct stages:

1. *Product development* begins when the company finds and develops a new-product idea. During product development, sales are zero and the company's investment costs mount.

2. *Introduction* is a period of slow sales growth as the product is being introduced in the market. Profits are non-existent in this stage because of the heavy expenses of product introduction.

3. *Growth* is a period of rapid market acceptance and increasing profits.

4. *Maturity* is a period of slowdown in sales growth because the product has achieved acceptance by most potential buyers. Profits level off or decline because of increased marketing outlays to defend the product against competition.

5. *Decline* is the period when sales fall off and profits drop.

Not all products follow the product life cycle. Some products are introduced and die quickly; others stay in the mature stage for a long, long time. Some enter the decline stage and are then cycled back into the growth stage through strong promotion or repositioning.

The PLC concept can describe a product class (petrol-engined cars), a product form (people-carrier) or a brand (the Fiat Punto). The PLC concept applies differently in each case. Product classes have the longest life cycles. The sales of many product

Product life cycle (PLC)

The course of a product's sales and profits over its lifetime. It involves five distinct stages: product development, introduction, growth, maturity and decline.

Figure 14.2

Sales and profits over the product's life from inception to demise

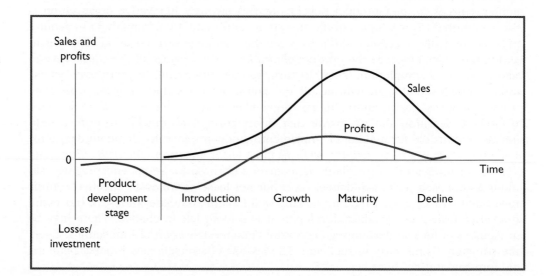

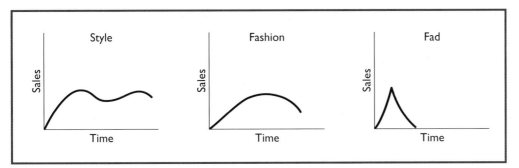

classes stay in the mature stage for a long time. Product forms, in contrast, tend to have the standard PLC shape. Product forms such as 'cream deodorants', the 'dial telephone' and 'phonograph records' passed through a regular history of introductions, rapid growth, maturity and decline. A specific brand's life cycle can change quickly because of changing competitive attacks and responses. For example, although teeth-cleaning products (product class) and toothpaste (product form) have enjoyed fairly long life cycles, the life cycles of specific brands have tended to be much shorter.

The PLC concept can also be applied to what are known as styles, fashions and fads. Their special life cycles are shown in Figure 14.3. A **style** is a basic and distinctive mode of expression. For example, styles appear in British homes (Edwardian, Victorian, Georgian); clothing (formal, casual); and art (realistic, surrealistic, abstract). Once a style is invented, it may last for generations, coming in and out of vogue. A style has a cycle showing several periods of renewed interest.

A **fashion** is a currently accepted or popular style in a given field. For example, the 'preppie look' in the clothing of the late 1970s and 1980s gave way to the 'loose and layered' look of the 1990s. Fashions tend to grow slowly, remain popular for a while, then decline slowly.

Fads are fashions that enter quickly, are adopted with great zeal, peak early and decline very fast. They last only a short time and tend to attract only a limited following. Fads often have a novel or quirky nature, as when people start buying Rubik's cubes, 'pet rocks' or yo-yos. Fads appeal to people who are looking for excitement, a way to set themselves apart or something to talk about to others. Fads do not survive for long because they normally do not satisfy a strong or lasting need or satisfy it well.[21] However, some fads, like Ty Inc.'s Beanie Babies, may begin life as fads but later become sought-after products that fetch a high price. Beanie Babies were originally children's toys. The craze has now passed over to adults who now make up 70 per cent of collectors. They trade the 212-strong range of animals on the secondary market (Beanies that sell for a few euros can trade for thousands), take out insurance policies in case their Beanies are stolen and write in for legal advice about how to split their collections if they get divorced. The Beaniex.com auction site for beanies has featured 'Peanut', a royal blue elephant, for close to €5,500 and 'Brownie Brown Bear' for over €2,500.[22]

The PLC concept can be applied by marketers as a useful framework for describing how products and markets work. But using the PLC concept for forecasting product performance or for developing marketing strategies presents some practical problems.[23] For example, managers may have trouble identifying which stage of the PLC the product is in, pinpointing when the product moves into the next stage and determining the factors that affect the product's movement through the stages. In practice, it is difficult to forecast the sales level at each PLC stage, the length of each stage and the shape of the PLC curve.

Using the PLC concept to develop marketing strategy can also be difficult because strategy is both a cause and a result of the product's life cycle. The product's current PLC position suggests the best marketing strategies, and the resulting marketing

Style
A basic and distinctive mode of expression.

Fashion
A current accepted or popular style in a given field.

Fads
Fashions that enter quickly, are adopted with great zeal, peak early and decline very fast.

strategies affect product performance in later life-cycle stages. Yet when used carefully, the PLC concept can help in developing good marketing strategies for different stages in the product life cycle.

We looked at the product development stage of the product life cycle in the first part of the chapter. Now let us look at strategies for each of the other life-cycle stages.

introduction stage

Introduction stage
The product life-cycle stage when the new product is first distributed and made available for purchase.

The **introduction stage** starts when the new product is first launched. Introduction takes time, and sales growth is apt to be slow. Well-known products such as instant coffee, personal computers and mobile telephones lingered for many years before they entered a stage of rapid growth.

In this stage, as compared to other stages, profits are negative or low because of the low sales and high distribution and promotion expenses. Much money is needed to attract distributors and build their inventories. Promotion spending is relatively high to inform consumers of the new product and get them to try it. Because the market is not generally ready for product refinements at this stage, the company and its few competitors produce basic versions of the product. These firms focus their selling on those buyers who are the readiest to buy – usually the higher-income groups. For radical product technologies, such as the video cassette recorder (VCR), electronic calculators and mobile telecommunications, business or professional users were the earliest targets.

A company might adopt one of several marketing strategies for introducing a new product. It can set a high or low level for each marketing variable, such as price, promotion, distribution and product quality. Considering only price and promotion, for example, management might *skim* the market *slowly* by launching the new product with a high price and low promotion spending. The high price helps recover as much gross profit per unit as possible, while the low promotion spending keeps marketing spending down. Such a strategy makes sense when the market is limited in size, when most consumers in the market know about the product and are willing to pay a high price (these consumers are typically called the 'innovators'), and when there is little immediate potential competition. If, however, most consumers in the limited market are unaware and know little about the innovation, and require educating and convincing, a high level of promotion spending is required. A high-price, high-promotion strategy also helps the firm to *skim rapidly* the price-insensitive end of the market in the early stages of the new product's launch.

On the other hand, a company might introduce its new product with a low price and heavy promotion spending (a *rapid penetration* strategy). This strategy promises to bring the fastest market penetration and the largest market share, and it makes sense when the market is large, potential buyers are price sensitive and unaware of the product, there is strong potential competition, and the company's unit manufacturing costs fall with the scale of production and accumulated manufacturing experience. A low-price, but low promotion spend (or *slow penetration* strategy) may be chosen instead if buyers are price conscious, but the firm wants to keep its launch costs down because of resource constraints.

A company, especially the *market pioneer*, must choose a launch strategy consistent with its intended product positioning. It should realise that the initial strategy is just the first step in a grander marketing plan for the product's entire life cycle. If the pioneer chooses its launch strategy to make a 'killing', it will be sacrificing long-run revenue for the sake of short-run gain. As the pioneer moves through later stages of the life cycle, it will have continuously to formulate new pricing, promotion and other marketing strategies. It has the best chance of building and retaining market leadership if it plays its cards correctly from the start.[24]

growth stage

If the new product meets market needs or stimulates previously untapped needs, it will enter a **growth stage**, in which sales will start climbing quickly. The early adopters will continue to buy, and later buyers will start following their lead, especially if they hear favourable word-of-mouth. Attracted by the opportunities for profit, new competitors will enter the market. They will introduce new product features, improve on the pioneer's product and expand the market for the product. The increase in competitors leads to an increase in the number of distribution outlets, and sales jump just to build reseller inventories. Prices remain where they are or fall only slightly. Companies keep their promotion spending at the same or a slightly higher level. Educating the market remains a goal, but now the company must also meet the competition.

Profits increase during the growth stage, as promotion costs are spread over a large volume and as unit-manufacturing costs fall. The firm uses several strategies to sustain rapid market growth as long as possible. It improves product quality and adds new product features and models. It enters new market segments and tries to grow sales further by selling through new distribution channels. It shifts some advertising from building product awareness to building product conviction and purchase, and it lowers prices at the right time to attract more buyers.

In the growth stage, the firm faces a trade-off between high market share and high current profit. By spending a lot of money on product improvement, promotion and distribution, the company can capture a dominant position. In doing so, however, it gives up maximum current profit, which it hopes to make up in the next stage.

Growth stage
The product life-cycle stage at which a product's sales start climbing quickly.

maturity stage

At some point, a product's sales growth will slow down and the product will enter a **maturity stage**. This maturity stage normally lasts longer than the previous stages, and it poses strong challenges to marketing management. Most products are in the maturity stage of the life cycle, and, therefore, most of marketing management deals with the mature product.

The slowdown in sales growth results in many producers with many products to sell. In turn, this overcapacity leads to greater competition. Competitors begin to cut prices, increase their advertising and sale promotions, and raise their R&D budgets to find better versions of the product. These steps lead to a drop in profit. Some of the weaker competitors start dropping out of the industry, and the industry eventually contains only well-established competitors.

Although many products in the mature stage appear to remain unchanged for long periods, most successful ones stay alive through continually evolving to meet changing consumer needs. Product managers should do more than simply ride along with or defend their mature products – a good offensive is the best defence. They should stretch their imagination and look for new ways to innovate in the market (market development), or to modify the product (product development) and the marketing mix (marketing innovation).

Maturity stage
The stage in the product life cycle where sales growth slows or levels off.

■ Market development

Here, the company tries increase the consumption of the current product. It repositions the brand and aims it at new users or market segments which the company is not currently serving, as when Johnson & Johnson targeted the adult market with its baby powder and shampoo. The company may want to reposition the brand to appeal to a larger or faster-growing segment, as Lucozade did when it introduced its new line of drinks aimed at younger users, not convalescents, the original target segment for the brand.

Adding value to a product in the late stage of its PLC is important. Swatch, eager to demonstrate their commitment to finding solutions to consumer problems, never cease to innovate.

Source: Swatch AG

■ Product development

The company might try to modify the product by changing characteristics, such as quality, features or style, to attract new users and to inspire more usage. It might improve the product's quality and performance – its durability, reliability, speed, taste. In an attempt to maintain its dominance of the world computer-games markets, five years after the launch of Playstation 1, Sony introduces PlayStation 2 (PS2), which offers a jump in performance and versatility. The PS2 incorporates two new semiconductor chips, the 'Emotion engine' 128-bit processor and the massively parallel 'Graphics Synthesiser', which give far richer and more detailed graphics than the first-generation machine. Its digital video disc (DVD) player also shows recorded films, and with a software upgrade, users can plug it into digital cable networks, transforming the Playstation into a broadband Internet-access device that can download games, films and music produced by the company's other business divisions.[25]

The firm might add new features that expand the product's usefulness, safety or convenience. For example, Nokia keeps adding new functions to its line of mobile phones, the mobile communications network operator Orange adds new services to inspire more usage of its network and Sony keeps adding new styles and features to its Walkman and Discman lines. Club Med has modified some of its holiday villages around the world to cater for business training clients. Finally, firms can improve the product's styling and attractiveness. Thus car manufacturers restyle their cars to

Club Med diversifies into the business training market.
SOURCE: Club Med

attract buyers who want a new look. The makers of consumer food and household products frequently introduce new flavours, colours, ingredients or packages to revitalise consumer buying.

■ Marketing innovation

Marketers can also try to modify the marketing mix – improving sales by changing one or more marketing-mix elements. Price cuts attract new users and competitors' customers. They can launch a better advertising campaign or use aggressive sales promotions – trade deals, discounts, premiums and contests. The company can also move into larger market channels as Dell Computers did when it pioneered telephone selling of personal computers. Or they can use mass merchandisers, if these channels are growing. Finally, the company can deliver even better value by offering new or improved services to buyers. For example, as the European market for MBA degree programmes matures, many European Business Schools are seeking to develop a competitive advantage through offering highly specific and custom-tailored management education and training programmes for corporate customers. By forging ongoing cooperation agreements, joint ventures and 'learning' partnerships with major business clients, institutions like IMD in Lausanne, Switzerland, INSEAD in Fontainebleau, France, and Manchester Business School in the United Kingdom, among others, seek to attract and retain customers by offering products and services that meet their needs more precisely than rival management schools. Others, like Cambridge University's Judge Institute of Management, are capitalising on digital education delivery technologies and the Internet and offering online distance learning masters programmes through joint ventures with external partners.[26]

decline stage

The sales of most product forms and brands eventually dip. This is the **decline stage**. The decline may be slow, as in the case of oatmeal cereal, or rapid, as in the case of phonograph records. Sales may plunge to zero, or they may drop to a low level where they continue for many years.

Sales decline for many reasons, including technological advances, shifts in consumer tastes and increased competition. As sales and profits decline, some firms withdraw from the market. Those remaining may reduce the number of their product offerings. They may drop smaller market segments and marginal trade channels, or they may cut the promotion budget and reduce their prices further.

Carrying a weak product can be very costly to a firm, and not just in profit terms. There are many hidden costs. A weak product may take up too much of management's time. It often requires frequent price and inventory adjustments. It requires advertising and sales force attention that might be better used to make 'healthy' products more

Decline stage
The product life-cycle stage at which a product's sales decline.

profitable or to create new ones. A product's failing reputation can cause customer concerns about the company and its other products. The biggest cost may well lie in the future. Keeping weak products delays the search for replacements, creates a lopsided product mix, hurts current profits and weakens the company's foothold on the future.

For these reasons, companies need to pay more attention to their ageing products. The firm should identify those products in the decline stage by regularly reviewing sales, market shares, costs and profit trends. Then management must decide whether to maintain, harvest for cash or drop each of these declining products.

Management may decide to *maintain* its brand without change in the hope that competitors will leave the industry. For example, Procter & Gamble made good profits by remaining in the declining liquid soap business as others withdrew. Alternatively, management may decide to reposition the brand in hopes of moving it back into the growth stage of the product life cycle. Or management may find new ways to revitalise the business as in the case of book clubs, a business that has recently reinvented itself by using the Internet for its own ends (see Marketing Highlight 14.3).

marketing highlight 14.3

Bertelsmann's Doubleday Direct: how the Internet breathes new life in the old club

The march of technology leaves its mark on many industries. Consumers' insatiable appetite for the latest gadget often rapidly obsoletes old technologies and companies' means of delivering consumer benefits. As the saying goes, 'New technology often kills old business.'

The birth of online book retailing would seem to spell the demise of the long-established book club business. Whereas book clubs demand a commitment from their members to buy in order to benefit from discounts, Internet bookshops, such as Amazon and others like it, don't. Moreover, the big online retailers outflanked the old, general-interest book clubs on product range and discounted bestsellers. For Bertelsmann, the largest book-club company in the world, with 25 million members, the problem was patently clear. Doubleday Direct, one of America's biggest book club companies, which it owns, experienced a 10 per cent fall in customer enrolment over 1998–9.

Bertelsmann responded to the Internet challenge by using the new technology for its own ends. In order to launch into online retailing, it acquired a 50 per cent stake in Barnesandnoble.com and introduced bol.com in Europe in 1999. Doubleday Direct Literary Guild and Time Warner's Book of the Month Club later joined forces on the Internet. Doubleday Direct employed Seth Radwell, an e-commerce man who helped launch Bertelsmann's online retailing, to redesign the book club for the Web.

Online book clubs like Doubleday Direct may still find it difficult to compete head-on with big Internet retailers such as Amazon on range and lower-price bestsellers. However, book clubs will do better in special-interest niches, particularly where newspaper reviews and bestseller lists are irrelevant and recommendations, instead, are more important. Book clubs use people, not software, to make recommendations. Amazon's automated 'people-who-bought-that-also-bought-this' system is therefore unsatisfactory for customers in special-interest categories. Book clubs are also not mere distributors, but are licensed by publishers to produce their own editions, which allows them to discount all books, not just bestsellers. Moreover, as the Internet enables book clubs to reach small audiences more easily, they are now able to launch specialist clubs at much lower costs. Hence Doubleday Direct is able to revitalise its business through offering new niche products such as Venus, which covers erotica for women, Black Expressions (for black families), Mango (titles for young women), Rhapsody (for romance) and a gay-and-lesbian club.

Doubleday Direct's online recruitment is picking up fast. Although management expected 5,000 new members to enrol in the three months after it went online, the figure was closer to 30,000. While enrolment through traditional technology continues to fall, online uptake is rising, accounting for some 20 per cent of new enrolments to the book club.

Hope has replaced panic at Bertelsmann. For now, the Internet is breathing new life into the old club.

SOURCES: Adapted from 'New life in the old club', *The Economist* (26 February 2000), p. 104.

Management may decide to harvest the product, which means reducing various costs (plant and equipment, maintenance, R&D, advertising, sales force) and hoping that sales hold up. If successful, harvesting will release cash and increase the company's profits in the short run. Or management may decide to drop the product from the line. It can sell it to another firm or simply liquidate it at salvage value. For example, declining real ale sales in the UK have caused dozens of regional brewers to close down over the past decade. More recently, two of the country's largest brewers, Bass and Whitbread, have sold off their brewing interests to the Belgian group, Interbrew.[27]

Importantly, before divesting an old product, management should carefully consider if the product or technology can be revived at all. As some firms have found, ditching old technologies completely can be a mistake because technologies dismissed as yesterday's habit may turn out to be not such old hat after all.

Consider the following examples. Clockwork, once a standard technology used to power clocks, watches and children's toys, was made obsolete by battery-powered gadgets. However, as the power needed by modern circuitry decreases, clockwork is becoming a feasible power source once more. Wind-up torches and radios are on sale and the US military is even considering hand-cranked satellite navigation devices and landmine detectors that would save soldiers from carrying bulky battery packs.

Electronic devices containing valves, then transistors and finally microprocessors displaced mechanical components used in calculators some decades ago. Now, microscopic mechanical components are also staging a comeback. These are used in a new class of silicon chips which perform functions that electronic devices cannot, such as tiny silicon arms and levers that act as compact filters, timekeepers, optical switches and sensors.[28]

Table 14.2 summarises the key characteristics of each stage of the product life cycle. The table also lists the marketing objectives and strategies for each stage.[29]

summary

Organisations must develop new products and services. Their current products face limited life spans and must be replaced by newer products. But new products can fail – the risks of innovation are as great as the rewards. The key to successful innovation lies in a total-company effort, strong planning, a marketing focus and a *systematic new-product development process*.

We examined the new-product development process which covers nine stages. The process starts with determining the *new-product strategy*, which provides direction for the new-product development effort. Next, the company must find new-product ideas. *Idea generation* may stem from internal sources and from external sources, such as customers, competitors, distributors, suppliers and others. Next comes *idea screening*, which reduces the number of ideas based on the company's defined criteria. Ideas that pass the screening stage continue through product *concept development*, in which a detailed version of the new-product idea is stated in meaningful consumer terms. In the next stage, *concept testing*, new-product concepts are tested with a group of target consumers to determine if the concepts have strong consumer appeal. Strong concepts proceed to *marketing strategy development*, in which an initial marketing strategy for the new product is developed from the product concept. In the *business analysis* stage, a review of the sales, costs and profit projections for the new product is undertaken to determine whether it is likely to satisfy the company's

	Introduction	Growth	Maturity	Decline
Characteristics				
Sales	Low sales	Rapidly rising sales	Peak sales	Declining sales
Costs	High cost per customer	Average cost per customer	Low cost per customer	Low cost per customer
Profits	Negative	Rising profits	High profits	Declining profits
Customers	Innovators	Early adopters	Middle majority	Laggards
Competitors	Few	Growing number	Stable number beginning to decline	Declining number
Marketing *objectives*	Create product awareness and trial	Maximise market share	Maximise profit while defending market share	Reduce expenditure and milk the brand
Strategies				
Product	Offer a basic product	Offer product extensions, service, warranty	Diversify brand and models	Phase out weak items
Price	Use cost-plus	Price to penetrate market	Price to match or beat competitors	Cut price
Distribution	Build selective distribution	Build intensive distribution	Build more intensive distribution	Go selective: phase out unprofitable outlets
Advertising	Build product awareness among early adopters and dealers	Build awareness and interest in the mass market	Stress brand differences and benefits	Reduce to level needed to retain hard-core loyals
Sales promotion	Use heavy sales promotion to entice trial	Reduce to take advantage of heavy consumer demand	Increase to encourage brand switching	Reduce to minimal level

Source: *Marketing Management: Analysis, planning, implementation, and control*, 9th Edition by Philip Kolter, © 1997. Reprinted by permission of Pearson Education, Inc., Upper Saddle River, NJ: NJ07458.

Table 14.2

Summary of product life-cycle characteristics, objectives and strategies

objectives. Positive results here moves the concept into *product development*, which now calls for a large jump in investment. As the product becomes more concrete, it is subjected to functional and customer tests. If it passes these tests, the product moves to *test marketing*, at which the product and marketing programme are tested in a more realistic market setting. The company goes ahead with *commercialisation* if test-market results are positive. The purpose of each stage is to decide whether the idea should be further developed or dropped.

Each product has a *life cycle* marked by a changing set of problems and opportunities. The sales of the typical product follow an S-shaped curve made up of five stages. The cycle begins with the *product development* stage when the company finds and develops a new-product idea. The *introduction stage* is marked by slow growth and low profits as the product is distributed to the market. If successful, the product enters a *growth stage*, which offers rapid sales growth and increasing profits. Next comes a *maturity stage*, when sales growth slows down and profits stabilise. The company seeks strategies to revitalise sales growth, including market, product and marketing-mix modification. Finally, the product enters a *decline stage*, in which sales and profits dwindle. Management must decide whether to maintain the brand, without change, hoping competitors will drop out of the market; harvest, by reducing costs and maintaining sales; or drop the product, selling it to another firm or liquidating it at salvage value.

discussing the issues

1. Ericsson, the Swedish telecommunications group, increased its spending on new product development over the 1990s. Its chief executive, Lars Ramqvist, extols the power of innovation: invest to the utmost in new products or services, forget about short-term profits and be willing to take risks. Ericsson soon came to dominate the world market for mobile phone systems and digital cellular equipment. Why do you think a willingness to take risks is so important when making heavy investments in developing new products and services? Is technology alone sufficient for success? What other factors do you think facilitate the successful commercialisation of new products and technologies?

2. Various studies suggest that less than a third of new-product ideas come from the customer. Does this low percentage conflict with the marketing concept's philosophy of 'find a need and fill it'? Why or why not?

3. Many businesses have formal new-product development systems. Yet recent studies suggest that most successful new products were those that had kept away from the formal system. Why might this be true?

4. What factors must be considered when testing new-product ideas and concepts with potential customers? How might the Internet assist marketers in these efforts to gauge new-product appeal to potential customers?

5. Do you think that the product life-cycle concept is a useful marketing-planning tool? Why or why not?

applying the concepts

1. Go to a grocery store you normally shop at. Make a list of ten items that appear to be new products. If you prefer, you can visit an online retail store and perform the exercise. In either case, note any information provided by the store or product packaging concerning the new offering. Rate each product for its level of innovation: give a '10' score for extremely novel and highly innovative products and '1' for a very minor change such as an improved package or fragrance. How truly new or innovative are these products overall? Do you think companies are being too risk averse because 'pioneers are the ones who get shot'?

2. 'Danger, Will Robinson! Danger!' might be one of the most memorable phrases ever uttered by a robot. However, today, the phrase would more likely be 'Buy Me! Take Me Home!' Who will offer the first practical, affordable home robot? NASA? Intel? Sony? Lego? Did you say Lego? Yes, the same little company that developed those great plastic building blocks has now developed several models of home robots (such as the R2-D2 model from *Star Wars*) that sell for as little as €250. These Lego model kits contain Lego pieces, light and touch sensors, gears and a minicomputer brick that forms the core of the system. The small, efficient robots already perform many hard-to-believe tasks (without complaining), and Lego is making daily upgrades. Copycat competitors have already begun a modification frenzy that will one day produce an awesome personal assistant. See www.lego.com, www.legomindstorms.com, www.lugnet.com and www.crynwr.com/lego-robotics for more information.

    (a) Who might the first customers be for a Lego robot? Explain.

    (b) Project the product life cycle for this new product. Explain your thinking.

    (c) Outline a strategy for positioning this product away from the toy category and into the 'personal-device' category.

    (d) Design a quick test market study for the Lego robot. Where would you administer the test?

references

1. Allyson L. Stewart, '"Innovative" products introduced in Europe', *Marketing News* (10 April 2000), pp. 19–20.

2. Adapted from 'Once more, with Elan', *The Economist* (11 December 1999), p. 93.

3. Fiona Harvey, 'High-tech ballpoint pen gets the message across', *Financial Times* (7 April 2000), p. 4.

4. Philip Kotler, *Kotler on Marketing* (New York: Free Press, 1999), p. 51; Robert G. Cooper, 'New product success in industrial firms', *Industrial Marketing Management*, **21** (1992), pp. 215–23; William Bolding, Ruskin Morgan and Richard Staelin, 'Pulling the plug to stop the new product drain', *Journal of Marketing Research* (February 1997), pp. 164–76.

5. For an excellent review, see Mitzie M. Montoya-Weiss and Roger Calantone, 'Determinants of new product performance: a review and meta-analysis', *Journal of Product Innovation Management*, 11 (1994), pp. 397–417. See also Don H. Lester, 'Critical success factors for new product development', *Research-Technology Management* (January–February 1998), pp. 36–43; Michael Song and Mark E. Parry, 'A cross-national comparative study of new product development processes: Japan and United States', *Journal of Marketing* (April 1997), pp. 1–18; Jerry Wind and Vijay Mahajan, 'Issues and opportunities in new product development', *Journal of Marketing Research* (February 1997), pp. 1–12; Robert G. Cooper and Elko J. Kleinschmidt, *New Product: The key factors in success* (Chicago, IL: American Marketing Association, 1990); Axel Johne and Patrician Snelson, *Successful Product Development: Lessons from American and British firms* (Oxford: Blackwell, 1990).

6. C. Merle Crawford, *New Products Management*, 4th edn (Boston, MA: Irwin, 1994), Ch. 3.

7. See Rosbeth Moss Kanter, 'Don't wait to innovate', *Sales and Marketing Management* (February 1997), pp. 22–4; Greg A. Steven and James Burley, '3,000 raw ideas equals 1 commercial success!', *Research-Technology Management* (May–June 1997), pp. 16–27.

8. See 'Listening to the voice of the marketplace', *Business Week* (21 February 1983), p. 90; Eric von Hipple, 'Get new products from consumers', *Harvard Business Review* (March–April 1982), pp. 117–22.

9. Lisa Wirkkala, 'Sibelius? No, it's my mobile', *The European Magazine* (17–23 April 1997), p. 7.

10. Andrew Baxter, 'Heineken wins the battle of the tainted bottle', *Financial Times* (11 May 2000), p. 24.

11. Philip Kotler, *Kotler on Marketing* (New York: Free Press, 1999), pp. 43–4.

12. See 'DaimlerChrysler plans '04 launch of fuel cell car', *Ward's Auto World* (April 1999), p. 25; and William J. Cook, 'A Mercedes for the future', *U.S. News & World Report* (29 March 1999), p. 62.

13. For more on product concept testing, see William L. Moore, 'Concept testing', *Journal of Business Research*, **10** (1982), pp. 279–94; David A. Schwartz, 'Concept testing can be improved – and here's how', *Marketing News* (6 January 1984), pp. 22–3.

14. 'Taking the toxin out of teeth', *Innovation and Technology Transfer*, **1** (January 2000), pp. 7–8. More information on the Innovation Relay Centre, IRC Northern Sweden, can be obtained by visiting their website: www.uminovacenter.umu.se.

15. See Howard Schlossberg, 'IRI, Nielsen slug it out in "Scanning Wars"', *Marketing News* (2 September 1991), pp. 1, 47.

16. For more on simulated test markets, see Kevin Higgins, 'Simulated test marketing winning acceptance', *Marketing News* (1 March 1985), pp. 15, 19; Howard Schlossberg, 'Simulated vs traditional test marketing', *Marketing News* (23 October 1989), pp. 1–2.

17. David Short, 'Microsoft goes hard sell', *The European* (24–30 August 1995), p. 17; Malcom Laws and Peggy Salz-Trautman, 'Stores are braced for launch of Windows 95', *The European* (24–30 August 1995), p. 21.

18. Don G. Reinertsen, 'The search for new product killers', *Electronic Business* (July 1983), pp. 62–6.

19. Hirotake Takeuchi and Ikujiro Nonaka, 'The new product development game', *Harvard Business Review* (January–February 1986), pp. 137–46; Bro Uttal, 'Speeding new ideas to market', *Fortune* (2 March 1987), pp. 62–5; Craig A. Chambers, 'Transforming new product development', *Research-Technology Management* (November–December 1996), pp. 32–8; Srikant Datar, Jordan C. Clark, Sundre Kekre, Surendra Rajiv and Kannan Srinivasan, 'Advantages of time-based new product development in a fast-cycle industry', *Journal of Marketing Research* (February 1997), pp. 36–49.

20. See Jerry Wind and Vijay Mahajan, 'Issues and opportunities in new product development', *Research-Technology Management* (May–June 1997), pp. 16–27; Vittorio Chiesa, Paul Coughlan and Chris A. Voss, 'Development of a technical inovation audit', *Journal of Product Innovation Management*, **13**

(1996), pp. 105–36; Robert G. Cooper and Elko J. Kleinschmidt, 'Benchmarking the firm's critical success factors in new product development', *Journal of Product Innovation Management*, **12** (1995), pp. 374–91; Shona L. Brown and Kathleen M. Eisenhardt, 'Product development: past research, present findings, and future directions', *Academy of Management Review* (April 1995), p. 343.

21. See David Stipp, 'The theory of fads', *Fortune* (14 October 1996), pp. 49–52; John Grossmann, 'A follow-up on four fabled frenzies', *Inc.* (October 1994), pp. 66–7.

22. 'You've Beanie had', *The Economist* (4 September 1999), p. 78.

23. See George S. Day, 'The product life cycle: analysis and applications issues', *Journal of Marketing* (Fall 1981), pp. 60–7; Chuck Ryan and Walter E. Rigg, 'Redefining the product life cycle: the five-element product wave', *Business Horizons* (September–October 1996), pp. 33–40.

24. For a discussion of how brand performance is affected by the product life cycle stage at which the brand enters the market, see Venkatesh Shankar, Gregory S. Carpenter and Lekshman Krishnamurthi, 'The advantages of entry in the growth stage of the product life cycle: an empirical analysis', *Journal of Marketing Research* (May 1999), pp. 269–76.

25. 'In their dreams', *The Economist* (26 February 2000), pp. 99–100.

26. See Linda Anderson, 'Cambridge at a distance', *Financial Times* (17 July 2000), p. 14; 'Financial Times Survey: Business Education', *Financial Times* (3 April 2000), pp. I–VIII (or visit their website at www.ft.com/ftsurveys/); Michael Rowe, 'Joint ventures keep up with change', *The European* (7–13 March 1996), p. 29; Joshua Jampol, 'French schools link food firms', *The European* (20–6 June 1996), p. 31.

27. 'Battling brewers', *The Economist* (18 March 2000), pp. 89–90; 'Brewer's droop', *The Business FT Weekend Magazine* (29 July 2000), pp. 34–6.

28. 'In praise of old technology', *The Economist* (17 April 1999), p. 22.

29. For a more comprehensive discussion of marketing strategies over the course of the product life cycle, see Philip Kotler, *Marketing Management*, The Millennium Edition (Upper Saddle River, NJ: Prentice Hall, 2000), Ch. 10, pp. 303–16.

case 14

The Swatchmobile: any colour combination, including black

If someone asked you what a Swatch watch and a Mercedes-Benz car have in common, you would probably answer, 'not much'. Perhaps you'd think the question was the lead-in to a joke. After all, the Swatch is a disposable €40–50 fashion watch made on assembly lines from plastic parts. Mercedes, by contrast, prides itself on making the 'best engineered cars in the world' – highly complex machines designed by engineers who cut no corners and make no compromises.

An unlikely marriage

Well, that's all true, but the Swiss Corporation for Microelectronics and Watchmaking Industries (SMH) and Mercedes do have one thing in common – the Swatchmobile. In 1994, the two companies announced that they would jointly develop an innovative, subcompact, economy car designed to reach speeds of up to 130 km per hour while getting 115 km per gallon. The idea behind the joint venture was to combine Mercedes' knowledge of how to design and build cars with SMH's knowledge of microtechnology design and automated production.

From the drawing board

Although he was an engineer, Nicolas Hayek of SMH does not design Swatches; nor will he design Swatchmobiles. He saw marketing energy and style as his strength. Hayek aimed to employ dozens of designers and artists as well as engineers to work on the Swatchmobile. 'Expect it to be offered in any colour – and any combination of colours – you want, *including* black', says Hayek.

The Swatchmobile concept eventually resulted from the work of several dozen young jeans-and-sweatshirt-clad engineers who laboured around the clock for three years in a secret garage in Biel, Switzerland. Its lightweight plastic body was designed to carry two people and their shopping through dense city traffic. It would be about 20 per cent smaller than a typical subcompact – you could park it sideways in a typical parking space! It would be a super-environmentally efficient car, with a fuel consumption rate half that of today's average family car. The two-seater would also combine the safety features of a Mercedes with the funkiness of a Swatch watch. According to Hayek, the Swatchmobile will be 'an

effort to change people's habits because it is only a two-seater'.

To help accomplish all this, the engineers designed a 600 cc, three-cylinder engine that would run on petrol, electricity, or a combination of the two and weigh one-tenth the amount of a typical petrol engine while achieving equal power.

Please. Not another European carmaker

Some saw Hayek's ideas as foolhardy. There was already overcapacity in the world car market. Bankers and other potential backers were openly critical of the venture. It was one step too far at the wrong time and in the wrong market. Some industry observers were not impressed either. Was it one diversification too far for both Mercedes and Swatch? How could the flamboyant Hayek work with Mercedes' technocrats? Would the Swatch and Mercedes brand names fit together?

However, others thought that the unlikely marriage was the result of market realities. Swatch, following its success in watches, was searching for something else on which to put its name. It had tried telephones, pager watches and sunglasses – all without much success. In the meantime, Mercedes watched its sales plummet 11 per cent in the early 1990s because of stiff Japanese competition in the luxury car market. Mercedes also intended to change itself from a luxury carmaker into a full-range producer by broadening its product range to cover four-wheel-drive sports/recreational vehicles, people carriers and small cars. The company plans to build 200,000 small family cars a year in Germany. It had already announced plans to introduce a compact, four-seat model called the 'Vision A' at a price of €20,000 in 1997.

A MORI survey sheds another light on the changing market. The study showed that 85 per cent of drivers still saw their car as an essential part of their lives. But security and environmental friendliness topped the new car-buyer's agenda, especially for women and the young. Top speed dropped was less important. Most wanted airbags, anti-locking brakes and catalytic converters in their next car, and would trade up to get them. The report heralded the 'light green' consumers, who want a car but care about its environmental impact. Moreover, European Commission pressure on the motor industry has escalated, and car manufacturers were expected to reduce emissions from the current average of 7 litres per 100 km to 5 litres per 100 km by 2005. Many car companies were already working on concepts for smaller cars powered with electric engines.

The Swatchmomerc?

Mercedes set up with SMH a joint-venture company, called Micro-Compact-Car (MCC), to develop the new car. Hayek initially owned 49 per cent of the company with Mercedes owning 51 per cent. MCC is headquartered in Biel, where it has 80 people on its staff. It also has a technical centre in Renningen, Germany, where it employs 170 people. The company changed the car's name to 'Smart' – a combination of Swatch, Mercedes, and art. However, the Smart car hit serious trouble just as it was about to be launched at the Frankfurt Motor Show in September 1997. Hayek bowed to pressure from shareholders, announcing that he would not participate in a Sfr200 million capital injection into the Smart joint venture, cutting SMH's stake from 49 per cent to 19 per cent. Mercedes has since purchased the remaining interest in the company so that it now owns 100 per cent.

MCC has invested about Sfr915 million for research and development on the new car, and its suppliers have invested another Sfr915 million for new plant and equipment. MCC will produce the car in Hambach, France. The company planned to have an initial production of 100,000–150,000 cars a year and to reach full capacity by 1999. At full capacity, the plant will employ 2,000 people and produce 200,000 cars per year.

The Smart car targets single people aged 18–36 and childless, dual-income couples living in urban areas who want a second car. The company wants to position the car as a fun but useful means of transportation in crowded cities. Although the car is small, it offers the crash protection of a Mercedes-Benz saloon.

Since the initial conception, the designers have abandoned the electric engine, because of the lack of adequate batteries, in favour of a small petrol engine. Instead of using a conventional assembly line, assemblers will snap the cars together, much as you would a child's toy model car, using five subassembly modules that come from suppliers' factories located immediately around the assembly site in Hambach. Workers can assemble the car in just four and a half hours. Because the car snaps together, the company will offer customers the ability to change the cars' features. For example, if after a month or so the customer does not like the car's colour, he or she can simply replace the panels with others of another colour. The car's overall length is 2.49 metres. Even though it is small on the outside, engineers say it is roomy on the inside. The Smart gets 47 to 49 miles per gallon with its 44–54 horsepower engines and has a top speed of 84 mph. Maintenance stops are guaranteed to take less than two hours.

The company expected to begin selling the car in March 1998. However, the launch was delayed for six months in order to rectify safety and production problems. The Smart car was eventually launched in September 1998 at a price between €11,190 and €13,568. The dealer margin is typically 16 per cent. Dealers offer a leasing package that includes the rental of a larger car for two weeks per year when the customer might want more seats and room for luggage. Financing, licensing and insurance are available on site, so purchasing a Smart takes less than an hour.

MCC began signing up dealers in 1997, with a target of signing up 100 in Europe (excluding the United Kingdom) in the first phase of developing distribution. Although it will give preference to Mercedes dealers, it has also advertised for interested entrepreneurs. Even Mercedes dealers, however, would have to set up separate dealerships to handle Smart. The second phase of distribution is scheduled to begin in 2001, covering the United Kingdom, Japan and other right-hand-drive countries and the United States. However, the UK launch was brought forward by 12 months due to a sharp rise in 'grey imports' by independent car dealers supplying Smart cars from continental Europe. The move was also part of a programme to lift Smart car sales by 20 per cent to 100,000 in 2000.

Dealers for the Smart Car will have to invest about €6 million to open a 'Smart Centre'. MCC prefers that dealers build on land located near suburban shopping centres. The dealer will get an assigned geographic area capable of generating 1,000 unit sales per year with sales forecast to increase to 1,300 units per year by 2001. The dealer will need a staff of 15 people initially with the expectation that it will sell 1,000 units in the first year.

The franchise agreement imposes tight restrictions on showroom design and customer service. Dealers who violate provisions in the agreement can lose their franchise quickly. The agreement requires that the dealer pay a fee of €85 per new car and €43 per used car to MCC to support marketing campaigns, as well as about €49,000 to support marketing research.

Dealers will also have to establish two other locations where consumers can get information about the car. One location will have to be in an airport or railway station, and a second location will have to be in a shopping centre.

Prior to the car's launch in France, MCC began a €59 million 'street awareness' campaign in October 1997 that featured promotion teams handing out postcards which merely read, 'Reduce to the max', without mentioning the car's name. Early ads just depicted the car operating in urban environments.

MCC projects that after five years, the typical dealer will have sales of about €21.5 million, with a gross profit on sales of 15 per cent, and a net return of 4–5 per cent of sales, about €862,750.

Will the Smart car fly?

Needless to say, there are plenty of sceptics who do not believe a tiny, two-seater car with almost no luggage space will make it in the highly competitive car market. They question its chances of succeeding against four-seater microcars from Fiat, Volkswagen, Renault and Rover. It would not be easy taking on established rivals like Renault's successful Twingo and Volkswagen's new City car. Twingo is selling 230,000 a year, about 2 per cent of the west European car market. Ford, which believes that tiny cars will eventually account for about one-third of the market, has a factory in Valencia, Spain, that is already producing 200,000 Ka models per year, and it plans to increase capacity.

Mercedes has to date invested nearly DM2bn (€1.02 billion) in the project. According to Andreas Renschler, chief executive of Smart, the Smart car is not expected to make a profit before 2003. The question is: Does he still believe that Smart can sell 200,000 cars a year and make a profit in five or six years? According to one Mercedes executive, 'Smart has been one sure-fire way of losing a lot of money!'.

Now, it will be up to consumers to determine whether the sceptics were right.

Questions

1. Hayek was able to make such a great success of Swatch. How transferable is the Swatch brand to other products in other markets, including cars?

2. What is Hayek's role in the new-product development process? Assess the effectiveness of the Hayek–Mercedes venture.

3. Is the Smart car a market-driven idea? What market research should be conducted? Is there now any justification for not basing new products on marketing research?

4. Critically assess the new product launch decisions that MCC has made for the Smart car.

5. Should Mercedes rethink its ambitions in the small-car segment? What are the chances that the Smart car will be a commercial success?

6. Can the Smart car sustain a competitive advantage in the highly competitive microcar market? What marketing recommendations would you make to MCC?

SOURCES: Tony Lewis, 'What's safe, green and doesn't go too fast?', *The European* (4–10 February 1994), p. 12; Kevin Done, 'Mercedes and Swatch in minicar venture', *Financial Times* (23 February 1994), p. 1; 'Decision on "Swatchmobile" site', *Financial Times* (29 November 1994), p. 3; 'Smaller cars, bigger profits? European cars', *The Economist* (9 November 1996), p. 82; Luca Ciferri, 'Smart to get first dealers this spring', *Automotive News* (11 March 1996), p. 20; Stefan Schlott, 'Get Smart', *Automotive Industries* (August 1997), p. 75; Haig Simonian, 'Mercedes-Benz may play it smart: Luxury carmaker hints at developing tiny two-seater into a "second brand"', *Financial Times* (6 October 1997), p. 1; 'Smart car builds street awareness', *Euromarketing Via E-mail* (17 October 1997); 'Caught in a moose trap', *The European* (6–12 November 1997), pp. 28–9; 'Final sales countdown looms for Swatch's clockwork car', *The European* (4–10 September 1997), pp. 24–5; 'Not so Smart', *The Economist* (6 September 1997), p. 81; Haig Simonian, 'Daimler delays Smart car over safety worries', *Financial Times* (19 December 1997), p. 1; 'Daimler-Chrysler plays early Smart card in sales bid', *Financial Times* (2 March 2000), p. 4.

€1 = Sfr1.52 = DM1.96

internet exercises

Internet exercises for this chapter can be found on the student site of the MYPHLIP Web Site at www.booksites.net/kotler.

chapter fifteen

Marketing services

Chapter objectives *After reading this chapter, you should be able to:*

- ✦ Define a *service*.

- ✦ Explain the uniqueness of marketing services and the characteristics that affect the marketing of a service.

- ✦ Identify the additional marketing considerations for services.

- ✦ Define strategies for marketing services, including differentiation, quality and productivity.

introduction

One of the major world trends in recent years has been the phenomenal growth of services. This shift towards a service economy has largely arisen because of rising affluence, more leisure time and the growing complexity of products that require servicing. In the major European countries, America and Japan, more people are employed in services than in all other sectors of the economy put together. Both public and private sector services in these countries account for between 60 and 75 per cent of gross domestic output. In international trade, services make up nearly a quarter of the value of all international trade.[1] In fact, a variety of service industries – from banking, insurance and communications to transportation, travel and entertainment – now account for well over 60 per cent of the economy in developed countries around the world. In some countries, service occupations have been forecast to contribute to all net job growth in the next five years.[2]

Service jobs include not only those in service industries – hotels, airlines, banks, law firms, telecommunications and others – but also service jobs in product-based industries, such as corporate lawyers, medical staff and sales trainers. Product-based companies also market tangible goods with accompanying services. BMW and Ford offer more than just motor vehicles. Their offer also includes repair and maintenance services, warranty fulfilment, showrooms and other support services. Consumer services are marketed to individuals and households, while industrial services are those offered to business and other organisations.

The increase in demand for consumer and industrial services has been attributed to a number of factors. First, rising affluence has increased consumers' desire to

preview case

Lufthansa: listening to customers

A Lufthansa ad runs as follows: 'When an airline has a young fleet, experienced pilots, attentive cabin crew and the pickiest ground technicians in the world, it is free to concentrate on what is really important: you.'

A decade ago, this German airline company could never make such claims to offering the customer its undivided attention and care. Today, it remains one of the world's largest airline operators and the most pro-fitable carrier in Europe, despite tough times in an industry hit by global excess capacity and the recent war in the Balkans. Lufthansa is taking great pride in its well-earned reputation – not just for quality, but also for being a 'good listener'. It knows that superior-quality service pays off. Most importantly, everyone in Lufthansa recognises that doing what the customer wants is the key to customer retention.

Lufthansa takes the pursuit of customer satisfaction seriously. Extensive, comprehensive passenger surveys are undertaken to research the views and gather com-ments from the thousands of air travellers who fly with them and other airlines. However, it is not so much the survey results that are noteworthy, but Lufthansa's com-mitment to respond to what customers want.

One early survey of international business trav-ellers highlighted a 'wish[want]-list' for a better flight: business passengers wanted more leg-room and elbow-room, designated lounges and non-smoking aircraft, and separate check-ins and passport control.

Lufthansa responded by redesigning business-class seats to make them wider. Heavy demand on business class often means an overspill into economy class. The redesign allowed any overspill into economy class to be met by telescoping seats on one side of the aisle and extending them on the other to make the seats wider. In economy class, the centre seat of the three can be removed by telescoping it into two. On the right of the aisle, the usual three seats could be extended into wider ones. Other conveniences (e.g. modern communications systems and credit-card-operated telephones) were also incorporated in the arms of the new seats.

To ensure that Lufthansa got things right first time, from the design of the new seats to the introduction of new in-flight services, processes are carefully thought out. For example, when redesigning or improving seats, the airline seat manufacturer commissioned to do the redesign is typically brought in to work with Lufthansa's marketing and technical staff.[3]

Finding out what target customers require or desire is one thing. Responding to these demands and to the satisfaction of customers is another. But as the story above shows, a customer focus can benefit service busi-nesses. To improve service quality, the firm must listen to what customers want and then commit resources to deliver precisely that. Marketing developed initially for selling physical products, such as toothpaste, cars, steel and equipment. However, marketing principles can also be applied to organisations that offer services, such as Lufthansa.

Questions

1. For a traveller flying with Lufthansa, what exactly constitutes the 'service offering'?

2. Identify the tangible and intangible aspects of the service.

3. What are the main aspects of the service that distinguish it from physical products?

4. What criteria might customers consider when selecting an airline for business travel?

5. For physical products, the buyer can touch, see or feel and compare alternative offers before deciding which brand to purchase. Taking into account the relative intangibility of airline services, how might an airline customer determine the choice of carrier?

6. How would the marketing of a service offering differ from that of physical products? Identify the main ways in which the service provider would adapt its marketing strategies to create a competitive advantage.

contract out mundane tasks such as cleaning, cooking and other domestic activities, giving rise to a burgeoning convenience industry. Second, rising incomes and more leisure time have created greater demand for a whole array of leisure services and sporting activities. Third, higher consumption of sophisticated technologies in the home (e.g. home computers, multimedia entertainment equipment, security systems) has increased the need for specialist services to install and maintain them. In the case of business customers, more complex markets and technologies have triggered companies' need for the expertise and knowledge of service organisations, such as market research agencies, marketing and technical consultants. Furthermore, the rising pressure on firms to reduce fixed costs means that many are buying in services rather than incur the overheads involved in performing specialised tasks in-house. The need to remain flexible has also led to firms hiring services that provide use without ownership. Finally, an increasing number of firms are keen to focus on their core competences. They are beginning to contract out non-core activities, such as warehousing and transportation, thus stimulating the growth of specialist business service organisations. All these developments have, in turn, led to a growing interest in the special problems of marketing services.

Service industries vary greatly. In most countries, the *government sector* offers services: for example, legal, employment, health care, military, police, fire and postal services, schools and regulatory agencies. The *private non-profit* sector offers services such as museums, charities, churches, colleges, foundations and hospitals. A large part of the *business organisations* includes profit-oriented service suppliers like airlines, banks, hotels, insurance companies, consulting firms, medical and law practices, entertainment companies, advertising and research agencies and retailers.

As a whole, selling services presents some special problems calling for special marketing solutions. Let us now examine the nature and special characteristics of service organisations that affect the marketing of services.

nature and characteristics of a service

defining services and the service mix

A **service** is any activity or benefit that one party can offer to another which is essentially intangible and does not result in the ownership of anything. Its production may or may not be tied to a physical product.

Activities such as renting a hotel room, depositing money in a bank, travelling on an aeroplane, visiting a doctor, getting a haircut, having a car repaired, watching a professional sport, seeing a movie, having clothes cleaned at a dry cleaner and getting advice from a solicitor all involve buying a service. Service businesses are also popping up on the Internet. Everything from online betting and video replays of crucial scores of Manchester United to real-time stocks and shares information feeds are new services that people seem to be willing to pay for. The market research company Datamonitor suggests that the e-services market worldwide will reach some $1 billion by 2002, with Europe currently accounting for 11.7 per cent of the global market for Internet-based customer service solutions.[4]

Generally, a company's offering to customers often includes some services. The service component can be a minor or major part of the total offering. As such, there is rarely such a thing as a pure service or pure good. In trying to distinguish between goods and services, it may be more appropriate to consider the notion of a goods–service continuum, with offerings ranging from tangible-dominant to intangible-dominant (see Figure 15.1).

Firms can create a differential advantage by moving along the continuum, seeking to alter the balance of tangible and intangible elements associated with their offering. Five categories of offerings can be distinguished:

1. The offering consists of a *pure tangible good*, such as soap, toothpaste or salt – no services accompany the product.

Service
Any activity or benefit that one party can offer to another which is essentially intangible and does not result in the ownership of anything.

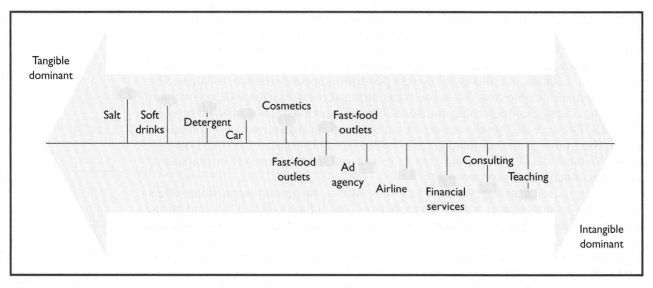

Figure 15.1

The tangible–intangible continuum for goods and services

2. The offering consists of a *tangible good with accompanying services* – the sales of technologically sophisticated products such as computers and cars are often dependent on the quality and availability of accompanying customer services (e.g. display rooms, delivery, repair and maintenance, user training programmes, installation advice and warranty fulfilment).

3. Many service providers also supply physical products along with their basic service. A *hybrid offer* consists of equal parts of goods and services. For example, people patronise restaurants for both their food and service.

4. A *service with accompanying minor goods* consists of a major service along with supporting goods. For example, British Airways and other airline passengers primarily buy transportation service, but the trip also includes some tangibles such as food, drinks and an airline magazine. The service also requires a capital-intensive good – an aeroplane – but the primary offer is a service.

5. The offering is a *pure service*, consisting primarily of a service such as a massage, babysitting, a doctor's examination or financial services.[5]

Because the service mix varies, it is difficult to generalise about services without further distinctions. One distinction is the nature of ownership – that is, whether they are private (e.g. warehousing and distribution firms, banks) or public (e.g. police, state-run hospitals) sector organisations. Another is the type of market – consumer (e.g. household insurance policy provider, retailer) or industrial (e.g. computer bureaux). Services can also involve high customer contact, where the service involves the customer's presence, as in the case of hairdressing and health care. Or there is low customer contact, as in dry cleaning and car repair, where the services are directed at objects. Services can be people-based (e.g. consultancies, education) or equipment-bound (e.g. automated car washes, vending machines, bank cash dispensers). People-based services can be further distinguished according to whether they rely on highly professional staff, such as legal advisers and medical practitioners, or unskilled labour, such as window cleaning, porters and caretakers.

The wide variety of service offerings means that service providers must address the problems specific to their particular service when seeking to create and maintain a competitive advantage. Despite this heterogeneity across sectors, there are a number of characteristics that are unique to services.

service characteristics

A company must consider five main service characteristics when designing marketing programmes: *intangibility, inseparability, variability, perishability* and *lack of ownership*. We will look at each of these characteristics in the following sections.[6]

■ Intangibility

Service intangibility means that services cannot be readily displayed, so they cannot be seen, tasted, felt, heard or smelt before they are bought. A buyer can examine in detail before purchase the colour, features and performance of an audio hi-fi system that he or she wishes to buy. In contrast, a person getting a haircut cannot see the result before purchase. Airline passengers have nothing but a ticket and the promise that they and their luggage will arrive safely at the intended destination, hopefully at the same time.

Because service offerings lack tangible characteristics that the buyer can evaluate before purchase, uncertainty is increased. To reduce uncertainty, buyers look for 'signals' of service quality. They draw conclusions about quality from the place, people, equipment, communication material and price that they can see. Therefore, the service provider's task is to 'manage the evidence' – they try to 'tangibilise the service' or the benefits offered in one or more ways. Whereas product marketers are challenged to add intangibles (e.g. fast delivery, extended warranty, after-sales service) to their tangible offers, service marketers try to add tangible cues suggesting high quality to their intangible offers.[7]

Consider a bank that wants to convey the idea that its service is quick and efficient. It must make this positioning strategy tangible in every aspect of customer

Service intangibility
A major characteristic of services – they cannot be seen, tasted, felt, heard or smelt before they are bought.

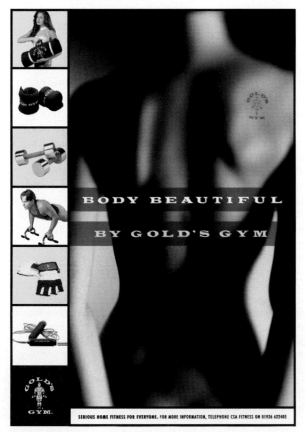

Gold's tangibilises its service by advertising the Gym's equipment line.
SOURCE: Gold's Gym/LGR International

contact through a number of marketing tools. The *place* or bank's physical setting must suggest quick and efficient service: its exterior and interior should have clean lines; internal traffic flow should be planned carefully; and waiting lines should seem short. The bank's staff (i.e. *people*) should be busy and properly dressed. There should be a sufficient number of staff to manage the workload. The *equipment* – computers, photocopiers, desks – should look modern. The bank's *communication materials* should suggest efficiency, with clean and simple designs and carefully chosen words and photos that communicate the bank's positioning. The bank should choose a name and *symbol* for its service that suggest speed and efficiency. Because service intangibility increases purchase risk, buyers tend to be more influenced by word-of-mouth, which gives credibility to the service, than by advertising messages paid for by the service provider. As such, the service marketer (the bank in this case) should stimulate word-of-mouth communication by targeting opinion leaders who could be motivated to try its services, and satisfied customers who could be encouraged to recommend its service(s) to peers and friends. Its *pricing* for various services should be kept simple and clear. It may even consider advertising its commitment to speed – ads may promise to deposit €10 in the account of any customer who waits in line for more than five minutes.

marketing highlight 15.1

Last orders for banks

'A Finnish customer pushes a trolley up to a robot till in the supermarket. The till uses a remote sensor to make up the bill which is sent to the customer's mobile phone. The buyer selects on-screen whether to pay by credit card, debit card or electronic cash, all of which is stored on the chip in the phone. There are no wallets, no loose change, no bank brand! The phone replaces the plastic card, but the bank's name is nowhere to be seen. The company behind all this could be one of today's banks, or it could be another company running the IT systems behind the phone. Customers would only deal with one firm – Vodafone, France Télécom or whoever.'

This is a 'bank-less world' scenario recently tested in Finland, which is currently leading the European Internet banking revolution, and home of MeritaNordbanken, Europe's biggest Internet bank. Indeed, it is a scenario that worries traditional bricks-and-mortar banks as telecoms companies' mobile phone SIM cards are substitutes for credit cards and cash.

Until recently, banks had to have a physical presence close to the customer in the form of a branch network where transactions were done. Things are changing. Thanks to the Internet, digital television and mobile telephones, online and virtual banking are now a reality. Traditional banks face increasing pressure to ask what makes them visible in a virtual world. Financial transactions are for the most part intangible. And, as people do not see a credit card payment, touch a mortgage or feel

a fund transfer, what features are there left in traditional banks to allow them to survive in the long run? Moreover, technology is making it easier for non-banks, like retailers, and new Internet banks, like Egg (UK) and UnoFirst (Spain), to enter the business. What makes banks special any more? As Bill Gates of Microsoft said: 'the world needs banking but it does not need banks'.

These are worrying concerns for traditional banks. They must rethink their business. Much of the time, a bank's role is not as much about managing money, but processing information. It may be that, one day, they will be relegated to the back-room, providing systems for supermarkets, airlines or television channels. Or branches will be transformed from transaction to information and advisory centres. Those that fear the worst are fast expanding into offering new services. MeritaNordbanken now runs a virtual shopping mall, and Spanish bank BBVA, which partly owns First-e, sells everything from books to groceries. The bank is dead. Long live the bank!

SOURCES: Christopher Brown-Humes, 'Internet banking. Clients engaged in revolution', in Financial Times Survey: Finland, *Financial Times* (10 July 2000), p. VI; James Mackintosh, 'The bank is dead . . .', in FT Life on the net, Chapter 8, p. 14, *Financial Times* (5 September 2000); John Wilmon, 'Branch equity', *Financial Times* (7 July 2000), p. 18; For an excellent survey of online finance, see 'A survey of online finance. The virtual threat', *The Economist* (20 May 2000). Also, further details are available from www.ft.com/lifeonthenet.

Although retail bank branches on high streets have traditionally served as conduits for delivering banking services to consumers, the problem presented by service intangibility is increasingly exacerbated by a fast-changing market environment. The Internet and new wireless application protocol (WAP) technology are creating new virtual banks, and together with increasing deregulation, have opened the floodgates to non-banks, which are making inroads into the business (see Marketing Highlight 15.1).

For some services, like football clubs, the problem of intangibility has been solved in a number of ways. Most noteworthy is the selling of replica football kits, home or away. Witness, for example, the recent, and much hyped, launch of a new replica kit by Manchester United, the UK's most commercially successful football club. The club's new strip (costing £60 for the complete kit of shirt, shorts and socks) heralded football's latest marketing blitz on the high street. Advanced orders for ManU's new kit reached record levels and sales in 2000 were set to generate a substantial portion of the country's annual £210 million kit market.[8]

■ Inseparability

Physical goods are produced, then stored, later sold and still later consumed. In contrast, services are first sold, then produced and consumed at the same time and in the same place. **Service inseparability** means that services cannot be separated from their providers, whether the providers are people or machines. If a service employee provides the service, then the employee is a part of the service. A rock concert is an example. The pop group or band is the service. It cannot deliver the service without the members of the band being present. A school or college teacher is a part of the education service provided and has to be present to deliver the service to students. Moreover, the rock group cannot deliver the service without the consumers (the audience) being present. A teacher cannot conduct the teaching session if there are no students attending class. Because the customer is also present as the service is produced, *provider–customer interaction* is a special feature of services marketing. Both the provider and the client affect the service outcome. How a doctor treats her patient or how a legal adviser relates to his client, for example, influences the client's judgement of the overall service delivered. The extent to which a teacher is able to develop a rapport with her students will influence the quality of their learning experience. Thus, it is important for service staff to be trained to interact well with clients.

A second feature of the inseparability of services is that other customers are also present or involved. The concert audience, students in the class, other passengers in a train, customers in a restaurant, all are present while an individual consumer is consuming the service. Their behaviour can determine the satisfaction that the service delivers to the individual customers. For example, an unruly crowd in the restaurant would spoil the atmosphere for other customers dining there and reduce satisfaction. The implication for management would be to ensure at all times that customers involved in the service do not interfere with each other's satisfaction.

Because of the simultaneity of service production and consumption, service providers face particular difficulty when demand rises. A goods manufacturer can make more, or mass-produce and stock up in anticipation of growth in demand. This is not possible for service operators like restaurants or a law firm. Service organisations have therefore to pay careful attention to managing growth, given the constraints. A high price is used to ration the limited supply of the preferred provider's service. Several other strategies exist for handling the problem of demand growth. First, the service provider can learn to work with larger groups, so that more customers are serviced simultaneously. For example, bigger sites or premises are used by retailers to accommodate larger numbers of customers, and a pop concert will cater for a larger audience if held in an open-air sports arena than in an enclosed concert hall.

Service inseparability
A major characteristic of services – they are produced and consumed at the same time and cannot be separated from their providers, whether the providers are people or machines.

Second, the service provider can learn to work faster. Productivity can be improved by training staff to do tasks and utilise time more efficiently. Finally, a service organisation can train more service providers.

■ Variability

Service variability
A major characteristic of services – their quality may vary greatly depending on who provides them and when, where and how.

As services involve people in production and consumption, there is considerable potential for variability. **Service variability** means that the quality of services depends on who provides them, as well as when, where and how they are provided. As such, service quality is difficult to control. For example, some hotels have reputations for providing better service than others. Within a given hotel, one registration-desk employee may be cheerful and efficient, whereas another, standing just a few metres away, may be unpleasant and slow. Even the quality of a single employee's service varies according to his or her energy and frame of mind at the time of each customer contact. For example, two services offered by the same solicitor may not be identical in performance.

The ability to satisfy customers depends ultimately on the behaviour of front-line service employees. A brilliant marketing strategy will achieve little if they do their job badly and deliver poor quality service. Service firms can take several steps towards quality control.[9] First, they can hire and train their personnel carefully. Airlines, banks and hotels, for example, invest large sums of money in training their employees to give good service. They train their front-line people so that they are empowered to take actions or do anything else to ensure that customers are treated well and any complaints are dealt with satisfactorily. However, training in many companies often boils down to little more than pep talks. In order for training to make a real difference to employees' behaviour, companies ensure that training focuses on helping employees to develop essential skills to do their jobs well. Consider the following example:

> Denmark's ISS is one of the world's leading international commercial cleaning businesses. In an industry characterised by low-skilled workers and high staff turnover, ISS trains its staff relentlessly. Commercial cleaning involves far more than just running a vacuum cleaner over the carpet. ISS serves big clients – factories, hospitals and offices. To do this well and profitably, employees must do their job efficiently. This means conserving time and cleaning supplies, improving quality and avoiding accidents and injuries. This is difficult enough in ordinary office buildings. At hospitals, chemical plants and factories, the equipment and skills needed can be tricky. Employees must also be able to spot and deal instantly with idiosyncratic customers they come across in the job. In the first six months on the job, employees are given training in cleaning techniques, such as knowing which chemicals to use for specific stains and surfaces, and in safety. The next six months, employees move on to applied economics – they learn to interpret client's contracts, how profitable a contract is and how the client's profitability contributes to that of ISS's local branch. This is invaluable if the employee is promoted to team leader, which can occur after a year. Once employees become a team leader, they receive training on how to deal with customers, coach junior staff in the team and management techniques that will help them meet performance targets, based on both profitability and customer retention. All this training helps ISS staff to do their jobs well.

Knowing how to do something well and being motivated to do it are different things. The second step towards quality control is to motivate staff by providing employee incentives that emphasise quality, such as employee-of-the-month awards or bonuses based on customer feedback.

ISS relies on a number of mechanisms to motivate its staff. One is the use of teamwork and peer pressure to motivate employees to do their best. For example, although most of the clients can be handled by a single person, ISS groups its cleaners into two- or three-person hit-squads rather than sending one person to each site. The squad works together and travels from site to site. Although seemingly inefficient, the extra motivation more than offsets the costs. ISS also encourages employees to stay loyal to the firm by paying them a little more. Managers are sometimes asked not to compete on wage costs even if it means that the division will lose some bids. The company believes that by retaining staff, all the training it has invested in is not wasted. As quality improves, the company continues to win new business, despite the higher costs. A major account won recently includes a contract to clean hotel rooms at Disneyland Paris.

A third mechanism to improve quality is by making service employees more visible and accountable to consumers – car dealerships can let customers talk directly with the mechanics working on their cars. A firm can check customer satisfaction regularly through suggestion and complaint systems, customer surveys and comparison shopping. When poor service is found, it is corrected.

In the case of ISS, management views contact between ISS supervisors and its clients' site managers as crucial. If clients are dissatisfied with the service, superiors get to know about it. In order to generate more contact with customers, ISS rescheduled many of its clients so that its teams overlap for half and hour or so with office workers, making it easier for clients to voice their complaints.[10]

Fourth, service firms can increase the consistency of employee performance by substituting equipment for staff (e.g. vending machines, automatic cash dispensers), and through standardising the service-performance process. This is done by developing a service blueprint which spells out events and processes or job procedures in a flowchart, alerting employees to potential fail points with the aim of ensuring activities are done properly (e.g. Walt Disney's theme parks, McDonald's and Club Med).

■ Perishability

Service perishability means that services cannot be stored for later sale or use. In some countries, dentists and general practitioners charge patients for missed appointments because the service value existed only at that point and disappeared when the patient did not show up. The perishability of services is not a problem when demand is steady. However, when demand fluctuates, service firms often have difficult problems. For example, public transportation companies have to own much more equipment because of rush-hour demand than they would if demand were even throughout the day.

Service firms can use several strategies for producing a better match between demand and supply. On the demand side, differential pricing – that is, charging different prices at different times – will shift some demand from peak periods to off-peak periods. Examples are cheaper early-evening movie prices, low-season holidays and reduced weekend train fares. Airline companies offer heavily discounted 'stand-by' tickets to fill unbooked seats. Or non-peak demand can be increased, as in the case of business hotels developing mini-vacation weekends for tourists. Complementary services can be offered during peak times to provide alternatives to waiting customers, such as cocktail lounges to sit in while waiting for a restaurant table and automatic tellers in banks. Reservation systems can also help manage the demand level – airlines, hotels and doctors use them regularly.

Service perishability
A major characteristic of services – they cannot be stored for later sale or use.

Services are perishable: empty seats at slack times cannot be stored for later use during peak periods.

On the supply side, firms can hire part-time employees to serve peak demand. Schools add part-time teachers when enrolment goes up, and restaurants call in part-time waiters and waitresses to handle busy shifts. Peak-time demand can be handled more efficiently by rescheduling work so that employees do only essential tasks during peak periods. Some straightforward tasks can be shifted to consumers (e.g. packing their own groceries). Or providers can share services, as when several hospitals share an expensive piece of medical equipment. Finally, a firm can plan ahead for future expansion, as when an airline company buys more wide-bodied jumbo jets in anticipation of future growth in international air travel or a theme park may buy surrounding land for later development. Service firms have to consider using any of the above strategies for achieving a better match between demand and supply. Some businesses have come up with novel solutions to perishability problems. Consider the following examples:

Club Med operates hundreds of Club med 'villages' (resorts) around the world. Unsold rooms and airline packages mean lost revenues. In addition to relying on travel agents to sell last-minute packages, the company now uses e-mail to notify people in its database early to midweek on rooms and air seats available for travel that weekend. These 'unsold inventory' are heavily discounted – typically 30 to 40 per cent below the standard package. With an average of 1.2 per cent response to these offers every month, e-mail sales of last-minute holidays are a great way of helping Club Med to deal with the perishability problem.[11]

The Dutch flower auctions in Holland provide an example of state-of-the-art auctions, where nearly 60 per cent of the world's cut flowers are sold annually. Because flowers are perishable, these auctions are designed for speed. Daily, millions of flowers are shipped to Amsterdam's Schiphol airport. They are swiftly taken to nearby auction centres. By the end of the day, over 34 million flowers and 3 million potted plants will have been purchased, covering some 60,000 transactions. Most of the flowers will then be rushed to the airport for immediate export. Over a 24-hour period, flowers are shipped to an auction centre, purchased by a wholesaler, sold to a retailer and bought by a New Yorker! The key to the process is to start with a high price set by the auctioneer, unlike the English auction in which bidders push the price up from below. The price then drops until a buyer signals he wants the goods. Each transaction takes only about four seconds. The speed is ideal for selling a large quantity of easily evaluated goods that are perishable and must be sold quickly. Since 1995, the auction houses have established an electronic system, allowing buying-at-a-distance. Online buyers can participate in several auctions simultaneously and gain a better feel for pricing and supply.

The Dutch auction has been adopted by a number of e-businesses. Intermodalex.com, for example, uses the system to lease container space on oceangoing vessels. Container space, like flowers, is perishable and is lost once the vessel casts off.[12]

■ Lack of ownership

When customers buy physical goods, such as cars and computers, they have personal access to the product for an unlimited time. They actually own the product. They can even sell it when they no longer wish to own it. In contrast, service products lack that quality of ownership. The service consumer often has access to the service for a limited time. An insurance policy is yours only when you have paid the premium and continue to renew it. A holiday is experienced and, hopefully, enjoyed, but after the event, it remains ephemeral, unlike a product in the hand. Because of the lack of ownership, service providers must make a special effort to reinforce their brand identity and affinity with the consumer by one or more of the following methods:

1. They could offer incentives to consumers to use their service again, as in the case of frequent-flyer schemes promoted by British Airways and Travel Passes offered by Scandinavian airlines.

2. They could create membership clubs or associations to give an impression of ownership (e.g. British Airways' executive clubs for air travellers, IKEA's family club membership).

Gives you control around the clock

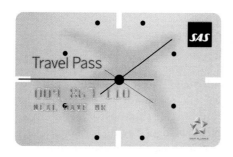

Reinforcing service brand identity and affinity with customers: SAS offers frequent travellers a ticketless Travel Pass, preloaded with 10, 20, 30 or an unlimited number of business class flights to a choice of Scandinavian cities.

Source: Scandanavian Airlines.
Agency: Admaker

Do you want to be in total control of your travel arrangements to Scandinavia? Do you want the flexibility of a 24-hour booking service? Then it's time to look into our unique pocket-size, ticketless Travel Pass. Preloaded with 10, 20, 30 or an unlimited number of Business Class flights to a choice of Scandinavian cities, it's made for the frequent traveller. It smooths your way through check-in. Enables you to book from anywhere, at any time - via the Internet, our interactive phone line or through your travel agent. For more information contact us on 020 8990 7100 E-mail: tpinfouk@sas.dk www.scandinavian.net

Now available from Birmingham as well as Heathrow, Manchester, Stansted, and Aberdeen.

It's Scandinavian

SAS
Scandinavian Airlines

A STAR ALLIANCE MEMBER

With Mariott Rewards, customers earn free flights or nights with miles or points accumulated for every pound spent at a Mariott hotel.
Source: Marriott Hotels, Resorts and Suites. *Agency:* McCann-Erikson, London

3. Where appropriate, service providers might turn the disadvantage of non-ownership into a benefit: for example, an industrial design consultant might argue that, by employing his or her expertise, the customer would actually be reducing costs, given that the alternative would be for that customer to employ a full-time designer with equally specialised knowledge. Paying for access to services rather than performing the activities in-house (e.g. warehousing) reduces capital cost, while also giving greater flexibility to a business.

marketing strategies for service firms

Until recently, service firms lagged behind manufacturing firms in their use of marketing. Many service businesses are small (shoe repair shops, barber shops, dry cleaners) and often consider formal management and marketing techniques unnecessary or too costly. Some service organisations (e.g. schools, churches) were at one time so much in demand that they did not need marketing until recently. Others (e.g. legal, medical and accounting practices) believed that it was unprofessional to use marketing. Still others who sell sensitive services did not contemplate using marketing techniques in the past, because it was not discreet to do so, but are increasingly realising the power of marketing tools (see Marketing Highlight 15.2).

marketing highlight 15.2

Marketing funerals: how about an all-singing, all-dancing casket?

The multi-billion-dollar funeral market has been changing fast in recent years. Slowing death rates and increasing competition have forced many of the larger funeral houses to grow profits by buying up smaller, independent, mom-and-pop funeral parlours. For example, when America's Service Corporation International (SCI) acquired Britain's Great Southern and Plantsbrook, in the early 1990s, it snapped up 15 per cent share of the funeral parlour and pre-need (prepaid) funeral market.

Customers are also increasingly seen to expect something more than black crêpe and tasteful wreaths for the few thousand euros they are paying out. On average a burial in the United Kingdom would cost nearly £1,000 and a cremation around £810; a burial in France costs in excess of £1,102; in Germany, £1,127; and in Belgium, £1,159. In the US, costs are as high as £3,500.

A greater understanding of what the *target customer wants* is now regarded as important. Some people may want to delay their purchase of a headstone. Others may want a proper funeral for the deceased. Some are cutting back on flowers. Others may want jazz funerals. People's attitudes regarding death are also changing; they are becoming more conscious of 'dying costs' and are, therefore, more willing to think and plan ahead than ever before. Educating the public to consider funerals in advance is hard going.

Arguably, the European invasion of US corporate titans like SCI and the Loewen Group has blown chilly winds of commercialism over the sensitive business of dying. Companies are deploying *innovative* practices to maintain and increase market share. These include pre-paid funeral schemes, to encourage customers to plan ahead, thus allowing undertakers to price their service in advance, or tactics have been deployed to persuade the bereaved to trade up to more expensive funerals. How about a traditional, Victorian-style send-off?

There is a fine line between savvy marketing and unsavoury sales tactics. Recent allegations made against the UK operations of SCI concerning hard-sell tactics, over-charging, even disrespectful treatment of the dead, have attracted adverse publicity from UK commentators. Since an Office of Fair Trading enquiry, the company has introduced a number of initiatives to display greater transparency of its ownership of UK businesses and pricing, as well as launched a customer charter that clearly sets out customers' rights and service standards that they can expect from all of the company's funeral homes. A hot-line to senior management is also set up for complaints.

Essentially, funeral directors use a variety of methods to *promote* their service. TV advertising and other media advertising and telemarketing are used to create awareness of prepayment schemes. These are established ways of signing up new pre-need customers in the US, although somewhat taboo still in the UK, where direct mail and newspapers are increasingly popular. The Co-operative Funeral Service (CFS), the UK market leader, holds 'open days' at its funeral homes, where visitors are greeted with a video, say, and literature about the work carried out in preparing for a funeral. It also has a free helpline, offering bereavement counselling. It uses local press and sponsorship of community-based activities such as bowling clubs to market its message – 'We understand'. But, while companies accept the inevitability of increased use of marketing tools such as these, good marketers maintain that personal recommendation or word-of-mouth is the best publicity.

More recently, however, funeral directors are importing new US schemes to *E-mmortalise* clients' loved ones. For a fee of between £25 and £250, the bereaved can commemorate loved ones through the Internet. Traditionalists may find this absolutely appalling, and reminiscent of the tasteless funeral practices satirised in Evelyn Waugh's classic novel, *The Loved One*, or the murky world of undertaking brought to bear in Jessica Mitford's bestseller, *The American Way of Death*. Nonetheless, InMemoryOf.co.uk is understatedly British in the style of its navigation pages – you'll find no flashing banner ads, no animated angels blowing trumpets or lots of fluffy white clouds. SCI too now boasts 'permanent' memorial websites. Its dignitymemorial.com website allows visitors to find their nearest funeral home. In the future, globe-trotting consumers will even be able to buy a standard plan over the Web that can be delivered at any of its 3,800 funeral homes worldwide!

For now, new-style undertakers appear to be paying more attention to 'deathstyle' and savvy marketing techniques to resurrect their market share. However, these may simply offer customers more options. Winners will ultimately be firms that respect customers and give them what they want in dignified ways that meaningfully differentiate their service from those of others.

SOURCES: Caroline Southey, 'Plantsbrook advances 8 per cent despite fall in death rate', *Financial Times* (9 September 1994), p. 20; Jean Eaglesham, 'The £5bn business of death', *Financial Times* (14/15 February 1998), p. 3; Nicholas Timmins, 'Watchdog to target funeral industry', *Financial Times* (16/17 May 1998), p. 6; Robert Dwek, 'Death and the salesmen', *Marketing Business* (March 1999), pp. 12–15; Jonathan Guthrie, 'Undertakers offer internet memorials', *Financial Times* (3 May 2000), p. 2; 'Staying alive', *The Economist* (5 August 2000), pp. 77–8.

Just like manufacturing firms, smart service businesses use marketing to position themselves strongly in chosen target markets. Budget-priced airlines like Go and easyJet position themselves as no-frills, low-cost carriers. Global data communications service provider NTT positions itself as a 'trusted partner' that can bring one-stop network solutions to western businesses operating in Asia. These and other service firms establish their positions through traditional marketing-mix activities.

However, because service firms differ from tangible products, they require additional marketing approaches. In a product business, products are fairly standardised and can sit on shelves waiting for customers. But in a service business, the customer and front-line service employee interact to create the service. Thus service providers must work to interact effectively with customers to create superior value during service encounters. Effective interaction, in turn, depends on the skills of front-line service staff, and on the service production and support processes backing these employees.

the service–profit chain

Successful service companies focus their attention on both their employees and customers. They understand the *service–profit chain*, which links service firms' profits with employee and customer satisfaction. This chain consists of five links:[13]

1. Internal service quality – superior employee selection and training, a quality work environment and strong support for those dealing with customers, which results in . . .
2. Satisfied and productive service employees – more satisfied, loyal and hard-working employees, which results in . . .
3. Greater service value – more effective and efficient customer value creation and service delivery, which results in . . .
4. Satisfied and loyal customers – satisfied customers who remain loyal, repeat purchase and refer other customers, which results in . . .
5. Healthy service-profits and growth – superior service firm performance.

Therefore, reaching service profits and growth goals begins with taking care of those who take care of customers. All of this suggests that in order to achieve favourable service outcomes, service marketing requires more than just traditional external marketing using the four Ps. Figure 15.2 shows that service marketing also requires both *internal marketing* and *interactive marketing*.

Figure 15.2

Three types of marketing in service industries

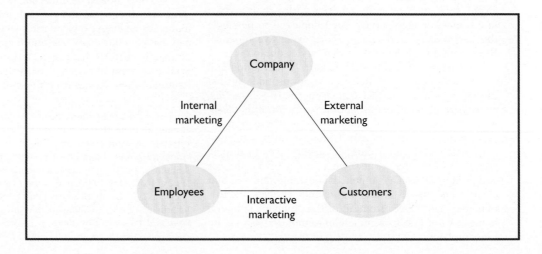

Internal marketing means that the service firm must invest heavily in employee quality and performance. It must effectively train and motivate its customer-contact employees and all the supporting service people to work as a *team* to provide customer satisfaction. For the firm to deliver consistently high service quality, everyone must practise a customer orientation. It is not enough to have a marketing department doing traditional marketing while the rest of the company goes its own way. Marketers must also encourage everyone else in the organisation to practise marketing. In fact, internal marketing must *precede* external marketing. It makes little sense to advertise excellent service before the company's staff is ready, willing and able to provide it. Thus, the service organisation must orient its employees carefully, instill in them a sense of pride and motivate them by recognising and rewarding outstanding service deeds.

Interactive marketing means that perceived service quality depends heavily on the quality of the buyer–seller interaction. In product marketing, product quality often depends little on how the product is obtained. But in services marketing, especially in high-contact and professional services, service quality depends on both the service deliverer and the quality of the delivery. Effective service deliverer–customer interaction is important for achieving a satisfactory service transaction. Service marketers cannot assume that they will satisfy the customer simply by providing good technical service. This is because the customer judges service quality not just on *technical quality* (e.g. the success of the surgery, the tastiness of the food served in the restaurant), but also on its *functional quality* (e.g. whether the surgeon showed concern and inspired confidence, whether the waiter was friendly and polite). Also, each interaction is a 'moment of truth' for the provider, where not just the service encounter, but also the organisation, will be decisively judged by the customer. Thus, professionals cannot assume that they will satisfy the client simply by providing good technical service. They have to master interactive marketing skills or functions as well.[14]

Effective buyer–seller interaction may help to secure a satisfied customer. However, to retain customers over the long term, many service providers have to develop *relationship marketing* skills for managing customer relationships. The topic of relationship marketing was dealt with in greater detail in Chapter 11.

Today, as competition and costs increase, and as productivity and quality decrease, more marketing sophistication is needed. Service companies face three major marketing tasks: they want to increase their *competitive differentiation*, *service quality* and *productivity*.

managing differentiation

In these days of intense price competition, service marketers often complain about the difficulty of differentiating their services from those of competitors. Service differentiation poses particular problems. First, service intangibility and inseparability mean that consumers rarely compare alternative service offerings in advance of purchase in the way that potential buyers of products do. Differences in the attractiveness or value of competing services are not readily obvious to the potential buyer. Moreover, to the extent that customers view a service as fairly homogeneous, they care less about the provider than the price. Witness, for example, the recent growth in online banking. Customers are lured to bank online not only because of the advantages of 24-hour service but also the tempting deals (for example, higher savings rates or lower transaction costs) that the online banks can offer them. Similarly, budget airlines are mushrooming because many fliers care more about travel costs than service. Service providers therefore often use pricing to differentiate their offering. However, pricing strategies (e.g. price cuts) are quickly emulated by competitors. Furthermore, intense price competition erodes margins and does not create a sustainable differential advantage over the long term.

Internal marketing
Marketing by a service firm to train and effectively motivate its customer-contact employees and all the supporting service people to work as a team to provide customer satisfaction.

Interactive marketing
Marketing by a service firm that recognises that perceived service quality depends heavily on the quality of buyer–seller interaction.

The solution to price competition is to develop a differentiated *offer*, *delivery* or *image*. The offer can include *innovative features* that set one company's offer apart from its competitors' offers.

> For example, Virgin mobile differentiates its mobile telephone service by offering advanced services such as the facility to surf music and to send and receive three-page e-mails. Airlines such as British Airways offer international business and first-class travellers a sleeping compartment, hot showers and cooked-to-order breakfasts. Virgin Atlantic Airways introduced such innovations as in-flight movies, advance seating, air-to-ground telephone service and frequent-flyer awareness programmes to differentiate their offers. Following British Airways, Virgin Atlantic has recently introduced reclining business-class seats that convert into a bed. The ability to offer this extra luxury to business travellers puts these two carriers into a dimension of comfort way beyond all other competitors. In addition, Virgin Upper Class cabin now has a private area for its beauty and massage treatments.[15]

Unfortunately, service differentiation exposes a second problem – service innovations cannot be patented and are easily copied. Still, the service company that innovates regularly will usually gain a succession of temporary advantages and an innovative reputation that may help it keep customers who want to go with the best.

Third, the variability of services suggests that standardisation and quality are difficult to control. Consistency in quality is generally hard to obtain, but firms that persistently cultivate a customer orientation and execute sound internal marketing schemes will increase their ability to differentiate their brand by offering superior-quality service *delivery*.

The service company can differentiate its service *delivery* in three ways: through *people*, *physical environment* and *process*. These are often referred to as the additional three *P*s in service marketing. The company can distinguish itself by having more able and reliable customer-contact people to deliver its service. The enthusiasm and smart appearance of front-line customer-contact staff also helps. More importantly, as mentioned earlier, the service business that emphasises an internal marketing approach, combined with customer-focused staff training and education, can succeed in improving employee quality and performance that will sustain superiority in service delivery. Ultimately, the commitment and performance of front-line staff, backed by the support of people involved in the operational processes, is vital to the success of service production and delivery. In turn, this affects customer relationships and the organisation's success.

The firm can develop a superior physical environment in which the service product is delivered. Hotels and restaurants, for example, will pay a great deal of attention to interior décor and ambience to project a superior service to target customers. Some retailers, such as The Body Shop and Harrods, have effectively managed the physical environment, giving very distinctive identities to their outlets.

Or it can design a superior delivery process. For example, banks offer their customers home banking as a better way to use banking services than by having to drive, park and wait in line.

Finally, service intangibility and variability mean that a consistent service brand image is not easily built. Brand image also takes time to develop and cannot be copied by competitors. Service companies that work on distinguishing their service by creating unique and powerful images, through symbols or branding, will gain a lasting advantage over competitors with lack-lustre images. For example, the Ritz, Sheraton, Hard Rock Café, British Airways and Citibank all enjoy superior brand positioning which has taken years of effort to develop. Amidst a technological revolution and rising competition, differentiation through branding has also become a priority for

marketing highlight 15.3

Telcos: working harder to win recognition

In the past, when telecommunications carriers were monopolies, few devoted much attention to developing and nurturing their image. Today, things are different. Deregulation and increased local and global competition have forced telecoms companies (telcos) to work harder to establish and differentiate their brands. 'You have to differentiate yourself – and that means creating a brand', says Chris Nuttall, communications director of I-21, an advanced fibre-optic network provider. 'The market is very uncertain at the moment. That's why it is very important to establish a brand for your company so that customers think of you first when they start to look for a solution to their problems . . . Nowadays, it's all about satisfying customer demands', echoes Han van der Zwan, communications director of Concert, the BT and AT&T global networking joint venture.

The point is not lost on any serious telco players. Cable & Wireless, for example, spent some £2 million on a UK national advertising campaign to promote itself as a provider of business-to-business IP products, and to change its old-fashioned image as a low-cost cable entertainment and telephony service company. But tomorrow's telecommunications brand may not necessarily be that of an incumbent telecom carrier.

Richard Branson's Virgin Telecom represents one among a new breed of telcos that could turn incumbents into dinosaurs. Virgin Telecom has entered into a high-profile agreement with the Deutsche Telekom-owned mobile network operator, One-2-One, to resell One-2-One's services. But, as far as consumers are concerned, they see the service as a Virgin product! Virtual telcos like Virgin which do not have their own networks, but resell capacity on those owned by others, are sprouting on a daily basis.

One has only to look at success stories like Orange to appreciate the value of superior brand recognition in the telecoms market. The mobile network operator, recently bought by France Télécom for £26 billion, has built Europe's strongest telecoms brand, according to analysts at 3I's communications group, which invests in telecoms companies. When Orange was launched in 1995, the concept of branding in mobile phones was virtually non-existent. Rather, it was the handset manufacturers like Nokia, Ericsson and Motorola that had the greater brand recognition. Crucially, Orange created an interesting brand, which was about service to customers, not technology. Orange was, and still is, about lifestyle, freedom, choice and independence – the Orange proposition is a wirefree handset that could be used by anyone, to keep in touch any time, any place. The promise was something new, unconventional, special and optimistic, conveyed through advertising using visual images of birth and awakening. Orange became an offering with a distinctive brand name, a vision (the future), a look and a set of values which quickly captured the imagination of users. Within nine months of launch, the brand's spontaneous awareness soared ahead of the established mobile network operators, Vodafone and Cellnet. Over the years, Orange has also protected the brand name despite its involvement in partnerships and joint ventures around the world – one reason why it attracted a premium when it was sold.

How's it all done? 'Developing the Orange brand is not rocket science', according to Hans Snook, chief executive of Orange. 'It's very simple. It's about treating people with respect and giving them what they want in ways they can understand. Brands are about values. . . . Brands are particularly important in telecommunications because when everything is the same, how you feel about a service is what makes you choose one over another.'

In a service business, the foremost delivery is through experience. The challenge for telcos, new and old, whose services are largely ephemeral and consumed invisibly, is to find and deliver an experience that differentiates the company meaningfully in the eyes of the customer.

SOURCES: Peter Purton, 'Telcos reinvent their businesses' and 'The virtual telco', FT Telecoms Survey, *Financial Times* (21 June 2000), p. v and p. vi respectively; Joia Shillingford, 'How to build a telecoms brand', Financial Times Survey, ibid, p. vi.

telecommunication service companies (see Marketing Highlight 15.3). Organisations such as Lloyd's Bank (which adopted the black horse as its symbol of strength), McDonald's (personified by its Ronald McDonald clown) and the International Red Cross have all differentiated their images through symbols.

managing service quality

One of the principal ways in which a service firm can differentiate itself is by delivering consistently higher quality than its competitors. Like manufacturers before them, many service industries have now joined the total quality management revolution. Recent years have seen the rapid adoption of service quality standards and awards such as the BS5750/ISO9000 international standard, the Malcolm Baldridge National Quality Award in the USA, the European Foundation for Quality Management Award and similar schemes in other countries. In Scandinavian countries, and particularly Sweden, service quality management is a topic of national concern, with the government taking a lead role through initiatives such as the Swedish Customer Satisfaction Barometer.

In the UK, local councils are facing increasing increasing pressure to deliver higher quality services to the local communities they serve.

> The Best Value programme, introduce by local government minister, Hilary Armstrong, in 1998, aims to achieve continuous improvements in local council performance. This puts emphasis on 'revolutionising' and 'modernising' the management of services, with an overriding focusing on customer satisfaction. Underpinning the initiative is the argument that, for the public, the ultimate test of a local authority is whether its services are any good. An evaluation scheme was developed involving council members and senior managers and academics, to facilitate measurement of 'best value' services to the public. The scheme points to the need for close monitoring of 'best value', supported through performance plans and service review mechanisms within councils. Importantly, Best Value compels councils to improve their understanding of what their public values, to better involve the public in the services they receive and enhancing their 'power as consumers'. Radical though it may sound, the days of consumer power are here to stay. The search for value begins with the needs of people in the community, and then giving them the quality services they want and value.[16]

Many service companies are finding that outstanding quality can give them a potent competitive advantage that leads to superior sales and profit performance. True, offering greater service quality results in higher costs. However, investments usually pay off because greater customer satisfaction leads to increased customer retention and sales.[17]

The key is to exceed the customer's service quality expectations. As the chief executive at American Express puts it, 'Promise only what you can deliver and deliver more than you promise!'[18] These expectations are based on past encounters and experiences, word-of-mouth and the firm's advertising. If *perceived service* of a given firm exceeds *expected service*, customers are apt to use the service provider again. Customer retention is, perhaps, the best measure of quality and reflects the firm's ability to hang on to its customers by consistently delivering value to them. Thus, where the manufacturer's quality target might be 'zero defects', the service provider's goal is 'zero customer *defections*'.

To meet quality targets, the service provider needs to identify the expectations of target customers concerning service quality. Unfortunately, quality in service industries is harder to define, judge or quantify than product quality. It is hard to quantify service quality because intangibility means that there are seldom physical dimensions, like performance, functional features or maintenance cost, which can be used as benchmarks and measured. It is harder to get agreement on the quality of a haircut than on that of a hair dryer, for instance. The inseparability of production and consumption means that service quality must be defined on the basis of both the process in which the service is delivered and the actual outcome experienced by the customer.

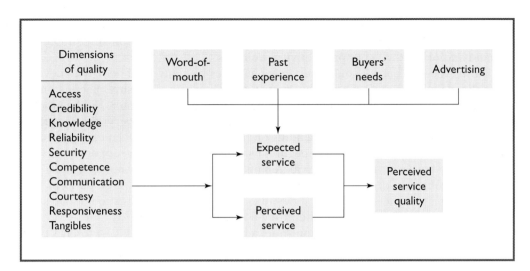

Figure 15.3

Key determinants of perceived service quality

Again, it is difficult to quantify standards or reference points against which service delivery process and performance outcomes are measured. We will look at service quality dimensions in greater detail later in the chapter.

To measure service quality, in practice, the provider has to determine how customers of the service *perceive* quality. Studies suggest that customer assessments of service quality are the result of a comparison of what they expect with what they experience.[19] Any mismatch between the two is a 'quality gap'. The service quality manager's goal is therefore to narrow the quality gap, taking into account that what is being measured is perceived quality, which is always a judgement by the customer. Hence, what the customer thinks is reality, is reality; quality is whatever the customer says it is. To improve quality, service marketers have to identify: the key determinants of service quality (that is, the key criteria customers use to judge quality); what target customers' expectations are; and how customers rate the firm's service in relation to these criteria against what they expected.

What are the criteria that typically reflect service quality? An important study highlights ten key determinants of perceived service quality.[20] Figure 15.3 summarises these dimensions: *access* (is the service easy to get access to and delivered on time?); *credibility* (is the company credible and trustworthy?); *knowledge* (does the service provider really understand customers' needs?); *reliability* (how dependable and consistent is the service?); *security* (is the service low-risk and free from danger?); *competence* (are staff knowledgeable and in possession of the skills required to deliver good service?); *communication* (how well has the company explained its service?); *courtesy* (are staff polite, considerate and sensitive to customers?); *responsiveness* (are staff willing and quick to deliver the service?); and *tangibles* (does the appearance of staff, the physical environment and other tangible representations of the service reflect high quality?). The first five are concerned with the quality of the *outcome* of service provided, while the last five are related to the quality of the delivery *process*. By focusing on the dimensions that are important to customers, the service firm can ensure that customers' expectations are fully met.

To a large extent, aspects such as good understanding of customers' needs and the ability to provide consistent and dependable service are achieved through internal marketing and continual investment in employee quality and performance. The reputation and credibility of the service provider and customers' perceived risk are interrelated. If the consumer trusts the service provider, he or she expects that the service is free from danger or perceives little risk in using the service. Credibility can be improved through effective communication of service quality through advertising and/or satisfied customers. Access can be improved by having multi-site locations (e.g. Pizza Hut, McDonald's), and waiting times can be reduced through synchronising supply and demand and/or tackling staff productivity problems.

During the past decade, many service companies have invested heavily to develop streamlined and efficient service delivery systems. They want to ensure that customers will receive consistently high-quality service in every service encounter. Unlike product manufacturers, which can adjust their machinery and inputs until everything is perfect, service quality will always vary, depending on the interactions between employees and customers. Problems will inevitably occur. Mistakes are a critical part of every service. Hard as they try, even the best service companies can't prevent the occasional late delivery, burnt steak, or grumpy employee. The fact is, in services, often performed in the customer's presence, errors are inevitable. Therefore companies should take steps to recover from service mistakes when they do occur.[21]

The first step is to *empower* front-line service employees – that is, to give them the authority, responsibility and incentives to recognise, care about and tend to customer needs, even going beyond their normal jobs to solve customer problems. Such empowered employees can act quickly and effectively to keep service problems from resulting in lost customers.

Studies in well-managed service companies show that they share a number of common virtues regarding service quality. These are summarised below:

1. Top service companies are '*customer obsessed*'. They have a clear sense of their target customers and their needs. They have developed a distinctive strategy for satisfying customer needs that wins enduring customer loyalty. At British Telecom, liaison panels are set up which demonstrate management commitment to listen to customers and ensure that the ethos of customer care is embedded in the whole company.

2. They have a history of *top management commitment to quality*. Management at companies such as Marks & Spencer, American Express, Swissair and McDonald's look not only at financial performance, but also at service performance. They develop a quality culture that encourages and rewards good service delivery.

3. The best service providers *set high service quality standards*. Swissair, for example, aims to have 96 per cent or more of its passengers rate its service as good or superior; otherwise, it takes action. The standards must be set *appropriately* high. A 98 per cent accuracy standard may sound good, but using this standard, 64,000 Federal Express packages would be lost each day, ten words would be misspelt on each page, 400,000 prescriptions would be misfilled daily, and drinking water would be unsafe eight days a year. Top service companies do not settle merely for 'good' service, they aim for 100 per cent defect-free service.[22]

4. Top service firms *watch service performance closely* – both their own and that of competitors. They communicate their concerns about service quality to employees and provide performance feedback. They use methods such as comparison shopping, customer surveys, suggestion schemes and customer complaint programmes. Customers like to see things right first time. But if things go wrong, customer complaints are an opportunity for companies to remedy poor service. When companies are responsive and deal with poor service promptly and effectively, they can recover customer confidence and loyalty. Most firms, however, are bad at handling customer complaints, if indeed they deal with them at all. Leading firms, on the other hand, view customer care in service-recovery situations as a source of unrivalled

competitive advantage. They establish effective complaint procedures to capture these opportunities. Because only a small minority of dissatisfied customers ever complain, the firm should proactively attract complaints from disenchanted customers. Channels of communication should be kept open to give customers access and to make it easy for them to offer feedback. Free telephone calls, regular follow-up of customer surveys and staff training all help. Customers themselves may use different channels of complaint: telephone, fax, letter, e-mail or personal visit to the store. Companies also have systems and procedures installed to offer a high level of customer service and care in service-recovery situations, giving the company another chance to offer service and satisfaction to the dissatisfied customer. Finally, service-conscious organisations develop a non-threatening culture – they do not penalise staff responsible for the 'mistake' in order to encourage them to analyse, resolve and learn from complaints. In addition to practising a 'no-blame policy', staff are rewarded for creating service-recovery opportunities.

5. Well-managed service companies *satisfy employees as well as customers*. They believe that good employee relations will result in good customer relations. Management clearly defines and communicates service level targets so that, first, its employees know what service goals they must achieve, and second, its customers know what to expect to receive from their interaction with the service provider.

    Management also execute internal marketing and create an environment of employee support, and reward good performance. Management regularly monitors employee job satisfaction. For example, the Danish-based international cleaning services giant ISS stresses good working relations and utilisation of human resources. Staff are encouraged to join trade unions. Total quality management is firmly upheld – staff are trained so that they can do their jobs well and derive satisfaction from them – happy satisfied customers yield happy employees. It has also gone to the extreme of moving into palatial new headquarters in a wooded country estate in northern Copenhagen – an absence of air-conditioning or dust-hugging carpets, together with soothing colours, reflect management's belief that scientific cleaning can help reduce staff illness.

managing productivity

Rising costs put service firms under great pressure to increase service productivity. The problem is particularly acute where the service is labour intensive. Productivity can be improved in several ways:

1. The service providers can train current employees better, or they can hire new ones who will work harder or more skilfully for the same pay.

2. The service providers can increase the quantity of their service by giving up some quality (e.g. doctors having to handle more patients by giving less time to each).

3. The provider can 'industrialise the service' by adding equipment and standardising production, as in McDonald's production-line approach to fast-food retailing. Commercial dishwashing, jumbo jets and multiple-unit cinemas (i.e. cineplexes and megaplexes) all represent the use of technological advances to increase service output.

4. Service providers can also increase productivity by designing more effective services. How-to-quit-smoking clinics and health-and-fitness recommendations may reduce the need for expensive medical services later on.

5. Providers can also give customers incentives to substitute company labour with their own labour. For example, business firms that sort their own mail before delivering it to the post office pay lower postal rates. Self-service restaurants are another case in point. Pay-and-display facilities in car parks alleviate the need to employ attendants (as well as reducing waiting time). Providers can harness the power of technology to save time and costs and make service workers more productive. A well-designed website can allow customers to obtain buying information, narrow their purchase options or even make a purchase directly, saving service provider time. For example, personal computer buyers can visit the Dell website (www.Dell.com), review the characteristics of various Dell models, check out prices and organise their questions ahead of time. Even if they choose to call a Dell telesales representative rather than buying via the website, they are better informed and require less personal service.

6. Service providers that have to deal with fluctuating demand can increase productivity by increasing flexibility and reshaping demand. Supplier flexibility – the ability to improve supply capacity – is increased by using part-time workers and shared facilities, and by rescheduling peak-time facilities and work. Demand movements are reshaped by differential pricing, reservation systems and stimulating non-peak usage.

However, companies must avoid pushing productivity so hard that doing so reduces perceived quality. Some productivity steps help standardise quality, increasing customer satisfaction. But other productivity steps lead to too much standardisation and can rob consumers of a customised service. Attempts to industrialise a service or to cut costs can make a service company more efficient in the short run, but reduce its longer-run ability to innovate, maintain service quality and flexibility, or respond to consumer needs and desires. In some cases, service providers accept reduced productivity in order to create more service differentiation or quality.[23]

We have looked at strategies for handling the particular marketing problems that service organisations face, given the specific characteristics of services. Importantly, to be successful, service firms must practise internal and interactive marketing, in addition to adopting an external marketing focus. The key lies in management's ability to develop a quality culture and to operationalise effectively an extended marketing mix that results in superior service differentiation and quality.

international services marketing

An Italian sportswear manufacturer calls her advertising agency in London to confirm plans for new billboards in Venezuela. A German businessman checks into his hotel room in Atlanta – the hotel is owned by a British company and managed by an American firm. The Zürich branch of a Japanese bank participates in a debt offering for an aircraft-leasing company in Ireland. A British construction firm builds an airport in Japan, and an American insurance company sells its products in Germany. These are just a few examples of the thousands of service transactions that take place each day around the globe.

A lot of trade no longer involves putting things into a crate and sending them abroad on ships! More and more, the global economy is dominated by services. The World Trade Organisation estimates that commercial-service trade is now worth over one trillion euros, almost one-quarter of the value of trade in goods. Indeed, a variety of service industries – from banking, insurance and communications to transportation, travel and entertainment – now account for well over 60 per cent of the economy in developed countries around the world. The worldwide growth rate for services (16 per cent in the past decade) is almost double the growth rate of manufacturing.[24] The internationalisation of services is very apparent when one travels around the world. Service firms like Hertz, Avis, DHL, McDonald's, Burger King, Holiday Inn and Ibis are found all over the world. Indeed, there are so many McDonald's restaurants in Budapest that it looks as if you are in the US.[25]

Some industries have a long history of international operations. For example, the commercial banking industry was one of the first to grow internationally. Many banks had to provide global services in order to meet the foreign exchange and credit needs of their home-country clients wanting to sell overseas. The Dutch ABN AMRO Bank established the first foreign bank in Saudi Arabia in response to the demand from Moslem clients in the then Nederlandsch Indië (now Indonesia) to change money in the country on their pilgrimage to Mecca. In recent years, however, as the scope of international financing has broadened, many banks have become truly global operations. Germany's Deutsche Bank, for example, has branches in over 41 countries. Thus, for its clients around the world that wish to take advantage of growth opportunities created by German reunification, Deutsche Bank can raise money not just in Frankfurt, but also in Zürich, London, Paris and Tokyo.

The travel industry also moved naturally into international operations. American hotel and airline companies grew quickly in Europe and the Far East during the economic expansion that followed World War II. Credit card companies soon followed – the early worldwide presence of American Express has recently been matched by Visa and MasterCard. Business travellers and holidaymakers like the convenience and they have now come to expect that their credit cards will be honoured wherever they go.

Professional and business services industries such as accounting, management consulting and advertising have only recently started operating on a worldwide scale. The international growth of these firms followed the globalisation of the manufacturing companies they serve. For example, increasingly globalised manufacturing firms have found it much easier to have their accounts prepared by a single accounting firm, even when they operate in two dozen countries. This set the stage for rapid international consolidation in the accounting industry. During the late 1980s, established accounting companies around the world quickly merged with America's 'Big Eight' to become the international 'Big Six' almost overnight. Similarly, as their client companies began to employ global marketing and advertising strategies, advertising agencies and other marketing services firms responded by globalising their own operations.[26]

Retailers are among the latest service businesses to go global. As their home markets become saturated with stores, retailers such as Wal-Mart, Toys 'R' Us and Disney have expanded into faster growing markets in Europe and Asia. European retailers are making similar moves. Carrefour of France is the leading retailer in Brazil and Argentina. Asian shoppers now buy western products in Dutch-owned Makro stores, now South-east Asia's biggest store group with sales in the region of more than $2 billion. Similarly, Japanese retailers like Yaohan now operates the largest shopping centre in Asia, the 21-story Nextage Shanghai Tower in China.[27]

International expansion opportunities abound for service businesses, including even those that are traditionally viewed as basic public services. Consider the following example:

Retailers are among the latest service businesses to go global. Here Asian shoppers buy American products in a Dutch-owned Makro store in Kuala Lumpur, Malaysia.

Post offices are generally regarded as national entities serving communities' postal needs across local and regional centres. Most postal deliveries in the EU are made nationally and only 4 per cent are sent across borders. Postal operators in the EU have typically enjoyed monopolies over all national letter deliveries and parcels up to 350g. With a view to full liberalisation by 2003, the European Commission has proposed new measures that will open the letters market in member countries to more competition. Moves to liberalise letter delivery around the world are also on the way. Three operators from different countries – the UK's Post Office, TNT Post Group (TPG), which is the quoted Dutch mail and logistic company, and Singapore Post – are joining forces to offer a global mail delivery service, in direct competition with national operators. The alliance partners are expected to pool their deliveries for letters and piggy-back on each other's infrastructure in an attempt to build a global network. TPG's global network was built up following its acquisition of Australian parcel and logistics company TNT in 1996, while Singapore Post will give the venture a strong Asian base. Although representing a small proportion of mail sent, the market for international mail, currently valued at £4.4 billion (€7.21 billion), is expected to grow. Whereas volume of personal letters is declining due to e-mails and faxes, the business mailshot market is growing. There are therefore tremendous opportunities for national postal service operators who are quick to take advantage of the increased commercial freedom brought by market liberalisation to expand their operations abroad.[28]

The rapidly expanding international marketplace provides many attractive opportunities for service firms. It also creates some special challenges, however. Service companies wanting to operate in other countries are not always welcomed with open arms. Whereas manufacturers usually face straightforward tariff, quota or currency restrictions when attempting to sell their products in another country, service providers are likely to face more subtle barriers. In some cases, rules and regulations affecting international services firms reflect the host country's traditions. In others, they appear to protect the country's own fledgling service industries from large global competitors with greater resources. In still other cases, however, the restrictions seem to have little purpose other than to make entry difficult for foreign service firms.

> Most of the industrialised nations want their banks, insurance companies, construction firms and other service providers to be allowed to move people, capital and technology around the globe unimpeded. Instead they face a bewildering complex of national regulations, most of them designed to guarantee jobs for local competitors. A Turkish law, for example, forbids international accounting firms to bring capital into the country to set up offices and requires them to use the names of local partners, rather than prestigious international ones, in their marketing. To audit the books of a multinational company's branch in Buenos Aires, an accountant must have the equivalent of a high school education in Argentinian geography and history. India is perhaps the most [difficult] big economy in the world [to enter] these days . . . New Delhi prevents international insurance companies from selling property and casualty policies to the country's swelling business community or life insurance to its huge middle class.[29]

Clearly, service organisations face many difficulties when seeking to enter foreign markets. The Uruguay round of the General Agreement on Tariffs and Trade (GATT), ending in 1993 (see Chapter 5), began to address some of these problems by extending international trade rules to cover services in addition to manufactured goods. Since then, new service agreements should ease the barriers that limit such trade. Thus, despite the difficulties in international service marketing, the trend towards growth of global service companies will continue, especially in banking, telecommunications and professional services. Today, service firms are no longer simply following their manufacturing customers. Instead, many are taking the lead in international expansion.

summary

Marketing has been broadened in recent years to cover services.

As we move towards a *world service economy*, marketers need to know more about marketing services. *Services* are products that consist of activities, benefits or satisfactions offered for sale that are essentially intangible. Services are characterised by five key characteristics. First, services are *intangible* – they cannot be seen, tasted, felt, heard or smelt. Services are *inseparable* from their service providers. Services are *variable* because their quality depends on the service provider as well as the environment surrounding the service delivery. Services are also *perishable*. As a result they cannot be stored, built up or back-ordered. Finally, service products often *do not result in* the *ownership* of anything. Each characteristic poses problems and requires strategies. Marketers have to find ways to make the service more tangible; to increase the productivity of providers who are inseparable from their products; to standardise the quality in the face of variability; and to improve demand shifts and supply capacities in the face of service perishability.

Successful service companies focus attention on *both* customers and employees. They understand the *service–profit chain*, which links service firm profits with employee and customer satisfaction. Services marketing strategy calls not only for external marketing, but also for *internal marketing* to motivate employees and *interactive marketing* to create service delivery skills among service providers. To succeed, service marketers must create *competitive differentiation*, offer high service *quality* and find ways to increase *service productivity*.

discussing the issues

1. Why is demand for services growing? How would marketers gain a competitive advantage by satisfying the growing demand for increased services?

2. How can a theatre deal with the intangibility, inseparability, variability and perishability of the service it provides? Give examples.

3. Wresting an apology from an airline for a delayed flight or persuading your telecom service provider that it has overcharged is often easier said than done. Many firms do not have easy channels for customers to register complaints. How important is it for firms to have established procedures for capturing customer complaints? Suggest ways in which firms should go about improving their capacity to deal with customer complaints and converting dissatisfied customers into satisfied customers through effective service-recovery.

4. Marketing is defined as satisfying needs and wants through exchange processes. What exchanges occur in marketing non-profit organisations, such as a museum, the Red Cross or other charities?

5. What are internal and interactive marketing? Give examples of how firms or organisations might use these concepts to increase the effectiveness of their services marketing. How might these concepts be linked to service differentiation?

applying the concepts

1. The core service in the airline industry is transportation. The 'problem-solving' benefit for the customer is travel from one place to another. To differentiate their services, airlines provide many additional benefits. If you intend to fly from one country to another within Europe you might consider KLM Royal Dutch Airlines, British Airways or Lufthansa. Review the websites of these airlines and complete the table to evaluate their services.

	KLM ROYAL DUTCH AIRLINES www.klm.com	BRITISH AIRWAYS www.british-airways.com	LUFTHANSA www.lufthansa.com
Many destinations?			
Attractive frequent-flyer programme?			
Other service features			
Evidence of service quality			
Evidence of competitive positioning strategy			
Ways customers can give feedback to company at site			

(a) How would you classify airlines using consumer product categories: convenience, shopping, speciality or unsought products?

(b) Which airline brand name best conveys a quality image to you?

(c) How does each airline differentiate itself from the others: KLM? British Airways? Lufthansa?

(d) Which airline would you choose for your European travel? Why?

2. Perishability is very important in the airline industry: unsold seats are gone for ever, and too many unsold seats mean large losses. With computerised ticketing, airlines can easily use pricing to deal with perishability and variations in demand.

✦ Call a travel agent or use an online service that is accessible to check airline fares. Get prices on the same route for 60 days in advance, two weeks, one week and today. Is there a clear pattern to the fares?

✦ When a store is overstocked on ripe fruit, it may lower the price to sell out quickly. What are airlines doing to their prices as the seats get close to 'perishing'? Why? What would you recommend as a pricing strategy to increase total revenues?

references

1. 'The manufacturing myth', *The Economist* (19 March 1994), pp. 98–9; Ronald Henkoff, 'Service is everybody's business', *Fortune* (27 June 1994), pp. 48–60.

2. See Ronald Henkoff, 'Service is everybody's business', *Fortune* (27 June 1994), pp. 48–60; Adrian Palmer and Catherine Cole, *Services Marketing: Principles and practice* (Upper Saddle River, NJ: Prentice Hall, 1995), pp. 56–60; Valerie Zeithaml and Mary Jo Bitner, *Services Marketing* (New York: McGraw-Hill, 1996), pp. 8–9; and Michael van Biema and Bruce Greenwald, 'Managing our way to higher service-sector productivity', *Harvard Business Review* (July–August 1997), pp. 87–95.

3. Kevin Done, 'Lufthansa leads European profits', *Financial Times* (5 May 2000), p. 35; Tony Patey, 'Lufthansa lends an ear to passengers', *The European* (29 April–5 May 1994), p. 22; for more information about Lufthansa Airline's operations visit their website: http://www.lufthansa.com

4. Philip Manchester, 'A golden opportunity for internet-based services', FT-IT Review E-Business: Services, *Financial Times* (3 May 2000), p. XVI.

5. See Christopher H. Lovelock, *Services Marketing*, 3rd edn (Upper Saddle River, NJ: Prentice Hall, 1996) for further classifications of services.

6. See Leonard L. Berry, 'Services marketing is different', *Business* (May–June 1980), pp. 24–30; Karl Albrecht, *At America's Service* (Homewood, IL: Dow-Jones-Irwin, 1988); William H. Davidow and Bro Uttal, *Total Customer Service: The ultimate weapon* (New York: Harper & Row, 1989). For more on definitions and classifications of services, see John E. Bateson, *Managing Services Marketing: Text and readings* (Hinsdale, IL: Dryden Press, 1989); Christopher H. Lovelock, *Services Marketing* (Englewood Cliffs, NJ: Prentice Hall, 1991).

7. See Theodore Levitt, 'Marketing intangible products and product intangibles', *Harvard Business Review* (May–June 1981), pp. 94–102.

8. Matthew Garrahan, 'Man United kicks off replica kit blitz', *Financial Times* (2 August 2000), p. 4.

9. For more discussion, see James L. Heskett, 'Lessons in the service sector', *Harvard Business Review* (March–April 1987), pp. 122–4; E. Gummesson, *Quality Management in Service Organisations* (New York: International Service Quality Association, St John's University, 1993).

10. 'Service with a smile', *The Economist* (25 April 1998), pp. 85–6.

11. Carol Krol, 'Case study: Club Med uses e-mail to pitch unsold, discount packages', *Advertising Age* (14 December 1998), p. 40.

12. Eric van Heck, 'The cutting edge in auctions', *Harvard Business Review* (March–April 2000), p. 189; John-Paul Flintoff, 'Pay and bouquet', *The Business FT Weekend Magazine* (16 September 2000), pp. 24–5.

13. R. T. Rust and A. J. Zahorik, 'Customer satisfaction, customer retention, and market share', *Journal of Retailing*, **69**, 2 (Summer 1993), pp. 193–215; James L. Heskett, Thomas O. Jones, Gary W. Loveman, W. Earl Sasser, Jr and Leonard A. Schlesinger, 'Putting the service–profit chain to work', *Harvard Business Review* (March–April 1994), pp. 164–74.

14. For more reading on internal and interactive marketing, see Christian Gronroos, 'A service quality model and its marketing implications', *European Journal of Marketing*, **18**, 4 (1984), pp. 36–44; Christian Gronroos, 'Internal marketing – theory and practice', in T. M. Bloch, G. D. Upah and V. A. Zeithaml (eds), *Services Marketing in a Changing Environment* (American Marketing Association, 1985); Richard J. Varey, 'A model of internal marketing for building and sustaining a competitive advantage', *Journal of Marketing Management*, **11** (January/February/April 1995), pp. 41–54.

15. Amon Cohen, 'Bed time at Virgin', *Financial Times* (24 July 2000), p. 19.

16. Alan Pike, 'The search for value in town halls', *Financial Times* (12 February 1998), p. 10.

17. See Joseph Cronin, Jr and Steven A. Taylor, 'Measuring service quality: a re-examination and extension', *Journal of Marketing* (July 1992), pp. 55–68; David Ballantyne, Martin Christopher and Adrian Payne, 'Improving the quality of services marketing: service (re)design is the critical link', *Journal of Marketing Management* (January/February/April 1995), pp. 7–24; Valerie A. Zeithaml, Leonard L. Berry and A. Parasuraman, 'Services competitiveness: an Anglo-US study', *Business Strategy Review*, **8**, 1 (1997), pp. 7–22.

18. John Paul Newport, 'American Express: service that sells', *Fortune* (20 November 1989), p. 20; Frank Rose, 'Now quality means service too', *Fortune* (22 April 1991), pp. 97–108.

19. C. Gronroos, *Strategic Management and Marketing in the Service Sector* (Bromley: Chartwell-Bratt, 1985), pp. 38–40; A. Parasuraman, Valarie A. Zeithaml and Leonard L. Berry, 'A conceptual model

of service quality and its implications for future research', *Journal of Marketing*, **49** (Fall 1985), pp. 41–50; Valerie Zeithaml, Leonard L. Berry and A. Parasuraman, *Delivering Service Quality: Balancing customer perceptions and expectations* (New York: Free Press, 1990); and Parasuraman, Zeithaml and Berry, 'Reassessment of expectations as a comparison standard in measuring service quality: implications for further research', *Journal of Marketing*, **58** (January 1994), pp. 111–24.

20. Parasuraman *et al.*, 'A conceptual model', op. cit.

21. See Erika Rasmusson, 'Winning back angry customers', *Sales & Marketing Management* (October 1997), p. 131; and Stephen S. Tax, Stephen W. Brown, and Murali Chandrashekaran, 'Customer evaluations of service complaint experiences: Implications for relationship marketing', *Journal of Marketing* (April 1998), pp. 60–76.

22. See James L. Heskett, W. Earl Sasser, Jr and Christopher W.L. Hart, *Service Breakthroughs* (New York: Free Press, 1990).

23. See Leonard A Schlesinger and James L. Heskett, 'The service-driven service company', *Harvard Business Review* (September–October 1991), pp. 72–81, and Michael van Biema and Bruce Greenwald, 'Managing our way to higher service-sector productivity', *Harvard Business Review* (July–August 1997), pp. 87–95.

24. Tom Hayes, 'Services go international', *Marketing News* (14 March 1994), pp. 14–15; 'Schools brief: trade winds', *The Economist* (8 November 1997), pp. 124–5; 'Trade in services', *The Economist* (5 February 2000), pp. 95–6.

25. For an international perspective on services marketing management see Hans Kasper, Piet van Helsdingen and Wouter de Vries Jr, *Services Marketing Management* (Chichester: Wiley, 1999).

26. Michael R. Czinkota and Ilkka A. Ronkainen, *International Marketing*, 2nd edn (Chicago, IL: Dryden, 1990), p. 679.

27. Tony Lisanti, 'Europe's abuzz over Wal-Mart', *Discount Stores News* (3 May 1999), p. 11; 'Top 200 global retailers', *Stores* (January 1998), pp. S5–S12.

28. See Louella Miles, 'Let the battle commence', *Marketing Business* (September 2000), pp. 16–18; Thorold Barker, 'Post Office set for global alliance', *Financial Times* (9 March 2000), p. 25.

29. Lee Smith, 'What's at stake in the trade talks', *Fortune* (27 August 1990), pp. 76–7.

case 15

NSPCC: misunderstood

When the National Society for the Prevention of Cruelty to Children (NSPCC) released its year-end annual accounts in December 2000, it promptly received a clip round the ear.

The revelation that the charity spent more on fundraising, publicity, campaigning and administration than on direct services to children (£43m or €70.5m compared with £32m or €52.5m) was a sign of complete incompetence, according to Gerald Howarth, Conservative MP for Aldershot. He brusquely vowed to stop backing Full Stop, the high-profile NSPCC campaign launched in March 1999.

According to Quentin Anderson, chief executive of Addison, the corporate marketing arm of WPP Group, such swift dismissal of the NSPCC strategy is unwise and fails to recognise the professional makeover many charities have undertaken in recent years. Charities are now highly organised operations. In line with environmental and social pressure groups they have adopted a more businesslike approach, which is essential if they are to survive in a crowded sector. When arguing how big the various components of the NSPCC's budget should be, detractors must remember that there is a total of £75m to disburse. Charities need highly skilled staff to manage such funds.

The NSPCC's campaign makes sense. The charity has stated that its long-term objectives are to raise social awareness of child cruelty and to raise £250m through the 'Full Stop' initiative. If people do not understand what the charity's directors are trying to achieve in the long term, they will judge them on short-term results. With the NSPCC, these include a £13.5m overspend for the last financial year. The NSPCC needs to ensure that people understand what it is trying to achieve because it needs their help. It needs to show that it is awake, reacting to change and anticipating it.

Marketing is also ideally suited to the task the charity has set itself. In crude terms, its route to market is not so obvious as those of other charities. For example, it is comparatively easy for 'Meals on Wheels' to identify where its services are needed and to dedicate the majority of its expenditure to staff and the resources they require. By contrast, the NSPCC has defined its audience as the whole population. By communicating clearly with all communities, it hopes, no doubt, to enlist many more foot soldiers than direct action ever would.

And the campaign has got a lot right. To achieve its aim the NSPCC decided to use celebrities to back its central message that to reduce cruelty to children you need to raise awareness of child cruelty and challenge social attitudes. To reach those at risk it has focused on teenage media. This translates to television, radio, magazines and the Internet.

As a result, visitors to its website will find messages from Madonna, Naomi Campbell and Ross Kemp. Other male and female icons, such as Alan Shearer and the Spice Girls, have also been highly visible in their support for the 'Full Stop' campaign.

Matching your brand to a superstar is a successful marketing technique and need not be a cause for controversy. Nike pays Tiger Woods handsomely but obviously believes it gets value for money. The NSPCC would be foolish not to exploit celebrities willing to donate their time free of charge. Without the Spice Girls, would the Full Stop campaign receive front-page exposure in the magazines teenagers read?

Because the charity has advertised its brand effectively, victims are more likely to know they can go direct to the 'Kidszone' at its website and obtain professional advice.

In short, the NSPCC should not be criticised for spending money and talking about it. The charity understands that dissemination of better information creates confidence in the community. This leads to many benefits, including greater loyalty from donors and a more secure position in the sector. It also avoids the accusation of hoarding funds that has been levelled at many charities.

The negative reaction to the publication of the NSPCC accounts is a sign not that its marketing strategy is failing but that its communications policy is. A first principle for all good communicators is to evolve messages defining what the organisation does and what its aims are. The NSPCC, it appears, has simply released its annual figures and allowed the public to draw its own conclusions.

The annual report, like every communication, should have a specific goal and add value to what has already been done. The NSPCC should have explained better the rationale behind its spending on marketing. It should have made clear that a high level of set-up costs in terms of administration and training is inevitably associated with a campaign such as Full Stop.

It should have demonstrated to donors and opinion-formers that it understands its campaign is expensive. But it should also have left them in no doubt that it thinks raising awareness is the only way to lobby for legislative change and – what really counts – to reach more victims of abuse.

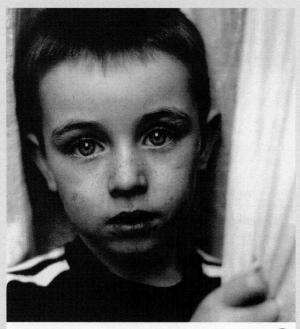

That cruelty to children exists at all in this country is horrifying enough – the shame of a civilised society. But the shocking truth is that you are more likely to be murdered in the year before your first birthday than at any other time.

Every week...
● At least one child dies following abuse.
● Over 9,000 children are on registers for physical abuse at any one time.
● Of these, 110 children who have been sexually abused are added to the Child Protection Register.
● The NSPCC Child Protection Helpline

receives over 100 reports of suspected child abuse.

Led by His Royal Highness the Duke of York, the NSPCC's Full Stop Campaign aims to end cruelty to children within a generation. It's the NSPCC's most ambitious challenge since it began protecting children more than 100 years ago. To achieve this, the NSPCC need to raise £250 million. The success of the campaign depends heavily on donations. If every *Tatler* reader were kind enough to give just £20, £5 million would be raised to help end the evil of child abuse and neglect. You can help us make a difference.

To make your donation, please:
Call the NSPCC credit card donations hotline on 0800 802020, or send a cheque made payable to 'NSPCC Registered Charity' to NSPCC 010402, FREEPOST WC1613, London EC2B 2NF, or donate online at www.nspcc.org.uk.

NSPCC ●
Cruelty to children must stop. FULL STOP.

The NSPCC's recently launched 'Full Stop' campaign.
SOURCE: NSPCC. *Photographer*: Matt. Harris

Questions

1. What are the main aspects of the service offered by a charity organisation such as the NSPCC?

2. Assess the role of marketing in assisting the charity to achieve its goals.

3. Who are the charity's target market?

4. Evaluate the NSPCC's current marketing strategy.

5. Has the charity got its current marketing strategy wrong? Or are the problems due to its communication policy?

6. How would the marketing of services offered by the NSPCC differ from that of other service offerings? Suggest ways in which the NSPCC could distinguish its service from that of other charities.

SOURCE: Quentin Anderson, 'INSIDE TRACK: In defence of the NSPCC: VIEWPOINT QUENTIN ANDERSON: The furore over the charity's allocation of funds rests on a misunderstanding of its long-term goals', *Financial Times* (14 December 2000), p. 19. Information about the charity's Full Stop appeal available from the NSPCC's website: www.nspcc.org.uk (May 2000).

internet exercises

Internet exercises for this chapter can be found on the student site of the MYPHLIP Web Site at www.booksites.net/kotler.

part five

Price

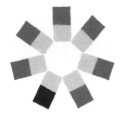

'Price: value plus a reasonable sum for the wear and tear of conscience in demanding it.'

AMBROSE PIERCE

part introduction

In Part Five we cover an element of the marketing mix that is both easy and expensive to manipulate – price.

Price cutting is an easy way to attract customers quickly, but a poor route to long-term market success. The reason is that giving a 10 per cent price cut to a customer can mean taking a 50 per cent cut in profits. The industrialist Philip Armour explained that businesses often resort to price-cutting: 'Anybody can cut prices, but it takes brains to make a better article.'

Many internal and external pressures influence the price decision, from internal costs to government legislation. The examination of these in Chapter 16 leads to *value-based pricing*, where a customer's perception of price, rather than costs, drives price. Chapter 17 then looks at pricing strategies under a variety of situations, such as when launching a product, when changing prices and when pricing within a product range.

Chapter 16

Pricing considerations and approaches

Chapter 17

Pricing strategies

chapter sixteen

Pricing considerations and approaches

Chapter objectives *After reading this chapter, you should be able to:*

✦ Understand the internal and external factors affecting price.

✦ See how market structures influence price setting.

✦ Explain the impact of cost on price.

✦ Compare and evaluate the general approaches to price setting.

introduction

All products and services have a price, just as they have a value. Many non-profit and all profit-making organisations must also set prices, be they for crossing some water (as in the preview case opposite) or the price of Madonna's Brixton Academy comeback celebration-cum-concert tickets for those who cannot get them officially. *Pricing* is controversial and goes by many names:

> Price is all around us. You pay *rent* for your apartment, *tuition* for your education and a *fee* to your physician or dentist. The airline, railway, taxi and bus companies charge you a *fare*; the local utilities call their price a *rate*; and the local bank charges you *interest* for the money you borrow . . . The guest lecturer charges an *honorarium* to tell you about a government official who took a *bribe* to help a shady character steal *dues* collected by a trade association. Clubs or societies to which you belong may make a special *assessment* to pay unusual expenses. Your regular lawyer may ask for a *retainer* to cover her services. The 'price' of an executive is a *salary*, the price of a salesperson may be a *commission* and the price of a worker is a *wage*. Finally, although economists would disagree, many of us feel that *income taxes* are the price we pay for the privilege of making money.[1]

In the narrowest sense, **price** is the amount of money charged for a product or service. More broadly, price is the sum of all the values that consumers exchange for the benefits of having or using the product or service.

Price
The amount of money charged for a product or service, or the sum of the values that consumers exchange for the benefits of having or using the product or service.

preview case

The Oresund Bridge: over or under, down and out, again and again

MARIA DEL MAR SOUZA FONTAN*

This time it was supposed to be different. Governments have no problem commissioning grand projects that go under or over the sea but they do have problems keeping costs down and getting people to use them. Within a year of being opened it looked like the Oresund Bridge, which crosses the Oresund Straits between Copenhagen in Denmark and Malmö in Sweden, was going the way of similar attempts to join up bits of land.

The poor management structure during the construction of the Channel Tunnel linking England and France resulted in a two-year delay and a cost that reached €11 billion compared with the originally estimated €4.7 billion. Forecasts of the level of traffic using the tunnel were too optimistic, resulting in financial problems for Eurotunnel, the Channel Tunnel's operator. London & Continental, the consortium awarded the contract to build and operate the high-speed railway between London and the Channel Tunnel, was also in trouble, the number of passengers between London, Paris and Brussels being 50 per cent below forecasts. Embarrassing as they are, the Chunnel's problems were minor compared with Japan's recent bridge building.

Inaugurated in 1998, the Akashi Kaikyo Bridge is the longest suspension bridge in the world. It crosses the Akashi Straits and connects the city of Kobe to Awaji Island, and cost ¥800 billion (€8.5 billion). However, spectacular as it is to behold, locals and Japanese taxpayers wonder what it is for. Authorities claimed that some 37,000 cars would use the bridge each day, although only 100–200 a day ever used the ferry between Kobe and Awaji Island. The bridge was to bring all manner of economic opportunities to the residents of Awaji and the equally impoverished island of Shikoku. Although a great aesthetic and engineering success, people still do not want to go to Awaji. After an initial burst of enthusiasm, daily use remains little above the numbers who used the ferry.

Shortly after opening, it looked like the Oresund bridge-cum-tunnel was going the same way as its predecessors. Not only was its use far below forecast but also it looked like its use could go even lower. Novo Nordisk, a Danish drug firm that moved its HQ to Malmö to take advantage of the 'bridge effect', is urging its Danish staff to limit their trips to Malmö by working more from home. Swedish furniture chain IKEA has gone even further and banned its employees from using the bridge on company business. They are told to make the crossing using the ferry. The ferry is a lot slower than the bridge but also a lot less expensive.

The Danish and Swedish governments initiated the Oresund Bridge project in 1991. The aim was to build a fixed link across the Oresund Region, which comprises Zealand, Lolland-Falster and Bornholm, on the Danish side, as well as Scania and Sweden. The construction of this bridge was to provide stronger and more intense cooperation regarding economy, education, research and culture between the two nations, as well as constituting the link to the European mainland for Sweden. In July 2000, the €1.5 billion bridge-cum-tunnel opened to traffic. The investment was to be recouped from the thousands of cars crossing the bridge every day. The link is changing local life. More Swedes are visiting the cafés and galleries of Copenhagen although Malmö does not seem so attractive to the Danes.

Economic reality is proving to be well short of expectations. Peaking at 20,000 crossings a day soon after opening, traffic has now fallen to 6,000. Seventy-five per cent more people cross the straits than did before the construction but numbers are way below target. An advertising campaign has been launched to attract more people to use the bridge but price seems to be the problem. With many fewer cars than expected crossing the bridge, the Danish and Swedish governments have to find a route to a better possible return on investment, by changing their pricing strategy.

There are currently two types of fares, depending on whether drivers pay at the toll station or whether they sign an agreement which offers discounts for frequent travellers. Motorists who cross the bridge only a few times a year will pay 'the cash price', whilst those who use the bridge regularly will be in position to benefit considerably from a subscription agreement (Table 1).[2]

* Aston Business School, England

Vehicle type	Length	Price (€)
Motorcycles		16.35
Private vehicles	Up to 6 m	30.38
Private vehicles including trailers, minibuses or small trucks	Up to 9 m	65.43
Coaches		130.87
Heavy Goods Vehicles (HGVs)	From 9 m to 12 m	79.41
HGVs	From 12 m to 16.5 m	94.89
HGVs	Over 16.5 m	111.25

Table 1 Oresund Bridge pricing

Questions

1. Why do you think the forecasts for national or international prestige projects, including the Anglo-French Concorde, Britain's Millennium Dome and Humber Bridge, are so far off target? Is price *the* problem?

2. Since it looks like these prestige projects will never cover their costs, never mind produce a financial return on investment made, what criteria should be used in evaluating pricing alternatives?

3. Suggest an alternative pricing schedule for the Oresund Bridge, giving the reasons for your pricing decision.

How are prices set? Historically, buyers and sellers usually bargained with each other to set prices. Sellers would ask for a higher price than they expected to get and buyers would offer less than they expected to pay. Through bargaining, they would arrive at an acceptable price. Individual buyers paid different prices for the same products, depending on their needs and bargaining skills.

Today, most sellers set *one* price for *all* buyers. Large-scale retailing led to the idea at the end of the nineteenth century. F.W. Woolworth and other retailers advertised a 'strictly one-price policy' because they carried so many items and had so many employees. Historically, price has been the most significant factor affecting buyer choice. This is still true in poorer nations, among poorer groups and with commodity products. However, non-price factors have become more important in buyer-choice behaviour in recent decades. Price is the only element in the marketing mix that produces revenue; all other elements represent costs. Price is also one of the most flexible elements of the marketing mix. Unlike product features and channel commitments, price can be changed quickly.

Many companies do not handle pricing well. The most common mistakes are: pricing that is too cost-oriented; prices that are not revised often enough to reflect market changes; pricing that does not take the rest of the marketing mix into account; and prices that are not varied enough for different products, market segments and purchase occasions.

In this and the next chapter, we focus on the problem of setting prices. This chapter looks at the factors that marketers must consider when setting prices and at general pricing approaches. In the next chapter, we examine pricing strategies for new-product pricing, product mix pricing, price changes and price adjustments for buyer and situational factors.

factors to consider when setting prices

A company's pricing decisions are affected both by internal company factors and by external environmental factors (see Figure 16.1).[3]

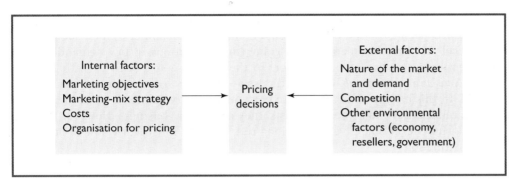

Figure 16.1

Factors affecting price decisions

internal factors affecting pricing decisions

Internal factors affecting pricing include the company's marketing objectives, marketing-mix strategy, costs and organisation.

■ Marketing objectives

Before setting price, the company must decide on its strategy for the product. If the company has selected its target market and positioning carefully, then its marketing-mix strategy, including price, will be fairly straightforward. For example, if Toyota decides to produce its Lexus cars to compete with European luxury cars in the high-income segment, this suggests charging a high price. Travelodge positions itself as motels that provide economical rooms for budget-minded travellers, a position that requires charging a low price. Thus pricing strategy is largely determined by past decisions on market positioning.

At the same time, the company may seek additional objectives. The clearer a firm is about its objectives, the easier it is to set price. Examples of common objectives are *survival, current profit maximisation, market-share maximisation* and *product-quality leadership*.

Marketing objectives: the price that Ford has set for its Luxuryka car has to be consistent with its positioning as 'the more luxurious small car'.

SOURCE: Ford Motor Company. *Agency:* Young & Rubicam

Companies set *survival* as their fundamental objective if they are troubled by too much capacity, heavy competition or changing consumer wants. Many steel-makers sell at a loss to keep a plant going through periods of low demand, hoping to increase prices when prices recover. In the public sector, such as with Britain's Millennium Dome, *survival* becomes the issue when government tire of demands for subsidy. In this case, profits are less important than survival. As long as their prices cover variable costs and some fixed costs, they can stay in business. However, survival is only a short-term objective. In the long run, the firm must learn how to add value or face extinction.[4]

Many companies use *current profit maximisation* as their pricing goal. They estimate what demand and costs will be at different prices and choose the price that will produce the maximum current profit, cash flow or return on investment. In all cases, the company wants current financial results rather than long-run performance. Other companies want to obtain *market-share leadership*. They believe that the company with the largest market share will enjoy the lowest costs and highest long-run profit. To become the market-share leader, these firms set prices as low as possible.

A variation of this objective is to pursue a specific *market-share gain*. Say the company wants to increase its market share from 10 per cent to 15 per cent in one year. It will search for the price and marketing programme that will achieve this goal.

Digital television transmission is set to make the current analogue television as outdated as 16 mm cine film or vinyl albums. It produces cinema quality pictures while cramming hundreds of channels through the wave bands needed for a dozen analogue transmissions. Seeing the mould-breaking potential of digital TV satellite television company, BSkyB and terrestrial BDB are set to battle for market leadership of digital television transmission. BSkyB's consortium of BT, HSBC and Matsushita aims to subsidise its TV set-top converters by €1 billion, almost giving them away although they cost over €500 to produce.

In pricing its set-top boxes below cost BSkyB is aiming to increase its market share and long-term profitability by considering the long-term cash flows that result from the customer's subscription. In this case the income will come from access charges to BSkyB's channels. In other cases, such as free Internet services, consumers pay indirectly. Marketing Highlight 16.1 details some of these free services.

A company might decide that it wants to achieve *product-quality leadership*. This normally calls for charging a high price to cover such quality and the high cost of R&D:

For example, Jaguar's limited edition XJ220 sold for £400,000 (€600,000) each, but had wealthy customers queuing to buy one. Less exotically, Pitney Bowes pursues a product-quality leadership strategy for its fax equipment. While Sharp, Canon and other competitors fight over the low-price fax machine market with machines selling at around €600, Pitney Bowes targets large corporations with machines selling at about €6,000. As a result, it captures some 45 per cent of the large-corporation fax niche.[5]

A company might also use price to attain other more specific objectives. It can set prices low to prevent competition from entering the market or set prices at competitors' levels to stabilise the market:

Leading grocery retailers Sainsbury and Tesco used 'Essentials' and 'Everyday super value range' campaigns to counter the attack of discounters Aldi and Netto on the UK market. Originally projected to take 20 per cent of the grocery market by 2000, forecasters later predicted the discounters would take only 12 per cent.[6]

marketing highlight 16.1

Is a free launch a free lunch?

Economists tell us that there is no such thing as a free lunch. Well, perhaps, but it certainly seems that many personal computer and Internet companies are trying to give them and it's paying off. So successful is giving it for free that in December 2000 Wanadoo, the Internet service provider (ISP) of France Télécom, paid £1.6 billion (€2.4 billion) for Freeserve, Britain's leading Internet provider. The deal takes Wanadoo, with its 4 million customers, to the number two slot, behind Germany's T-Online, in Europe's ISP market.

When the electronics retailer Dixons created Freeserve, a free ISP, in a low-profile launch in September 1998, many observers dismissed it as a marketing scam. Maybe a sales promotion designed to attract customers into their store to be sold PCs. Yet, within 5 months of its launch Freeserve had 1 million users. Not a surprising gain given that the other leading providers, such as AOL, charge for their service after an initial free trial period.

Dixon's success came from their decision to pioneer truly free Internet access for the mass market. But how could they make money by giving it away free when even the start-up disk and its packaging, never mind the server, must cost money? Freeserve's method is to charge its users nothing but to obtain 45 per cent of its income from a share of the normal British Telecom (BT) costs users incur to log onto the Internet. The system works because telecommunications have a high fixed cost, minimal cost of operation and much underutilised capacity when consumers are likely to use the Internet. Freeserve also made money when customers click on products or services they advertise. 'The average Freeserve customer accesses ninety-two pages of content per month. These are where we make advertising and e-commerce money from', says Freeserve's chief executive John Pluthero. The long-term plan, he says, has always been to ditch its ISP business to focus on offering its Internet portal as a Yahoo!-style shopping mall.

Although Freeserve was the 'free lunch' that launched scores of other free ISPs, the price-free option is nothing new when selling products to consumers or businesses. Companies make returns on the lifetime cost of ownership or cash flows that they receive because of the initial transaction. That is why it pays Scotch to provide three rolls of its Magic Tape with a free sticky tape dispenser for £2.99 (€4.53) when single rolls are priced at 99p. People have limited capacity to store the free dispensers and when they have a Scotch dispenser they are more likely to buy Scotch tape. Similarly, when aero-engine manufacturers give their engines to leading airlines for close to nothing, they are anticipating the income from years of spares and maintenance.

Or maybe there is no such thing as a free lunch. Before its sale to Wanadoo, financiers were concerned about Freeserve's continued losses and ever-diminishing reserves. Having got customers hooked, Freeserve found the free service expensive to provide. Faced with BT's wholesale SurfTime product, which halves Freeserve's revenues, the company needs to move its original 'free' customers to a monthly flat rate that covers Internet access and telephone. So far only 350,000 customers have taken up the offer of paying for what they already appear to get for free – and they are proving expensive. Maybe there is no such thing as a free lunch after all!

SOURCES: Chris Ayers, 'Freeserve chief set to ride out storm', *The Times* (17 March 2000), p. 33; 'Trawling for surfers', *The Economist* (1 May 1999), p. 95; Thorold Barker, 'Freeserve taken over for £1.6bn', *Financial Times* (7 December 2000), p. 27; Thorold Barker, 'Freeserve sale looks a good deal for Dixons', *Financial Times* (7 December 2000), p. 30.

Prices can be set to keep the loyalty and support of resellers or to avoid government intervention. Prices can be reduced temporarily to create excitement for a product or to draw more customers into a retail store. One product may be priced to help the sales of other products in the company's line. Thus pricing may play an important role in helping to accomplish the company's objectives at many levels.

Non-profit and public organisations may adopt a number of other pricing objectives. A university aims for *partial cost recovery*, knowing that it must rely on private gifts and public grants to cover the remaining costs. A non-profit hospital may aim for *full cost recovery* in its pricing. A non-profit theatre company may price its productions to fill the maximum number of theatre seats. A social service agency may set a *social price* geared to the varying income situations of different clients.

■ Marketing-mix strategy

Price is only one of the marketing-mix tools that a company uses to achieve its marketing objectives. Price decisions must be coordinated with product design, distribution and promotion decisions to form a consistent and effective marketing programme. Decisions made for other marketing-mix variables may affect pricing decisions. For example, producers using many resellers that are expected to support and promote their products may have to build larger reseller margins into their prices. The decision to position the product on high performance quality will mean that the seller must charge a higher price to cover higher costs. The perfume houses argue that their high margins, expensive advertising and exclusive distribution are essential to the brands and in the public interest.[7]

Companies often make their pricing decisions first and then base other marketing-mix decisions on the prices that they want to charge. Here, price is a crucial product-positioning factor that defines the product's market, competition and design. The intended price determines what product features can be offered and what production costs can be incurred.

Many firms support such price-positioning strategies with a technique called **target costing**, a potent strategic weapon. Target costing reverses the usual process of first designing a new product, determining its cost and then asking 'Can we sell it for that?' Instead, it starts with a target cost and works back:

Target costing
A technique to support pricing decisions, which starts with deciding a target cost for a new product and works back to designing the product.

> When starting up, Swatch surveyed the market and identified an unserved segment of watch buyers who wanted 'a low-cost fashion accessory that also keeps time'. Armed with this information about market needs, Swatch set out to give consumers the watch they wanted at a price they were willing to pay, and it managed the new product's costs accordingly. Like most watch buyers, targeted consumers were concerned about precision, reliability, and durability. However, they were also concerned about fashion and affordability. To keep costs down, Swatch designed fashionable simpler watches that contained fewer parts and that were constructed from high-tech but less expensive materials. It then developed a revolutionary automated process for mass producing the new watches and exercised strict cost controls throughout the manufacturing process. By managing costs carefully, Swatch was able to create a watch that offered just the right blend of fashion and function at a price consumers were willing to pay. As a result of its initial major success, consumers have placed increasing value on Swatch products, allowing the company to introduce successively higher-priced designs.[8]

Other companies de-emphasise price and use other marketing-mix tools to create *non-price* positions. Often, the best strategy is not to charge the lowest price, but rather to differentiate the marketing offer to make it worth a higher price.

> London's City Airport and the airlines that fly from there do not compete on price. Instead they offer the retailing, speed of processing and convenience wanted by frequent flying executives. In this case less means more. City's compact terminal has no burger bars, no video arcades and no air bridges. Surveys show that City Airport's regular users prefer using the aircraft's own stairs and braving the English weather rather than wait, hunched under luggage racks while air bridges are connected.[9]

Thus the marketer must consider the total marketing mix when setting prices. If the product is positioned on non-price factors, then decisions about quality, promotion and distribution will strongly affect price. If price is a crucial positioning factor, then price will strongly affect decisions made about the other marketing-mix elements. In most cases, the company will consider all the marketing-mix decisions together when developing the marketing programme.

Gucci's very strong image and reputation as a prestigious brand means that customers are willing to pay for the fashion house's expensive fragrances.

■ Costs

Costs set the floor for the price that the company can charge for its product. The company wants to charge a price that both covers all its costs for producing, distributing and selling the product, and delivers a fair rate of return for its effort and risk. A company's costs may be an important element in its pricing strategy. Many companies work to become the 'low-cost producers' in their industries. Companies with lower costs can set lower prices that result in greater sales and profits.

Types of cost A company's costs take two forms, fixed and variable. **Fixed costs** (also known as overhead) are costs that do not vary with production or sales level. For example, a company must pay each month's bills for rent, heat, interest and executive salaries, whatever the company's output. In many industries, such as airlines, fixed costs dominate. If an airline has to fly a sector with few passengers on board it can only save on the 15 per cent of its costs accounted for by cabin crew and passenger service. All other costs, including flight crew (7 per cent), fuel (15 per cent) and maintenance (10 per cent), are fixed.[10]

Variable costs vary directly with the level of production. Each personal computer produced involves a cost of computer chips, wires, plastic, packaging and other inputs. These costs tend to be the same for each unit produced. They are called variable because their total varies with the number of units produced.

Fixed costs
Costs that do not vary with production or sales level.

Variable costs
Costs that vary directly with the level of production.

Part of the cost of a CD is an agreed amount paid to artists for each unit sold. When CDs were introduced, recording companies renegotiated a lower rate than for vinyl recordings to allow them to recoup their costs. George Michael mounted an unsuccessful legal case against Sony Music, complaining that the rates were too low.

The lingering resentment of many artists over this 'deal' is now becoming important as recording companies try to agree rates to apply to electronically distributed music where customers play music on demand or download music on to their PC. With the possibility of no packaging, manufacturing, wholesaling or retailing costs, the artists' share of the asking price for this format could be high. Legal and illegal home copying through MP3.com, where users are only asked to confirm that they own the CD they want to copy, are making the resolution of this conflict critical to the industry.[11]

Total costs

The sum of the fixed and variable costs for any given level of production.

Total costs are the sum of the fixed and variable costs for any given level of production. Management wants to charge a price that will at least cover the total production costs at a given level of production. The company must watch its costs carefully. If it costs the company more than competitors to produce and sell its product, the company will have to charge a higher price or make less profit, putting it at a competitive disadvantage.

Costs at different levels of production To price wisely, management needs to know how its costs vary with different levels of production. Glen Dimplex, the Irish domestic appliances company that owns Morphy Richards, Dimplex and Belling, has taken over Roberts, a maker of high-quality radios. As part of its plan to add new and innovative products to the Roberts range, it could build a plant to produce 1,000 Roberts luxury travel clocks per day. Figure 16.2A shows the typical short-run average cost curve (SRAC). It shows that the cost per clock is high if Roberts' factory produces only a few per day. But as production moves up to 1,000 clocks per day, average cost falls. This is because fixed costs are spread over more units, with each one bearing a smaller fixed cost. Roberts can try to produce more than 1,000 clocks per day, but average costs

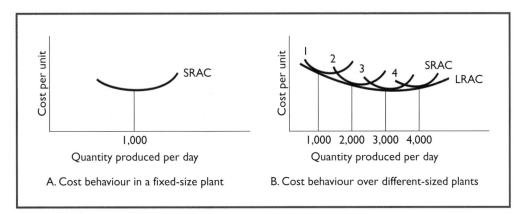

Figure 16.2

Cost per unit at different levels of production

will increase because the plant becomes inefficient. Workers have to wait for machines, the machines break down more often and workers get in each other's way.

If Roberts believed it could sell 2,000 clocks a day, it should consider building a larger plant. The plant would use more efficient machinery and work arrangements. Also, the unit cost of producing 2,000 units per day would be lower than the unit cost of producing 1,000 units per day, as shown in the long-run average cost (LRAC) curve (Figure 16.2B). In fact, a 3,000-capacity plant would be even more efficient, according to Figure 16.2B. But a 4,000 daily production plant would be less efficient because of increasing diseconomies of scale – too many workers to manage, paperwork slows things down and so on. Figure 16.2B shows that a 3,000 daily production plant is the best size to build if demand is strong enough to support this level of production.

Costs as a function of production experience Suppose Roberts runs a plant that produces 3,000 clocks per day. As Roberts gains experience in producing hand-held clocks, it learns how to do it better. Workers learn short cuts and become more familiar with their equipment. With practice, the work becomes better organised and Roberts finds better equipment and production processes. With higher volume, Roberts becomes more efficient and gains economies of scale. As a result, average cost tends to fall with accumulated production experience. This is shown in Figure 16.3.[12] Thus the average cost of producing the first 100,000 clocks is €10 per clock. When the company has produced the first 200,000 clocks, the average cost has fallen to €9. After it's accumulated production experience doubles again to 400,000, the average cost is €7. This drop in the average cost with accumulated production experience is called the **experience curve** (or **learning curve**).

If a downward-sloping experience curve exists, this is highly significant for the company. Not only will the company's unit production cost fall; it will fall faster if the company makes and sells more during a given time period. But the market has to stand

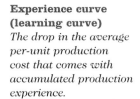

Experience curve (learning curve)
The drop in the average per-unit production cost that comes with accumulated production experience.

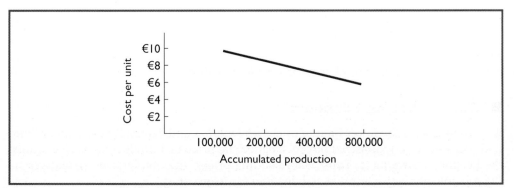

Figure 16.3

Cost per unit as a function of accumulated production: the experience curve

ready to buy the higher output. And to take advantage of the experience curve, Roberts must get a large market share early in the product's life cycle. This suggests the following pricing strategy. Roberts should price its clocks low; its sales will then increase and its costs will decrease through gaining more experience, and then it can lower its prices further.

Some companies have built successful strategies around the experience curve. For example, during the 1980s, Bausch & Lomb consolidated its position in the soft contact lens market by using computerised lens design and steadily expanding its one Soflens plant. As a result, its market share climbed steadily to 65 per cent. Yet a single-minded focus on reducing costs and exploiting the experience curve will not always work. Experience curves became somewhat of a fad during the 1970s and, like many fads, the strategy was sometimes misused. Experience-curve pricing carries some serious risks. The aggressive pricing might give the product a cheap image. The strategy also assumes that competitors are weak and not willing to fight it out by meeting the company's price cuts.

> An 'experience curve war' broke out between the Japanese makers of DRAM (dynamic random-access memory) chips, the semiconductor memory devices used in computers. Hitachi, Toshiba, NEC and Mitsubishi reduced the price of their 4-megabyte DRAMs from Yen 12,000 (€128) to Yen 2,500 within a year of its launch, at the same time spending heavily to develop the next generation's 16-megabyte DRAM. Within two years 1-megabyte DRAM sold for Yen 1,600, probably too low to recoup the cost of the production lines needed to make them.[13]

Finally, while the company is building volume under one technology, a competitor may find a lower-cost technology that lets it start at lower prices than the market leader, who still operates on the old experience curve.

■ Organisational considerations

Management must decide who within the organisation should set prices. Companies handle pricing in a variety of ways. In small companies, prices are often set by top management rather than by the marketing or sales departments. In large companies, pricing is typically handled by divisional or product line managers. In industrial markets, salespeople may be allowed to negotiate with customers within certain price ranges. Even so, top management sets the pricing objectives and policies, and it often approves the prices proposed by lower-level management or salespeople. In industries in which pricing is a key factor (such as in aerospace, railways, oil), companies will often have a pricing department to set the best prices or help others in setting them. This department reports to the marketing department or top management. Others who have an influence on pricing include sales managers, production managers, finance managers and accountants.

external factors affecting pricing decisions

External factors that affect pricing decisions include the nature of the market and demand, competition and other environmental elements.

■ The market and demand

Whereas costs set the lower limit of prices, the market and demand set the upper limit. Both consumer and industrial buyers balance the price of a product or service against the benefits of owning it. Thus, before setting prices, the marketer must understand the relationship between price and demand for its product.

In this section, we explain how the price–demand relationship varies for different types of market and how buyer perceptions of price affect the pricing decision. We then discuss methods for measuring the price–demand relationship.

Pricing in different types of market The seller's pricing freedom varies with different types of market. Economists recognise four types of market, each presenting a different pricing challenge.

Under **pure competition**, the market consists of many buyers and sellers trading in a uniform commodity such as wheat, copper or financial securities. No single buyer or seller has much effect on the going market price. A seller cannot charge more than the going price because buyers can obtain as much as they need at the going price. Nor would sellers charge less than the market price because they can sell all they want at this price. If price and profits rise, new sellers can easily enter the market. In a purely competitive market, marketing research, product development, pricing, advertising and sales promotion play little or no role. Thus sellers in these markets do not spend much time on marketing strategy.

Under **monopolistic competition**, the market consists of many buyers and sellers that trade over a range of prices rather than a single market price. A range of prices occurs because sellers can differentiate their offers to buyers. Either the physical product can be varied in quality, features or style or the accompanying services can be varied. Each company can create a quasi-monopoly for its products because buyers see differences in sellers' products and will pay different prices for them. Sellers try to develop differentiated offers for different customer segments and, in addition to price, freely use branding, availability, advertising and personal selling to set their offers apart. For example, Ty's Beanie Babies compete in the toy market for attention but have cultivated a distinctive appeal that has both stimulated demand and seen the price of some Beanies rocket.[14]

Under **oligopolistic competition**, the market consists of a few sellers that are highly sensitive to each other's pricing and marketing strategies. The product can be uniform (steel, aluminium) or non-uniform (cars, computers). There are few sellers because it is difficult for new sellers to enter the market. Each seller is alert to competitors' strategies and moves. If a steel company slashes its price by 10 per cent, buyers will quickly switch to this supplier. The other steel makers must respond by lowering their prices or increasing their services. An oligopolist is never sure that it will gain anything permanent through a price cut. In contrast, if an oligopolist raises its price, its competitors might not follow this lead. The oligopolist would then have to retract its price increase or risk losing customers to competitors.

In a **pure monopoly**, the market consists of one seller. The seller may be a government monopoly (a postal service), a private regulated monopoly (a power company) or a private non-regulated monopoly (Microsoft Windows). Pricing is handled differently in each case. A government monopoly can pursue a variety of pricing objectives. It might set a price below cost because the product is important to buyers who cannot afford to pay full cost. Or the price might be set either to cover costs or to produce good revenue. It can even be set quite high to slow down consumption or to protect an inefficient supplier. In a regulated monopoly, the government permits the company to set rates that will yield a 'fair return', one that will let the company maintain and expand its operations as needed. Non-regulated monopolies are free to price at what the market will bear. However, they do not always charge the full price for a number of reasons: for example, a desire not to attract competition, a desire to penetrate the market faster with a low price, or a fear of government regulation. The different pricing objectives lead to huge differences in monopolistic prices. NTT, Japan's huge telecoms monopoly, charges twice the local interconnection charge as does the France Télécom monopoly and six times the rate in the US's competitive market.[15]

Pure competition
A market in which many buyers and sellers trade in a uniform commodity – no single buyer or seller has much effect on the going market price.

Monopolistic competition
A market in which many buyers and sellers trade over a range of prices rather than a single market price.

Oligopolistic competition
A market in which there are a few sellers that are highly sensitive to each other's pricing and marketing strategies.

Pure monopoly
A market in which there is a single seller – it may be a government monopoly, a private regulated monopoly or a private non-regulated monopoly.

Consumer perceptions of price and value   In the end, the consumer will decide whether a product's price is right. When setting prices, the company must consider consumer perceptions of price and how these perceptions affect consumers' buying decisions. Pricing decisions, like other marketing-mix decisions, must be buyer-oriented.

When consumers buy a product, they exchange something of value (the price) to get something of value (the benefits of having or using the product). Effective, buyer-oriented pricing involves understanding how much value consumer's place on the benefits they receive from the product and setting a price that fits this value. These benefits can be actual or perceived. For example, calculating the cost of ingredients in a meal at a fancy restaurant is relatively easy. But assigning a value to other satisfactions such as taste, environment, relaxation, conversation and status is very hard. And these values will vary both for different consumers and for different situations.

> Functional confectionery, such as Clorets or Fisherman's Friend, offers tangible problem solutions that customers value. These products may cost little more to make than conventional sugar-based confectionery, such as Polo Mints or Rowntree's Fruit Pastilles, but customers value their physical performance. Makers of these products do not rely on consumers' perception of their brand's value, but convey the products on the pack and by promotions. For instance, the flavour, strength and packaging of Hall's Mentho-Lyptus is fine-tuned for local markets but remains true to its core benefit: throat soothing.

Thus the company will often find it hard to measure the values that customers will attach to its product. But consumers do use these values to evaluate a product's price. If customers perceive that the price is greater than the product's value, they will not buy the product. If consumers perceive that the price is below the product's value, they will buy it, but the seller loses profit opportunities.

Marketers must therefore try to understand the consumer's reasons for buying the product and set the price according to consumer perceptions of the product's value. Because consumers vary in the values they assign to different product features, marketers often vary their pricing strategies for different segments. They offer different sets of product features at different prices. For example, Philips offers €250 small 41 cm portable TV models for consumers who want basic sets and €1,200 68 cm 100-Hz Nicam stereo models loaded with features for consumers who want the extras.

Analysing the price–demand relationship   Each price the company might charge will lead to a different level of demand. The relation between the price charged and the resulting demand level is shown in the demand curve in Figure 16.4A. The demand curve shows the number of units that the market will buy in a given time

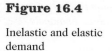

Figure 16.4

Inelastic and elastic demand

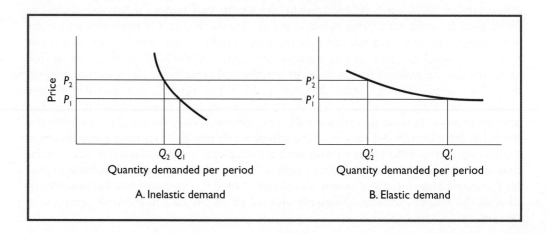

period at different prices that might be charged. In the normal case, demand and price are inversely related: that is, the higher the price, the lower the demand. Thus the company would sell less if it raised its price from P_1 to P_2. In short, consumers with limited budgets will probably buy less of something if its price is too high.

In the case of prestige goods, the demand curve sometimes slopes upward. Consumers think that higher prices mean more quality.

> When Gibson Guitars lowered its prices to compete more effectively with
> Japanese rivals like Yamaha and Ibanez the result was not what they expected.
> Gibson found that its instruments didn't sell as well at lower prices. 'We had an
> inverse [price–demand relationship]', noted Gibson's chief executive officer.
> 'The more we charged, the more product we sold.' Gibson's slogan promises:
> 'The world's finest musical instruments'. It turns out that low prices simply aren't
> consistent with 'Gibson's century old tradition of creating investment-quality
> instruments that represent the highest standards of imaginative design and
> masterful craftsmanship'.[16]

However, even for prestige products, if the price is too high, demand will reduce.

Most companies try to measure their demand curves by estimating demand at different prices. The type of market makes a difference. In a monopoly, the demand curve shows the total market demand resulting from different prices. If the company faces competition, its demand at different prices will depend on whether competitors' prices stay constant or change with the company's own prices. Here, we will assume that competitors' prices remain constant. Later in this chapter, we will discuss what happens when competitors' prices change.

In measuring the price–demand relationship, the market researcher must not allow other factors affecting demand to vary. For example, if Philips increased its advertising at the same time that it lowered its television prices, we would not know how much of the increased demand was due to the lower prices and how much was due to the increased advertising. The same problem arises if a holiday weekend occurs when the lower price is set – more gift-giving over some holidays causes people to buy more portable televisions. Economists show the impact of non-price factors on demand through shifts in the demand curve rather than movements along it.

Price elasticity of demand Marketers also need to know **price elasticity** – how responsive demand will be to a change in price. Consider the two demand curves in Figure 16.4. In Figure 16.4A, a price increase from P_1 to P_2 leads to a relatively small drop in demand from Q_1 to Q_2. In Figure 16.4B, however, a similar price increase leads to a large drop in demand from Q'_1 to Q'_2. If demand hardly changes with a small change in price, we say the demand is *inelastic*. If demand changes greatly, we say the demand is *elastic*. The price elasticity of demand is given by the following formula:

Price elasticity
A measure of the sensitivity of demand to changes in price.

$$\text{Price elasticity of demand} = \frac{\%\text{ change in quantity demanded}}{\%\text{ change in price}}$$

Suppose demand falls by 10 per cent when a seller raises its price by 2 per cent. Price elasticity of demand is therefore −5 (the minus sign confirms the inverse relation between price and demand) and demand is elastic. If demand falls by 2 per cent with a 2 per cent increase in price, then elasticity is −1. In this case, the seller's total revenue stays the same: that is, the seller sells fewer items, but at a higher price that preserves the same total revenue. If demand falls by 1 per cent when the price is increased by 2 per cent, then elasticity is −$^1/_2$ and demand is inelastic. The less elastic the demand, the more it pays for the seller to raise the price.

Table 16.1

How discounts influence sales and profits

Action	Regular price	10% discount	Percentage change
Sales			
Price (€)	1.00	0.90	
Sales volume	100	105	
Sales value (€)	100.00	94.50	(5.5)
Cost of goods sold			
Unit cost (€)	0.50	0.50	
Sales (units)	100	105	
Cost (€)	50.00	52.50	5.0
Gross profit	50.00	42.00	(16.0)
Other trading expenses	40.00	40.00	0.0
Net profit	10.00	2.00	(80.0)
Return on sales (%)	10.0	2.1	

What determines the price elasticity of demand? Buyers are less price sensitive when the product they are buying is unique or when it is high in quality, prestige or exclusiveness. They are also less price sensitive when substitute products are hard to find or when they cannot easily compare the quality of substitutes. Finally, buyers are less price sensitive when the total expenditure for a product is low relative to their income or when another party shares the cost.[17]

If demand is elastic rather than inelastic, sellers will consider lowering their price. A lower price will produce more total revenue. This practice makes sense as long as the extra costs of producing and selling more do not exceed the extra revenue.

> Yorkshire Chemicals, a dyes and specialist chemicals manufacturer, shrugged off the effects of a depressed European market by 'producing and selling more at lower price levels'. Investments in extra efficient capacity allowed the dyestuffs division to keep profits constant after cutting prices 5 per cent and increasing sales 8 per cent.[18]

Price influence on profits Increasing *sales volume* in items sold is the driving force behind much marketing activity. There are good reasons for this: increased sales show success and a growing company, increased market share shows competitive success and, if sales do not match production, capacity will be underused or customers disappointed.

Unfortunately, when price is used to increase sales volume, *sales value* – the proceeds from sales – may reduce. *Sales value* and *sales volume* do not always move hand in hand. A company that increases sales by 5 per cent by cutting prices by 10 per cent increases sales volume but reduces sales value, as the example in Table 16.1 shows.

Gross profit is the difference between net proceeds from sales and the cost of goods sold. The costs are the variable costs incurred each time a product is made. They typically include raw materials, labour, energy and so on. The interplay between gross profit and price is dramatic. The once popular idea of 'everyday low prices' increased sales volumes and value, but not always by enough to cover lost margins. The example in Table 16.1 shows that the 10 per cent price cut has much more impact on *gross profits* than do sales.

Net profit is the surplus remaining after all costs have been taken. The gross profit shows the contribution made to the company by each unit sold, but neglects many other trading expenses incurred by a company. These included fixed costs like rates and staff, and strategic expenditure like research and development. Interest paid on debts is sometimes not included because this depends upon the capital structure of the company. The fixed cost means that *net profit* is more volatile than *gross profit* (see Table 16.1). This sensitivity encourages companies to convert some of their fixed costs into variable ones: for example, hiring trucks rather than buying them.

Return on sales (or *margin*) measures the ratio of profit to sales:

$$\text{Return on sales} = \frac{\text{Net profit}}{\text{Sales}}$$

This is useful in comparing businesses over time. During a four-year period a company may find both sales and net profit increasing, but are profits keeping pace with sales? In Table 16.1 the 10 per cent price promotion gives an increase in sales volume, but a big reduction in return on sales. The interplay between price, sales, profits and investment makes these and other ratios central to marketing decision making and control. Marketing Highlight 16.2 introduces *Economic Value Added* (EVA), a measure that has become increasingly important in recent years.

> **Net profit**
> *The difference between the income from goods sold and all expenses incurred.*

marketing highlight 16.2

Economic Value Added

Return on capital employed (ROCE)

Some companies, such as grocery chains, have low returns on sales but are profitable. They achieve this because the critical measure is return on capital employed. This is the product of return on sales (ROS) and the speed at which assets are turned over (the activity ratio):

$$\text{ROCE} = \text{ROS} \times \text{ACTIVITY} = \frac{\text{NP}}{\text{Sales}} \times \frac{\text{Sales}}{\text{Assets}}$$

By turning over its assets four times each year, a supermarket can achieve a 20 per cent return on capital employed although its return on sales is only 5 per cent, while an exclusive clothes shop has very high margins but turns its assets over slowly.

$$\text{Supermarket ROCE} = \frac{5}{100} \times \frac{100}{25} = 20 \text{ per cent}$$

$$\text{Clothes shop ROCE} = \frac{40}{100} \times \frac{100}{300} = 13.3 \text{ per cent}$$

These are powerful ratios that can define how a company can do business. Aldi, the German discount grocery chain, succeeds with margins half those of many grocers. Its margins are very low (2–3 per cent), but it keeps its return on capital employed high by high stock turnover and keeping its other assets low.

There are two benefits from increasing asset turnover: improved return on capital employed, and reduced fixed costs. The firm that hires trucks rather than buying them reduces its fixed costs and, therefore, its sensitivity to volume changes. Also, by reducing its assets it increases its activity ratio and return on capital employed. Increased asset turnover is one of the direct benefits of just-in-time (JIT) and lean manufacturing. JIT cuts down the assets tied up in stock, and improves quality while lean manufacturing reduces investment in plant.

Capital cost covered (C³)

Assets cost money and return on capital costs takes that into account. It is a powerful tool because it combines three critical business ratios:

$$C^3 = \text{ROS} \times \text{ACTIVITY} \times \text{CAPITAL EFFICIENCY}$$

$$= \frac{\text{NP}}{\text{Sales}} \times \frac{\text{Sales}}{\text{Assets}} \times \frac{\text{Assets}}{\text{Cost of capital}}$$

The cost of capital is the average cost of debt and shareholder equity. For a supermarket the figure is

10 per cent per year. With assets of €25 million, the cost of capital is €25m × 0.10 = €2.5m, giving:

$$C^3 = \frac{5}{100} \times \frac{100}{25} \times \frac{25}{2.5} = \frac{NP}{CC} = 2.0$$

In other words, the net profit is double the capital cost – the company is healthy. This ratio is more discriminating than the familiar distinction between profit and loss. If the capital cost covered is below zero, a firm is making a loss. A capital cost covered above zero indicates a profit. However, capital cost covered between zero and 1 shows that a firm is in profit but not adding value – its profit does not cover its cost of capital.

Economic Value Added (EVA)

EVA makes a direct comparison between the cost of capital and net profits. It is a simple idea that has hugely increased the value of companies using it. Many leading companies see EVA as a way of examining the value of their investments and strategy.

The supermarket's EVA is:

EVA = Net profit – Cost of capital = 5 – 2.5 = €2.5m

Profit, economic value added and capital cost covered are related concepts: profit shows how a company's trading is going, economic value added shows a company's wealth creation in monetary terms, while capital cost covered gives the rate of wealth creation.

Category	C^3	EVA	NP	Economic state
I	>1	>0	>0	A profitable company which is adding economic value
II	1>0	<0	>0	A company whose profits do not cover the cost of capital
III	<0	<0	<0	A loss-making company

The supermarket is a clear category I company. This contrasts with the clothes store whose capital, at 16.25 per cent, is more expensive because the clothes market is cyclical and fashion-dependent. Assets of €300 million give a capital cost of €48.75 million.

	C^3	EVA (€m)	NP (€m)	Category
Supermarket	2.0	2.5	5	I
Clothes store	0.8	(9.5)	40	II

Many of the dot bombs (.com companies that went bust) never strayed beyond being category III companies, never making any net profits (NP<0) after having a high advertising spend with low margins and sales volume.

SOURCES: Alan Wolfe, 'Price wars', *Marketing Business* (November 1991), pp. 37–9; Shawn Tully, 'The real key to creating wealth', *Fortune* (20 September 1993), pp. 24–30; Neil Buckley, 'Potential cost of selling it cheap every day', *Financial Times* (24 March 1994), p. 17; Neil Buckley, 'Waging war over bread and baked beans', *Financial Times* (20 October 1994), p. 11; 'Valuing companies: a star to sail by?', *The Economist* (2 August 1997), pp. 61–3.

■ Competitors' costs, prices and offers

Another external factor affecting the company's pricing decisions is competitors' costs and prices, and possible competitor reactions to the company's own pricing moves. A consumer who is considering the purchase of a Canon camera will evaluate Canon's price and value against the prices and values of comparable products made by Nikon, Minolta, Pentax and others. In addition, the company's pricing strategy may affect the nature of the competition it faces. If Canon follows a high-price, high-margin strategy, it may attract competition. A low-price, low-margin strategy, however, may stop competitors or drive them out of the market.

Canon needs to benchmark its costs against its competitors' costs to learn whether it is operating at a cost advantage or disadvantage. It also needs to learn the price and quality of each competitor's offer. Canon might do this in several ways. It can send out comparison shoppers to price and compare the products of Nikon, Minolta and other competitors. It can get competitors' price lists and buy competitors' equipment and take it apart. It can ask buyers how they view the price and quality of each competitor's camera.

Once Canon is aware of competitors' prices and offers, it can use them as a starting point for its own pricing. If Canon's cameras are similar to Nikon's, it will have to price close to Nikon or lose sales. If Canon's cameras are not as good as Nikon's, the firm will not be able to charge as much. If Canon's products are better than Nikon's, it can charge more. Basically, Canon will use price to position its offer relative to the competition.

Low price is one of the strategies that Energis use against BT, the dominant competitor.

SOURCE: Energis

■ Other external factors

When setting prices, the company must also consider other factors in its external environment. *Economic conditions* can have a strong impact on the firm's pricing strategies.[19] Economic factors such as boom or recession, inflation and interest rates affect pricing decisions because they affect both the costs of producing a product and consumer perception of the product's price and value. The company must also consider what impact its prices will have on other parties in its environment. How will *resellers* react to various prices? The company should set prices that give resellers a fair profit, encourage their support and help them to sell the product effectively. The *government* is another important external influence on pricing decisions. Finally, *social concerns* may have to be taken into account. In setting prices, a company's short-term sales, market share and profit goals may have to be tempered by broader societal considerations.

general pricing approaches

The price that the company charges will be somewhere between one that is too low to produce a profit and one that is too high to produce any demand. Figure 16.5 summarises the primary considerations in setting price. Product costs set a floor to the price; consumer perceptions of the product's value set the ceiling. The company must consider competitors' prices and other external and internal factors to find the best price between these two extremes.

Companies set prices by selecting a general pricing approach that includes one or more of these three sets of factors – costs, consumer perception and competitors' prices.

Figure 16.5

Primary considerations in price settings

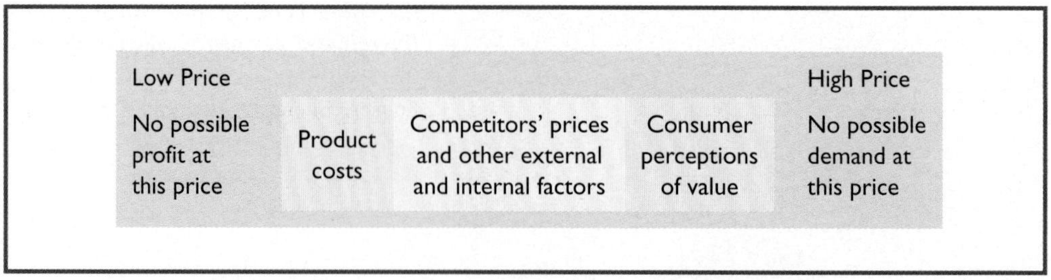

Low Price				High Price
No possible profit at this price	Product costs	Competitors' prices and other external and internal factors	Consumer perceptions of value	No possible demand at this price

We will examine the following approaches: the *cost-based approach* (cost-plus pricing, break-even analysis and target profit pricing); the *buyer-based approach* (perceived-value pricing); and the *competition-based approach* (going-rate and sealed-bid pricing).

cost-based pricing

■ Cost-plus pricing

Cost-plus pricing
Adding a standard mark-up to the cost of the product.

Mark-up/mark-down
The difference between selling price and cost as a percentage of selling price or cost.

The simplest pricing method is **cost-plus pricing** – adding a standard mark-up to the cost of the product. Construction companies, for example, submit job bids by estimating the total project cost and adding a standard mark-up for profit. Lawyers, accountants and other professionals typically price by adding a standard mark-up to their costs. Some sellers tell their customers they will charge cost plus a specified **mark-up**: for example, aerospace companies price this way to the government.

To illustrate *mark-up* pricing, suppose a toaster manufacturer had the following costs and expected sales:

Variable cost	€10
Fixed cost	€300,000
Expected unit sales	50,000

Then the manufacturer's cost per toaster is given by:

$$\text{Unit cost} = \text{Variable cost} + \frac{\text{fixed costs}}{\text{unit sales}} = €10 + \frac{€300,000}{50,000} = €16$$

Now suppose the manufacturer wants to earn a 20 per cent mark-up on sales. The manufacturer's mark-up price is given by:

$$\text{Mark-up price} = \frac{\text{unit cost}}{(1.0 - \text{desired return on sales})} = \frac{€16}{(1.0 - 0.2)} = €20$$

The manufacturer would charge dealers €20 a toaster and make a profit of €4 per unit. The dealers, in turn, will mark up the toaster. If dealers want to earn 50 per cent on sales price, they will mark up the toaster to €40 (€20 + 50 per cent of €40). This number is equivalent to a *mark-up on cost* of 100 per cent (€20/€20).

Does using standard mark-ups to set prices make logical sense? Generally, no. Any pricing method that ignores demand and competitors' prices is not likely to lead to the best price. Suppose the toaster manufacturer charged €20 but only sold 30,000 toasters instead of 50,000. Then the unit cost would have been higher, since the fixed costs are spread over fewer units and the realised percentage mark-up on sales would have been lower. Mark-up pricing works only if that price actually brings in the expected level of sales.

Still, mark-up pricing remains popular for a number of reasons. First, sellers are more certain about costs than about demand. By tying the price to cost, sellers simplify pricing – they do not have to make frequent adjustments as demand changes. Second, when all firms in the industry use this pricing method, prices tend to be similar and price competition is thus minimised. Third, many people feel that cost-plus pricing is fairer to both buyers and sellers. Sellers earn a fair return on their investment, but do not take advantage of buyers when buyers' demand becomes great.

■ Break-even analysis and target profit pricing

Another cost-oriented pricing approach is **break-even pricing** or a variation called **target profit pricing**. The firm tries to determine the price at which it will break even or make the target profit it is seeking. Target pricing is used by General Motors, which prices its cars to achieve a 15–20 per cent profit on its investment. This pricing method is also used by public utilities, which are constrained to make a fair return on their investment. Target pricing uses the concept of a *break-even chart*, which shows the total cost and total revenue expected at different sales volume levels. Figure 16.6 shows a break-even chart for the toaster manufacturer discussed here. Fixed costs are €300,000 regardless of sales volume. Variable costs are added to fixed costs to form total costs, which rise with volume. The total revenue curve starts at zero and rises with each unit sold. The slope of the total revenue curve reflects the price of €20 per unit.

The total revenue and total cost curves cross at 30,000 units. This is the *break-even volume*. At €20, the company must sell at least 30,000 units to break even: that is, for total revenue to cover total cost. Break-even volume can be calculated using the following formula:

$$\text{Break-even volume} = \frac{\text{fixed cost}}{(\text{price} - \text{variable cost})} = \frac{€300,000}{(€20 - €10)} = 30,000$$

If the company wants to make a target profit, it must sell more than 30,000 units at €20 each. Suppose the toaster manufacturer has invested €1,000,000 in the business and wants to set a price to earn a 20 per cent return or €200,000. In that case, it must sell at least 50,000 units at €20 each. If the company charges a higher price, it will not need to sell as many toasters to achieve its target return. But the market may not buy even this lower volume at the higher price. Much depends on the price elasticity and competitors' prices.

Break-even pricing (target profit pricing)
Setting price to break even on the costs of making and marketing a product; or setting price to make a target profit.

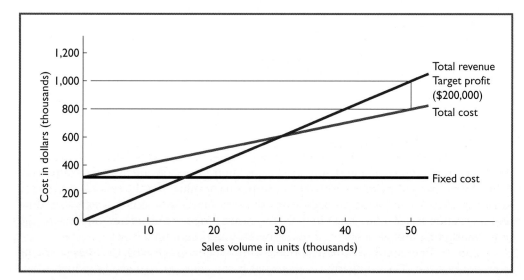

Figure 16.6

Break-even chart for determining target price

(1) Price (€)	(2) Unit demand needed to break even (000)	(3) Expected unit demand at given price (000)	(4) Total revenues = (1) × (3) (€000)	(5) Total cost* (€000)	(6) Profit = (4) − (5) (€000)
14	75	71	994	1,100	–16
16	50	67	1,072	970	102
18	37.5	60	1,080	900	180
20	30	42	840	720	120
22	25	23	506	530	–24

* Assumes a fixed cost of €300,000 and a constant unit variable cost of €10.

Table 16.2

Break-even volume and profits at different prices

The manufacturer should consider different prices and estimate break-even volumes, probable demand and profits for each. This is done in Table 16.2. The table shows that as price increases, break-even volume drops (column 2). But as price increases, demand for the toasters also falls off (column 3). At the €14 price, because the manufacturer clears only €4 per toaster (€14 less €10 in variable costs), it must sell a very high volume to break even. Even though the low price attracts many buyers, demand still falls below the high break-even point and the manufacturer loses money. At the other extreme, with a €22 price the manufacturer clears €12 per toaster and must sell only 25,000 units to break even. But at this high price, consumers buy too few toasters and profits are negative. The table shows that a price of €18 yields the highest profits. Note that none of the prices produces the manufacturer's target profit of €200,000. To achieve this target return, the manufacturer will have to search for ways to lower fixed or variable costs, thus lowering the break-even volume.

Airbus Industries base their forecasts for their superjumbo A3XX on the superior breakeven that it will offer airlines who buy it. Although much larger than its major competitor, the Boeing B747-400, the A3XX operating cost means that it breaks even at a fraction of its total capacity.[20]

Aircraft	Boeing 747-400	Airbus A3XX
Passenger capacity	413	555
Break even: passengers	290	323
Profitable seats: beyond breakeven	123	232
Break even: percentage of capacity	70%	58%

value-based pricing

Value-based pricing
Setting price based on buyers' perceptions of product values rather than on cost.

An increasing number of companies are basing their prices on the product's perceived value. **Value-based pricing** uses buyers' perceptions of value, not the seller's cost, as the key to pricing. Value-based pricing means that the marketer cannot design a product and marketing programme and then set the price. Price is considered along with the other marketing-mix variables *before* the marketing programme is set.

Figure 16.7 compares cost-based pricing with value-based pricing. Cost-based pricing is product driven. The company designs what it considers to be a good product, totals

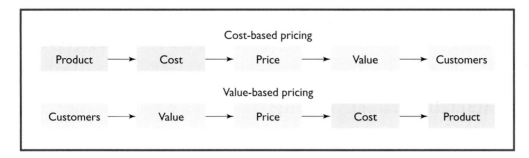

Figure 16.7

Cost-based versus value-based pricing

SOURCE: *The Strategy and Tactics of Pricing*, 2nd edn by Thomas T. Nagle and Reed K. Holden (1995). Reprinted by permission of Pearson Education, Inc., Upper Saddle River, NJ 07458.

the costs of making the product and sets a price that covers costs plus a target profit. Marketing must then convince buyers that the product's value at that price justifies its purchase. If the price turns out to be too high, the company must settle for lower mark-ups or lower sales, both resulting in disappointing profits.

Value-based pricing reverses this process. The company sets its target price based on customer perceptions of the product value. The targeted value and price then drive decisions about product design and what costs can be incurred. As a result, pricing begins with analysing consumer needs and value perceptions and a price is set to match consumers' perceived value:

> Consider Thorn selling its 10W 2D energy-saving electric light bulbs to a hotel manager. The SL18 costs far more to make than a conventional 60-watt tungsten light bulb, so a higher price has to be justified. Value pricing helps by looking at the hotel manager's total cost of ownership rather than the price of electric light bulbs. The life-cycle costs of the manager using a tungsten bulb for the 1,000 hours that they last includes the price of the bulb (60c), the labour cost of replacing it (50c) and electricity (€4.80). The life-cycle cost of the tungsten bulb is therefore €5.90. The Thorn 10W 2D bulb uses a sixth of the electricity of a conventional bulb and lasts eight times longer. Its life-cycle cost must therefore be compared with the cost of owning eight tungsten bulbs: 8 × €5.90 = €47.20. To work out the value of the Thorn bulb, its cost of ownership is also considered: changing the bulb 50c and electricity €6.40 (one-sixth the electricity costs of eight tungsten bulbs). The maximum value-based price of the Thorn bulb to the hotel manager is therefore:
>
> $$\text{Maximum value-based price} = \text{competitor's cost of ownership} - \text{own operating costs}$$
> $$= €47.20 - (€6.40 + 50c)$$
> $$= €40.30$$

> Using this evidence, Thorn can argue that it is worth the hotel manager paying a lot more than 60c to buy the energy-saving bulb. It is unrealistic to think that the manager would pay the full €40.30, but based on these figures, the actual price of €10.00 for the Thorn energy-saving bulb looks very reasonable. At first sight it seems hard to justify replacing a 60c tungsten bulb with a €10.00 energy-saving one, but value-based pricing shows the hotel manager is saving €30.00 by doing so. The value-based pricing using life-cycle costs can be used to justify paying a premium price on products: from low energy light bulbs to airliners.[21]

A company using perceived-value pricing must find out what value buyers assign to different competitive offers. However, measuring perceived value can be difficult. Sometimes consumers are asked how much they would pay for a basic product and for each benefit added to the offer. Or a company might conduct experiments to test the perceived value of different product offers. If the seller charges more than the buyers' perceived value, the company's sales will suffer. Many companies overprice their products and their products sell poorly. Other companies underprice. Underpriced products sell very well, but they produce less revenue than they would if prices were raised to the perceived-value levels.

competition-based pricing

Consumers will base their judgements of a product's value on the prices that competitors charge for similar products. Here, we discuss two forms of competition-based pricing: *going-rate pricing* and *sealed-bid pricing*.

■ Going-rate pricing

Going-rate pricing
Setting price based largely on following competitors' prices rather than on company costs or demand.

In **going-rate pricing**, the firm bases its price largely on *competitors'* prices, with less attention paid to its *own* costs or to demand. The firm might charge the same as, more, or less than its chief competitors. In oligopolistic industries that sell a commodity such as steel, paper or fertiliser, firms normally charge the same price. The smaller firms follow the leader: they change their prices when the market leader's prices change, rather than when their own demand or costs change. Some firms may charge a bit more or less, but they hold the amount of difference constant. Thus, minor petrol retailers usually charge slightly less than the big oil companies, without letting the difference increase or decrease.

Nationwide positions itself away from the competition by offering an Internet current account with higher interest on credit balances and free of many of the charges that rival banks require.

Source: Nationwide

INTERNET BANKING   

If your Internet current account hits you
with painful charges - it's medieval

If you're being hit from all angles with barbaric bank charges it can really start to hurt. Get an Internet current account from Nationwide - you'll find us a little more civilised. We don't charge for day-to-day services, for arranging an overdraft or to use 500,000 cash machines worldwide. We don't over charge on overdrafts and we offer ten times more interest on credit balances than most of the banks. You can even choose the way you bank with us - from Internet, branch and telephone banking.

So, hit your bank where it hurts, get out of the dark ages and get in touch today.

www.nationwide.co.uk | 0500 30 20 10 | call into your local branch

Going-rate pricing applies to complex products as well as commodities. Fierce competition between aerospace producers cut world aircraft prices by a fifth between 1996 and 1998. Manfred Bischoff, chief executive of Daimler-Benz's Dasa, cites Boeing as the chief culprit. 'There is a crumbling of prices in certain markets', he says. 'The price is dictated by Boeing. We are followers in this case.'[22]

Although it gives firms little control of their revenue, going-rate pricing can be quite popular. When demand elasticity is hard to measure, firms feel that the going price represents the collective wisdom of the industry concerning the price that will yield a fair return. They also feel that holding to the going price will prevent harmful price wars.

■ Auctions

Until the advent of the Internet, haggling (one-to-one negotiations) and a non-negotiable price had grown to dominate pricing. Auctions existed in specialised markets, such as commodities, some specialised financial services, fine art and antiques. Sealed bid pricing, where buyers submit secret bids, has always been common in business-to-business (B2B) marketing and some consumer markets, such as Scottish house buying. Now, led by eBay.com, online auctions for Beanie Babies and much more have become one of the most influential Internet innovations. Whereas conventional auctions needed the

marketing highlight 16.3

What am I bid?

In the late nineteenth century the French economist Léon Walras likened the entire pricing mechanism to the operation of a 'Walrasian auctioneer' who calls out a price, sees how many buyers and sellers there are and, if they do not balance, makes adjustments until demand equals supply. In the non-negotiable price setting that dominated C2C markets, the 'adjustments' take place over time to match supply and demand. In auctions, as in haggling where buyers and sellers negotiate a price or walk away, prices are set during each transaction. Economists see auctions as an efficient way of matching supply and demand but they do introduce uncertainty into transactions. The sellers do not know the price they will receive and buyers have no guarantee of making a purchase. One of the most common forms of auction, sealed bid pricing, is an example.

First-price sealed-bid pricing occurs in two ways. Potential buyers may be asked to submit sealed bids, and the item is awarded to the buyer who offers the highest price. Conversely, firms may have to bid for a contract to supply goods or services that is awarded to the contender with the lowest price.

In sealed-bid pricing, a firm bases its bid price on how it thinks competitors will bid. To win a contract, a contender has to price below other firms. Yet the firm cannot set its price below a certain level. It cannot price below cost without harming its position. In contrast, the higher the company sets its price above its costs, the lower its chance of getting the contract.

The net effect of the two opposite pulls can be described in terms of the *expected profit* of the particular bid (see Table 1). Suppose a bid of €9,500 would yield a high chance (say, 0.81) of getting the contract, but only a low profit (say, €100). The expected profit with this bid is therefore €81. If the firm bid €11,000, its profit would be €1,600, but its chance of getting the contract might be reduced to 0.01. The expected profit would be only €16. Thus the company might bid the price that would maximise the expected profit. According to Table 1, the best bid would be €10,000, for which the expected profit is €216.

Using expected profit as a basis for setting price makes sense for the large firm that makes many bids. In playing the odds, the firm will make maximum profits in the long run. But a firm that bids only occasionally or needs a particular contract badly will not find the

---

First-price sealed-bid pricing Potential buyers submit sealed bids, and the item is awarded to the buyer who offers the best price.

Company's bid (€)	Profit if bid wins (€) (1)	Assumed probability of bid winning (2)	Expected profit (€) (3) = (1) × (2)
9,500	100	0.81	81
10,000	600	0.36	216
10,500	1,100	0.09	99
11,000	1,600	0.01	16

Table 1 Effects of different bids on expected profit

expected-profit approach useful. The approach, for example, does not distinguish between a €100,000 profit with a 0.10 probability and a €12,500 profit with a 0.80 probability. Yet the firm that wants to keep production going would prefer the second contract to the first.

In **English auctions** the price is raised successively until only one bidder remains. This is the most common auction form, familiar from scenes of rare items, be it a Van Gogh or a pair of Madonna's pants, being sold by one of the great auction houses, such as Sotheby's or Christie's. These have joined eBay as providers of online auctions aimed at its network of regular dealers (sothebys.com) or, for smaller collectables ($100 to $100,000), at consumers (sothebys.amazon.com). One of the largest European operators, qxl.com, operates both B2C and C2C while on holidayauctions.net customers can bid for bargain late-break holidays.

In **Dutch auctions** prices start high and are lowered successively until someone buys. These auctions originated in the Dutch wholesale flower markets. B2B online traders, such as Bidbusiness.co.uk and constrauction.com, use both English and Dutch auctions to sell industrial products.

In **collective buying** increasing numbers of customers agree to buy as prices are lowered to the final bargain. The more customers join in, the lower the price becomes until a minimum demand is met. Letsbuyit.com and adabra.com offer each auction over a limited period for each option, then move on to the next batch. These sites often offer batches of products, say several items of kitchen equipment that are most suited to B2B markets.

In a **reverse auction** customers name the price that they are willing to pay for an item and seek a company willing to sell. In pioneering their online service priceline.com takes advantage of two major trends: first, most industries being in a continual state of excess capacity and, second, customers being 'brand neutral' if they can get a good deal. Most of Priceline's business is in travel services and mortgages but it is moving into life insurance, groceries and second-hand goods.

The 'moist hand'

Although economists see auctions as close to Adam Smith's 'invisible hand' that drives markets, there are few cool hands at auctions. Major art auctions are social, news worthy and exciting events. Jim Rose, of QXL, has no doubt about why online auctions are similarly popular: 'They're fun, they're entertaining, and people describe it as "winning" something rather than "buying" it.' The 'winner's curse' is very apparent in some South-east Asian markets where to 'win', contenders pay more than high street prices. And how many people can attend an auction and not walk away with something they had no intention of buying! The **second-price sealed bid** method can reduce some of the stress. In this, sealed bids are submitted but the buyer pays a price equal to the second-best bid.

Sources: 'The heyday of the auction', *The Economist* (24 July 1999), pp. 79–80; 'The price is right', *The Economist* (29 July 2000), p. 24; 'Bidding to win', *e.Business* (May 2000), pp. 36–49; Stuart Derrick, 'Putting a price on Europe', *e.Business* (December 2000), pp. 57–9.

English auctions   Price is raised successively until only one bidder remains.

Dutch auctions   Prices start high and are lowered successively until someone buys.

Collective buying   An increasing number of customers agree to buy as prices are lowered to the final bargain price.

Reverse auction   Customers name the price that they are willing to pay for an item and seek a company willing to sell.

Second-price sealed bid   Sealed bids are submitted but the contender placing the best bid pays only the price equal to the second-best bid.

market to gather for an auction or have simultaneous telephone contact, the Internet's global reach and simultaneity are putting auctions at the centre of trading. If forecasters are correct, auctions are set to become an increasingly common part of everyone's life. B2B is currently the dominant form but consumer-based auctions, both B2C and C2C, are now running at an estimated €6 billion a year, and by 2003 the figure is expected to be over €20 billion. Marketing Highlight 16.3 looks at some of the developments.

summary

Despite the increased role of non-price factors in the modern marketing process, *price* remains an important element in the marketing mix. Many internal and external factors influence the company's pricing decisions. *Internal factors* include the firm's *marketing objectives*, *marketing-mix strategy*, *costs* and *organisation for pricing*.

The pricing strategy is largely determined by the company's *target market and positioning objectives*. Common pricing objectives include survival, current profit maximisation, market-share leadership and product-quality leadership.

Price is only one of the marketing-mix tools that the company uses to accomplish its objectives, and pricing decisions affect and are affected by product design, distribution and promotion decisions. Price decisions must be carefully coordinated with the other marketing-mix decisions when designing the marketing programme.

Costs set the floor for the company's price – the price must cover all the costs of making and selling the product, plus a fair rate of return. Management must decide who within the organisation is responsible for setting price. In large companies, some pricing authority may be delegated to lower-level managers and salespeople, but top management usually sets pricing policies and approves proposed prices. Production, finance and accounting managers also influence pricing.

External factors that influence pricing decisions include the nature of the market and demand; competitors' prices and offers; and factors such as the economy, reseller needs and government actions. The seller's pricing freedom varies with different types of market. Pricing is especially challenging in markets characterised by monopolistic competition oligopoly.

In the end, the consumer decides whether the company has set the right price. The consumer weighs the price against the perceived values of using the product – if the price exceeds the sum of the values, consumers will not buy the product. Consumers differ in the values they assign to different product features and marketers often vary their pricing strategies for different price segments. When assessing the market and demand, the company estimates the demand curve, which shows the probable quantity purchased per period at alternative price levels. The more *inelastic* the demand, the higher the company can set its price. *Demand* and *consumer value perceptions* set the ceiling for prices.

Consumers compare a product's price to the prices of *competitors'* products. A company must learn the price and qualities of competitors' offers and use them as a starting point for its own pricing. With the advent of the Internet, online auctions look like becoming an increasingly common means of price setting.

The company can select one or a combination of three general pricing approaches: the *cost-based approach* (cost-plus pricing, break-even analysis and target profit pricing); the *value-based approach* (value-based pricing); and the *competition-based approach* (going-rate, sealed-bid pricing or auctions).

discussing the issues

1. Certain 'inexpensive' products that waste energy, provide few savings per package or require frequent maintenance may cost much more to own and use than products selling for a higher price. How would marketers use this information on 'true cost' to gain a competitive edge in pricing and promoting their products?

2. Sales of a brand of malt whisky increased when prices were raised by 20 per cent over a two-year period. What does this tell you about the demand curve and the elasticity of demand for this whisky? What does this suggest about using perceived-value pricing in marketing alcoholic drinks?

3. Genentech, a high-technology pharmaceutical company, developed a clot-dissolving drug called TPA that would halt a heart attack in progress. TPA saves lives, minimises hospital stays and reduces damage to the heart itself. It was initially priced at €2,500 per dose. What pricing approach does Genentech appear to have been using? Is demand for this drug likely to be elastic with price? Why or why not?

4. Like Amazon.com and egg, the Internet bank, most e-commerce operations offer prices well below those in the high street or mall and are making huge losses. What are the Internet businesses hoping to achieve with their aggressive pricing and is their price advantage likely to be maintained?

5. Select a personal care product or cosmetic item that you regularly use. Notice the price of the item. What are the main benefits you are looking for in using this product? Does the price communicate the total benefits sought? Does the product's price suggest good value? Do you think the manufacturer or retailer is overcharging or undercharging consumers for this product? Why or why not? What pricing approach do you think is most appropriate for setting the price for this product?

applying the concepts

1. Compare the price schedule for the Oresund Bridge in preview case 16 with those of other over- or under-water constructions. You will find details of some at hsba.go.jp, cheapest-channel-crossing.co.uk and humberbridge.co.uk. Explain the reasons for the huge differences in the prices charged.

2. You are faced with setting the price for an automatic car wash. Your annual fixed costs are €50,000 and variable costs are €0.50 per vehicle washed. You think customers would be willing to pay €2.50 to have their car washed. What would be the break-even volume at that price? What opportunities are there for pricing high? What might be the most significant constraints on your pricing decision?

references

1. See David J. Schwartz, *Marketing Today: A basic approach*, 3rd edn (New York: Harcourt Brace Jovanovich, 1981), pp. 270–3.

2. 'A not-so-popular Nordic bridge', *The Economist* (7 October 2000), p. 61; 'Asia: The bridge to nowhere in particular', *The Economist* (4 April 1998), p. 42; 'Welcome to Oresund Region', www.oresundnetwork.com/uk/englishintro.html; 'A bridge to the world', www.oresundnetwork.com/uk/englishnyheder.html; 'The Oresund Crossing', www.america.edu/projects/mandala/TED/ORESUND.HTM;

www.discovery.com/stories/technology/buildings/brdg.congest.html. For prices and traffic information see www.oresundskonsortiet.com/guide/bonus.htm, www.oresundskonsortiet.com/guide/prices.htm, www.oresundskonsortiet.com/guide/cash.htm.

3. For discussions of factors affecting pricing decisions, see Thomas T. Nagle and Reed K. Holden, *The Strategy and Tactics of Pricing*, 2nd edn (Englewood Cliffs, NJ: Prentice Hall, 1995), Ch. 1; Margaret C. Campbell, ' "Why did you do that?" The important role of inferred motive in perceptions of price fairness', *The Journal of Product & Brand Management*, 8, 2 (1999),

pp. 145–53, Thomas C. Lawton, 'The limits of price leadership: Needs-based positioning strategy and the long-term competitiveness of Europe's low fare airlines', *Long Range Planning*, **32**, 6 (1999), pp. 573–86.

4. Michiyo Makamoto, 'Weak Japanese recovery hits results at steelmakers', *Financial Times* (14 November 1994), p. 21; 'Millennium Dome: Doomed', *The Economist* (16 September 2000), p. 37.

5. Norton Paley, 'Fancy footwork', *Sales and Marketing Management* (July 1994), pp. 41–2.

6. Helen Slingsby, 'Discounters lose at their own game', *Marketing Week* (23 September 1994), pp. 21–2; Neil Buckley, 'Sainsbury launch price war campaign', *Financial Times* (10 October 1994), p. 8.

7. 'A funny smell from the scent counter', *Independent* (12 November 1993), p. 17.

8. See Timothy M. Laseter, 'Supply chain management: The ins and outs of target costing', *Purchasing* (12 March 1998), pp. 22–25. Also the Swatch Web page at www.swatch.com; Archie Lockamy III and Wilbur I. Smith, 'Target costing for supply chain management: criteria and selection', *Industrial Management & Data Systems*, **100**, 5 (2000), pp. 210–18; Margaret L. Gagne and Richard Discenza, 'Target costing', *Journal of Business & Industrial Marketing*, **10**, 1 (1995), pp. 16–22.

9. David Humphries, 'Niche airports for high-flyers', *How To Spend It* (Financial Times, London: 2000), pp. 8–10.

10. Yann Cochennec, 'The profitability problem', *Interavia* (June 2000), pp. 26–31.

11. Alice Rawsthorn, 'Discord over online music royalties', *Financial Times* (21 January 1998), p. 4; James Harding, 'Online battle of the bands', *Financial Times* (9 May 2000), p. 27; David Murphy, 'Music to whose ears?', *Marketing Business* (July/August 2000), p. 12.

12. Here accumulated production is drawn on a semi-log scale, so that equal distances represent the same percentage increase in output. For further work on experience curves see Stuart Chambers and Robert Johnston, 'Experience curves in services: macro and micro level approaches', *International Journal of Operations & Production Management*, **20**, 7 (2000), pp. 842–59, G. J. Steven, 'The learning curve: from aircraft to spacecraft?', *Management Accounting*, **77**, 5 (1999), pp. 64–5.

13. 'Japan's chip makers: falling off the learning curve', *The Economist* (23 February 1991), pp. 84–5. Also see K. Sivakumar, 'Understanding price-tier competition: methodological issues and their managerial significance', *The Journal of Product & Brand Management*, **9**, 5 (2000), pp. 291–303.

14. 'You've beanie had', *The Economist* (4 September 1999), p. 78; also see Beaniex.com, a Beanies website where you can get a royal blue elephant called Peanut for a cool $5,200 (€5,900)!

15. 'Cutting off NTT', *The Economist* (13 May 2000), pp. 83–4.

16. Joshua Rosenbaum, 'Guitar maker looks for a new key', *Wall Street Journal* (11 February 1998), p. B1; www.gibson.com (February 2000).

17. Nagle and Holden, *Strategy and Tactics of Pricing*, op. cit., Ch. 4.

18. Tim Burt, 'Yorkshire Chemicals ahead 19%', *Financial Times* (3 August 1994), p. 20.

19. For an operable example of this, see Kai Kristenson and Hans Jorn Juhl, 'Pricing and correspondence to market conditions: some Danish evidence', *European Journal of Marketing*, **24**, 5 (1989), pp. 50–5.

20. Kevin Done, 'Building the superjumbo', *Financial Times* (2 November 2000), p. 21; Rebecca Hoar, 'Fight for the skies', *EuroBusiness* (May 2000), pp. 68–72.

21. Values taken from 'Energy-saving light bulbs', *Which?* (May 1993), pp. 8–10; also see 'Low energy light bulbs', *Which?* (October 1999).

22. Graham Bowley, 'Aircraft prices down a fifth, says Dasa', *Financial Times* (21 January 1998), p. 27; Oliver Sutton, 'What's in a price hike?', *Interavia* (December 1998), pp. 36–8.

case 16

*EasyJet, easy Go**

Kevin Done

Michael O'Leary is on a roll. The ebullient chief executive of Ryanair, the leading low-cost airline in Europe, is raking in the money at a rate that can only make his rivals wilt.

'We make money with falling air fares. And we make stinking piles of money with rising fares', he says. Looking at the cash pile accumulating on the Ryanair balance sheet, he says: 'We could be a monster, it's scary.'

If you get it right, the low-cost formula is a route to high rewards in an airline industry better known for chronic lossmakers.

It has worked for 20 years for Southwest Airlines in the US, the original low-cost pioneer. And Ryanair has established itself as one of the world's most profitable airlines.

It trades on a racy forward price/earnings ratio of more than 36, a level normally reserved for growth companies, not airlines.

Others are trying to hang on to Ryanair's coat tails, notably Stelios HajiIoannou's EasyJet.

The entrepreneur and son of a wealthy Greek shipowner hopes to close the flotation of his five-year-old airline on the London Stock Exchange next week, raising about £200m of new money.

Go, British Airways' three-year experiment in the low-cost sector, also came on the market this week with a history of two years of heavy losses but a pledge to make 'a small profit' in the current year.

A trade sale, a management buy-out, even a flotation, all options are open, says Rod Eddington, the new broom at BA, who has decided that Go does not fit in with his vision of running a profitable (high-cost) full service airline.

There have been enough casualties along the way to show that the low-cost model is far from being a one-way bet, however. Debonair in the UK collapsed last year, and in the US the highly successful ValuJet was ruined by a fatal crash, although its operations continued under another owner.

Elsewhere in Europe, Virgin Express, Sir Richard Branson's Brussels and Nasdaq-listed attempt at setting up a no-frills carrier, provided further proof this week of the pitfalls waiting for operators that fail to control their costs.

Its losses are still mounting. In contrast to its fast-growing rivals it is being forced to retrench by cutting routes and selling aircraft. And it has just lost its second managing director in little over a year.

'In this business it's low-cost that wins', says Mr O'Leary.

'Ninety-nine per cent of people want the cheapest price. They don't want awards for the in-flight magazine or the best coffee. The brand, who cares? It has to be safe, on time and cheap. It's a bus service, it's transport.'

Not surprisingly EasyJet is comparing itself with Ryanair rather than Virgin Express.

Famous for its brash orange marketing and endless publicity stunts, it has tried to put on a more sober suit in recent days to convince institutional investors that their money will be safe in EasyJet stock.

It is doing some last-minute strengthening of its board to help allay possible investor concerns about future corporate governance. A board previously top-heavy with directors from the airline's executive management and from Mr HajiIoannou's inner core of advisers within EasyGroup has been bolstered by three non-executives with a fourth to be appointed shortly.

The EasyJet pathfinder prospectus is enough to set the pulse of prospective investors racing.

Thirteen pages are devoted to the risk factors of investing in the airline.

Its high aircraft utilisation rate makes it especially vulnerable to delays; it may face difficulties protecting its name and branding; the business is subject to strong seasonal variations; it may not meet its growth targets; rapid growth may be difficult to manage; it will incur significant costs acquiring additional aircraft; it is exposed to fuel price fluctuations; and there are the well-publicised problems with landing charges at Luton airport, its main hub.

Then there is the 'chairman's reputation'. Hitherto an asset, could it become a liability?

The prospectus says that Mr HajiIoannou has still not entirely shaken off the charges of manslaughter and shipwreck that were levelled at him in Italy in the wake of the sinking in 1991 off Genoa of an oil tanker managed by his father's shipping company in which he was a director at the time.

---

* This case is a reproduction of Kevin Done (with additional reporting by Mark Odell), 'Budget airlines lured by hope of sky high profits', *Financial Times* (11 November 2000), p. 20.

The charges were dismissed in the court of first instance and also dismissed on appeal, but the public prosecutor filed a further appeal two weeks ago with the Italian Supreme Court. Mr HajiIoannou's lawyers say the action will again be 'vigorously defended'.

Rather more esoteric is another outstanding charge in Greece of 'bribery during election' arising from EasyJet advertisements in the Athens press in 1998, inviting those who wanted to 'avoid the hassle of the election' to fly to London with EasyJet. Mr HajiIoannou has been advised the action is unlikely to succeed.

Whatever the risks put forward by careful investment bankers, most aviation analysts believe that it is EasyJet, rather than Go, Virgin Express, or Buzz (the Dutch airline KLM's experiment in the sector), that is the low-cost carrier most likely to emulate Ryanair.

Both airlines operate solely Boeing 737 fleets and they keep operations simple by offering no free food. But Ray Webster, EasyJet chief executive, says there are important differences.

Whereas Dublin-based Ryanair has flourished during much of its first decade using older second-hand aircraft, EasyJet has chosen to use new aircraft believing in the cost advantages to be gained from lower maintenance needs, the ability to achieve high utilisation levels, quick turnround times and greater reliability of service.

Ryanair has been ruthless about offering the lowest fares available, and a vital part of its strategy is to fly to secondary airports with much lower charges. It has also been expanding its network to more leisure destinations.

By contrast EasyJet uses more main airports that people want to use and that attract higher-paying business passengers as well as leisure travellers, says Mr Webster.

As a result he is currently seeking to add greater depth to the network by using the growing fleet to increase frequencies rather than destinations.

Because it started later than Ryanair, EasyJet has also been able to avoid using travel agents as a key way of keeping distribution costs low.

Mr O'Leary is just as devoted a believer in the power of the internet to cut sales and marketing costs, but says that at Ryanair these savings are still feeding through to the bottom line, whereas they have already been booked at EasyJet.

The web also gives an 'amazing capacity to fill our aircraft very quickly and we can sell with very little advertising', says Mr O'Leary, who is planning to add more routes next year to secondary airports, where the costs are low.

'There is a huge floating population in London that just wants to fly somewhere. If you make it very cheap they just go for a weekend anyway', he says.

Publicly he pours scorn on his rivals' strategies, but perhaps even Ryanair would be forced to admire the EasyJet low-cost toilet strategy.

Both airlines are adding new Boeing 737 aircraft at a rapid pace to meet forecast 25 per cent a year growth rates.

In the EasyJet case they order the aircraft with one toilet removed in order to cram in one more seat. 'There are no free meals or free drinks on board', says Mr Webster.

'If people have to pay, they consume less. There is less waste, the cabin crew themselves can do the clean-up. We don't have to stock the galleys and clean the aircraft at the airport.

'And people use the toilets less, so we can take one out.'

Questions

1. What is stimulating the growth of budget airlines?

2. What is allows Europe's new budget airlines to keep their costs down and which operator do you see as having the advantage?

3. Does the Internet have a distinct role in the budget airlines' operations?

4. Are the budget airlines in competition with conventional airlines or stimulating new demand?

5. Referring to Chapters 10, 11 and 12 in this text, how would you describe the competitive position of Go, EasyJet and Ryanair compared with (a) each other, (b) the major European airlines – BA, KLM, Air France, etc. – and (c) the state-owned airlines of Greece, Hungary, Italy and Spain struggling to survive in Europe?

internet exercises

Internet exercises for this chapter can be found on the student site of the MYPHLIP Web Site at www.booksites.net/kotler.

chapter seventeen

Pricing strategies

Chapter objectives   *After reading this chapter, you should be able to:*

+ Understand new-product pricing strategies and know when to use them.

+ Explain how pricing decisions are influenced by the product mix.

+ Appreciate price adjustment strategies and how to make price changes.

+ Differentiate between geographical pricing strategies and know their implications.

introduction

In this chapter, we will look at the complex dynamics of pricing. As Amaizer illustrates in the preview case opposite, price setting involves balancing conflicting interests and can be used to achieve a range of objectives. Even more, a company does not set a single price, but rather a *pricing structure* that covers different items in its line. This pricing structure changes over time as products move through their life cycles. The company adjusts product prices to reflect changes in costs and demand, and to account for variations in buyers and situations. As the competitive environment changes, the company considers when to initiate price changes and when to respond to them.

This chapter examines the dynamic pricing strategies available to management. In turn, we look at *new-product pricing strategies* for products in the introductory stage of the product life cycle, *product-mix pricing strategies* for related products in the product mix, *price-adjustment strategies* that account for customer differences and changing situations, and *strategies for initiating and responding to price changes*.[1]

new-product pricing strategies

Pricing strategies usually change as the product passes through its life cycle. The introductory stage is especially challenging. We can distinguish between pricing a product that imitates existing products and pricing an innovative product that is patent protected.

preview case

Amaizer: it tastes awful, but we're working on it

Amaizer is a new savoury snack made from maize. Its method of manufacture is similar to Cornflakes breakfast cereal, but it is to be sold as a savoury snack. Amaizers look like potato crisps, but are more golden and regular in shape. Raw materials and manufacturing costs are higher than for potato crisps, but they are healthier – in their basic form, they contain the same calories, but are low in saturates and cholesterol.

Amaizer is sweeter than potato crisps, but it can be flavoured. Unfortunately, consumer trials showed that the Amaizer versions of popular crisp flavours – salt and vinegar, cheese and onion, etc. – 'taste awful'. The R&D department was still working on the taste of these flavours. Meanwhile, the aim was to launch the product with four flavours that consumers did like: regular, sweet and sour, honey roasted ham and '1,000 Islands' dressing.

Although originally designed to use spare breakfast cereal capacity, the developed product needed dedicated plant. This produces Amaizer for a direct cost of €1,500 per tonne, excluding the cost of capital. With potato snacks selling for €3,000 per tonne, the brand manager was confident about the product's profitability.

The brand manager's confidence crashed, however, when sales, finance and market research each came up with recommended prices. The finance officer demanded that the price be set to cover the usual 100 per cent overhead charge plus a 20 per cent margin. His suggested price of €3,600 per tonne gave a very satisfactory €180,000 profit for the targeted 300 tonne annual sales.

Unfortunately, the finance officer's view conflicted with the sales manager's, who wanted the price to be €100 per tonne below potato crisps already sold by the company and several competitors. The sales manager claimed that only with a price advantage could they achieve the target sales against the established competition. The sales manager added that a low initial price would also compensate traders for the extra shelf space Amaizer used. Amaizer was bulkier than potato crisps and therefore needed about 20 per cent extra shelf space.

The marketing researcher's contribution to the pricing debate confused the brand manager even more. Rather than giving a price, the researcher gave a string of prices and sales and, to the annoyance of the finance officer, some financial information:

Price (€000)	2.5	3.0	3.5	4.0	4.5
Sales (tonnes)	400	350	280	200	100

The researcher also estimated €300,000 annual fixed operating cost for the product and capital investment that depended upon the annual volumes produced:

Annual sales (tonnes)	400	350	280	200	100
Capital investment (€000)	2,250	2,000	1,650	1,200	600

'I assume you know that our average cost of capital is 15 per cent', commented the finance officer.

'All very impressive', said the brand manager, 'but what price should we charge?'

'That all depends on what you want to achieve', replied the researcher.

Questions

1. Evaluate the pricing suggestions of the sales, finance and market research officers.

2. What criteria should be used to select the best price?

3. Calculate the prices that give the highest gross margins, return on investment, economic value added (EVA), net contribution, sales value and sales volume (Marketing Highlight 16.2 shows how to calculate these). Based on these results, what price would you choose and why? What do you notice about the room to manoeuvre around the optimum prices?

SOURCES: Adapted from in-company information. Names and figures have been changed for commercial reasons.

Figure 17.1

Four price-positioning
strategies

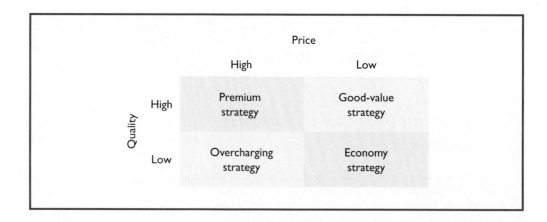

A company that plans to develop an imitative new product faces a product-positioning problem. It must decide where to position the product versus competing products in terms of quality and price. Figure 17.1 shows four possible positioning strategies. First, the company might decide to use a *premium pricing* strategy – producing a high-quality product and charging the highest price. At the other extreme, it might decide on an *economy pricing* strategy – producing a lower-quality product, but charging a low price. These strategies can coexist in the same market as long as the market consists of at least two groups of buyers, those who seek quality and those who seek price. Thus, Tag-Heuer offers very high-quality sports watches at high prices, whereas Casio offers digital watches at almost throwaway prices.[2]

The *good-value* strategy represents a way to attack the premium pricer. A leading grocery chain always uses the **strapline**: 'Good food costs less at Sainsbury's'. If this is really true and quality-sensitive buyers believe the good-value pricer, they will sensibly shop at Sainsbury's and save money – unless the premium product offers more status or snob appeal. Using an *overcharging* strategy, the company overprices the product in relation to its quality. In the long run, however, customers are likely to feel 'taken'. They will stop buying the product and will complain to others about it. Thus this strategy should be avoided.[3]

Companies bringing out an innovative, patent-protected product face the challenge of setting prices for the first time. They can choose between two strategies: *market-skimming pricing* and *market-penetration pricing*.

market-skimming pricing

Many companies that invent new products initially set high prices to 'skim' revenues layer by layer from the market. Intel is a prime user of this strategy, called **market-skimming pricing**. When Intel first introduces a new computer chip, it charges the highest price it can, given the benefits of the new chip over competing chips. It sets a price that makes it *just* worthwhile for some segments of the market to adopt computers containing the chip. As initial sales slow down and as competitors threaten to introduce similar chips, Intel lowers the price to draw in the next price-sensitive layer of customers.[4]

Strapline
A slogan often used in conjunction with a brand's name, advertising and other promotions.

Market-skimming pricing
Setting a high price for a new product to skim maximum revenues layer by layer from the segments willing to pay the high price; the company makes fewer but more profitable sales.

Maaväl was launched in Sweden at Skr12 (€1.40), more than twice the price of ordinary yoghurt. Developed by Scotia and a consortium of 1,300 Swedish farmers, Maaväl contains Olibra, a 'nutriceutical' made of a patent combination of palm oil extract, oat oil and water. It encourages the small intestine to release chemicals that tell the brain that enough has been eaten, giving a 'prolonged feeling of fullness'. The high price indicates the product's uniqueness and special properties, and allows

Market-penetration pricing: With its new high-speed Internet service, Freeserve aims to penetrate the market quickly, by offering a 'competitively priced, fixed monthly-cost service, with no other Internet call charges'.

SOURCE: Dixons Group/Advertising Archives

quicker recovery of development costs. Similar value-added, functional foods have proved profitable. Finland's Rasio has seen its share price increase tenfold since it launched Benecol, a cholesterol-lowering margarine. The success stimulated a follow up with Benecol 'cream cheese type spread' and Flora pro.activ, a 'me-too' from Van den Bergh Foods.[5]

market-penetration pricing

Rather than setting a high initial price to skim off small but profitable market segments, some companies use **market-penetration pricing**. They set a low initial price in order to *penetrate* the market quickly and deeply – to attract a large number of buyers quickly and win a large market share. The high sales volume results in falling costs, allowing the company to cut its price even further. For example, Dell and dan used penetration pricing to sell high-quality computer products through lower-cost mail-order channels. Their sales soared when IBM, Compaq, Apple and other competitors selling through retail stores could not match their prices. The Bank of Scotland and Winterthur of Switzerland used their Direct Line, Privilege and Churchill subsidiaries to grab profits and share in the motor insurance market by selling direct to consumers at market-penetrating prices. The high volume results in lower costs that, in turn, allow the discounters to keep prices low.[6]

Several conditions favour setting a low price. First, the market must be highly price sensitive, so that a low price produces more market growth. Second, production and distribution costs must fall as sales volume increases. Finally, the low price must help keep out the competition – otherwise the price advantage may be only temporary. For example, Dell faced difficult times when IBM and Compaq established their own direct distribution channels. However, competitive market-penetration pricing to gain

Market-penetration pricing
Setting a low price for a new product in order to attract large numbers of buyers and a large market share.

share can be withering. Almost all the US's leading Internet service providers, including Mindspring, PSINet, Earthlink, BBN and Netcom, are losing money as they fight for market share and new customers.[7]

product-mix pricing strategies

The strategy for setting a product's price often has to be changed when the product is part of a product mix. In this case, the firm looks for a set of prices that maximises the profits on the total product mix. Pricing is difficult because the various products have related demand and costs, and face different degrees of competition. Five *product-mix pricing* situations are summarised in Table 17.1.

product line pricing

Product line pricing

Setting the price steps between various products in a product line based on cost differences between the products, customer evaluations of different features, and competitors' prices.

Companies usually develop product lines rather than single products. For example, Merloni's sells Indesit, Ariston and Scholte appliances with price and status ascending in that order. There are full ranges of Indesit to Ariston appliances, from washing machines to freezers, covering the first two price bands, while Scholte sells expensive built-in kitchen equipment. Kodak offers not just one type of film, but an assortment including regular Kodak film, higher-priced Kodak Royal Gold film for special occasions, and a lower-priced, seasonal film called Funtime that competes with store brands. Each of these brands is available in a variety of sizes and film speeds. In **product line pricing**, management must decide on the price steps to set between the various products in a line.

The price steps should take into account cost differences between the products in the line, customer evaluations of their different features and competitors' prices. If the price difference between two successive products is small, buyers will usually buy the more advanced product. This will increase company profits if the cost difference is smaller than the price difference. If the price difference is large, however, customers will generally buy the less advanced products.

In many industries, sellers use well-established *price points* for the products in their line. Thus record stores might carry CDs at five price levels: budget, mid-line, full-line and imports ascending in price and with discounted special promotions on current chart albums. The customer will probably associate low to high-quality recordings with the first three price points. Even if the prices are raised a little, people will normally buy CDs at their own preferred price points. The seller's task is to establish perceived quality differences that support the price differences.

Table 17.1

Product-mix pricing strategies

PRODUCT LINE PRICING	OPTIONAL-PRODUCT PRICING	CAPTIVE-PRODUCT PRICING	BY-PRODUCT PRICING	PRODUCT-BUNDLE PRICING
Setting price steps between product line items	Pricing optional or accessory products sold with the main product	Pricing products that must be used with the main product	Pricing low-value by-products to get rid of them	Pricing bundles of products sold together

optional-product pricing

Many companies use **optional-product pricing** – offering to sell optional or accessory products along with their main product. For example, a Toyota Yaris customer may choose to add satellite navigation, CD autochanger or roof spoiler. Pricing these options is a sticky problem. Car companies have to decide which items to include in the base price and which to offer as options. BMW's basic cars once came famously underequipped. Typically the 318i is about €20,000, but the customer then has to pay extra for a radio (prices vary), electric windows (€350), sun roof (€900) and security system (€550). The basic model is stripped of so many comforts and conveniences that most buyers reject it. They pay for extras or buy a better-equipped version. More recently, however, American and European car makers have been forced to follow the example of the Japanese carmakers and include in the basic price many useful items previously sold only as options. The advertised price now often represents a well-equipped car.

captive-product pricing

Companies that make products that must be used along with a main product are using **captive-product pricing**. Examples of captive products are razors, camera film and computer software. Producers of the main products (razors, cameras and computers) often price them low and set high mark-ups on the supplies. Thus Polaroid prices its instant cameras low (€40 for a Barbie Cam) because it makes its money on specialised films they need (€10). And Gillette sells low-priced razors, but makes money on the replacement blades.

The strategy used by the cellular operators is called **two-part pricing**. The price of the service is broken into a *fixed fee* plus a *variable usage rate*. Thus a telephone company charges a monthly rate – the fixed fee – plus charges for calls beyond some

Captive-product pricing: Gillette's strategy consists of making profit from the replacement blades that have to be used together with the razors.

SOURCE: The Gillette Company/ Advertising Archives.
Agency: BDDO New York

minimum number – the variable usage rate. Amusement parks charge admission plus fees for food and some rides. The service firm must decide how much to charge for the basic service and how much for the variable usage. The fixed amount should be low enough to induce usage of the service, and profit can be made on the variable fees.

by-product pricing

By-products
Items produced as a result of the main factory process, such as waste and reject items.

By-product pricing
Setting a price for by-products in order to make the main product's price more competitive.

In producing processed meats, petroleum products, chemicals and other products, there are often **by-products**. If the by-products have no value and if getting rid of them is costly, this will affect the pricing of the main product. Using **by-product pricing**, the manufacturer will seek a market for these by-products and should accept any price that covers more than the cost of storing and delivering them. This practice allows the seller to reduce the main product's price to make it more competitive. By-products can even turn out to be profitable. For example, many lumber mills have begun to sell bark chips and sawdust profitably as decorative mulch for home and commercial landscaping.

Sometimes companies don't realise how valuable their by-products are. For example, most zoos don't realise that one of their by-products – their occupants' manure – can be an excellent source of additional revenue. But the Zoo-Doo Compost Company has helped many zoos understand the costs and opportunities involved with these by-products. Zoo-Doo licenses its name to zoos and receives royalties on manure sales. 'Many zoos don't even know how much manure they are producing or the cost of disposing of it', explains president and founder Pierce Ledbetter. Zoos are often so pleased with any savings they can find on disposal that they don't think to move into active by-product sales. However, sales of the fragrant by-product can be substantial. So far novelty sales have been the largest, with tiny containers of Zoo Doo (and even 'Love, Love Me Doo' valentines) available in 160 zoo stores and 700 additional retail outlets. For the long-term market, Zoo-Doo looks to organic gardeners who buy 15 to 70 pounds of manure at a time. Zoo Doo is already planning a 'Dung of the Month' club to reach these lucrative by-product markets.

product-bundle pricing

Product-bundle pricing
Combining several products and offering the bundle at a reduced price.

Using **product-bundle pricing**, sellers often combine several of their products and offer the bundle at a reduced price. Thus theatres and sports teams sell season tickets at less than the cost of single tickets; hotels sell specially priced packages that include room, meals and entertainment; computer makers include attractive software packages with their personal computers. Price bundling can promote the sales of products that consumers might not otherwise buy, but the combined price must be low enough to get them to buy the bundle.

In other cases, *product-bundle pricing* is used to sell more than the customer really wants. Obtaining a ticket to a rock event is sometimes difficult, but tickets to international concerts bundled with flights, accommodation, etc., are often widely available.[8]

price-adjustment strategies

Companies usually adjust their basic prices to account for various customer differences and changing situations. Table 17.2 summarises seven price-adjustment strategies:

DISCOUNT AND ALLOWANCE PRICING	SEGMENTED PRICING	PSYCHOLOGICAL PRICING	VALUE PRICING	PROMOTIONAL PRICING	GEOGRAPHICAL PRICING	INTERNATIONAL PRICING
Reducing prices to reward customer responses such as paying early or promoting the product	Adjusting prices to allow for differences in customers, products and locations	Adjusting prices for psychological effect	Adjusting prices to offer the right combination of quality and service at a fair price	Temporarily reducing prices to increase short-run sales	Adjusting prices to account for the geographical location of customers	Adjusting prices in international markets

Table 17.2

Price adjustment strategies

discount and allowance pricing, segmented pricing, psychological pricing, promotional pricing, value pricing, geographical pricing and *international pricing*.

discount and allowance pricing

Most companies adjust their basic price to reward customers for certain responses, such as early payment of bills, volume purchases and off-season buying. These price adjustments – called *discounts* and *allowances* – can take many forms.

A **cash discount** is a price reduction to buyers who pay their bills promptly. A typical example is '2/10, net 30', which means that although payment is due within

Cash discount
A price reduction to buyers who pay their bills promptly.

Quantity discount: The Dutch magazine Men's Health *offers a special price to customers who buy five magazines altogether.*

SOURCE: Weekblodpers, Men's Health (Dutch)

30 days, the buyer can deduct 2 per cent if the bill is paid within 10 days. The discount must be granted to all buyers meeting these terms. Such discounts are customary in many industries and help to improve the sellers' cash situation and reduce bad debts and credit-collection costs.

A **quantity discount** is a price reduction to buyers who buy large volumes. A typical example is Pilot Hi-Tecpoint pens from Staples Office supplies at €6 for a pack of three, €10 for six and €18 for 12. Wine merchants often give '12 for the price of 11' and Makro, the trade warehouse, automatically gives discounts on any product bought in bulk. Discounts provide an incentive to the customer to buy more from one given seller, rather than from many different sources. Price does not always decrease with the quantity purchased. More often than realised, people pay a **quantity premium**, a surcharge paid by buyers who purchase high volumes of a product. Marketing Highlight 17.1 relates when and why prices sometimes increase disproportionately with volume.

Quantity discount
A price reduction to buyers who buy large volumes.

Quantity premium
A surcharge paid by buyers who purchase high volumes of a product.

marketing highlight 17.1

Want more? Pay even more!

A quantity premium is sometimes charged to people buying higher volumes. In Japan it often costs more per item to buy a 12-pack of beer or sushi than smaller quantities because the larger packs are more giftable and therefore less price sensitive. Quantity surcharges can also occur when the product being bought is in short supply or in sets – for example, several seats together at a 'sold-out' rock concert or sports event – and some small restaurants charge a premium to large groups. Similarly, in buying antiques, it costs more to buy six complete place settings of cutlery than a single item. In this case the price will continue to increase with volume, eight place settings costing more than six, and 12 place settings costing more than eight.

Quantity premiums are more common than people imagine, and that is why they work. Consumers expect prices to decrease with volume and so do not check unit prices. This allows retailers to slip in high-margin items. Quantity surcharge increases with the variety and complexity of pack sizes and, in some markets, over 30 per cent of ranges include some quantity surcharging.

As with 12-packs of beer and sushi, it is giftability that really drives up prices. Christmas is the time when this really hots up, when people are out trying to buy things for other people that they either do not have, can have more of or use more of: hence gift packs or selections of consumables, from confectionery to condoms, where buying individual items would cost less than the gift pack. Manufacturers often do not make more money when selling gift packs. The packaging is expensive, requiring special production process; 'seasonals' are as prone to success or failure as any new product and often have a severely truncated saleable life. However, along

with consumers, manufacturers have to play the game. Half the annual sales and all the profits of many giftable items, such jewellery and fragrances, are taken in the six-week run-up to Christmas.

The gift battle is driven by the psychology and ignorance involved in gift-giving. People exchange gifts as a demonstration of their commitment to a relationship but this often involves the buyer operating in a market they do not understand: for example, men buying women's fragrances or almost anyone buying socks or ties as a gift. Uncertainty of the appropriateness of a gift is overcome by buying stock gift items or buying something that looks extra special. Check out any overseas Chinese house and you'll find bottle upon bottle of smooth-tasting, but exquisitely expensive, Remy Martin XO Cognac.

Gift-giving may solder relationships but, by themselves, the exchanges are far from economic. A survey in the US found that the gift receivers would have paid an average of only €318 for the gifts they receive, although they estimated that the donor would have paid €438 for them. The difference is what Joel Waldfogel calls 'the deadweight loss of Christmas'.

Sources: S. M. Widrick, 'Measurement of incidence of quantity surcharge among selected grocery products', *Journal of Consumer Affairs* (Summer 1979); Yiorgos Zotos and Steven Lysonski, 'An exploration of the quantity surcharge concept in Greece', *European Journal of Marketing*, **27**, 10 (1993), pp. 5–18; Joel Waldfogel, 'The deadweight loss of Christmas', *American Economic Review*, **83**, 5 (December 1993); John Kay, 'Waldfogel's unwanted gift', *Financial Times* (13 December 2000), p. 20.

A trade **discount** (also called a **functional discount**) is offered by the seller to trade channel members that perform certain functions, such as selling, storing and record keeping. Manufacturers may offer different functional discounts to different trade channels because of the varying services they perform, but manufacturers must offer the same functional discounts within each trade channel.

A **seasonal discount** is a price discount to buyers who buy merchandise or services out of season. For example, lawn and garden equipment manufacturers will offer seasonal discounts to retailers during the autumn and winter to encourage early ordering in anticipation of the heavy spring and summer selling seasons. Hotels, motels and airlines will offer seasonal discounts in their slower selling periods. Seasonal discounts allow the seller to stabilise capacity utilisation during the entire year.

Allowances are another type of reduction from the list price. For example, **trade-in allowances** are price reductions given for turning in an old item when buying a new one. Trade-in allowances are most common in the car industry, but are also given for other durable goods. **Promotional allowances** are payments or price reductions to reward dealers for participating in advertising and sales-support programmes.

In stable markets, price adjustments have traditionally been relatively infrequent changes made as part of a strategy marketing or promotional programme. The Internet is changing that. In online trading, the ink on sticker prices often has no time to dry. Prices can change from hour to hour and from customer to customer. Marketing Highlight 17.2 looks at these new pricing dynamics.

segmented pricing

Companies will often adjust their basic prices to allow for differences in customers, products and locations. In **segmented pricing**, the company sells a product or service at two or more prices, even though the difference in prices is not based on differences in costs. Segmented pricing takes several forms:

✦ *Customer-segment pricing*. Different customers pay different prices for the same product or service. Museums, for example, will charge a lower admission for young people, the unwaged, students and senior citizens. In many parts of the world, tourists pay more to see museums, shows and national monuments than do locals.

✦ *Product-form pricing*. Different versions of the product are priced differently, but not according to differences in their costs. For instance, the Dutch company Skil prices its 6434H electric drill at €100, which is €60 more than the price of its 6400H. The 6434H is more powerful and has more features, yet this extra power and features cost only a few more euros to build in.

✦ *Location pricing*. Different locations are priced differently, even though the cost of offering each location is the same. For instance, theatres vary their seat prices because of audience preferences for certain locations and EU universities charge higher tuition fees for non-EU students.

✦ *Time pricing*. Prices vary by the season, the month, the day and even the hour. Public utilities vary their prices to commercial users by time of day and weekend versus weekday. The telephone company offers lower 'off-peak' charges, electricity costs less at night and resorts give seasonal discounts.

For segmented pricing to be an effective strategy, certain conditions must exist. The market must be segmentable and the segments must show different degrees of demand. Members of the segment paying the lower price should not be able to turn round and resell the product to the segment paying the higher price. Competitors should not be able to undersell the firm in the segment being charged the higher price.

Functional discount (trade discount)
A price reduction offered by the seller to trade channel members that perform certain functions, such as selling, storing and record keeping.

Seasonal discount
A price reduction to buyers who buy merchandise or services out of season.

Trade-in allowance
A price reduction given for turning in an old item when buying a new one.

Promotional allowance
A payment or price reduction to reward dealers for participating in advertising and sales-support programmes.

Segmented pricing
Pricing that allows for differences in customers, products and locations. The differences in prices are not based on differences in costs.

marketing highlight 17.2

Back to the future: pricing on the Web

At one time all prices were negotiated. The Web seems to be taking us back – into a new age of fluid pricing. 'Potentially, [the Internet] could push aside stickier prices and usher in an era of dynamic pricing', says *Business Week* writer Robert Hof, 'in which a wide range of goods would be priced according to what the market will bear – instantly, constantly.' Here's how.

Lower prices, higher margins Web buying and selling can lower costs. Thanks to their Internet connections, buyers and sellers around the world can connect at almost no cost. Reduced inventory and distribution costs add to the savings. For example, by selling online and making its computers to order, Dell Computer reduces inventory costs and eliminates retail mark-ups. It passes on its savings as 'lowest price per $ for performance'.

Tailor offers to individuals Web merchants can target prices to specific customers. For example, Amazon.com can assess each visitor's 'click-stream', the way the person navigates the website, then tailor products and prices to that shopper's behaviour. If visitors behave like a price-sensitive shopper, they may be offered a lower price. The Internet also lets sellers give some customers access to special prices. For example, CDnow e-mails a special website address with lower prices to certain buyers. If you don't know the secret address, you pay full price.

Change prices according to changes in demand or costs With printed catalogues, such as Lands' End or Hawkshead, a price is a price until the next catalogue is printed. In contrast, online sellers can change prices hourly. This allows sellers to adjust to changing costs, offer promotions on slow-moving items or nudge prices upwards on hot-selling goods. Many business marketers use their extranets, the private networks that link them with suppliers and customers, to get a precise handle on inventory, costs and demand at any given moment and adjust prices instantly.

Negotiate prices online Want to sell that antique pickle jar? Post it on eBay, the world's biggest online flea market. Want to dump that excess stock? Try adding an auction feature to your own website. Sharper Image claims it's getting 40 per cent of retail for excess goods sold via its online auction site, compared with only 20 per cent from liquidators.

Get instant price comparisons from thousands of vendors Web shoppers can quickly compare information about products and vendors almost anywhere. New online comparison guides, such as Shopsmart and PriceScan, give product and price comparisons at the click of a mouse. Shopsmart lets consumers compare prices posted by more than 1,200 retailers. Other sites offer intelligent shopping agents. MySimon, for instance, takes a buyer's criteria for a camcorder or collectable, then roots through sellers' sites to find the best match at the best price.

Negotiate lower prices With market information and access comes buyer power. In addition to simply finding the vendor with the best price, customers armed with price information can often negotiate lower prices.

UTC tried something new last year. Instead of haggling with dozens of individual vendors to secure printed circuit boards for various subsidiaries worldwide, it put the contract out on FreeMarkets, an online marketplace for industrial goods. Bids poured in from 39 suppliers, saving UTC over €11 million off its initial €27 million estimate.

Will dynamic pricing sweep the marketing world? 'Not entirely', says Hof. 'It takes a lot of work to haggle – which is why fixed prices happened in the first place.' However, he continues, 'Pandora's E-box is now open, and pricing will never be the same.'

Sources: Quotes and extracts from Robert D. Hof, 'Going, going, gone', *Business Week* (12 April 1999), pp. 30–2; Robert D. Hof, 'The buyer always wins', *Business Week* (22 March 1999), pp. EB26–EB28; and Stephen Manes, 'Off-Web dickering', *Forbes* (5 April 1999), p. 134. Also see Amy E. Cortese, 'Good-bye to fixed pricing?', *Business Week* (4 May 1998), pp. 71–84; Scott Woolley, 'I got it cheaper than you', *Forbes* (2 November 1998), pp. 82–4; Scott Woolley, 'Price war!', *Forbes* (14 December 1998), pp. 182–4; and Michael Krauss, 'Web offers biggest prize in product pricing game', *Marketing News* (6 July 1998), p. 8; Hazel Ward, 'Top of the shops', *e.business* (April 2000), pp. 69–71.

Nor should the costs of segmenting and watching the market exceed the extra revenue obtained from the price difference. The practice should not lead to customer resentment and ill will. Finally, the segmented pricing must be legal.

psychological pricing

Price says something about the product. For example, many consumers use price to judge quality. A €100 bottle of perfume may contain only €3 worth of scent, but some people are willing to pay the €100 because this price indicates something special.

In using **psychological pricing**, sellers consider the psychology of prices and not simply the economics. For example, one study of the relationship between price and quality perception of cars found that consumers perceive higher-priced cars as having higher quality.[9] By the same token, higher-quality cars are perceived as even higher priced than they actually are. When consumers can judge the quality of a product by examining it or by calling on past experience with it, they use price less to judge quality. When consumers cannot judge quality because they lack the information or skill, price becomes an important quality signal. Psychological pricing is particularly apparent in airport duty-free shops where people buy expensive items in unfamiliar categories. In such outlets, exquisite malt whiskies are often sold inexpensively but inexperienced buyers are attracted by grandly packaged and overpriced blended whiskies.

Another aspect of psychological pricing is **reference prices** – prices that buyers carry in their minds and refer to when looking at a given product. The reference price might be formed by noting current prices, remembering past prices or assessing the buying situation. Sellers can influence or use these consumers' reference prices when setting price. For example, a company could display its product next to more expensive ones in order to imply that it belongs in the same class. Department stores often sell women's clothing in separate departments differentiated by price: clothing found in the more expensive department is assumed to be of better quality. Companies also can influence consumers' reference prices by stating high manufacturer's suggested prices, by indicating that the product was originally priced much higher or by pointing to a competitor's higher price.

Even small differences in price can suggest product differences. Consider a stereo priced at €400 compared to one priced at €399. The actual price difference is only €1, but the psychological difference can be much greater. For example, some consumers will see the €399 as a price in the €300 range rather than the €400 range. Whereas the €399 is more likely to be seen as a bargain price, the €400 price suggests more quality. Complicated numbers, such as €347.41, also look less appealing than rounded ones, such as €350. Some psychologists argue that each digit has symbolic and visual qualities that should be considered in pricing. Thus, 8 is round and even and creates a soothing effect, whereas 7 is angular and creates a jarring effect.[10]

Psychological pricing
A pricing approach that considers the psychology of prices and not simply the economics; the price is used to say something about the product.

Reference prices
Prices that buyers carry in their minds and refer to when they look at a given product.

promotional pricing

With **promotional pricing**, companies will temporarily price their products below list price and sometimes even below cost. Promotional pricing takes several forms. Supermarkets and department stores will price a few products as *loss leaders* to attract customers to the store in the hope that they will buy other items at normal mark-ups. Sellers will also use *special-event pricing* in certain seasons to draw in more customers. Thus linens are promotionally priced every January to attract weary Christmas shoppers back into the stores. Manufacturers will sometimes offer *cash rebates* to consumers who buy the product from dealers within a specified time; the manufacturer sends the

Promotional pricing
Temporarily pricing products below the list price, and sometimes even below cost, to increase short-run sales.

rebate directly to the customer. Rebates have recently been popular with carmakers and producers of durable goods and small appliances. Some manufacturers offer *low-interest financing*, *longer warranties* or *free maintenance* to reduce the consumer's 'price'. This practice has recently become a favourite of the car industry. Or the seller may simply offer *discounts* from normal prices to increase sales and reduce stocks.

value pricing

Value-based pricing
Setting price based on buyers' perceptions of product values rather than on cost.

During the slow-growth 1990s, many companies have adjusted their prices to bring them into line with economic conditions and with the resulting fundamental shift in consumer attitudes towards quality and value. More and more, marketers have adopted **value-pricing** strategies – offering just the right combination of quality and good service at a fair price. In many cases, this has involved the introduction of less expensive versions of established, brand name products. Thus Campbell introduced its Great Starts Budget frozen-food line, Holiday Inn opened several Holiday Express budget hotels, Revlon's Charles of the Ritz offered the Express Bar collection of affordable cosmetics, and McDonald's offered 'value menus'. In other cases, value pricing has involved redesigning existing brands in order to offer more quality for a given price or the same quality for less.

In many business-to-business marketing situations, the pricing challenge is to find ways to adjust the value of the company's marketing offer in order to escape price competition and to justify higher prices and margins. This is especially true for suppliers of commodity products, which are characterised by little differentiation and intense price competition. In such cases, many companies adopt *value-added* strategies. Rather than cutting prices to match competitors, they attach value-added services to differentiate their offers and thus support higher margins.

> When General Electric expanded a no-frost refrigerator, it needed more shipping boxes fast. The Irish packaging supplier Smurfit Corporation assigned a co-ordinator to juggle production from three of its plants – and sometimes even divert products intended for other customers – to keep GE's Decatur plant humming. This kind of value-added hustling helped Smurfit win the GE appliance unit's 'Distinguished Supplier Award'. It has also sheltered Smurfit from the struggle of competing only on price. 'Today, it's not just getting the best price but getting the best value – and there are a lot of pieces to value', says a vice president for procurement at Emerson Electric Company, a major Smurfit customer that has cut its supplier count by 65 per cent.[11]

geographical pricing

Geographical pricing
Pricing based on where customers are located.

A company must also decide how to price its products to customers located in different parts of the country or the world. Should the company risk losing the business of more distant customers by charging them higher prices to cover the higher shipping costs? Or should the company charge all customers the same prices regardless of location? We will look at five **geographical pricing** strategies for the following hypothetical situation:

> Tromsø a.s. is a Norwegian paper products company selling to customers all over Europe. The cost of freight is high and affects the companies from whom customers buy their paper. Tromsø wants to establish a geographical pricing policy. It is trying to determine how to price a Nkr1,000 order to three specific customers: Customer A (Oslo); Customer B (Amsterdam) and Customer C (Barcelona).

One option is for Tromsø to ask each customer to pay the shipping cost from the factory to the customer's location. All three customers would pay the same factory price of Nkr1,000 (€806), with Customer A paying, say, Nkr100 for shipping; Customer B, Nkr150; and Customer C, Nkr250. Called **FOB-origin pricing**, this practice means that the goods are placed *free on board* (hence, *FOB*) a carrier. At that point the title and responsibility pass to the customer, who pays the freight from the factory to the destination.

FOB-origin pricing
A geographic pricing strategy in which goods are placed free on board a carrier; the customer pays the freight from the factory to the destination.

Because each customer picks up its own cost, supporters of FOB pricing feel that this is the fairest way to assess freight charges. The disadvantage, however, is that Tromsø will be a high-cost firm to distant customers. If Tromsø's main competitor happens to be in Spain, this competitor will no doubt outsell Tromsø in Spain. In fact, the competitor would outsell Tromsø in most of southern Europe, whereas Tromsø would dominate the north.

Uniform delivered pricing is the exact opposite of FOB pricing. Here, the company charges the same price plus freight to all customers, regardless of their location. The freight charge is set at the average freight cost. Suppose this is Nkr150. Uniform delivered pricing therefore results in a higher charge to the Oslo customer (who pays Nkr150 freight instead of Nkr100) and a lower charge to the Barcelona customer (who pays Nkr150 instead of Nkr250). On the one hand, the Oslo customer would prefer to buy paper from another local paper company that uses FOB-origin pricing. On the other hand, Tromsø has a better chance of winning over the Spanish customer. Other advantages of uniform delivered pricing are that it is fairly easy to administer and it lets the firm advertise its price nationally.

Uniform delivered pricing
A geographic pricing strategy in which the company charges the same price plus freight to all customers, regardless of their location.

Zone pricing falls between FOB-origin pricing and uniform delivered pricing. The company sets up two or more zones. All customers within a given zone pay a single total price; the more distant the zone, the higher the price. For example, Tromsø might set up a Scandinavian zone and charge Nkr100 freight to all customers in this zone, a northern Europe zone in which it charges Nkr150 and a southern Europe zone in which it charges Nkr250. In this way, the customers within a given price zone receive no price advantage from the company. For example, customers in Oslo and Copenhagen pay the same total price to Tromsø. The complaint, however, is that the Oslo customer is paying part of the Copenhagen customer's freight cost. In addition, even though they may be within a few miles of each other, a customer just barely on the south side of the line dividing north and south pays much more than one that is just barely on the north side of the line.

Zone pricing
A geographic pricing strategy in which the company sets up two or more zones. All customers within a zone pay the same total price; the more distant the zone, the higher the price.

Using **basing-point pricing**, the seller selects a given city as a 'basing point' and charges all customers the freight cost from that city to the customer location, regardless of the city from which the goods are actually shipped. For example, Tromsø might set Oslo as the basing point and charge all customers Nkr100 plus the freight from Oslo to their locations. This means that a Copenhagen customer pays the freight cost from Oslo to Copenhagen, even though the goods may be shipped from Tromsø. Using a basing-point location other than the factory raises the total price for customers near the factory and lowers the total price for customers far from the factory.

Basing-point pricing
A geographic pricing strategy in which the seller designates some city as a basing point and charges all customers the freight cost from that city to the customer location, regardless of the city from which the goods are actually shipped.

If all sellers used the same basing-point city, delivered prices would be the same for all customers and price competition would be eliminated. Industries such as sugar, cement, steel and cars used basing-point pricing for years, but this method has become less popular today. Some companies set up multiple basing points to create more flexibility: they quote freight charges from the basing-point city nearest to the customer.

Finally, the seller that is anxious to do business with a certain customer or geographical area might use **freight-absorption pricing**. Using this strategy, the seller absorbs all or part of the actual freight charges in order to get the desired business. The seller might reason that if it can get more business, its average costs will fall and more than compensate for its extra freight cost. Freight-absorption pricing is used for market penetration and to hold on to increasingly competitive markets.

Freight-absorption pricing
A geographic pricing strategy in which the company absorbs all or part of the actual freight charges in order to get the business.

international pricing

Companies that market their products internationally must decide what prices to charge in the different countries in which they operate. In some cases, a company can set a uniform worldwide price. For example, Airbus sells its jetliners at about the same price everywhere, whether in the United States, Europe or a Third World country. However, most companies adjust their prices to reflect local market conditions and cost considerations.

The price that a company should charge in a specific country depends on many factors, including economic conditions, competitive situations, laws and regulations, and development of the wholesaling and retailing system. Consumer perceptions and preferences may also vary from country to country, calling for different prices. Or the company may have different marketing objectives in various world markets, which require changes in pricing strategy. For example, Sony might introduce a new product into mature markets in highly developed countries with the goal of quickly gaining mass-market share – this would call for a penetration pricing strategy. In contrast, it might enter a less developed market by targeting smaller, less price-sensitive segments – in this case, market-skimming pricing makes sense.

Costs play an important role in setting international prices. Travellers abroad are often surprised to find that goods, which are relatively inexpensive at home, may carry outrageously higher price tags in other countries. A pair of Levi's selling for $30 (€34) in the US goes for about $63 in Tokyo and $88 in Paris. A McDonald's Big Mac selling for a modest $2.25 in the US costs $5.75 in Moscow. A Britney Spears CD sells for $15.99 in the US, but costs about $20 in the UK. Conversely, a Gucci handbag going for only $60 in Milan, Italy, fetches $240 in the US. In some cases, such price escalation may result from differences in selling strategies or market conditions. In most instances, however, it is simply a result of the higher costs of selling in foreign markets – the additional costs of modifying the product, higher shipping and insurance costs, import tariffs and taxes, costs associated with exchange-rate fluctuations and higher channel and physical distribution costs.[12]

For example, Campbell found that its distribution costs in the UK were 30 per cent higher than in the US. US retailers typically purchase soup in large quantities – 48-can cases of a single soup by the dozens, hundred or carloads. In contrast, English grocers purchase soup in small quantities – typically in 24-can cases of *assorted* soups. Each case must be hand-packed for shipment. To handle these small orders, Campbell had to add a costly extra wholesale level to its European channel. The smaller orders also mean that English retailers order two or three times as often as their US counterparts, bumping up billing and order costs. These and other factors caused Campbell to charge much higher prices for its soups in the UK.[13] Thus international pricing presents some special problems and complexities that are discussed in more detail in Chapter 5.

price changes

After developing their price structures and strategies, companies often face situations in which they must initiate price changes or respond to price changes by competitors.

initiating price changes

In some cases, the company may find it desirable to initiate either a price cut or a price increase. In both cases, it must anticipate possible buyer and competitor reactions. Customers' sensitivity to price changes was illustrated by the furore and direct action taken by hauliers, farmers and fishermen across Europe in the face of fuel price increases in 2000. Protesters complained about the overall price of fuel although, in real terms, the cost of motoring in 2000 has changed little since 1975. In contrast, disposable income had almost doubled over the same period and public transport prices inflated by between 50 and 80 per cent! In reality, motoring costs in 2000 were the lowest they had ever been but the demonstrators' reaction to sudden fuel price changes was enough to panic governments.[14]

■ Initiating price cuts

Several situations may lead a firm to consider cutting its price. One such circumstance is excess capacity. In this case, the firm needs more business and cannot get it through increased sales effort, product improvement or other measures. It may drop its follow-the-leader pricing – charging about the same price as its leading competitor – and aggressively cut prices to boost sales. But as the airline, construction equipment and other industries have learned in recent years, cutting prices in an industry loaded with excess capacity may lead to price wars as competitors try to hold on to market share.

Another situation leading to price changes is falling market share in the face of strong price competition. Several industries – cars, consumer electronics, cameras, watches and steel, for example – lost market share to Japanese competitors who offered high-quality products at lower prices than Western competitors. In response, defending companies resorted to more aggressive pricing to hold on to their markets.

A company may also cut prices in a drive to dominate the market through lower costs. Either the company starts with lower costs than its competitors or it cuts prices in the hope of gaining market share that will further cut costs through larger volume. Bausch & Lomb used an aggressive low-cost, low-price strategy to become an early leader in the competitive soft contact-lens market.

■ Initiating price increases

In contrast, many companies have had to *raise* prices in recent years. They do this knowing that customers, dealers and even their own sales force may resent the price increases. Yet a successful price increase can greatly increase profits. For example, if the company's profit margin is 3 per cent of sales, a 1 per cent price increase will increase profits by 33 per cent if sales volume is unaffected.

A considerable factor in price increases is cost inflation. Rising costs squeeze profit margins and lead companies to make regular rounds of price increases. Companies often raise their prices by more than the cost increase in anticipation of further inflation. Another factor leading to price increases is over-demand: when a company cannot supply all its customers' needs, it can raise its prices, ration products to customers or both.

Companies can increase their prices in a number of ways to keep up with rising costs. Dropping discounts and adding higher-priced units to the line can raise prices almost invisibly. Or prices can be pushed up openly. Companies have learned to take care when passing price increases on to customers. The price increases should be supported with a company communication programme telling customers why prices are being increased. The company sales force should help customers find ways to economise. However, as the 2000 fuel-price protest showed, customers are not always willing to listen.

Where possible, the company should consider ways to meet higher costs or demand without raising prices. For example, it can shrink the product instead of raising the price, as confectionery manufacturers do. Or it can substitute less expensive ingredients or remove certain product features, packaging or services. Or it can 'unbundle' its products and services, removing and separately pricing elements that were formerly part of the offer. IBM, for example, now offers training and consulting as separately priced services.

In this ad, Abbey National encourages potential customers to move their bank accounts from competitor banks to Abbey National by offering economic advantages. The company must, however, be aware of the reactions of competitor banks.

SOURCE: Abbey National plc.
Agency: Euro RSCG WNEK Gosper

■ Buyer reactions to price changes

Whether the price is raised or lowered, the action will affect buyers, competitors, distributors and suppliers, and may interest government as well. Customers do not always interpret prices in a straightforward way. They may view a price *cut* in several ways. For example, what would you think if Sony were suddenly to cut its DVD prices in half? You might think that these DVDs are about to be replaced by newer models or that they have some fault and are not selling well. You might think that Sony is in financial trouble and may not stay in the business long enough to supply future parts. You might believe that quality has been reduced. Or you might think that the price will come down even further and that it will pay to wait and see.

Similarly, a price *increase*, which would normally lower sales, may have some positive meanings for buyers. What would you think if Sony *raised* the price of its latest DVD model? On the one hand, you might think that the item is very 'hot' and may be unobtainable unless you buy it soon. Or you might think that the recorder is unusually good value. On the other hand, you might think that Sony is greedy and charging what the traffic will bear.

■ Competitor reactions to price changes

A firm considering a price change has to worry about the reactions of its competitors as well as its customers. Competitors are most likely to react when the number of firms involved is small, when the product is uniform and when the buyers are well informed.

How can the firm figure out the likely reactions of its competitors? If the firm faces one large competitor and if the competitor tends to react in a set way to price changes, that reaction can be easily anticipated. But if the competitor treats each price change as a fresh challenge and reacts according to its self-interest, the company will have to figure out just what makes up the competitor's self-interest at the time.

The problem is complex because, like the customer, the competitor can interpret a company price cut in many ways. It might think that the company is trying to grab a larger market share, that the company is doing poorly and trying to boost its sales or that the company wants the whole industry to cut prices to increase total demand.

When there are several competitors, the company must guess each competitor's likely reaction. If all competitors behave alike, this amounts to analysing only a typical competitor. In contrast, if the competitors do not behave alike – perhaps because of differences in size, market shares or policies – then separate analyses are necessary. However, if some competitors will match the price change, there is good reason to expect that the rest will also match it.

responding to price changes

Here we reverse the question and ask how a firm should respond to a price change by a competitor. The firm needs to consider several questions: Why did the competitor change the price? Was it to make more market share, to use excess capacity, to meet changing cost conditions or to lead an industry-wide price change? Is the price change temporary or permanent? What will happen to the company's market share and profits if it does not respond? Are other companies going to respond? What are the competitor's and other firms' responses to each possible reaction likely to be?

Besides these issues, the company must make a broader analysis. It has to consider its own product's stage in the life cycle, its importance in the company's product mix, the intentions and resources of the competitor and the possible consumer reactions to price changes. The company cannot always make an extended analysis of its alternatives at the time of a price change, however. The competitor may have spent much time preparing this decision, but the company may have to react within hours or days. About the only way to cut down reaction time is to plan ahead for both possible price changes and possible responses by the competitor.

Figure 17.2 shows the ways that a company might assess and respond to a competitor's price cut. Once the company has determined that the competitor has cut its price and that this price reduction is likely to harm company sales and profits, it might simply decide to hold its current price and profit margin. The company might believe that it will not lose too much market share or that it would lose too much profit if it reduced its own price. It might decide that it should wait and respond when it has more information on the effects of the competitor's price change. For now, it might be willing to hold on to good customers, while giving up the poorer ones to the competitor. The argument against this holding strategy, however, is that the competitor may get stronger and more confident as its sales increase and the company might wait too long to act.

> By keeping the appeal of their products ahead of the competition and keeping costs down, Nokia has not only maintained profitability but increased its market share of the mobile phone market. According to Jorma Ollila, Nokia's chief executive: 'There was a belief among some in the market that new players entering the market place would disrupt the formula, but that has not happened.'[15]

If the company decides that effective action can and should be taken, it might make any of the following four responses:

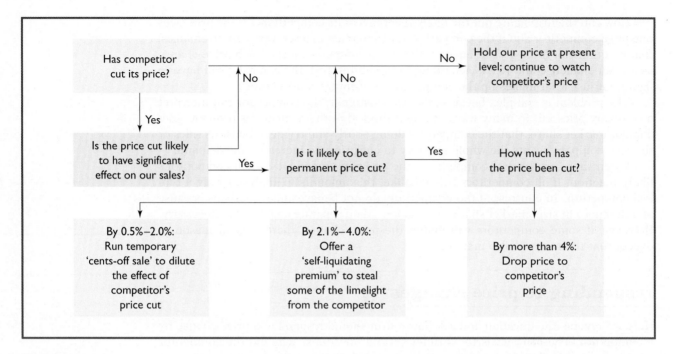

Figure 17.2

Price reaction programme for meeting a competitor's price cut

SOURCE: Redrawn with permission from a working paper by Raymond J. Trapp, Northwestern University, 1964.

1. *Reduce price*. The leader might drop its price to the competitor's price. It may decide that the market is price sensitive and that it would lose too much market share to the lower-priced competitor. Or it might worry that recapturing lost market share later would be too hard. Cutting price will reduce the company's profits in the short run. Some companies might also reduce their product quality, services and marketing communications to retain profit margins, but this ultimately will hurt long-run market share. The company should try to maintain its quality as it cuts prices.

2. *Raise perceived quality*. Like Nokia, a company might maintain its price but strengthen the perceived value of its offer. It could improve its communications, stressing the relative quality of its product over that of the lower-price competitor. The firm may find it cheaper to maintain price and spend money to improve its perceived quality than to cut price and operate at a lower margin.

3. *Improve quality and increase price*. The company might increase quality and raise its price, moving its brand into a higher price position. The higher quality justifies the higher price, which in turn preserves the company's higher margins. Or the company can hold the price on the current product and introduce a new brand at a higher price position.

4. *Launch low-price 'fighting brand'*. One of the best responses is to add lower-price items to the line or to create a separate lower-price brand. This is necessary if the particular market segment being lost is price sensitive and will not respond to arguments of higher quality. Thus, when attacked on price by Fuji, Kodak introduced low-priced Funtime film. When challenged on price by store brands and other low-priced entrants, Nestlé turned a number of its brands into fighting brands, including Fussell's condensed milk. In response to price pressures, Miller cut the price of its High Life brand by 20 per cent in most markets and sales jumped 9 per cent in less than a year.[16]

Pricing strategies and tactics form an important element of a company's marketing mix. In setting prices, companies must carefully consider a great many internal and external factors before choosing a price that will give them the greatest competitive advantage in selected target markets. However, companies are not usually free to charge whatever prices they wish. Several laws restrict pricing practices and a number of ethical considerations affect pricing decisions. Pricing strategies and tactics also depend upon the way that we pay for things. Increasingly, what we spend does not depend on how much money we have on us or how much we earned that week. These days our money is rarely something we see or feel; it is the electronic transmission of data between files within banks or on the Internet. Marketing Highlight 17.3 tells more about how money is changing.

marketing highlight 17.3

Excuse me, but do you accept money?

Cash is going out of style. Increasingly, people pay, for even small transactions, by credit card, debit card, pre-paid smart cards or e-cash. People are as uninterested in seeing their money as they are in viewing the petrol they buy. Money, and the constraints it imposes, is disappearing. The spending of both households and companies is becoming less determined by immediate income or money in the bank than by their expected wealth. Even the resistance of ultra-conservative Germany and Marks & Spencer has crumbled.

People and companies are turning to trading their skills and produce without using money. Want a plumbing job done? Fred will do it if you will mow his lawn for a week and babysit one night. What if the plumber does not want anything you can provide? In that case, clubs exist to trade credits. The plumber does the job for you, but he can use his credits to get goods or services from someone else. These tax-free networks are growing so fast that governments are starting to worry about them. The government's concerns are not new; England's King Athelstan tried to ban such tax dodging dealing 1,070 years ago.

London's Capital Barter Corporation (CBC) orchestrates third-party deals for companies that offer their services for trade credits rather than cash. CBC's deals range from a £15 (€22) restaurant meal to a £15,000 stock of computers. The most popular items are airline tickets, photocopiers and computers. Barter is not just for small deals between small firms – Lufthansa, Playtex and US Networks have all had deals worth €2 million or more.

CBC and other barter companies, including The Bartering Company and Eurotrade, debit and credit their members' accounts in 'trade pounds'. Each member has a credit limit depending upon the size of the company and the tradability of its products. But why barter rather than get money instead? The marketing manager of Konica Business machines explains: 'A lot of companies, when they find out how much a fax machine is in trade pounds, say they can get a better deal by getting a discount in cash. But if they think how much it would cost to generate that cash, they would find it cheaper to do the deal in barter.' The value of bartering is best when the incremental cost of serving an extra client is low, explains the chief executive of the International Reciprocal Trade Association. Letting a room on barter, for example, costs the hotel only the price of laundry and cleaning, since all the other costs are fixed. But the buying power it earns in trade pounds is equal to the full retail value of the room.

The Internet now has its own money. Punching in credit card numbers is the most common way of paying online but many customers feel that the method is insecure and lacks the anonymity of cash. Early e-money systems (e-cash 1.0), such as DigiCash and CyberCash, have bombed in the same way as many B2C dotcom companies. New attempts (e-cash 2.0), including 1ClickCharge and Qpass, have a big advantage over credit cards and e-cash 1.0 in costing retailers little and allowing 'micropayments' down to €0.001.

There are also more creative variants on e-cash 2.0. Flooz uses gift certificates while Beenz.com enables users to trade in the beenz they earn simply by being online. More mundane is PayMyBills which specialises in the electronic payment of subscribers' household bills. Most exotic of all is e-gold, where customers fund their online accounts by buying gold or other precious metals. Once purchased, this libertarian commodity is free of currency, purchases being paid for in units of weight of the metals.

SOURCES: Neil Buckley, 'M & S close to accepting debit card payments', *Financial Times* (29 August 1994), p. 6; Motoka Rich, 'Abracadabra! It's the barter magicians', *Financial Times* (1–2 October 1994), p. 4; Michael Lindemann, 'Germany flexible at last on credit cards', *Financial Times* (11 November 1994), p. 3); 'Bill payment on the Internet: for whom the bill tolls', *The Economist* (4 September 1999), p. 103; 'E-money revisited', *The Economist* (22 July 2000), p. 106; 'E-cash 2.0', *The Economist* (19 February 2000), p. 77; Simon Jenkins, 'The Year 1000' (Abacus, London: 2000).

summary

Pricing is a dynamic process. Companies design a *pricing structure* that covers all their products. They change this structure over time and adjust it to account for different customers and situations.

Pricing strategies usually change as a product passes through its life cycle. The company can decide on one of several price-quality strategies for introducing an imitative product. In pricing innovative new products, it can follow a *skimming policy* by initially setting high prices to 'skim' the maximum amount of revenue from various segments of the market. Or it can use *penetration pricing* by setting a low initial price to win a large market share.

When the product is part of a product mix, the firm searches for a set of prices that will maximise the profits from the total mix. The company decides on *price steps* for items in its product line and on the pricing of *optional products*, *captive products*, *by-products* and *product bundles*.

Companies apply a variety of *price-adjustment strategies* to account for differences in consumer segments and situations. One is *discount and allowance pricing*, whereby the company establishes cash discounts, quantity discounts, functional discounts, seasonal discounts and allowances. A second is *segmented pricing*, whereby the company sets different prices for different customers, product forms, places or times. A third is *psychological pricing*, whereby the company adjusts the price to communicate better a product's intended position. A fourth is *promotional pricing*, whereby the company decides on loss leader pricing, special-event pricing and psychological discounting. A fifth is *value pricing*, whereby the company offers just the right combination of quality and good service at a fair price. A sixth is *geographical pricing*, whereby the company decides how to price to distant customers, choosing from such alternatives as FOB pricing, uniform delivered pricing, zone pricing, basing-point pricing and freight-absorption pricing. A seventh is *international pricing*, whereby the company adjusts its price to meet different conditions and expectations in different world markets.

When a firm considers initiating a *price change*, it must consider customers' and competitors' reactions. The meaning that customers see in the price change influences customers' reactions. Competitors' reactions flow from a set reaction policy or a fresh analysis of each situation. The firm initiating the price change must also anticipate the probable reactions of suppliers, intermediaries and government.

The firm that faces a price change initiated by a competitor must try to understand the competitor's intent as well as the likely duration and impact of the change. If a swift reaction is desirable, the firm should pre-plan its reactions to different possible price actions by competitors. When facing a competitor's price change, the company might sit tight, reduce its own price, raise perceived quality, improve quality and raise price, or launch a fighting brand.

discussing the issues

1. In the run-up to Christmas 2000, online retailers were failing to achieve their growth in sales anticipated a year earlier. Also, the major gains were being made by 'bricks-and-byte' retailers who had to bear the cost of both online and 'bricks-and-mortar' stores. Given the cost advantage and lower prices of purely online traders, why are bricks and bytes beating the dotcoms?

2. American Express offers three tiers of 'product' to customers – a green card, a gold card and a platinum card. The membership fee (price) rises from €100 for the green card to €200 for the gold and €300 for the platinum. What pricing strategy is AmEx adopting? Do you think this type of strategy is effective? Why or why not?

3. A leading brand of room spray is priced at €2.50 for a 150 ml bottle. A close competitor launched a similar product priced at €1.99 for 300 ml and quickly became the no. 1 brand. Discuss the psychological aspects of this pricing. What sort of company image do you think the competitor possesses to allow the use of this superb-value strategy? Would a similar strategy work for the leading no. 1 brand? Why or why not?

4. The formula for household chlorine bleaching agents is virtually identical for all brands. One brand, Clorox, charges a premium price for this same product, yet remains an unchallenged market leader in some national markets. What does this imply about the value of a brand name? Are there ethical issues involved in this type of pricing?

5. A Bodum coffee percolator sells for under £20 (€33) in a department store in London. The same device is priced at £80 in Tang's, a local department store in Singapore. What do you think accounts for the discrepancy in price? Can you list other products or services that would reflect a similar international pricing pattern?

applying the concepts

1. Visit the online shopping sites of major retailers in Europe and the US and compare the prices of identical products for sale in both areas. (Examples to choose are CDs by European and American artists sold by Amazon.com in the US and the same CDs sold by their European operations, such as Amazon.co.uk.) How different are the prices and to what extent do the prices reflect the country of origin of the products? What are the barriers to the prices being forced to converge by people online shopping across borders? How do the prices compare with high-street prices and those from online price comparison websites, such Shopsmart or PriceScan, mentioned in Marketing Highlight 17.2?

2. You are probably familiar with the seasonal sales that take place at certain times of the year. Examples are the 'summer sales', 'Christmas sales' and 'New Year sales'. Why do retailers run these sales each year? Would it be more effective for a retailer to differentiate from others by offering discounts outside, rather than during, the conventional seasonal sales periods? Why or why not? In general, how effective are discount and allowance pricing strategies?

references

1. For a comprehensive discussion of pricing strategies, see Thomas T. Nagle and Reed K. Holen, *The Strategy and Tactics of Pricing*, 2nd edn (Englewood Cliffs, NJ: Prentice Hall, 1995).

2. John Parry, 'Times are changing for Tag-Heuer', *The European* (11–17 November 1994), p. 32; Ian Fraser, 'Don't crack under the pressure', *European Business* (June 1994), pp. 66–8. For more discussion see Kenneth N. Thompson and Barbara J. Coe, 'Gaining sustainable competitive advantage: selecting a perceived value price', *Pricing Strategy & Practice*, **5**, 2 (1997), pp. 70–9; Charles R. Duke, 'Matching appropriate pricing strategy with markets and objectives', *Journal of Product & Brand Management*, **3**, 2 (1994), pp. 15–27.

3. Bridget Williams, *The Best Butter in the World: A history of Sainsbury's* (London: Ebury, 1994).

4. David Kirkpatrick, 'Intel goes for broke', *Fortune* (16 May 1994), pp. 62–8; Andy Reinhardt, 'Pentium: the next generation', *Business Week* (12 May 1997), pp. 42–3; David Kirkpatrick, 'Intel's amazing profit machine', *Fortune* (17 February 1996), pp. 60–72.

5. Daniel Green, 'Yogurt may yield fat profit', *Financial Times* (9 January 1998), p. 16; Anna-Maija Tanttu, 'Spreading the benefits of science', *The European Magazine* (17 April 1997), pp. 10–11. For a study of pricing innovations see Biren Prasad, 'Analysis of pricing strategies for new product introduction', *Pricing Strategy & Practice*, **5**, 4 (1997), pp. 132–41; Ronald E. Goldsmith and Stephen J. Newell, 'Innovativeness and price sensitivity: managerial, theoretical and methodological issues', *Journal of Product & Brand Management*, **6**, 3 (1997), pp. 163–74.

6. Ralph Atkins, 'A certain lack of drive', *Financial Times* (25 November 1994), p. 18. For another example see Kay Atwal, 'New tactics cut soap giants down to size', *Marketing Week*, **19**, 25 (1996), p. 20.

7. Nicholas Denton, 'Higher costs in line for Internet users', *Financial Times* (13 February 1998), p. 4.

8. Susan Krafft, 'Love, Love Me Doo', *American Demographics* (June 1994), pp. 15–16; David Greenaway, Geoffrey Reed and Refaat Hassan, 'By-products and effective protection', *Journal of Economic Studies*, **21**, 6 (1994), pp. 31–6. 'Scrap tyre "cooking" becomes an economically viable proposition', *Professional Engineering*, **12**, 22 (1999), p. 9. Nagle and Holden, op cit., pp. 225–8; Sarah Toyne, 'Find your way through the mobile phone maze', *The Sunday Times* (21 November 1999), p. 3.

9. Gary M. Erickson and Johnny K. Johansson, 'The role of price in multi-attribute product evaluations', *Journal of Consumer Research* (September 1985), pp. 195–9.

10. For more reading on reference prices and psychological pricing, see Richard A. Briesch, Lakshman Krishnamurthi, Tridib Mazumdar and S. P. Raj, 'A comparative analysis of reference price models', *Journal of Consumer Research* (September 1997), pp. 202–14; Robert M. Schindler

and Patrick N. Kirby, 'Patterns of right-most digits used in advertised prices: implications for nine-ending effects', *Journal of Consumer Research* (September 1997), pp. 192–201; Ana María Angulo, José María Gil, Azucena Gracia and Mercedes Sánchez, 'Hedonic prices for Spanish red quality wine', *British Food Journal*, **102**, 7 (2000), pp. 481–93; Michel Wedel and Peter S. H. Leeflang, 'A model for the effects of psychological pricing in Gabor-Granger price studies', *Journal of Economic Psychology*, **19**, 2 (1998), pp. 237–60.

11. Jim Morgan, 'Value added: from cliché to the real thing', *Purchasing* (3 April 1997), pp. 59–61, pp. 51–2; Erika Rasmusson, 'The pitfalls of price cutting', *Sales and Marketing Management* (May 1997), p. 17; Leslie de Chernatony, Fiona Harris and Francesca Dall'Olmo Riley, 'Added value: its nature, roles and sustainability', *European Journal of Marketing*, **43**, 1/2 (2000), pp. 39–56.

12. David Wickers and Rob Ryan, 'America the booty full', *Sunday Times Travel* (14 November 1999), pp. 1–2; Peggy Hollinger, 'Britons pay most for popular Christmas presents, survey finds', *Financial Times* (17 November 2000), p. 7; 'Smuggling: the Belgian job', *The Economist* (8 May 1999), pp. 26–7. For a theoretical analysis of parallel imports, see B. Rachel Yang, Reza H. Ahmadi and Kent B. Monroe, 'Pricing in separable channels: the case of parallel imports', *Journal of Product & Brand Management*, **7**, 5 (1998), pp. 433–40.

13. Philip R. Cateora, *International Marketing*, 7th edn (Homewood, IL: Irwin, 1990), p. 540; see also S. Tamer Cavusgil, 'Pricing for global markets', *Columbia Journal of World Business* (Winter 1996), pp. 66–78.

14. 'Transport: Prescott's prize', *The Economist* (22 June 2000), p. 33; 'Standstill Britain', *The Economist* (16 September 2000), pp. 35–6; Mark Inglefield, 'Pump action', *The Times* (15 September 2000), p. 22.

15. Greg McIvor, 'Nokia shrugs off price pressure', *Financial Times* (13 February 2000), p. 29; Jaanis Kerkis, 'Talk of the worlds', *Financial Times Weekend Magazine* (9 October 1999), pp. 15–18.

16. Jonathon Berry and Zachary Schiller, 'Attack of the fighting brands', *Business Week* (2 May 1994), p. 125.

case 17

Pricing Imperial's oil

MARCEL COHEN*

The Imperial is the UK retailing arm of Imperial Oil, a global group with interests in oil exploration, production, refining and marketing. The Imperial's name is highly respected and its logo is one of the world's most recognised. In the UK Imperial Oil has 3,000 petrol stations and proudly boasts that 80 per cent of UK consumers are within 10 minutes' driving time from an Imperial petrol station. Although Imperial has only 15 per cent of the county's petrol stations, it is market leader with 30 per cent share of the UK market.

Nigel Bamby

Imperial Oil's UK retail operation division is a profit centre that is independent in all but name. Like most of Imperial's employees, Mr Nigel Bamby, the division's chief executive, has spent all of his working life with the company. When Mr Bamby took over Imperial it was about to announce its third year in succession of low and declining profits. The good old days of brand loyalty had gone. To motorists, 'petrol is petrol'! There was too much capacity chasing too little demand. Competition was rife. Whenever price increases were tried, prices came tumbling down as competitors tried to undercut each other. Invariably, all competitors priced at almost the same rock-bottom price. There were well-publicised confrontations in which competitors publicly 'gunned each other down'.

A recent shoot-out involved Amoil, an American company only recently established in the UK. However, its new refinery took advantage of the latest technology, giving it a cost advantage of 0.25 pence (€0.0015) per litre of petrol. Amoil vowed to keep prices 0.2 pence per litre cheaper than that of its competitors and said that it would not tolerate any competitor trying to match its price.

Since this was a frontal attack on their market leadership, Imperial retaliated by matching Amoil's prices in one region of the UK. Prices in the region immediately dropped so ridiculously low that the police had to disperse the queue of motorists scrambling for the bargain. The price war escalated until, scarred, the contenders retreated to their usual, not quite so low, prices.

Mike Lewis

Mike Lewis knew nothing about petrol when Mr Bamby recruited him. Mike had spent most of his working life marketing for a variety of companies. He viewed petrol as 'the world's largest and longest laboratory experiment'. It provided him and his team with a lot of statistics. They calculated that Imperial's demand-price elasticity was one-third that of Hispanoil, an aggressive competitor that had recently joined the market. In other words, Imperial's sales were a lot less price sensitive than Hispanoil's.

Based on the elasticity and cost information, Mike established that the optimum price for Imperial was 0.75 p/litre above the market price. This would have the added advantage, he predicted, of arresting the weekly erosion of the market price, which by that time was falling at a rate of 0.25 p/litre per week. 'It is worth a try', agreed Mr Bamby. Imperial prices were immediately raised and held at 0.75p above competitors, and petrol prices stabilised almost immediately. With the higher price Imperial sacrificed some market share but this was more than offset by the additional profits. Profits improved but remained far from covering the cost of the capital employed in the business.

If Imperial's offer was in some way superior to that of its competitors, then the market share forfeited through the premium pricing strategy could be kept to a minimum. In this way Imperial would benefit from higher margins without sacrificing so much market share. Mike had short-term and long-term answers.

Promotions, promotions, promotions

Mike's idea for the short term was to offer free gift promotions. This would not only attract more business but, if the gifts were collectable items, it would also retain that business when prices were increased. A whole series of free gift promotions were devised – tumblers, wine glasses, coffee mugs and commemorative coins. Soon after the first Imperial promotion, competitors began to offer gift promotions too. Nevertheless, as a direct result of these promotions, market share and profits were maintained despite Imperial's premium price strategy.

* Management School, Imperial College, London. Based on the case Imperial Oil (B) by the same author.

Product quality

Although the promotions were a success, Mike recognised that they were a short-term expedient. The only lasting advantage would be an improvement to the core product, Imperial. On various occasions in the past Imperial and its competitors had tried to gain a competitive advantage by improving the offer to the consumer. Unfortunately, motorists were generally cynical of oil company developments. One competitor tried to introduce talking pumps, warning customers that the fuel being dispensed from the pump was diesel and that it was not suitable for petrol engines. The company was trying to be helpful but the media voiced the motorist reaction as 'another gimmick at the forecourt'. When Sigma Oil dug up their forecourts to install more pipelines to accommodate unleaded petrol, the cry was: 'You, the motorist, will have to pay for this!'

The Imperial Group had been working on a global initiative to improve the quality of Imperial's petrol. Their scientists had formulated an additive that reduced the harmful emissions from car exhausts and improved fuel consumption by an average of 5 per cent. Local operating companies were in theory free to reject this initiative but Imperial Oil made it clear that they expected adoption. Mike felt uncomfortable with Imperial Oil's proposal. His preference was to spend money on improving the petrol station environment rather than the petrol itself. After all, he argued, they were badly in need of refurbishment and the changes he envisaged would make customers more disposed to accept his diversification ideas.

Diversification

Mike had begun working on diversification soon after joining Imperial. Initially, he had involved colleagues from various arms of the company. However, he found them unreceptive. They regarded him as an outsider and resented his intrusion. In any case, they felt that it was almost beneath them to consider being involved in anything other than the oil business. To counter the rejection, Mike formed a team that would work in secrecy. Once his ideas were properly formed, he could persuade his colleagues that he was right and that they were wrong.

When the team had completed their projects, Mike was very proud. He felt that they would give Imperial the long-term advantage that it was looking for, solve some emerging competitive problems and give Imperial an opportunity to diversify away from oil.

Teleshopping

Imperial should develop a shopping unit given to housewives free of charge. The unit would consist of a screen, joystick and small number of control buttons. It would have a built-in television aerial, a radio link to the housewife's telephone line and, most important of all, would use CDs to enable housewives to view video sequences. Using the equipment, the housewife could take a simulated walk around a store, scan the shelves, zoom in to a particular product, display information about the item and, if desired, order it. The TV link ensured that prices were current, while the telephone line transmitted orders.

A third party would manage teleshopping on Imperial's behalf. They would source, assemble and pack the order and deliver it to an Imperial petrol station. The order would be ready for collection within 8 hours of it being placed. At the same time as the order was being collected, the customer could seize the opportunity to refuel.

Banking

With 25 per cent of petrol sales being paid for by payment cards, Mike was concerned at the power held by banks and other card operators. He feared that the card issuers would one day wield their power in a damaging way. They could, for instance, threaten to direct motorists to Imperial's competitors unless Imperial made concessions. It was clear to Mike that Imperial had to issue its own payment card. Indeed, it was most probable that Imperial's competitors had recognised the same threats and were ready to launch their own cards. Oil companies in Scandinavia and the US had already done so. 'Could Imperial afford *not* to launch a card?', Mike quizzed.

Mike knew that an Imperial payment card offered the additional benefit of customer loyalty. Mike hoped to attract consumers by offering a unique contactless smart card. When a smart card is placed in its reader, contact is made and data transferred securely. A contactless smart card can transfer data without physical contact between the card and its reader. The development team's idea was to embed the smart card in a key fob. The team also proposed a series of financial services (e.g. cash dispensing, credit, debit, etc.) which, with the help of third-party agencies, enabled Imperial to offer full banking services. The proposal, therefore, gave Imperial an advantage over its competitors, arrested the power held by card issuers and was a diversification opportunity for Imperial.

Mr Bamby's reaction

Mike had demonstrated that he was a capable marketer, backing his proposals with fairly concrete analyses, but 'Were his proposals too big?' 'Were they too big even for a company as big as Imperial Oil?' If Mike's proposals could materialise then Imperial would stand to make a lot of money. On the other hand, if they were to fail, the

Imperial Board would come down on him 'like a ton of bricks'. Mr Bamby knew that he would get the Imperial Board's support for fuel improvements. After all, if the fuel improvements failed, no one would kick up a fuss. In view of the commercial as well as the political risks, Mr Bamby decided to put Mike's ideas 'on hold'. At the next Imperial Board meeting, Mr Bamby proposed that Imperial should continue with promotions while they prepared for a launch of the 'improved' petrol. The Imperial Board applauded Mr Bamby's sensible proposals and gave him the go-ahead.

In reality, launching the improved fuel took longer than anticipated and, meanwhile, promotions become a way of life for both competitors and consumers. It proved extremely difficult for Imperial, or indeed any of its competitors, to cease offering them. Indeed promotions were insufficient to combat the rise of a new breed of competitors: hypermarkets.

Hypermarkets

One or two food retailers had begun to sell petrol from their hypermarkets a decade earlier. Since supply exceeded demand in the oil industry, hypermarkets were able to obtain petrol from refiners at marginal cost. The hypermarkets used petrol as a 'loss leader', pricing their petrol well below that of conventional petrol stations. In their first five years of operation hypermarkets had increased their share of the UK petrol market from 1 to 5 per cent. As their petrol business grew, the hypermarkets started importing fuel rather than using UK refineries. The hypermarket petrol stations were popular with motorists. So much so that their throughput per site was seven times the national average. They could also share their costs with the hypermarket, rather than operating small independent sites on main roads. Their cost advantage allowed them to make profits on petrol even at loss leader prices. The number of hypermarkets offering petrol accelerated until they held 18 per cent of retail petrol sales. The hypermarkets had also become sophisticated petrol retailers. They were innovators as well as low-cost operators, for example leading the market in credit card payment for petrol at the pump.

In response to the hypermarkets, Amoil announced that it would match hypermarket prices. If Imperial were to follow, a terrible price war could erupt. Another oil company had decided to concentrate on selling groceries, not petrol! Once again, price was centre stage.

Questions

1. Why is the petrol market so prone to price competition? If consumers are so price sensitive to petrol prices, why do customers respond to sales promotions that must push up the cost of petrol in order to pay for 'free' gifts?

2. Why is Imperial Oil so keen on avoiding price competition while other competitors feel keen to cut prices?

3. If consumers believe 'petrol is petrol', how and why is Imperial able to charge more than other oil companies for their product and how do you think they achieve a market share out of proportion to their number of petrol stations?

4. Debate Mike's preference for diversification or spending on the refurbishment of petrol station rather than improving the product itself.

5. Suggest alternative courses of action for Imperial to respond to the increasing impact of the hypermarkets and the willingness of some competitors to cut prices in order to compete. Evaluate the options in terms of the likely long- and short-term risks and returns for Imperial.

internet exercises

Internet exercises for this chapter can be found on the student site of the MYPHLIP Web Site at www.booksites.net/kotler.

part six

Promotion

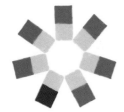

'Promise, large promise, is the soul of an advertisement.'

DR JOHNSON (WRITER AND LEXICOGRAPHER)

part introduction

IN PART SIX WE COVER the third element of the marketing mix – promotion. We show how organisations communicate and reach their various target markets.

Being able to design and develop a product or service that has all the features that attract customers is one thing. Getting the message across to them, and ultimately capturing or retaining a customer is quite a different matter; consequently, marketers must learn how to communicate effectively with their customers. Chapter 18 shows how to do this and gives an overview of the types of marketing communication or the promotion mix. There is no one best communication tool or approach to use; rather, marketers must employ a combination of tools and coordinate their strategies for each.

Chapter 19 addresses three mass communication tools – advertising, sales promotion and public relations efforts. We see how they help to achieve different types of response from consumers. Furthermore, we explore the opportunities and the barriers facing marketers seeking to communicate to customers worldwide.

Moving on from the discussion of indirect, non-personal forms of communication, Chapter 20 examines the role of direct, personal communications – that is, the use of a sales force to reach the firm's customers. Increasingly, the sales force is seen by firms as a source of value creation, not just as order takers. Through them, customer relationships can be forged and sustained. As a result, new forms of sales organisation, such as key account management, have arisen to allow firms to maximise the returns from investment in personal selling.

chapter eighteen

Integrated marketing communication strategy

Chapter objectives *After reading this chapter, you should be able to:*

✦ Name and define the four tools of the promotion mix.

✦ Discuss the process and advantages of integrated marketing communications.

✦ Outline the steps in developing effective marketing communications.

✦ Explain the methods for setting the promotion budget and factors that affect the design of the promotion mix.

introduction

Modern marketing calls for more than just developing a good product, pricing it attractively, and making it available to target customers. Companies must also *communicate* with current and prospective customers, and what they communicate should not be left to chance.

To communicate well, companies often hire advertising agencies to develop effective ads, sales promotion specialists to design sales-incentive programmes, direct-marketing specialists to develop databases and interact with customers and prospects by mail and telephone, and public relations firms to develop corporate images. They train their salespeople to be friendly, helpful and persuasive. For most companies, the question is not *whether* to communicate, but *how much to spend* and *in what ways*. All of their communications efforts must be blended into a consistent and coordinated communications programme.

A modern company has to communicate with its intermediaries, consumers and various publics. Its intermediaries communicate with their consumers and publics. Consumers have word-of-mouth communication with each other and with other publics. Meanwhile, each group provides feedback to every other group. The company therefore has to manage a complex marketing communications system (see Figure 18.1).

A company's total marketing communications mix – also called its **promotion mix** – consists of the specific blend of advertising, personal selling, sales promotion, public

Promotion mix
The specific mix of advertising, personal selling, sales promotion and public relations that a company uses to pursue its advertising and marketing objectives.

624

preview case

Volvo Trucks: the best drive in the game

Volvo Trucks, the truck division of Swedish AB Volvo, has been selling trucks in markets around the world for several decades. Its early trucks lacked quality, were sold under a variety of names in different countries, at relatively low prices, and had gained a reputation as low-status 'fleet trucks'. In recent years, however, Volvo Trucks had consolidated its various nameplates under the Volvo brand and had developed a new line of premium trucks – the VN Series – which were superior to competing premium brands in overall quality, design, safety and driving comfort. Now, all that remained was to raise Volvo Trucks' old low-status image to match the new high-quality reality. That task would take something dramatic to pull off.

The target market for heavy-duty trucks consists of truck fleet buyers and independent owner-operators. However, truck drivers themselves are an important buying influence. Firms perceived as having better-performing, more comfortable, higher-status trucks have a big edge in attracting and holding good drivers. Hence, truck buyers are swayed by driver perceptions. Volvo Truck's communications goal must seek to improve the image of Volvo's VN Series trucks, not just among truck buyers, but also truck drivers.

The key task was to determine how to reach this audience in its key European markets. It was important to get as much impact as possible per euro spent.

The marketing director came up with the following proposal which could be adapted for different country markets. Although mass advertising (e.g. ads on television, radio) was not an obvious tool to achieve this – no other heavy-duty truck manufacturer was advertising on television, he reckoned that this channel should not be ruled out. The key was to secure a slot in a major sports event – like the Soccer Cup Final – watched by a high proportion of truck drivers. Research, for example, suggests that nearly half of truck drivers watch some or all of an average European finals game.

Still, a single ad, by itself, wasn't likely to have much lasting impact on buyer and driver perceptions. An integrated promotional campaign, with Cup Final advertising as the centre-piece, would be required. The campaign (aptly called 'The Best Drive') would involve a sales promotion offering truck drivers a chance to win a new Volvo truck. The promotion would use a wide range of carefully coordinated media, including trucker magazines and radio stations. Drivers could enter the sweepstakes by responding to print or radio ads, visiting a Volvo Truck dealer or participating truck stop or by clicking onto the Volvo Trucks website (truckers use the Internet to schedule loads). To create additional interest, Volvo Trucks would visit major truck stops around the country, encouraging truck drivers to enter the Best Drive sweepstakes and giving them a chance to experience a new Volvo VN770 first-hand.

Each entrant would receive an entry card with one of 40 'Volvo Truths' printed on it – each emphasising a key VN770 positioning point. If the phrase on a driver's card matched the winning phrase revealed in the Soccer Finals commercial, the driver became a finalist eligible for the grand prize. To further encourage drivers to watch the commercial, Volvo Trucks would sponsor Soccer Finals parties at selected truck stops around the country. It would also have Volvo VN770s at each truck stop so that drivers could see the truck that was causing all the commotion.

The Volvo Trucks ad itself would used soft humour to make the quality point. It would feature an experienced and approachable professional driver, driving a new Volvo VN770 down a highway. The ad would show both the sleek, handsome exterior of the truck and its luxurious interior. The winning phrase, 'Volvo – Drive Safely', would appear on the screen as the commercial ended. The commercial, importantly, would portray professional truck drivers and their huge, sometimes scary trucks in a positive light.

Would the ad get the drivers buzzing about the VN770 truck and the winning phrase? In all, the Best Drive campaign would cost Volvo Trucks several million euros, much of this going to the ad alone. Was it worth the cost?[1]

Questions

1. Identify the different forms of communication used by Volvo Trucks to reach its target customers and the key objectives of these communication tools.

2. What are the key factors that must be considered by Volvo Trucks in order to ensure that the Best Drive campaign will achieve lasting impact in the marketplace?

3. To what extent do you think Volvo Truck's Best Drive campaign can be universally applied across European markets? Explain.

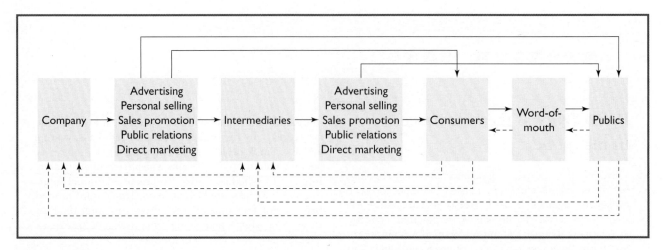

Figure 18.1

The marketing communications system

Advertising

Any paid form of non-personal presentation and promotion of ideas, goods or services by an identified sponsor.

Personal selling

Personal presentation by the firm's sales force for the purpose of making sales and building customer relationships.

Sales promotion

Short-term incentives to encourage purchase or sales of a product or service.

Public relations

Building good relations with the company's various publics by obtaining favourable publicity, building up a good 'corporate image', and handling or heading off unfavourable rumours, stories and events. Major PR tools include press relations, product publicity, corporate communications, lobbying and counselling.

relations and direct marketing tools that the company uses to pursue its advertising and marketing objectives. Let us define the five main promotion tools:

✦ **Advertising**. Any paid form of non-personal presentation and promotion of ideas, goods or services by an identified sponsor.

✦ **Personal selling**. Personal presentation by the firm's sales force for the purpose of making sales and building customer relationships.

✦ **Sales promotion**. Short-term incentives to encourage the purchase or sale of a product or service.

✦ **Public relations**. Building good relations with the company's various publics by obtaining favourable publicity, building up a good 'corporate image', and handling or heading off unfavourable rumours, stories and events.

✦ **Direct marketing**. Direct connections with carefully targeted individual consumers to both obtain an immediate response and cultivate lasting customer relationships – the use of telephone, mail, fax, e-mail, the Internet and other tools to communicate directly with specific consumers.[2]

Although direct marketing is now commonly regarded as one of the elements of the promotions mix, direct marketing tools behave not only as communication devices, but are also *sales channels* in their own right. For example, many companies use direct channels to sell their products. A wide range of products and services, including computers, software, financial services, jewellery, clothing and household appliances, can be purchased by phone, mail and the Internet.

Each category in the promotions mix involves specific tools. For example, advertising includes print, radio and television broadcast, outdoor and other forms. Personal selling includes sales presentations, fairs and trade shows, and incentive programmes. Sales promotion includes activities such as point-of-purchase displays, premiums, discounts, coupons, competitions, speciality advertising and demonstrations. Direct marketing includes catalogues, telemarketing, fax, kiosks, the Internet and more. Thanks to technological breakthroughs, people can now communicate through traditional media, such as newspapers, radio, telephone and television, as well as through newer types of media (e.g. fax machines, cellular phones, pagers and computers). The new technologies have encouraged more companies to move from mass communication to more targeted communication and one-to-one dialogue.

At the same time, communication goes beyond these specific promotion tools. The product's design, its price, the shape and colour of its package, and the stores that sell it – *all* communicate something to buyers. Thus, although the promotion

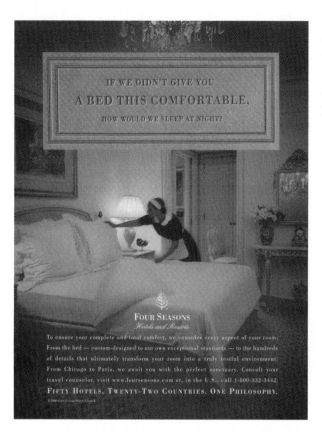

Four Seasons Hotels consider every aspect of its rooms – including custom-designed beds – as part of its communications strategy.
SOURCE: Four Seasons Hotels and Resorts. *Agency*: Ammirati Paris Limited

mix is the company's primary communication activity, the entire marketing mix – promotion *and* product, price and place – must be coordinated for greatest communication impact.

In this chapter, we begin by examining (a) the rapidly changing marketing communications environment that has resulted from shifting marketing strategies and advances in computers and information technologies; (b) the concept of integrated marketing communications and the communication process; (c) the factors that marketing communicators must consider in shaping an overall communications mix; and (d) the legal, ethical and social responsibility issues in marketing communications.

In Chapter 19, we will look at *mass-communication tools* – that is, advertising, sales promotion and public relations. Chapter 20 examines the sales force as a communication and promotion tool. Given the 'hybrid' role of direct marketing, we will review developments in *direct and online marketing* and address the implications for the firm's communications as well as distribution strategies in Chapter 22.

Direct marketing
Direct connections with individual customers to obtain an immediate response and generate lasting customer relationships.

integrated marketing communications

During the past few decades, companies around the world have perfected the art of mass marketing – selling highly standardised products to masses of customers. In the process, they have developed effective mass-media advertising techniques to support their mass-marketing strategies. These companies routinely invest huge sums of money in the mass media, reaching tens of millions of customers with a single ad. However, as we move into the twenty-first century, marketing managers are facing some new marketing communications realities.

the changing communications environment

Two major factors are changing the face of today's marketing communications. First, as mass markets have fragmented, marketers are shifting away from mass marketing. More and more, they are developing focused marketing programmes designed to build closer relationships with customers in more narrowly defined micromarkets. Second, vast improvements in computer and information technology are speeding the movement towards segmented marketing. Today's information technology helps marketers to keep closer track of customer needs – more information is available about customers at the individual and household levels than ever before. New technologies also provide new communications avenues for reaching smaller customer segments with more tailored messages.

The shift from mass marketing to segmented marketing has had a dramatic impact on marketing communications. Just as mass marketing gave rise to a new generation of mass-media communications, so the shift towards one-to-one marketing is spawning a new generation of more specialised and highly targeted communications efforts.[3]

Given this new communications environment, marketers must rethink the roles of various media and promotion-mix tools. Mass-media advertising has long dominated the promotion mixes of consumer-product companies. However, although television, magazines and other mass media remain very important, their dominance is declining. Market fragmentation has resulted in media fragmentation – in an explosion of more focused media that better match today's targeting strategies. For example, back in the 1970s and 1980s, in many developed countries, the three or four major TV networks attracted a majority of the nation's viewing audience. By the mid-1990s, that number had dropped significantly as cable television and satellite broadcasting systems offered advertisers dozens or even hundreds of alternative channels that reach smaller, specialised audiences. It's expected to drop further over the coming years.[4] Similarly, there has been a proliferation of special-interest magazines in recent decades, reaching more focused audiences. Beyond these media channels, companies are making increased use of new, highly targeted media, ranging from video screens on supermarket shopping trolleys to CD-ROM catalogues and websites on the Internet. As we move towards a 'wireless' world, there will be increasing opportunity to create more and more targeted communications. Consider the following:

> Thanks to new technologies such as wireless access protocol (WAP), which enables mobile devices to access information that previously only was available through wired Internet connections, marketers increasingly will serve up text or audio advertisements and promotions to wireless devices. These wireless ads and promotions can be directed at target customers, based on their locations, personal tastes and preferences. They will be used to drive users to visit their nearby stores or to prompt them to make a phone call or link to an advertiser's wireless website. US start-up firm, GeePS.com Inc., has recently rolled out its service across several major cities in the country, which allows brick-and-mortar businesses, from large retail chains to mom-and-pop restaurants, to drive traffic to their storefronts by sending promotions, coupons and price comparisons directly to the handheld wireless devices of willing prospects. GeePS.com claims that the technology is now available to reach their audience anywhere, anytime.
>
> Besides wireless advertising, the technology also offers sponsorship opportunities for wireless content and services. For example, a free daily diary service provider reminds users of important dates such as wedding anniversaries or birthdays, may carry an ad from a sponsoring florist who offers to deliver flowers to the special person at a discount. In a number of countries in Europe, which has a highly developed wireless market, agencies have already launched marketing trials that

direct users to wireless content sites and microsites, where users can view a company's ads without having to leave the original site. Analysts predict that, in a few years' time, there will be an explosion of wireless text and audio ads. According to Ovum Ltd, a London-based technology consultancy, wireless advertising is forecast to hit over $16 billion worldwide by 2005, accounting for nearly 20 per cent of overall Internet advertising spending.

Currently, wireless advertising remains a fledgling industry, with many unanswered questions, ranging from consumer protection and privacy, to standards and advertising measurement. It is, however, expected to garner response rates 2–3 times higher than standard Internet banner ads. As a senior consultant at Ovum notes, 'With wireless advertising, it's an immediate call to action. Consumers can respond on the spot, which makes ads very effective.'[5]

More generally, advertising appears to be giving way to other elements of the promotion mix. In the glory days of mass marketing, consumer-product companies spent the lion's share of their promotion budgets on mass-media communications. For example, Unilever and Procter & Gamble, the world's biggest advertisers, have both been cutting their television advertising. Over the last 12 months, P&G has reduced its advertising spending on network TV by 7 per cent, while Unilever cut its network TV spending by 24 per cent.

Today, media advertising captures a much reduced proportion of the total promotion spend. Companies are not giving up on advertising, but are seeking ways to get better value for money by switching to other promotion tools.[6] For example, many are placing greater emphasis on sales promotion activities, which can be focused more effectively on individual consumer and trade segments. They are using a richer variety of focused communication tools in order to reach their diverse target markets.

In Britain, for example, Unilever's Comfort Refresh, a clothing and fabric deodorant spray, is advertised in the women's lavatories of clubs and pubs, because its target audience of young females, who use it to remove the smell of cigarette smoke from their clothing, are more likely to be out partying than sitting at home watching television for hours at a time. Refresh also sponsors a TV series that appeals to young females. In keeping with the assumption that the company can no longer expect to communicate efficiently with consumers through a mere 30-second TV commercial, when the company launched Comfort Easy Iron spray, product demonstrations were staged in shopping malls across the country.[7]

In all, companies are doing less *broadcasting* and more *narrowcasting*.

the need for integrated marketing communications

The shift from mass marketing to targeted marketing, and the corresponding use of a richer mixture of communication channels and promotion tools, poses a problem for marketers. Consumers are being exposed to a greater variety of marketing communications from and about the company from a broader array of sources. However, customers do not distinguish between message sources in the way marketers do. In the consumer's mind, advertising messages from different media such as television, magazines or online sources blur into one. Messages delivered via different promotional approaches – such as advertising, personal selling, sales promotion, public relations or direct marketing – all become part of a single overall message about the company. Conflicting messages from these different sources can result in confused company images and brand positions.

All too often, companies fail to integrate their various communications channels. The result is a hodgepodge of communications to consumers. Mass advertisements

Figure 18.2

Integrated marketing communications

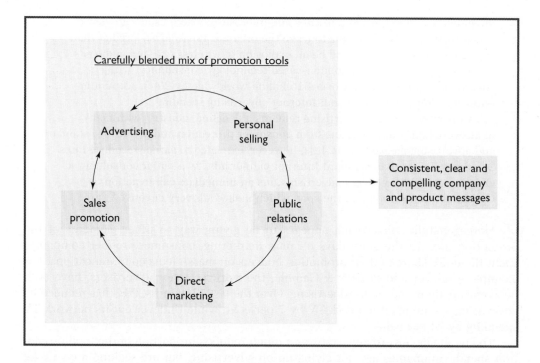

say one thing, a price promotion sends a different signal, a product label creates still another message, company sales literature says something altogether different and the company's website seems out of sync with everything else.

The problem is that these communications often come from different company sources. Advertising messages are planned and implemented by the advertising department or advertising agency. Personal selling communications are developed by sales management. Other functional specialists are responsible for public relations, sales promotion, direct marketing, online sites and other forms of marketing communication. Recently, such functional separation has been a major problem for many companies and their Internet communications activities, which are often split into separate organisational units. Moreover, members of various departments often differ in their views on how to split the promotion budget. The sales manager would rather hire a few more salespeople than spend a few hundred thousand euros more on a single television commercial. The public relations manager feels that he or she can do wonders with some money shifted from advertising to public relations.

In the past, no one person was responsible for thinking through the communication roles of the various promotion tools and coordinating the promotion mix. Today, however, more companies are adopting the concept of **integrated marketing communications** (IMC). Under this concept, as illustrated in Figure 18.2, the company carefully integrates and coordinates its many communications channels – mass-media advertising, personal selling, sales promotion, public relations, direct marketing, packaging and others – to deliver a clear, consistent and compelling message about the organisation and its products.[8] It builds a strong brand identity in the marketplace by tying together and reinforcing all the company's messages, positioning and images, and identity, coordinating these across all its marketing communications venues. It means that your PR materials say the same thing as your direct mail campaign, and your advertising has the same 'look and feel' as your website.

The IMC approach calls for recognising all contact points where the customer may encounter the company, its products and its brands. Each *brand contact* will deliver a message, whether good, bad or indifferent. The company works out the roles that the various promotional tools will play and the extent to which each will be used to deliver a consistent and positive message at all contact points. It carefully coordinates the

Integrated marketing communications

The concept under which a company carefully integrates and coordinates its many communications channels to deliver a clear, consistent, and compelling message about the organisation and its products.

promotional activities and the timing of when major campaigns take place. It keeps track of its promotional expenditures by product, promotional tool, product life-cycle stage and observed effect in order to improve future use of the promotion-mix tools. Finally, to implement integrated marketing communications, some companies appoint a marketing communications director – or *marcom manager* – who has overall responsibility for the company's communications efforts. Essentially, in order for the firm's external communications to be integrated effectively, it must first integrate its internal communications activities.

Integrated marketing communications produces better communications consistency and greater sales impact. It places the responsibility in someone's hands – where none existed before – to unify the company's image as it is shaped by thousands of company activities. It leads to a total marketing communication strategy aimed at showing how the company and its products can help customers solve their problems.

a view of the communication process

Integrated marketing communications involves identifying the target audience and shaping a well-coordinated promotional programme to elicit the desired audience response. Too often, marketing communications focus on overcoming immediate awareness, image or preference problems in the target market. This approach to communication has limitations: it is too short term and costly, and most messages of this nature fall

283 television channels.

292 radio stations.

8,500 magazines.

2 million websites.

Only one letterbox.

Royal Mail tries to convince businesses that direct mail is the best medium to reach their target audience.

SOURCE: Royal Mail. *Agency:* Bates UK

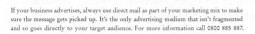
If your business advertises, always use direct mail as part of your marketing mix to make sure the message gets picked up. It's the only advertising medium that isn't fragmented and so goes directly to your target audience. For more information call 0800 885 887.

Royal Mail
www.royalmail.com/whydm

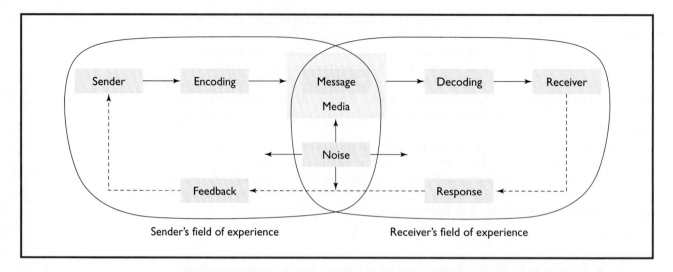

Figure 18.3

Elements in the communication process

on deaf ears. Today, marketers are moving towards viewing communications as *the management of the customer buying process over time*, during the pre-selling, selling, consuming and post-consumption stages. Because customers differ, the firm's communications programmes need to be developed for specific segments, niches and even individuals. Importantly, given the new interactive communications technologies, companies must ask not only 'How can we reach our customers?', but also 'How can we find ways to let our customers reach us?'.

Thus, the communication process should start with an audit of all the potential interactions that target customers may have with the product and company. For example, someone buying a new personal computer may talk to others, see television commercials, read articles and advertisements in newspapers and magazines, visit various websites and try out computers in one or more stores. The marketer needs to assess the influence that each of these communications experiences will have at different stages of the buying process. This understanding helps marketers to allocate their communication budget more effectively and efficiently.

To communicate effectively, marketers need to understand how communication works. Communication involves the nine elements shown in Figure 18.3. Two of these elements are the major parties in a communication – the *sender* and the *receiver*. Another two are the essential communication tools – the *message* and the *media*. Four more are primary communication functions – *encoding, decoding, response* and *feedback*. The last element is *noise* in the system. We will explain each of these elements using an ad for Hewlett-Packard colour copiers.

◆ *Sender*. The *party sending the message* to another party – in this case, Hewlett-Packard.

◆ *Encoding*. The process of *putting the intended message or thought into symbolic form* – Hewlett-Packard's advertising agency assembles words and illustrations into an advertisement that will convey the intended message.

◆ *Message*. The *set of words, pictures or symbols* that the sender transmits – the actual HP copier ad.

◆ *Media*. The *communication channels* through which the message moves from sender to receiver – in this case, the specific magazines that Hewlett-Packard selects.

◆ *Decoding*. The process by which the receiver *assigns meaning to the symbols* encoded by the sender – a consumer reads the HP copier ad and interprets the words and illustrations it contains.

+ *Receiver*. The *party receiving the message* sent by another party – the home office or business customer who reads the HP copier ad.
+ *Response*. The reactions of the receiver after being exposed to the message – any of hundreds of possible responses, such as the customer is more aware of the attributes of HP copiers, actually buys an HP copier or does nothing.
+ *Feedback*. The part of the *receiver's response communicated back to the sender* – Hewlett-Packard's research shows that consumers like and remember the ad, or consumers write or call HP praising or criticising the ad or HP's products.
+ *Noise*. The *unplanned static or distortion* during the communication process, which results in the receiver getting a different message than the one the sender sent – for example, the customer is distracted while reading the magazine and misses the HP copier ad or its key points.

For a message to be effective, the sender's encoding process must mesh with the receiver's decoding process. Thus, the best messages consist of words and other symbols that are familiar to the receiver. The more the sender's field of experience overlaps with that of the receiver, the more effective the message is likely to be. Marketing communicators may not always *share* their consumers' field of experience. For example, an advertising copywriter from one social stratum might create an ad for consumers from another stratum – say, blue-collar workers or wealthy business executives. However, to communicate effectively, the marketing communicator must understand the consumer's field of experience.

This model points out the key factors in good communication. Senders need to know what audiences they want to reach and what responses they want. They must be good at encoding messages that take into account how the target audience decodes them. They must send messages through media that reach target audiences and they must develop feedback channels so that they can assess the audience's response to the message.

steps in developing effective communication

We now examine the steps in developing an effective integrated communications and promotion programme. The marketing communicator must do the following: identify the target audience; determine the communication objectives; design a message; choose the media through which to send the message; and collect feedback to measure the promotion's results. Let us address each of these steps in turn.

identifying the target audience

A marketing communicator starts with a clear target audience in mind. The audience may be potential buyers or current users, those who make the buying decision or those who influence it. The audience may be individuals, groups, special publics or the general public. The target audience will heavily affect the communicator's decisions on *what* will be said, *how* it will be said, *when* it will be said, *where* it will be said and *who* will say it.

Figure 18.4

Buyer readiness stages

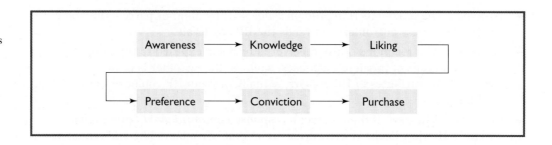

determining the communication objectives

Once the target audience has been defined, the marketing communicator must decide what response is sought. Of course, in many cases, the final response is *purchase*. But purchase is the result of a long process of consumer decision making. The marketing communicator needs to know where the target audience now stands and to what state it needs to be moved. To do this he or she must determine whether or not the customer is ready to buy.

The target audience may be in any of six **buyer-readiness stages** – the stages that consumers normally pass through on their way to making a purchase. These stages are *awareness, knowledge, liking, preference, conviction* and *purchase* (see Figure 18.4). They can be described as a *hierarchy of consumer response stages*. The purpose of marketing communication is to move the customer along these stages and ultimately to achieve final purchase.

Buyer-readiness stages
The stages that consumers normally pass through on their way to purchase, including awareness, knowledge, liking, preference, conviction and purchase.

■ Awareness

The communicator must first know how aware the target audience is of the product or organisation. The audience may be totally unaware of it, know only its name or know one or a few things about it. If most of the target audience is unaware, the communicator tries to build awareness, perhaps starting with just name recognition. This process can begin with simple messages that repeat the company or product name. For example, when Orange introduced its mobile phone network, it began with an extensive 'teaser' advertising campaign to create name familiarity. Initial ads for Orange created curiosity and awareness by emphasising the brand name, but not the service.

■ Knowledge

The target audience might be aware of the existence of the company or of the product, but not know much more. The company needs to learn how many people in its target audience have little, some or much knowledge about its offering. At launch, Orange ads created knowledge by informing potential buyers of the company's service and innovative features.

■ Liking

Assuming target audience members *know* the product, how do they *feel* about it? Once potential buyers knew about Orange, the company's marketers would want to move them along to the next stage – to develop favourable feelings about the brand. If the audience looks unfavourably on the brand, the communicator has to find out why, and then resolve the problems identified before developing a communications campaign to generate favourable feelings.

■ Preference

The target audience might *like* the product, but not *prefer* it to others. In this case, the communicator must try to build consumer preference by promoting the product's quality, value and other beneficial features. The communicator can check on the campaign's success by measuring the audience's preferences again after the campaign. If Orange finds that many potential customers like its service offering, but prefer other mobile phone operators' brands, it will have to identify those areas where its offerings are not as good as competing deals and where they are better. It must then promote its advantages to build preference among prospective clients, while redressing its weaknesses.

■ Conviction

A target audience might *prefer* the product, but not develop a *conviction* about buying it. Thus some customers may prefer Orange to other mobile phone network brands, but may not be absolutely sure that it is what they should subscribe to. The communicator's job is to build conviction that the offering is the best one for the potential buyer. A combination of the promotion-mix tools should be used to create preference and conviction. Advertising can be used to extol the advantages offered by the brand. Press releases and public relations activities would be used to stress the brand's specific features, such as its innovativeness or performance.

Direct marketing tools could be used or dealer salespeople could also be encouraged to educate potential buyers about the product or service options, value or after-sales service.

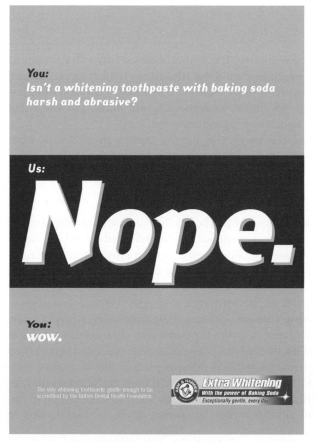

Conviction: Arm & Hammer is 'the only whitening toothpaste gentle enough to be accredited by the British Dental Health Foundation'.

SOURCE: Food Brokers Ltd. *Agency:* Scholz and friends

■ Purchase

Finally, some members of the target audience might have *conviction*, but not quite get around to making the *purchase*. Potential buyers might have decided to wait for more information or for the economy to improve. The communicator must lead these consumers to take the final step. Actions might include offering special promotional prices, rebates or premiums. Salespeople might call or write to selected customers, inviting them to visit the sales outlet for a special demonstration or product trial.

In discussing buyer readiness stages, we have assumed that buyers pass through *cognitive* (awareness, knowledge); *affective* (liking, preference, conviction); and *behavioural* (purchase) stages, in that order. This *'learn–feel–do'* sequence is appropriate when buyers have high involvement with a product category and perceive brands in the category to be highly differentiated, such as the purchase of a car. But consumers often follow other sequences. For example, they might follow a *'do–feel–learn'* sequence for high-involvement products with little perceived differentiation, such as a central heating system. Still a third sequence is the *'learn–do–feel'* sequence, where consumers have low involvement and perceive little differentiation, as is the case when they buy a product such as salt.

Furthermore, marketing communications alone cannot create positive feelings and purchases for the product. So, for example, Orange must provide superior value to potential buyers. In fact, outstanding marketing communications can actually speed the demise of a poor product. The more quickly potential buyers learn about the poor product, the faster they become aware of its faults. Thus, good marketing communications calls for 'good deeds followed by good words'. Nonetheless, by understanding consumers' buying stages and their appropriate sequence, the marketer can do a better job of planning communications.

designing a message

Having defined the desired audience response, the communicator turns to developing an effective message. Ideally, the message should get *Attention*, hold *Interest*, arouse *Desire* and obtain *Action* (a framework known as the AIDA model). In practice, few messages take the consumer all the way from awareness to purchase, but the AIDA framework suggests the desirable qualities of a good message.

In putting the message together, the marketing communicator must decide what to say (*message content*) and how to say it (*message structure and format*).

■ Message content

Rational appeals
Message appeals that relate to the audience's self-interest and show that the product will produce the claimed benefits; examples are appeals of product quality, economy, value or performance.

The communicator has to figure out an appeal or theme that will produce the desired response. There are three types of appeal: rational, emotional and moral. **Rational appeals** relate to the audience's self-interest. They emphasise the functional benefits – better performance, higher quality, outstanding economy or value – of the product. Thus, in its ads, Mercedes offers automobiles that are 'engineered like no other car in the world', stressing engineering design, performance and safety. One Volvo ad gives 'a whole stack of reasons' for buying the car – it has a rigid passenger safety cage, front and rear absorbing crumple zones, a catalytic converter that always works at peak efficiency, and many more reasons stressing design, safety and economy. When pitching computer systems to business users, IBM salespeople talk about quality, performance, reliability and improved productivity. One E. I. du Pont de Nemours ad tells customers how the company's fibres use a system that is similar to polar bear fur. Du Pont's fibres are so resistant to cold that they 'let people work, play and relax in sub-zero temperature'. The ad depicting a mother bear and her offspring resting snuggly in arctic snow assures customers that 'the miracles of science' can 'make humans as comfortable in the arctic as everyone else'.

Emotional appeals attempt to stir up either negative or positive emotions that can motivate purchase. These include fear, guilt and shame appeals that get people to do things they should (brush their teeth, invest in a pension plan, buy new tyres) or to stop doing things they shouldn't (smoke, drink too much, eat fatty foods). For example, a recent Crest ad invoked mild fear when it claimed, 'There are some things you just can't afford to gamble with' (cavities). So did Michelin tyre ads that featured cute babies and suggested 'Because so much is riding on your tyres'.[9] Communicators of industrial goods can also use emotional appeals, as in the case of Andersen Consulting's 'Are you making the most of all your strengths?' campaign which plays on managers' fear of undercapitalising the company's potential to take advantage of marketplace opportunities. The ad goes on to tell managers that Andersen Consulting, with its vast experience in strategy, technology, process and people, can help organisations capture their potential.

Advertisers also use positive emotional appeals such as love, humour, pride, promise of success and joy. Consider the following examples:

> British Telecom's 'Make someone happy with a phone call' and 'It's good to talk' campaigns stir a bundle of strong emotions. Ad campaigns for Häagen-Dazs equate ice-cream with pleasure (foreplay, to be more precise): one classic ad tells consumers how 'It is the *intense* flavour of the finest ingredients combined with *fresh* cream that is essentially Häagen-Dazs', and is followed by the strapline: 'Now it's on everybody's lips'. The firm claimed that the ad was a tremendous success. During the three months it advertised in newspapers and their supplements, brand awareness doubled while sales in big outlets rose by a third. Over the year, the particular campaign had boosted sales by 59 per cent.[10]

Moral appeals are directed to the audience's sense of what is 'right' and 'proper'. They are often used to urge people to support social causes such as a cleaner environment, better race relations, equal rights for women and aid to the disadvantaged.

■ Message structure

The communicator must decide *how* to say it. This requires the communicator to handle three message-structure issues. The first is whether to draw a conclusion or to leave it to the audience. Early research showed that drawing a conclusion was usually more effective where the target audience is less likely to be motivated or may be incapable of arriving at the appropriate conclusion. More recent research, however, suggests that in many cases where the targets are likely to be interested in the product, the advertiser is better off asking questions to stimulate involvement and motivate customers to think about the brand, and then letting them come to their own conclusions.

The second message structure issue is whether to present a one-sided argument (mentioning only the product's strengths), or a two-sided argument (touting the product's strengths while also admitting its shortcomings). Usually, a one-sided argument is more effective in sales presentations – except when audiences are highly educated or likely to hear opposing claims or when the communicator has a negative association to overcome. The third message-structure issue is whether to present the strongest arguments first or last. Presenting them first gets strong attention, but may lead to an anticlimactic ending.[11]

Emotional appeals
Message appeals that attempt to stir up negative or positive emotions that will motivate purchase; examples are fear, guilt, shame, love, humour, pride and joy appeals.

Moral appeals
Message appeals that are directed to the audience's sense of what is right and proper.

■ Message format

The communicator also needs a strong *format* for the message. In a print ad, the communicator has to decide on the headline, copy, illustration and colour. To attract attention, advertisers can use: novelty and contrast; eye-catching pictures and headlines; distinctive formats; message size and position; and colour, shape and movement. If the message is to be carried over the radio, the communicator has to choose words, sounds and voices. The 'sound' of an announcer promoting a used car should be different from one promoting quality furniture.

If the message is to be transmitted on television or conveyed in person, then all these elements plus body language have to be planned. Presenters plan their facial expressions, gestures, dress, posture and even hairstyle. If the message is carried on the product or its package, the communicator has to watch texture, scent, colour, size and shape. For example, colour plays an important communication role in food preferences.

> When consumers sampled four cups of coffee that had been placed next to brown, blue, red and yellow containers (all the coffee was identical, but the consumers did not know this), 75 per cent felt that the coffee next to the brown container tasted too strong; nearly 85 per cent judged the coffee next to the red container to be the richest; nearly everyone felt that the coffee next to the blue container was mild; and the coffee next to the yellow container was seen as weak.

Thus, if a coffee company wants to communicate that its coffee is rich, it should probably use a red container along with label copy boasting the coffee's rich taste.[12]

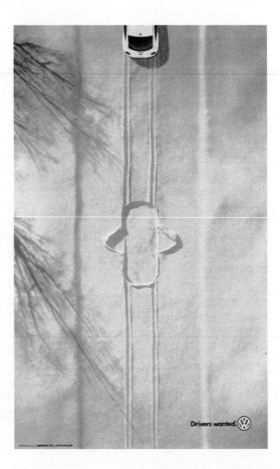

Message format: To attract attention, advertisers can use distinctive formats, novelty and eye-catching pictures, as in this award-winning Volkswagen ad.

Source: Volkswagen of America, Inc.

Even when an individual is exposed to a message, he or she may pay no attention to the message because it is either boring or irrelevant. The communicator increases the chances of the message attracting the attention of the target audience by taking into consideration the following factors:

✦ The message must have a practical value to the target audience because individuals are in the market for the product (for example, advertising pension schemes to undergraduates is a waste of time as they are likely to find such policies irrelevant to them for the time being).

✦ The message must interest the target group.

✦ The message must communicate new information about the product or brand. Consumers pay more attention to new messages.

✦ The message must reinforce or help to justify the buyer's recent purchase decisions – if you have recently bought a personal computer, it is likely that you will notice or your attention will be quickly drawn to ads for the PC (the phenomenon is called cognitive dissonance reduction).

✦ The presentation of the message must be impactful. As explained above, this objective can be achieved by paying attention to message formats and stressing creativity in the way the copy, artwork/illustrations and physical layout or presentation are delivered.

While advertisers' basic aim is to get their ads noticed, they must be sensitive to, and comply with, codes of practice operated by the industry watchdogs or country regulators. Messages should be designed to create maximum impact but without causing public offence and irritation (see Marketing Highlight 18.1).

choosing media

The communicator must now select *channels of communication*. There are two broad types of communication channel: *personal* and *non-personal*.

■ Personal communication channels

In **personal communication channels**, two or more people communicate directly with each other. They might communicate face to face, over the telephone, through the mail or even through an Internet 'chat'. Personal communication channels are effective because they allow for personal addressing and feedback.

Some personal communication channels are controlled directly by the communicator, as in the case of company salespeople who contact buyers in the target market. Other personal communications about the product may reach buyers through channels not directly controlled by the company. These might include independent experts – consumer advocates, consumer buying guides and others – making statements to target buyers. Or, they might be neighbours, friends, family members and associates talking to target buyers. This last channel, known as **word-of-mouth influence**, has considerable effect in many product areas.

Personal influence carries great weight for products that are expensive, risky or highly visible. For example, buyers of cars and major appliances often go beyond mass-media sources to seek the opinions of knowledgeable people. Companies can take steps to put personal communication channels to work for them. For example, they can create *opinion leaders* – people whose opinions are sought by others – by supplying certain

Personal communication channels
Channels through which two or more people communicate directly with each other, including face to face, person to audience, over the telephone, or through the mail.

Word-of-mouth influence
Personal communication about a product between target buyers and neighbours, friends, family members and associates.

Communications: the fine line between attraction and irritation

Very few advertisers set out deliberately to trick, mislead, insult or offend the public. Those that break a country's code of advertising practices invariably face a backlash from consumers and other parties, or are debarred at source from the means to publicise their messages due to media rejection.

Teasers: good campaigns get the punters talking, a bad one attracts complaints

Getting viewers to solve a puzzle in an advertisement is fair game in advertising. However, campaigns can backfire. Britvic Soft Drinks aired a 'Still Tango' ad which appealed to consumers to report any sightings of an apparently unlicensed product in the ad. Thirty thousand consumers responded, but were told that it was all a joke – they'd been 'Tango'd'! Sixty-three of those 'Tango'd' were so annoyed that they complained to the Independent Television Commission (ITC), which accused Britvic and its agency of undermining the credibility and authority of the medium – TV – and misleading consumers. People felt used, expressing irritation with the company for playing a prank on them. Britvic's teaser grabbed the audience's attention, but it ended up getting the wrong kind of publicity!

A campaign of a different kind caused uproar in Spain. An agency in Madrid sent out love letters to 50,000 young mothers in a direct-marketing campaign for Fiat's Cinquento car. A second batch of letters was then sent revealing the Cinquento as the secret admirer. Rather than this being seen as an amusing piece of junk mail, it caused a storm of protest. The Spanish Women's Institute denounced the campaign. Some women were so troubled, apparently, they were scared to leave the house.

There is a fine dividing line between attracting and irritating consumers. For most of the time, people are prepared to enjoy a light-hearted puzzle. A little intrigue adds interest. But the intrigue can only be stretched so far.

Bad taste ads?

Established brands using 'shock tactics' can also do as much damage, although observers argue that it is really a question of what is socially intolerable and a matter of taste. The RSPCA (Royal Society for the Prevention of Cruelty to Animals) campaign drew attention to the plight of horses exported for consumption by using a harrowing image of a dead pony hanging from a hook. The advertising watchdog, the ASA, upheld complaints against the ad, though it had no intention to frustrate the RSPCA's public enlightening efforts, but the visual image used was deemed misleading and grossly offensive.

More noteworthy is the controversy that dogged Italian clothing designer and manufacturer Benetton's 'United Colors' ads throughout the 1990s. Public opinion forced it to withdraw an early campaign showing a black woman breastfeeding a white child. Another campaign showing a blood-smeared newborn baby received hundreds of complaints to the UK's ASA, criticising Benetton for provoking public distress and outrage, and displaying a conspicuous disregard for public sensitivities. Benetton withdrew the ad after magazine publishers and poster contractors refused space to the advertiser. Other Benetton ads – a black child depicting a devil contrasting with a white cherub, an AIDS victim, a baby's bottom stamped 'HIV positive', the Queen of England as a black woman, the bloodied uniform of a dead Bosnian soldier, a nun kissing a priest, a black stallion mounting a white mare – consistently created furore. Benetton argued that the campaigns were not about pushing sales. Nor were they intended to insult or hurt. Rather they were designed to capture people's interest, promote tolerance and provoke reflection.

There is little doubt that Benetton's shocking ads created worldwide publicity and kept its name on everybody's lips. But over the years, its campaigns have been rejected in a number of countries, from Germany to Belgium, following protests from the firm's retailers and billboard operators. Benetton has changed its style, dropping its 'shock' posters in favour of more subtle ways of communicating its business philosophy to target audiences.

The lesson: keep it pleasant, please!

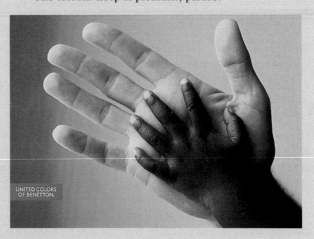

Benetton has backed away from its confrontational pitch after almost universal criticism.

Source: Benetton Group SPA

Sources: Claire Murphy, 'When the teasers become unbearable', *Marketing Week* (15 July 1994), p. 21; 'As you sow, so shall you reap' and 'Benetton cover story', *Marketing Week* (3 February 1995), pp. 5 and 21 respectively; Francine Cunningham, 'Mounting pressure', *The European* (15–21 August 1996), p. 15; Stephanie Bentley, 'Benetton risks fresh outrage', *Marketing Week* (13 September 1996), p. 9.

people with the product on attractive terms. They could work through community members such as local radio personalities, heads of local organisations or community leaders. They can also use influential people in their advertisements or develop advertising that has high 'conversation value'.

■ Non-personal communication channels

Non-personal communication channels are channels that carry messages without personal contact or feedback. They include major media, atmospheres and events. Important **media** consist of print media (newspapers, magazines, direct mail); broadcast media (radio, television); display media (billboards, signs, posters) and online media (online services, websites). **Atmospheres** are designed environments that create or reinforce the buyer's leanings towards buying a product. Thus lawyers' offices and banks are designed to communicate confidence and other factors that might be valued by their clients. **Events** are occurrences staged to communicate messages to target audiences. For example, public relations departments arrange press conferences, grand openings, shows and exhibits, public tours and other events to communicate with specific audiences (see Marketing Highlight 18.2).

Non-personal communication affects buyers directly. In addition, using mass media often affects buyers indirectly by causing more personal communication. Communications first flow from television, magazines and other mass media to opinion leaders and then from these opinion leaders to others. Thus opinion leaders step between the mass media and their audiences and carry messages to people who are less exposed to media. This suggests that mass communicators should aim their messages directly at opinion leaders, letting them carry the message to others. Pharmaceutical firms direct their new drugs promotions at the most influential doctors and medical experts first – the 'thought leaders' in the profession; if they are persuaded, their opinions have an impact upon the new product's acceptance by others in the field. Thus opinion leaders extend the influence of the mass media. Or they may alter the message or not carry the message, thus acting as gatekeepers.

■ Selecting the message source

In either personal or non-personal communication, the message's impact on the target audience is also affected by how the audience views the communicator. The credibility and attractiveness of the **message source** – the company, the brand name, the spokesperson for the brand or the actor in the ad who endorses the product – must therefore be considered.

Messages delivered by highly credible sources are more persuasive. Pharmaceutical firms want doctors to tell about their products' benefits because doctors rank high on expertise in their field, so they have high credibility. Many food companies promote to doctors, dentists and other healthcare experts to motivate these professionals to recommend their products to patients. For example, Sensodyne Toothpaste has, for years, promoted the product in dental surgeries, and ads use endorsements by dental practitioners to persuade target users to adopt the brand. To remain credible, however, the source must be perceived by the target audience as being an expert where the product is concerned, and trustworthy: that is, objective and honest in his or her opinion of the benefits claimed for the product.

Marketers also use celebrities to speak for their products. For example, as Internet firms deluge TV and radio with ads to establish brand awareness, some are roping in movie stars for advertisements. *Star Trek*'s William Shatner was used to tout the marvels of Priceline.com, in an ad campaign which promoted the company's latest line of bargain products. Whoopi Goldberg appeared in TV ads for flooz.com which sells gift vouchers.[13]

Non-personal communication channels
Channels that carry messages without personal contact or feedback, including media, atmospheres and events.

Media
Non-personal communications channels including print media (newspapers, magazines, direct mail); broadcast media (radio, television); and display media (billboards, signs, posters).

Atmospheres
Designed environments that create or reinforce the buyer's leanings towards consumption of a product.

Events
Occurrences staged to communicate messages to target audiences; examples are news conferences and grand openings.

Message source
The company, the brand name, the salesperson of the brand, or the actor in the ad who endorses the product.

marketing highlight 18.2

Celebrity parties: business with a serious side!

Parties are meant to be fun affairs. In early times, according to anthropologists, parties were occasions when people gathered for rituals, trading, finding partners and the sheer excitement of being in a larger group. Indeed, royal and celebrity parties were often given with a purpose – sometimes for fun, at times, to publicise starlets, or as showcases to impress. In May 1664, Louis XIV treated his 600 guests to a week of 'Pleasures of the Enchanted Island', arguably the bash of the millennium gone. Its purpose was to dazzle Europe. Or, perhaps, to keep entertained people who might otherwise plot in their castles against their king!

Today, royal and celebrity partying is taken no less seriously than before, not because modern-day monarchs have to guard against schemers and plotters, but because parties have become a business with a serious side to them.

Parties fall into two categories – the ones people join and the ones people go to. The latter apparently are the ones that excite and delight, create jobs and change the world. Many celebrity and business parties are put on to achieve precisely that. Aurelia Cecil, a London public relations diva, is noted for her glitzy bashes. The fashion house Versace and De Beers, the Goliath of the diamond business, approached her independently to help stage a big event, three weeks apart. Ms Cecil brought the two together, added a third name – Krug – to do the champagne and dusted the trio with a handful of 'famous' jewellers. Bon Jovi, the rock group, provided the music. Donatella Versace took care of the 'look' of the venue – London's Syon House, a stately home, boasting a Robert Adam interior and 30 acres of gardens landscaped by Capability Brown. This was just the start. Lining up her celebrity guests was not difficult – after all, Donatella Versace is a world-class celebrity herself, and so are her best friends, including Prince Charles, who was the star guest of the party. The bash raised £250,000 (€410,000) for charity, an impressive record

for an evening, and by London's standard, according to Ms Cecil. More importantly, the sponsoring companies benefited from the attendance of the constellation of celebrities, who guaranteed media coverage in every newspaper and on every television channel around the world. In all, some $20 million (€22.4 million) worth of publicity was generated.

Undoubtedly, many of the most lavish parties are carefully judged commercial events. They serve to raise money, attract publicity for sponsors and do favours that call for other favours in the future. According to *Vanity Fair*, the American magazine that has thrown celebrity parties, including ones to celebrate the Oscar awards, they are huge publicity opportunities and business positioning events. Not only do spectacular parties make great news, making a great impact on magazine sales, they attract global coverage, creating, in a sense, a showcase event, much like Louis XIV's Versailles bash in 1664.

Anthropologist William Ury, a specialist on partying patterns among humans, and an associate director of research at Harvard Law School, may have some important lessons to share with modern business managers. He argues that businesses are increasingly relationship-driven today, dominated by alliances, mergers and teams. Ury professes: 'Parties play a horizontal bridging role, giving people a different context in which to relate. They are rich venues for building new and unexpected relationships.' They 'create emotional capital', leading to people who have met each other at a party to be more willing in future to trust each other. So, it follows that, in an increasingly electronically connected world, parties should become more important for business people seeking to build trust.

Well, what are we waiting for? Let's go and party! But not to the ones people join!

SOURCES: Based on 'What fun?', *The Economist* (18 December 1999), pp. 71–2. See also William Ury, *Getting to Peace* (London: Viking, 1999); and Munro Price, *Preserving the Monarchy; the Comtede Vergennes 1774–87* (Cambridge: Cambridge University Press, 1995).

Celebrities are effective when they personify a key product attribute, but there can be a backlash, as in the case of Michael Jackson and O.J. Simpson, who were caught up in unsavoury publicity, which tarnished their credibility and esteem with the audience.

Attractiveness is associated with the prestige of the source, his or her similarity with the receiver, or the physical or personal attractiveness of the source. It is also

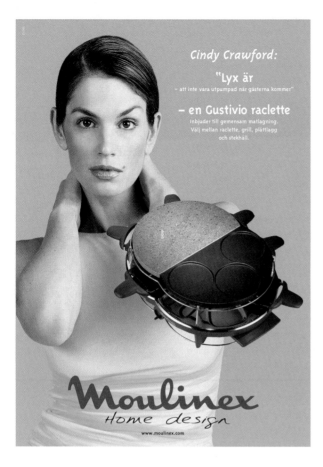

Moulinex promotes its product in association with the top model and actress Cindy Crawford.

SOURCE: Moulinex. *Agency:* DDB Needham Denmark

likely that the more attractive the source, the more he or she will be liked by the audience. It is therefore not surprising that many advertisers use well-known film stars, fashion models and top sports people to endorse their products.

collecting feedback

After sending the message, the communicator must research its effect on the target audience. This involves asking the target audience members whether they remember the message, how many times they saw it, what points they recall, how they felt about the message, and their past and present attitudes towards the product and company. The communicator would also like to measure behaviour resulting in the message – how many people bought a product, talked to others about it or visited the store.

Figure 18.5 shows an example of feedback measurement for two hypothetical brands. Looking at Brand A, we find that 80 per cent of the total market is aware of it, that 60 per cent of those aware of it have tried it, but that only 20 per cent of those who tried it were satisfied. These results suggest that although the communication programme is creating *awareness*, the product fails to give consumers the *satisfaction* they expect. Therefore, the company should try to improve the product while staying with the successful communication programme. In contrast, only 40 per cent of the total market is aware of Brand B, only 30 per cent of those aware of Brand B have tried it, but 80 per cent of those who have tried it are satisfied. In this case, the communication programme needs to be stronger to take advantage of the brand's power to obtain satisfaction.

Figure 18.5

Feedback measurements
for two brands

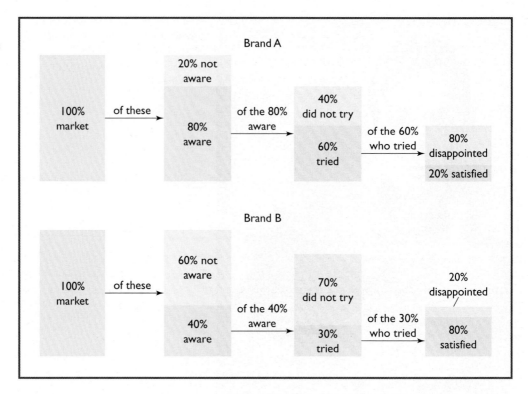

setting the total promotion budget and mix

We have looked at the steps in planning and sending communications to a target audience. But how does the company decide on the total *promotion budget* and its division among the major promotional tools to create the *promotion mix*? By what process does it blend the tools to create integrated marketing communications? We now look at these questions.

setting the total promotion budget

One of the hardest marketing decisions facing a company is how much to spend on promotion. John Wanamaker, an American department store magnate, once said: 'I know that half of my advertising is wasted, but I don't know which half. I spent $2 million for advertising, and I don't know if that is half enough or twice too much.' It is not surprising, therefore, that industries and companies vary widely in how much they spend on promotion. Promotion spending may be 20–30 per cent of sales in the cosmetics industry and only 2 or 3 per cent in the industrial machinery industry. Within a given industry, both low and high spenders can be found.

How does a company decide on its promotion budget? There are four common methods used to set the total budget for advertising: the affordable method, the percentage-of-sales method, the competitive-parity method and the objective-and-task method.[14]

■ Affordable method

A common 'rule-of-thumb' used by many companies is the **affordable method**: they set the promotion budget at the level they think the company can afford. They start with total revenues, deduct operating expenses and capital outlays, and then devote some portion of the remaining funds to advertising.

Unfortunately, this method of setting budgets completely ignores the effect of promotion on sales. It tends to place advertising last among spending priorities, even in situations where advertising is critical to the firm's success. It leads to an uncertain annual promotion budget, which makes long-range market planning difficult. Although the affordable method can result in overspending on advertising, it more often results in underspending.

■ Percentage-of-sales method

In the **percentage-of-sales method**, marketers set their promotion budget at a certain percentage of current or forecast sales. Or they budget a percentage of the unit sales price. Automotive companies usually budget a fixed percentage for promotion based on the planned car price. Fast-moving consumer goods companies usually set it at some percentage of current or anticipated sales.

The percentage-of-sales method has advantages. It is simple to use and helps managers think about the relationship between promotion spending, selling price and profit per unit. The method supposedly creates competitive stability because competing firms tend to spend about the same percentage of their sales on promotion.

Despite these claimed advantages, however, there is little to justify the method. It wrongly views sales as the *cause* of promotion rather than as the *result*.[15] The budget is based on availability of funds rather than on opportunities. It may prevent the increased spending sometimes needed to turn around falling sales. It fails to consider whether a higher or lower level of spending would be more profitable. Because the budget varies with year-to-year sales, long-range planning is difficult. Finally, the method does not provide any basis for choosing a *specific* percentage, except what has been done in the past or what competitors are doing.

■ Competitive-parity method

Other companies use the **competitive-parity method**, setting their promotion budgets to match competitors' outlays. They watch competitors' advertising or get industry promotion-spending estimates from publications or trade associations, and then set their budgets based on the industry average.

Two arguments support this method. First, competitors' budgets represent the collective wisdom of the industry. Second, spending what competitors spend helps prevent promotion wars. Unfortunately, neither argument is valid. There are no grounds for believing that the competition has a better idea of what a company should be spending on promotion than does the company itself. Companies differ greatly in terms of market opportunities and profit margins, and each has its own special promotion needs. Finally, there is no evidence that budgets based on competitive parity prevent promotion wars.

■ Objective-and-task method

The most logical budget-setting method is the **objective-and-task method**, whereby the company sets its promotion budget based on what it wants to accomplish with promotion. The method entails: (1) defining specific objectives; (2) determining the tasks needed to achieve these objectives; and (3) estimating the costs of performing these tasks. The sum of these costs is the proposed promotion budget.

Affordable method
Setting the promotion budget at the level management thinks the company can afford.

Percentage-of-sales method
Setting the promotion budget at a certain percentage of current or forecast sales or as a percentage of the sales price.

Competitive-parity method
Setting the promotion budget to match competitors' outlays.

Objective-and-task method
Developing the promotion budget by (1) defining specific objectives; (2) determining the tasks that must be performed to achieve these objectives; and (3) estimating the costs of performing these tasks. The sum of these costs is the proposed promotion budget.

The objective-and-task method forces management to spell out its assumptions about the relationship between amount spent and promotion results. But it is also the most difficult method to use. Managers have to set sales and profit targets and then work back to what tasks must be performed to achieve desired goals. Often it is hard to figure out which specific tasks will achieve specific objectives. For example, suppose Sony wants 95 per cent awareness for its latest camcorder model during the six-month introductory period. What specific advertising messages and media schedules would Sony need in order to attain this objective? How much would these messages and media schedules cost? Sony management must consider such questions, even though they are hard to answer. By comparing the campaign cost with expected profit gains, the financial viability of the promotions campaign can be determined.

The main advantage of this method is that it forces managers to define their communication objectives, to determine the extent to which each objective will be met using selected promotion tools and the financial implications of alternative communication programmes.

setting the promotion mix

The company must divide the total promotion budget among the main promotion tools – advertising, personal selling, sales promotion, public relations and direct marketing. The concept of integrated marketing communications suggests that it must blend the promotion tools carefully into a coordinated *promotion mix*. But how does the company determine what mix of promotion tools it will use? Companies within the same industry differ greatly in the design of their promotion mixes. For example, Compaq Computer relies on advertising and promotion to dealers, whereas Dell Computer uses only direct marketing.

Companies are always looking for ways to improve promotion by replacing one promotion tool with another that will do the same job more economically. Many companies have replaced a portion of their field sales activities with telephone sales and direct mail. Other companies have increased their sales promotion spending in relation to advertising to gain quicker sales.

Designing the promotion mix is even more complex when one tool must be used to promote another. Thus when British Airways decides to offer Air Miles for flying with the company (a sales promotion), it has to run ads to inform the public. When Lever Brothers uses a consumer advertising and sales promotion campaign to back a new washing powder, it has to set aside money to promote this campaign to the resellers to win their support.

Many factors influence the marketer's choice of promotion tools. We now look at these factors.

■ The nature of each promotion tool

Marketers have to understand the unique characteristics and the costs of each promotion tool in deciding the promotion mix. Let us examine each of the major tools.

Advertising The many forms of advertising make it hard to generalise about its unique qualities. However, several qualities can be noted:

+ Advertising can reach masses of geographically dispersed buyers at a low cost per exposure. For example, TV advertising can reach huge audiences.

+ Beyond its reach, large-scale advertising by a seller says something positive about the seller's size, popularity and success.

+ Because of advertising's public nature, consumers tend to view advertised products as standard and legitimate – buyers know that purchasing the product will be understood and accepted publicly.

+ Advertising enables the seller to repeat a message many times, and it lets the buyer receive and compare the messages of various competitors.

+ Advertising is also very expresssive, allowing the company to dramatise its products through the artful use of print, sound and colour.

+ On the one hand, advertising can be used to build up a long-term image for a product (such as Coca-Cola ads). On the other hand, advertising can trigger quick sales (as when a department store advertises a weekend sale).

Advertising also has some shortcomings:

+ Although it reaches many people quickly, advertising is impersonal and cannot be as persuasive as company salespeople.

+ Advertising is only able to carry on a one-way communication with the audience, and the audience does not feel that it has to pay attention or respond.

+ In addition, advertising can be very costly. Although some advertising forms, such as newspaper and radio advertising, can be done on smaller budgets, other forms, such as network TV advertising, require very large budgets.

Personal selling   Personal selling is the most effective tool at certain stages of the buying process, particularly in building up buyers' preferences, convictions and actions. Compared to advertising, personal selling has several unique qualities:

+ It involves personal interaction between two or more people, so each person can observe the other's needs and characteristics and make quick adjustments.

+ Personal selling also allows all kinds of relationships to spring up, ranging from a matter-of-fact selling relationship to a deep personal friendship. The effective salesperson keeps the customer's interests at heart in order to build a long-term relationship.

+ Finally, with personal selling the buyer usually feels a greater need to listen and respond, even if the response is a polite 'no thank you'.

These unique qualities come at a cost, however. A sales force requires a longer-term commitment than does advertising – advertising can be turned on and off, but sales force size is harder to change. Personal selling is also the company's most expensive promotion tool, costing companies several hundred euros on average per sales call.

Sales promotion   Sales promotion includes a wide assortment of tools – coupons, contests, price reductions, premium offers, free goods and others – all of which have many unique qualities:

+ They attract consumer attention and provide information that may lead to a purchase.

+ They offer strong incentives to purchase by providing inducements or contributions that give additional value to consumers.

+ Moreover, sales promotions invite and reward quick response. Whereas advertising says 'buy our product', sales promotion offers incentives to consumers to 'buy it now'.

With personal selling, the customer feels a greater need to listen and respond, even if the response is a polite 'no thank you'.

Companies use sales promotion tools to create a stronger and quicker response. Sales promotion can be used to dramatise product offers and to boost sagging sales. Sales promotion effects are usually short-lived, however, and are not effective in building long-run brand preference. To work, manufacturers must carefully plan the sales promotion campaign and offer target customers genuine value. Only then will they enhance perceived brand image, build sales and maintain customer loyalty.

Public relations Public relations or PR offers several unique qualities. It is all those activities that the organisation does to communicate with target audiences which are not directly paid for.

+ PR is very believable: news stories, features and events seem more real and believable to readers than ads do.
+ Public relations can reach many prospects who avoid salespeople and advertisements, since the message gets to the buyers as 'news' rather than as a sales-directed communication.
+ And, like advertising, PR can dramatise a company or product. The Body Shop is one of the few international companies that have used public relations as a more effective alternative to mass TV advertising.

Marketers tend to underuse public relations or to use it as an afterthought. Yet a well-thought-out public relations campaign used with other promotion-mix elements can be very effective and economical.

Direct marketing Although there are many forms of direct marketing – direct mail, telemarketing, electronic marketing, online marketing and others – they all share four distinctive characteristics.

+ Direct marketing is non-public as the message is normally addressed to a specific person.

+ Direct marketing is immediate as messages can be prepared very quickly.

+ Direct marketing can be customised, so messages can be tailored to appeal to specific customers.

+ Direct marketing is interactive: it allows a dialogue between the communicator and the consumer, and messages can be altered depending on the consumer's response.

Thus, direct marketing is well suited to highly targeted marketing efforts and to building one-to-one customer relationships.

■ Factors in setting the promotion mix

Companies consider many factors when developing their promotion mixes: namely, the type of product/market, the use of a push or pull strategy, the buyer-readiness stage and the product life-cycle stage.

Type of product/market   The importance of different promotional tools varies between consumer and business markets (see Figure 18.6). Consumer-goods companies usually put more of their funds into advertising, followed by sales promotion, personal selling and then public relations. Advertising is relatively more important in consumer markets because there are a larger number of buyers, purchases tend to be routine, and emotions play a more important role in the purchase-decision process. In contrast, industrial-goods companies put most of their funds into personal selling, followed by sales promotion, advertising and public relations. In general, personal selling is used more heavily with expensive and risky purchases, and in markets with fewer and larger sellers.

Although advertising is less important than sales calls in business markets, it still plays an important role. Advertising can build product awareness and knowledge, develop sales leads and reassure buyers. Similarly, personal selling can add a lot to consumer-goods marketing efforts. It is simply not the case that 'salespeople put products on shelves and advertising takes them off'. Well-trained consumer-goods salespeople can sign up more dealers to carry a particular brand, convince them to give more shelf space and urge them to use special displays and promotions.

Figure 18.6

Relative importance of promotion tools in consumer versus industrial markets

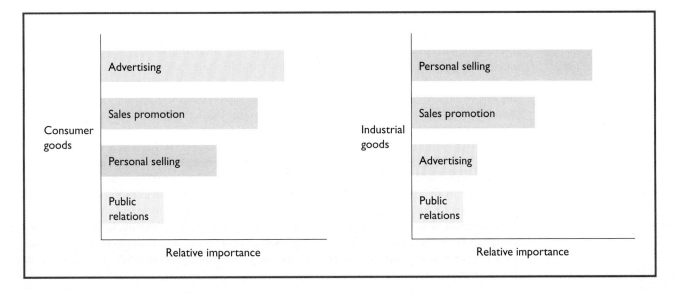

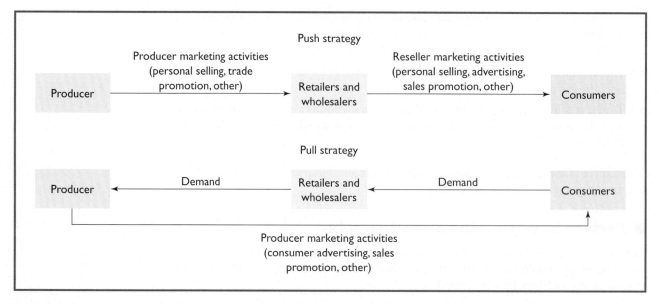

Figure 18.7

Push versus pull
promotion strategy

Push strategy

*A promotion strategy
that calls for using the
sales force and trade
promotion to push
the product through
channels. The producer
promotes the product
to wholesalers, the
wholesalers promote
to retailers, and the
retailers promote to
consumers.*

Pull strategy

*A promotion strategy
that calls for spending a
lot on advertising and
consumer promotion
to build up consumer
demand. If the strategy
is successful, consumers
will ask their retailers
for the product, the
retailers will ask the
wholesalers, and the
wholesalers will ask
the producers.*

Push versus pull strategy The promotional mix is influenced by whether the company chooses a *push* or *pull* strategy. Figure 18.7 contrasts the two strategies. A **push strategy** involves 'pushing' the product through distribution channels to final consumers. The firm directs its marketing activities (primarily personal selling and trade promotion) towards channel members to induce them to carry the product and to promote it to final consumers. Using a **pull strategy**, the producer directs its marketing activities (primarily advertising and consumer promotion) towards final consumers to induce them to buy the product. If the pull strategy is effective, consumers will then demand the product from channel members, who will in turn demand it from producers. Thus under a pull strategy, consumer demand 'pulls' the product through the channels.

Some small industrial-goods companies use only push strategies; some direct-marketing companies use only pull. However, most large companies use some combination of both. For example, Lever Brothers uses mass-media advertising to pull consumers to its products and a large sales force and trade promotions to push its products through the channels.

In recent years, consumer-goods companies have been decreasing the pull portions of their promotion mixes in favour of more push. There are a number of reasons behind this shift in promotion strategy. One is the rising cost of mass-media campaigns. Many firms have also found advertising less effective in recent years. Companies are increasing their segmentation efforts and tailoring their marketing programmes more narrowly, making national advertising less suitable than localised retailer promotions. In these days of heavy brand extensions and me-too products, many companies are finding it difficult to feature meaningful product differentiations in advertising. Instead, they differentiate their brands through price reductions, premium offers, coupons and other promotions aimed at the trade.

The growing strength of retailers is also a key factor influencing the shift from pull to push. Big retail chains in Europe have greater access now than ever before to product sales and profit information. They have the power to demand and get what they want from suppliers. And what they want is margin improvements – that is, more push. Mass advertising bypasses them on its way to the consumers, but push promotion benefits them directly. Consumer promotions give retailers an immediate sales boost and cash from trade allowances pads retailer profits. So, manufacturers are compelled to use push promotions just to obtain good shelf space and advertising support from their retailers.

However, reckless use of push promotion leads to fierce price competition and a continual spiral of price slashing and margin erosion, leaving less money to invest in the product R&D, packaging and advertising that is required to improve and maintain long-run consumer preference and loyalty. Robbing the advertising budget to pay for more sales promotion could mortgage a brand's long-term future for short-term gains. While push strategies will remain important, particularly in packaged-goods marketing, companies that find the best mix between the two – consistent advertising to build long-run brand value and consumer preference and sales promotion to create short-run trade support and consumer excitement – are most likely to win the battle for loyal and satisfied customers.[16]

Buyer-readiness stage   The effects of the promotional tools vary for the different buyer-readiness stages. Advertising, along with public relations, plays the leading role in the awareness and knowledge stages, more important than that played by 'cold calls' from salespeople. Customer liking, preference and conviction are more affected by personal selling, which is closely followed by advertising. Finally, closing the sale is mostly done with sales calls and sales promotion. Clearly, advertising and public relations are the most cost effective at the early stages of the buyer decision process, while personal selling, given its high costs, should focus on the later stages of the customer buying process.

Product life-cycle stage   The effects of different promotion tools also vary with stages of the product life cycle. In the introduction stage, advertising and public relations are good for producing high awareness, and sales promotion is useful in getting early trial. Personal selling efforts must be geared to persuading the trade to carry the product. In the growth stage, advertising and public relations continue to be powerful influences, whereas sales promotion can be reduced because fewer incentives are needed. In the mature stage, sales promotion again becomes important relative to advertising. Buyers know the brands and advertising is needed only to remind them of the product. In the decline stage, advertising is kept at a reminder level, public relations is dropped and salespeople give the product only a little attention. Sales promotion, however, might continue at a high level in order to stimulate trade and prop up sales to customers.

integrating the promotion mix

Having set the promotion budget and mix, the company must now take steps to see that all of the promotion mix elements are smoothly integrated. Here is a checklist for integrating the firm's marketing communications.

Analyse trends – internal and external – that can affect your company's ability to do business: Look for areas where communications can help the most. Determine the strengths and weaknesses of each communications function. Develop a combination of promotional tactics based on these strengths and weaknesses.

Audit the pockets of communications spending throughout the organisation: Itemise the communications budgets and tasks and consolidate these into a single budgeting process. Reassess all communications expenditures by product, promotional tool, stage of the life cycle, and observed effect.

Identify all contact points for the company and its brands: Work to ensure that communications at each point are consistent with your overall communications strategy and that your communications efforts are occurring when, where and how your *customers* want them.

Team up in communications planning: Engage all communications functions in joint planning. Include customers, suppliers and other stakeholders at every stage of communications planning.

Create compatible themes, tones and quality across all communications media: Make sure each element carries your unique primary messages and selling points. This consistency achieves greater impact and prevents the unnecessary duplication of work across functions.

Create performance measures that are shared by all communications elements: Develop systems to evaluate the combined impact of all communications activities.

Appoint a director responsible for the company's persuasive communications efforts: This move encourages efficiency by centralising planning and creating shared performance measures.[17]

socially responsible marketing communication

In shaping its promotion mix, a company must be aware of the large body of legal and ethical issues surrounding marketing communications. Most marketers work hard to communicate openly and honestly with consumers and resellers. Still, abuses may occur, and public policy makers have developed a substantial body of laws and regulations to govern advertising, personal selling, sales promotion and direct marketing activities. In this section, we discuss the issues regarding advertising, sales promotion and personal selling. Issues concerning direct marketing will be addressed in Chapter 22.

advertising and sales promotion

By law, companies must avoid false or deceptive advertising. Advertisers must not make false claims, such as suggesting that a product cures something when it does not. They must avoid ads that have the capacity to deceive, even though no one may actually be deceived. A car cannot be advertised as getting 45 km per gallon unless it does so under typical conditions, and a diet bread cannot be advertised as having fewer calories simply because its slices are thinner.

Sellers must avoid bait-and-switch advertising or deceptive sales promotions that attract buyers under false pretences. For example, a large retailer advertised a dishwashing machine at €250. However, when consumers tried to buy the advertised machine, the seller downplayed its features, placed faulty machines on showroom floors, understated the machine's performance and took other actions in an attempt to switch buyers to a more expensive machine. Such actions are both unethical and illegal.

International advertisers must also observe local rules. For example, in the United States, direct-to-consumer advertising is allowed for prescription drugs. Pharmaceutical firm Eli Lilly uses magazine advertisements to boost public awareness of its $2.4 billion (€2.7 billion) per year anti-depressant, Prozac (see Marketing Highlight 18.3). Heavy consumer promotion pushed up sales of cholesterol-lowering drugs, such as Bristol-Myers Squibb's Pravachol, Warner-Lambert's Lipitor and Merck's Zocor.[18] In Europe, such advertisements are illegal. Prescription drugs can be promoted only in medical journals and other publications where qualified physicians are presumed to browse.

marketing highlight 18.3

Promoting drugs on the Internet: for whose eyes only?

Health has overtaken pornography as the number one reason people log on to the Internet. So what? Well, for a start, European governments are facing uncharted waters where legislating for drug promotions is concerned. They are finding it impossible to impose national rules upon what is essentially a borderless medium – the Internet.

Here is an exercise. Try it and one can see why EU heads are having their minds blown in a regulatory minefield. Eli Lilly, the US pharmaceuticals company, makes the world's best-selling anti-depressant – Prozac. If you log on to the Internet, you can visit their website at www.prozac.com. The website allows you to take a test to see if you are depressed. Click and you can learn more about depression and a few other illnesses. Viewers have the opportunity to scan material about Prozac. Useful tips are just another click away – such as how to take control of the predicament, maximising the patient's recovery and caring for a loved one suffering from depression. If you like, you can even send a page to a friend!

Herein lies the problem. Throughout Europe, promotion of prescription drugs to the general public is illegal. That applies as much to the Internet as it does to television, radio or print media. Unlike in the US, promotions of these products can only be targeted at medical professionals, not prospective patients. True, a few words in fine print appear on the first page to remind viewers that 'This information is intended for U.S. residents only.'! But who's to stop European residents from scanning the material and what can authorities do if they ignore the somewhat discreet warning?

Regulators have tried banning websites. Recently, the UK regulatory body, the Medicines Control Agency, banned websites set up by Biogen and Schering, manufacturers of beta-interferon, a drug for treating multiple sclerosis, which is underutilised (and expensive) in Britain. The sites were campaigning for greater access by patients to the drug, but were deemed 'promotional' by the regulator.

Pharmaceutical firms see e-communication as a golden opportunity to strike up a dialogue with potential patients. There really is no stopping now. Companies are deciphering how best to exploit the new medium. Corporate websites typically bore customers with reams of information about their medicines. And most patients are unlikely to tap into individual companies to fish out information about their illness. Rather, more and more firms are using (more often than not, sponsoring) third parties that run disease-specific sites, like diabetes.com, mybackpain.com, sleepeasy.com and what have you.com to reach potential customers.

The regulatory loophole is a catalyst for pharmaceutical companies to redefine their communication spheres. According to Charles Beever, a consultant with Booz, Allen & Hamilton, the issue now is who owns consumers' eyeballs. Drug firms would do well to rethink ways to own the consumer, within the legal confines. Meanwhile, more and more pharmaceutical companies are set to exploit the loophole in a regulatory vacuum, which seems to suit firms fine.

Finally, if you've passed the test (i.e. clinically, you're far from depressed), give a sigh of relief! Log out, spirits up and keep smiling.

SOURCES: 'Advertising drugs. Pill pushers', *The Economist* (9 August 1997), pp. 62–3; David Pilling, 'Prozac online lifts drug sector spirits', *Financial Times* (3–4 June 2000), p. 15; insights also gained from the Eli Lilly and Company website (14 September 2000), at www.prozac.com.

A company's trade promotion activities are also closely regulated. For example, in some countries, sellers cannot favour certain customers through their use of trade promotions. They must make promotional allowances and services available to all resellers on proportionately equal terms.

Beyond simply avoiding legal pitfalls, such as deceptive or bait-and-switch advertising, companies can invest in communications to encourage and promote socially responsible programmes and actions. For example, earth-moving equipment manufacturer Caterpillar is one of several companies and environmental groups forming the Tropical Forest Foundation, which is working to save the great Amazon rainforest. It uses advertising to promote the cause and its involvement. British Telecom's sponsorship of a *Swimathon*, one of Europe's largest participatory sporting events, combined a swimming challenge with charity fundraising – the 46,000 swimmers who registered for the event raised £1.39 million (€2.28 million).[19]

personal selling

A company's salespeople must follow the rules of 'fair competition'. Some countries have enacted deceptive sales acts that spell out what is not allowed. For example, salespeople may not lie to consumers or mislead them about the advantages of buying a product. To avoid bait-and-switch practices, salespeople's statements must match advertising claims.

In business-to-business selling, salespeople may not offer bribes to purchasing agents or to others who can influence a sale. They may not obtain or use technical or trade secrets of competitors through bribery or industrial espionage. And salespeople must not disparage competitors or competing products by suggesting things that are not true.

No doubt, the laws governing sales and marketing practices differ across countries. Thus, international marketers must be fully aware of the laws and regulations governing sales and marketing communications practices, and how they differ across the countries in which they operate, when designing cross-border communications programmes. Beyond understanding and abiding by these laws and regulations, companies should ensure that they communicate honestly and fairly with consumers and resellers.

summary

Modern marketing calls for more than just developing a good product, pricing it attractively and making it available to target customers. Companies must also *communicate* with current and prospective customers, and what they communicate should not be left to chance. For most companies, the question is not *whether* to communicate, but *how much to spend* and *in what ways*.

In this chapter, we defined the company's total *marketing communications mix* – also called *promotion mix* – as the specific blend of *advertising*, *personal selling*, *sales promotion*, *public relations* and *direct marketing* tools that the company uses to pursue its advertising and marketing objectives. Advertising includes any paid form of non-personal presentation and promotion of ideas, goods or services by an identified sponsor. Personal selling is any form of personal presentation by the firm's sales force for the purpose of making sales and building customer relationships. Firms use sales promotion to provide short-term incentives to encourage the purchase or sale of a product or service. Public relations focuses on building good relations with the company's various publics by obtaining favourable unpaid publicity. Finally, firms seeking immediate response from targeted individual customers use direct marketing tools to communicate with customers.

We addressed nine elements of the communication process and how the process works: the *sender* and *receiver* are the two main parties in a communication; the *message* and *media* are the major communication tools; *encoding*, *decoding*, *response* and *feedback* are the major functions performed; and *noise* is the unplanned distortion during the process.

This chapter also identified major changes in today's marketing communications environment. First, recent shifts in marketing strategy from mass marketing to targeted or one-on-one marketing, coupled with advances in computers and information technology, have had a dramatic impact on marketing communications. Although still important, the mass media are giving way to a profusion of smaller, more focused media. Companies are doing less *broadcasting* and more *narrowcasting*. As marketing communicators adopt richer but more fragmented media and promotion mixes to reach their diverse markets, they risk creating a communication hodgepodge for consumers. To prevent this, more companies are adopting the concept of *integrated marketing communications*, which calls for carefully integrating all sources of company communication to deliver a clear and consistent message to target markets. To integrate its external communications effectively, the company must first integrate its internal communications activities. The company then works out the roles that the various promotional tools will play and the extent to which each will be used. It carefully coordinates the promotional activities and the timing of when major campaigns take place. Finally, to help implement its integrated marketing strategy, the company appoints a *marketing communications director* who has overall responsibility for the company's communications efforts.

Next, we outlined the steps involved in developing effective marketing communication. In preparing marketing communications, the communicator's first task is to *identify the target audience* and its characteristics. Next, the communicator has to define the response sought, whether it be *awareness, knowledge, liking, preference, conviction* or *purchase*. Then a *message* should be constructed with an effective content and structure. *Media* must be selected, for both personal and non-personal communication. Finally, the communicator must collect *feedback* by watching how much of the market becomes aware, tries the product and is satisfied in the process.

We moved on to explain the methods that marketers use for setting the promotion budget and factors that affect the design of the promotion mix. The most popular approaches are to spend what the company can afford, to use a percentage of sales, to base promotion on competitors' spending or to base it on an analysis and costing of the communication objectives and tasks.

The company has to divide the *promotion budget* among the major tools to create the *promotion mix*. Companies can pursue a *push* or a *pull* promotional strategy, or a combination of the two. The best blend of promotion tools depends on the type of product/market, the desirability of the buyer's readiness stage and the product life-cycle stage.

Finally, people at all levels of the organisation must be aware of the many legal and ethical issues surrounding marketing communications today. Companies must work hard and proactively at communicating openly, honestly and agreeably with their customers and reseller.

discussing the issues

1. The shift from mass marketing to targeted marketing, and the corresponding use of a richer mixture of promotion tools and communication channels, poses problems for many marketers. Using all of the promotion-mix elements suggested in the chapter, propose a plan for integrating marketing communications for the following:

    ◆ A clothing retailer that sells smart, casual attire aimed at young professional men and women.

    ◆ The launch of Nokia's new, WAP-enabled mobile communications system.

    ◆ A university's Business Studies department seeking to attract more overseas students on a master's degree programme.

    ◆ A fund-raising campaign to raise millions of euros to support development and emergency projects in less developed countries in Asia and eastern Europe.

    ◆ A new pop group.

2. List and briefly describe each of the six buyer-readiness stages through which consumers pass on their way to making a purchase. Provide your own example to illustrate how a consumer passes through these stages.

3. The marketing communicator can use one or more types of appeals or themes to produce a desired response. (a) What are these types of appeals?

(b) When should each be used? (c) Provide an example of each of type of appeal using three different magazine ads.

4. Consider a consumer-goods company that has historically set the promotion budget as a percentage of anticipated sales. Make out a case for changing the method, indicating your preferred method, and explain why.

5. Michael Jordan, Tiger Woods, Jeff Gordon and numerous Olympic athletes have had a huge impact on advertising and endorsements. Explain the positive and negative consequences of using celebrity sports figures to promote a company's products or services. What impact does the use of sports celebrity endorsers have on the average person? Is this different from the impact of other types of celebrity endorsers?

applying the concepts

1. Think of a nationally advertised product or service that has been running an advertising message for a while. Go to a bookshop, newsagent and/or the library and seek out magazines and other relevant print media that may contain print advertising for the brand you have selected. Where possible, copy examples of the ads from current and back issues of the magazines and the printed material you have accessed. Now examine the ads closely.

   ✦ How consistent are the message content, structure and format?

   ✦ Which response(s) do you think the campaign is seeking: awareness, knowledge, liking, preference, conviction or purchase?

   ✦ Do you think the ad campaign is successful in achieving the desired response? Why or why not?

2. The markets for personal and handheld computers are exploding. However, tomorrow's computers will probably be as different from today's as today's laptops are from yesterday's old 'punch card' machines. But how do you tell consumers in plain terms what they need to know about new generations of products without boring them? Computer manufacturers have learned that most consumers do not respond well to the detailed descriptions that are often needed to explain complex technological features and differences. Experts predict that more and more consumers will be surfing the Web for product information and that fewer will use traditional information sources. Select five computer manufacturers and examine their websites (for example, you can visit Sharp (www.sharp.com), IBM (www.ibm.com), NEC Computer Systems (www.nec.com), Casio (www.casio.com), Apple (www.apple.com) or Sony (www.sony.com)).

   ✦ How are the marketing communications at these websites different from those found in traditional advertising media? Develop a grid that compares and critiques the two forms of marketing communication. Assess the advantages and disadvantages of each form. Which of these websites is the most effective? Explain.

   ✦ After reviewing each site, pick a product that you might like to own (such as a laptop or handheld computer). Based solely on the websites above, which company and product most grabs your attention and purchasing interest? What information was most useful? How could the communication be improved? Would you be willing to purchase the product via the Internet? Why or why not?

references

1. Adapted from Philip Kotler and Gary Armstrong, *Principles of Marketing*, 9th edn (Upper Saddle River, NJ: Prentice Hall, 2000), Ch. 14; case material also based on information supplied by Volvo Trucks.

2. For these and other definitions, see Peter D. Bennett, *Dictionary of Marketing Terms* (Chicago, IL: American Marketing Association, 1995).

3. See Don E. Schultz, Stanley I. Tannenbaum and Robert F. Lauterborn, *Integrated Marketing Communication* (Chicago, IL: NTC, 1992), pp. 11, 17; Larry Percy, *Strategies for Implementing Integrated Marketing Communications* (Chicago, IL: NTC, 1997); and James R. Ogdan, *Developing a Creative and Innovative Integrated Marketing Communications Plan* (Upper Saddle River, NJ: Prentice Hall, 1998).

4. Michael Kubin, 'Simple days of retailing on TV are long gone', *Marketing News* (17 February 1997), pp. 2, 13.

5. Dana James, 'It'll be a wireless, wireless, wireless, wireless world', *Marketing News* (17 July 2000), pp. 25, 29.

6. Judann Pollack, 'Trade promotion luster dims for marketers, retailers', *Advertising Age* (7 April 1997), p. 18.

7. Richard Tomkins, 'End of spin and grin', *Financial Times* (2 June 2000), p. 16.

8. Schultz, Tannenbaum and Lauterborn, *Integrated Marketing Communication*, op. cit., Chs 3 and 4; Don E. Schultz, 'The inevitability of integrated communications', *Journal of Business Research* (November 1996), pp. 139–46; John F. Yarborough, 'Putting the pieces together', *Sales and Marketing Management* (September 1996), pp. 69–77.

9. For more on fear appeals, see Punam Anand Keller and Lauren Goldberg Block, 'Increasing the persuasiveness of fear appeals: the effect of arousal and elaboration', *Journal of Consumer Research* (March 1996), pp. 448–59.

10. 'Repent, ye sinners, repent', *The Economist* (24 April 1993), pp. 87–8; *Financial Times* (16 March 1992), p. 9.

11. For more on message content and structure, see Leon G. Schiffman and Leslie Lazar Kanuk, *Consumer Behavior*, 6th edn (Upper Saddle River, NJ: Prentice Hall, 1997), Chs 10, 12; Alan G. Sawyer and Daniel J. Howard, 'Effects of omitting conclusions in advertisements to involved and uninvolved audiences', *Journal of Marketing Research* (November 1991), pp. 467–74; Cornelia Pechmann, 'Predicting when two-sided ads will be more effective than one-sided ads: the role of correlational and correspondent inferences', *Journal of Marketing* (November 1992), pp. 441–53.

12. Philip Kotler, *Marketing Management: Analysis, planning, implementation and control*, 10th edn (Upper Saddle River, NJ: Prentice Hall, 2000), p. 559.

13. Garth Alexander, 'Advertising fever grips e-commerce', *The Sunday Times* (21 November 1999), p. 9.

14. For a more comprehensive discussion on setting promotion budgets, see J. Thomas Russell and W. Ronald Lane, *Kleppner's Advertising Procedure*, 14th edn (Upper Saddle River, NJ: Prentice-Hall, 1998), Ch. 6.

15. David Allen, 'Excessive use of the mirror', *Management Accounting* (June 1996), p. 12; Laura Petrecca, '4A's will study financial returns on ad spending', *Advertising Age* (April 1997), pp. 3, 52; Dana W. Hayman and Don E. Schultz, 'How much should you spend on advertising?', *Advertising Age* (26 April 1999), p. 32.

16. Louis Therrien, 'Brands on the run', *Business Week* (April 1993), pp. 26–9; Karen Herther, 'Survey reveals implications of promotion trends for the 90's', *Marketing News* (1 March 1993), p. 7; David Short, 'Advertisers come out to spend again', *The European* (12–18 August 1994), p. 21.

17. Based on Matthew Gonring, 'Putting integrated marketing communications to work today', *Public Relations Quarterly* (Fall 1994), pp. 45–8.

18. 'Pill pushers', *The Economist* (9 August 1997), pp. 62–3.

19. 'The ESCA Pan-European award nominations: corporate sponsorship', *Marketing Week* (14 February 1997).

case 18

Absolut Vodka: absolutely successful

PONTUS ALENROTH, ROBERT BJORNSTROM, JOAKIM ERIKSSON AND THOMAS HELGESSON*

Absolut Vodka's worldwide sales of 6.9 million nine-litre cases are small compared with those of the world's three leading Vodka brands, Stolichnaya (55m nine-litre cases), Moskovskaya (33m) and Russkaya (17.6m), all from the huge, Russian VAO Sojuzlodoimport. As number six in the world's sales ranking, Absolut's sales volumes are also well below those of the west's leading brand, Diageo's Smirnoff (15.9m). Absolut's trailing position is hardly surprising given it comes from Sweden, a country with highly restrictive licensing laws that do not allow spirits to be advertised. However, in the last two decades, Absolut has grown from being a little-known brand made in a country with no reputation in the spirits market to the world's leading premium brand of vodka and the leading brand in the huge US market.

When Lars Olsson Smith, Sweden's 'King of Vodka', introduced a new kind of 'Absolut Rent Brännvin' (Absolutely Pure Vodka) in 1879, little did he realise it would become the world's leading premium vodka a century later. In the nineteenth century the self-made spirits tycoon introduced a revolutionary rectification/ continuous distillation method, which is still used in producing Absolut Vodka. The result was a clear, high-quality vodka, free from dangerous and bad-tasting by-products. As its label shows, Absolut Vodka trades on its heritage:

ABSOLUT
Country of Sweden

VODKA
*This superb vodka
was distilled from grain grown
in the rich fields of Sweden.
It has been produced by the famous
old distilleries of Shus
in accordance with more than
400 years of Swedish tradition.
Vodka has been sold under the name
Absolut since 1879.*

Absolut's website (www.absolut.com) allows every aspect of the label's claims to be explored.

Despite its long traditions, Absolut Vodka's success was late in coming. In 1979, Vin & Sprit, the Swedish state-owned alcohol monopoly, decided to export the vodka to the US. After objections from American authorities, the name Absolutely Pure Vodka was changed to Absolut Vodka. Consultants had surveyed the US spirits market and found 'a clearly discernible consumer trend towards 'white spirits' [such as vodka, gin and white rum] as opposed to 'brown spirits' [brandy, whisky and dark rum]; white spirits are seen as being purer and healthier'. Vin & Sprit had no marketing or product design experience, so it employed outside teams of marketing and management experts to create a product for the newly discovered market.

The bottle continues to be the centrepiece in recent campaigns like 'Absolut Magic'. This ad reinforces the vodka's aura of exclusiveness, timelessness and sheer magic.

---

* Halstad University, Sweden. The authors wrote the original case 'Absolut Vodka: Absolutely Successful' on which this case is based.

The design of the bottle was recognised at an early stage as crucial to success. Absolut's Gunner Broman had the idea when he saw some eighteenth-century medicine bottles in a Stockholm antique shop. The bottles were elegant, different, simple and very Swedish. In reality, vodka was sold as a medicine in similar bottles during the eighteenth and nineteenth centuries. Broman argued his case for more than a year until the bottle was finally approved and the manufacturing problems were overcome. The resulting Absolut bottle was very different from that of competitors. It was considered a masterpiece in glass design; a timeless shape with fine lines and the exceptionally clear glass that distinguish Absolut from other premium vodkas.

Absolut's acceptance in the US market did not come easy. When Absolut's team first presented their ideas to New York agency NW Ayer, some of the agency's staff were thrilled but most shook their heads thinking 'who wants to drink a vodka from Sweden anyway?'. But, after many meetings, they agreed on the theme of 'Absolut Country of Sweden Vodka'. The bottle should be made of clear glass with silver text on it. They tested their idea by putting their bottles among the other big brands to see how it looked.

One of the people working with the Absolut account, Myron Poloner, fell in love with the bottle. He could sit and watch the 'medicine bottle' for hours and one night it struck him. The bottle should have no label at all. You should be able to see right through it. The vodka should be a premium vodka for well-educated people with a high income who could afford to eat out. They liked to hold parties at their home and to show off.

Attempts to sell the idea to US distributors met with the same cool reaction as the early meetings with the ad agency. 'Who has ever heard of a Swedish vodka? And it doesn't have a label. It'll disappear on the shelf. It will never sell!'

Carillion Importers Ltd, based in Manhattan, had a different view. Carillion's leader, Al Singer, accepted 'the challenge' the moment he saw the product. However, the company only had one salesman, Michel Roux, but he was to play a leading role in the success of Absolut Vodka. Singer did not want to work with a big New York agency, preferring instead Martin Landey Arlow. Landey and Singer also wanted to change the bottle, making it taller and with a thicker bottom. One day, as a joke, one of Broman's employees put a coin on the bottle's shoulder. The Americans loved it, so his staff decided to create a seal. They tried shields, swords, guns, naked women, men's heads etc. Broman's office was coincidentally located in Absolut's founder Lars Olsson Smith's old house. While there he thought, why not put 'The king of vodka's' head on the seal? The president of Vin & Sprit AB, Lars Lindmark, decided that the ABSOLUT VODKA letters should be blue for the 80 proof bottles and red for the 100 proof ones. And so the bottle changed to that we know today.

Unfortunately, Martin Landey had to stop acting for Carillion because of a conflict of interest with another, more profitable client in the spirits business. TBWA, another New York agency, heard about Carillion, contacted Singer and got the account. Geoff Hayes and Graham Turner were assigned to Absolut. One evening Hayes was sketching while watching TV. Trying to find a symbol of purity and simplicity, he made a halo. Soon his floor was covered with different ad-ideas, all with a humorous twist. The next day, he showed his ads to Turner. They changed the name for the Absolut Purity ad to Absolut Perfection. Absolut Heaven showed the bottle with wings. Fifteen minutes later they had a dozen different Absolut 'something' ads.

The Absolut, Carillion and TBWA staff loved the idea 'All advertising should centre around the bottle, the product should not be identified with any particular lifestyle, and the approach should have a timeless yet contemporary feel to it.' Every advertisement has two features in common: the depiction of an Absolut bottle and a two- or three-word caption beginning with the word 'Absolut'. It hit the US market in 1979 and Absolut soon became the biggest-selling imported vodka brand.

The innovative way of marketing Absolut contrasted directly with that of the established brands. As David Wachsman points out, the advertising of spirits in the United States used 'one of three formats: a roomful of exceedingly happy people, a celebrity holding a glass or old-fashioned settled family life'. Then came 'Absolut Perfection' and hundreds of different ads.

Absolut Vodka is a highly premium priced vodka and therefore has an aura of up-market exclusiveness. Considering the target market and the early magazine ads (Absolut Perfection, etc.), a tie-up with the arts world was inevitable. The first step in this direction was taken in 1985 when the New York cult pop artist Andy Warhol was commissioned to paint the Absolut Vodka bottle. Today Absolut cooperates with artists and designers in all the contemporary arts. 'The purity and clarity' of the product, says Gären Lundquist, President of The Absolut Company, a part of the Vin & Sprit Group, is a 'timeless source of inspiration'. There are now over 3,000 works in the Absolut collection. All feature some aspect of the bottle or its label. Like other very successful campaigns, the marketing is so sensational that the product receives a huge amount of free media exposure. In Absolut's case this has even occurred in markets, like Sweden, that did not allow alcohol advertising.

Absolut's unconventional marketing has generated demand for its ads – the advertising agency receives thousands of requests for ad reprints. The ads have become a modern icon. Besides winning the Effie and the Kelly awards, Absolut was honoured with an induction into America's Marketing Hall of Fame. That seal of approval confirmed Absolut's success and impact on the American lifestyle, especially since the only other brands that have received such an honour are Coke and Nike. 'Absolut Art' is also achieving international recognition. Warhol's and other key US works, together with others specially commissioned from French artists Bosser and Delprat, were shown at Paris's prestigious Lavignes-Bastille Gallery. From there, the exhibition moved to London's Royal College of Art, where new works by British artists, including Peter Blake, were added. The exhibition then travelled to Berlin, Munich and Milan. Over 350 artists and fashion designers have now produced Absolut ads. Their cult status is reflected in home3.swipenet.se and www.absolutad.org, websites dedicated to Absolut art.

An ingenious bottle and creative marketing played a crucial part in the Absolut saga, but Vin & Sprit's distribution partnership was also crucial to its success. However, Absolut had to bid farewell to Carillion, its original distributor. After a long and fruitful relationship, Absolut had outgrown Carillion. The new choice was the Canadian company Seagram, one of the world's leading alcohol distributors with a distribution network spanning 150 countries. With Seagram's help the Absolut Company intended to reinforce Absolut's presence in new markets, notably in Russia and Europe. It also hoped to increase its penetration in the more than 100 countries where Absolut is already present.

The Absolut Akademi aims to create 'a competitive edge through people'. 'The goal is to build a quality culture around a quality product.' Another tool in marketing is the *Absolut Reflexions* magazine, which is distributed in all markets. Used as a PR tool, *Absolut Reflexions* spreads news of the brand, its advertising and activities to consumers all over the world.

Vin & Sprit hopes to follow Absolut's success in the US with attacks on the European, Asian and Pacific markets. Compared with the United States, the European market is slow growing, fragmented and conservative. Europe has many leisure drinking cultures, but these vary from region to region and there are well-established traditions everywhere. Except for countries where vodka is the national drink, the European vodka market is underdeveloped. Vodka is drunk by only 4 per cent of consumers in Europe, compared to 21 per cent of Americans. To repeat its American success, Absolut will need clever and innovative strategies tailored specifically for each of Europe's submarkets. Vin & Sprit is bullish about Absolut's chances in Europe. 'We have built up a wide experience of operating abroad and we are confident we can meet the competition', says Vin & Sprit's Margareta Nyström. The company believes that wherever there is a demand for premium vodka, Absolut Vodka is the optimal choice. 'Absolut Vodka proves itself time and time again as more than just a fine vodka: it's an idea. And nothing can stop an idea whose time has come.'

Unfortunately, it appears that, while Absolut's 'time has come', Seagram's has gone. After years as one of the world's leading spirits distributors, Seagram has decided to dump Absolut, alongside its other spirits brands, to concentrate on entertainment. Pernod and Diageo agreed to pay $8.15bn (€9.2bn) to carve up Seagram's drinks business between them. For the $3bn it contributed, Pernod obtained Chivas Regal scotch, Martell cognac and Seagram's Gin and many smaller brands. Absolut's distribution rights will be part of a separate deal. Both Pernod and Bacardi are eyeing the Absolut account, which Vin & Sprit expects to go for $700m to $800m. Pernod is keen: 'We intend to enlarge our own distribution network by adding Seagram people. We have 45 people at the moment and will increase that to about 75. At this stage we are open to every possibility.'

Questions

1. What is the foundation of Absolut Vodka's success? Is it the vodka, the bottle, the distribution or the promotion?

2. How does Absolut's marketing build upon American trends in the late 1980s and early 1990s? Is Absolut a fashion product that will decline with the trends?

3. Do you believe that Absolut Vodka 'is an idea whose time has come' and that nothing can stop its success?

4. Vin & Sprit's European campaign uses ads in the same style that has been so successful in the United States. Do you think the US approach will work in other regions?

5. Since Absolut Vodka is such a lifestyle product, would you recommend that Vin & Sprit should extend the brand into other markets in the same way as Virgin has extended into video games, PCs, cola and vodka?

6. Absolut's successful advertising has benefited greatly from the publicity it generated. Can advertising campaigns be designed to create such media attention or is their success just good fortune?

SOURCES: Andrew Edgecliff-Johnson, 'Drinks disposal leave Seagram with hangover', *Financial Times* (20 November 2000), p. 36; John Thornhill, 'Trying to make selling spirits seriously easy', *Financial Times* (1 September 2000), p. 16; Damian Reece, 'Pernod set to win Absolut vodka war', *Electronic Telegraph* (24 December 2000), Issue 2039; www.absolut.com; www.absolutad.org; home3.swipenet.se.

internet exercises

Internet exercises for this chapter can be found on the student site of the MYPHLIP Web Site at www.booksites.net/kotler.

chapter nineteen

Mass communications: advertising, sales promotion and public relations

Chapter objectives *After reading this chapter, you should be able to:*

✦ Define the roles of advertising, sales promotion and public relations in the promotion mix.

✦ Describe the main decisions involved in developing an advertising programme.

✦ Explain how sales promotion campaigns are developed and implemented.

✦ Explain how companies use public relations to communicate with their publics.

introduction

The questions in the preview case overleaf get us to think about the alternative mass-marketing options open to marketers seeking to communicate with their target customers and to evoke desired responses. In this chapter, we address the major non-personal forms of communication and promotion. Personal selling is discussed in Chapter 20, whereas direct marketing and online approaches are examined in Chapter 22.

Companies must do more than offer good products or services. They must inform consumers about product or service benefits and carefully position these in consumers' minds. To do this, they must skilfully use the mass-promotion tools of *advertising*, *sales promotion* and *public relations*. In this chapter, we take a closer look at each of these tools.

advertising

Advertising can be traced back to the very beginnings of recorded history. Archaeologists working in the countries around the Mediterranean Sea have dug up signs announcing various events and offers. The Romans painted walls to announce gladiator fights, and the Phoenicians painted pictures promoting their wares on large

preview case

Barclays' bloomers

If Charles Colbet is correct and 'Imitation is the sincerest form of flattery', Barclays Bank must be pleased with Sara Dunlop's 60-second film *Big*. In it, Johnny introduces the big things in his life: mortgage, family and debts. In a series of tracking shots, we see his unsavoury world in London's West End, until he floats ghostlike through a swish foyer, takes a lift and climbs up on the roof. He's ready for 'the big drop' and it's at this point that any laughs are choked. The film is shown to support the sale of the *Big Issue*, a magazine sold by London's homeless. She shot the film in a day, using the ad agency Bartle Bogle Hegarty's reception area as the swanky foyer, and gave the movie to the *Big Issue*. The hard-hitting film was short-listed for the Switch2.net Short Film which is partly sponsored by Barclays.

Sara Dunlop's shot is a far cry from the Barclays' own big-budget, 'big is best' campaign starring Oscar-winning Sir Anthony Hopkins and made by Tony (Top Gun) Scott. The TV advert, which closes with the slogan 'A Big World Needs a Big Bank', positions Barclays as one of the world's largest banks. The 'big is best' was part of Barclays' response to low-cost Internet banks, Barclays being Britain's leading bricks-and-bytes Internet bank.

Barclays chose to boast of its bigness after 30 years in which it had declined from being one of the world's largest banks to a follower in the UK market. It is hard to exaggerate how far Barclays' eye had been off the banking ball. A story from a book by Martin Weyer gives some idea:

> In the late 1960's, two of Barclays' most senior executives from the London head office decreed that fish be eaten with two forks, 'in the manner of East Anglian Quakers'. Later, while the two were on holiday, a manager decided to modernise by allowing people to eat fish with a knife and fork. When the grandees returned from holiday, the offending manager was given a posting thousands of miles from London.

Like many other banks, Barclays' declining fortunes followed a series of risky loans to homeowners, small business, US banks, Russia and Robert Maxwell. London's 'Big Bang' deregulation gave the Bank a chance to consolidate its misfortunes by founding BZW, an investment bank. One of Barclays' employees noted: 'This new vision was a wonderful way of finding jobs for our people. But it had one weakness . . . we did not have the right people.'

After years of decline, Barclays now has a new, uncompromising chief executive, Matthew Barrett: 'We are an economic enterprise, not a government agency, and therefore have obligations to conduct our business in a way that provides a decent return to the owners of the business. We will continue to make value-maximising decisions without sentimentality or excuse.'

Mr Barrett's statement, in a letter to Barclays' employees, came at the start of a public outcry fired by their 'big is best' campaign and other unpopular actions:

+ Having lots of branches, the bank had many automatic teller machines (ATM) that were being increasingly used by users of Internet banks who had no such facility. Under an old agreement, Barclays charged the customer's bank for each of these transactions, who themselves often recharged their own customer a 'disloyalty charge' of up to £1.50. Barclays' idea was to charge the customer £1 (€1.64) directly.

+ Closing down 171 small branches on the same day. This still had Barclays closing fewer branches than competitors, but in one big bang. The result was Barclays being seen as deserting, since Barclays' branches were often the only ones left in rural communities.

+ The disclosure that Barclays' chairman's salary had quadrupled and Mr Barrett was to be paid £1.3m for three months' work.

This led Mr Weyer to exclaim: 'Barclays is no longer a "big bank" except in the way it pays its chairman and chief executive.' Sir Anthony Hopkins had to defend himself: 'I'll just have to set the record straight by saying that I do not run Barclays Bank.'

The self-proclaimed big bank was soon eating humble pie:

+ The proposed ATM charges were withdrawn.

+ In a deal with other banks, Barclays agreed to pay to enable Post Offices to provide a service where most branches had closed.

+ A £1m 'environmental regeneration' scheme was launched at 120 sites around the country.

At their annual general meeting Barclays' chairman, Sir Peter Middleton, admitted: 'Our execution and PR has not been of the best.' He was, however, able to report a 24 per cent increase in the retail division's profits.[1]

Questions:

1. Given Barclays' profits outturn, was Barclays 'big is best' campaign successful?

2. Account for Barclays' choice of personality and slogan in their campaign.

3. Comment on Sir Peter's admission that: 'Our execution and PR has not been of the best.'

rocks along parade routes. A Pompeii wall painting praised a politician and asked for votes. During the Golden Age in Greece, town criers announced the sale of cattle, crafted items and even cosmetics. An early 'singing commercial' went as follows: 'For eyes that are shining, for cheeks like the dawn. For beauty that lasts after girlhood is gone. For prices in reason, the woman who knows will buy her cosmetics from Aesclyptos.'

Modern advertising, however, is a far cry from these early efforts. In the EU, advertisers now run up an estimated annual advertising bill of more than $75 billion (€84 billion); worldwide ad spending exceeds $414 billion.[2] We define **advertising** as any paid form of non-personal presentation and promotion of ideas, goods or services through mass media such as newspapers, magazines, television or radio by an identified sponsor. Advertising is used by business firms, non-profit organisations, professionals and social agencies to communicate specific messages to various target publics. Advertising is a good way to inform and persuade, whether the purpose is to build brand preference for Nokia mobile phones worldwide, to get consumers in a developing country to drink more milk or to encourage smokers to give up the habit. Advertising is used in order to stimulate a response from the target audience. The response may be perceptual in nature: for example, the consumer develops specific views or opinions about the product or brand, or these feelings are altered by the ad. The response could be behavioural: for instance, the consumer buys the product or increases the amount that he or she buys.

Advertising
Any paid form of non-personal presentation and promotion of ideas, goods or services by an identified sponsor.

important decisions in advertising

Marketing management must make five important decisions when developing an advertising programme (see Figure 19.1).

setting objectives

The first step in developing an advertising programme is to set *advertising objectives*. These objectives should be based on decisions about the target market, positioning and marketing mix, which define the job that advertising must achieve in the total marketing programme.

Figure 19.1

Main advertising decisions

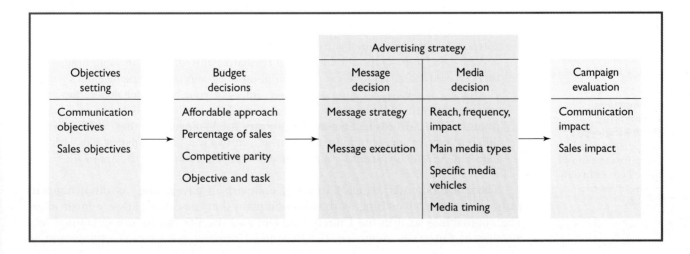

Table 19.1

Possible advertising objectives

To inform
+ Telling the market about a new product.
+ Suggesting new uses for a product.
+ Informing the market of a price change.
+ Explaining how the product works.

+ Describing available services.
+ Correcting false impressions.
+ Reducing buyers' fears.
+ Building a company image.

To persuade
+ Building brand preference.
+ Encouraging switching to your brand.
+ Changing buyer perceptions of product attributes.

+ Persuading buyers to purchase now.
+ Persuading buyers to receive a sales call.

To remind
+ Reminding buyers that the product may be needed in the near future.
+ Reminding buyers where to buy the product.

+ Keeping the product in buyers' minds during off seasons.
+ Maintaining top-of-mind product awareness.

Advertising objective
A specific communication task to be accomplished with a specific target audience during a specific period of time.

Informative advertising
Advertising used to inform consumers about a new product or feature and to build primary demand.

Persuasive advertising
Advertising used to build selective demand for a brand by persuading consumers that it offers the best quality for their money.

Comparison advertising (knocking copy)
Advertising that compares one brand directly or indirectly to one or more other brands.

An **advertising objective** is a specific communication task to be accomplished with a specific target audience during a specific period of time.[3] Advertising objectives can be classified by purpose: that is, whether their aim is to inform, persuade or remind. Table 19.1 lists examples of each of these objectives.

Informative advertising is used heavily when introducing a new product category. In this case, the objective is to build primary demand. Thus producers of compact disc players first informed consumers of the sound and convenience benefits of CDs. **Persuasive advertising** becomes more important as competition increases. Here, the company's objective is to build selective demand. For example, when compact disc players became established and accepted, Sony began trying to persuade consumers that its brand offered the best quality for their money.

Some persuasive advertising has become **comparison advertising**, in which a company directly or indirectly compares its brand with one or more other brands:

Among the most frequent users of comparison advertising or *knocking copy* is the car industry. In the UK, Korean car maker Hyundai sought to raise awareness of its cars with a series of light-hearted efforts: 'Even a kettle has a longer guarantee than Rover'. Another example was the war of words between two yellow-fat manufacturers. Van den Bergh, part of Unilever, provoked a battle with a campaign for its low-fat spread, Delight, that made taste comparisons with St Ivel Gold, produced by Unigate, and parodied some of its ad lines. St Ivel retaliated with an ad for its Gold brand that targeted Flora, another Van Den Bergh product, and turned one of Flora's catchlines, 'For your blooming generation', into 'For your ballooning generation'. The argument was that Flora contained twice as much fat as Gold. This led to a telling-off from the UK's Advertising Standards Authority (ASA) on grounds that, as Flora was a different type of spread (a full-fat margarine), St Ivel was not comparing like with like. The ASA finally urged both advertisers to refrain from using the approach.[4]

There are potential dangers in using comparison advertising. As often happens with comparison advertising, both sides complain that the other's ads are misleading. The approach is legal in the United Kingdom and the US, but its use is banned in a number of European countries. Belgium and Germany regard it as tantamount to

Comparative advertising: this ad reflects the 'war of words' between St Ivel (Gold) and Van den Bergh (Flora).

SOURCE: UNIQ plc

unfair competition. For example, a relatively innocuous Carlsberg commercial with the tagline 'Probably the best lager in the world' could not be run in those countries because it implicitly identified with products offered by rivals. Similarly, the car-hire company Avis's 'We try harder' ad would not be allowed in Germany because, although nobody is named, Hertz, the no. 1, is presumed to be the only real competitor. Efforts to produce a European directive to harmonise rules on comparative advertising across the EU have been relatively unsuccessful to date. Until such a directive is issued, however, advertisers in the region must remain sensitive to individual nations' codes of practice and legislation. This style of communication will probably always exist in one form or another, as most advertising is essentially comparative – after all, the aim of the advertiser is to persuade the consumer to respond to one product offering rather than another.[5]

Reminder advertising is important for mature products as it keeps consumers thinking about the product. Expensive Coca-Cola ads on television are often designed to remind people about Coca-Cola, not merely to inform or persuade them.

Advertisers might also seek to assure existing customers that they have made the right choice. For example, car firms might use reinforcement advertising that depicts satisfied owners enjoying some special feature of their new car.

Reminder advertising
Advertising used to keep consumers thinking about a product.

setting the advertising budget

After determining its advertising objectives, the company next sets its *advertising budget* for each product. The company wants to spend the amount needed to achieve the sales goal. Four commonly used methods for setting promotion budgets were discussed in Chapter 18. Here we describe some specific factors that should be considered when setting the advertising budget:

+ *Stage in the product life cycle*. New products typically need large advertising budgets to build awareness and to gain consumer trial. Mature brands usually require lower budgets as a ratio to sales.

+ *Market share*. High-market-share brands usually need more advertising spending as a percentage of sales than do low-share brands. Building the market or taking share from competitors requires larger advertising spending than does simply maintaining current share.

+ *Competition and clutter*. In a market with many competitors and high advertising clutter, a brand must be advertised more heavily to be noticed above the noise in the market.

+ *Advertising frequency*. When many repetitions are needed to present the brand's message to consumers, the advertising budget must be larger.

+ *Product differentiation*. A brand that closely resembles other brands in its product class (coffee, laundry detergents, chewing gum, beer, soft drinks) requires heavy advertising to set it apart. When the product differs greatly from competitors, advertising can be used to point out the differences to consumers.[6]

No matter what method is used, setting the advertising budget is no easy task. How does a company know if it is spending the right amount? Some critics maintain that large consumer packaged-goods firms tend to overspend on advertising, while industrial companies generally underspend on advertising. They also claim that, on the one hand, the large consumer companies use lots of image advertising extensively without really knowing its effects, overspending as a form of 'insurance' against not spending enough. Furthermore, what these companies decide to spend is based on traditional rules-of-thumb, such as what can be afforded or normal industry advertising/sales ratios, which have little local validity.[7] On the other hand, industrial advertisers tend to rely too heavily on their sales forces to bring in orders, underestimating the power of the company and product image in pre-selling to industrial customers. Thus they do not spend enough on advertising to build customer awareness and knowledge.

Companies have built sophisticated statistical models to determine the relationship between promotional spending and brand sales, and to help determine the 'optimal investment' across various media. Still, because so many factors affect advertising effectiveness, some controllable and other not, measuring the results of advertising spending remains an inexact science. In most cases, managers must rely on large doses of judgement along with more quantitative analysis when setting advertising budgets.[8]

advertising strategy

Advertising strategy covers two major elements: creating the advertising messages and selecting the advertising media. In the past, most companies developed messages and media independently. The creative department first created the ad, then the media department selected the best media for carrying the advertisements to the desired target audiences. Separation of the functions often caused friction between creatives and media planners.

Today, however, media fragmentation, soaring media costs and more focused target marketing strategies have promoted the importance of the media planning function. In some cases, an advertising campaign might begin with a good message idea followed by the choice of appropriate media. In other cases, however, a campaign might begin with a good media opportunity, followed by advertisements designed to take advantage of that opportunity. Increasingly, companies are realising the benefits of planning these two important activities jointly.

Thus, more and more advertisers are orchestrating a closer harmony between their messages and the media that deliver them. Media planning is no longer an after-the-fact complement to a new ad campaign. Media planners are now working more closely than ever with creatives to allow media selection to help shape the creative process, often before a single ad is written. In some cases, media people are even initiating ideas for new campaigns.

Among the more noteworthy ad campaigns based on tight media-creative partnerships is the pioneering campaign for Absolut vodka, marketed by Seagram.

The Absolut team and its ad agency meet once each year with a slew of magazines to set Absolut's media schedule. The schedule consists of up to 100 magazines, ranging from consumer and business magazines to theatre playbills. The agency's creative department is charged with creating media-specific ads. The result is a wonderful assortment of very creative ads for Absolut, tightly targeted to audiences of the media in which they appear. For example, an 'Absolut Bravo' ad in playbills has roses adorning a clear bottle, whereas business magazines contain an 'Absolut Merger' foldout. In some cases, the creatives even developed ads for magazines not yet on the schedule, such as a clever 'Absolut Centerfold' ad for *Playboy* magazine. The ad portrayed a clear, unadorned playmate bottle ('11-inch bust, 11-inch waist, 11-inch hips'). In all, Absolut has developed more than 500 ads for the almost two-decade-old campaign. At a time of soaring media costs and cluttered communication channels, a closer cooperation between creative and media people has paid off handsomely for Absolut. Largely as a result of its breakthrough advertising, Absolut now captures a 63 per cent share of the imported vodka market.[9]

■ Creating the advertising message

No matter how large the budget, advertising can succeed only if commercials gain attention and communicate well.

The changing message environment Good advertising messages are especially important in today's costly and cluttered advertising environment. The average consumer has numerous television channels and radio stations and thousands of magazines to choose from. Add the countless catalogues, direct-mail and online ads and a continuous barrage of other out-of-home media. Consumers are bombarded with ads at home, at work and at all points in between!

If all this advertising clutter bothers some consumers, it also causes big problems for advertisers – it is very costly. Network TV advertisers could pay tens to hundreds of thousands of euros for a 30-second slot during a popular prime-time TV programme. Also, their ads are sandwiched in with a clutter of other commercials, announcements and network promotions in any viewing hour.

Until recently, television viewers were pretty much a captive audience for advertisers. Viewers had only a few channels to choose from. But with the growth in cable TV, video cassette recorders and remote-controlled technologies, today's audience can also tune out ads by either watching commercial-free channels or 'zapping' commercials by pushing the 'fast-forward' button during taped programmes. With remote-control, they can instantly turn off the sound during a commercial or 'zip' around channels to see what else is on.

Thus, just to gain and hold attention, today's advertising messages must be better planned, more imaginative, more innovative, more entertaining and more rewarding to consumers. Creative strategy, even intentionally controversial ads, will play an increasingly important role in helping advertisers break through the clutter and gain attention for their products.

Message strategy The first step in creating effective advertising messages is to decide what general message will be communicated to consumers – to plan the *message strategy*. Generally, the purpose of advertising is to get target consumers to think about or react to the product or company in a certain way. People will respond only if they believe they will benefit from doing so. Thus, developing an effective message strategy usually begins with identifying target customer *benefits* that can be used as advertising appeals. Ideally, advertising message strategy follows directly from the company's broader positioning strategy.

Message strategy statements tend to be plain, straightforward outlines of benefits and positioning points that the advertiser wants to stress. The advertiser must develop a compelling *creative concept* – or '*big idea*' – that will bring the message strategy to life in a distinctive and memorable way. At this stage, simple message ideas become great ad campaigns. Usually, a copywriter and art director will team up to generate many creative concepts, hoping that one of these concepts will turn out to be the big idea. The creative concept may emerge as a visualisation, a phrase or a combination of the two.[10]

How should advertising planners evaluate advertising messages? Generally, the creative concept should guide the choice of specific appeals to be used in an ad campaign. Advertising appeals should have three characteristics. First, they should be *meaningful*, pointing out benefits that make the product more desirable or interesting to target customers. Second, appeals must be *believable*. This objective is difficult because many consumers doubt the truth of advertising in general. One study found that a full one-third of the public rates advertising messages as 'unbelievable'.[11] Advertisers also argue that the most meaningful and believable benefits may not be the best ones to feature. However, more recently, a number of companies have challenged conventional wisdom and successfully used advertising that stresses honesty in selling to consumers. Consumer scepticism is not surprising since many ads sell the notion that the product is bigger, better, brighter or far longer-lasting than rival offerings. Companies such as IKEA and Guinness have recently adopted a different tack – they aknowledge that their service or product is not perfect, and then, they turn these 'failures' into winning advertising copy (see Marketing Highlight 19.1).

Nonetheless, appeals should be *distinctive* in terms of telling consumers how the product is different from competing brands. For example, the most meaningful benefit of owning a wristwatch is that it keeps accurate time, yet few watch ads feature this benefit. Instead, based on the distinctive benefits they offer, watch advertisers might select any of a number of advertising concepts. For years, Timex has been the affordable watch that 'Takes a lickin' and keeps on tickin'. In contrast, Swatch has featured style, fun and fashion, whereas Rolex stresses luxury and status. Advertisers should therefore pre-test each ad to determine that it has the maximum impact, believability and appeal.

Message execution The advertiser now has to turn the 'big idea' into an actual ad execution that will capture the target market's attention and their interest. The impact of the message depends not only on *what* is said, but also on *how* it is said.

The creative people must find the best style, tone, words and format for executing the message. Any message can be presented in different *execution styles*, such as the following:

✦ *Slice of life.* This style shows one or more people using the product in a normal setting (e.g. the 'Oxo' gravy commercials which show the role of the mother who is tolerant of the domestic impositions of other members of her family).

✦ *Lifestyle.* This style shows how a product fits in with a particular lifestyle. For example, the 'After Eight' mints UK advertisement (elegant dinner party in a period house) appeals to aspirations more than anything else.

marketing highlight 19.1

Honesty – our best policy!

There is a saying that goes: Honesty is the best policy. Well, that is precisely what Swedish furniture retailer IKEA wants to communicate to its target audience in a recent ad campaign that tries to explain the retailer's shortcomings.

In a bold new campaign, IKEA tells people the truth about IKEA stores. The ad features a tattooed giant who shouts about the furniture store's long queues, its lack of assistants and the hassle of self-assembly. He makes it clear that if IKEA built everything, gave great service and home deliveries, then it wouldn't be IKEA! Al Young, from IKEA's ad agency, St Luke's, explains that customers have service expectations. But IKEA, to be honest, is not about service. You only need to look at its 'hellishly overcrowded' stores to appreciate this, according to Young. Customers are therefore spared all that 'better, bigger, brighter' advertising hype and told the truth and why IKEA is like it is. So far, IKEA thinks that it is working and business remains buoyant, so much so that the retailer is set to open 20 more stores in the UK in the coming years.

Another example of this new culture of honesty is seen in Guinness's latest attempt to advertise one of the most annoying things about drinking stout – the long pouring time. Drinkers get fed up waiting for Guinness to be poured. The company therefore decided to tackle this in its recent ad campaign using the strapline, 'Good things come to those who wait'.

Finally, Skoda has also rolled up to the 'truth zone'. According to a spokesperson from Fallon, its advertising agency, Skoda has a strong engineering heritage, but although many people have heard of the brand, Skoda suffers from a poor image. There was a need to address the gap between reality and perception. The agency addressed this essential truth about the product and came up with a down-to-earth campaign that says apologetically: 'It's a Skoda. Honest.' In the UK, the British self-deprecating sense of humour did help. The campaign seems to be proving a success as sales are improving and, for the first time in its history, a waiting list exists for one of its models.

Why stress failure? According to these companies, their brand has essential benefits to offer target consumers. These campaigns reflect a confidence that the brand can overcome its weakness and negative perceptions. Moreover, differentiating the brand using 'truthful advertising' not only sets them apart from major rivals, but enables them to compete with limited marketing budgets. For example, IKEA's £6 million (€9.84 million) advertising budget in the UK is miniscule, compared to that of competitors such as DFS, which spends £30 million on advertising a year. Skoda's £36 million is dwarfed by the spends of brands such as Volkswagen (its parent), which has an outlay of £52 million for promoting its VW-branded vehicles. 'When you can't beat them, why join 'em?' is the sentiment that lies at the heart of this new culture of honesty that is making inroads into the marketing mix. Glossy ads will not sell, but truth will.

So, advertising your faults may indeed be the best policy!

SOURCE: Based on Emma Halls, 'Roll up to the truth zone', *The Times* (7 July 2000), p. 30.

✦ *Fantasy.* This style creates a fantasy around the product or its use. For instance, many ads are built around dream themes. Gap introduced a perfume named Dream. Ads show a woman sleeping blissfully and suggests that the scent is 'the stuff that clouds are made of'.

✦ *Mood or image.* This style builds a mood or image around the product, such as beauty, love or serenity. No claim is made about the product except through suggestion. Timotei shampoo employs the mood for nature and simplicity – a strategy that has worked successfully in many countries across the globe.

✦ *Musical.* The ad is built around a song or some well-known music, so that emotional responses to the music are associated with the product. For example, one of the most famous ads in history was a Coca-Cola ad built around the song, 'I'd like to teach the world to sing'.

✦ *Personality symbol.* This style creates a character that represents the product. The character might be *animated* (e.g. the Jolly Green Giant, Garfield the Cat) or *real* (e.g. Eric Cantona and Les Ferdinand for Nike's 'Kick It' campaign).

✦ *Technical expertise.* This style shows the company's expertise in making the product. Thus Maxwell House shows one of its buyers carefully selecting the coffee beans, and Audi cars implies superiority with 'Vorsprung durch Technik'.

✦ *Scientific evidence.* This style presents survey or scientific evidence that the brand is better or better liked than one or more other brands. For years, Crest toothpaste has used scientific evidence to convince buyers that Crest is better than other brands at fighting cavities. In Elida Gibbs' relaunch of the skin-care brand Pond's, the advertisement referred to the 'Pond's Institute' where women were shown having their skin analysed, the ad emphasising the brand's scientific problem-solving qualities.

✦ *Testimonial evidence or endorsement.* This style features a highly believable or likable source endorsing the product. It could be a celebrity, like sports personality Will Carling, the former England rugby captain who was used to endorse Ericsson's Wap-enabled mobile phone, or ordinary people saying how much they like a given product.

The advertiser must also choose a *tone* for the ad. Positive appeals that evoke happiness, feelings of achievement, fun and excitement tend to be more effective than negative tones. By contrast, negative appeals that evoke fear may discourage viewers from looking at the advertisement, and so would be counterproductive.

The advertiser must also use memorable and attention-getting words in the ad.

This simple but impacting Peugeot car ad is a good example of how an efficient copy should be, concise but meaningful. The ad conveys the 'abnormal power' of the 206 GTi.

SOURCE: Peugeot Motor Company Plc.
Agency: Euro RSCG WNEK Gosper

PEUGEOT 206 GTi. ABNORMAL POWER.

0–60mph in 7.1 sec! 'The greatest GTi of all time' (Auto Express). From £13,695 MRRP.

This ad makes use of imagery and mood to promote Jean Paul Gaultier fragrances.

SOURCE: J.P. Gaultier/Advertising Archives

For example, rather than claiming simply that 'a BMW is a well-engineered car', BMW uses more creative and high-impact phrasing: 'The ultimate driving machine'. Instead of saying that Häagen-Dazs is 'a good tasting ice-cream', its ads say that it is, 'Our passport to indulgence: passion in a touch, perfection in a cup, summer in a spoon, one perfect moment'. It's not that 'Philishave gives optimum shaving satisfaction due to its high quality and advanced technology'. Rather, use the shaver 'For a better, closer shave'. And Stella Artois is not simply a high-price, high-quality beer, but instead, 'Stella Artois (is) – reassuringly expensive'.

Finally, *format* elements make a difference to an ad's impact as well as its cost. A small change in ad design can make a big difference to its effect. The *illustration* is the first thing the reader notices – it must be strong enough to attract attention. Next, the *headline* must effectively entice the right people to read the copy. Finally, the *copy*, which is the main block of text in the ad, must be simple but strong and convincing.

Importantly, all the elements – style, tone, words, format – must effectively work *together*. Even then, less than 50 per cent of the exposed audience will notice even a truly outstanding ad: about 30 per cent will recall the main point of the headline; about 25 per cent will remember the advertiser's name; and less than 10 per cent will have read most of the copy. Less than outstanding ads, unfortunately, will not achieve even these results.

■ Selecting advertising media

The advertiser must next decide upon the media to carry the message. The main steps in media selection are: (1) deciding on *reach*, *frequency* and *impact*; (2) choosing among chief *media types*; (3) selecting specific *media vehicles*; and (4) deciding on *media timing*.

Reach
The percentage of people in the target market exposed to an ad campaign during a given period.

Frequency
The number of times the average person in the target market is exposed to an advertising message during a given period.

Media impact
The qualitative value of an exposure through a given medium.

Deciding on reach, frequency and impact   To select media, the advertiser must decide what reach and frequency are needed to achieve advertising objectives. **Reach** is a measure of the *percentage* of people in the target market who are exposed to the ad campaign during a given period of time. For example, the advertiser might try to reach 70 per cent of the target market during the first three months of the campaign. **Frequency** is a measure of how many *times* the average person in the target market is exposed to the message. For example, the advertiser might want an average exposure frequency of three. The advertiser must also decide on the desired **media impact** – that is, the qualitative value of a message exposure through a given medium. For example, for products that need to be demonstrated, messages on television may have more impact than messages on radio because television uses sight and sound. The same message in a national newspaper may be more believable than in a local daily.

In general, the more reach, frequency and impact the advertiser seeks, the higher the advertising budget will have to be.

Choosing among chief media types   The media planner has to know the reach, frequency and impact of each of the major media types. The leading media have advantages and limitations, as shown in Table 19.2.

How do advertisers select appropriate media from the range of media available? Media planners consider many factors when making their media choices. The *media habits of target consumers* will affect media choice: for example, radio and television

Table 19.2

Profiles of major media forms

Medium	Advantages	Limitations
Newspapers	Flexibility; timeliness; local market coverage; broad acceptance; high believability.	Short life; poor reproduction quality; small pass-along audience.
Television	Good mass-market coverage; low cost per exposure; combines sight, sound and motion; appealing to the senses.	High absolute cost; high clutter; fleeting exposure; less audience selectivity.
Radio	Good local acceptance; high geographic and demographic selectivity; low cost.	Audio presentation only; low attention (the 'half-heard' medium); fleeting exposure; fragmented audience.
Magazines	High geographic and demographic selectivity; credibility and prestige; high-quality reproduction; long life; good pass-along readership.	Long ad purchase lead time; high cost; some waste circulation; no guarantee of position.
Direct mail	High audience selectivity; flexibility; no ad competition within the same medium; allows personalisation.	Relatively high cost per exposure; 'junk mail' image.
Outdoor	Flexibility; high repeat exposure; low cost; low message competition; good positional selectivity.	No audience selectivity; creative limitations.
Internet	High selectivity; low cost; immediacy; interactive capabilities.	Small, demographically skewed audience; relatively low impact; audience controls exposure.

are the best media for reaching teenagers. So will the *nature of the product*: fashions, for example, are best advertised in colour magazines and car performance is best demonstrated on television. Different *types of message* may require different media: for instance, a message announcing a big sale tomorrow will require radio or newspapers; a message with a lot of technical data might require magazines or direct mailings or an online ad and website. *Cost* is also an important consideration in media choice: whereas television is very expensive, newspaper advertising costs much less but also reaches fewer consumers. The media planner looks at both the total cost of using a medium and the cost per thousand exposures – that is, the cost of reaching 1,000 people using the medium.

Media impact and cost must be re-examined regularly. For a long time, television and magazines dominated in the media mixes of national advertisers, with other media often neglected. Recently, however, the costs and clutter of these media have gone up, audiences have dropped and marketers are adopting strategies aimed at narrower segments.[12] As a result, advertisers are increasingly turning to alternative media, ranging from cable TV and outdoor advertising to parking meters, taxis and shopping trolleys, that cost less and target more effectively.

Selecting specific media vehicles   The media planner must now choose the best **media vehicles** – that is, specific media within each general media type. In most cases, there is an incredible number of choices. For radio and television, and in any one country, there are numerous stations and channels to choose from, together with hundreds, even thousands, of programme vehicles – the particular programmes or shows where the commercial should be broadcast. Prime-time programmes are the favourites; the costs, however, tend to escalate with the popularity of the programme.

Media vehicles
Specific media within each general media type, such as specific magazines, television shows or radio programmes.

In the case of magazines, the media planner must look up circulation figures and the costs of different ad sizes, colour options, ad positions and frequencies for specific magazines. Each country has its own high- or general-circulation magazines (for example, TV guides) which reach general audience groups. There is also an array of special-interest publications that enable advertisers to reach special groups of audience (for instance, business magazines to reach business executives). The planner selects the media that will do the best job in terms of reaching the target customer group – that is, in terms of their selectivity towards the target. Then he or she must evaluate each magazine on factors such as credibility, status, reproduction quality, editorial focus and advertising submission deadlines. The media planner ultimately decides which vehicles give the best reach, frequency and impact for the money.

Media planners have to compute the cost per thousand persons reached by a vehicle. For example, if a full-page, four-colour advertisement in *The Economist* costs £30,000 and its readership is 3 million people, the cost of reaching each group of 1,000 persons is about £10. The same advertisement in *Business Week* may cost only £20,000 but reach only 1 million persons, giving a cost per thousand of about £20. The media planner would rank each magazine by cost per thousand and favour those magazines with the lower cost per thousand for reaching target consumers. Additionally, the media planner considers the cost of producing ads for different media. Whereas newspaper ads may cost very little to produce, flashy television ads may cost millions. Media costs vary across different countries, so care must be taken not to generalise the figures.

Thus the media planner must balance media cost measures against several media impact factors. First, the planner should balance costs against the media vehicle's *audience quality*. For a mobile telephone ad, business magazines would have a high-exposure value; magazines aimed at new parents or woodwork enthusiasts would have a low-exposure value. Second, the media planner should consider *audience attention*. Readers of *Vogue*, for example, typically pay more attention to ads than do *Business Week* readers. Third, the planner should assess the vehicle's *editorial quality*. For example, the *Financial Times* and *Wall Street Journal Europe* are more credible and prestigious than the *News of the World*.

Deciding on media timing   The advertiser must also decide how to schedule the advertising over the course of a year. Suppose sales of a product peak in December and drop in March. The firm can vary its advertising to follow the seasonal pattern, to oppose the seasonal pattern, or to be the same all year. Most firms do some seasonal advertising. Some do *only* seasonal advertising: for example, many department stores advertise – usually their seasonal sales – in specific periods in the year, such as Christmas, Easter and summer. Finally, the advertiser has to choose the pattern of the ads. **Continuity** means scheduling ads evenly within a given period. **Pulsing** means scheduling ads unevenly over a given time period. Thus 52 ads could either be scheduled at one per week during the year or pulsed in several bursts. The idea is to advertise heavily for a short period to build awareness that carries over to the next advertising period. Those who favour pulsing feel that it can be used to achieve the same impact as a steady schedule, but at a much lower cost. However, some media planners believe that although pulsing achieves minimal awareness, it sacrifices depth of advertising communications.

Recent advances in technology have had a substantial impact on the media planning and buying functions. Today, for example, new computer software applications called *optimisers* allow media planners to evaluate vast combinations of television programmes and prices. Such programmes help advertisers to make better decisions about which mix of networks, programmes, and day parts will yield the highest reach per ad euro.[13]

Continuity
Scheduling ads evenly within a given period.

Pulsing
Scheduling ads unevenly, in bursts, over a certain time period.

evaluating advertising

The advertising programme should regularly evaluate both the communication impact and the sales effects of advertising. Measuring the communication effects of an ad or **copy testing** tells whether the ad is communicating well. Copy testing can be done before or after an ad is printed or broadcast. Before the ad is placed, the advertiser can show it to consumers, ask how they like it, and measure recall or attitude changes resulting from it. After the ad is run, the advertiser can measure how the ad affected consumer recall or product awareness, knowledge and preference.

But what sales are caused by an ad that increases brand awareness by 20 per cent and brand preference by 10 per cent? The sales effects of advertising are often harder to measure than the communication effects. Sales are affected by many factors besides advertising – such as product features, price and availability. Despite the difficulty of accounting for sales, advertising effects must be monitored. Figure 19.2 shows the levels of communication effect that advertisers are likely to monitor and measure with respect to a campaign:

Copy testing
Measuring the communication effect of an advertisement before or after it is printed or broadcast.

+ The change in brand awareness is determined by the number of customers who were previously *unaware* of the brand and the number who *notice* the advertisement and are now *aware* of the brand, or by the difference in the number of customers who are aware that the brand exists before and after the campaign. If there has been little increase or even a decline in brand awareness, the advertiser has to determine whether the reason is the poor impact achieved by the communications campaign or that customers *forget* because of poor recall or inadequate advertising investment.

+ The nature of consumers' attitudes towards a brand can be ascertained before and after a campaign. An informative ad allows consumers to *learn* more about product/brand benefits. If the message is poorly targeted, or conveys an undesirable or unbelievable message, consumers are *antipathetic* towards the brand. They do not develop any liking for the product. Advertisers

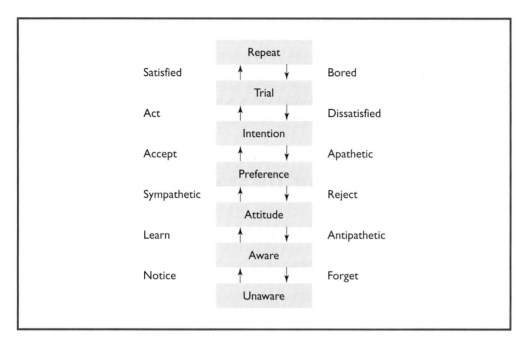

Figure 19.2

Advertising: measuring communications and sales effectiveness

may have to redesign the copy to generate greater interest among customers or improve message content in order to enhance the level of comprehension of brand benefits among target customers.

◆ Consumers who are *sympathetic* towards advertised brand benefits would manifest their favourable response in the form of stated brand preference. Similarly, before-and-after (the campaign) studies would enable changes in consumer brand preference to be determined. Reasons for brand *rejection* should be identified so that communication weaknesses can be redressed.

◆ An advertising campaign may be used to turn preference among customers into more definite *intention* to buy. Again, this response can be measured and changes in the level of buying intent may be determined.

◆ It is usually difficult to measure the sales effect of a campaign. Questions such as 'What sales are caused by an ad that increases brand awareness by 20 per cent and brand preference by 10 per cent?' are not easy to answer. Sales or *trials* are affected by many factors besides advertising, such as product features, price and availability. One way to measure the sales effect of advertising is to compare past sales with past advertising expenditures. Another way is through experiments. For example, to test the effects of different advertising levels, Pizza Hut could vary the amount it spends on advertising in different market areas and measure the differences in resulting sales levels. It could spend the normal amount in one market area, half the normal amount in another area, and twice the normal amount in a third area. If the three market areas are similar, and if all other marketing efforts in the area are the same, then the differences in sales in the three cities could be related to advertising level. More complex experiments could be designed to include other variables, such as differences in the ads or media used.

◆ If the customer is *satisfied* with the brand he or she has bought, this will lead to *repeat* purchase on another buying occasion. The extent to which advertising or a specific 'reminder' campaign affects repeat purchase is difficult to measure because of the difficulty of separating out the immediate and long-term effects of advertising. 'Before-and-after' type studies and controlled experiments can be used, nonetheless, to detect changes in purchase and usage frequency. Again, advertisers should obtain consumer feedback to increase their understanding of the impact of communications on repeat purchase. Advertising may not be blamed for non-repeat sales due to the nature of product consumption: for example, consumers get *bored* with the same product and want variety. In this case, advertising is not powerful enough to arrest that desire. Few of us would relish the thought of surviving on an uninterrupted diet of Heinz beans, Heinz soup and Heinz sausages all year round!

organising for advertising

Different organisations handle advertising in different ways. In small and medium-sized companies, advertising might be handled by someone in the sales or marketing department. Large companies might set up advertising departments whose job it is to set the advertising budget, work with the ad agency and handle dealer displays and other advertising not done by the agency. Most companies, small or large, tend to use outside advertising agencies because they offer several advantages:

✦ Agencies have specialists who can perform specialist functions (e.g. research, creative work) better than a company's own staff.

✦ Agencies bring an outside point of view to solving a company's problems, along with years of experience from working with different clients and situations.

✦ Agencies have more buying power in media than the firm. They are also paid partly from media discount, which would cost the firm less.

There are disadvantages in relinquishing the advertising function to an outside agency: loss of total control of the advertising process, a reduction in flexibility, conflicts arising when the agency dictates working practices, and client inability to exercise control or coordination. Despite the potential problems, however, most firms find that they benefit from employing the specialised expertise of agencies.

How does an advertising agency work? Advertising agencies were started in the mid-to-late nineteenth century by salespeople and brokers who worked for the media and received commission for selling advertising space to companies. As time passed, the salespeople began to help customers prepare their ads. Eventually they formed agencies and grew closer to the advertisers than to the media.

Some ad agencies are huge – McCann-Erickson and BBDO Group have annual billings (the value of advertising placed for clients) of more than $5 billion. In recent years, many agencies have grown by gobbling up other agencies, thus creating huge agency holding companies. An 'agency mega-group' such as the Omnicom Group includes several large advertising, public relations and promotion agencies – DDB Needham, BBDO, TBWA and several others – with combined worldwide gross income of $4.8 billion on billings exceeding $37 billion.[14]

Most large agencies have staff and resources to handle all phases of an ad campaign for their clients, from creating a marketing plan to developing campaigns and preparing, placing and evaluating ads. Agencies usually have four departments: creative, which develops and produces ads; media, which selects media and places ads; research, which studies audience characteristics and wants; and business, which handles the agency's business activities. Each account is supervised by an account executive and people in each department are usually assigned to work on one or more accounts.

Ad agencies have traditionally been paid through commission and fees. Higher commissions are paid to the well-recognised agencies for their ability to place more advertisements in media. However, both advertisers and agencies are becoming more and more unhappy with the commission system. Larger advertisers complain that they have to pay more for the same services received by smaller ones simply because they place more advertising. Advertisers also believe that the commission system drives agencies away from low-cost media and short advertising campaigns. Agencies, on the other hand, are unhappy because they perform extra services for an account without getting more pay. The commission formula also tends to overlook important emerging media such as the Internet. As a result, new agency payment methods may now include anything from fixed retainers or straight hourly fees for labour to incentives keyed to performance of the agencies' ad campaigns or some combination of these.

Another trend is affecting the agency business. Many agencies have sought growth by diversifying into related marketing services. These new diversified agencies offer a one-stop shop – a complete list of integrated marketing and promotion services under one roof, including advertising, sales promotion, marketing research, public relations and direct and online marketing. Some have added marketing consulting, television production and sales training units in an effort to become full 'marketing partners' to their clients.

Some companies favour buying marketing services from a consolidated one-stop shop. They argue that there are a number of benefits – it increases their clout with the agency; it is more efficient to deal with one 'contractor' than with many; it greatly simplifies the advertising for their products, including gaining the convenience of having to negotiate fees once only; it ensures that their marketing will be consistent worldwide; and a big international broad-line agency can help carry good ideas into many country markets quickly.

However, many agencies are finding that advertisers do not want much more from them than traditional media advertising services plus direct marketing, sales promotion and sometimes public relations. Client companies may want to keep a few agencies on call in a state of perpetual competition. Some, like Coca-Cola, seek creative variety, so they scatter the work to many different small and large agencies. Others, like Philips, the Dutch electronics group, are looking for a single specialist to design their entire global advertising media strategy. Still others, such as Procter & Gamble, Unilever and Nestlé, tend to keep a 'club' of three to six agencies on call to cover one agency's weak spots by drawing on the ideas of another with more talent in a particular market or service.[15] Thus, many agencies have recently dropped unrelated activities in order to focus more on traditional services or their core expertise. Some have even started their own 'creative boutiques' – smaller and more independent agencies that can develop creative campaigns for clients free of large-agency bureaucracy.[16]

international advertising

We have discussed advertising decisions in general. International advertisers face many complexities not encountered by domestic advertisers. When developing advertising for international markets, a number of basic issues must be considered.

standardisation or differentiation

The most basic issue concerns the degree to which advertising should be adapted to the unique characteristics of various country markets. Some large advertisers have attempted to support their global brands with highly standardised worldwide advertising,

Gillette Sensor Excel for Women ads are almost identical worldwide, with only minor adjustments to suit the local culture.
SOURCE: © The Gillette Company

with campaigns that work as well in Bangkok as they do in London. For example, Ericsson spent $100 million on a standardised global television campaign with the tag line 'make yourself heard', which featured Agent 007, James Bond. Coca-Cola's Sprite brand uses standardised appeals to target the world's youth. Gillette's ads for its Sensor Excel for Women are almost identical worldwide, with only minor adjustments to suit the local culture.

Standardisation produces many benefits, such as lower advertising costs, greater coordination of global advertising efforts and a more consistent worldwide company or product image. However, standardisation also has drawbacks. Most importantly, it ignores the fact that country markets, not just across the continents, but also within supposedly 'harmonised' trading communities, such as the European Union, differ greatly in their cultures, demographics and economic conditions. Pan-European advertising, for example, is complicated because of the EU's cultural diversity as reflected in the differences in circumstances, language, traditions, music, beliefs, values and life-styles among member nations. Ironically, the English have more in common with the Australians, who live on the opposite side of the globe, than with the Germans or the French, their closer neighbours. Cultural differences also exist across Asian countries (Japanese and Indonesian consumers are as alike as the Germans and Italians), as they do among emerging European markets. For example, the three Baltic states – Estonia, Latvia and Lithuania – are far from being a common market, with each displaying different languages, currencies and consumer habits.

Although advertising messages might be standardised, their executions cannot be, as culture invariably dominates communications.[17] Indeed, a survey in Europe among 210 pan-European brand managers showed that a majority (57 per cent) believe it is difficult to standardise advertising execution.[18] Thus, most international advertisers 'think globally, but act locally'. They develop global advertising *strategies* that make their worldwide advertising efforts more efficient and consistent. Then they adapt their advertising *programmes* to make them more responsive to consumer needs and expectations within local markets. In many cases, even when a standard message is used, execution styles are adapted to reflect local moods and consumer expectations.

Successful standardised advertising is most likely to work for capital goods or business-to-business marketing, where targets are more homogeneous in their needs and buy the product for the same reasons. For example, whether it be a European, Asian or American construction company, the purchase of bulldozers is governed by similar economic rationality (for example, productivity, lifetime cost of running the equipment, parts delivery). Consumer-goods advertising is less amenable to cross-cultural standardisation. However, considerable similarities are found in segments, such as the world's rich to whom lifestyle goods and brands like Cartier, Mont Blanc, Mercedes and Hugo Boss appeal. Similarly, youth culture across the globe may be targeted with a common message. Brands such as Nike, Pepsi and Jeep are advertised in much the same way globally; Jeep has created a worldwide brand image of ruggedness and reliability; Nike urges Americans, Africans, Asians and Europeans alike to 'Just do it'; Pepsi uses a standard appeal to target the world's youth.

centralisation or decentralisation

Global advertisers are concerned with the degree to which advertising decision making and implementation should be centralised or decentralised. This decision is directly linked to the decision about whether to follow a standardised or differentiated advertising approach. Five key factors influence the choice between centralisation and decentralisation of the responsibility for international advertising decisions and implementation:

1. *Corporate and marketing objectives*. A company whose global marketing objectives dominate over domestic objectives is likely to centralise advertising and communications decisions.

2. *Product uniformity*. The more similar the product or service marketed across different countries, the greater the feasibility of a uniform approach, which allows for centralised management of advertising.

3. *Product appeal*. Underpinning the product's appeal are the reasons why customers use the product, which may differ among different cultures, whatever the demographic or psychographic characteristics of consumers. Golf club membership is a status purchase in Singapore; in the United Kingdom it is a moderate leisure activity, without the same label of exclusivity attached. Where underlying appeals vary significantly, decentralised decision making makes better sense.

4. *Cultural sensitivities*. Where a product's usage and appeal are culture-bound in terms of the local attitudes towards consumption, habits and preferences, as in the case of drinks and food products, more decentralisation is necessary.

5. *Legal constraints*. Individual country rules and regulations affect advertising decisions and their implementation. Decentralisation of responsibility, with the aim of tapping local wisdom and knowledge, is necessary where strict country regulations apply. In the European Union, until real 'harmonisation' exists, cross-border advertisers must remain alert to subtle differences in nations' rules and codes of practice in order to avoid costly mistakes.

The modes used by firms vary. Some organisations exert tight control from the centre and executionary changes for local culture and conditions are closely monitored. Some corporations grant local management some degree of freedom to develop advertising within broad strategic guidelines, but with central directives on agencies and media buying groups. Yet others may give local management total autonomy in both strategy determination and local implementation of advertising strategies.

worldwide advertising media

The international media comprise an extensive mix:

+ *Newspapers.* Faster and more efficient circulation is possible with new technologies, such as satellite printing, which allows advertising copy to be sent by satellite to the printers. Many international newspapers (e.g. *International Herald Tribune, Financial Times, Asahi Shimbun, Wall Street Asian, Wall Street Journal*) are printed simultaneously in more than one country. In general, there have been enormous developments in local and global press, and more newspapers have gone global to reach specific audiences.

+ *Magazines.* There are some national and international journals which carry ads that target regional, international or global customers (e.g. *Fortune, Newsweek, Time, The Economist*). Women's magazines, such as *Cosmopolitan, Elle, Vogue* and *Harper's Bazaar*, are printed in different editions for readers in different target countries/regions. And there are other international magazines such as *Reader's Digest* and men's magazines like *Playboy* and *Penthouse.*

+ *Professional and technical magazines.* In Europe alone, there are more than 15,000 titles, and the number is rising yearly.

+ *Cinema.* This is a relatively popular medium for reaching younger viewers, such as teenagers. In developing and less developed nations, cinema remains important.

+ *Television.* There are few country markets where television is not available or where advertising is not carried via that medium. Satellite and cable opportunities have expanded enormously and accelerated the use of TV for international advertising. A few stations – notably CNN, NBC Super Channel and Eurosport – are well-recognised international media channels. Other international TV channels include Dow Jones's European Business News, BBC Worldwide and NBC's CNBC.

+ *Outdoor advertising and transport advertising.* This medium is used throughout the world. In the western developed markets, advertisers are expanding their repertoire of outside media (e.g. park benches, trucks, taxis, bus stop shelters). This medium is used as an alternative in cases where the product category cannot be advertised on TV, as in the case of tobacco and alcoholic products. In some countries, such as India and the People's Republic of China, outdoor advertising has become more important.

+ *Interactive communication media.* Interactive systems, such as videotext and pay-TV, have gained importance as cable TV continues to develop. Not only is the Internet a new channel for advertising, so are novelties such as TiVo, which allow viewers to store and play back TV programmes in real time. Interactive TV services are also emerging that increasingly give viewers control over what they watch and when they watch it, fragmenting further the mass television audience.

+ *Radio.* As a medium for international advertising, radio is constrained by availability in the sense that most commercial radio is regional. Radio

Luxembourg, the international European station, transmits ads in several languages and reaches the whole of Europe.

✦ *Place-based media*. This is a worldwide development and advertisers are increasingly deploying the medium to reach audiences wherever they happen to be – at work, the fitness centre, the supermarket, airports and in the aeroplane.

✦ *Trade fairs and exhibitions*. These can be costly, but are useful media for international communications.

✦ *Sponsorship*. Sponsorship of sports or art events, like the Olympic Games and the soccer World Cup, offers vast audience reach. However, such global audiences are rare and the effectiveness of the initiatives is not easy to measure.

✦ *Other media*. Point-of-sale materials are not easy to reproduce internationally. Invariably, they have to be adapted to local conditions, specifically the language, regulations and distribution outlets. Direct mail is used in many countries, but it is primarily a local technique. As postal services vary from country to country, including within the EU, the medium has yet to be applied internationally. Nonetheless, credit card companies that have an international customer database can exploit this medium for worldwide communications. Online media such as the Internet are gaining recognition and organisations are increasingly investing in this channel given its potential to reach a global audience (Chapter 22 discusses online marketing in greater detail).

media planning, buying and costs

International media planning is more complicated than local media planning as the media situation differs from country to country. To plan effectively, international advertisers require high-quality, reliable cross-country media and audience research data. In some countries, there is inadequate media research. Moreover, research techniques and measurement standards vary greatly across countries, making cross-country comparisons of media research data almost impossible. Unless reliable inter-country comparisons can be made, international advertisers will find it difficult to evaluate and quantify international media effectiveness. In the EU, the European Association of Advertising Agencies has been working on the harmonisation of data to help pan-European media researchers. Recent pan-European research projects, funded jointly by advertisers, agencies and print and TV media, have generated a range of data that help media planners go some way towards building more effective campaigns across Europe as well as in individual territories.[19]

Prices and preference for certain media also may vary greatly across countries. For example, one survey suggests that, in the Scandinavian countries, print media dominate as an advertising medium, with two in three consumers polled voicing positive attitudes towards print advertising; only one in five held the same opinion of TV advertising. The preference for the printed word has important implications for advertising media choice.[20]

Thus, firms that advertise their products in different country markets must decide on what media to use based on a consideration of their target groups, the budget available and an understanding of the media scene and relative media cost efficiencies in these countries.

international advertising regulations

Countries also differ in the extent to which they regulate advertising practices. Many countries have extensive systems of laws restricting how much a company can spend on advertising, the media used, the nature of advertising claims and other aspects of the advertising programme. The most important laws currently under discussion in Europe are those governing marketing to children and the advertising of tobacco and alcohol.

In Sweden, Norway and Denmark, TV advertising to children under 12 is banned. Moreover, Sweden is lobbying to extend that ban to all EU member countries. To play it safe, McDonald's advertises itself as a family restaurant in Sweden. Advertising to children is also restricted in Belgium, Ireland, Holland and Austria, and under consideration in Italy and Poland. Greece bans TV ads for toys before 10 p.m. The country is even considering banning all TV ads aimed at the under-18s!

As regards tobacco advertising, the European Commission requires its member states to ban all tobacco promotion by 2006. These bans will be phased in gradually, with cinema, radio, posters and direct mail going by July 2001, followed by print in 2002, sponsorship in 2003, and worldwide sponsorships such as Formula One going after 2006.

For alcohol advertising, Sweden and Finland impose strict limitations, while France is the most restrictive – all forms of alcohol advertising are banned. Denmark and the UK are calling for health warnings to be placed on packaging. Germany, too, is calling for stricter regulations.

Comparative ads, while acceptable and even common in the United States and Canada, are less commonly used in the United Kingdom, unacceptable in a number of EU countries as well as in Japan, and illegal in India and Brazil. PepsiCo found that its comparative taste test ad in Japan was refused by many television stations and actually led to a lawsuit. China has restrictive censorship rules for TV and radio advertising; for example, the words *the best* are banned, as are ads that 'violate social customs' or present women in 'improper ways'. On the latter front, advertisers in Europe also have faced restrictions. Such restrictions often require that advertisers adapt their campaigns from country to country, which can add to the costs of shooting commercials. For example, Heineken decided to use a highly successful Dutch TV commercial for the non-alcoholic beer, Buckler, across Europe. In the advertisement, a woman crawls along the bar of a crowded saloon to reach her boyfriend. In some countries it had to be reshot for being sexually overt.[21]

In the EU, the Internal Market Commission continues in its ongoing efforts to resolve the patchwork of national advertising regulations in an attempt to bring order into the EU's multi-billion-euro advertising industry. The advent of online interactive media and electronic commerce means that cross-border advertising will develop further. However, until the problem of different rules is ironed out, advertising campaigns can never be truly pan-European. Thus although advertisers may develop standardised strategies to guide their overall advertising efforts, specific advertising programmes and executions must usually be adapted to meet local cultures and customs, media characteristics and advertising regulations.

Having discussed advertising in the previous sections, let us now examine sales promotion.

sales promotion

Sales promotion
Short-term incentives to encourage purchase or sales of a product or service.

Sales promotion consists of short-term incentives, in addition to the basic benefits offered by the product or service, to encourage the purchase or sale of a product or service. Whereas advertising offers reasons to buy a product or service, sales promotion offers reasons that would achieve immediate sales. It seeks to motivate the customer to buy *now*.

Sales promotion tools are used by most organisations, including manufacturers, distributors, retailers, trade associations and non-profit institutions. They are targeted towards the consumer or final buyer, business customers, the trade or retailer and the company's sales force. **Consumer promotions** include money-off, coupons, premiums, contests and others. **Trade promotions** range from special discounts, free goods and loyalty bonuses to training. **Business promotions** include many of the same tools used for consumer or trade promotions such as conventions and trade shows, as well as sales contests. **Sales force promotions** include bonuses, commissions, free gifts and competitions.

rapid growth of sales promotion

Several factors have contributed to the rapid growth of sales promotion, particularly in consumer markets:

1. Inside the company, product managers face greater pressures to increase their current sales, and promotion is increasingly viewed as an effective short-run sales tool. In mature markets, manufacturers are striving to maintain market share through a balance between longer-term 'share-of-voice' gained from advertising and shorter-term incentives for the consumer.

2. Externally, the company faces more competition, and competing brands are less differentiated. Increasingly, competitors are using sales promotion to help differentiate their offers.

3. Advertising efficiency has declined because of rising costs, media clutter and legal restraints. Sales promotion used in conjunction with other communications, such as direct mail, can offer a more cost-effective route to reach target consumers.

4. Consumers have become more promotion oriented and retailers are demanding more deals from manufacturers.

5. Developments in information technology, the reduction in data storage and retrieval costs, and the increased sophistication of targeting techniques have facilitated implementation and enabled more effective measurement and control of sales promotion efforts.

The growing use of sales promotion has resulted in *promotion clutter*, similar to advertising clutter. Consumers who are continually bombarded with promotions are increasingly 'tuning out' promotions, weakening their ability to trigger immediate purchase. To capture the attention and interest of customers, manufacturers are now searching for ways to rise above the clutter, such as offering larger coupon values, creating more dramatic point-of-purchase displays or developing more creative campaigns that stand out from the crowd.

In using sales promotion, a company must set objectives, select the right tools, develop the best programme, pre-test and implement that programme, and evaluate the results. We will examine each of these issues in turn.

setting sales promotion objectives

Sales promotion objectives vary widely. Let us take *consumer promotions* first. Sellers may use consumer promotions to: (1) increase short-term sales; (2) help build long-term

---

Consumer promotion
Sales promotion designed to stimulate consumer purchasing, including samples, coupons, rebates, prices-off, premiums, patronage rewards, displays, and contests and sweepstakes.

Trade (or retailer) promotion
Sales promotion designed to gain reseller support and to improve reseller selling efforts, including discounts, allowances, free goods, cooperative advertising, push money, and conventions and trade shows.

Business promotion
Sales promotion designed to generate business leads, stimulate purchase, reward business customers and motivate the salesforce.

Sales force promotion
Sales promotion designed to motivate the sales force and make sales force selling efforts more effective, including bonuses, contests and sales rallies.

market share; (3) entice consumers to try a new product; (4) lure consumers away from competitors' products; (5) encourage consumers to 'load up' on a mature product; or (6) hold and reward loyal customers.

Objectives for *trade promotions* include: (1) motivating retailers to carry new items and more stock; (2) inducing them to advertise the product and give it more shelf space; and (3) persuading them to buy ahead.

For the *sales force*, objectives may be to: (1) prompt more sales force support for current or new products; or (2) stimulate salespeople to sign up new accounts.

Sales promotions are usually used together with advertising or personal selling. Consumer promotions are normally advertised and can add excitement and pulling power to ads. Trade and sales force promotions support the firm's personal selling process. Objectives, however, should be measurable. Rather than stating that the promotion aims to increase sales, the objective should be specific about the level of increase, who the main targets are and whether increased sales are expected to come from new trialists or from current consumers who are loading up or bringing forward their purchase.

Consumer relationship-building promotions
Sales promotions that promote the product's positioning and include a selling message along with the deal.

In general, sales promotions should be **consumer relationship building**. Rather than creating only short-term sales volume or temporary brand switching, they should help to reinforce the product's position and build long-term relationships with customers. Increasingly, marketers are avoiding the 'quick fix', price-led promotions in favour of promotions designed to build brand equity. Even price promotions can be designed to build customer relationships. Examples include all the 'frequency marketing programmes' and 'clubs' that have mushroomed in recent years. If properly designed, every sales promotion tool has the potential to build consumer relationships.

Sales promotions have certain limitations. Sellers need to recognise that new triers at whom their promotions are targeted consist of consumers of the product category, loyal users of another brand and users who frequently switch brands. Sales promotions often attract the last group – *brand switchers* – because non-users and users of other brands do not always notice or act on a promotion. Brand switchers are looking mostly for low price or good value. Sales promotions are unlikely to turn them into loyal brand users. Moreover, when a company uses price promotion for a brand too much of the time, consumers begin to think of it as a cheap brand. Or many consumers will buy the brand only when there is a special offer. Most analysts believe that sales promotion activities do not build long-term consumer preference and loyalty, as does advertising. Instead, they only boost short-term sales that cannot be maintained over the long run. Marketers therefore rarely use sales promotion for dominant brands because it would do little more than subsidise current users.[22]

Despite the dangers, many consumer packaged-goods companies continue to use sales promotions. These marketers assert that sales promotions benefit manufacturers by letting them adjust to short-term changes in supply and demand and to differences in customer segments. Sales promotions encourage consumers to try new products instead of always staying with their current ones. They lead to more varied retail formats, such as the everyday-low-price store or the promotional-pricing store, which give consumers more choice. Finally, sales promotions lead to greater consumer awareness of prices, and consumers themselves enjoy the satisfaction of taking advantage of price specials.[23]

selecting sales promotion tools

Many tools can be used to accomplish sales promotion objectives. The promotion planner should consider the type of market, the sales promotion objectives, the competition and the cost-effectiveness of each tool. Descriptions of the main consumer and trade promotion tools follow.

■ Consumer promotion tools

The main consumer promotion tools include samples, coupons, cash refunds, price packs, premiums, advertising specialities, patronage rewards, point-of-purchase displays and demonstrations, and contests, sweepstakes and games.

Samples are offers of a trial amount of a product. Some samples are free; for others, the company charges a small amount to offset its cost. The sample might be delivered door to door, sent by mail, handed out in a store, attached to another product or featured in an ad. Sampling is the most effective, but most expensive, way to introduce a new product.

Coupons are certificates that give buyers a saving when they purchase specified products. They can stimulate sales of a mature brand or promote early trial of a new brand. However, as a result of coupon clutter, redemption rates have been declining in years. Thus, most major consumer goods companies are issuing fewer coupons and targeting them more carefully. In the past, marketers have relied almost solely on mass-distributed coupons delivered through the mail or on free-standing inserts or ads in newspapers and magazines. Today, however, marketers are increasingly distributing coupons through shelf dispensers at the point of sale, by electronic point-of-sale printers or through 'paperless coupon systems' that dispense personalised discounts to targeted buyers at the checkout counter in stores. Some companies are now offering coupons on their websites or through online coupon services.

Cash refund offers (or **rebates**) are like coupons except that the price reduction occurs after the purchase rather than at the retail outlet. The consumer sends a 'proof of purchase' to the manufacturer, which then refunds part of the purchase price by mail.

Price packs or reduced prices offer consumers savings off the regular price of a product. The reduced prices are marked by the producer directly on the label or package. Price packs can be single packages sold at a reduced price (such as two for the price of one) or two related products banded together (such as a toothbrush and toothpaste). Price packs are very effective – even more so than coupons – in stimulating short-term sales.

Premiums are goods offered either free or at low cost as an incentive to buy a product, ranging from toys included with kids' products to phone cards, compact discs and computer CD-ROMs. A premium may come inside the package (in-pack) or outside the package (on-pack) or through the mail. Premiums are sometimes mailed to consumers who have sent in a proof of purchase, such as a box top. A *self-liquidating premium* is a premium sold below its normal retail price to consumers who request it.

Advertising specialities are useful articles imprinted with an advertiser's name and given as gifts to consumers. Typical items include pens, calendars, key rings, matches, shopping bags, T-shirts, caps and coffee mugs. Such items can be very effective. In a recent study, 63 per cent of all consumers surveyed were either carrying or wearing an ad speciality item. More than three-quarters of those who had an item could recall the advertiser's name or message before showing the item to the interviewer.[24]

Patronage rewards are cash or other awards offered for the regular use of a certain company's products or services. For example, airlines offer 'frequent flyer plans', awarding points for miles travelled that can be turned in for free airline trips. Some international hotels like Holiday Inn and Marriott Hotels have an 'honoured guest' plan that awards points to users of their hotels.

Point-of-purchase (POP) promotions include displays and demonstrations that take place at the point of purchase or sale. Unfortunately, many retailers do not like to handle the hundreds of displays, signs and posters they receive from manufacturers each year. Manufacturers have responded by offering better POP materials, tying them in with television or print messages, and offering to set them up.

Competitions, sweepstakes, lotteries and games give consumers the chance to win something, such as cash, trips or goods, by luck or through extra effort. A *competition*

Samples
Offers to consumers of a trial amount of a product.

Coupons
Certificates that give buyers a saving when they purchase a product.

Cash refund offers (rebates)
Offers to refund part of the purchase price of a product to consumers who send a 'proof of purchase' to the manufacturer.

Price packs
Reduced prices that are marked by the producer directly on the label or package.

Premiums
Goods offered either free or at low cost as an incentive to buy a product.

Advertising specialities
Useful articles imprinted with an advertiser's name, given as gifts to consumers.

Patronage rewards
Cash or other awards for the regular use of a certain company's products or services.

Point-of-purchase (POP) promotions
Displays and demonstrations that take place at the point of purchase or sale.

Contests, sweepstakes and games
Promotions that offer customers the chance to win something – cash, goods or trips – by luck or extra effort.

calls for consumers to submit an entry – a jingle, guess, suggestion – to be judged by a panel that will select the best entries. A *sweepstake* calls for consumers to submit their names for a draw. For a *lottery*, consumers buy tickets which enter their names into a draw. A *game* presents consumers with something, such as bingo numbers or missing letters, every time they buy, which may or may not help them win a prize. A sales contest urges dealers and sales force to increase their efforts, with prizes going to the top performers.

■ Sales promotions in Europe

The sales promotion industry is relatively more developed in the United Kingdom than in the other EU member states. Supermarket retailing in the United Kingdom is dominated by a few key players and decisions regarding acceptance of manufacturers' sales promotion activities are centralised. Cost-effectiveness is increased as the sales promotion handling house is able to use the retailing groups' own administrative processes.

Cultural differences affect consumers' acceptance of different sales promotion techniques. An incentive that is desirable in one country may have little appeal in another. Household items, especially electrical goods, are very popular in Germany. Beach towels, sunglasses and T-shirts are more popular in Spain and Portugal, while in France, it is pens, lighters and watches. In Italy, brand association is important – if the merchandise features a designer name, a recognised brand name or a football club, the chances are that it will be well received.

Like advertising, sales promotion techniques also face different legal constraints across Europe. In countries such as the UK, Ireland, Portugal and Spain, sales promotion activities are relatively free from legal constraints. By contrast, legal controls are stricter in the Benelux countries, Germany, France and, notably so, in Norway. Germany's laws governing unfair competition make it hard for companies to use promotions as sales incentives. Premiums, free draws, coupons or discounts of more than 3 per cent are not allowed, nor is sampling for a product that is not new. In the Netherlands, premiums must not exceed 4 per cent of the value of the main purchase, while in Belgium the ceiling is 5 per cent. In France, premiums are limited in value to no more than 7 per cent of the host product. Outside the EU, countries like Poland, Hungary, Russia and the Czech Republic have relatively liberal policies on promotions and incentives, whereas Switzerland appears to be the most restrictive.[25]

Countries in favour of tighter promotional legislation claim they have consumers' interests at heart, whereas proponents of greater liberalisation argue that increased regulation makes it more difficult for consumers as less information is made available. However, the extent to which directives can truly protect consumers is now a hotly debated issue as sellers turn increasingly to the Web to market products and services. Consider the following example:

> Amazon, the online book seller, has opened online outlets in the UK and Germany, from where buyers can purchase US, English or German publications. However, the German outlet now offers all publications postage free. Paul Schuchhard of Cabinet Stewart, a lobbyist group representing the European Promotional Marketing Alliance (EPMA), in favour of retention of sales promotion techniques as practised in the UK, points to the contradiction posed by online sellers that engage in cross-border marketing activities. Is the free postage to be deemed a discount, which in this case will exceed the 3 per cent factor allowed by German law? Even if this is illegal, few German consumers are likely to object. And how can legislators possibly check all incoming online transactions? And is there a basis for prosecution? According to Mr Schuchhard, when it comes to electronic commerce, decisions about legality of sales promotions could be

Pan-European sampling: Johnson & Johnson's pH5.5 sampling campaign worked on the basis of common packaging, with the language being changed for each different market.

based upon the the 'country-of-origin' and 'mutual recognition' approach. This means promotions deemed legal in the source country should automatically be accepted in other member states. Clearly, EU legislators in the 21st century face a 'doublethink' – in holding the view that it is their right to protect 'home' consumers from overly persuasive marketing tactics (e.g. the manipulative evils of discounts and premiums), they have apparently ignored the common knowledge that e-commerce is truly a borderless, global phenomenon. Little can be done, for now, to deny consumers the pleasure of endless 'illegal' promotional offers over the Internet.[26]

For now, the European market for sales promotion remains fragmented and, until true harmonisation is achieved, marketers must retain a sensitivity to national constraints and adapt strategies to fit individual country markets. Even if legislative harmonisation is achieved, the cultural, linguistic and climatic differences mean that if pan-European campaigns are employed, these will be based on a central or core theme, which is slightly adapted to each territory.

Ingenuity can help agencies to create pan-European sales promotions, with only slight adaptations in each country.

Promotional Campaigns Group (PCG) ran a campaign for Iomega, aimed at encouraging customers to buy multipacks of Zip 100 disks rather than single items. The promotion gets customers to 'Win all the stuff you buy today! When purchasing a multipack of Zip disks.' The mechanics of the promotion were adapted to comply with different rules in France, Germany and the UK, where the campaigns were run. In France, scratch cards were inserted into promotional multipacks with on-pack stickers. In the UK, instant-win scratch cards were issued by check-out staff, or customers could enter into a free prize draw. In Germany, retailers ran a competition involving a leaflet entry to win their day's purchases. In each participating country, the promotional campaign was deemed highly successful, with retailers recording sales increase.[27]

■ Trade promotion tools

Trade promotion can persuade retailers or wholesalers to carry a brand, give it shelf space, promote it in advertising and push it to consumers. Shelf space is so scarce these days that manufacturers often have to offer price discounts, allowances, buy-back guarantees or free goods to retailers and wholesalers to get on the shelf and, once there, to stay on it.

Discount

A straight reduction in price on purchases during a stated period of time.

Allowance

(1) Reduction in price on damaged goods. (2) Promotional money paid by manufacturers to retailers in return for an agreement to feature the manufacturer's product in some way.

Manufacturers use several trade promotion tools. Many of the tools used for consumer promotions – contests, premiums, displays – can also be used as trade promotions. Alternatively, the manufacturer may offer a straight **discount** off the list price on each case purchased during a stated period of time (also called a *price-off*, *off-invoice* or *off-list*). The offer encourages dealers to buy in quantity or to carry a new item. Dealers can use the discount for immediate profit, for advertising or for price reductions to their customers.

Manufacturers may also offer an **allowance** (usually so much off per case) in return for the retailer's agreement to feature the manufacturer's products in some way. An *advertising allowance* compensates retailers for advertising the product. A *display allowance* compensates them for using special displays.

Manufacturers may offer *free goods*, which are extra cases of merchandise, to intermediaries that buy a certain quantity or that feature a certain flavour or size. They may offer *push incentives* – cash or gifts to dealers or their sales force to 'push' the manufacturer's goods. Manufacturers may give retailers free *speciality advertising items* that carry the company's name, such as pens, pencils, calendars, paperweights, matchbooks, memo pads and ashtrays.

■ Business promotion tools

Companies also promote to industrial customers. These business promotions are used to generate business leads, stimulate purchases, reward customers and motivate salespeople. Business promotion includes many of the same tools used for consumer or trade promotions. Here, we focus on two of the main business promotion tools – conventions and trade shows, and sales contests.

Conventions and trade shows   Many companies and trade associations organise conventions and trade shows to promote their products. Firms selling to the industry show their products at the trade show. Vendors receive many benefits, such as opportunities to find new sales leads, contact customers, introduce new products, meet new customers, sell more to present customers and educate customers with publications and audiovisual materials.

Trade shows also help companies reach many prospects not reached through their sales forces. Business managers face several decisions, including which trade shows to participate in, how much to spend on each trade show, how to build dramatic exhibits that attract attention, and how to follow up on sales leads effectively.[28]

Sales contests   A *sales contest* is a contest for salespeople or dealers to urge their sales force to increase their efforts over a given period. Sales contests motivate and recognise good company performers, who may receive trips, cash prizes or other gifts. Sales contests work best when they are tied to measurable and achievable sales objectives (such as finding new accounts, reviving old accounts or increasing account profitability) and when employees believe they have an equal chance of winning. Otherwise, employees will not take up the challenge.

developing the sales promotion programme

The marketer must make several other decisions in order to define the full sales promotion programme. First, the marketer must decide on the *creative idea* and the *mechanics* of the promotion. The creative idea concerns adding some kind of value to the product. It is often difficult to generate an innovative idea which sets a sales promotion apart, since it is easy for competitors to copy price reductions, free products or gifts,

marketing highlight 19.2

Hoover: sucking up the mess

An infamous campaign put the Hoover name on every-body's lips – but for the wrong reason. The promotion offering consumers two free return flights to Europe or America if they bought any of its vacuum cleaners, washing machines or other household appliances worth more than £100 (€164) was dreamed up to tempt people to buy a new appliance. The consumer incentive pro-gramme was intended to raise cash on extra sales, at a time when the UK market for household appliances was depressed, with costs that did not have to be incurred until later, in the form of heavily discounted air tickets, when the appliance market would have improved. Hoover expected many consumers to be attracted by the promise of free flights, but to be deterred from redeem-ing their air tickets by the offer's small print, which laid down conditions about available dates for flights and choice of hotel accommodation, including one-application-per-household restrictions.

Unfortunately, the company (and no fewer than the three sales promotions agencies, which were involved in originating and costing the promotion) had miscalculated. As it happened, most consumers bought cheap vacuum cleaners that cost as little as £120. The cheapest pair of return air tickets to New York cost about £500. The firm was inundated with as many as 200,000 applications for free flights within the first ten months of the campaign, but managed to issue about 6,000 tickets within that same period. Although the travel agents, hired by Hoover, were also alleged to be unfairly dissuading consumers from taking up the offer, angry customers waited adamantly for their tickets. The miscalculation left Hoover with a huge bill. Maytag, its parent company, had to come up with a rescue package of nearly £20 million to honour Hoover's commitment to customers. Hundreds of other disgruntled consumers also sought compensation and many were awarded sums of over £450 where the com-pany was found guilty of abusing the rules. Until recently, Hoover was still busy sucking up the mess created by its free-flight campaign, as new cases and fresh allegations of misconduct brought before the courts opened the floodgates to more claims. The fiasco had cost Hoover well over £48 million, but in the UK, Hoover's name became a sick joke to millions of consumers and the company also attracted column inches of bad publicity.

The lessons? Do not underestimate one's spending on the sales promotion. Cost the sales promotion and carefully evaluate take-up rates before deciding on the *size of the incentive*. Then determine what it would cost the company given the size or attractiveness of the incentive. Over-generous incentives trigger an extreme rate of redemption that could financially cripple the firm. Other examples show how ill-thought-out sales promotion cam-paigns can cause untold damage. A highly publicised Cadbury's Golden Egg treasure hunt caused irrepar-able damage to archaeological sites and monuments around the country. There's also the wildly generous incentive from Mercury of free worldwide phone calls on Christmas day when purchasing a mobile phone – not surprisingly, it caused their network to crash!

In a way, like the Hoover fiasco, these disasters are also in fact examples of campaigns that did too well for their own good. To avoid the fiascos, companies must therefore advocate more planning (forethought) and objective enthusiasm for their incentive campaigns.

SOURCES: Mandy Thatcher, 'Back to basics', *Marketing Business* (September 2000), pp. 32–4; David Reed, 'Holiday programme', *Marketing Week* (5 July 1996), pp. 39–42; Natalie Cheary, 'Hoover fails to shake off free flights horror', *Marketing Week* (1 May 1997), p. 22.

and in-store demonstrations. The marketer must ensure that the promotion genuinely offers extra value and incentives to targets. A certain minimum incentive is necessary if the promotion is to succeed; a larger incentive will produce more sales response. Importantly, the promotion must not be misleading, and the firm must have the ability to honour redemptions. If not, the campaign could backfire, exposing the firm to bad publicity which damages its reputation and brand image (see Marketing Highlight 19.2).

The marketer must also set *conditions for participation*. Incentives might be offered to everyone or only to select groups. Conditions, such as the proof of purchase or closing date of the offer, must be clearly stated.

The marketer must then decide how to *promote and distribute the promotion* programme itself. A money-off coupon could be given out in a package, at the store, by mail or in an advertisement. Each distribution method involves a different level of reach and cost. Increasingly, marketers are blending several media into a total campaign concept.

The *length of the promotion* is also important. If the sales promotion period is too short, many prospects (who may not be buying during that time) will miss it. If the promotion runs for too long, the deal will lose some of its 'act now' force.

The marketer also must decide on the *response mechanism*: that is, the redemption vehicle to be used by the customer who takes part in the promotion. Immediate reward – for example, a price reduction, or a free gift attached to the product on offer – often yields a higher response. If the incentive requires further action to be taken by the consumer – for instance, to make another purchase or to collect the required number of tokens in promotion packs and then post these off to claim a gift or free product – the redemption rate can be reduced.

pre-testing and implementing

Whenever possible, sales promotion tools should be *pre-tested* to find out if they are appropriate and of the right incentive size. Consumer sales promotions can be pre-tested quickly and inexpensively. For example, consumers can be asked to rate or rank different possible promotions, or promotions can be tried on a limited basis in selected geographic areas.

Companies should prepare implementation plans for each promotion, covering lead time and sell-off time. *Lead time* is the time necessary to prepare the programme before launching it. *Sell-off time* begins with the launch and ends when the promotion ends.

evaluating the results

Evaluation is also very important. Many companies fail to evaluate their sales promotion programmes, while others evaluate them only superficially. Manufacturers can use one of many evaluation methods. The most common method is to compare sales before, during and after a promotion. Suppose a company has a 6 per cent market share before the promotion, which jumps to 10 per cent during the promotion, falls to 5 per cent right after and rises to 7 per cent later on. The promotion seems to have attracted new triers and more buying from current customers. After the promotion, sales fall as consumers use up their stocks. The long-run rise to 7 per cent means that the company gained some new users. If the brand's share had returned to the old level, then the promotion would have changed only the *timing* of demand rather than the *total* demand.

Consumer research would also show the kinds of people who responded to the promotion and what they did after it ended. *Surveys* can provide information on how many consumers recall the promotion, what they thought of it, how many took advantage of it and how it affected their buying. Sales promotions can also be evaluated through *experiments* that vary factors such as incentive value, timing, duration and distribution method.

Clearly, sales promotion plays an important role in the total promotion mix. To use it well, the marketer must define the sales promotion objectives, select the best tools, design the sales promotion programme, pre-test and implement the programme, and evaluate the results. Moreover, sales promotion must be coordinated carefully with other promotion mix elements within the integrated marketing communications programme.

public relations

Another important mass-promotion technique is **public relations**. This concerns building good relations with the company's various publics by obtaining favourable publicity, building up a good 'corporate image' and handling or heading off unfavourable rumours, stories and events. Public relations (PR) departments perform any or all of the following functions:

✦ *Press relations or press agency.* Creating and placing newsworthy information in the news media to attract attention to a person, product or service.

✦ *Product publicity.* Publicising specific products.

✦ *Public affairs.* Building and maintaining local, national and international relations.

✦ *Lobbying.* Building and maintaining relations with legislators and government officials to influence legislation and regulation.

✦ *Investor relations.* Maintaining relationships with shareholders and others in the financial community.

✦ *Development.* Public relations with donors or members of non-profit organisations to gain financial or volunteer support.

Public relations is used to promote products, people, places, ideas, activities, organisations and even nations. Trade associations have used public relations to rebuild interest in declining commodities such as eggs, apples, milk and potatoes. Even nations have used public relations to attract more tourists, foreign investment and international support. Companies can use PR to manage their way out of crisis, as in the case of Johnson & Johnson's masterly use of public relations to save Tylenol from extinction after its product-tampering scare.

Public relations can have a strong impact on public awareness at a much lower cost than advertising. The company does not pay for the space or time in the media. Rather, it pays for staff to develop and circulate information and to manage events. If the company develops an interesting story, it could be picked up by several different media, having the same effect as advertising that would cost a lot more money. It would have more credibility than advertising. Public relations results can sometimes be spectacular.

Despite its potential strengths, public relations, like sales promotions, is often described as a marketing stepchild because of its limited and scattered use. The public relations department is usually located at corporate headquarters. Its staff is so busy dealing with various publics – stockholders, employees, legislators, city officials – that public relations programmes to support product marketing objectives may be ignored. Moreover, marketing managers and public relations practitioners do not always talk the same language. Many public relations practitioners see their job as simply communicating. In contrast, marketing managers tend to be much more interested in how advertising and public relations affect sales and profits.

This situation is changing, however. Many companies now want their public relations departments to manage all their activities with a view to marketing the company and improving the bottom line. They know that good public relations can be a powerful brand-building tool. Anita Roddick built The Body Shop into a major international brand with hardly any advertising. Instead she travelled the world on a relentless quest for publicity!

Thus, some companies are setting up special units to support corporate and product promotion and image making directly. Many companies hire marketing public

Public relations
Building good relations with the company's various publics by obtaining favourable publicity, building up a good 'corporate image', and handling or heading off unfavourable rumours, stories and events. Major PR tools include press relations, product publicity, corporate communications, lobbying and counselling.

The birth of a brand is often accomplished with public relations, not advertising. For example, Beanie Babies have been highly successful with virtually no advertising.

relations firms to handle their PR programmes or to assist the company public relations team.

important public relations tools

There are a number of PR tools. One essential tool is *news*. PR professionals find or create favourable news about the company and its products or people. Sometimes news stories occur naturally. At other times, the PR person can suggest events or activities that would create news.

Speeches also create product and company publicity. Increasingly, company executives must field questions from the media or give talks at trade associations or sales meetings. These events can either build or hurt the company's image.

Another common PR tool is *special events*, ranging from news conferences, press tours, grand openings and firework displays to laser shows, hot-air balloon releases, multimedia presentations and star-studded spectaculars, or educational programmes designed to reach and interest target publics. Richard Branson, the chief executive of Virgin Group, offers a good example of a practitioner who has perfected the art of deploying both speeches and special events for self- and corporate promotion.

Public relations people also prepare *written materials* to reach and influence their target markets. These materials include annual reports, brochures, articles and company newsletters and magazines.

Audiovisual materials, such as films, slide-and-sound programmes and video and audio cassettes, are being used increasingly as communication tools.

Corporate-identity materials also help create a corporate identity that the public immediately recognises. Logos, stationery, brochures, signs, business forms, business cards, buildings, uniforms and even company cars and trucks make effective marketing tools when they are attractive, distinctive and memorable.

Companies might improve public goodwill by contributing money and time to *public service activities*: campaigns to raise funds for worthy causes – for example, to fight illiteracy, support the work of a charity, or assist the aged and handicapped – help to raise public recognition.

Sponsorship is any vehicle through which corporations gain public relations exposure. In Europe, the sponsorship industry is growing, with many firms committing huge sums of money around the world to the sponsorship of sport and the arts because it makes good sense as a marketing tool. Common trends are emerging in almost all European countries, according to the Comité Européen pour le Rapprochement de l'Economie et de la Culture (Cerec). There are professional sponsorship associations in most countries in Europe, and Cerec fosters closer ties between business and the arts and coordinates the network of sponsorship associations and its own business members. In Germany, however, due to high public subsidy for the arts and punishing levels of taxation, businesses play a lesser role. Those that do participate, like Daimler-Benz, BMW and Lufthansa, do seek public recognition and media coverage for their efforts.[29]

A company's *website* can also be a good public relations vehicle. Consumers and members of other publics can visit the site for information and entertainment. Websites can also be ideal for handling crisis situations. As more and more people look to the Net for information, not salesmanship, a real opportunity now unfolds for public relations (see Marketing Highlight 19.3).

main public relations decisions

As with the other promotion tools, in considering when and how to use product public relations, management should set PR objectives, choose the PR messages and vehicles, implement the PR plan and evaluate the results.

■ Setting public relations objectives

The *objectives* for public relations are usually defined in relation to the types of news story to be communicated, the communication objectives to be achieved (for instance, awareness creation, knowledge dissemination, generation of specific publicity for target groups) and the specific target audiences.

Public relations involves many functions beyond product publicity, including public affairs, lobbying and investor relations. For example, most company websites feature special sections for current and potential investors – like this one from Ericsson.

SOURCE: http://www.ericsson.com/investors.shtml

marketing highlight 19.3

Interactive PR: changing the face of publicity

The emergence of the World Wide Web is changing the way marketing is conducted in organisations, big and small. Not least is the scope of the Internet's potential to affect companies' public relations activities.

The PR industry faces a 'web' of opportunities to connect directly with customers and other target audiences. Company websites are now used to post testimonials from satisfied buyers; to make new product announcements; and to allow the organisation to respond publicly to events, particularly crises, swiftly and to a broad audience at relatively low cost. The direct-to-consumer nature of corporate websites means that firms' PR departments and their agencies have greater control over the message to be communicated. In the pre-Web era, journalists would be relied upon to write 'stories' about the organisation, its product or an employee to make the organisation or event newsworthy. It was the only way to win credibility.

One of the most important benefits of using company websites for public relations is a greater control of message consistency. Publications and editorials may not always give the intended 'spin' or prominent placement sought by the company. Moreover, publicity material can be geared up as sales vehicles, where appropriate. For example, since an online press release is going straight to the consumer, rather than journalists, links to sales or customer enquiries can be effected. Consumers' response and feedback can be got instantaneously.

The independence that the Internet brings to companies who use it as a channel of communication does not, however, mean they can forget schmoozing journalists and reporters. To the contrary, PR experts (agency representatives and their clients alike) have to work as hard as ever at media relations. Consumers are not morons, but have a critical eye. There have been a rising number of Internet scams, where offending firms and their less than credible messages have served to heighten people's scepticism about company-generated messages (advertising and publicity included). The UK's Advertising Standards Association (ASA), for example, has recently upheld complaints against start-up iglu.com, for falsely claiming to be the 'world's number one supplier of wintersport holidays'; Slammer.com for failing to live up to its price promises; and LineOne.com, the Internet service provider, for wrongly claiming to be the country's largest free content provider. Media relations remain important, since journalists still have the upper hand in matters of implied credibility. First, while journalists are dependent on the Web for background information and sources for story ideas, most remain wary of most sites. Headlines and press releases do not always capture journalists' attention either. And many will not even open e-mail attachments for fear of contracting nasty viruses. The solution is for PR representatives and their clients to make the effort to get to know reporters and journalists personally. Back to good, old-fashioned communications and media relations.

There is little question that the Internet will change the fundamentals of public relations work. A few simple rules may help professionals and clients alike when using the Web for communications. Journalists are not dead. So, do not bypass them. No other form of communication carries the same impact as journalism. Instead supplement online communications with journalists and other opinion-formers with direct communications such as face-to-face meetings and phone calls. Tracking is key. Keep pace with and respond to the online media by using online services such as news-trackers to filter relevant news items to target users' personal computers. Technology will continue to dazzle the PR world. Real-time devices such as instant messaging, online press conferences and 'Executive chats' will present untold opportunities for rapid movement of information, which can also be easily brought up to date.

Looking ahead, PR will go multimedia. Imagine the possibilities – audio and video clips attached to e-mails and websites that combine sound, animation and three-dimensional imaging. One reminder though. If you make the morning news, you should ensure your website flags your viewpoint. Otherwise, why bother with a medium that is so easy to update?

SOURCES: Based on Steve Jarvis, 'How the internet is changing the fundamentals of publicity', *Marketing News* (17 July 2000), pp. 6–7; Carlos Grande and Caroline Daniel, 'The high and lows of online shopping', *Financial Times* (16 May 2000), p. 9.

■ Choosing public relations messages and vehicles

Message themes for the public relations exercise should be guided by the organisation's PR objectives. In some cases the choice of PR messages and tools will be clear-cut. In others, the organisation has to create the news rather than find it by sponsoring noteworthy events. Creating events is especially important in publicising fund-raising drives for non-profit organisations. In the past, fund-raisers have created a large set of special events, ranging from art exhibits, auctions and dinners, to marathons, walkathons and swimathons.

■ Implementing the public relations plan

Implementing public relations requires care. For example, a *great* story is easy to place, but, unfortunately, most stories are not earth shattering and would not get past busy editors. Thus public relations people have to acquire a feel for what media editors want to feature in their papers and magazines as well as establish good relationships with them. They view media editors as a market to be satisfied so that editors will continue to use their stories.

■ Evaluating public relations results

Public relations results are difficult to measure because PR is used with other promotion tools and its impact is often indirect. Ideally, the company should measure the change in product awareness, knowledge and attitude resulting from the publicity campaign. Assessing the change requires measuring the before-and-after-the-campaign levels of these measures. Finally, sales and profit impact, if obtainable, is the best measure of public relations effort. If advertising and sales promotion were also stepped up during the period of the PR campaign, their contribution has to be considered.

Increasingly, companies, particularly high-media-profile organisations such as banks, food, chemicals and pharmaceuticals firms, invest in longer-term media tracking to help public relations managers to design and implement more effective PR programmes. They employ specialist media analysis and evaluation agencies or PR consultants to conduct in-depth media analyses which include coverage in both electronic and print media, and identify issues and public perceptions about the organisation's reputation, products and services and those of their competitors, as well as tracking legislative initiatives. They generate 'management intelligence' to determine the effectiveness of an organisation's PR activities and to help forward planning of communications and customer/public relationship building, including how management should react in a crisis management situation.

> For example, the charity organisation Barnardo's conducted media content analyses to identify if the public's perception of Barnardo's was consistent with the modern aspects of Barnardo's work. The charity was concerned that people still thought of Barnardo's as an outfit that runs orphans' homes, whereas the last one closed in the early 1980s, and they are now tackling modern childcare issues. By systematically tracking all reference to Barnardo's work currently in the press, the organisation found that the analyses proved that its initial strategy was working. When Shell UK faced adverse publicity over the disposal of its defunct oil rig, Brent Spar, Shell hired experts to provide in-depth analyses of media coverage and public opinion. The information helped the company deliver a strategic counter-attack once management understood the issues embedded in the crisis: who the opposition was and the nature of its agenda.[30]

Finally, like the other communications tools, public relations should be blended smoothly with other promotion activities within the company's overall integrated marketing communications effort.

summary

Companies must do more than deliver good products and services – they have to inform customers about product benefits and carefully position these in customers' minds. They do this by skilfully employing mass promotions to target specific buyers. The three mass-promotion tools are *advertising*, *sales promotion* and *public relations*.

Advertising is the use of paid media by a seller to inform, persuade and remind target audiences about its products or organisation. It is a powerful promotion tool which takes many forms and has many uses. *Sales promotion* covers a wide variety of purchasing incentives – coupons, premiums, contests, buying allowances – designed to stimulate final and business consumers, the trade and the company's own sales force. In many countries, sales promotion spending has been growing faster than advertising spending in recent years. *Public relations* – gaining favourable publicity and creating a favourable company image – is the least used of the major promotion tools, although it has great potential for building consumer awareness and preference.

Advertising decision making involves decisions about the objectives, the budget, the message, the media and, finally, the evaluation of results. Advertisers should set clear *objectives* as to whether the advertising is supposed to inform, persuade or remind buyers. The advertising *budget* can be based on what is affordable, on a percentage of sales, on competitors' spending, or on the objectives and tasks. *Message* decisions involve planning the message strategy – designing messages, evaluating and selecting them – and executing them effectively. The *media decision* calls for a definition of reach, frequency and impact goals; choosing chief media types; selecting media vehicles; and deciding on media timing. Finally, *evaluation* calls for evaluating the communication and sales effects of advertising before, during and after the advertising is placed.

Companies that advertise their products in different country markets can apply the basic principles relating to domestic advertising, but they must take into account the complexities involved in international advertising. They must address the similarities and differences in customer needs and buying behaviour, as well as cultural, socio-economic, political and regulatory environments across country markets, which will affect the decision to standardise or differentiate advertising strategies and executions.

In general, sales promotions should be about consumer relationship building. Sales promotion calls for setting sales promotion objectives, selecting tools, developing, pre-testing and implementing the sales promotion programme, and evaluating the results.

Organisations use *public relations* to obtain favourable publicity, to build up a good 'corporate image' and to handle or head off unfavourable rumours, stories and events. Public relations involves setting PR objectives, choosing PR messages and vehicles, implementing the PR plan and evaluating PR results. To accomplish these goals, PR professionals use a variety of tools, such as news, speeches and special events. Or they communicate with various publics through written, audiovisual and corporate identity materials, and contribute money and time to public relations activities.

discussing the issues

1. Comparison advertising is not permitted in some countries. What are some of the benefits and drawbacks of comparison advertising? Which has more to gain from using comparison advertising – the leading brand in a market or a lesser brand? Why?

2. Surveys show that many people are sceptical of advertising claims. Do you mistrust advertising? Why or why not? What should advertisers do to increase credibility?

3. What factors call for more *frequency* in an advertising media schedule? What factors call for more *reach*? How can you increase one without sacrificing the other or increasing the advertising budget?

4. Companies often run advertising, sales promotion and public relations efforts at the same time. Can their efforts be separated? Discuss how a company might evaluate the effectiveness of each element in this mix.

5. The Internet is the latest public relations frontier. Web users now routinely share their experiences and problems with a company's products, service, prices and warranties on electronic bulletin boards and chat rooms and at various websites. What kinds of special public relations problems and opportunities does the Internet present to today's marketers? How can companies use their own websites to deal with these problems and opportunities? Find a good example of a company that uses its website as a public relations tool.

applying the concepts

1. Buy a Sunday paper and sort through the colour advertising and coupon inserts. Find examples that combine advertising, sales promotion and/or public relations. For instance, a manufacturer may run a full-page ad that also includes a coupon and information on its sponsorship of a charity event.

   ✦ Do you think these approaches using multiple tools are more or less effective than a single approach? Why?

   ✦ Try to find ads from two direct competitors. Are these brands using similar promotional tools in similar ways?

2. Try to log into the websites of tobacco companies such as Philip Morris (www.philipmorris.com), RJ Reynolds (www.rjrt.com), BAT (www.bat.com) or Brown and Williamson (www.brownandwilliamson.com). Navigate to the tobacco area. You may encounter links to news about the tobacco industry, documents containing harsh criticisms from anti-smoking lobbies, as well as a host of other pro- and anti-tobacco material. RJ Reynolds tells you that 'it manufactures products that have significant and inherent health risks'

though it still urges you to report and protest about 'unfair' anti-smoking bans. On its website, Philip Morris admits that 'cigarette smoking is addictive'. Others, like Brown and Williamson, enable you to link to their 'courthouse' section so you can keep an exact count of the legal assaults upon the company. For years tobacco firms like Philip Morris have operated under a siege mentality, closing themselves off from the questions and criticisms coming from the outside world. Recently, however, this culture has slowly begun to change, with companies facing increasing pressure to change their image. However, being a responsible corporate citizen and changing the company's culture, products and image will not be easy.

   (a) What public relations issues do cigarette manufacturers such as BAT, Philip Morris and RJ Reynolds face?

   (b) What kind of public relations advantages does admission of tobacco's health risks create? What problems?

   (c) Outline a public relations programme for gaining public trust and shareholder interest.

references

1. Martin Vander Weyer, *Falling Eagle: the decline of Barclays Bank* (London: Weidenfeld and Nicolson, 2000); 'Barclays' big ambitions', *The Economist* (18 November 2000), pp. 46–9; John Williams, 'Barclays boosted by 24% retail profit rise', *Financial Times* (4 August 2000), p. 21; James Mackintosh, 'Barclays learns a lesson in keeping customers satisfied', *Financial Times* (4 July 2000), p. 4; 'Barclays learns belatedly that the consumer is king', *The Independent* (4 July 2000), p. 19; 'So, what's the big idea then?', *The Independent* (28 July 2000), p. 12; 'Sites revival by Barclays', *The Evening Standard* (8 May 2000), p. 40; 'Barclays admits bungle over site closures', *The Independent* (27 April 2000), p. 4; 'Big fee, big disclaimer', *The Guardian* (28 April 2000), p. 29.

2. 'Advertising expenditure by country and medium' in *European Marketing Pocket Book 2000* (Henley-on-Thames: NTC Publications, 2000), p. 24.

3. See Russell H. Colley, *Defining Advertising Goals for Measured Advertising Results* (New York: Association for National Advertisers, 1961). In this well-known book, Colley lists 52 possible advertising objectives. He outlines a method called DAGMAR (after a book's title) for turning advertising objectives into specific measurable goals. For a more complete discussion of DAGMAR, see M. L. Rothschild, *Advertising* (Lexington, MA: D. C. Heath, 1987), pp. 142–55.

4. Roger Trapp, 'Ads that hit raw nerves', *The Independent* (18 August 1994), p. 16.

5. See Patricia Nacimiento, 'Germany: Higher court takes new view on comparative advertising', *International Commercial Litigation* (July/August 1998), p. 47; John Shannon, 'Comparative ads call for prudence', *Marketing Week* (22 May 1999), p. 32.

6. See Donald E. Schultz, Dennis Martin and William P. Brown, *Strategic Marketing Campaigns* (Chicago, IL: Crain, 1984), pp. 192–7.

7. See C. Gilligan, 'How British advertisers set budgets', *Journal of Advertising Research* (17 February 1977).

8. See Andrew Ehrenberg, Neil Barnard and John Scriven, 'Justifying our advertising budgets', *Marketing & Research Today* (February 1997), pp. 38–44; and Dana W. Hayman and Don E. Schultz, 'How much should you spend on advertising?', *Advertising Age* (26 April 1999), p. 32.

9. Information from Gary Levin, '"Meddling" in creative more welcome', *Advertising Age* (9 April 1990), pp. S4, S8; Lynne Roberts, 'New media choice: Absolut Vodka', *Marketing* (9 April 1998), p. 12;

Eleftheria Parpis, 'TBWA: Absolut', *Adweek* (9 November 1998), p. 172; and the Q&A section at www.absolutvodka.com (March 2000).

10. See also Judith Corstjens, *Strategic Advertising: A practitioner's handbook* (Oxford: Heinemann Professional Publishing, 1990).

11. See Faye Rice, 'How to deal with tougher customers', *Fortune* (3 December 1990), pp. 38–48.

12. See, for example, R. Dunn, 'Greater freedom of the airwaves and advertising cost-effectiveness', *Admap*, **25**, 6 (1989).

13. See Gary Schroeder, 'Behavioral optimization', *American Demographics* (August 1998), pp. 34–36; and Erwin Ephron, 'Ad world was ripe for its conversion to optimizers', *Advertising Age* (22 February 1999), p. S16.

14. Information on advertising agency income and billings obtained online at http://adage/dataplace (December 1999); and from *The European Marketing Pocket Book 2000* (Henley-on-Thames: NTC Publications, 2000), p. 18.

15. 'Star turn', *The Economist* (11 March 2000), pp. 91–2.

16. 'A passion for variety', *The Economist* (30 November 1996), pp. 104–7.

17. Greg Harris, 'Factors influencing the international advertising practices of multinational companies', *Management Decision*, **34**, 6 (1996), pp. 5–11; Nikolaos Papavassiliou and Vlasis Stathakopoulos, 'Standardization versus adaptation of international advertising strategies: towards a framework', *European Journal of Marketing*, **31**, 7 (1997), pp. 504–27.

18. J. N. Kapferer and Eurocom, 'How global are global brands?', ESOMAR Seminar on the Challenge of Branding Today and in the Future, Brussels, 28–30 October 1992.

19. Boris Kaz, 'Researching the pan-European media market', *Admap* (July–August 1996), pp. 31–2; John Shannon, 'Research boost for pan-Euro TV', *Marketing Week* (19 April 1996), p. 29.

20. John Shannon, 'TV ads struggle in Scandinavia', *Marketing Week* (20 September 1996), p. 26.

21. James Curtis, 'Legal muscles from Brussels', *Marketing Business* (September 2000), pp. 44–5; 'Coca-Cola rapped for running competition in India', AdAgeInternational.com (February 1997); David Short and Hilary Clarke, 'Undoing the

patchwork of advertising laws', *The European* (16–22 May 1996), p. 25; For more on EU legislation visit: http://europa.eu.int/eur-lex/en/.

22. Louise O'Brien and Charles Jones, 'Do rewards really create loyalty?', *Harvard Business Review* (May–June 1995), pp. 75–82; Graham R. Dowling and Mark Uncles, 'Do customer loyalty programs really work?', *Sloan Management Review* (Summer 1997), pp. 71–82.

23. See John Philip Jones, 'The double jeopardy of sales promotions', *Harvard Business Review* (September–October 1990), pp. 145–52.

24. See Chad Kaydo, 'Your logo here', *Sales & Marketing Management* (April 1998), pp. 65–70; J. Thomas Russell and Ronald Lane, *Kleppner's Advertising Procedure*, 13th edn (Englewood Cliffs, NJ: Prentice Hall, 1996), pp. 453–6; 'Power to the key ring and T-shirt', *Sales and Marketing Management* (December 1989), p. 14.

25. A more extensive discussion of the legal position of sales promotion methods across EU states and developments towards EU harmonisation is found in: *European Promotional Legislation Guide*, 3rd edn (London: Institute of Sales Promotion, 1992); *European Code of Sales Promotion Practice* (London: Institute of Sales Promotion, March 1991); R. Lawson,

'Key problems in Europe: can you implement a pan-European promotion?', Incorporated Society of British Advertisers' Conference on 'Controlling Sales Promotion: Getting it Right is a Joint Responsibility', London, July 1991.

26. Mandy Thatcher, 'Abroad beyond', *Marketing Business* (February 2000), pp. 42–4; the EPMA comprises three organisations – The British Promotional Merchandise Association (BPMA), The European Federation of Sales Promotion (EFSP) and The Institute of Sales Promotion (ISP); further details from: Cabinet Stewart European Affairs, Rue d'Arlon 40, Brussels.

27. Mandy Thatcher, op cit.

28. Richard Szathmary, 'Trade shows', *Sales and Marketing Management* (May 1992), pp. 83–4. Srinath Gopalakrishna, Gary L. Lilien, Jerome D. Williams and Ian Sequeira, 'Do trade shows pay off?', *Journal of Marketing* (July 1995), pp. 75–83.

29. Louella Miles, 'Get noticed', *Marketing Business* (March 1992), pp. 30–3; Terry Eccles, 'Why $9 billion is put on board the sponsorship bicycle', *The European* (6–12 May 1994), p. 20.

30. Jo-Anne Walker, 'News analysis', *Marketing Week* (24 November 1996), p. 39.

case 19

Promotions in a digital age

The new millennium market bid dipper years for the dotcom companies and the advertising industry that consumed much of their cash. One commentator described the dotcom revolution as the fastest-ever transfer of money from the pockets of entrepreneurs to the pockets of the advertising industry. While dotcom companies rose and fell, the advertising industry benefited from the huge campaigns that the dotcom companies ran. With the mania quelled, advertising agencies face two dilemmas. First, they have to get used to lower advertising spends as e-businesses will behave more like real businesses and spend what they can afford. Second, they face the realisation that e-commerce and the digital age have changed media and the way people use them, for ever. Was the dotcom boom the final party for the dream factories of Madison Avenue and Berkeley Square? These two articles, which appeared six months apart in the *Financial Times,* illustrate the switchback that was 2000 – from boom to bewilderment.

Dotcom advertising: abstract ads keep audiences guessing[1]

Tired of watching dull television advertisements for dotcoms? There could soon be more. Research from market analyst AC Nielsen MMS shows that dotcom spending on TV advertising is rising substantially. But too many ads follow a predictable format – a series of quirky or just plain baffling images, followed by the company's website address. In many cases, it is unclear exactly what the dotcom is selling.

Doug Hamilton, creative director of London-based branding company Wolff Olins, says: 'Too many Internet advertising campaigns are like the Titanic. We have the launch, then they disappear. To build a brand you need a consistent message and a sustained campaign. Your brand needs to be the same everywhere, whether you are advertising online or offline.'

Mr Hamilton believes that online bookseller Amazon.com is one of the few companies to achieve this. 'Lastminute.com promises to do things better and cheaper. But when you try it, [you find] it doesn't', he says. 'A clear message is important. That's why LetsBuyIt.com's message – that if we all band together we can drive down prices – works.' Another example of successful branding is budget airline easyJet. 'The

message is about lowering cost by taking out things that people don't need', Mr Hamilton says.

There are several reasons behind the poor quality of some Internet companies' advertising. First, dotcoms are a new type of company – and marketeers are still finding out how to promote them best. Second, some companies have inexperienced managers who fail to get the best out of their advertising agencies. And third, many have limited advertising budgets.

Good or bad, spending on dotcom TV ads keeps increasing. According to AC Nielsen MMS, Internet-based companies in the UK spent £3.2m (€5.25) on mainstream advertising from March to May 1999; £7.8m the next quarter; £28.9m the quarter after that, and a massive £43.5m for the quarter to February 2000. The most popular media used by dotcom advertisers are TV and the press, accounting for a third and a quarter of all spend respectively, followed by direct mail (mainly used by financial services companies such as Egg), outdoor billboards and radio. But it is unclear whether dotcoms will continue to increase their TV ad spend.

Some agencies believe that advertising expenditure will shift away from conventional media and towards the Internet. Fletcher Research, for example, estimates that as much as 50 per cent of dotcoms' advertising budgets will eventually be spent online once their brands are sufficiently established, with UK online advertising revenues soaring from £50m at the end of 1999 to £625m by 2004. Most of this will be at the expense of direct marketing – which it expects to drop by a third – but outdoor, radio and press advertising will also be hit.

However, Jeremy Ridgway of AC Nielsen MMS points out that online advertisers are not going to find it easy to win and retain customer loyalty on an Internet that hosts millions of different websites 'surfed by disloyal, impatient consumers. They are likely to have to use existing media to build brand-awareness.' He predicts: 'Direct mail, in particular, may actually benefit from the dotcom explosion, by offering well-defined target audiences in an increasingly diverse digital advertising world.'

Online advertising has its limitations, such as falling 'click-through' rates. With this in mind, some companies prefer users to be referred via links from other companies' sites. Stephen Cole, managing director of Streets Online, which sells books, music, films and computer games, says: 'With partners such as Freeserve – which has invested £6m – Marbles, GWR, Egg, Which?Online

---

1. Joia Shillingford, 'Abstract ads keep audiences guessing: dotcom advertising', *Financial Times* (7 June 2000), p. 6.

and LineOne, we have substituted huge ad expenditure for a small commission fee to the site that directs the traffic.'

The secret, says Mr Hamilton, is for dotcom companies to go back to basics and choose the one thing that they want to be known for and a good product name. 'They must get away from being too postmodern', he says. 'If you see a website called Fish, then probably the last thing it sells is fish.' He also advises dotcoms not to blow all their money on TV advertising if they cannot afford to follow up their first big splash.

Mr Hamilton says there is still scope for doing something different to draw people to a website. For example, he is a proponent of viral marketing – a way of reaching a target audience by letting a small number of people spread the word about the product and brand. 'I really love Lomo.com', says Mr Hamilton. 'It's a Russian camera site where they are building up a database of photos of people doing crazy things. It has become a worldwide cult.' And his recipe for advertising dotcoms successfully? 'Commonsense – and as little money as possible.'

Digital media: advertising industry at a crossroads[2]

Joe Soap sits in front of the television set watching his favourite show. Fifteen minutes into the programme, he stretches out an arm, picks up the remote, and with a few dabs of his thumb on the QuickSkip button, turns the advertising world upside down. He has just zapped out the commercials.

Visions such as this are sending a shiver through the advertising industry as it tries to make sense of a future that has been thrown into uncertainty by new technology. For as long as most people can remember, the industry's prospects have been determined largely by the state of the economy. When the good times roll, profits soar. In a recession, they slump. But now, unless the promise of digital technology has become wildly exaggerated, the industry could be about to undergo the biggest change it has experienced since the introduction of television half a century ago.

'The advertising industry is at a crossroads, facing more fundamental change than at any time in the last 50 years', says Andrew Brown, director-general of the Advertising Association, a UK industry body. 'Trying to form a view of what the media landscape is going to be like over the next 10 years is very difficult. The tendency to extrapolate from one year to the next will become more open to challenge as new technology starts to bite.'

If broad economic trends were all the advertising industry had to worry about, some would argue that its outlook had never been better. Indeed, just as some pundits have argued that the economic cycle has been abolished, others suggest the advertising cycle has ended – meaning that advertising has entered an era in which it will grow more quickly than gross domestic product, whatever the state of the economic cycle. Increased competition underpins this argument. Generally, the greater the competition, the more companies need to advertise: and most industries are now operating in a more competitive environment than at any time in their history.

Globalisation and deregulation have helped increase competitive pressures. In addition, the wide availability of low-cost technology means that it is difficult for any company to maintain a technological lead over its competitors. So marketing and branding have taken over as the main way of differentiating one company's product from another's. Even so, a worry for traditional advertisers and their agencies is that digital technology will accelerate the fragmentation of the mass market, consigning old-established methods of advertising to the dustbin of history. For example, in the UK and other countries, analogue television will soon be replaced by digital television, greatly increasing the number of channels available to viewers and encouraging a multitude of niche audiences to emerge. Interactivity is driving fragmentation, too, because it allows advertisers to learn about people's individual tastes and preferences and send them customised messages instead of one-size-fits-all advertisements.

The Internet has already established itself as an important interactive medium; and now, interactive television is on the horizon, too, combining many of the characteristics of digital television and the Internet. When interactive television is established, set-top boxes will merge details of people's viewing habits with knowledge of what movies or games they download, what extra information services they demand, and what they buy through their interactive shopping channel – all opening the way for targeted advertising. And if these developments were not significant enough, there is also the new generation of interactive digital video recorders offered by companies such as TiVo and ReplayTV that allow viewers to skip past the commercials when playing recorded material.

Predictions that digital video recorders will bring the end of television advertising – and with it, the end of commercial television – are almost certainly unjustified. People will continue to watch much of their television live, and as long as they do so, they will be unable to skip the commercials even if they want to. Yet, the machines do raise some concerns. They make recording far simpler than is possible with the existing generation of video cassette recorders. And the ability to pause live programmes – for example, to answer the telephone – could tempt viewers to catch up with the

---

2. 'Digital media: advertising industry at a crossroads', *FT Creative Business* (14 November 2000), p. 28.

live action by skipping the advertisements. Because these machines automatically pick out and record the viewer's favourite shows, offering a form of customised programming, they will also encourage the trend towards fragmentation and targeted advertising.

The arrival of interactive communications is not necessarily bad news for the advertising industry. New media require new forms of advertising, which in turn will bring new areas of growth. But what is not yet clear is how far the growth of advertising in new media will be incremental to traditional mass market advertising, or how far it will become a substitute for it. A few weeks ago, Volvo Cars of North America, part of Ford Motor, raised eyebrows in the US advertising industry by launching its latest car, the S60, entirely online. It bought no television commercials nor any advertisements in the print media, except for two or three specialist car magazines. Partly, that was because Volvo's advertising budget was under strain, so it seemed an opportune moment to test the effectiveness of new media. And it is planning to do some traditional media advertising for the car next year. Yet, partly in response to the soaring cost of television airtime, big advertisers such as Procter & Gamble and Unilever have also been cutting their spending on television advertising even as they increase their budgets for interactive media and below-the-line marketing.

This week, at a ceremony in London, the Institute of Practitioners in Advertising announced the winners of its advertising effectiveness awards, which set out to identify Britain's most effective advertising campaigns. But to put the question provocatively, what is the point of the traditional advertising campaign if the whole world of advertising is about to be turned on its head?

'With every new medium and every new gadget, it is predicted that mass advertising will curl up and die, but it never does', says Rupert Howell, the IPA's president. 'And the reason it doesn't is that it is still the most cost-effective means of communication.' The problem with one-to-one marketing, says Howell, is that it is 'fiendishly expensive'. So although it is growing, it is as an addition to, not as a substitute for, mass advertising.

Howell says mass advertising still works because people like advertising. Apart from the fact that some of it is funny and entertaining, it helps people make choices in an over-supplied world; it introduces people to new and improved products and services; and it makes things famous, which appeals to people's curious obsession with famous things. 'There is no demise, there will be no demise and there never has been a demise', says Howell. 'Advertising has grown consistently for 2,000 years, and it will continue to do so.'

Questions

1. Do you think the forecast 'online advertising revenues soaring from £50m at the end of 1999 to £625m by 2004' still holds or is it a reflection of dotcom euphoria?

2. What accounts for the extraordinary levels of expenditure and content of dotcom advertising referred to in the first article?

3. Could or should advertising agencies have been more responsible in guiding the content and extraordinary levels of dotcom advertising?

4. Has advertising arrived at Andrew Brown's 'crossroads' or, as Rupert Howell intimates, will it continue to grow 'consistently'? For another 2,000 years?

5. If mass advertising is to decline, will the trend be global, will it reflect a reduction in overall promotional expenditure or will other media take its place?

6. Evaluate Rupert Howell's claim that the reason mass advertising still works is because 'it is still the most cost-effective means of communication . . . [and] people like advertising. Apart from the fact that some of it is funny and entertaining, it helps people make choices in an over-supplied world.'

Sources: See also: Lucy Killgren, 'Advertising; Adding to uncertainty', *FT Creative Business* (16 January 2001), p. 5; Thorold Barker, 'Yahoo! forecasts advertising slump', *Financial Times* (12 January 2001), p. 25; Richard Tomkins, 'Adverts spending fall in real terms', *Financial Times* (11 January 2001), p. 1.

internet exercises

Internet exercises for this chapter can be found on the student site of the MYPHLIP Web Site at www.booksites.net/kotler.

chapter twenty

Personal selling and sales management

Chapter objectives *After reading this chapter, you should be able to:*

- Discuss the role of a company's salespeople in creating value for customers and building customer relationships.

- Explain how companies set sales force strategy and structure.

- Explain how companies recruit, select and train salespeople.

- Describe how companies compensate and supervise salespeople and how they evaluate their effectiveness.

- Discuss the personal selling process, distinguishing between transaction-oriented marketing and relationship marketing.

introduction

The questions in the preview case overleaf reflect some of the critical issues that management must address when determining sales force strategy and structure. Indeed, the decisions called for are relevant not only for MD Foods, as in the preview case, but also for any firm that uses a sales force to help it market its goods and services. This chapter looks at the role and nature of personal selling and examines the key issues in managing the sales force.

Robert Louis Stevenson once noted that 'everyone lives by selling something'. We are all familiar with the sales forces used by business organisations to sell products and services to customers around the world. Sales forces are found in non-profit as well as profit organisations. Churches use membership committees to attract new members. Hospitals and museums use fund-raisers to contact donors and raise money. In this chapter, we examine the role of personal selling in the organisation, sales force management decisions and the basic principles of personal selling.

preview case

MD Foods AMBA: rethinking its sales force strategy and structure

MD Foods AMBA, owned by 8,728 Danish farmers, is Denmark's largest dairy cooperative. Production facilities are spread across the country. Through MD Foods International (MDI), MD operates its production and distribution facilities in England. Cooperative arrangements with counterparts such as Arla in Sweden and Arla's sales force in Finland have enabled MD to establish a strong presence in the Scandinavian markets. In milk tonnage terms, MD is now the fourth largest dairy in Europe. MD also has sales subsidiaries in England, France, Germany, Greece, Italy, Poland, Norway, Sweden and the Middle East.

Europe's dairy industry is dominated by national producers. Generic products are typically marketed by product type, such as brie, feta, camembert and so forth, which are internationally known. MD faces increasing competition not only from national and local producers but also from international companies with a track record in product development and branding.

A number of important changes have occurred in the European market environment in the past few years. These include the withdrawal of EU subsidies to the export of dairy products to non-EU countries in 1996, the increasing concentration of food retailers in Europe and the increasing centralisation in retailers' buying decision making as well as product mix planning. MD accounts for a third of total EU exports of feta cheese. The end of subsidies to exports to markets such as the Middle East has had a big impact on MD's profits, putting heavy pressure on the company to shift milk used for feta production to other products (such as milk powders and yellow cheeses) for EU customers.

Apart from deciding which product group(s) to emphasise, another major problem confronting MD is how to develop a more effective sales and marketing structure to compete cost-effectively in these market situations.

In the past, MD has based its sales organisation on geographical and national considerations. Moreover, the focus of the sales force was on individual stores rather than retail chains or key accounts. With the emerging retail concentration and centralisation of buying and planning functions in customers' organisations, MD recognises the need to respond to these pressures and to consider the options for managing the sales function, from analysing sales to managing key accounts. The time was right for dramatic action.

A key opportunity arose when one customer – a large international retailer – introduced the idea of key account management to MD. This one customer's European turnover from MD exceeded the turnover of many of MD's subsidiaries, making it more important than some of MD's geographic markets. MD decided to introduce key account management in its sales and marketing organisations, starting in Denmark, where retail concentration is high and MD has a dominant market position. Essentially, three key account managers were appointed to serve specific key accounts, divided into FDB, the Danish cooperative; DS, a private retail group together with Aldi, part of a German retail group; and other retailers. The key account managers worked as a team with three trade managers (who have in-store marketing and space management expertise) in relation to the specific key accounts. The Sales Director coordinated the key account managers, while the trade managers reported to the national trade marketing manager. In this way, MD could achieve optimisation of the sales force, while also ensuring that know-how is shared through coordination of trade marketing.

The organisational change piloted in Denmark was later introduced in Sweden, but reactions from both MD's subsidiary and major Swedish retailers were less positive. At headquarters, MD has been contemplating what steps to take next. What should MD's sales force strategy and organisational structure for sales be? Should the key account management format be applied in other markets? Should the key account managers be responsible for the sales force assigned to their key account? Existing sales forces also vary in size, from 15 to four people. Large sales forces dealing with stores with more autonomous management see to tasks such as sales, merchandising, displays, placing signs and posters and new campaigns. Smaller sales forces serve the highly centralised retailers and handle merchandising and displays. New developments must also take into account different workloads, skills and career developments for sales forces and key account managers serving different retailers and geographic markets. What will satisfy customer and employee requirements? Finally, can the new structure that is evolved be successfully applied to MD's operations across Europe?[1]

Questions

1. Why does MD Foods rely on a sales force to sell its products?

2. What are the key considerations that MD Foods needs to take into account in setting its sales force's objectives, strategy, structure and compensation? Identify the trade-offs involved in each of these decisions.

3. What are the key challenges facing MD Foods in developing and implementing an organisational structure that will satisfy both customers and employees (sales force, marketing and key account managers)? Recommend and justify a strategy for MD Foods.

SOURCE: Based on Mogéns Bjerre, 'MD Foods AMBA: A new world of sales and marketing', in *Understanding Marketing: A European Casebook*, Celia Phillips, et al. (eds). Reproduced with permission, © John Wiley & Sons, Ltd, 2000.

the role of personal selling

There are many types of personal selling jobs, and the role of personal selling varies greatly from one company to another. Here, we look at the nature of personal selling positions and at the role the sales force plays in modern organisations.

the nature of personal selling

Selling is one of the oldest professions in the world. The people who do the selling go by many names: *salespeople, sales representatives, account executives, sales consultants, sales engineers, field representatives, agents, district managers* and *marketing representatives*, to name a few.

People hold many stereotypes of salespeople. 'Salesman' may bring to mind the image of Arthur Miller's pitiable Willy Loman in *Death of a Salesman* or Meredith Willson's cigar-smoking, back-slapping, joke-telling Harold Hill in *The Music Man*. Both examples depict salespeople as loners travelling their territories trying to foist their wares on unsuspecting or unwilling buyers.

However, modern salespeople are a far cry from these unfortunate stereotypes. Today, most salespeople are well-educated, well-trained professionals who work to build and maintain long-term relationships with customers by listening to their customers, assessing customer needs and organising the company's efforts to solve customer problems.

Consider Airbus, the aerospace company that markets commercial aircraft. It takes more than a friendly smile and a firm handshake to sell expensive computer systems. Selling high-tech aircraft that cost tens of millions of euros a copy is complex and challenging. A single big sale can run into billions of euros. Airbus salespeople head up an extensive team of company sales specialists – sales and service technicians, financial analysts, planners, engineers – all dedicated to finding ways to satisfy airline customer needs. The salespeople begin by becoming experts on the airlines. They find out where each airline wants to grow, when it wants to replace planes and details of its financial situation. The team runs Airbus and rival planes through computer systems, simulating the airline's routes, cost per seat and other factors to show that their planes are most efficient. Then the high-level negotiations begin. The selling process is nerve-rackingly slow – it can take two to three years from the first sales presentation to the day the sale is announced. Sometimes top executives from both the airline and the company are brought in to close the deal. After getting the order, salespeople must stay in almost constant touch to keep track of the account's equipment needs and to make certain the customer stays satisfied. Success depends on building solid, long-term relationships with customers, based on performance and trust.

The term **salesperson** covers a wide range of positions. At one extreme, a salesperson might be largely an *order taker*, such as a department store salesperson standing behind the counter. At the other extreme are the *order getters*, salespeople whose job demands the *creative selling* of products and services ranging from appliances, industrial equipment or aeroplanes to insurance, advertising or consulting services. Other salespeople engage in *missionary selling*, whereby they are not expected or permitted to take an order, but only build goodwill or educate buyers. An example is a

Salesperson
An individual acting for a company by performing one or more of the following activities: prospecting, communicating, servicing and information gathering.

This Regent Hong Kong advertisement focuses on the hotel's people (its sales force) as one of the main selling propositions.

SOURCE: Regent International Hotels

salesperson for a pharmaceutical company who calls on doctors to educate them about the company's drug products and to urge them to prescribe these products to their patients. In this chapter, we focus on the more creative types of selling and on the process of building and managing an effective sales force.

the role of the sales force

Personal selling is the interpersonal arm of the promotion mix. Advertising consists of one-way, non-personal communication with target consumer groups. In contrast, personal selling involves two-way personal communication between salespeople and individual customers – whether face to face, by telephone, through videoconferences or by other means. As such, personal selling can be more effective than advertising in more complex selling situations. Salespeople can probe customers to learn more about their problems. They can adjust the marketing offer to fit the special needs of each customer and can negotiate terms of sale. They can build long-term personal relationships with key decision makers.

The role of personal selling varies from company to company. Some firms have no salespeople at all – for example, organisations that sell only through mail-order catalogues or through manufacturers' representatives, sales agents or brokers. In most firms, however, the sales force plays a major role. In companies that sell business products, such as ABB or Du Pont, the salespeople may be the only contact. To these customers, the sales force *is* the company. In consumer product companies, such as Adidas or Unilever, that sell through intermediaries, final consumers rarely meet salespeople or even know about them. Still, the sales force plays an important behind-the-scenes role. It works with wholesalers and retailers to gain their support and to help them to be more effective in selling the company's products.

The sales force serves as the critical link between a company and its customers. In many cases, salespeople serve both masters – the seller and the buyer. First, they *represent the company to customers*. They find and develop new customers and communicate information about the company's products and services. They sell products by approaching customers, presenting their products, answering objections, negotiating prices and terms, and closing sales. In addition, they provide services to customers, carry out market research and intelligence work, and fill out sales call reports.

At the same time, salespeople *represent customers to the company*, acting inside the firm as a 'champion' of customers' interests. Salespeople relay customer concerns about company products and actions back to those who can handle them. They learn about customer needs and work with others in the company to develop greater customer value. Thus, the salesperson often act as an *'account manager'* who manages the relationship between the seller and buyer.

As companies move towards a stronger market orientation, their sales forces are becoming more market focused and customer oriented. The old view was that salespeople should worry about sales and the company should worry about profit. The current view holds that salespeople should be concerned with more than just producing sales – they also must know how to produce customer satisfaction and profit. Today, organisations expect salespeople to look at sales data, measure market potential, gather market intelligence and develop marketing strategies and plans. They should know how to orchestrate the firm's efforts towards delivering customer value and satisfaction. A market-oriented rather than a sales-oriented sales force will be more effective in the long run. Beyond winning new customers and making sales, it will help the company to create long-term, profitable relationships with customers. As such, the company's sales team can be a central force in an organisation's relationship marketing programme. The topic concerning relationship marketing is discussed in greater detail in Chapter 11.

managing the sales force

We define **sales force management** as the analysis, planning, implementation and control of sales force activities. It includes setting sales force objectives, designing sales force strategy and structure, recruiting, selecting, training, supervising and evaluating the firm's salespeople. The primary sales force management decisions are shown in Figure 20.1. Let us take a look at each of these decisions next.

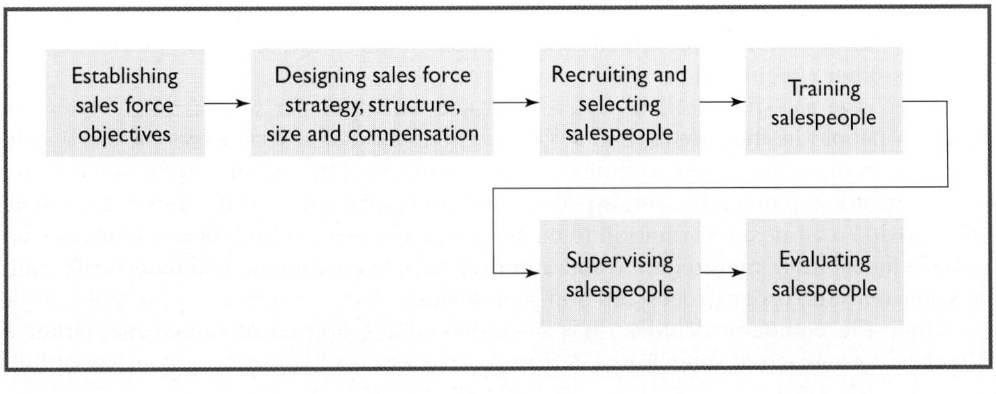

Sales force management
The analysis, planning, implementation and control of sales force activities. It includes setting sales force objectives; designing sales force strategy; and recruiting, selecting, training, supervising and evaluating the firm's salespeople.

Figure 20.1

Primary steps in sales force management

setting sales force objectives

Companies set different objectives for their sales forces. Salespeople usually perform one or more of the following tasks:

+ *Prospecting*. They find and develop new customers.
+ *Communicating*. They communicate information about the company's products and services.
+ *Selling*. They sell products by approaching customers, presenting their products, answering objections and closing sales.
+ *Servicing*. In addition, salespeople provide services to customers (e.g. consulting on problems, providing technical assistance, arranging finance).
+ *Information gathering*. Salespeople carry out market research and intelligence work, and fill out sales call reports.

Some companies are very specific about their sales force objectives and activities. For example, a company may advise its salespeople to spend 80 per cent of their time with current customers and 20 per cent with prospects, and 85 per cent of their time on current products and 15 per cent on new products. The company believes that if such norms are not set, salespeople tend to spend almost of all of their time selling current products to current accounts and neglect new products and new prospects.

designing sales force strategy and structure

Marketing managers face several sales force strategy and design questions. How should salespeople and their tasks be structured? How big should the sales force be? Should salespeople sell alone or work in teams with other people in the company? Should they sell in the field or by telephone? How should salespeople be compensated? And how should performance be rewarded where selling tasks are shared across members within the sales team? We address these issues below.

■ Sales force strategy

Every company competes with other firms to get orders from customers. Thus it must base its strategy on an understanding of the customer buying process. A company can use one or more of several sales approaches to contact customers. An individual salesperson can talk to a prospect or customer in person or over the phone, or make a sales presentation to a buying group. Similarly, a sales *team* (such as a company executive, a salesperson and a sales engineer) can make a sales presentation to a buying group. In *conference selling*, a salesperson brings resource people from the company to meet with one or more buyers to discuss problems and opportunities. In *seminar selling*, a company team conducts an educational seminar about state-of-the-art developments for a customer's technical people.

Often, the salesperson has to act as an account manager who arranges contacts between people in the buying and selling companies. Because salespeople need help from others in the company, selling calls for teamwork. Others who might assist salespeople include top management, especially when big sales are at stake; technical people who provide technical information to customers; customer service representatives who provide installation, maintenance and other services to customers; and office staff, such as sales analysts, order processors and secretaries.

Once the company decides on a desirable selling approach, it can use either a direct or a contractual sales force. A *direct* (or *company*) *sales force* consists of full-

or part-time employees who work exclusively for the company. This sales force includes *inside salespeople*, who conduct business from their offices via telephone or visits from prospective buyers, and *field salespeople*, who travel to call on customers. A *contractual sales force* consists of manufacturers' reps, sales agents or brokers who are paid a commission based on their sales.

■ Sales force structure

Sales force strategy influences the structure of the sales force. The sales force structure decision is simple if the company sells only one product line to one industry with customers in many locations. In that case the company would use a *territorial sales force structure*. If the company sells many products to many types of customer, it might need either a *product sales force structure* or a *customer sales force structure*, or a combination of the two.

Territorial sales force structure   In the **territorial sales force structure**, each salesperson is assigned to an exclusive territory in which to sell the company's full line of products or services. This simple sales force structure has many advantages. First, it clearly defines the salesperson's job, and because only one salesperson works the territory, he or she gets all the credit or the blame for territory sales. Second, the territorial structure increases the salesperson's desire to build local business relationships that, in turn, improve the salesperson's selling effectiveness. Finally, because each salesperson travels within a small geographic area, travel expenses are relatively small.

Territorial sales force structure
A sales force organisation that assigns each salesperson to an exclusive geographic territory in which that salesperson carries the company's full line.

Product sales force structure   Salespeople must know their products. The task is not easy if the company's products are numerous, unrelated and technically complex. To overcome this problem, many companies adopt a **product sales force structure**, in which the sales force sells along product lines. For example, Kodak uses different sales forces for its film products and its industrial products. The film products sales force deals with simple products that are distributed intensively, whereas the industrial products sales force deals with complex products that require technical understanding.

The product structure can lead to problems, however, if a given customer buys many of the company's products. For example, a hospital supply company has several product divisions, each with a separate sales force. Several salespeople might end up calling on the same hospital on the same day. This means that they travel over the same routes and wait to see the same customer's purchasing agents. These extra costs must be measured against the benefits of better product knowledge and attention to individual products.

Product sales force structure
A sales force organisation under which salespeople specialise in selling only a portion of the company's products or lines.

Customer sales force structure   More and more companies are using a **customer sales force structure**, whereby they organise the sales force along customer or industry lines. Separate sales forces may be set up for different industries, for serving current customers versus finding new ones, and for large accounts versus regular accounts.

Organising its sales force around customers can help a company to become more customer focused. For example, giant ABB, the Swiss-based industrial equipment maker, changed from a product-based to a customer-based sales force. The new structure resulted in a stronger customer orientation and improved service to clients:

Customer sales force structure
A sales force organisation under which salespeople specialise in selling only to certain customers or industries.

> David Donaldson sold boilers for ABB . . . After 30 years, Donaldson sure knew boilers, but he didn't know much about the broad range of other products offered by ABB's Power Plant division. Customers were frustrated because as many as a dozen ABB salespeople called on them at different times to peddle their products. Sometimes representatives even passed each other in customers' lobbies without realising that they were working for the same company. ABB's bosses decided that

this was a poor way to run a sales force. So, David Donaldson and 27 other power plant salespeople began new jobs. [Donaldson] now also sells turbines, generators, and three other product lines. He handles six major accounts . . . instead of a [mixed batch] of 35. His charge: Know the customer intimately and sell him the products that help him operate productively. Says Donaldson: 'My job is to make it easy for my customer to do business with us . . . I show him where to go in ABB whenever he has a problem.' The president of ABB's power plant businesses [adds]: 'If you want to be a customer-driven company, you have to design the sales organisation around individual buyers rather than around your products.'[2]

Complex sales force structures   When a company sells a wide variety of products to many types of customer over a broad geographical area, it often combines several types of sales force structure. Salespeople can be specialised by customer and territory, by product and territory, by product and customer, or by territory, product and customer. A salesperson might then report to one or more line and staff managers. No single structure is best for all companies and situations. Each organisation should select a structure that best serves the needs of its customers and fits its overall marketing strategy.

■ Sales force size

Once the company has set its strategy and structure, it is ready to consider *sales force size*. Salespeople constitute one of the company's most productive – and most expensive – assets. Therefore, increasing their number will increase both sales and costs.

The past few years have seen a reduction in sales force size. Advances in selling technology, such as selling on the Internet or the use of account management software, make salespeople more efficient in handling customers and can even replace salespeople altogether. The recent merger mania has also contributed to shrinking sales force size. When sellers merge, they rarely need a doubled sales force size. Similarly, when customer organisations merge, it means fewer customers, and fewer customers mean that fewer salespeople are needed to call on them.[3]

Workload approach
An approach to setting sales force size, whereby the company groups accounts into different size classes and then determines how many salespeople are needed to call on them the desired number of times.

Many companies use some form of **workload approach** to set sales force size. The company groups accounts according to size, account status or other factors related to the amount of effort required to maintain them. It then determines the number of salespeople needed to call on them the desired number of times. The logic is as follows. Suppose we have 1,000 Type-A accounts and 2,000 Type-B accounts. Type-A accounts require 36 calls a year and Type-B accounts require 12 calls a year. In this case, the sales force's *workload*, as defined by the number of calls it must make per year, is 60,000 calls [(1,000 × 36) + (2,000 × 12) = 36,000 + 24,000 = 60,000]. Suppose our average salesperson can make 1,000 calls a year. The company thus needs 60 salespeople (60,000/1,000).

■ Other sales force strategy and structure issues

Sales management also have to decide who will be involved in the selling effort and how various sales and sales support people will work together.

Outside sales force
Outside salespeople (or field sales force) who travel to call on customers.

Inside sales force
Salepeople who service the company's customers and prospect from their offices via telephone or visits from prospective customers.

Outside and inside sales forces   The company may have an **outside sales force** (or field sales force), an **inside sales force** or both. Outside salespeople travel to call on customers, whereas inside salespeople conduct business from their offices via telephone or visits from prospective buyers.

To reduce time demands on their outside sales forces, many firms have increased the size of their inside sales team, which includes technical support people, sales assistants and telemarketers. Technical support people provide technical information and answers

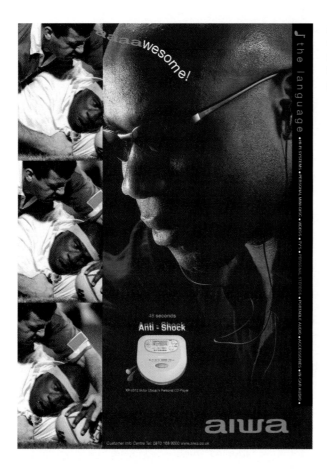

Inside sales force: Aiwa provides a Customer Information Centre telephone number to deal with customers' questions.

SOURCE: Aiwa

to customers' questions. Sales assistants provide clerical back-up for outside salespeople. They call ahead and confirm appointments, conduct credit checks, follow up on deliveries and answer customers' queries when salespeople cannot be reached. Telemarketers use the phone to find new leads and qualify prospects for the field sales force or to sell and service accounts directly.

The inside sales force frees salespeople to spend more time selling to major accounts and finding major new prospects. Depending on the complexity of the product and customer, a telemarketer can make 20–30 decision-maker contacts a day, compared to the average of 4 that an outside salesperson can make. For many types of product and selling situation, **telemarketing** can be as effective as a personal sales call, but much less expensive. For example, whereas a typical personal sales call can cost well over £200, a routine industrial telemarketing call costs between £5 and £20 depending on the complexity of the call. For example, chemicals company Du Pont uses experienced former field salespeople as telemarketing reps to help sell the company's complex chemical products. The telemarketers handle technical questions from customers, smooth out product and distribution problems, and alert field sales representatives to 'hot' prospects. According to Du Pont management, the inside–outside approach pays off, with some 80 per cent of the leads passed on to the field force converted into sales.[4]

Just as telemarketing is changing the way that many companies go to market, the Internet offers explosive potential for restructuring sales forces and conducting sales operations. More and more companies are now using the Internet to support their personal selling efforts, ranging from selling and training salespeople to conducting sales meetings and servicing accounts. Electronic negotiations are also taking root, with more and more organisations using the Web to conduct sales negotiations (see Marketing Highlight 20.1).

Telemarketing
Using the telephone to sell directly to consumers.

marketing highlight 20.1

E-negotiations?

There is little doubt that the Internet is changing the face of selling. An extreme example is found in the soccer world. Lately, managers of some of the world's biggest football clubs – including Manchester United, Eindhoven, Olympique Marseille, Inter Milan and the entire Brazilian first division – are negotiating transfers of players using a private (members-only) business-to-business (B2B) site, run by InterClub (developed by the German consultancy realTech and communications systems company InterClubNet). Similar marketplaces are being developed with other big-money sports such as ice hockey and basketball.

Not only are soccer club managers uncovering the benefits of managing some of their player signings through the e-marketplace, which provides for anonymity during the initial negotiation phases, but a raft of other firms are uncovering the potential of the Web as a negotiation channel. Sceptics, not surprisingly, argue that negotiations are more likely to go well if conducted face to face. There is that much one can accomplish in an exchange through keyboards and screens. Proponents, however, note that e-negotiations can be facilitated by the brief getting-to-know-you telephone call. And there is nothing to stop the negotiators from breaking the ice by swapping photographs and personal details before negotiations commence. Moreover, not all electronic negotiations take place between strangers, and studies have shown that e-negotiations go well when the parties involved already know each other.

Heidi Roizen, an executive at SoftBank Venture Capital, thinks that e-negotiation has its merits. For a start, the e-mails last for ever. The *durability* of e-mails enables Ms Roizen to keep track of negotiations with each of the half a dozen or more companies that she has to deal with at the same time. A second advantage is the *instant record-keeping* that e-negotiations entail.

According to Richard Hill, an IT manager and mediator with the Swiss-based consultancy Hill & Associates, which has developed online mediation services for clients, e-mails are increasingly likely to be used for negotiations. Although the telephone is cheaper and faster and can convey more information than a quick e-mail, there are distinct advantages for negotiators using e-mail or electronic sites. The negotiations can be done at a time that is convenient for the parties involved. The overall cost is also lower.

One word of caution though. The durability and instantaneity of e-mails mean that each piece of correspondence must be re-read and double-checked to minimise confusion, misunderstanding and embarrassment. It is much more difficult for the negotiator to retract information or 'emotions' once he or she has 'hit the send button'. Ms Roizen offers one piece of advice. Taking from the lessons learnt by every Victorian letter-writer, the best policy is: 'when in doubt, leave it overnight'. There is no better filter to apply to an angry note than a good night's sleep.

SOURCES: Amaya Guillerma, 'A league of their own', *Connectis* (Issue 5, October 2000), p. 22; 'Negotiating by e-mail', *The Economist* (8 April 2000), p. 85.

Team selling

Using teams of people from sales, marketing, production, finance, technical support, and even upper management to service large, complex accounts.

Team selling   For years, the customer has been solely in the hands of the salesperson. The salesperson identified the prospect, arranged the call, explored the customer's needs, created and proposed a solution, closed the deal and turned cheerleader as others delivered what he or she promised. For selling relatively simple products, this approach can work well. But if the products are more complex and the service requirements more demanding, the salesperson simply cannot go it alone. Instead, most companies are now using **team selling** to service large complex accounts.

Sales teams can unearth problems, solutions and sales opportunities that no individual salesperson could. Such teams might include people from sales, marketing, technical and support services, R&D, engineering, operations, finance and others. In team selling situations, the salesperson shifts from 'soloist' to 'orchestrators' who help coordinate a whole-company effort to build profitable relationships with key customers.[5]

Team selling does have its pitfalls. Selling teams can confuse and overwhelm customers who are used to working with only one salesperson. Salespeople who are used to having customers all to themselves may have trouble learning to work with and trust others on a team. Finally, difficulties in evaluating individual contributions to the team selling effort can create some sticky compensation issues.

Still, team selling can produce dramatic results. For example, Dun & Bradstreet, the world's largest marketer of business information and related services, recently established sales teams made up of representatives from its credit, collection and marketing business units, which up to then had worked separately. Their mission was to work as a team to call on higher-ups in customer organisations, learn about customer needs and offer solutions. The teams concentrated on D&B's top 50 customers.

> When one of the D&B sales teams asked to meet with the chief financial officer of a major telecommunications company, the executive responded, 'I'm delighted you asked, but why talk?'. He found out after a one-hour meeting. The D&B team listened as he discussed problems facing his organisation, and by the end of the information-seeking session, the team had come up with several solutions for the executive and had identified over $1.5 million in D&B sales opportunities from what had been a $900,000 customer. More teams met with more clients, creating more opportunities. About a year after the programme started, D&B's marketing department had targeted $200 million in sales opportunities, about half of which would not have been found under the old system. Now these teams are getting together with D&B's top 200 customers.[6]

Key account management Continuing relationships with large customers dominate the activities of many sales organisations. For makers of fast-moving consumer goods the relationship is with major retailers such as Tengelmann, Carrefour, Tesco or Ahold. The importance of these retailers has changed the way marketing as a whole is being organised. *Account managers* often orchestrate the relationship with a single retailer, although some will manage several smaller retailers or a class of independent outlet. Any major retailer will probably always be carrying major manufacturers' brands, so the account manager's role is one of increasing the profitability of sales through the channel. In this arrangement a great deal of sales promotions effort and advertising is customised for retailers that want exclusive lines or restrict the sort of promotions that they accept.

The situation is very similar in industrial sales organisations when a supplier has to sell components, raw materials, supplier or capital equipment in the concentrated markets described in Chapter 8. Even when a prospect is not a client, there are regular contacts at all levels between the organisations. When the client or prospect is particularly important, key account managers are responsible. These aim for a mutually beneficial relationship between the seller and buyer. The buyer benefits from traceability of supplies, smart purchasing, and lean supply and facilities management, while the seller gains market knowledge and profitable sales.

In most companies, account managers are like brand managers in not having formal or informal teams working for them. This means the key account managers compete for the resources to serve their client. Their role is to maintain smooth but creative relationships between the buying and selling teams.[7]

recruiting and selecting salespeople

At the heart of any successful sales force operation is the recruitment and selection of good salespeople. The performance difference between an average salesperson and a top salesperson can be substantial. In a typical sales force, the top 30 per cent of the salespeople might bring 60 per cent of the sales. Thus careful salesperson selection can greatly increase overall sales force performance.

Beyond the differences in sales performance, poor selection results in costly turnover. When a salesperson quits, the costs of finding and training a new salesperson, plus the costs of lost sales, could be considerable. Also, a sales force with many new people is less productive than one with a stable membership.[8]

■ What makes a good salesperson?

Selecting salespeople would not be a problem if the company knew what traits to look for. If it knew that good salespeople were outgoing, aggressive and energetic, for example, it could simply check applicants for these characteristics. Many successful salespeople, however, are also bashful, soft-spoken and laid back.

Still, the search continues for the magic list of traits that spells sure-fire sales ability. One survey suggests that good salespeople have a lot of enthusiasm, persistence, initiative, self-confidence and job commitment. They are committed to sales as a way of life and have a strong customer orientation. Another study suggests that good salespeople are independent and self-motivated and are excellent listeners. Still another study advises that salespeople should be a friend to the customer as well as persistent, enthusiastic, attentive and, above all, honest. They must be internally motivated, disciplined, hard working and able to build strong relationships with customers. Still other studies suggest that good salespeople are team players, not loners.[9]

How can a company find out what traits salespeople in its industry should have? A good start is to look at the job *duties* involved, which would suggest some of the traits a company should look for. For instance, is a lot of paperwork required? Does the job call for much travel? Will the salesperson face a lot of rejections? Will the salesperson be working with high-level buyers? The successful sales candidate should possess qualities ideally suited to these duties. The company should also look at the characteristics of its most successful salespeople for clues to needed traits.

■ Recruiting procedures and selection

After management has decided on needed traits, it must *recruit* the desired candidate. The human resources department looks for applicants by getting names from current salespeople, using employment agencies and placing classified ads. Another source is to attract top salespeople from other companies. Proven salespeople need less training and can be immediately productive.

Recruiting will attract many applicants, from which the company must select the best. The selection procedure can vary from a single informal interview to lengthy testing and interviewing. Many companies give formal tests to sales applicants. Tests typically measure sales aptitude, analytical and organisational skills, personality traits and other characteristics.[10] Companies generally take test results seriously. Gillette, for example, claims that tests have reduced turnover by 42 per cent and that test scores have correlated well with the later performance of new salespeople. But test scores provide only one piece of information in a set that includes personal characteristics, references, past employment history and interviewer reactions.

training salespeople

Many companies used to send their new salespeople into the field almost immediately after hiring them. They would be given samples, order books and general instructions. To many companies, a training programme translated into considerable expense for instructors, materials, space and salary for a person who was not yet selling, and a loss of sales opportunities because the person was not in the field.

Companies spend hundreds of millions of euros to train their salespeople in the art of selling.

Today's new salespeople, however, may spend anything from a few weeks or months to a year or more in training. Training programmes have several goals. Salespeople need to know and identify with the company, so most companies spend the first part of the training programme describing the company's history and objectives, its organisations, its financial structure and facilities, and its chief products and markets. Because salespeople also need to know the company's products, sales trainees are shown how products are produced and how they work. Salespeople also need to know the characteristics of competitors and customers, including distributors, so the training programme teaches them about competitors' strategies and about different types of customer and their needs, buying motives and buying habits. Because salespeople must know how to make effective presentations, they are trained in the principles of selling. Finally, salespeople need to understand field procedures and responsibilities. They learn how to divide time between active and potential accounts and how to use an expense account, prepare reports and route communications effectively.

■ Compensating salespeople

To attract salespeople, a company must have an attractive compensation plan. These plans vary greatly both by industry and by companies within the same industry. The level of compensation must be close to the 'going rate' for the type of sales job and needed skills. To pay less than the going rate would attract too few quality salespeople; to pay more would be unnecessary.

Compensation is made up of several elements – a fixed amount, a variable amount, expenses and fringe benefits. The fixed amount, usually a salary, gives the salesperson some stable income. The variable amount, which might be commissions or bonuses based on sales performance, rewards the salesperson for greater effort. Expense allowances, which repay salespeople for job-related expenses, let salespeople undertake needed and desirable selling efforts. Fringe benefits, such as paid vacations, sickness or accident benefits, pensions and life insurance, provide job security and satisfaction.

Management must decide what *mix* of these compensation elements makes the most sense for each sales job. Different combinations of fixed and variable compensation give rise to four basic types of compensation plans – straight salary, straight commission, salary plus bonus and salary plus commission.

Table 20.1

The relationship between overall marketing strategy and sales force compensation

	STRATEGIC GOAL		
	To gain market share rapidly	To solidify market leadership	To maximise profitability
Ideal salesperson	◆ An independent self-starter	◆ A competitive problem solver	◆ A team player ◆ A relationship manager
Sales focus	◆ Deal making ◆ Sustained high effort	◆ Consultative selling	◆ Account penetration
Compensation role	◆ To capture accounts ◆ To reward high performance	◆ To reward new and existing account sales	◆ To manage the product mix ◆ To encourage team selling ◆ To reward account management

Source: Adapted from Sam T. Johnson, 'Sales compensation: In search of a better solution,' *Compensation & Benefits Review*, November–December 1993, pp. 53–60. Copyright © 1998 American Management Association, NY, http://www.amanet.org.

The sales force compensation plan can both motivate salespeople and direct their activities. If sales management wants salespeople to emphasise new account development, it might pay a bonus for opening new accounts. Thus, the compensation plan should direct the sales force towards activities that are consistent with overall marketing objectives.

Table 20.1 shows how a company's compensation plan should reflect its overall marketing strategy. If the overall marketing strategy is to grow rapidly and gain market share, the compensation plan should be to reward high sales performance and encourage salespeople to capture new accounts, suggesting a larger commission coupled with new account bonuses. In contrast, if the marketing goal is to maximise profitability of current accounts, the compensation plan might contain a larger base salary component, with additional incentives based on current account sales and customer satisfaction. In fact, more and more companies are moving away from high commission plans that may drive salespeople to make short-term grabs for business. They may even ruin a customer relationship because they were pushing too hard to close a deal. Instead, companies are designing compensation plans that reward salespeople for building customer relationships and growing the long-run value of each customer.[11]

supervising salespeople

New salespeople need more than a territory, compensation and training – they need *supervision*. Through supervision, the company *directs* and *motivates* the sales force to do a better job.

■ Directing salespeople

How much should sales management be involved in helping salespeople manage their territories? It depends on everything from the company's size to the experience of its sales force. Hence, companies vary widely in how closely they supervise their salespeople.

Developing customer targets and call norms   Many companies help their salespeople in identifying customer targets and setting call norms. Generally, salespeople may call weekly on accounts with large sales or potential, but only infrequently on small accounts. Companies often specify how much time their sales force should spend prospecting for new accounts. If left alone, many salespeople will spend most of their time with current customers, which are better-known quantities. Moreover, whereas a prospect may never deliver any business, salespeople can depend on current accounts for some business. Therefore, unless salespeople are rewarded for opening new accounts, they may avoid new-account development.

Using sales time efficiently   Companies also direct salespeople in how to use their time efficiently. One tool is the *annual call schedule* which shows which customers and prospects to call on in which months and which activities to carry out. Activities include taking part in trade shows, attending sales meetings and carrying out marketing research. Another tool is *time-and-duty analysis*. In addition to time spent selling, the salesperson spends time travelling, waiting, eating, taking breaks and doing administrative chores. Figure 20.2 shows how salespeople spend their time. Because of the tiny portion of the day most sales staff actually spend selling or negotiating and talking face to face with potential customers, companies must look for ways to save time. This can be done by getting salespeople to use phones instead of travelling, simplifying record-keeping forms, finding better call and routing plans, and supplying more and better customer information.

Many firms have adopted sales force automation systems, computerised sales force operations for more efficient order-entry transactions, improved customer service and better salesperson decision-making support. Salespeople use computers to profile customers and prospects, analyse and forecast sales, manage accounts, schedule sales calls, enter orders, check inventories and order status, prepare sales and expense reports, process correspondence and carry out many other activities. Sales force automation not only lowers sales force calls and improves productivity; it also improves the quality of sales management decisions.

Perhaps the fastest-growing sales force technology tool is the Internet. As more and more organisations and individuals embrace Internet technology, salespeople are

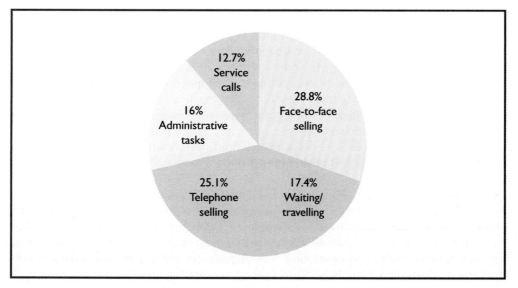

Figure 20.2

How salespeople spend their time

SOURCE: Reprinted with permission from Dartnell Corporation, © 1998, 360 Hiatt Drive, Palm Beach Gardens, FL 33418. All rights reserved. For more information on our customer service products please call 1-800-621-5463.

Here, American Express suggests that companies reward outstanding sales performers with high-tech Persona Select cards – electronically pre-paid reward cards that allow recipients to purchase whatever they want most.

SOURCE: American Express Incentive services

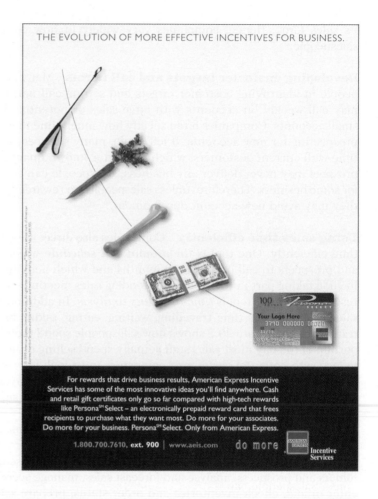

THE EVOLUTION OF MORE EFFECTIVE INCENTIVES FOR BUSINESS.

For rewards that drive business results, American Express Incentive Services has some of the most innovative ideas you'll find anywhere. Cash and retail gift certificates only go so far compared with high-tech rewards like Persona℠ Select – an electronically prepaid reward card that frees recipients to purchase what they want most. Do more for your associates. Do more for your business. Persona℠ Select. Only from American Express.

1.800.700.7610, ext. 900 | www.aeis.com   do more   Incentive Services

beginning to use the Internet regularly in their daily selling activities. The most common uses include gathering competitive information, monitoring customer websites and researching industries and specific customers. As more and more companies provide their salespeople with Web access, experts expect explosive growth in sales force Internet usage in the coming decade.[12]

■ Motivating salespeople

Some salespeople will do their best without any special urging from management. To them, selling may be the most fascinating job in the world. But selling can also be frustrating. Salespeople usually work alone, and they must sometimes travel away from home. They may face aggressive, competing salespeople and difficult customers. They sometimes lack the authority to do what is needed to win a sale and may thus lose large orders that they have worked hard to obtain. Therefore, salespeople often need special encouragement to do their best.

Management can boost sales force morale and performance through its organisational climate, sales quota and positive incentives.

Organisational climate   Organisational climate reflects the feeling that salespeople have about their opportunities, value and rewards for a good performance within the company. Some companies treat salespeople as if they are not very important. Other companies treat their salespeople as their prime movers and allow virtually unlimited opportunity for income and promotion. Not surprisingly, a company's attitude towards its salespeople affects their behaviour. If they are held in low esteem, there is high turnover and poor performance. If they are held in high esteem, there is less turnover and higher performance.

Sales quotas   Many companies set **sales quotas** for their salespeople. Sales quotas are standards stating the amount they should sell and how sales should be divided among the company's products. Compensation is often related to how well salespeople meet their quotas.

Positive incentives   Companies also use several incentives to increase sales force effort. *Sales meetings* provide social occasions, breaks from routine, chances to meet and talk with 'company brass', and opportunities to air feelings and to identify with a larger group. Companies also sponsor *sales contests* to spur the sales force to make a selling effort above what would normally be expected. Other incentives include honours, merchandise and cash awards, trips and profit-sharing plans.

Sales quotas
Standards set for salespeople, stating the amount they should sell and how sales should be divided among the company's products.

evaluating salespeople

So far we have described how management communicates what salespeople should be doing and motivates them to do it. This process requires good feedback, which means getting regular information from salespeople to evaluate their performance.

■ Sources of information

Management gets information about its salespeople in several ways. The most important source is the *sales report*, including weekly or monthly work plans and longer-term territory marketing plans. The *work plan* describes intended calls and routing. From this report, the sales force plans and schedules activities. It also informs management of the salespeople's whereabouts and provides a basis for comparing plans and performance. Salespeople can then be evaluated on their ability to 'plan their work and work their plan'. Sometimes, managers contact individual salespeople to suggest improvements in work plans. The *annual territory marketing plan* outlines how new accounts will be built and sales from existing accounts increased.

Salespeople write up their completed activities on *call reports*. Call reports keep sales managers informed of the salesperson's activities, show what is happening with each customer's account and provide information that might be useful in later calls. Salespeople also turn in *expense reports* for which they are partly or wholly repaid. Additional information comes from personal observation, customers' letters and complaints, customer surveys and talks with other salespeople.

Qualitative evaluation of salespeople   The sales manager might begin with a *qualitative evaluation*, looking at a salesperson's knowledge of the company, products, customers, competitors, territory and tasks. Personal traits like manner, appearance, speech and temperament can be rated. The sales manager can also review any problems in motivation or compliance. Each company must decide what would be most useful to know. It should communicate these criteria to salespeople, so that they understand how their performance is evaluated and can make an effort to improve it.

■ Formal evaluation of performance

Using sales force reports and other information, sales management *formally evaluates* members of the sales force. Formal evaluation produces four benefits. First, management must develop and communicate clear standards for judging performance. Second, management must gather well-rounded information about each salesperson. Third, salespeople receive constructive feedback that helps them to improve future performance. Finally, salespeople are motivated to perform because they know that they will have to sit down with the sales manager and explain their performance.

Comparing salespeople's performance   One type of formal evaluation compares and ranks the sales performance of different salespeople. Such comparisons can be misleading, however. Salespeople may perform differently because of differences in territory potential, workload, level of competition, company promotion effort and other factors. Furthermore, sales are not usually the best indicator of achievement. Management should be more interested in how much each salesperson contributes to net profits, a factor that requires analysis of each salesperson's sales mix and expenses.

Comparing current sales with past sales   A second type of formal evaluation is to compare a salesperson's current performance with past performance. Such a comparison should directly indicate the person's progress. Table 20.2 provides an example.

The sales manager can learn many things about Chris Bennett from this table. Bennett's total sales increased every year (line 3). This does not necessarily mean that

Table 20.2

Evaluating people's sales performance

TERRITORY: MIDLAND	SALESPERSON: CHRIS BENNETT			
	1997	1998	1999	2000
1. Net sales product A	£251,300	£253,200	£270,000	£263,100
2. Net sales product B	£423,200	£439,200	£553,900	£561,900
3. Net sales total	£674,500	£692,400	£823,900	£825,000
4. Percentage of quota product A	95.6	92.0	88.0	84.7
5. Percentage of quota product B	120.4	122.3	134.9	130.8
6. Gross profits product A	£50,260	£50,640	£54,000	£52,620
7. Gross profits product B	£42,320	£43,920	£53,390	£56,190
8. Gross profits total	£92,580	£94,560	£109,390	£108,810
9. Sales expense	£10,200	£11,100	£11,600	£13,200
10. Sales expense to total sales (%)	1.5	1.6	1.4	1.6
11. Number of calls	1,675	1,700	1,680	1,660
12. Cost per call	£6.09	£6.53	£6.90	£7.95
13. Average number of customers	320	324	328	334
14. Number of new customers	13	14	15	20
15. Number of lost customers	8	10	11	14
16. Average sales per customer	£2,108	£2,137	£2,512	£2,470
17. Average gross profit per customer	£289	£292	£334	£326

Bennett is doing a better job. The product breakdown shows that Bennett has been able to push the sales of product B further than those of product A (lines 1 and 2). According to the quotas for the two products (lines 4 and 5), the success in increasing product B sales may be at the expense of product A sales. According to gross profits (lines 6 and 7), the company earns twice as much gross profit (as a ratio to sales) on A as it does on B. Bennett may be pushing the higher-volume, lower-margin product at the expense of the more profitable product. Although Bennett increased total sales by £1,100 between 1999 and 2000 (line 3), the gross profits on these total sales actually decreased by £580 (line 8).

Sales expense (line 9) shows a steady increase, although total expense as a percentage of total sales seems to be under control (line 10). The upward trend in Bennett's total expenses, in money terms, does not seem to be explained by any increase in the number of calls (line 11), although it may be related to his success in acquiring new customers (line 14). However, there is a possibility that in prospecting for new customers, Bennett is neglecting present customers, as indicated by an upward trend in the annual number of lost customers (line 15).

The last two lines on the table show the level and trend in Bennett's sales and gross profits per customer. These figures become more meaningful when they are compared with overall company averages. If Bennett's average gross profit per customer is lower than the company's averages, he may be concentrating on the wrong customers or may not be spending enough time with each customer. Looking back at the annual number of calls (line 11), Bennett may be making fewer calls than the average salesperson. If distances in the territory are not much different, this may mean he is not putting in a full workday, he is poor at planning his routing or minimising his waiting time, or he spends too much time with certain accounts.

We have looked at the key issues surrounding sales force management – designing and managing the sales force. Next we will address the principles of personal selling.

principles of personal selling

Here, we address the actual personal selling process. Personal selling is an ancient art that has spawned a large literature and many principles. Effective salespeople operate on more than just instinct – they are highly trained in methods of territory analysis and customer management.

the personal selling process

Effective companies take a *customer-oriented approach* to personal selling. They train salespeople to identify customer needs and to find solutions. This approach assumes that customer needs provide sales opportunities, that customers appreciate good suggestions and that customers will be loyal to salespeople who have their long-term interests at heart. By contrast, those companies that use a *sales-oriented approach* rely on high-pressure selling techniques. They assume that the customers will not buy except under pressure, that they are influenced by a slick presentation and that they will not be sorry after signing the order (and that, even if they are, it no longer matters). The problem-solver salesperson fits better with the marketing concept than does the hard-sell salesperson or the glad-handing extrovert. Buyers today want solutions, not smiles; results, not razzle-dazzle. They want salespeople who listen to their concerns, understand their needs and respond with the right products and services.

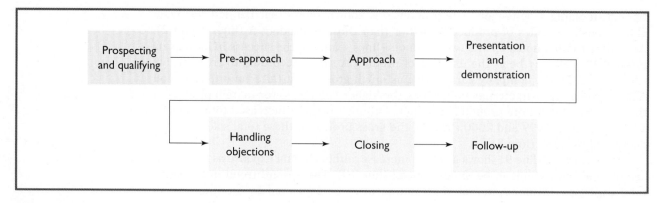

Figure 20.3

Primary steps in effective selling

steps in the selling process

Selling process
The steps that the salesperson follows when selling, which include prospecting and qualifying, pre-approach, approach, presentation and demonstration, handling objections, closing and follow-up.

Most training programmes view the **selling process** as consisting of several steps that the salesperson must master (see Figure 20.3). These steps focus on the goal of getting new customers and obtaining orders from them. However, many salespeople spend much of their time maintaining existing accounts and building long-term customer relationships. We will address the relationship aspect of the personal selling process in the final section of this chapter. A fuller discussion of key account management and its importance in sustaining customer relationships is found in Chapter 11.

■ Prospecting and qualifying

Prospecting
The step in the selling process in which the salesperson identifies qualified potential customers.

The first step in the selling process is **prospecting** – identifying qualified potential customers. The salesperson must approach many prospects to get just a few sales. Although the company supplies some leads, salespeople need skill in finding their own. They can ask current customers for referrals. They can build referral sources, such as suppliers, dealers, non-competing salespeople and bankers. They can join organisations to which prospects belong, or can engage in speaking and writing activities that will draw attention. They can search for names in newsletters or directories and use the telephone and post to track down leads. Or they can drop in unannounced on various offices (a practice known as 'cold calling').

Salespeople need to know how to *qualify* leads: that is, how to identify the good ones and screen out the poor ones. Prospects can be qualified by looking at their financial ability, volume of business, special needs, location and possibilities for sales growth.

■ Pre-approach

Pre-approach
The step in the selling process in which the salesperson learns as much as possible about a prospective customer before making a sales call.

Before calling on a prospect, the salesperson should learn as much as possible about the organisation (what it needs, who is involved in the buying) and its buyers (their characteristics and buying styles). This step is known as the **pre-approach**. The salesperson can consult standard industry and online sources, acquaintances and others to learn about the company. The salesperson should set *call objectives*, which may be to qualify the prospect, to gather information or to make an immediate sale. Another task is to decide on the best approach, which might be a personal visit, a phone call or a letter. The best timing should be considered carefully because many prospects are busiest at certain times. Finally, the salesperson should give thought to an overall sales strategy for the account.

■ Approach

During the **approach** step, the salesperson should know how to meet and greet the buyer, and get the relationship off to a good start. The salesperson's appearance, his or her opening lines and the follow-up remarks have a great deal of impact on relationship building in this early phase of the sales process. The opening lines should be positive: 'Mr Johnson, I am Chris Henderson from the Alltech Company. My company and I appreciate your willingness to see me. I will do my best to make this visit profitable and worthwhile for you and your company.' This opening might be followed by some key questions to learn more about the customer's needs, or the showing of a display or sample to attract the buyer's attention and curiosity.

Approach
The step in the selling process in which the salesperson meets and greets the buyer to get the relationship off to a good start.

■ Presentation and demonstration

The **presentation** is that step in the selling process where the salesperson tells the product 'story' to the buyer, showing how the product will make or save money. The salesperson describes the product features, but concentrates on presenting *customer benefits*. Using a *need-satisfaction approach*, the salesperson starts with a search for the customer's needs by getting the customer to do most of the talking. This approach calls for good listening and problem-solving skills.[13] The qualities that purchasing agents dislike most in salespeople include being pushy, and unprepared and disorganised. The qualities they value most include empathy, honesty, dependability, thoroughness and follow-through.[14]

Sales presentations can be improved with product samples or demonstrations. If buyers can see or handle the product, they will better remember its features and benefits. Visual aids can show how a product performs and provide other information about it. Booklets and brochures remain useful as 'leave-behinds' for customer reference. Today, advanced presentation technologies allow for full multimedia presentations to only one or a few people. Audio and video cassettes, laptop computers with presentation software and online presentation technologies have replaced the flip chart.

Presentation
The step in the selling process in which the salesperson tells the product 'story' to the buyer, showing how the product will make or save money for the buyer.

■ Handling objections

Customers almost always have objections during the presentation or when asked to place an order. The problem can be either logical or psychological, and objections are often unspoken. In **handling objections**, the salesperson should use a positive approach,

Handling objections
The step in the selling process in which the salesperson seeks out, clarifies and overcomes customer objections to buying.

In the sales presentation, the salesperson tells the product story to the buyers.
SOURCE: Reproduced courtesy of GettyOne

seek out hidden objections, ask the buyer to clarify any objections, take objections as opportunities to provide more information, and turn the objections into reasons for buying. Every salesperson should be trained in the skills of handling objections.

■ Closing

Closing
The step in the selling process in which the salesperson asks the customer for an order.

After handling the prospect's objections, the salesperson now tries to close the sale. Some salespeople do not get around to **closing** or do not handle it well. They may lack confidence, feel guilty about asking for the order or fail to recognise the right moment to close the sale. Salespeople should know how to spot closing signals from the buyer, including physical actions, comments and questions. For example, the customer might sit forward and nod approvingly or ask about prices and credit terms. Salespeople can use one of several closing techniques. They can ask for the order, review points of agreement, offer to help write up the order, ask whether the buyer wants this model or that one, or note that the buyer will lose out if the order is not placed now. The salesperson may offer the buyer special reasons to close, such as a lower price or an extra quantity at no charge.

■ Follow-up

Follow-up
The last step in the selling process, in which the salesperson follows up after the sale to ensure customer satisfaction and repeat business.

The last step in the selling process – **follow-up** – is necessary if the salesperson wants to ensure customer satisfaction and repeat business. Right after closing, the salesperson should complete any details on delivery time, purchase terms and other matters. The salesperson should then schedule a follow-up call when the initial order is received to make sure there is proper installation, instruction and servicing. This visit would reveal any problems, assure the buyer of the salesperson's interest and reduce any buyer concerns that might have arisen since the sale.

■ International selling

The typical sales process can be applied in international selling. However, intercultural trade always requires special efforts in tailoring sales and negotiation approaches (see Marketing Highlight 20.2).

relationship marketing

The principles of personal selling as described are *transaction oriented*, in that their aim is to help salespeople close a specific sale with a customer. But in many cases, the company is not seeking simply a sale: it has targeted a major customer that it would like to win and keep. The company would like to show the customer that it has the capabilities to serve the customer over the long haul, in a mutually profitable relationship.

Relationship marketing
The process of creating, maintaining and enhancing strong, value-laden relationships with customers and other stakeholders.

More companies today are moving away from transaction marketing, with its emphasis on making a sale. Instead, they are practising **relationship marketing**, which emphasises maintaining profitable long-term relationships with customers by creating superior customer value and satisfaction. They realise that, when operating in maturing markets and facing stiffer competition, it costs a lot more to wrest new customers from competitors than to keep current ones.

Today's customers are large and often global. They prefer suppliers that can sell and deliver a coordinated set of products and services to many locations. They favour suppliers which can quickly solve problems that arise in different parts of the nation or world, and who can work closely with customer teams to improve products and processes. For these customers, the sale is only the beginning of the relationship.

marketing highlight 20.2

Selling across cultures: in search of universal values

Face-to-face selling is the least easily controlled part of international marketing. Academics and consultants have drawn up numerous lists of 'do's and don'ts' based on examining negotiations within particular cultures. Increasingly, international marketers are turning to both culture-specific negotiation studies and general cultural research in an attempt to understand the cultural values that influence negotiation behaviour and how best to adapt their selling styles.

One popular tool is the Geert Hofstede 'five universal values' framework for defining national culture. These include:

Time orientation. This is a culture's sense of immediacy. Generally, Asians have longer time orientations than western cultures and tend to spend a longer time establishing a personal relationship at the start of the negotiation process. It is one reason why western business people found *karaoke* sessions rewarding when negotiating with Japanese and Korean executives! Because the relationship is the *content* of the negotiation, and the basis of the longer-term benefits derived from the deal, as opposed to the short-term aspects of the deal in progress, the 'relationship approach' will better fit Asian cultures than it would western cultures. The lesson: when selling to someone with a long-term orientation culture, expect to spend more time on forming the client-relationship, rather than merely focusing on the contract.

Aversion to uncertainty. The level of risk that negotiators will bear is partly a function of the level of uncertainty that they are used to in their culture. For countries where people reflect a higher tolerance of ambiguity, such as the UK and Denmark, the salesperson may spend less time probing the buyer's needs before closing the deal. In countries such as France, where people have lower tolerance of uncertainty, the French salesperson may take longer to clarify exactly what it is that the customer needs.

Acceptance of unequal power. The level of inequality that people expect and accept in their jobs and lives – also called 'power distance' by Hofstede – also affects negotiation style. In high power distance cultures, subordinates would only approach high-level superiors with a problem of great importance. By contrast, in low power distance cultures, staff at a lower level in the corporate hierarchy are more accustomed to being treated like equals by their superiors, with whom they feel they can discuss matters directly. So, when negotiating with a buyer used to weighting status heavily, the seller organisation should ensure that salesperson seniority matches that of the buyer.

Individualism or collectivism. This reflects the person's level of independence and degree of freedom. The US and UK are generally regarded as individualistic societies which value freedom and independence. In collectivistic cultures, such as Japan and China, people's sense of value is derived from belonging to a group. Consequently, negotiators influenced by the latter culture may take more time and effort to reach consensus and closure.

Masculinity and femininity. Achievement and possessions reflect masculine values, while the social environment and helping others tap femininity. People tend to lie along the masculinity–femininity continuum. In masculine cultures, exemplified by Austria in Hofstede's study, salespeople use an assertive style, which can be off-putting if applied in feminine cultures, such as Denmark. The latter would place more emphasis on partnership to achieve both parties' desired outcomes. Those in the middle of this continuum would value the establishment of good relationships with clients as much as hard facts and contractual details.

The five universal values offer a base for addressing cross-cultural settings in international selling and the need for adaptation of the selling approach. However, neither Hofstede nor advocates of his model suggest that successful international negotiation comes from following the old adage, 'when in Rome, do as the Romans do'. Rather, the experts argue that negotiators do not negotiate with someone from their own culture in the same way that they negotiate with someone from another culture. So, knowing how Swedish people negotiate with each other seldom gives much help in predicting how they will negotiate with their Japanese counterpart. Moreover, as an increasing proportion of international executives are educated abroad or have broad overseas experiences, they may adapt their cultural styles to show familiarity with their foreign negotiators' cultural values. Imagine a German salesperson adopting the French 'win–win' approach when negotiating with her French client and the French client using 'win–lose' techniques typically associated with German negotiation style. The key, therefore, lies not so much in *mimicking* the foreign client's cultural values, but in subtle *adaptation* to fit the other negotiator's style.

SOURCES: Anne Macquin and Dominique Rouziés, 'Selling across the culture gap' in *Financial Times*, FT Mastering Global Business, Part Seven (1997), pp. 10–1; Geert Hofstede, *Cultures and Organisations: Software of the mind* (London: McGraw-Hill, 1991); Geert Hofstede, *Culture's Consequences: International differences in work-related values* (London: Sage Publications, 1981); Sergey Frank, 'Global negotiating', *Sales and Marketing Management* (May 1992), pp. 64–9; J. C. Morgan and J. J. Morgan, *Cracking the Japanese Market* (New York: Free Press, 1991).

Relationship marketing: Geneva's Private Bankers remarks the importance of the human relations values of confidence, proximity, responsiveness, trust and understanding towards its clients.

Source: Geneva's Private Bankers.
Agency: The Creative Factory

❝We've been working *online* for 200 years; in other words talking directly with our clients.❞

GENFER PRIVATBANKIERS
FREI · UNABHÄNGIG · VERANTWORTLICH

I t goes without saying that we can master the most up-to-date data and communications technologies: we have always wanted the best for our clients. But these technological innovations are only there to reinforce the human relations values of confidence, proximity and responsiveness, that are the very essence of our business. We know that even with the most advanced technologies in the world, successful long-term asset management is, first and foremost, a matter of trust and understanding.

BORDIER & CIE - DARIER HENTSCH & CIE - LOMBARD ODIER & CIE - MIRABAUD & CIE - PICTET & CIE
(1844)   (1796)   (1798)   (1819)   (1805)

www.genevaprivatebankers.com

Unfortunately, many companies are not set up for these developments. They often sell their products through separate sales forces, each working independently to close sales. Their technical people may not be willing to lend time to educate a customer. Their engineering, design and manufacturing people may have the attitude that 'it's our job to make good products and the salesperson's to sell them to customers'. However, the more successful companies recognise that winning and keeping accounts requires more than making good products and directing the sales force to close lots of sales. It requires a carefully coordinated, whole-company effort to create value-laden, satisfying relationships with important customers.

Relationship marketing is based on the premise that important accounts need focused and ongoing attention. Studies have shown that the best salespeople are those who are highly motivated and good closers, but more than this, they are customer-problem solvers and relationship builders. Salespeople working with key customers must do more than call when they think a customer might be ready to place an order. They also study the account and understand its problems. They call or visit frequently, work with the customer to help solve the customer's problems and improve its business, and take an interest in customers as people. Taking care of customers by offering them gifts, free entertainment or corporate hospitality may, however, be questioned by outsiders who equate such activities with bribery. Companies must therefore set guidelines for their managers and employees on where to draw the line (see Marketing Highlight 20.3).

The importance of relationship marketing is now widely recognised. Companies find that they earn a higher return from resources invested in retaining customers than from money spent to attract new ones. Increasingly, companies also recognise the importance of establishing strategic partnerships with valued customers, making skilled relationship marketing essential.

marketing highlight 20.3

Corporate hospitality: drawing the line on freebies

Corporate entertaining or hospitality is an expected part of business life. But when does an all-expenses-paid golfing trip, a free weekend in Paris or a case of finest Moët & Chandon stop being part of corporate life and begin to look like sleaze?

Freebies, such as a calendar or a fountain pen carrying the supplier's logo, are usually accepted by clients without a second thought. A nice dinner to keep in touch with a valued customer rarely raises an eyebrow, but is a free trip for a client and an accompanying partner to somewhere warm improper inducement, or merely a relaxing opportunity to build relations?

What should businesspeople do when faced with freeloading opportunities? In the absence of clear corporate or standard guidelines, how would managers decide if a gift, meal or trip is acceptable or sleazy?

Some experts offer the following simple guidelines:

1. The first test is the 'means test'. It draws the line at entertainment 'way beyond the level the person would normally be able to afford themselves'. It also depends on the level of superiority or importance of the individual. A steak in a wine bar at lunchtime is not beyond the means of most ordinary managers. However, if you want to talk business with the chief executive officer of a big company, you may have to meet him in more expensive surroundings.

2. The second test is the 'wow test'. When you open an envelope containing an invitation, you may say 'how nice' (or you may groan and say 'I suppose I had better be there!'). However, if you find yourself saying 'Wow!', then you had better think twice.

3. The third test is the reciprocity test. It is worthwhile occasionally to check that entertaining is reciprocal – suppliers buy you lunch, but you also buy them lunch back sometimes. That way, the relationship does not become too oppressive.

Corporate hospitality can be costly. At top sporting events – such as the football Cup Final at Wembley, or a day at Epsom for the horse racing – the cost could be astronomical. It costs something upwards of £1,500 per head to entertain at the Wimbledon men's tennis finals, but businesspeople will pay that if they have big international customers coming into the city to talk over deals that are worth millions of pounds. And don't ask what a meal for four in a Tokyo geisha club would amount to.

Is corporate entertaining necessary? Some managers argue that such events serve a purpose. The idea is to get the client out for a good time. They feel good about you, and the next time you or your sales representatives call, they will receive you ahead of the competition. Furthermore, a night at the theatre or opera, with a ticket for an accompanying partner, is quite useful when overseas visitors need to be entertained in the evening. Weekend outings for clients and potential customers allow the company to buy a little of a contact's private time to talk about business. In some business cultures (e.g. Japan, Malaysia, Thailand and most countries in the Far East), offering and accepting hospitality is part of work. Contacts or customers often see it as a way of establishing relationships.

Some companies actively discourage all employees from accepting hospitality. Some have no qualms about offering or receiving freebies. For those that have a problem on the morality or ethics side of all this, the experts have this to say: look at whether a mention of the hospitality arrangement – meal, trip or gift – in the press would cause embarrassment; try the 'means' test; do the wow test.

SOURCES: Anil Bhoyrul, 'A man for all seasons', *BusinessAge Magazine*, **4**, 49 (1994), pp. 104–6; Diane Summers, 'Hitching a ride on the corporate gravy train', *Financial Times* (24 October 1994), p. 7.

summary

Selling is one of the world's oldest professions. People who do the selling are called by a variety of names, including *salespeople, sales representatives, account executives, sales consultants, sales engineers, agents, district managers* and *marketing representatives*.

Regardless of their titles, members of the sales force play a key role in modern marketing organisations.

The term salesperson covers a wide spectrum of positions. Salespeople may be *order takers*, such as the department store salesperson who stands behind the counter. Or they may be *order getters*, salespeople engaged in the *creative selling* of products and services such as appliances, industrial equipment, advertising, or consulting services and so forth. Other salespeople do *missionary selling*, in which they are not involved in taking an order but in building goodwill or educating buyers. To be successful in these more creative forms of selling, a company must first build and then manage an effective sales force.

Most companies use salespeople, and many companies assign them the key role in the marketing mix. For companies selling business products, the firm's salespeople work directly with customers. Often, the sales force is the customer's only direct contact with the company and, therefore, may be viewed by customers as representing the company itself. In contrast, for consumer product companies that sell through intermediaries, consumers usually do not meet salespeople or even know about them. But the sales force works behind the scenes, dealing with wholesalers and retailers to obtain their support and helping them become effective in selling the firm's products.

As an element of the marketing mix, the sales force is very effective in achieving certain marketing objectives and carrying out such activities as prospecting, communicating, selling and servicing, and information gathering. But with companies becoming more market oriented, a market-focused sales force also works to produce *customer satisfaction* and *company profit*. To accomplish these goals, the sales force needs skills in marketing analysis and planning in addition to the traditional selling skills.

The high cost of the sales force calls for an effective sales management process consisting of six steps: setting sales force objectives; designing sales force strategy, structure, size and compensation; recruiting and selecting; training; supervising; and evaluating.

In designing a sales force, sales management must address issues such as: what type of sales force structure will work best (territorial, product, customer or complex structured); how large the sales force should be; who should be involved in the selling effort and how its various sales and sales-support people will work together (inside or outside and team selling). Sales management must also decide how the sales force should be compensated in terms of salary, commissions, bonuses, expenses and fringe benefits.

To hold down the high costs of hiring the wrong people, salespeople must be *recruited* and *selected* carefully. In recruiting salespeople, a company may look to job duties and the characteristics of its most successful salespeople to suggest the traits it wants in its sales force. *Training* programmes familiarise new salespeople not only with the art of selling, but with the company's history, its products and policies, and the characteristics of its market and competitors. All salespeople need *supervision*, and many need continuous encouragement in view of the many decisions they have to make and the many frustrations they invariably face. Periodically, the company must *evaluate* their performance to help them do a better job. Salespeople evaluation relies on information regularly gathered through sales reports, personal observations, customers' letters and complaints, customer surveys and conversations with other salespeople.

The art of selling involves a seven-step *selling process*: *prospecting and qualifying*, *pre-approach*, *approach*, *presentation and demonstration*, *handling objections*, *closing* and *follow-up*. These steps help marketers close a specific sale and, as such, tend to be *transaction-oriented*. However, a seller's dealings with customers should be guided by the larger concept of *relationship marketing*. The company's sales force should help to orchestrate a whole-company effort to develop profitable long-term relationships with key customers based on superior customer value and satisfaction.

discussing the issues

1. One of the most pressing issues that sales managers face is how to structure salespeople and their tasks. Evaluate the methods described in the text. For each method, provide (a) a brief description of its chief characteristics, (b) an example of how it is used, and (c) a critique of its effectiveness.

2. Telemarketing and Web-based selling provide marketers with opportunities to reach customers at work and in their homes. Critique each of these approaches, discussing the advantages and disadvantages of each. Provide an example of product or service marketing that uses each approach and discuss how the selling process works in these examples.

3. What is team selling and what are its advantages and disadvantages? How would recruiting and training for a sales team differ from recruiting and training for individual selling?

4. List and briefly describe the steps involved in the personal selling process. Which step do you think is most difficult for the average salesperson? Which step is the most critical to successful selling? Which step do you think is usually done most correctly? Explain each of your choices.

5. Explain the meaning of relationship marketing. Describe how relationship marketing might be used in (a) selling a personal computer to a final consumer, (b) selling a new car, (c) providing a student with a university education, and (d) selling season tickets to a local drama theatre.

applying the concepts

1. Helen Adolph was excited about her new job as a personal communication consultant for Nokia (www.nokia.com), the giant phone producer that captures a quarter of the global market and half the profits. Rivals such as Ericsson (www.ericsson.se), Vodafone (www.vodafone. com), Panasonic (www.panasonic.com) and Motorola (www.motorola.com) have vowed to make things tougher for Nokia in the coming year. They've developed new designs, communications applications and strategic alliances between hardware and software makers in an effort to lure fickle consumers away from Nokia.

   ✦ Adolph is attempting to sell Nokia's latest model personal communication device to Shell Oil in the UK (several thousand phones). What sales strategy and plan should Adolph recommend? In your answer, consider the advantages and disadvantages of Nokia's product.

   ✦ Would you recommend that Nokia employ individual selling or team selling? Explain.

   ✦ Which step of the sales process do you think will be most critical to Adolph's success?

   ✦ What could Adolph do to establish a strong relationship with local Shell representatives?

2. In years past, young stockbroker trainees received extensive training on the technical workings of the stock market and the characteristics of potential clients. One of the most difficult tasks for new brokers was finding and developing clients.

This involved long and often discouraging hours on the telephone 'prospecting' and 'cold-calling' potential clients. Today, however, the rapid expansion of investment and information alternatives have made the broker's job more challenging. Most major investment services brokerages are now online and brokers can now help information-hungry investors in ways that would have been unimaginable only a few years ago. Visit the following websites: Selftrade (www.selftrade.com), Sharepeople (www.sharepeople.com), Inter-Alliance (www.inter-alliance.com), E*Trade (www.E*Trade.com; or E*Trade.co.uk) (for the UK online broker), Comdirect (www.comdirect.com), Fidelity Investments (www.fidelity.com), Charles Schwab (www.schwab-europe.com), State Street (www.statestreet.com) and Waterhouse (www.waterhouse.com; www.tdwaterhouse.co.uk) (for the UK online broker).

   ✦ How have such sites changed the brokerage business? How is the selling function in the brokerage business changing?

   ✦ How can online brokerage services help the average broker to be a more effective salesperson? What sales strategies appear to be most appropriate for the broker who wishes to use personal contact and online connections to do business?

   ✦ Which website did you find to be the most 'user friendly'? Why? Which of the sites would make it easiest for you to get in touch with a broker in your local area? How could the local broker find out that you had been using his or her company's online service?

◆ Compare the above sites on sales stimulation, information services, cost, graphic design, responsiveness, security and relationship marketing. Which site is best? Why?

references

1. Based on Mogens Bjerre, 'MD Foods amba: A new world of sales and marketing', in *Understanding Marketing: a European casebook*, Celia Phillips, Ad Pruyn and Marie-Paule Kestemont (eds) (Chichester, UK: © John Wiley & Sons, Ltd, 2000), pp. 30–41. Reproduced with permission.

2. Patricia Sellers, 'How to remake your salesforce', *Fortune* (4 May 1992), pp. 96–103; see also Charles Fleming and Leslie Lopez, 'The corporate challenge – no boundaries: ABB's dramatic plan is to recast its structure along global lines', *Wall Street Journal* (28 September 1998), p. R16; further information also obtained from 'Employing over 2,000,000 people in over 100 countries', accessed online at www.abb.com (September 1999); for a discussion of sales force management control systems, sales territory design and sales organisation effectiveness, see Emin Babakus, David W. Cravens, Ken Grant, Thomas N. Ingram and Raymond W. LaForge, 'Investigating the relationships among sales, management control, sales territory design, salesperson performance, and sales organisation effectiveness', *International Journal of Research in Marketing*, **13**, 2 (October 1996), pp. 345–60.

3. Melinda Ligos, 'The incredible shrinking sales force', *Sales & Marketing Management* (December 1998), p. 15.

4. See Martin Everett, 'Selling by telephone', *Sales and Marketing Management* (28 June 1993), pp. 75–9; Simon Rines, 'Forcing change', *Marketing Week* (8 March 1996), special supplement on sales forces.

5. Richard C. Whiteley, 'Orchestrating service', *Sales and Marketing Management* (April 1994), pp. 29–30.

6. Christopher Meyer, 'How the right measures help teams excel', *Harvard Business Review* (May–June 1994), pp. 95–103; Michelle Marchetti, 'Why teams fail', *Sales & Marketing Management* (June 1997), p. 91; Donald W. Jackson Jr, Scott M. Widmier, Ralph Giacobbe and Janet E. Keith, 'Examining the use of team selling by manufacturers' representatives; a situational approach', *Industrial Marketing Management* (March 1999), pp. 155–64.

7. For an innovative, thoughtful and thorough discussion of key account management, see Malcolm McDonald and Beth Rogers, *Key Account Management* (Oxford: Butterworth-Heinemann, 1998); see also Bill Donaldson, *Sales Management*, 2nd edn (London: Macmillan, 1998).

8. Thomas R. Wotruba and Pradeep K. Tyagi, 'Met expectations and turnover in direct selling', *Journal of Marketing* (July 1991), pp. 24–35; and Chad Kaydo, 'Overturning turnover', *Sales & Marketing Management* (November 1997), pp. 50–60.

9. Bill Kelley, 'How to manage a superstar', *Sales and Marketing Management* (November 1988), pp. 32–4; Geoffrey Brewer, 'Mind reading: what drives top salespeople to greatness?', *Sales and Marketing Management* (May 1994), pp. 82–8; Barry J. Farber, 'Success stories for salespeople', *Sales and Marketing Management* (May 1995), pp. 30–1.

10. See Robert G. Head, 'Systemizing salesperson selection', *Sales and Marketing Management* (February 1992), pp. 65–8; 'To test or not to test', *Sales and Marketing Management* (May 1994), p. 86.

11. Geoffrey Brewer, 'Brain power', *Sales and Marketing Management* (May 1997), pp. 39–48; Don Peppers and Martha Rogers, 'The money trap', *Sales and Marketing Management* (May 1997), pp. 58–60; and Don Peppers and Martha Rogers, 'The price of customer service', *Sales & Marketing Management* (April 1999), pp. 20–1.

12. 'Nearly 20 per cent of salespeople are now online', www.dartnellcorp.com (May 1997); Melinda Ligos, 'Point, click and sell', *Sales & Marketing Management* (May 1999), pp. 51–6.

13. Stephen B. Castleberry and C. David Shepherd, 'Effective interpersonal listening and personal selling', *Journal of Personal Selling and Sales Management* (Winter 1993), pp. 35–49; John F. Yarbrough, 'Toughing it out', *Sales and Marketing Management* (May 1996), pp. 81–4.

14. Rosemary P. Ramsey and Ravipreet S. Sohi, 'Listening to your customers: the impact of perceived salesperson listening behavior on relationship outcomes', *Journal of Academy of Marketing Science* (Spring 1997), pp. 127–37.

case 20

Britcraft Jetprop: whose sale is it anyhow?*

On 14 April 1997, Bob Lomas, sales administration manager at Britcraft Civil Aviation (BCA), received a telephone call from Wing Commander Weir, the air attaché for the United Kingdom in a European nation. The wing commander had found out that the national air force (NAF) of the European nation (hereafter Country) was looking for a lighter, utility/transport aircraft to replace its ageing freight/transport aircraft for intra-European operations. The air attaché thought the Britcraft Jetprop, BCA's top-selling aircraft, was a suitable candidate.

Britcraft Aviation

Britcraft Aviation is owned by Britcraft Group Ltd, a British company with global engineering interests. Before being bought by Britcraft, BCA was a differently named independent company, known for designing and producing many famous military aircraft in the past. Military and executive aircraft were sold by Britcraft Aviation (BMA) and Britcraft Executive Aviation (BEA), located at a different site from that of the civil division.

The Jetprop's major rival was a similar aircraft made by Fokker, a Dutch company that was Britcraft's main competitor. The Jetprop was designed as a regional airliner, particularly for developing countries. Unlike the Fokker, the Jetprop was a low-winged aircraft, with an unobstructed passenger area, which gave it aerodynamic, structural and maintenance advantages. All components used on auxiliary services were selected for proven reliability, long overhaul life and ease of provisioning, enabling the aircraft to achieve the primary design objective of low maintenance costs and high operator utilisation. The aircraft was fully fail-safe, whereby any failure due to fatigue developed sufficiently slowly for it to be detected during routine inspection before it became dangerous. The Jetprop also gave short take-off and landing (STOL) performance from semi-prepared runways. The primary design objectives remained the main selling features of the aircraft.

Sales organisation

BCA's sales organisation, which covered civil and military sales, was responsible for selling the Jetprop. A number of these sales became VIP transports for heads of state. Each year, markets were analysed and a list was made of the most likely sales prospects for the coming 12 months. Area sales managers received 'designated areas' comprising several prospective customers grouped geographically. There were exceptions due to special relationships that a salesperson had developed in the past. With time, new prospects were added to the designated areas.

Doug Watts, whose designated area included the air forces of Malaysia, Thailand, Zaire (now the Democratic Republic of Congo) and Germany, was the area sales manager eventually responsible for the NAF prospect. Like several other area sales managers, he had joined Britcraft after a distinguished career in the UK's Royal Air Force (RAF). A few area sales managers without RAF experience had previously worked in the company's technical departments. In the company the Sales Department had a very high status, occupying a series of ground-floor offices at the front of the Jetprop factory.

The sales engineers were all technically qualified, a number having postgraduate degrees. They were responsible for providing technical support to the Sales Department and did considerable routine work associated with the sales effort. Although they were not working directly for the area sales managers, their work usually related to one part of the world, requiring frequent contact with one or two people in the Sales Department, which was located close to the Sales Engineering Department.

Ian Crawford, the marketing director of Britcraft, worked at Britcraft's HQ in London. He was responsible for marketing for the whole of Britcraft Aviation in the United Kingdom and overseas. He also managed Britcraft Aviation's regional executives – senior executives strategically based to cover all the world's markets.

The opening phase

After receiving the telephone call from Wing Commander Weir, Bob Lomas circulated news of the prospect. Doug Watts took overall responsibility for it. Although BCA had agents in the Country, these had either not heard of the NAF requirement or failed to tell the company about it. BCA therefore made direct contact with the national authorities in the Country. Following a visit to Herr Hans Schijlter, the defence secretary, Bob Lomas sent copies of the standard Jetprop military brochure directly to the Ministry of Defence, which was acknowledged by

---

* This case is based on in-company records and documents. For this reason the identity of the buyer and the seller and the names of the people in the case have been disguised.

Lieutenant Colonel Schemann, junior defence secretary. The next contact made was with Lieutenant General Baron von Forster, defence attaché to the Country's embassy in London, whom Bob Lomas had met at the Hanover Air Show. The general confirmed the NAF's interest in new equipment and asked for details of the Jetprop to pass on to the authorities.

On 6 July, Air Commodore Netherton informed John Upton of Britcraft that the NAF probably had a requirement for a state VIP aircraft. The retired RAF air commodore had lived in the capital of the Country for eight years, where he had been responsible for the Queen's Flight. He founded Eilluft AG, a group that dominated civil aircraft maintenance and light aircraft operations in the Country. He was an *ad hoc* agent for the prospective sale of Britcraft's fighter aircraft. As an accredited agent for BMA, he became an agent in the Country for BCA. The sales organisations of BEA, which produced the Britcraft executive jet for VIPs, and BCA were told of the sales opportunity.

In response, Geoff Lancaster, deputy sales manager of BCA, sent copies of the Jetprop brochure to Air Commodore Netherton to pass on to the prospective customer. As the air commodore was not familiar with the Jetprop, a letter enclosed with the brochures outlined some of the selling points (e.g. the size of the accommodation, low price, full galley and toilet facilities, uses short air fields, available credit terms) that he could use. The letter also mentioned that the Country's minister of defence had recently flown in a Jetprop of the Queen's Flight and was favourably impressed.

On 10 July, Air Commodore Netherton met the officer in charge of the Operations Requirements Branch of the NAF, who confirmed plans to replace several types of transport aircraft. Simultaneously, Wing Commander Weir contacted Ron Hill, the executive director of marketing for BCA, requesting the company to contact the Long Term Planning Department of the NAF directly about its requirement. Major Graff or, alternatively, Colonel Beauers and Lieutenant Colonel Horten, were suitable contacts there.

Work in Iran prevented Ron Hill from attending a meeting arranged on behalf of Doug Watts by Brian Cowley, the Jetprop sales manager. Instead, Steve Williams, his executive assistant, took his place. The discussions – between Steve Williams, Air Commodore Netherton, Major Graff (the officer in command of re-equipment evaluations) and Lieutenant Colonel Horten (the second in command of the Planning Department) – went well. They noted that the Jetprop was among the replacements considered. Fokker had, however, already demonstrated its aircraft, which many in the NAF favoured. The final requirement would be for two or three general transport aircraft plus possibly one for the paratroop training school at NAF-Graz. A Short Skyvan had already given a demonstration as a paradrop aircraft and the Canadians wanted to demonstrate their aircraft.

The Jetprop's demonstration to the NAF would be on 20 October. Major Graff asked for further evidence to support the Jetprop. The advantages of the Jetprop over the Fokker aircraft were highlighted, which were lack of bonding and spot welding, no pneumatics, fail-safe design, progressive maintenance and rough-airfield performance. During the visit they met briefly with Colonel Beauers, the officer commanding the Long Term Planning Department, whom Air Commander Netherton had known well for a number of years, but who was soon to move to NATO HQ. After the meeting the air commodore expressed the hope that, provided the presentation in October went well and the NAF wanted the aircraft, the political people would agree to the purchase. He added that the sale of the paradrop aircraft seemed likely to depend upon support from Colonel Smit, the commanding officer of NAF-Graz, while the main issue, he thought, would be the aircraft's ability to operate safely, fully loaded for a parachute-training mission, from the NAF-Graz airstrip, which was grass and only 650 metres long.

Following the visit, Ernie Wentworth, a senior sales engineer, managed the technical selling effort. Through the Sales Department customer specifications engineer, the Production Planning Department was asked for a delivery schedule and the Estimating Department was requested to cost the aircraft. Other technical departments also became involved in supplying cost and performance evaluations. The Contracts Department would finally negotiate a price for the package of aircraft, spares, guarantees, and after-sales services required.

Major Graff later requested details of the take-off and landing performance of the Jetprop at NAF-Graz. Since it was marginal, Air Commodore Netherton concluded that the only course was to convince the airfield's commanding officer to extend the runway.

Before the scheduled demonstration took place, a number of the NAF personnel – Lt Col Horten (chief of Plans and Studies), Lt Col Wabber (chief of Pilot Training), Major Bayer and Major Graff (Plans and Studies) – were invited to attend the UK's biennial Farnborough Air Show where they were entertained by Britcraft. The meeting progressed well. Nine NAF officers visited BCA for the demonstration of the Jetprop in October, including officers from NAF Planning, Plans and Studies, Avionics, Technical Section, Supply/Spares and HQ Transport.

During the visit, technical specialists looked after most of the NAF officers, while the Long Term Planning Department people discussed contractual details. Prices for the basic version and additional options – strengthened floor for cargo operations, and large freight door – were also presented. The cost of avionics, spares and other equipment that allowed the aircraft to perform a wide variety of roles would be additional.

On the whole, the demonstration and presentation went very well, although Major von Betterei, 'from whom it was difficult even to wring a smile', was evidently 'Fokker oriented'. Air Commodore Netherton and he had been able to talk separately with the senior officer present, with whom they had a 'long and useful discussion about compensation'.

The second phase

Compensation or offset is an increasingly common part of large international sales. It usually involves a provision being made for the vendor or the vendor's country to buy goods from the customer's country. The discussion with Colonel Zvinek, of NAF Planning, Plans and Studies, during the demonstration marked the first occasion when offset appeared accompanying the NAF's procurement of transport aircraft.

The BEA advised the BCA that the offset was critical. In the past, the BEA had lost to the French, who offered very high offset, in the sale of two executive jet aircraft to the NAF. Meanwhile, BMA warned BCA not to use any of the compensation it had already earmarked for a possible sale of military trainer aircraft.

Air Commodore Netherton sought clarification from Herr Maximilian, an under-secretary in the Ministry of Economic Affairs, who was responsible for advising the Country's ministerial committee on offset. Herr Maximilian said offset had recently been between 60 and 70 per cent of the value of a contract and had been completed by the delivery date of the last aircraft. He felt that ideally the work should relate directly to the major project being considered, but should not involve the manufacture of main subassemblies such as wings, air frames or engines. He concluded by saying that negotiations were the responsibility of the vendor alone, who should not increase prices as a result of the required activities.

Soon after his visit to Herr Maximilian, the NAF gave the replacement top priority with a schedule for finalising the requirement in March 1998, signing of letter of intent by mid-1998, contract and deposit payment in late 1998 and delivery and full payment in 1999.

Colonel Zvinek, who originally doubted the Jetprop, was converted since the demonstration, together with all the other important NAF officers concerned. All that was necessary was to assemble an acceptable offset.

Some time passed with little further progress being made with the sale. It became evident that Fokker was offering a very substantial offset, aided by its shareholding in Baden GmbH, which owned Nationale Flugzeugwerke AG (NFW), the Country's largest airframe manufacturer, and which already manufactured Fokker parts.

Early in 1998, Kevin Murphy, the contracts manager for BCA, sent a firm proposal to Colonel Zvinek, with the Sales Engineering Department offering new performance and weight information that showed Jetprop in a better light.

Some days later an urgent fax came from Roger Woods of Britcraft, who had met Colonel Horten at a cocktail party in the capital, noting that Fokker's exceptional offset looked like losing Britcraft the deal. Air Commodore Netherton talked to Colonel Horten and then confirmed that the offset was 'not big business'. Further, Messrs Jones and Bedwell of BMA, who were in the Country at that time negotiating a large offset deal with the Ministry of Economic Affairs, found that 'offset would not really be involved on such a small order'.

In a subsequent meeting in April 1998, Major Graff informed Air Commodore Netherton that there was a feeling that the Jetprop was inferior to the Fokker on several technical grounds and the price of £1,393,000 compared unfavourably with the Fokker offer. The total cost, including the price of spares, was more than the amount budgeted. A new formal offer of £1,323,000, entailing a reduction in the number of roles the aircraft had to perform, went to the Country before the end of April.

At the Paris Air Show on 13 June, Doug Watts met Major Graff who emphasised that the offset was important, and that the NAF wanted to change the aircraft specifications and a new quotation would be necessary. Steve Williams had left Britcraft, so Geoff Lancaster took over negotiations. Wing Commander Weir was contacted who said he would probably be able to help in arranging some offset deal, but added that diplomatic circles generally felt that it was 'Britain's turn' to obtain a contract.

On 16 July Geoff Lancaster, Major Graff and Air Commodore Netherton visited Herr Maximilian at the Ministry of Economic Affairs. Four alternative offset arrangements were discussed:

1. Bought-out equipment for the Jetprop could be purchased from the Country's firms.

2. Basic aircraft could be flown to the Country to be finished and new avionics fitted by a NAF contractor.

3. Britcraft's vendors could subcontract work into the Country.

4. The Country's industry could build a future batch of Jetprops.

Herr Maximilian's response to the suggestion was not enthusiastic. He underlined his government's concern about offset being related directly to the contract or involving the NAF or the government. He quoted that, in the recent sale of two Boeing aircraft to the Country's national airline, Boeing had agreed to place £3,000,000 of work with the Country's industry in the first year and £15,000,000 over the next ten years. The figures suggested that the offset was far more than the price of the two aircraft.

After leaving the ministry, Geoff Lancaster told Major Graff the consequence of further delay in placing a firm order. Delays would reduce the likelihood of Britcraft being able to supply at the original price. Several customers were also on the verge of signing contracts for Jetprops. Major Graff worried about the delay, but said there was little he could do. His recommendations for purchase would go on to General Petsch, which would constitute the official NAF requirements. They would then go through a sequence of decision-makers: the air force adviser, the defence secretary, Hans Schijlter, who would examine the report closely but not consider offset, and the minister of defence, the Prime Minister and the minister for economic affairs, would make the final decision. Before Geoff Lancaster left the Country it was agreed to arrange for a group of NAF officers to visit Schiller Aviation, an independent airline which had recently bought some Jetprops. Air Commodore Netherton escorted the group on the visit and later reported that the airline was 'very complimentary' about the aircraft and Britcraft support.

The offset

In an attempt to arrange the necessary offset, several channels were investigated. A team of Britcraft design and production engineers investigated what work could be 'put out' to subcontractors in the Country. Negotiations with a number of companies did not come to fruition. Eventually, a company, Coles & Turf, offered to buy £4,500,000 worth of the Country's goods for a commission of 10 per cent. Britcraft felt that the commission rate requested left no room for them to make a profit on the contract, and eventually got Coles & Turf to agree to £1,500,000 of offset.

On 16 October there came a blow to the NAF deal. A Brazilian operator signed a contract with BCA for six aircraft. This meant that the NAF aircraft would be from the more expensive batch 15 rather than the original batch 14 and would cost more – £1,470,000. The NAF reluctantly accepted the price increase and signed a letter of intent in November. Roden AG agreed to accept £450,000 worth of specified subcontract work.

As April approached, a team at Britcraft was preparing to make a trip to the Country for final negotiations and contract signing. A day before they were due to leave, Dick Drake, the commercial director, received a fax from the Country's authorities. It read:

> Department of Economic Affairs urgently expect more precision about your commitment and also a sensible increase of work for national industry. It is quite obvious that the 10 per cent offset is absolutely unsatisfactory. A reply is expected by 29 April.

A copy of the message went to Air Commodore Netherton, to which Dick Drake added:

> It is virtually certain that it will be necessary for me to reply on Friday that we regret we are unable to increase our commitment and the only other offset is that which they already know about from the aero-engine supplier. However, before replying, I would like to know whether Weir still believes it is Britain's turn.

Questions

1. Trace the stages in the buying process and how the Country's interests changed from one stage to the next. Why were the Country's interests changing and was Britcraft keeping pace with the changes?

2. How well did the strengths of the Jetprop match the needs of the NAF?

3. Identify the players in the buying centre and gauge their role and influence. How well did Britcraft manage the complexity of the buying centre and their diverse needs?

4. Discriminate between the sales roles of the people in Britcraft.

5. Did Britcraft's structure help or hinder its sales campaign? How could it be changed for the better?

6. What were Britcraft's main failings and strengths? Do you think it will win the sale or is it too out of touch with the needs of the NAF and the Country's government? What could it do at this late stage? Is it still 'Britain's turn'?

internet exercises

Internet exercises for this chapter can be found on the student site of the myPHLIP Web Site at www.booksites.net/kotler.

part seven

Place

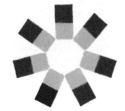

'To open a shop is easy; to keep it open is an art.'

CONFUCIUS (PHILOSOPHER)

part introduction

Chapter 21

Managing marketing channels

Chapter 22

Direct and online marketing: the new marketing model

THE FINAL PART OF THIS text comprises two chapters covering the fourth element of the marketing mix – place. It will help you to understand the decisions and actions that companies take in order to bring products and services to customers. It also considers how new information and communication technologies are transforming distribution and retailing functions.

How products and services are delivered to customers for final usage or consumption can make a difference to how customers perceive the quality and value of the overall offering. Speed of delivery, guaranteed supply and availability, convenience to shoppers and so forth can enhance buyer–seller relationships and increase customer satisfaction. Consequently, firms are increasingly paying greater attention to how they manage their distribution channels to deliver goods and services that customers want at the right time, right place and right price. Chapter 21 shows what channel organisations and their functions are, and how firms can build more cost-effective routes to serving and satisfying their target markets.

The last decade has seen a revolution taking place in the field of communications and telecommunications technology, which has had a significant impact on marketing activities. Telephones, televisions and computers are becoming important channels for selling products and services; these media are increasingly used not just for communicating messages to customers, but for interacting with and doing business with customers. Chapter 22 explores the ways in which direct, non face-to-face forms of marketing can help organisations reach specific target markets quickly. TV Web boxes, the Internet and wireless technologies are posing new challenges and opportunities – from virtual shopping to mobile commerce – for firms. In this final chapter we see how organisations conduct direct and online marketing, and we speculate on future directions for this new marketing model.

737

chapter twenty-one

Managing marketing channels

Chapter objectives   *After reading this chapter, you should be able to:*

✦ Explain why companies use marketing channels and discuss the functions these channels perform.

✦ Discuss how channel members interact and how they organise to perform the work of the channel.

✦ Identify the major channel alternatives open to a company and the key issues that

managers consider when setting up marketing channel systems.

✦ Discuss the nature and importance of retailers, wholesalers and physical distribution.

✦ Explain integrated logistics, including how it may be achieved and its benefits to the company.

introduction

In this chapter, we will take a closer look at an important, albeit often neglected, component of the marketing mix – place – and focus on decisions and activities relating to distribution channels and logistics management.

Marketing channel decisions are among the most important decisions that management faces. A company's channel decisions are linked with every other marketing decision. The company's pricing depends on whether it uses mass merchandisers or high-quality speciality stores. The firm's sales force and advertising decisions depend on how much persuasion, training and motivation the dealers or resellers need. Whether a company develops or acquires certain new products may depend on how well those products fit the abilities of its channel members.

Companies often pay too little attention to their distribution channels. Managers who see channel functions merely as the physical transportation, storage and distribution of finished goods to the end-user fail to utilise the channel of distribution as a competitive weapon. In contrast, many companies have used imaginative distribution systems to *gain* a competitive advantage. At one extreme, we see how a technology such as print-on-demand (see preview case overleaf) could potentially transform the nature of competition in the publishing industry. In others, such as personal computers, Dell Computer revolutionised its industry by selling personal computers directly to consumers rather than through retail stores.

preview case

Xlibris

For publishers and the book trade, the channel war is only just beginning. Book authors typically depend on their publisher to produce and market their creations and on bookstores, libraries and other retail outlets to make these available to their target audiences. However, information technology and the Internet are changing the way bookstores and publishers create and deliver value to customers. One theory is that multimedia will kill off traditional bookstores – consumers have less time to read in the wake of rising forms of entertainment such as digital TV channels and surfing the Internet. Those who read will increasingly buy their books from online retailers. Then, there is publishing's nemesis in the guise of Xlibris.

Xlibris is best described as an online publisher with a difference. It uses print-on-demand technology to bring the paper and electronic worlds of publishing together. This is how it works. A customer visiting an online bookstore – say, Amazon – clicks on the 'order' button for an Xlibris book. This sends a message to a printer which prints and binds the one copy and sends it off to the customer. No longer does the publisher need to print tens of thousands of the book to be profitable. Further back in the book supply chain are the authors, who upload their manuscript to Xlibris's website. The 'book' will subsequently be made available on the websites of online book retailers such as Amazon and Barnes & Noble.

Acting as an intermediary, Xlibris helps authors to bring to market their ideas. Except for works with graphics and diagrams, which incur a fee, authors get to publish their work free. Because large print-runs are unnecessary to make a book profitable, anyone who writes can publish on the site.

Xlibris is not alone in this new world of publishing. Groups such as iUniverse and MightyWords offer varying forms of online publishing services. For example, iUniverse will print whatever the customer wants in its portfolio – from entire books to selections from book series and guides. MightyWords specialises in delivering content that is off-size – too long for a magazine or too short for a book – and any knowledge that customers are willing to pay for. They also publish works of previously published authors and publishers seeking to boost sales of their authors' works. Online Originals publishes high-quality work that is uncommercial to print and deliver using traditional production and distribution.

Xlibris is receiving some 500 new titles a month. Whether or not people are actually buying or reading these titles is another matter. Although this is a question pondered by traditional publishers and booksellers, one thing seems certain. Plunging publishing costs and the combination of convenience and vast range offered by online book retailers are likely to increase the market share of the new online businesses. In response to the Internet challenge, bookstore chains such as Waterstones and Blackwells, in Britain, are turning visiting a bookshop into a leisure activity. They are opening new, fashionable mega-stores carrying over 200,000 titles and a million books. The new-style megastores have in-house cafés, juice bars and restaurants. In order to outwit the online stores, they are trying to turn book-buying into a pleasurable experience. If you visit the Waterstone's store, an old Simpson department store in London's Piccadilly, you could spend the whole day browsing. No, not the Internet, but read books without buying them (and eat blueberry muffins) to your heart's content.

Traditionally, authors rely on publishers to produce and market their works and bookstores to sell them. The authors, publishers, booksellers and other retail outlets all form part of a chain in the supply of books from its source of creation to customer ownership. With the rise of new online booksellers and as more online groups, such as Xlibris, find ways to bring publishing to the Internet and direct delivery to the customer, traditional channels in publishing and bookselling will have to seek new ways of creating value for customers.[1]

Questions

1. Taking books as an example, identify the supply chain and explain the channel service needs of (a) book authors and (b) the publisher.

2. How, and to what extent will new online publishing models reflected by Xlibis impact on traditional book publishing and retailing businesses?

3. Suggest potential channel strategies for traditional channel members that would enable them to sustain a competitive advantage in the changing publishing and bookselling industries.

Distribution channel decisions often involve long-term commitments to other firms. For example, companies such as Volvo, Nokia or Benetton can easily change their advertising, pricing or promotion programmes. They can scrap old products and introduce new ones as market tastes demand. But when they set up distribution channels through contacts with franchises, independent dealers or large retailers, they cannot readily replace these channels with company-owned stores if conditions change. Therefore, management must design its channels carefully, with an eye on tomorrow's likely selling environment as well as today's.

This chapter examines the following questions concerning marketing channels:

+ What is the nature of marketing channels?
+ How do channel firms organise to do the work of the channel?
+ What problems do companies face in designing and managing their channels?
+ What role does physical distribution play in attracting and satisfying customers?
+ How are marketing channels changing and what are their implications for marketers?

the nature of distribution channels

Distribution channel (marketing channel)
A set of interdependent organisations involved in the process of making a product or service available for use or consumption by the consumer or industrial user.

Most producers use third parties or intermediaries to bring their products to market. They try to forge a **distribution channel** – a set of interdependent organisations involved in the process of making a product or service available for use or consumption by the consumer or business user.[2] The channel of distribution is therefore all those organisations through which a product must pass between its point of production and consumption.[3]

why are marketing intermediaries used?

Why do producers give some of the selling job to intermediaries? After all, doing so means giving up some control over how and to whom the products are sold. The use of intermediaries results from their greater efficiency in making goods available to target markets. Through their contacts, experience, specialisation and scale of operation, intermediaries usually offer the firm more than it can achieve on its own.

Figure 21.1 shows how using intermediaries can provide economies. Part A shows three manufacturers, each using direct marketing to reach three customers. This system requires nine different contacts. Part B shows the three manufacturers working through one distributor, which contacts the three customers. This system requires only six contacts. In this way, intermediaries reduce the amount of work that must be done by both producers and consumers.

From the economic system's point of view, the role of marketing intermediaries is to convert the assortments of products made by producers into the assortments wanted by consumers. Producers make narrow assortments of products in large quantities, but consumers want broad assortments of products in small quantities. In the distribution channels, intermediaries buy the large quantities of many producers and break them down into the smaller quantities and broader assortments wanted by consumers. As such, intermediaries play an important role in matching supply and demand.

The concept of distribution channels is not limited to the distribution of tangible products. Producers of services and ideas also face the problem of making their output available to target populations. In the private sector, retail stores, hotels, banks and

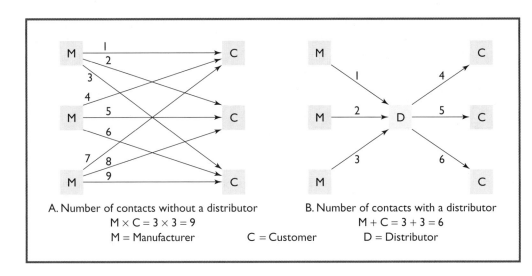

Figure 21.1

How a marketing intermediary reduces the number of channel transactions and raises economy of effort

other service providers take great care to make their services conveniently available to target customers. In the public sector, service organisations and agencies develop 'educational distribution systems' and 'healthcare delivery systems' for reaching sometimes widely dispersed populations. Hospitals must be located to serve various patient populations, and schools must be located close to the children who need to be taught. Communities must locate their fire stations to provide rapid response to fires and polling stations must be placed where people can vote conveniently.

marketing channel functions

A distribution channel moves goods from producers to consumers. It fills the main time, place and possession gaps that separate goods and services from those who would use them. Members of the marketing channel perform many key functions. Some help to complete transactions:

◆ *Information*. Gathering and distributing marketing research and intelligence information about actors and forces in the marketing environment needed for planning and facilitating exchange.

◆ *Promotion*. Developing and spreading persuasive communications about an offer.

◆ *Contact*. Finding and communicating with prospective buyers.

◆ *Matching*. Shaping and fitting the offer to the buyer's needs, including such activities as manufacturing, grading, assembling and packaging.

◆ *Negotiation*. Reaching an agreement on price and other terms of the offer, so that ownership or possession can be transferred.

Others help to fulfil the completed transactions:

◆ *Physical distribution*. Transporting and storing goods.

◆ *Financing*. Acquiring and using funds to cover the costs of the channel work.

◆ *Risk taking*. Assuming the risks of carrying out the channel work.

The question is not *whether* these functions need to be performed, but rather *who* is to perform them. To the extent that the manufacturer performs these functions, its costs go up and its prices have to be higher. At the same time, when some of these functions are shifted to intermediaries, the producer's costs and prices may be lower, but the intermediaries must charge more to cover the costs of their work. In dividing the work of the channel, the various functions should be assigned to the channel members that can perform them most efficiently and effectively to provide satisfactory assortments of goods to target consumers.

Channel level
A layer of intermediaries that performs some work in bringing the product and its ownership closer to the final buyer.

Direct-marketing channel
A marketing channel that has no intermediary levels.

Figure 21.2

Consumer and business marketing channels

number of channel levels

Distribution channels can be described by the number of channel levels involved. Each layer of marketing intermediaries that performs some work in bringing the product and its ownership closer to the final buyer is a **channel level**. Because the producer and the final consumer both perform some work, they are part of every channel. The *number of intermediary levels* indicates the *length* of a channel. Figure 21.2A shows several consumer distribution channels of different lengths.

Channel 1, called a **direct-marketing channel**, has no intermediary levels. It consists of a manufacturer selling directly to consumers. For example, Tupperware sells its products door-to-door or through home and office sales parties. Wine clubs, such as Bordeaux Direct and The Wine Society in the UK, sell their wines through mail order, telephone or at their websites. And Marks & Spencer sells its products through its own stores, offline and online, as well as through mail order and telephone. Direct sales of

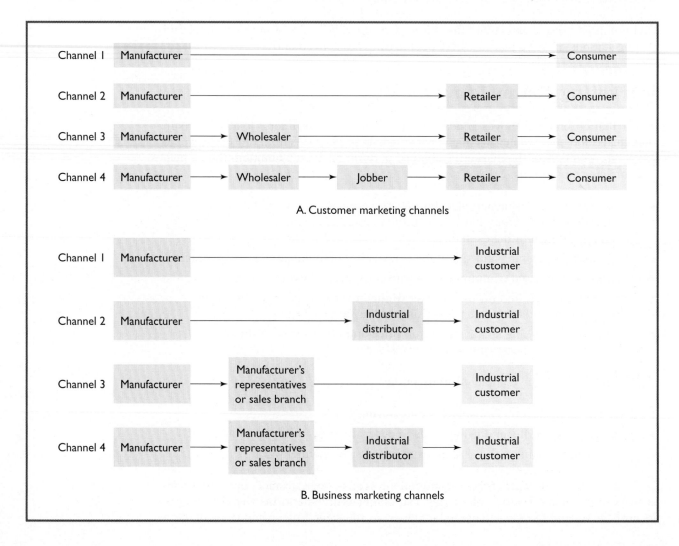

A. Customer marketing channels

B. Business marketing channels

consumer goods in some European countries have enjoyed record growth in recent years. In Chapter 22, we examine in greater detail the methods organisations use to market directly to consumers.

The remaining channels in Figure 21.2A are *indirect*-marketing channels. Channel 2 contains one intermediary level. In consumer markets, this level is typically a retailer. For example, the makers of televisions, cameras, furniture, major appliances and many other products sell their goods directly to large retailers, which then sell the goods to final consumers. Channel 3 contains two intermediary levels, a wholesaler and retailer. This channel is often used by manufacturers of food, drugs, hardware and other products. Channel 4 contains three intermediary levels. In the meat-packing industry, for example, jobbers usually come between wholesalers and retailers. The jobber buys from wholesalers and sells to smaller retailers, which generally are not served by larger wholesalers. Distribution channels with even more levels are sometimes found, but less often. From the producer's point of view, a greater number of levels means less control and greater channel complexity.

Figure 21.2B shows some common industrial or business distribution channels. The business marketer can use its own sales force to sell directly to business customers. It can also sell to industrial distributors, which in turn sell to business customers. It can sell through manufacturers' representatives or its own sales branches to business customers, or it can use these representatives and branches to sell through industrial distributors. Thus business markets commonly include multilevel distribution channels.

In summary, channel institutions play an important role in making products or services available to customers. All of these institutions are connected by several types of flows. These include the *physical flow* of products, the *flow of ownership*, the *payment flow*, the *information flow* and the *promotion flow*. These transfers can make even channels with only one or a few levels very complex. The types of intermediary channel will be discussed in greater detail in a later section.

channel behaviour and organisation

Distribution channels are more than simple collections of firms tied together by various flows. They are complex behavioural systems in which people and companies interact to accomplish individual, company and channel goals. Some channel systems consist only of informal interactions among loosely organised firms, while others consist of formal interactions guided by strong organisational structures. Moreover, channel systems do not stand still – new types of intermediary surface and whole new channel systems evolve. Here we look at channel behaviour and at how members organise to do the work of the channel.

channel behaviour

A distribution channel consists of firms that have banded together and are dependent on each other to achieve a common goal. For example, a Volvo dealer depends on the manufacturer to design cars that meet consumer needs. In turn, Volvo depends on the dealer to attract consumers, persuade them to buy Volvo cars, and service cars after the sale. The Volvo dealer also depends on the other dealers to provide good sales and service that will uphold the reputation of Volvo and its dealer body. In fact, the success of individual Volvo dealers depends on how well the entire Volvo distribution channel competes with the channels of other car manufacturers.

Each channel member plays a role in the channel and specialises in performing one or more functions. For example, Philips' role is to produce hi-fi equipment that consumers will like and to create demand through national and worldwide advertising. The role of the specialist shops, department stores and other independent outlets that stock and sell Philips' products is to display these items in convenient locations, to answer buyers' questions, to close sales and to provide a good level of customer service. The channel will be most effective when each member is assigned the tasks it can do best.

marketing highlight 21.1

Lego man's brand new retail experience: should toy retailers be impressed?

'We're not out just to create a new toy store. We are aiming for a new mind-set expression – or, a total brand value expression, showing a much broader range of what Lego is, and what it can do', says Karl Kalcher, the managing director of Lego Lifestyle International Ltd, and the force behind Lego's new retail concept store, recently launched in Bluewater, Kent (UK).

Lego already has ten licensed children's-wear stores across Europe, two United Nations-themed stores in the US, park stores in Denmark, Windsor and California, an airport store in Copenhagen and a number of other shopping stores throughout Europe. So, what is unique about the Bluewater store? According to Lego Lifestyle's director of Brand Retail, Paul Denham, the Bluewater store represents Lego's ultimate retail experience. When consumers visit the store, they should experience everything – all the values – that Lego, the brand, stands for. Underpinning the new retail store concept is the Lego Group's desire to become the leading brand amongst families and children. Lego values are translated throughout – from the construction of the building to the whole shopping experience.

Take the store shelves, for example. There are no sharp edges – expensive and impractical, from a construction perspective, but extremely important for the safety and enjoyment of children in the store. Other Lego values – the pleasures, educational stimulations and developmental benefits – to be experienced by target consumers are manifested through the 'high-touch element' that the Lego store allows. Interactivity is designed into the store environment. These include vending machines, store-front 'rocket race' interactives, incorporating LED codes which players have to memorise in order to activate the rocket, eye-level entertainment (for the vertically challenged), so children can be intrigued without needing adult intervention. Not least is the 'wow' factor offered by the raft of Lego models which never fail to add the wonder touch to the store. And, there are other pleasures – low toilet seats, big door handles, clear signs and little chance of getting locked in the loos!

Kalcher believes that the concept store sets a standard of retail innovation which ordinary retailers alone would not be able to achieve. The Bluewater model, in a way, is about investing time and effort in inspiring high-street retailers. Yet, this goal is far from doing what it sets out to achieve. Far from being inspired, many of Lego's current retailers have objected to the potential impacts on their own businesses. Many have been concerned about having to cut price to compete with the store. Some feel they have been undervalued or devalued as Lego stockists. Lego management are quick to reassure concerned channel members that its 'new retail experience' will not at all threaten traffic in the conventional retail outlets. Kalcher claimed that the Lego store is about building and sustaining a superior standard for the brand, which in turn promotes the esteem of the company's products for *all* Lego retailers. Sales within a 50-mile radius of Legoland, UK lifted after opening the park store. Lego product sales have risen above industry trends since its Minneapolis store opened. Besides, Lego's strategy has been to build an armoury of retailing experiences which would be transferred to its retail customers through franchise operations. Essentially, both manufacturer and retailer can satisfy consumers more effectively through building upon Lego's tradition for quality, heritage and innovation.

For the little consumer though, the real test is whether they will give an arm and a leg for the ultimate Lego experience.

Sources: Adapted from Claire Irwin, 'Construction site', *Marketing Business* (September 1999), pp. 36–9.

Ideally, because the success of individual channel members depends on overall channel success, all channel firms should work together smoothly to secure healthy margins or profitable sales. They should understand and accept their roles, coordinate their goals and activities and cooperate to attain overall channel goals. By cooperating, they can more effectively sense, serve and satisfy the target market.

Unfortunately, individual channel members rarely take such a broad view. They are usually more concerned with their own short-run goals and their dealings with those firms closest to them in the channel. Cooperating to achieve overall channel goals sometimes means compromising individual company goals. Although channel members are dependent on one another, they often act alone in their own short-term best interests. They often disagree on the roles that each should play – that is, on who should do what and for what rewards. Such disagreements over goals and roles generate **channel conflict**. Conflict can occur at two levels.

Horizontal conflict is conflict among firms at the same level of the channel. For instance, Volvo dealers in a particular region may complain about other dealers in the region that steal sales from them by being too aggressive in their pricing and advertising, or by selling outside their assigned territories.

Vertical conflict is even more common and refers to conflicts between different levels of the same channel. For example, some personal computer manufacturers created conflict with their high street dealers when they opened online stores to sell PCs directly to customers. Dealers, not surprisingly, complained. To resolve the conflict, manufacturers had to develop communication campaigns to educate dealers on how online efforts would assist dealers rather than hurt sales.

Some conflict in the channel takes the form of healthy competition (see Marketing Highlight 21.1). Without such competition, channel members could become passive and non-innovative. For the channel as a whole to perform well, each channel member's role must be specified and channel conflict must be managed. The channel will perform better if it includes a firm, agency or mechanism that has the power to assign roles, secure channel cooperation and manage conflict. Let us take a look at how channel members organise to do the work of the channel.

Channel conflict
Disagreement among marketing channel members on goals and roles – who should do what and for what rewards.

channel organisation

Historically, distribution channels have been loose collections of independent companies, each showing little concern for overall channel performance. These *conventional distribution channels* have lacked strong leadership and have been troubled by damaging conflict and poor performance. One of the biggest recent channel developments has been the *vertical marketing systems* that have emerged to challenge conventional marketing channels.

■ Vertical marketing systems

Figure 21.3 contrasts the two types of channel arrangement.

A **conventional distribution channel** consists of one or more independent producers, wholesalers and retailers. Each is a separate business seeking to maximise its own profits, even at the expense of profits for the system as a whole. No channel member has much control over the other members and no formal means exists for assigning roles and resolving channel conflict.

In contrast, a **vertical marketing system (VMS)** consists of producers, wholesalers and retailers acting as a unified system. One channel member owns the others, has contracts with them, or wields so much power that they all cooperate. The VMS can be dominated by the producer, wholesaler or retailer. Vertical marketing systems came into being to control channel behaviour and manage channel conflict. For example,

Conventional distribution channel
A channel consisting of one or more independent producers, wholesalers and retailers, each a separate business seeking to maximise its own profits even at the expense of profits for the system as a whole.

Vertical marketing system (VMS)
A distribution channel structure in which producers, wholesalers and retailers act as a unified system. One channel member owns the others, has contracts with them, or has so much power that they all cooperate.

Figure 21.3

A conventional
marketing channel
versus a vertical
marketing system

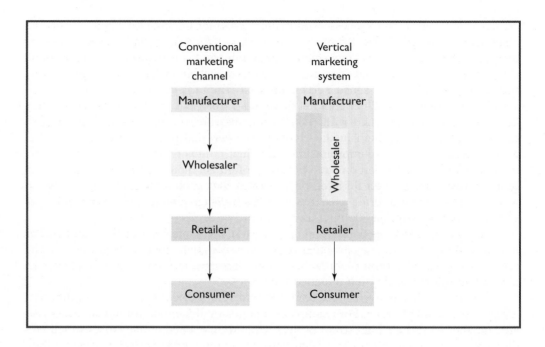

Figure 21.4

Main types of vertical
marketing system

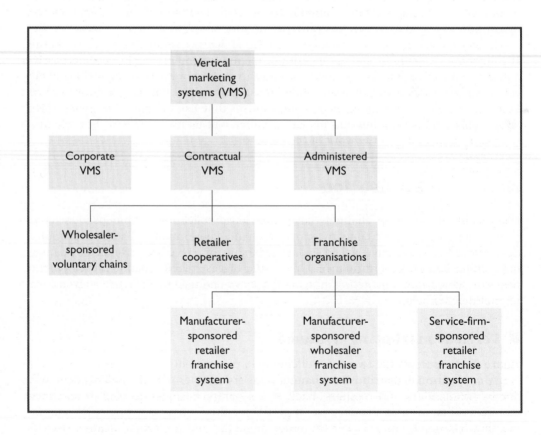

some pharmaceutical drugs manufacturers and distribution companies sought to increase control over the channel system either through acquiring a distributor or through cooperative alliance arrangements.

We now look at the three main types of VMS shown in Figure 21.4. Each type uses a different means for setting up leadership and power in the channel.

Corporate VMS   A **corporate VMS** combines successive stages of production and distribution under single ownership. Coordination and conflict management are attained through regular organisational channels. Petrol distribution through chains of petrol stations owned by the oil company is an example of delivery and control achieved by such a system. Breweries that sell beer through public houses under their ownership provide another example. In the car rental market, vehicle makers have established dominant positions in most of the world's leading vehicle rental groups. Retail organisations have also taken advantage of corporate VMS.

> For example, Ahold, the Dutch supermarket chain, and the number two grocery retailer in the US, acquired US Foodservice, the second largest American food distributor. Foodservice would allow Ahold not only to shift from a retailing focus to food supply (to eating establishments), reflecting a global consumer trend towards eating out, but also to realise synergies in areas of food purchasing, physical distribution and technology. Integrating operations with US Foodservice, which reaches 85 per cent of the US from 40 distribution centres, gives Ahold access to new territories on the West Coast and southern US.[4]

Contractual VMS   A **contractual VMS** consists of independent organisations at different levels of production and distribution who join together through contracts to obtain more economies or sales impact than each could achieve alone. Coordination and conflict management are attained through the legal arrangements agreed among channel members. There are three types of contractual VMSs: wholesaler-sponsored voluntary chains, retailer cooperatives and **franchise** organisations.

In *wholesaler-sponsored voluntary chains*, wholesalers organise voluntary chains of independent retailers to help them compete with large chain organisations. The wholesaler develops a programme in which independent retailers standardise their selling practices and achieve buying economies that let the group compete effectively with chain organisations.

In **retailer cooperatives**, a group of independent retailers band together to own wholesale operations jointly, or to conduct joint wholesaling and possibly production. The Swiss Migros, with its dozen or so cooperatives, and the UK's Cooperative Societies have tried to exploit group buying and promotion economies through setting up such marketing arrangements. Members buy most of their goods through the retailer co-op and plan their advertising jointly. Profits are passed back to members in proportion to their purchases.

A franchise is a contractual association between a franchiser – a manufacturer, wholesaler or service organisation – and an independent channel member (the franchisee), which buys the right to sell the franchiser's branded product or service. The franchisee links several stages in the production–distribution system. The franchiser typically provides a brand identity and start-up, marketing and accounting assistance as well as management know-how to the franchisee. In return, the franchiser gets some form of compensation, such as an initial fee and a continuing royalty payment, lease fees for equipment and a share of the profits. Franchising has been a fast-growing retailing form in recent years. Almost every kind of business has been franchised – from hotels and fast-food restaurants to dental and garden maintenance services, from wedding consultants and domestic services to funeral homes and fitness centres.

Franchising offers a number of benefits to both the franchiser and franchisee. The main advantages for the franchiser are as follows:

✦   The franchiser secures fast distribution for its products and services without incurring the full costs of setting up and running its own operations. Franchising also enables the franchiser to expand a successful business more rapidly than by using its own capital.

Corporate VMS
A vertical marketing system that combines successive stages of production and distribution under single ownership – channel leadership is established through common ownership.

Contractual VMS
A vertical marketing system in which independent firms at different levels of production and distribution join together through contracts to obtain more economies or sales impact than they could achieve alone.

Franchise
A contractual association between a manufacturer, wholesaler or service organisation (a franchiser) and independent businesspeople (franchisees) who buy the right to own and operate one or more units in the franchise system.

Retailer cooperatives
Contractual vertical marketing systems in which retailers organise a new, jointly owned business to carry on wholesaling and possibly production.

♦ The franchiser gets very highly motivated management as the franchisees are working for themselves rather than a salary.

♦ The contractual relationship ensures that franchisees operate to and maintain franchisers' standards.

The main advantages for franchisees are as follows:

♦ They are buying into a proven system if selling an established brand name (e.g. McDonald's, Shell, The Body Shop, Interflora).

♦ They can start a business with limited capital and benefit from the experience of the franchiser. This way they reduce the costs and risks of starting a new business.

♦ Franchisees also get the benefits of centralised purchasing power – since the franchisers will buy in bulk for the franchisees.

♦ They get instant expertise in operational issues such as advertising, promotions, accounts and legal matters, and can rely on franchisers' help should things go wrong.

Franchise systems have several disadvantages:

♦ Franchisers invariably have to forfeit some control when operating through franchisees.

♦ The franchisees may not all perform exactly to franchisers' operating standards, and inconsistencies in service levels can tarnish the brand name.

♦ Franchisees may not always have a good deal, in that they have to work extremely hard to meet sales and financial targets to make the business pay, and although they have already paid their initial fee, they have to meet continuing management services or royalty payments.

There are three forms of franchise. The first form is the *manufacturer-sponsored retailer franchise system*, as found in the car industry. BMW, for example, licenses dealers to sell its cars; the dealers are independent businesspeople who agree to meet various conditions of sales and service. Shell, the oil company, adopts a franchising system on many of its forecourts in the United Kingdom. French designer garden furniture company, Jardin en Plus, has relied greatly on franchising to expand into other European markets. The second type of franchise is the *manufacturer-sponsored wholesaler franchise system*, as found in the soft-drinks industry. Coca-Cola, for example, licenses bottlers (wholesalers) in various markets, which buy Coca-Cola syrup concentrate and then carbonate, bottle and sell the finished product to retailers in local markets. The third franchise form is the *service-firm-sponsored retailer franchise system*, in which a service firm licenses a system of retailers to bring its service to consumers. Examples are found in: the car rental business (Hertz, Avis, Europcar); the fast-food service business (McDonald's, Burger King); and the hotel business (Holiday Inn, Ramada Inn, Balladins).

The fact that most consumers cannot tell the difference between contractual and corporate VMSs shows how successfully the contractual organisations compete with corporate chains.

Administered VMS
A vertical marketing system that coordinates successive stages of production and distribution, not through common ownership or contractual ties, but through the size and power of one of the parties.

Administered VMS An **administered VMS** coordinates successive stages of production and distribution, not through common ownership or contractual ties, but through the size and power of one of the parties. Manufacturers of a top brand can obtain strong trade cooperation and support from resellers. For example, in the fast-moving consumer-goods market, companies like Nestlé, Unilever and Procter & Gamble can command unusual cooperation from resellers regarding displays, shelf space, promotions and price policies. In the consumer electronics sector, Sony can obtain a great deal of trade support from retail stores for its top-selling brands. Similarly, large retailers like IKEA can exert strong influence on the manufacturers that supply the products they sell. Consider IKEA.

> In just over four decades, IKEA, the privately owned Swedish furniture and home furnishings retailer, grew from a single store in Sweden's backwoods to become one of the most successful international retailers in the world. It now has 158 stores in 29 countries around the world, taking over 7.7 billion euros a year in sales. Its success formula was based on reinventing the furniture-retailing business. Traditionally, selling furniture was a fragmented affair, shared between department stores and small family-owned shops. All sold expensive products and delivered up to two or three months after a customer's order. IKEA, however, sells most of its furniture as knocked-down kits for customers to take home and assemble themselves. IKEA also trims costs to a minimum while still offering products that are durable and distinguished by design and quality. It does this by using global sourcing, working with key suppliers around the world that can supply high quality raw materials at low prices. In return these suppliers get technical advice and leased equipment from the company. IKEA's designers also work closely with manufacturers to find smart ways to reduce product costs from the outset. Other savings come from the huge economies of scale from operating in cheap out-of-town stores and from enormous production runs made possible by selling the same furniture all around the world. IKEA's success also means success for its suppliers. But they must operate to IKEA's terms and enable the global firm to fulfil its promise of quality merchandise at low cost to customers worldwide.[5]

■ Horizontal marketing systems

Another channel development is the **horizontal marketing system**, in which two or more companies at one level join together to follow a new marketing opportunity. By combining their capital, production capabilities or marketing resources, companies can accomplish more than any one company working alone. Companies might join forces with competitors or non-competitors.[6] They might work with each other on a temporary or permanent basis, or they may even create a separate company. Such channel arrangements also work well globally.

Horizontal marketing systems
A channel arrangement in which two or more companies at one level join together to follow a new marketing opportunity.

> For example, Nestlé and Coca-Cola formed a joint venture to market ready-to-drink coffee and tea worldwide. Coke provided worldwide experience in marketing and distributing beverages, and Nestlé contributed two established brand names – Nescafé and Nestea. Similarly, Coca-Cola and Procter & Gamble have created distribution systems linking Coca-Cola soft drinks and Pringles potato crisps in global markets.[7]

■ Hybrid marketing systems

In the past, many companies used a single channel to sell to a single market or market segment. Today, with the proliferation of customer segments and channel possibilities, more and more companies have adopted *multichannel distribution systems* – often called **hybrid marketing channels**. Such multichannel marketing occurs when a single firm sets up two or more marketing channels to reach one or more customer segments.

Figure 21.5 shows a hybrid channel system. In the figure, the producer sells directly to consumer segment 1 using direct-mail catalogues and telemarketing, and

Hybrid marketing channels
Multichannel distribution, as when a single firm sets up two or more marketing channels to reach one or more customer segments. A variety of direct and indirect approaches are used to deliver the firm's goods to its customers.

Figure 21.5

Hybrid marketing
channel

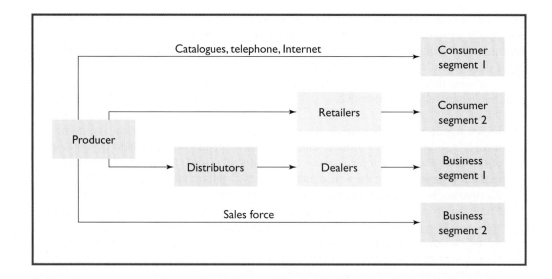

reaches consumer segment 2 through retailers. It sells indirectly to business segment 1 through distributors and dealers, and to business segment 2 through its own sales force.

Sony maintains a wide distribution coverage by adopting a hybrid marketing system. For example, Sony sells its consumer products through exclusive retail outlets such as the Sony Centres, through mass merchandisers like electrical chain stores (e.g. Comet, Dixons) and catalogue shops (e.g. Index, Argos) and by using direct marketing channels, such as mail-order catalogues operated by direct marketers.

Hybrid channels offer many advantages to companies facing large and complex markets. With each new channel, the company expands its sales and market coverage, and gains opportunities to tailor its products and services to the specific needs of diverse customer segments. But such hybrid channel systems are harder to control, and they generate conflict as more channels compete for customers and sales. For example, when IBM began selling personal computers directly to customers at low prices through catalogues and telemarketing and its own website, many of its dealers cried 'unfair competition' and threatened to drop the IBM line or give it less emphasis. Many outside salespeople felt they were being undercut by the new 'inside channels'.

■ Changing channel organisation

Changes in technology and the explosive growth of direct and online marketing are having a profound impact on the nature and design of marketing channels. One major trend is toward **disintermediation** – a big term with a clear message and important consequences. Disintermediation means that more and more, product and service producers are bypassing intermediaries and going directly to final buyers, or that radically new types of channel intermediaries are emerging to displace traditional ones.

Thus, in many industries, traditional intermediaries are dropping by the wayside. For example, companies like Dell Computer sell directly to final buyers, eliminating retailers from their marketing channels. E-commerce merchants are growing rapidly in number and size, displacing traditional bricks-and-mortar retailers. Today, consumers can buy flowers, books, videos, CDs, toys, household products, groceries, clothes, consumer electronics and many other goods and services without ever visiting a store.

Disintermediation presents problems and opportunities for both producers and intermediaries. To avoid being swept aside, traditional intermediaries must find new ways to add value in the supply chain. To remain competitive, product and service producers must develop new channel opportunities, such as Internet and other direct

Disintermediation

The elimination of a layer of intermediaries from a marketing channel or the displacement of traditional resellers by radically new types of intermediaries.

channels. However, developing these new channels often brings them into direct competition with their established channels, resulting in conflict. To ease this problem, companies often look for ways to make going direct a plus for both the company and its channel partners.

Going direct is rarely an all-or-nothing proposition. For example, to trim costs and add business, Hewlett-Packard opened three direct-sales websites: Shopping Village (for consumers), HP Commerce Centre (for businesses buying from authorised resellers) and Electronic Solutions Now (for existing contract customers). However, to avoid conflicts with its established reseller channels, HP forwards all its Web orders to resellers, who complete the orders, ship the products and get the commissions. In this way, HP gains the advantages of direct selling but also boosts business for resellers.

However, although this compromise system reduces conflicts, it also creates inefficiencies. HP is spending a fair chunk of change to set this up, plus the business partner still wants '8 per cent margins for getting the product to the customer'. To be really efficient in the long run, HP eventually will have to find ways for its resellers to add value or drop them from the direct channel.[8]

channel design decisions

We now look at several channel decisions facing manufacturers. In designing marketing channels, manufacturers struggle between what is ideal and what is practical. A new firm usually starts by selling in a limited market area. Deciding on the *best* channels might not be a problem: the problem might simply be how to convince one or a few good intermediaries to handle the line.

If the new firm is successful, it might branch out to new markets. Again, the manufacturer will tend to work through the existing intermediaries, although this strategy might mean using hybrid marketing channels. In smaller markets, the firm might sell directly to retailers; in larger markets, it might sell through distributors. In one part of the country, it might grant exclusive franchises because that is the way merchants normally work; in another, it might sell through all outlets willing to handle the merchandise. In one country it might use international sales agents; in another, it might partner a local firm.

Thus channel systems often evolve to meet market opportunities and conditions. However, for maximum effectiveness, channel analysis and decision making should be more purposeful. Designing a channel system calls for:

+ Analysing customer service needs.
+ Defining the channel objectives and constraints.
+ Identifying the major channel alternatives.
+ Evaluating those alternatives.

analysing customer service needs

Like most marketing decisions, designing a channel begins with the customer. Marketing channels are viewed as *customer value delivery systems* in which each channel member adds value for the customer. Thus designing the distribution channel starts with finding out what consumers want from the channel. Do customers want to buy from nearby locations or are they willing to travel to more centralised locations? Would they rather buy in person or over the phone, through the mail or via the Internet?

Do they value immediate delivery or are they willing to wait? Do they want breadth of assortment or do they prefer specialisation? Do customers want many add-on services (delivery, credit, repairs, installation) or will they obtain these elsewhere? The more decentralised the channel, the faster the delivery and the greater the assortment provided. Additionally, the more add-on services supplied, the greater the channel's service level. Generally, customer service is determined by the interaction of all these factors that affect the process of making the product or service available to the customer.

However, providing the fastest delivery, the greatest assortment and the most comprehensive services may not be possible or practical. The company and its channel members may not have the resources or skills needed to provide all the desired services. Also, providing higher levels of service results not only in higher costs for the channel, but also in higher prices for consumers. The company must balance consumer service needs against the feasibility and costs of meeting these needs as well as customer price preferences. Generally, customers tend to make trade-offs between service quality and other purchase dimensions, such as price. For example, consumers who shop at off-price and discount retail outlets, such as Aldi, Lidl, Kwik Save or Makro, are often willing to accept lower service levels if this means lower prices.

setting channel objectives and constraints

Channel objectives should be stated in terms of the desired service level of target customers. The company should identify if there are segments wanting different levels of channel service, decide which ones to serve and the best channels to use in each case. The company should aim to minimise the total channel cost of supplying customers in target segments, while also meeting their service requirements.

The company's channel objectives are also influenced by the nature of its products, company policies, marketing intermediaries, competitors and the environment. For example, companies selling perishable products require more direct marketing to avoid delays and too much handling. The company's size and financial situation determine which marketing functions it can handle itself and which it must give to intermediaries. In some cases, a company may want to compete in or near outlets that carry competitors' products. Thus companies may want their brands to be displayed next to competing brands: in town or city centres, Burger King wants to locate near McDonald's; Sony, Panasonic and Philips audio-video systems all compete for floor space in similar retail outlets; Nestlé and Mars confectionery brands want to be positioned side by side, and aggressively compete for shelf space, in the same grocery outlets. In other cases, producers may avoid the channels used by competitors. Avon, for example, decided not to compete with other cosmetics makers for scarce positions in retail stores and, instead, set up a profitable door-to-door selling operation in the home and overseas markets. Finally, *environmental factors*, such as economic conditions and legal constraints, affect channel design decisions. For example, in a depressed economy, producers want to distribute their goods in the most economical way, using shorter channels and dropping unneeded services that add to the final price of the goods. Legal regulations prevent channel arrangements that may lessen competition substantially or create a monopoly.

identifying major alternatives

When the company has defined its channel objectives, it should next identify its major channel alternatives in terms of the *types* and *number* of intermediaries to use and the *responsibilities* of each channel member.

■ Types of channel alternatives

A number of options exist:

+ *Direct marketing*. A number of **direct marketing** approaches can be used, ranging from direct-response selling via advertisements in print media, on radio or television, by mail order and catalogues to telephone and Internet selling. These methods are discussed further in Chapter 22.

+ *Sales force*. The company can sell directly through its own sales force or deploy another firm's sales force. Alternatively, a contract sales force might be used. The use of a company sales force to sell to customers is discussed in Chapter 20.

+ *Intermediaries*. **Intermediaries** are independent organisations that will carry out a number of activities. They include *wholesalers* and *retailers* who buy, take title to and resell the firm's goods. We will first address the nature of wholesalers.

Wholesalers   **Wholesalers** engage in wholesaling activity – selling goods and services to those buying for resale or business use. A producer uses wholesalers because they are often better at performing one or more channel functions. Wholesalers sales forces help to reach many small customers at a low cost. The wholesaler has many contacts and is often more trusted by the buyer than the distant manufacturer. Wholesalers can select items and build assortments needed by their customers, thereby saving the consumers a considerable amount of work. They save their customers money by buying in huge lots and breaking bulk (breaking large lots into small quantities). Wholesalers hold inventories, thereby reducing the inventory costs and risks of suppliers and customers. Wholesalers can provide quicker delivery to buyers because they are closer than the producers. They finance their customers by giving credit, and they finance their suppliers by ordering early and paying bills on time. Wholesalers absorb risk by taking title and bearing the cost of theft, damage, spoilage and obsolescence. They give information to suppliers and customers about competitors, new products and price developments. Wholesalers also provide management services and advice – they often help retailers train their sales assistants, improve store layouts and displays, and set up accounting and inventory control systems.

There are many types of wholesaler (see Table 21.1). They fall into three major groups: *merchant wholesalers*, *brokers and agents* and *manufacturers' sales branches and offices*. **Merchant wholesalers** include two broad types: full-service wholesalers and limited-service wholesalers. *Full-service wholesalers* provide a full set of services, whereas *limited-service wholesalers* offer fewer services to their suppliers and customers. The several different types of limited-service wholesalers perform varied specialised functions in the distribution channel.

Brokers and **agents** differ from merchant wholesalers. First, they do not take title to goods, and perform only a few functions. Like merchant wholesalers, they generally specialise by product line or customer type. A broker brings buyers and sellers together and assists in negotiation. Agents represent buyers or sellers on a permanent basis. Manufacturers' agents, also called manufacturers' representatives, are a common type of agent wholesaler. The third type of wholesaling is that done in manufacturers' sales branches and offices by sellers or buyers themselves rather than through independent wholesalers.

Although wholesalers play an important channel role, **retailers** are also critical intermediaries as they provide the final link between the consumer and provider. *Non-store retailing* has been growing much faster than has store retailing. Non-store retailing includes selling to final consumers through direct mail, catalogues, telephone, home TV shopping shows, home and office parties, door-to-door contact, vending

---

Direct marketing
Marketing through various advertising media that interact directly with consumers, generally calling for the consumer to make a direct response.

Intermediaries
Distribution channel firms that help the company find customers or make sales to them, including wholesalers and retailers that buy and resell goods.

Wholesaler
A firm engaged primarily in selling goods and services to those buying for resale or business use.

Merchant wholesaler
Independently owned business that takes title to the merchandise it handles.

Broker
A wholesaler who does not take title to goods and whose function is to bring buyers and sellers together and assist in negotiation.

Agent
A wholesaler who represents buyers or sellers on a relatively permanent basis, performs only a few functions, and does not take title to goods.

Retailers
Businesses whose sales come primarily from retailing.

TYPE	DESCRIPTION
Merchant wholesalers	Independently owned businesses that take title to the merchandise they handle. In different trades they are called *jobbers*, *distributors* or *mill supply houses*. Include full-service wholesalers and limited-service wholesalers.
Full-service wholesalers	Provide a full line of services: carrying stock, maintaining a sales force, offering credit, making deliveries and providing management assistance. There are two types:
Wholesale merchants	Sell primarily to retailers and provide a full range of services. *General-merchandise wholesalers* carry several merchandise lines, whereas *general-line wholesalers* carry one or two lines in greater depth. *Speciality wholesalers* specialise in carrying only part of a line. Examples: health food wholesalers, seafood wholesalers.
Industrial distributors	Sell to manufacturers rather than to retailers. Provide several services, such as carrying stock, offering credit, and providing delivery. May carry a broad range of merchandise, a general line or a speciality line.
Limited-service wholesalers	Offer fewer services than full-service wholesalers. Limited-service wholesalers are of several types:
Cash-and-carry wholesalers	Carry a limited line of fast-moving goods and sell to small retailers for cash. Normally do not deliver. Example: A small fish store retailer may drive to a cash-and-carry fish wholesaler, buy fish for cash and bring the merchandise back to the store.
Truck wholesalers (or truck jobbers)	Perform primarily a selling and delivery function. Carry a limited line of semi-perishable merchandise (such as milk, bread, snack foods), which they sell for cash as they make their rounds to supermarkets, small groceries, hospitals, restaurants, factory cafeterias and hotels.
Drop shippers	Do not carry inventory or handle the product. On receiving an order, they select a manufacturer, who ships the merchandise directly to the customer. The drop shipper assumes title and risk from the time the order is accepted to its delivery to the customer. They operate in bulk industries, such as coal, lumber and heavy equipment.
Rack jobbers	Serve grocery and drug retailers, mostly in non-food items. They send delivery trucks to stores, where the delivery people set up toys, paperbacks, hardware items, health and beauty aids, or other items. They price the goods, keep them fresh, set up point-of-purchase displays and keep inventory records. Rack jobbers retain title to the goods and bill the retailers only for the goods sold to consumers.
Producers' cooperatives	Owned by farmer members and assemble farm produce to sell in local markets. The co-op's profits are distributed to members at the end of the year. They often attempt to improve product quality and promote a co-op brand name.
Mail-order wholesalers	Send catalogues to retail, industrial and institutional customers. Maintain no outside sales force. Orders are filled and sent by mail, truck or other transportation.
Brokers and agents	Do not take title to goods. Main function is to facilitate buying and selling, for which they earn a commission on the selling price. Generally, specialise by product line or customer types.
Brokers	Chief function is bringing buyers and sellers together and assisting in negotiation. They are paid by the party who hired them, and do not carry inventory, get involved in financing or assume risk. Examples: food brokers, real estate brokers, insurance brokers and security brokers.
Agents	Represent either buyers or sellers on a more permanent basis than brokers do. There are several types:
Manufacturers' agents	Represent two or more manufacturers of complementary lines. A formal written agreement with each manufacturer covers pricing, territories, order handling, delivery service and warranties, and commission rates. Often used in such lines as clothing, furniture and electrical goods. Most manufacturers' agents are small businesses, with only a few skilled salespeople as employees. They are hired by small manufacturers who cannot afford their own field sales forces, and by large manufacturers who use agents to open new territories or to cover territories that cannot support full-time salespeople.
Selling agents	Have contractual authority to sell a manufacturer's entire output. The manufacturer either is not interested in the selling function or feels unqualified. The selling agent serves as a sales department and has significant influence over prices, terms and conditions of sale.
Purchasing agents	Generally have a long-term relationship with buyers and make purchases for them, often receiving, inspecting, warehousing and shipping the merchandise to the buyers. They provide helpful market information to clients and help them obtain the best goods and prices available.

TYPE	DESCRIPTION
Commission merchants	Take physical possession of products and negotiate sales. Normally, they are not employed on a long-term basis. Used most often in agricultural marketing by farmers who do not want to sell their own output and do not belong to producers' cooperatives. The commission merchant takes a truckload of commodities to a central market, sells it for the best price, deducts a commission and expenses and remits the balance to the producer.
Manufacturers' and retailers' branches and offices	Wholesaling operations conducted by sellers or buyers themselves rather than through independent wholesalers. Separate branches and offices can be dedicated to either sales or purchasing.
Sales branches and offices	Set up by manufacturers to improve inventory control, selling and promotion. Sales branches carry inventory. Sales offices do not carry inventory.
Purchasing offices	Perform a role similar to that of brokers or agents but are part of the buyer's organisation. Many retailers set up purchasing offices in major market centres.

Table 21.1

Major types of wholesalers

machines, online services and the Internet, and other direct retailing approaches. We discuss such direct-marketing approaches in detail in Chapter 22. In this chapter, we focus on store retailing.

Retail stores come in all shapes and sizes, and new retail types keep emerging. Generally, they can be distinguished by the amount of service they offer, the breadth and depth of their product lines, the relative prices charged and how they are organised.

■ Amount of service

Different products require *different amounts of service* and *customer service preferences* vary. **Self-service retailers** cater for customers who are willing to perform their own 'locate–compare–select' process to save money. Self-service is the basis of all discount operations and is typically used by sellers of convenience goods (e.g. supermarkets) and nationally branded, fast-moving shopping goods (e.g. discount stores). **Limited-service retailers**, such as department stores, provide more sales assistance because they carry more shopping goods about which customers need information. Their increased operating costs result in higher prices. **Full-service retailers**, such as speciality stores and up-market department stores, assist customers in every phase of the shopping process. They usually carry more speciality goods and slower-moving items, such as cameras, jewellery and fashions, for which customers like to be 'waited on'. They provide more services, resulting in much higher operating costs, which are invariably passed along to customers as higher prices.

■ Product line

Retailers vary in the *length and breadth of their product assortments*. A **speciality store** carries a narrow product line with a deep assortment within that line. Examples are stores selling fashion wear, outdoor leisure garments, furniture, books, cosmetics, jewellery, electronics, flowers or toys (e.g. Hennes & Mauritz, Naf-Naf, The Body Shop, Gap, Benetton, Foyles, Interflora). Today, speciality stores are flourishing for several reasons. The increasing use of market segmentation, market targeting and product specialisation has resulted in a greater need for specialist stores that focus on specific products and segments.

Self-service retailers
Retailers that provide few or no services to shoppers; shoppers perform their own locate–compare–select process.

Limited-service retailers
Retailers that provide only a limited number of services to shoppers.

Full-service retailers
Retailers that provide a full range of services to shoppers.

Speciality store
A retail store that carries a narrow product line with a deep assortment within that line.

Department store
A retail organisation that carries a wide variety of product lines – typically clothing, home furnishings and household goods; each line is operated as a separate department managed by specialist buyers or merchandisers.

Convenience store
A small store located near a residential area that is open long hours seven days a week and carries a limited line of high-turnover convenience goods.

Supermarkets
Large, low-cost, low-margin, high-volume, self-service stores that carry a wide variety of food, laundry and household products.

Superstore
A store almost twice the size of a regular supermarket that carries a large assortment of routinely purchased food and non-food items and offers such services as dry cleaning, post offices, film developing, photo finishing, cheque cashing, petrol forecourts and self-service car-washing facilities.

Category killers
A modern 'breed' of exceptionally aggressive 'off-price' retailers that offer branded merchandise in clearly defined product categories at heavily discounted prices.

Hypermarkets
Huge stores that combine supermarket, discount and warehouse retailing; in addition to food, they carry furniture, appliances, clothing and many other products.

A **department store** carries a wide variety of product lines. Examples of well-known department stores are Harrods and Harvey Nichols (in the United Kingdom), Sogo, Takashimaya and Isetan (in Japan and south-east Asia), Saks Fifth Avenue and Bloomingdale (in the United States), El Corte Inglés (in Spain), Galeries Lafayette (in France) and Karstadt (in Germany). In recent years, department stores have been squeezed between more focused and flexible speciality stores on the one hand, and more efficient, low-priced discounters on the other. In response, many have added 'bargain basements' and promotional events to meet the discount threat. Others have set up store brand programmes, 'boutiques' and 'designer shops' (such as Polo, Dolce and Gabana, Salvatore Ferragamo or DKNY shops within department stores) and other store formats that compete with speciality shops. Still others are trying mail-order, telephone or website selling. Service, invariably, remains the key differentiating factor.

Convenience stores are small stores that carry a limited line of high-turnover convenience goods. Examples are Happy Shopper, Spar, Mace and VG stores. These are located near residential areas and remain open for long hours. In countries where retail laws are more relaxed and there is less restriction in store opening hours, convenience stores may be opened for seven days a week. They satisfy an important consumer need in a niche segment – shoppers in this segment use convenience stores for emergency or 'fill-in' purchases outside normal hours or when time is short, and they are willing to pay for the convenience of location and opening hours.

Supermarkets are the most frequently shopped type of retail store. Today, however, they are facing slow sales growth and an increase in competition from convenience stores, discount food stores and superstores. Thus, supermarkets have to make improvements to attract more customers. In the battle for 'share of stomachs', some of the larger supermarkets, for example, have moved up-market, providing in-store bakeries, gourmet deli counters and fresh seafood departments. Others are cutting costs, establishing more efficient operations and lowering prices in order to compete more effectively with food discounters.

Superstores are much larger than regular high street supermarkets and offer a large assortment of routinely purchased food products, non-food items and services, ranging from dry cleaning, post offices and film developing and photo finishing, to cheque cashing, petrol forecourts and self-service car-washing facilities. Superstores are located out of town, frequently in retail parks, with vast free car parks. In recent years, many are cutting costs, establishing more efficient and effective operations through rigid quality control, centralised distribution and electronic technologies, and lowering prices in order to compete more effectively with discount stores (see later section).

The 1990s saw explosive growth of superstores that are actually giant speciality stores, the so-called **category killers**. They feature stores the size of aircraft hangars that carry a very deep assortment of branded products belonging to a particular line, with a knowledgeable staff. Their predatory pricing strategy – pile them high, sell them cheaper than the competition – and ability to decimate much of the competition in their sector explains their name. Category killers have been prevalent in a wide range of categories, including books, toys, electronics, furniture, home improvement products, sporting goods and even pet supplies. However, in increasingly competitive and saturating markets, many, including the US Toys 'R' Us, have seen declining sales and profitability in their key European markets.

Another superstore variation, **hypermarkets**, are even bigger, perhaps as large as six football fields. They carry not just routinely purchased goods, but also sell furniture, appliances, clothing and many other things. Carrefour, the number one grocery retailer in France (and number two worldwide), opened the world's first 'hypermarché' at Ste-Geneviève-des-Bois, near Paris, in 1963. Since then, the concept quickly took off in France and the company now operates hundreds of these giant stores in Europe, South America and Asia. Other examples of hypermarkets include Real in Germany, Pyrca in Spain and Meijers in the Netherlands. Although hypermarkets have dominated

Cité Europe: New shopping concepts like this offer a new experience for shoppers.

SOURCE: (left) Prentice Hall Europe

in some countries, such as France, Italy, the Netherlands and the US, the concept has enjoyed mixed success in the UK. Those that have succeeded with hypermarkets in the UK – Sainsbury's Savacentres, Asda and Tesco Extra – have had to invest heavily in making the stores look nice and adding facilities such as crèches, cafés, clean toilets and carefully designed car parks.[9]

■ Relative prices

Retailers can also be classified according to the prices they charge. Most retailers charge regular prices and offer normal quality goods and customer service. Others offer higher quality goods and services at higher prices. The retail stores that feature low prices include discount stores, off-price retailers and catalogue showrooms.

A **discount store** sells standard merchandise at lower prices by accepting lower margins and selling higher volume. Examples include the German Aldi, Norma and Lidl, the Danish Netto, the French Carrefour and Matalan and Peacock in the UK. The early discount stores cut expenses by offering few services and operating in warehouse-like facilities in low-rent, heavily travelled districts. In recent years, facing intense competition from other discounters and department stores, many discount retailers have 'traded up'. They have improved décor, added new lines and services and opened suburban branches, which have led to higher costs and prices.

When the major discount stores traded up, a new wave of **off-price retailers** moved in to fill the low-price, high-volume gap. Ordinary discounters buy at regular wholesale prices and accept lower margins to keep prices down. In contrast, off-price retailers buy at less-than-regular wholesale prices and charge consumers less than retail. One type of off-price retailer is the factory outlet. **Factory outlets** sometimes group together in *factory outlet malls* and *value-retail centres*, where dozens of outlet stores offer prices 30–50 per cent below retail on a wide range of items. Whereas outlet malls consist primarily of manufacturers' outlets, value-retail centres combine manufacturers' outlets with off-price retail stores and department store clearance outlets. Factory outlet malls have recently taken off. A growing number of factory outlets now feature brands such as Donna Karan, Esprit, Calvin Klein, Reebok and Nike, causing department stores to protest to the manufacturers of these brands. Given their higher costs, the department stores have to charge more than the off-price outlets. Manufacturers counter that they send last year's merchandise and seconds to the factory outlet malls, not the

Discount store
A retail institution that sells standard merchandise at lower prices by accepting lower margins and selling at higher volume.

Off-price retailer
Retailer that buys at less-than-regular wholesale prices and sells at less than retail.

Factory outlet
Off-price retailing operation that is owned and operated by a manufacturer and that normally carries the manufacturer's surplus, discontinued or irregular goods.

new merchandise that they supply to the department stores. For example, Marks & Spencer offers a mix of slow-selling stock, ranges from the previous season and items specifically manufactured for factory outlet malls. The malls are also located far from urban areas, making travel to them more difficult. Still, the department stores are concerned about the growing number of shoppers willing to make weekend trips to stock up on branded merchandise at substantial savings.[10]

Warehouse club (wholesale club, membership warehouse)
Off-price retailer that sells a limited selection of brand-name grocery items, appliances, clothing and a hodgepodge of other goods at deep discounts to members who pay annual membership fees.

Another off-price retail format is the **warehouse club** (also known as *wholesale club* or *membership warehouse*), which operates in huge, draughty, warehouse-like facilities and offers few frills. Customers themselves must wrestle furniture, heavy appliances and other large items to the checkout line. Such clubs make no home deliveries. The policy is 'cash and carry' as they accept no credit cards, but they do offer rock-bottom prices. For example, Makro, owned by Germany's number one retailing group, Metro, operates vast warehouses across Europe, selling food, beverages, wines and spirits, confectionery, household goods, clothes and other assortments to members – consumers and trade (resellers/retailers) who pay a membership fee. Warehouse clubs saw tremendous growth over the 1980s, but growth has slowed considerably in the 1990s as a result of increasing competition among warehouse store chains and effective reactions by supermarkets and discount stores. In the UK, the warehouse club Costco has managed to expand its stores, but some, like Cargo Club, quickly fell by the wayside.

■ Retail organisations

Although many retail stores are independently owned, an increasing number are banding together under some form of corporate or contractual organisation. The major types of retail organisations include *corporate chains*, *voluntary chains* and *retailer cooperatives*, *franchise organisations*, and *merchandising conglomerates*.

Chain stores are two or more outlets that are commonly owned and controlled. They have many advantages over independents. Their size allows them to buy in large quantities at lower prices. They can afford to hire corporate-level specialists to deal with areas such as pricing, promotion, merchandising, inventory control and sales forecasting. Corporate chains gain promotional economies because their advertising costs are spread over many stores and over a large sales volume.

The great success of corporate chains caused many independents to band together in one of two forms of contractual associations. One is the *voluntary chain* – a wholesaler-sponsored group of independent retailers that engages in group-buying and common merchandising. The other form of contractual association is the *retailer cooperative* – a group of independent retailers that band together to set up a jointly owned, central wholesale operation and conduct joint merchandising and promotion efforts. These organisations give independents the buying and promotion economies they need to meet the prices of corporate chains. Another form of contractual retail organisation is a franchise. The main difference between franchise organisations and other contractual systems (voluntary chains and retail cooperatives) is that franchise systems are normally based on some unique product or service; on a method of doing business; or on the trade name, goodwill, or patent that the franchiser has developed. Franchising, which we discussed in an earlier section, has been prominent in fast foods, video stores, health or fitness centres, haircutting, auto rentals, motels, travel agencies, real estate, and dozens of other product and service areas.

Finally, *merchandising conglomerates* are corporations that combine several different retailing forms under central ownership. Examples include Arcadia, Dixons and the Kingfisher Group. Arcadia operates Principles (middle- to upmarket clothing for professional men and women), Dorothy Perkins (middle-market apparel for younger females), Top Shop (high fashion, mid-priced clothing for young, trendy segment), and Evans (larger-sized clothing or outsizes for the older female). The Kingfisher Group owns numerous speciality chains and variety chain stores, including B&Q (Do-it-yourself, DIY store), Comet (electrical and home appliances), Superdrug (discount toiletries), Charlie Brown's (auto spare parts and accessories), and Woolworth (general merchandise and variety store). Diversified retailing, which provides superior management systems and economies that benefit all the separate retail operations, is likely to increase in the new millennium.

We have discussed the types of channel members. Next we look at decisions concerning the number of channels to use.

■ Number of marketing intermediaries

Companies must also decide on *channel breadth*: that is, how extensive their market coverage should be and, therefore, the number of channel members to use at each level. Three strategies are available: intensive distribution, exclusive distribution and selective distribution.

Producers of convenience products and common raw materials typically seek **intensive distribution** – a strategy whereby they stock their products in as many outlets as possible. These goods must be available where and when consumers want them. For example, sweets, chewing gum, disposable razors, soft drinks, batteries, camera film and other similar items are sold in myriad outlets to provide maximum brand exposure and consumer convenience. Bic, Coca-Cola, Nestlé, Duracell, Fuji, Kodak and many consumer-goods companies distribute their products in this way.

By contrast, some producers purposely limit the number of intermediaries handling their products. The extreme form of this practice is **exclusive distribution**, in which the producer gives only a limited number of dealers the exclusive rights to distribute its products in their territories. Exclusive distribution is often found in the distribution of luxury cars (e.g. Rolls-Royce, Lexus) and prestige clothing for men and women (e.g. Giorgio Armani, Hugo Boss, Yves St Laurent, Christian Dior). By granting exclusive distribution, the manufacturers gain strong selling support from the outlet and more control over dealer prices, promotion, credit and services. Exclusive distribution also enhances brand image and allows for higher mark-ups.

Between intensive and exclusive distribution lies **selective distribution** – the use of more than one, but fewer than all of the intermediaries that are willing to carry a company's products. Most electronic products, furniture and small household appliance brands are distributed in this manner. For example, Philips-Whirlpool, Braun, Electrolux and Hoover sell their major appliances through dealer networks and selected large retailers. By using selective distribution, they do not have to spread their efforts over many outlets, including many marginal ones. They can develop good working relationships with selected channel members and expect a better-than-average selling effort. Selective distribution gives producers good market coverage with more control and less cost than does intensive distribution.

Intensive distribution
Stocking the product in as many outlets as possible.

Exclusive distribution
Giving a limited number of dealers the exclusive right to distribute the company's products in their territories.

Selective distribution
The use of more than one, but less than all of the intermediaries that are willing to carry the company's products.

■ Responsibilities of channel members

The producer and its intermediaries need to agree on the terms and responsibilities of each channel member. The producer should establish a list price and a fair set of discounts for intermediaries. It must define each channel member's territory, and it should be careful about where it places new resellers. Mutual services and duties need to be spelled out carefully, especially in franchise and exclusive distribution channels. For example, McDonald's provides franchisees around the world with promotional support, a record-keeping system, training and general management assistance. In turn, franchisees must meet company standards for physical facilities, cooperate with new promotion programmes, provide requested information, and buy specified food products.

evaluating the main alternatives

Suppose a company has identified several channel alternatives and wants to select the one that will best satisfy its long-run objectives. The firm must evaluate each alternative against *economic*, *control* and *adaptive* criteria.

Using economic criteria, the company compares the likely profitability of different channel alternatives. It estimates the sales that each channel would produce and the costs of selling different volumes through each channel. The company must also consider control issues. Using intermediaries usually means giving them some control over the marketing of the product, and some intermediaries take more control than others. Other things being equal, the company prefers to keep as much control as possible. Finally, the company must apply adaptive criteria. Channels often involve long-term commitments to other firms and loss of flexibility, making it hard to adapt the channel to a changing marketing environment. The producer wants to keep the channel as flexible as possible. To be considered, a channel involving long-term commitment should be greatly superior on economic or control grounds.

channel management decisions

Channel management calls for selecting and motivating individual channel members and evaluating their performance over time.

selecting channel members

Producers vary in their ability to attract qualified marketing intermediaries. Some producers have no trouble signing up channel members. For example, Toyota had no trouble attracting new dealers for its Lexus line. In fact, it had to turn down many would-be resellers. In some cases, the promise of exclusive or selective distribution for a desirable product will draw plenty of applicants.

At the other extreme are producers that have to work hard to line up enough qualified intermediaries. When Reckitt & Colman first launched its new 'green' detergent brand, Down to Earth, in the UK market, access was restricted to one supermarket chain – Tesco. The Belgian firm Ecover managed to acquire sole rights for distribution in Asda stores, and in Sainsbury's, Safeway and the Co-op when it launched its radical 'green' detergents at the height of green consumerism in the United Kingdom. A rival green brand, Ark, secured distribution in specialist retail outlets, but with sales declining over the 1990s, it is no longer able to secure distribution at any of the major grocery outlets. Similarly, many small food and grocery producers that own marginal brands often have difficulty getting retailers to carry their products.

When selecting intermediaries, the company should determine what characteristics distinguish the better ones. It will want to evaluate the channel members' years in business, other lines carried, growth and profit record, level of cooperation and reputation. If the intermediaries are sales agents, the company will want to evaluate the number and character of other lines carried and the size and quality of the sales force. If the intermediary is a retail store that wants exclusive or selective distribution, the company will want to evaluate the store's customers, location and future growth potential.

motivating channel members

Channel members must be continuously motivated to do their best. The company must sell not only *through* the intermediaries, but *to* them. Most producers see their intermediaries as first-line customers. Some use the 'carrot-and-stick' approach. At times, they offer *positive* motivators such as higher margins, special deals, premiums, cooperative advertising allowances, display allowances and sales contests. At other times they use *negative* motivators, such as threatening to reduce margins, to slow down delivery or to end the relationship altogether. A producer using this approach has usually failed to do a good job of studying the needs, problems, strengths and weaknesses of its channel members.

More advanced companies try to forge long-term partnerships with their intermediaries to create a marketing system that meets the needs of both the manufacturer and the intermediary. Thus, manufacturers such as Unilever and P&G work together with grocery retailers to create superior value for final consumers. They jointly plan merchandising goals and strategies, inventory levels and advertising and promotion plans. Similarly, construction equipment manufacturer JCB and automobile producers such as Ford and Toyota have to work closely with their dealers to help them be successful in selling the company's products. In managing its channels, a company must convince distributors and retailers that they can make their money by being part of an advanced vertical marketing system.[11]

evaluating and controlling channel members

The producer must regularly monitor the channel's performance against agreed targets such as sales quotas, average inventory levels, customer delivery time, treatment of damaged and lost goods, cooperation in company promotion and training programmes, and services to the customer. The company should recognise and reward intermediaries that are performing well. Those which are underperforming should be helped, remedial actions should be taken or, as a last resort, the intermediary should be replaced. The firm must periodically 'requalify' its intermediaries and prune the weak performers, allowing only the best ones to carry its products.

Finally, manufacturers need to be sensitive to their dealers. Those who treat their dealers lightly risk not only losing their support, but also causing legal problems. Disputes with dealers are counterproductive. The key to profitable channel management lies in creating win–win outcomes for all in the channel system – a symbiotic relationship that yields cooperation, not conflict, among channel participants will invariably result in higher channel performance.

physical distribution and logistics management

In today's global marketplace, selling a product is sometimes easier than physically getting it to customers. Companies must decide on the best way to store, handle and move their products and services, so that they are available to customers in the right assortments, at the right time and in the right place. Logistics effectiveness will have a significant impact on both customer satisfaction and company costs. A poor distribution system can destroy an otherwise good marketing effort. Here we consider the nature and importance of *marketing logistics*, goals of the *logistics system*, *major logistics functions*, *choosing transportation modes* and the importance of *integrated logistics management*.

nature and importance of physical distribution and marketing logistics

Physical distribution (marketing logistics)
The tasks involved in planning, implementing and controlling the physical flow of materials and final goods from points of origin to points of use to meet the needs of customers at a profit.

To some managers, physical distribution means only trucks and warehouses. But modern logistics is much more than this. **Physical distribution** or **marketing logistics** involves planning, implementing and controlling the physical flow of materials, final goods and related information from points of origin to points of consumption to meet customer requirements at a profit. In short, it involves getting the right product to the right customer in the right place at the right time.

Traditional physical distribution has typically started with products at the plant and tried to find low-cost solutions to get them to customers. However, *marketing logistics* thinking starts with the marketplace and works backwards to the factory. Logistics addresses the problem of outbound distribution (moving products from the factory to customers) and that of inbound distribution (moving products and materials from suppliers to the factory). It involves the management of entire *supply chains*, value-added flows from suppliers to final users, as shown in Figure 21.6. Thus the logistics manager's task is to coordinate the whole channel physical dis-tribution system – the activities of suppliers, purchasing agents, marketers, channel members and customers. These activities include forecasting, purchasing, production planning, order processing, inventory management, warehousing and transportation planning.

Companies today are placing greater emphasis on logistics for several reasons:

✦ Customer service and satisfaction have become the cornerstones of marketing strategy in many businesses, and distribution is an important customer service element. Companies are finding that they can win and keep more customers by giving faster delivery, better service or lower prices through more effective logistics.

✦ Logistics is a major cost element for most companies. About 15 per cent of an average product's price is accounted for by shipping and transport alone. Poor logistics decisions result in higher costs whereas improvements in efficiency can yield tremendous cost savings for both the company and its customers.

✦ The explosion in product variety has created a need for improved logistics management. For example, in the early part of the twentieth century, the typical grocery store carried only 200–300 items. The store manager could keep track of this inventory on about ten pages of notebook paper stuffed in a shirt pocket. Today, the average store carries a bewildering stock of ten to twenty thousand items. Ordering, shipping, stocking and controlling such a variety of products presents a sizeable logistics challenge.

✦ Finally, improvements in information technology have created opportunities for positive gains in distribution efficiency. The increased use of computers, electronic point-of-sale scanners, uniform product codes, satellite tracking, electronic data interchange (EDI) and electronic funds transfer (EFT) has allowed companies to create advanced systems for order processing, inventory control and handling, and transportation routing and scheduling.

Figure 21.6

Marketing logistics: managing supply chains

Suppliers

Manufacturers

Wholesalers

Retailers

Customers

Value-added flows of materials, final goods and related information through coordination of forecasting, information systems, purchasing, production planning, order processing, inventory, warehousing and transportation

goals of the logistics system

The starting point for designing a marketing logistics system is to study the service needs of customers. Unfortunately, few companies can achieve the logistic objective of *both* maximising customer service *and* minimising distribution costs. Maximum customer service implies rapid delivery, large inventories, flexible assortments, liberal returns policies and a host of other services – all of which raise distribution costs. In contrast, minimum distribution cost implies slower delivery, small inventories and larger shipping lots – which represent a lower level of overall customer service.

The goal of the marketing logistics system should be to provide *a targeted level of customer service at the least cost*. The company must first research the importance of various distribution services that customers require and then set desired service levels for each segment. The company will want to offer at least the same level of service as its competitors do. The ultimate objective is to maximise *profits*, not sales. Therefore, the company must weigh the benefits of providing higher levels of service against the costs. Some companies offer less service than their competitors and charge a lower price. Other companies offer more service and charge higher prices to cover higher costs.

major logistics functions

Given a set of logistics objectives, the company is ready to design a logistics system that will minimise the cost of attaining these objectives. The major logistics functions are order processing, warehousing, inventory management and transportation.

■ Order processing

Orders can be submitted in many ways – by mail or telephone, through salespeople, or via computer and electronic data interchange (EDI). Once received, orders must be processed quickly and accurately. Both the company and its customers benefit when the order-processing steps are carried out efficiently. Most companies now use computerised order-processing systems to speed up the order–shipping–billing cycle. Moreover, today's computing systems enable firms to reduce distribution costs, while speeding up activities and increasing the level of service to customers.

■ Warehousing

Every company must store its goods while they wait to be sold. To ensure it can meet orders speedily, it must have stock available. A storage function is needed because production and consumption cycles rarely match. For example, a lawnmower manufacturer must produce all year long and store up its products for the heavy spring and summer buying season. The storage function overcomes differences in needed quantities and timing.

A company must decide on *how many* and *what types* of warehouses it needs, and *where* they will be located. The company might use storage warehouses, which store goods for moderate to long periods. Or, they may use **distribution centres**, which are designed to move goods rather than just store them. They are large and highly automated warehouses designed to receive goods from various plants and suppliers, take orders, fill them efficiently, and deliver goods to customers as quickly as possible. In these warehouses, only a few employees are needed. Computers read orders and direct fork-lift trucks, electric hoists or robots to gather goods, move them to loading docks and issue invoices. These warehouses have reduced worker injuries, labour costs, theft and breakage and have improved inventory control. In the European market, more and more producers of industrial and consumer goods are looking to incorporate pan-European distribution networks to provide consistently high standards of service and flexibility. For example, British Steel (now part of Corus), in the face of stiff competition in mainland European markets, set up regional distribution centres to be closer to customers, while also developing information-technology links between production plants, distribution operators and customers in an attempt to improve service efficiency.[12]

Distribution centre
A large, highly automated warehouse designed to receive goods from various plants and suppliers, take orders, fill them efficiently, and deliver goods to customers as quickly as possible.

■ Inventory

Inventory levels also affect customer satisfaction. The major problem is to maintain the delicate balance between carrying too much inventory and carrying too little. Carrying too much inventory results in higher-than-necessary inventory carrying costs and stock obsolescence. Carrying too little may result in stock-outs, costly emergency shipments or production, customer dissatisfaction or lost sales as unserved customers defect to a competitor. In making inventory decisions, management must balance the costs of carrying larger inventories against resulting sales and profits.

During the past decade, many companies have greatly reduced their inventories and related costs through *just-in-time* (JIT) logistics systems. Through such systems, producers and retailers carry only small inventories of parts or merchandise, often only enough for a few days of operations. New stock arrives at the factory or retail outlet exactly when needed, rather than being stored in inventory until being used. JIT

Robocom Systems International's RIMS warehouse management system is an essential part of today's warehouse - improving the flow of critical information and optimizing the use of all warehouse assets.

RIMS '01 Users' Conference

Click for **Robocom Careers**

Warehousing: Robocom Systems is a warehouse management software vendor and systems integrator, specialising in the design and implementation of automated warehouse systems with diverse commercial applications.

SOURCE: Robocom Systems, (http://www.robocom.com)

systems require accurate forecasting along with fast, frequent and flexible delivery, so that new supplies will be available when needed. However, these systems result in substantial savings in inventory carrying and handling costs.

■ Transportation

Transportation decisions have a critical impact on logistics costs. The choice of transportation carriers affects the pricing of products, delivery performance and condition of the goods when they arrive – all of which will ultimately affect customer satisfaction.

In shipping goods to its warehouses, dealers and customers, the company can choose among five transportation modes: road, rail, water, pipeline and air.

Road   Trucks are highly flexible in their routing and time schedules. They are efficient for short hauls of high-value merchandise. In the EU, the bulk of goods traded is moved by road vehicles. The Conference of European Transport Ministers (CEMT) reported that transport volumes in the EU have risen by more than 50 per cent in the last 20 years.[13] The gradual deregulation and removal of restrictive practices in the road transport market in the EU is expected to increase intra-EU haulage competition, with a downward pressure on rates. Also, there will be greater freedom for international hauliers to transport goods between destinations within one country, thereby raising the efficiency in use of trucks.

Rail   Railroads are one of the most cost-effective modes for shipping large amounts of bulk products – coal, sand, minerals, farm and forest products – over long distances. The EU's efforts to speed up the development of rail freight and combined road/rail transport services throughout Europe – including the opening up of networks in eastern Europe – are pushing rail transport much more firmly into the general distribution spotlight. However, collaboration and standardisation among Europe's railways is necessary to reinforce rail's presence on main cross-border routes. The revitalisation of rail freight is ongoing, backed by an optimism among authorities and politicians who agree that it is not a simple question of road versus rail – Europe must have both.[14]

Water   In countries favourably served by coastal and inland waterways, a large amount of goods can be moved by ships and barges. Although the cost of water transportation is very low for shipping bulky, low-value, non-perishable products such as sand, coal, grain, oil and metallic ores, water transportation is the slowest mode and is affected by the weather.

In the EU, waterways' share of freight transport volume is low compared to rail and roads. Its full potential, however, cannot be realised without harmonisation of European shipping and port policies and pricing systems, and the further removal of restrictive and unnecessary legislation.

Pipeline Pipelines are a specialised means of shipping raw commodities such as petroleum, natural gas and chemicals from sources to markets. Most pipelines are used by their owners to ship their own products.

Air Although the use of air carriers tends to be restricted to low-bulk goods, they are becoming more important as a transportation mode. Air-freight rates are much higher than rail or truck rates, but air freight is ideal when speed is needed or distant markets have to be reached. Among the most frequently air-freighted products are perishables (fresh fish, cut flowers) and high-value, low-bulk items (technical instruments, jewellery). Companies find that air freight also reduces inventory levels, packaging costs and the number of warehouses needed.

choosing transportation modes

In choosing a transportation mode for a product, shippers must balance many considerations: speed, dependability, availability, cost, capability and others. Thus, if a shipper needs speed, air and truck are the prime choices. If the goal is low cost, then water or pipeline might be best. In practice, firms may rely on a combination of transportation methods which would best enable them to meet logistics objectives cost-effectively.

designing international distribution channels

International marketers face many additional complexities in designing their channels. Each country has its own unique distribution system that has evolved over time and changes very slowly. For instance, in food and drinks retailing, contract distributors play a far more important role in the delivery of goods from producer to retailer in the United Kingdom than in other EU countries like Germany, France, Spain and Italy. Also, multiple retailer dominance of the grocery market is more pervasive in the United Kingdom than in the latter countries. Thus global marketers must usually adapt their channel strategies to the existing structures within each country.

There are other challenges. For example, international logistics have become a critical area for global businesses, whose inbound supply movements are shifting from domestic sources to global ones, and whose outbound supplies undergo an equally international trade flow. Sophisticated computer-based technologies, such as computer-integrated logistics (CIL), are used to enable international companies and logistics service providers to manage the supply chain and specific logistics functions. International logistics place even greater demands on good integration of logistics operations and systems between supplier/manufacturer and others involved in moving supplies or goods along the supply chain across national borders. In the European market, increasing competitive pressures and the continuing drive for greater efficiency have forced

The Japanese distribution system has remained remarkably traditional. A profusion of tiny retail shops are supplied by an even greater number of small wholesalers.

SOURCE: Stock Boston/ Charles Gupton

distribution service providers to focus more heavily on service quality improvement or risk losing out on invitations to bid for new business.

In some overseas markets, the distribution system is complex and hard to penetrate, consisting of many layers and large numbers of intermediaries. For example, in Japan, the distribution system encompasses a wide range of wholesalers, agents, brokers and retailers, differing more in number than in function from their European or American counterparts.[15]

Many western firms have had great difficulty breaking into the closely knit, tradition-bound Japanese distribution network. However, Japan's archaic 'Large Scale Retail Law', which controlled planning consent for new stores and opening hours in order to protect small retailers from new high-street competitors, has been deregulated. Retailing law reforms have enabled foreign retailers, such as Toys 'R' Us, to break the links between the manufacturers and the high-street stores. Boots, the UK retailer of health and beauty products, has also succeeded in setting up shop in this protected market.[16]

At the other extreme, distribution systems in developing countries may be scattered and inefficient, or altogether lacking. For example, although China and India each contain hundreds of millions of people, these markets are much smaller than the population numbers suggest. Their inadequate distribution systems mean that most companies can profitably access only the small portion of the population living in the most affluent cities.[17]

Thus international marketers face a wide range of channel alternatives. Designing efficient and effective channel systems between and within various country markets poses a difficult challenge.

channel trends

We have examined the major channel and logistics decisions facing managers. Finally, let us look at the major changes occurring in distribution channels.

integrated logistics management

Integrated logistics management
A physical distribution concept that recognises the need for a firm to integrate its logistics system with those of its suppliers and customers. The aim is to maximise the performance of the entire distribution system.

Today, companies are increasingly adopting the concept of **integrated logistics management**. This concept recognises that providing better customer service and trimming distribution costs require *teamwork*, both inside the company and among all the marketing channel organisations. Inside the company, the various functional departments must work closely together to maximise the company's own logistics performance. Outside, the company must integrate its logistics system with those of its suppliers and customers to maximise the performance of the entire distribution system.

■ Cross-functional teamwork inside the company

In most companies, responsibility for various logistics activities is assigned to many different functional units – marketing, sales, finance, manufacturing, purchasing. Too often, each function tries to optimise its own logistics performance without regard for the activities of the other functions. However, transportation, inventory, warehousing and order-processing activities interact, often in an inverse way. For example, lower inventory levels reduce inventory carrying costs. But they may also reduce customer service and increase costs from stock-outs, backorders, special production runs and costly fast-freight shipments. Because distribution activities involve strong trade-offs, decisions by different functions must be coordinated to achieve superior overall logistics performance.

Thus the goal of integrated logistics management is to harmonise all of the company's distribution decisions. Close working relationships among functions can be achieved in several ways. Some companies have created permanent logistics committees made up of managers responsible for different physical distribution activities and for setting policies for improving overall logistics performance.

Companies can also create management positions that link the logistics activities of functional areas. Many companies have created 'supply managers', who manage the full supply chain activities for each of the company's product categories. Some have a senior executive for logistics with cross-functional authority.[18] The important thing is that the company coordinates its logistics and marketing activities to create high market satisfaction at a reasonable cost.

■ Building channel partnerships

The members of a distribution channel are linked closely in delivering customer satisfaction and value. One company's distribution system is another company's supply system. The success of each channel member depends on the performance of the entire supply chain. For example, a big supermarket like Wal-Mart can charge the lowest prices at retail only if its entire supply chain – consisting of thousands of merchandise suppliers, transport companies, warehouses and service providers – operates at maximum efficiency.

Companies must do more than improve their own logistics. They must also work with other channel members to improve whole-channel distribution. Today, clever companies are coordinating their logistics strategies and building strong partnerships with suppliers and customers to improve customer service and reduce channel costs.[19]

These channel partnerships can take many forms. Many companies have created *cross-functional, cross-company teams*. Other companies partner through *shared projects*. For example, many larger retailers are working closely with suppliers on in-store programmes. Channel partnerships may also take the form of *information sharing* and *continuous inventory replenishment* systems. Companies manage their supply chains through information. Suppliers link up with customers through EDI systems to share information and coordinate their logistics decisions. Benetton, the Italian company, gained a competitive advantage in the past through its management of total supply or throughput time. It uses direct feedback from its franchised outlets to monitor sales trends, links this information into its computer-aided design and manufacturing system and, making use of its highly flexible manufacturing processes, quickly produces (even small quantities) to order.[20]

Today, more and more companies are also beginning to exploit information technology and the Internet to develop sophisticated electronic, business-to-business (B2B) marketplaces, where companies can build collaborative global trading networks. These B2B exchanges have initially focused on bringing together manufacturers and their suppliers for online sourcing, raw materials procurement, auctions and other services (see Marketing Highlight 21.2).

Today, as a result of partnerships, many companies have switched from *anticipatory-based distribution systems* to *response-based distribution systems*.[21] In anticipatory distribution, the company produces the amount of goods called for by a sales forecast, holding stocks at various supply points such as the plant, distribution centres and retail outlets, and reordering automatically when its order point is reached. A response-based distribution system, in contrast, is *customer-triggered*. The producer continuously builds and replaces stock as orders arrive. It produces what is currently selling.

> For example, in the global motor car industry, manufacturers are coming under increasing pressure to increase the speed of customer response, while also tailoring products to consumer needs, in order to strengthen customer loyalty. Toyota, Ford and GM are all trying out the concept of BTO (build-to-order) or OTD (order-to-delivery). BTO is a system pioneered by Dell. When a customer goes online or calls a freephone number to order his personal computer, Dell assembles the tailored product and ships it to the customer within days. A car is far more complex than a PC, but many car manufacturers believe that they can reduce order-to-delivery time to less than two weeks compared to the three or more months they currently have to wait. Essentially, a customer will pick her preferred package and, within seconds, the transaction reaches a central database which checks that the order meets an approved design; the car is then scheduled for assembly, based on the earliest date the parts can be shipped. The system should reduce not only the transaction cost, but also take costs out of the inventory process. The 'dream' is for customers to get all but the most unusual packages within a matter of days![22]

Some large appliance manufacturers, such as Philips-Whirlpool and clothing retailers such as Benetton, use a *quick-response system*. Benetton dyes its sweaters and garments in the 'in' colours that are currently selling, instead of trying to guess long in advance which colours people will want. Producing for order rather than for forecast substantially cuts down inventory costs and risks.

Partnerships in logistics are expected to grow in importance in the years ahead. Furthermore, some companies are outsourcing more and more of their logistics functions to third-party logistics providers (e.g. FedEx Logistics, Emory Global Logistics) that they believe can do the jobs more efficiently and at lower cost, leaving them free to focus more intensely on their core business.[23] Finally, managers argue that integrated logistics companies understand increasingly complex logistics environments. This can be extremely helpful to companies seeking to expand their global coverage. For example, companies distributing their products across Europe face a bewildering array of environmental restrictions that affect logistics, from product packaging standards, truck size and weight limits to noise and emissions pollution controls. By outsourcing, it can gain a complete pan-European distribution system without incurring the costs, delays and risks associated with setting up their own system.

marketing highlight 21.2

B2B: the attraction of online partnerships

Over 750 business-to-business online markets have sprouted around the world. Some, like the early tie-up between Wal-Mart and General Electric, seek to conduct procurement online in order to cut cost and speed supplies. Another form involves third-party exchanges set up by independent firms that bring together many buyers and sellers to conduct exchanges online, again with the aim of slashing time and margins out of each transaction. More recently, things have moved on. Many giants of an industry are forming online 'consortia' to create virtual marketplaces. In automotives, GM, Ford, DaimlerChrysler, Toyota, Renault and its Japanese affiliate, Nissan, and others have joined forces, creating the world's biggest online market – Covisint – which amounts to some $240 billion-worth of parts sales from tens of thousands of suppliers. Six of the largest 'tier one' automotive parts suppliers – Delphi Automotive, Dana, Eaton, TRW, Motorola and Valeo – have also combined forces to use e-commerce technologies to improve management of their supply chain, after-market activities and customer support. In the retail sector, Ahold, the Dutch supermarket chain, J. Sainsbury, the UK supermarket group, and Metro of Germany have joined GlobalNetXchange, the global B2B marketplace recently launched by two of the world's largest retailers, France's Carrefour and America's Sears, and Oracle, a software group. Other retailers – Kroger, Safeway and Tesco – are also set to take stakes in the venture, which would enable members to buy, sell, trade or auction goods and services, a market that is worth over $5,000 billion (€5,600 billion). The online exchange should lead to cost savings for partners as they streamline their supply chains.

In agribusiness, Cargill, DuPont and Cenex Harvest, the American farm cooperative, have also set up an online market, Roster.com, to extract greater supply chain efficiencies. Then there has also been the recent authorisation by the European Commission of the aerospace products and services joint venture – MyAircraft.com, set up by the two largest aircraft after-market parts suppliers, United Technologies Corporation and Honeywell International Inc. This has been set up to provide a 'one-stop shop' and supply management functions to the aerospace industry.

Finally, not to be left behind, the consumer-goods world has spawned its own online collaborative venture – Transora. Transora brings together some fifty of the world's largest branded consumer goods groups, including Coca-Cola, Cadbury Schweppes, Kraft, Unilever, Heineken and Procter & Gamble. The aim? Just like the other independent online exchanges, members not only hope to reduce supplier costs, but also to improve supply chain efficiency. However, Transora aspires to achieve a 'deep connectivity between manufacturers' internal planning systems and their suppliers', according to Judith Sprieser, chief executive of Transora. Some $1,000 billion of inventory held throughout the consumer-goods industry can be eliminated by integrating suppliers, manufacturers, wholesalers and retailers via this kind of exchange.

There is just one catch. Savings made by Internet exchange would eventually have to be passed on to the consumer, which further squeezes supplier and manufacturer margins. So, Transora would, instead, seek to become a B2B 'information hub', turning valuable data brought to the exchange into subscription services as well as offering members auxiliary services ranging from financing to advertising. Because technology would become more interlinked, the online exchange would enable members to take more control of their supply chain process. If it works, it would mean that companies, rivals and suppliers alike, may get on with the job that is, and has always been, most important in business – focusing on how to add value and then delivering it.

SOURCES: Carlos Grande, 'Exchange of the big brands', *Financial Times* (21 July 2000), p. 16; Andrew Edgecliffe-Johnson, 'Top 50 consumer groups go online', *Financial Times* (17 March 2000), p. 36; 'Seller beware', *The Economist* (4 March 2000), pp. 85–6; Susanna Voyle, 'Sainsbury and Metro join net exchange', *Financial Times* (24 March 2000), p. 26; Ian Bickerton, 'Ahold acquires US Foodservice', *Financial Times* (8 March 2000), p. 32; Nikki Tait, 'Part suppliers to examine e-commerce', *Financial Times* (4 April 2000), p. 34.

retailing and wholesaling trends

■ Retailing trends

Retailers operate in a harsh and fast-changing environment, which offers threats as well as opportunities. For example, in many countries, the industry suffers from chronic overcapacity, resulting in fierce competition for customers. Consumer demographics, lifestyles and shopping patterns are changing rapidly, as are retailing technologies. To be successful, then, retailers will have to choose target segments carefully and position themselves strongly. They will have to take the following retailing developments into account as they plan and execute their competitive strategies.

New retail forms and shortening retail life cycles New retail forms continue to emerge to meet new situations and consumer needs, but the life cycle of new retail forms is getting shorter. Department stores took about 100 years to reach the mature stage of the life cycle; more recent forms, such as warehouse stores, reached maturity in about ten years. In such an environment, seemingly solid retail positions can crumble quickly.

Many retailing innovations are partially explained by the **wheel of retailing** concept. According to this concept, many new types of retailing forms begin as low-margin, low-price, low-status operations. They challenge established retailers that have become 'fat' by letting their costs and margins increase. The new retailers' success leads them to upgrade their facilities, carry higher-quality merchandise and offer more services. In turn, their costs increase, forcing them to increase their prices. Eventually, the new retailers become like the conventional retailers they replaced. The cycle begins again when still newer types of retailer evolve with lower costs and prices. The wheel of retailing concept seems to explain the initial success and later troubles of department stores, supermarkets and discount stores, and the recent success of off-price and no-frills retailers.[24] Thus retailers can no longer sit back with a successful formula. To remain successful, they must keep adapting and reshaping their business accordingly.

While the wheel of retailing explains the evolution and development of new types of retail store, the concept of the **retailing accordion** can be used to explain the intermittent changes in the depth of retailers' merchandise or the breadth of their operations. Typically, retailers begin by selling a wide assortment of products. They are followed by retailers offering a narrower or more specialised range of products, which in turn are eventually superseded by broad-line mass merchandisers. The theory suggests that retailers pass through a *general–specific–general cycle*. It adequately tapped the evolution of the American retail scene, where the nineteenth-century general stores gave way to the twentieth-century specialist retailers, which were then superseded by the postwar mass merchandisers. The accordion concept may be used to describe the more recent *specific–general–specific cycle* of retailing observed in some sectors.

For instance, some retailers begin by selling a narrow range or special type of goods, as in a grocery store that carries mainly food, drinks and convenience items. As sales expand, the store manager tends to add new merchandise, such as household goods, stationery, cosmetics and non-prescription drugs, to his or her portfolio. As it grows further, extra services and amenities – for example, delicatessen, fresh-fish-and-seafood counter, in-store bakery, credit card and cheque facilities – are added. This is the path reflected by large supermarkets, which started as narrow-line grocery retailers, stretching out, over the years, into broad-line superstores. More recently, further growth in edge-of-town superstores is slowing down and out-of-town shopping centres are reaching saturation point. Some of the larger supermarkets are moving

Wheel of retailing
A concept of retailing which states that new types of retailer usually begin as low-margin, low-price, low-status operations, but later evolve into higher-priced, higher-service operations, eventually becoming like the conventional retailers they replaced.

Retailing accordion
A phenomenon describing how the width of retailers' product assortment or operations shifts over time: there tends to be a general–specific–general cycle. However, it is possible that many retailing businesses evolve along a specific–general–specific cycle.

back into the high streets. In the UK, Sainsbury's and Tesco reintroduced small town-centre formats, Metro and Central respectively, which are able to trade more profitably now than they could ten years ago through the supermarkets' increased buying power and efficiency.[25]

Growth of non-store retailing Although most retailing still takes place the old-fashioned way across countertops in stores, consumers now have an array of alternatives, including mail order, television, phone and online shopping. Although such advances may threaten some traditional retailers, they offer exciting opportunities for others. Most store retailers are now actively exploring direct retailing channels.

Increasing inter-type competition Today's retailers increasingly face competition from many different forms of retailers. For example, a consumer can buy CDs at speciality music stores, discount music stores, electronics superstores, general merchandise discount stores, video-rental outlets and through dozens of websites. They can buy books at stores ranging from independent local bookstores to discount stores, superstores or websites. When it comes to brand-name appliances, department stores, discount stores, off-price retailers and electronics superstores all compete for the same customers.

The rise of mega-retailers The rise of huge mass merchandisers and speciality superstores, the formation of vertical marketing systems and buying alliances, and a rash of retail mergers and acquisitions have created a core of superpower mega-retailers. In the grocery sector, for example, the battle for global power among the 80 large supermarket groups in Europe has created a superleague of eight heavyweight retailers (see Figure 21.7).

Through their superior information systems and buying power, these giant retailers are able to offer better merchandise selections, good service, and strong price savings to consumers. As a result, they grow even larger by squeezing out their smaller, weaker competitors. The mega-retailers also are shifting the balance of power between retailers and producers. A relative handful of retailers now controls access to enormous numbers of consumers, giving them the upper hand in their dealings with manufacturers.

The growing importance of retail technology Retail technologies are becoming critically important as competitive tools. Progressive retailers are using computers to produce better forecasts, control inventory costs, order electronically from suppliers, send e-mail between stores, and even sell to customers within stores. They are adopting checkout scanning systems, online transaction processing, electronic funds transfer, electronic data interchange, in-store television, and improved merchandise-handling systems. The key to lasting success is *efficient consumer response (ECR)* – slicing time out of the entire supply process and working in partnership with their suppliers to deliver goods consumers want whenever and wherever they want them.[26]

Perhaps the most startling advances in retailing technology concern the ways in which today's retailers are connecting with customers. In the past, retailers connected with their customers through stores, through their salespeople, through the brands and packages they sold, and through direct mail and advertising in the mass media. But today, life is more complex. There are dozens of new ways to attract and engage consumers. Indeed, even if one omits the obvious – the Web – retailers are still surrounded by technical innovations that promise to redefine the way they and manufacturers interact with customers. Consider touch-screen kiosks, electronic shelf labels and signs, handheld shopping assistants, smart cards, self-scanning systems, virtual reality displays and intelligent agents. So, if we ask the question, 'Will technology change the way retailers interface with customers in the future?', the answer has got to be yes.[27]

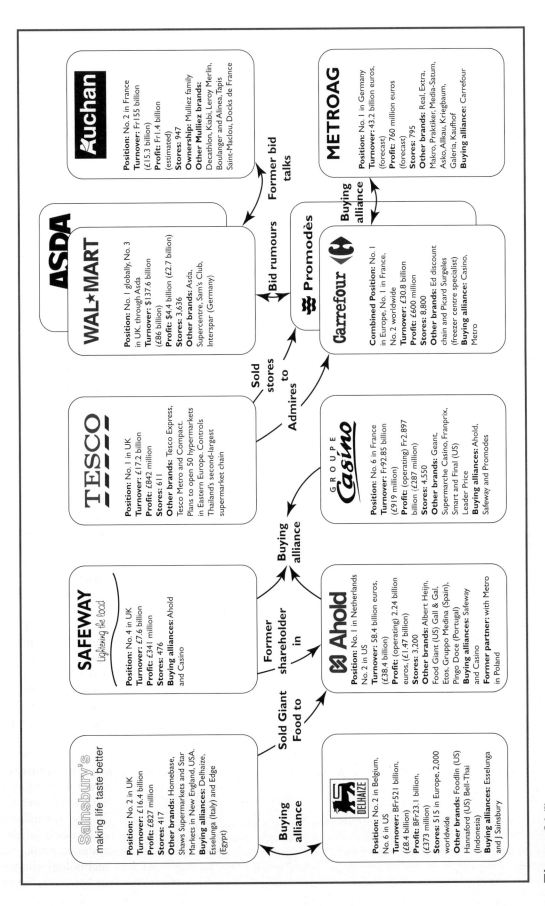

Figure 21.7

Grocery retailers in Europe: the superleague

SOURCE: *The Times* (1 September 1999), p. 29.

marketing highlight 21.3

Retail giants: coming to terms with the global marketplace

As major store retailers within national boundaries have consolidated into corporate giants and domestic markets have become ever more crowded, the big players have been crossing borders for growth opportunities. However, store retailing is a business that is proving difficult to transfer across national frontiers. Even for those whose international businesses are already well advanced – notably, the Dutch C&A (arguably the oldest retail chain in Europe) – getting things right in international markets is not easy.

First, consider the recent experience of the world's largest retailer, America's Wal-Mart, in Germany. Through its acquisition of the Wertkauf hypermarket in 1997 and Interspar in 1998, Wal-Mart Germany became the country's fourth largest hypermarket chain. Although this move initially sent shockwaves through the European retail industry, the German venture is proving to be performing poorly, losing $200 million–$300 million (€224 million–€333 million) a year.

Volker Barth, head of Wal-Mart Germany, noted that management did not underestimate the difficulty involved in succeeding in Europe's most competitive food retail market. But they did make mistakes. The most serious one was disregarding the German food retailing distribution structure. To control the distribution to stores, the company centralised procurement rather than left it to suppliers. This resulted in delivery chaos and stock-out rates as high as 20 per cent compared with a 7 per cent average for the industry. Although sizeable, with 10 per cent of the hypermarket sector, Wal-Mart Germany has less than 2 per cent of the food retail market. It lacked the purchasing muscle to dictate to suppliers and distributors, unlike Edeka and Rewe, with a combined market share of 30 per cent. Moreover, in a sector already dominated by hard discounters, Wal-Mart's 'low-price message' was nothing new. Rivals quickly matched its price-cuts. High renovation costs and the complexity of Germany's planning and social regulations have also delayed planned refurbishment of stores, with many remaining unattractive or in the wrong locations. Poor quality staff and sloppy customer service at its Interspar stores have not helped either.

Wal-Mart also acknowledged misjudging corporate culture. Filling the top positions at the German stores with US expatriates prompted an exodus of German managers, which denied the group local expertise.

Wal-Mart's losses in Germany may be reconcilable, given the venture is in its infancy. IKEA waited eight years until its US store eventually went into profit. However, C&A, the Dutch clothing chain, for all of its 159 years of retail experience, from the Republic of Ireland to the Czech Republic, has taken an age to wake up to the reality of international marketing.

C&A's European turnover dipped €500 million over 1999–2000. It has shut the UK and Danish chains and three stores in the Netherlands. Management attribute the rapid decline to the firm's decision to reduce costs by centralising purchasing in Düsseldorf and Brussels. Unfortunately, centralised buying resulted in a clothing range that was not tailored to the vast differences in tastes across the 12 countries that the retailer supplied. When it is sunny enough for bikinis in Spain, it is chilly and damp in Rotterdam. Young teens in Frankfurt may want to wear Flintstones T-shirts but 14-year olds in Birmingham would not be caught dead in one!

In addition to offering a 'homogeneous' collection for an 'idealised' European customer, the retailer succeeded in alienating core customers. Its designer-driven styles sought to woo the more fashion-conscious suburbanites. Unfortunately, the clothes it sold were being increasingly pitched at mainstream, price-conscious mums who neither wanted nor expected them. Lucas Brenninkmeijer, chairman and chief executive of C&A, laments the firm's neglect of the simple principle – fashion is global, but business is local. He acknowledged: 'We learned the hard way that England is not mainland Europe and English tastes are not European tastes.' C&A currently struggles to revamp its image and to adapt products and distribution to specific markets. However, changing now may be too little, too late for a store losing £1 million (€1.64 million) a week.

Sources: Richard Tomkins, 'Wal-Mart makes foray into Europe with Wertkauf buy', *Financial Times* (19 December 1997), p. 21; Fraser Nelson, 'Grocers must play their cards right', *The Times* (1 September 1999), p. 9; 'Shopping all over the world', *The Economist* (19 June 1999), pp. 83–9; Bertrand Benoit, 'Wal-Mart finds German failures hard to swallow', *Financial Times* (12 October 2000), p. 25; Peggy Hollinger and Chris Tighe, 'C&A was forced down market and now out', *Financial Times* (16 June 2000), p. 3; Ian Bickerton, 'A victim of fashion', *Financial Times* (27 June 2000), p. 18; Peggy Hollinger, 'A shopping market stacked with difficulties', *Financial Times* (2 August 2000), p. 19.

Global expansion of retailers Retailers with unique formats and strong brand positioning are increasingly moving into other countries. Many are expanding internationally to escape mature and saturated home markets. Over the years, several giant US retailers – McDonald's, Gap, Toys 'R' Us, Wal-Mart – have become prominent in countries around the world as a result of their great marketing prowess. However, European and Asian retailers are ahead of the US when it comes to global expansion. Only 18 per cent of the top US retailers operate globally, compared to 40 per cent of European retailers and 31 per cent of Asian retailers. Among the European retailers that have gone global are Britain's Marks & Spencer, Italy's Benetton, France's Carrefour hypermarkets and Sweden's IKEA home furnishings stores.[28] Although many retailers appear to have caught globalisation fever, not all have done well. Despite the enthusiasm, retailers are finding it hard to make a success of the transition from national to multinational (see Marketing Highlight 21.3).

■ Trends in wholesaling

Progressive wholesalers constantly watch for better ways to meet the changing needs of their suppliers and target customers. They recognise that, in the long run, their only reason for existence comes from adding value by increasing the efficiency and effectiveness of the entire marketing channel. To achieve this goal, they must constantly improve their services and reduce their costs.

The distinction between large retailers and large wholesalers continues to blur. Retailers that operate formats such as wholesale clubs and hypermarkets perform many wholesale functions. In return, many large wholesalers are setting up their own retailing operations. A prime example of this type of *hybrid* operator is the cash-and-carry self-service wholesaler, Makro, which, in one sense, is a limited-service wholesaler, selling primarily to the trade – that is, to small shopkeepers/retailers. In another sense, Makro is also a large retailer in that many of the 'trade visitors' who purchase goods from its warehouse are not resellers but individuals bulk-buying for personal consumption.[29]

Wholesalers will continue to increase the services they provide to retailers – retail pricing, cooperative advertising, marketing and management information reports, accounting services, online transactions and others. Rising costs on the one hand, and the demand for increased services on the other, will put the squeeze on wholesaler profits. Wholesalers who do not find efficient ways to deliver value to their customers will soon drop by the wayside. However, the increased use of computerised, automated and Internet systems will help wholesalers to contain the costs of ordering, shipping and inventory holding, boosting their productivity.

Finally, facing slow growth in their domestic markets and the trend towards globalisation, many large wholesalers are now going global, thus creating new challenges for the wholesaling industry worldwide. To survive, players must learn to adapt to their changing environment. Like their customers – the resellers or retailers, whose success relies on their ability to capture and retain customers by offering better value than the competition can – wholesalers must consistently add to that value-creation process. For all channel partners, wholesalers and retailers alike, nothing happens until a sale takes place, until customers buy. And there are no long-term rewards unless these customers come back for more!

summary

Marketing channel decisions directly affect every other marketing decision. Each channel system creates a different level of revenues and costs, and reaches a different segment of target customers. Most producers try to forge a *distribution channel* – a set of interdependent organisations involved in the process of making a product or service available for use or consumption by the consumer or business user. Through their contacts, experience, specialisation and scale of operation, intermediaries usually offer the firm more than it can achieve on its own.

Marketing channels perform many key functions: *information gathering and dissemination; communication and promotion; contact work; matching offers to buyers' needs; negotiation; physical distribution; financing;* and *risk taking.*

The channel is most effective when each member is assigned the tasks it can do best and all members work together smoothly. In recent years, new types of channel organisation have appeared that provide stronger leadership and improved performance.

Each firm needs to identify alternative ways to reach its market. These vary from direct marketing channels to using one, two, three or more intermediary *channel levels.* Marketing channels face continuous change. Three of the most important trends are the growth of *vertical, horizontal* and *hybrid marketing systems.* These trends affect channel cooperation, conflict and competition.

Channel design begins with assessing customer channel-service needs and company channel objectives and constraints. The company then identifies the main channel alternatives in terms of the *types* of intermediary, the *number* of intermediaries and the *channel responsibilities* of each.

There are many types of channel intermediary, ranging from wholesalers, brokers and agents to retailers. *Wholesaling* includes all the activities involved in selling goods or services to those who are buying for the purpose of resale or for business use. Wholesalers perform many functions, including selling and promoting, buying and assortment building, bulk-breaking, warehousing, transporting, financing, risk bearing, supplying market information and providing management services and advice. Wholesalers fall into three groups: *merchant wholesalers* take possession of the goods; *agents* and *brokers* do not take possession of the goods, but are paid a commission for facilitating buying and selling; and *manufacturers' sales branches and offices* are wholesaling operations conducted by non-wholesalers to bypass the wholesalers.

Retailers perform activities involved in selling goods and services directly to final consumers for their personal use. Retailers can be classified as *store retailers* and *non-store retailers.* They can be further classified by the *amount of service* they provide (e.g. self-service, limited service or full service); *product line sold* (e.g. speciality store, department store, supermarket, convenience store, superstores); and their *relative price emphasis* (e.g. discount store, category killer, off-price retailers). Today, more chains and retailer cooperatives are banding together in corporate and contractual retail organisations (e.g. corporate chains, voluntary chains and retailer cooperatives, franchise organisations and merchandising conglomerates).

Each channel alternative must be evaluated according to economic, control and adaptive criteria. Channel management calls for selecting, motivating and periodically evaluating qualified intermediaries. Companies operating in different geographic markets can apply the key principles of channel management, but must adapt approaches to the conditions in individual markets.

More business firms are now paying attention to *physical distribution* or *marketing logistics.* Marketing logistics involves coordinating the activities of the entire *supply chain* to deliver maximum value to customers. No logistics system can both maximise customer service and minimise distribution costs. Instead, the goal of logistics management is to provide a *targeted* level of service at the least cost. The primary logistics functions include *order processing, warehousing, inventory management* and *transportation.*

Increasingly, companies are adopting the *integrated logistics concept,* recognising that improved logistics requires close working relationships across functional areas inside the company, and across various organisations in the supply chain. Companies achieve logistics harmony among functions by creating cross-functional logistics teams, integrative supply manager positions and senior-level logistics executives with cross-functional authority. Channel partnerships can take the form of cross-company teams, shared projects and information-sharing systems. Through such partnerships, many companies have switched from *anticipatory-based distribution systems* to customer-triggered *response-based distribution systems*. Today, some companies are outsourcing their logistics functions to third-party logistics providers to reduce costs, increase efficiency and gain faster and more effective access to global markets.

Higher cost pressures, increasingly demanding customers, globalisation and the rising impact of technologies affect not just the way producers must manage channel activities, but also how channel intermediaries should adapt their services to satisfy the needs of target customers.

discussing the issues

1. Describe the kinds of horizontal and vertical channel conflict that might occur in one of the following: (a) the personal computer industry, (b) the automobile industry, (c) the music industry, or (d) the clothing industry. How would you remedy the problems you have just described?

2. What is disintermediation? Give an example other than those discussed in the chapter. What opportunities and problems does disintermediation present for traditional retailers? Explain.

3. In only the past few years, online retailing has boomed. (a) How will retailers going online change the competitive balance between retailers, direct and catalogue marketers, wholesalers and manufacturers? (b) What are the major advantages of online retailing? The pitfalls? (c) What do you think is the future of online retailing?

4. 'Category killers' and discounters provide tough price competition to other retailers. Will large retailers' growing power in distribution channels affect manufacturers' willingness to sell to category killers and other discounters? What policy should Sony have regarding selling to these retailers?

5. Many European and US retailers are seeking to expand globally. (a) What key factors might govern successful international expansion? (b) Thinking of examples of local retailers, explain which of these might be well positioned for global expansion. (c) How will online retailing affect global retail expansion? (d) Study Sweden's IKEA home furnishings stores (www.ikea.com). Why has IKEA been so successful in expanding into overseas markets?

applying the concepts

1. You know about the Internet, but have you ever heard of an extranet? An extranet occurs when a company opens part of its own internal network (or intranet) to trusted suppliers, distributors and other selected external business partners. Via such extranets, a company can communicate quickly and efficiently with its partners, complete transactions and share data. A supplier might analyse the customer's inventory needs. Partners might swap customer lists for interrelated products and services or share purchasing systems to gain savings through more efficient purchasing. These 'virtual partners' communicate in nanoseconds about shifting supply and demand situations, customer requests and opportunities, and just-in-time inventory needs.

Purchase processing times can be reduced from weeks to minutes at enormous cost savings, which can then be passed along to consumers. (a) What role will extranets play in distribution decisions for retailers, wholesalers, and manufacturers? (b) Discuss the potential dangers and benefits of an extranet system. (c) How might large retailers employ an extranet in their dealings with suppliers? What types of activities and information might be shared on this extranet? How might this save time and costs?

2. In this exercise you are going to build your own online store. Yahoo! Store is a comprehensive solution for small businesses seeking to establish

an online storefront. Visit Yahoo! Store at store.yahoo.com. Go ahead and create a free online store (it expires in ten days). You can sell anything you want at your store, but don't worry, no one can place a real order. Once you have created the store, make a printout of the home page. Note the URL, which will read like this: store.yahoo.com/yourusername. Next, list the retail functions (e.g. Web store design, Web store hosting, order processing, merchandising, customer service, and others) provided by Yahoo! Store. Define your

retail operation in terms of the amount of service offered and product line. (a) Who is your target market and what position will you occupy for this store? (b) What is the cost of running a store on Yahoo! Store? (c) Who are some of Yahoo! Store's more prominent clients? (d) What steps would you take to advertise your store? Yahoo! Store domain names are store.yahoo.com/mystore. For an additional charge you can register a domain name such as www.mystore.com. Which approach would be better for your business? Why?

references

1. Paul Talacko, 'Novel practices on the net', *Financial Times* (6 October 2000), p. 14; 'The book trade. Pile 'em high', *The Economist* (18 September 1999), pp. 36 and 39.

2. Louis Stern and Adel I. El-Ansary, *Marketing Channels*, 5th edn (Upper Saddle River, NJ: Prentice Hall, 1996), p. 3.

3. For alternative levels of definition of a channel of distribution, see Michael J. Baker, *Macmillan Dictionary of Marketing and Advertising*, 2nd edn (London: Macmillan, 1990), pp. 47–8.

4. Ian Bickerton, 'Ahold acquires US Foodservice', *Financial Times* (8 March 2000), p. 32.

5. 'Furnishing the world', *The Economist* (19 November 1994), pp. 101–2; details also obtained from IKEA's website: www.ikea.com (pages covering 'facts and figures', 'our vision', and 'press room', October 2000).

6. This has been called 'symbiotic marketing'. For further reading, see Lee Adler, 'Symbiotic marketing', *Harvard Business Review* (November–December 1966), pp. 59–71; P. 'Rajan' Varadarajan and Daniel Rajaratnam, 'Symbiotic marketing revisited', *Journal of Marketing* (January 1986), pp. 7–17; Gary Hamel, Yves L. Doz and C. D. Prahalad, 'Collaborate with your competitors and win', *Harvard Business Review* (January–February 1989), pp. 133–9.

7. See Allan J. Magrath, 'Collaborative marketing comes of age again', *Sales and Marketing Management* (September 1991), pp. 61–4; Lois Therrien, 'Café au lait, à croissant and trix', *Business Week* (24 August 1992), pp. 50–1; Judann Pollack and Louise Kramer, 'Coca-Cola and Pringles eye global brand link-up', *Advertising Age* (15 June 1998), pp. 1, 73.

8. Rochelle Garner, 'Mad as hell', *Sales & Marketing Management* (June 1999), pp. 55–9.

9. 'Killing off the competition', *Marketing Business* (April 1994), pp. 11–14; *Category Killers: Prospects for the year 2000* (London: Euromonitor, 1994); Alex Spillius, 'Invasion of the category killers', *Observer Life* (27 February 1994), pp. 6–7; Sarah Cunningham, 'The seduction of the hyper-sensitive Brits', *The Times* (19 June 1999), pp. 28–9; Matthew Barbour, 'Rolling in the aisles at Tesco', *The Times* (19 June 1999), p. 29.

10. Duke Ratliff, 'Evolution of off-price retailers', *Discount Merchandising* (March 1996), pp. 22–30; and Howard Banks, 'The malling of Europe', *Forbes* (22 February 1999), p. 66; Peggy Hollinger, 'M&S moves into factory outlets', *Financial Times* (13 July 2000), p. 25.

11. Nirmalya Kumar, 'The power of trust in manufacturer–retailer relationships', *Harvard Business Review* (November–December 1996), pp. 92–106; James A. Narus and James C. Anderson, 'Rethinking distribution', *Harvard Business Review* (July–August 1996), pp. 112–20; James C. Anderson and James A. Narus, *Business Market Management* (Upper Saddle River, NJ: Prentice Hall, 1999), pp. 276–88.

12. Michael Terry, 'Drive for greater efficiency', *Financial Times* (3 September 1992), p. IV.

13. Tom Todd, 'The new ground rules', *EuroBusiness* (May 1994), pp. 43–4.

14. 'Rays of hope and prophecies of doom', *EuroBusiness* (May 1994), pp. 46–7.

15. Subhash C. Jain, *International Marketing Management*, 3rd edn (Boston: PWS-Kent Publishing, 1990), pp. 489–91; Emily Thornton, 'Revolution in Japanese retailing', *Fortune* (7 February 1994), pp. 143–7; 'Ever-shorter channels – wholesale industry restructures', *Focus Japan* (July–August 1997), pp. 3–4.

16. Bayan Rahman, 'The Japanese face of Boots', *Financial Times* (4 October 2000), p. 15.

17. See Philip Cateora, *International Marketing*, 7th edn (Homewood, IL: Irwin, 1990), pp. 570–1; Dexter Roberts, 'Blazing away at foreign brands', *Business Week* (12 May 1997), p. 58.

18. Shlomo Maital, 'The last frontier of cost reduction', *Across the Board*, **31**, 2 (February 1994), pp. 51–2.

19. See D. Shipley, 'What British distributors dislike about manufacturers', *Industrial Marketing Management*, **16** (1987), pp. 153–62; Robert D. Buzzell and Gwen Ortmeyer, 'Channel partnerships streamline distribution', *Sloan Management Review* (22 March 1995), p. 85.

20. Martin Christopher, 'From logistics to competitive advantage', *Marketing Business* (August 1989), pp. 20–1.

21. For a general discussion of improving supply chain performance, see Marshall L. Fisher, 'What is the right supply chain for your product?', *Harvard Business Review* (March–April 1997), pp. 105–16.

22. 'Car making', *The Economist* (26 August 2000), pp. 68–70.

23. Martha Celestino, 'Choosing a third-party logistics provider', *World Trade* (July 1999), pp. 54–6.

24. See Malcolm P. McNair and Eleanor G. May, 'The next revolution of the retailing wheel', *Harvard Business Review* (September–October 1978), pp. 81–91; Eleanor G. May, 'A retail odyssey', *Journal of Retailing* (Fall 1989), pp. 356–67; Stephen Brown, 'The wheel of retailing: past and future', *Journal of Retailing* (Summer 1990), pp. 143–9; Sachiko Sakamaki, 'Simple success', *Far Eastern Economic Review* (21 August 1997), p. 75.

25. S. C. Hollander, 'Notes on the retail accordion', *Journal of Retailing*, **42**, 2 (1966), p. 24; Neil Buckley, 'Still shopping as the margins drop', *Financial Times* (4 August 1994), p. 15; Cathy Hart, 'The retail accordion and assortment strategies: an exploratory study', *International Review of Retail Distribution and Consumer Research*, **9** (April 1999), pp. 111–26.

26. Alan Mitchell, 'Serving up a logistical philosophy', *Marketing Week* (24 May 1996), pp. 26–7; Francis J. Mulhern, 'Retail marketing: from distribution to integration', *International Journal of Research in Marketing*, **14** (1997), pp. 103–24.

27. Regina Fazio Maruca, 'Retailing: confronting the challenges that face bricks-and-mortar stores', *Harvard Business Review* (July–August 1999), pp. 159–68.

28. Carla Rapoport, 'Retailers go global', *Fortune* (20 February 1995), pp. 102–8; Joseph H. Ellis, 'Global retailing's winners and losers', *Chain Store Age* (December 1997), pp. 27–9.

29. Various Makro (UK) Newsletters (Leeds: Makro self-service wholesalers, 1995, 1996, 1997); see also *Cash and Carry Outlets* (Hampton, Middx: Keynote Publications, 1992).

case 21

Pieta luxury chocolates

Peter Abel, the young managing director of his family's firm, was pleased with the way he had revitalised the firm after he took over ten years ago. Since being formed in 1923, Pieta had sold its luxury Belgian chocolates through its own small shops. It had a high reputation within the trade and many devoted customers. It was the country's largest luxury chocolate manufacturer, but until Peter took over, the company had stagnated. In his opinion, Pieta should be more like other leading family firms such as Cadbury, Ferrero and Mars.

When he took over, he launched the company into new ventures. Franchising widened distribution to some small shops which now had corners devoted to Pieta's range. He felt these did not compete with Pieta's own shops because the franchisees were CTNs (confectioners, tobacconists and newsagents), where people made many impulse purchases. These contrasted with Pieta's shops, which people visited to make purchases for a special occasion or as an indulgence. Other distribution channels that were developed included own-label to Marks & Spencer in the United Kingdom, direct mailing for special occasions and exporting (see Exhibit 21.1).

There were some new Pieta shops and 20 per cent of the old ones were refurbished. The refurbishment rate was slower than he would have liked, for he knew that many of the shops were poorly located, cluttered and overcrowded. The well-sited shops often had queues trailing out of their doors when they were busy, but most did not do so well. The company had not kept pace with changes in shopping and geodemographics. Most of Pieta's shops were on secondary sites in declining industrial towns. Other new channel opportunities, such as 'shop-in-shop' outlets and international expansion, had also been largely ignored.

However, the product range was now wider. The chocolate market was seasonal, so the shops sold ice-creams to help summer sales. The outlets also carried a range of greetings cards and Pieta gift vouchers to make them more of a one-stop shop. Soon he would be introducing countlines aimed at the mass market.

As a result of his efforts, Peter was able to present a dynamic set of results to his family shareholders (see Exhibit 21.2). He was angry to find that some shareholders were not as supportive as they had been. Some worried about the company's reputation being spoilt by it becoming less exclusive. Others were anxious about the new injection of equity he was requesting. He thought it odd that the strategy they had supported and backed financially two years ago was now in question. He reminded them how well the firm had done despite the tough economic climate over the last few years (see Exhibit 21.3). The company was now more professional than it had ever been. He had just introduced a new tier of senior people to manage the day-to-day operations of the company. These were not family members, but were bright and very well qualified and had broad experience within the industry. With them in place he would have more time to think about and initiate other ways of developing the company.

Questions

1. Comment on Abel's expansion strategy and Pieta's performance since he took over.

2. Argue the case for further expansion wanted by Abel.

EXHIBIT 21.1 CHANNEL PERFORMANCE

Year	SALES TONNAGE					
	OWN SHOPS	CTN FRANCHISE	M&S OWN LABEL	DIRECT MAIL	EXPORT	NUMBER OF OWN SHOPS
1994	6,049	1	3	3	3	128
1995	7,203	92	255	136	11	130
1996	8,351	392	661	167	24	130
1997	9,933	1,002	636	172	149	132
1998	11,845	1,303	462	205	184	138
1999	14,753	1,259	868	205	167	148
Gross margin (%)	55	45	37	35	33	
Net profit (%)	6	14	7	3	(6)	

EXHIBIT 21.2 COMPANY PERFORMANCE (Bfr m)

YEAR	SALES	GROSS PROFIT	NET PROFIT	NET ASSETS	EQUITY	DEBT
1989	2,262	1,285	282	1,218	809	409
1990	2,222	1,215	308	1,305	885	420
1991	2,783	1,568	387	1,503	1,043	460
1992	3,461	1,961	636	1,896	1,241	655
1993	4,270	2,405	723	2,373	1,488	885
1994	5,653	3,005	779	2,931	1,735	1,196
1995	7,091	4,066	951	3,425	2,002	1,423
1996	8,821	4,696	793	4,228	2,217	2,011
1997	10,887	5,803	975	4,749	2,661	2,088
1998	12,826	6,891	1,123	6,201	2,594	3,607
1999	15,551	9,064	1,372	7,515	3,113	4,402

EXHIBIT 21.3 ECONOMIC PERFORMANCE

YEAR	RETAIL (INDEX)	CTN (INDEX)	COST OF LIVING (INDEX)	COST OF DEBT (%)	COST OF EQUITY (%)
1989	100	100	100	11	13
1990	108	107	109	9	12
1991	133	121	117	11	17
1992	151	131	128	14	18
1993	175	155	148	16	23
1994	208	191	184	17	28
1995	238	223	213	17	21
1996	271	257	251	12	20
1997	310	285	274	13	26
1998	345	297	311	16	23
1999	389	351	360	16	25

3. What is the scope for channel innovation in the industry?

4. How is Abel's strategy endangering Pieta's future performance and brand image? What, if anything, has Abel been neglecting?

5. Track the changes in C^3 (capital cost covered) and EVA (economic value added) for Pieta over the last ten years. **Marketing Highlight 16.2** shows how to do this.

6. Comment on the C^3 and EVA trends and compare them with the impression given by the growth in profits and sales. What strategies of Abel's explain the performance that the C^3 and EVA reveal? Should the trend be changed and, if so, how could it be changed?

SOURCE: From company records. All dates, figures and names have been changed for commercial reasons.

internet exercises

Internet exercises for this chapter can be found on the student site of the MYPHLIP Web Site at www.booksites.net/kotler.

chapter twenty-two

Direct and online marketing: the new marketing model

Chapter objectives *After reading this chapter, you should be able to:*

+ Discuss the benefits of direct marketing to customers and companies and the trends fuelling its rapid growth.

+ Define a customer database and list the four ways in which companies use databases in direct marketing.

+ Identify the major forms of direct marketing.

+ Compare the two types of online marketing channel and explain the effect of the Internet on electronic commerce.

+ Identify the benefits of online marketing to consumers and marketers, and the ways in which marketers can conduct online marketing.

+ Discuss the public policy and ethical issues facing direct marketers.

introduction

The case of Dell (see preview case opposite) gets us to think about the role that direct marketing methods play in achieving market performance. In this chapter, we look at the nature of direct marketing and how it can be used by organisations to reach target customers more effectively and efficiently.

Many of the marketing tools we examined in previous chapters were developed in the context of *mass marketing*: targeting broad markets with standardised messages and offers distributed through intermediaries. Today, however, with the trend towards more narrowly targeted or one-to-one marketing, more and more companies are adopting *direct marketing*, as a primary marketing approach or as a supplement to other approaches. Increasingly, companies are turning to direct marketing in an effort to reach carefully targeted customers more efficiently and to build stronger, more personal, one-to-one relationships with them.

In this chapter, we examine the nature, role and growing applications of direct marketing and its newest form, online marketing and e-commerce. We address the

preview case

Dell Computer Corporation

When 19-year-old Michael Dell began selling personal computers out of his college dorm room in 1984, few would have bet on his chances for success. In those days, most computer makers sold their PCs through an extensive network of all-powerful distributors and resellers. Michael Dell has proved the sceptics wrong. In little more than a decade, he turned his dorm-room mail-order business into a burgeoning, $22 billion computer empire. Dell is now the world's largest direct marketer of computer systems. Dell became the world's fastest-growing computer manufacturer and overtook IBM to become the number two PC maker by 1998. Direct buyers now account for nearly a third of all PC sales and Dell's once-sceptical competitors are now scrambling to build their own direct marketing systems.

Dell's stunning success has been due to the company's radically different business model – *the direct model*. Dell's direct marketing approach delivers greater customer value through an unbeatable combination of product customisation, low prices, fast delivery and award-winning customer service. A customer can order by phone a fully customised, state-of-the-art PC to suit his or her special needs and have the machine delivered to his or her doorstep within 48 hours – all at a price that's 10–15 per cent below competitors' prices. Dell also backs its products with high-quality service and support.

Michael Dell's initial idea was to serve individual buyers by letting them customise machines with the special features they wanted at low prices. However, this one-to-one approach also appeals strongly to corporate buyers, because Dell can so easily pre-configure each computer to precise requirements. Dell routinely preloads machines with a company's own software and even undertakes such tedious tasks as pasting inventory tags on to each machine so that computers can be delivered directly to a given employee's desk. As a result, nearly two-thirds of Dell's sales now come from large corporate, government and educational buyers.

Because Dell builds machines to order, it carries barely any inventory. Dealing one-to-one with customers helps the company react immediately to demand shifts, so Dell does not get stuck with PCs that no one wants. Finally, by selling directly, Dell has no dealers to pay off. As a result, on average, Dell's costs are 12 per cent lower than those of Compaq, its leading PC competitor.

Dell knows that time is money, and the company is obsessed with 'speed'. Dell has long been a model of lean, just-in-time manufacturing and efficient supply-chain management. It has also mastered the intricacies of today's lightning-fast electronic commerce. All these enable Dell to convert the average sale to cash in less than 24 hours compared to the days, even weeks, taken by rival companies which sell primarily through dealers. And because Dell does not order parts until an order is booked, it can take advantage of ever-falling component costs. On average, Dell is 60 days further down the price curve, gaining a 6 per cent profit advantage from parts costs alone.

With more and more competitors now following Dell's successful strategy of direct selling, the company has extended its direct marketing model to the Internet. 'The Internet', says Michael Dell, 'is the ultimate direct model. [Customers] like the immediacy, convenience, savings and personal touches that the [Internet] experience provides. Not only are some sales done completely online, but people who call on the phone after having visited Dell.com are twice as likely to buy.'

The direct marketing pioneer now sells over $30 million worth of computers daily from its website, accounting for over 40 per cent of revenues. 'The Internet is like a booster rocket on our sales and growth', Michael Dell proclaims. 'Our vision is to have *all* customers conduct *all* transactions on the Internet, globally.'

This time, competitors are not scoffing at Michael Dell's vision of the future.[1]

Questions

1. Taking the case of Dell Computer Corporation, outline the major advantages of direct marketing for (a) the manufacturer and (b) the customer.

2. Identify the organisational and operational factors that govern successful implementation of direct methods of selling products such as PCs.

3. As more and more computer companies seek to emulate Dell's direct marketing model, there is increasing threat to the company's competitive advantage in terms of speed and low cost. Taking into account the main advantages and limitations of Dell's direct model, recommend a strategy for Dell that will help the company to create and sustain a competitive advantage in the future.

following questions: What is direct marketing? What are its benefits to companies and their customers? How do customer databases support direct marketing? What channels do direct marketers use to reach individual prospects and customers? What marketing opportunities do online channels provide? How can companies use integrated direct marketing to create a competitive advantage? What public and ethical issues do direct and online marketing raise?

what is direct marketing?

Once, all marketing was of the direct sort: the salesperson confronted customers face to face, one 'doorstep' at a time. This technique was steadily replaced by mass marketing, whereby mass marketers spread a standard message to millions of buyers through the mass media – newspapers, magazines, radio and then television. Thus, companies typically promoted products with a single message, hoping that millions nationwide would learn the message and buy the brand. They did not need to know their customers' names or anything specific about them, only that they have certain needs that their products might help to fulfil. Under this mass-marketing model, most marketing communications consisted of one-way communication directed *at* consumers, not two-way communication *with* them.

Direct marketing
Marketing through various advertising media that interact directly with consumers, generally calling for the consumer to make a direct response.

In contrast, **direct marketing** consists of direct communications with carefully targeted individual customers to obtain an immediate response and cultivate lasting customer relationships. Using detailed databases, they tailor their marketing offers and communications to the needs of narrowly defined segments or even individual buyers. Beyond brand and image building, they usually seek a direct, immediate and measurable consumer response. For example, Dell Computer interacts directly with customers, by telephone or through its Web page, to design systems that meet their individual needs. Buyers order directly from Dell, which then quickly and efficiently delivers the new computers to their homes or offices.

the new direct-marketing model

Early direct marketers – catalogue companies, direct mailers and telemarketers – gathered customer names and sold their goods mainly through the post and by telephone. Today, fired by rapid advances in database technologies and new marketing media – especially the Internet and other electronic channels – direct marketing has undergone a dramatic transformation.

In previous chapters, we have discussed direct marketing as direct distribution, as marketing channels that contain no intermediaries. We have also included marketing as one element of the marketing communications mix – as an approach for communicating directly with customers. In fact, direct marketing is both these things. Most companies still use direct marketing as a supplementary channel or medium for marketing their goods. Thus, companies such as Nokia and Lexus market mostly through mass-media advertising and their dealer networks but also supplement these channels with direct marketing. Their direct marketing includes promotional materials mailed directly to prospective buyers and their Web pages which provide customers with information about their products, financing (in the case of Lexus) and dealer locations. Similarly, many department stores and banks sell the majority of their merchandise or services off their 'bricks and mortar' outlets as well as via telemarketing and the Internet.

However, for many companies today, direct marketing – especially Internet marketing and e-commerce – constitutes a new and complete model for doing business.

For companies like Nokia, direct marketing and the Web supplement other marketing efforts. But for e-corporations, such as CoShopper.com, they constitute a new and complete model for doing business.

SOURCE: (top) Nokia (http://www.nokia.com) (bottom) CoShopper Ltd. (http://www.coshopper.com)

'The Internet is not just another marketing channel; it's not just another advertising medium; it's not just a way to speed up transactions', says one strategist. 'The Internet is the foundation for a new industrial order. [It] will change the relationship between consumers and producers in ways more profound than you can yet imagine.'[2] This new *direct model*, suggests another analyst, is 'revolutionizing the way we think about . . .

how to construct relationships with suppliers and customers, how to create value for them, and how to make money in the process; in other words, [it's] revolutionizing marketing'.[3]

Whereas most companies use direct marketing and the Internet as supplemental approaches, firms employing the direct model use it as the *only* approach. Examples include online bookseller Amazon.com; CoShopper.com, a Norwegian Internet shopping company; Framfab, the Swedish Internet consultancy; Direct Line, the insurance company; and Dell. Many strategists have hailed direct marketing as the marketing model of the new millennium. They envisage a day when all buying and selling will involve direct connections between companies and their customers. The new model will fundamentally change customers' expectations about convenience, speed, comparability, price and service. Those new expectations will reverberate throughout the economy, affecting every business. Even those offering more cautious predictions agree that the Internet and e-commerce will have a tremendous impact on future business strategies.

growth and benefits of direct marketing

Whether used as a complete business model or as a supplement to a broader integrated marketing mix, direct marketing brings many benefits to both buyers and sellers. As a result, direct marketing has grown very rapidly.

the benefits of direct marketing

Direct marketing benefits buyers in many ways. First, it is *convenient*. Customers do not have to battle through traffic, find parking spaces and trek through stores and aisles to find and examine products. They can do comparative shopping by browsing through mail catalogues and or surfing websites. Buying is *easy* and *private*. Customers confront fewer buying hassles and do not have to face salespeople or open themselves up to persuasion and emotional pitches. Business customers can learn about available products and services without waiting for and tying up time with salespeople.

Direct marketing often gives shoppers greater product *access* and *selection*. For example, the world's the limit for the Web. Cyberstores such as Amazon, CDNow and others can offer an almost unlimited selection compared to the more meagre assortments of counterparts in the bricks-and-mortar world.

Beyond a broader selection of sellers and products, online and Internet channels also give buyers access to a wealth of comparative *information*, information about companies, products and competitors. Good websites often provide more information in more useful forms than even the most solicitious salesclerk can. CDNow, for example, offers best-seller lists and record reviews.

Finally, direct marketing – especially online buying – is *interactive* and *immediate*. Customers can often interact with the seller's site to create exactly the configuration of information, products or services they desire, then order or download them on the spot. Furthermore, the Internet and other forms of direct marketing give customers a greater measure and sense of control. For example, a rising proportion of car buyers 'shop online', arming themselves with information about car models and dealer costs before showing up at a dealership.

Direct marketing also yields many benefits to seller. First, direct marketing is a powerful tool for *customer relationship building*. They can build or buy databases containing detailed information about potentially profitable customers. Using these databases, they build strong, ongoing customer relationships. With today's technology, a direct marketer can select small groups or even individual consumers, personalise offers to their special needs and wants, and promote these offers through individualised communications.

Direct marketing can also be timed to reach prospects at just the right moment. For example, Nestlé's baby food division maintains a database of new parents and mails them six personalised packages of gifts and advice at key stages in the baby's life. And, because they reach more interested consumers at the best times, direct marketing materials receive higher readership and response. Direct marketing also permits easy testing of alternative media and messages.

Because of its one-to-one, interactive nature, the Internet is an especially potent direct-marketing tool. Companies can interact online with customers to learn more about specific needs and wants. In turn, online customers can ask questions and volunteer feedback. Based on this ongoing interaction, companies can increase customer value and satisfaction through product and service refinements. For example, in a recent TV advertising campaign, Marmite invited consumers to e-mail their reasons for either loving or hating the product. The company saw this as a cost-effective way of reaching the 18 to 24s audience and to build a one-to-one relationship. The pay-off comes from being able to understand, and, therefore, meet consumers' needs better by developing an intimacy with the consumer.

Direct marketing via the Internet and other electronic channels yields additional advantages, such as *reducing costs* and *increasing speed and efficiency*. Online marketers avoid the expense of maintaining a store and the accompanying costs of rent, insurance and utilities.

By using the Internet to link directly to suppliers, factories, distributors and customers, businesses can wring waste out of the system and pass on savings to customers. Recently, there has been a tremendous growth of business-to-business trade on the Internet (also called business-to-business or B2B exchanges). More than 40 online B2B exchanges now serve the motor industry, and initiatives are now found in the aerospace, petroleum, chemicals, food, energy, pharmaceuticals and many more industries. Such exchanges can bring cost savings and efficiencies on many levels to buyers. These range from sourcing or identifying new sources of supply, negotiating (through e-mail or auctions), carrying out transactions and payments, supply chain management functions such as production line planning and collaborative product design and development. An increasing number of manufacturers, for example, have been able to accelerate the product development process by using the Internet to share designs for component or assemblies with suppliers or to pass design work on from teams in one time zone to another.[4] Hence, the Internet is also a truly *global* medium that allows buyers and sellers to click from one country to another in seconds.

Online marketing also offers greater *flexibility*, allowing the marketer to make ongoing adjustments to its offers and programmes. For example, once a paper catalogue is mailed, the products, prices and other catalogue features are fixed until the next catalogue is sent. However, an online catalogue can be adjusted daily or even hourly, adapting product assortments, prices and promotions to match changing market conditions.

the growth of direct marketing

Sales through traditional direct marketing channels (catalogues, direct mail and telemarketing) have been growing rapidly. In the past five years, the annual rate of growth in spending on conventional direct marketing channels (e.g. direct mail) has outstripped that for mass-marketing channels.[5] While direct marketing through traditional channels is growing rapidly, online marketing is growing explosively. The 'information superhighway' or **Internet** promises to revolutionise commerce.

Internet (the Net)
A vast global computer network that enables computers, with the right software and a modem (a telecommunications device that sends data across telephone lines), to be linked together so that their users can obtain or share information and interact with other users.

According to one source, Internet adoption by households across Europe grew from less than 10 million in 1995 to more than 50 million in 2000, and will rise to a projected 100 million by 2004. Internet access via mobile phones is also becoming common. According to another source, mobile terminal access in Europe will increase to 300 million users, compared to 200 million users using PC-based access by 2004.[6]

The proportion of Internet users who conduct online shopping remains relatively low at the moment, but e-commerce is growing very fast.[7] Previously dominated by technically oriented, young, male users, the Internet is now attracting more females and more users in the 25–35 age group.

Additionally, more and more companies around the world are launching websites. The US dominates with over 24 million Internet hosts (websites and other computers sitting permanently on the Internet). The US currently also accounts for some 90 per cent of all commercial websites in the world. However, there are many websites in Europe. When we look at the number of Internet hosts per thousand inhabitants, Finland leads the pack, with the US in second position (see Figure 22.1).[8] We will examine online marketing in greater detail later in this chapter.

What are the factors that are driving the growth in direct marketing? In the consumer market, the extraordinary growth of direct marketing is a response to the new marketing realities discussed in previous chapters. Market 'demassification' has resulted in an ever-increasing number of market niches with distinct preferences. Direct marketing allows sellers to focus efficiently on these minimarkets with offers that better match specific consumer needs.

Other trends have also fuelled the rapid growth of direct marketing in the consumer market. Higher costs of driving, traffic congestion, parking headaches, lack of time, a shortage of retail sales help and long queues at checkout counters all encourage at-home shopping. Consumers are responding favourably to direct marketers' freephone numbers, their willingness to accept telephone orders 24 hours a day,

Figure 22.1

Internet hosts: wiring up for e-commerce (per 1,000 inhabitants, July 1999)

Source: 'E-commerce survey', © The Economist Newspaper Ltd., London, p. 35, 26 February 2000.

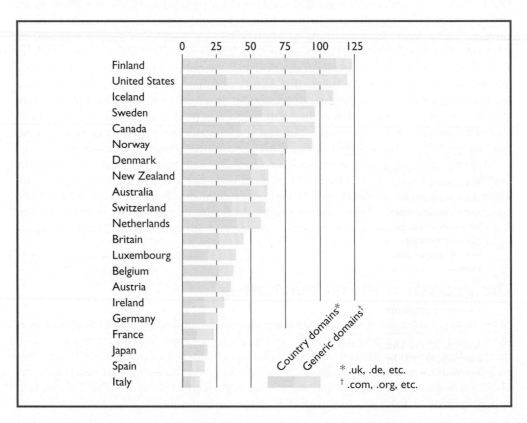

7 days a week, and their growing commitment to customer service. The growth of 24-hour and 48-hour delivery via express carriers such as Federal Express, UPS, DHL and others has made direct shopping fast and easy. Finally, the growth of affordable computer power and customer databases has enabled direct marketers to single out the best prospects for any product they wish to sell.

Direct marketing has also grown rapidly in business-to-business marketing, partly in response to the ever-increasing costs of reaching business markets through the sales force. When personal sales calls cost several hundred euros per contact, they should be made only when necessary and to high-potential customers and prospects. Lower cost-per-contact media – such as telemarketing, direct mail and the newer electronic media – often prove more cost-effective in reaching and selling to more prospects and customers.

customer databases and direct marketing

Table 22.1 lists the main differences between mass marketing and so-called *one-to-one marketing*.[9] Companies that know about individual customer needs and characteristics can customise their offers, messages, delivery modes and payment methods to maximise customer value and satisfaction. Today's companies have a very powerful tool for accessing the names, addresses, preferences and other pertinent information about individual customers and prospects: the customer database.

Successful direct marketing begins with a good customer database. The **customer database** is an organised collection of comprehensive data about individual customers or prospects, including geographic, demographic, psychographic and buying behaviour data. The database can be used to locate good potential customers, tailor products and services to the special needs of targeted consumers, and maintain long-term customer relationships. *Database marketing* is the process of building, maintaining and using customer databases and other databases (products, suppliers, resellers) for the purpose of contacting and transacting with customers.

Customer database
An organised collection of comprehensive data about individual customers or prospects, including geographic, demographic, psychographic and buying behaviour data.

Table 22.1

Mass marketing versus one-to-one marketing

Mass marketing	One-to-one marketing
Average customer	Individual customer
Customer anonymity	Customer profile
Standard product	Customised market offering
Mass production	Customised production
Mass distribution	Individualised distribution
Mass advertising	Individualised message
Mass promotion	Individualised incentives
One-way message	Two-way messages
Economies of scale	Economies of scope
Share of market	Share of customer
All customers	Profitable customers
Customer attraction	Customer retention

Source: Adapted from *The One-to-One Future* by Don Peppers and Martha Rogers, Ph.D, copyright © 1993 by Don Peppers and Martha Rogers, Ph.D. Used by permission of Doubleday, a division of Random House, Inc.

Although many companies are now building and using customer databases for targeting marketing communications and selling efforts at the individual customer, data protection regulations in some countries may slow down growth in database marketing practices. For example, usage in the United States and the United Kingdom is far more widespread, with data laws being much more open compared to the rest of Europe. But the international race is on to exploit database marketing and few businesses can afford to ignore this important vehicle for competitive success. As Tom Peters comments in *Thriving on Chaos*, 'A market has never bought things. Customers buy things. That's why database marketing's ability to target the individual customer in the crowded marketplace is so valuable.'[10]

Many companies confuse a customer mailing list with a customer database. The former is simply a set of names, addresses and telephone numbers. A customer database contains much more information. In business-to-business marketing, the salesperson's customer profile might contain information such as the products and services that the customer has bought; past volumes and prices; key contacts (and their ages, birthdays, hobbies and favourite foods); competitive suppliers; status of current contracts; estimated customer expenditures for the next few years; and assessments of competitive strengths and weaknesses in selling and servicing the account. In consumer marketing, the customer database might contain a customer's demographics (age, income, family members, birthdays), psychographics (activities, interests and opinions), buying behaviour (past purchases, buying preferences) and other relevant information. Companies must distinguish between *transaction-based* and *custom-built* marketing databases. Transactional databases are put in by an accounts department for the purpose of sending invoices/bills out and getting money back. By contrast, custom-built databases focus on what the firm's marketing people need to know to serve and satisfy customers profitably and better than the competition can – for example, the most cost-effective way to reach target customers, the net worth of a transaction, customers' requirements and lifetime values, lapsed customers and why they departed, why competitors are making inroads and where.

Business-to-business marketers and service retailers (e.g. hotels, banks and airlines) are among the most frequent users of database marketing. Increasingly, however, consumer packaged-goods companies and other retailers are also employing database marketing. Armed with the information in their databases, these companies can identify small groups of customers to receive fine-tuned marketing offers and communications.

forms of direct marketing

The major forms of direct marketing include face-to-face selling, direct mail marketing, catalogue marketing, telemarketing, direct-response television (DRTV) marketing and online shopping. Many of these techniques were first developed in the United States, but have become increasingly popular in Europe. In the EU, some forms of direct marketing – notably direct mail and telemarketing – are forecast to grow. In practice, however, the impact of a unified Europe has been limited by the labyrinth of legislation across the Union, which means that certain direct marketing techniques are feasible in some countries but not others.

For example, telemarketing is widely practised in some countries, but virtually illegal in Germany. Differences in postal systems, standards and rates across countries pose problems for pan-European direct-mailing programmes. Direct mail is strong in countries with efficient and inexpensive postal systems (e.g. the UK, Sweden) and weak where the post is slow and delivery unreliable (e.g. Spain, Italy). Even etiquette is a problem. The bright, brash American-style direct-mail methods used in the UK would be considered anything but courteous in France. On the other hand, the flowery phrases of a formal letter in France would definitely be *de trop* in the UK.

Face-to-face selling

The original and oldest form of direct marketing is the sales call, which we examined in Chapter 20. Most business-to-business marketers rely heavily on a professional sales force to locate prospects, develop them into customers, build lasting relationships and grow the business. Or they hire manufacturers' representatives and agents to carry out the direct selling task. Consumer companies also use a direct selling force to reach final consumers. In the UK, Avon leads in the face-to-face selling and direct-to-door distribution of cosmetics and personal care products. Vacuum cleaner manufacturer Electrolux has a direct sales business in Europe. Others, notably Tupperware, Ladybird Books and Oriflame Cosmetics, have also helped to popularise home selling, through home-sales parties or *party plans*, in which several friends and neighbours attend a party at a private home where products are demonstrated and sold directly to a group of people.

Direct-mail marketing

Direct-mail marketing involves mailings of letters, ads, samples, fold-outs and other 'salespeople on wings' sent to prospects on mailing lists. The mailing lists are developed from customer lists or obtained from mailing-list houses that provide names of people fitting almost any description – the super-rich, veterinarians, pet owners, the typical catalogue purchaser and many, many others.

Direct mail is well suited to direct, one-on-one communication. It permits high target-market selectivity, can be personalised, is flexible and allows easy measurement of results (the firm can count the responses it gets and the value of those responses to the business). Whereas the cost per thousand people reached is higher than with mass media such as television or magazines, the people who are reached are much better prospects, since direct-mail marketers target individuals according to their personal suitability to receive particular offerings and promotions. Direct mail has proved very successful in promoting all kinds of products, from books, magazine subscriptions and insurance to gift items, clothing, gourmet foods, consumer packaged goods and industrial products. Direct mail is also used heavily by charities, such as Oxfam and Action Aid, which rely on correspondence selling to persuade individuals to donate to their charity.[11]

The direct-mail industry constantly seeks new methods and approaches. For example, videocassettes and CDs are now among the fastest-growing direct-mail media. Some direct marketers even mail out computer diskettes. Until recently, all direct mail was paper-based and handled by postal and telegraphic services and other mail carriers. Recently, however, fax mail, e-mail and voice mail have become popular.

These new forms deliver direct mail at incredible speeds, compared to the post office's 'snail mail' pace. Yet, much like mail delivered through traditional channels, they may be resented as 'junk mail' if sent to people who have no interest in them. For

Direct-mail marketing
Direct marketing through single mailings that include letters, ads, samples, fold-outs and other 'salespeople on wings' sent to prospects on mailing lists.

this reason, direct marketers must carefully identify their targets to avoid wasting huge sums of money or the recipient's time.

catalogue marketing

Catalogue shopping once started almost as explosively as the Internet, though few of us might remember this. Cataloguers' sales pitch was remarkably similar too – no need to struggle to the store, vast choice, lower prices. Today, the growth in catalogue shopping has slowed but catalogues are increasingly used by store retailers, which see them as an additional medium for cultivating sales. Most consumers enjoy receiving catalogues and will sometimes even pay to get them. Many catalogue marketers are now even selling their catalogues at bookstores and magazine stands. Many business-to-business marketers also rely heavily on catalogues.

Catalogue marketing
Direct marketing through print, video or electronic catalogues that are mailed to select customers, made available in stores or presented online.

Rapid advances in technology, however, along with the move to personalised one-to-one marketing, have resulted in dramatic changes in **catalogue marketing**. With the stampede to the Internet, although printed catalogues remain the primary medium, more and more catalogues are going electronic. Many traditional print or mail-order catalogue firms have added Web-based catalogues to their marketing mixes and a variety of Web-only cataloguers have emerged. For example, Web-based sales account for 10 per cent of the turnover at Quelle, the German mail-order company. Quelle expects half of the group's sales to come via the Net within the next five years. Other mail-order companies such as 3 Suisses and La Redoute in France, and Lands' End anticipate at least 15 per cent of sales to be generated online by 2005.[12]

Along with the benefits, however, Web-based catalogues also present challenges. Whereas a print catalogue is intrusive and creates its own attention, Web catalogues are passive and must be marketed. It is much more difficult to attract new customers with a Web catalogue. And the online cataloguers have to use advertising, linkage and other means to drive traffic to their sites.

telemarketing

Telemarketing
Using the telephone to sell directly to consumers.

Telemarketing uses the telephone to sell directly to consumers. It has become a primary direct marketing tool. Marketers use *outbound* telephone marketing in a proactive way to generate and qualify sales leads, and sell directly to consumers and businesses. Calls may also be for research, testing, database building or appointment making, as a follow-up to a previous contact, or as part of a motivation or customer-care programme.

Marketers use *inbound* freephone numbers to receive orders from customers. These calls are usually made in response to an advertisement in the press, on radio or television, in a door drop or direct mailing, in catalogues or via a mixture of these media. Marketers also use the telephone in a reactive way for inbound calls involving customer enquiries and complaints.

In Europe, telemarketing is more established in the UK and Netherlands than in Germany, which has the toughest telemarketing laws. For example, telemarketing in Germany is impossible because the consent of the prospects or consumers is needed before they can be contacted. If someone buys a shovel from a garden centre in winter, even if they gave their name and telephone number, the centre cannot telephone them in the spring with a special offer on bulbs because that would be illegal. Contrast the situation in Holland, where, for example, before an election, political parties are permitted to ring voters to gain their support.[13]

The recent explosion in unsolicited telephone marketing has annoyed many consumers who object to 'junk phone calls' that pull them away from the dinner table

Web-based catalogues:
most catalogue
companies now present
merchandise and take
orders over the Internet.

SOURCE: 3 Suisses France
(http://www.3suisses.fr)
La Redoute
(http://www.redoute.co.uk)

or clog up their answering machines. Laws or self-regulatory measures have been introduced in different countries in response to complaints from irate customers. At the same time, some consumers may appreciate the genuine and well-presented offers they receive by telephone. When properly designed and targeted, telemarketing provides many benefits, including purchasing convenience and increased product and service information.[14]

direct-response television marketing

Direct-response television marketing (DRTV)
The marketing of products or services via television commercials and programmes which involve a responsive element, typically the use of a freephone number that allows consumers to phone for more information or to place an order for the goods advertised.

Direct-response television marketing (DRTV) takes one of two main forms. The first is *direct-response advertising*. Direct marketers air television spots, 60 or 120 seconds long, that persuasively describe a product or service and give customers a freephone number for ordering. Direct-response television advertising can also be used to build brand awareness, convey brand/product information, generate sales leads and build a customer database.

Television viewers may encounter longer advertising programmes, or 'infomercials', for a single product. An infomercial is a themed TV programme, typically 30 minutes long, during which the features or virtues of a product – say, an exercise machine or multipurpose kitchen device – are discussed by 'experts' before an audience. These are selling programmes which are presented in an entertaining manner to attract the target audience. In Europe, infomercials are broadcast on existing pan-European satellite stations such as NBC Super Channel and Eurosport. The infomercial industry has grown, with companies such as Quantum International and TV Shop airing programmes across countries in Europe.

Direct-response advertising is growing in popularity. Organisations ranging from mail order (e.g. Sounds Direct), leisure (e.g. Scandinavian Seaways) and financial services (e.g. Direct Line, AA Insurance Services) to cars (e.g. Daewoo, Fiat), fast-moving consumer goods (e.g. Britvic, Martini, McVitie's) and government departments (e.g. the British army, US navy) have been using DRTV marketing. DRTV marketing has also been used by charities and fund-raising campaigners to persuade viewers to offer donations or volunteer services. Examples include the 'Live Aid' campaign that captured the imagination of millions of people across the globe, 'Children in Need' and many other international fund-raising events.[15]

Home-shopping channels, another form of direct-response television marketing, are TV programmes or entire channels dedicated to selling goods and services.

In the US, home-shopping channels are very well established. Quality Value Channel (QVC) and the Home Shopping Network (HSN) broadcast 24 hours a day, and almost every day of the year. The programmes offer bargain prices on products ranging from jewellery, lamps, collectible dolls and clothing, to power tools and consumer electronics – usually obtained by the home-shopping channel at close-out prices. The presentation of products is upbeat and a theatrical atmosphere is created, often with the help of celebrity guests, and up-to-date information can be given on product availability, creating further buying excitement. QVC and other US-spawned TV shopping channels are now operating in Europe. These compete with large European electronic home-shopping businesses such as TV Shop. TV Shop operates across Europe, of which Germany is the biggest market. While infomercials account for some 60 per cent of the firm's turnover, its activities are wide ranging. It produces commercial videos and TV programmes, operates TVG, its own Swedish shopping channel, and runs electronic shopping malls as well as other Internet-based sales operations in Europe.

Access to TV shopping channels has been restricted to homes with satellite or cable TV. In Europe, Germany, Sweden and the Netherlands lead in terms of household penetration of cable systems. However, over the next few years, the reach of TV shopping channels will increase as the cable and satellite market grows. TV shopping channel operators believe that countries such as the United Kingdom, France, Spain and Italy, with a lower level of satellite and cable penetration, offer great potential for growth. Web TV boxes are already making inroads into the market, allowing more and more consumers to surf the Internet on their TV screen without the need for a computer.[16]

online marketing and electronic commerce

Online marketing is conducted through interactive online computer systems, which link consumers with sellers electronically. There are two types of online marketing channel: commercial online services and the Internet.

Commercial online services offer online information and marketing services to subscribers who pay a monthly fee. Examples include America Online (AOL), CompuServe, Demon and Prodigy.[17] These online services provide subscribers with information (news, libraries, education, travel, sports, reference), entertainment (fun and games), shopping services, dialogue opportunities (bulletin boards, forums, chat boxes) and e-mail.

After growing rapidly through the mid-1990s, the commercial online services are now being overtaken by the Internet as the primary online marketing channel. In fact, all of the online service firms now offer Internet access as a primary service. The Internet is a vast and burgeoning global web of computer networks. It was created by the US Defense Department during the 1960s, initially to link government labs, contractors and military installations. Today, this huge, public computer network links computer users of all types all around the world. Those who log on to the Internet can obtain or share information on almost any subject and interact with other users.[18]

Internet usage has surged with the recent development of the user-friendly **World Wide Web** access standard and Web browser software such as Netscape Navigator and Microsoft Internet Explorer. Today, even novices can surf the Net and experience fully integrated text, graphics, images and sound. Users can send e-mail, exchange views, shop for products and access news, food recipes, art and business information.

rapid growth of online marketing

The online information and shopping services industry has its roots in the United States. However, in recent years, Internet penetration has been increasing rapidly in countries across western Europe and the more affluent Asian economies. Although still in its infancy, Internet usage and online marketing has been forecast to continue to grow explosively.

Although most of the world's online marketing takes place in the United States and the Internet is still some way from becoming the dominant promotion medium, European marketers are no longer ignoring the technology.[19] In time, the biggest opportunity will be for sales or service delivery across national borders.

> For example, QXL.com, designed to cope with different languages and currencies, offers a string of auction sites across Europe. 27 per cent of the sales of the US Internet bookshop Amazon.com are abroad, frequently to customers who would otherwise be unable to find the book they were looking for. Virgin Radio's online radio station offers a live audio-feed direct to the computers of Internet users, allowing them to hear the material played to them over the Net. The service (www.virgin.co.uk) can be accessed from anywhere in the world.[20]

The explosion of Internet usage heralds the dawning of a new world of *electronic commerce*. **Electronic commerce** is the general term for a buying and selling process that is supported by electronic means. *Electronic markets* are 'market spaces' in which sellers offer their products and services electronically, and buyers search for

Online marketing
A form of direct marketing conducted through interactive online computer services, which provide two-way systems that link consumers with sellers electronically.

Commercial online services
Companies that offer online information, entertainment, shopping and other marketing services to subscribers who pay the company a monthly fee. They make use of their own dedicated networks and operate their own computers which are connected to the Internet, thus offering somewhat better security than the Internet.

World Wide Web (WWW or the Web)
A part of the Internet that uses a standard computer language to allow documents containing text, images, sound and video to be sent across the Internet.

Electronic commerce
A general term for a buying and selling process that is supported by electronic means.

information, identify what they want and place orders using a credit card or other means of electronic payment.

E-commerce can be conducted by both businesses and consumers. At present, the biggest volume of trade by far over the Internet is business-to-business transactions. Consider, for example, the following business-to-business market exchanges:

Electronic Euromarket (www.e-euromarket.com) is a B2B meeting place run by Confirm, a Swedish company that creates online trading platforms. Businesses are allocated a page to display goods and services and to publish their advertisements and newsletters. Products are grouped by code, which enables detailed requests to be sent to all businesses which stock the relevant items.

Antwerpes (www.antwerpes.de) is a Neuer Markt-listed Internet services company that specialises in producing healthcare sites for pharmaceutical firms. It owns DocCheck.com, a password service that grants medical professionals such as Bayer, Henkel, Novartis Pharma and Pfizer in Holland, access to more than 200 sites, avoiding the need to register each one individually.

BuyEnergyHere (www.buyenergyhere.com) is a marketplace where businesses buy energy and energy-related products. This e-market, financed by Norsk Hydro, operates in Norway, Sweden and the UK. Members view the full range of energy contracts, choose the type they want and set a deadline. At close of auction, the buyer is sent the five most competitive bids. The buyer is contacted directly when the supplier is selected and the order completed.[21]

B2B transactions currently account for around 80 per cent of all e-commerce. According to Forrester Research, online B2B trade totalled over $150 billion in 1999; the figure is predicted to grow to over $3 trillion by 2003.

There are also other segments of e-commerce: business-to-consumer (B2C), consumer-to-business (C2B) and consumer-to-consumer (C2C) (see Table 22.2).

B2C entails online retail activities such as bookselling by Amazon or PC selling by Dell. C2B refers to transactions initiated by the consumer: for example, would-be passengers bidding for airline tickets on priceline.com, leaving the airlines to decide whether or not to accept the bid. C2C entails consumers' auctions, such as QXL, Alando.de and eBay, that can aggregate bidders around the world, which gives the market space a huge advantage over traditional offline, local 'flea markets'.[22]

A recent study found that 39 per cent of all Net users have searched for product information online prior to making a purchase. The proportion of Net users who have

Table 22.2

The e-commerce matrix

	BUSINESS	CONSUMER
Business	**B2B** Covisint (Ford, GM, DaimlerChrysler and others) E-euromarket	**B2C** Amazon Dell
Consumer	**C2B** Priceline Accompany	**C2C** QXL eBay

SOURCE: 'A survey of e-commerce. Shopping around the web', © *The Economist Newspaper* Ltd., London (26 February 2000), p. 9.

actually purchased a product or service online varies across countries, but the numbers remain modest. Nonetheless, US e-commerce trends suggest that the Internet will gain around 5 per cent of the retail market, and could be worth some $185 billion by 2004. Analysts are also predicting that other affluent nations in Europe are likely to follow in its wake, with consumer-based e-commerce accounting for 15–20 per cent of retail sales by 2010. While the percentage is forecast to increase in the years ahead, analysts also issue cautionary words to aspiring online business-to-consumer operators. They have to take stock of the lessons to be learnt from the recent upheaval among many 'dotcommers' and the crash in Internet stocks (see Marketing Highlight 22.1).

Early attempts to develop online shopping and electronic shopping malls has also been held back by consumers' concerns about security, fraud and missing or damaged products. But consumer confidence is expected to grow, as improvements in secure payment systems, standards and services are being achieved to make online transactions a mainstay of twenty-first century commerce.[23] Technological change to increase speed and capacity will come in the form of broadband Internet connections to the home. Broadband will proliferate as more and more people acquire cable modems or DSL lines, both of which are much faster than today's dial-up modems, offering much quicker access to the Web. E-commerce will also be boosted by the current growth in mobile telephone usage as well as the emergence of a host of other electronic devices that are ousting the PC as the dominant internet access device (Marketing Highlight 22.2).

In summary, business-to-business Internet commerce is exploding and business buyers are by far the largest Web users. However, despite the teething problems, business-to-consumer e-commerce will grow in significance which will impact on traditional intermediaries and offline retail businesses.[24]

the online consumer

When people think of the typical Internet user, many mistakenly imagine a pasty-faced computer nerd or 'cyberhead'. Others imagine a young, techy, upscale male professional. Although such stereotypes are sadly outdated, the Net population does differ demographically from the general population.

As a whole, the Internet population is still younger, more affluent, better educated and more male than the general population.[25] However, as more and more people find their way on to the Net, the cyberspace population is becoming more mainstream and diverse. Increasingly, the Internet provides online marketers with access to a broad range of demographic segments. For example, 46 per cent of Internet users are women, up from 37 per cent in 1996. Although more than half of all users are professionals or managers, this percentage is decreasing.[26]

Net users come from all age groups. For example, the populations of almost 9 million 'Net kids' and more than 8 million teens (will reach almost 22 million and 17 million, respectively, by the early 2000s) have attracted a host of online marketers. America Online offers a 'Kids Only' area featuring homework help and online magazines along with the usual games, software and chat rooms. The Microsoft Network site carries Disney's Daily Blast, which offers kids games, stories, comic strips with old and new Disney characters and current events tailored to pre-teens. BeingGirl.com is a site for teens, offering information on relationships, boys, periods and much more. Leading girls' entertainment software publishers also joined forces to offer a special website (just4girls.com) that promotes stories, games, dolls and accessories targeted at 8–12-year-old girls.[27]

Although Internet users are younger on average than the population as a whole, seniors aged 55 to 64 make up less than a quarter of today's online households and the number is expected to grow to around 40 per cent by 2003. Whereas younger groups

Dot.bombs: lessons for dot.coms

The Internet is a fast, exciting world. No one can deny that, not least yesterday's dotcom stars. 'Here today, gone tomorrow' seems to best describe the pace of cyber activity and the lifespan of many of Europe's once optimistic Internet start-ups.

At the height of dotcom fever in 1999, hundreds of 'newly-minted' Internet companies had high hopes about taking on the world. Credulous investors, thinking that dot.commers were sure-fire winners, and 'fast-talking 'rock-star' analysts fuelled a frenzy of speculation. Up until April 2000, almost anybody in Europe could raise funds for an Internet venture. But, as fast as it boomed, the Internet bubble burst. The crash in Internet stocks, high-profile collapses and cash-burning, loss-making ventures sent investors fleeing the sector. Boo.com (sportswear), Boxman.com (CDs) and Clickmango.com (healthcare business) are among the high-profile business-to-consumer casualties. Others, such as World Online (Internet service provider) and KB toys' dot.com division, faced disastrous flotations or delayed plans for a public offering in the wake of disinterested financial markets.

Established online retailers, such as Amazon.com, and traditional offline retailers who jumped on the Web bandwagon have also taken their knocks. Toy sites backed by corporate giants such as Walt Disney and Viacom were closed in 1999. In 2000, Toys 'R' Us failed to deliver many presents in time for Christmas. Since then, Amazon and Toys 'R' Us have combined their online toy stores.

Many Internet companies, from e-tailers to online media companies and B2B marketplaces, are now rationalising, merging or going out of business. A more resilient breed of competitors appears to surface. To succeed, there are a number of pointers to take on board, as these competitors begin to re-invent themselves.

✦ *United you stand, divided you fall*. Online fledglings may have attractive growth prospects, but their balance sheets, cost control and meagre pricing power are not appealing to most investors. Substantial consolidation may be necessary to avoid extinction. E-tailers like Boo.com, Amazon and others have discovered that assets such as an established infrastructure for customer service and order fulfilment cost a fortune to build. That has helped established catalogue retailers such as Quelle and Lands' End to exploit the Internet. Either e-tailers adjust their ambitions, or they partner with others with the cash or established track record.

✦ *Convergence is the new religion*. Make the best of the virtual and real worlds. This means tapping the power of integrated channels, which combine stores, Internet catalogues, telephone and television. Real-world retailers are in a stronger position to knit offline and physical worlds together. For example, Wal-Mart has huge buying power with established suppliers that enables it to keep prices low and to compete with pure Web retailers claiming a price advantage. It also has the cash to subsidise a website in its early years. Multi-channel retailing is also driving offline retailers' investments in smaller dotcom businesses. Kingfisher in the UK has taken a stake in ThinkNatural.com, a healthcare products business, which brings to the company technological know-how, knowledge about how consumers shop online and publishing (content and editing) skills. Meanwhile, pure online retailers are moving offline. For example, Alloy.com, which sells clothes and accessories, became a hit only after it launched a print catalogue: the day after the launch, its servers crashed as teenagers flocked to the site.

✦ *Brand loyalty*. Building a brand from nothing overnight is expensive. Here is one area where many Internet companies were parting with money faster than they earned it. Boo.com spent a fortune on public relations to get on magazine covers. According to The Boston Consulting Group, Internet-only companies were spending 80 per cent of online revenue on gaining new customers, more than twice what it costs their multi-channel counterparts. Aspiring dotcommers, beware! Develop realistic business plans. There are no cheap routes to building brand loyalty.

The e-revolution is not over. As the storm calms, the dotcom industry wakes up to a new challenge. This time the battle will be fought and won where real and virtual worlds unite.

Sources: Thorold Barker, 'B2C claims another victim', *Financial Times* (11 October 2000), p. 29; Carlos Grande, 'Crash of dotcom stars recalls "curse of *Hello!*"', *Financial Times*, 30 May 2000), p. 3; James Harding, 'World Online "lost interest" in contract with duchess', *Financial Times* (21 June 2000), p. 1; Carlos Grande, 'Bubble bursts at dotcom but designers stay in the pink', *Financial Times* (3 August 2000), p. 3; Andrew Edgecliffe-Johnson, 'E-revolution shelved', *Financial Times* (3 August 2000), p. 16; Susanna Voyle, 'E-tailers find their perfect partner on the high street', *Financial Times* (7 April 2000), p. 25; 'The real Internet revolution', *The Economist* (21 August 1999), pp. 59–60; 'Europe's dot.bombs', *The Economist* (5 August 2000), p. 20; 'Lies, damned lies and web valuations', in 'The Internet revolution. Special report', *Financial Times* (13 October 2000), p. 16; 'Only the strong survive after the storm', in 'The Internet revolution, Special report', *Financial Times* (16 October 2000), p. 14; 'Wannabes widen the net', in 'The Internet revolution, Special report', *Financial Times* (11 October 2000), p. 15.

marketing highlight 22.2

Getting ready for M-commerce

Just as fixed e-commerce, conducted through Internet access via a PC or interactive television, is taking off, the merging of wireless systems such as mobile phones, palm computers and other portable devices with the Internet is ready to cast the net of *mobile e-commerce* (m-commerce). The idea of being able to gain access to a wealth of information on the Internet, transact business, log on to corporate intranets and do it all instantly, wherever you may be, is compelling.

Already, the race is on to make the technology work. Companies such as Nokia, Ericsson and Motorola have launched Internet-enabled mobile phones based on wireless application protocol (WAP) technology. But WAP technology is not fast enough for surfing the Web and is clumsy because you have to tap buttons on a tiny keypad. However, the data wave has begun in Europe with the launch of GPRS (general packet radio service) in late 2000, which is twice as fast as 56K fixed-line dial-up modems. EDGE (enhanced data rate for GSM evolution) comes in 2001, which is seven times faster than today's dial-up. UMTS (universal mobile telecommunications system), the third generation (3G) mobile, will be in service in Europe and Japan by 2004, and in America by 2006. 3G will bring genuine broadband capacity and is 200 times faster than today's dial-up. Moreover, voice-enabled mobile phones and 'talking websites' are already paving the way for mobile *voice-commerce* (v-commerce). Hundreds of companies have supported the development of VoiceXML (voice extens-

ible mark-up language), a standard voice browser technology. Others, like Lernout and Hauspie, the Belgian speech and language technology company, and Intel, are developing intelligent e-commerce Web servers that people can talk to.

Meanwhile, Nokia, Motorola and Ericsson have joined forces to develop a world m-commerce standard to allow safe credit card payments using mobile phones. It also avoids customer confusion caused by a proliferation of standards which would delay global adoption of mobile-commerce. These companies expect that some 600 million Internet-enabled mobile phones will be sold between 2002 and 2006 and the m-commerce market will be worth between $13 billion and $28 billion in Europe alone by 2002.

Although the cultural base and usage of wireless phones is not as advanced in the US as in Europe, fast-footed American Internet software providers are tapping the huge growth opportunities offered by the wireless Web. For example, Inktomi, the US Internet software group, and Nokia have struck a partnership, whereby Nokia will use Inktomi's software for mobile Internet applications. America OnLine (AOL) Europe has partnered with Nokia and Ericsson to test technology for a wireless portal for mobile-phone users. Microsoft, through MSN, and Yahoo! are also doing the same. Others, such as banks and retailers, also want to roll out their own mobile Internet services.

Despite all this enthusiasm from the supplier side, m-commerce has still a long way to go. Early adopters are somewhat disappointed that, beyond looking up or

EXHIBIT 1 TYPES OF SERVICE SUITED TO FIXED AND MOBILE ECOMMERCE

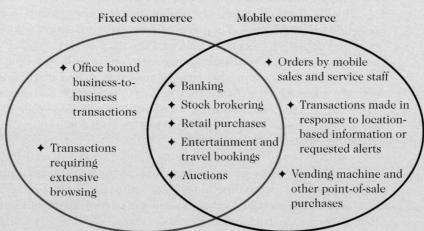

SOURCE: Analysys 2000. Reprinted by permission of Katrina Bond, Analysys.

listening to weather forecasts, checking share prices and e-mails, or finding out which restaurants are nearby, there is not more to do on a WAP-phone. However, companies are investing heavily to increase the range of services available. Advances in technology are also promising to deliver e-commerce to users, at Internet speed, anytime, anywhere.

Analysts, however, suggest that not all services are appropriate for m-commerce (see Exhibit 1). Moreover, mobile firms will find their business model fragmenting as new services come from anybody and are connected to anyone.

The e-revolution isn't over yet. Just as firms begin to embrace the opportunities created by a *wired-up world*, changes are fast engulfing the *wireless* one, posing firms fresh and daunting challenges. The winners will be firms that remain at the centre of the partnership webs and joint ventures that put all the pieces of a service together. But, because everything is happening at Internet velocity, firms will need to move at lightning speed to capture a meaningful size of the value that is ultimately created.

Sources: 'Vodafone-Mannesmann. What next?', *The Economist* (12 February 2000), pp. 88 and 91; Peter Thal Larsen, 'A digital Rosetta stone', *Financial Times* (19 May 2000), p. 21; Carlos Grande, 'Demand low for mobiles linked to internet', *Financial Times* (9 November 2000), p. 2; Lucas van Grinsven, 'Triple alliance seeks fast track for m-commerce', *Financial Times* (12 April 2000), p. 1; Joia Shillingford, 'Plenty more to come for mobile net enthusiasts', FT Telecoms. Financial Times Survey, p. XVII in *Financial Times* (21 June 2000); George Cole, 'Word of mouth spreads the net of m-commerce', *Financial Times* (12 April 2000), p. 15; information obtained at CIM website: www.cim.co.uk, 'Get ready for m-commerce' (January 2000).

are more likely to use the Internet for entertainment and socialising, older Net surfers go online for more serious matters. For example, 24 per cent of 50–64-year-olds use the Net for investment purposes, compared with only 3 per cent of those between 25 and 29. Figure 22.2 shows the main uses of the Internet and the major purchases of online consumers. Interestingly, individuals go on the Internet primarily for using e-mail and search engine sites and browsing.

Internet users also differ psychographically from the general consumer population. Forrester Research and SRI Consulting have developed approaches for measuring attitudes, preferences and behaviour of online service and Internet users. SRI Consulting's website (www.future.sri.com/VALS/survey/html) allows visitors to take their values, attitude and lifestyle (VALS 2) questionnaire and get immediate feedback on their VALS 2 type. The firm has identified ten different psychographic segments ranging from Wizards, skilled users who identify strongly with the Internet, to Socialites, who are strongly oriented towards social aspects of the Internet.[28]

Finally, Internet consumers differ in their approaches to buying and in their responses to marketing. They are empowered consumers who have greater control over the marketing process. People who use the Net place greater value on information and tend to respond negatively to messages aimed only at selling. Whereas traditional marketing targets a somewhat passive audience, online marketing targets people who actively select which websites they will visit and which ad banners they will click on. They decide which marketing information they will receive about which products and services and under what conditions. Thus, in online marketing, the consumer, not the marketer, controls the interaction.

Internet 'search engines', such as Yahoo!, Infoseek and Excite, give consumers access to varied information sources, making them better informed and more discerning shoppers. In fact, online buyers are increasingly creators of product information, not just consumers of it. As greater numbers of consumers join Internet interest groups that share product-related information, 'word-of-Web' is joining 'word-of-mouth' as an important buying influence. Thus, the new world of e-commerce will require new marketing approaches.

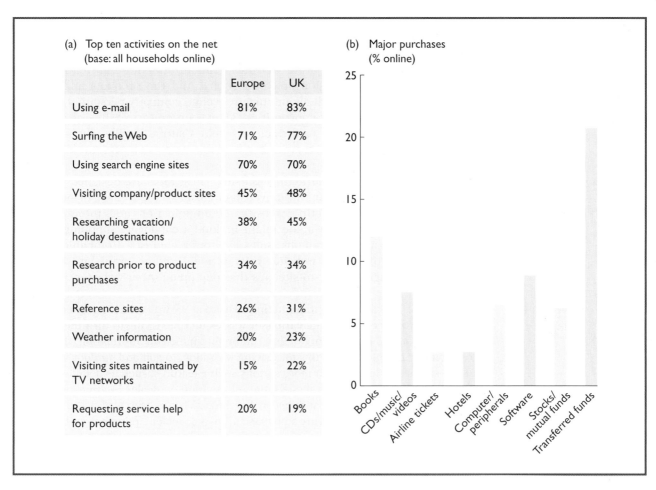

(a) Top ten activities on the net
(base: all households online)

	Europe	UK
Using e-mail	81%	83%
Surfing the Web	71%	77%
Using search engine sites	70%	70%
Visiting company/product sites	45%	48%
Researching vacation/ holiday destinations	38%	45%
Research prior to product purchases	34%	34%
Reference sites	26%	31%
Weather information	20%	23%
Visiting sites maintained by TV networks	15%	22%
Requesting service help for products	20%	19%

(b) Major purchases (% online)

Figure 22.2

Internet activities and major purchases

SOURCE:
www.ebusiness.uk.com

conducting online marketing

Marketers can conduct online marketing in four ways: by creating an electronic storefront; placing ads online; participating in Internet forums, news groups or 'Web communities'; or using online e-mail or Webcasting. Let us take a look at these channels next.

■ Creating an electronic online presence

In opening an electronic storefront, a company has two choices: it can buy space on a commercial online service or it can open its own website. Buying a location on a commercial online service involves either renting storage space on the online service's computer or establishing a link from the company's own computer to the online service's shopping mall. A retailer, for example, can link to AOL or CompuServe, gaining access to the millions of consumers who subscribe to these services. The online services typically design the storefront for the company and introduce it to their subscribers. For these services, the company pays the online service an annual fee plus a small percentage of the company's online sales.

In addition to buying a location on an online service, or as an alternative, thousands of companies have now created their own websites. These sites vary greatly in purpose and content. The most basic type is a **corporate website**. These sites are designed to handle interactive communication *initiated by the consumer*. They seek to build customer goodwill and to supplement other sales channels rather than to sell

Corporate website
A site set up by a company on the Web, which carries information and other features designed to answer customer questions, build customer relationships and generate excitement about the company, rather than to sell the company's products or services directly. The site handles interactive communication initiated by the consumer.

the company's products directly. For example, the corporate websites of IKEA and Nokia typically offer a rich variety of information and other features in an effort to answer customer questions, build closer customer relationships and generate excitement about the company. Corporate websites generally provide information about the company's history, its mission and philosophy, and the products and services that it offers. They might also tell about current events, company personnel, financial performance and employment opportunities. Many corporate websites also provide exciting entertainment features to attract and hold visitors. Finally, the site might also provide opportunities for customers to ask questions or make comments through e-mail before leaving the site.

Marketing website
A site on the Web created by a company to interact with consumers for the purpose of moving them closer to a purchase or other marketing outcome. The site is designed to handle interactive communication initiated by the company.

Other companies create a **marketing website**. These sites are designed to engage consumers in an interaction that will move them closer to a purchase or other marketing outcome. With a marketing website, communication and interaction are *initiated by the marketer*. Such a site might include a catalogue, shopping tips and promotional features such as coupons, sales events or contests. Companies aggressively promote their marketing websites in traditional, offline, print and broadcast advertising, and through 'banner-to-site' ads that pop up on other websites.

For example, Toyota operates a marketing website at www.toyota.com. Once a potential customer clicks in, the carmaker wastes no time trying to turn the enquiry into a sale. The site offers plenty of entertainment and useful information, from cross-country trip guides and tips for driving with kids, to golf and outdoor events. But the site is also loaded with more serious selling features, such as detailed descriptions of current Toyota models and information on dealer locations and services, complete with maps and dealer Web links. Visitors who want to go further can use the Shop@Toyota feature to choose a Toyota, select equipment and price it, then contact a dealer and apply for credit. Or they fill out an online order form for brochures and a free interactive CD-ROM that shows off the features of Toyota models. The chances are good that before the CD-ROM arrives, a local dealer will call to invite the prospect in for a test drive.[29]

Business-to-business marketers also make good use of marketing websites. For example, corporate buyers can visit Sun Microsystems' website (www.sun.com), select detailed descriptions of Sun's products and solutions, request sales and service information and interact with staff members. Customers visiting FedEx's website (www.fedex.com) can schedule their own shipments, request a courier and track their packages in transit.

Creating a website is one thing; getting people to *visit* the site is another. The key is to create enough value and excitement to get consumers to come to the site, stick around and come back again. This means that companies must create sites that are easy to read and navigate as well as constantly update their sites to keep them fresh and exciting. Doing so involves time and expense, but the expense is necessary if the online marketer wishes to cut through the increasing online clutter. In addition, many online marketers believe that they cannot build a brand simply on the Internet, but have to spend heavily on good old-fashioned advertising and other offline marketing avenues to attract visitors to their sites. At the same time, one study reported that 37 per cent of online purchases were through referred websites and 13 per cent through e-mail marketing, compared to only 6 per cent being inspired by offline advertisements. These results imply that marketers need to create a core of Net users who can spread the word about the company or its brands through the Internet itself.[30]

For some types of product, attracting visitors is easy. Consumers buying new cars, computers or financial services will be open to information and marketing initiatives from sellers. Marketers of lower-involvement products, however, may face a difficult

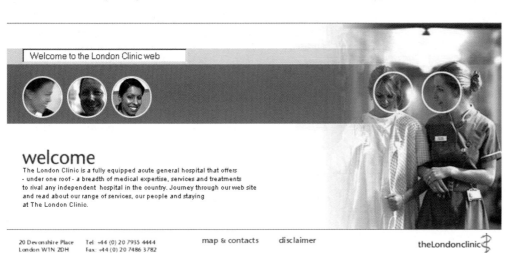

| Services | About your Stay | Recruitment | Consultants | News | General Guide | Site Index |

Welcome to the London Clinic web

welcome

The London Clinic is a fully equipped acute general hospital that offers
- under one roof - a breadth of medical expertise, services and treatments
to rival any independent hospital in the country. Journey through our web site
and read about our range of services, our people and staying
at The London Clinic.

20 Devonshire Place   Tel: +44 (0) 20 7935 4444   map & contacts   disclaimer   theLondonclinic
London W1N 2DH   Fax: +44 (0) 20 7486 3782

Companies launching websites recognise that they have to promote their Internet presence: here the London Clinic turns its 'virtual press centre' into a goldmine of information for target audiences, from harried reporters to prospective employees.

SOURCE: The London Clinic (http://www.thelondonclinic.co.uk)

challenge in attracting website visitors. As one veteran notes: 'If you're shopping for a computer and you see a banner that says, 'We've ranked the top 12 computers to purchase', you're going to click on the banner. [But] what kind of banner could encourage any consumer to visit dentalfloss.com?'[31] For such low-interest products, the company should create a corporate website to answer customer questions and build goodwill, using it only to supplement selling efforts through other marketing channels.

Next, let us take a look at how advertisements are placed online.

■ Placing advertisements online

There are a growing number of ways to advertise online. **Online ads** appear while Internet users are surfing online services or websites. Such ads include *banner* ads, pop-up windows, 'tickers' (banners that move across the screen) and 'roadblocks' (full-screen ads that users must pass through to get to other screens they wish to view). Other forms of online advertising appear as *permanent buttons* which are smaller than banners, are an enduring feature of a site and, typically, sit close to a relevant site. For example, the online broker E*Trade can put its button next to a share tip on a financial site. Banners and most buttons are not interactive, taking viewers away from the website if they click on them. Banners and buttons account for some 60 per cent of all online advertisements. Although their use is widespread, they are least likely to yield a response, compared to buttons whose response rates can reach 15 per cent (see Figure 22.3).

Interstitials are ads that pop up on their own screen, like 'roadblocks', in between content pages, but viewers usually cannot click on them. They offer audiovisual features, but are losing popularity because they take as long as two minutes to download, annoying users. *Superstitials* are new interstitials that allow the content to be downloaded in the browser's short-term memory to avoid interrupting the user. Recently, banners have been given a new lease of life on the Web by rich-media technology. Using technology such as Java, Shockwave, Flash and Enliven, *rich-media expanding banners* allow online advertisers to deliver multimedia presentations, which viewers can click on without leaving the original site. The banners take live website information to viewers, enabling them to shop, register for information and interact, without leaving the original site. However, they are prone to crashing the website. Next time you click on a moving icon that sings, swims, parachutes and bungee-jumps

Online advertising
Placing advertisements on the Internet in special sections offered by commercial online services, as banner ads that pop up while computer subscribers are surfing online services or websites, or in Internet news groups that have been set up for commercial purposes.

Figure 22.3

Online advertising: techniques for attracting visitors

Source: 'Netymology', © The Economist Newspaper Ltd., London, 9 October 1999.

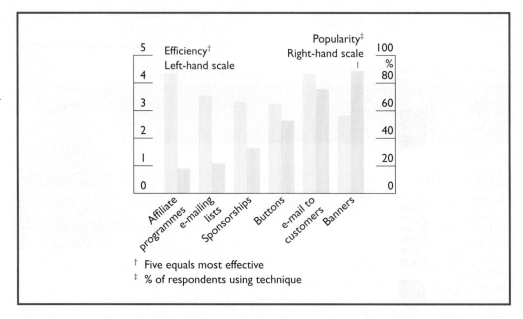

around your computer screen, beware – such banners have been deliberately designed to crash websites for fun, and all because the advertiser wants to grab your 'eyeball' attention.

Affiliate deals are gaining in popularity. Essentially these deals split the advertiser's revenues with the site in exchange for free advertising. Or the site providing the link gets a payment for each click-through or a commission on each sale. Companies can also use sponsorships or co-branded deals involving an up-front payment, irrespective of a sale, to buy advertising slots in cyberspace. For example, Procter & Gamble joined forces with Yahoo! to market Pringles crisps, Pepto-Bismol medicine and Pampers nappies. Or, in return for registering with CBS.Sportsline.com, users have the chance to win a signed Reebok shoe belonging to basketball star Shaquille O'Neal.

Web advertising is on the increase. According to Forrester Research, online ad spending is forecast to rise from $3.3 billion in 1999 to $33 billion by 2004, about 8 per cent of all advertising. This represents only a tiny fraction of overall advertising media expenditures. Many marketers still question its value as an effective advertising tool. Costs are reasonable compared with those of other advertising media. For example, Netscape, the popular Web-browser site, charges about $360,000 per year and delivers an estimated 1 million impressions. Still, Web surfers can easily ignore these banner ads, and often do. Moreover, the industry has yet to develop good measures of advertising impact – of who clicks on Web ads and how the ads affect them. Thus, although many firms are experimenting with Web advertising, it still plays only a minor role in their promotion mixes. Nonetheless, to make the best use of the Internet as a communications tool, marketers and advertisers alike have to devise ways to harness fully the Internet's interactivity and potential for ultra-precise targeting – two of its most potent qualities.[32]

■ Participating in forums, newsgroups and Web communities

Companies may decide to participate in or sponsor Internet forums, newsgroups and bulletin boards that appeal to specific special interest groups. Such activities may be

Banner ads: while booking a holiday on lastminute.com, site visitors are exposed to ads from hotels, restaurants, credit card companies and others. However, such ads are easily overlooked.

SOURCE: Lastminute.com (http://www.lastminute.com)

organised for commercial or non-commercial purposes. *Forums*, discussion groups located on commercial online services, may operate a library, a 'chat room' for real-time message exchanges and even a classified ad directory. For example, America Online boasts some 14,000 chat rooms, which account for a third of its members' online time. It also provides 'buddy lists', which alert members when friends are online, allowing them to exchange instant messages.[33] Most forums are sponsored by interest groups. Thus, a major musical instruments manufacturer such as Yamaha might start a forum on classical music.

Newsgroups are the Internet version of forums. Unlike commercial forums, newsgroups are made up of groups of people posting and reading messages on a specified topic of interest to them, rather than managing libraries or conferencing. Internet users can participate in newsgroups without subscribing. There are thousands of newsgroups dealing with every imaginable topic, from healthy eating, home repairs and caring for your Bonsai tree to collecting antique cars or exchanging views on the latest soap opera happenings.

Bulletin board systems (BBSs) are specialised online services that centre on a specific topic or group. These deal with a wide range of topics, such as holidays, health and computer games. Marketers might want to identify and participate in newsgroups and BBSs that attract subscribers who fit their target markets. However, newsgroups and BBS users often resent commercial intrusions on their Net space, so the marketer must tread carefully, participating in subtle ways that provide real value to participants.

The popularity of forums and newsgroups has resulted in a rash of commercially sponsored websites called *Web communities*. Such sites allow members to congregate online and exchange views on issues of common interest. They are 'the cyberspace equivalent to the bar, where everybody knows your e-mail address'. For example, iVillage is a Web community in which 'smart, compassionate real women' can obtain information and exchange views on families, fitness, relationships, travel, finances or just about any other topic. The site reaches 7.3 million unique visitors per month, greater than the combined monthly average paid circulation of *Cosmopolitan, Glamour, Vogue* and *Marie Claire* magazines. Tripod is an online hangout for twenty-somethings, offering chat rooms and free home pages for posting curriculum vitae.

Visitors to these Net neighbourhoods or *cyberhoods* develop a strong sense of community. Such communities are attractive to advertisers because they draw consumers with common interests and well-defined demographics. Moreover, cyberhood consumers visit frequently and stay online longer, increasing the chance of meaningful exposure to the advertiser's message.

■ Using e-mail and Webcasting

A company can encourage prospects and customers to send questions, suggestions and complaints to the company via e-mail. Customer service representatives can quickly respond to such messages. The company may also develop Internet-based electronic mailing lists of customers or prospects. Such lists provide an excellent opportunity to introduce the company and its offerings to new customers and to build ongoing relationships with current ones. Using the lists, online marketers can send out customer newsletters, special product or promotion offers based on customer purchasing histories, reminders of service requirements or warranty renewals or announcements of special events. E-mailing is one of the cheapest and most effective means of bringing an offer or product information direct to customers, with response rates of between 5 and 10 per cent.

Webcasting (push programming)
Process whereby the online marketer sends advertisements or information over the Internet directly to the desktops of target customers. Companies can also sign on with Webcasting service providers, which automatically download customised information to the personal computers of subscribers to their services.

Companies can also sign on with any of a number of **Webcasting** services, such as Pointcast and Ifusion, which automatically download customised information to recipients' PCs. For a monthly fee, subscribers to these services can specify the channels they want – news, company information, entertainment and others – and the topics they're interested in. Then, rather than spending hours scouring the Internet, they can sit back while the Webcaster automatically delivers information of interest to their desktops.

Webcasting, also known as 'push' programming, affords an attractive channel through which online marketers can deliver their Internet advertising or other information content. The major commercial online services are also offering Webcasting to their members. For example, AOL offers a feature called Driveway that fetches information, Web pages and e-mail based on members' preferences and automatically deliver it to their PCs.

However, as with other types of online marketing, companies must be careful that they do not cross the fine line between adding value and exploiting relationships with customers by intrusive e-mails, which can cause resentment among Internet users who are already overloaded with 'junk e-mail'. Netiquette, the unwritten rules that guide Internet etiquette, suggests that marketers should ask customers for permission to e-mail marketing pitches – and tell recipients how to opt-out if they prefer not to receive any e-mail promotions at any time.

■ The promise and challenges of online marketing

Online marketing offers great promise for the future. Its most ardent apostles envision a time when the Internet and electronic commerce will replace magazines, newspapers and even stores as sources for information and buying. Yet despite all the hype and promise, online marketing may be years away from realising its full potential. And even then, it is unlikely to fulfil such sweeping predictions. To be sure, online marketing will become a full and complete business model for some companies: Internet businesses such as Amazon, eBay, Yahoo! and Netscape; and direct marketing companies such as Dell Computer. But, for most companies, online marketing will remain just one important approach to the marketplace that works alongside other approaches in a fully integrated marketing mix.

Although novel and exhilarating, online marketing has yet to carve out a central role in consumers' lives. For many online marketers, including Internet superstars such as Amazon.com, the Web is still not a money-making proposition – according to one report, less than half of today's websites are profitable.[34] Here are just some of the challenges that online marketers face:

- *Limited consumer exposure and buying.* Although expanding rapidly, online marketing still reaches only a limited market-space. Moreover, many Web users do more window browsing than actual buying. One source estimates that although 65 per cent of current Internet users have used the Web to check out products and compare prices before a purchase decision, only 14 per cent of Internet users have actually purchased anything online. Still fewer used their credit cards.[35]

- *Skewed user demographics and psychographics.* Online users tend to be more upscale and technically oriented than the general population. This makes online marketing ideal for marketing computer hardware and software, consumer electronics, financial services and certain other classes of product. However, it makes online marketing less effective for selling mainstream products.

- *Chaos and clutter.* The Internet offers up millions of websites and a staggering volume of information. Thus, navigating the Internet can be frustrating, confusing and time consuming for consumers. In this chaotic and cluttered environment, many Web ads and sites go unnoticed or unopened. Irrelevant and distracting advertisements are also seen as a nuisance. Even when they are noticed, marketers will find it difficult to hold consumer attention. One study found that a site must capture Web surfers' attention within eight seconds or lose them to another site. That leaves very little time for marketers to promote and sell their goods. By contrast, TV commercials and infomercials offer a narrative that the Internet cannot, and the marketer is able to control the pace and sequence of the advertisement.

- *Security.* Consumers worry that unscrupulous snoopers will eavesdrop on their online transactions or intercept their credit card numbers and make unauthorised purchases. In turn, companies doing business online fear that others will use the Internet to invade their computer systems for the purposes of commercial espionage or even sabotage. Online marketers are developing solutions to such security problems. However, there appears to be a 'never-ending competition between the technology of Internet security systems and the sophistication of those seeking to break them'.[36]

- *Ethical concerns.* Privacy is a primary concern. Marketers can easily track website visitors, and many consumers who participate in website activities provide extensive personal information. This may leave consumers open to information abuse if companies make unauthorised use of the information in marketing their products or exchanging electronic lists with other companies. There are also concerns about segmentation and discrimination. The Internet currently serves upscale consumers well. However, poorer consumers have less access to the Net, leaving them increasingly less informed about products, services and prices.[37]

Despite these challenges, companies large and small are quickly integrating online marketing into their marketing mixes. As it continues to grow, online marketing will prove to be a powerful tool for building customer relationships, improving sales, communicating company and product information, and delivering products and services more efficiently and effectively.

integrated direct marketing

Too often, a company's individual direct marketing efforts are not well integrated with one another or with other elements of its marketing and promotion mixes. For example, a firm's media advertising may be handled by the advertising department working with a traditional advertising agency. Meanwhile, its direct mail and catalogue business activities may be handled by direct marketing specialists while its website is developed and operated by an outside Internet firm. Within a given direct marketing campaign, too many companies use a 'one-shot' approach to reach and sell a prospect or a single vehicle in multiple stages to trigger purchases. For example, a magazine publisher might send a series of four direct-mail notices to a household to get a subscriber to renew before giving up. A more powerful approach is **integrated direct marketing**, which involves using multiple-vehicle, multiple-stage campaigns to improve response. Whereas a direct-mail piece alone might generate a 2 per cent response, adding a website and freephone number can raise the response rate by 50 per cent. A well-designed outbound telemarketing effort might lift response by another 500 per cent. Suddenly a 2 per cent response has grown to 15 per cent or more by adding interactive marketing channels to a regular mailing.

Integrated direct marketing
Direct marketing campaigns that use multiple vehicles and multiple stages to improve response rates and profits.

More elaborate integrated direct-marketing campaigns can be used. Consider the following multimedia, multistage marketing campaign:

Paid ad with a response channel → Direct mail → Outbound telemarketing → Face-to-face sales call

Here, the paid ad to target customers creates product awareness and stimulates enquiries. The company immediately sends direct mail to those who enquire. Within a few days, the company follows up with a phone call seeking an order. Some prospects will order by phone or via the firm's website; others might request a face-to-face sales call. In such a campaign, the marketer seeks to improve response rates and profits by adding media and stages that contribute more to additional sales than to additional costs.

public policy and ethical issues in direct marketing

Direct marketers and their customers usually enjoy mutually rewarding relationships. Occasionally, however, a darker side emerges. The aggressive and sometimes shady tactics of a few direct marketers can bother or harm consumers, giving the entire industry a black eye. Abuses range from simple excesses that irritate consumers to instances of unfair practices or even outright deception and fraud. During the past few years, the direct marketing industry has also faced growing concerns about invasion of privacy.[38]

irritation, unfairness, deception and fraud

Direct marketing excesses sometimes annoy or offend consumers. Most of us dislike direct-response TV commercials that are too loud, too long and too insistent. Especially bothersome are dinner-time or late-night phone calls. Beyond irritating consumers, some direct marketers have been accused of taking unfair advantage of impulsive or less sophisticated buyers. TV shopping shows and programme-long 'infomercials' seem to be the worst culprits. They feature smooth-talking hosts, elaborately staged demonstrations, claims of drastic price reductions, 'while they last' time limitations, and unequalled ease of purchase to inflame buyers who have low sales resistance.

Worse yet, 'heat merchants' design mailings and write copy intended to mislead buyers. Other direct marketers pretend to be conducting research surveys when they are actually asking leading questions to screen or persuade consumers. Fraudulent schemes, such as investment scams or phoney collections for charity, have also multiplied in recent years. Crooked direct marketers can be hard to catch: direct marketing customers often respond quickly, do not interact personally with the seller, and usually expect to wait for delivery. By the time buyers realise that they have been duped, the thieves are usually somewhere else, plotting new schemes.

invasion of privacy

Invasion of privacy is perhaps the toughest public policy issue now confronting the direct marketing industry. These days, it seems that almost every time consumers order products by mail or telephone, enter a sweepstake, apply for a credit card or take out a magazine subscription, their names are entered into some company's already bulging database. Using sophisticated computer technologies, direct marketers can use these databases to 'microtarget' their selling efforts.

Consumers benefit from such database marketing if they receive more offers that are closely matched to their interests. However, many critics worry that marketers may know *too* much about consumers' lives, and that they may use this knowledge to take unfair advantage of consumers. At some point, they claim, the extensive use of databases intrudes on consumer privacy.

For example, they ask, should telecom network operators be allowed to sell marketers the names of customers who frequently call the free (e.g. 0800) numbers of, say, catalogue companies? Is it right for credit bureaux to compile and sell lists of people who have recently applied for credit cards – people who are considered prime direct-marketing targets because of their spending behaviour?

In their drives to build databases, companies sometimes get carried away. For example, Microsoft caused substantial privacy concerns when it introduced its Windows 95 software. It used a 'Registration Wizard' which allowed users to register their new software online. However, when users went online to register, without their knowledge, Microsoft took the opportunity to 'read' the configurations of their PCs. Thus, the company gained instant knowledge of the major software products running on each customer's system. When users learned of this invasion, they protested publicly. The enraged outcry led Microsoft to abandon such snooping. However, such actions have spawned a quiet but determined 'privacy revolt' among consumers and public policy makers.[39]

The direct marketing industry in a number of countries is addressing issues of ethics and public policy. For example, in the United Kingdom, faced with the threat of legislation, including wider EU directives, the industry has adopted stringent self-regulation measures to restrain unsavoury practices and to bring the 'cowboys' into line. Similarly, in the case of the Internet, there is rising user concern about malpractice, ranging from the flood of unsolicited 'junk cybermail' to intrusion of privacy. So, while

marketing highlight 22.3

The wild, wild, Web: music piracy

How far can Internet entrepreneurs push the law in developing new business models? For the moment, neither politicians nor the legal experts have the answer. But many fear that, without regulation of some sort, the Web is fast becoming a land where anyone, anywhere can do or say anything! Yet, while some cry out to the law for protection, others have found alternative solutions for dealing with so-called Web offenders. The recent legal tussles between the Recording Industry Association of America (RIAA) and online upstarts like MP3.com and Napster, the music world's most wanted Web outlaws, are a case in point.

MP3.com has been attacked for creating a database of over 80,000 CDs which enables registered users to listen to their CD collection on the Net (My.MP3.com). MP3 is a compression technology which allows songs to be downloaded from the Internet in a few minutes instead of a few hours. MP3.com argues that it has not violated copyright laws. Registered users can only listen to a CD they own – by placing it in their computer's CD-ROM drive – before they can listen from other locations to a digital copy of the music made by MP3.com. Napster is a digital music exchange service which allows users to swap music online. Its server contains a list of digital songs that registered Napster users have stored on their hard disks. A user searching for a song goes to the Napster website and types in the title. Napster connects the searcher's PC to its server. From there, it sends the searcher directly to a user who has stored the song on his or her hard disk. Napster claims that what it does is not illegal: it does not store or copy music data on its own computers. Neither does it control or supervise materials transmitted between users. Both argue that online music swapping or exchange, with suitable safeguards, will stimulate music listening, benefiting consumers and the recording industry in the long run.

The Big Five record companies – EMI, Universal Music, Warner, Sony and BMG – are not amused. They desperately want to protect their intellectual property and tried-and-tested, albeit outdated, distribution channels. Joining forces, and with the RIAA representing them, they have deluged MP3.com with lawsuits, charging the company with enabling Internet piracy. Rather than seeking its closure, or imposing punitive financial damages, however, all except Universal have accepted out-of-court settlements. MP3 paid $20 million in damages to each company and agreed to reform its service. In exchange, the record labels would make their catalogue available to the company. Universal opted to seek $120 million in damages.

In the case of Napster, supporters say that the company has merely invented a tool which customers use for non-commercial purposes. Current copyright law does not cover this situation. Copyright, therefore, needs a radical rethink. In any case, the RIAA detected some 4,500 free music download websites carrying copyright songs in the first half of 2000 alone. How far can the RIAA take their legal wrangling with so many bandits out there? A victory over Napster is pyrrhic given the scale of the activity. Even if the RIAA wins the case, music-downloading sites would go underground. Some sites such as Gnutella and Freenet have the technology to make swaps virtually anonymous, hence untraceable.

There is an alternative solution that record companies might contemplate. If you can't beat them, join them. This is precisely what the German Bertelsmann Music Group (BMG), in a strategic alliance with Napster, has done. BMG struck a strategic alliance with the renegade online music service in November 2000. The idea is to develop a 'file-sharing' or 'peer-to-peer' model together under which consumers would pay a subscription every month to use a legitimate version of the Napster system. Although the other four rival music companies were initially sceptical and attacked the Napster–Bertelsmann deal, most concede that the time has come to review their options. The big players agree that, after all, technology and partnership, not the law, will prove better in defeating music piracy on the wild, wild, Web.

Sources: Patti Waldmeir, 'MP3.com shares fall 42% on music copyright ruling', *Financial Times* (29–30 April 2000), p. 1; 'Technology may prove better than the law in defeating music piracy', *Financial Times* (1 May 2000), p. 6; Thomas Clark and Helen Laube, 'Going for a song', *Connectis* (October 2000), pp. 34–8; Chris Parkes, 'Peer-to-peer pressure', *FT Creative Business* (7 November 2000), pp. 4–5; James Harding and Christopher Grimes, 'A musical outlaw plays it straight', *Financial Times* (2 November 2000), p. 29; James Harding and Christopher Grimes, 'Bertelsmann–Napster deal attacked', *Financial Times* (2 November 2000), p. 1; and 'Napster nabbed', *Financial Times* (2 November 2000), p. 28.

the Internet offers vast potential as a multimedia, global communication channel to marketers, firms should seek to police themselves, operating within acceptable codes of practice. The recent cases of MP3 and Napster, both of which have been accused of enabling music piracy over the Web, are unusual and extreme examples showing just how far individuals or organisations can push the law (see Marketing Highlight 22.3). In these cases, corporations, not consumers, claim they have been wronged.

Direct marketers know that, left untended, unethical conduct will lead to increasingly negative consumer attitudes, lower response rates, and calls for more restrictive legislation. More importantly, most direct marketers want the same things that consumers want: honest and well-designed marketing offers targeted only towards consumers who will appreciate and respond to them. Direct marketing is just too expensive to waste on consumers who don't want it.

Mass marketers have typically tried to reach millions of buyers with a single product and a standard message communicated via the mass media. Consequently, most mass-marketing communications were one-way communications directed *at* consumers rather than two-way communications *with* consumers. Today, many companies are turning to direct marketing in an effort to reach carefully targeted customers more efficiently and to build stronger, more personal, one-to-one relationships with them.

summary

We discussed the benefits of direct marketing to customers and companies, and the trends fuelling its rapid growth. Customers benefit from direct marketing in many ways. For consumers, home shopping is fun, convenient, saves time and gives them a bigger selection of merchandise. It allows them to compare shop offers using mail catalogues and online shopping services, then to order products and services without dealing with salespeople. Sellers also benefit. Direct marketers can buy mailing lists containing names of nearly any target group, customise offers to special wants and needs, and then use individualised communications to promote these offers. Direct marketers can also build a continuous relationship with each customer; time offers to reach prospects at the right moment, thereby receiving higher readership and response; and easily test alternative media and messages. Finally, direct marketers gain privacy because their offer and strategy are less visible to competitors.

Various trends have led to the rapid growth of direct marketing. Market 'demassification' has produced an increasing number of market niches with specific preferences. Direct marketing enables sellers to focus efficiently on these mini-markets with offers that better match particular consumer wants and needs. Other trends encouraging at-home shopping include higher costs of driving, traffic congestion, parking headaches, lack of time, a shortage of retail sales help and long lines at checkouts. Consumers like the convenience of direct marketers' freephone numbers, their acceptance of orders round the clock and their commitment to customer service. The growth of quick delivery via express carriers has also made direct shopping fast and easy. The increased affordability of computers and customer databases has allowed direct marketers to single out the best prospects for each of their products. Finally in business-to-business marketing, lower cost-per-contact media have proven more cost-effective in reaching and selling to more prospects and customers than using a sales force.

We also looked at the ways companies use databases in direct marketing. A *customer database* is an organised collection of comprehensive data about individual customers or prospects, including geographic, demographic, psychographic and behavioural data. Companies use databases to identify prospects, form relationships with target customers and deepen customer loyalty, decide which customers should receive a particular offer and reactivate customer purchases.

Next we addressed the main forms of direct marketing, including *face-to-face selling*, *direct-mail marketing*, *catalogue marketing*, *telemarketing*, *direct-response television marketing* and *online marketing*. Most companies today continue to rely heavily on *face-to-face selling* through a professional sales force, or they hire manufactures' representatives and agents. *Direct-mail marketing* consists of the company sending an offer, announcement, reminder or other item to a person at a specific address. Recently, three new forms of mail delivery have become popular – *fax mail*, *e-mail* and *voice mail*. Some marketers rely on *catalogue marketing*, or selling through catalogues mailed to a select list of customers or made available in stores. *Telemarketing* consists of using the telephone to sell directly to consumers. *Direct-response television marketing* has two forms: (1) *direct-response advertising* or *infomericials* and (2) *home-shopping channels*. *Online marketing* involves online channels and electronic commerce, and is usually conducted through interactive online computer systems, which electronically link consumers with sellers.

We examined the two types of online marketing channel – *commercial online services* and the *Internet* – and explained the effect of the Internet on electronic commerce. *Commercial online services* provide online information and marketing services to subscribers for a monthly fee. The *Internet* is a vast global and public web of computer networks. In contrast to commercial online services, use of the Internet is free. The explosion of Internet usage has created a new world of *electronic commerce*, a term that refers to the buying and selling process that is supported by electronic means. In this process, *electronic markets* become 'marketspaces' in which sellers offer products and services electronically, while cyberbuyers search for information, identify their wants and needs, and then place orders using a credit card or other form of electronic payment.

The growth in online marketing can be appreciated when we examine the benefits of Internet technology. For consumers, online marketing is beneficial because it is *interactive* and *immediate*, and provides access to an abundance of comparative *information* about products, companies and competitors. Marketers also benefit from online marketing. For them, it helps *consumer relationship building*, *reduces costs*, *increases efficiency*, provides more *flexibility*, and is, in the form of the Internet, a *global* medium that enables buyers and sellers in different countries to interact with each other in seconds. Marketers can conduct online marketing by creating an electronic storefront, placing ads online, participating in Internet forums, newsgroups or Web communities, or using online e-mail or Webcasting.

Finally, direct marketers have to address a variety of public policy and ethical issues. Direct marketers and their customers have typically forged mutually rewarding relationships. However, there remains a potential for customer abuse, ranging from irritation and unfair practices to deception and fraud. There also have been growing concerns about invasion of privacy, perhaps the most difficult public policy issue currently facing the direct marketing industry.

discussing the issues

1. The chapter suggests that a new direct-marketing model has been created. Answer the following questions: (a) What is direct marketing? (b) How is it different from other forms of marketing delivery? (c) How will the new direct-marketing model impact on the emerging electronic marketplace?

2. Make a list of products or services that you have purchased via direct marketing channels. What were the factors that influenced your decision to buy direct? If these products or services could also be purchased from a reseller or retail outlet, would the buying experience be different? How?

3. Identify some organisations that have used direct-response television advertising to promote their offering. What types of response are typically sought by the advertisers? What are some of the key issues concerning response handling that users of DRTV must consider to ensure an effective outcome for the campaign?

4. Companies that know about individual customer needs and characteristics can customise their offers, messages, delivery modes and payment methods to maximise customer value and satisfaction. Select an organisation that operates within each of the following sectors: (a) home insurance, (b) computers, (c) charity, (d) automotive, and (e) personal finance. What information should these organisations keep in their customer databases? Where would they get this information? How might they use the databases? How much would it cost to build such databases?

5. In the past year there has been a dramatic increase in the number of Web communities (commercially sponsored websites). If you were (a) Adidas, (b) Nokia, (c) British Airways or (d) Fuji, what type of Web communities would you be interested in sponsoring? What would be the possible advantages and disadvantages of doing this? Find a Web community and evaluate its site. Discuss your conclusions.

applying the concepts

1. Online marketing can bring benefits to customers that other channels cannot. A good example is online music stores, where customers can listen to clips of selected tracks before buying a CD. Other online benefits are ease of communication with customers and adaptability to marketplace changes. Visit CDNow (www.cdnow.com) and look up three CDs of your choosing. For each CD, record below the total number of tracks on that CD and the number of tracks that CDNow will let you sample.

   ✦ Does CDNow offer other benefits that you might not find at a traditional retail music store? If so, what are they?

   ✦ If you were to purchase a CD, how could CDNow use the information from your visit to develop a one-to-one relationship with you?

   ✦ How could traditional music stores offer some of the same benefits as CDNow? Would it be cost-effective for them to do so?

   ✦ Do you think CDNow should open a traditional store in addition to its online store? Why or why not?

2. Watch a satellite or cable television shopping channel or tune into a television shopping show. Where feasible, you might surf the Internet and 'tour' a specialist retailer's site. Or you might sample Virgin's radio station by clicking on icons, accessing features such as playlists and DJ biographies.

   ✦ How are the TV shows attempting to reach target buyers? Do they mix product lines (e.g. fine china with sports equipment) or do they target more carefully?

   ✦ How do online communications attempt to reach target buyers?

   ✦ What are the main differences in the way the TV shopping channels and Internet retailers attempt to evoke a response from target consumers?

references

1. Quotes from Gary McWilliams, 'Whirlwind on the Web', *Business Week* (7 April 1997), pp. 132–6; Bill Robbins and Cathie Hargett, 'Dell Internet sales top $1 million a day', press release, Dell Computer Corporation (4 March 1997). See also Tom Foremski, 'Hard act to follow', in Financial Times Survey. E-Business: ERP and beyond, *FT-IT Review Series* (19 July 2000), p. V; 'Didn't Delliver', *The Economist* (20 February 1999), pp. 82–3; 'Dell PC sales via Internet doubling', Reuters Ltd (18 June 1997); 'Michael Dell's plan for the rest of the decade', *Fortune* (9 June 1997), p. 138; Andrew E. Serwer, 'The hottest stock of the '90s', *Fortune* (8 September 1997), p. 16.

2. Gary Hamel and Jeff Sampler, 'The E-Corporation: More than just web-based, it's building a new industrial order', *Fortune* (7 December 1998), pp. 80–92.

3. Alan Mitchell, 'Internet zoo spawns new business models', *Marketing Week* (21 January 1999), pp. 24–5.

4. Emma Charlton, 'Business-to-business online exchanges. A case of first come, first served', FT-IT Review, Manufacturing in the Internet age, *Financial Times* (1 November 2000), p. II; Andrew Baxter, 'Internet heralds new era of collaboration', FT-IT Review, Manufacturing in the Internet age, *Financial Times* (1 November 2000), p. V; additional information on B2B exchanges accessed at www.ft.com/ftit.

5. 'Hi ho, hi ho, down the data mine we go', *The Economist* (23 August 1997), pp. 55–6.

6. Figures given by The Gartner Group and reported *in FT Telecommunications Survey, Financial Times* (21 June 2000), p. X.

7. Zenith Media, 'Satellite watch', *Marketing Week* (5 April 1996), p. 16; John Shannon, 'Building brands on the Internet', *Marketing Week* (3 May 1996), p. 22; see also Kim Benjamin, 'Internet technologies grow in Europe', *e.business* (February 2000), pp. 18–19; statistics provided by Forrester Research.

8. Figures given by *The Economist World in Figures 2000*. Also reported by York Membery, 'World Netheads', *The Business FT Weekend Magazine* (29 April 2000), p. 45; James Champy, 'The cyber-future is now', *Sales and Marketing Management* (September 1997), p. 28.

9. See Don Peppers and Martha Rogers, *The One-to-One Future* (New York: Doubleday/Currency, 1993).

10. Tom Peters, *Thriving on Chaos* (New York: Knopf, 1987).

11. Tony Coad, 'Distinguishing marks', *Marketing Business* (October 1992), pp. 12–14.

12. Constance Legrand, 'A marriage made in cyber-heaven', *Connectis* (October 2000), pp. 40–1.

13. A. Burnside, 'Calling the shots', *Marketing* (25 January 1990), p. 40; Anne Massey, 'Ring my bell', *Marketing Business* (June 1992), pp. 35–9; Kevin R. Hopkins, 'Dialing into the future', *Business Week* (28 July 1997), p. 90.

14. See Martin Everett, 'Selling by telephone', *Sales and Marketing Management* (December 1993), pp. 75–9; John F. Yarbrough, 'Dialing for dollars', *Sales and Marketing Management* (January 1997), pp. 61–7.

15. See Martin Croft, 'Right to reply', *Marketing Week* (12 April 1996), pp. 37–42; Paul Gander, 'Tele vision', *Marketing Week* (23 August 1996), pp. 29–34; David Reed, 'Double vision', *Marketing Week* (17 April 1997), pp. 59–62.

16. See Frank Rose, 'The end of TV as we know it', *Fortune* (23 December 1996), pp. 58–68; Elizabeth Lesly and Robert D. Hof, 'Is digital convergence for real?', *Business Week* (23 June 1997), pp. 42–3; Torin Douglas, 'A case of sofa not so good', *Marketing Week* (30 September 1994), p. 17; David Short, 'QVC loses out in UK screen test', *The European* (9–15 September 1994), p. 21; Miroslav Cerovic, 'Sofa so good for home shopping', *Marketing Week* (16 August 1996), p. 24; Hale Richards, 'Europe turns on to TV shopping', *The European* (2–8 January 1997), p. 19.

17. See Michael H. Martin, 'What's online: how to get on the Net without AOL', *Fortune* (14 April 1997), p. 174; Catherine Arnst and Peter Elstrom, 'CompuServe: too little, too late?', *Business Week* (19 May 1997), p. 118G.

18. For more on the basics of using the Internet, see Raymond D. Frost and Judy Strauss, *The Internet: A new marketing tool – 2000* (Upper Saddle River, NJ: Prentice Hall, 2000).

19. Richenda Wilson, 'Security alarm', *Marketing Week* (26 January 1996), pp. 49–53; Amy Cortese, 'Census in cyberspace', *Business Week* (5 May 1997), p. 84. For the most recent statistics, check the results of an ongoing survey of Internet usage conducted by CommerceNet and Nielsen Media Research, www.commerce.net/nielsen/. See also Edith Coron, 'Le web: Jospin orders the French to log on', *The European* (26 January–1 February 1998), p. 22.

20. 'Virgin starts Europe's first live on-line radio', *Marketing Week* (15 March 1996), p. 15.

21. See Liz Bassett, 'e-business websites', *Connectis* (October 2000), p. 25.

22. 'Define and sell', in A survey of e-commerce, p. 9, *The Economist* (26 February 2000).

23. 'The once and future mall', *The Economist* (1 November 1997), pp. 92, 97; 'Startling increase' in Internet shopping reported in *New CommerceNet/ Nielsen Media Research Survey*, CommerceNet press release, www.commerce.net/nielsen/press-97.html (12 March 1997).

24. Information provided by Forrester Research, August 1999; also, see Laura Cohn, 'B2B: The hottest net bet yet', *Business Week* (17 January 2000), pp. 36–7.

25. Amy Cortese, 'A census in cyberspace', op. cit., p. 84; James Champy, 'The cyber-future is now', *Sales and Marketing Management* (September 1997), p. 28.

26. 'Females lead online growth spurt', CommerceNet and Nielsen Media Research (17 June 1999), accessed online at www.cyberatlas.com.

27. Richard Tomkins, 'Long arm of commerce touches the newsroom', *Financial Times* (16 October 2000), p. 18; B.G. Yovovich, 'Girls in cyberspace', *Marketing News* (8 December 1997), pp. 8, 12; Paul M. Eng, 'Cybergiants see the future and it's Jack and Jill', *Business Week* (14 April 1997), p. 44.

28. See Rebecca Piirto Heath, 'The frontiers of psychographics', *American Demographics* (July 1996), pp. 38–43; and the SRI Consulting website (www.Future.sri.com), June 1999.

29. See Kathy Rebello, 'Making money on the Net', *Business Week* (23 September 1996), pp. 104–18; Melanie Berger, 'It's your move', *Sales & Marketing Management* (March 1998), pp. 45–53.

30. Robert McLuhan, 'Target marketing', *e.business* (June 2000), pp. 34–8.

31. John Deighton, 'The future of interactive marketing', *Harvard Business Review* (November–December 1996), pp. 151–62.

32. 'Advertising that clicks', *The Economist* (9 October 1999), pp. 101–2 and 105.

33. Robert D. Hof, 'Internet communities', *Business Week* (5 May 1997), pp. 64–80.

34. Heather Green, 'Cyberspace winners; how they did it', *Business Week* (22 June 1998), pp. 154–60; Michael D. Donahue, 'Adapting the internet to the needs of business', *Advertising Age* (2 February 1998), p. 26; Shikhar Ghosh, 'Making business sense of the Internet', *Harvard Business Review* (March–April 1998), pp. 126–35; Lisa Bransten, 'E-commerce (A special report) – A new model – the bottom line: if they built it, will profits come?', *Wall Street Journal* (12 July 1999), p. R8.

35. 'eCommerce: consumers and shopping online', accessed at www.emarketer.com/estats/ec shop.html (September 1999).

36. John Deighton, op cit., p. 158. See also Richenda Wilson, 'Security alarm', op. cit.

37. See Edward C. Braig, Marcia Stepanek and Neil Gross, 'Privacy: the internet wants your personal information. What's in it for you?', *Business Week* (5 April 1999), pp. 84–90; Ira Teinowitz, 'Internet privacy concerns addressed', *Advertising Age* (16 June 1997), p. 6, and 'Net privacy debate spurs self-regulation', *Advertising Age* (9 June 1997), p. 36.

38. Parts of this section are based on Terrence H. Witkowski, 'Self-regulation will suppress direct marketing's downside', *Marketing News* (24 April 1989), p. 4. See also Katie Muldoon, 'The industry must rebuild its image', *Direct* (April 1995), p. 106.

39. 'Hi ho, hi ho, down the data mine we go', op. cit.; John Hagel III and Jeffrey F. Rayport, 'The coming battle for customer information', *Harvard Business Review* (January–February 1997), pp. 53–65.

case 22

Cool Diamonds: are they forever?

The company

After meeting his British wife, Michel Einhorn moved from Antwerp to London where he has been working as a diamond dealer in London's famous Hatton Garden for 14 years. Three hundred members of his family also currently work in the diamond business based in Belgium. Besides his in-depth knowledge about diamonds, Michel is also mad about computers. In his spare time, he designs and builds robots. Recently, with everybody talking about the Internet, Michel figured that it must be easier to set up shop online than building a robot. Together with partner Chris O'Farrell, they formed Cool Diamonds. It took three months to design and set up the website, using market research to refine it.

E-diamonds: luxury that won't cost the earth

Diamonds are the ultimate symbol of love, with each stone unique, valued for its rarity, lasting qualities and the ability to dazzle as it reflects the light. Diamond jewellery makes a breathtaking gift. But they're not just a girl's best friend. Today, young trendies – from Britney Spears and Mel C to David Beckham and Denise Van Outen – are flashing their belly-button studs and ear studs.

The Internet is changing the face of diamond purchasing. By harnessing the latest digital technology, cooldiamonds.com gives customers a realistic view of a piece of diamond jewellery. 'Virtual reality' enables a quality diamond ring to be rotated before the visitor, just as if the ring was being displayed right in front of their eyes. According to Michel, 'With just one click of the mouse, you can drag the piece from the left and to the right as it rotates before your eyes – the only thing you cannot do is touch it!' However, it is also possible for the potential customer to make an appointment to visit the Hatton Garden offices if a personal viewing is preferred.

On cooldiamonds.com, visitors can also choose from a variety of rings, earrings, necklaces and body jewellery, such as belly studs. Importantly, Cool Diamonds takes the mystique out of diamond buying. The interactive website offers detailed guidelines to help the novice buyer to choose the size, grade, design and budget of a piece of jewellery. So, customers can specify the stone according to the 4 Cs: cut (shape), clarity (from flawless to severely blemished), colour (from white to dirty yellow) and carat (size). There is a fifth C – cost. If they click on 'more expensive', it will go up first by size. If it is too expensive, they can change the clarity or the colour. They can select a piece of diamond jewellery 'off-the-peg' or have Cool Diamonds create a bespoke piece just for them.

Cool Diamonds now offers a stunning choice of designer labels, including Lisando, Jo Lagoon, Alisa, Galio (winner of the award for innovation), Liz Taylor (winner of the best design at the UK jewellery awards) and MJD. Prices range from £90 to half a million. With some 72,000 different variations, ranging from the classic to the cool, young and trendy, it gives the customer a choice that no traditional offline jeweller can match. If Michel does not have a particular stone, he acquires one from his father or any of the 300 family members in the trade. The company supports the condemnation by the London Diamond Bourse and Club (LDBC), one of 23 diamond Bourses worldwide, of the 'conflict diamond' trade. The latter has profiteered on the back of violence and human suffering in the war-torn diamond-producing countries of Sierra Leone and Congo. As such, the company's purchasing policy is restricted to diamonds from only the most respected source, diamond conglomerate De Beers.

However, choice is not the only benefit that Cool Diamonds offers customers. Traditionally, diamond jewellery is sold from prestigious premises in the high street and carries a huge mark-up. Prices paid typically reflect the cost of centrally located outlets, massive stocks and the long chain of middlemen (dealers, cutters, jewellery manufacturers) involved in the trade (also called the diamond pipeline). While the cut and polished diamond jewellery may seem like 'timeless beauty' to the lucky owner, and worth the huge mark-up, rough diamonds are a commodity, whereby a stone of any given weight, colour, clarity and cut has a wholesale price. This is the same in Antwerp, London, New York or Tokyo. Sadly, diamonds purchased from a high-street jeweller depreciate like a stone! A £10,000 pair of diamond earrings on sale in a local high-street store will be worth approximately half to one-third this amount the moment the buyer walks out of the shop. By selling direct to buyers, Cool Diamonds has no expensive overheads, such as prestigious retail premises, to maintain. Moreover, the stock does not need to be duplicated as it is kept in one central location. As such, it can offer the public better value – about 40 per cent of high-street prices. These prices are close to wholesale value, making the diamond not only affordable, but also a great investment as the shrewd buyer can avoid the usual depreciation suffered.

Then, there is the convenience of buying online – customers have the opportunity to buy something unique without even having to walk out of their front door. The site also features special sale items and advice about diamonds. Customers can pay with a credit card over the Internet, which is simple and secure, or they can make a purchase by telephoning Cool Diamonds direct. All diamonds are certified by a De Beers guarantee and purchases have a 10-day money back guarantee if customers change their mind.

Consumers no longer dazzled by the Internet

According to Cool Diamonds, people are becoming more familiar with the Internet and increasingly relaxed about buying online. Engagement rings are among the most popular purchases, but body jewellery is also becoming desirable. A measure of the improved confidence in the Internet is found in the following trends observed by Cool Diamonds:

◆ Six months ago, 85 per cent of Cool Diamonds' customers collected the goods in person, to reassure themselves of the quality of the merchandise. Today, this has fallen to 45 per cent.

◆ Average purchase has risen from £500 to £2,700, with purchases of £5,000 an almost weekly occurrence.

◆ Of the 460,000 hits a month, a large percentage of these are women who are buying their own jewellery rather than waiting for their nearest-and-dearest to buy them something.

◆ The most popular purchase is a diamond ring. The most valuable to date has been a £17,000 two-carat solitaire diamond ring, closely followed by a classy diamond navel stud, which, in one month, attracted more sales than earrings and pendants put together.

Cool Diamonds: are they forever?

'Diamonds are forever', so the saying goes. But now, buying them won't burn a hole in your pocket, thanks to Cool Diamonds. However, the competition is hotting up with more manufacturers, wholesalers, retailers and even mining companies (e.g. Rex Mines) beginning to sell diamond jewellery online. A growing number of US companies are already selling loose diamonds at discount prices. These include mondera.com, diasource.com, diamonds4u.com and nydex.com. Diamondring.com, which claims to be 'the diamonds portal', has links to many similar sites. In the UK, which

accounts for nearly 98 per cent of Cool Diamonds' sales, competitors are popping up all over the Web. Simon Lewis, a Hatton Garden diamond jewellery manufacturer, sells stones direct to the public through thediamondshop.co.uk. Others straddling the middle range of the market, such as Beaverbrooks, Jewellery WebShop, Sovereign Diamonds and Gordon Stoker, are all offering a lot more carat for buyers' money on the Internet. At the top end of the market are companies such as VanPeterson.com which specialises in luxury diamond and platinum jewellery costing thousands. Not all of the competitors match Cool Diamonds' staggering choice and chic selection. Nor do all have interactive sites that navigate as smoothly and speedily as Cool Diamonds or give buyers instant quotes. Moreover, Cool Diamonds benefited from the positive endorsement given by the UK's Consumer Association in its *Which?* magazine, which reported on the findings of their recent survey of Web traders. Cool Diamonds have restricted their advertising spend, relying mainly on word-of-mouth (or word-of-Web) recommendations and PR which generates news stories in the national press (e.g. *Financial Times*, *Daily Express*), as well as features in glossy magazines like *Vogue*, *Tatler* and *Cosmopolitan*, to communicate their 'sparkle' to the public.

Cool Diamonds is opening an office in France in a bid to replicate the success it has had in the UK. It is moving steadily and cautiously, though. The founding partners believe that there are lessons to be learnt from the rapid decline of pan-European e-tailer Boo.com – mismanagement as well as trying to expand too quickly without taking time to build local teams. Should their expansion prove successful, Cool Diamonds will plan for a full European rollout. Meanwhile, as business booms, Michel Einhorn has to determine how best to proceed to ensure Cool Diamonds, like their stones, will be there forever.

Cool Diamonds

SOURCE: Molly McKellar Public Relations, London.

Questions

1. How do customers and Cool Diamonds each benefit from online marketing?

2. Identify the factors that influence the success of Cool Diamonds' online marketing approach to date.

3. What problems do you see with its strategy?

4. What marketing recommendations would you make to Cool Diamonds, taking into account ways in which Cool Diamonds can get more people to visit and buy expensive diamond jewellery through its site?

5. What are the major challenges facing Cool Diamonds in the future?

6. Recommend a strategy for Cool Diamonds. Explain how it will enable the company to sustain a differential advantage in an increasingly competitive market.

SOURCES: Based on company data provided by Cool Diamonds; materials supplied by Molly McKellar Public Relations, London; see also Simon London, 'Don't let diamonds get you down', *Financial Times* (31 May 2000), p. 18; John-Paul Flintoff, 'Diamond geezers', *Weekend FT* (18 August 2000), pp. 18–22; David Andrews, 'A discount on screen gems', *Daily Express* (14 June 2000), p. 19; Sarah Williams, 'Diamonds are forever', *Internet Investor* (October 2000), pp. 76–7.

internet exercises

Internet exercises for this chapter can be found on the student site of the MYPHLIP Web Site at www.booksites.net/kotler.

glossary

Accessibility The degree to which a market segment can be reached and served.

Actionability The degree to which effective programmes can be designed for attracting and serving a given market segment.

Actual product A product's parts, quality level, features, design, brand name, packaging and other attributes that combine to deliver core product benefits.

Adapted marketing mix An international marketing strategy for adjusting the marketing-mix elements to each international target market, bearing more costs but hoping for a larger market share and return.

Administered VMS A vertical marketing system that coordinates successive stages of production and distribution, not through common ownership or contractual ties, but through the size and power of one of the parties.

Adoption The decision by an individual to become a regular user of the product.

Adoption process The mental process through which an individual passes from first hearing about an innovation to final adoption.

Advertising Any paid form of non-personal presentation and promotion of ideas, goods or services by an identified sponsor.

Advertising objective A specific communication task to be accomplished with a specific target audience during a specific period of time.

Advertising specialities Useful articles imprinted with an advertiser's name, given as gifts to consumers.

Affordable method Setting the promotion budget at the level management thinks the company can afford.

Agent A wholesaler who represents buyers or sellers on a relatively permanent basis, performs only a few functions, and does not take title to goods.

Allowance (1) Reduction in price on damaged goods. (2) Promotional money paid by manufacturers to retailers in return for an agreement to feature the manufacturer's product in some way.

Alternative evaluation The stage of the buyer decision process in which the consumer uses information to evaluate alternative brands in the choice set.

Annual plan A short-term plan that describes the company's current situation, its objectives, the strategy, action programme and budgets for the year ahead, and controls.

Approach The step in the selling process in which the salesperson meets and greets the buyer to get the relationship off to a good start.

Aspirational group A group to which an individual wishes to belong.

Atmospheres Designed environments that create or reinforce the buyer's leanings towards consumption of a product.

Attitude A person's consistently favourable or unfavourable evaluations, feelings and tendencies towards an object or idea.

Augmented product Additional consumer services and benefits built around the core and actual products.

Available market The set of consumers who have interest, income and access to a particular product or service.

Balance sheet A financial statement that shows assets, liabilities and net worth of a company at a given time.

Basing-point pricing A geographic pricing strategy in which the seller designates some city as a basing point and charges all customers the freight cost from that city to the customer location, regardless of the city from which the goods are actually shipped.

Behavioural segmentation Dividing a market into groups based on consumer knowledge, attitude, use or response to a product.

Belief A descriptive thought that a person holds about something.

Benchmarking The process of comparing the company's products and processes to those of competitors or leading firms in other industries to find ways to improve quality and performance.

Benefit segmentation Dividing the market into groups according to the different benefits that consumers seek from the product.

Brand A name, term, sign, symbol or design, or a combination of these, intended to identify the goods or services of one seller or group of sellers and to differentiate them from those of competitors.

Brand equity The value of a brand, based on the extent to which it has high brand loyalty, name awareness, perceived quality, strong brand associations, and other assets such as patents, trademarks and channel relationships.

Brand extension Using a successful brand name to launch a new or modified product in a new category.

Brand image The set of beliefs that consumers hold about a particular brand.

Break-even pricing (target profit pricing) Setting price to break even on the costs of making and marketing a product; or setting price to make a target profit.

Broker A wholesaler who does not take title to goods and whose function is to bring buyers and sellers together and assist in negotiation.

Business analysis A review of the sales, costs and profit projections for a new product to find out whether these factors satisfy the company's objectives.

Business buying process The decision-making process by which business buyers establish the need for purchased products and services, and identify, evaluate and choose among alternative brands and suppliers.

Business market All the organisations that buy goods and services to use in the production of other products and services, or for the purpose of reselling or renting them to others at a profit.

Business portfolio The collection of businesses and products that make up the company.

Business promotion Sales promotion designed to generate business leads, stimulate purchase, reward business customers and motivate the salesforce.

Buyer The person who makes an actual purchase.

Buyer-readiness stages The stages that consumers normally pass through on their way to purchase, including awareness, knowledge, liking, preference, conviction and purchase.

Buying centre All the individuals and units that participate in the business buying-decision process.

By-product pricing Setting a price for by-products in order to make the main product's price more competitive.

By-products Items produced as a result of the main factory process, such as waste and reject items.

Capital items Industrial goods that partly enter the finished product, including installations and accessory equipment.

Captive-product pricing Setting a price for products that must be used along with a main product, such as blades for a razor and film for a camera.

Cash cows Low-growth, high-share businesses or products; established and successful units that generate cash that the company uses to pay its bills and support other business units that need investment.

Cash discount A price reduction to buyers who pay their bills promptly.

Cash refund offers (rebates) Offers to refund part of the purchase price of a product to consumers who send a 'proof of purchase' to the manufacturer.

Catalogue marketing Direct marketing through print, video or electronic catalogues that are mailed to select customers, made available in stores or presented online.

Category killers A modern 'breed' of exceptionally aggressive 'off-price' retailers that offer branded merchandise in clearly defined product categories at heavily discounted prices.

Causal research Marketing research to test hypotheses about cause-and-effect relationships.

Channel conflict Disagreement among marketing channel members on goals and roles – who should do what and for what rewards.

Channel level A layer of intermediaries that performs some work in bringing the product and its ownership closer to the final buyer.

Closed-end questions Questions that include all the possible answers and allow subjects to make choices among them.

Closing The step in the selling process in which the salesperson asks the customer for an order.

Co-brand The practice of using the established brand names of two different companies on the same product.

Cognitive dissonance Buyer discomfort caused by postpurchase conflict.

Collective buying An increasing number of customers agree to buy as prices are lowered to the final bargain price.

Commercial online services Companies that offer online information, entertainment, shopping and other marketing services to subscribers who pay the company a monthly fee. They make use of their own dedicated networks and operate their own computers which are connected to the Internet, thus offering somewhat better security than the Internet.

Commercialisation Introducing a new product into the market.

Communication adaptation A global communication strategy of fully adapting advertising messages to local markets.

Company and individual brand strategy A branding approach that focuses on the company name and individual brand name.

Comparison advertising (knocking copy) Advertising that compares one brand directly or indirectly to one or more other brands.

Competitive advantage An advantage over competitors gained by offering consumers greater value, either through lower prices or by providing more benefits that justify higher prices.

Competitive strategies Strategies that strongly position the company against competitors and that give the company the strongest possible strategic advantage.

Competitive-parity method Setting the promotion budget to match competitors' outlays.

Competitor analysis The process of identifying key competitors; assessing their objectives, strategies, strengths and weaknesses, and reaction patterns; and selecting which competitors to attack or avoid.

Competitor-centred company A company whose moves are mainly based on competitors' actions and reactions; it spends most of its time tracking competitors' moves and market shares and trying to find strategies to counter them.

Competitor intelligence Information gathered that informs on what the competition is doing or is about to do.

Complex buying behaviour Consumer buying behaviour in situations characterised by high consumer involvement in a purchase and significant perceived differences among brands.

Concentrated marketing A market-coverage strategy in which a firm goes after a large share of one or a few submarkets.

Concept testing Testing new product concepts with a group of target consumers to find out if the concepts have strong consumer appeal.

Confused positioning A positioning error that leaves consumers with a confused image of the company, its product or a brand.

Consumer buying behaviour The buying behaviour of final consumers – individuals and households who buy goods and services for personal consumption.

Consumer market All the individuals and households who buy or acquire goods and services for personal consumption.

Consumer-oriented marketing A principle of enlightened marketing which holds that a company should view and organise its marketing activities from the consumers' point of view.

Consumer product A product bought by final consumers for personal consumption.

Consumer promotion Sales promotion designed to stimulate consumer purchasing, including samples, coupons, rebates, prices-off, premiums, patronage rewards, displays, and contests and sweepstakes.

Consumer relationship-building promotions Sales promotions that promote the product's positioning and include a selling message along with the deal.

Consumerism An organised movement of citizens and government agencies to improve the rights and power of buyers in relation to sellers.

Contests, sweepstakes and games Promotions that offer customers the chance to win something – cash, goods or trips – by luck or extra effort.

Continuity Scheduling ads evenly within a given period.

Contract manufacturing A joint venture in which a company contracts with manufacturers in a foreign market to produce the product.

Contractual VMS A vertical marketing system in which independent firms at different levels of production and distribution join together through contracts to obtain more economies or sales impact than they could achieve alone.

Convenience product A consumer product that the customer usually buys frequently, immediately, and with a minimum of comparison and buying effort.

Convenience store A small store located near a residential area that is open long hours seven days a week and carries a limited line of high-turnover convenience goods.

Conventional distribution channel A channel consisting of one or more independent producers, wholesalers and retailers, each a separate business seeking to maximise its own profits even at the expense of profits for the system as a whole.

Copy testing Measuring the communication effect of an advertisement before or after it is printed or broadcast.

Core product The problem-solving services or core benefits that consumers are really buying when they obtain a product.

Core strategy The identification of a group of customers for whom the firm has a differential advantage, and then positioning itself in that market.

Corporate brand licensing A form of licensing whereby a firm rents a corporate trademark or logo made famous in one product or service category and uses it in a related category.

Corporate brand strategy A brand strategy whereby the firm makes its company name the dominant brand identity across all of its products.

Corporate VMS A vertical marketing system that combines successive stages of production and distribution under single ownership – channel leadership is established through common ownership.

Corporate website A site set up by a company on the Web, which carries information and other features designed to answer customer questions, build customer relationships and generate excitement about the company, rather than to sell the company's products or services directly. The site handles interactive communication initiated by the consumer.

Cost-plus pricing Adding a standard mark-up to the cost of the product.

Countertrade International trade involving the direct or indirect exchange of goods for other goods instead of cash.

Forms include barter compensation (buyback) and counterpurchase.

Coupons Certificates that give buyers a saving when they purchase a product.

Critical success factors The strengths and weaknesses that most critically affect an organisation's success. These are measured relative to competition.

Cultural environment Institutions and other forces that affect society's basic values, perceptions, preferences and behaviours.

Culture The set of basic values, perceptions, wants and behaviours learned by a member of society from family and other important institutions.

Current marketing situation The section of a marketing plan that describes the target market and the company's position in it.

Customer-centred company A company that focuses on customer developments in designing its marketing strategies and on delivering superior value to its target customers.

Customer database An organised collection of comprehensive data about individual customers or prospects, including geographic, demographic, psychographic and buying behaviour data.

Customer delivered value The difference between total customer value and total customer cost of a marketing offer – 'profit' to the customer.

Customer lifetime value The amount by which revenues from a given customer over time will exceed the company's costs of attracting, selling and servicing that customer.

Customer Relationship Management (CRM) systems IT-based applications that integrate a company's information about customers with the knowledge of how to use that information.

Customer sales force structure A sales force organisation under which salespeople specialise in selling only to certain customers or industries.

Customer satisfaction The extent to which a product's perceived performance matches a buyer's expectations. If the product's performance falls short of expectations, the buyer is dissatisfied. If performance matches or exceeds expectations, the buyer is satisfied or delighted.

Customer value The consumer's assessment of the product's overall capacity to satisfy his or her needs.

Customer value analysis Analysis conducted to determine what benefits target customers value and how they rate the relative value of various competitors' offers.

Customer value delivery system The system made up of the value chains of the company and its suppliers, distributors and ultimately customers, who work together to deliver value to customers.

Cycle The medium-term wavelike movement of sales resulting from changes in general economic and competitive activity.

Decider The person who ultimately makes a buying decision or any part of it – whether to buy, what to buy, how to buy, or where to buy.

Deciders People in the organisation's buying centre who have formal or informal powers to select or approve the final suppliers.

Decision-and-reward systems Formal and informal operating procedures that guide planning, targeting, compensation and other activities.

Decision-making unit (DMU) All the individuals who participate in, and influence, the consumer buying-decision process.

Decline stage The product life-cycle stage at which a product's sales decline.

Deficient products Products that have neither immediate appeal nor long-term benefits.

Demands Human wants that are backed by buying power.

Demarketing Marketing to reduce demand temporarily or permanently – the aim is not to destroy demand, but only to reduce or shift it.

Demographic segmentation Dividing the market into groups based on demographic variables such as age, sex, family size, family life cycle, income, occupation, education, religion, race and nationality.

Demography The study of human populations in terms of size, density, location, age, sex, race, occupation and other statistics.

Department store A retail organisation that carries a wide variety of product lines – typically clothing, home furnishings and household goods; each line is operated as a separate department managed by specialist buyers or merchandisers.

Derived demand Business demand that ultimately comes from (derives from) the demand for consumer goods.

Descriptive research Marketing research to better describe marketing problems, situations or markets, such as the market potential for a product or the demographics and attitudes of consumers.

Desirable products Products that give both high immediate satisfaction and high long-run benefits.

Differentiated marketing A market-coverage strategy in which a firm decides to target several market segments and designs separate offers for each.

Direct investment Entering a foreign market by developing foreign-based assembly or manufacturing facilities.

Direct-mail marketing Direct marketing through single mailings that include letters, ads, samples, fold-outs and other 'salespeople on wings' sent to prospects on mailing lists.

Direct marketing Marketing through various advertising media that interact directly with consumers, generally calling for the consumer to make a direct response.

Direct-marketing channel A marketing channel that has no intermediary levels.

Direct-response television marketing (DRTV) The marketing of products or services via television commercials and programmes which involve a responsive element, typically the use of a freephone number that allows consumers to phone for more information or to place an order for the goods advertised.

Discount A straight reduction in price on purchases during a stated period of time.

Discount store A retail institution that sells standard merchandise at lower prices by accepting lower margins and selling at higher volume.

Disintermediation The elimination of a layer of intermediaries from a marketing channel or the displacement of traditional resellers by radically new types of intermediaries.

Dissonance-reducing buying behaviour Consumer buying behaviour in situations characterised by high involvement but few perceived differences among brands.

Distribution centre A large, highly automated warehouse designed to receive goods from various plants and suppliers, take orders, fill them efficiently, and deliver goods to customers as quickly as possible.

Distribution channel (marketing channel) A set of interdependent organisations involved in the process of making a product or service available for use or consumption by the consumer or industrial user.

Dogs Low-growth, low-share businesses and products that may generate enough cash to maintain themselves, but do not promise to be large sources of cash.

Durable product A consumer product that is usually used over an extended period of time and that normally survives many uses.

Dutch auctions Prices start high and are lowered successively until someone buys.

Economic environment Factors that affect consumer buying power and spending patterns.

Electronic commerce A general term for a buying and selling process that is supported by electronic means.

Electronic Data Interchange (EDI) Custom-built systems that link the computer systems of major buyers to their suppliers to enable them to coordinate their activities more closely.

Embargo A ban on the import of a certain product.

Emotional appeals Message appeals that attempt to stir up negative or positive emotions that will motivate purchase; examples are fear, guilt, shame, love, humour, pride and joy appeals.

Emotional selling proposition (ESP) A non-functional attribute that has unique associations for consumers.

Engel's laws Differences noted over a century ago by Ernst Engel in how people shift their spending across food, housing, transportation, health care, and other goods and services categories as family income rises.

English auctions Price is raised successively until only one bidder remains.

Enlightened marketing A marketing philosophy holding that a company's marketing should support the best long-run performance of the marketing system; its five principles are consumer-oriented marketing, innovative marketing, value marketing, sense-of-mission marketing and societal marketing.

Environmental management perspective A management perspective in which the firm takes aggressive actions to affect the publics and forces in its marketing environment rather than simply watching it and reacting to it.

Environmental sustainability A third environmentalism wave in which companies seek to produce profits for the company while sustaining the environment.

Environmentalism An organised movement of concerned citizens and government agencies to protect and improve people's living environment.

Ethnic segmentation Offering products or marketing approaches that recognise the special strengths or needs of an ethnic community.

Events Occurrences staged to communicate messages to target audiences; examples are news conferences and grand openings.

Exchange The act of obtaining a desired object from someone by offering something in return.

Exchange controls Government limits on the amount of its country's foreign exchange with other countries and on its exchange rate against other currencies.

Exclusive distribution Giving a limited number of dealers the exclusive right to distribute the company's products in their territories.

Experience curve (learning curve) The drop in the average per-unit production cost that comes with accumulated production experience.

Experimental research The gathering of primary data by selecting matched groups of subjects, giving them different treatments, controlling related factors and checking for differences in group responses.

Exploratory research Marketing research to gather preliminary information that will help to better define problems and suggest hypotheses.

Export department A form of international marketing organisation that comprises a sales manager and a few assistants whose job is to organise the shipping out of the company's goods to foreign markets.

External audit A detailed examination of the markets, competition, business and economic environment in which the organisation operates.

Externalities Activities or facilities that are external to an organisation but affect its performance.

Factory outlet Off-price retailing operation that is owned and operated by a manufacturer and that normally carries the manufacturer's surplus, discontinued or irregular goods.

Fads Fashions that enter quickly, are adopted with great zeal, peak early and decline very fast.

Family life cycle The stages through which families might pass as they mature over time.

Fashion A current accepted or popular style in a given field.

Financial intermediaries Banks, credit companies, insurance companies and other businesses that help finance transactions or insure against the risks associated with the buying and selling of goods.

First-price sealed-bid pricing Potential buyers submit sealed bids, and the item is awarded to the buyer who offers the best price.

Fixed costs Costs that do not vary with production or sales level.

FOB-origin pricing A geographic pricing strategy in which goods are placed free on board a carrier; the customer pays the freight from the factory to the destination.

Focus group A small sample of typical consumers under the direction of a group leader who elicits their reaction to a stimulus such as an ad or product concept.

Follow-up The last step in the selling process, in which the salesperson follows up after the sale to ensure customer satisfaction and repeat business.

Forecasting The art of estimating future demand by anticipating what buyers are likely to do under a given set of conditions.

Fragmented industry An industry characterised by many opportunities to create competitive advantages, but each advantage is small.

Franchise A contractual association between a manufacturer, wholesaler or service organisation (a franchiser) and independent businesspeople (franchisees) who buy the right to own and operate one or more units in the franchise system.

Freight-absorption pricing A geographic pricing strategy in which the company absorbs all or part of the actual freight charges in order to get the business.

Frequency The number of times the average person in the target market is exposed to an advertising message during a given period.

Full-service retailers Retailers that provide a full range of services to shoppers.

Functional discount (trade discount) A price reduction offered by the seller to trade channel members that perform certain functions, such as selling, storing and record keeping.

Gatekeepers People in the organisation's buying centre who control the flow of information to others.

Gender segmentation Dividing a market into different groups based on sex.

General need description The stage in the business buying process in which the company describes the general characteristics and quantity of a needed item.

Geodemographics The study of the relationship between geographical location and demographics.

Geographic segmentation Dividing a market into different geographical units such as nations, states, regions, counties, cities or neighbourhoods.

Geographical pricing Pricing based on where customers are located.

Global firm A firm that, by operating in more than one country, gains R&D, production, marketing and financial advantages that are not available to purely domestic competitors.

Global industry An industry in which the strategic positions of competitors in given geographic or national markets are affected by their overall global positions.

Global marketing Marketing that is concerned with integrating or standardising marketing actions across different geographic markets.

Global organisation A form of international organisation whereby top corporate management and staff plan worldwide manufacturing or operational facilities, marketing policies, financial flows and logistical systems. The global operating unit reports directly to the chief executive, not to an international divisional head.

Going-rate pricing Setting price based largely on following competitors' prices rather than on company costs or demand.

Government market Governmental units – national and local – that purchase or rent goods and services for carrying out the main functions of government.

Growth stage The product life-cycle stage at which a product's sales start climbing quickly.

Habitual buying behaviour Consumer buying behaviour in situations characterised by low consumer involvement and few significant perceived brand differences.

Handling objections The step in the selling process in which the salesperson seeks out, clarifies and overcomes customer objections to buying.

Horizontal marketing systems A channel arrangement in which two or more companies at one level join together to follow a new marketing opportunity.

Human need A state of felt deprivation.

Human want The form that a human need takes as shaped by culture and individual personality.

Hybrid marketing channels   Multichannel distribution, as when a single firms sets up two or more marketing channels to reach one or more customer segments. A variety of direct and indirect approaches are used to deliver the firm's goods to its customers.

Hypermarkets   Huge stores that combine supermarket, discount and warehouse retailing; in addition to food, they carry furniture, appliances, clothing and many other products.

Idea generation   The systematic search for new-product ideas.

Idea screening   Screening new-product ideas in order to spot good ideas and drop poor ones as soon as possible.

Implausible positioning   Making claims that stretch the perception of the buyers too far to be believed.

Income segmentation   Dividing a market into different income groups.

Individual marketing   Tailoring products and marketing programmes to the needs and preferences of individual customers.

Industrial product   A product bought by individuals and organisations for further processing or for use in conducting a business.

Industry   A group of firms that offer a product or class of products that are close substitutes for each other. The set of all sellers of a product or service.

Inelastic demand   Total demand for a product that is not much affected by price changes, especially in the short run.

Influencer   A person whose views or advice carries some weight in making a final buying decision; they often help define specifications and also provide information for evaluating alternatives.

Information search   The stage of the buyer decision process in which the consumer is aroused to search for more information; the consumer may simply have heightened attention or may go into active information search.

Informative advertising   Advertising used to inform consumers about a new product or feature and to build primary demand.

Initiator   The person who first suggests or thinks of the idea of buying a particular product or service.

Innovation   An idea, service, product or technology that has been developed and marketed to customers who perceive it as novel or new. It is a process of identifying, creating and delivering new-product or service values that did not exist before in the marketplace.

Innovative marketing   A principle of enlightened marketing which requires that a company seek real product and marketing improvements.

Inside sales force   Salepeople who service the company's customers and prospect from their offices via telephone or visits from prospective customers.

Institutional market   Schools, hospitals, nursing homes, prisons and other institutions that provide goods and services to people in their care.

Integrated direct marketing   Direct marketing campaigns that use multiple vehicles and multiple stages to improve response rates and profits.

Integrated logistics management   A physical distribution concept that recognises the need for a firm to integrate its logistics system with those of its suppliers and customers. The aim is to maximise the performance of the entire distribution system.

Integrated marketing communications   The concept under which a company carefully integrates and coordinates its many communications channels to deliver a clear, consistent, and compelling message about the organisation and its products.

Intensive distribution   Stocking the product in as many outlets as possible.

Interactive marketing   Marketing by a service firm that recognises that perceived service quality depends heavily on the quality of buyer–seller interaction.

Intermediaries   Distribution channel firms that help the company find customers or make sales to them, including wholesalers and retailers that buy and resell goods.

Internal audit   An evaluation of the firm's entire value chain.

Internal marketing   Marketing by a service firm to train and effectively motivate its customer-contact employees and all the supporting service people to work as a team to provide customer satisfaction.

Internal records information   Information gathered from sources within the company to evaluate marketing performances and to detect marketing problems and opportunities.

International division   A form of international marketing organisation in which the division handles all of the firm's international activities. Marketing, manufacturing, research, planning and specialist staff are organised into operating units according to geography or product groups, or as an international subsidiary responsible for its own sales and profitability.

Internet (the Net)   A vast global computer network that enables computers, with the right software and a modem (a telecommunications device that sends data across telephone lines), to be linked together so that their users can obtain or share information and interact with other users.

Internet exchanges   Web-based bazaars, often shared by buyers, where suppliers bid against requirements posted on the Internet.

Introduction stage   The product life-cycle stage when the new product is first distributed and made available for purchase.

Invention   A new technology or product that may or may not deliver benefits to customers.

Joint ownership   A joint venture in which a company joins investors in a foreign market to create a local business in which the company shares joint ownership and control.

Joint venturing   Entering foreign markets by joining with foreign companies to produce or market a product or service.

Leading indicators   Time series that change in the same direction but in advance of company sales.

Learning   Changes in an individual's behaviour arising from experience.

Licensed brand   A product or service using a brand name offered by the brand owner to the licensee for an agreed fee or royalty.

Licensing   A method of entering a foreign market in which the company enters into an agreement with a licensee in the foreign market, offering the right to use a manufacturing process, trademark, patent, trade secret or other item of value for a fee or royalty.

Life-cycle segmentation   Offering products or marketing approaches that recognise the consumer's changing needs at different stages of their life.

Lifestyle   A person's pattern of living as expressed in his or her activities, interests and opinions.

Limited-service retailers   Retailers that provide only a limited number of services to shoppers.

Line extension   Using a successful brand name to introduce additional items in a given product category under the same brand name, such as new flavours, forms, colours, added ingredients or package sizes.

Long-range plan   A plan that describes the principal factors and forces affecting the organisation during the next several years, including long-term objectives, the chief marketing strategies used to attain them and the resources required.

Macroenvironment   The larger societal forces that affect the whole microenvironment – demographic, economic, natural, technological, political and cultural forces.

Management contracting   A joint venture in which the domestic firm supplies the management know-how to a foreign company that supplies the capital; the domestic firm exports management services rather than products.

Manufacturer's brand (national brand)   A brand created and owned by the producer of a product or service.

Mark-up/mark-down   The difference between selling price and cost as a percentage of selling price or cost.

Market   The set of all actual and potential buyers of a product or service.

Market-centred company   A company that pays balanced attention to both customers and competitors in designing its marketing strategies.

Market challenger   A runner-up firm in an industry that is fighting hard to increase its market share.

Market follower   A runner-up firm in an industry that wants to hold its share without rocking the boat.

Market leader   The firm in an industry with the largest market share; it usually leads other firms in price changes, new product introductions, distribution coverage and promotion spending.

Market nicher   A firm in an industry that serves small segments that the other firms overlook or ignore.

Market-penetration pricing   Setting a low price for a new product in order to attract large numbers of buyers and a large market share.

Market positioning   Arranging for a product to occupy a clear, distinctive and desirable place relative to competing products in the minds of target consumers. Formulating competitive positioning for a product and a detailed marketing mix.

Market segment   A group of consumers who respond in a similar way to a given set of marketing stimuli.

Market segmentation   Dividing a market into distinct groups of buyers with different needs, characteristics or behaviour, who might require separate products or marketing mixes.

Market-skimming pricing   Setting a high price for a new product to skim maximum revenues layer by layer from the segments willing to pay the high price; the company makes fewer but more profitable sales.

Market targeting   The process of evaluating each market segment's attractiveness and selecting one or more segments to enter.

Marketing   A social and managerial process by which individuals and groups obtain what they need and want through creating and exchanging products and value with others.

Marketing audit   A comprehensive, systematic, independent and periodic examination of a company's environment, objectives, strategies and activities to determine problem areas and opportunities, and to recommend a plan of action to improve the company's marketing performance.

Marketing concept   The marketing management philosophy which holds that achieving organisational goals depends on determining the needs and wants of target markets and delivering the desired satisfactions more effectively and efficiently than competitors do.

Marketing control   The process of measuring and evaluating the results of marketing strategies and plans, and taking corrective action to ensure that marketing objectives are attained.

Marketing environment The actors and forces outside marketing that affect marketing management's ability to develop and maintain successful transactions with its target customers.

Marketing implementation The process that turns marketing strategies and plans into marketing actions in order to accomplish strategic marketing objectives.

Marketing information system (MIS) People, equipment and procedures to gather, sort, analyse, evaluate and distribute needed, timely and accurate information to marketing decision makers.

Marketing intelligence Everyday information about developments in the marketing environment that helps managers prepare and adjust marketing plans.

Marketing intermediaries Firms that help the company to promote, sell and distribute its goods to final buyers; they include physical distribution firms, marketing-service agencies and financial intermediaries.

Marketing management The analysis, planning, implementation and control of programmes designed to create, build and maintain beneficial exchanges with target buyers for the purpose of achieving organisational objectives.

Marketing mix The set of controllable tactical marketing tools – product, price, place and promotion – that the firm blends to produce the response it wants in the target market.

Marketing process The process of (1) analysing marketing opportunities; (2) selecting target markets; (3) developing the marketing mix; and (4) managing the marketing effort.

Marketing research The function that links the consumer, customer and public to the marketer through information – information used to identify and define marketing opportunities and problems; to generate, refine and evaluate marketing actions; to monitor marketing performance; and to improve understanding of the marketing process.

Marketing services agencies Marketing research firms, advertising agencies, media firms, marketing consulting firms and other service providers that help a company to target and promote its products to the right markets.

Marketing strategy The marketing logic by which the business unit hopes to achieve its marketing objectives.

Marketing strategy statement A statement of the planned strategy for a new product that outlines the intended target market, the planned product positioning, and the sales, market share and profit goals for the first few years.

Marketing website A site on the Web created by a company to interact with consumers for the purpose of moving them closer to a purchase or other marketing outcome. The site is designed to handle interactive communication initiated by the company.

Mass customisation Preparing individually designed products and communication on a large scale.

Mass marketing Using almost the same product, promotion and distribution for all consumers.

Materials and parts Industrial products that enter the manufacturer's product completely, including raw materials and manufactured materials and parts.

Maturity stage The stage in the product life cycle where sales growth slows or levels off.

Measurability The degree to which the size, purchasing power and profits of a market segment can be measured.

Media Non-personal communications channels including print media (newspapers, magazines, direct mail); broadcast media (radio, television); and display media (billboards, signs, posters).

Media impact The qualitative value of an exposure through a given medium.

Media vehicles Specific media within each general media type, such as specific magazines, television shows or radio programmes.

Membership groups Groups that have a direct influence on a person's behaviour and to which a person belongs.

Merchant wholesaler Independently owned business that takes title to the merchandise it handles.

Message source The company, the brand name, the salesperson of the brand, or the actor in the ad who endorses the product.

Microenvironment The forces close to the company that affect its ability to serve its customers – the company, market channel firms, customer markets, competitors and publics, which combine to make up the firm's value delivery system.

Micromarketing A form of target marketing in which companies tailor their marketing programmes to the needs and wants of narrowly defined geographic, demographic, psychographic or behavioural segments.

Mission statement A statement of the organisation's purpose – what it wants to accomplish in the wider environment.

Modified rebuy A business buying situation in which the buyer wants to modify product specifications, prices, terms or suppliers.

Monopolistic competition A market in which many buyers and sellers trade over a range of prices rather than a single market price.

Moral appeals Message appeals that are directed to the audience's sense of what is right and proper.

Motive (drive) A need that is sufficiently pressing to direct the person to seek satisfaction of the need.

Multibrand strategy A strategy under which a seller develops two or more brands in the same product category.

Multiple niching   Adopting a strategy of having several independent offerings that appeal to several different subsegments of customer.

Natural environment   Natural resources that are needed as inputs by marketers or that are affected by marketing activities.

Need recognition   The first stage of the buyer decision process in which the consumer recognises a problem or need.

Net profit   The difference between the income from goods sold and all expenses incurred.

New product   A good, service or idea that is perceived by some potential customers as new.

New-product development   The development of original products, product improvements, product modifications and new brands through the firm's own R&D efforts.

New task   A business buying situation in which the buyer purchases a product or service for the first time.

Niche marketing   Adapting a company's offerings to more closely match the needs of one or more subsegments where there is often little competition.

Non-durable product   A consumer product that is normally consumed in one or a few uses.

Non-personal communication channels   Channels that carry messages without personal contact or feedback, including media, atmospheres and events.

Non-tariff trade barriers   Non-monetary barriers to foreign products, such as biases against a foreign company's bids or product standards that go against a foreign company's product features.

Objective-and-task method   Developing the promotion budget by (1) defining specific objectives; (2) determining the tasks that must be performed to achieve these objectives; and (3) estimating the costs of performing these tasks. The sum of these costs is the proposed promotion budget.

Observational research   The gathering of primary data by observing relevant people, actions and situations.

Occasion segmentation   Dividing the market into groups according to occasions when buyers get the idea to buy, actually make their purchase, or use the purchased item.

Off-price retailer   Retailer that buys at less-than-regular wholesale prices and sells at less than retail.

Oligopolistic competition   A market in which there are a few sellers that are highly sensitive to each other's pricing and marketing strategies.

Online advertising   Placing advertisements on the Internet in special sections offered by commercial online services, as banner ads that pop up while computer subscribers are surfing online services or websites, or in Internet news groups that have been set up for commercial purposes.

Online marketing   A form of direct marketing conducted through interactive online computer services, which provide two-way systems that link consumers with sellers electronically.

Open-end questions   Questions that allow respondents to answer in their own words.

Operating control   Checking ongoing performance against annual plans and taking corrective action.

Operating statement (profit-and-loss statement or income statement)   A financial statement that shows company sales, cost of goods sold and expenses during a given period of time.

Opinion leaders   People within a reference group who, because of special skills, knowledge, personality or other characteristics, exert influence on others.

Optional-product pricing   The pricing of optional or accessory products along with a main product.

Order-routine specification   The stage of the business buying process in which the buyer writes the final order with the chosen supplier(s), listing the technical specifications, quantity needed, expected time of delivery, return policies and warranties.

Outside sales force   Outside salespeople (or field sales force) who travel to call on customers.

Overpositioning   A positioning error referring to too narrow a picture of the company, its product or a brand being communicated to target customers.

Packaging   The activities of designing and producing the container or wrapper for a product.

Packaging concept   What the package should be or do for the product.

Patronage rewards   Cash or other awards for the regular use of a certain company's products or services.

Penetrated market   The set of consumers who have already bought a particular product or service.

Percentage-of-sales method   Setting the promotion budget at a certain percentage of current or forecast sales or as a percentage of the sales price.

Perception   The process by which people select, organise and interpret information to form a meaningful picture of the world.

Perceptual maps   A product positioning tool that uses multidimensional scaling of consumers' perceptions and preferences to portray the psychological distance between products and segments.

Performance review   The stage of the business buying process in which the buyer rates its satisfaction with suppliers, deciding whether to continue, modify or drop them.

Personal communication channels   Channels through which two or more people communicate directly with each other, including face to face, person to audience, over the telephone, or through the mail.

Personal influence   The effect of statements made by one person on another's attitude or probability of purchase.

Personal selling   Personal presentation by the firm's sales force for the purpose of making sales and building customer relationships.

Personality   A person's distinguishing psychological characteristics that lead to relatively consistent and lasting responses to his or her own environment.

Persuasive advertising   Advertising used to build selective demand for a brand by persuading consumers that it offers the best quality for their money.

Physical distribution (marketing logistics)   The tasks involved in planning, implementing and controlling the physical flow of materials and final goods from points of origin to points of use to meet the needs of customers at a profit.

Physical distribution firms   Warehouse, transportation and other firms that help a company to stock and move goods from their points of origin to their destinations.

Place   All the company activities that make the product or service available to target customers.

Planned obsolescence   A strategy of causing products to become obsolete before they actually need replacement.

Pleasing products   Products that give high immediate satisfaction but may hurt consumers in the long run.

Point-of-purchase (POP) promotions   Displays and demonstrations that take place at the point of purchase or sale.

Political environment   Laws, government agencies and pressure groups that influence and limit various organisations and individuals in a given society.

Portfolio analysis   A tool by which management identifies and evaluates the various businesses that make up the company.

Postpurchase behaviour   The stage of the buyer decision process in which consumers take further action after purchase based on their satisfaction or dissatisfaction.

Potential market   The set of consumers who profess some level of interest in a particular product or service.

Pre-approach   The step in the selling process in which the salesperson learns as much as possible about a prospective customer before making a sales call.

Premiums   Goods offered either free or at low cost as an incentive to buy a product.

Presentation   The step in the selling process in which the salesperson tells the product 'story' to the buyer, showing how the product will make or save money for the buyer.

Price   The amount of money charged for a product or service, or the sum of the values that consumers exchange for the benefits of having or using the product or service.

Price elasticity   A measure of the sensitivity of demand to changes in price.

Price packs   Reduced prices that are marked by the producer directly on the label or package.

Primary data   Information collected for the specific purpose at hand.

Primary demand   The level of total demand for all brands of a given product or service – for example, the total demand for motor cycles.

Private brand (middleman, distributor or store brand)   A brand created and owned by a reseller of a product or service.

Problem recognition   The first stage of the business buying process in which someone in the company recognises a problem or need that can be met by acquiring a good or a service.

Product   Anything that can be offered to a market for attention, acquisition, use or consumption that might satisfy a want or need. It includes physical objects, services, persons, places, organisations and ideas.

Product adaptation   Adapting a product to meet local conditions or wants in foreign markets.

Product-bundle pricing   Combining several products and offering the bundle at a reduced price.

Product concept   The idea that consumers will favour products that offer the most quality, performance and features, and that the organisation should therefore devote its energy to making continuous product improvements.

Product development   Developing the product concept into a physical product in order to ensure that the product idea can be turned into a workable product.

Product idea   An idea for a possible product that the company can see itself offering to the market.

Product image   The way consumers perceive an actual or potential product.

Product innovation charter (PIC)   A new-product strategy statement formalising management's reasons or rationale behind the firm's search for innovation opportunities, the product/market and technology to focus upon, and the goals and objectives to be achieved.

Product invention   Creating new products or services for foreign markets.

Product life cycle (PLC)   The course of a product's sales and profits over its lifetime. It involves five distinct stages: product development, introduction, growth, maturity and decline.

Product line   A group of products that are closely related because they function in a similar manner, are sold to the same customer groups, are marketed through the same types of outlet, or fall within given price ranges.

Product line filling   Increasing the product line by adding more items within the present range of the line.

Product line pricing   Setting the price steps between various products in a product line based on cost differences between the products, customer evaluations of different features, and competitors' prices.

Product line stretching   Increasing the product line by lengthening it beyond its current range.

Product mix (product assortment)   The set of all product lines and items that a particular seller offers for sale to buyers.

Product position   The way the product is defined by consumers on important attributes – the place the product occupies in consumers' minds relative to competing products.

Product quality   The ability of a product to perform its functions; it includes the product's overall durability, reliability, precision, ease of operation and repair, and other valued attributes.

Product sales force structure   A sales force organisation under which salespeople specialise in selling only a portion of the company's products or lines.

Product specification   The stage of the business buying process in which the buying organisation decides on and specifies the best technical product characteristics for a needed item.

Product-support services   Services that augment actual products.

Production concept   The philosophy that consumers will favour products that are available and highly affordable, and that management should therefore focus on improving production and distribution efficiency.

Profitable customer   A person, household or company whose revenues over time exceed, by an acceptable amount, the company's costs of attracting, selling and servicing that customer.

Promotion   Activities that communicate the product or service and its merits to target customers and persuade them to buy.

Promotion mix   The specific mix of advertising, personal selling, sales promotion and public relations that a company uses to pursue its advertising and marketing objectives.

Promotional allowance   A payment or price reduction to reward dealers for participating in advertising and sales-support programmes.

Promotional pricing   Temporarily pricing products below the list price, and sometimes even below cost, to increase short-run sales.

Proposal solicitation   The stage of the business buying process in which the buyer invites qualified suppliers to submit proposals.

Prospecting   The step in the selling process in which the salesperson identifies qualified potential customers.

Psychographic segmentation   Dividing a market into different groups based on social class, lifestyle or personality characteristics.

Psychographics   The technique of measuring lifestyles and developing lifestyle classifications; it involves measuring the chief AIO dimensions (activities, interests, opinions).

Psychological pricing   A pricing approach that considers the psychology of prices and not simply the economics; the price is used to say something about the product.

Public   Any group that has an actual or potential interest in or impact on an organisation's ability to achieve its objectives.

Public relations   Building good relations with the company's various publics by obtaining favourable publicity, building up a good 'corporate image', and handling or heading off unfavourable rumours, stories and events. Major PR tools include press relations, product publicity, corporate communications, lobbying and counselling.

Pull strategy   A promotion strategy that calls for spending a lot on advertising and consumer promotion to build up consumer demand. If the strategy is successful, consumers will ask their retailers for the product, the retailers will ask the wholesalers, and the wholesalers will ask the producers.

Pulsing   Scheduling ads unevenly, in bursts, over a certain time period.

Purchase decision   The stage of the buyer decision process in which the consumer actually buys the product.

Pure competition   A market in which many buyers and sellers trade in a uniform commodity – no single buyer or seller has much effect on the going market price.

Pure monopoly   A market in which there is a single seller – it may be a government monopoly, a private regulated monopoly or a private non-regulated monopoly.

Push strategy   A promotion strategy that calls for using the sales force and trade promotion to push the product through channels. The producer promotes the product to wholesalers, the wholesalers promote to retailers, and the retailers promote to consumers.

Qualified available market   The set of consumers who have interest, income, access and qualifications for a particular product or service.

Qualitative research   Exploratory research used to uncover consumers' motivations, attitudes and behaviour. Focus-group interviewing, elicitation interviews and repertory grid techniques are typical methods used in this type of research.

Quality The totality of features and characteristics of a product or service that bear on its ability to satisfy stated or implied needs.

Quantitative research Research which involves data collection from a sufficient volume of customers to allow statistical analysis.

Quantity discount A price reduction to buyers who buy large volumes.

Quantity premium A surcharge paid by buyers who purchase high volumes of a product.

Question marks Low-share business units in high-growth markets that require a lot of cash in order to hold their share or become stars.

Quota A limit on the amount of goods that an importing country will accept in certain product categories; it is designed to conserve on foreign exchange and to protect local industry and employment.

Range branding strategy A brand strategy whereby the firm develops separate product range names for different families of product.

Rational appeals Message appeals that relate to the audience's self-interest and show that the product will produce the claimed benefits; examples are appeals of product quality, economy, value or performance.

Reach The percentage of people in the target market exposed to an ad campaign during a given period.

Reference groups Groups that have a direct (face-to-face) or indirect influence on the person's attitudes or behaviour.

Reference prices Prices that buyers carry in their minds and refer to when they look at a given product.

Relationship marketing The process of creating, maintaining and enhancing strong, value-laden relationships with customers and other stakeholders.

Reminder advertising Advertising used to keep consumers thinking about a product.

Resellers The individuals and organisations that buy goods and services to resell at a profit.

Retailer cooperatives Contractual vertical marketing systems in which retailers organise a new, jointly owned business to carry on wholesaling and possibly production.

Retailers Businesses whose sales come primarily from retailing.

Retailing accordion A phenomenon describing how the width of retailers' product assortment or operations shifts over time: there tends to be a general–specific–general cycle. However, it is possible that many retailing businesses evolve along a specific–general–specific cycle.

Reverse auction Customers name the price that they are willing to pay for an item and seek a company willing to sell.

Role The activities a person is expected to perform according to the people around him or her.

Sales force management The analysis, planning, implementation and control of sales force activities. It includes setting sales force objectives; designing sales force strategy; and recruiting, selecting, training, supervising and evaluating the firm's salespeople.

Sales force promotion Sales promotion designed to motivate the sales force and make sales force selling efforts more effective, including bonuses, contests and sales rallies.

Sales promotion Short-term incentives to encourage purchase or sales of a product or service.

Sales quotas Standards set for salespeople, stating the amount they should sell and how sales should be divided among the company's products.

Salesperson An individual acting for a company by performing one or more of the following activities: prospecting, communicating, servicing and information gathering.

Salutary products Products that have low appeal but may benefit consumers in the long run.

Sample A segment of the population selected for market research to represent the population as a whole.

Samples Offers to consumers of a trial amount of a product.

Seasonal discount A price reduction to buyers who buy merchandise or services out of season.

Seasonality The recurrent consistent pattern of sales movements within the year.

Second-price sealed bid Sealed bids are submitted but the contender placing the best bid pays only the price equal to the second-best bid.

Secondary data Information that already exists somewhere, having been collected for another purpose.

Segment marketing Adapting a company's offerings so they more closely match the needs of one or more segments.

Segmented pricing Pricing that allows for differences in customers, products and locations. The differences in prices are not based on differences in costs.

Selective attention The tendency of people to screen out most of the information to which they are exposed.

Selective demand The demand for a given brand of a product or service.

Selective distortion The tendency of people to adapt information to personal meanings.

Selective distribution   The use of more than one, but less than all of the intermediaries that are willing to carry the company's products.

Selective retention   The tendency of people to retain only part of the information to which they are exposed, usually information that supports their attitudes or beliefs.

Self-concept   Self-image, or the complex mental pictures that people have of themselves.

Self-service retailers   Retailers that provide few or no services to shoppers; shoppers perform their own locate–compare–select process.

Selling concept   The idea that consumers will not buy enough of the organisation's products unless the organisation undertakes a large-scale selling and promotion effort.

Selling process   The steps that the salesperson follows when selling, which include prospecting and qualifying, pre-approach, approach, presentation and demonstration, handling objections, closing and follow-up.

Sense-of-mission marketing   A principle of enlightened marketing which holds that a company should define its mission in broad social terms rather than narrow product terms.

Sequential product development   A new-product development approach in which one company department works individually to complete its stage of the process before passing the new product along to the next department and stage.

Served market (target market)   The part of the qualified available market that the company decides to pursue.

Service   Any activity or benefit that one party can offer to another which is essentially intangible and does not result in the ownership of anything.

Service inseparability   A major characteristic of services – they are produced and consumed at the same time and cannot be separated from their providers, whether the providers are people or machines.

Service intangibility   A major characteristic of services – they cannot be seen, tasted, felt, heard or smelt before they are bought.

Service perishability   A major characteristic of services – they cannot be stored for later sale or use.

Service variability   A major characteristic of services – their quality may vary greatly depending on who provides them and when, where and how.

Services   Activities, benefits or satisfactions that are offered for sale.

Shopping product   A consumer product that the customer, in the process of selection and purchase, characteristically compares with others on such bases as suitability, quality, price and style.

Simultaneous product development   An approach to developing new products in which various company departments work closely together, overlapping the steps in the product development process to save time and increase effectiveness.

Single-source data systems   Electronic monitoring systems that link consumers' exposure to television advertising and promotion (measured using television meters) with what they buy in stores (measured using store checkout scanners).

Social classes   Relatively permanent and ordered divisions in a society whose members share similar values, interests and behaviours.

Societal marketing   A principle of enlightened marketing which holds that a company should make marketing decisions by considering consumers' wants, the company's requirements, consumers' long-run interests and society's long-run interests.

Societal marketing concept   The idea that the organisation should determine the needs, wants and interests of target markets and deliver the desired satisfactions more effectively and efficiently than competitors in a way that maintains or improves the consumer's and society's well-being.

Specialised industry   An industry where there are many opportunities for firms to create competitive advantages that are huge or give a high pay-off.

Speciality product   A consumer product with unique characteristics or brand identification for which a significant group of buyers is willing to make a special purchase effort.

Speciality store   A retail store that carries a narrow product line with a deep assortment within that line.

Stalemate industry   An industry that produces commodities and is characterised by a few opportunities to create competitive advantages, with each advantage being small.

Standardised marketing mix   An international marketing strategy for using basically the same product, advertising, distribution channels and other elements of the marketing mix in all the company's international markets.

Stars   High-growth, high-share businesses or products that often require heavy investment to finance their rapid growth.

Statistical demand analysis   A set of statistical procedures used to discover the most important real factors affecting sales and their relative influence; the most commonly analysed factors are prices, income, population and promotion.

Status   The general esteem given to a role by society.

Straight product extension   Marketing a product in a foreign market without any change.

Straight rebuy A business buying situation in which the buyer routinely reorders something without any modifications.

Strapline A slogan often used in conjunction with a brand's name, advertising and other promotions.

Strategic business unit (SBU) A unit of the company that has a separate mission and objectives and that can be planned independently from other company businesses. An SBU can be a company division, a product line within a division, or sometimes a single product or brand.

Strategic control Checking whether the company's basic strategy matches its opportunities and strengths.

Strategic group A group of firms in an industry following the same or a similar strategy.

Strategic plan A plan that describes how a firm will adapt to take advantage of opportunities in its constantly changing environment, thereby maintaining a strategic fit between the firm's goals and capabilities and its changing market opportunities.

Style A basic and distinctive mode of expression.

Subculture A group of people with shared value systems based on common life experiences and situations.

Substantiality The degree to which a market segment is sufficiently large or profitable.

Supermarkets Large, low-cost, low-margin, high-volume, self-service stores that carry a wide variety of food, laundry and household products.

Superstore A store almost twice the size of a regular supermarket that carries a large assortment of routinely purchased food and non-food items and offers such services as dry cleaning, post offices, film developing, photo finishing, cheque cashing, petrol forecourts and self-service car-washing facilities.

Supplier search The stage of the business buying process in which the buyer tries to find the best vendors.

Supplier selection The stage of the business buying process in which the buyer reviews proposals and selects a supplier or suppliers.

Suppliers Firms and individuals that provide the resources needed by the company and its competitors to produce goods and services.

Supplies and services Industrial products that do not enter the finished product at all.

Survey research The gathering of primary data by asking people questions about their knowledge, attitudes, preferences and buying behaviour.

SWOT analysis A distillation of the findings of the internal and external audit which draws attention to the critical organisational strengths and weaknesses and the opportunities and threats facing the company.

Systems buying Buying a packaged solution to a problem and without all the separate decisions involved.

Target costing A technique to support pricing decisions, which starts with deciding a target cost for a new product and works back to designing the product.

Target market A set of buyers sharing common needs or characteristics that the company decides to serve.

Target marketing Directing a company's effort towards serving one or more groups of customers sharing common needs or characteristics.

Tariff A tax levied by a government against certain imported products. Tariffs are designed to raise revenue or to protect domestic firms.

Team selling Using teams of people from sales, marketing, production, finance, technical support, and even upper management to service large, complex accounts.

Technological environment Forces that create new technologies, creating new product and market opportunities.

Telemarketing Using the telephone to sell directly to consumers.

Territorial sales force structure A sales force organisation that assigns each salesperson to an exclusive geographic territory in which that salesperson carries the company's full line.

Test marketing The stage of new-product development where the product and marketing programme are tested in more realistic market settings.

Time-series analysis Breaking down past sales into their trend, cycle, season and erratic components, then recombining these components to produce a sales forecast.

Total costs The sum of the fixed and variable costs for any given level of production.

Total customer cost The total of all the monetary, time, energy and psychic costs associated with a marketing offer.

Total customer value The total of the entire product, services, personnel and image values that a buyer receives from a marketing offer.

Total market demand The total volume of a product or service that would be bought by a defined consumer group in a defined geographic area in a defined time period in a defined marketing environment under a defined level and mix of industry marketing effort.

Total quality management (TQM) Programmes designed to constantly improve the quality of products, services, and marketing processes.

Trade (or retailer) promotion Sales promotion designed to gain reseller support and to improve reseller selling efforts, including discounts, allowances, free goods, cooperative advertising, push money, and conventions and trade shows.

Trade-in allowance A price reduction given for turning in an old item when buying a new one.

Transaction   A trade between two parties that involves at least two things of value, agreed-upon conditions, a time of agreement and a place of agreement.

Trend   The long-term, underlying pattern of sales growth or decline resulting from basic changes in population, capital formation and technology.

Two-part pricing   A strategy for pricing services in which price is broken into a fixed fee plus a variable usage rate.

Underpositioning   A positioning error referring to failure to position a company, its product or brand.

Undifferentiated marketing   A market-coverage strategy in which a firm decides to ignore market segment differences and go after the whole market with one offer.

Uniform delivered pricing   A geographic pricing strategy in which the company charges the same price plus freight to all customers, regardless of their location.

Unique selling proposition (USP)   The unique product benefit that a firm aggressively promotes in a consistent manner to its target market. The benefit usually reflects functional superiority: best quality, best services, lowest price, most advanced technology.

Unsought product   A consumer product that the consumer either does not know about or knows about but does not normally think of buying.

Users   Members of the organisation who will use the product or service; users often initiate the buying proposal and help define product specifications.

Value analysis   An approach to cost reduction in which components are studied carefully to determine if they can be redesigned, standardised or made by less costly methods of production.

Value-based pricing   Setting price based on buyers' perceptions of product values rather than on cost.

Value chain   A major tool for identifying ways to create more customer value.

Value marketing   A principle of enlightened marketing which holds that a company should put most of its resources into value-building marketing investments.

Value positioning   A range of positioning alternatives based on the value an offering delivers and its price.

Variable costs   Costs that vary directly with the level of production.

Variety-seeking buying behaviour   Consumer buying behaviour in situations characterised by low consumer involvement, but significant perceived brand differences.

Vertical marketing system (VMS)   A distribution channel structure in which producers, wholesalers and retailers act as a unified system. One channel member owns the others, has contracts with them, or has so much power that they all cooperate.

Volume industry   An industry characterised by few opportunities to create competitive advantages, but each advantage is huge and gives a high pay-off.

Warehouse club (wholesale club, membership warehouse)   Off-price retailer that sells a limited selection of brand-name grocery items, appliances, clothing and a hodgepodge of other goods at deep discounts to members who pay annual membership fees.

Webcasting (push programming)   Process whereby the online marketer sends advertisements or information over the Internet directly to the desktops of target customers. Companies can also sign on with Webcasting service providers, which automatically download customised information to the personal computers of subscribers to their services.

Wheel of retailing   A concept of retailing which states that new types of retailer usually begin as low-margin, low-price, low-status operations, but later evolve into higher-priced, higher-service operations, eventually becoming like the conventional retailers they replaced.

Wholesaler   A firm engaged primarily in selling goods and services to those buying for resale or business use.

Word-of-mouth influence   Personal communication about a product between target buyers and neighbours, friends, family members and associates.

Workload approach   An approach to setting sales force size, whereby the company groups accounts into different size classes and then determines how many salespeople are needed to call on them the desired number of times.

World Wide Web (WWW or the Web)   A part of the Internet that uses a standard computer language to allow documents containing text, images, sound and video to be sent across the Internet.

Zone pricing   A geographic pricing strategy in which the company sets up two or more zones. All customers within a zone pay the same total price; the more distant the zone, the higher the price.

subject index

company index